Warman's
ANTIQUES
AND THEIR PRICES

23rd Edition

*The Standard Price Reference for antiques
and collectibles, for collectors, dealers
and professionals in the trade.*

Edited by
Harry L. Rinker

**Completely illustrated
and authenticated**

**Warman Publishing Co., Inc.
Willow Grove, PA, 19090**

ISBN: 0-911594-15-9
ISSN: 0196-2272
Library of Congress Catalog Card No. 82-643542
Printed in the United States of America

Additional copies of this book may be obtained from your bookstore or directly from the publisher, Warman Publishing Co., P.O. Box 1112, Dept. 23, Willow Grove, PA 19090. Enclose $12.95 plus $2.00 for postage and handling. Pennsylvania residents please add 78¢ state sales tax.

EDITORIAL STAFF, 23rd EDITION

Craig Dinner
P. O. Box 455
Valley Stream, NY
11582
(516) 825-0145
Doorstops

Robert A. Doyle
Doyle Auctioneers &
Appraisers
R. D. 3, Box 137
Osborn Hill Rd.
Fishkill, NY 12524
(914) 896-9492
Razors

Arthur M. Feldman
1815 St. Johns Avenue
Highland Park, IL 60035
(312) 432-2075
Judaica

Regis and Mary Ferson
122 Arden Rd.
Pittsburgh, PA 15216
(412) 563-1964
Milk Glass

Mildred Fishman
37 Canaan Close
New Canaan, CT 06840
(203) 966-0748
*Goss and Crested
Wares*

Doug Flynn and Al
Bolton
Holloway House
P. O. Box 210
Lititz, PA 17543
(717) 627-4567
*British Royalty
Commemoratives*

Ron Fox
Fox-Terry Steins, Inc.
416 Throop St.
N. Babylon, NY 11704
(516) 669-7232
Mettlach, Steins

Walter Glenn
Geode Ltd.
3393 Peachtree Rd.
Atlanta, GA 30326
(404) 261-9346
Frankart

Dan Golden
5375-C Avenida Encinas
Carlsbad, CA 92008
(619) 438-8383
Telephones

Ted Hake
Hake's Americana &
Collectibles
P. O. Box 1444
York, PA 17405
(717) 848-1333
*Disneyana, Political
Items*

Peg Harrison
Harrison's Antiques
2417 Edgewater Dr.
Orlando, FL 32804
(305) 425-6481
Haviland China

John High
415 E. 52nd St.
New York, NY 10022
(212) 758-1692
Stevengraphs

Alda Horner
Whitehall Shop
1215 E. Franklin St.
Chapel Hill, NC 27514
(919) 942-3179
Linens

Joan Hull
1376 Nevada
Huron, SD 57350
(605) 352-1685
Hull Pottery

David and Sue Irons
Irons Antiques
R. D. 4, Box 101
Northampton, PA 18067
(215) 262-9335
Irons

William J. Jenks
Golden Webb Antiques,
Inc.
P. O. Box 1274
Wilkes-Barre, PA 18703
(717) 288-3039
Pattern Glass

Judy Knauer
1224 Spring Valley Lane
West Chester, PA 19380
(215) 431-3477
Toothpicks

Edward W. Leach
381 Trenton Ave.
Paterson, NJ 07503
(201) 684-5398
Shaving Mugs

Ron Lieberman
The Family Album
R. D. 1, Box 42
Glen Rock, PA 17327
(717) 235-2134
*Books, Modern
American First
Editions*

Elyce Litts
P. O. Box 394
Morris Plains, NJ 07950
(201) 361-4087
 Geisha Girl

Elaine J. Luartes
Athena Antiques
100 Beta Drive
Franklin, TN 37064
(615) 377-3442
 Jewelry

Clarence and Betty
Maier
The Burmese Cruet
P. O. Box 432
Montgomeryville, PA
18936
(215) 855-5388
 Burmese Glass, Crown
 Milano, Royal Flemish

James S. Maxwell, Jr.
P. O. Box 367
Lampeter, PA 17537
(717) 464-5573
 Banks, Mechanical

Joan Collett Oates
5912 Kingsfield Dr.
W. Bloomfield, MI
48322
(313) 661-2335
 Phoenix Bird Pattern

Evalene Pulati
National Valentine
Collectors Association
P. O. Box 1404
Santa Ana, CA 92702
 Valentines

Darryl K. Reilly
Dendara's Antiques
P. O. Box 1203
Pepperel, MA 01463
(508) 433-8718
 Pattern Glass

Ferill J. Rice
302 Pheasant Run
Kaukauna, WI 54130
(414) 766-9176
 Fenton

Julie Rich
Tea Leaf Readings
9720 Whiskey Run
Laurel, MD 20707
(301) 490-7604
 Tea Leaf Ironstone
 China

Connie Rogers
1733 Chase St.
Cincinnati, OH 45223
 Willow Ware

Mark Supnick
8524 NW 2nd St.
Coral Springs, FL 33071
(305) 755-3449
 Shawnee Pottery

George Theofiles
Miscellaneous Man
Box 1776
New Freedom, PA 17349
(717) 235-4766
 Posters

Margaret L. Tyrell
117 North 40th St.
Allentown, PA 18104
(215) 395-9364
 Children's Books

Bill Wheeler
The Oarhouse
P. O. Box 3434
Clearwater Beach, FL
33515
(813) 733-7447
 Nautical, Scrimshaw,
 Whaling

Kathy Wojciechowski
P. O. Box 230
Peotone, IL 60468
 Nippon

INTRODUCTION

"Warman's Is The Key"

Warman's provides the keys needed by auctioneers, collectors, and dealers to open the doors to understanding and dealing with the complexities of the antiques market. A price list is only one of the many keys needed today. **Warman's** 23rd Edition contains many additional keys including histories, reference books, periodicals, collectors' clubs, and museums. Useful buying and collecting hints also are provided.

Warman's has been designed to be your first key to the exciting world of antiques. As you use the keys provided to advance beyond this book into specialized collecting areas, **Warman's** hopes you will remember with fondness where you received your start. When you encounter items outside your area of speciality, remember **Warman's** remains your key to unlocking the information you need, just as it has for over forty years.

ORGANIZATION

Listings: Objects are listed alphabetically by category, beginning with ABC Plates and ending with Zsolnay Pottery. If you have trouble identifying the category in which your object belongs, use the extensive index in the back of the book. It is designed to guide you to the proper category.

We have attempted to make the listings descriptive enough so that specific objects can be identified. We also have placed emphasis on those items which are actively being sold in the marketplace. Nevertheless, some harder-to-find objects are included in order to demonstrate the market spread.

Each year as the market changes, we carefully consider which categories to include, which to drop, and which to add. **Warman's** is a direct response to the developing trends in the marketplace. To further help collectors and dealers, **Warman** has published *Warman's Americana & Collectibles*, an excellent source for information and prices on 20th century collectibles and items of nostalgia.

History: Every collector should know something about the history of his object. We have presented a capsule background for each category. In many cases the background contains collecting hints or tips to spot reproductions.

References: Special references are listed for each category to help collectors learn more about their objects. Included are author, title, publisher [if published by a small firm or individual, we have indicated "published by author"], and date of publication or most recent edition.

Finding these books may present a problem. The antiques and collectibles field is blessed with a dedicated core of book dealers who stock these specialized publications. You will find them at flea markets, antiques shows, and advertised in leading publications in the field. Many dealers publish annual or semi-annual catalogs. Ask to be put on their mailing lists. Books go out-of-print quickly, yet many books printed over twenty-five years ago remain the standard work in a field. Used book dealers often can turn up many of these valuable reference materials.

Periodicals: Generally, the newsletter or bulletin of a collectors' club focuses on the specific publication needs within a category. However, there are other publications, not associated with collectors' clubs, of which the collector and dealer should be aware. These are covered under specific categories.

In addition, there are general interest newspapers and magazines which deserve to be brought to our user's attention. These are:

Antique Review, P. O. Box 538, Worthington, OH 43085
Antique Showcase, Amis Gibbs Publications, Ltd., Canfield, Ontario, Canada, N0A 1C0
Antique Trader Weekly, P. O. Box 1050, Dubuque, IA 52001
Antique Week, P. O. Box 90, Knightstown, IN 46148
Antiques (The Magazine Antiques), 551 Fifth Avenue, New York, NY 10017
Antiques Journal, 4 Church St., Ware, MA 01082
Antiques & Collecting Hobbies, 1006 S. Michigan Ave., Chicago, IL 60605
Collector News, Box 156, Grundy Center, IA 50638
Collectors' Showcase, 1018 Rosecrans, San Diego, CA 92106
Maine Antique Digest, P. O. Box 358, Waldoboro, ME 04572
MidAtlantic Antiques Magazine, P. O. Box 908, Henderson, NC 27536
New York-Pennsylvania Collector, Drawer C, Fishers, NY 14453
Southern Antiques, P. O. Box 1550, Lake City, FL 32055
West Coast Peddler, P. O. Box 5134, Whittier, CA 90607

It is impossible to list all the national and regional publications in the antiques and collectibles field. The above is merely a sampling. A check with your local library will bring many other publications to your attention.

Collectors' Clubs: The large number of collectors' clubs adds vitality to the antiques and collectibles fields. Their publications and conventions produce knowledge which often cannot be found anywhere else. Many of these clubs are short-lived; others are so strong that they have regional and local chapters.

Museums: The best way to study a specific field is to see as many documented examples as possible. For this reason, we have listed museums where significant collections in that category are on display. Special attention must be directed to the complex of museums which make up the Smithsonian Institution in Washington, D.C.

Reproductions: Reproductions are a major concern to all collectors and dealers. Most reproductions are unmarked; the newness of their appearance is often the best clue to uncovering them. Specific objects known to be reproduced are marked within the listings with an asterisk (*).

Index: A great deal of effort has been expended to make our index useful. Always try to find the most specific reference. For example, if you have a piece of china, look first for the maker's name and second for the type. The key is to ask the right questions of yourself.

Photographs: You may encounter a piece you cannot identify well enough to use the index. Consult the photographs and marks. If you own the last several editions of **Warman's**, you have assembled a valuable photographic reference to the antiques and collectibles field.

PRICE NOTES

In assigning prices we assume the object is in very good condition. If otherwise, we note this in our description. It would be ideal to suggest that mint, or unused, examples of all objects do exist. The reality is that objects from the past were used, whether they be glass, china, dolls, or toys. Because of this, some normal wear must be expected. In fact, if an object such as furniture does not show wear, its origins may be more suspect than if it does show wear.

Whenever possible, we have tried to provide a broad listing of prices within a category so you have a "feel" for the market. We emphasize the middle range of prices within a category, while also listing some objects of high and low value to show the market spread.

We do not use ranges because they tend to confuse rather than help the collector and dealer. How do you determine if your object is at the high or low end of the range? There is a high degree of flexibility in pricing in the antiques field. If you want to set ranges, add or subtract 10% from our prices.

One of the hardest variants with which to deal is the regional fluctuations of prices. Victorian furniture brings widely differing prices in New York, Chicago, New Orleans, and San Francisco. We have tried to strike a balance. Know your region and subject before investing heavily. If the best prices for cameo glass are in Montreal or Toronto, then be prepared to go there if you want to save money or add choice pieces to your collection. Research and patience are key factors to building a collection of merit.

Another factor that affects prices is a sale by a leading dealer or private collector. We have tempered both dealer and auction house figures.

PRICE RESEARCH

Everyone asks—where do we get our prices? They come from many sources.

First, we rely on auctions. Auction houses and auctioneers do not always command the highest prices. If they did, why do so many dealers buy from them? The key to understanding auction prices is to know when a price is high or low in the range. We think we do this and do it well.

Second, we work closely with dealers. We screen our contacts to make certain they have a full knowledge of the market. Dealers make their living from selling antiques; they cannot afford to have a price guide which is not in touch with the market.

Over thirty antiques magazines, newspapers, and journals come into our office regularly. They are excellent barometers of what is moving and what is not. We don't hesitate to call an advertiser and ask if their listed merchandise sold.

When the editorial staff is doing field work, we identify ourselves. Our conversations with dealers and collectors around the country have enhanced this book. Teams from **Warman's** are in the field at antiques shows, flea markets, and auctions recording prices and taking photographs.

Collectors work closely with us. They are specialists whose devotion to research and accurate information is inspiring. Generally, they are not dealers. Whenever we have asked them for help, they have responded willingly and admirably.

BOARD OF ADVISORS

Our Board of Advisors are specialists, both dealers and collectors, who feel a commitment to accurate information. You'll find their names listed in the front of the book. Several have authored a major reference work on their subject.

Members of the Board of Advisors file lists of prices in their categories. They help select and often supply the photographs used. If you wish to buy or sell an object in their field of expertise, drop them a note along with an SASE. If time or interest permits, they will respond.

BUYER'S GUIDE, NOT SELLER'S GUIDE

Warman's is designed to be a buyer's guide to what you would have to pay to purchase an object on the open market from a dealer or collector. **It is not a seller's guide to prices.** People frequently make this mistake. In doing so, they deceive themselves. If you have an object listed in this book and wish to sell it to a dealer, you should expect to receive approximately fifty percent (50%) of the listed value. If the object is not anticipated to be resold quickly, expect to receive even less.

A private collector may pay more, perhaps seventy to eighty percent of our list price. Your object will have to be something needed for his or her collection. If you have an extremely rare object or an object of exceptionally high value, these guidelines do not apply.

Examine your piece as objectively as possible. As an antiques appraiser, I spend a great deal of time telling people their treasures are not ''gold'' at all, but items readily available in the marketplace.

In respect to buying and selling, a simple philosophy is that a good purchase occurs when the buyer and seller are happy with the price. Don't look back. Hindsight has little value in the antiques field. Given time, things tend to balance out.

COMMENTS INVITED

Warman's Antiques and Their Prices continues to be the leader in the antiques and collectibles price guide field because we listen to our readers. Readers are encouraged to send their comments and suggestions to our Editorial Office, P. O. Box 265, Zionsville, PA 18092.

ACKNOWLEDGEMENTS

As Warman Publishing Company, Inc., celebrates its fortieth birthday, it is appropriate to honor those individuals who shaped *Warman's Antiques And Their Prices* for the past four decades. First and foremost is Edwin G. Warman, our founder, who guided our book through its first fifteen editions.

Ellen L. Schroy, Senior Editor, shoulders principal responsibility for schedules, research, copy, and computerization. She is ably assisted by Terese Oswald, Assistant Editor.

Finally, special thanks to two key groups: (1) those individuals who submitted price lists and letters of information to us, allowed their material to be photographed, and took the time to discuss the antiques business on the telephone and in the field and (2) you, our users.

It is the pledge of the entire editorial staff to exceed in the decade ahead the quality that you have found in *Warman's Antiques And Their Prices* during the past four decades. Happy antiquing.

Editorial Office   Harry L. Rinker
Warman Publishing Co., Inc.   Editor
P. O. Box 265
Zionsville, PA 18092
January 1989

STATE OF THE MARKET

"Auction madness" dominated the 1988 antiques and collectibles market. The New York auction houses, as well as many regional houses, have developed pre-auction hype to the point where there is more publicity about an auction or sale before it happens than afterward. The auction or sale is an event unto itself. The objects are lost among the reporters, television cameras, and necks straining to see "who bought it."

Nothing illustrated this better than the Warhol auction and Perelman sale. At the Warhol auction cookie jar forms that could be bought on the open market from fifty dollars to a few hundred dollars averaged $1,250 plus. It is time to question how much extra value should be attached to a piece because it was owned by a famous individual. Is this added value greatly distorted in the present market? In a hundred years will Margaret Hamilton's witch's hat or Marilyn Monroe's dress not only retain their present value, but increase at a rate greater than inflation?

The use of the tag sale method of selling is increasing. The tag sale has always been popular in portions of the south and southwest. Now, it is developing nationwide appeal. The Perelman toy collection sale is a clear indication that the tag sale has achieved national impact.

Another trend in the auction arena is the grouping of material into large lots with a minimum expected bid of five hundred or a thousand dollars. More and more auction houses are catering to the lot-buying dealer rather than the individual collector, especially for less expensive merchandise. The lower and middle buyer who might want to add a piece or two to his or her collection is left out.

If you are planning to sell, this is the time. A cloud of optimism covers the entire antiques and collectibles market. Investors are bullish; speculators abound. Few think the good times are going to end. Even more spectacular is the fact that "good times fever" spreads throughout all levels of the antiques and collectibles market. Many think serious technical corrections in the market are long overdue.

The hottest new trend is Victoriana. Material from the Victorian era, 1837-1901, is in demand. Several new magazines with a Victorian theme have been launched within the past year. In America, much of the Victorian focus is on the post-Civil War period. Within the past month, talks with country dealers indicate that many are liquidating their country inventory and going into Victoriana.

The decline of American Country appears to have ended. Prices are now stable. Further, the concept of "country" has changed. When interior decorators want a country look, they no longer turn to American Country but rather the continental country look from rural France, Germany, or the Scandinavian countries.

Interest in modernism, the period from the mid-1930s through the 1950s, continues to grow. 1988 saw a marked increase in the number of specialized modernism shows and dealers. At the moment, there is confusion in respect to defining modernism and how its pieces should it be valued. Much of this should clear up in the year ahead.

The vast majority of collecting categories in the antiques and collectibles field enjoy a stable pricing structure, i.e., prices do not rise or fall more than five percent of the norm. However, there always are areas gaining and declining in value. You may not agree with my conclusions, but you would be well advised to think about them.

Gaining	*Declining*
American Flyer trains	Architectural elements
Banks, mechanical	Art Deco
Character & personality items	Clothing, vintage
Compacts, vintage	Folk Art, regional
Continental country	Lionel trains
Games, especially McLoughlin and television era	Opalescent glass
Jewelry of the 1940s and 1950s	Radios, Catalin from the 1930s and 1940s
Metalsmiths, Twentieth Century	Redware
Modernist pieces with strong design elements	Satsuma
Posters	Staffordshire, Historical, light views
Toys, especially post-World War II	
Victoriana	

In last year's State of the Market report, attention was called to the fact that European buyers would be coming to the United States to buy their country's products and take them back home. Well, they arrived and they are buying. One of the principal reasons for this is a renewed collecting interest in Europe. The Germans and French always had a strong collecting bent. But, the big news is the English. Yes, the English are actually collecting their own material with emphasis on objects from the nineteenth and early twentieth centuries. The "container" flow is being reversed, good news for America's trade deficit.

The decade of the 1980s saw two major shifts in the way business was conducted in the antiques and collectibles field. The outdoor flea market was replaced by the indoor dealer cooperative and mall. Although flea markets will linger, their heyday is over.

The second trend was the growth of the mail order auction. Whether conducted from formally issued catalogs or through advertisements in specialized trade papers, the mail auction has come of age. The mail auction is an unlicensed, unregulated form of business. Here rests both its strengths and weaknesses.

Will the buoyancy of the late 1980s will be sustained as we enter the 1990s? The test will come in fall 1989. Get ready.

AUCTION HOUSES AND DEALERS

The following auction houses and dealers cooperated with Warman Publishing Co. by providing catalogs of their auctions and/or sales. This support is most appreciated.

Sanford Alderfer Auction
501 Fairgrounds Rd.
Hatfield, PA 19440
(215) 368-5477

W. Graham Arader III
1000 Boxwood Court
King of Prussia, PA
19406
(215) 825-6570

Ark Antiques
Box 3133
New Haven, CT 06515
(203) 387-3754

Arman Absentee
Auctions
RR 1 Box 353A
Woodstock, CT 06281
(203) 928-5838

Arthur Auctioneering
R. D. 2
Hughesville, PA 17737
(717) 584-3697

Noel Barrett Antiques
and Auctions Ltd.
Carversville, PA 18913
(215) 297-5109

Robert F. Batchelder
1 West Butler Avenue
Ambler, PA 19002
(215) 643-1430

Richard A. Bourne Co.
Corporation St.
P. O. Box 141
Hyannis, MA 02647
(617) 775-0797

Butterfield's
1244 Sutter St.
San Francisco, CA
94109
(415) 673-1362

Christie's
502 Park Avenue
New York, NY 10022
(212) 546-1000

Christie's East
219 E. 67th St.
New York, NY 10021
(212) 546-1000

Marvin Cohen Auctions
Box 425, Rts 20 & 22
New Lebanon, NY
12125
(518) 794-7477

Marlin G. Denlinger
RR 3, Box 3775
Morrisville, VT 05661
(802) 888-2774

Robert A. Doyle
Doyle Auctioneers &
Appraisers
R. D. 3, Box 137
Fishkill, NY 12524
(914) 896-9492

William Doyle Galleries
175 E. 87th St.
New York, NY 10028
(212) 427-2730

Early Auction Co.
123 Main St.
Milford, OH 45150
(513) 831-4833

Fine Arts Co. of
Philadelphia, Inc.
2317 Chestnut St.
Philadelphia, PA 19103
(215) 564-3644

Ron Fox
F. T. S. Inc.
416 Throop St.
N. Babylon, NY 11704
(516) 669-7232

Garth's Auction, Inc.
2690 Stratford Rd.
P. O. Box 369
Delaware, OH 43015
(614) 362-4771 or 369-
5085

Glass-Works Auctions
P. O. Box 187
East Greenville, PA
18041
(215) 679-5849

Guerney's
Tuxedo Park, NY 10987
(212) 794-2280

Hake's Americana and
Collectibles
P. O. Box 1444
York, PA 17405
(717) 848-1333

Harmer Rooke Galleries
3 East 57th St.
New York, NY 10022
(212) 751-1900

Harris Auction Galleries
873-875 N. Howard St.
Baltimore, MD 21201
(301) 728-7040

Norman C. Heckler &
Company
Bradford Corner Rd.
Woodstock Valley, CT
06282
(203) 974-0682

Leslie Hindman, Inc.
215 West Ohio St.
Chicago, IL 60610
(312) 670-0010

James D. Julia, Inc.
Route 209
RFD 1, Box 830
Fairfield, ME 04937
(207) 453-7904

Mid-Hudson Auction
Galleries
One Idlewild Ave.
Cornwall-On-Hudson,
NY 12520
(914) 534-7828

Milwaukee Auction
Galleries
4747 West Bradley Rd.
Milwaukee, WI 53223
(414) 355-5054

Neal Alford Company
4139 Magazine St.
New Orleans, LA 70115
(504) 899-5329

New England Auction
Gallery
Box 8087
East Lynn, MA 01904
(617) 581-5366

New Hampshire Book
Auctions
Woodbury Rd.
Weare, NH 03281
(603) 529-1700

Nostalgia Publications
21 South Lake Dr.
Hackensack, NJ 07601
(201) 488-4536

Pettigrew Auction
Company
405 S. Nevada Ave.
Colorado Springs, CO
80903

Phillips
406 East 79th St.
New York, NY 10021
(212) 570-4830

David Rago Arts &
Crafts
P. O. Box 3592 Station E
Trenton, NJ 08629
(609) 585-2546

Lloyd Ralston Toys
447 Stratfield Rd.
Fairfield, CT 06432
(203) 366-3399 or 335-
4054

R. Niel & Elaine
Reynolds
Box 133
Waterford, VA 22190
(703) 882-3574

Roan Bros. Auction
Gallery
R.D. 3, Box 118
Cogan Station, PA 17728
(717) 494-0170

Savoia's Auction
Services
Route 23
South Cairo, NJ 12482
(518) 622-8000

Robert W. Skinner Inc.
Bolton Gallery
Route 117
Bolton, MA 01740
(617) 779-5528

Smith House Toy Sales
26 Adlington Rd.
Eliot, ME 03903
(207) 439-4614

Sotheby's
1334 York Avenue
New York, NY 10021
(212) 472-8424

Swann Galleries, Inc.
104 E. 25th St.
New York, NY 10010
(212) 254-4710

George Theofiles
Miscellaneous Man
Box 1776
New Freedom, PA 17349
(717) 235-4766

Waverlys Auctions
7649 Old Georgetown Rd.
Bethesda, MD 20814
(301) 951-0919

Winter Associates
21 Cooke St. Box 823
Plainville, CT 06062
(203) 793-0288

Wolf's Auction Gallery
13015 Larchmere Blvd.
Shaker Heights, OH
44120
(216) 231-3888

Woody Auction
Douglass, KS 67039
(316) 746-2694

ABBREVIATIONS

The following are standard abbreviations which we have used throughout this edition.

ah =	applied handle	litho =	lithograph
C =	century	ls =	low standard
c =	circa	MIB =	mint in box
circ =	circular	mkd =	marked
cov =	cover	MOP =	mother of pearl
d =	diameter or depth	NE =	New England
dec =	decorated	No. =	number
DQ =	Diamond Quilted	opal =	opalescent
emb =	embossed	orig =	original
ext. =	exterior	os =	orig stopper
FE =	first edition	pat =	patent
ftd =	footed	pcs =	pieces
ground =	background	pr =	pair
h =	height	rect =	rectangular
hp =	hand painted	sgd =	signed
hs =	high standard	sngl =	single
imp =	impressed	SP =	silver plated
int. =	interior	SS =	Sterling silver
irid =	iridescent	sq =	square
IVT =	inverted thumbprint	w =	width
j =	jewels	yg =	yellow gold
K =	karat	# =	numbered
l =	length		

ABC PLATES

History: The majority of early ABC plates were manufactured in England, imported into the United States, and achieved their greatest popularity from 1780 to 1860. Since a formal education was limited in the early 19th century, the ABC plate was a method of educating the poor for a few pennies.

ABC plates are found in glass, pewter, porcelain, pottery, and tin. Porcelain plates range in diameter from 4⅜ to slightly over 9½ inches. The rim usually contains the alphabet and/or numbers; the center features animals, great men, maxims, or nursery rhymes.

Reference: Susan and Al Bagdade, *Warman's English & Continental Pottery & Porcelain, 1st Edition,* Warman Publishing Co., Inc., 1987; Mildred L. and Joseph P. Chalala, *A Collector's Guide to ABC Plates, Mugs and Things,* Pridemark Press, 1980.

GLASS

6"

Garfield, frosted center	110.00
Hen and Chicks	45.00
Star Medallion, pattern glass	40.00
Thousand Eye, blue, clock center, pattern glass	65.00
Westward Ho, pattern glass	50.00
6¼", Christmas Morning, frosted center scene, stippled alphabet border	165.00
6¾", Independence Hall, 1776–1876	135.00
7", clear, clock, sq, stippled, ruffled edge	15.00

PORCELAIN OR POTTERY

5½"

Children, dog, parrot, and verse, multicolored transfer center, emb alphabet border	30.00
Gathering Cotton, raised alphabet border, multicolored center scene, Staffordshire	200.00
5¾", girls in flower garden, black transfer center, emb alphabet border, marked "J. & G. Meakin," 1851	50.00

6"

Fox and Grapes, black and white, red trim, marked "J. Meir & Son, Tunstall, England"	38.00
Franklin Maxim Proverb, "If You Would Know The Value Of Money Try To Borrow Some - Creditors Have Better Memories Than Debtors," two men in an office	110.00
Hesitation, Matrimonial Ladder, lady and gentleman strolling through park, Staffordshire	200.00

Robinson Crusoe On The Raft	140.00
The Drive, raised alphabet border, center scene of couple in open horse drawn carriage, Staffordshire	110.00
6½", Noah and the Ark, religious transfer center, emb alphabet border	40.00

6¾"

Canary, Bullfinch and Goldfinch, polychrome transfer of birds, emb alphabet border	60.00
Franklin Maxim Proverb, "He That Hath A Trade Hath An Estate - Industry Pays Debts While Despair Increases Them," blacksmith scene, relief letter border	145.00
My Face Is My Fortune, bulldog sitting in grass, brown and white, marked "C. A. & Son, England," c1890–1912	50.00
7", Teddy Bears Playing Tennis, multicolored transfer center, printed alphabet border	100.00
7½", Cricket Game, multicolored, Staffordshire	125.00
7¾", Who Killed Cock Robin	40.00
8", Stable Yard, horse and foal	50.00

Tin, 7⅞" d, Who Killed Cock Robin, $48.00.

TIN

3"

Girl and boy rolling hoop	140.00
Tom Thumb	30.00
4¼", Sir Colin Campbell, KCB, emb man riding horse in center, alphabet border	200.00
5½", Liberty	55.00
6", two kittens playing with yarn	35.00
6¼", Victoria and Albert	60.00

8"

Monkey on Barrel, litho	60.00

Peter Rabbit, litho, colorful center
scene, alphabet border **45.00**
9", Hey Diddle Diddle **45.00**

ADAMS ROSE

History: Adams Rose, made c1820–40 by Adams and Son in the Staffordshire district of England, is decorated with brilliant red roses and green leaves on a white ground.

G. Jones and Son, England, made a variant known as "Late Adams Rose." The colors are not as brilliant and the ground is a "dirty" white. It commands less than the price of the early pattern.

Reference: Susan and Al Bagdade, *Warman's English & Continental Pottery & Porcelain, 1st Edition,* Warman Publishing Co., Inc., 1987.

Plate, 7¼" d, early, $145.00.

Bowl, 9", early, mint, rare size **450.00**
Creamer, 5¾", early **300.00**
Cup and Saucer, handleless
  Early **200.00**
  Late, rose dec on saucer, blue spatter **75.00**
Plate
  8", vine border, early, imp mark **225.00**
  8,½", early **180.00**
  9", early **200.00**
  9¼", emb scalloped rim, late **60.00**
Platter
  12" l, late **85.00**
  17⅝" l, emb scalloped rim, early . . . **435.00**
Soup Plate
  10¼", early **200.00**
  10½", late **55.00**
Sugar, cov early **300.00**
Tea Bowl and Saucer, early **175.00**
Teapot, cov
  Early **600.00**
  Late **200.00**
Vegetable, early
  10¾" l **100.00**
  12⅝" l, cov **500.00**

ADVERTISING

History: Before the days of mass media, advertisers relied on colorful product labels and advertising giveaways to promote their products. Containers were made to appeal to the buyer by the use of stylish lithographs and bright colors. Many of the illustrations used the product in the advertisement so that even an illiterate buyer could identify a product.

Advertisements were put on almost every household object imaginable and were constant reminders to use the product or visit a certain establishment.

References: Al Bergevin, *Food And Drink Containers And Their Prices,* Wallace-Homestead, 1988; Ray Klug, *Antique Advertising Encyclopedia,* Vol. 1 (1978) and Vol. 2 (1985), L-W Promotions; Ralph and Terry Kovel, *Kovels' Advertising Collectibles Price List,* Crown Publishers Inc., 1986; Robert W. and Harriet Swedberg, *Tins "n" Bins,* Wallace-Homestead, 1985.

Collectors' Clubs: The Ephemera Society of America, 124 Elm Street, Bennington, VT 05021.; National Association of Paper and Advertising Collectibles, P. O. Box 500, Mount Joy, PA 17552.; Tin Container Collectors Association, 11650 Riverside Drive, North Hollywood, CA 91602.

Additional Listings: See *Warman's Americana & Collectibles* for more examples.

Almanac, The Diamond Dye Almanac, 1888, 6 x 8¼", $17.50.

Ashtray
  Bengal Gin, ceramic, tiger **35.00**
  Hardwick Stove Co., skillet, porcelain
    over cast iron, 4", black, white letters, marked **20.00**
  Mountain States Telephone, porcelain **85.00**
Bank
  Hershey's Chocolate **10.00**

Swank Shoe Polish, telephone shape ... **35.00**

Banner
Blue Lick Health Water, Blue Lick Springs, KY, 12 x 48", yellow and white, blue canvas **45.00**
Occident Flour, cloth **275.00**

Bill Clamp, Wingold, Baystate Milling Co, celluloid, multicolored **20.00**

Blotter, unused
Green River Whiskey **20.00**
Reid's Ice Cream, pretty lady **35.00**

Bookmark
Carnation Milk, celluloid **25.00**
Mr. Peanut **15.00**
Poole Piano, celluloid **12.50**

Bottle Carrier, Pepsi Cola, cloth **50.00**

Butter Crock, blue Meadowbrook Butter adv, Red Wing **60.00**

Button Hook, Bond Street Spats **20.00**

Calendar
Garr-Scott Thresher Co, 1911 ..... **225.00**
Osborne Machinery Co, 1909 ..... **85.00**
Singer Sewing Machine, tin, green and white, yellow trim, lady using her Singer, cardboard back, complete set of day, number, and month cards, 19 x 13½" **200.00**
Walter A. Wood Mowing & Reaping Machine Co, 1890 .... **75.00**

Carpet, Roberts Men's Shoes, 27 x 60" **55.00**

Change Receiver, Don Diego Cigars, glass **25.00**

Change Tray
Century Beer, Schneider Brewing Co, Trinidad, CO **135.00**
White Rock Table Water, rect, semi nude **95.00**

Clock
Activator Shoes, light up type, black dial, white numbers and hands, black border with white lettering top, white border with red lettering bottom **250.00**
Orange Crush, electric, Art Deco, reverse painting on glass **500.00**
Vision Baking Powder, short drop regulator style, 25" l **225.00**

Cookie Cutter, Davis Baking Powder, tin, marked, set **40.00**

Cooler
Pepsi Cola, raised bottle cap logo, 1940s **200.00**
7-Up **45.00**

Corkscrew, Kentucky Taylor Whiskey, 3½", wood handle **15.00**

Delivery Box, wood, lacquered, 18 x 26 x 8", sides marked "Property of General Baking Co," ends marked "Bond Rolls 5-52" **50.00**

Dish, Clark's Teaberry Gum, amethyst **45.00**

Dominos, Marlboro Cigarette, eighteen pcs **30.00**

Door Push
Camel Cigarettes, tin, dancing cigarette packs **45.00**
Millbrook Bread, enamel over steel, blue and white, loaf shaped center brown bag front, "Thanks! Call Again" on back, 30" l **25.00**
Red Rose Tea **120.00**

Egg Separator, South Bend Range, tin **6.00**

Fan, hand
The Winchester Store, P.A. Krause & Sons, Fullerton, NE **35.00**
20 Mule-Team Borax **75.00**
Zig-Zag Candy, honeycomb inside, makes designs **40.00**

Box, Grandpa's Wonder Soap, Beaver Soap Co., Dayton, OH, 2½ x 4¼ x 1½", $12.50.

Sign, Burger Beer, Cincinnati's Famous Beer, 8 x 14¼", $75.00.

Fishing Bobber, Kikkoman All Purpose Soy Sauce, wood, Japanese fan, bamboo, and fish underwater **10.00**

Game, Champion Spark Plug, board, 1930s **40.00**

Humidor, cov
Bagdad Tobacco, china, pictures Turkish soldier 30.00
Imperial Tobacco, colorful college flags 35.00
Jar
Rexall, window display, porcelain . . 45.00
Sunshine Coffee, lion logo, replaced lid 18.00
Jug, stoneware
J.H. Kerns Sunnyside Saloon, black adv, cream ground, 2 gallons 75.00
Litha Spring Water, Londonderry, NH, cobalt slip longhand dec, 3 gallons 385.00
Standard Bottling, Denver 35.00
Letter Opener
Dioxogen Chemical Co., celluloid handle 15.00
GE 15.00
Lunch Box
Blue Tiger Tobacco, tin, tiger at each end, two handles 160.00
Salerno Finest Cookies, tin, oak handles 45.00
Match Holder
De Laval Cream Separator 240.00
Laxets, tin 110.00
Moxie 330.00
Menu Board, Budweiser, reverse painting on glass 425.00
Milk Bottle Crate, B & B Dairy, Brookhaven, MS, emb, weathered wood slats, metal bottom, 16 x 13 x 11" . . 20.00
Mirror
Ceresota Flour 35.00
Mascot Tobacco 45.00

Button, Shoot Peters Shells and Cartridges, ⅞″ d, celluloid, gold, blue, and red, $25.00.

Mixing Bowl, Levitz Furniture Co, 8″ d . 30.00
Mug
A & W Root Beer, small 20.00
Hires Root Beer, boy with mug, Mettlach 150.00
Needle Kit, Aunt Jemima Flour 23.00
Paper Dolls, Kis-Me Gum, uncut 30.00
Paperweight
Dutch Boy Paints, lead, raised Dutch Boy on front 25.00
New York Telephone Company, Local & Long Distance Telephone, glass, cobalt, gray enamel lettering, 3″ h 100.00
Pencil Sharpener, Baker Chocolate, figural, lady 35.00
Pocket Mirror
American Line Steamship, Philadelphia 65.00
Applegarth's Oysters, 3½″ d 20.00
Bell's Coffee 45.00
Horlick's Malted Milk Extra Fine . . . 65.00
Panama Carbon Paper, 3½″ d 20.00
Poster
Haig Scotch, 50 x 90″, Uncle Sam, Lady Liberty, Spirit of St. Louis '27 1,600.00
Mentor Bicycles, young girls riding, c1890 . . . . 750.00
Zwieback, comical baby 425.00
Pot Scraper, tin
Junket Powder 125.00
Red Wing Milling Co 300.00
Royal Granite Ware 240.00
Puzzle, Campfire Marshmallow, orig adv mailer 10.00
Rolling Pin, "Guenthers Sells It For Less, Phone No. 1, Lake City, Iowa," stoneware 165.00
Salt and Pepper Shakers, pr, Kool Cigarettes, plastic, penguins Millie and Willie 10.00
Shoe Horn, Shinola Shoe Polish, metal, 1907 . . . . 30.00
Sifter, tin, wood handle
Browmwell's Flour, yellow handle . . 15.00
Calumet Baking Powder 10.00
Perfect Flour 10.00
Sign
Banquet Ice Cream, cardboard, diecut, woman and child eating ice cream, woman's arms move 750.00
Budweiser, pool table type, electrical 235.00
Canadian Frontenac Ale 145.00
Fairbanks Scales, porcelain 130.00
Kis-Me Gum, tin, red headed woman, self framed 800.00
L.C. Smith & Bros. Typewriters, tin, emb, horseshoe, horse, and typewriter 750.00
Meerschaum Tobacco, diecut, cats . 85.00
Newport Kentucky Whiskey, tin, fortune teller, woman reading cards, self framed 2,500.00

Tobacco Tin, Chicago Cubs Chewing Tobacco, Rock City Tobacco Co, Quebec, 6⅜ x 4⅜ x 4", eagle, blue border, gold ground, $125.00.

Orange Crush, 1940	**65.00**
Splendid Varnish, emb, Victorian room scene	**575.00**
Tape Measure, celluloid	
Crown Flour	**30.00**
John Deere, 1¾" d	**35.00**
Tea Bag Holder, Servit Tea, figural ½ cup, china	**20.00**
Thermometer	
Cleo Cola, round, reverse painting on convex glass, 10"	**600.00**
Dad's Root Beer, tin, emb, gold, red and blue lettering and label, brown bottle, dad on label, glass rod, 26" h, 10"w	**60.00**
Honey Krust Bread, 16", tin, red and blue loaf, white ground	**85.00**
Kayo Chocolate, tin	**100.00**
Peters Weatherbird Shoes, porcelain, 27" h	**150.00**

Tin Container, Shamokin Packing Co., 2 pound pail, 4¾" d, 4¾" h, wire handle, Indian motif, blue ground and top, $30.00.

T. G. Buckley Moving Company, green metal case, yellow face, black adv, green and white moving van, 9" d	**40.00**
Tin	
Addingley's Liquorice, 3 x 4"	**15.00**
Continental Cubes, pocket, 5" h . . .	**110.00**
Cornell Tobacco	**40.00**
Sure Shot Chewing Tobacco, litho, 16" w, 11" d	**375.00**
Sweet Cuba, litho, 8" w	**95.00**
Tray, litho, tin	
Crown Baking Powder, litho, 10" . . .	**175.00**
Esso, Tony the Tiger	**20.00**
Martha Washington Wine, Texas . . .	**95.00**
Rainier Beer, 13"	**110.00**
Red Raven, little girl and red raven .	**450.00**
Tray, tip	
Cottolene Lard, blacks picking cotton	**150.00**
Lemon-Kola	**90.00**
Stegmaier Beer, 4¼"	**35.00**
Taka Cola, litho, tin	**75.00**
Washboard, Quapaw Zinc Products, metal	**60.00**
Watch Fob	
Bartlett, Shotts, & Wilson Millwork, Pittsburgh, black on yellow, enameled	**20.00**
Du Pont Workers, celluloid photo, Hopewell, #5391	**25.00**
GE Erie Works, blue and white enamel	**15.00**
Windshield Visor, car shape, garage adv	**30.00**
Whistle	
Aunt Jemima, dated 1919	**100.00**
Dairy Queen, cone shape, plastic . .	**15.00**
Jack & Jill Gelatin, tin, litho	**30.00**
Wrench, AC Filter Service	**35.00**

ADVERTISING TRADE CARDS

History: Advertising trade cards are small, thin cardboard cards made to advertise the merits of a product and usually bear the name and address of a merchant.

With the invention of lithography, colorful trade cards became a popular advertising media in the late 19th and early 20th centuries. They were made especially to appeal to children. Young and old alike collected and treasured them in albums and scrapbooks. Very few are dated; 1880 to 1893 were the prime years for trade cards; 1810 to 1850 cards can be found, but rarely. By 1900 trade cards were rapidly losing their popularity. By 1910 they had all but vanished.

References: Kit Barry, *The Advertising Trade Card*, Book 1, Iris Publishing Co., 1981; John and Margaret Kaduck, *Advertising Trade Cards*, privately printed; Robert Jay, *The Trade Card In*

Nineteenth-Century America, University of Missouri Press, 1987;

Jim and Cathy McQuary, *Collectors Guide To Advertising Cards,* L-W Promotions, 1975; Murray Card (International) Ltd., *Cigarette Card Values: Murray's 1988 Guide To Cigarette & Other Trade Cards,* published by author, 1988.

Periodical: *Trade Card Journal,* 86 High Street, Brattleboro, VT 05301. Quarterly.

Additional Listings: See *Warman's Americana & Collectibles* for more examples.

CLOTHING

Beals, Torrey & Co., Boots and Shoes, Palmer Cox brownies	6.50
Edwin Burt Fine Shoes, children's tea party scene	5.00
M.V. Prevost, Fine Millinery, diecut, fan shape, comical animals	1.00
Star Braid, girl driving butterfly chariot	6.00
Wheeler & Wilson, two ladies making dress	5.00

COFFEE

Banan-Nutro, mechanical, woman raises cup to her lips, white, yellow, brown, purple, and red	15.00
Great Atlantic & Pacific Tea Co., Dinah praises A & P teas and coffees, black landlord and renter's conversation on bottom, adv on back, 1884, 8 x 9″	20.00
Victor Coffee, four horses pulling chariot	6.00

FARM MACHINERY

Enterprise Raising Seeder	10.00
McCormick, diecut, hand shape	10.00
Princess Plow Co., Canton, OH, The Princess of Wales Plow, full color, 4 page, Princess on cover, illus of farm plows on 3 pgs	12.00
Sharples Bros., Philadelphia, cream separator, chromolitho of girl and bunny	12.00

FOOD

Arm & Hammer Baking Soda, bird series, set of 15	10.00
Dixon's Ice Cream, Kearny Statue in Military Park	6.00
Hecker's Buckweat, hold to light	18.00
Heinz Pickles, child carrying products in wicker basket, logo on hat	3.00
Homogenized Bond Bread, movie star series, set of 52	25.00
Pillsbury's Flour, three ladies on a top, wearing flowing gowns	7.00
Ridge's Food, child shakes rattle over baby's head	4.00

Food, Pillsbury XXXX Best Flour, two black children floating in tub, flour sack for sale, multicolored, printed by A. Hoen & Co, Baltimore, $7.00.

Scheuer's Kew-Bee Bread, mechanical, child, eyes move, 3⅛ x 4″	20.00
Thurber's Canned Vegetables	5.00
Wilson's Beef, Indian plans ambush to steel beef	7.00

Soap, French Laundry Soap, diecut frog, 3⅝ x 2¹³⁄₁₆″, adv on back, printed by Kendall Manuf Co., Providence, RI, $4.50.

LAUNDRY AND SOAPS

Geneva Hand Fluter, young lady fluting her petticoat, two kittens playing under table, 3¾″	5.00
Niagara Starch, well dressed, long haired lady holding box, full color, 3 x 4½″	4.00
Packer's Tar Soap, mother washing baby, full color	2.00

Star Soap, The Best For Family Use,
elegantly dressed lady, full color . . .   **2.00**

MEDICINE

Ayers Pills, lovely lady taking pill	**8.00**
Dr Seth Arnold's Cough Killer, girl holding puppy	**5.00**
Evarosa, portrait of woman	**3.00**
Krauter Bitters, 3 folds, elaborate center panel	**3.50**
Quaker Bitters, The Brighton Belle . . .	**7.50**
Schenk's Pulmonic Syrup, hold to light scene, sleeping children and kitten .	**10.00**

MISCELLANEOUS

Agate Iron Ware, chromolitho of children beating on pots and pans	**20.00**
Buckingham's Dye For The Whiskers, metamorphic, gentleman with chest length white beard changes to black beard, adv on back, 3 x 3½" closed	**10.00**
Dutch Boy Paints, mechanical, feet move, diecut, blue, white, yellow, and red, 6" h	**12.00**
McAuslan & Wahelin Co. Toyland, Holyoke, MA, mechanical, Santa writes on blackboard, black, white, and red, adv on back	**35.00**
Metropolitan Life, diecut chromolitho of three little girls having tea party, boy wearing baker's hat, c1900	**25.00**
Nevius & Haviland Shades, hunting dog	**8.50**
New Home, hold to light, rags to riches	**8.00**
Royal Glue, Capitol building, Washington DC	**6.00**

PIANOS AND ORGANS

Jesse French & Sons Piano Co., bookmark, lady, rose in hair, full color, black and white vignette of factory .	**5.00**
Patterson Organs, parlor scene	**4.00**
Waterloo Organs, Malcolm Love & Co., lady seated in front of ornate parlor organ, full color	**5.00**

STOVES AND RANGES

Dixon's Stove Polish, child listening to watch	**6.00**
Happy Thought Range, diecut jelly roll	**4.00**
Noble Cook Stoves, early wood stove, happy chef	**10.00**

THREAD AND SEWING

J & P Coats, Nancy Hanks, famous trotting mare	**9.50**
Merrick's Thread, titled "In Search of the North Pole," hot air balloon	**5.00**

Wheeler & Wilson, delivery of sewing
machine by buggy to prosperous rural
family, full color, black and white illus
on back with adv, horizontal, 3 x 5" .   **6.00**

TOBACCO

Allen & Ginter, fish series, booklet of 50	**75.00**
Horsehead Tobacco, horse's head, plug in mouth	**8.50**
King Bull 3¢ Cigar, risque metamorphic, diecut opening, adv on back, 3 x 5½" closed	**25.00**
Lang's Plug, barometer card, before and after chewing	**8.00**
Newsboy Plug, "Where is Mother," five puppies	**5.00**
Vetern Tobacco, soldier, windmill	**8.00**

AGATA GLASS

History: Agata glass was invented in 1887 by Joseph Locke of the New England Glass Company, Cambridge, Massachusetts.

Agata glass was produced by using a piece of peachblow glass, coating it with metallic stain, spattering the surface with alcohol, and firing. The result was a high gloss, mottled appearance of oil droplets floating on a watery surface. Shading usually ranged from opaque pink to dark rose. Pieces are known in a pastel opaque green. A few pieces have been found in a satin finish.

Vase, 8", extended neck, $1,800.00.

Bowl, 4⅛" d, green opaque	**275.00**
Celery, 6½" h, crimped top	**1,750.00**
Finger Bowl, ruffled top	**875.00**
Lemonade, 1⅝" d base, 2½" d top, 5⅛" h, NE peachblow shading, pronounced mottling, gold tracery	**1,250.00**
Plate, 6⅝" d, ribbon candy fluted rim .	**850.00**

Punch Cup, green opaque	285.00
Spooner, 4⅛" d, 3¾" h, green opaque, mottled band with gold border	950.00
Toothpick, bulbous, pinched in scalloped rim	800.00
Tumbler, green opaque, fine mottling and gold	750.00
Vase, 8½" h, bulbous stick	700.00

AMBERINA GLASS

History: Joseph Locke developed Amberina glass in 1883 for the New England Glass Works. "Amberina," a trade name, describes a transparent glass which shades from deep ruby to amber color. It was made by adding powdered gold to the ingredients for an amber glass batch. A portion of the glass was reheated later to produce the shading effect. Usually it was the bottom which was reheated to form the deep red; however, reverse examples have been found.

Most early Amberina is of flint quality glass, blown or pattern molded. Patterns include Diamond Quilted, Daisy and Button, Venetian Diamond, Diamond and Star, and Thumbprint.

In addition to the New England Glass Works, the Mt. Washington Glass Company of New Bedford, Massachusetts, copied the glass in the 1880s and sold it at first under the Amberina trade name and later as "Rose Amber." It is difficult to distinguish pieces from these two New England factories. Boston and Sandwich Glass Works never produced the glass.

Amberina glass also was made in the 1890s by several Midwest factories, among which was Hobbs, Brockunier & Co. Trade names included "Ruby Amber Ware" and "Watermelon." The Midwest glass shaded from cranberry to amber and resulted from a thin flashing of cranberry applied to the reheated portion. This created a sharp demarkation between the two colors. This less expensive version caused the death knell for the New England variety.

In 1884 Edward D. Libbey was assigned the trade name "Amberina" by the New England Glass Works. Production occured in 1900, but ceased shortly thereafter. In the 1920s Edward Libbey renewed production at his Toledo, Ohio, plant for a short period. The glass was of high quality. Amberina from this era is marked "Libbey" in script on the pontil.

Reproduction Alert: Reproductions abound.

NEW ENGLAND

Basket, 7" h, handle, marked "Libbey"	1,500.00
Bowl	
4⅞", DQ, Mt Washington	175.00
5", ruffled, marked "Libbey"	145.00
7½", DQ	275.00

Punch Cup, Baby Thumbprint pattern, applied clear reeded handle, attributed to New England, $100.00.

8", rolled, turned down, scalloped rim, deep ribbing, three applied amber feet, Libbey	800.00
Bride's Basket, ribbed, ruffled, SP holder	650.00
Butter Pat, 3½" d, paneled	175.00
Carafe	
8¼", IVT, reverse color, applied amber dec at neck	175.00
8½", DQ, Sandwich	200.00
Celery Vase	
6¾" h, 4" d base, Venetian Diamond, sq scalloped top, polished pontil, Mt Washington	335.00
7", DQ, scalloped top	375.00
Champagne, 4", hollow stem	200.00
Cologne Bottle, 6", Daisy and Button, orig stopper	2,225.00
Creamer, 5½", IVT	285.00
Cruet	
5", Sawtooth, applied amber handle, orig stopper, Mt Washington	375.00
6¾", Thumbprint, reverse color, applied amber handle, orig faceted stopper	265.00
Finger Bowl	
5", DQ, reverse color, Sandwich	90.00
5½ x 2¾", fluted	225.00
Jug, 5¾", IVT, applied reeded amber handle, Mt Washington	350.00
Lamp Shade, 8½" d, 4⅜" fitter ring, Daisy and Button	250.00
Lemonade, DQ, applied ring handle	275.00
Marmalade, cov, 5½", IVT, white metal cov, Mt Washington	165.00
Perfume Bottle, 4¾" h, bulbous, long dauber stopper, sgd "Libbey," orig paper label	600.00
Pitcher	
5", Melon Herringbone, sq, applied amber handle	235.00

6½", IVT, sq mouth, applied clear
reeded handle 435.00
7", DQ, tankard, round mouth, applied
amber handle 325.00
Punch Cup, DQ, deep color, applied
amber reeded handle 100.00
Rose Bowl, 5⅛", paneled, ftd, Mt Wash-
ington 300.00
Sherbet, 5" d, 5" h, sgd "Libbey," 1917 365.00
Spooner, 3⅛ x 4½", DQ, sq scalloped
top 240.00
Sugar, cov, 4¼", IVT 350.00
Tumble-Up, 8½", DQ, reverse color . . 550.00
Tumbler, 3¾" h, DQ, Sandwich 150.00
Vase
5⅜", DQ, deep color, attributed to Mt.
Washington 250.00
7", lily shape, paneled 150.00
Whiskey, 2⅝", DQ 125.00

MIDWESTERN

Bowl
4½", DQ, three applied feet 115.00
5", Daisy and Button, sq 85.00
Bride's Basket, 10" d, hobnail, amber
handle, enamel clover dec 350.00
Celery, Inverted Coinspot 65.00
Creamer, 4½", Hobnail, applied clear
reeded handle 175.00
Decanter, 11", orig amber bubble stop-
per 150.00
Finger Bowl, Coinspot 125.00
Jack-In-The Pulpit Vase, 9⅞", heavy
gold enamel flowers, blue enamel dec 225.00
Lamp, hanging, hall, 9 x 10", hobnail,
ornate brass trim and fittings 350.00
Pickle Castor, 2⅞" d, IVT 165.00
Pitcher, 8½", melon ribbed, applied am-
ber strap handle 200.00
Punch Cup, Expanded Diamond, ap-
plied amber handle 85.00
Salt Shaker, Baby IVT, reverse color,
pewter top 170.00
Spooner, DQ, reverse color 115.00
Sugar, cov, 5¼ x 4½", Thumbprint, two
handles, ribbed, quatrefoil top 150.00
Tumbler, Swirl, heavy enamel floral dec 85.00
Vase, 8⅛", Swirl, fan top, amber edge,
applied amber wishbone feet 125.00

AMBERINA GLASS—PLATED

History: The New England Glass Company,
Cambridge, Massachusetts, first made Plated Amberina in 1886; Edward Libbey patented the process for the company in 1889.

Plated Amberina was made by taking a gather
of chartreuse or cream opalescent glass, dipping
it in Amberina and working the two, often utilizing
a mold. The finished product had a deep amber to
deep ruby red shading, a fiery opalescent lining,
and often vertical ribbing for enhancement. Designs ranged from simple forms to complex pieces
with collars, feet, gilding, and etching.

A cased Wheeling glass of similar appearance
had an opaque white lining, but is not opalescent
and the body is not ribbed.

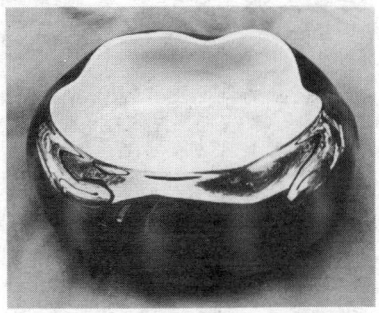

**Bowl, 7¾ x 3¾", bulbous, scalloped
top, New England Glass Co., $2,750.00.**

Bowl, 8" d, 3¼" h, ruffled 1,650.00
Creamer, squatty, applied clear amber
handle 3,000.00
Cruet, 6¼" h, deeply ribbed, trefoil top,
amber handle and faceted stopper . 3,600.00
Pitcher, 6½", paneled, applied clear am-
ber handle 4,500.00
Salt Shaker, ribbed 900.00
Spooner, 4", paneled, ground pontil . . 2,000.00
Tumbler, 3¾" 1,850.00
Vase, 3¼", bulbous 2,400.00

AMPHORA

History: The Amphora Porcelain Works was
one of several pottery companies located in the
Teplitz-Turn region of Bohemia in the late 19th
and early 20th centuries. It is best known for art
pottery, especially Art Nouveau and Art Deco
pieces.

Several markings were used, including the
name and location of the pottery and the Imperial
mark which included a crown. Prior to WWI Bohemia was part of the Austro-Hungarian Empire so
the word "Austria" may appear as part of the mark;

after WWI the word "Czechoslovakia" may be part of the mark.

Reference: Susan and Al Bagdade, *Warman's English & Continental Pottery & Porcelain, 1st Edition,* Warman Publishing Co., Inc., 1987.

Additional Listings: Teplitz.

Vase, 6″ h, dragon fly dec, sgd, $100.00.

Basket
7½″, double handles, flower dec, sgd	**65.00**
12″ h, bearded man, imp "Imperial, Amphora"	**175.00**

Bowl, 8″, beige, raised apples, vines, and leaves, ftd **165.00**

Bust, 16″ h, woman, low cut dress, ruffled neckline, marked "Turn Teplitz-Bohemia" and "Amphora, Austria, RS & K" **275.00**

Compote, double handles, applied blackberries, Imperial mark **200.00**

Ewer
7½″, bulbous, pinched, blown out cobalt floral top, mottled green and brown, large red and green leaves, flowing leaf handles, imp crown mark **175.00**
9″, hp, mosaic panels, marked "Amphora-Teplitz" **75.00**
15″, pear shape, purple and cream flowers, green ground, applied root handle **125.00**

Mug, 5¾″, fox and bear, imp crown mark, c1891 .... **100.00**

Pitcher, 10½″, cat, whimsical, red ribbon, marked "Amphora, Austria" ... **165.00**

Rose Bowl, white, cobalt trim, enamel flowers and leaves **85.00**

Vase
6″, floral dec, artist sgd	**200.00**
9″, Art Deco incised bird and flowers	**120.00**
13¼″, swelled cylindrical, beige pebbled bodies, panel of birds on branch, mauve and blue band at neck, low blue foot, pr	**200.00**

16½ x 9½″, emb basketweave, applied blackberries, c1920 .... **400.00**

ARCHITECTURAL ELEMENTS

History: Architectural elements are those items which have been removed or salvaged from buildings, ships, or gardens. Many are hand crafted. Frequently they are carved in stone or exotic woods. Part of their desirability is due to the fact that it would be almost impossible to duplicate the items today.

The current trend of preservation and recycling architectural elements has lead to the establishment and growth of organized salvage operations who specialize in removal and resale of elements. Special auctions are now held to sell architectural elements from churches, mansions, office buildings, etc. Today's decorators often design an entire room around one architectural element, such as a Victorian marble bar or mural, or use several as key accent pieces.

References: J. L. Mott Iron Works, *Mott's Illustrated Catalog of Victorian Plumbing Fixtures For Bathrooms and Kitchens,* Dover Publications, 1987; Alan Robertson, *Architectural Antiques,* Chronicle Books, 1987; J. P. White's Pyghtle Works, Bedford, England, *Garden Furniture And Ornament,* Apollo Books, 1987.

Additional Listings: Stained Glass.

Arch, 96 x 206″, Eastlake, cornice, dentils, anthemion leaf brackets, incised panels, fluted columns, paneled base **475.00**

Architectural Ornament
Art Deco, 35¼ x 38¾″, cast aluminum, scene of farmer sharpening scythe, plate glass mirror backing **900.00**

Eagle
33½″, cast iron, seated, closed wings, American, late 19th C .. **800.00**
68″, cast iron, orig finish, spread wings, perched on half globe base, Gettysburg, PA cemetery gate type, American, c1870 .. **4,000.00**

Barn Door, 39½ x 71″, pine, three boards, two wide battens, orig wrought iron strap hinges, mid section with seven slots cut with curved scallop, traces of old red paint, PA . **95.00**

Bathtub, cast iron, ball and claw feet . **50.00**

Ceiling Medallion, 31″ d, plaster, acanthus leaf dec **100.00**

Door
Front, entrance, spiderwebbed paneled transom, five beveled glass panes on each side, carved moldings **650.00**
Interior, 36¾ x 77″, poplar, paneled, orig flame graining in imitation of mahogany, white moldings **65.00**

Pocket, sliding, etched glass panels of wheat and grapes, pr **400.00**

Eagle, 24" wingspread, 11¾" h, sculptured pine, orig gilt, American, early 19th C, old repairs to wings **850.00**

Fire Grate, 20½ x 18½", cast nickel steel, Minerva head dec, early 20th C **285.00**

Fireboard, punched birds and grapes, Victorian **1,600.00**

Flooring, 152 sq ft, oak, 2¼" w **1,200.00**

Floor Register, 8 x 12", cast iron, scrolling vines **25.00**

Fountain, 64" d, 48" h, cast iron, fluted bowl, everted rim, lappets, pedestal base of four cranes **375.00**

Garden Furniture
Bench
48" l, cast iron, rococo, American, mid 19th C **1,500.00**
49" l, cast iron, rustic branches and foliage, joints welded, old gray repaint, light rust **1,100.00**
Chair, arm, cast iron, rustic branches and foliage, American, mid 19th C **650.00**
Table, cast iron, Gothic style, marble top, American, mid 19th C **500.00**

Garden Figure
Crane, bronze, Italian, late 19th C, base sgd "Campaiola" **900.00**
Woman, 67¼", ceramic, classical dress, 20th C, weathered **200.00**

Garden Pedestal, 50" h, wrought iron, painted gray-green, pr **175.00**

Garden Urn
17 x 34", cast iron, rect base, open grill work panels, florentine handles **425.00**
21½ x 37", iron, painted, pedestal base, florentine dec, marked "C. Ewal, Buffalo" **400.00**

Gate
24 x 59½", picket fence, paneled section in base, various sized spires, orig cast iron hardware and latch, Southern, weathered **100.00**
34½ x 38", wooden, picket, orig wrought iron hinges and latch, traces of old white paint **175.00**

Hitching Post, cast iron
Elephant, standing on drum base, long curving trunk meets base to form hitching ring **1,200.00**
Horse Head, 57½", mounted on wood post **850.00**

Lightning Rod, 65" h, wrought iron, tripod stand **45.00**

Mantel
44" w, 47½" h, 9¼" d x 44 l" shelf, 24⅜ w x 35 h" opening, poplar, applied folk art dec, worn brown graining, ebonized areas, yellow striping **250.00**
54¾" w, 48½" h, 8¾" d x 66 l" shelf, 37¼" w x 37¾" h opening, pine,

marbleized red paint, cream ground **400.00**
61" w, 6¼" d, 92" h, 42¼" w x 37" h opening, natural woods, molded columns and eagles at corners, fretwork bands, dentil border, corresponding upper panel, American, late 18th C **1,000.00**
63" w, 6" d, 48½" w x 43" h opening, Adam, deal pine, relief urns, swags, birds, oak leaf foliage **600.00**
71¼" w, 7" d, 53" w x 40⅜" h opening, Adam, deal pine, relief urns, swags, wheat sheaves, grapes, and foliage, beaded opening, dentil borders, English, late 18th C **1,250.00**

Valance, Art Deco, bronzed cast iron, 24¼" l, 5½" h, 4 pcs, marked, $400.00

72⅛" w, 10" d, 51¼" h, 25½" w x 32¾" h opening, carved pumpkin pine, sunburst motifs and molding, removed from Towle House, Middlesex, VT, late 18th C **2,000.00**

Niche, 24 x 66", plaster, Gothic, finger molded arch, brackets, marble shelf **175.00**

Pedestal
26½", folk art, multicolored mosaic tiles of glass, pottery shards, frog at base **130.00**
28½", folk art, base and column cov with material tooled to resemble bottle caps, mottled daubs of red, green, and yellow green paint, rect top painted red, wavy black line lattice **175.00**
44" h, marble, green, carved details **325.00**
56" h, 10¼" d top, mahogany, double open spiral stem, tripod base, old dark finish, early 20th C **225.00**

Pediment, exterior, 9'4" l, 46" h, tin, paneled arch, heart shaped shell, small shells on ends, raised date 1881, orig red paint **1,700.00**

Post Finial, 14 x 17 x 17", cast iron, corner, cut outs on 2 sides, raised star, dated 1883 . . . . **50.00**

Radiator, cast iron **100.00**

Roof Ornament, 22" h, cast iron, figural, hawk, found in Marietta, PA, c1875 . **1,200.00**

Safe, 16½" sq, 20½" h, iron, orig dec, landscape, flowers, wading birds, and butterfly, orig combination, 19th C . . **1,400.00**

Sink, pedestal, oval bowl, fluted column	50.00
Staircase, Victorian, 21 steps, curved, newel post, 52 spindles	1,000.00
Wainscoting, 28 units, 16″ on center . .	400.00

Window
18 x 123″, bay, double hung, orig hardware, four panels, four louvers recessed into sides **250.00**
34 x 63″, louvered shutters, louvered fan top, worn green paint **475.00**
37½ x 45½″, pine, hinged shutters, double arch frame, stripped **250.00**
Window Valance, 30 x 59″, printed floral design on red velvet, tassel trim . . . **40.00**

Woodwork
Dining Room, bracket plate rack on wainscoting, three windows, glass paneled doors, swinging door, beamed ceiling, built in china breakfront with triangular pediment and Corinthian pilasters **850.00**
Living Room, pine, paneling, two fireplaces, four doors, doorways **5,250.00**

ART DECO

History: The Art Deco period was named for an exhibition, "L'Exposition Internationale des Arts Decoratifs," held in Paris in 1927. It is a later period than Art Nouveau, but sometimes the two styles overlap since they were closely related in time.

Art Deco designs are angular and of simple lines. This was the period of skyscrapers, movie idols, and the cubists works of Picasso and Legras. It was used for every conceivable object being produced in the 1920s and 1930s, including ceramics, furniture, glass, and metals, not only in Europe, but in America as well.

References: Victor Arwas, *Glass: Art Nouveau To Art Deco*, Rizzoli, 1977; Lillian Baker, *Art Nouveau & Art Deco Jewelry: An Identification & Value Guide*, Collector Books, 1981; Bryan Catley, *Art Deco And Other Figures*, Antique Collectors' Club; Katherine Morrison McClinton, *Art Deco: A Guide For Collectors*, reprint, Clarkson N. Potter, 1986.

Additional Listings: Furniture and Jewelry. Also check glass, pottery, and metal categories.

Architectural Element
Gate, two panels, scalloped top, pierced and wrought iron, flowers and stems against geometric trellises, fluted rect base band, American, attributed to Lansha Studios, c1930 . . . . **2,200.00**
Panel, etched glass, egret and steamboat on Mississippi River, sgd "Denis Abbe, NY," from New Orleans restaurant **1,200.00**

Bookends, pr, 5″ l base, 5″ h, Spalter, bronze wash, celluloid faces, marble base, $400.00.

Bookends, pr
3½ x 5″, figural kneeling nudes, metal, gold satin finish **65.00**
7″, figural nudes, arched back, long flowing hair, metal, bronze wash finish **80.00**
8″, female archer, large bow, painted cast iron **55.00**
Camera, Kodak, 8¼″ leather case, hinged cov, enameled medium and dark brown and orange geometric devices, chrome trim, orig rect 8^{13}/₁₆″ cedar presentation box with enamel dec, metal tag inscribed "No. 1A Gift Kodak/Made in USA By/Eastman Kodak Co/Rochester, NY," designed by Walter Dorwin Teague, c1930 . . . . . **2,860.00**
Chandelier
16⅞″ l, sq wrought iron ceiling plate, deep apron, conforming rect standard, shade of rect alabaster shapes, Pierre Chareau, c1930, pr **18,000.00**
27″ l, molded glass, silvered metal, three lights, molded Muller Freres signature **450.00**
Cigarette Box, 5¼ x 6½″, rect, classical figure carrying grapes, bronze, Rockwell Kent, c1920 . . . . **500.00**
Cigarette Case, 3⅝″, sq, lacquered, black, Chinese red, and khaki, gilt metal, clasp imp "Jean Dunand" . . . **900.00**
Clock, mantel, marble, sq face enameled red and black, stepped stone base, 10″ h **2,150.00**
Cocktail Shaker, dumbbell shape, cobalt blue glass, chrome trim **110.00**
Dresser Tray, 9 x 12″, cobalt blue glass handles and center, silver lcart type woman and dog in center **45.00**
Figure, 15½″, seminude, maiden, shell and wave, earthenware, marked "Fieldings, England" **200.00**

Compact, 2¼ x 2¼", blue, white, and chrome, $20.00.

Fruit Bowl, 9 x 9", figural, swan, cobalt blue, triangular bowl, outstretched wings, "S" curved head and neck .. **75.00**

Furniture

Bar, 56¾" w, 59¾" h, bleached burled walnut, upright rect center, fluted doors, illuminated shelved int., mirrored peach glass and sliding shelf over two cupboard doors, flanked by two lower rect sections set with cupboard door, shelved int., raised on scrolling U form support, rect plinth, attributed to Ray Hille, c1930 **1,550.00**

Cabinet, vitrine, 32¾" w, 67¾" h, rect, marble top, glazed front and side panels, wrought iron scallops and leaf tips, mirrored back and shelves, stylized drop crest, raised toupie feet, French **3,850.00**

Chair, side, carved walnut, open rounded back set with wide I form gridwork, carved blossoms, buds, and foliage, rounded rect seat, shallow grooved apron, tapering sq legs, acanthus terminals, attributed to Paul Follot **4,000.00**

Dining Suite, 52" l table with X form base, two armchairs, eight straight chairs, buffet with floral marquetry panel, Ebene de Macassar **11,000.00**

Hall Tree, 51¼" w, 75" h, wrought iron, rect, top set with shallow open hat shelf above octagonal mirror, shallow verde antico shelf raised on angled supports, straight bands and coils, two rect sections with three coat hooks, outset rect umbrella stands, imp scrolls and geometric devices, French, c1925 ... **12,100.00**

Mirror, cheval, ebonized, swivel rect mirror, rounded edges, low sq mount, German, artist sgd, 70" h . **300.00**

Settee, 61" l, walnut, rect back, inset upholstered back, two partially up-

holstered scrolling arms, rect seat, wide U form support, four short legs, white muslin upholstery, French, c1930 .... **3,300.00**

Table

Center, 22" d, 29⅜" h, circular veined black marble top, four scrolling wrought iron supports, applied vertical tendrils, hammered ball and raised block form support, four gently scrolling tapering feet, French **3,850.00**

Console, 43" l, 33" h, wrought iron, rect marble top, curved front, shallow apron, five outward scrolling supports, strung iron "rope" dec, stepped rect base, attributed to Raymond Subes, c1925 .... **7,150.00**

Dresser Set, nail file box, shoe horn, two cov boxes, amber bases, pearlized tops with black flower and leaf dec, $25.00.

Goblet, 4⅞", SS, trumpet shaped knob stem, circular bowl, applied floral roundels, Tiffany & Co. **100.00**

Hat Box, 12½ x 12¾", wood, drawer, pedestal, orig blue paint, c1920 ... **45.00**

Perfume, green glass cube top and ground stopper, sq green glass body, fluted corners **35.00**

Piano, 37¾" h, 54½" w, 52" d, Amboyna Strohmenger, D section form case, three arched supports jointed by black ovoid housing two pedals, narrow ovoid bench on U support, oval white trimmed base, c1930 .... **13,200.00**

Pitcher, 5" d, 11" h, pottery, Celtic Harvest pattern, honey glaze, raised sheaves of wheat, orange flowers, fruited orange, yellow, and green handle, marked "Clarice Cliff" **200.00**

Sconce

12″ l, plaster, extended hand form, rounded triangular cup shade, mirrored glass reflector liners, designed by Alberto Giacometti for Jean-Michel Frank, pr **2,500.00**

24¼″, demilune form, etched radiating stylized papyrus blossoms, chrome mounts, intaglio sgd "Daum Nancy, France," croix de Lorraine mark, pr **2,400.00**

Toothpick Holder, 1¾″ d, 2¾″ h, light amber glass, flower shape, diamond cut base **55.00**

Vase

4¾″ d, 12½″ h, Raised Parakeets pattern, blue and cream ground, emb green, yellow, and blue parakeets, marked "Newport Pottery, Clarice Cliff" **175.00**

5″ d, 7″ h, My Garden pattern, salmon pink ground, raised pink, blue, and purple flowers, marked "Newport Pottery, Clarice Cliff" **100.00**

6½″ d, 8½″ h, Heavy Raised Florals pattern, blue and cream ground, raised pink, blue, and purple flowers, marked "Newport Pottery, Clarice Cliff" **165.00**

13″, cylindrical, enameled bell flowers, matte yellow ground, sgd "Swultmont, Belgium" **210.00**

Wall Pocket, 9″, china, figural, woman, marked "Germany" **100.00**

ART NOUVEAU

History: Art Nouveau is the French term for the "new art" which had its beginning in the early 1890s and continued for the next 40 years. The flowing and sensuous female forms used in this period were popular in Europe and America. Among the most recognized artists of this period were Galle, Lalique, and Tiffany.

Art Nouveau can be identified by its flowing, sensuous lines, floral forms, insects, and the feminine form. These designs were incorporated on almost everything produced at that time, from art glass to furniture, silver, and personal objects.

References: Victor Arwas, *Glass: Art Nouveau To Art Deco*, Rizzoli, 1977; Lillian Baker, *Art Nouveau & Art Deco Jewelry: An Identification & Value Guide*, Collector Books, 1981; Giovanni Fanelli and Ezio Godoli, *Art Nouveau Postcards*, Rizzoli International Publication, Inc., 1987; Don Fredgant, *Collecting Art Nouveau: Identification And Values*, Books Americana, 1982; Albert Christian Revi, *American Art Nouveau Glass*, reprint, Schiffer Publishing, 1981.

Additional Listings: Furniture and Jewelry. Also check glass, pottery, and metal categories.

Bonboniere, 10¾″ h, porcelain, figural, oval flaring box, fluted sides, deep coral sides with silver overlay and stylized acanthus leaves dec, silver overlay finial in form of two ballet dancers and stylized tree, sgd in underglaze blue "Richard/Ginori," partial orig paper label, c1925 . . . . **10,000.00**

Bowl

7⅜″, pottery, int. dec with mermaid holding shell, ext. with bands of leaves and swags, silver luster, deep blue and apple-green ground, short cylindrical foot, inscribed "RB" (Rene Buthard), c1925 . . . . **825.00**

13″, SS, everted rim, applied grapevine dec, hammered, made by Gorham Mfg Co., Providence, RI, retailed by F W Drosten, c1905, 49 ozs, 8 dwts **1,225.00**

Candlesticks, pr, 12″, bronze, bobeche suspended on baluster tripod standard, leaf form legs **750.00**

Clock

Mantel, 14⅞″, gilt bronze, arched top, undulating sides, cast high relief, poppy blossoms and leaves, openwork feet, center black painted arabic numerals above visage of young woman, crowned by blossom, matted ground, inscribed "Charles Honchery," c1900 . . . . . **3,850.00**

Wall, 15″ l, silvered bronze, circular chapter ring, cast Roman numerals, center blossoms, supported by pair of doves and bowed ribbons, inscribed "A Binquet Sculpteur 1928" **1,150.00**

Crumber Set, French, SP, handled 8″ l tray, raised floral motif, imp "O Gallia" **400.00**

Figure

8¾″, ivory, young woman, poised on right foot, nude, drapery length, ebony base, inscribed "R Middegaels," c1925 . . . . **2,750.00**

16⅜″, polychromed bronze, woman, head tilted back, eyes closed, holding cov urn, dark green drapery length with gilt flowers around hips, falling over crossed legs, flaring rect marble base, titled "Idol," inscribed "Marcel Bouraine," c1925 **1,210.00**

18¾″, polychromed bronze, woman, long flowing skirt, close fitting patterned blouse, body arched, poised on right foot, carved ivory hands and face, stepped onyx base, titled "Dancer, Ayouta," inscribed "D Chiparus," c1925 . . . . **12,100.00**

24¼″, bronze, slender nude figure, upswept hair, long snake trails down arm, drapery trailing to feet,

Vase, 12″ h, brass, grape leaves and vine motif, $275.00.

mottled green patina, sq black marble base, inscribed "E Saroldi," c1920 .... **3,000.00**

24½″ l, bronze, equestrian group, turbanned man, exotic costume, racing on horseback with young maiden, mustard, black, and brown patina, multicolored onyx base, inscribed "Niomel," c1920 .... **4,625.00**

Frame, picture, easel support

10¼″ h, SS, shaped rect, chased flowers, foliage, undulating ridges, wood backing, marked "JA & S, Birmingham," 1908 .... **800.00**

11½″, SS, arched crest, chased pendent husks, clusters of fruit, velvet cov back, marked "Walker & Hall, Birmingham," 1911 .... **1,120.00**

12⅜″ h, SS, shaped rect, chased herons, water lilies, cattails, undulating tendrils, wood backing, marked "W Aitken, Birmingham, England," 1905 .... **2,750.00**

Furniture

Cabinet

Burl walnut, jewel cabinet, single frieze drawer over two doors, carved and applied fruit, twenty short int. drawers, single deep drawer, gilt bronze mounts, Ecole de Nancy, Louis Majorelle type, 56″ h **3,000.00**

Fruitwood, inlaid overall floral and figural marquetry, shaped upper section, two doors flanked by two shelves, attributed to Emile Galle, 78″ h **12,000.00**

Fruitwood, vitrine, upper section with arched crest, single glazed door, lower section with single door, marquetry dec, Ecole de Nancy, 68″ l **3,200.00**

Chair, side

English, oak, orig finish, old worn black leatherized cloth upholstery **75.00**

French, walnut, tall pierced foliate back, sq seat, straight legs, spade feet, 24″ h, set of 4 .... **500.00**

Desk, lady's, carved fruitwood, slanted writing surface, shaped corners, carved organic motifs, Ecole de Nancy, 24″ l **1,150.00**

Settee, painted white, Louis Majorelle, Les Pins pattern, 56″ l **1,500.00**

Table

Occasional, carved walnut, two tiers, 34″ l **500.00**

Side, marquetry, burlwood three sided top, inlaid columbine dec, three slender fluted triangular legs, inlaid "Galle," 29″ h **700.00**

Goblet, 6⅝″ h, Russian silver, gilt int., "N.C." maker, and Moscow hallmarks, c1890 .... **75.00**

Handbag, 10¼″ l, rect, leather, diamond shaped studs on edges, monogrammed, gilt metal hammered emb and chased surface with beadwork, florets, faux tortoiseshell fittings, braided leather handle, suede int., Tiffany & Co, NY, c1880 .... **825.00**

Inkwell, 9¼″, metal, oval dish, cov well with glass insert at end, low relief, head and bust of youth, ivy garlands, French, molded initials "GF" (Georges de Feure) **200.00**

Mirror, lady's, hand

Bronze, 13⅞″, circular back, intaglio cast, branching thistles, two heavy buds, long tapering handle, brown patina, stamped "Lalique" **11,000.00**

Nickel Silver, undulating lines **80.00**

Panel, 35⅝ x 20⅝″, rect, marquetry, inlaid garden landscape, bird on twig, Cristallerie Galle paper label **400.00**

Print, lithograph, printed in color

Mucha, Alphonse, "Job," bottom marked "F Champeonis, Paris, 1898," margins, framed **5,500.00**

Rhead, Louis John, "Panneau Decoratif," c1896, published by La Plume, full margins **2,420.00**

Tray, 19¾″, octagonal, two carved griffins handles, marquetry, church ruins in forest landscape, inlaid "Galle" .. **700.00**

Urn, 16½″, bronze, figural, ovoid, waisted neck, C scroll handle, cast full relief, nude woman seated on river bank, drawing fishing net, neck cast as gushing waves, gnarled tree handle, rich brown patina, inscribed "A

Vibert," imp circular seal "Siot Decauville/Fondeur/Paris," c1900 .... **3,500.00**

Vase

13", SS, wavy rim, emb and chased daisies and foliage, hammered surface, stamped "Martele," over spread winged eagle, Gorham Mfg Co., Providence, RI, c1898, 35 ozs, 12 dwts **3,525.00**

13⅛", bronze, expanding cylindrical neck, truncated body, cast high relief, nude water nymph sipping water, two lug handles cast as fruiting vines, base with lotus blossoms and leaves, brown patina, inscribed "J Ofner," c1900 .... **12,000.00**

14⅝", gilt bronze, glass liner, ovoid, two undulating S scroll handles, medium and high relief, nude woman cavorting with playful putti, theatrical masks, inscribed "Joseph Cheret," foot inscribed "E Soleau, Paris," c1904 .... **2,100.00**

18½", parcel gilt bronze, flaring cylindrical, cast low relief, two nude female figure playing hide and seek among iris leaves, irregular neck cast with four silvered bronze iris blossoms, inscribed "Peyre," c1900 .... **3,600.00**

24¼", parcel gilt bronze, ovoid, cast overlapping leaves, elongated tulip buds, one gilt blossom opening over lip, gilt nude woman on side, brown patina, inscribed "Ch Louchet," c1900 .... **3,000.00**

ART PEWTER

History: Pewter objects produced during the Art Nouveau, Arts and Crafts, and Art Deco periods are gaining in popularity. These mostly utilitarian objects, e.g., tea sets, trays, and bowls, were elaborately decorated and produced in the Jugendstil manner by German firms, such as Kayserzinn, and Austrian companies, such as Orivit. In England, Liberty and Company marketed Tudric Pewter, which often had a hammered surface and was embellished with enameling or semi-precious stones. Most pieces of art pewter contain the maker's mark.

ETAIN D'ART

Chamberstick, 6", handled **50.00**

IMPERIAL ZINN

Vase, 13", three iris at top, triangular base, marked "Imperial Zinn" **125.00**

Bowl, cov, 7½" d, sunflowers dec, ftd, handled, bulbous sides, marked "Kayserzinn," numbered, **$125.00**.

KAYSERZINN

Bowl, 10", scalloped, water lily center, dragonflies **75.00**

Inkwell, pen holder, frog sitting on top . **375.00**

Knife Rest, dachshund **60.00**

Plate, 8½", lattice design with scrolls and strawberries in relief **75.00**

ORIVIT

Pitcher, 10½" h, emb grapes and leaves **125.00**

Vase, 7", Art Nouveau flowers and vines **80.00**

TUDRIC

Clock, 6½" h, tapering rect body, sq peaked top, circular copper clock face with blue-green enameled center, curvilinear blue, green, and deep red enameled medallion. designed by Archibald Knox for Liberty & Co, stamped "Tudric, Made In England" **1,500.00**

Money Clip, Art Nouveau **25.00**

Vase, 9⅞", two leafy handles, floriform, designed by Archibald Knox for Liberty & Co, c1903, circular foot stamped "Tudric" **500.00**

WOODHULL

Punchbowl, 19" d, 10⅞" h, flared rim, three sq feet, stepped circular base, engraved panels of armorial crests, log cabins, farmers, matching ladle, inscribed "W C Woodhull" **350.00**

ART POTTERY (GENERAL)

History: The period of art pottery reached its zenith in the late 19th and early 20th century. Over a hundred companies produced individually designed and often decorated wares which served a utilitarian as well as an aesthetic purpose. Artists moved about from company to company, some forming their own firms.

Quality of design, beauty in glazes, and condition are the keys in buying art pottery. This category covers companies not found elsewhere in the guide.

References: Paul Evans, *Art Pottery of the United States, Second Edition,* Feingold & Lewis Publishing Co., 1987; Lucile Henzke, *Art Pottery of America,* Schiffer Publishing; Ralph and Terry Kovel, *The Kovels' Collector's Guide to American Art Pottery,* Crown Publishers, Inc., 1974.

Additional Listings: See Cambridge, Clewell, Clifton, Cowan, Dedham, Fulper, Grueby, Jugtown, Marblehead, Moorcroft, Newcomb, North Dakota School of Mines, Ohr, Owens, Paul Revere, Peters and Reed, Rookwood, Roeville, Van Briggle, Weller, and Zanesville.

Arequipa Pottery (1913–18), Fairfax, CA
Bowl, 9 x 4¾", light blue glossy glaze, molded flower and leaf dec, rolled over rim, marked	25.00
Vase, 5⅝", matte green, marked	50.00

California Faience Co. (1916–30), Berkeley, CA
Bowl, 4½", medium blue, glossy glaze	115.00
Flower Frog, 6" h, Oriental laundry woman, multicolored	175.00
Vase, 5" h, 7" d, pumpkin shape, luminous turquoise glaze, marked	90.00

Chelsea Keramic Art Works (1872–89), Chelsea, MA
Jug, 5 x 3½", bulbous, deep olive green high glaze, incised "CKAW"	200.00
Pitcher, 7¾", blended moss green glaze, metal shape, imp geometric dec, overglaze painting of birds on flowering branch, pre 1880 3 line mark	300.00
Tea Set, 4¾" cov teapot, 3" h creamer, 4⅜" h cov sugar, dark blue spotted olive green, lions' heads masks on feet	725.00

Jervis Pottery, (1908–1912), Oyster Bay, NY
Bowl, 3 x 6¼", bisque royal blue glaze, dec rim band, incised geometric pale blue and white, pattern, die stamped "Jervis"	550.00
Pot, 8 x 12", bulbous, six carvings, curving handles reaching from rim to base tolled with stylized leaf forms, green matte glaze, vertically incised "Jervis" and "62"	2,000.00
Vase, 5 x 3", cylindrical body, stepped in neck and collar rim, incised line tree motif, mocha brown, green and blue horizon line, white clouds and geometric pattern	800.00

Kenton Hills (1939–42), Erlanger, KY
Ashtray, 7¼ x 6½", bright turquoise high glaze, horse's head, marked	40.00
Bowl, 3½", olive green glossy glaze, marked	100.00
Vase, 4¼", intense medium blue, glossy glaze	60.00

Norse, (1903–13), Edgerton, WI, and Rockford, IL
Bowl, otter handles, sunburst design on sides	110.00
Candlestick, 11", marked Shape 54	60.00
Ewer, 4½", matte black, green incised dec, handled, marked	35.00
Vase, gunmetal gold	100.00

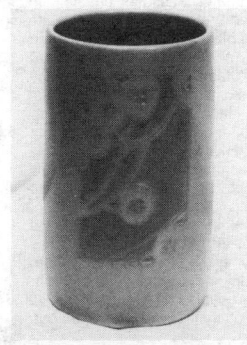

Overbeck, vase, 5¾", cylindrical, beige ground, pale green, marked "Thrown by Elizabeth, decorated by Mary F.," $850.00.

Overbeck Pottery (1911–55), Cambridge City, IN
Figure
2 x 3¼", dog, turquoise body, large black dots, lavender ears, unmarked	225.00
7 x 5½", woman, white and pink southern belle dress, pink wide brimmed hat, bouquet, incised "OBK"	250.00
Trivet, 6½" d, incised design of two galloping lilac ponies, black manes, cream, turquoise, and periwinkle blue ground, incised "OBK" and "EF"	425.00
Vase, 5½ x 5", bulbous, wide flared neck, matte olive green, carve dec, wide band of light olive green fish, sea plants, brown ground, incised "OBK" and "EH"	1,400.00

Pisgah Forest (1913–present), Mt. Pisgah, NC

Bowl, 5", turquoise crackle glaze, pink int. **50.00**
Creamer and Sugar, 2½", mottled turquoise glaze, pink int. **15.00**
Vase, Crackle, trumpet shape, dark plum high glaze, white int., 1949 . **65.00**

Stockton Art Pottery (1890–95, 1896–1900), Stockton, CA

Ewer, 7", underglaze painting, large creamy to yellow blossoms, shaded brown ground, tree branch handle, marked "Rekston" **150.00**
Vase, floral **100.00**

Teco (1886–1930) Terra Cotta, IL

Lamp, 18 x 10", bulbous base, four vertical buttresses ending in flanged feet, medium green matte glaze, black feathering, orig leaded glass shade with three stylized burnt orange and white slag glass flowers, green leaded squares, clear glass chimney, die stamped "Teco," incised "271" **6,000.00**
Pitcher, 8¾ x 5¼", corset shape, flowing wishbone handle, rich gloppy gunmetal to green matte glaze, imp mark **150.00**
Vase, 7 x 4¼", bulbous, four vertical buttresses forming pierced handles at top, ending as flanges at base, medium matte green, black highlights, double imp "Teco" mark . . **650.00**

Volkmar Pottery (1882–1903), Tremont, NY

Mug, 6", light gray-green glaze, metallic gray runs, marked **45.00**
Oil Lamp Base, 8 x 5½", brown and light green intermingled runs, high gloss majolica-like glaze, marked . **35.00**
Vase, 4", semi-gloss deep green, light green fine striations around rim . . **100.00**

Walrath Pottery, (1908–1921), Rochester, NY

Bowl, 6 x 7", centerpiece, crouched nude woman in center, light pea green matte **300.00**
Tumbler, 4½", greenish brown, stylized chestnut dec in gold and light green **315.00**

ARTS AND CRAFTS MOVEMENT

History: The Arts and Crafts Movement in American decorative arts took place between 1895 and 1920. Leading proponents of the movement were Elbert Hubbard and his Roycrofters, the brothers Stickley, Frank Lloyd Wright, Charles and Henry Greene, George Niedecken, and Lucia and Arthur Mathews.

The movement was marked by individualistic design (although the movement was national in scope) and re-emphasis on handcraftsmanship and appearance. A reform of industrial society was part of the long range goal. Most pieces of furniture favored a rectilinear approach and were made of oak.

References: David M. Cathers, *Furniture Of The American Arts and Crafts Movement,* New American Library, 1981; Paul Evans, *Art Pottery Of The United States, 2nd Edition,* Feingold & Lewis Publishing, 1987; Bruce Johnson, *The Official Indentification And Price Guide To Arts And Crafts,* House of Collectibles, 1988; Wendy Kaplan, *The Art That Is Life: The Arts And Crafts Movement In America 1875-1920,* Boston Museum of Fine Arts, 1987; Coy L. Ludwig. *The Arts and Crafts Movement In New York State, 1890s–1920s,* Gallery Association of New York State, 1983.

Periodical: *Arts and Crafts Quarterly,* P.O. Box 3592, Station E, Trenton, NJ 08629.

Museum: Museum of Modern Art, New York, NY.

Additional Listings: Roycroft Items, Stickleys, and art pottery categories.

Andirons, 22" h, hammered metal, dark brown patina, pr **200.00**
Ashtray, metal, grapes, enamel, underplate, marked "Sascha Brastoff" . . . **40.00**
Bookends, pr, 4 x 8", Batchelder tan bisque tiles, brass, marked "Potter Studio" **200.00**
Bowl, 3½, hammered copper, darkened patina **150.00**
Box, 4⅜ x 5⅜", rect, copper, domed rect lid, central aqua and lavender enamel cabochon, silver heart shaped clasp, hammered silver feet and corners, stamped marks for Birmingham, England, 1904, and "A E J" **500.00**
Clock, 19", dark fumed oak, metal hardware, broadly flattened nailheads dec, paper label, "Maria/Eight Day Mission Strike/Manufactured by/Wm. L. Gilbert Clock Co." **250.00**
Compote, 7 x 6 x 5½", hammered aluminum, seahorse standard, marked "Cellini Craft" **20.00**
Dresser Set, SS, hand mirror, two hair brushes, two clothes brushes, shoe horn, button hook, cylindrical box, and tray, strapwork, maiden, and tulips dec, copper rivets, marked "Goldsmiths & Silversmiths Co., Ltd., London," 1900, 9 pcs **3,525.00**
Fireplace Equipment
Log Basket, Mission oak **125.00**
Screen, 17½ x 28", copper, hand crafted large repousse Viking ship in full sail, riveted, aged patina . . **400.00**

Tankard, 14″ h, copper and brass, pewter lined, wheat designs, $350.00.

Flatware Service, SS, service for six (dinner knife, dinner fork, soup soon, teaspoon, butter spreader, cocktail fork, and demitasse spoon) plus serving pcs, hammered pointed handles, applied gilt monogram, Lebolt, Chicago, c1930 .... **1,800.00**

Furniture

Cabinet, vitrine, honey stained oak, sgd "Gustav Stickley," 56″ h **2,250.00**

Chair, arm, Mission oak, cleaned, seat recovered in vinyl, Stickley type **75.00**

Clothes Tree, 43″, child's, fumed oak, Mission style **50.00**

Commode, bedside, oak, one drawer, brass strap hinged cupboard door **200.00**

Cupboard, 80″ h, single door, copper hinges, marquetry inlay of peacocks with spreading feathers, pierced carved gallery, retailer "Story & Triggs, London" label .. **3,400.00**

Rocker, Mission oak, cleaned, seat recovered in vinyl, branded "Stickley Bros Co., Grand Rapids, No. 504" **150.00**

Table

Center, stained oak, H form stretcher with tenons, Gustav Stickley type, 40″ l **950.00**

Game, orig leather top, four mortise and tenon legs, joined by X stretcher, sgd "Gustav Stickley," 48¼″ d, 30″ h **5,000.00**

Humidor, cov, 6″, brass, acid etched dec, sailing ships, glass liner, marked "Silver Crest" **50.00**

Jewelry, pendant, 1¼″, SS, hammered openwork quatrefoil body, central MOP panel, matching chain, Guild of Handicraft, Ltd, c1905 .... **300.00**

Lamp, table, 16¼″ h, tapering four sided leaded shade, brown cattails and green bullrushes dec, sq columnar standard, sq ft **400.00**

Lamp Shade, 16¼ x 8¼″, brass mesh, octagonal, flocked and painted, brown and tan **75.00**

Mirror, 42 x 24″, rect, hammered copper, emb roundels at corners, emb sides, sq pods, English **600.00**

Paperweight, 2¼″, pewter figural dog, dark brown hammered copper base, marked "Avon Coppersmith Shop" . **75.00**

Sconces, pr, 7¾″ h, brass, 2 candleholders, dark patina **25.00**

Tea Service, silver, 4½″ h teapot, cov sugar, creamer, waste bowl, hammered bands, American, approx 25 ozs **800.00**

Tray, 11¼″, heavy copper, hammered, tight concentric circles spiral from center, aged patina, marked "E.T.C. Fish, Tioga, PA" **75.00**

Vase, 9¾″, sgraffito dec, swallows in flight, medium brown, green, and tan, light gray ground, marked "Martin Bros," 1890 .... **400.00**

AUSTRIAN WARE

History: Over a hundred potteries were located in the Austro-Hungarian Empire in the late 19th and early 20th centuries. Although Carlsbad was the center of the industry, the factories spread as far as modern day Czechoslovakia.

Many of the factories were either owned or supported by Americans; hence, their wares were produced mainly for export to the United States. Responding to the 1891 law that imported products must be marked as to country of origin, many wares do not have a factory mark, but only the word "Austrian."

Reference: Susan and Al Bagdade, *Warman's English & Continental Pottery & Porcelain, 1st Edition,* Warman Publishing Co., Inc., 1987.

Additional Listings: Amphora, Carlsbad, Royal Dux, and Royal Vienna.

Bowl

9″, fruit and leaves dec, sgd "Koch" **30.00**

10″, Thistle pattern **20.00**

Chocolate Pot, cov, grapes dec, gold mark **50.00**

Creamer

7⅛″, blue glaze, floral dec panel ... **40.00**

7¼″, ivory ground, floral dec **45.00**

Demitasse Cup and Saucer, Alhambra pattern **45.00**

Dish, 10⅛″ l, 9″ w, triangular, opalescent, overshot, applied strawberries,

Bowl, 11″ d, 2⅞″ h, white porcelain, scalloped edge, swirl and shell relief, two rose floral motifs, gilt trim, $70.00.

blossoms, stems, leaves, and amber
feet **200.00**
Dresser Set, tray, two boxes, pin tray,
multicolored **110.00**
Fish Set, eight plates, platter, sauce
boat **225.00**
Jar, cov, 5⅜″ h, rect, pebbled pale green
glass, gold oil spot dec, SP rim,
domed SP cov **200.00**
Pitcher
13½″, applied gold lizard handle,
flowers, cream ground, sgd "Stellmacher No. 228" **165.00**
15″, tankard, grapes and leaves dec,
marked "Vienna" **200.00**
Plate
7″, hp, Falstaff and Mrs. Ford, dark
green border, 1″ gold trim **60.00**
8″, red raspberries and green foliage,
soft shaded pastel ground, gold
trim, set of 8 .... **120.00**
8½″, grape cluster dec, sgd "Koch" . **32.00**
Portrait Plate
8½″, medallions of Josephine, Maria
de Medici, and Duchess de Bourgogne, floral medallions, scalloped
gilt edge **65.00**
9½″, Amicitia, brunette woman, gold
trim, blue underglaze beehive mark **175.00**
10″, Queen Louise, beehive mark .. **110.00**
Salt, hp, open pink roses, green leaves,
gold feet, set of 4 .... **60.00**
Sugar Shaker
Bluebird dec, marked "Victoria-Carlsbad" **40.00**
Grapes dec **85.00**
Teapot, relief scrolls, hp flowers,
marked "Carlsbad, Austria 1892" .. **55.00**
Tray, 15″, pierced handles, beaded rim,
ornate gold, green, and purple grape
clusters, sgd "Koch" **85.00**
Vase
4¾″ h, 4¾″ bulbous base, scalloped
flared top, decal portrait of blonde

women, russet brown ground, gold
trimmed handle **30.00**
9″ h
Bulbous, blue luster, bronze holder **200.00**
Stick, ruby, heavy gold and white
enamel dec **200.00**
12 x 5½″, portrait of Bohemian girl,
lavender and blue flower dec, gold
handles, marked "Victoria, Crown,
Austria" **225.00**

AUTOGRAPHS

History: Autographs occur in a wide variety of formats—letters, documents, photographs, books, and cards, etc. Most collectors focus on a particular person, country, or category, e.g. signers of the Declaration of Independence.

The condition and content of letters and documents bears significantly on value. Collectors should know their source since forgeries abound, and copy machines compound the problem. Further, some signatures of recent presidents and movie stars are done by machine rather than by the persons themselves. A good dealer or advanced collector can help one spot the differences.

The leading auction sources for autographs are Swann Galleries, Sotheby's, Christie's, and Phillips, all located in New York City.

References: Mary A. Benjamin, *Autographs: A Key To Collecting*, reprint, Dover, 1986; Bob Benett, *A Collector's Guide To Autographs With Prices*, Wallace-Homestead, 1986; Charles Hamilton, *American Autographs*, University of Oklahoma Press, 1983; George Sanders, Helen Sanders, Ralph Roberts, *The Price Guide To Autographs*, Wallace-Homestead, 1988.

Collectors' Clubs: Manuscript Society, 350 Niagara Street, Burbank, CA 91505; Universal Autograph Collectors Club, P. O. Box 467 Rockville Center, NY 11571.

Additional Listings: See *Warman's Americana & Collectibles* for more examples.

The following abbreviations denote type of autograph material and their sizes.

ADS	Autograph Document Signed
ALS	Autograph Letter Signed
AQS	Autograph Quotation Signed
CS	Card Signed
DS	Document Signed
LS	Letter Signed
PS	Photograph Signed
TLS	Typed Letter Signed

Sizes (approximate):

Follo	12 x 16 inches
4to	8 x 10 inches
8vo	5 x 7 inches
12mo	3 x 5 inches

COLONIAL AMERICA

Adams, Andrew, signer of Articles of Confederation, ALS, 1 pg 4to, Litchfield, Oct 27, 1792 to Timothy Pitkin on financial matters **200.00**

Bassett, Richard, signer of Constitution, full pg folio, August 1772, attorney for defendant Jesse Beauchamp, being sued for 16 pounds by William Manlowe **850.00**

Blair, John, singer of Constitution, ALS, 1 pg oblong 8vo, to U S Treasurer Samuel Meredith, Williamsburg, July 8, 1794, matted and framed with Blair portrait **850.00**

Dickinson, John, ADS, 1½ pg folio, to Hugh McDowell, leases of house and plantation in Kent County, Delaware, Nov 11, 1786 . . . .   **650.00**

Fitzsimons, Thomas, signer of Constitution, ALS 2 pgs 4to, to John Anderson, concerning land in Pennsylvania, Philadelphia, Aug 2, 1792 . . . .   **200.00**

Huntington, Samuel, signer of Declaration of Independence, ADS, 1 pg 8vo, ordering the Sheriff of Windham County to summon John Ripley to the court of common pleas, Norwich, Nov 12, 1789 . . . .   **225.00**

Ross, George, signer of Declaration, ADS, 1 pg folio, attorney for Peter Lane, being sued by Jacob Erbe for 20 pounds, April 25, 1757 . . . .   **325.00**

EUROPEAN

De Gaulle, Charles, TLS, 1 pg 4to, to an American girl, Paris, Jan 8, 1948, orig envelope **300.00**

De Lesseps, Ferdinand, ALS, 1 pg 8vo, to an admiral written in French, Paris, June 4, 1862 . . . .   **250.00**

Hugo, Victor, French author, ALS 1 pg 4to, to Grand Chancellor of France, accepting award of Chevalier of the Legion of Honor of France, Paris, May 12, 1838 . . . .   **500.00**

Jung, Carl Gustav, Swiss psychiatrist, TLS, 1 pg 4to, to Everett Bleiler of MA, thank you letter, Zurich, April 15, 1946 . . . .   **650.00**

Louis Philippe, last King of France, ALS, 1 pg 4to, to Comte de Berenger, advising next session of the Assembly open on July 26, Paris, July 16, 1842   **200.00**

Napoleon I, ADS, 1 pg folio, awarding fusil d'honneur or brevet commission to Citoyen Debevre for part in battle at Marengo, Nov 19, 1800 . . . .   **950.00**

Potter, Beatrix, CS, "With every good wish/from Beatrix Heelis/Dec 20, '39"   **300.00**

Sullivan, Sir Arthur, English composer, ALS, 1 pg 8vo, to Miss DaCosta, London, Nov 15, 1893 . . . .   **775.00**

Wagner, Richard, German composer, ALS, 2 pgs 8vo, to Mr. Anderson, concerning a score for performance at Royal Court London, Zurich, Dec 12, 1857 . . . .   **1,300.00**

GENERAL

Barton, Clara, American Red Cross Founder, PS, standing in her garden holding flowers, professionally matted, sgd "Very Sincerely yours, Clara Barton, Sept 27, 1911" lower margin   **475.00**

Burns, William J, TLS, 1 pg 4to, to H H McClure, agency letterhead, Chicago, July 30, 1911 . . . .   **200.00**

Morse, Samuel F B, PS, 4 x 6", bold "Saml F B Morse" **975.00**

Peary, Robert E, ALS, 1 pg 4to, to SS McClure, Etah, Greenland, Aug 28, 1899 . . . .   **250.00**

Penn, William, ADS, folio, granting 1500 acres to Thomas Church, April 4, 1695 . . . .   **3,500.00**

Rockwell, Norman, TLS, to Mr. Rosenthal with pen and ink drawing of small dog, Aug 8, 1973 . . . .   **900.00**

San Martin, Jose De, South American statesman and soldier, ADS, vignette at top, passport for man sailing from port of Callero on ship Hercules, Lima, Dec 13, 1822 . . . .   **500.00**

Smith, Jessie Wilcox, pen and ink drawing, inscribed and sgd "Marching on to a great future! Jessie Wilcox Smith" **350.00**

Tom Thumb (Chas S Stratton), small piece lined paper, "Charles S. Stratton/known as/Genl Tom Thumb" . . .   **175.00**

Wright, Orville, PS, Kitty Hawk, Orville lying on plane, and Wilbur standing, sgd on lower left, 1928 2¢ stamp honoring International Civil Aeronautics Conference upper left **900.00**

LITERATURE

Capote, Truman, 1 pg 4to, typescript, "In Cold Blood" **200.00**

Christie, Agatha, TLS, 1 pg 4to, to Mr. Stanhope, July 22, 1970 . . . .   **200.00**

Day, Clarence S, ALS 2 pgs 4to, to Mr. Nock, New York, Sept 22, 1935 . . .   **200.00**

Dickens, Charles, ALS, 1 pg 8vo, to Mr. Knight, London, June 15, 1858 . . . .   **750.00**

Ferber, Edna, TLS, 1 pg 4to, to Orr (probably her brother), saw movie "So Big" based on her novel and thinks it is rotten, Monday Dec 29, 1924 .... **125.00**

Holmes, Oliver Wendell, AQS, 4to, poem to commemorate seventieth birthday of poet John Greenleaf Whittier, Nov 1, 1881 .... **500.00**

Longfellow, Henry Wadsworth, ALS, 1 pg 8vo, Cambridge, March 26, 1881 **225.00**

Stowe, Harriett Beecher, AQS, 1 pg 12mo, May 18, 1893 .... **2,500.00**

Whittier, John Greenleaf, ALS, 4 pgs 8vo, reflecting his seventy years of life, Oak Knoll, Dec 22, 1877 ..... **250.00**

MUSIC

Berlin, Irving, TLS, 1 pg 4to, to Leon Leonidoff of Radio City Music Hall Theater, NY, Nov 6, 1962 .... **150.00**

Caruso, Enrico, PS, 6½ x 8½", sepia, seated in tuxedo, boldly inscribed, sgd, and dated 1914 .... **775.00**

Crawford, Robert, sheet music, Off we go, into the wild blue yonder, "To my gracious hostess Elizabeth Weaver with deep appreciation, Robert Crawford, Maxwell Field, 1939" **200.00**

Dorsey, Jimmy, postcard, black and white photograph of Dorsey as young man, inscribed and sgd **45.00**

Farrar, Geraldine, postcard, shows her in Juliet costume, Metropolitan Opera debut, boldly sgd green ink **100.00**

Gershwin, George, TLS, 1 pg 4to, to Walter W Clark, RCA Victor Co, New York, Sept 14, 1931 .... **2,000.00**

McCartney, Paul, PS, 4 x 6", seated on brick wall, boldly sgd **120.00**

PRESIDENTIAL, AMERICAN

Buchanan, James, ALS, 1 pg 4to, to Department of State, requesting three letters from Nicholas Trist concerning Mexican War, March 16, 1848 ..... **650.00**

Cleveland, Grover, ADS, warrant served to Peter McArdle, 2 pgs folio, includes notarized document that warrant was duly served, July 20, 1883, sgd as Governor, NY **325.00**

Grant, Ulysses S, DS, 1 pg 4to, authorizing Secretary of State to affix the US Seal to "Proclamation to suppress domestic violence in the State of Arkansas," May 14, 1874 .... **1,800.00**

Harrison, Benjamin, TLS, 1 pg 4to, to publisher S S McClure, Indianapolis, May 28, 1898 .... **300.00**

Johnson, Andrew, note, 1 pg, 8vo, referred to Sec of War for consideration when a vacancy occurs **800.00**

Johnson, Lyndon B, TLS, 1 pg 4to, to

Commander W I Causey of New Orleans, concerning application of Charles Zivley for commission as lieutenant in the Naval Reserves, US House of Representatives, Committee on Naval Affairs letterhead, July 8, 1940 .... **325.00**

Kennedy, John F, TLS, 1 pg 4to, to Frederick Broch of Cambridge, MA, concerning claim against government of Yugoslavia, Congress of US letterhead, May 25, 1950 .... **900.00**

Lincoln, Abraham, ALS, 1 pg 8vo, to K Clark, request of his autograph, Springfield, Nov 8, 1860, sgd as President-elect, matted with steel engraving of Lincoln, gold wood frame ... **2,300.00**

McKinley, William, ADS, folio, appointing William Barnard a Notary Public, May 28, 1895, sgd as Governor ... **200.00**

Monroe, James, ADS, 1 pg folio, land grant to James Barr in Illinois, July 6, 1818, upper left corner vignette **375.00**

Roosevelt, Theodore, ADS, 1 pg folio, appointing Jacob F Kreps Major of Infantry in the US Army, Sept 4, 1906, matted and framed **450.00**

Taft, William H, ADS, 1 pg folio, appointing Lewis C Lucas Lieutenant Colonel in US Marine Corps, Dec 1, 1909, attached lower left blue seal **300.00**

Van Buren, Martin, ADS, 2 pgs folio, sgd as Attorney General of NY, 1817 ... **200.00**

Wilson, Woodrow, TLS, 1 pg 4to, to John Phillips of McClure's Magazine, concerning problems he is having finding time to write essay, Princeton, March 5, 1898 .... **400.00**

SHOW BUSINESS

Chevalier, Maurice, PS, 4to, sgd "Beaucoup good wishes, Maurice Chevalier" **100.00**

Dietrich, Marlene, PS, 4to, boldly sgd "Dietrich," c1936 .... **85.00**

Flynn, Errol, PS, 4to, sepia, sitting in chair, inscribed and sgd "To Peggy, best wishes, Errol Flynn, 1939" **350.00**

Harlow, Jean, PS, framed, 11¼ x 15", creased **65.00**

Hepburn, Katharine, PS, 12vo, black and white, bold signature **120.00**

Leigh, Vivien, postcard, black and white, dressed as Scarlett O'Hara **775.00**

Russell, Lillian, postcard, photograph, sgd "Very truly yours, Lillian Russell," 1897 .... **150.00**

Valentino, Rudolph, PS, 18th C French costume, framed, 10 x 12¼" **35.00**

Weissmuller, Johnny, PS, 8vo, showing him as Tarzan swimming, sgd "Sin-

cerely yours, Johnny "Tarzan" Weiss-
muller" **150.00**

SPORTS

Camp, Walter, ALS, 2 pgs 8vo, to
McClure's Magazine, concerning H T
Webster's "Boyhood Ambitions" car-
toons, Atlantic City **200.00**
Johnson, Walter P, baseball pitcher,
small card **250.00**

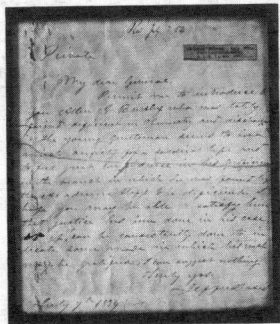

**Jefferson Davis, ALS, letter of intro-
duction, 8¼ x 9¼", $600.00.**

STATESMEN, AMERICAN

Boone, Thomas, Governor of New Jersey and South Carolina, ADS, 1 pg
folio, ordering Provincial Treasurer to
pay Samuel Smith 262 pounds, July
7, 1761, sgd as Governor of New Jer-
sey **125.00**
Clinton, DeWitt, ALS, 1½ pgs 4to, to M
Carey, Erie Canal business, Albany,
Jan 13, 1826 . . . .   **400.00**
Johnston, Samuel, Governor, ALS, 1 pg
4to, to his sister, family matters, Her-
mitage, June 4, 1800 . . . .   **200.00**
Lincoln, Robert T, TLS, 2 pgs 8vo, to
publisher SS McClure, June 25, 1900   **150.00**
Pierce, William, ADS, 1 pg 4to, certifi-
cation to quantity and value of sugar
and coffee from Philadelphia mer-
chant, Savannah, Jan 6, 1786 . . . .   **500.00**
Washington, Bushrod, Associate Jus-
tice of Supreme Court, ADS, 1 pg
8vo, promissory note for 1248 dollars
to George C Washington, Jan 26,
1815 . . . .   **450.00**
Webster, Daniel, ALS, 1 pg 4to, to Al-
exander Ross, Washington, Feb 1,
1851 . . . .   **150.00**

AUTOMOBILES

History: Automobiles can be classified into several categories. In 1947 the Antique Automobile
Club of America devised a system whereby any
motor vehicle (car, bus, motorcycle, etc.) made
prior to 1930 is an "antique" car. The Classic Car
Club of America expanded the list focusing on
luxury models from 1925 to 1948. The Milestone
Car Society developed a list for cars in the 1948
to 1964 period.

Some states, such as Pennsylvania, have devised a dual registration system for older cars—
antique and classic. Models from the 1960s and
1970s, especially convertibles and limited production models, fall into the "classic" designation depending how they are used.

References: Quentin Craft, *Classic Old Car
Value Guide, 21st Edition,* published by author,
1987; *The Official Price Guide To Collector Cars,
7th Edition,* House of Collectibles, 1986.

Periodicals: *Hemmings Motor News,* Box 100,
Bennington, VT 05201; *Old Cars Price Guide,* 700
E. State Street, Iola, WI 54990; *Old Cars Weekly,*
700 E. State Street, Iola, WI 54990.

Collectors' Clubs: Antique Automobile Club of
America, 501 W. Governor Road, Hershey, PA
17033; Classic Car Club of America, P. O. Box
443, Madison, NJ 07940; Milestone Car Society,
P. O. Box 50850, Indianapolis, IN 46250.

Note: The prices below are based upon a car
in running condition, with a high percentage of
original parts, and somewhere between 60 and
80% restored. *Prices can vary by as much as 30%
in either direction.*

Many older cars, especially if restored, now exceed $15,000.00. Their limited availability makes
them difficult to price. Auctions, more than any
other source, are the true determinant of value at
this level. Especially helpful are the catalogs and
sale bills of Kruse Auctioneers, Inc., Auburn, Indiana, 46706.

AUTOMOBILES

Alfa-Romeo, 1954, Model 1900,
T.I.Super, Sedan, four door, 4 cyl. . .   **6,500.00**
Anderson, 1924, Model 50-E, Touring . **10,000.00**
Apperson, 1914, Runabout Jackrabbit   **12,400.00**
Auburn, 1929, Model 76, Cabriolet, 6
cyl. **25,000.00**
Austin-American, 1935, Bantam,
Roadster, 4 cyl. **9,000.00**
Baker Electric, 1913, Coupe **9,000.00**
Bentley, 1951–52, Abbott, Fixed Head
Coupe, 6 cyl. **15,000.00**
Brewster, 1914, Convertible, Limou-
sine **28,000.00**
Buick
1907, Model D, Touring, 4 cyl. **9,500.00**
1941, Special Series 40-A, Sport
Coupe, 8 cyl. **7,250.00**

1965, Skylark, Sedan, four door, V-6 **2,000.00**

Cadillac

1916, Phaeton, 5 pass, V-8 . . . . . . **20,000.00**
1932, Series 370-B, Convertible, V-12 . . . . **60,000.00**
1938, Series 60, Touring Sedan, V-8 . . . . **17,500.00**
1951, Series 75 Fleetwood, 8 pass Imperial **7,500.00**

Chandler, 1921, Sport Touring Model 20 . . . . **10,000.00**

Checker, 1964, Marathon, Sedan **2,000.00**

Chevrolet, 1931, Model AE, two door sedan, 6 cylinder, $10,000.00.

Chevrolet

1917, Series F2, Roadster, 4 cyl. . . **10,500.00**
1927, Model AA, Cabriolet, 4 cyl. . . **7,500.00**
1933, Standard 4D Sedan **6,500.00**
1940, Master 85, Station Wagon, 6 cyl. **7,250.00**
1942, Coupe Fleetmaster **5,000.00**
1956, Corvette, Convertible, V-8 . . **15,000.00**
1961, Corvair, Series 700, Sedan, 6 cyl. **2,200.00**

Chrysler

1926, Series G-70, Phaeton, 6 cyl. . . **11,750.00**
1933, Convertible Sedan, 6 cyl. . . . **15,750.00**
1938, Imperial Custom, Sedan, five pass, 8 cyl. **4,500.00**
1942, Town and Country, Station Wagon, woody **18,000.00**
1952, New Yorker, Convertible, 8 cyl. **8,500.00**

Columbia, 1905, Roadster, electric . . . **7,000.00**
Crosley, 1941, Convertible, 2 cyl. **2,150.00**
Cunningham, 1924, Cabriolet, 8 cyl. . . **26,000.00**
Dagmar, 1927, Sedan, 6 cyl. **9,500.00**
Datsun, 1960, Fairlady Roadster SPL 212, 4 cyl. **2,650.00**

DeSoto

1934, Airflow SE, Sedan, 6 cyl. **4,500.00**
1941, Club Coupe **3,600.00**
1958, Adventurer, Convertible, V-8 . **7,000.00**

Diana, 1927, Sedan, 8 cyl. **4,500.00**

Dodge

1917, Touring, 4 cyl. **5,000.00**
1931, Series DG, Convertible, rumble seat, 8 cyl. **14,000.00**

1951, Meadowbrook Series D42, Sedan, 6 cyl. **2,850.00**

Durant, 1928, Model M, Sedan, 4 cyl. . . **6,500.00**
Eagle, 1909, Roadster, air cooled, 2 cyl. **8,500.00**
Elcar, 1927, Touring **8,000.00**
Essex, 1924, Victoria Coupe **4,500.00**
Flint, 1926, Model 80, Brougham **7,000.00**

Ford

1912, Model T, Touring, 4 cyl. **9,000.00**
1926, Roadster Pickup **7,250.00**
1935, Model 48, Roadster, V-8 . . . . **15,000.00**
1940, Deluxe Coupe **8,750.00**
1953, Crestline, Station Wagon, 8 cyl. **3,250.00**
1959, Edsel, Ranger Series, Hardtop, four door, V-8 . . . . **3,000.00**
1960, Thunderbird, Hardtop, two door **5,750.00**

Franklin, 1912, Model M, Touring, 6 cyl. **18,000.00**
Frazer, 1948, Manhattan, Sedan, 6 cyl. **4,000.00**
Glide, 1915, Model 40, Touring, 4 cyl. **12,500.00**

Graham

1930, Cabriolet **16,500.00**
1936, Crusader Model 80, Sedan, four door, 6 cyl. **4,250.00**

Henderson, 1914, Roadster **7,500.00**

Hudson

1919, Super Six Series 0, Sedan, 6 cyl. **4,000.00**
1926, Phaeton, six pass **12,000.00**
1928, Super Six Series, Sedan, five pass **9,750.00**

Imperial, 1909, Touring **14,000.00**
Jeffrey, 1917, Roadster **8,500.00**
Kaiser, 1950, Traveler, Sedan, four door, 6 cyl. **4,000.00**
Koehler, 1913, Touring **8,000.00**
LaSalle, 1938, Series 50, Convertible, V-8 . . . . **26,500.00**

Lincoln

1923, Model L, Coupe, V-8 . . . . **16,000.00**
1938, Zephyr, Sedan, four door, V-12 **11,000.00**
1953, Capri, Convertible, V-8 . . . . . **7,500.00**
1970, Continental, Sedan, four door **3,500.00**

Marmon, 1921, Model 34, Touring, 4 pass, 6 cyl. **11,500.00**
Mercedes-Benz, 1952, Model 300, Club Coupe **29,000.00**

Mercury

1939, Coupe **7,200.00**
1946, Series 69M, Sedan, four door, V-8 . . . . **3,150.00**
1957, Montclair Series, Convertible, V-8 . . . . **5,750.00**

Metz, 1914, Speedster **7,250.00**
MG, 1932, J-2 Midget Roadster **6,500.00**

Nash

1923, Series 690, Sedan, 6 cyl. . . . **4,000.00**
1933, Standard Series, Roadster . . **8,500.00**
1953, Ambassador, Custom Country Club, 6 cyl. **3,000.00**

Oakland, 1914, Model 6-48, Touring, 6 cyl. **7,500.00**

AMX, 1968 Sports, hard top, $2,500.00.

Oldsmobile
    1909, Model D, Touring, 4 cyl. **12,000.00**
    1926, Sport Roadster, 6 cyl. **12,000.00**
    1936, Model L-36, Convertible, 8 cyl. **9,500.00**
    1941, Model 66, Sedan, four door .. **3,500.00**
    1953, Series 88, Sedan, four door, V-
    8 .... **3,250.00**
Opel, 1953, Rekord, Coupe, 1488cc .. **2,250.00**
Packard
    1912, Model NE, Coupe, 4 cyl. **11,500.00**
    1927, Single Eight (3rd Series),
    Phaeton, 8 cyl. **22,500.00**
    1951, 24th Series, Convertible **3,500.00**
Pierce Arrow, 1935, Model 845, Coupe,
    8 cyl. **28,000.00**
Plymouth
    1934, Standard PF, Business Coupe,
    6 cyl. **4,250.00**
    1941, Cabriolet **10,500.00**
    1950, DeLuxe, Coupe, 6 cyl. **3,250.00**
    1959, Belvedere, Convertible, V-8 .. **4,500.00**
Pontiac
    1927, Sport Roadster **11,000.00**
    1938, DeLuxe Model 6DA, Station
    Wagon, 6 cyl. **3,350.00**
    1950, Chieftain DeLuxe, Convertible,
    8 cyl. **6,000.00**
    1959, Catalina, Hardtop, four door, V-
    8 .... **3,000.00**
Porche, 1955, Model 356, Coupe, 4 cyl. **10,000.00**
Rambler, 1911, Model 63, Coupe, 4 cyl. **9,000.00**
Reo
    1920, Model T6, Touring, 6 cyl. **9,000.00**
    1929, Flying Cloud Sedan, S. M. **18,250.00**
Riker, 1900, Electric, Torpedo Racing . **20,000.00**
Rockne, 1932, Sedan, four door **8,000.00**
Rolls-Royce
    1923, Silver Ghost, Roadster, 6 cyl. **125,000.00**
    1924, Model 20, Limousine **18,200.00**
    1936, Model PIII, Sedan, 12 cyl. **25,000.00**
Saab, Model GT750, Sedan, two door,
    3 cyl. **2,250.00**
Sears, 1908, High Wheel Auto Buggy . **8,750.00**
Simplex, 1911, Speedster, 4 cyl. **35,000.00**
Star, 1924, Coupe, 4 cyl. **6,000.00**
Studebaker
    1915, Series 15, Model SD, Roadster,
    4 cyl. **7,500.00**

    1931, Studebaker Six, Model 53,
    Touring **12,500.00**
    1950, Commander Convertible, 6 cyl. **8,500.00**
    1957, Silver Hawk, Coupe, V-8 .... **3,000.00**
Stutz, 1924m Speedway Phaeton .. **25,000.00**
Thomas, 1909, Touring, 6 cyl. **65,000.00**
Triumph, 1955, Model TR-3, Roadster,
    4 cyl. **4,750.00**
Viking, 1929, Sedan, V-8 .... **8,000.00**
White, 1914, Model 30, Roadster **14,000.00**
Willys-Knight, 1921, Touring, 4 cyl. ... **8,200.00**

MISCELLANEOUS

Fire Engine
    Ahrens Fox, 1928, Combination Pum-
    per and Ladder **11,250.00**
    American LaFrance
        1915, Hook & Ladder **7,500.00**
        1928, Pumper **7,000.00**
        1951, 700 Series, 700 gpm Pumper **4,000.00**
    Chevrolet, 1931, Pumper **6,500.00**
    Ford, 1918, Model T **8,500.00**
    Mack
        1930, Pumper **6,000.00**
        1944, Fire Truck & Pumper **9,000.00**
        1946, Type 45, 500 gpm, Pumper **4,500.00**
    Peter Pirsch, 1945, 65', wood aerial
    ladder, all ground ladders **7,000.00**
    Seagrave
        1915, Chain Drive Pumper **7,250.00**
        1941, Fire Engine **5,000.00**
        1949, Model J, 1000 gpm cab Pum-
        per, V-12 .... **5,000.00**
Motorcycle
    Ariel, 1947, Red Hunter, 500 Twin .. **1,500.00**
    BMW, 1961, R50 .... **3,500.00**
    Harley, 1942, Model EL, sidecar ... **6,000.00**
    Indian, 1930, Scout, Model 101 .... **5,500.00**
    Triumph, 1970, Model TR6 .... **1,200.00**
    Vincent, 1951, Series C, Black
    Shadow **7,500.00**
Truck
    Chevrolet
        1932, ½ ton, Stake **6,400.00**
        1947, ½ ton, Pickup **5,000.00**
        1954, Sedan Delivery, 6 cyl. **5,000.00**
    Crosley, 1949, Panel, 4 cyl. **1,650.00**
    Diamond T, 1940, 1 ton, Pickup ... **5,750.00**
    Dodge
        1940, ¾ ton, 6 cyl. **2,500.00**
        1959, ½ ton, 6 cyl. **2,250.00**
    Federal, 1937, ¾ ton, Hercules,
    Pickup, 4 cyl. **6,250.00**
    Ford
        1933, Model 40, Delivery, V-8 ... **8,000.00**
        1940, Pickup, V-8 .... **3,250.00**
        1958, Model F100, Panel, V-8 ... **3,000.00**
    Graham, 1926, Hucksters **6,200.00**
    Hudson, 1937, Terraplane, Pickup, 6
    cyl. **3,500.00**

International Harvester, 1936, Pickup,
½ ton, 6 cyl. **2,650.00**
Mack
1916, Model AC, solid rubber . . . **12,000.00**
1929, Model AB, Pickup **6,500.00**
1937, Model BX, Diesel, Dump . . **5,000.00**
Stewart, 1½ ton, Stake **7,500.00**
Studebaker, 1948, ½ ton, 6 cyl. **2,000.00**
White, 1928, Model #15, 1½ ton
flatbed, 4 cyl. **5,000.00**

AUTOMOBILIA

History: The amount of items related to the
automobile is endless. Collectors seem to fit into
three groups—those collecting parts to restore a
car, those collecting information about a company
or certain model for research purposes, and those
trying to use automobile items for decorative purposes. Most material changes hands at the hundreds of swap meets and auto shows around the
country.

Reference: Scott Anderson, *Check The Oil:
Gas Station Collectibles With Prices,* Wallace-
Homestead, 1986.

Periodical: *Hemmings Motor News,* Box 100,
Bennington, VT 05201.

**Sign, Penn-Drake Motor Oil, 27⅞ x 9⅝″,
emb tin, litho, black ground, orange letters, made by H. L. Moore Co, Coch-
ranton, PA, $90.00.**

Advertising
Ashtray, Goodyear, tire, amber glass
wheel center 30.00
Blotter, Goodyear Tires 5.00
Mirror, Studebaker Vehicle Works,
South Bend, IN, 1910, 2¾″ oval . . 125.00
Sign
Dodge Brothers Service Station,
porcelain, c1930, 15 x 45″ 125.00
Ford Dealer's, neon 750.00
United Motor Dealer, neon outline
of early auto 1,250.00
Thermometer, Kendall Oil, round . . . 25.00
Ashtray, Buick, dash type 20.00
Bank, Phillips 66 Motor Oil, tin, 3½″ . . 15.00
Calendar, White Rose Gasoline, 1933 . 10.00
Carburetor, Buick, 1924–25 . . . . 25.00

Catalog
Auburn, 1935, part color, 9 x 16″, 16
pgs 35.00
Kissel Kar, 10 x 13″, 36 pgs 125.00
Chauffeur's Badge, 1936, Missouri . . . 15.00
Clock, Motor, "Luna," 8 day, luminous
dial, brass and bronze, 1914 . . . . . . 120.00
Display Case, Autolite, glass front, for
sparkplugs 125.00
Engine
Maxwell, 1914, complete 200.00
Packard, 1935 . . . . 800.00
Gas Pump Globe
Mobil, glass and metal 250.00
Standard Oil, crown, glass globe, one
piece, good paint 200.00
Gearshift Knob, glass swirl, blue and
white 15.00
Grill, Packard, 1941 . . . . 125.00
Headlamp, bullseye, Marchal, 12″, orig 700.00
Horn, Pierce Arrow, 1915-20, cowl
mounted, correct bracket 175.00
Hubcaps, Plymouth, 1939–40, set of 4 250.00
License Plate, 1933, North Dakota, orig
wrapper, pr 7.50
Literature
Owner's Manual, Ford, 1914, Model
T 15.00
Sales Brochure, Buick, 1933, Series
90, orig photos, 8 x 10″, black and
white 7.00
Shop and Parts Manual
Cadillac, 1941, ... 110.00
DeSoto, 1936, master 45.00
Magazine Advertisement, Wayne Cut
278, 1912 . . . . 85.00
Oil Can, Texaco, 1927, orig spout . . . 35.00
Ornament, radiator
Buick, front grill emblem, 1934 . . . . 30.00
Plymouth, 1933 . . . . 45.00
Pontiac, feather headdress, 1958 . . 15.00
Pinback Button, Buick, "Looking Fine
For 39" 45.00
Postcards, DeSoto, 1939, full color, one
with four door Sedan, other with two
door Sedan, pr 8.00
Poster, Buick, "Kansas City," 1921–22,
25 x 38″, black and white 85.00
Radio, Cadillac, 1937 . . . . 250.00
Trunk, Packard, pre-WWII, metal, 18 x
36″ 450.00

BACCARAT GLASS

History: The Sainte-Anne glassworks at Baccarat in the Voges, France, was founded in 1764

and produced utilitarian soda glass. In 1816 Aime-Gabriel d'Artiques purchased the glassworks, and a Royal Warrant was issued in 1817 for the opening of Verrerie de Vonuché Baccarat. The firm concentrated on lead crystal glass products. In 1824 a limited company was created.

From 1823 to 1857 Baccarat and Saint-Louis glassworks had a commercial agreement and used the same outlets. No merger occurred. Baccarat began the production of paperweights in 1846. In the late 19th century the firm achieved an international reputation for cut glass table services, chandeliers, display vases and centerpieces, and sculptures. Products eventually included all forms of glass ware. The firm still is active today.

Additional Listing: Paperweights.

Atomizer, 6″ h, amberina, $75.00.

Atomizer, 5″ h, 3½″ l, oval, etched crystal body, metal chrome top, marked .	85.00
Beverage Set, 4¼″ d, 9¾″ h pitcher, six 2½″ d, 4¾″ h tumblers, 11½″ d tray, Rose Tiente, marked	600.00
Biscuit Jar, 6″, etched ground, cranberry flowers, leaves, and vines, marked inside lid	400.00
Bookends, pr, 12″ h, crystal, serpentine tube on molded rocky form base, etched "Baccarat, France"	150.00
Bowl, 5½″, cameo, clear etched leaf ground, chartreuse floral dec	75.00
Brandy Snifters, gilded foliate cartouche, monogrammed N, set of 12 .	275.00
Candelabra, pr, 16″ h, ormolu mounts, early 19th C	1,800.00
Candlesticks, pr, 14½″, baluster form, spiral, dome base, clear, 19th C . . .	200.00
Cologne Bottle, 3¼ x 8″, Rose Tiente, pinwheel	85.00
Dish, oval, 3½ x 9½″, Rose Tiente . . .	75.00
Dresser Set	
5 pcs, Art Deco, amberina, swirl,	

brass rack with beveled mirror, marked	650.00
16 pcs, shaped rect molded glass case, all-over gilt vermicule pattern, removable gilt metal frame, six scent bottles with metal hinged cov, four gilt molded toilette bottles with stoppers, c1875	425.00
Epergne, 14″ h, twig and floriform SP mounts supporting fluted glass bowl and vase, c1900	300.00
Fairy Lamp, 5½ x 4½″, Rose Tiente, sunburst, matching base	230.00
Jar, cov, 6″ h, 3¼″ d, sapphire blue, swirl, marked	75.00
Liquor Bottle, 3½″ d, 10⅛″ h, lime green, gold flowers and leaves dec, three petal top, clear bubble stopper with gold dec, clear pedestal base, orig paper label	125.00
Mustard, 5 x 3″, cov, Rose Tiente, swirl	75.00
Perfume	
1½″ d, 4¼″ h, Rose Tiente, swirl, marked	65.00
5½″, amberina, shell pattern, orig stopper	65.00
Pitcher, water, 15″ tankard, deeply etched full length portrait of Napoleon in oval, wide ribbed base	400.00
Powder Jar, cov, 3½″ d, 4¼″ h, Rose Tiente, swirl, marked	100.00
Rose Bowl, 3″, cranberry, lace enamel dec	150.00
Tray, 9 x 13″, Rose Tiente	125.00
Tumbler, 3½″, Rose Tiente, marked . .	55.00
Vase	
9¼″, ovoid, cut, large thumbprint design, acid stamped factory mark .	190.00
12″, expanding circular section on short foot, opal, pale yellow enameled hummingbird, butterfly, and summer blossoms, border of pink thistle blossoms and gilt leaves, marked "Baccarat le 26 Septembre 1860"	1,000.00
Wine, Perfection pattern	45.00
Wine Coolers, pr, 9½″ h, tapered oct base, applied gilt bronze collar, loop handles	1,700.00

BANKS, MECHANICAL

History: Banks which display some form of action while utilizing a coin are considered mechanical banks. Although mechanical banks are known which date back to ancient Greece and Rome, the majority of collectors center their interests in those made between 1867 and 1928 in Germany, England, and the United States. Recently there has been an upsurge of interest in later types, some of which date into the 1970s.

Initial research suggested that approximately 250 to 300 different or variant designs of banks were made in the early period. Today that number has been revised to 2,000–3,000 types and varieties. The field remains ripe for discovery and research.

Over 80% of all cast iron mechanical banks produced between 1869 and 1928 were made by J.E. Stevens Co., Cromwell, Connecticut. Tin banks tend to be German in origin.

While rarity is a factor in value, appeal of design, action, quality of manufacture, country of origin, and history of collector interest also are important. Radical price fluctuations may occur with an imbalance of these factors. Rare banks may sell for a few hundred dollars while one of more common design with greater appeal will sell in the thousands.

The prices on our list represent fairly what a bank sells for in the specialized collectors market. Some banks are hard to find and establishing a price outside auction is difficult.

The prices listed are for original old mechanical banks with minor repairs, in sound operating condition, and with a majority of the original paint intact.

References: Al Davidson, *Penny Lane, A History Of Antique Mechanical Toy Banks,* Long's Americana; Bill Norman, *The Bank Book: The Encyclopedia of Mechanical Bank Collecting,* Collectors' Showcase, 1984.

Reproduction Alert: Reproductions, fakes, and forgeries exist for many banks. Forgeries of some mechanical banks were made as early as 1937, so age alone is not a guarantee of authenticity. In our listing two asterisks indicate banks for which serious forgeries exist and one asterisk indicates banks for which casual reproductions have been made.

Advisor: James S. Maxwell, Jr.

Eagle and Eaglets, iron, J & E Stevens Co, Cromwell, CT, Charles M. Henn designer, patent 1-23-1883, $575.00.

** Afghanistan, iron	1,150.00
African Native, tin	600.00
Alligator, pot metal, spring jawed	400.00
Artillery Bank, eight sided block house, cannon shoots	625.00
Aunt Dinah and the Good Fairy	20,000.00
Automatic Coin Savings, iron	1,500.00
Baby Elephant, unlocks at 10 o'clock, lead and wood	5,750.00
Bamboula, iron	750.00
Bank Teller, iron, tall man behind three sided lattice work grill	8,000.00
Bear, tin	900.00
** Bear and Tree Stump, iron	675.00
** Bill E. Grin, iron	650.00
** Bird on Roof, iron	875.00
Blacksmith, lead	2,875.00
Bow-ery, iron, wooden works	9,500.00
Bowling Alley, wood and iron, ball knocks down wooden pins and rings bell	16,000.00
** Boy and Bull Dog, brass	850.00
** Boy Robbing Bird's Nest, iron	1,350.00
Boy Scout with Tray, tin	950.00
Breadwinners, iron	5,500.00
** Bucking Mule, iron	1,050.00
** Bull and Bear, brass	5,000.00
Bulldog, tin, English type	550.00
** Bulldog Standing, coin on tongue	450.00
** Bull with Movable Horns, iron	450.00
Bureau, iron, Ideal	750.00
Bureau, wood, Lewando's toy savings	5,800.00
Bureau, wood, Serrill patent	975.00
** Butting Goat, tree stump	650.00
* Cabin, iron	275.00
Called Out, brass pattern	3,600.00
** Called Out, iron, painted	6,000.00
Calumet with Calumet Kid, cardboard and tin can	150.00
Calumet with Sailor, cardboard and tin can	350.00
Calumet with Soldier, cardboard and tin can	650.00
** Camera, iron	2,200.00
Carnival, iron	1,275.00
** Cat & Mouse, iron, cat stands on hands	980.00
Cat, pot metal, spring jawed	325.00
** Chief Big Moon, iron	845.00
Chinaman, coin on tongue	450.00
Chinaman in Boat, lead	7,600.00
Chinaman with Queue, tin	975.00
Circus, iron	4,450.00
Clever Dick, tin	850.00
Clown, tin, white faced	875.00
Clown Bust with Acorn Shaped Hat, iron	1,650.00
Clown on Lattice Base, tin clown with tray on iron base, does flip	5,800.00
Coasting, iron	7,500.00
Columbian Magic Savings, iron	460.00
* Creedmoor, iron	450.00
Crossed Legged Minstrel, tin	450.00
Cupola, iron, man in circular building	1,350.00
* Darktown Battery, iron	1,150.00
Darky Fisherman, lead	11,500.00

Dinah, iron	425.00
Ding Dong Bell, tin, windup	6,375.00
Dog on Turntable, iron	400.00
Dog Standing, tin, nods head	475.00
Droste's, tin	360.00
* Eagle and Eaglettes, iron	750.00
** Elephant, iron, Hannibal	540.00
Elephant, iron, made in Canada, trunk moves	625.00
** Elephant, iron, three stars	390.00
** Elephant, iron, tusks on wheels	1,250.00
Elephant, tin, safe deposit	4,200.00
* Elephant and Three Clowns	850.00
** Elephant with Howdah, iron, pull tail	300.00
Feed the Goose, pot metal	280.00
Feed the Kitty, pot metal	1,400.00
** Ferris Wheel, iron and tin, no markings (smaller than Bowen's Pat. model)	1,500.00
Five Cent Adding, iron	750.00
** Football, iron, boy and shed	1,900.00
Fortune Wheel, tin	875.00
Freedman, wood, pewter, cloth, etc., man sitting at desk	20,000.00
** Frogs, iron, two	550.00
Frogs on Rock, iron	270.00
** Gem, iron	350.00
Giant in Tower, iron	5,500.00
** Girl Skipping Rope, iron	6,000.00
** Glutton, iron, lifts turkey	725.00
** Goat, Frog, and Old Man, iron	2,800.00
Grenadier, iron	720.00
Guessing, lead and iron, woman's figure	7,800.00
Hall's Excelsior, iron and wood, monkey figure	200.00
Hall's Lilliput, Type I	450.00
Hall's Lilliput, Type III	350.00
Hall's Yankee Notion, iron	2,300.00
Hardwig and Vogel Candy Dispenser, tin	660.00
Hen and Chick, iron	1,125.00
** Hindu, iron	1,450.00
** Hold the Fort, iron, seven holes	1,500.00
Home, tin	240.00
Hoop-la, iron	950.00
** Horse Race, iron with tin horses, straight base	1,450.00
Horse Race Savings Bank, tin, Pat. Oct. 5, 1897	3,500.00
Huntley and Palmers Biscuit Tin, drawer pulls out	1,280.00
** I Always Did 'Spise A Mule, iron, jockey	650.00
* Indian and Bear, iron, brown bear	750.00
Indian Chief, aluminum, bust, black face with headdress	4,500.00
Japanese Ball Tosser, tin, windup	5,000.00
John Bull's Money Box, iron	8,000.00
** Jolly Nigger, aluminum, bar and screw side	165.00
** Jolly Nigger, aluminum, moves ears, high hat	250.00
** Jolly Nigger, aluminum, with fez	400.00
** Jolly Nigger, iron, butterfly tie	190.00
** Jolly Nigger, iron, fixed eyes	240.00
* Jonah and Whale, iron, rect base	950.00
** Jumbo, iron, elephant on wheels	975.00
Key, iron, Golden Gate Exposition	450.00
Kilte, iron	850.00
Lehmann London Tower, tin	1,700.00
Lighthouse, pot metal	600.00
Lion, tin	1,150.00
** Lion and Two Monkeys, iron	575.00
Little Jack Horner, tin, windup	5,000.00
Little Joe, iron	205.00
** Lost Dog, iron	725.00
** Magic Man, iron	750.00
Magic Safe, tin	675.00
Magie, tin	1,100.00
** Mama Katzenjammer, iron, 1905–08, dark blue dress painted to neck	2,750.00
Mammy and Child, iron	1,000.00
Man in Chair with Dog near Feet, wood	3,600.00
Man standing wearing Top Hat, wood	1,050.00
Memorial Liberty Bell, iron	750.00
** Merry-Go-Round, iron, semi-mechanical version	400.00
Mickey Mouse with Accordian, tin	2,700.00
** Milking Cow, iron	1,400.00
Model Railroad Drink Dispenser, tin	2,200.00
Model Railroad Ticket Dispenser, tin	2,200.00
** Monkey, iron, drop coin in stomach	1,250.00
Monkey Face	1,125.00
Moody and Sanky, iron and paper	700.00
Moonface, tin	1,150.00
Motor, iron, trolley car	3,750.00
Musical, tin	875.00
Musical Savings, wood and tin, Regina music box	4,500.00
Musical Savings, wood base	2,075.00
National, iron	1,000.00
New, iron, lever on side	400.00
North Pole, iron	5,500.00
Novelty, iron, Johnson's Pat	400.00
* Organ, iron, boy and girl	575.00
* Organ, iron, medium	625.00
Owl, iron, slot in book	425.00
* Owl, iron, turns head	270.00
Panorama, iron	1,800.00
Patronize the Blind Man, iron	1,600.00
** Pelican with Arab, iron	900.00
** Pelican with Man Thumbing Nose, iron	1,125.00
** Perfection Registering, iron, girl at blackboard	2,900.00
** Piano, iron, modern conversion to musical	1,600.00
Picture Gallery Bank	1,875.00
Pistol, cast iron	650.00
Popeye Knockout, tin	375.00
Preacher in Pulpit, iron	15,000.00
Presto, iron, small building with drawer	380.00
Preston, iron and sheet metal, 1930s house	750.00
Professor Pug Frog, iron	2,100.00
Punch and Judy, cast iron front, tin back	1,550.00

Punch and Judy, tin, beach scene . . .	300.00
Puss and Boots, iron	20,000.00
Queen Victoria, brass, bust	5,000.00
Rabbit, iron, small	475.00
Registering Dime Savings	475.00
Robot, aluminum	1,800.00
** Rooster, iron	315.00
Sailor Face, tin	850.00
Sambo, iron	625.00

Organ Bank, seated man with top hat, iron, Kyser & Rex, $400.00.

** Santa Claus, iron	780.00
Savo, tin, rect with lines	210.00
Savo, tin, rect with soldiers	275.00
Schley Bottling Up Cervera, iron	3,750.00
Seek Him Frisk, iron, dog chases cat up tree	18,000.00
Sentry, tin, raises bugle	1,200.00
Shoot That Hat, iron	12,000.00
Shoot the Chute, iron	6,500.00
** Smyth X-Ray, iron	3,750.00
** Snap It, iron	450.00
Springing Cat, lead	4,250.00
Squirrel, lead	550.00
Starkies Aeroplane	8,500.00
Stollwerk, tin, Vending	480.00
* Stump Speaker	875.00
** Tabby, iron	500.00
Tank and Cannon, iron	585.00
Target Building, iron	750.00
* Teddy and the Bear, iron	840.00
Thrifty Animal, tin	420.00
Tid-Bits Automatic Money Box, tin . . .	1,850.00
Time Is Money, iron, embossing of man bent over	2,400.00
Toad on Stump, iron	440.00
Tommy, iron	2,300.00
* Trick Dog, iron, six part base	540.00
** Trick Donkey, iron	625.00
Trick Savings, wood, end drawer	285.00
** Tricky Pig, iron, risque	1,800.00

** Turtle, iron	4,000.00
Twentieth Century Savings Bank	950.00
U. S., iron	1,250.00
Uncle Sam, iron, standing figure	1,000.00
** Uncle Tom, iron, no star	540.00
Uncle Tom, iron, no lapels	510.00
Village School Master, tin, windup . . .	3,750.00
Watch, tin, dime disappears, several varieties	675.00
Watch Dog Savings, wood	950.00
* William Tell, iron	650.00
Winner Savings, tin and glass, horse race	4,000.00
Wishbone, iron	12,500.00
Woodchopper, iron	810.00
Woodpecker, tin, 1940s	425.00
World's Fair, iron	775.00

BANKS, STILL

History: Banks with no mechanical action are known as still banks. The first still banks were made of wood, pottery, or from gourds. Redware and stoneware banks, made by America's early potters, are prized possessions of today's collectors.

Still banks reached a "golden age" with the arrival of the cast iron bank. Leading manufacturing companies include Arcade Mfg. Co., J. Chein & Co., Hubley, J. & E. Stevens and A. C. Williams. The banks often were ornately painted to enhance their appeal. During the cast iron era, banks and other businesses used the still bank as a form of advertising for attracting customers.

The tin lithograph bank, again frequently with advertising, did not reach its zenith until the 1930 to 1955 period. The tin bank was an important premium, whether it be a Pabst Blue Ribbon beer can bank or a Gerber's Orange Juice bank. Most tin advertising banks resembled the packaging shape of the product.

Almost every substance has been used to make a still bank–diecast white metal, aluminum, brass, plastic, glass, etc. Many of the early glass candy containers also converted to a bank when the candy was eaten. Thousands of varieties of still banks were made, and hundreds of new varieties appear on the market each year.

References: Earnest Ida and Jane Pitman, *Dictionary of Still Banks*, Long's Americana, 1980; Andy and Susan Moore, *Penny Bank Book, Collecting Still Banks*, Schiffer Publishing, Ltd., 1984; Hubert B. Whiting, *Old Iron Still Banks*, Forward's Color Productions, Inc. 1968, out of print.

Collectors' Club: Still Bank Collectors Club of America, P. O. Box 356, Bradford, VT 05033. *Penny Bank Post.*

Museum: Perelman Antique Toy Museum, Philadelphia, PA; Margaret Woodbury Strong Museum, Rochester, NY.

Wood, mahogany, 3¼ x 5 x 4¾", slant front writing desk shape, $100.00.

CHALK

Dove, 11" h, dove, worn green, red, and
yellow ochre paint 225.00
Pig, 7⅛" l, old white repaint, pink ears   85.00

GLASS

Bulldog, 4½", sitting, tin closure 35.00
Clock, 3¾", mantel type, painted, tin closure 25.00
Independence Hall, 7¼", clear, tin closure 225.00
Pig, 4¼" l, painted gold 25.00
Radio, clear 25.00

METAL. Cast Iron unless otherwise stated.

Advertising
Gem Heaters, 4⅝" h, figural, parlor
stove, marked "Abendroth Bros,
NY," bronze finish 185.00
Mellon Furnace, 3⅝" h, worn bronze
finish 115.00
Peter's Weatherbird Shoes, 2" h, tin
and printed paper 20.00
Animal
Bear, 7" h, stealing honey, brown japanning, gold trim 175.00
Bull
6" l, standing on rect base, worn
polychrome, pitted surface 175.00
7½" l, Aberdeen Angus, aluminum,
black paint 60.00
Cat
4¼", bow, polychrome 90.00
4¾", "Feed the Kitty," silvered lead   75.00
4⅞", "Lindy's Kat Bank," lead, silver gilt, trap missing 85.00

5⅝" l, ball, worn gold paint 315.00
Cockatoo
2⅞" h, ball, lead and tin, minor wear
to polychrome 175.00
5" h, white metal, polychrome . . .   250.00
Cow, milking, 7" l, nickel steel, polychrome 200.00
Dog
Boston Bull, 4⅜", polychrome . . .   150.00
Newfoundland, pack 75.00
Scottie, 2⅞", black paint 60.00
Donkey, 7½" h, on base, worn polychrome 425.00
Elephant
2½" h, swivel trunk, black, gold trim   180.00
3⅝" l, traces of bronze finish 75.00
Horse
4¼", standing under horseshoe,
marked "Good Luck", black and
gold 135.00
7½", rearing 75.00
Lion, 2⅝", minor wear to gold paint .   55.00
Owl, 4¼" h, polychrome 135.00
Pig
4⅜" l, "Decker's Iowana," minor
wear to gold paint 85.00
7" l, "All Hog Bank, Take All I Get,"
corkscrew tail, layers of gold and
black paint, ...   125.00
Turkey, 4¼" h, brown japanning, red
highlights 300.00
Beehive, 5½", combination bank and
string holder, worn bronze finish,
nickel plated brass finial 450.00
Bible, 3⅝" l, hinged cov, German inscription "Dein Reich Komme!" (Thy
Kingdom Come), black, gold trim, unpainted curved side replacement
piece 300.00
Bucket, 3¼" h, marked "White City Puzzle," nickel finish 100.00

Cast Iron, 5¾" h, emb "Give Me A Penny," black, red hat and coat, gold letters, turn pin, $150.00.

Building

Bank

3¼" h, cupola, worn polychrome, light rust **55.00**
4⅛" h, "Home Bank," traces of green paint **210.00**
4¼" h, "Deposit," worn japanning . **75.00**
Bungalow, 3¾" h, bronze finish **150.00**
Castle, 7" h, two towers, brown japanning **400.00**
Cottage, 3¾" l, half frame, silver plated, hinged lid, key lock **50.00**
Merry Go Round, 4⅝" h, nickel finish **215.00**
Mosque, 4⅛" h, "Jewel Bank," worn nickel finish **115.00**
Old South Church, 9¾" h, white metal, old gold repaint, professional repair to roof **575.00**
Pagoda, 5" h, silver, worn gold paint **265.00**
San Gabriel Mission, CSMS Bank, 4¾" h, worn polychrome **875.00**
Washington Monument, 6⅛" h, worn gold paint **125.00**
Westminster Abbey, 6⅝" h, traces of gold paint **165.00**

Character and Personality

Dot, 3⅞" h, nickel finish, very light rust **125.00**
Dutch Boy, 8¼" h, factory conversion from doorstop, worn polychrome repaint **200.00**
Foxy Grandpa, 5½" h, worn polychrome **55.00**
Golliwog, 6" h, unpainted aluminum . **100.00**
Mickey Mouse, 4⅝" l, playing mandolin, white metal, polychrome ... **150.00**
Mutt & Jeff, 5⅛" h, minor wear to gold paint **140.00**
Pirate, 5⅞" h, white metal, worn polychrome **35.00**
Roosevelt, F. D., 4¾" h, marked "F. D. Roosevelt, New Deal," minor wear to bronze and green paint .. **225.00**
Von Hindenburg, 9¼" h, bust, lead . **350.00**
Football, 3¼" l, "Official League Ball," worn nickel finish **175.00**
Gun Boat, 8½" l, painted blue and white, brown masts **850.00**
Jukebox, 3⅛" h, Wurlitzer, white metal, polychrome **50.00**

Liberty Bell

2¾" h, red paint, gold trim **155.00**
4½" h, marked "The Old Liberty Bell," green patina, worn nickel base, orig worn paper label **85.00**
7" h, white metal, dark finish, wood base **125.00**
Parlor Stove, 7" h, black, metallic trim . **225.00**
Radio, 3¼" h, blue paint, gold trim ... **115.00**
Safe, 4" h, combination lock, black, gold trim, nickel dial **75.00**
Tank, 8¼" l, worn brown japanning, gold trim, replaced screw and washer ... **225.00**

Treasure Chest, 2¾" l, minor wear to gold paint **70.00**
Zeppelin, 7⅞" l, Graf, minor wear to silver paint, nickel wheels **265.00**

PAPIER MACHE

Charlie McCarthy, "Feed Me...," worn polychrome **30.00**
Kewpie, 5" h, worn polychrome, no trap **35.00**
Scottie, 5⅛" h, black, orange eyes ... **18.00**

POTTERY

Acorn, adv "Acorn Stoves Will Save Half Your Fuel Money" **75.00**
Bag, 6" h, Oriental figures **30.00**
Colonial Woman, 2¼", polychrome enamel dec, Staffordshire **75.00**
Cottage, 4¾", polychrome enamel dec, Staffordshire **60.00**
Log Cabin, 3¾" l, "House in which Abraham Lincoln was Born..." **15.00**
Pig, 4" l, clear and brown marbleized glaze **18.00**

BARBER BOTTLES

History: Barber bottles, colorful glass bottles found on the shelves and counters in barber shops, held the liquids barbers used daily. A specific liquid was kept in a specific bottle which the barber knew by color, design, or lettering. The bulk liquids were kept in utilitarian containers under the counter or in a storage room. The attractive bottles held the place of honor.

Barber bottles are found in many types of glass: art glass with varied decoration, pattern glass, and commercially prepared and labeled bottles.

References: Richard Holiner, *Collecting Barber Bottles*, Collector Books, 1986; Ralph & Terry Kovel, *The Kovels' Bottle Price List*, Crown Publishers, Inc. 1984, 7th ed.

Note: Prices are for bottles without original stoppers unless otherwise noted.

Amber
6¾", Daisy and Button pattern, flared mouth **30.00**
7¼", melon shape, Coin Spot pattern, rolled lip, smooth base **45.00**
Amethyst
7½", Mary Gregory, white enamel figure **250.00**
7⅞", white enamel dec, woman with long flowing hair, rolled lip, pontil, label "VEGEDERMA" **385.00**
8", applied enamel floral dec, rolled lip, pontil **70.00**
8⅝", enamel and gilt Art Nouveau style dec, formed lip and pontil .. **150.00**

Blue
  7¼″, Coin Spot pattern, rolled lip, po-
    lished pontil 135.00
  8″, Thumbprint pattern, white enamel
    dec, woman surrounded by leaves
    and hollyhock wreaths, rolled lip,
    pontil 330.00
Clear, 7⅞″, light pink frosting, applied
  heavy enamel dec, lattice work and
  floral vines 275.00
Cobalt Blue, 8″, Loetz, irid purple
  streaks, sheared mouth, smooth
  base, 1870–1920 . . . . 170.00
Frosted, clear, 8¼″, inverted cone
  shape, painted lavender palm tree
  dec, tooled mouth, smooth base,
  1870–1920 . . . . 200.00
Hobnail
  Amethyst, orig stopper 100.00
  Canary, 7¼″, three pouring rings,
    round lip, smooth base 40.00
  Clear, 6¾″, opal hobnails, rolled lip,
    polished pontil 40.00
  Cranberry, 7¼″, rolled lip, polished
    pontil, three pouring rings 110.00
  Topaz, 7″, tooled mouth, smooth
    base, 1870–1920 . . . . 40.00

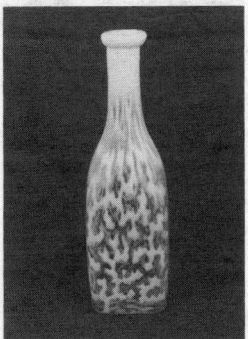

Opal, 8½″ h, seaweed pattern, $275.00.

Opalescent
  Cranberry, 8⅜″, sq, Spanish Lace,
    rolled lip, polished pontil 100.00
  Light Blue
    Fluted, 6⅞″, Coin Spot pattern,
      tooled mouth, smooth base . . . 80.00
    Round, 9¼″, rolled lip, Waffle pat-
      tern 75.00
    Square, 8¼″, Spanish Lace, rolled
      lip, polished pontil 210.00
  Sapphire Blue, 7¼″ h, white enamel
    Mary Gregory dec, young girl in sail-
    or's suit, sheared mouth, pontil 200.00

Spatter Glass, opal, polished mouth and
  base
  Cranberry, 8″ 55.00
  Light blue and white, 8¼″ 210.00
  Yellow-green, 7⅝″, Tiffany type, rolled
    lip and pontil 120.00
  Violet Blue, 8¹⁄₁₆″, applied Art Nouveau
    enamel dec 275.00

BAROMETERS

History: A barometer is an instrument which
measures atmospheric pressure which, in turn,
aids weather forecasting. Low pressure indicates
the coming of rain, snow, or storm; high pressure
signifies fair weather.

Most barometers use an evacuated and graduated glass tube which contains a column of mercury and are classified by the shape of the case.
An aneroid barometer has no liquid and works by
a needle connected to the top of a metal box in
which a partial vacuum is maintained. The movement of the top moves the needle.

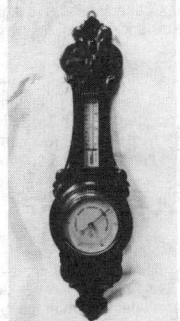

**Short and Mason, London, #2404,
26½″, $250.00.**

Aneroid
  5½″, Holosteric, brass, ring hanging
    mount, marked "France, USLH Es-
    tablishment" from New London
    Lighthouse 265.00
  6½″, hand carved oak frame 75.00
Banjo
  37″, rosewood, English, case fitted
    with hygrometer dial, arched ther-
    mometer, small mirror, round ba-
    rometer dial, 19th C 275.00
  38½″, mahogany, inlaid case, ther-
    mometer, and silvered dial, sgd
    "Pastorelli, Bowling St., Westmins-
    ter," Victorian 600.00

39½", mahogany, level, convex mirror, thermometer, and hydrometer, English **350.00**

45", Louis XIV, bouelle marquetry, ormolu dial, white enamel, surmounted by figure of Vanity, veneered pedestal, brass mounts, blue tortoiseshell ground **2,000.00**

50½", mahogany, 12" silvered scale, mercury thermometer, hygrometer, spirit level, inscribed "V. Zanetti, Manchester" **2,500.00**

Desk

6", gilt bronze, barometer, thermometer, clock, marked "Gustave Keller," c1900 . . . . **1,000.00**

Stick

36½", rosewood, George VI, rect silvered dial, waisted case, fluted pilaster form vial cov, demilune plinth, c1860 . . . . **1,600.00**

37", rosewood, William IV, waisted case, ivory scale with brass border, sgd "S A Caile, Newcastle," c1835 **1,600.00**

38", mahogany, George III, broken arch pediment, paper face **575.00**

38¾", inlaid mahogany case and dial, thermometer, sgd "Smith & Sons, Scarboro" **500.00**

39", mahogany, sgd "I Sordelli, London" **285.00**

42", mahogany, George III, broken pediment, waisted case, marquetry anthemion, hygrometer, rect barometer, and thermometer, London, c1775 . . . . **2,500.00**

58", mahogany, Georgian, split baluster, thermometer, 19th C **700.00**

Wheel

38", mahogany, thermometer and hydrometer, marked "S. Crocker, Kingston" **365.00**

39", late George III, inlaid mahogany, inlaid shell dec, sgd "Holbn, London," early 19th C **800.00**

40½", Victorian, walnut, sgd "Abraham & Co., Liverpool" **285.00**

BASKETS

History: Baskets were invented when man first required containers to gather, store, and transport goods. Today's collector, influenced by the country look, focuses on baskets made of splint, rye straw, or willow. Emphasis is placed on handmade examples. Nails or staples, wide splints which are thin and evenly cut, and a wire bail handle denote factory construction which can date back to the mid-19th century. Painted or woven decorated baskets rarely are handmade, unless American Indian.

Baskets are collected by (a) type–berry, egg, or field, (b) region–Nantucket or Shaker, and (c) composition–splint, rye, or willow. Stick to examples in very good condition; damaged baskets are a poor investment even at a low price.

References: Frances Thompson-Johnson, *Wallace-Homestead Price Guide To Baskets*, Wallace-Homestead, 1987; Don and Carol Raycraft, *Country Baskets*, Wallace-Homestead, 1982 (fourth printing); Frances Thompson, *Antique Baskets and Basketry*, Wallace-Homstead, 1985; Martha Wetherbee and Nathan Taylor, *Legend of the Bushwhacker Basket*, published by author, 1986; Christoph Will, *International Basketry For Weavers and Collectors*, Schiffer Publishing, 1985

Reproduction Alert: Modern reproductions abound, made by diverse groups ranging from craft revivalists to foreign manufacturers.

Market, early, 10½ x 9", braided rim, $15.00

Bread, 15" d, coil work, open handles, Pennsylvania **60.00**

Cheese, 26" d, hexagon weave, New England, mid 19th C **375.00**

Egg

11 x 13", woven splint, bentwood handle **350.00**

11½ x 13", woven splint, radiating ribs, handle, old yellow paint **95.00**

12 x 17", woven splint, bentwood handle **400.00**

12 x 21", oval, woven splint, radiating ribs, bentwood handle **65.00**

14 x 15", woven splint, radiating ribs, brown varnish finish, bentwood handle **85.00**

14 x 17½", woven splint, radiating ribs design, handle **175.00**

15 x 9", woven splint, radiating ribs design, bentwood handle, old orange varnish **125.00**

Field

22", oval, oak splint, plaited weaving pattern, carved hickory handle . . . **225.00**

28" d, checker work bottom 375.00
Fruit Drying, ash splint, pine frame, mortised ribs, pinned 350.00
Garden, 32 x 18 x 13", oak splint, rib construction, braided handle, late 19th C 275.00
Herb, oak splint, "X" wrapped rim, early 20th C, New England 125.00
Knife and Fork, 11 x 6½ x 5", oak splint, carved bow type handle, painted green, late 19th C 160.00
Market
 14 x 16", 9¼" h, woven reed and splint, oval rim, bentwood swivel handle, round base 75.00
 15" l, 6" h, woven splint, oval rim tapers to rect base, bentwood handle, painted dark green, 19th C . . 275.00
Melon
 5½", ash splint, rib construction, hickory splint handle 130.00
 14 x 17", 20 rib, woven splint, bentwood handle, worn finish 165.00
Miniature, woven oak splint, double rim, painted orange with black dec, carved handle, mid 19th C 375.00
Nantucket
 6¼" d, 2⅞" h, swivel handle, printed label "Light ship Basket, made by William D Appleton, Nantucket, Mass" 850.00
 14 x 16½", woven rattan sides, bentwood swing handles, wood base sgd "Made in Nantucket Jose Formoso Reyes" 2,550.00
Picnic, 10¼ x 16", 22 rib, woven natural and colored splint, bentwood handle, double hinged cov 175.00
Sewing, rib construction, demi-john bottom, double wrapped rim, hickory handles 140.00
Storage
 10" d, 3¼" h, open, woven splint, round top, sq base, wrapped rim, bentwood rim handles 225.00
 18 x 24", cov, woven splint, yellow, red, and natural, black potato print design 350.00
Utility, 13" d, tightly woven, ash splint, carved oak bows, rib construction, late 19th C 140.00
Weaver's, 10½ x 18", woven splint, orange and blue watercolor designs, divided int., rounded corners 175.00

BATTERSEA ENAMELS

History: Battersea enamel is a generic term for English enamel-on-copper objects of the 18th century.

In 1753 Stephen Theodore Janssen established a factory to produce "Trinkets and Curiosities Enamelled on Copper" at York House, Battersea, London. Here the new invention of transfer printing developed a high degree of excellence, and the resulting trifles delighted fashionable Georgian society.

Recent research has shown that enamels actually were being produced in London and the Midlands several years before York House was established. However, most enamel trinkets still are referred to as "Battersea Enamels," even though they were probably made in other workshops in London, Birmingham, Bilston, Wednesbury, or Liverpool.

All manner of charming items were made, including snuff and patch boxes bearing mottos and memory gems. (By adding a mirror inside the lid, a snuff box became patch box). Many figural whimsies, called "toys," were created to amuse a gay and fashionable world. Many other elaborate articles, e.g., candlesticks, salts, tea caddies, and bonbonnieres, were made for the tables of the newly rich middle classes.

Reference: Susan Benjamin, *English Enamel Boxes*, Merrimack Publishers Circle, 1978.

Advisors: Barbara and Melvin Alpren.

Box, 1⅜ x 1½ x 1", St. Ann's Well, Buxton, scenic, black letters and scene, gold trim, white ground, blue base, $450.00.

Bonbonniere
 Otter's head, natural colors, floral slip on lid, c1770, Bilston 2,500.00
 Spaniel, King Charles, oval, black and white, yellow ground, pastoral scene lid, c1770, Bilston 2,900.00
Candlestick, 10½" h, white ground, landscape vignettes within pink ground, gilt scroll borders, c1770, Bilston 3,900.00

Cloak Hooks, 2" l, oval, rose festooned anchors, white ground, c1775, South Staffordshire **500.00**

Counter Box, 1½" d, ivory, fanned playing cards top, center inscribed "Lady Luck," tortoise shell lined, c1770 ... **950.00**

Patch Box

¾", round, "Keep this for my Sake," slip lid, c1775, Bilston **350.00**

1¼", "Always the same," oval, love birds on white lid, pink base, c1780, Bilston **500.00**

1½", "A Trifle from Abroad," oval, white, blue ship, red wavy border, c1775, Bilston **550.00**

2¼", oval, red checked gingham, green raised ivy, c1770, Bilston .. **650.00**

Scent Bottle Holder, ½ x 1¼ x 2¼", pink all-over floral with trellis, leafy green, c1775, Bilston **350.00**

Snuff Box, 2½" l, white, lovers in pastoral setting, ruin background, c1780, Bilston **800.00**

BAVARIAN CHINA

History: Bavaria, Germany, was an important porcelain production center, similar to the Staffordshire district in England. The name Bavarian China refers to companies operating in Bavaria, among which were Hutschenreuther, Thomas, and Zeh, Scherzer & Co. (Z. S. & Co.). Very little of the production from this area was imported into the United States prior to 1870.

Reference: Susan and Al Bagdade, *Warman's English & Continental Pottery & Porcelain, 1st Edition,* Warman Publishing Co., Inc., 1987.

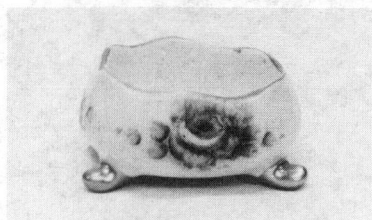

Salt, 2 x ¾", white int. and ext., two pink roses, green leaves, gold scalloped rim and feet, $20.00.

Ashtray, 5¼", sq, full figure Peter Pan seated on corner, legs extending to opposite corner, marked "Hutschenreuther" **145.00**

Berry Set, 6 pcs, small pink mums, marked "JS Bavaria" **45.00**

Bowl, 7¼", octagonal, decal, 2 parrots, reticulated lavender rim **35.00**

Cake Plate, 13", yellow and red roses, shaded green ground **60.00**

Candlesticks, pr, hp, forget-me-not dec **65.00**

Celery Tray, hp, multicolored parrots, white ground **32.50**

Chocolate Pot, cov, hp, pink flowers, green ground **85.00**

Creamer and Sugar, cov, violets dec, gold handles, sgd "Hirt," c1870 .... **45.00**

Cup and Saucer, pink roses, pink luster ground **40.00**

Dinner Set, hp, birds, blue, gray, and yellow ground, marked "Paul Mueller, Selb," 66 pcs **250.00**

Dish, 9½ x 10", sq, open handles, white, garlands of pink and tan roses, green leaves and stems, maroon border, gold dec **40.00**

Dresser Set, hp, pink, cream, and green, hp, 1914, 3 pcs **75.00**

Hair Receiver, pink roses, green leaves, gold trim, marked "Z. S. & Co." **25.00**

Marmalade Jar, 6", cov, underplate, 2 handles, hp, pink roses, black and gold trim, cream ground **100.00**

Mayonnaise Set, rose dec, cream ground, 3 pcs **65.00**

Mug, 5¾", hp, yellow and russet corn and husk dec, orange luster dragon form handle **45.00**

Perfume Doll, yellow, long dauber ... **85.00**

Pitcher, 9", bulbous, burnished gold lizard handle, hp blackberry dec, shaded ground, artist sgd **115.00**

Plate

6", geraniums dec, marked "Z. S. & Co." **18.00**

9½", peonies on cobalt blue center, gold foliage **45.00**

Powder Box, cov, figural woman holding rose bouquet, marked "Bavaria 3153" **80.00**

Syrup, decal, ivory roses, pale green ground **35.00**

Teapot, cov, hp, heavy silver overlay . **125.00**

Toothpick, pink flowers, green leaves, shaded ground, gold rim, marked "Versailles/R. C. Bavaria" **25.00**

Wall Pocket, figural, woman **80.00**

BELLEEK

History: Belleek, a thin, ivory colored, almost iridescent-type porcelain, was first made in 1857 in county Fermanagh, Ireland. Production continued until World War I, was discontinued for a period of time, and then resumed. The Shamrock pattern is most familiar, but many patterns were made, including, Limpet, Tridacna, and Grasses.

Irish Belleek has several identifying marks, e.g., the Harp and Hound (1865–80) and Harp, Hound, and Castle (1863–91). After 1891 the word "Ireland" or "Erie" was added. Some pieces are marked "Belleek Co., Fermanagh."

There is an Irish saying: If a newly married couple receives a gift of Belleek, their marriage will be blessed with lasting happiness.

Several American firms made a Belleek-type porcelain. The first was Ott and Brewer Co. Trenton, New Jersey, in 1884, followed by Willets. Other firms included The Ceramic Art Co. (1889), American Art China Works (1892), Columbian Art Co. (1893), and Lenox, Inc. (1904).

Reference: Mary Frank Aston, *American Belleek,* Collector Books, 1984.

Additional Listings: Lenox.

Abbreviations: 1BM = 1st Black Mark; 2BM = 2nd Black Mark; 3BM = 3rd Black Mark; 4GM = 4th Green Mark; 5GM = 5th Green Mark.

Advisor: Mary Beth Appert.

Cup and Saucer, white ground, gold dec, twig handle, Willetts, American, $100.00

AMERICAN

Bowl, 9"l, Wavecrest, cream, Lenox green wreath mark	45.00
Demitasse Cup, cream liner with gold rim, SS holder, Willets brown mark .	35.00
Cup and Saucer, 4"d, 3"h, white, gold trim, SS handled holder, Lenox green wreath mark, set of 12	2,500.00
Figure	
Swan	
4" l, pink, gold trim, Lenox green wreath mark	45.00
9" l, cream, Lenox green wreath mark	90.00

Lamp, 12"h, Armstrong vase base with swan handles, cream, Lenox green wreath mark	150.00
Pitcher, 8"h, 4"d, six handled 4" h mugs, hp, pale green ground, stem with leaves and orange apples, artist sgd, "C.F. Wyatt," 1926 Lenox pallette mark	300.00
Salt	
1" d, individual	
Cream, SS holder, Willets brown mark	25.00
Painted gold, Willets brown mark, artist sgd "M.B."	18.50
2" d, master, three feet, gold painted stem with leaves, gold rim, cream ground, Lenox pallette mark, dated October 11, 1905 on bottom	17.50
Tea Set, 6" h teapot, 4" h cov creamer and sugar, sq pedestal base, angular handles, gold trim, cream ground, monogrammed "B," Lenox palette mark	210.00
Vase	
5", horn of plenty form, violet vase, pink ground, white handle, Lenox green wreath mark	35.00
7", urn form, pedestal, Rose pattern, swan handles, Lenox green wreath mark	95.00
8", tree trunk form, pink, Lenox green wreath mark	90.00
12", elongated bulbous form, pedestal, gray ground, white flashing around bottom, Lenox green wreath	120.00

IRISH

Basket	
4½" d, Heart, floral dec, pearl finish, four strands, two pads imp "Belleek" and "Co. Fermanagh"	450.00
5" d	
Heart, floral dec, pearlescent luster, four strands, three pads imp "Belleek" and "Co. Fermanagh" & "Ireland"	550.00
Shamrock, three strands, pearlescent luster, one pad imp "Belleek, Co. Fermanagh," chips . .	425.00
5¼" d, Shamrock, floral dec, painted, four strands, two pads imp "Belleek R," "Co. Fermanagh"	400.00
6" d, Erne, applied floral rim, four strands, pearl finish, one pad imp "Belleek Co., Fermanagh"	475.00
8½" d, Twig, three strands, pearl finish, applied twig handles, applied floral dec around rim, two pads imp "Belleek" and "Co. Fermanagh," minor chip on one rose	2,250.00

9¼" d, Lily, applied lily flowers around rim, painted finish, four strands, two pads imp "Belleek, R" and "Ireland" **550.00**

10½" d, Sydenham Twig, applied floral rim dec, three strands, pearl finish, applied handles, one pad marked **1,400.00**

12½" l, oval, cov, handles, applied floral dec to cover, painted finish, four strands, two pads imp "Belleek R" & "Co. Fermanagh" **2,500.00**

13¼" d, Henshall's, applied center twig handle, applied floral dec on each side of handle, pearl finish, four strands, two pads imp "Belleek" and "Co. Fermanagh" **1,900.00**

Creamer

2¼" h, Grasses, painted, 1BM **200.00**
3", Echinus, tinted, 1BM **275.00**
4", Nautilus, pearl, 1BM **300.00**
5", Undine, cob luster, 3BM **80.00**
6", Ivy, painted, 1BM **100.00**

Creamer and Sugar

3¼" h, Lotus, cob luster, 3BM **80.00**
3½", Ribbon, painted and pearl, 2BM **150.00**
4¾", Ivy, pearl, 1BM **140.00**
Egg, 3¾" h, cob luster, 6GM **150.00**

Figure

3" h

Boxer on cushion, bisque and pearl finish, 6GM **80.00**
Spaniel on Cushion, bisque and pearl finish, 6GM **80.00**
6½" h, Greyhound, bisque and pearlescent finish, sitting on base, 3BM **375.00**

Frame, 12" x 11½", two photograph openings, elaborate applied floral dec, pearl finish, 1BM **4,500.00**

Kettle, 6½" d, Grass Tea Ware, painted finish, repaired spout, 1BM **450.00**

Plate, 10" d, United States Bicentennial, painted silver with gold finish, three strand basketweave, orig thirteen states names and flowers on pads, applied states flowers, center dec of American flag with thirteen stars and stripes, special mark **6,000.00**

Teapot

3¼" h, Tridacna, pearl luster, 1BM . **500.00**
3¾", Tridacna, tinted, 1BM **600.00**
4¼", Shamrock, 3BM **160.00**
4½", Neptune, cob luster, repaired, 2BM **175.00**
5½", Neptune, pearl luster, spout chipped, 2BM **150.00**
6", Limpet, cob luster, lid repaired, 3BM **250.00**
6½", Limpet, cob luster, 6GM **175.00**

Tea Set

Limpet, teapot with lid, cream and sugar, cob luster finish, 3BM **550.00**

Neptune, kettle with lid, cream and sugar, cob luster, 6GM **500.00**

Tobacco Box, 6½" x 3¾", Mask Tea Ware, cob luster, 3BM **275.00**

Vase

5½" h, Rock Spill, cob luster, 3BM . **100.00**
7¼", Aberdeen, applied foral dec, pearl finish, 2BM **550.00**
7¾", Rock Spill, cob luster, 6GM ... **70.00**
9"

Aberdeen, applied floral dec, left handled, pearl finish, 4GM **325.00**
Tulip, triple, painted, 2BM **1,400.00**
9¼", Rock Spill, pearl finish, 2BM .. **175.00**
12", Fish, double, painted and gilt finish, 1BM **1,000.00**
13½", Nile, pearl finish, 2BM **225.00**
15¾", Fish, triple, painted, minor chips, 1BM **3,250.00**

BELLS

History: Bells have been used for centuries for many different purposes. They have been traced as far back as 2697 B.C., though at that time they did not have any true tone. One of the oldest bells is the "crotal," a tiny sphere with small holes and a ball or stone or metal inside. This type now appears as sleigh bells.

True bell making began when bronze, the mixing of tin and copper, was discovered. There are now many types of materials of which bells are made—almost as many materials as there are uses for them.

Bells of the late 19th century show a high degree of workmanship and artistic style. Glass bells from this period are sometimes an example of the glass blower's talent and the glass manufacturer's product.

Collectors' Club: American Bell Association, Rt. 1, Box 286, Natronia Heights, PA 15065. *The Bell Tower* newsletter.

Additional Listings: See *Warman's Americana & Collectibles* for more examples.

Altar, brass, emb, angels and Latin script, 2½" **75.00**

Church

Gong, brass, 16" h **75.00**
Steeple, molded signature "Made by Meneeley Bell Co. at Troy, NY, 1911," mounting bracket, wooden base, 20" d **300.00**
Triple, graduated stand, domed, cross finial, 27" h **75.00**

Desk

Side tap, bronze, white marble base, c1875 .... **42.50**
Turtle, cast iron, operates by head or tail, 6½" l **200.00**
Twirler type, double chime, c1850 .. **70.00**

Glass, amber, 5″ h, etched floral dec, $30.00.

School, 6 x 10″, brass	80.00
Ship's, bronze, wooden stand, 30″	165.00
Sleigh, brass, leather strap	
33 bells, graduated	80.00
68 bells, 1″ wide strap	150.00
Table, SS, cupid blowing horn, figural handle, frosted finish, foliate strapwork border, Gorham Mfg Co, c1870, 4⅝″	725.00
Tap, brass, marble stand	125.00
Trolley Car, brass	125.00

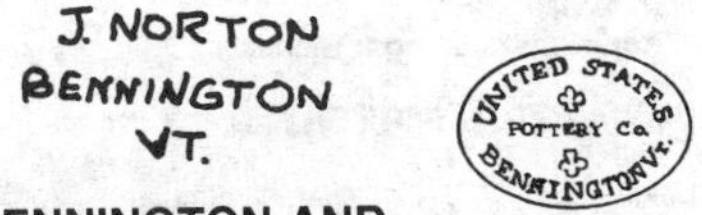

J. NORTON
BENNINGTON
VT.

BENNINGTON AND BENNINGTON-TYPE POTTERY

History: In 1845 Christopher Webber Fenton joined Julius Norton, his brother-in-law, in the manufacturing of stoneware pottery in Bennington, Vermont. Fenton sought to expand the company's products and glazes; Norton wanted to concentrate solely on stoneware. In 1847 Fenton broke away and established his own factory.

Fenton introduced the famous Rockingham glaze, developed in England and named after the Marquis of Rockingham, to America. In 1849 he patented a flint enamel glaze, "Fenton's Enamel," which added flecks, spots, or streaks of color (usually blues, greens, yellows, and oranges) to the brown Rockingham glaze. Forms included candlesticks, coachman bottles, cow creamers, poodles, sugar bowls, and toby pitchers.

Fenton produced the little known scroddled ware, commonly called lava or agate ware. Scroddled ware is composed of different colored clays, mixed with cream colored clay, molded, turned on a potter's wheel, coated with feldspar and flint, and fired. It was not produced in quantity, as there was little demand for it.

Fenton also introduced Parian ware to America. Parian was developed in England in 1842 and known as "Statuary ware." Parian is a translucent porcelain which has no glaze and resembles marble. Bennington made the blue and white variety in the form of vases, cologne bottles, and trinkets.

Five different marks were used, with many variations. Only about twenty percent of the pieces carried any mark; some forms were almost always marked, others never. Marks: (a) 1849 mark (4 variations) for flint enamel and Rockingham; (b) E. Fenton's Works, 1845–47, on Parian and occasionally on scroddled ware; (c) U. S. Pottery Co., ribbon mark, 1852–58, on Parian and blue and white porcelain; (d) U. S. Pottery Co., lozenge mark, 1852–58, on Parian; and (e) U. S. Pottery, oval mark, 1853–58, mainly on scroddled ware.

Fire Engine, chromed bronze, 12″	275.00
Hand	
Brass, figural	
Napoleon, raised scene of Battle of Waterloo around bell bowl, 6¼″	70.00
Queen Elizabeth, crown on head, high ruffled collar, 2⅝ x 5¼″	60.00
Sad Faced Queen Hemony, 6½″	175.00
Victorian Lady, plumed hat, 2 x 4¼″ h	75.00
Windmill, movable blades, 5″	50.00
Bronze, figural	
Dutch girl with jug, 4½″	125.00
Hat, Metropolitan Police, Queen Elizabeth initials, clapper inside hat	20.00
China	
Delftware, Dutch boy, girl, and windmill, marked "Holland," 4″	50.00
Dresden-Meissen, floral dec, intricate border	75.00
Limoges, hp roses	48.00
Copper, enameled designs, glass clapper	60.00
Glass	
Cranberry, wedding	115.00
Fostoria, American pattern	50.00
Moser, gold gilded Arabic dome top, green cut to clear, sgd, c1940, 5¼″	35.00
Overlay, pink ext., cream int., amber glass handle, rigaree and clapper, applied pink and cream flower, green glass leaves, 5″	175.00
Metal, R.A.F. Victory, 1939–45 R.A.F. Benevolent Fund, emb head of Stalin, Churchill, and F.D.R., 4½ x 6″	60.00
Locomotive, brass, mounting frame	650.00
Mechanical, figural, Colonial boy, turn knob to ring, 2½ x 4″	90.00
Saddle, Russian, pinwheels, outside clappers, c1850	140.00

The hound handled pitcher is probably the best known Bennington piece. Hound handled pitchers also were made by some 30 potteries in over 55 different variations. Rockingham glaze was used by over 150 potteries in 11 states, mainly the Mid-West, between 1830 and 1900.

References: Richard Carter Barret, *How To Identify Bennington Pottery,* Stephen Greene Press, 1964; Laura Woodside Watkins, *Early New England Potters And Their Wares,* Harvard University Press, 1950.

Museums: Bennington Museum, Bennington, VT; East Liverpool Museum of Ceramics, East Liverpool, OH.

Additional Listings: Stoneware.

BENNINGTON POTTERY

Baking dish, 7" d, flint enamel, circular,
   1849 mark **175.00**
Book Flask
   "Hermit's Companion," flint enamel,
    1849 mark **850.00**
   Untitled, flint enamel, Lyman Fenton
    Co circular mark, marked "L. F. &
    Co/Patent" on spine **500.00**

Bennington, book flask, untitled, 6" h, Fenton, $400.00.

Bust, 5" h, parian, girl with bird on shoulder **50.00**
Chamber Pot, 9⅛" d, flint enamel, scal-
   loped rib pattern **600.00**
Coffeepot, 12" h, flint enamel, scalloped
   rib pattern, crack in base **650.00**
Cuspidor
   8¼" d, scalloped rib pattern, 1849
    mark, tiny hole in one panel **100.00**
   9½" d, flint enamel, rare 1849 mark . **450.00**
Ewer, 7" h, parian, raised grapevines . **150.00**
Figure, poodles, 9½" l, 8¼" h, flint

enamel, one professionally repaired
   leg, one half of basket handle miss-
   ing, pr **5,500.00**
Jar, 4⅜" h, 4¼" d, parian, blue and
   white, acanthus leaf pattern, lid miss-
   ing **70.00**
Nameplate
   7⅞" l, white, numerals "702" **100.00**
   8" l, Rockingham glaze **125.00**
Paperweight, 5 x 3 x 2¾", flint enamel,
   imp 1849 mark **350.00**
Pipkin, 9" h, flint enamel, lid **2,600.00**
Pitcher
   6¼" h, brown, scroddle, alternate rib
    pattern, U.S. Pottery oval mark,
    age cracks **400.00**
   8¾" h, white, tulip and sunflower, U.S.
    Pottery ribbon mark **1,300.00**
   8⅞" h, white, cascade pattern, highly
    glazed, U.S. Pottery raised lozenge
    mark **300.00**
   10" h
    Flint enamel, tulip and heart pat-
     tern, sgd 1849 mark **600.00**
    Parian
     Pond Lily pattern, U.S. Pottery
      ribbon mark **175.00**
     Wild rose pattern, glazed int. . . **200.00**
   10½" h, flint enamel, octagonal
    paneled, imp 1849 mark **300.00**
Relish Dish, 10" l, Rockingham glaze . **350.00**
Snuff Jar, dark greenish-brown glaze,
   flint enamel, lidded, minor repair . . . **600.00**
Sugar Bowl, 3¾" h, parian, blue and
   white, repeated oak leaves pattern,
   raised grapevine dec lid **125.00**
Syrup, parian, blue and white, spinning
   wheel pattern, pewter lid **150.00**
Teapot, flint enamel, alternate rib pat-
   tern, pierced pouring spout, period lid **400.00**
Toby
   Ben Franklin, green, flint enamel,

Bennington-Type, pitcher, 6½" h, anchor, rope rim, medium brown glaze, marked "Trenton Pottery, NJ," $175.00.

boot handle, 1849 mark, hat rim repair **325.00**
Coachman, 10⅜" h, Rockingham glaze, honey colored, 1849 mark . **475.00**
General Stark, Rockingham glaze . . **1,200.00**
Toothbrush Holder, flint enamel, alternate rib pattern, lid **500.00**
Vase, 10" h, flint enamel, colorful glaze **600.00**

BENNINGTON-TYPE

Candlesticks, 9¼" h, Rockingham glaze, circular kiln separations, pr . . **725.00**
Curtain Tieback, 4¼" d, 4½" l, flint enamel **30.00**
Frame, 8 x 7", oval, Rockingham glaze **325.00**
Trinket Box, 5" l, natural colors, flowers and grapes dec **50.00**
Vase, 4" h, Majolica **275.00**

BISCUIT JARS

History: The biscuit or cracker jar was the forerunner of the cookie jar. They were made of various materials by leading glassworks and potteries of the late 19th and early 20th centuries.

Note: All items listed have silver plated mountings unless otherwise noted.

Crown Milano. bulbous, multicolored chrysanthemum dec, silverplated lid and ornate bail handle, sgd, $800.00.

Bristol, 6¼" h, 5¼" d, opaque, beige satin finish, pink roses, gold leaves, and gray foliage dec, SP top, rim, and handle **145.00**
Cameo Glass, unknown English maker 5½ x 6½", opaque white cyclamen and butterfly, red ground, emb SP lid and split bail handle **1,750.00**
5¾ x 5⅜", opaque white florals, deep frosted red ground, SP top **2,100.00**
Cased, 6¼" h, 5¼" d, blue, enameled pink roses and green leaves dec, SP top, rim, and handle **145.00**

Crown Milano, 7½" d, painted and enameled variegated multicolored flowers, heavy gold scrolls, lid marked "M.W.," floral band emb rim **950.00**
Cut Glass, hobstars, strawberry, diamond, and fan, SP lid, 1890s **235.00**
Limoges, roses, blue forget-me-nots, gold trim, handled **100.00**
Loetz, 6¼" h, 4¼" d, off-white translucent background, green splotches on bottom half, mother-of-pearl irid finish, melon sectioned swirl, SP top, rim, and handle, unmarked **195.00**
Mount Washington, 6½" d, peachblow, melon ribbed, pink and gold flowers, shadow leaves, floral emb lid **175.00**
Royal Bonn
7", sq, floral design, SP top and handle **85.00**
7½", red roses, SP top **100.00**
Royal Doulton, 5¼ x 7¼", Shakespeare Ware, Ophelia, SP top, rim, and handle **250.00**
Royal Worcester
6", floral design, SP top, rim, and handle **265.00**
7", swirl pattern, daises, and fuchsias, marked **275.00**
Satin Glass, 6" h, 4⅝" d, gold prunus dec, golden yellow overlay, heavy gold branches and flowers, large moth, white lining, SP top, rim, and handle **575.00**
Smith Bros, 5½" d, melon ribbed, pink carnations, gold outlines, SP lid and twisted bail, rampant lion mark **375.00**
Wave Crest
8", flowers and leaves, pastel shades **350.00**
10½", blue, emb floral dec, cover sgd "C.F. Monroe" **280.00**
Wedgwood, 7 x 5", Jasperware, tricolor, dark blue, light blue, and white, resilvered SP mountings, c1910 . . . . . . **375.00**

BISQUE

History: Bisque or biscuit china is the name given to wares that have been fired once and are not glazed.

Bisque figurines and busts were popular during the Victorian era, being used on fireplace mantels, dining room buffets, and end tables. Manufacturing was centered in the United States and Europe. By the mid-20th century the Japanese were the principal source of bisque items, especially character related items.

Reference: Susan and Al Bagdade, *Warman's English & Continental Pottery & Porcelain, 1st Edition,* Warman Publishing Co., Inc., 1987.

Figure, Getrude, 7¾" h, early movie star, beige and dark green dress, gold trim, marked "Germany," early 1900s, $40.00.

Bank, 3", fox head, wearing glasses	375.00
Bust, 15", Abraham Lincoln, polychrome enamel and gilt, detachable socle, Japanese, late 19th C	1,500.00
Cigar Holder, 4¼" h, tree stump, bird chasing insect, natural colors, German, c19th C	35.00

Figure

3" d, 7" h, Fat Boy from Dicken's Pickwick Papers, blue coat, yellow rim, black top hat, printed and imp "Heubach"	65.00
3½" d, 6" h, young man and woman under umbrella, pink, blue, lavender, peach, and gray, wire umbrella handle	175.00
4½" d, 5¾" h, young lady and man at well, bisque bucket on string, pink and white, gold trim	100.00
5 x 2½ x 5½", brown and white dog holding basket of three puppies, pink bows	100.00
7" l, 2⅞" h, boy with football, peach sweater, cream pants, imp "G Kraus Germany"	110.00
9", pastoral couple, binoculars, gold beading, pr	55.00
10½", bathing beauty, arched back, arms raised, white, imp "Germany"	155.00
11¾", youngsters, gold beading, fancy dress, marked "Paulux Japan," pr	60.00
Match Holder, 5½", girl holding doll	60.00
Nodder, 4¾", poodle and bulldog, oval base	140.00

Piano Baby

4", lying on back, left foot in air, white

gown, blue trim, Heubach sunburst mark **120.00**

5", crawling, right foot up, white gown, Heubach sunburst mark	140.00
Smoker Set, 6½" d, 6" h, gray dog and brown and white cat on fence, center cigar holder, match holder, and ash container, blue diamond with R mark	165.00
Vase, 8¼", girl standing by vase, shaded blue dress and hat, raised dots dec	115.00

BITTERS BOTTLES

History: Bitters, a "remedy" made from natural herbs and other mixtures with an alcohol base, often was viewed as the universal cure-all. The names given to various bitter mixtures were imaginative, though the bitters seldom cured what their makers claimed.

The manufacturers of bitters needed a way to sell and advertise their products. They designed bottles in many shapes, sizes, and colors to attract the buyer. Many forms of advertising, including trade cards, billboards, signs, almanacs, and novelties proclaimed the virtues of a specific bitter.

During the Civil War a tax was levied on alcoholic beverages. Since bitters were identified as medicines, they were exempt from this tax. The alcohol content was never mentioned. In 1907 when the Pure Foods Regulations went into effect, "an honest statement of content on every label" put most of the manufacturers out of business.

References: Carlyn Ring, *For Bitters Only,* 1980; J. H. Thompson, *Bitters Bottles,* Century House, 1947; Richard Watson, *Bitters Bottles,* Thomas Nelson and Sons, 1965.

Periodical: *Antique Bottle and Glass Collector,* P.O. Box 187, East Greenville, PA 18041

America's Suffolk Bitters Life Preserver, pig shape, amber, 9½" l	32.50
Ayer Restorative Bitters, Boston, rect, aqua	170.00
Baxter's Mandrake Bitters, Lord Bros, Burlington, VT, 12 sided, clear	35.00
Beggs Dandelion Bitters, Chicago, IL, sq, amber	150.00
Brophy's Bitters, Nokomix, IL, sq, aqua, ornate crescent and star trademark	185.00
Burdock Blood Bitters, rect, aqua	20.00
California Fig and Herb Bitters, San Francisco, sq, amber	125.00
Caroni Bitters, round, green	135.00
Dr J Samson's Strengthening Bitters, sq, amber	200.00
Dr Mampe's Herb Stomach Bitters, rect, aqua	80.00
Dr Stanley's South America Indian Bitters, sq, smooth base, yellow amber	130.00

Rohrer's Bitters, ¾ qt, rope sides, emb on four sides "Expectoral Wild Cherry Tonic, Lancaster, PA," plus emb beehive on two sides, Rohrer's oval rope trademark on other two sides, brown, $80.00

Electric Brand Bitters, H. E. Bucklen & Co., Chicago, IL, sq, amber	40.00
Gates Life of Man Bitters, rect, aqua	100.00
Gentiana Root and Herb Bitters, Seth C Clapp, Boston, sq, aqua	225.00
Hall's Bitters, figural, barrel, yellow-amber	160.00
Home Bitters, Jas A Jackson & Co., St Louis, MO, sq, amber	75.00
Iron Bitters, Brown Chemical Co, Baltimore, sq, amber	30.00
Johnson's Calisaya Bitters, Burlington, VT, sq, amber	125.00
Kaiser Wilhelm Bitters Co, Sandusky, OH, round, amber	100.00
Aqua	30.00
Kennedy's East India Bitters, Iler & Co, Omaha, NE, sq, clear	120.00
Lash's Bitters, sq, amber	25.00
Litthauer Stomach Bitters Invented 1964 by Joseph Loewenthal, Berlin, sq, case gin, milk glass	175.00
McKeever's Army Bitters, cannonballs on shoulders, amber, ¾ qt	1,725.00
New York Hop Bitters, emb flag, aqua	190.00
Old Dr Warner's Quaker Bitters, Flint & Co, Providence, RI, rect, aqua	80.00
Old Sachem Bitters and Wigwam Tonic, figural, barrel, golden amber	275.00
O'Leary's 20th Century Bitters, sq, amber	275.00
Paines Celery Compound, amber	20.00
Panknin's Hepatic Bitters, NY, dark amber	200.00
Peychaud's American Aromatic Bitter Cordial, New Orleans, round, amber	50.00
Pineapple, figural, amber	150.00
Plantation Bitters, S T Drakes, figural, log cabin, golden amber, 1860, 10½" h	125.00
Pond's Kidney and Liver Bitters, an Unexcellent Laxative, sq, orange-amber	50.00
Rising Sun Bitters, John C Hurst, Phila, sq, amber	160.00
Royal Amaranth Bitters, Alfred Savigear & Co, round, aqua, double collar	500.00
Royce's Sherry Wine Bitters, rect, smooth base, aqua	115.00
Solomon's Strengthening & Invigorating Bitters, Savannah, Georgia, sq, cobalt blue	425.00
Star Kidney and Liver Bitters, sq, amber, 8⅞"	50.00
Tonic Bitter, J T Higby, Milford, CT, sq, amber	150.00
Tonola Bitters, Phila, ornate trademark, sq, aqua	150.00
Vermo Stomach Bitters, Tonic and Appetizer, sq, clear	100.00
Wheat Bitters, rect, amber	125.00
Whitcomb's, Faith, Bitters, Boston, rect, aqua	150.00
Willard's Golden Seal Bitters, oval, aqua	100.00
Yochim Bros. Celebrated Stomach Bitters, sq, red-amber	80.00
Zu Zu Bitters, sq, aqua	175.00

BLOWN THREE MOLD

History: The Jamestown colony in Virginia introduced glass making into America. The artisans used a "free blown" method.

Blowing molten glass into molds was not introduced into America until the early 1800s. Blown three mold glass used a pre-designed mold that consisted of two, three, or more hinged parts. The glass maker placed a quantity of molten glass on the tip of a rod or tube, inserted it into the mold, blew air into the tube, waited until the glass cooled, and removed the finish product. The three part mold is the most common and lends its name to this entire category.

The impressed decorations on blown mold glass usually are reversed, i.e., what is raised or convex on the outside will be concave on the inside. This is useful in identifying the blown form.

By 1850 American made glassware was in relatively common usage. The increased demand led to large factories and the creation of a technology which eliminated the smaller companies.

Reference: George S. and Helen McKearin, *American Glass*, reprint, Crown Publishers, 1941, 1948.

Basket, pontil, solid applied handle Clear, 4" d, 4½" h, rayed base	275.00

Cobalt Blue, 3⅛″ d, 3½″ h, plain base,
gold rib dec traces **110.00**
Ruby Stained, 3¼″ d, 3⅛″ h, plain
base, gold rim and ribs dec **100.00**
Bottle, 9″ h, gold-amber **700.00**
Bowl, clear
4¼″ d, 1¾″ h, straight sided, sixteen
diamond base, pontil, outwardly
folded rim **210.00**
5″ d, 1⅝″ h, rounded sides, rayed
base, pontil, outwardly folded rim .   **155.00**
5″ d, 2⅛″ h, slightly rounded sides,
rayed base, pontil **375.00**
6″ d, 1¾″ h, straight slanting sides,
sixteen diamond base, pontil, out-
wardly folded rim **130.00**
6¼″ d
Twelve diamond base, pontil,
folded rim **185.00**
Rayed base, slanted sides, pontil,
folded rim **175.00**
6⅜″ d, 5¾″ h, folded rim, sixteen dia-
mond base, pontil, ftd, tilts to one
side, GII-18 . . . .   **4,800.00**
Carafe, 9¼″ h, dark yellow-green, rayed
base, deep pontil **2,300.00**
Cordial, 3″ h, clear, stemmed **750.00**

**Toilet Water Bottle, 6″ h, medium blue,
ribbed, McKearin GI-1, type 5, $200.00**

Creamer
2⅞″ h, clear, fifteen diamond base,
pontil, applied ribbed handle, tip
missing **100.00**
3¼″ h, clear, ringed base, formed
mouth and spout, applied solid
handle with curled end **375.00**
Cruet
Clear, 5⅜″ h, plain base, pontil,
formed pouring lip, GII-28 . . . . . .   **45.00**
Sapphire blue, rayed base, pontil,
molded neck rings, orig solid tam
stopper **450.00**

Cup Plate, 3⅞″ d, folded rim, rayed
base, pontil, three McKearin labels,
ex-collection George McKearin and
TMR Culbertson, GII-1 . . . .   **550.00**
Decanter
Clear
Pint, square, chamfered corners,
plain base, pontil, pressed stop-
per **235.00**
Quart, fourteen diamond base,
pontil, three applied double pour-
ing rings, orig acorn stopper . . .   **425.00**
Quarter pint, rayed base, pontil,
orig ribbed solid stopper **300.00**
Pale yellow-green, quart, rayed base,
pontil, flanged lip **800.00**
Dish, clear
5″ d **325.00**
5¾″ d, 1⅞″ h, rayed base, pontil,
folded rim **185.00**
6⅜″ d, folded rim, rayed base, iron
pontil **90.00**
7″ **475.00**
Flip, clear, 5⅝″ h, 4⅝″ d, eighteen dia-
mond base **130.00**
Hat
Clear
2⅛″ h, fifteen diamond base, pontil,
folded rim **275.00**
2¼″ h, swirled rayed base, pontil,
folded rim **110.00**
Sapphire blue, 2⅝″ h, 2¼″ d, folded
rim, ringed and pontil base **850.00**
Inkwell
Amber, 2¾″ d, 1⅞″ h, drum shape,
faint ringed base, pontil **110.00**
Amber, deep, 1⅝″ h, 2¼″ d, disc
mouth, plain base, pontil **90.00**
Olive amber, 1⅜″ h, 2¼″ d, disc
mouth, plain base, rough pontil . .   **95.00**
Lamp
Fluid, 6½″ h, clear, double paw
pressed base, orig brass collar,
marked "BTM font/Mr Vernon
Works/GI-30, ex-collection George
McKearin **800.00**
Sparking, 2⅞″ h, 2¼″ d, purple blue,
solid base, sheared, orig drop
burner, mouth roughness, GI-30 . .   **450.00**
Mustard, clear
3⅞″ h, flanged lip, iron pontil **25.00**
5″ h, solid sheared ball finial, flanged,
folded lip, pontil, orig matching cov   **120.00**
5¼″ h, plain base, pontil, orig pressed
finial finish hollow blown cov, GI-24   **85.00**
Pitcher
Clear
3¾″ h, bulbous shape, fifteen diamond base, pontil, solid applied
handle **275.00**
7″ h, rayed base, pontil, manipu-

lated mouth, hollow applied handle 230.00
Plate, clear, 5⅜" d, plain base, pontil, folded rim 150.00
Salt, master
Clear, hollow stem and base, pontil . 575.00
Purple blue, 2¼" h, rayed and ringed base, pontil 750.00
Sapphire blue, 2½" h, rayed base, pontil, galleried rim 1,600.00
Salt Shaker, clear
4⅝" h, pontil base, orig metal cap .. 65.00
5" h, sheared lip, orig metal cap and pontil 70.00
Toddy Plate, 4¼" d, clear, rayed base, pontil, folded rim 260.00
Toilet Bottle
Clear, rayed base, pontil, tam stopper 550.00
Cobalt Blue, plain base, pontil matching stopper, GI-7, ex-collection TMR Culbertson 350.00
Sapphire Blue, plain base, pontil, flanged folded lip 170.00
Violet, 6¾" h, smooth base, flanged lip, orig tam stopper 650.00
Yellow Green, 6⅝" h, tapering ovoid shape, plain base, pontil, orig matching stopper, GI-3, type-II, ex-collection Alan Hodges and William J. Elholz 2,600.00
Tumbler, clear
3⅛" h, ringed base, pontil, inwardly folded lip 220.00
3¼" h, barrel shape, rayed base, pontil 325.00
3½" h, barrel shape, rayed base, plain sheared lip, pontil 375.00
3⅜" h, ringed base, pontil, Sandwich Glass Co 275.00
Whimsey, hat shape
2" h, diamond base, pontil, folded rim 160.00
2¼" h, rayed and pontil base, folded rim 135.00
Whiskey Taster, 1⅝" h, clear, ringed base, pontil 185.00
Whiskey Tumbler, clear
2⅝" h, barrel shape, sixteen diamond base, pontil 210.00
2¾" h, plain base, pontil 275.00

BOHEMIAN GLASS

History: The once independent country of Bohemia, now a part of Czechoslovakia, produced a variety of fine glassware: etched, cut, overlay, and colored. Their glassware was first imported into America in the early 1820s and continues today.

Bohemia is known for its "flashed" glass that was produced in the familiar ruby color, and also in amber, green, blue, and black. Common patterns include "Deer and Castle," "Deer and Pine Tree," and "Vintage."

Most of the Bohemian glass encountered in today's market is from the 1875–1900 period. A Bohemian type glass also was made in England, Switzerland, and Germany.

Reproduction Alert.

Beaker
5½" h, amber flashed, engraved, animals and building, C scroll panels, flared foot, c1860 .... 80.00
6½" h, armorial, engraved coat of arms on shield, flower sprays and bands, dated "Anno 1791" 185.00
Bowl
3⅛ x 2", ftd, ten panels with grape etching, ruby and clear 48.00
7", gilt crystal and ruby overlay 200.00
9", Deer and Castle pattern, amber over clear, ftd 85.00
10" x 4¾", Vintage pattern, ruby, frosted, and clear 50.00
Box, 10¾" l, rect, clear and frosted, cobalt blue overlay, cut in hunting hound and game scenes, hinged bronze lid, applied bronze handles, c1900 .... 600.00
Castor Set, five bottles, ruby flashed cut to clear, SP holder 250.00

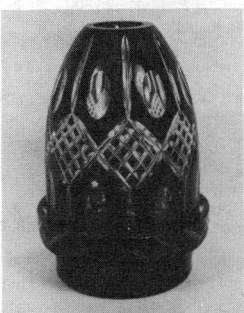

Fairy Lamp, ruby cut to clear, matching base, clear Clarke burner, 3½" d, 4¾" h, $165.00.

Champagne, Vintage pattern, ruby ... 90.00
Cologne Bottle
3 x 6¾", Vintage pattern, ruby and clear, orig steeple stopper 125.00
2½ x 7⅜", ruby circles and medallion with etched deer scene, cut scalloped base, ruby, frosted, and clear, ruby cut stopper 140.00
Compote, 7½ x 9½", white cut to green, multicolored enameled floral dec ... 85.00

Cruet, Deer and Castle pattern, ruby
and clear, orig stopper **85.00**
Decanter
11½", Deer and Pine Tree pattern,
amber, frosted, and clear **100.00**
11¾", Vintage pattern, ruby, frosted,
and clear, blown stopper **90.00**
15", Deer and Castle pattern, ruby cut
to clear, orig stopper **90.00**
Goblet
5", yellow overlay, carved animal car-
touches **100.00**
6", amethyst, gilt rim, etched blos-
soms, late 19th C **90.00**
7", octagonal, crystal, etched scene
of two deer feeding **85.00**
Jewel Box
5 x 3½", amber, etched animals,
birds, and trees, key **350.00**
6" w, oblong, blue, cut star top **175.00**
Mug, 5¼" h, red, etched Vintage pattern   **35.00**
Mustard Jar, Deer and Castle pattern,
ruby and clear **60.00**
Perfume Bottle, 8½", birds and flowers,
ruby and clear **65.00**
Pitcher, 5½", Deer and Castle pattern,
amber, frosted, and clear, gold trim .   **115.00**
Sugar Shaker, Deer and Castle pattern,
ruby and clear, SP top **60.00**
Toothpick Holder, Deer and Pine Tree
pattern, ruby and clear, c1900 . . . . .   **45.00**
Tumbler, 5¼", flared, pink ground, white
overlay, painted bouquets, cut med-
allions, gild trim, c1850 . . . .   **125.00**
Vase
5", flared, Diamond and Oval pattern,
cranberry cut to clear **150.00**
10¾" h, applied 3" sq base, cobalt
overlay cut to clear, star and geometric cutting, six panels on slender neck, petaled top, polished
pontil, pr **425.00**
12", flared rim, ftd, etched birds and
trees, ruby and clear **75.00**
13", white overlay cut to cranberry,
maiden in oval panel, gilt, late 19th
C **225.00**

BOOKS, MODERN FIRST EDITIONS

History: Collecting modern first editions can be
very financially and aesthetically rewarding. Speculators are cautioned about the volatility of the
market.

There is no easy method to identify a first edition. Collectors are urged to consult Blank's *Bib-
liography of American First Editions* or Tannen's
How to Identify & Collect American First Editions.

Modern first editions must be in fine condition

and complete with dust jacket to be of value. The
dust jacket is very important; books without it are
worth substantially less.

Most collectors will automatically reject book
club editions.

The following prices are for books in fine condition. Hints are given to help identify first editions.
These are called "points" by collectors.

Additional Listings: See *Warman's Americana
and Collectibles* for additional listings in Paperback Books, and Western Americana.

Advisor: Ron Lieberman

Albee, Edward, *The Zoo Story, The
Death of Bessie Smith, The Sandbox,*
New York, Coward-McCann, 1960,
158 pgs, orig cloth, dj **40.00**
Barth, John, *Giles Goat Boy,* New
York, 1966, 1st ed, cloth, slipcase . .   **75.00**
Beerbohm, Max, *A Peep Into the Past,*
privately printed, New York, 1923, 1st
ed **120.00**
Bellow, Saul, *The Adventures of Augie
March,* London, 1954 . . . .   **15.00**
Benet, Stephen Vincent, *John Brown's
Body,* Garden City, NY, 1928, 1st ed,
gilt stamped morocco, bookplate . . .   **125.00**
Bloch, Robert, *Psycho,* New York, 1959,
1st ed, dj **90.00**
Bowles, Paul, *Let It Come Down,* New
York, 1952, 1st ed, pictorial cov label,
dj **60.00**
Boyle, Kay, *American Citizen,* New
York, 1944k, paperwraps **25.00**
Capote, Truman, *In Cold Blood,* New
York, 1965, 1st ed, gilt stamped cloth,
dj **100.00**
Clemens, Samuel L.
The Innocents Abroad, Hartford,
American Publishing Co, 1869, 651
pgs, orig black cloth, gilt, frontis,
plates **125.00**
Roughing It, Hartford, American Pub-
lishing Co, 1872, 691 pgs, illus,
frontis **60.00**
Collins, Wilkie, *The Moonstone,* New
York, Harper, 1868, first American
edition, 223 pgs, orig dark blue-green
cloth, gilt, illus, frontis, plates **20.00**
De Vries, Peter, *Comfort Me With Ap-
ples,* Boston, 1956, review slip **20.00**
Dickens, Charles, *The Personal History
of David Copperfield,* London, Bradbury & Evans, 1850, 624 pgs, vignette title, frontis, plates, bound from
orig parts issue **290.00**
Dobie, J. Frank, *Coronado's Children,*
Dallas, Southwest Press, 1930, 367
pgs, cloth, dj **50.00**
Douglas, Norman, *Looking Back,* illus,
London, 1933, 1st ed, gilt lettered
cloth, dj **45.00**

Doyle, Sir Arthur Conan, *The Memoirs of Sherlock Holmes,* Sidney Paget, illus, London, 1894, 1st ed, gilt stamped cloth, gilt edges **500.00**

Durrell, Lawrence, *The Alexandria Quartet,* London, 1962, 1st ed, one volume, gilt stamped buckram and leather spine label, slip case **100.00**

Eliot, T. S., *Ash Wednesday,* New York, 1930, 1st ed, gilt stamped cloth, board slip case **225.00**

Emerson, Ralph Waldo, *Representative Men,* Boston, Phillips Sampson, 1850, 285 pgs, orig black cloth, gilt . **60.00**

Faulkner, William
A Green Bough, New York, 1933, cloth, dj **95.00**
Absalom, Absalom!, New York, 1936, 1st ed, gilt stamped cloth, dj **200.00**
The Mansion, New York, 1959, 1st ed, gilt lettered cloth, dj **70.00**

Fisher, Roy, *The Ship's Orchestra,* London, 1966, engraved wood illus **20.00**

Fitzgerald, F. Scott
All the Sad Young Men, New York, 1926, gilt stamped cloth, pictorial dj **400.00**
The Great Gatsby, New York, 1925, gilt lettered cloth **225.00**

Fleming, Ian
Diamonds are Forever, London, 1956, black boards, dj **125.00**
On Her Majesty's Secret Service, London, 1963, vellum, cloth **1,200.00**

Forster, E. M., *A Passage to India,* London, 1924, cloth **100.00**

Fowles, John, *The Magus,* London, 1966, cloth, dj **90.00**

Frost, Robert
A Masque of Mercy, New York, 1947, gilt buckram, glassine dj, slipcase **155.00**
West-Running Brook, New York, 1928, woodcut illus, cloth **70.00**

Galsworthy, John, *The Forsyte Saga,* London, 1922, folding genealogical table, gilt stamped green cloth **100.00**

Glasgow, Ellen, *The Battle-Ground,* New York, Doubleday, 1902, 512 pgs, orig cloth, gilt, frontis, plates **20.00**

Graves, Robert, *Good-bye to All That,* London, 1929, cloth, dj **180.00**

Gulik, Robert Van, *The Chinese Bell Murders,* London, 1958, illus by author, dj **150.00**

Harte, Bret
The Heritage Of Dedlow Marsh, Boston, 1889 . . . . **20.00**
The Luck Of Roaring Camp, Boston, Osgood, 1872, 75 pgs, first illus edition, orig green cloth, gilt, folio, frontis, plates **75.00**

Hemingway, Ernest
A Farewell to Arms, New York, 1929, cloth, dj **180.00**
Across the River and Into the Trees, New York, 1950, gilt stamped cloth, dj **125.00**
Death in the Afternoon, New York, 1932, gilt stamped cloth **150.00**
For Whom the Bell Tolls, New York, 1933, cloth, dj **150.00**

Holley, Marietta, *Samantha At The World's Fair,* New York, Funk & Wagnalls, 1893, 694 pgs, orig blue pictorial cloth, gilt, illus, frontis **20.00**

Hough, Emerson, *The Law Of The Land,* Indianapolis, 1904, 416 pgs, orig dec cloth, gilt **20.00**

James, Henry, *In The Cage,* Chicago, Herbert Stone, 1898, 229 pgs, orig slate cloth **125.00**

Joyce, James
Finnegan's Wake, London & New York, 1939, cloth, board slip case **1,200.00**
Letters, New York, 1957 . . . . **25.00**

Kilmer, Joyce, *Trees And Other Poems,* New York, Doran, 1914, 75 pgs, orig gray boards **40.00**

Kipling, Rudyard, *Kim,* New York, Doubleday, Page, 1901, 460 pgs, orig green cloth, frontis, plates **80.00**

Lea, Tom, *The Brave Bulls,* Boston, MA, 1949, 270 pgs, illus by author, cloth, dj **25.00**

Leacock, Stephen, *The Iron Man And The Tin Woman,* New York, 1929 . . **25.00**

London, Jack, *The Game,* New York, 1905, Henry Hutt and T. C. Lawrence, illus and dec, pictorial cloth **50.00**

Lowell, Amy, *East Wind,* Boston, Houghton Mifflin, 1926, 240 pgs **20.00**

Markham, Edwin, *The Man With The Hoe, New York, 1899, 134 pgs* . . . **20.00**

Meriwether, Lee, *The Tramp At Home,* New York, 1889, book plate **15.00**

Miller, Henry, *Tropic of Capricorn,* Paris, Obelisk Press, 1939, printed wrappers, errata slip laid in **200.00**

Mitchell, Margaret, *Gone With The Wind,* New York, 1936, cloth, dj **380.00**

Nabokov, Vladimir, *Lolita,* Paris, Olympia Press, 1955, printed wrappers . . **1,400.00**

Neville, James M., *Ladies Under Glass,* Philadelphia, 1938, 315 pgs **10.00**

Porter, Katherine Anne, *Flowering Judas,* New York, Harcourt Brace, 1929, 145 pgs, only 600 copies printed at Primavera Press, orig cloth back boards **75.00**

Queen, Ellery, *The Detective Short Story,* Boston, 1942, cloth, printed spine label, dj **50.00**

Rinehart, Mary Roberts, *The Yellow*

Room, New York, 1945, 248 pgs, dark
blue cloth, dj **20.00**
Rohmer, Sax, *Bimbashi Baruk of Egypt,*
New York, 1944, gilt lettered cloth,
pictorial dj **40.00**
Sage, Agnes Carr, *Two Girls Of Old
New Jersey,* New York, 1912, 195
pgs, pictorial cloth illus, frontis **20.00**
Salinger, J. D., *The Catcher in the Rye,*
Boston, 1951, cloth **200.00**
Santayana, George, *The Last Puritan,*
New York, 1936, dust wrapper **10.00**
Sayers, Dorothy L., *Lord Peter Views
the Body,* New York, 1928, cloth . . . **35.00**
Speyer, Leonora, *Fiddler's Farewell,*
New York, 1927, 2nd printing, dust
wrapper, inscribed by author **20.00**
Steinbeck, John, *The Grapes of Wrath,*
New York, 1939, pictorial cloth, dj . . **120.00**
Stevenson, Robert Louis
Kidnapped, London, Cassell, 1886,
311 pgs, first issue, orig tan cloth,
folding map **100.00**
Treasure Island, London, 1883, gilt
lettered cloth, frontispiece map . . **330.00**
Stoker, Bram, *Lady Athlyne,* London,
1908, cloth **70.00**
Susann, Jacqueline, *Every Night Jose-
phine!,* New York, 1963, 240 pgs, orig
cloth, dj **22.00**
Tarkington, Booth, *Penrod,* Garden
City, NY, 1914, Gordon Grant, illus,
pictorial cloth **130.00**
Thomas, Dylan, *Me And My Bike,* New
York, 1965, Leonora Box, illus, 1st
trade **20.00**
Trumbo, Dalton, *Johnny Got His Gun,*
Philadelphia, 1939, cloth, dj **75.00**
Walker, Jack, *Boomer's Gold,* Amarillo,
TX, 1978, 313 pgs, dj **10.00**
Wells, H. G., *The Wife of Sir Isaac Har-
man,* London, 1914 . . . . **25.00**
Wilder, Thorton
The Bridge of San Luis Rey, London,
1927, gilt lettered cloth, dj **85.00**
The Eighth Day, New York, Harper,
1967, 435 pgs, orig cloth, dj **15.00**
Zelevansky, Paul, *The Book Of Takes,*
New York, 1976, limited to 1000 cop-
ies, Jericho map **15.00**

BOOTJACKS

History: Bootjacks are metal or wooden devices
that facilitate the removal of boots. Bootjacks are
used by placing the heel of the boot in the "U"
shaped opening, putting a foot on the back of the
bootjack, and pulling the front boot off the foot.

Cast Iron
  Closed loop, large **65.00**

Heart, 12 " l, cast iron, $265.00

Double ended, ornate **75.00**
Downs & Co **85.00**
Intertwined scrolls form letter "M,"
  11½" l **25.00**
Musselman's Plug Tobacco adv . . . **130.00**
Ornate, raised heel holder **65.00**
Pheasants, two, brushes, 19" l **225.00**
Scissor action, marked "Pat 1877" . **85.00**
Try Me, emb **35.00**
V shape, ornate **45.00**
Wood
  Mahogany, folding, c1860 . . . . **35.00**
  Pine, 24" l, rose head nails, pierced
    for hanging **40.00**
  Walnut, 22" l, heart and diamond
    openwork **40.00**

BOTTLES, GENERAL

History: Cosmetic bottles held special creams,
oils, and cosmetics designed to enhance the
beauty of the user. Some also claimed, especially
on their colorful labels, to cure or provide relief
from common ailments.

A number of household items, e.g., cleaning
fluids and polishes, required glass storage containers. Many are collected for their fine lithograph
labels.

Mineral water bottles contained water from a
natural spring. Spring water was favored by health
conscious people between the 1850s and 1900s.

Nursing bottles, used to feed the young and
sickly, were a great help to the housewife because
of graduated measures, replaceable nipples, ease
of cleaning, sterilizing, and reuse.

References: Ralph & Terry Kovel, *The Kovels'
Bottle Price List,* Crown Publishers, Inc., 1984, 7th
ed.; Carlo & Dot Sellari, *The Illustrated Price
Guide To Antique Bottles,* Country Beautiful Corp,
1975.

Periodicals: *Antique Bottle And Glass Collector,* P.O. Box 187, East Greenville, PA 18041.

Additional Listings: Barber Bottles, Bitter Bottles, Figural Bottles, Food Bottles, Ink Bottles,
Medicine Bottles, Poison Bottles, Sarsaparilla Bottles and Snuff Bottles. Also see the bottle cate-

gories in *Warman's Americana & Collectibles* for more examples.

COSMETICS

Cam's Vegetable Hair Tonic, Boston, 7 x 3", glass stopper	275.00
Hinds' Honey and Almond Cream, 5½"	5.00
Ingrams Shaving Cream, 2¼", round, milk glass, screw top	5.00
Mrs. H E Wilsons Hair Regenerator, Tewdsbury & Wilson, aqua, open pontil	36.00
Violet Dulce Vanishing Cream, 2½", 8 panels	12.00

HOUSEHOLD

All-Bright Shoe Polish, 8"	4.00
E Z Stove Polish, #14, 6", aqua	10.00
Jennings Blueing, 7", aqua, blob top . .	5.00
Parsons Ammonia, aqua, 1882	17.00
Spaulding's Glue	20.00

Mineral Bottle, 11½" h, Adams Springs Mineral Water, Lake County, PA, Dr. W. R. Prather, Prop., light blue, c1895, $15.00.

MINERAL OR SPRING WATER

Clark & White Co, NY, olive green, qt .	30.00
Congress & Empire Spring Co, Saratoga, 7½", emerald green	475.00
Jubille Spring Water Co, 11½", aqua, emb "101" on bottom	25.00
Mineral Water Distributors, Dublin, ribbed, labeled	25.00
New Century Mineral Water, San Francisco, aqua	90.00
Renfros Mineral Water, Lexington, KY .	10.00
Tweddles Celebrated Soda Or Mineral	

Water, 7½", cobalt, graphite pontil, "Courtland Street, #38, NY" on back	75.00
Vermont Spring, 9¼", bubble burst, apricot	150.00
Wheeler & Co, Cromac Springs, Belfast, aqua, spoked circle	70.00
Wm W Lappeus Premium Soda-Mineral Waters, cobalt, iron pontil	150.00

NURSING

Burr Co, aqua, Boston, MA	40.00
Happy Baby, clear, boy and girl	15.00
Little Papoose, 8"	150.00
Nonpareil Nurser, 5½", aqua	20.00
Sunshine Dairy, picture of baby, nipple, 8 oz, orig cap	5.00
Universal Feeder	15.00

BRASS

History: Brass is a durable, malleable, and ductile metal alloy consisting mainly of copper and zinc. It achieved its greatest popularity for utilitarian and decorative art items in the eighteenth and nineteenth centuries.

References: Mary Frank Gaston, *Antique Brass: Identification and Values,* Collector Books, 1985; Peter, Nancy, and Herbert Schiffer, *The Brass Book,* Schiffer Publishing, Ltd, 1978.

Additional Listings: Bells, Candlesticks, Fireplace Equipment, and Scientific Instruments.

Reproduction Alert: Many modern reproductions are being made of earlier brass forms, especially in the areas of buckets, fireplace equipment, and kettles.

Andirons
17½", acorn finials, ball feet	210.00
29" h, neo-classical detail, 20th C . .	120.00

Candlestick, 9¼" h, solid, American, $175.00.

Belt Buckle, figural, buffalo, marked "Pan Am 1901" **60.00**

Bowl, 28 x 8½", tooled rim, Middle East **65.00**

Box
  1¾" d, miniature on ivory in lid, sgd . **95.00**
  4¾ x 5", gilt, miniature on ivory, sgd **245.00**

Candlestick
  7¾" h, pushup **150.00**
  8" h, scalloped bases, pushup, pr .. **550.00**
  12½" h, peacock stem, red and black enameling, Indian **50.00**

Card Holder, engraved Egyptian designs, Bradley & Hubbard **25.00**

Chafing Ball, 4¾", pierced, gimbaled burner, used as carriage hand warmer **75.00**

Chandelier, 23" d, 17" h, eight arms, electric candles, white silk shades, chain, 20th C, pr **410.00**

Chestnut Roaster, 23" l, reticulated detail, English, registry mark **150.00**

Clock, 13", sailing ship with cupid, marked "1904" **140.00**

Doorknob, lock, elaborate face plates, S.P.U. monogram, marked "Pat June 6, 1899," set **35.00**

Doorstop, 11½", sea horse **25.00**

Fireplace
  Fan, 25" h, 38" w, emb griffon base . **75.00**
  Fender
    40¹/₁₂" l, 10" h, pierced curved rill, cast paw feet **135.00**
    42" l, tubular rails, finials, late 19th C **150.00**
    54" l, two rails, columnar posts, Corinthian capitals, ball finials . **290.00**
  Tool Set, shovel, tongs, and poker, Irish, mid 19th C **125.00**

Inkwell, 3¼ x 4½ x 5", figural winged cupid depicted as blacksmith, forge well, cov, brown patina, Victorian, c1880 .... **225.00**

Jam Kettle, 11¼" d, Ansonia, Hayden, sgd **50.00**

Kettle Stand, 11½" h, 10½" d, tilt top table style, reticulated top, English . **225.00**

Lamp
  Hand, 4" h, tin bottom, removable sleeve on spout, marked "E.F. Rogers, Pat Jan 30, 1866" **175.00**
  Student, 25" h, double, cased green fluted umbrella shades, electrical . **425.00**
  Wax, 6½", fluted stem, double drop burners, dolphin handle, saucer base **250.00**

Lantern, hurricane, 10", chain hanger . **100.00**

Menorah, 19" h, heavy detail **200.00**

Mortar and Pestle, 6" h, 7" d, solid, English, 18th C **100.00**

Pail, 10½" d, 6¾" h, iron bail handle, stamped "The American Brass Kettle Manufacturers" **65.00**

Pot
  16½ x 15", repoussé line in circular cross section, floral devices, raised lion's paw feet, Georgian **800.00**
  Two iron handles, 19th C **150.00**

Scale, balance, English, 19th C **400.00**

Shelf
  9½ x 14", carved loop, emb **125.00**
  12½ x 23½ x 7', geometric design, reticulated top, baluster legs, English registry mark **150.00**

Skimmer, 23" l, butterfly shape bowl, English **65.00**

Snuff Box, 3⅛" l, engraved armorial design, crowned wheel, two rampant lions, marked "G. F." and "1765" .. **125.00**

Spoon, shaped handle, hanging hook, Pennsylvania, 1830, sgd "Schmidt" . **245.00**

Stamp Box, enamel dec **35.00**

Strainer, 9½" d, wrought iron handle .. **65.00**

Tankard, 7½" h, baluster shape, hinged domed lid, shaped handle, circular base, "IL" touchmark, England, 18th C **2,750.00**

Tea Kettle, 7" h, dovetailed, gooseneck spout, swivel handle, marked "4" .. **150.00**

Tea Strainer, spoon type, spring loaded **20.00**

Tobacco Box, oval, engraved railroad steam engine and tender, swag borders, hinged lid **270.00**

Tobacco Cutter, 6½" l, ornate, steel blade, Middle Eastern **20.00**

Trivet
  10¾", reticulated top, worn silvering **65.00**
  11½", wrought iron feet **45.00**

Umbrella Holder, 14¼ x 29', emb dog, people and furniture scene, 3 copper bands, high collar **350.00**

Vase, 11¾" h, lobed body, hand hammered, elongated oval bands, sgd "Jean Dunand," dated **1,980.00**

Warming Pan
  42" l, floral dec, turned wood handle, mid 19th C **275.00**
  44½" l, foliage, flowers, and long tailed bird, engraved lid, turned wood handle **475.00**

Watch Holder, American eagle, wings spread **135.00**

BREAD PLATES

History: Beginning in the mid-1880s, special trays or platters were made for serving bread and rolls. Designated by collectors as "bread plates," these small trays or platters can be found in porcelain, glass (especially pattern glass), and metals.

Bread plates often were part of a china or glass set. However, many glass companies made special plates which honored national heroes, commemorated historical or special events, offered a moral maxim, or supported a religious attitude. The theme on the plate could be either in a horizontal or vertical format. The favorite shape for these plates is oval, with a common length being ten inches.

Reference: Anna Maude Stuart, *Bread Plates And Platters*, published by author, 1965.

Additional Listings: Pattern Glass.

Liberty Bell pattern, 13¼″ l, Declaration of Independence 1776–1876 center, signatures border, $85.00.

Advertising, Pioneer White Wings Flour, china, 90th anniversary	65.00
Ironstone, sq, Tea Leaf pattern, closed handles, Alfred Meakin	55.00
Historical Glass	
Eagle and Constitution, GUTD	100.00
U.S. Grant, 9½″ d, Grant, "Let Us Have Peace," Maple Leaf border, blue	75.00
Liberty Bell, signers	65.00
Three Presidents, "In Remembrance"	100.00
Pattern Glass	
Actress, GUTDODB	70.00
Apollo, sq	27.50
Barberry	23.00
Basketweave, amber	35.00
Beaded Grape, 10 x 7″, green	40.00
Beaded Loop	25.00
Canadian, 10″ d, handled	50.00
Cane, amber	125.00
Chain With Star, handled	33.00
"Faith, Hope, Charity," double handle, pat. and dated 1875	45.00
Finecut and Panel, 13 x 9″, amber .	45.00
Fishscale	25.00
Frosted Stork, One Hundred One pattern border	60.00
Good Luck	40.00
Kansas, 10½″, oval, "Our Daily Bread"	40.00

Liberty Bell, 11½ x 7⅛″, "John Hancock," shell handles	150.00
US Coin, frosted coins	400.00
Scalloped Tape	35.00
Porcelain, 13½ x 6½″, rose dec, shaded green ground, double domed rim, R. S. Prussia	165.00
Majolica	
11½″ d, Etruscan, emb, fern leaves and wheat stocks on rim	250.00
13″ l, Pond Lily pattern	150.00
Toleware, 13″ w, 3¾″ h, ovoid, sloping sides, pierced handles, red floral dec, black ground, painted, American, 19th C	200.00

BRIDE'S BASKETS

History: A ruffled edge, glass bowl in a metal holder was a popular wedding gift in the 1880–1910 era, hence, the name of "bride's basket." The glass bowls can be found in most glass types of the period. The metal holder was generally silver plated with a bail handle, thus enhancing the basket image.

Over the years bowls and bases became separated, and married pieces resulted. When the base has been lost, the bowl is sold separately.

Reference: John Mebane, *Collecting Bride's Baskets And other Glass Fancies*, Wallace-Homestead, 1976.

Reproduction Alert: The glass bowls have been reproduced.

Note: Items listed have silver plated holder unless otherwise noted.

8½″, satin glass, DQ, MOP, blue	125.00
9″, peachblow, amber applied rim, shiny finish, SP holder marked "Wilcox" . .	175.00

Pink cased, 11½″ d bowl, blackberry dec, silverplated frame marked "Quadraplate," $265.00.

9½"

Pigeon blood, enamel floral dec, SP
holder **200.00**

Satin glass, moire, MOP, blue, SP
holder with applied strawberries
and leaves, marked "Simpson,
Hall, Miller Co." **350.00**

10"

Amberina, hobnail, amber handle and
ruffled rim **350.00**

Cased, pink int., blue and pink
enamel flowers, sq **85.00**

Spatter glass, silver flecked, pink
shaded to white, ruffled edge, shiny
finish **75.00**

10½", satin, DQ, MOP, pale blue, floral
and vine dec, shiny finish **100.00**

10½ x 23½", Burmese, acid finish, deep
ruffled top, ext. with enamel and yellow spider chrysanthemums, ornate
SP standard with three cherubs, ball
feet **1,600.00**

11", pink ext., gold stylized flowers,
peachblow int., ornate SP holder with
aquatic marine life motif, marked
"Pairpoint Mfg Co." **800.00**

13½ x 11½", satin, gold overlay, pink
and white flowers and leaves, orig SP
frame **525.00**

BRISTOL GLASS

History: Bristol glass is a designation given to
a semi-opaque glass, usually decorated with
enamel and cased with another color. Initially the
term referred only to glass made in Bristol, England, in the 17th and 18th centuries. By the Victorian era firms on the Continent and in America
were copying the glass and its forms.

**Vases, 11⅛" h, window and curtain
motif, lake scene in background,
flared, scalloped lid, gold band and
highlights, pedestal foot, pr, $75.00**

Biscuit Jar, 4¼" d, 7" h, gray-brown,
enameled running ostrich and stork,
florals, bail handle **275.00**

Box, hinged cov

1⅝ x 1", turquoise, gold dec **100.00**

3⅝ x 5¾", egg shape, white, pink,
cream, blue, and yellow floral dec **215.00**

Compote, fluted, hp, cat scene, metal
base **65.00**

Creamer and Sugar, cov, opaque white,
multicolored floral dec **60.00**

Decanter, 11½" h, rose shading to deep
rose, purple flowers, gilt butterfly on
neck, applied handle, marbleized
rose and white stopper **115.00**

Ewer, 11", white, gold floral dec **65.00**

Goblet, 10¾", pedestal base, opaque
blue, polychrome enamel floral dec,
gilt trim **85.00**

Mantel Lusters, 15⅝" h, 6¼" d, pink overlay, white lining, blue, yellow, and
white flowers, gold trim, prisms, pr . **850.00**

Pitcher, 3¼" d, 2¼" h, turquoise, gold
band, enameled yellow flowers and
leaves, applied turquoise handle ... **60.00**

Plate, 14½", hp, lavender and ochre
French lilacs, green leaves **75.00**

Ring Box, cov, 1¾" d, 1¾" h, turquoise,
gold flowers and leaves **45.00**

Sweetmeat Jar

3 x 5½", deep pink, enameled flying
duck, leaves, and blue flowers,
white lining, SP top, rim, and bail
handle **115.00**

5½ x 4½", green, garlands of flowers
and butterflies, SP top and bail .. **125.00**

Tumbler, 2¾ x 6¾", turquoise, gold and
white rope garlands, gold foot **70.00**

Vase

2" h, 1¼" d, turquoise, gold bands,
enameled yellow flowers and
leaves, pr **70.00**

9", satin, portrait of young boy and
girl, pr **150.00**

9⅝", hp, flowers, gold trim, raised
enameling, pr **100.00**

10"

Blue, cut out base, enamel floral
dec, pr **110.00**

White, brown neck, enamel floral
dec **35.00**

13", pink, gold, blue, and white dec,
pr **120.00**

17", 7" w, American cattle dec, artist
sgd, pr **235.00**

BRITISH ROYALTY
COMMEMORATIVES

History: British commemorative china, souvenirs to commemorate coronations and other royal

events, dates from the 1600s, with the early pieces being rather crude in design and form. The development of transfer printing, c1780, led to a much closer likeness of the reigning monarch on the ware.

Although few commemorative pieces predating Queen Victoria's reign are found today at popular prices, a number of items have been produced for recent royal events. They include the wedding of HRH Prince Andrew and Miss Sarah Ferguson and the subsequent birth of their daughter HRH Princess Beatrice.

Some British Royalty commemoratives are easily recognized by their portraits of past or present monarchs. Some may be in silhouette profile. Other royal symbols include crowns, dragons, royal coats of arms, national flowers, swords, sceptres, dates, messages, and initials.

References: Malcolm Davey and Doug Mannion, *50 Years of Royal Commemorative China 1887-1937,* Dayman Publications, *1988; John May, Victoria Remembered, A Royal History 1817–1861,* London, 1983: John and Jennifer May, *Commemorative Pottery 1780–1900, A Guide for Collectors,* Charles Scribner's Sons, 1972; Josephine Jackson, *Fired For Royalty,* Heaton Moor, 1977; David Rogers, *Coronation Souvenirs and Commemoratives,* Latimer New Dimensions, Ltd., 1975; Sussex Commemorative Ware Centre, *200 Commemoratives,* Metra Print Enterprises, 1979; Geoffrey Warren, *Royal Souvenirs,* Orbis, 1977; Audrey B. Zeder, *British Royal Commemoratives,* Wallace-Homestead, 1986.

Additional Listings: See *Warman's Americana & Collectibles* for more examples.

Advisors: Douglas Flynn and Alan Bolton.

Bowl, Elizabeth II, 1972, Silver Anniversary, 10″ d, 5½″ h, black and white portraits in well, limited edition of 500, Royal Worcester, $425.00

Beaker
Elizabeth II, 1953 Coronation, 3½″ h, Poole **29.00**
Elizabeth II, 60th Birthday, 4½″ h, limited edition 250, Caverswall **85.00**

George/Mary, 1911 Coronation, 3½″ h, Bishop and Stonier **75.00**
George VI/Elizabeth, 1937 Coronation, 4⅛″ h, Grindley **40.00**
Bowl
Edward VIII, 1937 Coronation, 6¼″ d, Grindley **40.00**
Elizabeth II, 1959 Canada Visit, 1½″ h, Royal Albert **50.00**
George VI/Elizabeth, 1937 Coronation, coat of arms, 5½″ d, Paragon **45.00**
Victoria, 1901, In Memoriam, 9½″ d, pressed glass **100.00**
Box, Elizabeth II, 1977 Jubilee, raised flowers, 1⅞″ d, Crown Staffordshire . **20.00**
Cake Plate, Victoria, 1897 Jubilee, sepia portraits, residences, Man of War, 10¾″ d **130.00**
Cup and Saucer
Andrew/Sarah, 1986 Wedding, Colclough **25.00**
Charles/Diana, 1981 Wedding, Duchess **30.00**
Edward VII/Alexandra, 1888 Silver Wedding Anniversary, coat of arms, oversize **175.00**
George VI/Elizabeth, 1937 Coronation, sepia portraits with Princess Elizabeth and Margaret, Welworth **45.00**
Jug
Elizabeth II, 1953 Coronation, emb crowning scene, 8¼″ h, Burleigh Ware **240.00**
George VI/Elizabeth, 1937 Coronation, musical, sepia portraits, Princess Elizabeth/Margaret on reverse, Shelley **260.00**
Lithophane
Alexandra, 1902, cup, crown, and cypher, 2¾″ h **180.00**
Edward VII, 1902, mug, crown, and cypher, 2¾″ h **85.00**
George V, 1911, mug, crown, and cypher, 2¾″ h **150.00**
Mary, 1911, cup, crown, and cypher, 2¾″ h **270.00**
Loving Cup
Andrew/Sarah, 1986 Wedding, color portraits in wedding attire, 2⅞″ h, Fenton **60.00**
Elizabeth II, 1972 Silver Wedding Anniversary, 3″ h, Paragon **175.00**
George VI/Elizabeth, 1937 Coronation, brown portrait, 3¼″ h, Marcus Adams, Sampson Smith **135.00**
Henry, 1984 Birth, 3″ h, Paragon ... **110.00**
Victoria, 1897 Jubilee, brown portrait, 4″ h, Victoria **175.00**
Mug
Charles, 1969 Investiture as Prince of Wales, gold dragon, feathers, black ground, 4″ h, Portmeirion Pottery . **60.00**

Duke/Duchess of Windsor, In Memoriam, black and white portraits, important dates, 3⅜″ h, Dorincourt . **55.00**

Edward VIII, 1937 Coronation, etched crystal, accession and coronation dates, T Goode & Co **140.00**

Elizabeth II, 40th "Ruby" Wedding Anniversary, color portraits, 3″ h, Coalport **45.00**

George/Mary, 1911 Coronation, sepia portraits, 4″ h, Ridgway **100.00**

Victoria, 1887 Jubilee, color beaded crown and ribbon, 3¼″ h, William Whiteley **90.00**

Victoria, 150th Anniversary of Coronation, 3⅝″ h, Caverswall **40.00**

Paperweight

Charles/Diana, 1981 Wedding, black and white portraits, 2¾″ d **25.00**

Edward VIII, 1937 Coronation, black and white portrait, 4¼ x 1⅛″ **20.00**

Victoria/Albert, black and white portraits, color and glitter, 2⅞″ **30.00**

Pin Tray

Edward VIII, 1937 Coronation, color portrait, 4″ d **25.00**

Edward VII/Alexandra, 1902 Coronation, sepia portraits, 4″ d **40.00**

George VI, 1937 Coronation, sepia portrait, 3″ sq, Royal Crown Derby **40.00**

Victoria, 1897 Jubilee, sepia portrait, 5″ d **45.00**

Pitcher

Elizabeth, 1953 Coronation, brown portrait, 6¼″ h, Royal Doulton . . . **185.00**

Victoria, 1887 Jubilee, black and white portrait, 5″ h **120.00**

Plate

Charles, 1969 Investiture as Prince of Wales, sepia portrait, 8″ d, Coronet **65.00**

Plate, George V and Mary, 1911 Coronation, multicolored coat of arms, crowns, partially hand painted, Late Foley Shelley. $125.00

Charles/Diana, 1981 Wedding, sepia portraits, 6¼″ d, Weatherby **20.00**

Edward VII/Alexandra, 1902 Coronation, color portraits, 7″ d **50.00**

Elizabeth II, 60th Birthday, large color portrait, limited edition 20,000, Coalport **80.00**

George VI/Elizabeth, 1937 Coronation, black and white portraits, 6″ d, Royal Doulton **50.00**

Princess Margaret, Birth, parakeets, flowers, 6″ d, Paragon **75.00**

Victoria, 150th Anniversary of Coronation, gold portrait, 10½″ d, limited edition 150, Caverswall **135.00**

Victoria, 1897 Jubilee, brown and white young and mature portraits, 7½″ d **70.00**

Plate, 9½″ d, Edward VII, 1902 Coronation, sepia portrait, Wedgwood, $140.00

Playing Cards

Andrew/Sarah, 1986 Wedding, color portraits, double deck, Waddingtons **30.00**

Edward VIII, 1919 Canada Visit, color portrait, single deck, C Goodall & Co **75.00**

Elizabeth II, 1977 Jubilee, sepia portrait, single deck, Waddingtons . . . **25.00**

George/Mary, 1911 Coronation, color portraits, double deck **75.00**

Shaving Mug

Edward VII/Alexandra, 1902 Coronation, color portraits, 3¾″ h **100.00**

Edward VIII, 1937 Coronation, sepia portrait, 4″ h **75.00**

Elizabeth II, 1953 Coronation, color portrait, 4″ h **70.00**

George VI/Elizabeth, 1937 Coronation, sepia portraits, 4½″ h, Shelley **95.00**

Teapot
 Charles/Diana, 1981 Wedding, sepia
  portraits, 5" h, Price . . . .　**55.00**
 Charlotte, In Memoriam, black and
  white dec, 6" h . . . .　**260.00**
 Edward VII/Alexandra, 1902 Corona-
  tion, color portraits, 4¾" . . . .　**65.00**
 Elizabeth II, 1953 Coronation, relief
  portraits, Jasperware, white on
  royal blue, 5" h, Wedgwood . . . . .　**225.00**
 George/Mary, 1911 Coronation, color
  portraits with Prince of Wales, 6" h,
  bone china . . . .　**255.00**
 Victoria, 1897 Jubilee, color portraits,
  4" h . . . .　**130.00**
 Victoria, 1897 Jubilee, color coat of
  arms, 6" h, Aynsley . . . .　**250.00**
Tea Set, Elizabeth II, 1953 Coronation,
 teapot, cream and sugar, relief portraits, Jasperware, white on royal
 blue, Wedgwood . . . .　**325.00**
Tin
 Andrew/Sarah, 1986 Wedding, color
  portraits, 8" d . . . .　**20.00**
 Edward VII/Alexandra, 1902 Corona-
  tion, color portraits, hinged lid, 4¼
  x 5½" . . . .　**65.00**
 Edward VII/Alexandra, 1902 Corona-
  tion, color portrait, 5 x 3½", Ridg-
  way Ltd. Tea . . . .　**95.00**
 Edward VIII, 1937 Coronation, color
  portrait, hinged lid, 5¾ x 3¾", Ri-
  ley's Toffee . . . .　**45.00**
 Elizabeth II, 1953 Coronation, color
  portrait, hinged lid, 5½ x 4¼",
  Rowntree . . . .　**25.00**
 George/Mary, 1935 Jubilee, color por-
  traits, 6¾ x 4½" . . . .　**45.00**
 George VI/Elizabeth, 1937 Corona-
  tion, gold portraits, 3" h, Oxo . . . .　**18.00**
 George VI/Elizabeth, 1937 Corona-
  tion, sepia Vandyk portrait, 5¾" h,
  4½ x 3¼" . . . .　**50.00**
 Princess Mary, 1914 Christmas,
  brass, emb profile, hinged lid, 4¾ x
  3 x 1" . . . .　**50.00**
 Princess Mary, 1922 Wedding, color
  portraits, 4¼ x 4" . . . .　**45.00**
 Victoria, 1897 Jubilee, color dec,
  accession picture on lid, 5½ x 3½
  x 3½" . . . .　**100.00**
 Victoria, color portrait on hinged lid,
  6¾ x 4½ x 3¼" . . . .　**75.00**

BRONZE

History Bronze is an alloy of copper, tin, and
traces of other metals. It has been used since
Biblical times not only for art objects, but also for
utilitarian purposes. After a slump in the Middle

Ages, bronze was revived in the 17th century and
continued in popularity until the early 20th century.
 Reference: Anita Jacobsen (ed.), *Jacobsen's
Painting and Bronze Price Guide,* published by
author.
 Notes: Do not confuse a "bronzed" object with
a true bronze. A bronzed object usually is made
of white metal and then coated with a reddish-
brown material to give it a bronze appearance.
 A signed bronze commands a higher market
price than an unsigned one. There also are
"signed" reproductions in the market. It is very
important to know the history of the mold and the
background of the foundry.

Animal
 Baboons, 8", Oriental, pr . . . .　**1,200.00**
 Dog, whippet, 20½" h, 27" l, full bod-
  ied, dark patina, good detail, pr . .　**1,050.00**
 Deer, 48", standing, Oriental, patina,
  pr . . . .　**5,500.00**
 Fu Dog, 10", Oriental, mounted as
  lamp bases, pr . . . .　**550.00**
 Horse, 11½" h, French, 19th C, sgd
  "Mene" . . . .　**2,400.00**
 Tiger, 13", seated, multicolored mar-
  ble base, sgd "Bonheur" . . . .　**1,000.00**
Basket, grapevine and perched bird on
 handle, gold finish, silver inlays . . . .　**250.00**
Blotter, rocker type, Zodiac pattern, sgd
 "Tiffany Studios" . . . .　**90.00**
Bowl, 11¾", polished ext., figural mark
 on int. bottom, Harry Dixson, San
 Francisco . . . .　**360.00**
Box, 8" l, Oriental, keg shape, mouse
 on lid, gold tassel, worn orig red fin-
 ish, gilt trim . . . .　**270.00**
Candelabra, 3 light, prisms, lion mas-
 ques, dark patina, c1830 . . . .　**180.00**
Candlesticks, pr
 7¾" h, floral form, green patina . . . .　**415.00**
 12½" h, slender stem, onion shape
  socket, flat bobeche, disc foot, Jar-
  vie, Chicago, IL, c1910 . . . .　**1,20.00**
Cigar Box, Grapevine pattern, cedar
 lined, green glass insets, sgd "Tiffany
 Studios" . . . .　**425.00**
Clock
 Carriage, Waterbury, c1880–90 . . . .　**100.00**
 Mantel, gothic design, French, mid
  19th C . . . .　**700.00**
Figure
 Arabian Equestrian, Vienna, c1880–
  85, sgd . . . .　**275.00**
 Athena, 8⅜", green marble base, re-
  placed spear . . . .　**195.00**
 Buddha, 6¼" h, sitting on lotus
  throne, black patina . . . .　**115.00**
 Cherubs, one reading, other writing,
  white marble bases, French,
  c1870, pr . . . .　**550.00**

Dancer, 22½", onyx plinth, green patina, marked "Lorenze, Austria" .. **850.00**

Satyr
Gilt, verde antico marble base, French, 1880 .... **275.00**
Stealing two goslings pursued by goose, black marble base, 15" l, sgd "Prof. V Seifest" **450.00**

Skater, 20½", posed on toe, black marble plinth **850.00**

Woman, black, seated, Vienna, c1880–85, sgd **150.00**

Figure, boy with lamb, attributed to Barye, $700.00.

Gong, 16", bell shape, mounted on stand **50.00**

Inkwell, 7½", sparrow on branch, painted, c1910 .... **350.00**

Jardiniere, 8" h, cast bacchanalian scenes, bacchus mask handles, stamped "Copyright by E Soleau, Paris, 1893," 19th C **880.00**

Lamp
Bouillotte, gilt, three scrolling arms, French, 19th C, repairs **850.00**
Floor, bell frame, columned, painted domical shade, Handel, c1900 ... **800.00**

Lantern, 24", 3 light, rococo style, arched panel **600.00**

Medal, George Washington, bust, emb, old patina **35.00**

Mortar, 5¼", two concentric bands of leaves under inscription, dolphin handles, dated 1636, Flemish **500.00**

Paperweight, elf on horseshoe **95.00**

Pen Tray, Pine Needle pattern, sgd "Tiffany Studios" **135.00**

Pitcher, 12½" h, oak leaves and acorns, nude figure form handle, legs form tree roots, golden brown patina, c1900 .... **1,050.00**

Plaque
Napoleon, rearing horse, glass frame, 19th C **210.00**
Theodore Roosevelt, 10 x 12¾", cast, quote, paper label on back, marked "Fraser 1920" **175.00**

Pot, 8" h, Oriental, birds and flowering branches in relief, dragon handles, old dark patina **90.00**

Sconce
3 light, frosted glass petal shades, gilt, pr **40.00**
4 light, wall, scrolling arms, gilt, c1830–35, pr **700.00**

Spoon Mold, dessert size **325.00**

Stamp Box, American Indian pattern, green and brown patina, sgd "Tiffany Studios" **175.00**

Statue, 26" h, girl with bow, green patina, bow end glued, artist sgd **800.00**

Stein, 6½", Palace of Electricity in relief **60.00**

Tiebacks, rococo, American, c1860–65, set of 4 .... **70.00**

Toy, 8", cannon, steel carriage, worn red and black paint **100.00**

Tray
6", Japanese beetles molded on handles, branches, late 19th C **250.00**
9" d, Abalone pattern, sgd "Tiffany Studios" **185.00**

Umbrella Stand, 26" h, hammered, high relief scenes, liner **185.00**

Urn, 25", animal scenes, brown patina **325.00**

Vase
6" h, Art Nouveau, gilded cherub faces in swirling sea, brown patina, marked "Louchet," artist sgd "Jules Meliedon 1896" **320.00**
12¾" h, baluster shape, nude maidens and cherubs amongst flowering draperies, obverse and reverse cast in relief, handled metal liner, sgd "Tiffany Studios, NY" **1,320.00**
19", animal scenes, Oriental, pr ... **525.00**

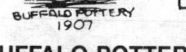

DELDARE WARE, UNDERGLAZE

BUFFALO POTTERY

History: Buffalo Pottery Co., Buffalo, New York, was chartered in 1901. The first kiln was fired in

October 1903. Larkin Soap Company conceived Buffalo Pottery to produce premiums for its extensive mail order business. Wares also were sold to the public by better department and jewelry stores. Elbert Hubbard and Frank L. Wright, who designed the Larkin Administration Building in Buffalo in 1904, were two prominent names associated with the Larkin Company.

Early production consisted mainly of dinner sets of semi-vitreous china. Buffalo was the first pottery in the United States to produce successfully the Blue Willow pattern, marked "First Old Willow Ware Mfg. in America." Buffalo also made a line of hand decorated, multicolored willow ware, called Gaudy Willow. Other early items include a series of game, fowl, and fish sets, pitchers, jugs, and a line of commemorative, historical, and advertising plates and mugs.

In 1908–09 and 1921–23, Buffalo Pottery produced the line for which it is most famous, Deldare Ware, The earliest of this olive green, semi-vitreous china depicts hand decorated scenes from the English artist Cecil Aldin's *Fallowfield Hunt*. Hunt scenes only were done in 1908–09. English village scenes also were characteristic and found throughout the series. Most are artist signed.

In 1911 Buffalo Pottery produced Emerald Deldare, which used scenes from Goldsmith's *The Three Tours of Dr. Syntax* and an Art Nouveau type border. Completely decorated Art Nouveau pieces also were made.

In 1912 Abino was born. Abino was done on Deldare bodies and showed sailing, windmill, and seascape scenes. The main color was rust. All pieces are artist signed and numbered.

In 1915 the pottery was modernized, giving it the ability to produce vitrified china. Consequently, hotel and institutional ware became their main production, with hand decorated ware de-emphasized. Buffalo china became a leader in producing and designing the most famous railroad, hotel, and restaurant patterns. These wares, especially railroad items, are eagerly sought by collectors.

In the early 1920s fine china was made for home use, e.g., the Bluebird pattern. In 1950 Buffalo made their first Christmas plate. They were given away to customers and employees from 1950–60. Hample Equipment Co. ordered some in 1962. The Christmas plates are very scarce.

The Buffalo China Company made "Buffalo Pottery" and "Buffalo China," the difference being one is semi-vitreous ware and the other vitrified. In 1956 the company was reorganized, and Buffalo China became the corporate name. Today Buffalo China is owned by Oneida Silver Company. The Larkin family no longer is involved.

Reference: Seymour and Violet Altman, *The Book Of Buffalo Pottery*, reprinted by Schiffer Publishing, 1987.

Note: Numbers in parenthesis refer to plates in the Altman's book.

Advisor: Seymour & Violet Altman.

Plate, 10", Niagara Falls, blue transfer on white, $45.00.

ABINO WARE

Dresser Tray, 10½ x 13¾", rect, herd of sheep on village street, blue highlights, 1913 (238)	**1,500.00**
Hair Receiver, sailing ship, blue highlights, 1913, sgd "WE Simpson" (237)	**600.00**
Pitcher, 7", Portland Head Light (256)	**950.00**
Plaque, 12¼", sailing ship (241)	**1,000.00**
Plate, 6½", bread and butter, windmill scene with ships (243)	**300.00**
Tile, 6", nautical scene (259)	**700.00**
Vase, 6¾", windmill scene (258)	**875.00**

BLUE AND GAUDY WILLOW

Blue Willow

Bowl, 14 oz	**18.00**
Cup and Saucer (26)	**25.00**
Plate, 9¼" (75)	**25.00**
Platter, 13 x 16" (24)	**60.00**
Teapot, round	**100.00**

Gaudy Willow

Butter Pat	**25.00**
Pitcher, 8" (C8)	**385.00**
Plate, 10½" (28)	**140.00**

CHRISTMAS PLATES

1953 (263)	**65.00**
1957 (267)	**40.00**
1960 (270)	**50.00**

COMMERCIAL SERVICES

Bowl, 8½", Ahwahnee, Yosemite Park (299)	**75.00**
Cake Plate, 10", Roycroft Inn (288)	**200.00**
Cup and Saucer, George Washington (276)	**275.00**

Plate
  9", Fairview Golf Club **80.00**
  10½", Skier **100.00**

Deldare, creamer, Village Life in Ye Olden Days, c1909, $200.00.

DELDARE

Bowl
  6½", Ye Olden Days (154) **250.00**
  9", Ye Village Tavern (152) **500.00**
Calling Card Tray, 7¾", Ye Lion Inn
  (173) **300.00**
Candlestick
  6¾", shield back, Art Nouveau dec
  (193) **1,000.00**
  9", bayberry motif, pr (192) **950.00**
Charger, 14", An Evening At Ye Lion Inn
  (170) **550.00**
Creamer, Scenes of Village Life In Ye
  Olden Days (138) **200.00**
Cup and Saucer
  Fallowfield Hunt (128) **250.00**
  Ye Olden Days (150) **225.00**
Dresser Tray, 9 x 12", Dancing Ye Min-
  uet (144) **575.00**
Humidor, 7", octagon, Ye Lion Inn (174) **700.00**
Mug
  2¼", I Give The Law To That Are Ow-
  ing (202) **500.00**
  4¼", Ye Lion Inn (178) **300.00**
Pitcher
  7", To Spare An Old Soldier (166) . . **500.00**
  10", A Noble Hunting Party (205) . . **1,200.00**
Plate
  6¼", Ye Lion Inn (172) **100.00**
  8½", Spanish Galleons (226) **450.00**
  10", Fallowfield hunt, Breaking Cover
  (124) **265.00**
  10", Yankee Doodle (219) **1,250.00**
Relish, 12 x 6½", The Fallowfield
  Hunt—The Dash (135) **475.00**
Sugar, cov, Village Scenes, 1925 (138) **225.00**
Tea Tray, 10½ x 12", Heirlooms, 1908
  (141) **675.00**
Teapot, 3¼", Village Life, 1909 (138) . **300.00**

DELDARE SPECIALS

Humidor, 8", There Was An Old Sailor
  (227) **875.00**
Salt and Pepper, Art Nouveau (194) . . **600.00**

EMERALD DELDARE

Cup and Saucer, Dr. Syntax At Liverpool
  (181) **400.00**
Fern Dish, 8", butterflies and flowers
  (186) **750.00**
Mug, 4¼", Dr. Syntax Again Filled Up
  His Glass (200) **450.00**
Plate, 8¼", Art Nouveau dec (214) . . . **375.00**
Plaque
  13½", Penn's Treaty With The Indi-
  ans, 1911 (217) **2,000.00**
  16½", The Garden Trio (211) **5,000.00**
Toothpick, 2¼", Art Nouveau dec (197) **385.00**
Vase, 8", kingfisher, dragonflies, iris,
  and waterlilies (188) **1,000.00**

GAME SETS

Plates, 9"
  Deer, Eastern White Tail Deer (67) . **50.00**
  Fish, Great Northern Pike (61) **50.00**
  Fowl, American Herring Gull (63) . . **75.00**
  Fowl, Wild Turkey (64) **75.00**
Platter
  Buffalo Hunt, 1907 (62) **350.00**
  Deer, sgd "RK Beck," 1909 (66) . . . **150.00**

HISTORICAL, COMMEMORATIVE, AND ADVERTISING WARE

Mug, 3½", Beechland Farms (112) . . . **95.00**
Plates, Commemorative, 7½"
  Gates Circle, Buffalo, NY (97) **125.00**
  George Washington (101) **250.00**
  Odd Fellows Hall, Cambridge, MA (96) **85.00**
  Trinity Church, New York City (94) . **85.00**
Plates, Historical, 10"
  Faneuil Hall, Boston (84) **60.00**
  Niagara Falls (81) **60.00**

MISCELLANEOUS

Cake Plate, 6" (324) **35.00**
Celery Tray, 11¾" (332) **45.00**
Chocolate Pot, 11½" (334) **150.00**
Creamer and Sugar, (332) **55.00**
Cup and Saucer (340) **50.00**
Dinner Sets, 100 pcs
  Maple Leaf (314) **400.00**
  Seneca (315) **400.00**
  Vienna (319) **500.00**
Feeding Dish, Mary Had A Little Lamb
  (331) **50.00**
Plate, 9"
  Dr. Syntax In Blue (363) **225.00**

Erie County SPCA, 1967	25.00
Rouge Lamelle, garden scene (349)	115.00
Rose Bowl, 3¾″ (358)	125.00
Tea Set, child's Baby Bunting (315) ..	250.00
Toilet Set, 11 pcs	
Chrysanthemum (326)	650.00
Hero (325)	650.00
Tea Rose	500.00
Vase	
10″, Sailing Ships (359)	375.00
10¼″, Rococo	100.00

BURMESE GLASS

History: Burmese glass is a translucent art glass originated by Frederick Shirley and manufactured by the Mt. Washington Glass Co., New Bedford, Massachusetts, from 1885 to c1891. Burmese glass shades from a soft lemon to a salmon pink. Uranium was used to attain the yellow color and gold was added to the batch so that on reheating one end turned pink. Upon reheating again, the edges would revert to the yellow coloring. The blending of the colors was so gradual that it was difficult to determine where one color ended and the other began.

Although some of the glass has a surface that is glossy, most of it is acid finished. The majority of the items were free blown, but some were blown molded in a ribbed, hobnail, or diamond quilted design.

American-made Burmese is quite thin, fragile, and brittle. The only factory licensed to make Burmese was Thos. Webb & Sons in England. Out of deference to Queen Victoria, they called their wares "Queen's Burmese."

Reproduction Alert: Reproductions abound in almost every form. Since uranium can no longer be used, some of the reproductions are easy to spot. In the 1950s Gunderson produced many pieces in imitation of Burmese.

MW = Mount Washington

Wb = Webb

a.f. = acid finish

s.f. = shiny finish

Advisors: Clarence and Betty Maier.

Biscuit Jar, 6″, Wb, a.f., round, bittersweet and butterfly dec	900.00
Bowl	
2½″, Wb, s.f., star shape opening ..	335.00
5½″ h, 7″ d, MW, a.f., Queen's design dec, berry pontil, 4 applied feet ..	1,650.00
5¾″, Wb, a.f., bittersweet and butterfly dec, SP holder	785.00
6″ d, Wb, s.f., dainty blue blossoms dec	375.00
Bride's Bowl, 10½″ d, 23½″ h, MW, a.f., ruffled, chrysanthemum dec, SP holder with three cherubs dec	1,600.00

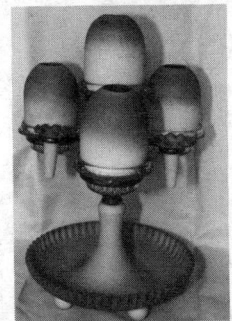

Epergne, 18″ h, Webb, acid finish, four fairy lamps with undecorated Burmese shades, clear glass bases; three Burmese bud vases, bowl base with crimped edge and four Burmese ball shaped feet, $2,575.00.

Condiment, MW, a.f.	
Cylindrical ribbed salt and pepper, fancy SP holder	375.00
Undecorated cylindrical oil bottle, faceted stopper	450.00
Undecorated cylindrical ribbed salt and pepper, mustard, and oil bottle, SP holder	600.00
Creamer and Sugar, MW, a.f., berry pontil, wishbone feet	1,450.00
Cruet, MW	
a.f., melon ribbed, undecorated	985.00
s.f., melon ribbed, undecorated	950.00
Fairy Lamp, Wb, a.f.	
Crimped edge bowl, undecorated shade, 2¼″ h, 4½″ d	550.00
Prunus blossom dec	
Fold-over base, matching shade .	2,450.00
Porcelain base sgd "Tunncliffe" ..	335.00
Muffineer, 4″, Wb, a.f., floral dec, SP top	675.00
Novelty	
Egg, 4½″, MW, a.f., hen and two chicks dec, date 1880 on reverse	1,750.00
Glass, lemonade, 5″, MW, a.f., applied handle	275.00
Plate, 6″, MW, a.f., Queen's design dec	1,450.00
Pitcher, MW, a.f.	
6″, squatty shape, undecorated, 2 qt	485.00
7¼″, tankard	575.00
Rose Bowl, 3″, Wb, a.f., prunus blossom dec	325.00
Salt, 2¹/₁₆″, MW, a.f., undecorated	385.00
Toothpick Holder, 2½″, MW, a.f., tiny yellow blossoms dec (Heacock #3) .	385.00
Tumbler, MW	
a.f.	285.00
s.f.	350.00

Vase

2¾″, MW, a.f., sq top, pine cone dec	**375.00**
4½″ h, MW, s.f., swallows dec, white dot band around top	**585.00**
5¾″, MW, a.f., flower form, gilt finish cupid holder, Pairpoint signature .	**485.00**
6¾″, MW, a.f., jack-in-pulpit, undecorated	**450.00**
8″	
Mb, a.f., bulbous, coralene dec . .	**450.00**
MW, s.f., bulbous, prunus blossom dec, dot band around top	**845.00**
10″, MW, a.f.	
Forget-me-not dec, long neck, bulbous base	**1,085.00**
Sacred Ibis dec, tapered	**1,450.00**
11½″, Wb, a.f., bulbous stick, ivy leaf dec, sgd	**900.00**

BUSTS

History: The portrait bust has its origins in pagan and Christian tradition. Greek and Roman heroes, and later images of Christian saints, dominate the early examples. Busts of the "ordinary man" first appeared in the Renaissance.

Busts of the nobility, poets, and other notable persons dominated the 18th and 19th centuries, especially those designed for use in a home library. Because of the large number of these library busts, excellent examples can be found at reasonable prices, depending on artist, subject, and material.

Reference: Anita Jacobsen (ed.), *Jacobsen's Painting and Bronze Price Guide,* published by author.

Additional Listings: Ivory, Parian Ware, Soapstone, and Wedgwood.

Bust, bronze, 8½″ h, William Penn, sgd "Greil," $300.00

Alabaster, Diana, classical style, 19th, 16½″	**100.00**
Bronze	
Art Nouveau lady, upswept hair, rosebud, hand held fan at base, brown patina, sgd "Ferrand," 15″ .	**625.00**
Woman, bun in hair, gray marble plinth, marked "Feldhoff," 15″ . . .	**110.00**
Chalkware	
Hiawatha, 1890s, 20″ h	**115.00**
Indian Brave, sgd "Sam Lord Wise," 1901 copyright	**125.00**
Majolica, Evangeline, full color, Minton, 16″	**600.00**
Marble	
Apollo, S Amore, Italian, 19th C, 15″	**275.00**
Woman, turned left, E H Baily, c1840, 14¾″	**1,100.00**
Young Augustus, white, Roman, 16″	**850.00**
Spelter, woman, good detail and patina, 11½″	**125.00**
Staffordshire, John Wesley, polychrome enamel, 12″	**300.00**
Terra Cotta	
Chinaman, braided hair, incised signature, impressed eagle and Paris address mark, 13″ h	**1,550.00**
Roman soldier, green brown finish, sgd base, 20th C, 26″	**200.00**
Victorian woman, playing mandolin, sgd, Athens, Greece, 1870	**350.00**
Wedgwood, Shakespeare, black basalt, marked, 10″	**115.00**
Wood, Duke of Wellington, boxwood, sgd and dated, 9″	**525.00**

BUTTER PRINTS

History: Butter prints divide into two categories: butter molds and butter stamps. Butter molds are generally of three piece construction—the design, the screw-in handle, and the case. Molds both mold and stamp the butter at the same time. Butter stamps are of one piece construction, sometimes two pieces if the handle is from a separate piece of wood. Stamps decorate the top of butter after it is molded.

The earliest prints were one piece and hand carved, often thick and deeply carved. Later prints were factory made with the design forced into the wood by a metal die.

Some of the most common designs are sheaves of wheat, leaves, flowers, and pineapples. Animal designs and Germanic tulips are difficult to find. Rare prints include unusual shapes, such as half-rounded and lollipop, and those with designs on both sides.

Reference: Paul E. Kindig, *Butter Prints And Molds,* Schiffer Publishing, 1986.

Reproduction Alert: Reproductions of butter prints date as early as the 1940s.

MOLD

Acorn, 1½″ d, wood, hand carved, two leaves	**55.00**
Cow, 4¼″ d, wood, hand carved	**75.00**
Daisy and Leaf, 3½″ d, wood, hand carved, 3 ribbed border	**65.00**
Fleur-de-lis, glass, wood handle	**45.00**
Musk Melon, wood, hand carved, ½ lb, c1830	**65.00**
Pineapple, 5 x 6½″, dovetailed case, dark patina	**195.00**
Rose, 4″ d, wood, hand carved, blossom, bud, and leaves	**95.00**
Tulip, 5 x 6⅝″, dovetailed case	**185.00**

Stamp, 3½″ d, leaf motif, $40.00

STAMP

Cow, 4½″ d, cherry, hand carved, knob handle, 18th C	**385.00**
Fern Leaf, wood, hand carved, knob handle, 19th C	**40.00**
Heart and Florals, 9 x 3¾″, wood, hand carved, almond shape	**435.00**
Knot design, 4½ x 4¾″, round, whittled handle	**60.00**
Leaf, 4⅞″ d, wood, hand carved	**75.00**
Pinwheel, 7¼″ l, lollipop, wood, hand carved	**550.00**
Sheaf of Wheat, 3¼ x 6¼″, half circle, wood, hand carved	**130.00**
Star, 4″ d, wood, hand carved	**125.00**
Tulip, 4¼″ d, wood, carved tulips and two stars, turned handle	**300.00**

CALENDAR PLATES

History: Calendar plates were first made in England in the late 1880s. They became popular in the United States after 1900, the peak years being 1909 to 1915. The majority of the advertising plates were made of porcelain or pottery with a calendar, the name of a store or business, and either a scene, portrait, animal, or flowers. Some also were made of glass or tin.

Additional Listings: See *Warman's Americana & Collectibles* for more examples.

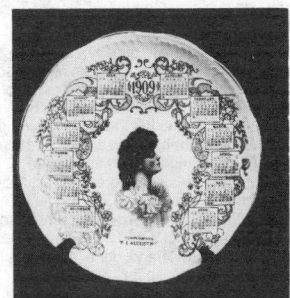

1909, 9½″ d, green transfer, multicolored portrait, white ground, gold trim, "Compliments T. J. Augustine, Gen. Merchandise, Addison, PA, 1909," $40.00.

1908, 7¼″, crossed American flags, Oyster Bay, NY	**35.00**
1909, 9″, portrait, NE adv	**24.00**
1909, 8″, red breasted bird, seasonal scenes	**25.00**
1909, 8½″, flower girl, souvenir, Abrams, WI	**40.00**
1909, 9½″, Gibson girl type portrait, calendar months, fruit, and floral border, WI adv	**25.00**
1910, 7½″, boxer dog, Somerville, NJ adv	**35.00**
1910, 9″, portrait, ME adv	**30.00**
1910, 9½″, bust of woman, large hat, calendar months, fruit, and floral border	**50.00**
1910, 10″, woman in garden center, calendar months border	**30.00**
1911, 8″, red open touring car, Buffalo Pottery	**38.00**
1912, 8¼″ d, Indian husking corn	**25.00**
1912, 8½″, hot air balloons	**75.00**
1912, 9″, glider plane	**25.00**
1913, 8″, calendar months center, rose garland and holly border	**20.00**
1913, 8¼″, sweet peas, pink and lavender ground	**45.00**
1914, 9¼″, Washington's Tomb, Milford, DE, artist sgd "A Smith"	**32.00**
1916, 8¼″, eagle with shield, American flag	**32.00**

1919, 8¼", American flag, John J Rutgers Co, Holland, MI adv	**38.50**
1919, 9", Walnut Grove, MN	**42.00**
1921, 8½", Tabor & Pukwana, SD	**60.00**

CALLING CARD CASES AND RECEIVERS

History: Calling cards, usually carried in specially designed cases, played an important social role in the United States from the period of the Civil War until the end of World War I. When making a formal visit, a caller left their card in a receiver (card dish) in the front hall. Strict rules of etiquette developed. For example, the lady in a family was expected to make calls of congratulations, visits to the ill, and condolence.

The cards themselves were small, embossed or engraved with the caller's name, and often carried a floral design. Many hand done examples, especially in Spencerian script, can be found. The cards themselves are considered collectible and range in price from a few cents to several dollars.

Note: Don't confuse a calling card case with a match safe.

American coin silver, 2¼ x 3⅜", scenic center, cartouche with mountain, and lake scene, scale and herringbone design, $85.00.

CALLING CARD CASES

Ivory	
Carved scene, French, c1880	**250.00**
William Tell tale scene, German	**185.00**
Mother-of-pearl, 2¾ x 3¾", diamond pattern, ivory trim	**40.00**
Silver	
Chinese Export	
2½ x 3½", repousse, Chinese life views, grapes and vines edges, oval monogrammed cartouche, matching silver chain, marked "W," c1860	**200.00**
2½ x 3¾", filigree, dragons on each side, rect cartouche on top inscribed "F.L.G.L./Dec 14th, 1852," orig silk embroidered case, mid 19th C	**160.00**
Sterling	
2½ x 3¾", applied flowers and butterfly, filigree border	**110.00**
3½ x 3½", curved, monogrammed	**75.00**

CALLING CARD RECEIVERS

Art Nouveau, 13 x 15½", 22K gold on pewter, nude sitting on leaf	**380.00**
China	
Hand Painted, 6" l, 3" w, scenic	**65.00**
Nippon, 7¾ x 6", mythical dragon and bird, blue maple leaf mark	**45.00**
Noritake, 3" h, Tree In The Meadow pattern, green ground, red stamped mark	**50.00**
Milk Glass, Jewish star in center	**25.00**
Porcelain, 4", figural, frog standing on large open shell, beige, matte finish, Royal Dux, pink triangle mark	**120.00**
Silver	
Plated, 2¼ x 6", rect, scroll border, Alvin	**125.00**
Sterling, handle, Reed & Barton	**150.00**

CAMBRIDGE GLASS

History: Cambridge Glass Company, Cambridge, Ohio, was incorporated in 1901. Initially the company made clear tableware, later expanding into colored, and engraved glass. Over 40 different hues were produced in blown and pressed glass.

Five different marks were employed during the production years, but not every piece was marked.

The plant closed in 1954. Some of the molds were later sold to the Imperial Glass Company, Bellaire, Ohio.

References: National Cambridge Collectors, Inc., *The Cambridge Glass Co., Cambridge, Ohio* (reprint of 1930 catalog and supplements through 1934), Collector Books, 1976; National Cambridge Collectors, Inc., *The Cambridge Glass co., Cambridge, Ohio, 1949 Thru 1953* (catalog reprint), Collector Books, 1976; National Cambridge Collectors, Inc., *Colors In Cambridge Glass*, Collector Books, 1984; Mark Nye, *Cambridge Stemware*, published by author, 1985.

Collectors' Club: National Cambridge Collectors, Inc., P. O. Box 416, Cambridge, OH 43725. *Crystal Ball* (monthly).

Ashtray
Apple Blossom, pink 65.00
Caprice, triangular 10.00
Heather, ftd 70.00
Rosepoint, 2½″, sq, crystal, etched . 55.00
Basket
Apple Blossom, 6″, pink 35.00
Cleo, 11″, blue 75.00
Gadroon 195.00
Bell, Rosepoint, orig chain and clapper 125.00
Bonbon, Caprice, blue, sq 24.00
Bookends, eagle, crystal, 6″ h, pr 165.00
Bowl
Acadia, 6¼″, crystal 12.50
Apple Blossom, 11″, pedestal, yellow 85.00
Azurite, 7¼″, gold border 40.00
Bashful Charlotte, 8″, pink, etched
gold rim 140.00
Caprice, 12½″, blue 40.00
Everglades, 10″, frosted, red 40.00
Primrose, 8¼″ 40.00
Rosepoint, 12″, ruffled 40.00
Seashell, 10″ 60.00
Brandy Set, green glass, ball jug, six
glasses, Farberware mountings, 7
pcs 60.00
Butter Dish, cov, Rosepoint 180.00
Cake Plate, Heatherbloom, orchid, han-
dles 45.00
Candlesticks, pr
Everglade, amber, two light 140.00
Grecian Columns, gold trim 110.00
Twist, 8½″, opaque jade 100.00
Candy Dish, cov
Caprice, pink 95.00
Rosepoint, 2 handled 300.00
Wildflower 45.00
Champagne, Elaine, etched 24.00
Centerpiece Bowl
Elaine, 13″, crystal, etched, gold trim 45.00
Everglade, 13 x 6″, moonlight blue . 200.00
Cigarette Set, Caprice, blue, cov box,
four ashtrays 65.00
Claret, nude stem
4½ oz, blue 100.00
5½ oz, green 90.00
Cocktail
Candlelight, oyster 27.50
Crown Tuscan, nude stem 75.00
Daffodil 27.50
Rosepoint 24.00
Tally-ho, amber 10.00
Cocktail Shaker
Portia 80.00
Rosepoint, SS base and top, 3 pcs . 135.00
Compote
Caprice, 6″, crystal 25.00
Crown Tuscan, 8″, nude stem 100.00
Faberware, amethyst bowl, nude
stem 125.00
Honeycomb, 6½″, rubina 120.00
Rosepoint, 7¾″, gold dec 85.00

Tomato, 7 x 5½″, yellow-green top
and base, shading to red 85.00
Console Set, Caprice, crystal, gold dec,
13½″ console bowl, 4″ candlesticks . 50.00
Cream Soup, Diane, crystal, etched . . 45.00
Creamer and Sugar
Chantilly 32.00
Decagon, amber 20.00
Lily of the Valley, etched 150.00
Rosepoint 40.00
Cruet, Caprice, blue, 3 oz 85.00
Cup and Saucer
Caprice 15.00
Martha Washington, red 28.00
Wildflower, crystal 35.00
Decanter
Caprice, crystal 130.00
Carman, golf ball stopper 45.00
Faber, amber glass, chrome fittings,
14¾″, 32 oz 50.00
Mt. Vernon, crystal, 40 oz 65.00
Figure, Eagle, crystal, wings spread, 6″
h 58.00
Flower Frog
Bashful Charlotte, 6″, light emerald . 95.00
Draped Lady, 9″, green 115.00
Mandolin Player, green 100.00
Rose Lady, 9″, emerald 200.00
Goblet
Cascade 8.00
Decagon, cobalt 35.00
Rosepoint 22.50
Ice Bucket
Chantilly 50.00
Decagon, amber 20.00
Gloria, pink 85.00
Iced Tea
Caprice, ftd 35.00
Wildflower 18.00

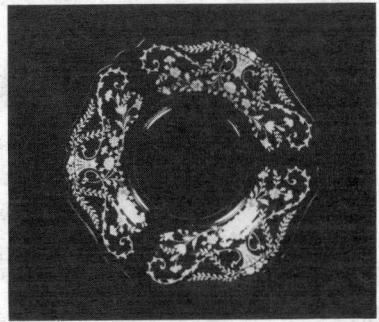

Plate, 8½″ d, Portia pattern, etched design, crystal, $12.00.

Ivy Ball, Crown Tuscan	50.00

Jug, 80 oz

Apple Blossom	150.00
Diane, ball, crystal	185.00
Lamp, Buddha, green, orig shade, pr	240.00
Marmalade and Underplate, Rosepoint	40.00
Mayonnaise Set, Wildflower, 3 pcs	45.00

Nut Dish

Peach-Blo, 3", light pink, c1920	10.00
Rosepoint, 5", crystal	65.00

Pitcher

Chantilly, etched, 76 oz	150.00
Chrysanthemum, cov, amber, etching	150.00
Tally Ho, tankard, 74 oz	100.00

Plate

Apple Blossom, 8½", light blue	30.00
Caprice	
8½", amber	9.00
10", crystal, dinner	14.00
Decagon, 8", blue	10.00
Portia, 8½", crystal	12.00
Willow Blue, 10½", needle etched	120.00
Punch Bowl, Tally Ho, red, clear ladle, 2 pcs	125.00

Relish

Diane, 3 part, 8", crystal	28.00
Gloria, 3 part, heatherbloom	85.00
Pristine, 3 part, crystal	18.00
Rose Bowl, 8", amber, iris, thumbprint	35.00

Salt and Pepper, pr

Caprice, blue	75.00
Tally-ho, red	125.00
Wildflower	32.50
Sandwich Server, Diane, etched, heath-erbloom, center handle	90.00

Sherbet

Candlelight, etched	20.00
Caprice, pink, tall	35.00
Decagon, blue, low	12.50
Rosepoint, low, ftd	18.00
Wildflower, low	12.00

Swan

Carmen, 3", orig label	100.00
Ebony, 3½"	40.00
Green, #1, 10½"	225.00
Mandarin Gold, 6"	90.00
Tray, Caprice, 6", blue	40.00

Tumbler

Caprice, crystal, ftd	20.00
Gloria, forest green	28.00
Rosepoint, ftd	25.00
Urn, Crown Tuscan, cov, 12"	275.00

Vase

Amberina, 6½", flared	100.00
Chantilly, 11", cornucopia, SS base	125.00
Rosepoint, 12", crystal, keyhole stem, etched	135.00

Wine

Bacchus, nude frosted stem	75.00
Ebony, nude stem	75.00

CAMBRIDGE

CAMBRIDGE POTTERY

History: The Cambridge Art Pottery was incorporated in Ohio in 1900. Between 1901 and 1909 the firm produced the usual line of jardinieres, tankards, and vases with underglazed slip decorations and glazes similar to other Ohio potteries. Line names included Terrhea, Oakwood, Otoe, and others.

In 1904 the company introduced Guernsey kitchenware. It was so well received that it became the plant's primary product. In 1909 the company's name was changed to Guernsey Earthenware Company.

All wares were marked.

Bowl, 8½" d, 5¾" h, matte green glaze, four sgd imp acorn marks, $100.00.

Bank, 6 x 3½", pig shape, brown mottled glaze	75.00
Bowl, 6½ x 3", Acorn, green glossy glaze, marked	48.00
Candlestick, 4", Terrhea, standard brown glaze	50.00
Ewer, 7½", Oakwood, cream, yellow, and green blended glaze, numbered	60.00
Inkwell, acorn stopper, Terrhea	100.00

Pitcher

6" h, 3 ftd, handle, dark brown ground, honeysuckle dec, sgd "DL," marked "Cambridge" and "CAP"	200.00

16½″, tankard, two ears of corn, incised signature, mold #263 . . . . . **700.00**
Tile, 6″, floral, high relief majolica type **18.00**
Vase
5½″, bulbous, yellow and green berries, high glaze, imp acorn mark . **150.00**
7¼″, bud, brown streaked, molded flowers, marked "Oakwood" **90.00**
8″, extended body, saucer base, applied shaped handles, Oakwood, blended yellow, green, and brown, high glaze, mold 235 . . . . **165.00**
9″, dog portrait, brown glaze, sgd "AV Lewis" **675.00**

CAMEO GLASS

History: Cameo glass is a form of cased glass. A shell of glass was prepared; then one or more layers of glass of a different color(s) was faced to the first. A design was then cut through the outer layer(s) leaving the inner layer(s) exposed.

This type of art glass originated in Alexandria, Egypt, 100-200 A.D. The oldest and most famous example of cameo glass is the Barberini or Portland vase which was found near Rome in 1582. It contained the ashes of Emperor Alexander Serverus who was assassinated in 235 A.D.

Emile Gallé is probably one of the best known artists of cameo glass. He established a factory at Nancy, France, in 1884. Although much of the glass bears his signature, he was primarily the designer. On many pieces assistants did the actual work, even to signing his name. Glass made after his death in 1904 have a star before the name Gallé. Other makers of French cameo glass include D'Argental, Daum Nancy, LeGras and Delatte.

English cameo does not have as many layers of glass (colors) and cuttings as do French pieces. The outer layer is usually white, and cuttings are very fine and delicate. Most pieces are not signed. The best known makers are Thomas Webb & Sons and Stevens and Williams.

References: Victor Arwas, *Glass Art Nouveau to Art Deco*, Rizzoli International Publications, Inc., 1977; Ray and Lee Grover, *English Cameo Glass*, Crown Publishers, Inc., 1980; Albert C. Revi, *Nineteenth Century Glass*, reprint, Schiffer Publishing, 1981.

AMERICAN

Tiffany
Vase
5¼″, spherical, finely carved Chinese red nasturtium blossoms and apple green leaves, translucent white sides, amber irid washed int., inscribed "L. C. Tiffany-Favrille," numbered, c1908 **3,500.00**

8½″, ovoid, flaring circular foot, shoulder band of meandering leafy vine with lotus leaves, amber irid, inscribed "L. C. Tiffany-Favrille" **3,350.00**

ENGLISH

Stevens and Williams
Perfume Bottle, 4″, bulbous, white trailing fuchsias, red ground, hinged spherical silvered metal cap, c1900 . . . . **365.00**
Vase, 4¾″, ovoid, flaring lip, white anemone blossoms and leaves, cornflower blue ground, c1895 . . . **500.00**
Unsigned
Biscuit Jar, 5¾ x 5⅜″, opaque white flowers, frosted deep red ground, SP top **2,100.00**
Bowl, 8¼ x 4″, opaque white flowers, leaves, and branches, frosted blue ground **2,250.00**
Inkwell, 3 x 4½″, sq, white florals, frosted citron ground, dome SS hinged top **1,350.00**
Lamp Shade, 2¼″ gaslight fitter ring, two white maidenhead fern sprays and border, powder blue ground, pr **1,500.00**
Sweetmeat Jar, 4¾″ d, 3″ h, frosted deep cranberry ground, opaque white carved apple blossoms and leaves, SP top, rim, and handle . . **995.00**
Vase
9″, pink and white morning glories on one side, grain on other, citron ground **1,850.00**
9⅛″, white Christmas roses, two large butterflies, blue ground . . **1,400.00**
12″ h, 5⅝″ d, cylindrical, white carved irises, frosted blue ground **2,250.00**
Thomas Webb and Sons
Bowl, 3½″ d, 4⅝″ d underplate, white flowers and butterflies, deep blue to deep red shaded ground, pr . . **2,675.00**
Cologne Bottle, 7⅝″, white grapes and leaves, raspberry red drapery ground, spring hinged repousse silver stopper **4,200.00**
Vase
7⅝″, ovoid, white flowering leafy branch and butterfly, pale cranberry ground, acid stamped "Thomas Webb & Sons," c1900 **1,650.00**
9¾″, cylindrical neck, bulbous body, salmon pink and white carved butterfly, blossoms, trailing vines, and tendrils, parakeet yellow ground, two horizontal neck bands, sgd in cameo "Thomas Webb & Sons," c1900 **2,860.00**

10¼", white wisteria and butterfly dec, blue ground, sgd "Thos. Webb & Sons" **2,300.00**

FRENCH

Arsall, sgd "Arsall" in cameo
Lamp, table, 15" d domical shade of yellow glass overlaid in brown, cut stag in wooded landscape, black patinated peasant couple on base, figural base cast from model by Bruno Zach, base inscribed "Zach Austria" **3,000.00**
Vase, 6", deep lavender lily of the valley dec, frosted white ground **475.00**
Burgun and Schverer, pieces sgd "Verrerie D'Art'De Lorraine/B/S/&/Co depose" within croix de Lorraine and thistle, c1900
Vase
6", ovoid, pale vanilla yellow overlay, wheel carved fuchsia blossoms and leafy branches, milk gray ground, sgd in enamel ... **2,000.00**
7⅝", baluster, violet overlay, carved branches of spring blossoms, sawtooth neck band, gray ground with violet splashes, traces of gilding, circular silvered metal repousse foot **2,400.00**

Daum Nancy, tumbler, 4¾" h, frosted ground, white floral dec, gold trim, $475.00.

Daum Nancy, pieces sgd "Daum Nancy" in gilt intaglio, croix de Lorraine mark
Bowl, 6¾", squatty ovoid, pale sky blue, lemon yellow and emerald green overlay, finely enameled pendant emerald green, purple, and charcoal bellflowers and leaves, clear mottled ground, gilt highlights, c1910 .... **4,510.00**
Cruet, 5½" h, lily of the valley, butterfly, and bee dec, opalescent textured ground **1,500.00**
Dresser Box, 3½" d, snow scene, brown trees, mottled gold ground . **350.00**
Lamp, 19" h, two ovoid shades, overlaid, cut, and enameled swags and bunches of violets, gold centers, green leaves, mottled shaded gray to deep violet glass, two scrolling bronze arms, cast acanthus leaves, paneled classical standard, lobed foot cast with blossoms and beading, shades sgd in cameo, c1900 .... **3,850.00**
Perfume Bottle, 4⅜" h, bulbous, band of rust, deep mauve, and white florals enameled on neck, carved wildflowers, apricot, olive green, and gray streaked ground, flattened bulbous carved stopper, c1900 .... **4,500.00**
Pitcher, tankard, blue and fuchsia, white frosted ground, ornate SP lid and handle **2,800.00**
Rose Bowl, 2¾" h, rose hips and leaves, autumn colors, mottled cream and yellow ground **650.00**
Vase
4¾" d, 2½" h, squatty, narrow neck, purple clusters of grapes, green leaves, frosted gold ground ... **1,500.00**
11½", burgundy and dark brown scenic trees, water, and mountains, frosted gold ground **2,500.00**
13¾", oval, scenic, dark green trees, lake, tree covered islands, pink and green mottled frosted ground **1,100.00**
16½", baluster, cut and enameled winter forest, silver birches, snow, mottled lemon yellow and salmon ground, sgd in enamel, c1910 .... **5,000.00**
19", light green and frosted ground, enamel enhanced dark blue, gold, brown, and green dec ... **2,400.00**
De Vez, pieces sgd "de Vez" in cameo, c1920
Tumbler, 5", barrel shape, red star flowers, green leaves, mottled amber frosted ground **775.00**
Vase
3¼ x 9⅝", sailboats scene, rose, dark and light green, three cuttings **750.00**
5¾", moonlight scenic, irid gold, rose, blue, and green **1,200.00**
8½", red poppies, satin citron ground **700.00**

Desire Christian Meisenthal, vase, swelling cylindrical neck, compressed bulbous body, deep lavender overlay, finely wheel carved sweet peas, pods, leaves, and scrolling tendrils, opal martele sides, 16¼", sgd in intaglio, c1900 .... **4,000.00**

Gallé, vase, 6⅜" h, reddish amber frosted ground, mahogany (dark red) Japanese Ginko leaves dec, sgd, $775.00.

Gallé, pieces sgd "Gallé" in cameo
 Bottle, 10½", three color full leaf and flower, purple and yellow **1,250.00**
 Chandelier, 21⅝" d, shallow domical shade, crimson and cherry red overlay, cut prunus blossoms and leaves, lemon yellow ground, int. overlay and cut back in pale ochre, gilt bronze mounts, c1900 ...... **19,800.00**
 Dresser Box, 4½", sq, burgundy pods and leaves, frosted gold ground .. **2,000.00**
 Ewer, 9¾", ribbed ovoid, irregular lip, finely cut and enameled mauve, olive green, mint green, aqua, and rust grasshopper, two poppy pods, and ferns, amber sides, gilt highlights, C form handle, whiplash terminal, c1900 .... **6,000.00**
 Lamp, 7⅞" h, conical 7⅞" d shade, spherical base, pink and olive green overlay, cut cherry blossoms and branches, gray ground, gilt bronze mounts, c1900 .... **9,130.00**
 Pitcher, 3¼" h, heavy enameled floral dec, green, mottled red, and brown ground, applied green serpent handle **1,650.00**
 Vase
  5½", pilgrim shape, lavender water lilies, pale blue frosted ground . **1,450.00**
  13½", stick, bun base, three color

flower and leaf dec, peach, green, frosty white **950.00**
  14¾", tapered, burgundy vintage pattern, mottled blue, yellow, and red frosted ground **7,000.00**
Le Gras, vase, 14", purple spider chrysanthemums and festoons, frosted textured ground, sgd **425.00**
Michel, J.
 Vase
  8¼", ovoid, navy blue and pumpkin orange river landscape, framed by pendant flowering branches in foreground, lemon yellow ground, sgd in cameo, c1920 .. **1,100.00**
  10", scenic, sailboats, birds, and mountains, green to red **1,300.00**
Muller Fres, pieces sgd "Muller Fres/ Luneville" in cameo
 Lamp, 18⅞" h, 10" d domical shade, baluster base, overlaid in pale coral, blue-gray, olive green, and deep chocolate brown, cut mountain landscape, tranquil lake, august firs in foreground, pale lemon yellow and coral streaked ground, wrought iron supports base, c1920 **16,000.00**
 Vase
  5½", triangular, yellow, brown and blue florals **900.00**
  6¼", bulbous, fuchsia poppies, mottled yellow and blue base, ivory ground **1,650.00**
  12", gold phlox and large brown leaves, birds perched on branches, mottled blue and pink frosted ground **2,600.00**
  13¾", globular, teal blue, amber, and brown, cut lake and mountains landscape, tall firs and rocky ledges in foreground, luminous amber ground, c1925 .. **8,250.00**
  14⅞", ovoid, teal blue and black cut poppy blossoms, buds, and leaves, luminous yellow mottled ground, c1925 .... **5,775.00**
Pantin, vase, 9½", red irid, florals ... **1,250.00**
Richard, vase, 15", bright orange ground, dark cobalt blue castle and mountains scene **1,550.00**
T. Michel-Paris
 Vase
  8", green and red sailing ship on scenic lake, hanging fuchsia at top, fire polished **1,000.00**
  10", stick, flared top, brown trees and ships, chartreuse ground .. **650.00**
Vesier, cordial, 5", green dec, white ground, sgd **200.00**

CAMERAS

History: The collecting of cameras, except in isolated instances, started about 1970. Although photography generally is considered to have had its beginning in 1839, it is very unusual to find a camera made before 1880. These cameras and others made before 1925 are considered to be antique cameras. Most cameras made after 1925 that are no longer in production are considered to be classic cameras. American, German, and Japanese cameras are found most often.

Value of cameras is affected by both exterior and mechanical conditions. Particular attention must be given to the condition of the bellows if cameras have them.

References: John F. Maloney, *An Identification And Value Guide To Vintage Cameras And Images,* Books Americana, 1981; *Jason Schneider On Camera Collecting, Book Three,* Wallace Homestead, 1985; David Sharbrough, *American Premium Guide To Olde Cameras,* Books Americana, 1983; M. Wolf, *Blue Book Illustrated Price Guide to Collectible & Useable Cameras, Second Master Edition,* Photographic Memorabilia, 1985.

Periodical: Photique Magazine, One Magnolia Hill, West Hartford, CT 06117.

Collectors' Clubs: American Photographic Historical Society, P. O. Box 1775, Grand Central Station, New York, NY 10163. *Photographica;* Leica Historical Society of America, 2314 W. 53rd Street., Minneapolis, MN 55410. National Steroscopic Association, P. O. Box 14801, Columbus, OH 43214. *Stereo World* (bimonthly).

Museum: George Eastman Museum, Rochester, NY; Smithsonian Institution, Washington, DC.

Additional Listings: See *Warman's Americana & Collectibles* for more examples.

Eastman Kodak, Brownie #2A, orig box, 3¼ x 5 x 6", $35.00.

Akeley, lightweight aluminum, hand crank, designed for wildlife photography, tripod, c1917	600.00
Ansco No 4, Model D, wood case	65.00
Baby Hawkeye, roll film box, c1897	160.00
Bell's Straight Working Panoram camera, BG 100, horizontal format, folding bellows, 5 panoramic exposure	250.00
Biflex, 35mm, 2cm f2.5 Tritar lens, 200 exposure, Mfg in Switzerland, Made for British intelligence, c1945	425.00
Ciro 35T, 35mm, Wollensak Anastigmat 50mm f2.8 coated lens, Rapax shutter, c1950	30.00
Conley Camera Co, Rochester, NY, Folding Plate Camera, 4 x 5", red bellows	70.00
Devin One-Shot Color Camera, 6.5 x 9 cm sheet film, Goerz Dogmar 5½" f4.5 lens, Compur dialset shutter, c1940	300.00
Eastman Kodak	
Petite, Model B, vest pocket, Meniscus lens, rotary shutter, 127 roll film, blue, brown, gray, green, or red, c1929–33	60.00
No 2, factory loaded, sixty exposures, 1890	225.00
Six-20 Camera, Kodak Anastigmat 10mm f4.5 coated lens, No 1 Diodak shutter, 620 roll film, c1932–37	15.00
3B Quick Focus, Meniscus Achromatic lens, rotary shutter, 125 roll film, c1906–11	125.00
Fallowfield Hand Camera, Moroccan crocodile skin valise, c1892	425.00
Franke	
Rollei 16S, subminiature, Tessar 25mm f2.8 lens, first Rollei with one lens, black	75.00
Rolleidoscop Reflex Stereo Camera, Zeiss Tessar 75mm f4.5 lenses, c1926	650.00
Rolleiflex New Standard 1939, Zeiss Tessar 75mm lens, Synchro-Compur shutter, c1939–41	50.00
Goerz	
Minicord, 16mm, Helgro 25mm f2.0 lens, 16mm cassettes film, eye level viewing through roof prism, c1951	150.00
Stereo Ango, Goerz Dagor 120mm f6.8 lens, film pack adapter, rising and sliding lens panel, c1906	225.00
Jumbo Century Studio Camera, No 4A, wood, lens, hand held rubber squeeze bulb, brass hardware, orig label, made by Folmer Graphflex Corp, Rochester, NY, 12½ x 25", 16½" h	100.00
Polaroid Land Camera, Model 95B, unused	50.00
J Robinson & Sons, England, Luzo Detective Camera, Aplanat 2½" f11 lens, variable speed sector shutter, used	

Eastman roll type film, first British made box camera, c1890 . . . . **1,500.00**

Ross Twin Lens Reflex, Ross Homocentric 7″ f6.3 lens, Bausch & Lomb pneumatic shutter, rotating back, c1891 . . . . **575.00**

Samei Sangyo, Japan, Samoca 35III, 35mm, c1957 . . . . **15.00**

Schmitz & Thienemann, Dresden, Germany, Uniflex, Unar 75mm f4.5 lens, self cocking Pronto shutter coupled to mirror, c1933 . . . . **120.00**

Scovill 4 x 5″ Vertical View Camera, R Morrison NY lens, rotating stops, holder and case, c1881 . . . . **225.00**

A G Taylor Tailboard Camera, brass clement Gilmer lens, mahogany finish, brass fittings, leather bellows, c1890 . . . . **250.00**

Universal Camera Corp (New York)
Iris, miniature, Ilex Vitar 50mm f7.9 lens, T B I shutter **10.00**

Mercury I, 35 mm half frame, Tricor 35mm f3.5 lens, rotary sector, c1947 . . . . **30.00**

Voigtlander A G, Braunschweig, Germany, Bergheil, Heliar 12cm f4.5 lens, Compur shutter, folding plate, c1930 **50.00**

Watson View Camera, Bush Rapid Symmetrical lens, Thornton Pickard behind lens shutter, mahogany finish, brass fittings, reversible and tilting back, c1890 . . . . **375.00**

Zeiss Contraflex, Walz filter kit, wide angle and telephoto lens, instruction book and case **250.00**

CAMPHOR GLASS

History: Camphor glass derives its name from its color. Most pieces have a cloudy white appearance, similar to gum camphor; the remainder has a pale colored tint. Camphor glass is made by treating the glass with hydrofluoric acid vapors.

Basket, 5″, ruffled, applied clear handle **25.00**

Biscuit Jar, cov, brass fittings **60.00**

Bookends, 7″, horse heads **80.00**

Bowl, 7½″ d, 3½″ h, flared, scalloped rim, ftd **75.00**

Goblet, 7″, butterscotch bowl, gold dec, blue ring, red jewels **90.00**

Hair Receiver, scroll dec **50.00**

Lemonade Set, pitcher and 8 tumblers **150.00**

Mustard, cov, Wild Rose and Bowknot **40.00**

Plate, hp
6½″, Easter Greeting **25.00**
7¼″, owl **28.00**

Powder Jar, cov, sq, blue, bird finial, c1920 . . . . **60.00**

Ring tree, 4½″ **15.00**

Pitcher, 2½″ h, "Souvenir of Youngstown, Ohio," gold lettering, $35.00.

Rose Bowl, hp, blue forget me nots, gold trim **45.00**

Salt and Pepper Shakers, 3½″ h, hand holding torch, orig tops, c1876 . . . . **75.00**

Scent Bottle, 8″, gold motif **45.00**

Shoe, 5″, lady's, Libbey Glass, World's Fair, 1893 . . . . **50.00**

Tray, 8 x 10½″, Wild Rose and Bowknot **30.00**

Vase, 8″, nude in relief **30.00**

CANDLESTICKS

History: The domestic use of candlesticks is traced to the 14th century. The earliest was a picket type, named for the sharp point to hold the candle. The socket type was established by the mid-1660s.

From 1700 to the present, candlestick design mirrored furniture design. By the late 17th century, a baluster stem was introduced, replacing the earlier Doric or clustered column stem. After 1730 candlesticks reflected rococo ornateness. Neoclassic styles followed in the 1760s. Each new era produced a new grouping of candlesticks.

However, some styles became universal and remained in production for centuries. For this reason, it is important to examine the manufacturing techniques of the piece when attempting to date a candlestick.

Reference: Margaret and Douglas Archer, *The Collector's Encyclopedia Of Glass Candlesticks*, Collector Books, 1983.

Brass
6¼″, panel stem, octagonal base . . **145.00**

6¾″ h, neoclassical design, rounded, columnar body, flared lip, tapered base, push-up **85.00**

7″ h, ball turned baluster, cylindrical candlecup, drip pan, domed circular foot, Dutch late 17th C, electrically fitted **825.00**

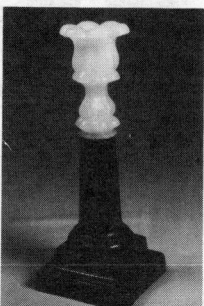

Doric Column, 8½″ h, clambroth petal socket, medium blue sand finish base, Lee 186-3, attributed to Sandwich, $275.00.

8¼″ h, turned columnar stem, flared socket, round dome base, Regency period, England, c1820, pr **225.00**

9½″ h, trumpet turned stem, cylindrical candlecup, lobed bobeche and circular base, George II, mid 18th C, pr **1,320.00**

Glass

Blown, 8¾″ h, hollow socket, flared rim, ring and column base, applied foot, 19th C **260.00**

Bohemian, Vintage pattern, ruby, engraved, c1860, pr **180.00**

Flint, 9⅜″ h, canary, columnar ribbed stem, petal socket, stepped base, pr **400.00**

Monart, 3″, mottled blue shading to lavender, pr **75.00**

Nash, 4″, blood red and gray Chintz, ball stem, sgd, pr **450.00**

Pairpoint, 11½″, amber, crystal bubble ball stems, bell shape base, pr **175.00**

Sandwich, 7⅞″, clear, flint, deep blown socket, hexagonal base . . . **100.00**

Iron, 6⅝″ h, hogscraper, push-up and hanging lip, marked "Shaw" **275.00**

Ormolu and Marble, French, neoclassical, 19th C, pr **1,100.00**

Pewter

5⅜″, capstan base, England, 18th C, pr **175.00**

10⅝″, baluster, standard, removable bobeche, pr **100.00**

Newcomb Pottery, 9½″ h, ivy dec, one with orig price tag, Henrietta Bailey, 1924, pr **1,200.00**

Silverplated

5½″, cylindrical, hand applied silver on copper, molded bases, English, late 18th C, pr **150.00**

8″, Corinthian columns, pr **210.00**

Rococo, c1860–70, pr **120.00**

Wood, 24″ h, turned, old dark finish, pr **135.00**

CANDY CONTAINERS

History: In 1876 Croft, Wilbur and Co. filled a small glass Liberty Bell with candy and sold it at the Centennial Exposition in Philadelphia. From that date until the 1960s glass candy containers remained popular and served to outline American and American transportation history.

Jeannette, Pennsylvania, a center for the packaging of candy in containers, was home for J. C. Crosetti, J. H. Millstein, T. H. Stough, and Victory Glass. Other early manufacturers included: George Borgfeldt, New York, New York; Cambridge Glass, Cambridge, Ohio; Eagle Glass, Wheeling, West Virginia; L. E. Smith, Mt. Pleasant, Pennsylvania; and, West Brothers, Grapeville, Pennsylvania.

Candy containers with original paint, candy, and closures command a high premium, but be aware of reproduced parts and repainting. The closure is a critical part of each container; its loss detracts significantly from the value.

Small figural perfumes and other miniatures often are sold as candy containers.

References: George Eikelberner and Serge Agadjanian, *The Compleat American Glass Candy Containers Handbook,* revised and published by Adele L. Bowden, 1986; Jennie Long, *An Album Of Candy Containers,* published by author, Volume I: 1978, Volume II: 1983.

Collectors' Club: Candy Container Collectors Of America, P.O. Box 1088, Washington, PA 15301. *The Candy Gram* (bimonthly).

Museums: Cambridge Glass Museum, Cambridge, OH; L. E. Smith Glass, Mt. Pleasant, PA.

Additional Listings: See *Warman's Americana & Collectibles* for more examples.

Airplane, 4⅛″ l, stippled clear glass body, red plastic wing, cap labeled "T H Stough Co, Jeannette, PA" **30.00**

Automobile

Hearse, 4¼″ l, clear pressed glass, windows with tassels, tin slide closure **325.00**

Sedan, 4¼″ l, pressed glass, plate glass windows, two open doors, red painted wheels, tin slide closure **60.00**

Baby, glass, nude **50.00**

Boat

Battleship, on waves, 5¼″ l, clear pressed glass, three sections, tin slide closure **100.00**

Cabin Cruiser, 4½″ l, emb "4" in circle, cardboard closure, J H Millstein . . **15.00**

Rabbit pulling basket, papier mache, pasteboard wheels, 9″ I, $50.00.

Cannon, 3¾″ I, pressed glass, red tin
carriage, two pierced wheels, tin
screw on cap 400.00
Chicken on egg, German 35.00
Church, 3½″ h, litho tin, white brick
walls, brown door and window, eight
cut out windows 125.00
Dog
Bulldog, 3¾″ h, clear pressed glass,
sitting, open base, inside flanges . 30.00
Scotty, clear pressed glass, head
down, open base, inside flanges . 20.00
Fire Engine, 4¾″, Little Boiler, blue
pressed glass, open base 50.00
Frog, 4¼″ h, milk glass, sitting upright,
green and brown traces, protruding
glass eyes, 1¾″ d base, tin screw on
cap 300.00
Globe, clear glass, raised degree lines
and continents, metal screw-on cap
over North America with raised concentric circles dec, and "OUR COUN-
TRY," globe spins in metal frame
stand, marked "Pat Appl'd For" 375.00
Golf Club, 4⅝″ I, clear glass, un-
threaded neck, marked "D R G M" . 40.00
Hat
2″ h, opaque white and stained
colors, screw on tin brim, card-
board closure 60.00
Uncle Sam, milk glass, painted stars
and stripes 85.00
Jack O'Lantern, 2½″ h, clear pressed
glass, ribbed, red intaglio nose and
mouth with raised white teeth, black
ringed protruding pop eyeballs, allover pumpkin yellow paint, wire bail,
slotted metal screw on cap 300.00
Jeep, 4⅜″ I, cardboard closure, emb
"Willy's JEEP/J H Millstein/Jeannette,
PA" 20.00
Kangaroo, 5¼″ h, clear pressed glass,
sitting holding cricket bat, black paint
traces, metal screw on cap 2,000.00
Locomotive, 4⅞″, emb 888 below win-

dows, cardboard closure, Victory
Glass Co 30.00
Mailbox, 3¼″ h, "Souvenir - Dubua IA"
in gilt, clear pressed glass, aluminum
painted, tin slide closure 125.00
Mug, 2¼″ h, 3½″ w, drum shape,
painted gold, emb eagle on one side,
slotted closure 200.00
Opera Glasses, 2⅞″ h, milk white, plain
panels, painted dec, screw on cap,
c1908 . . . . 135.00
Owl, paint traces, tin cap closure, unmarked, 1920s 70.00
Phonograph, 2⅞″ w, tin horn and re-
cord, inkwell type depression, tin clo-
sure on base 220.00
Pipe, 4¼″ h, ornate bowl, swirl stem
base 50.00
Powder Horn, 4⅞″, blown two part mold,
clear, rough lip, rubber like composi-
tion cork, metal screw on cap, marked
"Pat appd for" 40.00
Rabbit
Eating carrot, 4⅜″ h, c1947 . . . . . . 35.00
Playing golf, German 235.00
Rocking Horse and Clown, blue glass . 225.00
Rolling Pin, 7″ I, glass center, metal cap
ends, turned wood handles, marked
"VG Co Jnet Pa ¾ oz" 175.00
Santa
5″, German 175.00
Papier Mache, bust 35.00
Soldier, 5⅛″ h, clear pressed glass,
scarlet tunic, gray pants, silver sword
and scabbard, gilted belt and sword
sash, white painted helmet, un-
painted plinth type base, tin slide closure, marked "1¼. AV. OZ" 800.00
Table, 2⅛″ h, clear pressed glass, gilt
table edge and drawer outline, knob
feet, tin snap closure 650.00
Tank, 4⁵⁄₁₆″ I, World War I, paint, closure 110.00
Telephone, 4⅞″ h, wire hanger, wood
receiver, marked "Victory Glass Co,"
c1944 . . . . 35.00
Turkey, German 155.00
Wheel Barrow, 6″ I, tin closure top . . . 60.00
Windmill, 4⅞″ h, Dutch type, six sided
tower, tin arms, cardboard closure
marked "Pla-Toy Co," 1940s 60.00
Vacuum, 3 x 2¼″, tin wire handle,
wheels, and closure, emb "Dolly
Sweeper/West Bros/Grapeville, PA/
Serial No 2862" 350.00

CANES

History: Canes and walking sticks were important accessories in a gentleman's wardrobe in the
18th and 19th centuries. They often served both
a decorative and utilitarian function. Collectors fre-

quently view carved canes in wood and ivory as folk art and pay higher prices for them. Glass canes and walking sticks were glass makers' whimsies, ornamental rather than practical.

Reference: Catherine Dike, *Cane Curiosa*, published by author, 1983.

CANES

Bamboo, ivory handle, carved stag in forest	**165.00**
Ebony	
34", gold dog's head handle, pattern on neck, c1901	**600.00**
35", elephant head handle, ivory tusks and eyes, chip carved staff, horn tip, India	**500.00**
Glass	
30", amber, twisted handle and tip ..	**50.00**
34", clear, red and blue swirls, gilded int.	**250.00**
55¾". aqua. twisted handle and tip .	**85.00**
Ivory, 33½", inlaid geometric dec, incised pattern	**150.00**
Scrimshaw, 34½", whalebone shaft, whale ivory head, 19th C	**225.00**
Wood	
Mahogany, 36", inlay ebony band ..	**75.00**
Rosewood, 36", cherry stained horn handle, gold band	**110.00**
Zebrawood, 32", curved handle	**50.00**

Walking Stick, 35" l, walnut, ball and trap top, four twisted pieces, $90.00.

WALKING STICKS

African Wood, 36", carved, giraffe's head	**250.00**
Bamboo, 36", heavy, natural bark on handle	**15.00**
Blackthorn, 36½", vines twisted around shaft, root end handle	**70.00**
Ebony, 36½", horn tip, horn handle, carved hound, gold ferrule, owner name inscribed	**200.00**
Folk Art, 37½", tattoo type, primitive, pony, gazelle, fish, crane, lizard, and snake, knob handle	**30.00**
Horn, 35", variegated, SS top, brass tip	**80.00**
Walnut, 36", lady's, twisted shaft, two grooved sides	**25.00**

HANDLES

Celluloid, carved dog's head, glass eyes	**35.00**
Ivory, 3⅜", carved bearded black man	**250.00**
Scrimshaw, 5½", carved hand clutching spotted snake, turned wood base, 19th C	**650.00**
Silver, sterling, walking stick type, floral dec	**65.00**

CANTON CHINA

History: Canton china is a type of oriental porcelain made in the Canton region of China from the late 18th century and early 19th century to the present and produced largely for export. Canton china is hand decorated in light to dark blue underglaze on white. Design motifs include houses, mountains, trees, boats, and a bridge. A design similar to "willow china" is the most common.

Borders on early Canton feature a rain and cloud motif (a thick band of diagonal lines with a scalloped bottom). Later pieces usually have a straight line border. The markings "Made in China" and "China" indicate wares which date after 1891.

Reference: Sandra Andacht, *Oriental Antiques & Art: An Identification And Value Guide*, Wallace-Homestead, 1987.

Reproduction Alert: Several museum gift shops and private manufacturers are issuing reproductions of Canton china.

Cup and Saucer, loop handle, $75.00.

Basket, 9¾" l, reticulated fruit, matching undertray, c1850	**900.00**
Bowl	
4 x 10", sq, cut corners, early 1800s	**650.00**
8¾" l, rect, scenic center	**190.00**

9¾", bird and floral dec, gold and red,
c1820 . . . . **450.00**
10 x 9¾ x 4", scalloped corners, early
19th C **650.00**
12¾", Men Riding Mice pattern, cal-
ligraphy center, brown glaze rim,
unglazed foot, underglaze blue
Ch'eng Hua apocryphal seal **275.00**
Box, cov, 9¼, circular scene of 8 Daoist
immortals under large tree on cov, 6
shaped floral cluster reserves, yellow
scrolling foliate ground, blue 6 character Qianlong mark **275.00**
Butter Pat **85.00**
Candlesticks, pr, 7", trumpet shape, flat
bobeche **2,350.00**
Charger
21¾", village scene, unglazed base,
brass hanger, 19th C **350.00**
24¼", alternating shaped medallions
of figures and birds, flower strewn
ground **1,200.00**
Coffeepot, 10", domed lid **750.00**
Creamer, 5½", white, rose border, gold
trim **140.00**
Cup and Saucer
Butterflies, pastels **75.00**
Pagoda and willow tree dec **50.00**
Ginger Jar, cov
5½", Hawthorne pattern, double ring
base **200.00**
12", willow tree dec **400.00**
Jardiniere, 4½ x 10", rect, turquoise, cobalt blue, and red dec, c1890 . . . . **475.00**
Jug, 8½", Mandarin figures, precious artifacts, butterfly, and famille rose,
early 19th C **300.00**
Mug, 4", twisted handle **300.00**
Pitcher, 8", mountain and bridge scene **275.00**
Plate
8½", landscape, c1830 . . . . **160.00**
10", water edge scene, c1820 . . . . . **100.00**
10½", family scene **120.00**
12", floral, butterfly center, triangle
border **175.00**
Platter
12½", river and bridge scene, trellis
border, underglaze blue dec, c1820 **350.00**
14¼", octagonal, Isles of Blest pat-
tern, trellis border **250.00**
16 x 13", canted corners, rain cloud
border, c1800 . . . . **325.00**
Sauce Tureen, cov, 4¾ x 7½", boar's
head handles **400.00**
Soup Plate, 8¾", late **50.00**
Sugar, cov **225.00**
Tea Caddy, floral dec, 19th C **310.00**
Teapot, 6", branch handle **325.00**
Tile, hexagonal, tea house scene **200.00**
Undertray, 12⅜", Men Riding Mice pat-
tern, dragon center, brown glazed rim,

underglaze Ch'eng Hua apocryphal
seal **225.00**
Vase
13", birds and floral dec **500.00**
23½", crackle ivory glaze, figures and
floral dec **650.00**
Vegetable Dish, cov
8½ x 9½", oblong **200.00**
10½", diamond shape, figures in land-
scape, early 19th C **250.00**
11½", oval, strawberry finial, scal-
loped rim **500.00**
Warming Dish, 10¾", Isles of Blest pat-
tern, rain and cloud border, straight
sides, lotus clusters, pr **425.00**

CAPO-DI-MONTE

History: In 1743 King Charles of Naples established a soft paste porcelain factory near Naples
which made figures and dinnerware. In 1760 many
of the workmen and most of the molds were taken
to Buen Retiro, near Madrid, Spain. A new factory
opened in Naples in 1771 and added hard paste
porcelains. In 1834 the Doccia factory in Florence
purchased the molds and continued their production in Italy.

Capo-di-Monte was copied heavily by factories
in Hungary, Germany, France, and Italy. Many of
the pieces in today's market are of recent vintage.
Do not be fooled by the crown over the "N" mark;
it also was copied.

Reference: Susan and Al Bagdade, *Warman's
English & Continental Pottery & Porcelain, 1st Edition,* Warman Publishing Co., Inc., 1987.

**Figures, 6" h, girl reading, blue coat,
yellow pants, boy with garland, yellow
coat, pink garments, $500.00.**

Bowl
  12″ d, relief cherubs, center relief
    scene, pierced for hanging **80.00**
  14″ d, relief molded leopard scene,
    c1860 .... **175.00**
Candleholder, 3″, raised flowers and
  nude figure **95.00**
Chocolate Cup and Saucer, relief
  molded figures, cupid finial cov,
  c1870 .... **140.00**
Compote, 13″ d, shell shape, cherubs
  and classical figures in relief, scroll
  base **115.00**
Demitasse Cup and Saucer, maiden,
  dog, tree, and mountain scene, pastels, branch handle **65.00**
Figure
  African Crowned Crane, 14″, one foot
    in water, other held up, water
    plants, sgd "G. Armani" **150.00**
  Beggar, 12″, bisque, standing, um-
    brella under arm, box at side,
    mending his coat, crossed feathers
    mark, sgd "Benn" **150.00**
  Group, 9 x 7 ½″, bisque, seated man
    with cigar offering bone to dog,
    shoes being shined by kneeling
    man, blue apron, crossed feathers
    mark **125.00**
Jewel Box
  Musical motif dec, marked **275.00**
  Roman and Biblical motif on lid, 3 ¼″
    h **150.00**
Pastille Box, int. and ext. dec, relief
  molded nudes and putti cov **285.00**
Pitcher, 8″ h, polychrome enameling, gilt
  trim, relief molded satyrs and cherubs **65.00**
Plate
  Raised classical figure border, multi-
    colored, "crowned N" mark **200.00**
  Relief semi-nudes bathing beside
    brook, floral festoon border **95.00**
Platter, 19″, relief molded scene of la-
  dies **85.00**
Tile, paneled, relief molded, nude maid-
  ens at Roman bath scene **165.00**
Urn
  7″ h, relief molded white classical
    women and cherubs, gold trim and
    handles **165.00**
  15″, cov, pseudo underglaze mark, pr **500.00**
Vase, 11″ h, cherubs, pastel colors, pedestal base, pr **125.00**

CARLSBAD CHINA

History: Because of changing European boundaries, German–speaking Carlsbad found itself lo-

cated in the last hundred years first in the Austro-
Hungarian Empire, next in Germany, and currently
in Czechoslovakia. Carlsbad was one of the leading pottery manufacturing centers in Bohemia.

Wares from the numerous Carlsbad potteries
are lumped together under the term "Carlsbad
China." Most pieces on the market are post-1891,
although several potteries date to the early 19th
century.

Reference: Susan and Al Bagdade, *Warman's
English & Continental Pottery & Porcelain, 1st Edition,* Warman Publishing Co., Inc., 1987.

**Vase, 9½″ h, two handles, portrait cen-
ter, deep pink ground, gold trim, artist
sgd "Fr. Stahl," marked "Victoria,
Carlsbad, Austria," $90.00.**

Biscuit jar, cov, 5½ x 6⅜, multicolored
  florals, gold trim, marked "Victoria-
  Carlsbad" **50.00**
Bowl
  6¾ x 3¼″, irid gold, pink int., four gold
    handles, marked "Karlsbad, Aus-
    tria" **160.00**
  12 x 2″, sq, pale peach shading to
    pale blue, center transfer of five
    classical maidens, gold foliage,
    marked "Victoria-Carlsbad" **65.00**
  16 x 9″, oval, fluted top, hp, purple
    and blue flowers, gold trim **45.00**
Box, cov, diamond shape, amethyst cut
  to clear, marked **400.00**
Cake Plate, 12″, violets, pierced gold
  handles, marked "Victoria, Carlsbad,
  Austria" **40.00**
Chocolate Pot, 10″, multicolored daisies, gold trim, white ground, marked **100.00**
Dessert Set, 9½″ master bowl, twelve
  5½″ bowls, scalloped and fluted, four
  winter scenes, apple blossom
  boughs, cream ground, 13 pcs **165.00**
Gravy, 5⅝ x 9¼″, open handled under-

plate, yellow and pink roses, green leaves, gold rims, white ground, c1908 . . . . **65.00**

Miniature Lamp, 8½" h, porcelain base, Bristol glass shade, orange, blue, and lavender flowers, scrolling gold trim, nutmeg burner, marked "Victoria, Carlsbad, Austria" **425.00**

Mug, 4", decal portrait of monk, violin, marked "Victoria-Carlsbad" **6500**

Pitcher, 11", cobalt blue bands, gold trim, pink ground **100.00**

Plate, 7⅝", scalloped, spray of pink and yellow roses, green buds and leaves, gold trim, white ground, c1905 . . . . **30.00**

Portrait Plate, 9", portrait of blonde woman, heavy gold trim **50.00**

Relish, pierced handles, multicolored flowers, pink border, cream ground . **32.00**

Sugar Shaker, Bluebird pattern, marked "Victoria-Carlsbad" **40.00**

Teapot, cov, relief scrolls, hp, marked "Carlsbad 1892" **45.00**

Vase
   8½", portrait of monk reading newspaper, pink and gold, two handles, sgd "Carlsbad Victoria" **50.00**
   9", baluster, shaded pink and red roses, blue violets, green leaves, gold trim, cream ground **75.00**
   12½", custard glass, gourd shape, stick neck, blue, pink, and tan enamel floral dec, marked "Karlsbad-Tichy-R," c1910 . . . . **225.00**
   Graduated, hp, crazed glaze, artist sgd, set of 3 . . . . **100.00**

CARNIVAL GLASS

History: Carnival glass, an American invention, is colored pressed glass with a fired on iridescent finish. It was first manufactured about 1905 and was immensely popular both in America and abroad. Over 1,000 different patterns have been identified. Production of old carnival glass patterns ended in 1930.

Most of the popular patterns of carnival glass were produced by five companies—Dugan, Fenton, Imperial, Millersburg, and Northwood. Northwood patterns frequently are found with the "N" trademark. Dugan used a diamond trademark on several patterns.

In carnival glass color is the most important factor in pricing. The color of a piece is determined by holding the piece to the light and looking through it.

References: Bill Edwards, *The Standard Encyclopedia of Carnival Glass, Revised Second Edition,* Collector Books, 1988; Bill Edwards, *The Standard Carnival Glass Price Guide, 7th Edition,* Collector Books, 1987; Marion T. Hartung, *First Book of Carnival Glass to Tenth Book of Carnival Glass* [series of 10 books], published by author, 1968 to 1982; Thomas E. Sprain, *Carnival Glass Tumblers,* New and Reproduced, published by author, 1984.

Collectors' Club: American Carnival Glass Association, Box 3514, Plymouth, MA 02360. *American Carnival Glass News,* quarterly; Heart of America Carnival Glass Association, 3048 Tamarak Drive, Manhatten, KS 66502. *HOCGA,* monthly; International Carnival Glass Association, Inc., R.D. #1, Box 14, Mentone, IN 46539. *The Carnival Pump,* quarterly.

Acorn Burrs, Northwood
   Bowl, berry, 5", pastel **60.00**
   Butter Dish, cov, marigold **125.00**
   Creamer, dark **100.00**
   Spooner, marigold **75.00**
   Tumbler, purple **55.00**
Apple Blossom, Dugan
   Bowl, 7½"
      Marigold **25.00**
      Peach opal **125.00**
   Plate, 8¾", green **125.00**

Left: Acorn Burrs, tumbler, marigold, $55.00; center: Butterfly and Berry, bowl, 10" d, ftd, marigold, $85.00; right: Good Luck, bowl, ruffled, basketweave back, marigold, $125.00.

Apple Blossom Twigs, Dugan
Bowl, three in one edge, peach opal   85.00
Plate, marigold 75.00
Beaded Cable, Northwood
Candy Dish, ftd, marigold 45.00
Rose Bowl, aqua opal 285.00
Blackberry, Fenton
Compote, small, blue 60.00
Hat, marigold 40.00
Blackberry Spray, Fenton
Bonbon, green 50.00
Compote, marigold 38.00
Hat, marigold 40.00
Butterfly and Berry, Fenton
Tumbler, marigold 18.00
Vase, 6″, marigold 35.00
Water Set
7 pcs, blue 510.00
7 pcs, marigold 350.00
Butterfly and Fern, Millersburg
Pitcher, water, marigold 70.00
Tumbler, aqua 50.00
Carolina Dogwood, Westmoreland
Bowl, peach opal, piecrust edge . . .   115.00
Plate, white, irid 300.00
Circle Scroll, Dugan
Butter Dish, cov, marigold 215.00
Compote, amethyst 125.00
Spooner, marigold 150.00
Whimsey, 7″, purple 90.00
Diamond Ring, Imperial
Bowl, berry, 5″, amethyst 48.00
Fruit Bowl, 9″, marigold 40.00
Dutch Twins, Unknown Maker
Ashtray, marigold 25.00
Dresser Set, 5 pc, marigold 210.00
Fern Panels, Northwood
Hat, marigold 30.00
Floral and Grape, Fenton
Pitcher, water, blue 135.00
Tumbler, marigold 30.00
Fluffy Peacock, Fenton
Pitcher, water, blue 135.00
Tumbler, marigold 45.00
Water Set, 7 pc, blue 800.00
Flute, Imperial
Bowl, 9″, marigold 17.50
Flute, Millersburg
Vase, 9″, amethyst 82.00
Golden Grape, Dugan
Bowl, 7″, marigold 35.00
Rose Bowl, collar base, marigold . .   55.00
Good Luck, Northwood
Bowl, ruffled
Green, basketweave back 300.00
Marigold, basketweave back 125.00
Purple, ribbed back 165.00
Plate, 9″, purple 300.00
Grape, Imperial
Bowl, 4¾″, marigold 13.00
Tray, center handle, marigold 27.50
Water Set, 7 pcs, marigold 200.00

Grape and Cable, Fenton and North-wood
Banana Boat, green 275.00
Bonbon, two handles, marigold 35.00
Cup and Saucer, green 365.00
Hatpin holder, marigold, 7″ 200.00
Perfume Bottle, marigold 325.00
Pin Tray, purple 100.00
Plate, 9″, purple, sgd "Northwood" .   100.00
Sweetmeat, cov, purple 200.00
Table Set, cov butter, creamer, cov
sugar, and spooner, marigold 450.00
Tumbler, purple 37.50
Water Set, 7 pcs, purple 400.00
Whiskey Glass, amethyst 135.00
Grape Arbor, Northwood
Hat, blue 80.00
Pitcher, water, white 475.00
Tumbler, ice blue 140.00
Water set, 5 pcs, marigold 200.00
Grapevine Lattice, Dugan
Bowl, 7″, ruffled, marigold 28.00
Plate, 6″, white 80.00
Tumbler, purple 35.00
Greek Key, Northwood
Bowl, green 75.00
Pitcher, water, green 700.00
Tumbler, purple 75.00
Hearts and Flowers, Fenton
Bowl, 8″, blue, piecrust rim 425.00
Compote, white 150.00
Plate, marigold 300.00
Heavy Iris, Dugan
Pitcher, water, peach opal 1,000.00
Tumbler, white 175.00
Water set, 9 pcs, marigold 610.00
Kittens, Fenton
Bowl, cereal, blue 200.00
Cup and Saucer, marigold 225.00
Dish, marigold 80.00
Plate, 4½″, marigold 150.00
Toothpick Holder, blue 300.00
Leaf and Beads, Northwood
Candy Dish, ftd, green 75.00
Nut Bowl, purple 65.00
Rose bowl
Aqua opal 235.00
Marigold 65.00
Leaf Tiers, Unknown Maker
Bowl, 5″, ftd, marigold 25.00
Creamer, marigold 45.00
Lamp Shade, marigold 90.00
Tumbler, marigold 70.00
Lustre Flute, Northwood
Breakfast Set, creamer and sugar, in-dividual size
Green 85.00
Marigold 50.00
Creamer, green 48.00
Hat, green 35.00
Nappy, marigold 30.00
Punch Cup, green 16.00

Sugar, open, two handles, marigold .	27.50

Lustre Rose, Imperial
Bowl

7", stippled, marigold	45.00
8½", ftd, marigold	35.00
Butter Dish, cov, marigold	50.00
Creamer and Sugar, marigold	40.00
Fernery, blue	80.00
Pitcher, water, clambroth	70.00
Plate, 9", marigold	85.00
Sauce Dish, green	24.00
Spooner, marigold	35.00
Sugar, cov, amber	75.00
Water Set, 7 pcs, marigold	250.00

Octagon, Imperial

Bowl, 10" sq, green	48.00
Butter Dish, cov, marigold	110.00
Compote, jelly, green	75.00
Pitcher, water, 8", purple	450.00
Table Set, cov butter dish, creamer, cov sugar, and spooner, marigold .	225.00
Tumbler, purple	75.00

Open Rose, Imperial
Berry Set, master bowl, six sauces,

marigold	85.00
Bowl, amber	25.00

Plate, 9"

Amber	150.00
Green	70.00
Marigold	55.00
Rose Bowl, green	50.00
Tumbler, marigold	20.00

Orange Tree, Fenton

Bowl, 5½", ftd, purple	55.00
Compote, 5" d, blue	60.00
Creamer, ftd, white	50.00
Goblet, marigold	20.00
Hatpin Holder, purple	165.00
Loving Cup, white	200.00
Mug, amber	125.00
Plate, 9", clambroth	150.00
Powder Jar, cov, marigold	60.00
Punch Set, 9 pcs, blue	465.00
Tumbler, marigold	48.00

Water Set, 8 pcs, blue	500.00
Wine, marigold	24.00

Panther, Fenton

Bowl, berry, marigold	25.00
Bowl, centerpiece, marigold	600.00
Bowl, ruffled, 9" d, claw ftd, blue	250.00

Peach, Northwood
Berry Set, master bowl, four sauces,

white	400.00
Table Set, cov butter, creamer, cov sugar, spooner, white	575.00
Tumbler, blue	65.00

Peacock and Grape, Fenton

Bowl, 8", ruffled, violet	65.00
Bowl, 9", collared base, blue	60.00
Plate, 9", ftd, marigold	180.00

Peacock and Urn, Millersburg
Berry Set, master bowl, five sauces,

purple	750.00
Compote, 5½ x 5", aqua	325.00
Goblet, marigold	75.00
Ice Cream Bowl, master, stippled, ice blue	800.00
Plate, 9", marigold	165.00
Sauce, blue	125.00

Peacock at the Fountain, Northwood

Bowl, berry, master, marigold	90.00
Compote, blue	500.00
Creamer, purple	90.00
Orange Bowl, ftd, lavender	325.00
Punch Set, 6 pcs, marigold	500.00
Spooner, purple	80.00
Tumbler, purple	48.00

Peacocks on the Fence, Northwood
Bowl, ruffled, ribbed back

Marigold	185.00
Purple, piecrust rim	335.00
White, very irid	875.00
Plate, 9", ice green	325.00

Persian Medallion, Fenton

Bonbon, two handles, aqua	100.00
Bowl, scalloped edge, marigold	35.00
Compote, 6¼" h, blue, flared top	70.00
Fruit Bowl, 10" d, three feet, int. Per-	

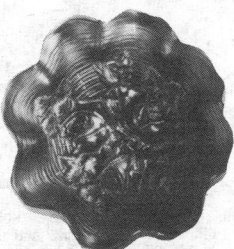
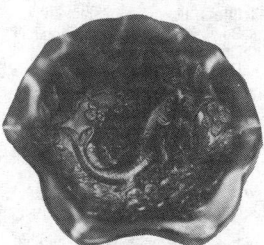

Left: Peacock and Urn, master berry bowl, purple, $225.00; center: Rose Show, bowl, marigold, $275.00; right: Trout and Fly, bowl, 8¾", marigold, $315.00.

sian Medallion, ext. Grape and Cable pattern, blue **160.00**
Plate, 6½", blue **60.00**
Polo, Unknown Maker
Ashtray, marigold **25.00**
Rose Show, Northwood
Bowl, marigold **275.00**
Plate, pastel **475.00**
Sailboat, Fenton
Bowl, 4", marigold **40.00**
Wine, marigold **15.00**
Seacoast, Millersburg
Pin Tray, green **275.00**
Smooth Rays, Westmoreland
Bowl, 8", dome base
Marigold **30.00**
Primrose **68.00**
Compote, green **75.00**
Springtime, Northwood
Butter Dish, cov, purple **210.00**
Creamer, marigold **125.00**
Spooner, marigold **120.00**
Sugar, cov, amethyst **200.00**
Stag & Holly, Fenton
Bowl, marigold **75.00**
Rose Bowl, ftd, green **400.00**
Star of David and Bows, Northwood
Bowl, 7", amethyst, ftd **75.00**
Stippled Rays, Northwood
Bonbon, blue **40.00**
Creamer and Sugar, marigold **65.00**
Plate, 7", amethyst **45.00**
Swirl Hobnail, Millersburg
Rose Bowl, scalloped rim
Marigold **225.00**
Purple **250.00**
Spittoon, marigold **575.00**
Three Fruit, Northwood
Bowl, 9" d, fluted, purple, marked .. **70.00**
Bonbon, marigold **50.00**
Plate, stippled, green **125.00**
Tree of Life, Imperial
Basket, marigold **40.00**
Perfume Bottle, marigold **45.00**
Plate, 8", marigold **27.00**
Tumbler, marigold **24.00**
Triplets, Dugan
Bowl, 7", scalloped, marigold **35.00**
Compote, marigold **30.00**
Hat, amethyst **40.00**
Trout and Fly, Millersburg
Bowl, 8¾", oval, marigold **315.00**
Bowl, 8¾" round
Green **450.00**
Marigold **325.00**
Vintage, Fenton
Card Tray, marigold **40.00**
Cup, green **35.00**
Epergne, amethyst **100.00**
Fernery, blue **45.00**
Plate, 11", ruffled, marigold **150.00**

Wishbone, Northwood
Bowl, 10"
Amethyst **85.00**
Marigold, dark **65.00**
Tumbler, green **125.00**
Wreath of Roses, Dugan
Rose Bowl, marigold **45.00**
Spittoon, amber **160.00**
Wreathed Cherry, Dugan
Bowl, berry, master, purple **125.00**
Bowl, berry, individual, purple **40.00**
Creamer, marigold **65.00**
Toothpick Holder, amethyst **150.00**
Tumbler, white **150.00**
Zipper Loop, Imperial
Lamp, oil, 8" h, smoke irid, small base
chip **450.00**

CAROUSEL FIGURES

History: By the late 17th century carousels were found in most capital cities of Europe. In 1867 Gustav Dentzel carved America's first carousel. Other leading American manufacturers include Charles I. D. Looff, Allan Herschell, Charles Parker, and William F. Mangels.

Original paint is not critical, since figures were repainted annually. Park paint indicates layers of accumulated paint; stripped means paint removed to show carving; restored involves stripping and repainting in the original colors.

References: Charlotte Dinger, *Art Of The Carousel,* Carousel Art, Inc., 1983; Tobin Fraley, *The Carousel Animal,* Tobin Fraley Studios, 1983; Frederick Fried, *The Pictorial History Of The Carousel,* Vestal Press, 1964; William Manns, Peggy Shank, and Marianne Stevens, *Painted Ponies: American Carousel Art,* Zon International Publishing, 1986.

Periodical: *Carrousel Art,* P.O. Box 992, Garden Grove, CA 92642.

Collectors' Clubs: The American Carousel Society, 470 South Pleasant Avenue, Ridgewood, NJ 07450; National Carousel Association, 7266 West Stanley Road, Flushing, MI 48433.

Bear, 34" l, simulated carved fur, carved saddle and bow tie, glass eyes, stripped and finished, J R Anderson, Bristol, England, c1875 .... **1,430.00**
Chariot, armored, three figures, Coney Island style, Charles Carmel **5,000.00**
Deer, prancing, closed mouth, eagle behind saddle, restored, Gustav Dentzel, c1885 .... **17,500.00**
Donkey, 43" l, nodding head, carved, saddle and blanket, gray, red, brown, yellow, and blue, brass handle grip, Bayol of Angers, France, c1880 ... **1,425.00**
Elephant, 26" h, 34" l, pine, carved, traces of gilding, black paint, glass

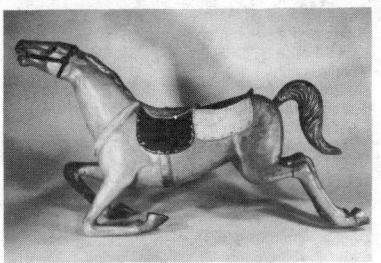

Horse, 38″ l, $1,800.00.

eyes, black trimmed red blanket on
back 3,300.00
Giraffe, 67″ h, 54″ l, wood, carved,
painted, Dentzel 14,000.00
Horse
  Jumper
    Inner row, carved, stripped, Aniel
      Muller-Gustav Dentzel 7,500.00
    Outside row, 57″ h, 48″ l, Armitage-
      Herschell, c1890 . . . . 2,250.00
  Prancer
    Inside row, 51″ h, 53″ l, Looff, late
      19th C 4,250.00
    Middle row, pin striping blanket dec,
      hand scraped orig factory paint,
      E J Morris 10,500.00
    Standing, outside row, carved jewels
      and mane, Charles Looff, c1880,
      restored 7,500.00
      73″ h, 64″ l, orig paint, iron stirrups,
      Stein and Goldstein, Brooklyn,
      NY, c1899–1900 . . . . .40,000.00
Ostrich, 56″ h, 58″ l, running, carved
  feathers and saddle, hinged neck, re-
  finished, Savages of King's Lynn,
  England, c1875 . . . . 3,300.00
Pig, leaping, wood, carved, painted,
  Philadelphia style, Dentzel, c1912,
  restored 9,350.00
Rooster, 38″ h, 32″ l, running, 19th C . 2,500.00
Tiger, walking, raised head, carved sad-
  dle, Gustav Dentzel-Daniel Muller,
  c1895, restored 23,000.00
Zebra, proud pose, fancy straps, parrot
  peeking beneath saddle, Gustav
  Dentzel, c1895, restored 23,000.00

CASTLEFORD

History: Castleford is a soft paste porcelain
made in Yorkshire, England, in the 1800s for the
American trade. The ware has warm, white
ground, scalloped rims (resembling castle tops),
and is trimmed in deep blue. Occasionally pieces

are decorated further with a coat of arms, eagles,
or Liberty.

Bowl, 5″, scalloped, white ground, blue
  bands 185.00
Creamer, 3½″, 3 brown oval medallions,
  one with white applied eagle and
  shield, second with Lady Liberty, and
  third with cherubs and eagle on cloud 300.00
Sugar, cov, round, mythological scenes,
  vertical panels, twisted rope band
  near top, scalloped edge with oval
  medallions, blue enamel lines, dome
  lid, floral knob 200.00

**Teapot, 7 x 10½″, saltglaze, cobalt blue
borders, $165.00.**

Teapot, cov, mythological scenes,
  flanked by floral panels, acanthus leaf
  borders top and bottom, blue enamel
  lines on body, lid, and handle, leaf
  shape spout, floret knob 250.00

CASTOR SETS

History: A castor set consists of matched condiment bottles within a frame or holder. The bottles
are for condiments such as salt, pepper, oil, vinegar, and mustard. The most commonly found castor sets consist of three to five glass bottles in a
silver plated frame.

Although castor sets were known as early as
the 1700s, most of the sets encountered today
date from the 1870 to 1915 period when they enjoyed great popularity.

2-bottle, sq cut glass bottles, bulbous
  faceted stoppers, SS stand, shaped
  rect base, chased acanthus leaves,
  central ribbon band laurel wreath support handle, marked "K. Faberge,"
  Imperial warrant, Moscow, c1910,
  10⅝″ h 2,850.00
3-bottle, Bristol glass, enameled flow-
  ers, SP holder 110.00

7 Bottles, ornate silverplated Sheffield holder and hallmarked stoppers, mismatched glass stoppers, $425.00.

3-bottle, IVT, amber, SP holder, brass ring handle	125.00
3-bottle, milk glass, salt and pepper shakers, mustard container, orig matching undertray	225.00
3-bottle, opaque, Mt Washington bottles, floral on salt and pepper, hummingbird on mustard, pastels, round hammered SP frame, marked "Pairpoint 724"	185.00
3-bottle, satin glass, white, ribbed, SP holder marked "Pairpoint"	225.00
4-bottle, blown-three mold, cruet with solid ball stopper, mustard with ribbed cov, 2 shakers with orig metal caps, red painted sq tin frame, GI-7	400.00
4-bottle, clear, oct paneled pressed glass bottles, pewter stand, attributed to Israel Trask, 7½"	200.00
4-bottle, Daisy and Button, blue, glass holder	100.00
4-bottle, milk glass, turquoise, Fenton .	75.00
4-bottle, Mt Washington, Burmese, acid finish, ribbed, salt, pepper, mustard, and vinegar, SP holder marked "F. B. Rogers"	625.00
5-bottle, Bellflower pattern, two bottles with ribbed period stoppers, pewter stand, 11¼" h	300.00
5-bottle, china, Blue Willow pattern, matching holder	125.00
5-bottle, cut glass, cut lunar and geometric cutting, SS mountings, SS stand, Warwick form, shell shaped foot, English, hallmarks, c1750, 8½"	600.00
5-bottle, Gothic pattern, one bottle replaced, pewter frame	125.00
5-bottle, Heavy Paneled Finecut pattern, SP holder	90.00
5-bottle, ivory, mahogany case, SP tops	150.00

5-bottle, vaseline, fern engraving, orig tops and stoppers, sgd Meriden handled frame	275.00
6-bottle, amberina, metal holder, marked "Aurora, 487," 18" d	2,000.00
6-bottle, cut glass, ribbed trim on pedestal base, deep skirt, bale handle holds bell and plunger, marked "Meriden B Co," 7" h	225.00
6-bottle, cut glass, Sheffield SP oval holder, baluster stem, loop handle, 9¾"	375.00
7-bottle, cut glass bottles, SS collars and caps, George III silver galleried canoe shaped tray, scroll feet, marked "Peter, Ann & William Bateman, London," 1801, 8½"	1,250.00

CATALOGS

History: The first American mail order catalog was issued by Benjamin Franklin in 1744. This popular advertising tool helped to spread inventions, innovations, fashions, and other necessities of life to rural America. Catalogs were profusely illustrated and are studied today to date an object, identify its manufacturer, study its distribution, and determine its historical importance.

References: Don Fredgant, *American Trade Catalogs: Identification and Value Guide,* Collector Books, 1984; Lawrence B. Romaine, *A Guide To American Trade Catalogs 1744–1900,* R. R. Bowker, 1960.

Additional Listings: See *Warman's Americana & Collectibles* for more examples.

AC Becken Wholesale Jewelers, 1915, 768 pgs	60.00
Aladdin Lamps, 1933, silk and leaded shades, 46 pgs	65.00

R. M. Kellogg Co, Three Rivers, MI, 1922, 67 pgs, $8.50.

Baker's Chocolate, 1923, recipes 18.00
Bausch and Lomb Binoculars, 1930, 32
  pgs 15.00
Bing's Toys and Miniature R.R. System,
  1910, 68 pgs 85.00
Butler Bros, 1930, Summer, 402 pgs . 35.00
Consumers Wholesale Groceries, 1900 20.00
Clayton-Mark Water Well Supplies,
  1939, 95 pgs 15.00
Cochran-Sargent Windmills, 1920, 230
  pgs 20.00
Crouse Hinds, 1926, 20 pgs 35.00
Dayton Jewelry, 1920, 35 pgs 15.00
Elkart Carriages and Harness Supplies,
  240 pgs 75.00
Fairbanks Scales, 1914, 236 pgs 60.00
Fuller-Morrison, Soda Fountain Requi-
  sites, 1920, 452 pgs 38.00
Garland Stoves, 1892, 168 pgs 120.00
Harrison Richards Arms Co, 1922 . . . 20.00
Herschell Carousel Horses, 1910, 24
  pgs 100.00
Hulman & Co Wholesale, Terre Haute,
  IN and Mattoon, IL, December, 1925,
  394 pgs 60.00
Indian Motorcycle, 1915 . . . . 50.00
Jackson & Newton Co Doors and Win-
  dows, 1911 . . . . 15.00
Johnson Smith Novelties, 1937 . . . . . 18.00
Marshall Field Floor Coverings & Fur-
  niture, 1924 . . . . 38.00
McDonald Well Supplies, 1933, 67 pgs 15.00
Montgomery Ward
  1910, Sewing Machines, 44 pgs . . . 35.00
  1931, Spring and Summer 40.00
  1951, Fishing and Hunting, 114 pgs 20.00
Oneida Carriage, 1895, 46 pgs 48.00
Samson Windmills, 1937, 4 pgs 5.00
Schoenhut's Toys, 1912, 16 pgs 75.00
Sears, 1911, Men's Wear, cloth samples 45.00
Spiegel, Christmas, 1927, 42 pgs 25.00
Structo Weaving Looms, c1920, 42 pgs 8.00
Thomas Rods, 1939 . . . . 30.00
Tinkertown Toys, 1930, color 20.00
Victor Records, 1940, Nipper on cov,
  500 pgs 20.00
Wallace Nutting Furniture, 1927, 56 pgs 75.00
Western Electric Supply, 1920, 1,000
  pgs 50.00
Willis Boat Supplies, 1940, 203 pgs . . 25.00
Witte Diesel Engines, 1941, 100 pgs . 10.00

CELADON

History: The term celadon, meaning a pale grayish green color, derives from a theatrical character Celadon, who wore costumes of varying shades of grayish green, in Honore d'Urfe's 17th century pastoral romance, "L'Astree." French Jesuits living in China applied it to a specific type of Chinese porcelain.

Celadon divides into two types. Northern celadon, made during the Sung Dynasty up to the 1120s, has a gray to brownish body, relief decoration, and monochrome olive green glaze.

Southern (Lung-ch'uan) celadon, made during the Sung Dynasty and much later, is paint decorated with floral and other scenic designs and found in forms which would appeal to the European and American export market. Many of the Southern pieces date from 1825 to 1885. A blue square with Chinese or pseudo-Chinese characters appears on pieces after 1850. Later pieces also have a larger and sparser decorative patterning.

Reproduction Alert.

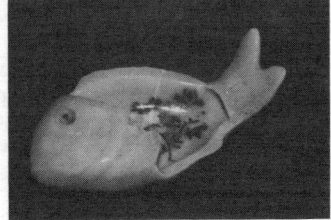

Condiment Dish, 5½" l, fish shaped, floral dec, $85.00.

Bowl
  8" h, bulbous, polychrome flowers
    and bird, wood lid 40.00
  10½" d, white raised enamel em-
    blems and scholar's implements,
    everted rim, cylindrical foot, 19th C 245.00
Charger, 14½" h, octagon shape, peacock and blossoms 200.00
Dish, 10½" d, incised peony blossom,
  crackled deep green glaze, everted
  rim, Ming Dynasty 250.00
Ewer, 3⅝", ovoid, ribbed, plain shoulder,
  loop handle, upright spout, blue-
  green glaze, burnt orange foot rim,
  Southern Sung Dynasty 900.00
Figure, elephant, 6" h, porcelain,
  Chinese 200.00
Jar
  5" h, globular form, pale green glaze,
    Yongzheng mark, 1723–35 . . . . . 4,950.00
  5½" h, relief molded, blue, pink, and
    red flowers, green leaves, gold
    trim, lid 95.00
Planter, 7", rect, blue, white scrolls, ftd 125.00
Platter, oval, floral and bird design, gold
  trim, 19th C 350.00
Rose Jar, 5¾ x 4¼", three part, bulbous,
  pink, relief red and blue flowers,
  green foliage, gold trim, cov 120.00

Sake Pot, 5¼" h, ribbed, dome cov,
    green foliage, pink flowers 75.00
Tureen, lid, rose medallion, Canton,
    19th C 1,150.00
Vase
    6" h, Moghul style, low relief carved
        Indian lotus motif, exotic bloom
        carved handles, surmounted lotus
        form knot cov 2,860.00
    7¼" h, stick type, incised dragon, ling-
        zhi and scrolling clouds, flared rim,
        rolled foot, 19th C 355.00
    11½" h, hand thrown, prunus blos-
        soms 75.00
    13" h, baluster, stepped neck, flaring
        mouth, carved and incised flowers
        and leaf scroll, crackled sea green
        glaze, Chinese 200.00
    28" h, double gourd, incised flowers
        panels, lotus scroll ground, soft pea
        green glaze, mounted as lamp, pr   2,800.00
Wall Pocket
    6", dark green branches, tiny white
        dots 95.00
    12", blue Iris design, Japan 60.00

CELLULOID ITEMS

History: In 1869 brothers J. W. Hyatt and I. S.
Hyatt developed celluloid, the world's first synthetic plastic, as an ivory substitute because elephant herds were being slaughtered for their ivory
tusks.

Known as "Ivorine" or "French Ivory," celluloid
was made of nitrocellulose and camphor. Early
pieces have a creamy color with stripes and
grooves to imitate the texture of ivory or bone. The
1897 Sears catalog featured celluloid items. Celluloid was used widely until synthetics replaced it
in the early 1950s. Celluloid often is used as a
generic term for all early plastics.

Animal
    Cat, 10", black and white 40.00
    Elephant, 3½", gray 25.00
Bookmark
    Girl on rocking horse 35.00
    Pan American Exposition, 1901 . . .   25.00
Bottle Opener, pipe wrench shape,
    Coes Wrench Company, c1910 . . . .   22.50
Charm, Cracker Jack, blue, chain 18.00
Compact, mirror, girl pictured, "Kremola
    Skin Cream" adv, dated 1915 . . . . .   15.00
Compass, 1¾", "Northfield Iron" adv .   32.00
Corkscrew, 4" l, nude mermaid, marked
    "Geschutz," Germany 320.00
Dresser Set, cov powder box, cov hair
    receiver, and hand mirror, green, pur-
    ple orchid dec, 3 pcs 18.00
Dresser Tray, 11¼" l 20.00
Frame, 7", oval, easel type 25.00

Advertising bookmark, Poole Pianos, 2
x 2⅝", made by Whitehead & Hoag Co,
Newark, NJ, $22.50.

Glove Box, roses, 1900 . . . .   30.00
Hair Receiver, cov, pearlized green . . .   6.00
Letter Opener, monkey, carved 38.00
Manicure Set, 15 pc, elephant skin case   55.00
Pencil Sharpener, airplane 35.00
Pin Cushion, 4" d, lift off plush cov top   10.00
Pinback Button, round, pictured Heinz
    Pickle 15.00
Rattle
    Doll, blue dress and pink hat, 1920–
        30 . . . .   15.00
    Turtle 20.00
Ring Box, 5" h, 3" d, cov, creamy ivory,
    ftd 15.00
Shoe Horn, creamy ivory, relief high but-
    ton shoe on handle, painted high-
    lights 22.00
String Holder, 3", Lydia Pinkham, black
    on white 35.00
Tape Measure
    People's National Bank adv 12.00
    Pig shape 25.00
Teething Ring, 5½" h, girl holding lamb
    and basket of flowers, pink and blue
    on white, emb "VCO USA" on back .   16.00
Toy, 4½" l, 4" h, Prince on pig, jointed
    legs 30.00
Vase, 6" h, pansy 30.00
Wall Plaque, scenic, c1930 . . . .   32.50

CHALKWARE

History: William Hutchinson, an Englishman, invented chalkware in 1848. It was a substance used
by sculptors to imitate marble. It also was used to
harden plaster of Paris, creating a confusion between the two products.

Chalkware often copied many of the popular
Staffordshire items of the 1820 to 1870 period. It

was cheap, gayly decorated, and sold by vendors. The Pennsylvania German "folk art" pieces are from this period.

Carnivals, circuses, fairs, and amusement parks used chalkware pieces as prizes during the late 19th and 20th centuries. They often were poorly made and gaudy. Don't confuse them with the earlier pieces. Prices for these chalkware items range from five to forty dollars.

References: Thomas G. Morris, *Carnival Chalk Prize*, Prize Publishers, 1985; Ted Soufe, *Midway Mania: A Collectors Guide To Carnival Plaster Figurines, Prizes, and Equipment 1900–1950*, L-W, Inc., 1985.

Additional Listings: See Carnival Chalkware in *Warman's Americana & Collectibles*.

Bust, 11¼″ h, woman on pedestal, titled "Micaela," painted, $135.00.

Bank

Apple, 3½″, worn red paint	125.00
Dove, 10½″, perched on stump	190.00
Bookends, pug dog, faces	60.00

Figures

Bulldog, 10″ h, 11¾″ l, polychrome dec, painted	195.00
Cat	
10″ h, seated with crouching mouse, octagonal base, blue ribbon collar, painted, repaired ear	150.00
15½″ h, seated, painted, yellow ears outlined in red, white coat, brown markings, red and blue ribbon around neck, molded base with brown and white dots, 19th C	8,800.00
Deer, 16″ h, 15″ l, two recumbent deer, painted, rect base	600.00
Dog, 5¾″, seated, red, green, and black	100.00
Doves, 11½″ h, perched on stump base, leaf and cherry dec, painted, late 19th C, pr	525.00

Fat Man, 10″, standing, arms folded behind back, hole in mouth for cigar	165.00
Horse, 10″ h, standing, raised foreleg, oval shrubbery form base, painted, late 19th C	285.00
Indian Chief, 27″, reclining	75.00
Rabbit, 5″, seated, orig paint	230.00
Lamp, Art Deco style, nude, frosted green shade	40.00
Nodder, cat, 9″ l, brown patina, orig painted features, c1800	450.00
Note Pad Holder, mammy, 10½″ h	35.00
String Holder, Scotty dog, 1910	50.00
Vase, 9″, squirrel holding nut, 1930s	25.00
Whistle, bird, molded folded feathers, painted yellow, orange, black, and white markings, American, 19th C	1,100.00

CHARACTER AND PERSONALITY ITEMS

History: The use of the "star" product endorser began in the late 19th and early 20th centuries. By the 1930s the system was entrenched.

Two groups evolved. The first was the characters found in cartoons or portrayed on radio, in the movies, or on television by actors. Some characters, e.g., Tony The Tiger, were created by the advertising industry solely for advertising use.

The second group consists of "real" people, e.g., actors, sports personalities, heroes, or political figures. The 1960s and 70s witnessed the pinnacle of star endorsed products.

References: Sandra Andacht, *Joe Franklin's Show Biz Memorabilia*, Wallace Homestead, 1985; David Longest, *Character Toys and Collectibles*, Collector Books, 1984; David Longest, *Character Toys And Collectibles, Second Series*, Collector Books, 1987; Anthony Slide, *A Collector's Guide To Movie Memorabilia With Prices*, Wallace Homestead, 1983.

Additional Listings: See *Warman's Americana & Collectibles* for expanded listings in Cartoon Characters, Cowboy Collectibles, Movie Personalities and Memorabilia, Shirley Temple, and Space Adventurers.

CHARACTERS

Betty Boop

Figure, 3″ h, bisque, holding French horn, "Fleischer Studios copyright and Made In Japan C407" stamped on back, c1930	175.00
Perfume, 3½″, glass, clear, figural, painted facial features, dark red plastic cap, c1930	50.00

Buck Rogers

Member Badge, brass	70.00
Watch, pocket, copper lightning bolt	

hands, one-eyed monster on reverse **300.00**

Buster Brown

Napkin Ring, celluloid, Buster Brown and Tige **30.00**

Whistle, 1 x 2⅝", litho tin, brown ground, yellow and green accents, c1920–30 .... **45.00**

Captain America, shield, brass, red and blue, 1941–42 .... **350.00**

Captain Midnight, figure, 6½", plaster, holster belt, aviator cap, and goggles detail, etched wing insignia, Captain Midnight and Wader Co copyright on base, 1940s **75.00**

Cracker Jack

Birthday Card, 3½ x 6½", red, white, and blue, textured paper, Cracker Jack box design, inked signature, Hallmark, 1940 copyright **50.00**

Prize

Magnifying Glass,¾ x 1¼", swing-out type, green plastic case, Sailor Jack and dog on one side, other "C J Co," marked "Made in Hong Kong," c1960 .... **15.00**

Wagon,¼ x 2 x 1", litho tin, red, white, and blue, fold-over wagon and horse, inscription "The More You Eat/The More You Want" on roof, c1930 .... **40.00**

Whistle,¾ x 2", tin, marked, 1930s **20.00**

Davey Crockett

Bank, 3 x 3½ x 5", metal copper colored, bust, frontier outfit with coonskin cap, Crockett on front base, Ohio bank imprint on reverse, mid 1950s **50.00**

Lamp, desk, 11" h, plaster, figure, holding rifle, 4½" d green accent color grass base, 10" d tan paper shade with continuous Crockett, Indians, and mountains scene, marked "Premco Co," 1955 copyright **200.00**

Ring, brass, name on band, portrait on top, adjustable, c1950 ...... **45.00**

Dick Tracy

Button, 1¼", back paper "Read Dick Tracy Every Day In The Chicago Tribune," Chester Gould signature, 1930s **30.00**

Flashlight, 5" l, plastic, black, dimensional plastic head on front glows when operated, 1975 copyright .. **20.00**

Ring, brass, star and shield design, Tracy portrait on top, green enamel paint, red enamel base, mid 1930s **150.00**

Tie Clip, 2½" l, silvered brass, blue lettering and center star **60.00**

Green Hornet, button, 1¼", red, blue, and black hornet center, yellow

Character, Howdy Doody, 7", bank, $40.00.

ground, yellow lettering with green ground rim **250.00**

Howdy Doody

Bank, 4 x 7", china, red and blue stripe shirt, blue neckerchief, rubber trap missing, unmarked, early 1950s **40.00**

Mask, 8 x 9", rubber, molded, orig red, white, and blue tag with Howdy, Clarabell, and Bob Smith copyright, c1948–51 .... **75.00**

Watch, silvered metal case, plastic crystal over Howdy dial, letters form numerals around face, diecut eyes slowly move clockwise, plaid fabric band, Bob Smith copyright, 1948–51 .... **150.00**

Little Orphan Annie

Mug, 3" h, plastic, Ovaltine premium **30.00**

Nodder, 4" h, bisque, Germany **100.00**

Pinback Button, 1¼" d, celluloid, "Little Orphan Annie Loves Red Cross Macaroni" **40.00**

Watch, brass, compass and sundial combination, Egyptian hieroglyphics on back, Ovaltine, 1938 ..... **50.00**

Lone Ranger

Badge, 2¼", white metal, red raised mask and lettering, late 1950s ... **35.00**

Ring, brass base, gray plastic six-gun on top, flint slot, 1948 .... **90.00**

School Bag, 10½ x 12", black grained vinyl, Lone Ranger and Tonto illus on silvery blue metallic ground, silvered metal studding dec, fabric lined int., carrying strap, 1950s .. **75.00**

Melvin Purvis, badge, brass, black and red details, 1936 .... **25.00**

Paladin, holster set, black, leather, 9" holsters with white trim and raised metal Paladin chess knight symbol, silvered metal belt buckle with western symbols, bullet clip and three plastic bullets, guns and tassel thongs missing **40.00**

Popeye
Egg Cup, figural, china **120.00**
Pencil Sharpener, tin, dated 1929 .. **30.00**

Red Ryder
Flashlight **35.00**
Gun
BB, Daisy Mfg, 1930s **40.00**
Clicker, tin, Wyandotte **10.00**

Reddy Kilowatt, pinback button, 7/8", red, white, and blue, 1930s **30.00**

Straight Shooter
Badge, silver, inset red, blue, and silver foil checkerboard **75.00**
Tin, make-up, 1 1/4", red and white checkerboard design, no contents, 1940, Ralston premium **20.00**

Superman, belt buckle, 1 x 1 1/2", brass, emb, hinged loop, Pioneer, c1940 .. **150.00**

The Shadow, ring, plastic, white, glows-in-the-dark, images of Shadow wearing mask and holding gun forms band, 1941 .... **375.00**

Tom Corbett
Badge, 2" d, silvered brass, diecut, emb, re-soldered **35.00**
Ring, plastic, blue, inset space suit celluloid disk, c1952 .... **15.00**

Uncle Wiggily, umbrella, black fabric, full color Wiggily and pig wearing beret under umbrella in downpour decal, curved wood hand grip, 24" d opened **75.00**

Wizard of Oz, puppet set, 10" h, vinyl heads and hands, Dorothy, Scarecrow, Tin Woodman, Cowardly Lion, Good Witch, and Bad Witch, c1960, set of 6 .... **75.00**

Yellow Kid, Stickpin, 3/4" h painted white metal diecut figure, 1 1/4" stickpin, c1896 .... **75.00**

PERSONALITIES

Jimmie Allen
Member Certificate, 8 x 11", parchment paper, green border design, red seal, "Full Fledged Pilot Member" Richfield Oil issue, c1934 ... **40.00**
Wings, brass, imprinted "Betsy Ross Bread" **40.00**

Amos and Andy, Toy, wind-up, taxicab, moves along, stops, and shakes violently, Amos driver and dog shakes back and forth, Andy mounted in back, horsehoe hood ornament, 3 1/2 x 5 x 8", Marx **550.00**

Jack Armstrong
Flashlight, 4 1/2", cardboard, black,

tube shape, metal caps ends, c1939 .... **15.00**
Pedometer, 2 3/4" d, dark blue outer rim, 1935 General Mills premium . **30.00**
Telescope, 8 1/4" opened, cardboard, black, metal cap ends, Wheaties premium, c1938 .... **20.00**

Gene Autry
Guitar, 31" l, plastic, tan, Autry portrait and western motifs, black fingerboard and neck, metal and nylon strings, twined carrying cord, trapezoid shape cardboard case with simulated brown alligator hide cov, tan plastic handle with brass mounted hinges, orig instruction book and Emenee catalog, early 1950s **200.00**
Pistol, cap, 9" l, silvered, die cast metal, Autry on each side, ivory color plastic grips with raised horse's head, box, Leslie-Henry Co, 1950s **125.00**

Eddie Cantor, game, "Tell It To The Judge," 20" sq board, soft portrait image in center, card to be worn around player's neck, currency, orig box, c1940 .... **50.00**

Charlie Chaplin
Doll, dressed, Louis Ambery & Son, 1920s **360.00**
Pinback Button, 2 1/2", figural, painted **45.00**
Toy, pull, 4", tin, tips hat when pulled, England **120.00**

Bing Crosby
Lobby Card, "Sing, Bing, Sing," 1933 **45.00**
Ring, plastic, gold, glossy black and white photo on top, c1940 ...... **15.00**

Dionne Quintuplets
Fan, 8 x 14", cardboard, babies playing in sand, 1936 .... **20.00**
Plate, 7", Annette, Cecille, and Yvonne as babies **25.00**
Poster, 14 1/2 x 32", full color, Quaker Oats adv, 1935 .... **75.00**

Clint Eastwood, lobby card, 11 x 14", *Where Eagles Dare* film scene, autographed **75.00**

Judy Garland
Mask, 7 x 9", face, paper, diecut, "Dorothy From Wizard of Oz, 1939" on back **20.00**
Paper Doll, two 12" cardboard dolls, one profile, other front view, clothing and 10 x 14" bed included, 1940 Whitman book #999 .... **45.00**

Gabby Hayes, coloring book, 11 x 13", full color Gabby illus on front and back cov, each page neatly colored by crayon, Abbot Publishing Co, 1954 copyright **40.00**

Sonja Henie, button, 1 3/4", blue drawing,

Personality, Judy Garland's ruby slippers, from The Wizard of Oz, size 6B, $165,000.00.

white letters, bright green ground, "Sonja Henie Ice Review," c1940 .. **20.00**

Bob Hope, sheet music, 9 x 12", 4 pgs, "A Thousand Violins," black and white Hope and Rhonda Fleming photo within red heart design cov, 1949 Paramount *The Great Lover* .. **15.00**

Laurel and Hardy

Poster, 14½ x 22¼", wearing police uniforms, "Bons a'Tout Bons a'Rien" movie title, printed in Brussels, Belgium, 1950s **75.00**

Roly Poly, 10½" h, Hardy, vinyl, musical, Transogram, 1966, Larry Harmon copyright, orig retail label taped to stomach **50.00**

Lennon Sisters, coloring book, 8½ x 11", full color photo front and back cov, 13 pages colored, Whitman, 1959 .... **15.00**

Shari Lewis, game kit, 10 game props with instructions, 33⅓ rpm record, orig box, Lowell Toy, 1962 copyright **50.00**

Charles Lindbergh, photograph, 8 x 10", brown tone, standing by plane, wearing dress suit, c1927 .... **25.00**

Pinky Lee, coloring book, health and safety, 80 pgs **25.00**

Jackie Robinson, doll, outfit, bat, comic, MIB, c1940 .... **325.00**

Roy Rogers

Binoculars, plastic and metal, black, Roy Rogers sticker on each hand grip, 4 x 40 lenses, leather carrying strap, yellow, black, and white design box, 1956 Roy Rogers-Frontiers copyright **100.00**

Ring, silvered brass, saddle with engraved seat, 1948 .... **150.00**

Wristwatch, green face, Roy and Trig-

ger, orig brown leather band, Ingraham, 1951 .... **65.00**

Babe Ruth

Pinback Button, 1³⁄₁₆", red, white, blue, and yellow, litho, tin, "Most Homeruns Per Season/60 In 1927" ... **20.00**

Wristwatch **95.00**

Shirley Temple

Pitcher, 4½" h, glass, clear blue, white portrait image on side, Wheaties premium, 1938 .... **50.00**

Ring, child's, size 4½, brass band, clear plastic covered black and white photo on top, 1930s **80.00**

Rudolph Valentino, candy container, 7½" d, 2½" h, tin, black, color litho portrait on lid **50.00**

Lawrence Welk, album, 8½ x 11", photos and features, 52 pgs, Skyline Features Publisher, 1956 copyright **15.00**

CHELSEA

History: Chelsea is a fine English porcelain designed to compete with Meissen. The factory began operating in the Chelsea area of London, England, in the 1740s. Chelsea products are divided into four periods: (1) Early period, 1740s, with incised triangle and raised anchor mark; (2) The 1750s, with red raised anchor mark; (3) The 1760s, the gold anchor period; and (4) The Derby period from 1770–1783. In 1924 a large number of the molds and models of figurines were found at the Spode-Copeland Works, and many items were brought back into circulation.

Reference: Susan and Al Bagdade, *Warman's English & Continental Pottery & Porcelain, 1st Edition,* Warman Publishing Co., Inc., 1987.

Plate, 9⅞" d, white ground, $95.00.

Bonbonniere, 2" l, lady's head, frilly white cap, black domino mask, painted int., hinged copper-gilt mount rim, c1755 . . . . **1,650.00**

Bowl, 7⅝", oval, lotus molded, rose, purple, blue, yellow, green, iron-red, and gray painted int., insect hovering beside floral bouquet, brown edged petal molded rim, red anchor mark . **990.00**

Charger, 13¾" d, exotic birds on branches center, gilt scroll and dentil rim, Mazarine blue border, c1760–65, gold anchor mark **360.00**

Cup and Saucer, striped pink tulip and columbine, yellow ground, gilt rim, scroll and puce foliage handle, c1760, gold anchor mark **325.00**

Dish
8¾" l, Sunflower, seed molded center, greenish yellow to brown, rows of yellow petals, dark green stem handle, red anchor mark **6,600.00**

9" l, Peony, lightly molded, brown center, small and large feathered petals, green stem handle, c1756 . . . **7,150.00**

9½" l, Cabbage Leaf, iron-red and green floral sprig painted center, rose colored molded veining, curled stem handle, pale yellow and grass green shaded rim, rose anchor mark **1,650.00**

Figure, 5½", boy and girl, seated, blue shades, white ground **200.00**

Patch Box, 1¹⁄₁₆" l, lady's face, black domino mask, rose-cut diamond mounted eyes, mounted pink stone mouth, faceted rock crystal cov, hinged gold mount rim, c1755 . . . . . **1,100.00**

Plate
8⅜" d, rose, iron-red, yellow, brown, blue, and green floral bouquet and sprigs dec, scalloped rim, brown edge, red anchor mark, pr **330.00**

8¹³⁄₁₆" d, green, puce, purple, iron-red, and yellow painted, peas, plum, and cherries center surrounded by foliate sprigs and two ladybirds, three fruit sprigs alternating with butterflies rim, rococo scroll molded edge, picked out in blue enamel and gold, 1760–65 . . . . **825.00**

9" d, striated purple blue and gray painted tulip, iron-red dotted center, brown edged scalloped rim, red anchor mark **7,700.00**

Seal, ¾" h, red molded squirrel, mounted on gilt metal ring, c1755 . . **275.00**

Soup Plate, 9¼" d, Hans Sloane, painted pink flowers, three red gooseberries, brown and turquoise feather molded rim, red anchor mark **430.00**

Teabowl and Saucer, iron-red, gold, and

blue, Queen Charlotte pattern, spiral fluted **180.00**

Vase, 8⅝" h, boy seated and standing holding fish, light green, yellow, and puce, oval shape rockwork base, c1765, red anchor mark **1,100.00**

"CHELSEA" GRANDMOTHER'S WARE

History: "Chelsea" Grandmother's ware identifies a group of tableware with raised reliefs of either grapes, sprigs of flowers, or thistles on a white ground. Some examples are lustered.

The ware was made in the first half of the 19th century in England's Staffordshire district by a large number of manufacturers. The "Chelsea" label is a misnomer, but commonly accepted in the antiques field.

Plate, 7" d, Vintage dec, copper luster dec, $20.00.

Bowl, 6½ x 3½", Sprig		18.00
Butter Pat, Thistle		15.00
Coffee Pot, Grape		150.00
Creamer, Grape		50.00
Cup and Saucer		
Grape, handleless		32.50
Shell & Scroll		25.00
Sprig, wishbone handle		30.00
Pitcher, 6¾", Scrolls and Medallions . .		75.00
Plate		
6¾", Staffordshire Knot, eagles and nest		12.00
7¼", Grape		15.00
8", Sprig		25.00
9", Grape		24.00
Sauce Boat, Grape		30.00
Sugar, cov, Grape		50.00
Teapot, cov, Thistle		125.00
Vegetable Bowl, Grape, oval		32.50

CHILDREN'S BOOKS

History: Because there is a bit of the child in all of us, collectors always have been attracted to children's books. In the 19th century books were popular gifts for children, with most of the children's classics written and published during this time. These books were treasured and often kept throughout a lifetime.

Developments in printing made it possible to include more attractive black and white illustrations and color plates. The work of these artists and illustrators has added value beyond the text itself.

References: Barbara Bader, *American Picture Books From Noah's Ark To The Beast Within,* Macmillan, 1976; Virginia Haviland, *Children's Literature, A Guide To Reference Sources,* Library Of Congress, 1966, first supplement, 1972, second supplement, 1977, third supplement, 1982.

Libraries: Free Library of Philadelphia, PA; Library of Congress, Washington, D.C.; Pierpont Morgan Library, New York, NY; Toronto Public Library, Toronto, Ontario, Canada.

Additional Listings: See *Warman's Americana & Collectibles* for more examples and an extensive listing of collectors' clubs.

Note: dj = dust jacket; wraps = paper covers; pgs = pages; unp = unpaged; n.d. = no date; teg = top edges gilt

Advisor: Margaret L. Tyrrell.

Alger, Horatio, *Lester's Luck,* Henry T. Coates, 1901, 1st ed	**130.00**
Anderson, Anne, *Old French Nursery Songs,* Harrap, n.d., 64 pgs, 1st ed, dj	**55.00**
Baum, L. Frank	
Mother Goose in Prose, Maxfield Parrish, illus, George M. Hill, 1901, 265 pgs	**400.00**
The Magic of Oz, John R. Neill, illus, Reilly & Lee, 1919, 266 pgs, 1st ed	**650.00**
Brett, David, *Baby's ABC,* Dean's Rag Books #80, 1949, 16 pgs	**30.00**
Carroll, Lewis, *Alice's Adventures In Wonderland,* Willy Pogany, illus, Dutton, 1929	**125.00**
Crane, Walter, *Pothooks & Perseverance: or the ABC-Serpent,* Marcus Ward, 1886, 24 pgs, 1st ed	**175.00**
Cox, Palmer, *The Brownies Through The Union,* Century, 1895, 144 pgs, 1st ed	**75.00**
DeBrunhoff, Jean, *Babar en Famille,* Hachette, 1938, 40 pgs, 1st ed	**125.00**
Dulac, Edmund, *A Fairy Garland,* Scribner's, 1929, 251 pgs, 1st U.S. ed	**100.00**
Godden, Rumer, *The Dolls House,* Tasha Tudor, illus, Viking, 1962, 136 pgs, dj, 1st ed	**45.00**
Greenaway, Kate, *Mother Goose or the*	

Old Nursery Rhymes, Warne, n.d., 52 pgs	**100.00**
Gruelle, Johnny, *The Magical Land of Noom,* Donohue, n.d., 157 pgs	**60.00**
Humphrey, Maud, *A Treasury of Stories, Jingles, and Rhymes,* Stokes, 1894	**85.00**
Kingsley, Charles, *The Water-babies,* W. Heath Robinson, illus, Houghton Mifflin, 1915, 320 pgs, 1st ed	**225.00**
Lear, Edward, *The Nonsense ABC,* Macmillan, 1928, 40 pgs, 1st ed	**175.00**
Lofting, Hugh, *The Story of Doctor Dolittle,* Frederick A. Stokes, 1920, 180 pgs, 1st ed, signed	**150.00**
MacDonald, George, *At The Back of the North Wind,* Jessie Willcox Smith, illus, David McKay, 1919, 342 pgs, 1st ed	**100.00**

Seaside Fun, 9 x 12″, pop-up, Dean's "Surprise Model," Series No. 3, London, inscribed 1897, $200.00.

May, Robert L., *Rudolph the Red-Nosed Reindeer,* Marion Build, illus, Maxton, 1950, 20 pgs, pop up	**40.00**
Moore, Clement C, *The Night Before Christmas,* Arthur Rackham, illus, George C. Harrap, 1931, 36 pgs, dj, 1st ed	**275.00**
Newell, Peter, *The Rocket Book,* Harper & Bros, 1912, unp, 1st ed	**100.00**
Pyle, Howard, *The Story of the Champions of the Roundtable,* Scribner's, 1905, 329 pgs, 1st ed	**100.00**
Potter, Beatrix, *Appley Dapply's Nursery Rhymes,* Frederick Warne, 1917, 53 pgs, 1st ed	**150.00**
Scott, Anna M., *A Year With The Fairies,* M. T. Ross, illus, P. F. Volland, 1914, 99 pgs, 1st ed	**95.00**
Sendak, Maurice, *Higglety Pigglety Pop!,* Harper & Row, 1967, 69 pgs, dj, 1st ed	**125.00**

Seuss, Dr., *The Cat In the Hat Comes Back*, Random House, 1958, 63 pgs, dj, 1st ed **200.00**
Stratton-Porter, Gene, *Laddie*, Herman Pfeifer, illus, Doubleday Page, 1913, 602 pgs, 1st ed **40.00**
Thompson, Ruth Plumly, *The Perhappsy Chaps*, Arthur Henderson, illus, P. F. Volland, 1918, 95 pgs, 1st ed **250.00**
Ungerer, Tomi, *Crictor*, Harper & Bros, 1958, 32 pgs, dj, 1st ed **50.00**
Upton, Bertha, *The Golliwogg's Fox Hunt*, Florence Upton, illus, Longmans Green, 1905, 66 pgs, stiff wraps **60.00**
Young, Miriam, *Miss Suzy*, Arnold Lobel, illus, Parents Magazine Press, 1964, 42 pgs, dj, 1st ed **40.00**

CHILDREN'S FEEDING DISHES

History: Unlike toy dishes meant for play, children's feeding dishes are the items actually used in the feeding of a child. Their colorful designs of animals, nursery rhymes, and children's activities are meant to appeal to the child and make meal times fun. Many plates have a unit to hold hot water, thus keeping the food warm.

Although glass and porcelain examples from the late 19th and early 20th centuries are most popular, collectors are beginning to seek some of the plastic examples from the 1920s to 40s, especially those with Disney designs on them.

References: Doris Anderson Lechler, *Children's Glass Dishes, China and Furniture*, Collector Books, 1983; Doris Anderson Lechler, *Children's Glass Dishes, China, Furniture, Series II*, Collector Books, 1986; Lorraine May Punchard, *Child's Play*, published by author, 1982; Margaret & Kenn Whitmyer, *Children's Dishes*, Collector Books, 1984.

Baby Feeding Dish
7⅜" d, decals of cats and rooster, marked "Roma" **50.00**
7¾", kewpies, sgd "Rose O'Neill, Royal Rudolstadt" **235.00**
8", seated dog, gray band, sgd "Roseville" **65.00**
8½", Nursery Rhyme, cobalt blue . . **18.00**
9", three parts, green crystal, "See Saw Margery Daw", scene of children, two dogs, cat, and pig on rim **25.00**
Bowl
6¼", Nursery Rhyme, cobalt blue . . **15.00**
7½", Dollie Dimples and Sammy, gold rim, marked "Buffalo Pottery" . . . **75.00**
Cereal Set, cereal bowl, mug, and plate
Bunnykins, marked "Royal Doulton" **100.00**
Nursery Rhyme, Jack and Jill, 6" plate, marked "Royal Bayreuth" . . **125.00**

Porcelain and metal, 10″ wide handle to handle, three chamber dish, hot water reservoir, base marked "GW Co," $55.00.

Snowbabies, two children and dog sledding, marked "Royal Bayreuth" **150.00**
Creamer, rabbit dressed in red jacket, green band, marked "Roseville" . . . **35.00**
Mug
2¼", black transfer of Faith and Hope, pink luster border **50.00**
3½", Nursery Rhyme, cobalt blue . . **18.00**
4½", barrel shape, blue and white, transfer "The Sisters," c1860 . . . . **125.00**
Staffordshire, multicolored, four children, VWX, "W" is for whipping . . **110.00**
Plate
6", polychrome transfer of sleeping girls and angels **60.00**
6½", Dr Franklin maxim, "It Is Hard For An Empty Bag To Stand Free," pawn shop scene, black line border **75.00**
7½", Sunbonnet babies washing, hanging clothes, marked "Royal Bayreuth" **125.00**

CHILDREN'S NURSERY ITEMS

History: The nursery is a place where children live in a miniature world. Things come in two sizes. Child scale designates items actually used for the care, housing, and feeding of the child. Toy or doll scale denotes items used by the child in play and for creating a fantasy environment which copies that of an adult or his own.

Cheap labor and building costs during the Victorian era enabled the nursery to reach a high level of popularity. Most collectors focus on items from the 1880 to 1930 period.

References: Doris Anderson Lechler, *Children's Glass Dishes, China, and Furniture*, Collector Books, 1983; Doris Anderson Lechler, *Children's Glass Dishes, China, Furniture, Series II*,

Collector Books, 1986; Lorraine May Punchard, *Child's Play,* published by author, 1982.

Additional Listings: Children's Books, Children's Feeding Dishes, Children's Toy Dishes, Dolls, Games, Miniatures, and Toys.

Alphabet and Counting Board, metal and wood, 1917	50.00
Baby Bassinet, 68", swinging, white iron, wire mesh, bedding, brass finial, wire arch with shade	250.00
Bed, 29 x 48 x 30½", country, Sheraton, turned legs and posts, wooden slat railings, old green paint	225.00
Blocks, set of 36, 1¾", polychrome, alphabet, animals, and stripes	110.00

Chair

22" h, Windsor, fan back, labeled "Stickley"	575.00
25" h, primitive, plank seat, comb back, old green paint	85.00
Chamber Set, china, washbowl and pitcher, slop jar, cov soap dish, cov toothbrush and comb holder, chamber pot, hp florals, white ground, marked "Germany"	180.00
Cupboard, child's size, pine, flat wall type, cut out feet, open top board and batten door base, refinished	250.00

Father Christmas Teether, 5¼" l, Santa Claus head, mother of pearl teether, sterling silver, English, $275.00.

Doll Carriage, 26 x 13 x 28", wicker, metal frame, spoked wheels, shade for head	175.00
Doll Trunk and Accessories, 14 x 14 x 15" wooden trunk, flowered paper lining and tray, 15 pcs of French fashion doll clothing, five small bonnets, ivory handled parasol, patchwork quilt, four small cardboard boxes with miniature accessories, three fashion purses, scissors, thimble, fashion hat, straw	

sewing basket, dresser set in orig package, c1870	4,200.00
Handkerchief, 12" sq, cotton, Red Riding Hood and Wolf, printed scene . .	25.00
Highchair, 33½" h, youth type, footrest, walnut, carved seat and back	175.00

Hobby Horse

42" l, dapple-gray, real leather saddle, Victorian	1,150.00
50¾", orig brown haircloth cov, removable wooden rocker base . . .	300.00
Ice Skates, 12" l, wooden, curved wrought iron blades, old worn orange paint	100.00
Parasol, red and white, ruffled	25.00
Pencil Box, 2½ x 7¾", wood, divided int., litho Mother Goose lid	15.00
Quilt, 60 x 68", pieced, cotton, blue, green, gray, white, and black, lavender border, blue binding, Amish, Susie Peachey, Mifflin County, PA, c1930	650.00

Rattle

Celluloid

Gander, long neck, 5¼" h	25.00
Puffin bird, 3½" h	10.00
Sterling Silver, coral ring teether . . .	375.00
Rocking Horse, 26" l, black leather seat between two wooden silhouettes, padded leather on head and neck, worn leather ears and harness, sheet metal teeth, marble eyes, old alligatored white paint, black spots	775.00
Rolling Pin, glass	125.00
Sewing Machine, blue floral dec, c1809, sgd "Lindstrom, Made in USA"	50.00

Sled

36" l, curved wooden iron tipped runners, cast iron swan finials, orig red paint, white striping, white center panel with red striping, black transfer of horse and Oriental woman .	200.00
41", oak, metal runners, orig label "Steermasters Bob Ski"	150.00
Sleigh, 36 x 36 x 21", dark red body, gold trim, cream and blue handle, black leather seat, wooden runners .	400.00
Soap Dish, cov, rabbit and sandpiper transfer, luster, ironstone	90.00
Tin Pail, 5½", stippled ground, raised flower and leaf, picture of ship, red, emb "A Good Child," 1897	30.00
Wagon, 17" l, wooden, old red paint, Daisy stenciled in black	250.00
Wheelbarrow, 8¾ x 29½ x 10", wooden, stenciled	175.00

CHILDREN'S TOY DISHES

History: Dishes made for children often served a dual purpose—play things and a means of learning social graces. Dish sets came in two sizes. The first was for actual use by the child when entertaining her friends. The second, a smaller size than the first, was for use with dolls.

Children's dish sets often were made as a side line to a major manufacturing line either as a complement to the family service or as a way to use up the last of the day's batch of materials. The artwork of famous illustrators, such as Palmer Cox, Kate Greenaway, and Rose O'Neill, can be found on porcelain sets.

References: Doris Anderson Lechler, *Children's Glass Dishes, China and Furniture,* Collector Books, 1983; Doris Anderson Lechler, *Children's Glass Dishes, China, Furniture, Series II* Collector Books, 1986; Lorraine May Punchard, *Child's Play,* published by author, 1982; Margaret & Kenn Whitmyer, *Children's Dishes,* Collector Books, 1984.

China, tea set, white porcelain, multi-colored transfer of woman and children, marked "Germany," $250.00.

Akro Agate
Cup and Saucer, Interior Panel, opaque, pumpkin	25.00
Plate, Oxblood and Lemonade, octagonal	18.00
Set, Trans-Optic, Interior Panel, jade, cov teapot, creamer, cov sugar, four cereal bowls, cups, saucers, and plates, 21 pcs	135.00

China
Creamer and Sugar, Willowware . . .	25.00

Dinner Set
Allerton, "Punch," teapot, creamer, sugar, six cups, saucers, and plates, 22 pcs	90.00
Geisha Girl, 17 pcs	75.00
Moss Rose, 29 pcs, orig box	115.00
Noritake, robin's egg blue dec, marked "M" in green wreath, 15 pcs, orig box	125.00
Plate, Blue Willow, grill	45.00

Tea Set, teapot, creamer, cov sugar, six cups and saucers
Geisha Girl, Japanese	100.00
White Patterned Ironstone, English, handleless cups	375.00
Willowware, blue, Japanese	250.00

Depression Glass
Creamer, Cherry Blossom, pink	25.00
Pitcher, Doric & Pansy, pink	25.00
Plate, Laurel, scotty decal	20.00

Set
Cherry, delphite, 14 pcs	190.00
Little Hostess, Hazel Atlas, 14 pcs, orig box	75.00

Graniteware
Coffeepot, blue and white	75.00
Plate, gray	15.00
Tea Set, blue and white, 21 pcs, orig box	275.00

Milk Glass
Mug, Gooseberry, 1⅞"	30.00
Punch Cup, Nursery Rhyme	25.00
Stein, Monk, rings on top	25.00
Table Set, Thumbelina, cov butter, creamer, and cov sugar	50.00

Pattern Glass
Berry Bowl, individual, Patte Cross .	12.00
Butter, cov, Tulip and Honeycomb . .	35.00
Cake Stand, Ribbon Candy, green, 6½" d, 3½" h	45.00
Castor Set, American Shield, four bottles	125.00

Creamer
Dewdrop	30.00
Grape Vine with Ovals	40.00
Michigan, clear, gold trim	35.00
Pennsylvania	16.00
Tappan, amethyst	35.00
Wee Branches	80.00

Mug
Hobnail, cranberry rim	35.00
Wee Branches	20.00
Pitcher, Waffle and Button	30.00
Punch Bowl, Thumbelina	30.00
Punch Cup, Wheat Sheaf	8.00
Saucer, Cat in Boot	22.50

Spooner
Hawaiian Lei	20.00
Pennsylvania	16.00

Sugar, cov
Colonial, Cambridge	40.00
Menagerie, blue	275.00
Michigan, clear, gold trim	40.00
Tappan, amethyst	45.00
Table Set, cov butter, creamer, cov sugar, and spooner	
Duncan and Miller #42	125.00
Sweetheart	85.00
Twist, white opal	600.00
Tumbler, Patte Cross	12.00

Tin
Mug, 2½", Little Bo Peep	15.00

Tea Set
    Dogs and Cats, red, blue, and
       white, marked "Germany," 9 pcs **75.00**
    Snow White, 1937, 15 pcs **135.00**

CHRISTMAS ITEMS

History: The celebration of Christmas dates back to Roman times. Several customs associated with modern Christmas celebrations date back to the early pagan rituals.

Father Christmas, believed to have evolved in Europe in the 7th Century, was a combination of the pagan god Thor, who judged both the good and punished the bad, and St. Nicholas, the generous Bishop of Myra. Kris Kringle originated in Germany and was brought to America by the Germans and Swiss who settled in Pennsylvania in the late 18th Century.

In 1822 Clement C. Moore wrote "A Visit From St. Nicholas" and developed the character of Santa Claus into what we know today. Thomas Nast did a series of drawings for *Harper's Weekly* from 1863 until 1886 and further solidified the character and appearance of Santa Claus.

Reference: Robert Brenner, *Christmas Past*, Schiffer Publishing, 1986; Francine Kirsch, *Christmas Collectibles*, Wallace-Homestead, 1985; Maggie Rogers and Peter R. Hallinan, *The Santa Claus Picture Book: An Appraisal Guide*, Dutton 1984; Maggie Rogers and Judith Hawkins, *The Glass Christmas Ornament, Old and New,* Timber Press, 1979; Nancy Schiffer, *Christmas Ornaments: A Festive Study,* Schiffer Publishing, 1984; Clara Johnson Scroggins, *Hallmark Keepsake Ornaments: A Collector's Guide, Second Edition,* Wallace-Homestead, 1985; Phillip V. Snyder, *The Christmas Tree Book*, Penguin Books, 1985.

Additional Listings: See *Warman's Americana & Collectibles* for more examples.

Advisor: Lissa L. Bryan-Smith and Richard M. Smith.

Tree Stand, cast iron, 9½″ sq, 5¾″ h, painted green, bell dec, $75.00.

Book
    Christmas With The Poets, Waed,
      Loch, Tyler, London, leather bound,
      tinted illus, ornamented letters . . . **25.00**
    "Santa Claus Comes to America,"
      Caroline Singer and Cyrus Leroy
      Baldridge, writers and illus, hard-
      back **18.00**
    The Christmas Stocking, Charles E.
      Graham & Co, three children hang-
      ing stockings on fireplace **8.00**
    The Night Before Christmas, Cupples
      & Leon Co, NY, 1913, hardback . . **12.50**
    The Romance Of A Christmas Card,
      Kate Douglas Wiggin, 1st ed, 1916 **10.00**
Candy Container
    Father Christmas, 4″ h, green glass,
      metal lid on bottom **225.00**
    Santa, 8″ h, red felt suit, pink com-
      position face, cotton beard, feet
      slide out for candy **90.00**
    Santa in sleigh, holding feather tree,
      red and blue felt suit, rabbit fur
      beard, removable head **195.00**
Christmas Fence
    3″ h, wood, folding, red and green . . **40.00**
    4″ h
      Cast Iron, 10 sections, dark green,
        gate **185.00**
      Wood, 3 sections, unpainted,
        picket, constructed from cheese
        boxes **75.00**
    5″, wood, 4 sections, blue, picket,
      gate **90.00**
Deer
    Art Glass, blown, 5″ h stag, 4″ h doe,
      silvered, Germany **70.00**
    Celluloid, 3″ h, white, antlers **7.00**
    Composition, 4½″ h, brown, wood
      legs, metal antlers, Germany **45.00**
    Metal, 5″ h, brown, marked "Ger-
      many" **35.00**
House
    Cardboard, 4″ h, white mica, cello-
      phane windows **5.00**
    Log Cabin, 5″ h, white mica roof,
      marked "Germany" **18.00**
    Set of 5, 1½″ h, cardboard and silver
      mica, orig box and hangers on
      each **12.00**
    Village, 5″ h, lithograph paper, five
      buildings, USA **25.00**
Light Bulbs
    Clown, 3″ h, blue suit, Japan **15.00**
    House, 2½″ h, pink and blue, Japan **10.00**
    Lantern, 4½″ h, Oriental, red, Japan **18.00**
    Santa, 3″ h, one leg in chimney, Ja-
      pan **25.00**
    Street Lamp, 2″ h, Japan **12.00**
Lights
    Bubble, orig box **35.00**

Celluloid, assortment of figures on large string 150.00

Ornament, 2½" h, glass, house, painted, red roof, door, and windows, $22.50.

Ornament
  Chromolithograph
    Angel
      7" h, dresden wings 80.00
      Resting on hands, tinsel trim . . 10.00
    Father Christmas
      8" h, brown cat, fur hat, toys at feet 25.00
      9" h, cotton batting coat, flat . . . 150.00
    Three children, 4" h, winter clothing, tinsel trim 15.00
  Cotton Batting
    Bird on clip, 3", white 25.00
    Boy, 4" h, white, composition face, brown cotton shoes, Germany . 120.00
    Carrot, orange and red, green paper top 17.50
    Girl, 4" h, Kewpie type, composition face, white legs, orange shirt . . 150.00
    Santa, 4" h, tomato red suit, black rim, legs and boots 40.00
  Dresden
    Dog, 4" h, setter type, silver, standing in green grass 50.00
    Doll Carriage, 3" h, three dimensional, gold 125.00
    Rooster, 6" h, flat, gold, red, and green 48.00
    Slipper, 5" h, flat, gold, netting, tinsel trim 40.00
    Zepplin, 3½" l, three dimensional, detailed trim 350.00
  Glass
    Barrel, gold and white, wire wrap, unsilvered, Victorian 60.00
    Basket, art glass, small glass oranges 85.00
    Bottle
      Victorian, red, wire wrap, unsilvered 35.00

Wine, red and pink, paper label "Malaga" 40.00
Clown, head, ruffle 45.00
Fish
  5" h, blue, red trim 90.00
  Porcupine type, blue and gold . 30.00
Goldilocks, blonde hair, red band and bow 160.00
House, elf peeking out door, gold, red trim 50.00
Mushroom on clip, red and white, unsilvered 42.00
Parrot on clip, blue, red, and silver 45.00
Windmill, blue, unsilvered 8.00
Wine Keg, red and silver, flowers . 20.00
Kugels
  Grapes, purple and blue 85.00
  Sphere, green, 4" d 42.00
Metal, basket, metal handle, 3" h . . 35.00
Wax, angel, early
  Large 85.00
  Small 42.00
Photograph, black and white
  3 x 5", three children holding tree, trimmed tree and toys background, c1910 . . . . 15.00
  5 x 7", girls, group dressed as angels in church, two ceiling high dec trees, c1920 . . . . 25.00
Pinback Button
  "Health for All," ½", Santa head and National Tuberculosis Assoc symbol 5.00
  "Joe, The Motorists Friend," 1½", Santa head, pack of toys, suspending red ribbon and bell 10.00
  "Meet Me At Kline, Eppinhimer and Co," ⅔", Santa head, white background 8.00
  "Merry Christmas, Butler Bros, Co," 1¼", Santa head, star background 8.00
Putz Animal
  Camel, 5" l, composition body, hide covering, wood legs, Germany . . . 38.00
  Cow, 4" h, celluloid, brown, Japan . . 10.00
  Donkey, 3", composition, hide covering wood legs, Germany 20.00
  Ram, 2" h, celluloid, tan, USA 7.00
Roly Poly, 6" h, Santa, red, green belt 250.00
Santa
  ¾" h, walking with staff in hand, celluloid 20.00
  1" h, celluloid, standing in cardboard sleigh, pulled by two brown reindeer 45.00
  2" h
    Chenille, green, composition face, Japan 18.00
    Cotton batting, standing by paper house, composition face 65.00
  5½", Santa on chimney, red suit, composition face 70.00

8¼" h, standing, composition legs and boots, felt coat, basket on back	**400.00**
9" h, Santa by chimney, egg carton .	**85.00**

Tree

2" h, brush, green, snow, Japanese .	**2.00**
8" h, paper, green, USA	**15.00**
48" h, feather, green, red berries, candle clip, sq white base with holly stencil, Germany	**400.00**
Elephant, 5" h, composition, hide covering, wood legs, Germany	**30.00**

CIGAR CUTTERS

History: Counter and pocket cigar cutters were used at the end of the 19th and the beginning of the 20th centuries. They were a popular form of advertising. Pocket-type cigar cutters often were a fine piece of jewelry that was attached to a watch chain.

COUNTER TOP

Advertising

Brunswick Havana Cigars	**325.00**
Flor de Melba, glass top, cuts three at once	**80.00**
Havana Cigars, "Tas Amantes," wood base, glass top	**150.00**
Hotel Sherman Co, figural street light, red globe in ornate base, marked "Reed & Barton"	**250.00**
Hyneman Bros, windup, wood box base	**225.00**
King Alfred 10¢ Cigar, 1901, cast iron, ornate Waterbury clock on top, mechanical	**575.00**

Figural

Horse Head, flowing mane, SP, 5¾"	**90.00**
Spearhead, cast iron, orig paint	**60.00**

Pocket, 1⅝" h, metal, man, arm swings to cut cigar, $85.00.

POCKET

Advertising

Bergner & Engel Brewing Co, mechanical	**50.00**
Morrel's Fine Hams	**25.00**
Brass, relief portrait, George Washington	**130.00**

Miniature

Boy using potty, chrome	**130.00**
Clown, leaping, spring action	**70.00**
Lady Acrobat, holding trapeze ring, squeeze action	**90.00**
Monkey, riding tricycle, swing action	**120.00**
Victorian Lady, large bust, spring action	**150.00**

Scissor Handle

MOP, marked "1902"	**50.00**
Sterling Silver, repousse	**40.00**

CIGAR STORE FIGURES

History: Cigar store figures were familiar sights in front of cigar stores and tobacco shops from about 1840. Figural themes included Sir Walter Raleigh, sailors, Punch figures, ladies, and Indians, the most popular.

Most figures were carved in wood, although figures also were made in metal and papier mache for a short time. Most carvings were life size or slightly smaller and brightly painted. A coating of tar acted as a preservative against the weather. Of the few surviving figures, only a small number have their original bases. Most replacements are due to years of wear and usage by dogs.

Use of figures declined when local ordinances were passed requiring shop keepers to move the figures inside at night. This soon became too much trouble, and other forms of advertising developed.

Reference: A.W. Pendergast and W. Porter Ware, *Cigar Store Figures*, The Lightner Publishing Corp., 1953.

Indian Chief

56½" h, pine, carved, painted, posed on tobacco bale, 19th C	**20,900.00**
64" h, carved, painted wood, highly detailed, holds bundle of cigars in one hand, tobacco leaves in other, fox pelt draped over right shoulder	**40,000.00**
Maiden, 41½", wearing headdress, tobacco in hand	**2,800.00**

Indian Princess

71" h, pine, carved, painted, holding block of tobacco in one hand, bunch of cigars in other, inscription "Geo W Joyce, Tobacconist Depot For" and "PARTIDOS, Sweet Catawba"	**67,500.00**

Indian Princess, 56½" h, yellow dress, blue feathers, red top, replaced green painted base, $4,000.00.

83" h, pine, carved, painted, feathered headdress, blue, yellow and green costume, red cloak, holding tobacco leaves bunch in right hand, wood base **23,100.00**
Indian Squaw, 57½" h, carved, painted wood, holds tobacco leaf in left hand **14,000.00**
Punch, 72" h, pine, carved, Pierrot collar, black and orange painted dec, sq roller base **77,000.00**
Sailor, 33" h, polychrome pin, carved, stands beside tobacco keg, inscription "Cigars" on front **16,500.00**

CINNABAR

History: Cinnabar is a ware made of numerous layers of a heavy mercuric sulfide and often referred to as vermillion, the red hue in which it is most commonly found. It was carved into boxes, buttons, snuff bottles, and vases. The best examples were made in China.

Reference: Sandra Andacht, *Oriental Antiques & Art: An Identification And Value Guide,* Wallace-Homestead, 1987.

Box
5" l, dragon design detail, blue enameled metal int. **300.00**
Cosmetic Box, 14⅞" w, dragons chasing flaming pearls, cresting waves, three drawers and two door compartments int., gilt handles, 19th C, restored **2,640.00**
Cup, 4½" d, dragon handles, c1900 . . **200.00**
Dish, 10¾" d, deeply carved, leafy melon vines int. and ext., black lacquer bottom **880.00**

Ginger Jar, 8½" h, landscape scene, red on cream ground, c1900 . . . . **275.00**
Incense Burner, pagoda style, Taoist mask design, c1900 . . . . **1,300.00**
Plate
8" d, scroll design, red on black, c1900 . . . . **120.00**
12¾" d, double dragon design **375.00**
13" d, floral scene, red on green, c1900 . . . . **450.00**
Tray, 15" l, bird and flower scene, reddish brown **625.00**

Box, 3¾ x 5⅜", Chinese figures in garden, $75.00.

Snuff Bottle, 3", carved, houses and tree scenes **65.00**
Vase
10" h, landscape design **120.00**
11½" h, landscape design, figures, and flowers, wood stands, pr **270.00**
Wine Pot, 7" h, rect, floral panels, lid . **425.00**

CLAMBROTH GLASS

History: Clambroth glass is a semi-opaque, grayish-white glass which resembles the color of the broth from clams. Pieces are found in both a smooth finish and a rough sandy finish. Sandwich Glass Co. and other manufacturers made clambroth glass.

Barber Bottle
7", emb "Bay Rum" in red, porcelain stopper, marked "M. A. Co." **30.00**
8" h, emb "Water" in red, porcelain stopper **25.00**
Box, cov, 5" l, tub shape, cut panels, polychrome enamel dec, engraved silver handles **70.00**
Candlestick, 11", acanthus, blue socket **475.00**
Curtain Tiebacks, 3" d, pewter shanks, pr **200.00**
Egg Cup, cov, Diamond Point, 5¾" . . . **200.00**

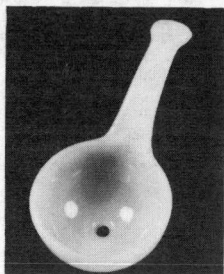

Ladle, 9½″ l, $30.00.

Goblet, Button Arches, souvenir	25.00
Mug, Lacy Medallion, souvenir	25.00
Pitcher, 8″, eight heavy pillar molded ribs, applied handle, curled end, polished pontil	600.00
Spooner, 5⅞″, Cable	185.00
Whiskey Taster, 2⅜″ h, seven arches and panels, iron pontil	100.00

CLEWELL POTTERY

History: Charles Walter Clewell was first a metal worker and second a potter. In the early 1900s he opened a small shop in Canton, Ohio, to produce metal overlay pottery.

Metal on pottery was not a new idea, but Clewell was perhaps the first to completely mask the ceramic body with copper, brass, "silvered" and "bronzed" metals. One result was a product whose patina added to the character of the piece over time.

Most of the wares are marked with a simple incised "CLEWELL" along with a code number. Because Clewell used pottery blanks from other firms, the names "Owens" or "Weller" are sometimes found.

Since Clewell operated on a small scale with little outside assistance, only a limited quantity of his art work exists. He retired at the age of 79 in 1955, choosing not to reveal his technique to anyone else.

References: Paul Evans, *Art Pottery of the United States, 2nd Edition,* Feingold & Lewis Publishing Corp., 1987; Ralph and Terry Kovel, *The Kovels' Collector's Guide To American Art Pottery,* Crown Publishers, Inc., 1974.

Ashtray, 3¼″, copper, circular imp mark, "Clewell, Canton, OH," 1922	165.00
Bowl, 4½″, riveted overlay finish, sgd, circular imp mark, "Clewell Coppers," seal	200.00

Candlesticks, pr, 10″ h, 4¼″ d, dark metallic glaze, green base patina, incised "Clewell" and "4115-2-6"	475.00
Tobacco Jar, 8″, cov, hammered and riveted dec, dark brown patina	600.00

Tankard Set, pitcher and mugs, riveted metal design, marked "Clewell, Canton, OH," $650.00.

Vase, 8″, bulbous, collar neck, rolled rim, brown to green to dark bround to orange patinated bronze coating, incised "Clewell" and "459-21"	450.00
Wine Jug, 10½″ h, 5½″ d, archaic form, scroll like handle undulating rim, relief design, brown and green patina, partial label	150.00

CLIFTON

CLIFTON POTTERY

History: The Clifton Art Pottery, Newark, New Jersey, was established by William A. Long, once associated with Londhuna Pottery, and Fred Tschirner, a chemist.

Production consisted of two major lines: Crystal Patina, which resembled true porcelain with a subdued crystal-like glaze, and Indian Ware or Western Influence, an adaptation of the American Indians' unglazed and decorated pottery with a high glazed black interior. Other lines included Robin's Egg Blue and Tirrube. Robin's Egg Blue is a variation of the crystal patina line but in blue-green instead of straw colored hues and with a less prominent "crushed crystal" effect in the glaze. Tirrube is on a terra cotta ground, features brightly colored, slip decorated flowers, and is often artist signed.

Marks are incised or impressed. Early pieces may be dated and shape numbers impressed. Indian wares are identified by tribes.

References: Paul Evans, *Art Pottery Of The United States*, Everbodys Press, Inc., 1974; Ralph and Terry Kovel, *The Kovels' Collector's Guide To American Art Pottery*, Crown Publishers, Inc., 1974.

Humidor, Indian Ware, brown, 4½" w, 4¼" h, \$50.00.

Bowl, 3½ x 2½", red clay body, feather design, glazed black int., Indian Ware	165.00
Candlesticks, pr, 9½" h, Indian Ware, incised "Pueblo Viejo, Arizona," artist sgd, c1906	135.00
Jar, cov, Indian Ware, artist sgd	90.00
Mug, 4", Indian Ware	60.00
Teapot, 8", tan drip dec, green ground	115.00
Vase	
6 x 8", bulbous, long cylindrical neck, creamy yellow flambe glaze unevenly over metallic crystal patina flambe, incised "Clifton" and "1906," stamped "164"	350.00
8", Indian Ware, brick red, black, white, geometric design, marked "Arkansas/205"	165.00
9 x 5", Tirrube	150.00
12", light green, 1905	75.00

CLOCKS

History: The sundial was the first man-made device for measuring time. Its basic disadvantage is well expressed in the saying: "Do like the sundial, count only the sunny days."

With need for greater dependability, man developed the water clock, oil clock, and the sand clock respectively. All these clocks worked on the same principle—time was measured by the amount of material passing from one container to another.

The wheel clock was the next major step. These clocks can be traced back to the 13th century. Many improvements on the basic wheel clock were made and continue to be made. In 1934 the quartz crystal movement was introduced.

Recently an atomic clock has been invented that measures time by the frequency of radiation and only varies one second in a thousand years.

Identifying the proper model name for a clock is critical in establishing price. Condition of works also is a critical factor. Examine the works to see how many original parts remain. If repairs are needed, try to include this in your estimate of purchase price. Few clocks are purchased purely for decorative value.

References: *Collectors Guide To Clocks Price Guide,* L-W Promotions, 1973 (revised 1986 price list); Roy Ehrhardt, *Clock Identification And Price Guide: Book I,* rev. ed., Heart of America Press, 1979; Roy Ehrhardt, *Clock Identification And Price Guide: Book II,* Heart of America Press, 1979; Roy Ehrhardt, ed., *The Official Price Guide To Antique Clocks,* House of Collectibles, Third Edition, 1985; Tran Duy Ly, *Clocks: A Guide To Identification and Prices,* Arlington Book Company, 1984; Alan and Rita Shenton, *The Price Guide To Clocks, 1840-1940,* Antique Collectors' Club, 1977.

Collectors' Club: National Association of Watch and Clock Collectors, Inc., P. O. Box 33, Columbia, PA 17512. Dues: \$20.00. *Bulletin* (bimonthly).

Museum: American Clock & Watch Museum, Bristol, CT; Museum of National Association of Watch and Clock Collectors, Columbia, PA.

MISCELLANEOUS

Advertising	
Belle Bourbon, shelf, metal bell shaped case, Roman numerals	250.00
Dr. Pepper, Drink & Bite To Eat, wall, Telechron, 15"	300.00
General Electric, shelf, figural, refrigerator, white heavy metal case, 5¼ x 9", electric	100.00
Goulding's Manuers, wall, 32" h, New Haven Clock Company, New Haven, CT, 1900, 8 day time movement, paper on zinc dial, label on back of case, minor staining on dial	800.00
Jolly Tar, Pastime, Tobacco Manufacturers, Louisville, KY, wall, 31" h, Baird Clock Co., Plattsburg, NY, 1895, Seth Thomas 8 day movement, lacks key	1,100.00
None Such Mince Meat, wall, cardboard and tin, pumpkin form, Arabic numerals, 9½" d	300.00

Alarm, Tom-Tom, 14¼ x 14¼ x 4½", 8 day, advertising "True Time Tellers, Octagon Alarms," New Haven Clock Co, c1920, $850.00

Alarm
   Attleboro, c1909, 36 hour, nickel plated case, owl dec 50.00
   Champion, 9", 30 hour, American movement, metal frame, ornamental feet, solid back brace 65.00
   Gilbert, Wm. L., Bi-Nite, 6½"', h, 4½" d, 4" black dial, luminous numerals and hands 7.50
   New Haven, c1900, 8", 30 hour, silver plated case, perfume shape, beveled glass mirror, removable cut glass scent bottle, beaded handle 175.00
   Thomas, Seth, Long Running Alarm Clock, 9" h, bronzed white metal case, with a 30 hour time and alarm lever movement, paper on zinc dial 80.00
   Tiger, La Sallita, one day, nickel plated brass case, 2" Ivorine dial, beveled crystal, self-centered wheels, western frictionless pivots 25.00
   Waterbury, Kremlin-Moselm, one day, calendar, alarm, 3¾" dial, hammered gilt case, brass winding and setting parts 45.00
Barometer with clock, probably European, c1900, 22" h, carved oak case in shape of an anchor with dolphins, an aneroid barometer in lower section, 8 day lever movement in upper section 350.00
Blinking Eye, figural
   Dog, German, patented 1928, 8" h, carved figure of dog with eyes revolving independently of each other to indicate time, 30 hour balance wheel movement 200.00
   Owl, unknown maker, c1920, 6½" h, nickel plated white metal front, green eyes, 30 hour level movement, hardwood case, paper dial,

nickel plated bezel, beveled glass, lacks key 325.00
Boat Clock
   Chelsea Clock Co., Boston, 1910, 10½" d, solid cast brass case, silvered dial with seconds indicator, 8 day time movement with lever escapement, lacks key 200.00
   Thomas, Seth, Thomaston, CT, 1880, 6¼" d, nickel plated brass case, painted dial with seconds indicator, 8 day double wind movement with lever escapement, lacks key 85.00
Garden Clock, French, c1875, 60" h, cast white metal figure of draped classical woman with raised arm carrying a clock, figure has fine old patina highlighted with bronze paint, 8-day time and strike lever movement, porcelain dial 2,100.00
Gas Night Light, Ansonia Clock Co, Ansonia, CT, c1900, milk glass dial, cast brass rim, 30 hour time movement, lever escapement, maker's name inscribed on movement, 6" 275.00
Glass, Lalique
   4½" h, molded opalescent glass sq case, medium relief of nude female naiads, long beaded hair, gilt metal clock face with engine turned ground, case molded "R. Lalique," c1932 . . . . 6,200.00
   8½" l, molded frosted glass demilune case, low and medium relief of lovebirds and foliage, circular clock face cast with stylized blossom, marked "Mascaras & Fils/Albi," case molded "R. Lalique," c1930 . 3,125.00
Gravity
   American, c1925, brass case, powered by weight of clock movement descending along two posts, lifting movement back winds the clock for another 24 hours, marked "Patented 8/2/21," 10¼" 175.00
   French, c1940, sold by Shreve, Crump & Low, Boston, 17" h, powered by the fall of the movement along the brass rails, rewinding accomplished by lifting the movement back to the top of rails, mahogany case with turned columns and brass finials, 30 hour movement, porcelain dial, encased in polished stone drum 800.00
Inkstand
   Ansonia, Good Luck, horseshoe, 10", 1 day, calendar, metal 250.00
   Gilbert, Wm. L., Parlor ink, 6½", bird on branch separates two bottles . 150.00
Novelty
   Automobile, Boston Clock Co., Bos-

ton, MA, c1911, 3½″ d, 8 day, 7 jeweled, Brequet hairsprings, compensation balances, polished brass water and dust proof adjustable case, attached by ratchet and back nut **175.00**

Birdcage

German, c1930, 8″ h, brass plated stand and cage dec with simulated diamonds and scrolled designs, time indicated by revolving dials in center of cage, bird swings back and forth in conjunction with balance wheel of 30 hour time and alarm lever movement **175.00**

Japanese, c1940, 11″ h, birdcage on stand, revolving globe inside birdcage, bird connected to escape wheel, marble base, winding key missing, marble base cracked and repaired **200.00**

Figural

Cathedral, European, c1875, 15½″ h, MOP, extremely intricate clock features a miniature cathedral constructed from hundreds of pieces of MOP, steeple is small clock movement with a visible pendulum and a MOP dial, 30 hour time only movement **400.00**

Dice, N. Shure Co., Chicago, 1934, 2⅞″ sq, 30 hour movement, composition, gilt hands **25.00**

Clock Peddler, probably German, c1900, 15″ h, painted figure of man carrying in one hand a pair of weights, a clock on his back, and a clock on his chest, 30 hour time movement **300.00**

Tennis Racquet, New Haven, c1900, 1 day time, gold plated finish, thermometer on handle . **125.00**

Lamp

Bradley, B., mechanism on top ignites small brass lamp when alarm strikes, solid walnut case, carved dec, 30 hour time and alarm movement, paper on zinc dial, orig brass pendulum, H. J. Davies, NY, 1865 movement, illuminating alarm mechanism by B. Bradley & Co, Boston, MA, orig paper label on back, 14½″ . **1,100.00**

Unknown Maker, American, c1900, lamp, brass case, revolving glass shade, 30 hour time movement wound by key on back of lamp, shade repainted, 12½″ **350.00**

Paperweight, Ideal Clock Co., New York, c1900, 2 x 3″, 1 day lever

time, imitation black polished marble case **85.00**

Welch, E. N., Bristol, CT, 1860, Briggs Rotary Patent, rotary escapement mounted on turned wood base, cast feet, orig glass dome, nickel plated pendulum ball, 8″ **300.00**

World's Fair, St. Louis Clock and Silver Ware Co., St. Louis, MO, 1904, 8½″, Cascades and Festival Hall, 1 day time, gold plated, 2″ porcelain dial **75.00**

Parade, Bradley & Hubbard, Meriden, CT, 1885, 14″, 30 hour time only balance wheel movement, case of stamped brass, embellished with assorted sizes of colored glass, translucent glass dial reveals time at night by a lighted candle inside of case, glass dial cracked **1,500.00**

Ship's Clock, Seth Thomas, Thomaston, CT, 1900, 8¾″ h, brass cased with upside-down movement striking ship's bells, silvered dial with seconds indicator, 30 hour level movement, lacks key **500.00**

Water, English, oak and brass, marked "B. Kindle-1651-Halifax," 30″ **200.00**

SHELF CLOCKS

Acorn

Brown, J. C., Bristol, CT, 25¼″, 8 day time and strike, driven by fusee spring, case and sidearms of laminated wood, fine old finish, laminations with alternating light and dark wood, orig glass tablet depicting scene in the city with carriages and buildings, maker's label on backboard, minor retouching on lower glass **15,000.00**

Forestville Manufacturing Co., Bristol, CT, c1849, 19¼″, 8 day brass time and strike movement with fusees, laminated case construction and rosewood veneered, sgd on dial, orig paper label, some retouching to glass **4,750.00**

Automation, Directorie, Le Remouleur, late 18th C, mantel, bronze and marble, rect case cross section with molded white marble top surmounted by grotesque figure sharpening knives, sharpening wheel in barrow, automated with the movement, frieze of peasant dancers centering hag's mask with open mouth revealing annual hour and minute bands, caryatid corners, plinth base, 15½ x 25″ **30,000.00**

Beehive

Ansonia, Tudor, 19″, 8 day, strike, veneered case, floral and Roman pillar motif **275.00**

Boardman, Chauncey, Bristol, CT, 1850, 19″, 8 day time and strike fusee movement, mahogany veneered case, door with tablet of "Bouston Springs," orig dial and paper label, hands replaced, one fusee wheel broken, ivory escutcheon missing from door **850.00**

Gilbert, Wm. L., Star Round Top Extra, 16¾″, 8 day spring, strike ... **175.00**

New Haven, Guide, 1 day, strike, castle scene in glass **150.00**

Smith & Brother, Philadelphia, PA, c1843, 21″ h, mahogany veneers, retains an eglomise tablet with marbleized background and geometric designs, painted wood dial, 30 hour time and strike movement, paper label **1,350.00**

Terry & Andrews, Bristol, CT, 1850, 19″ h, rosewood veneered case with a mirror, painted zinc dial, 8 day time and strike Lyre movement, paper label **350.00**

Welch, E. N., Bristol, CT, 1870, 18¾″ h, rosewood veneered case, door with painted tablet of rampant lions and crown, 30 hour time and strike movement, maker's label **175.00**

Shelf, cottage type, time and strike, 30 hour movement, 9¼″ h, Seth Thomas, Thomasville, CT, $175.00.

Box or Cottage

Atkins Clock Co., Bristol, CT, 12⅜″, miniature, octagon top, rosewood veneer, orig label on reverse **150.00**

German, 10″ h, c1880, softwood case, carved door, paper on zinc dial, 30 hour time and alarm movement, old pendulum and key, paper label on rear of case, hands replaced **125.00**

Gilbert, Wm. L., Favorite, 11⅛ x 13½″, 1 day, spring strike **100.00**

Terry, S. B., Terryville, CT, 10½″, orig frosted tablet, perfect zinc dial, 30-hour time ladder movement with alarm and pendulum bob, brass hands, paper label, lacks key ... **650.00**

Thomas, Seth, Plymouth Hollow, CT, 1860, rosewood veneered case, black and gold eglomise panel, painted zinc dial, fine paper label, 30 hour time movement, 9″ **120.00**

Bracket

George III

Arched Case, inlaid mahogany, free standing corner columns, brass finials, scalloped apron, bracket brass feet, 13″ **1,000.00**

Balloon Case, brass bracket feet, silvered dial and movement, c1775, 17″ **2,000.00**

Japanese, miniature, 7″ h, c1850, solid rosewood case, front and rear doors that slide up, 30 hour fusee time and strike movement with crown wheel escapement, engraved designs on back plate, revolving hour dial, small aperture in arch of dial indicating signs of the Zodiac, dial back has a hand painted scene on it **1,800.00**

Louis XV, Darville, Paris, mid 18th C, kingwood, balloon form case, asymmetrical ormolu crest, borders, and feet, circular enamel plaquette dial, sgd on dial and movement, 15½ x 35″ **1,200.00**

Regency Style, stepped hood, conforming door, circular silvered dial, arched plate sgd "Pietro del Moro," 15″ **600.00**

Loundes, Charles, Pall Mall, London, 4th quarter 17th C, 13″, verge movement, fitted engraved backplate, molded ebony case, gilt metal escutcheons **10,000.00**

Rimbault, Stephen, London, 1770, 14¾″, 8 day time and strike fusee movement with crown wheel escapement, ebonized oak-case, brass carrying handle, pierced fret, glazed front door opening to brass dial with maker's name inscribed, rear door opening to engraved movement, front door locked and key missing, molding missing from rear door, some damage to feet, 3 out of 4 glass panels replaced ... **2,500.00**

Calendar
  Davis Clock Co., Columbus, MS, Column Flat Top, 25″, 8 day, strike, 7″ dial 450.00
  Ingraham, 25″, Urania, 8 day, half hour strike, barometer and thermometer, oak case 275.00
  Ithaca Calendar Clock Co., Ithaca, NY, 1875
    No. 10 Farmer's Model, 26″ h, walnut case, 8 day time and strike movement by E. N. Welch, paper on zinc dials 700.00
    Shelf Steeple, 24½″, solid walnut case, turned finial and pierced fret surrounding dials, 8 day time and strike movement, calendar mechanism with day and month apertures, and date indicator, paper on zinc dials, movement manufactured by E. N. Welch .. 600.00
  Thomas, Seth, Empire, 30″, 8 day, strike, orig weight, Plymouth Hollow label 900.00
  Welch, Spring & Co., Forestville, CT, 1870, 19¾″ h, Italian Type, rosewood veneered case, turned columns, 8 day time and strike movement, hour dial has day indicator, lower dial has date and month indicator, "V"-type B.B. Lewis calendar mechanism mounted to back . 425.00
Carriage
  Boston Clock Company (Boston, MA, 1890), 6½″ h with handle up, fine brass case, porcelain dial, 8 day time movement, lever escapement, nickel plated plates 300.00
  Dent, E., Paris, mid-19th C, 5¾″, dial sgd 1,200.00
  French, unknown maker, 1880, 6½″ h with handle up, very fancy case with applied ormolu, porcelain dial, 8 day time and alarm movement, alarm movement strikes a bell in the bottom of the case 400.00
  Japy, France, c1840, 7½″ h with handle up, one piece case, porcelain dial, 8 day time, strike, and alarm, hour repeat, engraved platform and balance cock, movement inscribed by maker, alarm hand replaced .. 650.00
  Sandoz, Gve., Palais Royal, 3¾″, sides and back with polychrome enamel dec, later lever platform, molded sgd oval case 1,500.00
  Stillman, London, England, 1850, 5¼″ h with handle up, gilded brass case, 8 day time fusee movement with lever escapement of fine quality, porcelain dial inscribed by maker, engraved brass dial sur-

round, front and rear doors spring loaded and open by pushing buttons on case bottom, movement features maintaining power 1,000.00
  Waterbury Clock Co., Waterbury, CT, 1908, miniature, 3″ h with handle up, cast gilded brass case, porcelain dial, maker's trademark, 30 hour time movement, lever escapement 150.00
Crystal Regulator
  Ansonia, Emperor, 13″, 8 day, half hour strike, visible escapement, polished brass, gold ornaments, cloisonne inlay 1,500.00
  Gilbert, Wm. L., Tuscan, 19″, 8 day, half hour strike, ivory porcelain dial, visible escapement, Brazilian green onyx columns, ormolu gold finish, urn and wreath finial 850.00
  Waterbury, Orne, 13⅛″, 8 day, half hour strike, gong, visible escapement, cut glass columns 1,250.00

Shelf, figural, pot metal with gold finish, Art Deco, Golden Girl, wood base, Sessions, $250.00.

Figural
  Ansonia Clock Co., 1882, 21½″, French Empire style, cast detail with figures of hunter and fisherman, enameled dial with clear beveled glass, cast white metal with old gold and black repaint, some minor damage and old repair 325.00
  Elephant, gilt and patinated bronze, Louis XV style, 19th C, mantel, drum form case surmounted by chinois, held aloft by Indian elephant on scrolling rockwork base, circular brass dial, enameled numeral plaquette contained by beaded bezel, 22″ 3,750.00

Gilbert, Wm. L., c1910, 32″, Archer, half hour strike, 4″ ivory porcelain dial, beveled glass, bronze and gilt ... **600.00**

United Clock Co., 1955, Ship, walnut hull, chrome plated sails and rigging, lighted port holes, ship's wheel dial ... **90.00**

Urn, Louis XVI, late 18th C, gilt bronze, two putti bearing laurel branches as handles, truncated white marble columnar base, Roman hour and Arabic minute dials, 20″ ... **4.500.00**

French, mantel

Charles X, 2nd quarter 19th C, 11″, ormolu case, striking movement with a 3″ d white enamel dial marked "Maufsenet a Chalons sur Marne," depicting a young boy teaching a dog to mind, the rect base with a plaque inscribed "garde a vous" ... **800.00**

Napoleon III, 2nd half 19th C, 14½″, gilt bronze mounted white marble clock in style of Louis XVI, 4¼″ white enamel dial with Roman and Arabic numerals, inscribed "L. Leroy Cie. a Paris, 7 Bould. de la Madeleine," the movement striking on the hour and half hour on a single bell, modern wood base ... **900.00**

Neveux, Haas & Cie, c1920, molded as temple of love, movement contained within cornice, diamond studded handles above figure of cupid playing harp, silver gilt case with sky blue enamel, engine turned ground, orig leather carrying case, 11″ ... **7,000.00**

Garniture, French, 3 pcs

Louis XV style, late 19th C, 22½″, cloisonne enamel dial, gilt bronze case, cloisonne enameled candelabra, retailed by Overstrid, Rotterdam ... **1,600.00**

Louis XVI style, Lesteau Le Jeune, 19th C, Sevres porcelain and gilt bronze, after 18th C example by Kinable, lyre form clock surmounted by Apolline mask, enamel dial with gilt bronze bezel, paste brillians, companion anthenienne form garnitures with satyr masks, holding bouquets of roses as candelabra, 22″ h clock, 3 pcs ... **6,000.00**

Louis Philippe, 2nd/3rd quarter 19th C, gilt bronze and verde antico marble, stamped "G. Megnin," columned case surmounted by griffin finials and flower-filled basket, the flanking four light candelabra applied with female therms ... **1,325.00**

Gingerbread (Kitchen)

Ansonia

Louisiana, 22¾″, 8 day, strike, 6″ dial, black walnut case, filigree style tablet ... **190.00**

X-No. 6, 22½″, 8 day, hour and half hour strike, oak case ... **175.00**

Gilbert, Wm. L.

Forest, 24½″, 8 day strike, 7″ dial, oak case, tablet with bird and butterfly in marsh setting ... **200.00**

Leopard (Animal Series), 21″, 8 day movement, strike wire bell, walnut finish case, tablet shows bird in pond setting ... **185.00**

Ingraham, Mt. Vernon, 22″, 8 day, half hour strike, highly emb, octagon door, solid oak, relief of Mt. Vernon on crest, made for 1904 St. Louis World's Fair ... **300.00**

F. Kroeber Clock Co., Wanderer, 23″, 8 day gong strike, 6″ fancy dial, walnut case, elaborate geometric tablet ... **285.00**

New Haven Clock Company, Nereid, 23½″, 8 day strike, 6″ dial, oak case, tapered style, half round urn finial on crest ... **185.00**

Thomas, Seth

Newark, 23″, 8 day, spring, strike, wire bell, black walnut case, fleur-de-lis crown top finial, pierced carved leaf scroll attachments on side ... **250.00**

Ogden, 21½″, 8 day, spring, strike, alarm, cathedral gong, black walnut case, 2 finials flanking clock on base ... **200.00**

Waterbury Clock Company

Harding, 21½″, 1 day, spring, strike, fan motif in crest, floral motif on left side of tablet ... **175.00**

Seaford, 21⅛″, 8 day, half hour slow strike, gong, 6″ dial, black walnut case ... **200.00**

Welch, E. N.

Irving (part of the Actor series), 23″, 8 day, half hour strike, 6″ dial, oak case, two figures in classical costume on tablet ... **165.00**

Sampson (Admiral), 24″, 8 day, half hour strike, cathedral bell, 6″ dial, oak case, bust portrait of Sampson on crest, ship on tablet ... **275.00**

Lyre, gilt bronze and crystal

Charles X, sulphide bust portrait flanked by cut glass columns, elaborately chased with Neo-classical motifs, 25″ ... **7,500.00**

French Empire, mask with crown above lyre strings flanged by pair of facing swan heads holding swag over Roman numeral enamel dial, Baccarat crystal base with center ormolu mounted ribbon tied swag and trumpet, works by Archambult, Paris, 20" **2,250.00**

Mantel

American Renaissance, Edward F. Caldwell and Co, NY, first quarter 20th C, drum form marble case resting on cushion of scrolling satyre masks, plinth with angled feet as floral bouquets, gilt bronze mounts, circular enamel dial contained by reeded bezel, sgd on dial "Edward F. Caldwell & Co., New York," 16 x 12" **2,400.00**

Empire, Thomire & Cie, early 19th C, arched case flanked by two gilt bronze figures of Atlanta and Meleager, white marble plinth with hunt trophy, quivers, and arrows, circular enamel dial, sgd on dial "Thomire & Cie," 17½ x 28" **8,500.00**

Louis XVI Style, ormolu and white marble, female figure and cupid flanking circular clock face, white enamel dial, black Arabic numerals, oval plinth base with ormolu putti frieze, flattened bun feet, sgd "Leroy, H'er du Roi," 16½" l, 15" h **1,800.00**

Onyx

Boston Clock Co., c1890, 10" h, 8 day, half hour cathedral strike, 7 jeweled movement, bronze gilted ornaments **275.00**

Welch, E. N., c1890, 12" h, 8 day, half hour strike, diamond movement, visible escapement, tinted dial, gilt trim **200.00**

Wood, enameled

New Haven, 1900, 11" h, 8 day, half hour strike, cathedral gong, 6" MOP dial, bronze trim, scroll feet **150.00**

Russell & Jones, 10" h, 8 day, slow strike, 5" dial, Tennessee marble columns, marble finished wood . **125.00**

Welch, E. N., c1890, 11" h, 8 day, half hour cathedral strike, marbleized, black, 5" gilt dial, bronze feet, and side ornaments, gilt engraved **125.00**

Massachusetts Shelf

Balch, Daniel, Jr., Newburyport, MA, c1790, 28½ x 12 x 6", Federal, mahogany, two sets of reeded pilasters, lower door with keystone and arch, scrolled pediment, plinth with brass urn and flame finials, brass dial **12,000.00**

Sherwin, William, Buckland, MA, 1830, 29¾", time and strike 30 hour wooden works movement, maple

case, shaped crest, turned feet and turned columns flanking glazed door with mirror tablet, paper label, orig wood dial, orig weights, stenciling removed from crest and traces can be seen **900.00**

Tower, Reuben, Hingham, MA, c1836, 8 day, orig weights, stenciled tablet with lyre spandrels, dished painted metal dial **7,500.00**

Unknown, 8½", miniature, 30 hour time only movement with S. B. Terry patented torsion balance, marked "Oct 5th, 1852, iron case, MOP inlay, painted gold dec, orig dial **1,200.00**

Metal

Bronze

Ansonia, 4¼", 1 day time, Art Nouveau case **75.00**

Charles X, 19th C French gilt bronze, bronze winged maiden clasping torch, drawing back the "Veil of Night," rect base with relief chariot and putti, 20" **1,150.00**

Louis XVI, Louis Berthoud, flower filled urn with satyre mask carry handles, surmounted by snakes, waisted base, foliate cast plinth, circular enamel dial within beaded bezel, 19" **900.00**

Gilt Bronze

Art Nouveau, Charles Jonchery, c1900, arched top, undulating sides cast in high relief, poppy blossoms on leafy stems, openwork feet, clock painted Arabic numerals above visage of young woman crowned with blossom, matted ground, inscribed "Jonchery," 14⅞" **3,850.00**

Louis Philippe, Poirier and Bouge, Paris, early 19th C, circular engine turned dial within faux stone wall forming seat for figural cupid, green marble base, draped with flowers and ribbons, flower form feet, 12 x 5 x 19" .. **4,500.00**

Louis XV, Ferdinand Berthoud, mid 18th C, block form case surmounted by celestial globe, infant astronomer studying chart leans against case, molded guillouche ornamented base, circular enamel dial contained by guillouche bezel, sgd on dial and movement, 12 x 5 x 12" **6,250.00**

Louis XV, Gilbert, mid 18th C, balloon form case, foliage ornaments and wave work, surmounted by sunburst within clouds and seated figural cupid with quiver of arrows, circular enamel dial with Roman hours and Arabic minutes, bezel ring, marked on dial and plate "Gilbert a Paris," stamped with crowned C mark, 19½" **11,000.00**

Louis XVI, Lepaute, third quarter 18th C, figural, urn resting on fluted truncated column, draped with laurel and floral swags, surmounted by pine cone, twin annular rings at mid point, coiled serpent pointer, sgd on base "Lepaute," 19" h **28,000.00**

Iron

F. Kroeber Clock Co., Gothic, 12", 8 day, MOP inlay **190.00**

Pomeroy, N., Bristol, CT, c1865, cast iron case, MOP inlay, gold dec, 30 hour level movement inscribed by maker, painted zinc dial, nickel-plated balance wheel visible through opening in dial, orig pendulum, 10¼" **250.00**

Unknown Maker, CT or NY, c1860, iron front case, Gothic dec, MOP inlay, painted dec, paper on zinc dial and 30 hour time movement, old pendulum, back marked "T. Kennedy, Patent applied for 1856," lacks key, hour hand replaced, 12¼" **100.00**

Nickel, F. Kroeber Clock Co., NY, 1880, 6½", strike, carriage type, gilt front, glass sides **275.00**

Ormolu, Louis XV style, mantel, fully sculpted Bacchanalian scene, 21½" **1,500.00**

Pot Metal

Ansonia, 10" h, 30 hour movement, 3" gilt dec dial, beveled glass, Art Nouveau pedestal case, emb scrolled openwork, gold stippled finish **150.00**

N. Shure Co., c1934, 6¼", 30 hour movement, figural knight, silvered finish **75.00**

Mirror Side

Ansonia, Windsor, 21½", 8 day, strike, silvered cupids, bronze ornaments **375.00**

Gilbert, Wm. L., 8 day, walnut, cherubs **400.00**

Ogee

Ansonia, 26", 1 day, strike, alarm, veneered case, putti with garland in cameo reverse, orig weights **225.00**

Birge, John, Bristol, CT, 1840, 23¼", 8 day fusee powered time and strike, highly figured rosewood veneered case, ¾ size, door with mirror, orig dial and paper label, minor

veneer damage, damage to 1 fusee cone, minute hand missing **375.00**

Brewster, E. C., Bristol, CT, 28", 8 day time and strike driven movement with cast iron back plate, patented by Charles Kirk (Bristol), mahogany veneered case, door with orig glass and mirror, orig dial and paper label, one veneer chip **300.00**

Hill, Goodrich & Co., Plainville, CT, c1850, 31", 8 day brass time and strike movement with a cast iron back plate cased in a brass shell, veneered with choice mahogany, glazed door with painted tablet opening to gilted carved crest and columns, gilted columns with mirrors behind, orig dial and paper label, tablet repainted, mirror behind right column partially gone, minor veneer damage **700.00**

Johnson, Wm. S., New York, NY, c1845, 26 x 15¾ x 4½", mahogany veneer, painted flower basket on green ground **350.00**

New Haven, Weight No. 2, 26", 1 day, strike, zebra wood case **200.00**

Thomas, Seth, Plymouth Hollow, CT, 1865, mahogany and rosewood veneered case, black and gold eglomise panel with Masonic emblem, painted zinc dial, fine paper label, 30 hour time, strike, and alarm movement inscribed by maker, old pendulum, new key, minute hand replaced, 16½" **150.00**

Pillar and Scroll

Dohenes, Ephraim, Bristol, CT, c1830, 31 x 17½", Federal, carved mahogany, shaped crest, 3 brass urn finials above a hinged glazed door, eglomise panel with houses and pond, tapering columns, bracket feet **750.00**

North, Norris, Wolcottville, CT, 30⅜", swan's neck, 3 brass urn finials, painted dial with foliate spandrels, cottage in wood scene glass (repainted) **1,350.00**

Terry, Eli, Plymouth, CT, 1830, mahogany case, delicate scrolled crest and feet, 30 hour time and strike wood movement, painted wood dial, maker's label, fine orig eglomise tablet, three brass finials, old pendulum, key, and weights, replaced scroll crest, some restoration to eglomise, 31¼" **1,400.00**

Terry, Eli and Samuel, CT, 1830, mahogany case, delicate scrolled crest and feet, 30 hour time and strike wood movement, painted wood dial, maker's label, eglomise tablet, three brass finials, old pendulum and weights, 31½" **1,000.00**

Thomas, Seth, Plymouth, CT, c1820, 28½", 30 hour wood time and strike movement, painted wood dial, glass tablet of mansion with gilt foliate surround, oculus in painting center, orig finials and label, minor restoration to lower glass, replaced upper glass **2,500.00**

Porcelain or China Case

Ansonia Royal Bonn, 1901, La Bretagne, 15" h, 12½" w, 8 day, half hour gong strike, 5" dial, rococo sash, beveled glass, porcelain visible escapement, Roman numerals, dec in green and pastel floral motif **500.00**

German, cartouche form, four figural putti depicting seasons, surrounded by flowers, cartouche form base, 23" **700.00**

New Haven, 1900, 8¼", 1 day lever time, easel back, beveled glass, 2" dial, gilt and silver scrolls, hp florals **150.00**

Waterbury, 5¾", 1 day lever time, beveled glass, 2" dial, cobalt blue ground, hp florals, gilt scrolls **100.00**

Skeleton

English

11½", mid-19th C, brass, ornate scrolling frame, Arabic numerals **350.00**

18", brass, marble base, glass dome **650.00**

French, c1840, 23", weight driven, frame stamped "Augt. Moineau Roland Degrege" **3,500.00**

Shelf

Atkins Clock Co, Bristol, CT, 1860, figured rosewood veneers, regilded columns, two fine black and gold eglomise panels, paper label, 8 day time and strike movement, replaced painted dial, old pendulum bob, lacks key, 16½" **400.00**

Brown, J. C., Bristol, CT, 1860, 20", 8 day time and strike movement, rippled front, etched glass tablet opening to orig dial and paper label, finials missing **1,700.00**

Burr & Chittenden, Lexington, MA, 1835, "Groaner," mahogany veneered case, applied split columns, mirror tablet, painted wood dial paper label, 30 hour time and strike wood movement, old pendulum,, weights, and key, replaced crest and mirror, 35½" **350.00**

Hubbard, Daniel, Medfield, MA, c1820, 32¼", Federal, stenciled and eglomise bride's clock, foliate stenciled finial support surmounted by gilt acorn finial above a foliate and grape dec panel centering the inscription "Daniel Hubbard Medfld," opening to a dished white painted dial, a hinged door below with eglomise panel depicting a young girl presenting a bouquet to the married couple seated in horse drawn carriage, a foliate stenciled base below, gilt metal paw feet, pendulum and weight included, sections of case now painted black over the orig white paint **20,000.00**

Ingraham, E., and Co, Bristol, CT, 1870, "Grecian Model," rosewood veneered case, laminated and turned bezel and rosettes, painted zinc dial, 8 day time and strike movement inscribed by maker, door opens to paper label "Ernest Myer, Frederick, MD," green paper maker's label, old pendulum and key, 14½" **275.00**

Ives, C. & L. C., Bristol, CT, 1835, carved mahogany case, floral eglomise table, painted wood dial, paper label, large 8 day time and strike strap movement with roller pinions, orig iron weights and old pendulum, replaced carved crest, lacks key, 38½" **450.00**

Munger, Asa, Auburn, NY, 18309, mahogany case, three painted tablets, painted dial inscribed by maker with seconds indicator, 8 day time and strike movement, Flying Eagle pendulum, old key, lacks weights, second hand replaced, dial and movement not orig to case, 38" .. **400.00**

New Haven Clock Co., 1855, miniature sleigh front, 20½" h, 13¾" w, 8 day time and strike movement marked "New Haven Clock Co., Conn. U.S.A.," mahogany veneered case, half round columns, molded cornice, 2 doors, lower door with orig frosted glass opening to label of E. O. Goodwin (clock dealer, 1855), upper door with 2 orig painted tablets opening to painted dial, old finish, minor veneer chips, label rough, gong replaced **700.00**

Spencer, Hotchkiss & Co., Salem Bridge, CT, c1830, 28" high, 18" wide, 8 day time only "Salem Bridge" movement, mahogany veneer, turned feet, stenciled half round columns, molded cornice, door opens to fine dial with gold leaf and seconds bitt and a label, crest molding and two front feet are old replacement, some veneer loss, stenciled columns chipped . . **950.00**

Terry, Silas B., Plymouth, CT, c1830, 28½", time and alarm brass weight driven 8 day movement retaining both orig weights, mahogany case, carved eagle pediment, paw feet, glazed door flanked by half round mahogany columns, fine primitive painted tablet, orig wood dial and paper label, some flaking in tablet **3,500.00**

Terry, Silas B., Terryville, CT, c1840, 24", 30 hour weight driven brass time and strike movement, orig weights and pendulum bob, mahogany veneered, molded mahogany door, painted tablet of castle in forest scene, heart-shaped pendulum opening, orig paper dial backed with wood, very minor touch-up on glass and minor veneer chips **1,400.00**

Welch Manufacturing Co., E. N., Forestville, CT, c1870, 18½", 8 day time and strike movement, "patti," rosewood case with numerous dec of turned wood, orig glass, dial, and colored glass pendulum, orig paper label in back, minute hand broken in middle, small piece of wood chipped from back of left rear foot **900.00**

Steeple

Birge & Fuller, Bristol, CT, double steeple, 24¼", 30 hour brass time and strike movement, Joseph Ives patent spring lever, rosewood veneered case, 4 button feet, 4 steeple and 2 doors, upper door with painted tablet opening to orig dial, lower door with perfect orig tablet opening to patent spring lever, center tablet repainted on old glass, minor veneer damage, 1 fusee chain replaced, 1 button foot replaced **2,250.00**

Boardman, Chauncey, Bristol, CT, 1847, 20", triple fusee 30 hour time, strike, and alarm movement stamped "C. Boardman, Bristol, Conn, U.S.A., Patented 1847," mahogany veneered case, tablet depicting "Independence Hall," orig dial, paper label, minor flaking to glass and dial **400.00**

Brewster & Ingraham, Bristol, CT, 1845, round Gothic, mahogany veneered case, turned columns and finials, etched tablet, painted zinc dial inscribed by maker, fine paper label, 8 day time and strike movement, repeating strike mechanism

with rack and snail, old pendulum, door and winding keys, replaced minute hand, 19¾" **1,250.00**

Gilbert, Wm. L., 19¾", 8 day movement, mahogany veneer, painted glass with sailing ship and dial restored **250.00**

Jerome, Chauncey, New Haven, CT, 1845, 22¾", large steeple with rosewood veneered case, door with orig tablet of floral wreath, orig dial, paper label, cast iron spring barrels in the bottom of the case transferring power to the movement by cords, some veneer loss and replacement, minor wear on tablet **600.00**

Manross, Elisha, Bristol, CT, 1850, 19¾", 30 hour time and strike movement, mahogany veneered case, door with orig tablet depicting "Market Place, Quebec," orig dial and paper label, movement retains orig brass springs, minor veneer loss, orig tablet cracked **150.00**

Terry & Andrews, Bristol, CT, 1850

Double steeple, mahogany veneered case, two orig eglomise tablets, 8 day time, strike, and alarm lyre movement inscribed by maker, excellent paper label with large eagle, painted zinc dial, old pendulum and key, case refinished, alarm mechanism replaced, 25½" **1,700.00**

Gothic, sharp, rosewood and mahogany veneered case, turned columns and finials, eglomise tablet, painted zinc dial, fine paper label with eagle, 8 day time and strike movement inscribed by maker, orig brass movement springs, old pendulum, replaced tablet, refinished case, 19½" . . **750.00**

Waterbury Clock Co, Waterbury, CT, 1875, mahogany veneered case, floral transfer glass, painted zinc dial, paper label, 30 hour time and alarm movement, old pendulum, lacks key, glass tablet background repainted, minute hand replaced, 15" **250.00**

TALL CASE CLOCK

Aken, A. V., Dutch, 3rd quarter 18th C, 101", rococo burl walnut case, 12" arched brass dial matted within the steel chapter ring, subsidiary seconds dial and date aperture, regulations lever in the arch, 8 day with Dutch strike on two bells, caddy top hood with 2

Tall Case, Willard, Aaron, Hepplewhite, mahogany, French feet, string inlay fluted columns, rocking ship movement, sgd dial, orig paper label, $30,000.00.

finials of angels sounding trumpets flanking the figure of Atlas, the shaped arched hood with a molded cornice centered by carved cartouche cresting over a blind fret frieze, trunk with canted corners enclosed by a line inlaid paneled door, base with angled scrolled brackets continuing to supports **6,000.00**

Bramer, Paulus, Amsterdam, 18th C, choice walnut veneered slender case with inlays, engraved brass dial inscribed by maker, 8 day time and strike movement, hour and half hour strikes on different bells, old weights and pendulum, lacks key, replaced feet, door glass, 79" h **4,250.00**

Crosthwaite, John, Dublin, George III, last quarter 18th C, mahogany, shaped hood, broken pediment, waisted case, shaped and inlaid door, fluted quarter columns, sq base, bracket feet, circular silvered dial contained in sq brass plate, 19 x 9½ x 93" **3,600.00**

Du Chesne, Lourens, Amsterdam, mid 18th C, Baroque, walnut, hood surmounted by gilt figure of Atlas and two winged maidens, waisted case, paneled base, compressed ball feet, circular silvered chapter ring, arched brass dial with moon phase, subsidiary second hand, date, and day of the week apertures, 18 x 9¾ x 112½" .. **9,500.00**

Filber, John, York(town), PA, c1800, 98½", 30 hour, Chippendale, carved, cherrywood, white painted dial with bird and butterfly motif, date register, and inscription, bonnet with molded swan's neck pediment ending in carved rosettes, centering a turned finial, arched door with colonnettes, waisted case with arched door flanked by quarter columns, base with quarter columns and bracket feet .. **5,000.00**

Girand, Benois, Paris, Louis XV style, mounted kingwood, hood surmounted by gilt bronze figural Father Time, marquetry inlaid body with gilt bronze musical instruments, foliage scrolls, glazed cartouche with figural sunburst pendulum, plinth base, sgd white enamel face with Roman numerals, 28 x 15 x 106" **8,000.00**

Higoc, Irvin, Dutch, 1790, 99½", orig burl walnut case with molded and carved top, pierced fret, door with applied columns opening to brass dial with maker's name and moon phases, lower case with walnut veneers and line inlay, retains old weights and pendulum, movement and case married, pierced fret on hood replaced, minute hand missing, various minor case repairs **2,300.00**

Hill, Joakim, Flemington, NJ, c1815, 95", 8 day, Federal, inlaid mahogany, hood with molded swan's neck pediment ending in inlaid rosettes, 3 urn form finials, vine inlaid panel, arched glazed door, white painted dial fitted with minute and date registers, phases of moon, waisted case, flanked by fluted quarter columns, bracket feet **6,500.00**

Hopkins & Lewis, Litchfield, CT, 2nd quarter, 19th C, 92½", cherry, bonnet with freestanding columns and broken arch pediment, wooden face with yellowed varnish on a painted ground with delicate dec in black with red and gold, face has wear and is attached to bonnet, replaced brass works marked "Sessions Clock Company," chamfered edge waist with scrolled top door, paneled base, turned feet, some repairs to case, brass finials replaced **1,200.00**

Hutchins, Levi and Abel, Concord, NH, c1790, 83", Chippendale, maple case, broken arch hood with carved rosettes, 3 brass finials, 3 piece engraved brass dial inscribed by makers and featuring a calendar aperture, arched waist door, molded base on straight bracket feet, case refinished, feet reduced slightly, finials are period but not orig to case, minor repair to left hood molding **5,000.00**

Lamy, David, Hoorn, c1710, 95", 8 day brass movement with half hour strike and alarm mechanism, figured walnut veneered case, bell top with 3 carved finials and brass dec, sq glazed door opening to a brass dial with maker's name inscribed, lower case with long slender door with bull's-eye opening, molded and cross banded base with turned bun feet, old weights and pendulum, finials replaced, some brass dec missing on hood, replaced glass, some minor veneer damage **5,000.00**

McDowell, James, Duck Creek or Smyrna, DE, painted dial possibly by Beard and Weaver, Appoquinimonk, DE, c1785, 96½", Chippendale carved mahogany case, hood with molded and dentil-carved swan's neck crest ending in pierced terminals, centering orig carved and ribbed urn form finial above a pierced trellis panel, fret carved tympanum below, glazed door below opening to a white painted dial with phases of moon, minute and date registers, fluted colonnettes flanking, waisted case with scalloped paneled door flanked by fluted quarter columns, based with scalloped panel flanked by fluted quarter columns on ogee bracket feet, two weights, pendulum, key, and crank included **66,000.00**

Nutting, Wallace, case copied from John Goddard case, movement c1800 (name illegible), 8 day brass time and strike movement with moon phases, Chippendale, mahogany, 2 block and shells, broken arch hood with 3 flame finials, carved rosettes, fluted hood column, fluted quarter column, blocks and shells on waist, door, and base panel **7,250.00**

Owen & Sile, Chester, PA, c1790–1810, 97½", 8 day, Chippendale, carved mahogany, white painted dial, sgd "Owen & Sile Chester," painted moon face, bonnet with scrolled pediment with dentil molding and rosettes, centering an urn and leaf finial above trailing leafage, glazed arch door, and fluted colonnettes, waisted case with leaf carved molding over a shaped door flanked by fluted quarter columns, base with shield panel, ogee bracket feet, works may not be orig to case **17,500.00**

Schouten, Pieter, Amsterdam, 1710, 78", 8 day time and strike movement retaining old weights and pendulum,

walnut and walnut veneer case, molded top, finials, pierced fret, glazed door with twisted rope columns applied, brass dial with maker's name inscribed and moon dial aperture, lower case with rect door with bull's-eye opening, molded cross banded base, 2 moldings on waist door replaced, pierced fret on hood replaced, door glass replaced, dial bent, movement has replaced crutch wire and some poorly done repairs, bottom base molding is old replacement **4,000.00**

Seip, David, Bucks County, PA, 19th C, 19 x 12 x 96", Chippendale style, birch, arched hood with swan's neck and dentilated cornice, waisted case, fluted corner columns, French bracket feet, enamel dial with second hand, lunette dial **13,500.00**

Taber, S., New England, early 19th C, 20 x 12 x 83", Country Federal, grain painted, arched glazed door flanked by freestanding columns, flat top hood, waisted case with thumb molded door, molded base, short bracket feet, painted dial **1,600.00**

Tiffany & Company, New York, NY, c1900, 105", carved oak case in Renaissance style, glazed door enclosing a brass and silvered dial, quarter striking Westminster chimes **7,750.00**

Unknown Maker

American, Chippendale, PA, walnut, hood with molded swan's neck pediment, pinwheel rosettes, three brass ball turned and spire finials on fluted plinths, frieze of floral fretwork over arched glazed door, tapering columns, brass dial with seconds and calendar dial, waisted case, shaped cupboard door flanked by quarter columns, cove molding, base with applied purple panel, quarter columns, ogee bracket feet, dial sgd "C. Warner," 21 x 11 x 91" **4,500.00**

American, Federal style, 19th C 21 x 12 x 96", attributed by Berks County, PA, first half 19th C, painted maroon with gold details, hood with molded swan's neck pediment, ring turned rosettes, three fluted urn turned finials with fluted plinths, arched glazed door, baluster turned columns, white painted dial with calendar dial, waisted case, cock beaded arched cupboard door, chamfered corners, box base, bracket feet **2,675.00**

21 x 11 x 106", mahogany, arched glazed door flanked by stop fluted colonnettes surmounted by swan's neck pediment and banded bordered finials, waisted case, oval inlaid door, stop fluted quarter columns, conforming case with bracket feet, enamel dial with date indicator, lunette dial **6,750.00**

French, Empire, mahogany, dentil molding over circular glazed door, ormolu mounted lyre, foliate, and scroll dec, white enamel Roman numeral dial, plinth base, 81" h .. **4,500.00**

William and Mary, late 17th, early 18th C, dwarf, walnut, putto head spandrels, hooded case with spirally turned columnar supports, molded cornice, waisted case with marquetry inlay, molded base, brass dial with Roman hours, Arabic numerals, 12 x 8 x 67" **18,000.00**

Wady, James, Newport, RI, c1765, 90½", Queen Anne carved mahogany case, molded hood with shaped crest and two ball finials above a glazed door opening to an engraved brass dial, inscribed with the maker's name and NEWPORT above minute and date registers, waisted case with hinged door above a molded base, minor restoration to crest, pendulum and bob, door key, two weights, and crank included **9,000.00**

Wilder, Joshua, Hingham, MA, c1810, 45½" (dwarf size), 8 day brass weight driven time only movement, pine case with old finish, straight bracket feet, rect door, arched glazed door, pediment on top later addition, dial is a new replacement, movement is a banjo movement converted to fit case, new hands **3,500.00**

WALL

Art Deco, Albert Binquet, c1928, silvered bronze, circular chapter ring cast with Roman numerals centering profusion of blossoms, supported by pair of doves, center bowed ribbon, inscribed "A. Binquet Sculpteur 1928," 15" l **1,100.00**

Banjo

Brewster & Ingraham, Bristol, CT, 1860, mahogany and rosewood case, two black and gold eglomise tablets, painted zinc dial, 8 day time movement, maker's label, lacks key, minor replacements, c1880 movement, 31¼" **200.00**

Banjo, 34" l, mahogany, repainted dial, 8 day, dial marked "John Sawin, Boston," $1,500.00.

Cummens, William, Boston, MA, c1810, 34" (with finial), 8 day T-bridge movement, cross banded mahogany frames, painted tablets, sea creatures pulling shell boat with driver, old finish, orig brass finial **2,000.00**

Howard, E., & Co., Boston, MA, 1940, 40½" h, #95 Presentation Model, solid mahogany case, lower glass tablet of Mount Vernon, glasses sgd by D. J. Steele, 8 day time movement, nickel plated plates, maintaining power, and stop works, painted zinc dial, cast brass eagle finial, lead weight **2,150.00**

Munro, Concord, MA, c1820, 35", mahogany giltwood case, ball & eagle finial, foliate eglomise throat, brass fillets, eglomise panel depicting bucolic scene on hinged lower door **1,750.00**

New Haven Clock Company, New Haven, CT, 1930, miniature, 17½" h, mahogany case, 2 dec tablets with lower depicting Mount Vernon, silvered dial, 12 day lever movement, eagle finial **175.00**

Sessions, Wellfleet, 22½", 8 day, lever, 5" metal dial, green lacquer finished case, eagle finial, brass fillets, Mediterranean scene painted panel **200.00**

Terry, Eli, and Sons, Plymouth, CT, 1830, sq case, mahogany veneer, two fine eglomise tablets, painted wood dial, 30 hour time and strike wood movement, iron weights, old pendulum, lacks key, possibly Henry Terry, 34¾" **700.00**

Waltham, No. 1540, 40½", eagle finial, walnut case, foliate waist, brass fillets, rural village scene . . **1,350.00**

Willard, Aaron, Boston, MA, c1825, 41 x 10½", 8 day, weight driven movement, Federal, mahogany case, eglomise throat, white painted dial, giltwood acorn finial . **3,500.00**

Willard, Simon, Boston, MA, c1810, 34", 8 day, mahogany, cross banded, brass ball and eagle finial, eglomise throat panel depicting acanthus leaves, gold and white brass fillets flanking lower section with eglomise panel on hinged door, inscribed "S. Willard's Patent" **7,500.00**

Calendar

Ansonia, 10" Drop Octagon, 24", 8 day, strike, rosewood veneer with gilt molding **300.00**

Gilbert, Wm. L., Standard Admiral, 26½", 8 day, strike, octagonal, short drop **400.00**

Ithaca, No. 2 Bank, 61", 8 day, oak case **2,750.00**

Jerome & Co., Register, 33¾", 8 day **1,500.00**

New Haven, Ionic Figure, 29½", double dial, 8 day **1,350.00**

Prentiss, Empire, 60 day, 2 springs, walnut case **2,000.00**

Welch, E. N., St. Clair, 12" dial, oak case, short drop **400.00**

Cuckoo

American Clock Co., Philadelphia, PA, c1930, 17 x 14 x 7½", carved wood case, carved spread eagle at top, 8 day brass movement, cuckoo painted red, blue, and black **175.00**

German, Black Forest, c1881, 24", 1 day, quarter hour strike, carved ivy dec **400.00**

Keebler Clock Co., Philadelphia, PA, 1920, 5 x 4 x 1¾", pressed log design, leaves, flowers, nest of birds, brass spring pendulum **90.00**

Lux, 1942, 16" h, 10" w, hunting scene, synthetic carved wood deer head with glass eyes, spread antlers, 2 rifles, quail, and rabbit, half hour strike, 4" dial, white raised Roman numerals, 75" chain **250.00**

Gallery

Ansonia, Foyer No. 1, c1890, 39", 8 day, strike, 18" dial, oak case . . . **275.00**

Gilbert, Wm. L., Corridor, c1920, 24 x 15½", 8 day, varnished oak finish . **125.00**

Thomas, Seth, Engine Lever, c1888, 1 day, 6" dial, brass case **125.00**

Lyre

Unknown, MA, probably Boston, c1820, 43", 8 day time and strike movement with skeletonized plates striking on a belt inside the hood, orig lead weights, mahogany with full bodied carved and gilted eagle, ornate throat with figured mahogany panel, lower door frame of half round mahogany with a figured panel, glazed wood bezel opening to a mint orig dial, wood bezel and glass are old replacements, eagle has been painted over with gold paint **3,000.00**

Unknown, MA, c1825, 39" including finial, 8 day time movement, painted dial, mahogany case with carved throat, turned wood finials, brass bezel and reverse painted tablet of naval scene, inscribed "Willard's Patent," supported by molded bracket with finial, tablet not orig and cracked, both finials are replacements of orig, case refinished, minus key and weight . . **2,000.00**

Unknown, MA, 1825, 40½" including finial, painted iron dial 8 day brass movement, time only, true lyre clock without lower door, carved throat with 2 mahogany panels and carved finial, molded base with a bracket, orig weight, refinished . . **4,250.00**

Mirror

Collins, James, Goffstown, NH, 1835, 37" h, Empire-style Gothic case, veneered with choice mahogany veneers and a door with an orig pleated cloth math behind the door glass, 8 day time and strike movement, iron weights, painted zinc dial inscribed "James Collins, Goffstown," case refinished **4,500.00**

Jones, Abner, East Bloomfield, NY, 1833, 40" high, 20½" wide, 8 day time and strike movement, inner dial attached to movement and outer half is attached to rear of door, stenciled half columns applied to door, brass hands and large tin can weights, dials possibly very early repaint **2,500.00**

Miscellaneous

Dutch Hood Clock, Holland, c1825, 52" h, solid oak case, turned finials, applied brass mount revealing the motion of the pendulum, painted iron moon and calendar apertures, face with nautical scene, 30 hour time, strike, and alarm movement, turned pillars, brass weight, dial repainted, number of replaced parts **1,100.00**

Morbier, French, c1850, 60" h, pressed brass, lyre pendulum, porcelain dial, 30 hour time and strike

movement with calendar, upright
strike rack, retains period weights,
side door missing **550.00**
Swinger, Ansonia, Automatic Swing
No. 2, 8″, 1 day, male child swings
from tree **600.00**

Regulator

Ansonia

Office, 61″, 8 day, weight time, mahogany case, 18″ dial **1,800.00**
Parlor, 36″, 8 day hour and half
hour, gong, strike, walnut case,
8″ silvered dial, Roman numerals **450.00**
Gustav Becker, Vienna, 42″, walnut,
2 orig weights **800.00**
ECO Magneta Clock Co., Boston,
1895, Office, 70″ h, 23″ w, 8 day,
60 beats per minute, 14″ d dial .. **1,000.00**
German, c1908, 32″, 14 day, spring,
half hour strike, cathedral gong, 5″
dial, walnut case, elaborate carvings **275.00**
Gilbert, Wm. L., Railway, 105″ h, 33″
w, walnut, glass sides, brass
weight, gridiron pendulum, sweep
second hand, dead beat escape-
ment, 12″ porcelain dial **5,000.00**
Ingraham, c1905, 38½″, 8 day, strike,
calendar, 12″ d dial **500.00**
New Haven, c1880, 31″, 8 day time,
oak Figure 8 case, 12″ dial **325.00**
Sessions, c1929, 35½″, 8 day time,
oak case, 12″ dial **300.00**
Thomas, Seth, c1890, Regulator No.
18, 54″, mahogany and oak veneer,
8 day, weight, time, Graham dead
beat escapement, polished plates,
iron bracket, 14″ dial **1,850.00**

Waterbury

Figure 8, 22″, 8 day, half hour
strike, calendar, rosewood veneer case, 10″ dial **400.00**
Regulator No. 11, c1896, 52″, 8 day
time, cherry case, glass sides,
silver dial, 10″ brass weights .. **1,200.00**

School House

Ansonia, 24″, 8 day, strike, octagon
case, 12″ drop **325.00**
Atkins, Whiting & Co., Bristol, CT,
c1850–54, 25″ h, 17″ w, 30 day time
and strike movement powered by a
lever, rosewood veneered case,
hexagonal shaped top, rippled
molding around edge, lower door
has orig tablet and opens to expose
label from Atkins, Whiting & Co.,
minor touch up on dial, minute
hand replaced **2,000.00**
Gilbert, Wm. L., Janiero, 8 day, calendar, Figure 8 rosewood veneer
case **450.00**

Imperial, Regulator No. 4T120E,
34½″, oak case, electric **425.00**
Ingraham Co., Bristol, CT, 21¼″, 8
day time only movement, Figure 8,
orig company label, restored **475.00**
Jerome, c1850, 8 day, 12″ dial, octagon, mahogany and rosewood
case **300.00**
New Haven, 27″, 8 day time, 12″ dial,
oak case, scroll trim **225.00**
Russell & Jones, c1889, 26″, 8 day,
spring, 12″ dial, gilt glass, walnut
and oak case **350.00**

Waterbury

21″, 8 day, half hour strike, 10″ dial,
veneered zebra wood case ... **300.00**
27¾″, English Drop No. 2, 8 day,
time, calendar, veneered oak
case **450.00**
Welch, E. N., c1870, 24″, 8 day,
time, spring, 12″ dial, octagon,
veneered case **350.00**

Wag on Wall

Astragal, English, 19th C, painted
wood, painted stag above black
painted clock face, gilt corner dec,
white ground, 12″ h **200.00**
Dutch, 28″, 18th C, 30 hour time and
strike pull up movement, painted
and scroll front, pierced crest of
lions and flower vase, standing
lions flank face, angel dec at top
corners of face, retains old weights,
pendulum, and wall bracket, some
touch-up on paint, some repair and
damage to scroll **800.00**

CLOISONNÉ

History: Cloisonné is the art of enameling on
metal. The design is drawn on the metal body;
wires, which follow the design, then are glued or
soldered on the body. The cells thus created are
packed with enamel and fired; this step is repeated
several times until the level of enamel is higher
than the wires. A buffing and polishing process
brings the level of enamels flush to the surface of
the wires.

This art form has been practiced in various
countries since 1300 B.C. and in the Orient since
the early 15th century. Most cloisonne found today
is from the late Victorian era, 1870–1900, and was
made in China and Japan.

Bowl

5″, dragon, 1880 .... **75.00**
8″ d, 2½″ h, yellow dragons, flaming
pearl around rim and int., black
ground, brass stand **130.00**
14 x 4¼″, geometric design **150.00**

Vase, 5″ h, black ground, metallic base, pastel flowers, Japanese, $125.00.

Box, 4¾″ l, bird and flower design, red ground, marked "Made in China"	**85.00**
Brush Pot, 5″ h, butterfly and asters dec, light blue ground, sgd "Takeuchi," Japanese, c1875	**195.00**
Charger, 12″ d, pink and rose florals, green leaves, two gray flying birds and one sitting on branch, scalloped edge, turquoise blue ground	**400.00**
Dish, 9″, oval, blue lotus, 1880	**90.00**

Figure

Dignitary, 11½″, polychrome roundels and bats, ivory head and hands, coral ground robe	**150.00**
Horse, 9″, Tang style, c1880	**275.00**
Ginger Jar, 6¾″, yellow scaly dragon, dark blue ground, ornate carved wood base, marked "China"	**275.00**
Humidor, cov, 8″ h, 5¾″ d, colorful flowers, double "T" fret cloisonnés, light blue border, brick red ground, brass Foo dog finial, ornate teakwood base	**225.00**

Incense Burner

Lion, 10″, 1800	**400.00**
Multicolored floral dec, brass lid with cut-out butterflies, cobalt blue ground and 3 feet	**225.00**
Jar, cov, 4⅛″ d, 4½″ h, white, blue, green, and rust with flowers and butterflies panels around top, black, gold, blue, and flowers below	**290.00**
Jardiniere, 10″, multicolored dragon and floral motif, black ground, teakwood base, Chinese	**150.00**
Mirror, 17¾″, incised birds on flowering branch mirror, pedestal, floral scrolls, blue ground	**425.00**
Perfume, 2″, oval, red, gold, blue, and white florals, hanging loops	**75.00**

Plate

5″ d, multicolored, phoenix bird in tree	**140.00**
7¼″ d, mallard duck, blue ground, Chinese	**100.00**
Salt and Pepper Shakers, 2″ d, 2½″ h, pale blue fishscale ground, one with multicolored dragon, other with cranes, Japanese, pr	**225.00**
Sauceboat, turquoise artichoke dec, green handle, marked "China"	**110.00**
Teapot, cov, 3½″ h, double gourd shape, diagonal flower and butterflies bands, white and green interspersed with black and goldstone, Japanese	**245.00**
Tumbler, 3¾″ h, beaker shape, flared, iron red serpentine dragon, sky blue ground	**110.00**

Vase

2½ x 6″, celadon, transparent flower sprays and bird	**400.00**
3½″ d, 1¾″ d, multicolored peacock, silver wire flowers at bottom, white foil ground, Japanese	**650.00**
6″, multicolored floral design, yellow ground, multicolored floral design and medallion with dark blue ground	**250.00**
9¾″ h, 3¾″ d, exotic dragons on shield shaped panels, green with goldstone, butterflies around top, blue ground, Japanese	**395.00**
10″, pottery, 2 blue, turquoise, rust, and black panels, butterfly rim	**300.00**
31½″ h, compressed ovoid, birds in flight, blossoming peony cluster, and chrysanthemum scene, elaborate floral meanders shoulder framing bird and flower reserves, lotus and foliate tendril ground, pr	**1,650.00**

CLOTHING

History: While museums and a few private individuals have collected clothing for decades, it is only recently that collecting clothing has achieved a widespread popularity. Clothing reflects the social attitudes of an historical period.

Christening and wedding gowns abound and, hence are not in large demand. Among the hardest items to find are men's clothing from the 19th and early 20th centuries. The most sought after clothing is by designers, such as Fortuny, Poirret, and Vionnet.

Note: Condition, size, age, and completeness are critical factors in purchasing clothing. Collectors divide into two groups: those collecting for aesthetic and historic value and those desiring to wear the garment. Prices are higher on the west coast; major auction houses focus on designer clothes and high fashion items.

References: Maryanne Dolan, *Vintage Clothing 1880–1960*, Second Edition, Books Americana, 1987; Tina Irick-Nauer, *The First Price Guide to*

Antique and Vintage Clothes, E.P. Dutton, 1983; Sheila Malouff, *Clothing With Prices*, Wallace-Homestead, 1983; Terry McCormich, *The Consumer's Guide To Vintage Clothing*, Dembner Books, 1987.

Periodical: *Vintage Clothing Newsletter*, P.O. Box 1422, Corvallis, OR 97339.

Collectors' Club: The Costume Society of America, P.O. Box 761, Englishtown, NJ 07726.

Museums: Los Angeles County Museum (Costume and Textile Dept.), Los Angeles, CA; Metropolitan Museum of Art, New York, NY; Museum of Costume, Bath, England; Philadelphia Museum of Art, Philadelphia, PA; Smithsonian Institution (Inaugural Gown Collection), Washington, D.C.

Additional Listings: See *Warman's Americana & Collectibles* for more examples.

Bed Jacket, rayon, peach, quilted, c1940	15.00
Blouse	
Rayon, long sleeve, red and yellow	5.00
Silk chiffon, beaded front, c1915	25.00
Caftan, batiste	25.00
Camisole, cotton, white, 1 pc, lace, Victorian	60.00
Chemise, satin, pink, mauve colored lace	25.00
Christening Outfit, gown, slip, and cap, cotton, white, c1920	75.00

Bathing Suit, man's, black wool, $20.00.

Coat	
Evening, silk velvet, black	45.00
Fur	
Monkey, full length, large, 1930–40	900.00
Persian lamb, black, matching hat, medium, orig Petra Furriers - Waterloo, Iowa label	65.00
Duster	
Lawn, white, watteau back, lace trim, handmade, c1880	50.00

Linen	35.00
Dress	
Child's, net, white, cotton lace, embroidery on bodice and hem	15.00
Day	
Chiffon, print, medium	30.00
Linen, white, satin stitched embroidery, ¾ sleeves, Edwardian style	60.00
Silk, black, flapper, drop waist, belt, MOP buckle, ecru neck inset, c1920	24.00
Silk Faille, black, mourning, size 14, 1890	50.00
Evening	
Beaded, French, black dec on black net overdress, 1915	130.00
Lace, mauve overdress, mauve satin underskirt, V neck, keyhole back, sleeveless matching jacket trimmed in burgundy velvet	45.00
Net, 2 pc, black, satin appliques, c1890	98.00
Satin, apricot, rhinestone straps, 1930	85.00
Sequin studded, irid, gold embroidered net panel, short sleeves, sq neckline, c1915	125.00
Tea	
Batiste, white, long, lace and tucks	110.00
Lace, black matching jacket, c1920	25.00
Jacket, brocade, Chinese	35.00
Nightgown	
Cotton, white, crocheted bodice	25.00
Satin, pink, lace trim, medium	25.00
Silk, pink, Saks 5th Avenue label, large	20.00
Nightshirt, man's, cotton, white, long	25.00
Pajamas	
Satin, peach, medium	30.00
Silk, pink, ribbon rosettes, crochet trim, c1920	100.00
Taffeta, long jacket, web motif, harem pants, c1940	25.00
Pedal Pushers, poplin, side laces, unworn, c1950	25.00
Petticoat	
Cotton, brown, hand quilted	125.00
Flannel, small	15.00
Sateen, black	36.00
Viole, white, tucks, wide crocheted ruffle, Victorian	35.00
Riding Habit, lady's, wool, black, side saddle type, 2 pcs	125.00
Robe	
Cotton	
Breakfast, green print, medium, 1893	40.00
Man's, plaid, c1920	35.00
Satin, lime green, flocking, maribou trim on ¾ length sleeves	35.00
Velvet, green, sq cut, gilt printed, Bel-	

lini stylized foliate motif, Fortuny label **2,150.00**
Sacque, cotton, embroidered, Victorian **45.00**
Shirt, man's, homespun, c1890 ..... **40.00**
Shorts, man's, Prince Albert, 2 pr, MIB **18.00**
Skirt
   Felt, circular, brown, appliqued poodle, flowers, and beads, c1950 .. **10.00**
   Muslin, white, full length, deep tucks, ruffled flounce, hand embroidered **40.00**
Slacks, gabardine, brown, c1930 .... **18.00**
Slip
   Cotton, white, rows of tucks and lace inserts, crocheted top and flowers **25.00**
   Wool, homespun, baby size **10.00**
Suit, boy's, velvet pants, double breasted silk shirt, 1907 .... **40.00**
Swimsuit
   Spandex, shiny, back buttons, flared skirt, c1930 .... **45.00**
   Wool, green and wine, orig Bradley Wool Knitwear label, c1920 ..... **28.00**
Teddy
   Batiste, c1920 .... **10.00**
   Crepe, peach **20.00**
   Silk, peach, hairpin lace yoke **35.00**
Wedding Gown, satin, wax flowers, beaded hat, Victorian **175.00**

CLOTHING ACCESSORIES

References: Rod Dyer & Ron Spark, *Fit To Be Tied: Vintage Ties Of The Forties And Early Fifties,* Abbeville, 1987; Evelyn Haetig, *Antique Combs & Purses,* Gallery Graphics Press, 1983; Richard and Teresa Holiner, *Antique Purses,* Second Edition, Collector Books, 1987.

Additional Listings: See *Warman's Americana & Collectibles* for more examples.

Apron, cotton, hand sewn, patchwork design, ties **28.00**
Boa, 70″, ostrich feathers **50.00**

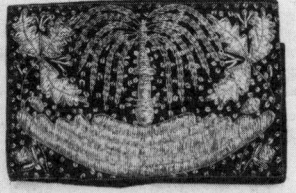

Handbag, Art Deco, 8 x 5½″ h, black velvet, silver embroidery, $45.00.

Bonnet
   Amish, deep blue, 10½″, c1880 .... **45.00**
   Cotton, sunbonnet **25.00**
Collar
   Beaded, pearls **12.50**
   Satin, peach, gold thread, pearl trim, c1920 .... **20.00**
Garters, child's, Lord Milford, orig card **5.00**
Gloves
   Kidskin, white, full length, buttons at wrist, c1950 .... **18.00**
   Leather, opera length **15.00**
   Suede, cream, small **7.50**
Handbag
   Alligator, made in Cuba **50.00**
   Beaded
      Multicolored, carpet design, small beads **165.00**
      Multicolored, 14K gold frame, jeweled clasp, Black Starr & Frost . **375.00**
      White, silk, opal beads and sequins **15.00**
   Brocade, clutch, lucite rim, rhinestones **35.00**
   Evening, mesh, 18K gold, chevron pattern, central oval cut diamond, graduated old mine cut diamonds, cabochon sapphire thumbpiece, gold link strap, 15½ oz **5,000.00**
   Linen, clutch **5.00**
   Mesh
      Enameled, gold, black, and white, curved frame, cabochon sapphire thumbpiece, foxtail tassel, seed pearls, mesh strap, enamel slide **1,000.00**
      Gold, 9 x 5″, Whiting Davis, matching change purse and mirror, rhinestone trim **45.00**
      Sterling Silver, snap closure, chain handle **48.00**
Handkerchief, silk **2.50**
Hat
   Amish, felt, black **40.00**
   Boy's, military, early 1900s **12.00**
   Lady's
      Silk, orange, cloche style, orig tag, c1920 .... **25.00**
      Straw, black, wide brim, cream and pink flowers **30.00**
      Velvet, black, wide brim, large feather, ribbon, c1914 .... **35.00**
   Man's, derby, black **35.00**
Muff, fur
   Mink, hanging tails, c1940 .... **115.00**
   Seal, child's **20.00**
Parasol, bamboo handle, ivory silk shade, woven with pink, lavender, and green flowers, leaves, and scrolls, ivory patterned silk gauze ruffles, SS tip, marked "Tiffany & Co," orig box, c1905 .... **350.00**
Scarf, India, fringe, 48″, reversible ... **25.00**

Shawl
  Kashmir, Indian red, blue, ecru,
    fringed, c1880 . . . .   **50.00**
  Silk, Chinese, ivory, embroidered
    flowering vines, knotted silk fringe   **85.00**
Shoes, silk brocade, flapper, rhinestone
    buckles **50.00**
Socks, Amish, man's, wool, tan, blue
    geometric border **45.00**
Stockings, nylon, orig package **35.00**
Stole, mink fur **150.00**
Sweater, white rabbit fur trim, beading   **35.00**
Veil, ecru net and lace, full length, 1918   **100.00**

COALPORT

History: In the mid-1750s Ambrose Gallimore established a pottery at Caughley in the Severn Gorge, Shropshire, England. Several other potteries, e.g., Jackfield, developed in the area.

About 1795 John Rose and Edward Blakeway built a pottery at Coalport, a new town founded along the right-of-way of the Shropshire Canal. Other potteries located adjacent to the canal were those of Walter Bradley and Anstice, Horton, and Rose. In 1799 Rose and Blakeway bought the "Royal Salopian China Manufactory" at Caughley. In 1814 this operation was moved to Coalport.

A bankruptcy in 1803 led to refinancing and a new name, John Rose and Company. In 1814 Anstice, Horton, and Rose was acquired. The South Wales potteries at Swansea and Nantgarw were added. The expanded firm made fine quality, highly decorated ware. The plant enjoyed a renaissance in the 1888 to 1900 period.

World War I, decline in trade, and shift of the pottery industry away from the Severn Gorge brought hard times to Coalport. In 1926 the firm, now owned by Cauldon Potteries, moved from Coalport to Shelton. Later owners included Crescent Potteries, Brain & Co., Ltd., and finally, in 1967, Wedgwood.

Reference: Susan and Al Bagdade, *Warman's English & Continental Pottery & Porcelain, 1st Edition,* Warman Publishing Co., Inc., 1987.

Additional Listings: Indian Tree Pattern.

Dessert Service, partial, assembled,
  Rock and Tree pattern, twelve plates,
  two pudding plates, oval 12⅜" fruit
  stand, three lozenge shaped dishes,
  sq dish, Imari palette, gilt edges,
  c1805–10, 19 pcs **3,575.00**
Dinner Service, partial, thirty-four
  plates, sixteen soup plates, two ob-

Tureen, cov, handled, 9" d, 10½" h, Imari type dec, polychromed finial, c1805–10, $1,200.00.

long 14⅝" l cov soup tureens, and
  other serving pcs, underglaze cobalt
  blue ground, center reserve with multicolored floral medallion, gilt scrollwork, gilt feather edged shell shaped
  panels alternating with reserved vase
  shaped panels with floral sprigs, gilt
  lion's head handles and knobs,
  c1805–10, 64 pcs **4,125.00**
Inkstand, 6⁷⁄₁₆" l, crescent shape, yellow
  foliage scroll border, gilt edged orange band, gold diamond devices
  border, gilt foliage dec on top, four
  pen holes, three larger apertures, two
  inkpots, pounce pot, c1805 . . . .   **375.00**
Mug, election, cylindrical, gilt inscription
  "Clive and Robinson" over spray of
  wheat, and Clive motto "Audacter Et
  Sincere," reverse painted en grisaille,
  gold and iron red arms and griffin
  Clive crest, band inscribed "Clive and
  Liberty" with boughs of gold oak
  leaves, yellow acorns, gilt rims,
  crowned cross batons and D mark,
  pattern number, painter's mark,
  c1806, pr **400.00**
Plate, 10⅜", dinner, green ground, three
  cartouches with floral bouquets on
  rim, white center with large floral bouquet, gilt bellflowers border, imp potter's mark, minor damage, set of 12,
  c1825 . . . .   **1,100.00**
Platter, 10¾", Tobacco Leaf pattern,
  Chinese export style, underglaze
  blue, turquoise, chartreuse, rose,
  iron-red, yellow, green, salmon, puce,
  and gold, scalloped rim with underglaze blue band, four underglaze blue
  flowering branches on underside,
  c1805, pr **2,475.00**
Tea Service, partial, Japan pattern, oval
  prow shaped teapot, cov, and stand,
  cov sugar bowl, gilt dolphin's mask

and ring handles, milk jug, cake plate, nine teacups and saucers, underglaze blue, iron-red, and gold dec, gilt edges, gold pattern number marks, c1807, 23 pcs **1,000.00**

COCA-COLA ITEMS

History: The originator of Coca-Cola was John Pemberton, a pharmacist from Atlanta, Georgia. In 1886 Dr. Pemberton introduced a patent medicine to relieve headaches, stomach disorders, and other minor maladies. Unfortunately, his failing health and meager finances forced him to sell his interest.

In 1888 Asa G. Candler became the sole owner of Coca-Cola. Candler improved the formula, increased the advertising budget, and widened the distribution. Accidentally, a "patient" was given a dose of the syrup mixed with carbonated water instead of still water. The result was a tastier, more refreshing drink.

As sales increased in the 1890s, Candler recognized that the product was more suitable for the soft drink market and began advertising it as such. From these beginnings a myraid of advertising items have been issued to invite all to "Drink Coca-Cola."

Dates of interest: "Coke" was first used in advertising in 1941. The distinctive shaped bottle was registered as a trademark on April 12, 1960.

References: Deborah Goldstein Hill, *Wallace-Homestead Price Guide to Coca-Cola Collectibles,* Wallace Homestead, 1983; Shelly and Helen Goldstein, *Coca-Cola Collectibles* (four volumes, plus index), published by author, 1970s; Allan Petretti, *Petretti's Coca-Cola Collectibles Price Guide,* The Nostalgia Company, 1984; Al Wilson, *Collectors Guide To Coca-Cola Items, Volume I,* (revised: 1987) and *Volume II,* (1987), L-W Book Sales.

Collectors' Club: The Cola Clan, 2084 Continental Drive N.E., Atlanta, GA 30345.

Additional Listings: See *Warman's Americana & Collectibles* for more examples.

Paperweight, clear, red ground, white lettering, $45.00.

Bag, vinyl, red, "Drink Coca-Cola In Bottles" **10.00**
Bank, 3½ x 4 x 8¼", plastic, red, cola dispensing machine design, three paper Coke labels, box, C & G Toys, c1960 . . . . **50.00**
Blotter
Girl wearing bathing suit, 1942 . . . . **20.00**
Pictures two 1916 bottles, 1920s . . . **15.00**
Bookmark, paper, 5" **225.00**
Bottle, aqua, emb, Coco-Cola Bottling Works, Toledo, OH **25.00**
Bottle Carrier, six pack, cardboard, patent 1933 . . . . **50.00**
Bottle Opener, knife, bone handle, 1908 **100.00**
Calendar, 1910, girl wearing picture hat **4,100.00**
Clock
Neon, white, 18" d **1,000.00**
Regulator, printed dial, 32" h, Ingraham Co **650.00**
Crate, wood, "Drink Coca-Cola In Bottles" **30.00**
Door Push, porcelain, white letters, red ground **70.00**
Globe, milk glass, 12" d, 9" h **600.00**
Ice Pick, wood handle, 1930s **12.50**
Key Chain, brass disc, red enameled, emb bottle and design, 1955 . . . . . . **6.00**
Knife
Pocket type, bone handle, 1908 . . . **105.00**
Table, "Drink Coca-Cola," ivory handle **35.00**
Light, bottle shape, painted milk glass, orig tin cap, cast metal base **3,640.00**
Lighter, 50th Anniversary, red, white bull's eye, "Drink Coco-Cola" **80.00**
Menu Board, wood, 26 x 36", December 1923 bottle, color **285.00**
Mirror, early 1950s **55.00**
Money Clip, knife on each side, enameled coke cup on front with "Enjoy Coca-Cola" **50.00**
Notebook, 3½ x 6", cardboard cov, red, white lettering, 1943 calendar inside cov **25.00**
Paperweight, mirrored, celluloid and glass **475.00**
Pencil Box, 75th Anniversary **55.00**
Plate, 7¼" . . . . : **275.00**
Playing Cards, 1943 . . . . **40.00**
Pocket Clip, bottle shape, silver **15.00**
Pretzel Dish, aluminum, three coke bottles legs, 1936 . . . . **40.00**
Radio, Coca-Cola vending machine shape, battery operated, red, white, and black, c1970 . . . . **45.00**
Sign
15½ x 24", cardboard, emb Coca-Cola bottle, Clark Gable and Joan Crawford **45.00**
20 x 28", tin, litho, metal frame, "Ice Cold Coca-Cola Sold Here" **225.00**

20 x 36", cardboard, double sided, blond woman in swimsuit for summer, majorette for fall, 1952 ..... **85.00**

36" h, tin, 1932 bottle shape, marked "Pat'd Dec 25, 1923" **105.00**

String Holder, "Take Home Coca-Cola in Cartons," six-pack in center **325.00**

Thermometer, metal, cigar shape, "Drink Coca-Cola-Sign of Good Taste," red and white, 30" h **90.00**

Thimble, glass, red **25.00**

Tip Tray, 6" l, 1917, pretty girl wearing large hat, holding glass of Coca-Cola, cigarette stains, $65.00.

Tray
  1914, Betty, oval **195.00**
  1920, Garden Girl, oval, 13¾ x 16½" **400.00**
  1928, girl with bobbed hair, oblong, 10½ x 13¼" **150.00**
  1931, farm boy with dog, oblong, 10½ x 13¼", Norman Rockwell **350.00**
  1936, Hostess, oblong, 10½ x 13¼" **100.00**
  1957, Umbrella girl **180.00**
Tray, tip, tin, litho
  1905 .... **275.00**
  1909 .... **120.00**
Vest, wool, zipper, 1940s **60.00**
Watch Fob, 1¼ x 1½", metal, relief girl in large hat drinking bottle,1917 ... **175.00**

COFFEE MILLS

History: Coffee mills or grinders are utilitarian objects designed to grind fresh coffee beans. Before the advent of stay-fresh packaging, coffee mills were a necessity.

The first home size coffee grinders were introduced about 1890 The large commercial grinders designed for use in stores, restaurants, and hotels often bear an earlier patent date.

Reference: Terry Friend, *Coffee Mills*, Collector Books, 1982.

COUNTERTOP (COMMERCIAL)

Charles Parker Co, Meriden, Ct, 12" h, wood base, orig red and blue paint, some orig stenciling **200.00**

Enterprise Manufacturing Co, Philadelphia, PA, 24" h, white wheels, wood base, orig red paint **175.00**

Fairbanks-Morse, 38" h, 2 wheels, brass finial, white paint **350.00**

Golden Rule, cast iron **195.00**

Swift, 12" wheels, cast iron **190.00**

FLOOR MODEL (COMMERCIAL)

John C. Dell & Sons, 66" h, 33" wheels, brass hopper, sand blasted and primed cast iron **900.00**

Enterprise, 72" h **400.00**

LAP (DOMESTIC)

C. P. Company, 6", sq **35.00**

Imperial, 5½" sq, dovetailed box **25.00**

Logan & Strobridge, machine dovetailed, cast iron hopper and handle, oak base **70.00**

Imperial No. 1 Mill, 6⅞" sq, 9½" h, manufactured by Arcade Co, Patented June 5, 1894, $85.00.

TABLE (DOMESTIC)

Arcade, sliding filler lid, orig except for decal, Pat June 5, 1884 .... **75.00**

Charles Parker Co, 14¼" h, cast iron handle and crank, tin top and filler **80.00**

Enterprise No. 0, 11½" h, clamp on style, cast iron **40.00**

Unmarked, 13" h, emb cast iron top, slide open hopper **70.00**

WALL (DOMESTIC)

Arcade, glass top, all orig **75.00**

Brighton, cast iron, mounted on wood board	65.00
Koffie, red glass canister, crank handle, measuring cup at base, mounted on board	75.00
Steinfeld #17, lacy iron grinder, glass canister	35.00
Universal	45.00

COIN OPERATED ITEMS

History: Coin operated items include amusement games, pinball, jukeboxes, slot machines, vending machines, cash registers and other items operated by coins.

The first jukebox was developed about 1934 and played 78 RPM records. Jukeboxes were important parts of teenage life before the advent of portable radios and television.

The first pinball machine was introduced in 1931 by Gottlieb. Pinball machines continued to be popular until the advent of solid state games in 1977 and advanced electronic video games.

The first three-reel slot machine, the Liberty Bell, was invented in 1905 by Charles Fey in San Francisco. In 1910, Mills Novelty Company copyrighted the classic fruit symbols. Improvements and advancements have lead to the sophisticated machines of today.

Vending machines for candy, gum, and peanuts, were popular from 1910 until 1940 and can be found in a wide range of sizes and shapes.

Because of the heavy usage these coin operated items received, many are restored and at the very least have been repainted by either the operator or manufacturer. Using reproduced mechanisms to restore pieces is acceptable in many cases, especially when the restoration will be able to perform as originally intended.

References: Jerry Ayliffe, *American Premium Guide To Jukeboxes And Slot Machines, Gumballs, Trade Stimulators, Arcade,* Books Americana, 1985; Rick Botts, *1983 Jukebox Collectors Directory,* published by author, 1983; Richard Bueschel, *An Illustrated Guide To 100 Collectible Pinballs,* Coin Slot Books, 2 volumes, 1983 and 1984; Nic Costa, *Automatic Pleasures: The History Of The Coin Machine,* Kevin Francis Publishing Ltd., 1988; Bill Enes, *Silent Salesmen: An Encyclopedia Of Collectible Gum, Candy & Nut Machines,* published by author, 1987; Stephen K. Loots, *The Official Victory Glass Price Guide To Antique Jukeboxes, 1988 (Third) Edition,* Jukebox Collector Newsletter, 1988; Richard D. and Barbara Reddock, *Price Guide To Antique Slot Machines,* Wallace-Homestead, 1981.

Periodical: *Jukebox Collector Newsletter,* 2545 SE 60th Street, Des Moines, IA 50317.

Additional Listings: See *Warman's Americana & Collectibles* for separate categories for Jukeboxes, Pinball Machines, Slot Machines, and Vending Machines.

GAME

Big Strike Bowling Game, 10¢, faux wood metal, silver case	80.00
Big Top Pin Ball, 25″ h, 15 x 8″, aluminum, glass, and wood, base	850.00
Chester Pollard, arcade, derby race, wheel mechanism moves horses around track, c1903	2,000.00
High Striker Strength Machine, 96″ h, arcade	1,000.00
Kicker & Catcher, Baker Novelty Co, c1935	200.00
Mill's Perfect Muscle Developer, 60″ h, arcade, restored	2,100.00
Tug-O-War, Callie	4,500.00

JUKEBOX

Capehart 28-G, 18 play mechanism, c1928	2,500.00
Rockola	
Counter type, 12 selection, 1939	750.00
Floor type, 1428, wood work, ornate trim, lights up	3,250.00
Seeberg Q 100, 100 selection	650.00
Western Electric Selectraphone, pneumatic driven record selector, 1928	3,000.00
Wurlitzer	
Model P12, 12 selection, 1935	1,150.00
Model 24, 24 selection, 1938	2,250.00
Model 800, 20 selection, visible turntable system, 1940	2,750.00
Model 1100, space age design, 1947	1,700.00

SLOT MACHINE

Buckley, 5¢, black and gold case, red highlights, restored	950.00
Caille Black Cat, 66″ h, upright, musical, c1902	18,000.00
Jennings, 25¢, Dutch boy and girl, c1930	950.00
Mills	
Bursting Cherry, 5¢, metal payout card on top, key, c1940	1,200.00
Hi Top, 50¢, 28″ h, orig	850.00
Pace, The Kitty, 25¢, countertop	3,500.00
Wattling, Blue Seal, 5¢, 24″, three reel, double jackpots, c1932, restored	1,500.00

VENDING

Beech-Nut, gum, 15″ h, 11″ w, cast metal, glass, and litho tin, seven column	600.00
Blinkey Eye, 1¢, gum, 17″ h, 6″ w, cast iron and wood, red ground, flesh colored face front, orig	5,200.00

Bull's Head, perfume, 15" h, cast iron
and glass, orig paint, paper directions **3,200.00**
Clawson Machine Co, 1¢, candy, cast
iron, tiger striped copper finish, pat
Oct 24, 1917 . . . . **1,250.00**
Diamond, 1¢, safety match, 13" h, bur-
gundy, gold lettering **160.00**
George E. Bayle Co, 5¢, peanuts, 27",
emb coin mechanism, George E.
Bayle Co, c1910 . . . . **750.00**
Jacob's, 5¢, cigar, 36" w, wood, glass,
and metal, accommodates three
brands, marked, pat 1907 . . . . **1,400.00**
Mack Vending Manufacturing Co, 5¢, ci-
gar, 21½" h, oak, pat Apr 3, 1900 . . **325.00**
National Dispenser Co, 1¢, mints, four
cylindrical glass columns, rotating
lazy-susan style, pre 1939 . . . . **125.00**
O.D. Jennings & Co, 5¢, mints, sheet
metal, three column, 1932 . . . . **250.00**
Scoopy, 1¢, gum, 20" h, animated, man
drops gum from scoop, 1¢ **1,300.00**
Wallace, 1¢, chocolate, 30½", l shape,
musical, American Automatic Vend-
ing Machine Co, c1890s **1,000.00**
Whiffs of Fragrance, perfume, 17" h, 14"
w, cast aluminum, orig polychrome
dec, paper instructions, and labels on
bottles, Mills Novelty Co, c1912 . . . **5,700.00**

**National Cash Register, Model 442, 20
x 16¾ x 23", small crank, $0.00 to $9.99,
bronze, mahogany base, 1912, $700.00.**

MISCELLANEOUS

Cash Register, National, Model 421, 23"
h, crank operated, receipt machine at
side, oak cash drawer **650.00**
Fortune, Mills Wizard Fortune Teller, 1¢,
six questions selection, c1920 . . . . . **450.00**
Knotty Peek, 1¢ **450.00**
Postage Stamp, 22" h, 10 w, aluminum
and wood, beveled mirror, 2, 4, and
5¢ stamps **1,700.00**

Weighing
National Automatic, 69" h, cast iron,
porcelain dial, ornate, nice patina,
period repaint in silver, 1¢ **1,000.00**
Watling, 71" h, "What is Yur Wate To-
day?", porcelainized cast iron, porcelain dial, 1¢, Pat 1920 . . . . **550.00**

CONTINENTAL CHINA AND PORCELAIN (GENERAL)

History: By 1700 porcelain factories existed in
large numbers throughout Europe. In the mid-18th
century the German factories at Meissen and
Nymphenburg were dominant. As the century
ended, French potteries assumed the leadership
role. The "golden age" of Continental china and
porcelains was from the 1740s to the 1840s.

Americans living in the last half of the 19th century eagerly sought the masterpieces of the European porcelain factories. In the early 20th century this style of china and porcelain was a "blue
chip" among the antiques collectors.

References: Susan and Al Bagdade, *Warman's
English & Continental Pottery & Porcelain, 1st Edition,* Warman Publishing Co, Inc, 1987; Rachael
Feild, *Macdonald Guide To Buying Antique Pottery & Porcelain,* Macdonald & Co., Ltd., 1987.

Additional Listings: France—Haviland, Limoges, Old Paris, Sarregeumines, and Sevres; German—Austrian Ware, Bavarian China, Carlsbad
China, Dresden/Meissen, Rosenthal, Royal Bayreuth, Royal Bonn, Royal Rudolstadt, Royal Vienna, Schlegelmilch, and Villeroy and Boch; Italy—Capo-di-Monte.

**Chantilly, figure, 13¼" h, pastel matte
colors, c1875, marked, $1,000.00.**

FRENCH

Chantilly
Box, 9¾" sq, cov, Kakiemon palette, figural Oriental seated on lid, iron red hunting horn mark, c1740 ... **23,760.00**
Dish, 9¾", quatrefoil, Kakiemon palette, chrysanthemum, chocolate rim, c1740 .... **200.00**
Figure, 11¼", white, woman, frilled bonnet, man wearing coat and long skirt, both carrying baskets on back, c1745, pr **5,000.00**
Plate, 9½", blue and white, carnations, basketwork border, blue hunting horn mark, c1745, set of 12 **750.00**
Pot de Creme, 4¼", tin glazed body, purple, blue, yellow, iron-red, and green flowers, brown sides, lavender twig handles, brown rim, iron-red hunting horn mark, c1750 ... **725.00**
Waste Bowl, 8⅛", Kakiemon palette, brown rim, iron-red hunting horn mark, c1740 .... **3,275.00**
Duc d'Angouleme, Vieux, urn, 17⅝", periwinkle blue ground, gilded neoclassical devices, foliate borders, c1800, pr **6,875.00**
Faience
Cake Plate, 8⅜", winged harvester, grapevine border, marked "Creil," c1815 .... **50.00**
Ewer, 10", Louis XIV, Euler, and cupid, c1815 .... **275.00**
Plate, 8⅛", French bucolic scene, polychrome transfer, c1800 .... **50.00**
Platter, 18¾", hp scene, floral rim, gilt trim, marked "VP" **175.00**
Urn, 17¾", polychrome, floral dec, matching reticulated lid, pr **250.00**
Mennency
Bouillon, cov, 4⅜", polychrome dec, birds, fruits, and foliage, leafy branches handles, pink edge border, imp DV, late 18th C **1,700.00**
Figure
6⅞" h, young man and woman, c1740, pr **2,850.00**
7", two children, yellow coat, puce breeches and bodice, blue striped skirt, yellow apron, flower encrusted rockwork base, c1735 **850.00**
Pot de Creme, 5⅞", scalloped shell and rocaille, rose and yellow, handles, mid 18th C, minor repairs, pr **6,875.00**
St. Cloud, cup and saucer, 2¾", white, branches of plum trees relief dec, mid 18th C, pr **1,700.00**
Samson
Cachepot, 5¾", Chinese famille verte chrysanthemums and baskets of flowers dec, late 19th C **450.00**

Dinner Service, Chinese Export armorial, magenta, iron red, bottle green, and black, gilding, late 19th C, service for 23 .... **10,000.00**
Humidor, 9", owl shape, modeled, sprigs of famille rose flowers, pseudo achievement, late 19th C, pr **2,500.00**
Jar, cov, 17", famille verte type dec, baskets of flowers under trailing canopies, late 19th C **800.00**
Urn, 16¼", polychrome, enamel floral dec, red cartouche mark, pr **500.00**
Vincennes
Bowl, 12¾" w, central floral medallion, three border bouquets, blue crowned L and Bourbon fleur-de-lis mark, c1752 .... **12,000.00**
Ewer and Basin, 14⅛ x 9½" **31,650.00**
Pot de Creme, 5¼", reserve medallion of flying birds, gilt, c1753 ... **3,000.00**
Potpourri Vase, 4¾" h, white, incised DV mark **300.00**
Teapot, 4⅜" h, conical, bleu lapis, reserve with birds and foliage, blue interlaced L marks, painter's mark "Thevenet," c1753 .... **1,750.00**
Watering Can, 7⅞", painted by Bardet, c1754 .... **46,000.00**

GERMAN

Berlin
Dinner Service, partial, scalloped gold rim, blue stylized sprays, Gotzkowsky's Factory and the Royal Factory, c1840, approx eleven settings and service pcs, 57 pcs **450.00**
Figure, 8½", group, grape harvest, white glazed porcelain, mid 19th C **150.00**
Frankenthal
Cup and Saucer, Chinoiserie, figures, three exotic birds, birdcage, landscape, gilt rococo scrolls, puce trailing flowers, c1765 .... **2,450.00**
Figure
5", Oriental Actor, pointed white and yellow hat, white jacket and pants, grotesque mask, c1776 . **3,500.00**
6⅝" w, group of lovers, chinoiserie, blue crowned CT mark **1,125.00**
6¾", Four Seasons, cherubs, shaped oval scroll, gilt, blue crowned interlaced CT mark, c1772 .... **1,500.00**
Plate, multicolored bouquets and scattered floral sprays, chocolate rim, pr **400.00**
Tea Caddy, 4¾", arched rect, cartouches of peasant figures, scat-

tered floral sprigs and sprays, c1765 .... **750.00**

Tureen, cov, 13⅞″, oval, naturalistic bouquets and summer floral sprays, molded borders, domed cov, sliced lemon finial, c1760 ... **1,750.00**

Furstenberg
Figure
6¼″, bird seller, modeled by Desoches, blue script F mark, c1775 .... **1,600.00**
7⅛″, lady musician, floral patterned skirt, pink bodice, white apron, yellow hat, and green shoes, c1775 .... **725.00**
Vase, cov, 16¾″, cylindrical body, sepia, oval panels of neoclassical figures, knob cracked, underglaze blue mark, c1790 .... **900.00**

Hoechst
Cup and Saucer, brilliant colors, peasant figures, landscape vignettes, branch handles, gilt, c1755 .... **1,500.00**
Figure
7″, boy and girl, Turkish costume, puce, yellow, white, and green, modeled by JP Melchior, blue wheel mark, c1775 .... **1,600.00**
7½″ w, sleeper, garlands, modeled by J P Melchior, blue wheel mark, c1770c **4,000.00**
Plate, 10″, nude Venus reclining on shell, riding waves, foliage garland, puce scale border, shaped rim, gilt, blue wheel mark, sgd "Joseph Angele," c1780 .... **2,000.00**
Tea Set, individual size, birds and landscapes, gilt scrollwork, purple bands, green laurel entwined border, gilt rims, 10 c, c1765 ...... **4,250.00**

Ludwigsburg
Figure
4⅛″, child, holding parrot on ring, chinoiserie, repaired hat, c1765 **475.00**
5⅛″, butcher, blue hat, blue edged jacket, iron-red waistcoat, maroon and yellow breeches, modeled by Pierre Francois Lejeune, c1770 .... **1,150.00**
Plate, 9¼″, famille rose style, two birds in landscape, iron-red rim scrolls, c1760 .... **3,700.00**
Tureen, cov, oval, 12½″ w, rococo dec, figural finial, two handles, blue crowned interlaced C mark, imp "IP," c1765 .... **3,800.00**

Nuremberg Faience, tankard, 8¼″, armorial, cobalt blue, pale blue ground, pewter lid marked "Johann Mehlin of Bamberg" **2,000.00**

Nymphenburg
Cup and Saucer, 3¾″, bell shaped bowl, Maximilian Joseph Platz, burnished gilt int. and scroll handle, c1835 .... **1,900.00**
Dish, 10⅝″, octafoil, Hoff service dec, imp "P2," c1760 .... **4,000.00**
Teapot, 4¾″, striated russet, brown, and pale yellow to imitate knotty wood, reserves of trompe l'oeil prints, painted en grisaille, worn gilt edges, c1780 .... **450.00**
Thuringian, vase, campana shape, molded bacchic mask handles, portrait medallions, garland borders, repaired base, late 18th C, pr **350.00**

ITALIAN

Deruta, jar, 7¼″ h, majolica, inscribed "Ghoma di Lava," scrollwork, grotesques and leaf forms **500.00**
Doccia
Charger, 15¾″, Imari style, cobalt blue, iron-red, and gold, branches of flowering prunus and peonies, trellis diaper and floral panel borders, c1755 .... **300.00**
Coffeepot, 8¾″ h, baluster, bird's head mask spout, floral dec, c1780 **450.00**
Tea Bowl, 3¼″, chinoiserie figures, c1770 .... **450.00**
Ginori, figure, 13″ l, 12½″ h, hunting group, fox hunter on horseback and hounds, hp, mid 20th C **150.00**
Naples, demitasse cups and stands, landscape panel, cobalt ground, gilt, Neo-classical, late 18th C, service for 6 .... **1,600.00**
Savona, compote, 14″ d, blue and white dec, floral border, pierced, blue lighthouse mark **1,200.00**

COPELAND

COPELAND AND SPODE

History: In 1749 Josiah Spode apprenticed to Thomas Whieldon and in 1754 worked for William Banks in Stoke-on-Trent. In the early 1760s Spode started his own pottery, making cream colored earthenware and blue printed whiteware. In 1770 he returned to Banks' factory as master, purchasing it in 1776.

Spode pioneered the use of steam powered pottery making machinery and mastered the art of transfer printing from copper plates. Spode opened a London shop in 1778 and sent William Copeland there about 1784. A number of larger London locations followed. At the turn of the century Spode introduced bone china. In 1805 Josiah Spode II and William Copeland entered into partnership for the London business. A series of partnerships between Josiah Spode II, Josiah Spode III, and William Taylor Copeland resulted.

In 1833 Copeland acquired Spode's London operations and the Stoke plants seven years later. William Taylor Copeland managed the business until his death in 1868. The business remained in the hands of Copeland heirs. In 1923 the plant was electrified; other modernizations followed.

In 1976 Spode merged with Worcester Royal Porcelain to become Royal Worcester Spode, Ltd.

References: Susan and Al Bagdade, *Warman's English & Continental Pottery & Porcelain, 1st Edition,* Warman Publishing, 1987; D. Drakard & P. Holdway, *Spode Printed Wares,* Longmans, 1983; L. Whiter, *Spode: A History Of The Family, Factory, And Wares, 1733–1833,* Barrie & Jenkins, 1970.

Creamer, 5½" w, 4¼" h, blue band, gold trim, ivory ground, No. 893, c1810, $75.00.

Basket
  8", reticulated, two handles, fruit, flowers, leaves, and branches, gray, c1815 .... **200.00**
  11 x 8½", white, shaded pink to white int., gold floral and leaf dec, intertwined pink handle, c1851–55 ... **210.00**
Bowl, 8½", fruit, Imari type, blue, green, and orange, pedestal base, scalloped edge, c1850 .... **85.00**
Chamberstick, 3¹⁵⁄₁₆", Japan pattern,

columnar, gilt edged circular drip pan, wing shaped thumbpiece, gilt ring handle, c1810 .... **325.00**
Coffeepot, 8", brown transfer **75.00**
Compote, 9½ x 2¾", white, floral dec, turquoise dots, gold, trim, lattice sides **225.00**
Cup and Saucer
  Fleur-de-lis, pink, blue mark, c1890 . **45.00**
  Royal Windsor, Spode **35.00**
  Tower pattern, blue and white, Spode **45.00**
Decanter, Edward VII 1902 Coronation, cobalt blue, raised relief royals cameo, flags, and coat of arms, crown stopper, marked "Spode Copeland," registry marks **275.00**
Dessert Service
  13 pcs, pierced 8½" basket, twelve 9¼" octagonal plates, multicolored central floral bouquet, three small sprigs in gilt dentil border, pink ground rim with four foliage devices, rim edge gold and white molded foliations and blossoms, gilt twig handles, basket marked "Spode," plates marked "Spode Felspar Porcelain," gold pattern number, imp potters' marks, c1828 **1,550.00**
  19 pcs, 13⅝" l fruit stand, two rect dishes, four shell shaped dishes, twelve plates, center botanical floral sprigs surrounded by smaller sprigs in panels, gilt floral and foliate scrollwork, apple green border, gilt edges, shell and scroll handles, some pieces marked with wreath "Spode Felspar Production," and potter's mark, c1826 .... **4,675.00**
Figure, 17½", mother with baby, "Go to Sleep," parian, Copeland, c1865 ... **525.00**
Game Plate, 12", 19th C reproduction of Chelsea-Derby, sculptured biscuitware, Chinese style pheasants and butterflies, gilt, claret ground, fake Chelsea marks, initials CAR surround fleur-de-lis, numbered **200.00**
Jug, 4", white, floral dec, c1830 ..... **100.00**
Oyster Plate, hp, insects and flowers . **20.00**
Pitcher
  4¼", royal blue, hunters, horses, dogs in white, high relief **40.00**
  6½", Tower pattern, blue transfer, Spode **65.00**
  8", large, limited edition, "Chicago," dark Wedgwood blue, applied white scenes, Chicago Fire, Mrs. O'Leary and her cow, Fort Dearborn, Father Marquette, three larger medallions of an Indian scene, frontier scene, and Miss Liberty, imp "Copeland England," stamped "Chicago Pitcher Designed by Frank Burley, Burley & Co," #92, c1890 ...... **500.00**

Plate
6″
 Flowers and birds, heavy gold dec **100.00**
 Tobacco Leaf pattern, c1850 . . . . **30.00**
 8″, Florence **14.00**
 9″
  Bird of Paradise center, floral bor-
   der **35.00**
  Floral center, cobalt blue and gold,
   scalloped edge **55.00**
 10″, all-over floral pattern, blue-gray,
  c1880 . . . . **30.00**
 10¼″, Marathon, white center, cream
  border with blue floral dec, gold trim **20.00**
Punch Bowl, 12½″, punch, multicolored,
 Chinese garden scene, gold trim
 c1810 . . . . **750.00**
Tea Service, partial, Japan pattern,
 shield shaped cov teapot, waste bowl,
 two cake dishes, eight teacups, seven
 coffee cups, seventeen saucers, underglaze blue, iron-red, and gold dec,
 oval pavilion vignettes surrounded by
 gilt foliate scrollwork, blue-ground
 rect panels, marked "Spode," and
 pattern numbers in iron-red or black,
 c1812–15, 36 pcs **2,000.00**
Tureen, cov, 7½″ d, blue and white,
 bridge scene with flowers, stand,
 c1820 . . . . **125.00**
Vase, 5″, Japan pattern, c1820 . . . . . . **95.00**
Vegetable, cov, 10″, Geisha pattern,
 blue **100.00**

COPPER

History: Copper objects, such as kettles, tea kettles, warming pans, measures, etc., played an important part in the 19th century household. Outdoors, the apple butter kettle and still were the two principal copper items. Copper culinary objects were lined with a thin protective coating of tin to prevent poisoning. They were relined as needed.

Great emphasis is placed by collectors on signed pieces, especially those by American craftsmen. Since copper objects were made abroad as well, it is hard to identify unsigned examples. Many modern reproductions also exist.

References: Mary Frank Gaston, *Antique Copper*, Collector Books, 1985; Henry J. Kauffman, *Early American Copper, Tin, and Brass*, Medill McBride Co., 1950.

Additional Listings: Arts and Crafts Movement and Roycroft.

Apple Butter Kettle, 35 gal **475.00**
Bed Warmer, punched bird design . . . **325.00**
Bowl, 16″, dovetailed, handled, po-
 lished, dented **75.00**
Candlestick, 5½ x 4½″, brass handle,
 19th C, pr **45.00**

Coffee Server, 16½″ h, iron stand, $325.00.

Coal Scuttle, 22″ l **100.00**
Dipper, 7½ x 26″, brass handle **125.00**
Egg Warmer, 10″ h, pewter trim, English
 Victorian **145.00**
Dish, lead flower handle, Nekrassoff . . **65.00**
Funnel, 5″ l **20.00**
Hot Water Bottle, 8½″, marked "WA-
 FAX" **65.00**
Letter Opener, hammered, strap handle,
 Arts & Crafts **20.00**
Measure, qt **40.00**
Mold
 Fruit basket, 10″ l, 20th C **90.00**
 Turk's head, geometric design, 10″ . **65.00**
Milk Pail, iron swing handle, England,
 19th C **200.00**
Pan, 10″ d, 3¾″ h, dovetail construction,
 applied strap handle **90.00**
Pitcher, 12″, dovetailed, classic design **110.00**
Pot, cov, applied rim handles with tulip
 ends, dovetailed bottom **295.00**
Punch Bowl, 14″ d, 6½″ h **85.00**
Roasting pan, 27 x 20 x 7″, diamond
 shape, English, 19th **360.00**
Tea Kettle, American
 10″ h, eagle mark, minor denting . . . **350.00**
 10½″ h, marked "J Kidd," minor dent-
  ing **500.00**
 10¾″ h, marked " I Roberts Phila" . **575.00**
 11¼″ h, marked "J Geddes/Balti-
  more," minor denting **850.00**
 11½″ h, marked "J Bollinger" **500.00**
 12¼″ h, marked "W Heyser/6/Cham-
  bersburg," minor denting **275.00**
Tray, 16¼″, hammered, loop handles,
 Gustav Stickley, c1905 . . . . **250.00**
Vase, 10½″, hammered, Gustav Stick-
 ley, No 26, c1905 . . . . **550.00**
Warming Pan, pierced floral design lid,
 orig turned wood handle, American . **600.00**
Wash Boiler, marked "Atlantic 11 gal" . **125.00**
Weathervane, 43″ l, horse, running,
 gilded **2,100.00**

CORALENE

History: Coralene is a glass or china object which has the design painted on the surface of the piece and tiny glass colorless beads applied with a fixative. The piece is placed in a muffle which fixes the enamel and sets the beads.

Several American and English companies made glass coralene in the 1880s. Seaweed or coral was the most common design. Other motifs were "Wheat Sheaf" and "Fleur-de-Lis." Most of the base glass was satin finished.

China and pottery coralene, made from the late 1890s to the post WW II era, is referred to as Japanese coralene. The beading is opaque and inserted into the soft clay. Hence, it is only half to three-quarters visible.

Reproduction Alert: Reproductions are on the market, some using an old glass base. The beaded decoration on new coralene has been glued and can be scraped off.

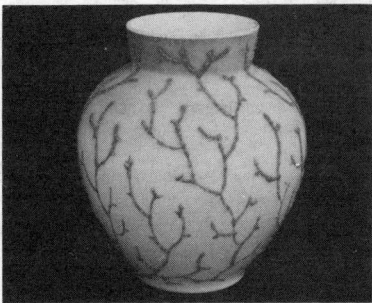

Vase, 6¼″ h, white shading to blue, yellow seaweed coralene dec, white cased int., c1880, $250.00.

CHINA

Bowl, 8″ d, blue matte ground, purple plums, green leaves, c1910 ...... **175.00**
Box, cov, 1½ x 2 x 3″, copper matte ground, pink, lavender, and green thistle, marked "Kinran Pat. 16132 Japan" **125.00**
Sugar Shaker, white ground, orange coralene seaweed dec, orig top ... **165.00**
Vase, 8″, bulbous, scalloped and fluted rim, shaded lavender to light blue ground, multicolored snapdragons, c1909 .... **225.00**

GLASS

Bowl, 4½″ d, blue, flowers and leaves, SP holder **150.00**

Pitcher, 7¾″, sq mouth, shaded pink satin ground, yellow coralene seaweed dec, applied frosted handle, Hobbs, Brockunier & Co. **750.00**
Sweetmeat, blue bowl, flowers and leaves, SP holder **400.00**
Tumbler, white, satin, acorns and leaves outlined in coralene **35.00**
Vase
5⅜″, golden yellow snowflake MOP satin ground, white ground, yellow wheat coralene dec **500.00**
7½″
Blue, bulbous, yellow coralene seaweed dec **250.00**
Peachblow, yellow coralene seaweed dec **375.00**
Yellow to white ground, yellow coralene seaweed dec **200.00**
8 x 5″, satin, alternating pink, white, and green stripes at top which shade to white, yellow coralane beading **500.00**

CORKSCREWS

History: The corkscrew is composed of three parts: (1) handle, (2) shaft, and (3) worm or screw. The earliest known reference to "a Steele Worme used for drawing corks out of bottles" is 1681. Samuel Henshall, an Englishman, was granted the first patent in 1795.

Elaborate mechanisms were invented and patented from the early 1800s onward, especially in England. However, three basic types emerged: "T" handle (the most basic, simple form), lever, and mechanism. Variations on these three types run into the hundreds. Miniature corkscrews, employed for drawing corks from perfume and medicinal bottles between 1750 and 1920, are among the most eagerly sought by collectors.

Nationalistic preferences were found in corkscrews. The English favored the helix worm and tended to coppertone their steel products. By the mid-18th century English and Irish silversmiths were making handles noted for their clean lines and practicality. Most English silver handles were hallmarked.

The Germans preferred the center worm and nickel plate. The Italians used chrome plate or massive solid brass. In the early 1800s the Dutch and French developed elaborately artistic silver handles.

Americans did not begin to manufacture quality corkscrews until the late 19th century. They favored the center worm and specialized in silver mounted tusks and carved staghorn for handles.

LEVER

Brass, rack and pinion type, double, steel shaft, center worm, cap lifter in handle, Italian, c1920 . . . . 30.00
Chrome, zig-zag design, 10½" extended, French 60.00
Steel, bronzed, helical worm, double lever patent, Heeley "A1" 60.00

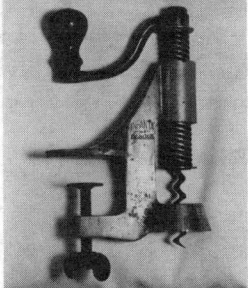

Table type, cast iron, nickel plating, double action, American, Infanta No. 8, Patented 1895, $350.00.

MECHANISM

Bone handle, English rack and pinion corkscrew, polished, brush and hanging ring, four plain post open barrel, narrow rack, long wire helix, side handle, sgd "Verinder," c1800 . . . . 400.00
Bronze Frame, rosewood handle with brush, marked "G Twigg's Patent," c1868 . . . . 400.00
Chrome Frame, cylindrical ebony wood handle, steel, cyphered worm, marked "Swiss Made, 2908A3" 130.00
Steel Frame, floral and leaf scrolling, clamp handles on base, raised steel arms, cyphered worm, marked "Yankee No 7," c1913 . . . . 160.00

MINIATURE

Chrome, elephant, trunk corkscrew . . . 40.00
Ivory handle, crescent shape, chromed turned steel shaft wire helix, c1790–1820 . . . . 70.00
Meissen, porcelain Johann Von Schiller head, uncyphered center worm, underglaze crossed swords mark, c1870 . . . . 375.00
MOP, carved palmette handle, helical worm 20.00

Nickel Plated Steel, folding boco, heart shape, fluted wire helix 35.00

NOVELTY

Brass, figural cat, tail corkscrew, 3¾" l 45.00
Celluloid, figural mermaid, brown, steel cyphered worm, H H & S Express . . 300.00
Pewter, triton blowing a shell, steel cyphered worm, 19th C 90.00
Silver, gaucho and horse, oblong platform handle, seal from sheath with scrolling, Archimedean screw 800.00

T-HANDLE

Brass, Thomason type, bone handle with brush, helical worm 150.00
Stag's horn handle, ornate SS cap . . . 100.00
Steel, "The Surprise," cage frame, marked "Registered by George Willetts, Birmingham, England," 1884 . . 95.00
Wood
   Shaped and turned handle, cyphered center worm, bell and wire cutter, cap lifter, "Williamson" on shaft, marked "Ptd 13 Dec 1898" 30.00
Wood handle, duck bill cap, simple Archimedean screw, German 80.00

COSMOS GLASS

History: Cosmos glass is a milk glass pattern made by the Consolidated Lamp and Glass Company, c1900.

Cosmos glass is identified by its distinctive pattern. The ground is a molded cross-cut design. Relief molded flowers are painted in pink, blue, and yellow. Cosmos glass comes in an extended tableware line which includes several sizes and shapes of lamps.

Syrup Pitcher, 6½" h, white ground, pink and yellow flowers, $200.00.

Butter Dish, cov, 7½" d	170.00
Cologne Bottle, 4½", orig stopper	100.00
Creamer	150.00
Miniature Lamp	
7", fish net ground	350.00
9", pink, yellow, and blue dec, electri-	
fied	75.00
Pickle Castor, pink band, ftd, SP frame	400.00
Pitcher, 5" h, milk	170.00
Salt and Pepper Shakers, pr	185.00
Spooner, pink flowers	130.00
Sugar, cov	175.00
Syrup, SP lid	200.00
Tumbler	85.00

COWAN POTTERY

History: R. Guy Cowan founded the Cowan Pottery in 1913 in Cleveland, Ohio. The establishment remained in almost continuous operation until 1931 when financial difficulties forced closure.

Early production was redware pottery. Later a porcelain-like finish was perfected with special emphasis placed on glazes. Lustreware is one of the most common types. Commercial wares marked "Lakeware" were produced from 1927 to 1931.

Early marks include an incised "Cowan Pottery" on the redware (1913–17), an impressed "Cowan," and an impressed "Lakewood". The imprinted stylized semicircle with or without the initials R. G. was later.

References: Paul Evans, *Art Pottery of the United States, 2nd Edition,* Feingold & Lewis Publishing Corp., 1987; Ralph and Terry Kovel, *The Kovels' Collector's Guide to American Art Pottery,* Crown Publishers, Inc., 1974.

Ashtray, shell shape, gunmetal glaze .	15.00
Bookends, pr, polar bears eating fish,	
ivory glaze	215.00
Candlesticks, pr, figural	
4½", seahorse, green	25.00
12", nude, ivory glaze	250.00
Cigar Tray, model of duck	28.00
Figure	
8", Spanish dancers, old ivory glaze,	
pr	375.00
11", flamingo, ivory glaze	200.00
12", peacock, turquoise glaze	75.00
Flower Frog	
5", mushroom	80.00
6½", Art Deco nude, white	35.00
Pitcher, pink luster glaze, quart	55.00

Matchholder, 3⅜" h, seahorse motif base, pink, $50.00.

Place Card Holder, 3", cream glaze, imp	
mark	18.00
Plate, 11½", hp, rabbit, blue and black	
glaze	500.00
Strawberry Jar, mint green glaze	75.00
Trivet, 6½", Louis Mora, red and yellow	
flowers, blue ground	200.00
Vase	
7" h, seahorse, green	35.00
10", handled, deep blue-green glaze	55.00
12", pillow, mythical figures, glossy	
royal blue crackle glaze	250.00

CRANBERRY GLASS

History: Cranberry glass is transparent and named for its color, achieved by adding powdered gold to a molten batch of amber glass which then is reheated at a low temperature to develop the cranberry or ruby color. The glass color first appeared in the last half of the 17th century, but was not made in American glass factories until the last half of the 19th century.

Cranberry glass was blown, mold blown, or pressed. Examples often are decorated with gold or enamel. Less expensive cranberry glass was made by substituting copper for gold and can be identified by its bluish-purple tint.

Reference: William Heacock and William Gamble, *Encyclopedia Of Victorian Colored Pattern Glass: Book 9, Cranberry Opalescent from A to Z,* Antique Publications, 1987.

Additional Listings: See specific categories, such as Bride's Baskets, Cruets, Jack-in-the-Pulpit Vases, etc.

Reproduction Alert: Reproductions abound. These pieces are heavier, off-color, and lack the quality of older examples.

Banana Bowl, 12 x 6½", boat shape,	
bronze ftd basket	575.00
Barber Bottle, 7", IVT, porcelain top . .	85.00

Bottle, 4" d, 10¼" h, blue and white enameled flowers, gold and silver leaves, clear bubble stopper with engraved flowers 165.00

Box, cov, hinged, round

3½ x 3½", gold band with pink and blue flowers, leaves, center with pink, blue and white flowers 210.00

3¾ x 2⅞", enameled pink and white flowers, green leaves 200.00

4¼ x 4¼", clusters of white flowers and leaves, two multicolored birds 250.00

Chalice, cov, 16" h, enamel portrait of girl, gold trim 175.00

Condiment Set, 4 x 7¼", open salt with spoon, pepper pot, and mustard jar, Swirl pattern, SP holder 165.00

Creamer, 2⅝ x 3⅝", two bands, enameled white dots and flower dec, applied clear handle 100.00

Cruet

3¾ x 7½", enameled white flowers and leaves, applied clear handle, clear bubble stopper 165.00

8", ribbed, gold band at base and top, gold dec on matching stopper ... 100.00

8¾", flattened bulbous vessel, pewter casing, figural cherub pewter stopper 200.00

9½", engraved flowers and leaves, applied clear handle and wafer foot, clear cut faceted stopper ... 160.00

13", three petal top, engraved flowers and leaves, applied clear handle and pedestal base, clear bubble stopper 165.00

Decanter, swirled, stylized enamel floral dec 225.00

Ewer, 9½", gold leaves, white enamel outlines, flowers, and branches, applied clear handle 150.00

Jam Jar, IVT, wild rose and fern enamel dec, SP top, fleur-de-lis finial 150.00

Jewel Box

5¾ x 5", gold enamel floral dec, brass mounts, ring handles, key 425.00

6" h, round, lid with enamel white slate roof, turret, and doves, blue enamel flowers, brass ring handles and ball feet 400.00

Lamp, finger, 4¼" d, 6" h, applied clear handle 150.00

Lamp Shade, 7¾ x 4¾", hobnail, ruffled rim 100.00

Perfume

2¼ x 5¾", sanded gold enameled leaves, white enameled flowers, clear ball stopper, gold trim 120.00

3⅜" l, ¾" oval, lacy filigree openwork ormolu, gilt collar, engraved, hinged lid, inner stopper, attached chains and finger ring 235.00

Pickle Castor, 10" h, melon shaped cranberry base, silverplated frame, marked "WR, New York, 482," $275.00.

Pickle Castor

Coin Spot, enamel dec, SP holder . 225.00

Inverted Thumbprint, double, gold enameled florals and scroll, Moser style, ornate ftd Wilcox frame and cov, braided handle, resilvered ... 400.00

Ribbed, enameled flowers, SP holder and tongs 275.00

Swirl, ornate SP holder 225.00

Pitcher

2¼ x 2⅝", bulbous, round mouth, applied clear handle, enameled green and white leaves, small yellow leaves, gold bands, applied red jewels 120.00

3¼", DQ, applied clear handle 65.00

4¼ x 6½", bulbous, round mouth, IVT, applied clear handle 115.00

5¼ x 8¼ x 5¾", clear ruffled applied leaves, triangular cranberry body, clear applied handle, hollow stem, and foot 300.00

7⅜", bulbous, round mouth, applied clear rope and braided handle ... 250.00

Ring Box, 1¾ x 1½", gold leaves, branches and buds, small enameled blue and white flowers, gold and white diamond dec on cov 75.00

Salt, Master

2¼ x 2⅛", Optic, applied clear wishbone feet 60.00

3¾ x 1¾", applied clear shell trim, fluted SP holder, orig spoon 100.00

Sugar Shaker, 5¾", paneled, SP top .. 60.00

Syrup, Baby IVT, applied clear handle, pewter lid 125.00

Toothpick, Fraizer 65.00

Tumble-Up, carafe and tumbler, IVT .. 80.00

Tumbler

3½", IVT 25.00

3¾", gold top band, enameled pink and white flowers, green leaves, gold scrolls 60.00

Vase

3½", blue enameled flower garland, white leaves, white dots and scrolls, gold rim band 60.00

4⅝ x 2⅝", IVT, applied crystal icicles 250.00

5 x 2½", enameled green, yellow, and white oak leaves and acorns, lacy gold foliage 225.00

6", flower petal shaped top, clear stem and pedestal base 60.00

9⅜ x 3¾", white enameled daisies and leaves, pr 225.00

9⅜ x 4¼", applied crystal leaves and rigaree, crystal pedestal foot 145.00

10¼ x 3⅝", three petal top, dainty blue enameled flowers, white scrolls, gold trim, green leaves, pr 325.00

10½ x 5½", gold scrolls and leaves, small blue and white flowers, pedestal base 225.00

10¾ x 4¼", blue and white floral dec, gold leaves, matching pr 375.00

11", enameled white, pink, and blue flowers, gold trim and foliage, pr . 375.00

CROWN MILANO

History: Crown Milano is an American art glass produced by the Mt. Washington Glass Works, New Bedford, Massachusetts. The original patent was issued in 1886 to Frederick Shirley and Albert Steffin.

Normally it is an opaque white satin glass finished with light beige or ivory color ground embellished with fancy florals, decorations, and elaborate heavy raised gold. When marked, pieces carry an entwined CM with crown in purple enamel on the base. Sometimes paper labels were used. The silver plated mounts often have "MW" impressed or a Pairpoint mark as both Mount Washington and Pairpoint supplied mountings.

Advisors: Clarence and Betty Maier.

Biscuit Jar

7½" d, multicolored flowers, gold scrolls, emb resilvered lid, rim, and bail 950.00

7½" h, Burmese color, gold autumn leaves and wild roses, emb SP lid and bail 675.00

Box, 6" d, round, all-over red blossoms and scrolls dec, emb SP rims, orig velvet lining, sgd 450.00

Vase, 11½" h, heavy raised gold dec, large fully opened chrysanthemum blossoms, buds, and foliage, shadow background of sepia colored chrysanthemum foliage, fancy gold embellishments on neck, brushed gold highlights on handles and rolled crown shaped top, $1,250.00.

Creamer and Sugar, cov, 4" h, dainty multicolored floral dec, gold finial and shell handles, sgd 5,250.00

Ewer, 10½" h, woman and sheep on obverse, birds and roses on reverse, both framed with raised laurel leaves garland, lilac and opal ground, gold rope handle, sgd "Crown Milano" and numbered 504 . . . . 2,650.00

Muffineer, 4½" h, melon ribbed, floral, pristine white ground, SP top, sgd . . 300.00

Salt Shaker

1½" h, fig shape, pink floral dec, cream ground, SP pronged top, sgd 185.00

3" h, cockle shell shape, yellow floral, white ground, SP pronged top . . . 275.00

Sweetmeat, 4¼" h, 4" d

Raised molded-in stars, enamel and jewel stylized starfish dec, gold and silver highlights, twig finial, emb crab on lid 850.00

Thistle and leaves with raised gold outline, twig finial, emb SP flowers and leaves lid 650.00

Syrup, 5¾" h, melon ribbed, Burmese colored, lotus blossom dec with raised gold outline, SP top and handle, "MW" on lid 985.00

Urn

11½" h, egg shape, overlaid gold roses, leaves, and branches dec, rose branch shadow background, gold neck and lid embellishments, finial repair, sgd 850.00

14½″ h, raised gold Peacock dec, jewel crest and tail, perched on foliated branch, sgd **4,950.00**

Vase

8″ h

Multicolored florals over shadow leaves and scrolls, gold scrolls around neck **745.00**

Square sided, oak leaves and acorns dec, raised gold shadow oak leaves background, 2 applied shell handles, orig paper-label **1,250.00**

11¼″ h, court lady and gentleman figures dec, surrounded by gold scrolls, top folds down to form handles, red crown surrounded by laurel leaves mark and Albertine signature **750.00**

CRUETS

History: Cruets are small glass bottles, used to hold oil, vinegar, wine, etc., for the table. The high point of cruet use was during the Victorian era when a myriad of glass manufacturers made cruets in a wide assortment of patterns, colors, and sizes. All cruets had stoppers; most had handles.

Reference: Dean L Murray, *More Cruets Only*, Killgore Graphics, Inc., 1973; William Heacock, *Encyclopedia of Victorian Colored Pattern Glass: Book 6, Oil Cruets From A To Z*, Antique Publications, 1981.

Additional Listings: Pattern Glass and specific glass categories such as Amberina, Cranberry and Satin.

Cranberry shading to white, opal hobnail, 6¼″ h, cased neck, tricorn lip, applied clear handle, orig clear hobnail ground stopper, Fenton, $65.00.

Amber

3¼″ d, 8½″ h, enameled blue, white, yellow, and green floral dec, gold trim, applied sapphire blue handle, cut faceted blue stopper **225.00**

4¾″ d, 9½″ h, engraved leaves and butterfly, flattened bulbous shape, applied blue handle, cut faceted blue stopper **250.00**

Amberina, 4½″ h, Coin Spot pattern, dainty blue enamel flowers, amber stopper **350.00**

Chocolate, Greentown Glass

Chrysanthemum Leaf **850.00**
Geneva pattern **1,000.00**
Wild Rose and Bowknot **300.00**

Cranberry, 3¾″ d, 7½″ h, enameled white flowers and leaves, applied clear handle, clear bubble stopper . . **165.00**

Custard Glass, Chrysanthemum Sprig, blue **650.00**

Opalescent

Flora pattern, 6½″ h, vaseline **425.00**
Hobb's Hobnail, cranberry, orig stopper **300.00**
Stripe pattern, 3½″ d, 6¾″ h, blue, three petal top, applied blue handle, cut faceted blue stopper **125.00**
Reverse Swirl, cranberry, chrysanthemum base **300.00**

Peachblow, 6½″ h, mahogany shading to cherry red to cream, white int., trefoil top, Wheeling **1,285.00**

Pattern Glass

Cottage **25.00**
Dice and Block, amber, orig stopper **85.00**
Florida, emerald green **110.00**
Nestor, amethyst, gold trim **95.00**
Shoshone, ruby stained **200.00**

Sapphire Blue, 4″ h, 7¾″ h, enameled white lilies of the valley, gold bands and trim, three petal top, applied blue handle, orig blue ball stopper **145.00**

Satin, 5″ h, DQ, MOP, pink, thorn handle and stopper **575.00**

Sevres, 8½″, pale green, gold scrolls and florals, clear free form handle, ball stopper with teardrop air-trap, orig paper label **435.00**

CUP PLATES

History: Many early cups and saucers were handless, with deep saucers. The hot liquid was poured into the saucer and sipped from it. This necessitated another plate for the cup, the "cup plate."

The first cup plates made of pottery were of the Staffordshire variety. In the mid-1830s to 40s, glass cup plates were favored. Boston and Sandwich Glass Company was one of the main contributors to the lacy glass type.

It is extremely difficult to find glass cup plates in outstanding (mint) condition. Collectors expect some marks of usage, such as slight rim roughness, minor chipping [best if under rim], and in rarer paterns a portion of a scallop missing.

Reference: Ruth Webb Lee and Robert Rose, *American Glass Cup Plates*, published by author, 1948, reprinted by Charles E. Tuttle Co., Inc. in 1985.

Notes: The numbers used are from the Lee-Rose book in which all plates are illustrated.

Prices are based on plates in "average" condition.

GLASS

LR 10, clear, 3⅜″, plain rim, New England	55.00
LR 13, deep blue, 3¾″, A-type mold, plain rim, New England	60.00
LR 22-A, clear, 3⁷/₁₆″, 15 scallops with shelves, New England or Sandwich origin	85.00
LR 28, clear, 3¼″, 17 even scallops, New England or Sandwich origin	30.00
LR 36, 3¼″, opal opaque, 17 even scallops	475.00
LR 46, lavender, 3½″, 15 even scallops, strawberry diamond pattern, eastern origin	125.00
LR 52, opalescent, 3¾″, 15 scallops with points between, eastern origin	200.00
LR 60, clear, 3⅜″, plain rope, cross hatching, eastern origin	200.00
LR 70, clear, 3⁷/₁₆″, plain rope, midwestern origin	125.00
LR 79, pink tint, 3¾″, rope top and bottom, New England origin	50.00
LR 82, opaque blue, 3⅝″, plain rim, 5 pointed star center, attributed to New England	275.00
LR 95, 3⅝″, opal opaque, 10 sided, rope top and bottom, 1 tiny under rim nick	150.00
LR 107, 3⅜″, clear, plain rim, attributed to Philadelphia area, slight underfill, trace of mold roughness	50.00
LR 120, clear, 3¹/₁₆″, 30 even scallops, midwestern origin	165.00
LR 135, clear, 3⁷/₁₆″, 24 bull's eyes, points between, attributed to midwestern origin	75.00
LR 148-C, 2⅞″, 17 scallops, points between, clear, one point and one scallop missing	75.00
LR 150-B, clear, 2¹⁵/₁₆″, plain, robe on bottom, midwest origin	50.00
LR 163, light green, 3¼″, 34 scallops, radial lines between, midwest origin	65.00
LR 179, lavender, 3⁷/₁₆″, 10 scallop, rope	

top and bottom, attributed to Philadelphia area	125.00
LR 183-B, deep blue, 3½″, octagonal rim, 7 scallops between corners, midwest origin	90.00
LR 200, clear, 3⅛″, 96 sawtooth scallops, midwest origin	35.00
LR 225-A, clear, 3½″, 12 large scallops, 4 small scallops between, attributed to Philadelphia area	50.00
LR 255, amethyst tint, 3⅝″, 24 bold scallops, divided by pairs of small scallops	20.00
LR 311, 3⅝″, 23 bold scallops, pairs of smaller scallops between each, Sandwich origin, amber stain on center design and border triangles, 2 scallops missing	300.00
LR 343-B, clear, 3⁷/₁₆″, plain, dotted below	45.00
LR 347, yellow 3¾″, 65 even scallops	115.00
LR 388, opaque white, 3⁵/₁₆″, plain, central star, attributed to Philadelphia area	35.00
LR 412, clear, 3³/₁₆″, 10 sided, star center, Sandwich origin	95.00
LR 425, 3⅜″, deep amethyst, unlisted color, 9 large scallops with hearts between on rim, trace of mold roughness	1,600.00
LR 430, clear, 3⅜″, 9 large scallops, hearts between diamond diapering, eastern origin	75.00
LR 455, opal, 3⅞″, 48 even scallops, Sandwich origin	265.00
LR 465-F, 3⅜″, violet blue, 63 even scallops, Sandwich origin, one scallop missing, 5 tipped	130.00

GLASS, HISTORICAL

LR 562, clear, 3⁷/₁₆″, Henry Clay, 18 large scallops, 2 smaller scallops between, Sandwich origin	75.00
LR 576, medium blue, 3⁹/₁₆″, 25 large scallops, 2 smaller scallops between, Sandwich origin	85.00
LR 580, clear, 3¾″, Victoria and Albert, 56 even scallops, English origin	250.00
LR 605-A, clear, 3½″, octagonal, ship, 3 scallops lightly tipped	275.00
LR 643, clear, 3⁹/₁₆″, Bunker Hill Monument, 53 even scallops, drape pattern shoulders, Sandwich origin	35.00
LR 653, clear, 3″, plain, eagle, laurel wreath, large chip	125.00
LR 668, clear, 3¹/₁₆″, 56 even scallops, attributed to midwestern origin	100.00
LR 676, clear, 3¹¹/₁₆″, 60 even scallops, Curling's Ft Pitt Glass Works	65.00

LR 691, 3³⁄₁₆″, clear, lyre center, 24 large beads with reels between, mold roughness **175.00**

Porcelain, Battery, NY, 3⅝″ d, dark blue, $300.00.

PORCELAIN OR POTTERY

Adam's Rose, 3¾″	75.00
Pink Luster	45.00
Staffordshire, Historical	
Conway, N Hampshire, 4⅛″, light colors, marked "American Scenery"	75.00
Oak Leaves, 4″, Rogers, dark blue, faint hairline	25.00
Valley Of The Sanandoch From Jefferson's Rock, light colors	75.00
Worcester Cathedral, 4″, Hall, tiny rub on rim	40.00
Staffordshire Romantic	
California, Podmore Walker & Co . .	75.00
Corinth, James Edwards	40.00
Damascus, Wm Adams and Sons, blue and white	50.00
Garden Scenery, Mayer, pink, 12 sided	30.00
Lozere, Edward Challinor	65.00

CUSTARD GLASS

History: Custard glass was developed in England in the early 1880s. Harry Northwood made the first American custard glass at his Indiana, Pennsylvania, factory in 1898.

From 1898 until 1915, many manufacturers produced custard glass patterns, e.g., Dugan Glass, Fenton, A. H. Heisey Glass Co., Jefferson Glass, Northwood, Tarentum Glass, and U.S. Glass. Cambridge and McKee continued the production of custard glass into the Depression.

The ivory or creamy yellow custard color is achieved by adding uranium salts to the molten hot glass. The chemical content makes the glass glow when held under a black light. The higher the amount of uranium, the more luminous the color. Northwood's custard glass has the smallest amount of uranium, creating an ivory color; Heisey used more, creating a deep yellow color.

Custard glass was made in patterned tableware pieces. It also was made as souvenir items and novelty pieces. Souvenir pieces are marked with place names or hand painted decorations, e.g., flowers. Patterns of custard glass often were highlighted in gold, enamel colors, and stains.

Reference: William Heacock, *Encyclopedia Of Victorian Colored Pattern Glass, Book IV: Custard Glass From A to Z,* Peacock Publications, 1980.

Reproduction Alert: L. G. Wright Glass Co. has reproduced pieces in the Argonaut Shell and Grape and Cable patterns. It also introduced new patterns, such as Floral and Grape and Vintage Band. Moser reproduced toothpicks in Argonaut Shell, Chrysanthemum Sprig, and Inverted Fan & Feather.

Additional Listings: Pattern Glass.

Creamer, 4½″ h, Chrysanthemum Sprig, gold drape dec, $90.00.

Banana Bowl, Louis XV	100.00
Berry Bowl, ind, Intaglio, green dec . .	55.00
Berry Bowl, master	
Argonaut Shell	100.00
Chrysanthemum Sprig, dec	135.00
Fan and Feather	110.00
Grape and Cable, nutmeg stain . . .	75.00
Winged Scroll	100.00
Butter, cov	
Intaglio, marked "N"	175.00
Tartentum's Victoria	125.00
Celery, Georgia Gem, gold dec	185.00
Compote, jelly	
Argonaut Shell	135.00
Everglades, green, gold dec	350.00
Ring Band, marked "Heisey"	125.00

Creamer

Chrysanthemum Sprig, gold dec . . .	90.00
Fan	125.00
Geneva	85.00
Maple Leaf, green, gold dec	125.00

Cruet

Argonaut Shell, 6½"	200.00
Chrysanthemum Sprig, blue	650.00
Inverted Fan, 6½" h, gold dec	600.00

Dresser Tray, Grape and Cable, nutmeg

stain	200.00

Goblet

Beaded Swag, rose dec, marked "Heisey"	60.00
Grape and Gothic Arches, souvenir .	50.00

Ice Cream Bowl, Peacock at the Urn,

nutmeg stain	200.00

Match Holder, Winged Scroll, gold dec	175.00

Pitcher, Diamond with Peg, 7½" h, roses

dec, marked "Krystol"	135.00

Plate

Fruits and Flowers, 7"	40.00
Grape and Cable, nutmeg stain . . .	45.00

Punch Cup, Diamond with Peg, roses

dec	50.00

Salt and Pepper Shakers, pr

Argonaut Shell	350.00
Intaglio, orig tops, marked "N"	150.00
Inverted Fan and Feather, SP tops .	400.00

Sauce

Cane Insert	20.00
Delaware, nutmeg stain	40.00
Wild Bouquet	60.00

Spooner

Chrysanthemum Sprig, green, pink, and gold, sgd "Northwood"	115.00
Georgia Gem, gold trim	65.00
Louis XV	85.00
Maple Leaf, gold dec	100.00
Wild Bouquet, dec	130.00

Sugar, cov

Intaglio, green dec	125.00
Louis XV	55.00
Victoria, floral dec	150.00
Winged Scroll	135.00

Table Set, cov butter, creamer, cov

sugar, and spooner, Louis XV	350.00

Toothpick Holder

Jefferson Optic, souvenir	50.00
Punty Band, rose dec	65.00
Ribbed Drape	100.00

Tumbler

Argonaut Shell	75.00
Cherry and Scale, nutmeg stain . . .	70.00
Little Gem, green dec	60.00

Water Set, pitcher, six tumblers, 7 pcs

Intaglio, green and gold trim	575.00
Inverted Fan and Feather	900.00

Wine

Beaded Swag, marked "Heisey" . . .	35.00
Honeycomb	60.00

CUT GLASS, AMERICAN

History: Glass is cut by the process of grinding decoration into the glass by means of abrasive-carrying metal wheels or stone wheels. A very ancient craft, it was revived in 1600 by Bohemians and spread through Europe, to Great Britain, and to America.

American cut glass came of age at the Centennial Exposition in 1876 and the World Columbian Exposition in 1893. The American public recognized American cut glass to be exceptional in quality and workmanship. America's most significant output of this high quality glass occurred from 1880 to 1917, a period now known as the "Brilliant Period."

About the 1890s some companies began adding an acid-etched "signature" to their glass. This signature may be the actual company name, its logo, or chosen symbol. Today, signed pieces can command a premium over unsigned pieces since the signature clearly establishes the origin.

However, caution should be exercised in regard to signature identification. Objects with forged signatures have been in existence for some time. To check for authenticity, run your finger tip or finger nail lightly over the area with the signature. As a general rule, a genuine signature cannot be felt; a forged signature exhibits a raised surface.

Many companies never used the acid-etched signature on the glass and may or may not have affixed paper labels to the items originally. Dorflinger Glass and the Meriden Glass Co. made cut glass of the highest quality, yet never acid-etched a signature on the glass. Furthermore, cut glass made before the 1890s was not signed. Many of these wood polished items, cut on blown blanks, were of excellent quality and often won awards at exhibitions.

Consequently, if collectors restrict themselves to signed pieces only, many beautiful pieces of the highest quality glass and workmanship will be missed.

References: E. S. Farrar & J. S. Spillman, *The Complete Cut & Engraved Glass Of Corning,* Crown Publishers [Corning Museum of Glass monograph],1979; J. Michael Pearson, *Encyclopedia Of American Cut & Engraved Glass,* Volumes I to III, published by author, 1975; Albert C. Revi, *American Cut & Engraved Glass,* Thomas Nelson, Inc., 1965; Martha Louise Swan, *American and Engraved Glass,* Wallace-Homestead, 1986; H. Weiner & F. Lipkowitz, *Rarities In American Cut Glass,* Collectors House of Books, 1975.

Collectors' Club: American Cut Glass Association, 1603 SE 19th, Suite 112, Edmond Professional Bldg., Edmond, OK 73013. *Hobstar* (10 times a year).

Museums: The Corning Museum of Glass, Corning, NY; High Museum of Art, Atlanta, GA; Huntington Galleries, Huntington, WV; Lightner

Museum, St. Augustine, FL; Toledo Museum Of
Art, Toledo, OH.

Basket, handle
  6 x 4¼ x 6″, diamond mitres, diamond
    points, small stars, pie crust rim,
    star base **225.00**
  8½ x 8½″, hobstars, double twist han-
    dle **425.00**
  14″, Spillane pattern, sgd Libbey,
    sabre mark **650.00**
Bell, 6″, Kalana Lily pattern, Dorflinger **100.00**
Biscuit Jar, cov
  5 x 6½″, arches, fans, small thumb-
    prints, vertical mitres, star bottom . **110.00**
  6½″, stars, fans, mitres, star bottom,
    SP rim, and reeded bail handle . . **120.00**
Bitters Bottle, 8½″, thumbprint cutting
  on shoulders, oval panel cut around
  base, side wreath etched "Bitters,"
  multi-faceted stopper **85.00**
Bonbon, 6″ d, triangular, Jewel pattern,
  handle, matching underplate, Clark . **150.00**

**Bowl, 5″ d, tab handles, Sinclaire
Glass, sgd, $100.00.**

Bowl
  6¼ x 2¾″, star, diamond, and swag
    mitres, pleated rays, piecrust rim,
    heavy blank **85.00**
  8″
    Buzz saw, fan, and fern variant,
      side cut edge, scallops **140.00**
    Glenda pattern, sgd Libbey **350.00**
    Hobstars and fans, sawtooth edge **85.00**
    Pinwheels and fan, scalloped ser-
      rated edge **115.00**
  8 x 4″, Radiant Star pattern, 6″ snow-
    flake center, allover cut, sgd Hins-
    berger **325.00**
  8¼″, deep cut, chain of hobstars, six
    point star, fold-in scalloped serrated
    rim **275.00**
  8½″, sq, Checkerboard pattern **350.00**

9″
  Hobstars, repouss SS rim marked
    Gorham **525.00**
  Maple City pattern, notched prism **300.00**
  Millicent pattern, sgd Hawkes . . . **250.00**
  Pinwheel, fan, and crosshatch,
    scalloped sawtooth rim **150.00**
10″
  Hobstars, dandelions, and butter-
    flies, scalloped serrated rim, sgd
    ST **375.00**
  Hobstars, single stars, and fern,
    scalloped sawtooth rim **350.00**
  17½ x 11¾″, oblong, ornate, hob-
    stars, nailhead, fan, stars, and
    cane, scalloped sawtooth rim **850.00**
Bread Tray
  Brilliant Period, 11½ x 8″ **475.00**
  Harvard pattern, 13½ x 8½″, intaglio
    cut center **115.00**
  Star and Feather pattern, 12 x 7½″,
    sgd Libbey **275.00**
Butter Dish, cov
  Harvard type pattern with florals . . . **315.00**
  Hobstars and prisms, blown blank . . **475.00**
Candlesticks, pr
  10½″, butterfly, rose, leaves, teardrop
    stem **275.00**
  12″, engraved over body, foot, and
    bowl, large teardrop stem, sgd Lib-
    bey **475.00**
Candy Dish, 4½″, hobstar within hobstar
  pattern, three corners, pedestal **175.00**
Carafe
  6¼ x 8″, pineapple and fan, notched
    panel neck, bulbous multi-rayed
    base **100.00**
  6¾ x 7¼″, hobstar within hobstar,
    fans, diamond fields, notched panel
    neck, multi-rayed base **115.00**
Castor Set, 8½″ h, four sq bottles, waffle
  pattern, Chippendale style SP stand **235.00**
Celery Dish
  11″, intaglio cut strawberries, center
    hobstar, sgd Hawkes **175.00**
  11¼ x 5⅛″, intaglio cut flowers and
    butterflies, polished leaf sprays,
    notched and scalloped rim **65.00**
  12 x 4″, fold-in, notched prism encir-
    cling oblong hobstar, serrated edge **200.00**
Celery Vase, 6½″, hobstars and fans . **250.00**
Cheese Dome, 7 x 7″, geometric cut-
  tings, 10″ d underplate **600.00**
Cheese and Cracker, 9½″ d, 4½″ h,
  Flute and Panel pattern, Sinclaire . . **265.00**
Clock
  4 x 6″, Russian pattern **225.00**
  5½ x 4″, Harvard pattern **600.00**
Cologne Bottle
  5″, pinwheel and flashed fan, cut hol-
    low stopper, sgd Clark **150.00**
  7 x 3″, Colonial pattern, Dorflinger . . **140.00**

Compote

6 x 5″, pinwheel, fan, and hobstars, six sided flared and scalloped base **100.00**

6 x 8″, hobstars, fan, and cane, eight sided teardrop stem, hobstar base, scalloped sawtooth rim, sgd Clark **200.00**

8″, Geometric pattern, intaglio, sgd Tuthill **325.00**

10½ x 8½″, Ambrosia, hobstars, fan, vesica variant, feather and strawberry diamond, 24 point hobstar base **650.00**

Condiment Bottle, chain of hobstars around top and bottom, engraved flowers and stars, SS cap **70.00**

Cordial, Princess pattern, sgd Libbey . **65.00**

Cordial Set, Notched Prism pattern, cranberry to clear **450.00**

Creamer and Sugar

Hobstar, fan, and cane, hobstar in base, scalloped rim, notched handles **150.00**

Intaglio, 7″, applied blue handles and base, sgd Libbey, pr **275.00**

Nailhead, hobstar, and fan, sgd Hawkes **150.00**

Box, hinged cov, Feather Stars, Heinz Brothers, c1900, $250.00.

Cruet

Art Deco, 8 paneled neck, horizontal wing flare cutting, tall flared stopper **35.00**

Hobstars and fans, orig stopper, notched handle, sgd Fry **165.00**

Petticoat, strawberry diamond, fan, and stars, hobstar base, triple notched handle, faceted stopper . **100.00**

Wheel cut petal flower, cane cut center, polished leaf sprays, rayed base, multi-faceted stopper, notched handle, panel neck **55.00**

Decanter

9½″, sq, chamfered corners, zipper,

fan, vesica, multi-faceted stopper, pr **350.00**

12″

Morning glory vine, deep cut, ten panels, painted stopper, cut leaves **125.00**

Pinwheel pattern **200.00**

13½″, Harvard and Floral pattern, bowling pin shape **435.00**

15″, deep intaglio engraved flowers and leaves, honeycomb faceted neck and stopper, bowling pin shape **125.00**

Dresser Box

4½ x 3 x 3″, large hobstar on top with expanding rays, prisms around lid, hinged **165.00**

8½ x 5½″, blown-out, hobstars and fan, hinged SS rim **1,100.00**

Dresser Tray, Sheraton pattern, 10 x 7″ oval, engraved medallions, triple mitre-cut bands alternating with strawberry diamond bands, sgd Hawkes **200.00**

Ferner

7¼ x 4″, hobstar in pinwheel, feathering between hobstar base, three small feet, metal liner **125.00**

8 x 4″, Harvard pattern sides, 3″ d flower center, small flowers, sgd Clark **245.00**

8½ x 4½″, Star and Feather pattern, peg legged, sgd Libbey **245.00**

Finger Bowl, 4¾″ d, 2¾″ h, Brilliant Period, Lotus pattern, Eggington **85.00**

Flower Center, 12″ d, Glenwood pattern, large hobstar base, sgd Bergen **1,225.00**

Goblet

Brunswick pattern, 6″ h **115.00**

Cross hatch and fan, cut six sided stem, star base **50.00**

Millicent, 7″ h **75.00**

Ice Bucket, Marlboro pattern, two handles, matching underplate, Dorflinger **1,450.00**

Ice Cream Set, Jewel pattern, 17 x 10″ tray, ten matching serving dishes, sgd "Libbey" **1,475.00**

Ice Cream Tray

11½ x 8″, Brilliant Period cutting **175.00**

14¼ x 7½″, deeply cut hobstars, prism, and nailhead **375.00**

Inkwell, 1⅜″ sq, polished bottom and sides, SP hinged filigree lid, stand and fancy pen rest **55.00**

Jewelry Box, 7 x 7″, heart shape, Russian cut sides, diamond cut on center top **600.00**

Jug, 9½″, cross cut diamond and fan, ornate handle, matching stopper **365.00**

Juice Tumbler

3½″, hobstars, cross-cut diamond and fan **40.00**

3⅞", Brunswick pattern, chain of hobstars, zipper type beading and flute, sgd Hawkes **75.00**

4", pinwheel, hobstars, fan, and mitre-cutting, flaring rim **25.00**

Knife Rest

Hobstars, fans, and crosshatching, 5½" **85.00**

Notch and Prism pattern **45.00**

Ladle, teardrop and notched handle, cut hobstars and fan **575.00**

Lamp

13" h, boudoir, mushroom shade, prisms, wheel cut flowers, polished leaves **385.00**

23" h, 10" d shade, ornate hobstars, cane, flashed fan, step-cut and prism stem, scalloped sawtooth base **2,800.00**

Loving Cup, three handles

8½", hobstars, fans, and strawberry diamonds, hobstar base, pedestal, honeycomb handles **3,250.00**

9 x 10", Block pattern **750.00**

Mayonnaise, hobstar, nailhead diamonds, and fans, matching underplate **245.00**

Medicine Bottle, hobstars, strawberry diamond, notched prism, hollow stopper **175.00**

Mint Tray

4½", pinwheel and fan, scalloped serrated rim, five panel standard . . . **75.00**

6" d, hobstars and nailhead, sawtooth and scalloped edge **100.00**

Napkin Ring, Brilliant Period cutting . . **85.00**

Nappy, intaglio cut tulip type flowers and butterflies, polished leaf spray, notched rim, ring handle **55.00**

Orange Bowl, 8" deep, Rayed Points pattern **225.00**

Perfume Bottle

4" l, lay down type, curved, int. stopper, ornate SS top **85.00**

12" l, Russian pattern, Gorham SS cap **265.00**

Pin Tray, 9", split vesica, star, rays, and floral **115.00**

Pitcher

7", Strawberry Diamond pattern, bulbous **225.00**

8⅛", Brilliant Period, hobstar within hobstar, notched strawberry fields, fans, double notched handle, rayed base **175.00**

9½", Brilliant Period, pinwheel, fans, and hobstars, triple notched handle **300.00**

9¾", emerald green cut to clear, notched prism pattern, applied clear handle, marked Sterling top, emb floral dec **475.00**

9⅞", tankard, pinwheel, nailhead, and

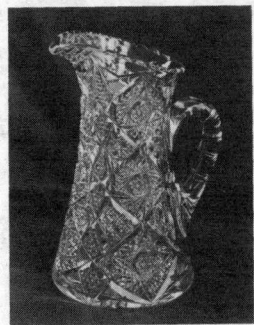

Pitcher, 10" h, cluster, O. F. Eggington, Corning, NY, c1910, $500.00.

hobstars, step-out spout, sgd Libbey **250.00**

12", tankard, swirled notched prism, SS rim marked Tiffany **450.00**

14", punties and chain of hobstars, hobstar base, triple notched handle **375.00**

14½", bulbous, notched prisms and hobstars, hobstar base, beaded SS top marked Wilcox **650.00**

Plate

10", star center surrounded by radiant threads, four assorted floral panels, alternating vintage and cut diamond panels, sgd Sinclaire **325.00**

10¼", Rosaceae, large hobstar center, intaglio cut floral and leaves surrounding star, chain of hobstars at rim, sgd Tuthill **700.00**

11½", service, Russian-type center, elaborate scalloped cutout rim . . . **925.00**

12", pinwheels and hobstars, scalloped serrated rim **250.00**

Powder Jar

4½ x 3¾", diamond mitres, star base, star cut lid, piecrust rim, knob finial **75.00**

5" d, Murillo pattern, butterflies and flowers, hinged, sgd Pairpoint . . . **245.00**

Punch Bowl, 14 x 13", two part, hobstars, cane, vesica, and fan, scalloped serrated rim and base, sgd with star in circle **1,400.00**

Punch Cup

Prism pattern **40.00**

Russian, hobstar foot **60.00**

Rose Bowl, engraved chrysanthemums, Sinclaire **125.00**

Salt, master, Parisian pattern, paperweight type, Dorflinger **95.00**

Spooner

Arlington pattern, 4½", Unger Bros . **200.00**

Brilliant Period, two handles **120.00**

Sugar Shaker
  5", pear shape, hobstars, thumbprint,
    notched prisms, SS top **175.00**
  5½", sq, Norwegian heavy cut, bev-
    eled diamonds, block base, blue
    enamel and vermeil screw on top,
    marked **175.00**
Syrup Pitcher
  Brilliant Period, 5½", allover hobstars,
    rows of hexagonal buttons in cross
    hatching, cut fans, cut notched
    handle and rayed base **200.00**
  Vertical notched prisms, SS hinged lid **120.00**
Tobacco Jar, 6 x 4", hobstars, large
  stopper with hobstar **350.00**
Toothpick Holder
  Chain of hobstars, strawberry dia-
    mond and fan, pedestal base,
    rayed foot **135.00**
  Fluted diamonds **40.00**
Tray
  6 x 9", Hunts Royal **225.00**
  10 x 7½", Colonna pattern, chain of
    hobstars, crosshatched triangle,
    star, strawberry diamond and fan,
    sgd Libbey **375.00**
  10½ x 17½", oblong, Kimberly pat-
    tern, large six point star surrounded
    by hobstars and fan, scalloped
    sawtooth rim, sgd Libbey **950.00**
  11 x 8 x 2", buzzsaws and fan, caning,
    sgd Libbey **125.00**
  11 x 8½", Corinthian pattern, Mt
    Washington **565.00**
  12", Venetian pattern, chain of hob-
    stars, star, strawberry diamond split
    vesicas and fan, sgd Hawkes . . . **1,250.00**
  13", round, six deeply cut entwined
    circles, alternating notched prisms,
    hobstars, and nailhead, scalloped
    rim, sgd Clark **1,550.00**
  14 x 8", Hobstar cluster **350.00**
Tumbler, water
  Brilliant Period, overall cutting, 24
    point star base, sgd Hoare **80.00**
  3⅞", pinwheel, diamond window-
    panes, deep mitres, star base, 9 oz
    blank, set of 6 . . . . **175.00**
Vase
  5⅜", purple cut to clear, allover
    grapes and leaves, notched 4¾" d
    rim, clear base, polished pontil . . **185.00**
  8", Brilliant Period, corset shape,
    scalloped and serrated rim, 12
    point rayed base **100.00**
  8½", Brilliant Period, bud, SS base . **75.00**
  11½", Millicent pattern, glass knob,
    SS foot, Hawkes **250.00**
  12"
    Brilliant Period, sgd Hawkes **225.00**
    Carolyn pattern, sgd Clark **375.00**
    Harvard pattern, ruby cut to clear,

      cross-cut diamond, fan, and
        strawberry diamond, Libbey . . . **750.00**
    Hobstars, bull's eye, notched
      prism, 24 point hobstar in base,
      scalloped serrated top **200.00**
    Lotus pattern, chain of hobstars,
      flashed fan, St Louis diamond,
      star, strawberry diamond and
      fan, Eggington **400.00**
    Russian and Pillar pattern, star but-
      ton, and swirl **900.00**
    Strawberry Diamond pattern, bud . **125.00**
  13", Block pattern, 3" swirl over 16
    point hobstar base **275.00**
  14", New York pattern, trumpet
    shape, ruffled free form rim, sgd
    Hoare **280.00**
  14½"
    Harvard pattern, three alternating
      panels of intaglio cut flowers, sgd
      Clark **225.00**
    Hobnail, flattened bulbous form,
      large hobstars, strawberry dia-
      mond and fan, paneled neck,
      scalloped rim **2,100.00**
  16", Easter pattern, trumpet shape,
    hobnail, flute, and fan, sgd Hawkes **500.00**
  20", Nassau pattern, engraved flow-
    ers, cane, hobstar, star, and straw-
    berry diamonds, Hoare **1,600.00**
Water Set, pitcher and tumblers
  Brilliant Period, sgd Libbey, 5 pcs . . **500.00**
  Butterfly and Daisy pattern, 4 pcs . . **250.00**
  Flowers, butterflies, polished leaf
    sprays, multi-rayed base, double
    notched handle, c1914, sgd Hall-
    mark, 6 pcs **300.00**
  Hobstar in pinwheel, fans, multi-rayed
    base, double notched handle and
    rim, 4 pcs **210.00**
  Poppy pattern, split vesicas of hob-
    stars and fan, star bases, double
    notched handle, sgd Tuthill, 7 pcs **1,100.00**
  Queens pattern, chain of hobstars,
    bull's eye and fan, sgd Hawkes, 10
    pcs **1,325.00**
Whiskey Jug, 5 x 8", Japan pattern,
  strap handle, sgd Fry **825.00**
Wine
  4", Hawkes, set of 11 . . . . **575.00**
  4¼", Diamond & Fan pattern, cran-
    berry to clear cross cut **150.00**

CUT VELVET

History: Several glass manufacturers made cut
velvet during the late Victorian era, c1870–1900.
An outer layer of pastel color was applied over a
white casing. The piece then was molded or cut
in a ribbed or diamond shape in high relief, ex-

posing portions of the casing. The finish had a satin velvety feel, hence the name "cut velvet."

Bottle, 8″, ribbed, shaded blue, white lining	165.00
Creamer	
3¼″, bulbous, DQ, blue, white lining, applied white satin glass handle	200.00
5¼″, butterscotch	100.00
Cruet, 5½″ h, blue, clear applied handle, blue stopper, shiny	250.00
Pitcher	
8″, blue, Honeycomb pattern, Webb	350.00
8½″ h, pink, sq mouth, frosted reeded twisted handle, rosettes and neck ring	425.00
Rose Bowl, 3¼″ d, egg shape, crimped top, DQ, rose, white lining	150.00
Tumbler, 3¾″ h, ribbed, medium pink, lighter striping	75.00

Vase, 7½″, ribbed, undulating crimped top, pink, white int., $225.00.

Vase	
6″, stick shape, blue	90.00
6½″, stick shape, DQ, rose, white lining	200.00
7″, gourd shape, peachblow, DQ	100.00
7⅛″, bulbous, pink, DQ	150.00

CZECHOSLOVAKIAN ITEMS

History: Objects marked "Made in Czechoslovakia" were produced after 1918 when the country claimed its independence from the Austro-Hungarian Empire. The people became more cosmopolitan, liberated, and expanded their scope of life. Their porcelains, pottery, and glassware reflect many influences.

A specific manufacturer's mark may be identified as being much earlier than 1918, but this only indicates the factory existed in the Bohemian or Austro-Hungarian Empire period.

Reference: Ruth A. Forsythe, *Made in Czechoslovakia,* Richardson Printing Corp., 1982.

Barber Bottles, pr, 7½″ h, amethyst ground, white, orange, and gold raised enamel daisy and dot pattern, $250.00.

GLASS

Box, 3 x 4″, cov, cut glass, engraved	40.00
Inkwell, 3¼ x 3¼″, clear, figural, sitting Scotty dog, SP collar, marked	65.00
Necklace	
Caramel, beveled glass, chrome links, Art Deco	35.00
Green, cut cubes, 15″, marked	65.00
Perfume Bottle	
2 x 2¼″, reticulated ormolu enameled florals, studded blue stones, screw on jeweled top, long dabber	55.00
5½″, pink cut glass, frosted floral stopper	50.00
8½″, amber, 8 panel cut, waisted, amber stopper	110.00
Vase	
6″ h, cased, blue ext., red ruffled top, marked	25.00
7⅛″ h, jack-in-the-pulpit, orange, black sponged design, sgd	48.00

POTTERY AND PORCELAIN

Bowl, 4″, crackle, hp floral dec	30.00
Candy Dish, multicolored spatter, black feet	45.00
Creamer, 4½″ h, cat handle, marked "Souvenir of Irish Hills, Michigan," and "Made in Czechoslovakia"	25.00
Figure	
Cockatoo, 17″, yellow and orange	135.00
Moose Head, high glaze, tan and green, marked	35.00

Pickle Dish, 9 x 4½", pierced handle, floral medallions, green leaves, red berries on white ground, gold trim, marked 18.00

Pin Dish, Pierrot, black and white 80.00

Plate, 10", Art Deco maiden, black and yellow, 1920s 50.00

Seafood Set, figural, crab, 5 pcs 65.00

Water Set, 9¾" pitcher, four tumblers, Art Deco pattern, red, green, and yellow, sgd "Ditmar Urbach" 100.00

DAVENPORT

History: John Davenport opened a pottery in Longport, Staffordshire, England in 1793. His ware was of high quality, light weight, and cream colored with a beautiful velvety texture.

The firm made soft-paste (Old Blue), lustre trimmed ware, and pink lustre with black transfer. There have been pieces of Gaudy Dutch and Spatterware found with the Davenport mark. Later Davenport became a leading maker of ironstone and early flow blue. His famous "Cyprus" pattern in mulberry became very popular. His heirs continued the business until the factory closed in 1886.

Reference: Susan and Al Bagdade, *Warman's English & Continental Pottery & Porcelain, 1st Edition,* Warman Publishing Co., Inc., 1987.

Biscuit Jar, 6½", Imari dec, SP cov and bail, c1870c 140.00

Bowl and Underplate, red flowers, green leaves, c1840 . . . . 60.00

Butter Pat, flow blue dec 18.00

Compote, 9", hp, pink flowers, gold trim, c1830 . . . . 90.00

Cup and Saucer
Clifford pattern 95.00
Green wreath, gold trim 60.00
Japan pattern, c1870 . . . . 45.00

Cup Plate, Friburg pattern 25.00

Dessert Service
20 pcs, multicolored floral sprays, scroll surrounds, gilt stylized foliage on green border, puce printed mark, c1850 . . . . 1,000.00
21 pcs, eleven dessert plates, two 7¼" sauce boats and stands, six shaped serving dishes, white ground, green and white floral dec, c1825 . . . . 1,200.00

Dish, 7⅜" d, rose dec, red and gold, marked "Davenport" 50.00

Ewer, 9", multicolored, flower dec, c1830 . . . . 175.00

Fruit Bowl, ftd, 2½ x 9½", hp roses, gold trim, c1865 . . . . 135.00

Gravy Boat, blue and white flowers . . 85.00

Pitcher, 6", tan transfer, serpent handle 175.00

Plate
7½", hexagonal, emb floral border, green transfer of child and cat . . . 85.00
8¾", Chantilly pattern, white with blue and orange floral dec, imp "Davenport," red anchor mark 50.00
9"
Hand painted, water scene in center, green border, gold scalloped edge, marked 38.00
Maroon and gold border, gold medallion center, marked "Davenport," anchor, c1850 . . . . 25.00

Platter
9 x 12½", Cyprus, mulberry 100.00
10 x 9", blue Oriental scene, c1820 . 75.00
10⅜" x 13⅝", Amory pattern, flow blue, rect, chamfered corners, incised "Amory," anchor mark 165.00

Teapot, Imari design 140.00

Tray, 11 x 9", cloverleaf design, c1850 130.00

Tureen, 10½", Cyprus pattern, mulberry 100.00

Urn, 6", white with blue and gold trim, classic figure, handled 250.00

Vegetable Dish, Berry pattern, imp signature, anchor mark 50.00

DECOYS

History: Carved wooden decoys, used to lure ducks and geese to the hunter have become widely recognized as an indigenous American folk art form in the past several years.

Cup and Saucer, 3¾" d cup, 6" d saucer, Amoy pattern, flow blue, incised name and anchor mark, $70.00.

Many decoys are from the 1880–1930 period when commercial gunners commonly hunted over rigs of several hundred decoys. Many fine carvers also worked through the 1930s and 1940s.

The value of a decoy is based on several factors: (1) fame of the carver, (2) quality of the carving, (3) species of wild fowl—the most desirable are herons, swans, mergansers, and shorebirds, and (4) condition of the original paint (o.p.).

The inexperienced collector should be aware of several facts. The age of a decoy, per se, is usually of no importance in determining value. Since very few decoys were ever signed, it will be quite difficult to attribute most decoys to known carvers. Anyone who has not examined a known carver's work will be hardpressed to determine if the paint on one of his decoys is indeed original.

Repainting severely decreases a decoy's value. In addition, there are many fakes and reproductions on the market and even experienced collectors are occasionally fooled.

Richard A. Bourne Co., Inc., Hyannis, Massachusetts, is one of the leading auctioneers of decoys.

Decoys listed below are of average wear unless otherwise noted. o.p. indicates original paint.

Reference: Henry A. Fleckenstein, Jr., *American Factory Decoys*, Schiffer Publishing; Art, Brad and Scott Kimball, *The Fish Decoy*, Aardvark Publications, Inc., 1986; Carl F. Luckey, *Collecting Antique Bird Decoys: An Identification & Value Guide*, Books Americana, 1983.

Periodicals: *Decoy Hunter Magazine*, 901 North 9th, Clinton, IN 47842, bimonthly; *Decoy Magazine*, P.O. Box 1900, Montego Bay Station, Ocean City, MD 21842, quarterly publication; *The Wild Fowl Art Journal*, Ward Foundation, 655 South Salisbury Blvd, Salisbury, MD 21801.

American Bittern, Thomas W Carlock, carved, painted, re-glued beak	**650.00**
Black Duck	
A Elmer Crowell, Iver Johnson Supreme brand on bottom	**5,250.00**
Clark Madara, hollow carved, head turned to left, old paint	**650.00**
Rhoades Truax, hollow carved, orig paint, branded "H W Cain" on back	**475.00**
Unknown Maker, hollow carved, head tucked down, 3 pc body construction, old paint	**575.00**
Black-Breasted Plover	
George Boyd, New Hampshire, orig paint, minor wear	**3,000.00**
John Dilley, Long Island, painted feather detail	**3,750.00**
Rhoades Truax, orig paint	**1,150.00**
Blue-Breasted Plover, unknown maker, Long Island, carved wings, split tail, old paint	**300.00**
Bluebill Drake	
G W Stevens Factory, Weedsport, NY,	

orig paint, replacement eyes, branded "G W Stevens"	**1,200.00**
Ira Hudson, orig paint	**1,500.00**
Bluebill Hen, Harry V Shourds, hollow carved, old paint, restored bill	**350.00**
Blue-Wing Teal Drake, solid body, branded " C H G C," attributed to John Blair, worn mostly to natural wood	**1,600.00**

Broadbill Drake, Standard Grade, glass eyes, Mason Decoy Co, Detroit, MI, $225.00.

Brant	
Lloyd Parker, hollow carved, old repaint	**800.00**
Nathan Cobb, Virginia, hollow carved, slightly turned head and cocked down, "V" detail, c1860	**5,500.00**
Nathan "Rowley" Horner, hollow carved, orig paint	**2,700.00**
Roy Maxwell, hollow carved, orig paint, from H W Cain rig	**1,600.00**
Bufflehead Drake, Doug Jester, orig paint	**275.00**
Canada Goose	
Dude Crane, hollow carved, orig paint	**600.00**
Harry V Shourds, carved, swimming position, shoe button eyes, paint worn mostly to natural wood	**1,050.00**
Hudson Family, flying, scratch feather paint, open bill, orig paint, needs re-gluing	**2,400.00**
Unknown Maker, hollow, carved wings, 3 pc body construction, old paint	**550.00**
Clapper Rail, Thomas W Carlock, carved feather detail	**400.00**
Common Loon, slightly turned head, sgd on bottom	**375.00**
Curlew	
A Elmer Crowell, Cape Cod, MA, carved feathers, wire legs, orig paint, oval brand on bottom, restored wing tips	**9,000.00**
Cobb Island area, carved F in bottom, orig paint	**2,600.00**
McNair, carved, raised wing tips, sgd, age split	**800.00**

Obidah Verity, carved eyes, deeply incised wings, orig paint, replaced bill **5,300.00**

Dowitcher, William Bowman, Long Island, carved wings, raised wing tips, split tail, slightly cocked head, muscled detail, orig paint, replaced bill . **7,500.00**

Eider Drake, Maine, sway back style, carved bill, inlet neck, patina, white worn paint, chip of wood missing on neck **1,100.00**

Eider Hen, Unknown maker, Maine, carved bill, inlet neck, orig paint, minor wear **900.00**

Goldeneye Drake, Harry V Shourds, hollow carved, orig paint **500.00**

Green-Wing Teal Hen, Wildfowler, balsa body, orig paint **300.00**

Gull, Bill Cranmer, hollow carved, orig paint, weathered **425.00**

Herring Gull, unknown maker, carved wings, detailed feather carving back and tail area, c1900 . . . . **2,400.00**

Kingfisher, Thomas Carlock, carved feathers **250.00**

Mallard Drake, Ira Hudson, flying, carved, scratch feather painting . . . **4,600.00**

Mallard Hen, premiere grade, swirl feather painting, branded "Fuller" on bottom, orig paint, minor wear and age splits **850.00**

Mergansers, unknown maker, Cape May, NJ, carved eyes, graceful carved body, old paint, c1890, pr . . . **6,250.00**

Pied Bill Grebe, Jim Polite, carved minnow in mouth, sgd and dated 1974 . **325.00**

Pintail Drake

Harry M Shourds, hollow carved, repainted **1,000.00**

John Blair, hollow carved, repainted **2,600.00**

McNair, hollow carved, sgd **800.00**

Wendell Gilley, Maine, sgd base . . . **850.00**

Wildfowler, cedar, hollow body, orig paint **275.00**

Red-Breasted Mergansers, Daniel Horn, old paint, age split **1,650.00**

Redhead, John McLoughlin, hollow carved, won 3rd place, 1968 International Decoy Contest in Davenport, Iowa, pr **2,100.00**

Ringbill Drake, Mark Whipple, orig paint **750.00**

Roothead Heron, unknown maker, old paint, 19th C **1,300.00**

Ruddy Turnstone, John Horn, orig paint **800.00**

Shoveller Hen, Bob Schaber **275.00**

Snowy Egret, branded "H Conklin" on bottom **400.00**

Squaw Drake, hollow carved, sgd "McNair" **850.00**

Swan, Madison Mitchell, solid body, keel, orig paint **2,900.00**

White Winged Scoter, Joe Lincoln, MA, canvas cov, professional restored bill **1,200.00**

Widgeon Hen, hollow carved, branded "W P Patton" on bottom, orig paint, attributed to John Blair **4,500.00**

Yellowlegs

Unknown Maker, Longport, NJ, tack eyes, graceful form, orig paint . . . **550.00**

Rhoades Truax, orig paint **650.00**

William Southard, carved wings and eyes, replaced bill **450.00**

DEDHAM POTTERY

History: Alexander W. Robertson established the Chelsea Pottery in Chelsea, Massachusetts, in 1860. In 1872 it was known as the Chelsea Keramic Art Works.

In 1895 the pottery moved to Dedham, and the name was changed to Dedham Pottery. Their principal product was gray crackleware dinnerware with a blue decoration, the rabbit pattern being the most popular. The factory closed in 1943.

The following marks help determine the approximate age of items: (1) Chelsea Keramic Art Works, "Robertson" impressed, 1876–1889; (2) C.P.U.S. impressed in a cloverleaf, 1891–1895; (3) Foreshortened rabbit, 1895–1896; (4) Conventional rabbit with "Dedham Pottery" stamped in blue, 1897; (5) Rabbit mark wtih "Registered", 1929–1943.

Reference: Lloyd E. Hawes, *The Dedham Pottery And The Earlier Robertson's Chelsea Potteries,* Dedham Historical Society, 1968.

Bowl

6", Rabbit **130.00**

7⅝", Rabbit **285.00**

9", Rabbit, wide border on outside rim **445.00**

Butter Dish, Rabbit **200.00**

Candlestick, Azalea, pr **175.00**

Creamer

2½", Rabbit **265.00**

3¼", Rabbit **225.00**

4⅞", "Morning and Night," pre 1929 **300.00**

Creamer and Sugar, Berry pattern . . . **400.00**

Cup and Saucer

Elephant **375.00**

Polar Bear **110.00**

Rabbit **150.00**

Celery Dish, Elephant **150.00**

Jug, 5", Azalea **120.00**

Mug, Rabbit **200.00**

Mush Set, 3½" cup, matching saucer, Rabbit **275.00**

Paperweight, 2¾", Rabbit **275.00**

Pitcher
Azalea **325.00**
Morning & Evening, rooster, hens,
and sun **575.00**

Plate, 8½" d, Grape pattern, $100.00.

Plate
6", Pond Lily **75.00**
6⅛"
Rabbit **100.00**
Turtle **265.00**
7¾", Turkey, post 1929 .... **175.00**
8¼", Moth, pre 1929 .... **350.00**
8⅝"
Magnolia, pre 1929 .... **100.00**
Tapestry Lion, pre 1929 .... **600.00**
8½"
Crab, pre 1929 .... **525.00**
Horse Chestnut, pre 1929 ...... **150.00**
Poppy, blue with white ground ... **400.00**
8⅝"
Lobster, post 1929 .... **425.00**
Poppy, white with blue ground ... **450.00**
Rabbit, pre 1929 .... **100.00**
Snow Tree, pre 1929 .... **225.00**
Turtle **395.00**
8¾", Rabbit, unusual short and
chubby rabbit, post 1929 .... **150.00**
9¾", Turkey, pre 1929 .... **350.00**
10"
Duck, light blue, pre 1929 ...... **250.00**
Grape **110.00**
Iris **125.00**
Lobster, sgd "Maude O. Daven-
port" between head and claws,
pre 1929 .... **700.00**
Pineapple, raised mark "CPUS" . **540.00**
Polar bear **185.00**
Rabbit
Dark blue, post 1929 .... **235.00**
Dark color, pre 1929 .... **175.00**
10⅛", Rabbit, raised **175.00**

12½"
Crab **260.00**
Rabbit **175.00**
Salt Shaker, 2¾", Rabbit **135.00**
Sugar, cov, 4½", Rabbit, double handles **225.00**
Tile
Magnolia **110.00**
Swan **140.00**
Vase
8", Volcanic, brown, green, and yel-
low, marked "HCR, Dedham Pot-
tery" **275.00**
8½"
Crackle glaze, marked "HCR and
BW, Dedham Pottery," blue this-
tle mark **600.00**
Volcanic, dark green, with brown,
blue, and light green, marked
"HCR and BW, Dedham Pottery" **300.00**

DELFTWARE

History: Delftware is pottery of a soft red clay
body with tin enamel glaze. The white, dense,
opaque color came from adding tin ash to lead
glaze. The first examples had blue designs on a
white ground. Polychrome examples followed.

The name originally applied to pottery made in
the region around Delft, Holland, beginning in the
16th century and ending in the late 18th century.
Tin came from the Cornish mines in England. By
the 17th and 18th centuries English potters in London, Bristol, and Liverpool were copying the glaze
and designs. Some designs unique to English potters also developed.

In Germany and France, the ware is known as
Faience and in Italy as Majolica.

Reference: Susan and Al Bagdade, *Warman's
English & Continental Pottery & Porcelain, 1st Edition,* Warman Publishing Co., Inc., 1987.

Reproduction Alert: Much souvenir Delft-type
material has been produced in the late 19th and
20th centuries to appeal to the foreign traveler.
Don't confuse these modern pieces with the older
examples.

Basket, 8¾", round, pierced interlaced
border, vase with flowers, table of
shrubs int., trailing flower branches
ext., Liverpool, c1760 .... **1,350.00**
Bottle, 9⅛", blue and white, vase of peacock feathers and fungi on pierced
rock surrounded by peonies, prunus,
chrysanthemums, and bamboo, tall
neck, blue border, leaf scrolls at rim,
mounted as lamp base, tall wood
base, Irish, c1755 .... **500.00**
Bowl, 10¾", manganese, floral spray
within diaper border, ochre line rim,
Lambeth, c1780 .... **450.00**
Butter Tub, 4½", polychrome, harbor

Charger, 12¾" d, blue and white windmill scene, $175.00.

scene on cov and sides, gold finial and handles, marked "VA," Dutch, c1740–60 .... 350.00
Charger, 13½", shaped border, chinoiserie foliage, arched border panels . 700.00
Dish, 13½", polychrome, center with row of flutes, painted yellow, blue, and green, bird perched among flowers, robust floral border on fluted and everted rim, Dutch, c1690 .... 825.00
Pastille Burner, 5¼", cottage with sign, "Inde Rokende Moor" 325.00
Plaque, 15", winter canal scene, sgd "Bonneville" 100.00
Plate
  9", blue and white, chrysanthemum on pierced rock work, "A. V., 1753" in center, Bristol, 1753 .... 600.00

12", powder blue ground, cartouche with Oriental seated beneath flowing tree, border with four leaf shaped panels of trailing branches, brown line rim, Bristol, c1750 .... 365.00
Platter, 15¼", octagonal, blue and white, shrubs and bamboo in fenced garden, pagoda on rocky, shrubby island, trellis and flowerhead border, ochre line rim, blue "F" mark, Dublin, c1765 .... 775.00
Punch Bowl, polychrome, blue ext. with two rows of iron-red, blue, and green floral roundels alternating with reserved iron-red leaves and astral devices, blue band, hatchwork borders, int. with blue floral spray, border of alternating scrollwork branches, blue edged rim, Bristol, c1725 .... 3,000.00
Tobacco Jar, cov, blue and white, pipe smoking Indian seated beside cargo, one labeled "St Domingo," other labeled "St Vincent," barrel of tobacco leaves and parcel monogrammed "VOC," Dutch ships in distance, brass cov, blue "B:P" marks, Dutch, mid 18th C, pr 3,850.00
Vase, 14⁵⁄₁₆", cov, octagonal beaker shape, blue and white, trellis diaper ground, large panel of Chinaman watching bird, smaller quatrefoil panels of leaves and floral panels, seated lion finial, Dutch, mid 18th C, pr 2,000.00
Wall Pocket, 7¾", blue and white, molded masks, scrolls, and foliage, Liverpool, c1770 .... 365.00

DEPRESSION GLASS

History: Depression glass is a glassware made during the period of 1920–40. It was an inexpensive machine-made glass, produced by several companies in various patterns and colors. The number of pieces within a pattern also varied.

Depression glass was sold through variety stores, given as premiums, or packaged with certain products. Movie houses gave it away from 1935 until well into the 1940s.

Like pattern glass, knowing the proper name of a pattern is the key to collecting. Collectors should be prepared to do research.

References: Gene Florence, *The Collector's Encyclopedia of Depression Glass, Eighth Edition,* Collector Books, 1988; Gene Florence, *Elegant Glassware of the Depression Era, Third Edition,* Collector Books, 1988; Gene Florence, *Very Rare Glassware Of The Depression Years,* Collector Books, 1987; Carl F. Luckey and Mary Burris, *An Identification & Value Guide to Depression Era Glassware, Second Edition,* Books Americana, 1986; Mark Schliesmann, *Price Survey, Second Edition,* Park Avenue Publications, Ltd, 1984; Hazel Marie Weatherman, *1984 Supplement & Price Trends for Colored Glassware Of The Depression Era, Book 1,* published by author, 1984.

Periodical: The Daze, Box 57, Ottisville, MI 48463.

Collectors' Club: National Depression Glass Association, Inc., P.O. Box 11128, Springfield, MO 65808.

Reproduction Alert: Send a self addressed stamped business envelope to *The Daze* and request a copy of their glass reproduction list. It is one of the best bargains in the antiques business.

Additional Listings: See *Warman's Americana & Collectibles* for more examples.

CAMEO, Ballerina or Dancing Girl, Hocking Glass Co., 1930–34. Made in crystal, green, pink, and yellow.

	Crystal	Green	Pink	Yellow
Bowl				
4¼", sauce	4.75	42.50	—	—
5½", cereal	4.00	18.00	—	—
7¼", salad	—	35.00	—	—
8¼", master berry	—	22.00	—	—
Butter Dish, cov	—	125.00	—	645.00
Cake Plate, 10", 3 legs	—	18.00	—	—
Candlesticks, pr, 4"	—	65.00	—	—
Candy Dish, cov, 4"	—	48.00	375.00	52.00
Champagne, 4"	—	20.00	—	—
Compote, 5"	—	18.00	—	—
Console Dish, 11", 3 legs. . .	—	50.00	20.00	—
Cookie Jar	—	38.00	—	—
Cream Soup, 4¾"	—	48.00	—	—
Creamer.	—	15.00	—	12.00
Cup and Saucer	—	15.00	—	10.00
Goblet, 6"	—	35.00	—	90.00
Ice Bucket	—	100.00	375.00	175.00
Mayonnaise, ftd.	—	20.00	—	—
Pitcher, 8½"	215.00	35.00	—	—
Plate				
6", sherbet.	2.25	3.00	45.00	12.00
7", salad	3.75	7.00	25.00	4.00
8", luncheon	4.50	7.50	25.75	5.50
9", dinner	—	12.00	40.00	—
10½", grill	—	35.00	—	12.00
Platter	—	15.00	32.50	8.00
Salt and Pepper Shakers, pr	—	50.00	—	—
Sherbet	—	32.00	24.00	18.00
Sugar.	—	14.00	12.00	12.00
Tumbler, 3 oz, juice, ftd	—	38.00	—	—
Vegetable, 10", oval.	—	17.00	—	—
Wine, 3½".	—	42.00	—	—

CAPRICE, Cambridge Glass Co, 1940s through early 1950s. Made in crystal, blue, amber, amethyst, pink, emerald green, cobalt blue, moonlight blue, and white. Prices listed are for crystal and blue, the most commonly found colors. Some molds (marked with an *) have been sold to Summit Art Glass Co. and are being reproduced. The reproductions are sometimes marked, and usually a little heavier in weight.

	Crystal	Blue		Crystal	Blue
* Ashtray, 3"	6.00	12.00	* Mayonnaise, cov, underplate,		
Bonbon, 6", oval, ftd	15.00	24.00	6½".	25.00	65.00
Bowl			Pitcher, 32 oz	75.00	245.00
8", 4 ftd.	25.00	45.00	Plate		
10", 4 ftd	18.00	30.00	6½", bread and butter . . .	8.00	12.00
* Butter Dish, cov, ¼ lb.	185.00	—	8½", luncheon	14.50	21.00
Cake Plate, 13", ftd	125.00	225.00	*9½", dinner	35.00	100.00
Candy Dish, 6", cov.	42.50	70.00	* Relish, 12", 3 pt, rect.	38.50	85.00
Cigarette Box, cov, 3½ x			Salt and Pepper Shakers, pr,		
2¼".	15.00	25.00	ball shape	35.00	75.00
Coaster, 3½"	10.00	18.00	Saucer	2.50	4.00
* Creamer, medium	8.00	15.00	Sugar, medium	10.00	15.00
Cup	10.00	14.00	Tray, 9", oval.	18.00	32.00
Decanter, stopper	130.00	185.00	Tumbler, 5 oz, ftd	20.00	40.00
Marmalade, cov	40.00	115.00	Vase, 6"	50.00	95.00

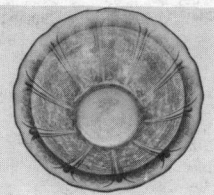

Left, Cameo, 6″ d plate, yellow, $12.00; center, Caprice, creamer and sugar, medium size, blue, $30.00; right, Florentine No. 1, bowl, 8½ x 2½″, pink, $24.00.

EMPRESS, A. H. Heisey Glass & Co., Blank #1401. Made in crystal, Flamingo pink, Sahara yellow, Moongleam green, cobalt and Alexandrite. Dolphin feet are characteristic of this extended table service.

	Crystal	Flamingo	Sahara	Moongleam	Alexandrite
Ashtray	30.00	55.00	75.00	175.00	165.00
Bonbon, 6″	10.00	15.00	18.00	25.00	—
Bowl					
5″, preserve	12.00	18.00	24.00	28.00	—
9″, floral, flared	30.00	70.00		50.00	—
10″, oval, dessert, two					
handles	32.00	45.00	58.00	65.00	—
Candy, cov, dolphin ftd, 6″ . .	32.50	80.00	85.00	115.00	—
Cream Soup, sq liner	15.00	25.00	28.00	40.00	150.00
Creamer, ftd	15.00	30.00	25.00	42.00	185.00
Cup	12.00	24.00	30.00	35.00	90.00
Mayonnaise, cov, ftd	20.00	35.00	45.00	50.00	150.00
Mustard, cov	28.00	58.00	62.00	75.00	—
Oyster Cocktail	15.00	20.00	25.00	30.00	—
Plate					
6″, sq, bread and butter, . .	5.00	8.00	12.00	15.00	32.50
8″, round, luncheon.	8.50	15.00	20.00	32.00	58.00
10½″, dinner	35.00	95.00	95.00	115.00	—
Relish, 7″, pt, handle	20.00	45.00	48.00	72.00	—
Salt and Pepper Shakers, pr.	40.00	75.00	100.00	115.00	225.00
Sandwich Tray, 12″, center					
handle	32.00	45.00	55.00	65.00	—
Saucer	2.00	6.00	14.00	15.00	—
Sugar, ftd, 3 handles	12.00	18.00	25.00	28.50	185.00
Tumbler, 8 oz	12.00	28.00	35.00	40.00	—
Vase, 9″, ftd	55.00	80.00	95.00	135.00	500.00

FLORENTINE NO. 1, Old Florentine, Poppy No. 1. Hazel Atlas Co., 1932–35. Made in cobalt blue, crystal, green, pink, and yellow. Limited production in cobalt blue.

	Crystal	Green	Pink	Yellow
Ashtray	8.00	18.00	25.00	36.00
Bowl				
5″, berry	6.75	9.75	14.00	8.00
6″, cereal	8.00	8.00	12.00	10.00
8½″, master berry	15.00	18.00	24.00	20.00
Coaster, 3¾″	14.00	15.00	24.00	20.00
Creamer, plain edge	8.00	10.00	12.00	9.75

	Crystal	Green	Pink	Yellow
Cup	4.25	7.00	9.00	8.00
Pitcher, 6½", ftd	45.00	55.00	65.00	45.00
Plate				
6", sherbet	5.25	5.00	4.75	4.00
8½", salad	6.75	7.00	8.75	9.75
10", dinner	15.00	15.00	14.00	15.00
10½", grill	9.25	9.00	10.50	12.00
Platter, 10½", oval	15.00	15.00	22.50	18.00
Salt and Pepper Shakers, pr	25.00	28.00	45.00	40.00
Saucer	2.00	2.00	3.00	3.00
Sherbet	8.00	9.00	8.75	9.75
Sugar, plain edge	9.00	4.75	10.00	8.00
Tumbler, 4¾", 10 oz, water,				
ftd	12.00	12.00	18.00	15.00

GLORIA, Cambridge Glass Co. Known as 3400 Line, dinnerware introduced 1930. Made in crystal, yellow (known as Gold Krystol), amber, pink, emerald green, and Heatherbloom. Add 50% for dark emerald green pieces and 75% for Heatherbloom.

	Crystal	Colors		Crystal	Colors
Basket, 6", two handles	12.00	18.00	Oyster Cocktail	10.00	15.00
Bonbon, 5½", ftd	15.00	18.00	Pickle, 9", tab handle	15.00	20.00
Bowl			Pitcher, 80 oz	100.00	185.00
6", cereal	8.00	16.00	Plate		
9½", salad, two handles . .	45.00	75.00	6", bread and butter	8.00	12.00
10", two handles	32.00	58.00	8½", luncheon	8.50	12.00
Cake Plate, 11", sq, ftd	45.00	115.00	9½", dinner	35.00	50.00
Candy Box, cov	42.50	70.00	Relish, 12", 5 pt	25.50	45.00
Cheese Compote, 11½"			Salt and Pepper Shakers, pr,		
cracker plate, tab handle .	25.00	42.50	glass top, tall	30.00	65.00
Cream Soup, sq saucer	15.00	28.00	Saucer	2.00	4.00
Creamer, ftd	10.00	15.00	Sugar, ftd	12.00	18.00
Cup	15.00	24.00	Sugar Shaker, glass top	75.00	150.00
Ice Bucket, metal handle and			Syrup, ftd	40.00	55.00
tongs	35.00	85.00	Tumbler, 8 oz, ftd	12.00	20.00
Mayonnaise, liner, ladle	35.00	55.00	Vase, 12"	45.00	80.00

HOLIDAY, Buttons & Bows, Jeanette Glass Co., 1947–49. Made in pink and a limited number of pieces in iridescent.

	Pink		Pink
Bowl		Pitcher, 6¾"	24.00
5⅛", berry	6.00	Plate	
7¾", flat soup	26.50	6", sherbet	3.00
8½", master berry	15.00	9", dinner	9.00
Butter Dish, cov	35.00	Platter	8.50
Cake Plate, 10½", 3 legs . . .	62.50	Saucer	2.50
Candlesticks, pr, 3"	50.00	Sherbert	5.00
Creamer, ftd	8.50	Sugar, cov	12.00
Cup	5.00	Tumbler, 4", ftd	25.00

JUNE, Fostoria Glass Company, 1928–44. Made in crystal, azure blue, topaz yellow, and rose pink. Topaz yellow and rose pink have approximately the same values.

	Crystal	Blue	Topaz
Ashtray	20.00	40.00	30.00
Baker, 9", oval	30.00	60.00	45.00
Bottle, dressing, SS top	155.00	300.00	250.00
Bowl, 10"	20.00	45.00	35.00
Candy Dish, cov, 3 part	48.00	225.00	75.00
Compote, 7"	20.00	60.00	38.50
Cordial, 4"	40.00	75.00	72.00
Cup, ftd	15.00	25.00	20.00
Grapefruit	25.00	55.00	40.00
Mayonnaise, liner	21.00	40.00	40.00
Mint Bowl	10.00	20.00	15.00
Parfait	20.00	50.00	45.00
Plate			
6", bread and butter	4.00	6.00	5.00
8¾", luncheon	6.50	12.25	12.00
10", grill	15.00	32.00	25.00
10¼", dinner	20.00	48.50	38.00
Platter, 12"	20.00	48.00	42.00
Relish, 8½"	15.00	20.00	18.00
Sauce Boat	32.50	100.00	70.00
Saucer	3.50	7.50	6.00
Sugar, ftd	12.00	24.00	20.00
Tray, 11", center handle	20.00	40.00	32.00
Tumbler, 5¼", ftd	15.00	25.00	22.50
Whipped Cream Pail	60.00	135.00	115.00

LORAIN, Basket, No. 615, Indiana Glass Co., 1929–32. Made in crystal, green, and yellow.

	Crystal	Green	Yellow
Bowl			
6", cereal	22.00	24.00	40.00
7¼", salad	25.00	27.00	35.00
8", master berry	75.00	75.00	100.00
Creamer, ftd	25.00	24.00	20.00
Cup	9.00	9.00	10.00
Plate			
5½", sherbet	4.00	3.75	7.50
7¾", salad	8.75	8.75	10.00
8¾", luncheon	16.50	12.75	20.00
10¼", dinner	30.00	35.00	38.00

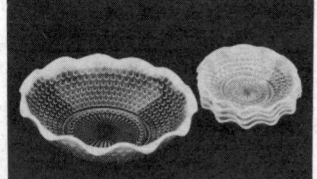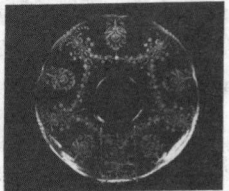

Left, Madrid, pitcher, 5¾" h, 32 oz, juice, amber, $30.00; center, Moonstone, master berry bowl, 9½ x 2½", $10.00, and small berry bowl, $7.50; right, Orchid, bowl, 13", floral, $65.00.

	Crystal	Green	Yellow
Platter, 11½″	20.00	18.00	28.00
Relish, 8″, 4 part	6.75	15.00	20.00
Saucer	3.50	3.50	4.00
Sherbet	15.00	15.00	28.00
Sugar, ftd	12.00	10.00	12.00
Tumbler, 4¾″, ftd	15.00	14.75	18.50

MADRID, Federal Glass Co., 1932 and 1939. Made in amber, blue, crystal, green, and pink. This pattern was reissued by Federal in 1976 and by Indiana Glass in the 1980s as "Recollection." The reissue was made using some of the original molds and with some variations to the original styles, colors, and marks.

	Amber	Blue	Crystal	Green	Pink
Ashtray, 6″ sq	130.00	—	120.00	75.00	—
Bowl					
5″, sauce	5.00	7.50	5.00	4.75	—
8″, salad	12.00	65.00	15.00	—	—
10″, oval, vegetable	14.00	20.00	14.00	15.50	14.00
Butter Dish, cov	65.00	—	65.00	72.50	—
Cake Plate, 11½″	15.00	—	165.00	22.50	10.00
Candlesticks, pr, 2¼″	18.00	—	15.00	—	15.00
Coaster	30.00	—	25.00	—	—
Cookie Jar	35.00	—	35.00	—	32.50
Cream Soup, 4¾″	15.00	—	15.00	—	—
Creamer,	6.00	14.00	5.00	8.75	—
Cup	4.00	12.00	3.75	6.50	5.75
Marmalade, cov	—	25.00	12.00	15.00	—
Pitcher, 80 oz, ice lip	50.00	—	48.00	175.00	—
Plate					
6″, sherbet	2.75	8.00	2.75	4.00	3.25
7½″, salad	8.00	12.75	8.00	8.00	8.50
8⅞″, luncheon	4.50	18.00	4.50	8.00	8.00
10½″, dinner	25.00	45.00	25.00	28.50	—
Salt and Pepper Shakers,					
3½″, ftd	60.00	115.00	60.00	85.00	—
Saucer	2.50	6.00	3.50	3.75	2.75
Sherbet	5.50	12.00	5.50	8.75	—
Sugar	25.00	75.00	25.00	28.50	—
Tumbler					
3⅞″, 5 oz	10.00	20.00	12.00	20.00	—
5½″, 10 oz, ftd	18.00	—	18.00	30.00	—

MOONSTONE, Anchor Hocking Glass Corp., 1941–46. Made in crystal with opalescent hobnails.

	Crystal		Crystal
Bonbon, heart shape	7.50	Goblet, 10 oz, water	15.00
Bowl		Plate	
5½″, berry	7.50	6¼″, sherbet	2.00
6½″, fruit, crimped, handle	5.00	8″, luncheon	6.50
7¾″, flat soup	8.50	10″, dinner	15.00
9½″, crimped	10.00	Relish, cloverleaf	10.00
Candlesticks, pr	15.00	Salt and Pepper Shakers, pr	45.00
Candy Dish, cov	15.00	Saucer	3.75
Cigarette Box, cov	16.50	Sherbet	5.25
Cologne Bottle	9.00	Sugar, cov	8.00
Creamer	7.50	Tumbler, ftd	15.00
Cup	5.50	Vase, bud	8.50

NAVARRE, Fostoria Glass Company, 1937–80. Made primarily in crystal.

	Crystal		Crystal
Bonbon, 7⅜", ftd	20.00	8½", luncheon	10.00
Bowl		9½", dinner	25.00
5", handle	12.00	Salt and Pepper Shakers, pr,	
10", oval, floating garden .	35.00	ftd.	65.00
Candlesticks, pr, 4"	20.00	Saucer	3.50
Celery Tray, 9"	18.50	Sherbert	12.00
Champagne, 6 oz	13.00	Sugar, ftd	10.00
Cheese Compote	25.00	Sweetmeat Bowl, 6", sq. . . .	15.00
Creamer, ftd	10.00	Tid Bit Tray, 8¼"	18.00
Cup	12.50	Torte Plate, 16".	48.00
Finger Bowl	18.00	Tumbler, 10 oz	15.00
Goblet	16.00	Vase, 5"	45.00
Pickle, 8"	20.00	Wine	25.00
Plate			
6", bread and butter	5.00		

ORCHID, A. H. Heisey & Co., 1940–1957. Made only in crystal.

	Crystal		Crystal
Ashtray, 3"	24.00	Goblet	40.00
Bell, dinner	120.00	Marmalade, cov	85.00
Bowl		Pitcher, 73 oz	150.00
7", salad	40.00	Plate	
8½", flared.	50.00	6", bread and butter	12.00
10½", floral, ftd	80.00	8", luncheon	15.00
Butter Dish, cov	125.00	10½", dinner	65.00
Candlesticks, pr, 2 lite, 5". . .	100.00	Salt and Pepper Shakers, pr,	
Celery Tray, 12"	55.00	ftd.	65.00
Cheese and Cracker Server,		Saucer	8.50
14" plate	125.00	Sherbet	25.00
Compote, 6", low standard. .	60.00	Sugar, ftd	30.00
Creamer	28.00	Tumbler, 12 oz	55.00
Cup	42.50	Vase, 8", ftd, bud.	125.00
Decanter, pint	275.00	Wine	65.00
Finger Bowl	50.00		

THUMBPRINTS, Pear Optic, Federal Glass Co., 1929–30. Made in green.

	Green		Green
Bowl		Salt and Pepper Shakers, pr	15.00
4¾", berry	2.50	Saucer	1.75
5", cereal.	2.75	Sherbet	4.00
8", berry	7.00	Sugar, ftd	5.00
Creamer, ftd	6.50	Tumbler	
Cup	2.50	4", 5 oz	4.00
Plate		5", 10 oz	4.50
6", sherbet.	2.00	5½", 12 oz.	5.75
8", luncheon	2.50	Whiskey, 2¼", 1 oz	4.00
9¼", dinner	5.00		

DISNEYANA

History: Walt Disney and the creations of the famous Disney Studios hold a place of fondness and enchantment in the hearts of people throughout the world. The release of "Steamboat Willie" featuring Mickey Mouse in 1928 heralded an entertainment empire.

Walt and his brother, Roy, showed shrewd business acumen. From the beginning they licensed the reproduction of Disney characters in products ranging from wristwatches to clothing. In 1984 Donald Duck celebrated his 50th birthday, and collectors took a renewed interest in material related to him.

The market in Disneyana has been established by a few determined dealers and auction houses. Hake's Americana and Collectibles of York, PA offers several hundred Disneyana items in each of their bimonthly mail and phone bid auctions. Sotheby's collector carousel auctions often include Disney cels, and Lloyd Ralston Toys auctions include Disney toys.

References: Robert Heide & John Gilman, *Cartoon Collectibles,* 1984 (only covers Disney material); Richard Schickel, *The Disney Version: The Life, Times, Art and Commerce of Walt Disney,* Avon Books, 1968; Michael Stern, *Stern's Guide to Disney Collectibles,* Collector Books, 1989; Tom Tumbusch, *Tomart's Illustrated Disneyana Catalog and Price Guide,* Vols. 1, 2, and 3, Tomart Publications, 1985.

Archives: Walt Disney Archives, 500 South Buena Vista Street, Burbank, CA 91521

Collectors' Club: Mouse Club, 2056 Cirone Way, San Jose, CA 95124

Additional Listings: See *Warman's Americana & Collectibles* for more examples.

Advisor: Ted Hake

Alice In Wonderland
    Dish Set, plastic, pink, impressed images, plates, tray, pr 2" h teacups and saucers, 2 sets knives, forks, and spoons, orig box, unused, Plastic Art Toy Corp of America, c1951, set 50.00
    Pocketbook, 5 x 7½ x 2", red, white, blue, and yellow plaid fabric, Alice chasing White Rabbit scene on emb front flap, red plastic strap, small black "100" on side of dress 40.00
Bambi
    Coloring Book, 8 x 11", brown flocked body on cov, unused, Whitman, 1966 . . . . 25.00
    Figure, 4 x 7 x 8", , "Evan K Shaw" foil label on back, c1940 . . . . 125.00
    Puzzle, 14 x 22" complete, Bambi sleeping next to mother, forest animals looking on, boxed, Jaymar . 15.00

Cinderella
    Bank, 6½" h, ceramic, yellow star in one hand, pastel coloring, pressed "Cinderella" and "1950 copyright" on back 45.00
    Sand Pail, 4" h, plastic, dark blue, Cinderella head and mice oval decal on side, red litho tin handle with Disney characters, incised Donald Duck head on bottom and Marx toys copyright 15.00
    Wrist Watch, white dial, pink letters and hands, plastic crystal, expansion band, US Time, 1950s 30.00
Davy Crockett, bag, 5 x 8½", vinyl, black, white, and tan fabric cov Davy and hat, Frontierland fort and Indian tepee scene, zipper with brass ring, 18 blue ink names on back, c1955 . 30.00
Donald Duck
    Bank, 3½ x 4½ x 7", plaster, carnival style figure, holding coin in hand, green base, c1950s 25.00
    Mug, 3" d, 3½" h, ceramic, white, glazed, raised image, early 1960s 15.00
    Patch, 2 x 3", oval, Donald with arms extended, blue edge, yellow ground, c1950s 8.00
    Toy, 7" h, rubber, squeaker, stamped Disney copyright "W D P" and "H H," c1950s 20.00
Dumbo
    Bank, 4", metal, three dimensional figure, standing, gray paint, red, white, and blue striped collar, blue and white hat, tin trap with locking mechanism, no key, "Made In USA" and Disney copyright on base 200.00
Goofy
    Figure, 6" h, vinyl, one day-glow pink, other yellow, Marx, pr 5.00
    Miniature, 1⅞" h, bisque, brown red, and green outfit, 1930s 30.00
Fantasia, souvenir book, 9½ x 12½", 32 pg, full color illus and making of the film, 1940 . . . . 40.00
Mickey Mouse
    Figure, 5¼", bisque, with banjo, black string tail missing 250.00
    Handkerchief, 8½" sq, cotton, white, 4 black, white, and orange pictures on corners 20.00
    Mask, 10½ x 12", linen, black and white, adult size 45.00
    Napkin Ring, 2½" l, SP, oval, Mickey's name and impressed full figure on top, c1930s 60.00
    Sand Sifter, 6" d, wire mesh screen, Mickey and Minnie at seashore on edge, tin handle, early 1930s 75.00
    Watch, pocket, 2" d, silvered brass

Hoppity Mickey Mouse, 23″ h, Walt Disney Productions, Sun Products Corp., $50.00.

case, black and white dial with Mickey running, red gloved hands point to numerals, second hand, Disney copyright, late 1960s 45.00

Minnie Mouse

Bowl, 6½″ d, divided, china, white, glazed, 3 sections, 2 transfer pictures, 1 decal, early 1930s 75.00

Container, 3½ x 3½ x 4″, china, heart shape, white, glazed, Minnie reclining on top, marked "Walt Disney Production/Japan" under lid and "Made In Japan" sticker under base, c1970s 10.00

Figure, 3½″, bisque, holding black and gold concertina, orig "Walter E. Disney" copyright sticker under base 40.00

Peter Pan

Figure, seated, green felt tunic, purple base, orig box 20.00

Puppet, hand, 10″ h, soft rubber head, red, white, blue, and green fabric body, felt hands, red bow, Gund label, c1953 .... 20.00

Pinocchio

Glass, 4¾″ h, clear, red illus, 4 line verse on back 15.00

Lunch Box, 5″ d, 6½″ h, tin, red, images on removable lid and sides, swivel handle, 1940 copyright ... 150.00

Puppet, hand, light blue velvet body, yellow velvet hands, three dimensional head, blue cloth bow tie, orig tag, 1939 Disney copyright 75.00

Salt and Pepper, 5″ h, ceramic, figures, one dark blue pants and green hat, other red pants and yellow hat, orig corks, marked "Hand-painted/Japan" under base, pr ... 50.00

Pluto

Figure, 1½ x 7 x 4″, hard rubber, red body, black and white facial details, tail missing, early 1930s 35.00

Puppet, hand, 4 x 5 x 6″, rubber head, fabric body, orig box, Gund, 1950s 20.00

Toy, wind-up, 4 x 10 x 10″, plastic, yellow, holds metal bell in each hand, rings loudly and he rocks back and forth, built-in key, black rubber tail missing, Marx 60.00

Sleeping Beauty, bubble wand, plastic, yellow, star shape wire end for making bubbles, orig bubble formula dried up, 4 x 16″ cardboard package, c1950s 15.00

Snow White

Comic Book, 5 x 7″, full color, 12 pgs, "Mystery Of the Missing Magic," A & P Food Store giveaway, copyright 1958 .... 20.00

Glass, 4¾″ h, clear, black illus, 5 line verse on back 15.00

Handkerchief, 8½″ sq, red, white, blue, and brown image, c1938 ... 15.00

Toothbrush Holder, 2 x 2 x 6″, china, figure, holds one brush, late 1930s 100.00

Three Little Pigs

Ashtray, 3 x 3½ x 3¼″, china, dark blue luster, pigs perched on back edge playing musical instruments, Japanese, early 1930s 75.00

Fan, 7″ h, wood and paper, 11″ w opened, three pigs color picture, green, yellow, and red design borders, brass handle, c1930s 40.00

Tinkerbell, doll, 13″ h, soft rubber, translucent plastic diecut wings with gold sparkles, velvet-like olive green dress, c1955 .... 25.00

Zorro

Flashlight, ½ x ⅞ x 3″, plastic, yellow, diecut, plastic hat and mask when pressed by button fly up to reveal Zorro's face, brass chain, paper label, c1960 .... 15.00

Hat, black straw, black felt mask, black and white chin strap and diecut label 20.00

DOLL HOUSES

History: Doll houses date from the 18th century to modern times. Early doll houses often were handmade, sometimes with only one room. The most common type was made for a young girl to fill with replicas of furniture scaled especially to fit into a doll house. Special sized dolls also were made for doll houses. All types of accessories and styles allowed a doll house to portray any historical period.

References: Flora Bill Jacobs, *Dolls' Houses in America: Historic Preservation in Miniature*, Charles Scribner's Sons, 1974; Donald and Helene Mitchell, *Dollhouses, Past and Present*, Collector Books, 1980; Stille, Eva, *Doll Kitchens 1800–1980*, Schiffer Publishing, 1988.

Blair Whitton (ed.), *Bliss Toys And Dollhouses*, Dover, 1979.

Museums: Margaret Woodbury Strong Museum, Rochester, NY; Washington Dolls' House and Toy Museum, Washington, D.C.

Arcade, folding, bedroom, orig cast iron
   furniture, c1927 . . . .   **400.00**
Bliss
  Four Rooms, two story, litho, wood,
    sides open, 24 x 20″ **1,500.00**
  Four Rooms, three story, litho, wood,
    metal, c1910, 25 x 20″ **1,800.00**
Converse, wood, cottage, hinged front,
   two int. rooms, 12″ **250.00**
Hacker, Christian, Nurnberg, Germany,
   painted, front facade stuccoed, five
   rooms, 2½ story, steepled roof, two
   chimneys, bay window, papered int.,
   FAO Schwarz label, 34″ **500.00**
Marx, metal, orig carton **50.00**
McLoughlin Bros, NY, cardboard, litho,
   folding, two rooms, two story, Victo-
   rian styling, 15 x 16″ **675.00**
Schoenhut
  Two rooms, two stories, wood and
    pressed board, red shingled roof,
    green shutters, decal on base, 16
    x 15 x 11″ **275.00**
  Eight rooms, attic, gray blocks,
    c1917, 28 x 23 x 23″ **1,200.00**
Victorian, country, wood, painted brick,
   four fireplaces, 25 x 21″ **700.00**
Wood
  Butcher Shop, one room, papered
    int., orig counter and bisque
    butcher doll, 13½ x 15 x 5″ **600.00**
  Cottage, one room, stenciled paper,
    red painted roof, black stenciled
    shingles, four turned wooden porch
    pillars, base stenciled as stone
    wall, front porch opens to stenciled
    living room, 8 x 11 x 12″ **200.00**

DOLLS

History: Dolls have been children's play toys for centuries. Dolls also have served other functions. During the 14th through 18th century doll making was centered in Europe, mainly in Germany and France. The French dolls produced in this era represented adults and were dressed in the latest couturier designs. They were not children's toys.

During the mid-19th century, child and baby dolls, made in wax, cloth, bisque, and porcelain, were introduced. Facial features were hand painted; wigs were made of mohair and human hair. They were dressed in baby or children's fashions.

Marks from the various manufacturers are found on the back of the head, neck, or back area. These marks are very important in identifying the doll and date of manufacture.

Doll making in the United States began to flourish in the 1900s with names like Effanbee, Madame Alexander, Ideal, and others.

References: Johana Gast Anderton, *More Twentieth Century Dolls From Bisque to Vinyl, Volume A-H, Volume I-Z, Revised Edition,* Wallace-Homestead, 1974; John Axe, *The Encyclopedia of Celebrity Dolls,* Hobby House Press Inc., 1983; Jean Bach, *Collecting German Dolls*, Main Street Press, 1983; Paul Fellows, *Doll Auction Prices*, Wallace-Homestead, 1985; Jan Foulke, *8th Blue Book Dolls and Values*, Hobby House Press Inc. 1987; Wendy Lavitt, *American Folk Dolls*, Alfred Knopf, Inc., 1982; Wendy Lavitt, *Dolls*, Alfred A. Knopf, 1983; Robert W. Miller, *Wallace-Homestead Price Guide To Dolls, 1986–87,* Wallace-Homestead, 1986; Patricia R. Smith, *Modern Collector's Dolls, Editions 1, 2, 3, 4, 5,* Collector Books, 1973, 1975, 1976, 1979, 1984; Patricia R. Smith, *The World of Alexander-kins,* Collector Books, 1985; Marjorie Victoria Sturges Uhl, *Madame Alexander, Ladies of Fashion,* Collector Books, 1982.

Periodicals: *Doll Reader*, Hobby House Press, Inc., 900 Frederick Street, Cumberland, MD 21502; *Dolls The Collector's Magazine*, Acquire Publishing Co., 170 Fifth Avenue, NY, NY 10010.

Collector's Clubs: Madame Alexander Fan Club, P. O. Box 146, New Lenox, IL 60451; United Federation of Doll Clubs, 2814 Herron Lane, Glenshaw, PA 15116.

Museums: Margaret Woodbury Strong Museum, Rochester, NY; Yesteryears Museum, Sandwich, MA.

Additional Listings: See *Warman's Americana & Collectibles* for more examples.

Adams, Emma, 29″, cloth head, jointed
   cloth body, oil paint features, curly
   brown hair, blue eyes, closed mouth,
   knitted gray and white wool dress,
   white cotton drawers, red cotton
   stockings, American, c1886 . . . . . .   **600.00**
Amberg, Louis, 14″, Orange Blossom,
   composition shoulderhead, cloth
   body, composition arms and legs,
   painted features, blue eyes, molded
   orange cap, orig orange dress,
   matching pantaloons, replaced shoes
   and socks, marks: L.A. & So., 1924 .   **325.00**
Arranbee Doll Co.
  10″, storybook, composition, swivel
    neck, jointed arms and legs,
    molded and painted hair and eyes,
    orig costume, c1930 . . . .   **150.00**

13", solid dome bisque head, composition body, painted hair, sleep eyes, recostumed, marks: Arranbee 375.00

Averill, Georgene

12", International, cloth, mask face, painted features, yarn hair, orig clothes, wrist tag, and box 60.00

16", infant baby, composition head, soft cloth body, composition hands, flange neck, painted hair, sleep eyes, closed mouth, marks: Genuine/Madame Hendren/Doll/522/ Made in USA 135.00

Belton

14", solid dome bisque socket head, flattened top, three stringing holes, early jointed body, straight wrists, cupped hands, new blonde mohair wig, brown bulging paperweight eyes, closed mouth, pierced ears, feathered brows and painted lashes, couturier type coat dress, matching bonnet, marks: 106 6 .. 800.00

23", solid dome bisque socket head, flattened top, three stringing holes, very pale bisque face, rosy cheeks, jointed composition body, straight wrists, brown mohair wig, blue bulgy paperweight eyes, feathered brows, painted lashes, open mouth, pierced ears, redressed, marks: 12 .... 2,100.00

Borgfeldt, George, 15", bisque socket head, five pc jointed composition body, blonde human hair wig, blue sleep eyes, feathered brows and painted lashes, open mouth, antique christening gown, lace trim petticoat, marks: GB 12 .... 425.00

Bru, 16", bisque swivel neck shoulder head, kid body, bisque lower arms, leather over wood upper arms, wood lower legs, blonde Rembrandt style wig over cork pate, blue paperweight stationary glass eyes, open mouth, pierced ears, white baby clothing, nursing mechanism, marks: Bru Jne/ 6 on head, Bru Jne/N 6T on shoulder, Bebe Bru Bte S. G. D. G./Tout Contrefacteur sera saisi et pour suivi/conformet a la Loi on paper label 4,000.00

Cameo Doll Co., 17", Little Annie Rooney, composition, jointed arms and legs, yellow yarn braids, painted round eyes, watermelon smile, painted black stocking legs, molded yellow shoes, gray velvet jacket, pink plaid skirt, c1920 .... 200.00

Chase, Martha, 16½", boy, cloth, oil paint features, molded head features, body jointed at shoulders and hips, applied ears, blonde hair, curl on forehead, blue eyes, closed mouth, black velvet suit, paint badly crazed, minor paint loss 450.00

Davis, M. S., 12", Gussie Decker, leather, center seam, black painted features, c1902 .... 325.00

Delcroix, H., 12½", bisque socket head, composition jointed French body, straight wrists, orig blonde mohair wig, blue paperweight eyes, shaded and feathered brows, pierced ears, closed mouth, antique blue silk dress, marks: PAN 2, c1887 .... 3,800.00

Demalcol, 10½", bisque socket head, composition five pc body, straight legs, brown mohair wig, brown glass side glancing inset googly eyes, painted lashes, closed mouth, orig white dress, green felt trim, green felt shoes and hat, orig box, marks: Demalcol 5/0 incised on head, My Playmate Doll Germany dress tag 1,200.00

Effanbee, 13½" h, Suzanne, brown sleep eyes, light hair, orig red and white dress, straw hat, four outfits and orig suitcase, bracelet tags, $200.00.

Effanbee

14", Skippy, composition, jointed at neck, shoulders, and hips, yellow molded and painted hair, blue painted side glancing eyes, closed mouth, redressed, marks: Effanbee Skippy P. L. Crosby 275.00

16", Patsy Joan, composition five pc body, straight legs, molded and painted hair, green sleep eyes, real and painted lashes, closed mouth, orig yellow dress, bonnet, and undergarments, shoes and stockings, orig heart bracelet, orig soiled box, marks: Effanbee Patsy Joan **700.00**

Ellis, Joel, 12″, wood, mortise and tenon joints, metal hands and feet, painted features, molded blonde hair, aqua painted boots, partial black paper band around waist, recostumed, light crazing and wear to paint **375.00**

French, 22″, bisque socket head, French wooden and composition body, brunette mohair wig, silk replica of orig dress, marked "A. Marque" in script on head and "12" in red ink script, c1899, $38,000.00.

French Fashion, unidentified maker
18″, bisque flange neck head, kid lined shoulderplate, wooden articulated body jointed at shoulders, elbows, hips, and knees, swivel waits, carved fingers and toes, blonde mohair wig over cork pate, blue glass inset eyes, closed mouth, antique green silk gown, beaded black trim, matching hat, marks: B/S on lower back shoulderplate **3,100.00**

18″, bisque socket head, kid lined shoulderplate, wooden articulated body, human hair wig over cork pate, blue glass paperweight eyes, painted lashes, closed mouth, pierced ears, antique purple dress, fringed shawl, matching velvet hat, marks: 4 on head and shoulderplate **2,600.00**

20″, bisque socket head, kid lined shoulderplate, kid gusset jointed fashion body, stitched fingers and toes, auburn human hair wig over cork pate, blue glass inset eyes,

closed mouth, pierced ears, light blue cotton two pc gown, unmarked **2,800.00**

Gautler, F. G., 15½″, fashion, bisque swivel head, bisque shoulderplate, kid leather body, brown hair wig, light blue paperweight eyes, closed mouth, pierced ears, marks: F. G. ... **1,250.00**

Greiner Patent, 30″, papier mache shoulderhead, homemade cloth body, painted black hair, cork screw curls to shoulders, blue painted eyes, exposed ears, dark blue floral print dress, varnish removed from face, composition crazed, c1858, marks: paper label "Greiner's Improved/Patent Heads **600.00**

Handwerck, Heinrich, 21″, bisque socket head, ball jointed composition body, brown human hair wig, brown glass sleep eyes, open mouth, teeth, pierced ears, white cotton dress, marks: Heinrich Handwerck-Halbig . **350.00**

Hartmann, Karl, 20″, bisque socket head, ball jointed composition body, auburn human hair wig, blue glass sleep eyes, antique cotton dress, lace trim, marks: H (K1) **275.00**

Hertel and Schwab
13½″, solid dome bisque socket head, composition five pc bent limb baby body, brush stroked hair with molded forelock, blue glass sleep eyes, open mouth, teeth, antique baby dress, knitted sweater, marks: Germany 151 incised on head ... **1,500.00**

18″, solid dome bisque socket head, composition bent limb baby body, separate hands, brush stroked blonde hair, gray glass sleep eyes, open mouth, two painted teeth, recostumed, body repainted, replacement hands, marks: 151 incised on head **375.00**

Heubach, Gebruder
11″, Coquette, bisque shoulderhead, cloth body, composition lower limbs, molded and painted features, black intaglio eyes, open mouth, light blue nylon dress, tiny chip on shoulder, marks: molded ribbon incised 3/0/78 Heubach in sq 50/Germany **250.00**

13″, Indian, bisque shoulderhead, cloth body, bisque lower arms, composition lower legs, black human hair wig, painted intaglio eyes, closed mouth, orig costume, leather jacket, fur collar and pants, high leather boots, marks: Heubach incised in sq, 9457 .... **1,600.00**

Horsman, 10½″, Billiken, molded composition character head, jointed mohair body, laughing face, standup brows, molded topknot, watermelon smile, marks: Copyright the Billiken Company, orig sq label on body ... **225.00**

Ideal

13", Shirley Temple, composition head, five pc jointed composition, straight limbs, blonde curly mohair wig, brown plastic sleep eyes, open mouth, plastic teeth, pleated organdy dress, pin, marks: Shirley Temple on head and torso, Genuine/Shirley Temple/Doll/Registered Pat. Off/Ideal Toy Co. on dress label **175.00**

20", Toni, hard plastic, jointed at neck, shoulders, and hips, dark brown nylon wig, blue sleep eyes, closed mouth, orig dress, orig box and contents **450.00**

Jumeau, Emile

15", bisque head, ball jointed composition French body, jointed wrists, orig brown hair wig, blue stationary glass eyes, closed mouth, pierced ears, red silk dress, matching bonnet, marked DEP and "6" **1,900.00**

16", bisque socket head, ball jointed wood composition French body, blonde mohair wig over cork pate, brown glass paperweight inset eyes, painted lashes, closed mouth, teeth, antique cotton dress, brown leather shoes, marks: Tete Jumeau Depose Bte SGDG 6 stamped in red on head, Jumeau Medaille Paris stamped in blue on torso **2,350.00**

18½", automated, 13" doll, 5" box, bisque socket head, one pc composition torso and legs, wire upper arms, bisque lower arms, blonde mohair wig over cork pate, blue glass inset paperweight eyes, closed mouth, pale green and white silk jacket and skirt, lace and flowered trim, box with small drawer cov in maroon fabric, celluloid fan moves as head turns from side to side, non functioning music box, marks: Depose Tete Jumeau Bte SGDG stamped in red on head .. **3,200.00**

19", bisque socket head, composition French jointed body, straight wrists, orig blonde mohair wig, blue paperweight eyes, closed mouth, applied pierced ears, redressed, one orig shoe, marks: 6 E. J. blue stamp on body, Jumeau, Medaille D'or, Paris **4,650.00**

25", bisque socket head, composition

French jointed body, early straight wrists, strawberry blonde mohair wig over cork pate, long face, blue glass paperweight eyes, painted lashes, blushed upper lips, closed mouth, applied pierced ears, pale green antique dress, matching bonnet, lace and ribbon trim, marks: II on head, Jumeau Medaille Dor Paris stamped in blue on torso . . **16,000.00**

Kamkins, 18", molded mask head, cloth stuffed body, jointed at neck, shoulders, and hips, painted features, short brown mohair wig, painted blue eyes, orig white cotton dress, marks: Kamkins, A Dolly Made To Love on red paper heart on chest **1,100.00**

Kammer and Reinhardt

19", bisque socket head, ball jointed composition body, blonde mohair wig, blue glass sleep eyes, open mouth, teeth, antique lined blue and white silk dress, lace and ruffles trim, matching bonnet, marks: K & R, Simon & Halbig/117n **900.00**

20", character, bisque socket head, jointed composition baby body, worn brown mohair wig, blue sleep eyes, open mouth, tremble tongue, marks: K & R, Simon & Halbig, Germany 126 .... **400.00**

27", Mein Leibling, bisque socket head, composition ball jointed body, dark blonde human hair wig, blue glass sleep eyes, real and painted lashes, closed mouth, antique cotton dress, eyelet trim, straw hat, marks: K & R, Simon & Halbig 117 incised on head, Excelaior Germany stamped in red on rear torso **8,000.00**

J. D. Kestner, 13″, Hilda, bisque socket head, composition bent limb baby body, molded baby features, blue glass sleep eyes, $3,000.00.

Kestner

15″, Gibson Girl, bisque shoulderhead, kid body, bisque lower arms,
cloth lower legs, dark brown mohair
wig over papier mache pate, blue
glass sleep eyes, painted and real
lashes, closed mouth, orig white
cotton blouse with tucks and lace
insets, black skirt, black straw hat
with feathers, marks: 172/1 on
head, remnants of paper label on
torso **1,700.00**

28″, bisque turned shoulderhead, kid
gusseted body, bisque lower arms,
blonde mohair wig, brown glass
sleep eyes, open mouth, teeth,
mauve two pc dress, body weak at
seams, sawdust loss, marks: 698½
Germany #13 .... **500.00**

29″, bisque socket head, wood and
composition ball jointed body,
blonde mohair wig, brown glass
eyes, open mouth, teeth, white cotton baby clothes, marks: stamped
red Germany/6 1′2 .... **475.00**

Kruse, Kathe

16″, molded muslin painted head,
cloth body jointed at shoulders and
hips, painted short brown hair,
brush stroked curls, painted blue-
gray eyes, closed pouty mouth, red
and white cotton dress, marks:
Kathe Kruse and numbers on sole
of foot **1,750.00**

16½″, molded muslin painted head,
cloth body jointed at shoulders and
hips, stitched toes and fingers, separate thumbs, light brown brush
stroked hair, painted brown eyes,
pink romper suit, coat, and matching bonnet, paint flake on tip of
nose **1,850.00**

Kuhnlenz, Gebruder, 24″, bisque socket
head, wood and composition ball
jointed body, brown wig, brown glass
eyes, open mouth, pink dress and
bonnet, white oil-cloth boots, marks:
incised 305/Gbr 165K/9/Germany .. **250.00**

Lenci, 11″, felt, molded head coated
with cellulose covering, cotton torso
and felt limbs, blonde mohair wig,
painted brown eyes, blue dress, purple shawl, wood clogs, yellow felt
goose under arm, marks: purple
stamp **150.00**

Linder, Louis, 10″, papier mache shoulderhead, kid body, wooden limbs,
molded and painted features, black
curly hair, plaid wool jacket, blue and
green plaid trousers, both feet missing **125.00**

Madame Alexander

8″

Alexander-kins, skater, hard plastic, bent knee walker, blonde hair,
blue eyes, orig dress, bonnet,
part orig box, marks: Alexander-
kins dress tag **135.00**

Bride, hard plastic, bent knee,
blonde hair, blue eyes, white tulle
gown, lace trim, veil, marks:
dress tag **250.00**

Little Women, five dolls, bent
knees, orig boxes, clothes, dress
tags, marks: Alexander-kins,
Amy, Meg, Jo, Beth, Marme ... **600.00**

Morocco, hard plastic, bent knee,
dark skin, gold brocade dress,
multi striped taffeta coat, maroon
sash and turban, marks: cloth
dress tag, orig wrist tag and box **225.00**

Southern Belle, blue eyes, powder
blue taffeta gown, lace trim,
matching blue poke bonnet, wrist
tag missing, orig box, marks:
Southern Belle dress tag **250.00**

12″, McGuffy Ana, composition head,
five pc jointed composition body,
blonde mohair plaited wig, blue
sleep eyes, orig tagged clothes,
face badly crazed, marks: Alexander on head **175.00**

Marseille, Armand

13½″, baby, 10½″ d solid dome bisque socket head, five pc bent limb
baby body, painted hair, blue stationary glass eyes, closed mouth,
body repainted, marks: AM/Ger-
many/341/3K incised on head ... **150.00**

14″, My Dream Baby, bisque solid
dome socket head, composition
five pc bent limb baby body, brown
painted baby hair, lightly molded
forelock, blue glass sleep eyes,
open mouth, two bottom teeth,
white baby dress, marks: AM Germany 351k incised on head **375.00**

40″, bisque socket head, ball jointed
composition body, blonde human
hair wig, brown glass sleep eyes,
real and painted lashes, open
mouth, teeth, antique white cotton
dress, eyelet trim, marks: Armand
Marseille Germany 390 incised on
head **1,500.00**

Moss, Leo, 26″, character, child, black,
sculpted papier-mache head, lower
arms and legs, cloth body, very curly
molded hair, brown glass inset eyes,
broad nose, full red lips, white baby
dress, unmarked **5,000.00**

Nancy Ann Storybook Doll

3½″, Christening Baby, hard plastic,

straight baby legs, jointed shoulders, and hips, molded painted yellow hair, closed mouth, marks: Storybook Dolls/USA/Trademark/Reg. 1952 . . . . **25.00**

5″, bisque, one pc body, painted eyes, Cinderella, mark: Story/Book/Doll/USA on back **30.00**

5½″, bisque, one pc body, painted features, Elsie Marley, 1942 . . . . . **25.00**

6″, hard plastic, black sleep eyes, Jeannie, marks: Storybook Dolls/USA/Trademark/Reg. 1952 . . . . . **25.00**

Newell, Edgar G., 24″, fabric mill cutout, cloth, litho printed, flat face, brown hair, blue eyes, white chemise, yellow boots, cotton dress, matching hat, marks: Feb 13, 1900 stamped on soles of boots **325.00**

Nippon, 20″, Hilda-type, bisque socket head, composition five pc bent limb baby body, brown wig, brown glass sleep eyes, open mouth, teeth, recostumed, marks: B9 RE Nippon incised on head **225.00**

Ohlhaver, Gebruder, 14″, bisque socket head, composition bent limb body, brown mohair wig, blue glass sleep eyes, open mouth, teeth, long white baby dress, marks: head incised with quarter circle/Revalo/Germany/2 4 . **200.00**

Perreau Paradise Infants, 18″, fashion, bisque swivel head, bisque shoulderplate, kid leather body, orig wig, blue glass stationary eyes, pierced ears, orig clothes, marks: Perreau Paradise Infants on body **3,500.00**

Putnam, Grace S., Bye Lo Baby

13″, solid dome bisque head, flange neck, cloth body, celluloid hands, lightly painted brown hair, molded forelock, blue glass sleep eyes, closed mouth, white gown and matching slip, non functioning cryer, marks: Copr. by Grace S. Putnam incised on head, Bye-Lo stamped on body **300.00**

16″, solid dome bisque head, flange neck, cloth body, celluloid hands, lightly painted brown hair, molded forelock, blue glass sleep eyes, closed mouth, christening gown and matching bonnet, non functioning crier, marks: Copr. by Grace S. Putnam incised on head, Bye-Lo stamped on body **325.00**

Recknagel, Theodor, 14½″, bisque socket head, ball jointed wood and composition body, brown mohair wig, stationary blue glass eyes, navy blue polka dot dress, marks: incised 1909/DEP/R4oA **150.00**

Schoenau & Hoffmeister

15″, solid dome head, bisque flange neck, cloth body, celluloid hands, blue glass stationary eyes, closed mouth, voice box, long white baby's dress, one eye cracked, marks: Made in Germany/S PB in star H/N.E. **650.00**

30″, bisque socket head, wood and composition ball jointed body, brown mohair wig, blue glass sleep eyes, open mouth, teeth, child's silk dress, marks: incised S PB in star, H/1906/15/Germany **400.00**

Schoenhut

21″, wooden head, wooden spring jointed body, carved hair, blue painted bow on back of head, small hole for cloth bow, painted blue intaglio eyes, closed mouth, recostumed white cotton sailor dress, head professionally repainted, marks: Schoenhut Doll Pat. Jan. 17th, 11, USA & Foreign Countries, incised on torso **1,000.00**

23″, wooden head, wooden spring jointed body, blonde mohair wig, decal eyes, painted open mouth, four painted teeth, orig jersey teddy, marks: oval Schoenhut paper label, Pat. Jan. 17th, 1911, USA **950.00**

Shaker, 12″, bisque shoulder head, kid body, bisque lower arms, blonde hemp wig, brown glass sleep eyes, open mouth, four teeth, cream wool Shaker dress, summer straw hat, dressed in 1908 by Mount Lebanon NY Shakers, marks: 16/0 Germany on head **250.00**

Simon and Halbig

13″, Oriental, bisque olive cast socket head, ball jointed composition body, orig black wig with flowers dec, brown glass sleep eyes, open mouth, teeth, pierced ears, Korea costume, marks: Simon & Halbig/Germany/1329/3 incised on head . **1,000.00**

17″, black, bisque socket head, composition ball jointed body, glued black wig, brown glass eyes, painted lashes, open mouth with teeth, pierced ears, old cotton dress, marks: SH 949 incised on head **575.00**

17½″, Santa, bisque socket head, ball jointed composition body, brown replaced wig, brown glass sleep eyes, open mouth, teeth, pierced ears, recostumed, possible hand replacements, marks: S & H 1249 DEP Santa **500.00**

18", bisque socket head, composition jointed body, orig mohair wig, blue sleep eyes, open mouth, pierced ears, antique dress, peplum jacket, fitted skirt, wired bonnet, ruffled edge, marks: S H 1039 8½ DEP . **625.00**

18", bisque solid dome socket head, two stringing holes, composition and wooden jointed body, replaced brown human hair wig, large brown glass inset eyes, closed mouth, applied pierced ears, white cotton antique dress, tucks and eyelet trim . **3,000.00**

Schmitt et Fils bebe, 28", bisque head, French composition body, orig blue silk outfit, $12,000.00.

Smith, Ella, 14½", Alabama Baby, cloth, oil paint features, molded head features, body jointed at shoulders and hips, brown hair, brown eyes, exposed ears, painted blue boots, brown and gray print romper, paint cracking, nose rub, marks: faint stamp "Mrs S. S. Smith/Manufacturer Of The Indestructible Doll/Alabama . **1,000.00**

Societe Francaise de Bebes et Jouets, 26", toddler, bisque socket head, composition French jointed toddler body, replaced human hair wig, blue glass sleep eyes, open laughing mouth, two molded upper teeth, recostumed in white cotton dress, marks: SFBJ 236 Paris incised on head **3,000.00**

Steiner

11½", Phenix Bebe, bisque head, composition jointed body, straight wrists, brown hair wig, blue stationary glass eyes, open mouth, pierced ears, marks: "82" on head, Bebe Steiner on body **1,850.00**

14½", bisque socket head, composition French jointed body, straight wrists, blonde mohair wig over cardboard pate, blue glass inset eyes, closed mouth, marks: Paris A 7-8 incised on head, Le Parisien stamped in red on head, Bebe Steiner Le Petit Parisien stamped in blue on body **2300.00**

18", bisque socket head, composition and wooden French jointed body, brown human hair wig, blue glass sleep eyes, open mouth, upper and lower teeth, pierced ears, working mama pull strings, dark blue cotton dress, marks: J Steiner Bte SGDG Paris Fire B incised on head, Le Petit Parisien Bebe Steiner stamped in blue on torso **2,250.00**

20½", bisque socket head, ball jointed French composition body, blonde mohair wig over cardboard pate, brown glass inset eyes, closed mouth, pierced ears, white eyelet dress, white leather shoes, marks: J. Steiner/B.S.G.D.G. Paris/C/Le Petit Parisien Bebe Steiner purple stamp on torso **4,100.00**

Swaine & Co., 12", character, bisque socket head, five pc bent limb composition baby body, short cropped blonde mohair wig, brown glass sleep eyes, white lawn toddler dress, brown leather shoes, marks: DIP/3 incised on head, green stamped Geschutz/S & Co./Germany in circle **500.00**

Terri Lee, 16", composition, jointed at neck, shoulders, and hips, orig brown wig, painted brown side glancing eyes, closed mouth, orig pink dress, orig tabs and booklet tied to wrist, crazing of painted surface, arms repainted, marks: Terri Lee Pat. Pending on rear torso **160.00**

Unis, 19", character, bisque head, jointed composition toddler body, brown human hair wig, blue open/close eyes, two molded upper teeth, marks: Unis 251 . . . . **1,500.00**

Verlinque, J., 20½", bisque socket head, wood and composition ball jointed body, red human hair wig, brown glass stationary eyes, open mouth, brown velvet hat, coat, light brown satin skirt, hands repainted, marks: incised Petite Francaise/JV/anchor/France/Liane/6 BIS **250.00**

Vogue, 7", Hansel and Gretel, hard plastic, jointed at neck, shoulders, and hips, blonde mohair wig, blue sleep eyes, orig clothing, orig "The Vogue

Doll Family'' 1958 booklet, marks:
Ginny/Vogue Dolls, pr **325.00**
Walkure, 30″, bisque socket head,
jointed composition body, orig blonde
human hair wig, molded and shaded
brows, painted lashes, blue sleep
eyes, open mouth, pierced ears, Victorian lace dress, marks: 6 Walkure
Germany **525.00**
Wislizenus, Adolf, 17″, bisque socket
head, ball jointed composition body,
replaced brown wig, brown glass
sleep eyes, open mouth, pierced
ears, recostumed, marks: AW W on
head **300.00**

DOOR KNOCKERS

History: Before the advent of the mechanical
bell or electrical buzzer and chime, a door knocker
was considered an essential door ornament to an-
nounce the arrival of visitors. Metal was used to
cast or forge the various forms; many cast iron
examples were painted. Collectors like to find
knockers with English registry marks.

**Parrot on branch, 4″ oval base, cast
iron, body painted pink and rose,
$35.00.**

BRASS

Anchor	55.00
Cat, arched back	50.00
Deer, 4″	45.00
Dog's head, 7″	65.00
Eagle, 8½″	60.00
Grecian Urn, 7″	30.00
Lady, hand holds mirror	35.00
Lion's head, 4″, ring knocker, c1880 . .	75.00
Pheasants	45.00

BRONZE

Fu Dog, large	100.00
Grecian Head, 4½″	80.00
Kissing Couple, 10½″	40.00

CAST IRON

Bat, flying	70.00
Butterfly	65.00
Horseshoe	40.00
Lady's hand, holding ball, ruffled cuff,
ring on finger, 6″	70.00
Mercury, figure	60.00
Parrot	20.00

DOORSTOPS

History: Doorstops became popular in the late
19th century. They can be found flat or three dimensional and were made in cast iron, bronze,
wood, and other material. Hubley, a leading toy
manufacturer, made many examples.

References: Jeanne Bertoia, *Doorstops: Identification And Values*, Collector Books, 1985; Marilyn Hamburger and Beverly Lloyd, *Collecting Figural Doorstops*, A.S. Barnes and Company,
1978.

Reproduction Alert: Reproductions are prolif-
erating as prices on genuine doorstops continue
to rise. There is usually a slight reduction in size
in a reproduced piece unless an original mold is
used at which time size remains the same. Reproductions have less detail, lack of smoothness to
the overall casting, and lack of detail in the paint.
If there is any bright orange rusting, this is strongly
indicative of a new piece. Beware. If it looks too
good to be true, it usually is.

Notes: Pieces described below contain at least
80% or more of the original paint and are in very
good condition. Repainting drastically reduces
price and desirability. Poor original paint is preferred over repaint.

All listings are cast iron and flatback castings
unless otherwise noted.

Doorstops marked with an asterick are currently
being reproduced.

B + H = Bradley and Hubbard.

Advisor: Craig Dinner.

Basket
11″ h, rose, ivory wicker basket, natural flowers, handle with bow, sgd
"Hubley 121" **135.00**
15⅜″ h, fruit, tan wicker basket, blue
ribbon and bow, Hubley **245.00**
Bellhop, black, 7½″ h, carrying satchel,
facing sideways, orange-red uniform
and cap **385.00**
Bowl, 7 x 7″, green-blue, natural colored
fruit, sgd "Hubley, 456" **115.00**

Petunias and Asters, 6½ x 9½", pink, blue, and yellow flowers, green leaves, orange and cream basketweave base, Hubley, $125.00.

Boy
>9⅜", "The Tiger," hands at side, riding outfit, cartoon like eyes, "FISH" on front, sgd "Hubley 269" **600.00**
>10⅝" h, wearing diapers directing traffic, police hat, red scarf, brown dog at side **400.00**
>11" h, full figure, Dutch, hands in pocket, blue jump suit and hat, red belt and collar, brown shoes, blonde hair **375.00**
>12¾" h, native wearing turban and leopard skin, one hand extended . **425.00**
>* Caddie, 8" h, carrying brown and tan bag, white, brown knickers, red jacket **375.00**

Cat
>* 7", male and female holding each others waist, dressed **285.00**
>* 8", black, red ribbon and bow around neck, on pillow **115.00**
>9½" h, 7" w, full figure, Persian, sitting, gray, light markings, sgd "Hubley" inside casting **160.00**
>10½" l, fireside, full figure, gray, light markings, sgd "Hubley" inside casting **150.00**

Child, 17" h, reaching, naked, flesh color, short curly brown hair **525.00**

Clown, 10" h, full figure, 2 sided, red suit, white collar, blue hat, black shoes **475.00**

Cottage
>6⅜" h, three dimensional garden, tan roof, 3 red chimneys, flowers, 2 pc casting, Ann Hathaway **275.00**
>8⅝" l, 5¾" h, Cape Cod type, blue roof, flowers, fenced garden, path, sgd "Eastern Specialty Mfg Co 14" **150.00**

Dancer
>8⅞" h, Art Deco couple doing Charleston, pink dress, black tux, red and black base, "FISH" on front, sgd "Hubley 270" **450.00**
>11⅛" h, black woman doing rhumba, red yellow and blue dress, red kerchief **365.00**

Dog
>Boston Bull
>>9" h, full figure, facing left, black, tan markings **125.00**
>>10½" h, facing right, black, white markings **90.00**
>Boxer, 8½ x 9", full figure, facing forward, brown, tan markings **165.00**
>Pekingese, 14½" l, 9" h, full figure, life-like size and color, brown, sgd "Hubley" **475.00**
>* Puppies, 7", three puppies in basket, natural colors, sgd "Copyright 1932 M Rosenstein, Lancaster, PA, USA" **350.00**
>Japanese Spaniel, 9" h, black and white, long curly hair, sgd "1267" . **225.00**
>Wire Haired Fox Terrier, 9 x 8", full figure, facing sideways, tan, brown markings **100.00**

Drum Major, 12⅝", full figure, ivory pants, red hat with feather, yellow baton in right hand, left hand on waist, sq base **325.00**

Duck, 7½", white, green bush and grass **225.00**

Elephant, 14", pulling coconut out of palm tree, natural color **165.00**

Fisherman, 6¼" h, standing at wheel, hand blocking sun over eyes, rain gear **175.00**

Fish, 9¾" h, three, fantail, orig paint, sgd "Hubley 464" **150.00**

Flower
>Goldenrods, 7⅛" h, natural color, sgd "Hubley 268" **170.00**
>Jonquil, 7" yellow flowers, red and orange cups, sgd "Hubley 453" . . . **175.00**

Frog, 3", full figure, sitting, yellow and green **50.00**

Girl
>9"
>>French, holding skirt out at sides, hat, sgd "Hubley 23" **150.00**
>>Sunbonnet, blue hat, pink dress . . **250.00**
>10⅞", bathing, yellow and red swimsuits, green and yellow bathing caps under umbrella, "FISH" on front, sgd "Hubley 250" **425.00**
>* 13¾" h, 9¾" l, white hat, flowing cape, holding orange jack-o-lantern with red cutout eyes, nose, and mouth **575.00**

* Golfer, 10" h, overhead swing, hat and ball on ground, Hubley **300.00**

Horse, 7⅞" h, jumping fence, jockey, sgd "Eastern Spec Co #790" **225.00**

House
5½" h, 8¼" l, 2 story, attic, path to door, shutters, sgd "Sophia Smith House" 225.00
6" h, woman walking up front stairs, grapevines, sgd "Easter Spec Co" .. 200.00
* Kitten, 7", 3 kittens in wicker basket, sgd "M Rosenstein, c1932, Lancaster, PA" 375.00
Lighthouse, 7¾" h, 9" l, three dimensional buildings and light house, base, Highland 275.00
* Mammy
8½" h, full figure, red dress, white apron, blue kerchief with white spots, sgd inside "Hubley 327" .. 150.00
12", full figure, blue dress, white apron, red kerchief with white spots, sgd "copyright Hubley" inside 325.00
Messenger Boy, 10" h, bouquet in hand, cap, rosy checks, front sgd "FISH" . 375.00
Monkey, 8⅜" h, on yellow and black barrel, green, yellow face, ears, tail and paws, sgd "Taylor Cook No 3, 1930" 375.00
Musician, 6⅞" h
Black man playing saxophone, white pants, red jacket 475.00
Black man playing drums, black paint 425.00
Owl, 9½" h, sits on books, sgd "Eastern Spec Co" 275.00
Pan, 7" h, with flute, sitting on mushroom, green outfit, red hat and sleeves, green grass base 150.00
Parrot, 13¾" h, in ring, two sided, heavy gold base, sgd "B & H" 240.00
Penguin, 10" h, full figure, facing sideways, black, white chest, top hat and bow tie, yellow feet and beak, unsgd Hubley 300.00
* Pheasant, 8½", brown, bright markings, green grass, sgd "Fred Everett" front, sgd "Hubley" back 275.00
Policeman, 9½" h, leaning on red fire hydrant, blue uniform and tilted hat, comic character face, tan base, "Safety First" on front 550.00
Popeye, 9" h, full figure, pipe in mouth, white hat, blue pants, black and red shirt, sgd "Hubley, 1929 King Features Syn, Made in USA" 625.00
* Quail, 7¼" h, 2 brown, tan, and yellow birds, green, white, and yellow grass, Fred Everett on front, sgd "Hubley 459," 285.00
Rabbit
8⅛" h, eating carrot, red sweater, brown pants 325.00
15¼" h, sits on hind paws, tan, green

grass, detailed casting, sgd "B & H 7800" 400.00
Ringmaster, 10½" h, full figure, hands clasped behind back, red jacket, green pants, top hat 650.00
Rooster
7", standing, black, colorful detail .. 185.00
12", full figure, black, red comb, yellow claws and beak 275.00
13" h, red comb, black and brown tail and chest, yellow stomach 285.00
Ship
5¼" h, clipper, full sails, American flag on top mast, wave base, 2 rubber stoppers, sgd "CJO" 75.00
11¼", three masts, full sail 55.00
Skier, 12½" h, full figure, woman, red scarf, gloves, and belt, blue ski suit and beret, wood skis at side 375.00
Squirrel, 9", sitting on stump eating nut, brown and tan 175.00
Stork, 13¾", white, yellow beak, orange feet, black markings, flowers and grass 285.00
Storybook
Huckleberry Finn, 12½" h, floppy hat, pail, stick, Littco Products label .. 500.00
Humpty Dumpty, 4½", full figure, sgd "661" inside 300.00
Little Miss Muffet, 7¾" h, sitting on mushroom, blue dress, blonde hair 160.00
Little Red Riding Hood
7½" h, 9½" w, sgd "NUYDEA" ... 425.00
9½", basket at side, red cape, tan dress with blue pattern, blonde hair, sgd "Hubley" 350.00
Mary Quite Contrary, 11⅜" h, blue hat, yellow dress and socks, green watering can, "Littco Products" label 450.00
Puss in Boots, flat back, head sticking out of boot, sgd "Creations Co 1930" 350.00
Tiger, 8½" h, tan, black stripes, baseball bat on shoulder, black base 350.00
* Windmill, 6¾" h, 6⅞" w, ivory, red roof, house at side, green base 125.00
Woman
8" h, Colonial, sgd "Hubley" 140.00
8½" h, minuet, one hand on hip ... 175.00
8¾" h, peasant, blue dress, black hair, fruit basket on head 140.00
* 11" h, flowers and shawl 160.00
12" h, carrying parasol and hat box in left hand, satchel with "Phoebe" in right hand, flowered hat 300.00
Zinnias, 11⅝" h, multicolored flowers, blue and black vase, detailed casting, 2 rubber stoppers, sgd "B & H" ... 200.00

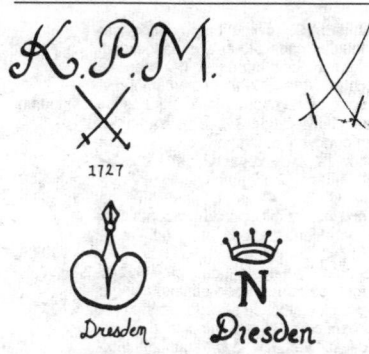

1727

Dresden
1883-93

N Dresden
MODERN MARK

Figurines, Dresden 8″ h, shepherd and shepherdess, multicolored, interlocking mark, pr., $200.00

DRESDEN/MEISSEN

History: Augustus II, Elector of Saxony and King of Poland, founded the Royal Saxon Porcelain Manufactory in the Albrechtsburg, Meissen, in 1710. Johann Frederick Boettger, an alchemist, and Tschirnhaus, a nobleman, experimented with kaolin clay from the Dresden area to produce porcelain. By 1720 the factory produced a whiter hard paste porcelain than that from the Far East. The factory experienced its golden age in the 1730–50s period under the leadership of Samuel Stolzel, kiln master, and Johann Gregor Herold, enameler.

Many marks were used by the Meissen factory. The first was a pseudo-oriental mark in a square. The famous crossed swords mark was adopted in 1724. A small dot between the hilts was used from 1763–74 and a star between the hilts from 1774 to 1814. Two modern marks are swords with a hammer and sickle and swords with a crown.

The Meissen factory was destroyed and looted by forces of Frederick the Great during the Seven Years' War (1756–1763). It was reopened, but never achieved its former greatness.

In the 19th century, the factory reissued some of its earlier forms. These later wares are called "Dresden" to differentiate them from the earlier examples. Further, there were several other porcelain factories in the Dresden region, and their products also are grouped under the "Dresden" designation of collectors.

Reference: Susan and Al Bagdade, *Warman's English & Continental Pottery & Porcelain, 1st Edition,* Warman Publishing Co., Inc., 1987.

DRESDEN

Charger, 18″, soldiers receiving provisions, flower garland border, black enamel pseudo AR cipher, 19th C .. **650.00**
Chocolate Set, rococo style, relief shell and scroll dec, deep brown and white

glaze, gilt, blue crossed swords mark, c1850, 17 pcs **400.00**
Fruit Stand, 9¼″ d, 11½″ h, hp, reticulated basket, applied flowers, matching baluster standard **150.00**
Loving Cup, 5½ x 6½″, three gold handles, red ground, ornate gold trim framing scenes of nymphs, marked . **325.00**
Mirror Frame, 26½″, circular, beaded border, applied high relief molded multicolored flowers, foliage, cherubs flanking a portrait of Marie Antoinette **1,200.00**
Plate, 8¼″, cupids in center, cobalt blue border, raised gold dec and flowers, pr **350.00**
Tile, 4″, draped young woman holding lyre, putti in tree playing violin, sgd "H Rock," framed **300.00**
Vase
8½″, cobalt blue, center medallion, courting scene, raised gold beading **325.00**
14″, baluster, landscape dec, ivory ground, inscribed mark, pr **750.00**

MEISSEN

Bowl, 10″, oval, shaped lip, reticulated border, molded base of swans and herons, late 18th C **1,000.00**
Cake Plate, 14½″ d, 5″ h, scalloped rim, alternating blue and gilt bands **85.00**
Centerpiece, 15″ l, water god with spirit in net, polychrome enameling, crossed swords mark **300.00**
Chocolate Pot, 6″, yellow ground, rustic landscape in shaped cartouche, angular handle, scroll molded spout, gilt, metal handle on cov, c1740 ...... **2,750.00**
Clock, 12″, white enameled 2¼″ dial, Roman and Arabic numerals, archi-

tectural form case, seated Eros figure, lovebirds finial **1,250.00**

Cream Jug, 3¼", pear shape, multicolored, figures in river landscape, gilt scroll rim, branch handle, 3 scroll feet, blue crossed swords and dot mark, c1765 . . . . **385.00**

Demitasse Cup and Saucer, white small floral sprays on cup, applied flowers and leaves, twig feet on saucer **120.00**

Figure

Actor, 6¼", hp, multicolored, mid 19th C **425.00**

Cat with snail, polychrome, crossed swords mark, 7⅜" **175.00**

Choir Girl, 5", hp, multicolored, mid 19th C **275.00**

Cupid, 7", hp, pouting, standing by tree trunk, wrapped in garlands of roses, missing some fingers, mid 19th C **275.00**

Pastoral lovers, seated beneath leafy tree, woman in floral dec skirt, laced bodice, holding lamb on lap, man dressed in shades of green, black hat, dog lying at feet, oval base, scroll molded border, gilt, underglaze blue crossed swords mark, imp letter and numerals marks **600.00**

Miniature, patch box, 1⁷⁄₁₆" l, modeled as lady's face, pale iron-red lips, finely detailed brown hair, flesh tones, black domino mask, rose-cut diamond eyes, yellow-streaked quartz cov, modern hinged gold mounting and loop, c1750 . . . . **1,500.00**

Plate

8¼", dessert, hp, reticulated border, central floralspray, late 19th C, set of 11 . . . . **385.00**

9¼", cobalt blue, scalloped rim, 24K gold medallions encircling flowers, blue crossed swords mark **200.00**

10", Kakiemon palette, scattered flower sprays and insects, brown line, shaped rim, blue crossed swords mark, c1740 . . . . **400.00**

Rose Box, 5¼", circular, molded overlapping puce petals, rosebud and green branch finial, imp W, c1755 . . **400.00**

Slipper, floral dec, turned up toe and open back, crossed swords mark . . **50.00**

Salts, master, 7" h, figural, African attending basketweave bowl, deutschbleumen ornamentation, late 18th C, pr **2,000.00**

Sugar, cov, 3¾", sea green ground, battle scenes, shaped quatrefoil cartouches, flowering branch finial, blue crossed swords mark, gilder's mark, c1740 . . . . **1,875.00**

Tankard, 9", cylindrical, hunting cartouche, gilded laub and bandelwerk, lid inscribed "Johann Christian Richter Ano 1729" commemorative coin, contemporary silver gilt base . **18,000.00**

Tea Bowl and Saucer, sea green ground, gilt burnished flower spray reserves, blue crossed swords mark, c1740 . . . . **900.00**

Tea Caddy, 4", rect, pale lavender ground, multicolored mountainous river landscapes, iron-red mark, c1740 . . . . **900.00**

Teapot, 7", baluster, quatrefoil, Kakiemon palette, arched panels, flowers, gilt, blue crossed swords mark, c1735 **3,100.00**

Tureen, cov, 14", two scroll handles with cauliflower and asparagus, multicolored clusters of fruit and flowers in ozier molded cartouches, cherub holding cornucopia finial on cov, blue crossed swords mark, c1755 . . . . . **825.00**

DUNCAN AND MILLER

History: George Duncan, Harry B. and James B., his sons, and Augustus Heisey, his son-in-law, formed George Duncan & Sons in Pittsburgh, Pennsylvania, in 1865. The factory was located just two blocks from the Monongahela River, providing easy and cheap access by barge for materials needed to produce glass. The men, from Pittsburgh's southside, were descendents of generations of skilled glass makers.

The plant burned to the ground in 1892. James E. Duncan, Sr., selected a site for a new factory in Washington, Pennsylvania, where operations began on February 9, 1893. The plant prospered, producing fine glassware and table services for many years.

John E. Miller, one of the stockholders, was responsible for designing many fine patterns, the most famous being "Three Face." The firm incorporated, using the name The Duncan and Miller Glass Company until its plant closed in 1955. The company's slogan was "The Loveliest Glassware in America." The U. S. Glass Co. purchased the molds, equipment, and machinery in 1956.

References: Gail Krause, *The Encyclopedia Of Duncan Glass*, published by author, 1984, 3rd printing; Gail Krause, *A Pictorial History Of Duncan & Miller Glass*, published by author, 1976; Gail Krause, *The Years Of Duncan*, published by author, 1980.

Collectors' Club: National Duncan Glass Society, P. O. Box 965, Washington, PA 15301. *National Duncan Glass Journal* (quarterly).

Additional Listings: Pattern Glass.

Ashtray

Pall Mall, figural, duck, clear, 7" l . . . **24.00**

Plaque, 14″ d, light green, sailing ship, $30.00.

Teardrop, individual size	**5.00**
Basket	
Sandwich pattern, clear, loop handle, 11½″ h	**100.00**
Floral etching, 6″, crystal	**25.00**
Bonbon, Terrace, rolled up handles, cobalt blue	**15.00**
Bowl	
Caribbean, 8½″, blue	**100.00**
Puritan, console, rolled edge, cutting, crystal	**30.00**
Sanibel, blue opal	**75.00**
Butter Pat, Pall Mall, clear	**15.00**
Candelabra, Sandwich, 16″, 3 lite	**275.00**
Candlesticks, pr	
First Love, 5¾″, 2 lite, clear	**60.00**
Language of Flowers, 2 lite, clear . .	**68.00**
Celery, Canterbury, 11″, crystal	**20.00**
Champagne	
First Love, saucer	**20.00**
Sandwich, 5¼″, 5 oz	**20.00**
Cheese Dish, Caribbean, blue	**30.00**
Cigarette Box, cov, Patio, green	**40.00**
Coaster, Sandwich	**10.00**
Cocktail, Sandwich, 4¼″, 3 oz	**12.50**
Cocktail Shaker, Chanticleer, 8″, frosted	**75.00**
Compote	
Buck and doe etching, 10 x 9¼″ . . .	**100.00**
Puritan, green	**15.00**
Condiment Set, Teardrop, crystal, 5 pc	**65.00**
Creamer and Sugar	
Canterbury, breakfast, tray, crystal, 3 pc	**18.00**
First Love	**35.00**
Sandwich	**12.00**
Cup and Saucer	
Canterbury, crystal	**14.00**
First Love	**20.00**
Spiral Flutes, amber	**7.00**
Epergne, 9½ x 4½″, Caribbean, blue .	**90.00**
Finger Bowl, Spiral Flutes, green	**7.50**

Goblet	
First Love, 10 oz	**18.00**
Theme, cut	**15.00**
Willow, cut	**8.00**
Ice Bucket, First Love, orig handle . . .	**75.00**
Juice, ftd	
Sandwich, 3¾″, 5 oz	**12.00**
Willow, cut	**15.00**
Mayonnaise, underplate, Teardrop . . .	**15.00**
Nappy, Sandwich, 5″	**5.00**
Olive, Teardrop, 2 part	**5.00**
Paperweight, duck, crystal	**55.00**
Plate	
Hostess, 16″	**85.00**
Nautical, 8½″	**15.00**
Sandwich, 8″	**10.00**
Willow, 8¾″	**12.00**
Punch Set, Caribbean, crystal, ruby handles, 15 pcs	**225.00**
Relish	
Canterbury, 3 handles, gold overlay .	**25.00**
First Love, 7″, 3 part	**25.00**
Salt and Pepper, First Love, pr	**25.00**
Sherbet	
Hobnail, crystal	**10.00**
Spiral Flutes, 4¾″, pink	**10.00**
Teardrop, low, ftd	**4.50**
Sugar, Puritan, green	**5.00**
Swan	
7″, avocado green neck and bowl . .	**25.00**
7½″, crystal, sylvan	**40.00**
Tumbler, Spiral Flutes, 5″, green, ftd . .	**17.50**
Urn, 7″, pattern 545, two handles	**65.00**
Vase	
Canterbury, 7¼″, inverted candle . . .	**110.00**
Cornucopia, 8″, three feathers	**75.00**
Hand, holding cornucopia, oval base, daisy and sq design, red buttons, red scalloped rim, red oval ribbed base	**125.00**

DURAND

History: Victor Durand (1870–1931), born in Baccarat, France, apprenticed at the Baccarat glass works where several generations of his family worked. In 1884 Victor came to America to join his father at the Whitall-Tatum & Co. in New Jersey. In 1897 father and son leased the Vineland Glass Manufacturing Company in Vineland, New Jersey. Products included inexpensive bottles, jars, and glass for scientific and medical purposes. By 1920 four separate companies existed.

When Quezal Art Glass and Decorating Company failed, Victor Durand recruited Martin Bach, Jr., Emil J. Larsen, William Wiedebine, and other Quezal men and opened an art glass shop at Vineland in December, 1924. Quezal style iridescent pieces were made. New innovations included cameo and intaglio designs, geometric Art Deco shapes, Venetian Lace, and oriental style pieces.

In 1928 crackled glass, called Moorish Crackle and Egyptian Crackle, was made.

Much of Durand glass is not marked. Some bears a sticker labeled "Durand Art Glass," some has the name "Durand" scratched on the pontil, or "Durand inside a large "V". Etched numbers may be part of the marking.

Durand died in 1931. The Vineland Flint Glass Works was merged with Kimble Glass Company a year later, and the art glass line discontinued.

Vase, 7" h, irid blue, white webbing, $375.00.

Bowl, 5" d, 2¾" h, Spanish yellow, paneled, fine green rim, ftd **50.00**
Compote, 6⅝" d, 5¾" h, pale amethyst, handle, sgd "Durand" within letter "V", numbered **225.00**
Ginger Jar, 7" h, green, silver King Tut dec, amber rosette finial **1,300.00**
Lamp
  Base, 9¾", green and opal feather dec, gold luster, threaded **175.00**
  Boudoir, 8½" d flared shade, opal pulled green feathers, gold threaded base **1,200.00**
  Night, 6½" d pointed green textured dome shade, 9" h, black marble base **375.00**
Perfume Bottle, 5⅛", teardrop, irid blue, applied handles, numbered **200.00**
Plate, 8" d, Feather pattern, unsgd
  Blue, opal, and clear **175.00**
  Ruby, opal, and clear **150.00**
Urn, 10", King Tut, gold Aurene, green feathers and plumes, gold threading, sgd **500.00**
Vase
  6⅜", lustered and cut, orig label . . .   **175.00**
  6⅞", swirled black, irid blue int. **425.00**
  8¾", gold, opal pulled feathers outlined in blue, gold threading, sgd "V. Durand" **800.00**

9¾", cylinder, irid gold, King Tut bluish green dec **525.00**
11", blue, opal hearts and vine dec .   **1,400.00**
13", gold, opal pulled feathers outlined in green, sgd **800.00**

ENGLISH CHINA AND PORCELAIN (GENERAL)

History: The manufacture of china and porcelain was scattered throughout England, with the majority of the factories located in the Staffordshire district. The number of potteries was over one thousand.

By the 19th century English china and porcelain had achieved a world wide reputation for excellence. American stores imported large amounts for their customers. The special production English pieces of the 18th and early 19th centuries held a position of great importance among early American antiques collectors.

References: Susan and Al Bagdade, *Warman's English & Continental Pottery & Porcelain, 1st Edition*, Warman Publishing, 1987; Peter Bradshaw, *18th Century English Porcelain Figures, 1745–1795*, Antiques Collectors' Club; Geoffrey A. Godden, *Godden's Guide To Mason's China And The Ironstone Wares*, Antique Collectors' Club; Geoffrey A. Godden, *Lowestoft Porcelain*, Antique Collectors' Club; R. K. Henrywood, *Relief Molded Jugs, 1820–1900*, Antique Collectors' Club; LLewellynn Jewitt, *The Ceramic Art Of Great Britain*, New Orchard Editions Ltd., distributed by Sterling Publishing Co., 1985 reprint of 1883 edition; Rachael Feild, *Macdonald Guide To Buying Antique Pottery & Porcelain*, Macdonald & Co., Ltd., 1987.

Additional Listings: Castleford, Chelsea, Coalport, Copeland and Spode, Liverpool, Royal Crown Derby, Royal Doulton, Royal Worcester, Historical Staffordshire, Romantic Staffordshire, Wedgwood, and Whieldon.

BOW

Candlestick, 7¹⁵⁄₁₆" h, Autumn, modeled as youthful Bacchus, wearing wreath of grape clusters and lavender nosed yellow leopard skin, standing beside putto, holding end of grapevine entwined around blue edged scroll, maroon and blue rococo scroll candlestick, maroon, puce, and blue edged scrolled molded base, black enamel stroke mark, c1760 . . . .   **2,000.00**
Creamer, 4¹³⁄₁₆", oval, fluted, iron-red, yellow, blue, puce, and green floral spray, yellow, rose, and green johnnyjump-ups, small blue morning glory, int. floral sprig, pink feathered border, rose foliate scrolls on foot, c1760, pr   **700.00**

Plate, 8¼" d, rose, blue, iron-red, gray, yellow, brown, purple, turquoise and green exotic birds and insects, brown edged scalloped rim, James Giles type painting, c1770 . . . . **400.00**

Sauceboat, 8" l, molded large spray of flowering prunus, rose, blue, yellow, and turquoise, scattered sprigs, int. rose and turquoise floral sprig and turquoise trellis diaper border, scroll handle, three paw feet, c1754, pr . . **3,200.00**

Teapot, cov, 4¹³⁄₁₆" h, white, flowering prunus blossom sprigs on both sides and under the spout, molded scallops and faceted thumbpiece, c1755 . . . **1,200.00**

CAUGHLEY

Dish, 7¾" l, shell shape, lobed rim, center floral sprig, four floral garlands, double line border, underglaze blue "S" mark, c1780 . . . . **225.00**

Milk Jug
   2½" h, Chelsea ewer shape, cluster and sprays of flowers and fruit, blue edged rim, c1790 . . . . **235.00**
   3⅞" h, fluted pear shape, Carnation pattern, int. cell diaper border, underglaze blue "S" mark, c1780 . . **250.00**

Plate, 8⅜", scalloped rim, Kakiemon pattern, orange, green, turquoise, blue, and gold, c1785, pr **275.00**

DERBY

Bough Pot, cov, 9⅝" w, D shaped body, teal-blue, brown, green, and rose view "A Calm," British ships and smaller boats, gilt foliage trelliswork ground, gilt foliate vine border, spreading foot and rim with gold and white shaded periwinkle blue borders, black shaded gilt stars and leaf sprigs, gilt edged lozenges, crescents, and circles on pierced cov, painted by George Robertson, blue enamel view inscription and crowned crossed batons and "D" mark, c1795 **2,350.00**

Dish, 12", lozenge shape, oval medallion of brown, green, gray, blue, and yellow view "On the Shore of Posilipo" (sic), figures in boats and on beach, castle, buildings, smoking Vesuvius in background, turquoise and gold bands, stylized floral devices, wider border, painted by John Brewer, topographical inscription, crowned crossed batons and "D" mark and numerals, c1805 . . . . **1,150.00**

Plate
   10", iron-red, rose, yellow, blue, purple, and green central cluster of flowers, small floral sprigs, pierced basketwork rim with gilding and four narrow cartouches of rose scalework, molded border of gilt bands and rose dashes, painting attributed to Leonard Lead, iron-red crowned "Bloor Derby" circular thumbprint marks, c1825–30, pr . . **2,750.00**

   10⅛", King's pattern, underglaze blue, iron-red, and gold, central prunus tree, peonies, and other flowers, elaborate grisaille cell diaper vignettes border, iron-red ground panels of white scrolls in underglaze blue and gilt foliate scrolls, gilt rim, iron-red crowned crossed batons and "D" mark, c1825, assembled set of 16 . . . . . **1,800.00**

Platter
   10½" l, oval, botanical, "Tall Blue Aster," blue, purple, puce, yellow, and green, shaped rim, painting attributed to William Pegg, blue enamel botanical inscription, crowned crossed batons and "D" mark, incised "7", c1796 . . . . **2,650.00**

   20⅛" l, oval, iron-red and green conjoined dots, two shades of underglaze blue, gilt highlights, central iron-red and gold patina, salmon ground, gilt edge, iron-red crowned crossed batons and "D" mark, underglaze blue marks on footrim, c1820 . . . . **1,450.00**

Sauce Tureen, matching stand, 10" l, 6" h, marked "Bloor Derby" **700.00**

FLIGHT, BARR AND BARR

Dessert Service, 13 pcs, scalloped 7³⁄₁₆" h sauce tureen, cov, and stand, tray, scalloped oval dish, two shell shaped dishes, milk jug, six plates, wide orange ground border, garland of oak leaves and acorns in shades of brown and gold, gilt bands, handles, and knobs, incised marks, c1800 . . . . . . **1,925.00**

Dinner Service, 36 pcs, 11" sq bowl, ten dinner plates, twelve dessert plates, ten soup plates, three oval 16⅝", 18", and 19⅞" platters, underglaze blue, iron-red, and orange Oriental floral dec, central iron-red sprig, gilt band border, imp crowned "FBB" marks, c1820 . . . . **2,250.00**

Dish, 11", armorial, iron-red, green, black, russet, and gray arms and crest of John Prendergast-Smyth, gray banderole inscribed "Vincit Veritas," scalloped rim with gilt palmettes and leaf scrolls border, imp crowned "BFB" mark, crowned and plumed brown "Barr Flight & Barr Royal Porcelain Works, Worcester" oval mark, c1804–09 .... **900.00**

Sauce Tureen, cov, 6⅝" h, circular, wide grisaille cell diaper border, iron-red whorl panels alternating with white scrolls, gilt stippled panels of turquoise diamonds, gilt highlighted cobalt blue foliate scrolls and pink, iron-red, blue, and green stylized blossoms and leaves, blue band and gold ball border, edged in bronze and gold, gilt eagle's head and ring handles, flame form knob, imp crowned "BFB" mark, c1810 .... **800.00**

Urn, 5" h, topographical, campaniform body, naturalistic shades, two small figures in gilt edged rect view, white beadwork band, gilt foliate border, gilt eagle handles, circular foot with gilt lyre, palmette, and foliage spray border between robin's egg blue bands, flaring rim with gilt banded and foliage borders, gilded sq foot, brown script view Birkleigh Vale near Plymouth inscription, crowned "Barr Flight & Barr Royal Porcelain Works Worcester" marks, c1810 .... **1,875.00**

Lowestoft, saucer, 4¾" d, Chinese style blue dec, $65.00.

LOWESTOFT

Creamboat, 3¾", Chelsea ewer shape, fluted oval body, purple, iron-red, rose, and olive-green fuchsias, roses, and flowers, turquoise edged rim, small int. purple sprig, base molded with leaves, c1775 .... **800.00**

Feeding Cup, 3¼" h, tapering cylindrical body, underglaze blue transfer print, flower spray, fruit, and floral sprig, underglaze blue hatched crescent mark, c1770–75 .... **300.00**

Pickle Dish, 4½" l, leaf shape, Mansfield pattern, underglaze blue, int. veined molded, c1768–72, pr **900.00**

Tea Caddy, 4⁵⁄₁₆" h, rect, imitation of Worcester Mansfield pattern, floral sprig knob, modern silver cov and neck mount, underglaze blue floral dec, underglaze blue crescent mark, c1780 .... **450.00**

Teapot, 5⅛" h, spherical, imitation of Worcester Mansfield pattern, underglaze blue floral dec, underglaze blue crescent mark, c1780 .... **675.00**

Waste Bowl, 3¼" h, Three Flowers pattern, underglaze blue transfer print, underglaze blue hatched crescent mark, c1770–75 .... **275.00**

MASON'S

Dinner Service, partial, seventeen dinner plates, twenty-one luncheon plates, twenty-five soup plates, eight cups and saucers, twelve salad crescents, eleven dessert plates, three oval platters, sauceboat, two stands, oval vegetable bowl, Imari type dec, marked "Masons Patented Ironstone" **2,800.00**

Platter, 18¾", chamfered rect, Willow pattern, underglaze blue transferprint, whorl border, marked crowned "Patent Ironstone China," c1820 ... **375.00**

Punch Bowl, 12¾", Lotus pattern, underglaze blue, iron-red, pink, green, turquoise, salmon, and gold, iron-red trellis diaper band, salmon luster edge, imp "Mason's Patent Ironstone China," c1815 .... **1,450.00**

Wine Cooler, campaniform body, cobalt blue, gold stylized peony blossom, chrysanthemums, and prunus, gilt mermaid handles, patterned gilt rim, molded leaf border, gilt bordered foot, pr, c1820–25 .... **1,800.00**

NEW HALL

Tea Service,

13 pcs, 8⁷⁄₁₆" cake dish, milk jug, five teacups, coffee cup, four saucers, Japan pattern, underglaze blue, iron-red, salmon, green, turquoise, and gilded flowering tree and plant, gilt edged rim, circular brown printed mark, c1815 .... **500.00**

18 pcs, ogee shaped oval cov teapot, stand, straight cov oval teapot, milk jug, waste bowl, teacup, three tea-

bowls, two coffee cans, four saucers, black printed and enameled Chinaman, blue robe, lady in green coat and rose robe, watching boy, iron-red double band border, minor damage and repairs, assembled, c1795 .... **725.00**

ENGLISH SOFTPASTE

History: Between 1820 and 1860 a large number of potteries in England's Staffordshire district produced decorative wares with a soft earthenware (creamware) base and a plain white or yellow glazed ground.

Design or "stick" spatterware was created by a cut-sponge (stamp), hand painting, or transfer. Blue was the dominant color. The earliest patterns were carefully arranged geometrics and generally covered the entire piece. Later pieces had a decorative border with a center motif, usually a tulip. In the 1850s Elsmore and Foster developed the Holly Leaf pattern.

King's Rose features a large, cabbage-type rose in red, pale red, or pink. The pink rose often is called "Queen's Rose." Secondary colors are pastels of yellow, pink, and occasionally green. The borders vary: a solid band, vined, lined, or sectional. The King's Rose exists in an oyster motif.

Strawberry China ware comes in three types: strawberries and strawberry leaves (often called strawberry luster), green feather-like leaves with pink flowers (often called cut-strawberry, primrose, or old strawberry), and a third type with the decoration in relief. The first two types are characterized by rust red moldings. Most pieces have a creamware ground. Davenport was one of the many potteries who made this ware.

Yellow-glazed earthenware (canary luster) has a canary yellow ground, transfer design which is usually in black, and occasional luster decoration. The earliest pieces date from the 1780s and have a fine creamware base. A few hand painted pieces are known. Not every piece has luster decoration.

Marked pieces are uncommon. Because the ground is softpaste, the ware is subject to cracking and chipping. Enamel colors and other types of decoration do not hold well. It is not unusual to see a piece with the decoration worn off.

Reference: Susan and Al Bagdade, *Warman's English & Continental Pottery & Porcelain, 1st Edition,* Warman Publishing Co., Inc., 1987.

Additional Listings: Adams Rose, Gaudy Dutch, Salopian Ware, Staffordshire Items.

DESIGN SPATTERWARE

Bowl
6¾", blue stick spatter, gaudy floral band, marked "Baker & Co, Ltd, England" **125.00**
9½, serrated rim, blue, white, and black trim **290.00**
Creamer, 4", purple spatter **75.00**
Cup and Saucer, floral, blue, green, ochre, and red **135.00**
Cuspidor, 7¼ x 5", blue and white dec **75.00**
Jug, 7", barrel shape, rosettes, fern prongs, blue **150.00**
Mug
4", geometric dec, red, green, and brown **90.00**
6", rosettes, blue, green bands **90.00**
Plate
8⅜", green stick spatter, gaudy four color floral center, red rim stripes . **125.00**
8½", black stick spatter border, center red and blue flower, green leaves **175.00**
8¾", red concentric center circles, narrow red line border with stars circled in blue **100.00**
9", stars in center, pin wheels around narrow red line border **100.00**
9¼", green flowers, red stick spatter center **115.00**
10½", tulip, purple and blue spatter, marked "Cotton & Barlow" **325.00**
Platter
12", red and green **175.00**
16", purple and green **230.00**
Sugar, cov, 5", white, blue, and red flowers, green leaves, closed ring and shell handles **100.00**
Teapot, cov, rosettes, blue **225.00**

KING'S ROSE

Bowl, 5⅝" **115.00**
Coffeepot, 12", pink, green, yellow, and red dec, dome lid, c1825, minor restoration **1,200.00**
Creamer, brick red rose, helmet shape **230.00**
Cup and Saucer, solid border **165.00**
Plate
6½", vine border, yellow puff balls .. **140.00**
7½", pink border **145.00**
Platter, 13" **300.00**
Sauce Boat, 6¾" **150.00**
Soup Plate, 9" **160.00**
Sugar, cov, pink rose **175.00**
Tea Set, cov teapot, four handleless cups and saucers, brick red rose, imp "Wood" **600.00**
Teapot, Queen Anne shape, minor chips on cov **450.00**

STRAWBERRY CHINA

Bowl, 6¼", pink luster, red and green enamel, wide strawberry border, c1820 .... **175.00**
Coffeepot, 11¼", Strawberry Luster, dome cov, strawberry finial **465.00**

Creamer, 6¼"	175.00
Cup and Saucer, handleless	100.00
Mug, 2½", applied handle	80.00
Plate	
6½", strawberries and morning glories, pink luster border	185.00
8¼", Cut Strawberry	185.00
10"	150.00
Relish, 8¾", shell shape	115.00
Soup Plate, 8¼"	175.00
Teapot, 4¼ x 9½"	375.00
Vegetable Dish, cov, octagonal	375.00

Yellow glazed earthenware, mug, 2⅝" h, 2¾" d, Schoolhouse pattern, pink luster trim, $350.00.

YELLOW GLAZED EARTHENWARE

Bowl, 7¼ x 3¼"	400.00
Cup and Saucer, 3" d handleless cup, 4¾" d saucer, brown transfer, couple at tea	300.00
Jug	
4½", silver luster border and round medallion of Peace as young girl	360.00
5¾", black transfer print, silver luster dec, inscribed "Accept this trifle from a friend whose love for thee shall never end" and "George Lawton, 1809" under spout	700.00
Mug, child's	
1⅞ x 2", silver luster trim	250.00
2", brown transfer, silver luster rim, boys flying kite, inscribed "For a favorite"	230.00
Pitcher, 3¾", red and orange flowers, wine dec on neck	625.00
Plate	
6¼", center inscribed "Thomas", bright green band, sponged border, c1820	425.00
7⅜", bright red and green floral dec, emb floral rim	300.00

8½", red transfer center scene, molded acanthus border, imp Wood	275.00
Potpourri Vase, 7½", 6 classical figures outlined in black enamel, flaming brazier, inscribed "Sacrifice A L'Hymen," silver luster lion head handles	425.00
Waste Bowl, 5⅜" x 2⅞", red and green floral dec, emb floral rim	250.00

FAIRINGS, MATCH-STRIKERS, AND TRINKET BOXES

History: Fairings are small, charming china objects which were purchased or given away as prizes at English fairs in the 19th century. Although fairings are generally identified with England, they actually were manufactured in Germany by Conte and Boehme of Possneck.

Fairings depicted an amusing scene either of courtship and marriage, politics, war, children or animals behaving as children. Over four hundred varieties have been identified. Most fairings bore a caption. Early examples, 1860–70, were of better quality than later ones. After 1890 the colors became more garish, and gilding was introduced.

The manufacturers of fairings also made match-strikers and trinket boxes. Some were captioned. The figures on the lids were identical to those of the fairings. The market for the match-strikers and trinket boxes was identical to that for the fairings.

Reference: Susan and Al Bagdade, *Warman's English & Continental Pottery & Porcelain, 1st Edition*, Warman Publishing Co., Inc., 1987.

Advisors: Barbara and Melvin Alpren.

5⅞" h, bisque, painted, Ladies of Llangollen, Welsh, $65.00.

FAIRINGS

"Baby's First Step," three children hand in hand	200.00

"Before Marriage," couple embracing
on sofa **250.00**
"Home Rule," couple by bed **250.00**
"The Delights of Matrimony," father
feeding infant on lap **200.00**

MATCH-STRIKERS

Crown and scepter, oval, applied flow-
ers on borders **250.00**
Drum and drumsticks, red, white, and
blue, gilt accents **250.00**
Tea Party, 3 ladies around tea table,
bright colors **300.00**

TRINKET BOXES

Baby
In highchair with his cat **200.00**
On dresser, pulling on socks, colorful **250.00**
Boy, on dresser, paddling himself in
bowl with a spoon **200.00**
Cavalier in canoe, colorful **200.00**
Pocket watch on dresser, bombe front **175.00**

FAIRY LAMPS

History: Fairy lamps, originating in England in
the 1840s, are candle burning night lamps. They
were used in nurseries, hallways, and dim corners
of the home.

Two leading candle manufacturers, the Price
Candle Company and the Samuel Clarke Company, promoted fairy lamps as a means to sell
candles. Both contracted with other manufacturers
of glass, porcelain, and metal to produce the
needed shades and cups. For example, Clarke
used Worcester Royal Porcelain Company, Stuart
& Sons, and Red House Glass Works in England,
plus firms in France and Germany. Clarke's trademark was a small fairy with a wand surrounded by
the words "Clarke Fairy Pyramid, Trade Mark."

Fittings were produced in a wide variety of
styles. Shades ranged from pressed to cut glass,
from Burmese to Nailsea. Cups are found in glass,
porcelain, brass, nickel, and silver plate.

American firms selling fairy lamps included Dia-
mond Candle Company of Brooklyn, Blue Cross
Safety Candle Co., and Hobbs-Brockunier of
Wheeling, West Virginia.

Fairy lamps are found in two pieces (cup and
shade) and three pieces (cup with matching shade
and saucer). Married pieces are common.

References: John F. Solverson, *Those Fascinating Little Lamps*, Antique Publications, 1988;
John F. Solverson (comp.), *Those Fascinating Little Lamps, Miniature Lamps Value Guide*, Antique
Publications, 1988.

Reproduction Alert: Reproductions abound.

**Cobalt Blue, Diamond Point pattern, 2
pcs, sgd "Geo. Davidson/Est 1867/
England," $90.00.**

Amber, 3 x 3⅝", pyramid, white opal
swirl glass shade, clear marked
"Clarke" base **100.00**
Baccarat, 5¼ x 4", Rose Tiente, Sun-
burst pattern, saucer base **235.00**
Bisque, figural, head
Kitten, gray, blue collar, green eyes . **485.00**
Monkey, 3½" h, natural coloring, am-
ber eyes **365.00**
Pekingese Pup, blue collar, amber
eyes, black nose **485.00**
Burmese
4½", clear pressed base, shade
marked "S. Clarke's, Patent,
Trademark, Fairy" **325.00**
6", Burmese candle insert, marked
"S. Clarke, Fairy" sgd "Thos. Webb
& Sons-Queen's Burmese" **1,550.00**
7 x 5⅜", Webb, acid finish, dome
shade, matching reversible ruffled
base, marked "Clarke" candle cup
and insert cup **550.00**
Cranberry, 4⅛" x 4", opaque white loop-
ing on shade, clear marked "Clarke"
base **150.00**
Lithophane, 4", white lithophane newel
post shade, clear marked "Clarke
Cricklite" base **450.00**
Mt Washington, 5¼", peachblow, clear
glass candle cup **250.00**
Nailsea
4½", blue, clear marked "Clarke
Cricklite" base **375.00**
4¾", citron, marked "Clarke Cricklite"
crystal base **175.00**
5", pink and white, clear marked
"Clarke Cricklite" base **190.00**
Opalescent, 3¾ x 2⅞", blue emb rib,
pyramid, clear marked "Clarke" base,
shade reg #130643 . . . . **85.00**

Opaline, 17", French blue, 4 large faceted jewels in purple and dark blue, filigree brass mountings **275.00**

Overshot

   3 x 3¾", pyramid, green overshot shade, clear marked "Clarke" base **110.00**

   3 x 4½", crown shaped cranberry overshot shade, clear marked "Clarke" base **200.00**

Peachblow, 6⅜", peachblow shade and base with blue, white, brown and green enamel dec, white int., clear marked "Clarke Cricklite" base **410.00**

Porcelain, 3 faced, owl, cat, and dog dec **150.00**

Pottery, 4¾ x 3¼", English, Art Deco cottage, orange roof, pierced windows and doors, green saucer base **110.00**

Satin Glass, 5½"

   DQ, MOP, pink, clear marked "Clarke" base **200.00**

   Swirled, rainbow, crimped top, clear marked "S. Clarke" base **450.00**

Spatter Glass

   4 x 14", Swirl pattern shade, gold, white, and pink spatter, white int., clear marked "Clarke" glass peg base, brass candlestick **425.00**

   13¾" d, 17¾" h, double, emb ribbed overlay shades, SP Cricklite base **450.00**

Stevens & Williams, 3⅞ x 4½, pink and white swirled striped, clear marked "Clarke" base **175.00**

Vaseline, 2⅞ x 3½", ribbed dome, green pressed "Clarke" base **165.00**

FAMILLE ROSE

History: Famille Rose is Chinese export enameled porcelain in which the pink color predominates. It was made primarily in the 18th and 19th centuries. Other porcelains in the same group are Famille Jaune (yellow), Famille Noire (black), and Famille Verte (green).

Decorations include courtyard and home scenes, birds, and insects. Secondary colors are yellow, green, blue, aubergine, and black.

Mid to late 19th century Chinese export wares similar to Famille Rose are identified as Rose Canton, Rose Mandarin, and Rose Medallion.

Reference: Sandra Andacht, *Oriental Antiques & Art: An Identification And Value Guide*, Wallace-Homestead, 1987.

Bowl

   6¾" d, four well painted circular medallions sides, pink ground, incised lotus and blossoms, Daoguang mark and period, pr **770.00**

   11¼" d, ext. genre scenes cartouche,

Dish, 6½" d, central peach medallion with heron, peaches, symbols of longevity, and immortals, gold rim, Tongzhi seal mark, $200.00

   int. pastoral scene with figures, gilt scroll and floral ground, mid 18th C **900.00**

Brushpot, 5" h, light blue, green, pink, and yellow enamel painted flowers on side panels, black and iron-red outlines **440.00**

Center Bowl, 15½" d, Canton, late 19th C **500.00**

Charger, 14½", Famille Verte, green and blue peacock, rose flowers and leaves, black ground, blue border with butterflies **365.00**

Clock, 23", mantel, gilt bronze, c1890 . **935.00**

Dish, 7¾", lady seated beside table holding fly wisk, cell pattern band, three peony cartouche, Yongzheng . **350.00**

Figure, group of ten peaches, various sizes up to 10" l, leafy stem, multicolored, 19th C **4,750.00**

Flowerpot, 10" h, birds and flowers alternating with raised leafy vines panel dec, pink and turquoise base, two braided handles, pierced cov, 18th C **1,540.00**

Garden Seat, 17¾" h, painted, dragon and phoenix, chrysanthemum, peony, and lotus blossoms, pale blue ground, pierced double-cash motif, raised bosses bands, lappet borders, pr **2,860.00**

Jar, 3⅛" h, globular form, painted rosettes and clouds sides, yellow ground, scrollwork band, leaf shape floral panels on pink diaper ground . **880.00**

Lamp Base, 26½", ovoid, convex flaring neck, bats and medallions, ornate borders, celadon ground, mounted as lamp, Chinese, 18th C **1,200.00**

Mug, 6¼", cylindrical body, flared base, pencilled leaf form swags with florets, vignettes of birds and flowers surrounded by leafy tendril ground, strap handle, late 18th C **500.00**

Plate, 8¼" d, woman seated with three children, flower head and diaper border, early 18th C **300.00**
Platter
14¾", foliate rim, turquoise prunus panels, 18th C **900.00**
17½" l, ribbon tied floral bouquet, 18th C **2,000.00**
Punch Bowl and Stand, figures in indoor settings panels alternating with birds and flowers panels, gilt ground, reserved on blue ground, lotus scrolls dec, dated inscriptions in Arabic script, dated **4,400.00**
Vase
15¼" h, painted side and neck well with figural bird and flower, landscape scene surrounded by gilt, gilt scrolls ground reserve, leafy peony scrolls dec shoulder on gilt ground, drilled and mounted as lamp **4,950.00**
23½" h, ovoid form, painted Qianlong style, raised fretwork shoulder, yellow ground, two imitation handles suspending gilt rings, raised cylindrical foot, Qianlong mark base .. **3,575.00**
Warming Dish, 10" d, detailed int. vignette, dragons, deer, birds, and butterflies border, pr **1,400.00**
Wine Cup and Saucer, 4½" d, eggshell porcelain, circular reserve panels of flowers, minute diaper ground, ruby enamel seal marks, Yongzhen period **2,500.00**

FENTON GLASS

History: The Fenton Art Glass Company began as a cutting shop in Martins Ferry, Ohio, in 1905. In 1906 Frank L. Fenton started to build a plant in Williamstown, West Virginia, and produced the first piece of glass in 1907. Early production included carnival, chocolate, custard, and pressed plus mold blown opalescent glass. In the 1920s stretch glass, Fenton dolphins, jade green, ruby, and art glass were added.

In the 1930s boudoir lamps, "Dancing Ladies," and various slags were produced. The 1940s saw crests of different colors being added to each piece by hand. Hobnail, opalescent, and two-color overlay pieces were popular items. Handles were added to different shapes, making the baskets they created as popular today as then.

Through the years Fenton has added beauty to their glass by decorating it with hand painting, acid etching, color staining, and copper wheel cutting. Several different paper labels have been used. In 1970 an oval raised trademark also was adopted.

References: Shirley Griffith, *A Pictorial Review Of Fenton White Hobnail Milk Glass,* published by author, 1984; William Heacock, *Fenton Glass: The First Twenty-Five Years,* O-Val Advertising Corp, 1978; William Heacock, *Fenton Glass: The Second Twenty-Five Years,* O-Val Advertising Corp, 1980.

Collectors' Club: Fenton Art Glass Collectors Of America, Inc, P. O. Box 2441, Appleton, WI 54911. *Butterfly Net* (bimonthly).

Additional Listings: Carnival Glass.
Advisor: Ferill J. Rice

Ashtray
French Opal, fan shape, 4" **10.00**
Silver Crest, coaster type, 7" **42.00**
Topaz Opal, fan shape, 4" **15.00**
Basket
Aqua Crest, dark aqua handle, 7" .. **38.00**
Hobnail, French Opal, 4" **32.00**
Macaroon, ruby **110.00**
Peach Crest, 6½" **50.00**
Silver Crest, crystal handle, 8" w ... **28.00**
Bonbon
Dolphin, green, two handles, 6½" .. **30.00**
Hobnail, French Opal, 6" **12.00**
Boot, Daisy and Button, blue milk glass, 4" **7.00**
Bowl
Blue Burmese, blue shaded to pink, ruffled, 8½" **35.00**
Diamond Optic, orchid, flared, 13" .. **30.00**
Dolphins, green swirl, 8½" **55.00**
Hobnail, deep cranberry, opal, 6" ... **45.00**
Peach Crest, 8" **30.00**
Candleholder
Aqua Crest, dark, cornucopia shape **25.00**
Silver Crest, ruffled, 3" **12.00**
Candlesticks, Hobnail, plum opal, 8" .. **90.00**
Candy Dish, cov
Diamond Optic, green, dolphin ftd, 4" **55.00**
Jade, ftd **30.00**
Compote
Aqua Crest, light, ftd, 6" **20.00**
Coin Spot, green, jelly **15.00**
Silver Crest, 4" **10.00**
Condiment Set
Hobnail, milk glass, 7 pcs **65.00**
Teardrop, milk glass **60.00**
Cracker jar, Hobnail, topaz opal **210.00**
Creamer and Sugar
Georgian, ruby **35.00**
Hobnail, French Opal, 3½" **20.00**
Cruet
Burmese, hp roses **65.00**
Hobnail, French Opal **22.00**
Decanter, cranberry opal **100.00**
Egg, pink blossom, pedestal base ... **32.00**
Epergne, Diamond Lace, emerald green, 4 pc **125.00**
Ewer, Hobnail, plum opal, 14", applied crystal handle **225.00**
Fairy Lamp, Persian Medallion, lime sherbet, 3 pc **25.00**
Goblet, Thumbprint, blue **8.00**

Epergne, 9½" h, 12" d, Diamond Lace pattern, French Opalescent, applied aqua rim, three lily vases, $160.00.

Hat

Coin Dot, green, 4"	28.00
Hobnail, French Opal, 2½"	12.00
Peach Crest, 4"	35.00
Violets in Snow, hp	50.00
Ivy Bowl, amber, milk glass base	38.00
Jug, Dot Optic, green opal, 9"	125.00

Lamp

Desk, Coin Dot, cranberry	70.00
Dresser, Hobnail, blue opal, pr	75.00

Lemonade Set, pitcher and tumblers

Floral Cutting, vaseline, 7 pcs	215.00
French Swirl, applied black handle, 5 pcs	300.00
Ring pattern, French Opal, applied black handles, 9 pcs	200.00

Marmalade Jar, cov

Block and Star, milk glass	45.00
Hobnail, white, milk glass	30.00
Mayonnaise, underplate, Silver Crest	22.50

Mustard, cov, Hobnail, blue opal, orig

spoon	24.00

Perfume Bottle

Dot Optic, blue opal	35.00
Melon, mulberry	75.00

Pitcher

Coin Dot, cranberry opal, water	165.00
Dot Optic, cranberry, 4"	40.00

Plate

Aqua Crest, dark, 6"	8.50
Silver Crest, 8"	10.00
Rose Bowl, Spiral, French Opal, 4½"	40.00

Salt and Pepper Shakers, pr

Block and Star, milk glass	24.00
Topaz Opal, orig label	50.00
Sherbet, Jade, ebony base, flared, 3"	20.00
Slipper, Hobnail, green, cat	12.00
Toothpick, Hobnail, pink, 2½"	11.00

Tumbler

Coin Dot, French Opal, 5¼"	20.00
Jade, ebony ftd, 5½"	25.00

Vase

Appleblossom	155.00
Coin Dot, green opal, 6½", tricorn	100.00
Ivory Crest, corncupia shaped, pr	135.00
Mandarin Red, flared, 6"	60.00
Peach Crest, tulip shape, 9"	40.00
Rose Crest, 6"	20.00
Silver Crest, apple tree, milk glass	75.00
Spatter Glass, blue and green, 4"	30.00

FIESTA

History: The Homer Laughlin China Company introduced Fiesta dinnerware in January, 1936, at the Pottery and Glass Show in Pittsburgh, Pennsylvania. Fredrick Rhead designed the pattern; Arthur Kraft and Bill Bensford molded it. Dr. A. V. Blenininiger and H. W. Thiemecke developed the glazes.

The original five colors were red, dark blue, light green (with a trace of blue), brilliant yellow, and ivory. A vigorous marketing campaign took place between 1939 and 1943. In 1938 turquoise was added; red was removed in 1943 because of the war effort and did not reappear until 1959. In 1951 light green, dark blue, and ivory were retired and forest green, rose, chartreuse, and gray added to the line. Other color changes took place in the late 1950s, including the addition of a medium green.

Fiesta ware was redesigned in 1969 and discontinued in 1972–73. In 1986 Fiesta was reintroduced by Homer Laughlin China Company. The new china body shrinks more than the old semi-vitreous and ironstone pieces, thus making the new pieces slightly smaller than the earlier pieces. The modern colors are also different in tone or hue. The cobalt blue is darker than the old blue. Other modern colors are black, white, apricot, and rose.

References: Linda D. Farmer, *The Farmer's Wife Fiesta Inventory and Price Guide,* published by author, 1984; Sharon and Bob Huxford, *The Collectors Encyclopedia of Fiesta,* Collector Books, 1987, 6th Edition.

Reproduction Alert.

Additional Listings: See *Warman's Americana & Collectibles* for more examples.

Ashtray, gray	32.50

Bowl

4¾", orange	14.00
5½", green	10.00
6¼", red	18.00
8", yellow	30.00

Utility Tray, turquoise, $14.00.

8½", tan	15.00
9½", orange	22.00
12", red	80.00
12¼", blue, ftd	40.00
Candleholder, ivory, bulb, pr	30.00
Casserole, cov	
Green	42.50
Yellow, French	70.00
Coffeepot	
Yellow	60.00
Red	68.00
Compote, large, cobalt	65.00
Cream Soup	
Red	25.00
Yellow	18.00
Creamer, red	18.00
Cup and Saucer	
Chartreuse	17.50
Dark green	25.00
Light green	16.00
Navy	20.00
Turquoise	16.00
Demitasse Cup and Saucer	
Navy	25.00
Red	40.00
Fruit Compote, 12", yellow	40.00
Gravy Boat, turquoise	25.00
Mug	
Chartreuse	25.00
Orange	45.00
Red	50.00
Turquoise	25.00
Pitcher, disc	
Chartreuse	65.00
Yellow	32.00
Pitcher, juice, yellow	25.00
Plate	
6", green	5.00
9", dark green	9.00
10", orange, grill	20.00
13", chop, red	22.00
Salt and Pepper, pr, orange, ftd	16.00
Sugar, cov, ivory	18.00
Syrup, turquoise	125.00
Teapot, medium green	125.00
Tumbler, juice, light green, 5 oz	15.00
Vase, 8", medium green	150.00

FIGURAL BOTTLES

History: Figural Bottles, made of porcelain either in glaze or bisque form, achieved popularity in the late 1800s and remained popular to the 1930s. The majority of figural bottles were made in Germany, with Austria and Japan accounting for the balance. They averaged in size from three to eight inches.

The figural bottles were shipped to the United States empty and filled upon arrival. They were then given away to customers by brothels, dance halls, hotels, liquor stores, and taverns. Some were lettered with the names and addresses of the establishment; others had paper labels. Many were used for holidays, e.g., Christmas and New Year.

Figural bottles also were made in glass and other materials. The glass bottles held perfumes, foods, or beverages.

References: Ralph & Terry Kovel, *The Kovels' Bottle Price List, 7th Edition,*, Crown Publishers, 1984; Otha D. Wearin, *Statues That Pour*, Wallace-Homestead, 1965.

Periodical: *Antique Bottle And Glass Collector*, P.O. Box 187, East Greenville, PA 18041.

Additional Listings: See *Warman's Americana & Collectibles* for more examples.

BISQUE

Boy, 3½", holding up night shirt, Germany	100.00
Elk, bark back, emb antlers	50.00
Fox, 6¼", standing, wearing brown suit	35.00
Sailor, 6½", cartoon type, high gloss front, white pants, blue blouse and hat, marked "Made in Germany"	110.00

Owl, 8" h, clear orange glass, painted face and feet, $60.00.

GLASS

Bear, 8½", aqua, applied face, sheared mouth	270.00
Bunker Hill Monument, 9⅛", milk glass	115.00
Christmas Tree, star stopper	175.00
Clam Shell, amber	65.00
Crane, 14½", clear	35.00
Eagle, 10", milk glass, tooled mouth, Europe, 1890–1920	20.00
Fat Man, 9¾", sapphire blue, wearing cape	330.00
John Bull, 12", golden amber, tooled mouth	130.00
Pistol, amber	35.00
Rolling Pin, 13¾", dark olive amber, white flecks	125.00
Turk, seated, clear	60.00
Walking Stick, red, white, and blue	100.00

PORCELAIN

Book, green, yellow, and blue, flint enamel glaze, titled "Battle of Bennington," c1849	900.00
Duck with cape, 12"	25.00
Man on a barrel, Jim Crow	45.00
Mermaid, 12", brown	40.00
Robert E Lee, Southern Comfort	100.00

FINDLAY ONYX GLASS

History: Findlay onyx glass, produced by Dalzell, Gilmore & Leighton Company, Findlay, Ohio, was patented in 1889 for the firm by George W. Leighton. Due to high manufacturing costs resulting from a complex manufacturing process, the glass was made only for a short time.

Layers of glass were plated to a bulb of opalescent glass through repeated dippings into a glass pot. Each layer was cooled and reheated to develop opalescent qualities. A pattern mold then was used to produce raised decorations of flowers and leaves. A second mold gave the glass bulb its full shape and form.

A platinum lustre paint, producing pieces identified as silver or platinum onyx, was applied to the raised decorations. The color was fixed in a muffle kiln. Other colors such as cinnamon, cranberry, cream, raspberry, and rose were achieved by using an outer glass plating which reacted strongly to reheating. For example, a purple or orchid color came from the addition of manganese and cobalt to the glass mixture.

Reference: James Measell and Don E. Smith, *Findlay Glass: The Glass Tableware Manufacturers, 1886-1902*, Antique Publications, 1986.

Bowl, 7" d, 2¾" h, silver	300.00
Butter Dish, cov, 5½" d, silver	800.00

Jar, 3⅞" d, creamy white, gold dec, $300.00.

Celery, 6¼" h, cream	250.00
Creamer, 4½" h, cream	525.00
Mustard, 3" h, cream	275.00
Salt and Pepper Shakers, pr, 3" h, platinum	550.00
Spooner, 4¼" h, raspberry	600.00
Sugar, cov, 5½" h, raspberry	650.00
Sugar Shaker, 6" h, silver	300.00
Syrup, 7" h, SP lid marked "Pat. March 28, 82," lid finial missing, silver	400.00
Toothpick, 2½" h, cream	375.00
Tumbler, raspberry, Floradine pattern	785.00

FIREARM ACCESSORIES

History: Muzzle loading weapons of the eighteenth and early nineteenth centuries varied in caliber and required the owner to carry a variety of equipment with him, including a powder horn or flask, patches, flints or percussion caps, bullets, and bullet molds. In addition, military personnel were responsible for bayonets, slings, and miscellaneous cleaning equipment and spare parts.

In the mid-19th century, cartridge weapons replaced their black powder ancestors. Collectors seek anything associated with early ammunition from the cartridges themselves to advertising material. Handling old ammunition can be extremely dangerous due to decomposition of compounds. Seek advice from an experienced collector before becoming involved in this area.

Military related firearm accessories generally are worth more than their civilian counterparts. See "Militaria" for additional listings.

Reproduction Alert: The amount of reproduction and fake powder horns is large. Be very cautious!

Bayonet
   Civil War Rifled Musket, blade of bayonet stamped "US," socket stamped "A," complete in orig black

leather scabbard with brass tip, brown leather frog for attachment to belt stamped in 2 ovals "N. LUTZ/U.S./ORD. DEPT/SUB INSPECTOR" **150.00**

U.S. Model 1816 Musket, blade deeply stamped "US/RJ," socket stamped with letter "S" **50.00**

Zouave Saber, blade nice and crisp but with some scattered age staining, brass hilt generally very sharp and crisp, light age patina, several minor handling marks, orig brass trimmed black leather scabbard in very fine condition **150.00**

Book

Sutherland, Robert Q., and R. L. Wilson, *The Book Of Colt Firearms*, dust jacket **700.00**

Wilson, R. L., *The Book Of Colt Engraving*, first edition, dust jacket .. **250.00**

Wilson, R. L., *The Book Of Winchester Engraving*, first edition, dust jacket **500.00**

Bullet Mould

American, brass, 12⅝" overall, 4½" turned wooden handles, casts 9 balls, bottom of mould engraved "A. Gladding," the left side engraved "Shot Mould 1 of 16 to a Pound,/6 of 18 and 2 of 20 to ditto," with intertwined initials "AG," the left side engraved "Providence December 18th, 1798" with slightly crude spread winged Federal eagle, handles with minor stress or grain cracks, brass mould with many nicks and little dents **3,200.00**

Colt Navy Gang, steel, walnut handles, brass ferrules, casting 6 conical bullets, cavities fine, outer surfaces moderately pitted overall .. **200.00**

Colt Police or Belt, all steel, side stamped "36B," usual "COLTS/PATENT" stamped on sprue cutter, casting round and conical bullets, about mint with 98% orig blue **600.00**

Cartridge belt, western, brown leather, 3" wide, made of doubled over leather stitched on one edge, the other edge slightly tooled to give a stitched effect, fitted with 40 leather loops for 44 caliber or 45 caliber cartridges, 34" without closing strap, heavy square 2¼" nickel plated buckle, late 19th or early 20th century **225.00**

Catalog, Merwin, Hulbert & Co., Catalog No. 30, issued August 1, 1886, 6½ x 11", faded green paper cover with black printing, 32 pgs listing various pistols and ammunition offered by the company, text in Spanish and English, spine strengthened with Scotch tape **325.00**

Charger, Colt Paterson shotgun, 8" overall, brass plunger nozzle, collar stamped "PATENT," lacquered copper body with 4 carrying rings, 75% orig lacquer finish, bottom seam split **1,800.00**

Grips, pair

Colt Navy, ivory, antique one piece style with wooden filler **250.00**

Colt Root, solid ivory, raised carved in extremely high relief on the left side with the American eagle standing on the shield clutching arrows and olive branches, the branches running in relief down the front side of the grip, the shield over a "LIBERTY" scroll, missing a tiny chip at the rear toe on each side . **650.00**

Colt Root, one piece antique checkered ivory **425.00**

Mervwin Hulbert Army, ivory, raised carved on right side with the Mexican eagle and snake **325.00**

Holster

Colt Model 1849, 6" pocket, brown leather, sparse leaf tooled pattern covering the front and flap coming over top of the pistol, missing loop that flaps fits into **25.00**

Colt Model 1851 KM, made for the Austrian Kreigs Marine Colt Navies, designed for the pistol with a pouch for the spare cylinder to the side and another pouch in front for the capper, brown leather, leather a bit dry, both closure straps broken but there **175.00**

Western style, brown, 10½" overall, tooled decoration around the pistol shape only, c1900, orig lined with red wood flannel, most of which is missing **250.00**

Flasks, Powder

Brass

8" overall, emb on both sides in an Art Nouveau style fluted pattern **50.00**

11½", body emb on both sides with a fluted pattern, lacquered finish, nickel plated top dispensing loader, adjustable to 6 "Drams," collar marked "PATENT APPLIED FOR" **150.00**

Brass and Horn, 8½" overall, pressed horn body, brass mounts, early 18th C, bottle design body **150.00**

Copper

8½" overall, emb on both sides with oak leaves and acorns, stag's head at top and face of fox at bottom, brass top stamped "G. & J. W. HAWKSLEY/SHEFFIELD" **100.00**

Batty Peace Flask, top marked "BATTY," dated "1848" and inspected "JAG," complete and orig throughout **250.00**

Horn, flattened, 11¼" overall, turned nozzle and hand carved rect wood plug, base cov with horn, fitted with 2 flattened iron carrying rings, old leather strap **75.00**

Rubber, pistol, 4⅝" overall, brass top, hard rubber body marked "GOODYEARS PATENT May.6.1851," exceptionally clear markings **100.00**

Flask, Shot, Leather

8¼", emb on both sides with large panel depicting a setter in the woods, one side marked 4 lbs. brass, top marked "AM. FLASK & CAP CO," near mint condition ... **60.00**

8½", emb on both sides with Highland scene showing a Scottish hunter alongside a fallen stag with 2 hounds, brass top **45.00**

Powder Horn, 8½" l, dec of man with pipe, dog, and deer, inscribed "Eagle 1858," $600.00.

Horn, Powder

9", relief carved ivory, body with scene of man with a boar spear surrounded by dogs which are attacking massive wild boar, spout with open mouth highly stylized monster's head which somewhat resembles a wild boar, base low grade silver with scalloped edges, bottom engraved "1746/Prael Colod," minor age cracks **750.00**

11", engraved with a large country house with a smaller house on each side, all looking down on an orchard scene with a stream or river below, many of the trees with a bird at the top, and with a scene showing 6 very stylized running dogs, round wooden base with wrought iron strap loop, 1st half of 19th C **350.00**

13", PA, early 19th C, engraved with a figure of a spread-winged American eagle with shield on its breast, grasping olive leaves and arrows in its talons, banner in beak inscribed "E Pluribus Unum," fully rigged sailing ship, interlacing hearts, figure of mermaid inscribed "Neptune," soldier on back of seahorse, compasses, horse tied up at stake, large fort-like building with mounted guns, faceted spout, raised ring .. **1,750.00**

17", military, wooden base with screw out filling plug, fitted with heavy brass rings at nozzle and base with brass sling swivel fittings for the orig 1⅜" wide dark brown leather carrying strap with iron buckle, typical of horns used by US and militia troops in early 19th C, strap broken **300.00**

Padlock, W. F. Ames & Co., solid brass, 3⅛" overall, stamped "W.F.&CO." on one side of hasp, other side stamped "AMES SWORD Co. CHICOPEE MASS. U.S.A./PAT. SEPT. 19, 1882," orig key **425.00**

Signal Cannon, Winchester, Deluxe, serial number D113, deluxe chrome finish overall, 10 gauge, orig pine shipping crate **325.00**

Sporan, Scottish, leather purse, brass trim, covered with very long black hair on the front, brass mounted white hair tassels attached, early 20th C **175.00**

Surgeon's Kit, presentation, brass bound walnut case, 18¾ x 9¾ x 3½", fancy name plate with scalloped edges on lid, engraved "Mr. Kirkland," lined with purple velvet, lid with orig silver plate reading "Presented to Mr. Kirkland/by/Sir George Beaumount/as a mark on his part of the very/great attention he received from him/while suffering from the effects of a/severe accident," int. with two trays of various medical tools, large saw not orig, approximately 35% of tools missing **700.00**

Tool, combination, military, 3 fittings for attachment to the ramrod, screwdriver, nipple pick, and mainspring vise **80.00**

FIREARMS

History: The 15th century arquebus was the forerunner of the modern firearm. The Germans refined the wheelock firing mechanism during the 16th and 17th centuries. English settlers arrived in

America with the smoothbore musket; German settlers had rifled arms. Both used the new flintlock firing mechanism.

A major advance was achieved when Whitney introduced interchangeable parts into the manufacturing of rifles. The warfare of the 19th century brought continued refinements in firearms. The percussion ignition system was developed by the 1840s. Minie, a French military officer, produced a viable projectile. By the end of the 19th century cartridge weapons dominated the field.

Two factors control pricing firearms—condition and rarity. The value of any particular antique firearm covers a very wide range. For instance, a Colt 1849 pocket model revolver with a 5″ barrel can be priced from $100.00 to $700.00 depending on whether or not all the component parts are original, whether some are missing, how much of the original finish (bluing) remains on the barrel and frame, how much silver plating remains on the brass trigger guard and back strap, and the condition and finish of the walnut grips. Be careful to note any weapons' negative qualities. A Colt Paterson belt revolver in fair condition will command a much higher price than the Colt pocket model in very fine condition. Know the production run of a firearm before buying it.

References: Norman Flayderman, *Flayderman's Guide To Antique American Firearms. And Their Values,* 4th ed., DBI Books, 1987; Joseph Kindig, Jr., *Thoughts On The Kentucky Rifle In Its Golden Age,* 1960, available in reprint; Russell and Steve Quetermous, *Modern Guns: Identification & Values, Revised 7th Edition,* Collector Books, 1989.

Periodical: *Gun List,* 700 East State Street, Iola, WI 54990.

FLINTLOCK PISTOLS - SINGLE SHOT

English, Blunderbuss, 29½″ overall, 14″ round iron barrel with Birmingham proofs, fitted with 12½″ triangular snap bayonet, walnut full stock with lightly engraved brass furniture, 2 ramrod pipes, butt plate, trigger guard, small shied shaped wrist plate, and 2 lock plate screw escutcheons, attributed to John Whitehouse, early 19th C, metal parts complete and orig throughout, missing sliver of wood along right side at muzzle **900.00**

English, Queen Anne, center hammer, 12¼″, 7″ round brass barrel with Birmingham proofs, cannon turned muzzle, brass box lock with floral engraving, walnut grip with floral emb hallmarked silver butt cap, inlaid silver dec **1,400.00**

French, military, 16″ overall length, 9″ round iron barrel, flat beveled lockplate with faceted pan fitted with flat beveled reinforced hammer, brass furniture, unmarked **750.00**

Halbach & Sons, Baltimore, MD, holster pistol, c1785 to early 1800s, 9″ brass part round/part octagon barrel, 65 caliber, lock marked "HALBACH & SONS," large brass butt cap with massive spread wing eagle (primitive) in high relief surrounded by cluster of 13 stars, large relief shell carving around tang of barrel, full walnut stock, pin-fastened **1,650.00**

Kentucky, 10″ octagonal iron barrel, 48 caliber, full curly maple stock with brass forend cap, brass trigger guard and ramrod pipes, lock marked "Ashmore/Warranted" **3,000.00**

Kentucky, 14½″, New York, 9¼″ round barrel, caliber 60, smoothbore iron barrel, silver blade foresight, flat beveled lock sgd "B. HOMER," goose neck hammer with roller frizzen spring, plain walnut stock with silver mounts, 2 ramrod pipes, escutcheons for the lockplate screws, escutcheons with light engraving on bow and engraved pineapple finial, shield shaped escutcheon with simple engraving about edges, orig ramrod with horn tip, complete and orig throughout, excellent condition **5,000.00**

U.S. Model 1808, Navy, Simeon North, Berlin, CT, c1808–10, 10⅛″ round barrel, 64 caliber, smoothbore, unmarked barrel, lock marked with spread eagle above U. STATES ahead of hammer and vertically at rear S. NORTH/BERLIN/CON., hickory ramrod with swelled tip, full walnut stock, pin-fastened, iron belt hook attached to left side of stock **3,000.00**

U.S. Model 1813, Army and Navy, Simeon North of Middletown, CT, c1813–15, 9¹⁄₁₆″ round barrel, 69 caliber, smoothbore, breech of barrel marked P/US on left side and inspector marking H.H.P. above touchhole, lock marked ahead of hammer S. NORTH over an American eagle motif with letters U and S at either side over bottom line MIDLN CON., hickory ramrod with swelled tip at one end and metal ferrule at other, iron mountings **1,750.00**

U.S. Model 1819, Simeon North, Middletown, CT, c1819–23, 10″ round barrel, 54 caliber, smoothbore, barrel marked at breech P/US, lock marked ahead of hammer S. NORTH over American eagle and shield motif with letters U and S at either side over bottom line MIDLTN CONN., date of production marked at rear of lock below safety bolt, swivel type ramrod, iron mountings, sliding safety bolt, brass blade front sight, oval shaped rear sight on tang **750.00**

PERCUSSION PISTOLS - SINGLE SHOT

Note: Conversion of flintlock pistols to percussion was common practice. Most English and U.S. military flintlock pistols listed above can be found in percussion. Values for these percussion converted pistols are from 40 to 60% of the flintlock values as given.

Blunt & Syms side hammer, Blunt & Syms, New York, NY, c1840s–50s, 6″ octagon barrel, 44 caliber, barrel marked "B & S NEW YORK," dec broad scroll engraving on frame, iron forend, ramrod mounted beneath, bag shaped handle, walnut grips . . . **300.00**

John Dickson & Son, cased set, breech loading, underlever target pistols, Serial Numbers 4230 and 4231, 17¼″ overall, 11″ round barrel, caliber 45, flat matted ribs, sgd "John Dikson & Sons, 63 Princess Street, Edinburgh," English scroll engraved steel butt caps, actions, trigger guards, and locks fitted with sliding half cock safeties and sgd "John Dickson & Son," well grained walnut stocks checkered at wrists, forends also checkered and fitted with horn tips, orig oak case 20¼ x 11½ x 3″, heavy brass trimmed corners, orig accessories, complete with outer leather carrying case . . . **5,500.00**

Elgin Cutlass Pistol, Morrill, Mosman & Blair, Amherst, MA, 4″ round barrel rifled with six grooves, 34 caliber, a bowie blade 10″ long and 1½″ wide fastened to the barrel and etched with a vase containing fruit surmounted by "ELGIN'S PATENT" in script in a rect and an eagle holding a pennant in his beak (right), vase containing fruit surmounted by "Morill/Mosman/& Blair/Amherst Mass" and eagle holding pennant in beak (left), leather scabbard **4,250.00**

Mule Ear, 9⅛″ overall, 5⅛″ octagon rifled barrel, caliber 44, large dovetailed brass front sight, open rear sight, simple mule ear lock with external mainspring, tiger striped full stock with simple brass forend cap and trigger guard, sear and corresponding notch of hammer restored, two small cracks in stock **500.00**

U.S. Model 1842, Henry Aston, Middletown, CT (also by Ira N. Johnson of Middletown, CT, and Palmeto Armory of Columbia, SC), c1845–52, 8½″ round barrel, 54 caliber, smoothbore, proof stamps on breech of barrel beneath which are inspector's initials, date stamping on barrel tang, lockplate marked US/H. ASTON forward of hammer, marked vertically at rear MIDDTN/CONN., swivel type steel ramrod, all brass mountings, brass blade front sight **575.00**

Waters, Single Shot, A. H. Waters & C., Millbury, MA, mid–1840s to 1849, round barrel, 54 caliber, smoothbore, flat flush fitted lockplate, marked "A. H. WATERS & Co./MILLBURY MASS." in center of lock, side lug nipple, iron furniture, brass blade front sight, oval shaped rear sight on tang **475.00**

PERCUSSION PISTOLS - MULTI-SHOT

Colt

Dragoon, Second Model, 7½″ part round, part octagonal barrel, 44 caliber, 6 shot, barrel stamped "ADDRESS SAML COLT NEW-YORK. COLT'S/PATENT" with ".U.S." centered beneath, one piece walnut grip, squareback trigger guard and rect cylinder stop slots, Texas Ranger and Indian fight scene roll engraved on cylinders **4,250.00**

Navy, Model 1861, 7½″ round barrel, 36 caliber, 6 shot, creeping style loading lever, barrel stamped ADDRESS COL. SAML COLT NEW-YORK, U.S. AMERICA - .36 CAL," cylinder roll scene depicts battle between Texas Navy and that of Mexico, one piece walnut grip . . . **1,000.00**

Paterson Belt Model, No. 2, 5½″ octagonal barrel, 31 caliber, 5 shot, barrel stamped "Patent Arms M'g Co Paterson NJ Colt's Pt.," engraved cylinder, disappearing trigger, no trigger guard, flared walnut grips **4,500.00**

Pocket, Model 1849, barrel lengths of 3″, 4″, 5″ and 6″, 31 caliber, 5 or 6 shot, octagon barrel with attached loading lever, barrel stamped "ADDRESS COL SAML COLT NEW-YORK U.S. AMERICA," cylinder engraved with stagecoach holdup scene, round trigger guard, walnut grips **500.00**

Remington

Belt, New Model, 6½″ octagon barrel, 36 caliber, 6 shot, barrel stamped "PATENTED SEPT. 14, 1856/E. REMINGTON 7 SONS, ILION,

NEW YORK U.S.A./NEW MODEL,"
round cylinder, threads visible at
breech end, safety notches on cylinder shoulders between nipples . **550.00**

Navy, 1861, 7⅜" octagon barrel, 36
caliber, 6 shot, barrel stamped
"PATENTED DEC 17, 1861/MAN-
UFACTURED BY REMINGTON'S
ILION, N.Y.," round cylinder, walnut
grips **650.00**

Remington-Beals 3rd Model Pocket
Revolver, cased, 4" octagon barrel,
31 caliber, 5 shot, barrel stamped
"BEAL'S PATENT 1856 7 57 758/
MANUFACTURED BY REMING-
TON'S ILION, N.Y.," orig cardboard
box with brass bullet mold, quantity
of bullets, eagle and shield flask,
mushroom shaped cleaning rod
with screw-in type extension, extra
pawl spring, can of Eley percussion
caps **2,250.00**

Other

Deringer and Deringer Type

Deringer, Henry, Philadelphia, PA,
c1830s-60s, medium pocket
model, 3½" barrel, 41 caliber,
barrel stamped "DERINGER/
PHILADELA," identical marking
appears on lockplate, checkered
walnut stock, German silver trigger guard and butt cap (Flayderman 7D-002) **800.00**

Robertson, Philadelphia, PA,
pocket, 4½" barrel, approx. 41
caliber, barrel stamped "ROB-
ERTSON, PHILA.," forends have
double wedges and escutcheons
and double ramrod pipes (Flayderman 7D-022) **525.00**

Pepperboxes

Bacon, Thomas K., Norwich, CT,
c1852–58, 4" ribbed barrel, 31
caliber, 6 shot, barrel stamped
"BACON & CO., NORWICH, CT"
and "CAST STEEL," single action, underhammer, engraved
nipple shield, blued finish, walnut
grips (Flayderman 7B-001) **350.00**

Pecare & Smith, Ten-Shot, Jacob
Pecare and Joseph Smith, NY,
late 1840s to early 1850s, 4" barrel, 28 caliber, 10 shot barrel
cluster, dec scroll engraving on
frame and barrel shield, semi-
concealed hammer visible from
top, trigger folds down, brass
frame, walnut grips (Flayderman
7B-013) **1,750.00**

Stocking & Co., Worcester, MA, late
1840s to early 1850s, 31 caliber,
6" barrel cluster, barrel stamped

"STOCKING & CO., WORCES-
TER" and "CAST STEEL WAR-
RANTED," dec scroll engraving
on iron frame and nipple shield,
trigger spur guard (Flayderman
7B-017) **350.00**

**Pistol, 36 caliber, Navy Revolver, E.
Whitney, New Haven, 6 cyl., $550.00.**

Revolvers

Alsop, C. R., Middletown, CT, Navy
Model, c1862–63, 6½" octagonal
barrel, 36 caliber, 5 shot, barrel
stamped "C.R. ALSOP MIDDLE-
TOWN CONN." and patent date,
round cylinder, wooden grips
(Flayderman 7A-002) **1,150.00**

Joslyn, Benjamin, Stonington, CT,
Army Model, c1861–62, 8" octagon barrel, 44 caliber, 5 shot,
barrel stamped "B.F. JOSLYN/
PATD.MAY 4, 1858," case hardened loading lever and hammer,
checkered walnut grips (Flayderman 7A-043) **700.00**

Nichols and Childs, Conway, MA,
Belt Model, late 1830s, approx 6"
barrel, approx 34 caliber, 6 shot,
frame stamped "NICHOLS &
CHILDS/PATENT/CONWAY/
MASS.," bag shaped walnut
grips, only about 25 known (Flayderman 7A-073) **5,000.00**

Walch, John, New York, NY, Pocket
Model, early 1860s, 3¼" octagon
barrel, 31 caliber, 10 shot cylinder with five chambers, barrel
stamped "WALCH-FIRE-ARMS
CO.NEW-YORK/PAT'D FEB. 8,
1859," brass frame, two piece
walnut grips (Flayderman 7A-
117) **750.00**

REVOLVERS (CARTRIDGE)

Colt

Camp Perry, caliber 22 long rifle, Serial Number 1714, 8" barrel, double
action, one-shot chamber, old but
non-factory 13 x 7 x 2½" walnut

case, fitted with custom carved wooden grips, 97-98% orig blue, excellent to mint bore (Flayderman 5B-210) **750.00**

Cloverleaf, House Model, caliber 41 RF, Serial Number 2123, 1½" octagonal barrel stamped "COLT" on left side, 4-shot cylinder, walnut grips, hammer, trigger, and barrel all with 98% orig blue, brass frame very sharp and crisp with 97-98% orig light silver plate (Flayderman 5B-151) **2,300.00**

Model 1878, "Alaskan," caliber 45, Serial Number 47766, stamped with U.S. inspection marked, dated 1902, most of the lightly age browned re-blue finish overall, Rampant Colt grips (Flayderman 5B-189) **450.00**

New Line 22, caliber 22RF, Serial number 19644, 7-shot cylinder, 2¼" barrel, varnished rosewood grips, nickel plate finish, all orig, blued barrel with etched panel and an even 75% blue, brass frame with 95% slightly dulled nickel plate (Flayderman 5B-165) **275.00**

Woodsman, caliber 22LR, Serial Number 153549, 4½" barrel, 99.5% orig pre-War blue finish, orig carton missing one-half of end label **550.00**

Harrington & Richardson

Blue Jacket No. 2, caliber 32RF, Serial Number 589, full factory engraved, deeper cuts highlighted with black paint or enamel, checkered hard rubber grips with head of dog at top, 99% plus orig nickel plate **175.00**

USRA Target, caliber 22, Serial Number 1669, 7" barrel, checkered walnut grips, orig labeled carton with instructions on lid, 20% blue on forestrap only, balance with 98% blue **650.00**

High Standard, Supermatic Trophy Auto, caliber 22 LR, Serial Number 236994, 7¼" barrel, spare 5½" barrel, orig foam plastic carton, blued, 99.9% brand new **400.00**

Hopkins & Allen XL Navy, Serial Number 952, caliber 38RF, 6½" round barrel, varnished grips, orig brown leather holster, leather flap replace during period with a piece of black oil cloth, cylinder with 80% nickel, blued trigger and case colored hammer (Flayderman 8A-065) **625.00**

Marlin No. 32 Standard, Serial Number 5417, caliber 32RF, 3" round tip-up barrel, five shot fluted cylinder, steel frame with spur trigger, full factory engraved, fitted with DeGress grips, light grip with scroll and foliage relief plus the "PAT. APR-28-74" marking around the screw hole, right with a 1½" figure of standing woman surrounded by foliage, 95% of orig nickel plate (Flayderman 5D-016) **800.00**

Mauser, Model 1914 Auto, caliber 32, Serial Number 263004, slide dated 1920, forestrap stamped with issue marks "L.Hi.116," one-piece wood grip, 90% plus orig blue **200.00**

Savage, Model 1917 Auto, caliber 32, Serial Number 255730, visible spur type hammer, ten-shot magazine, 3¾" barrel, dull blue-black finish, later production with model designation on left side of frame, 99% plus dull blue-black finish (Flayderman 8B-019) .. **200.00**

Smith & Wesson

Model 1½ Old, Serial Number 10322, caliber 32RF, 5-shot non-fluted cylinder, rosewood grips, 80% orig blue, left grip missing a small chip at rim (Flayderman 5G-027) **350.00**

Model 3, caliber 44 Russian, Serial Number 14964, 6½" barrel, 6-shot fluted cylinder, target sights, 99% orig old reblue finish (Flayderman 5G-125) **400.00**

32 Safety 1st Model DA, Serial Number 77788, caliber 32 S &W, 3" barrel, 5-shot fluted cylinder, bottom of left grip stamped with number 6304, black hard rubber "S & W" grips, over 95% orig blue, only hints of bright wear at edge (Flayderman 5G-043) **100.00**

38 Double Action Perfected, Serial Number 9296, caliber 38 S&W, 6" barrel, 5-shot fluted cylinder, "S&W" checkered hard rubber grips, about mint with bright case colored trigger and hammer, blued release catch at top of frame, balance of steel parts with 99.9% orig nickel plate (Flayderman 5G-080) **300.00**

Walther Air Pistol MDL. LP3, caliber .177, Serial Number 34960, orig foam carton, tools and instructions, brand new **225.00**

FLINTLOCK LONG ARMS

French, Model 1766 Charlesville Musket, orig barrel length 44¾", lockplate only partially legible "Charlesville," etc. markings, correct period and matching ramrod very slightly too short, top jaw and screw period replacements, otherwise complete and orig throughout **1,100.00**

Kentucky, N. Beyer, caliber 50, original smooth bore, 58½″ overall, 42½″ part round barrel, orig front sight mounted on light engraved brass oval, sgd in script "N. Beyer" on top flat and secured to stock with incise carving on the forend to the faceted brass tailpipe, 2 faceted brass ramrod pipes and brass forend cap, beveled brass sideplate, raised scroll carving about tang with lightly engraved silver oval wrist escutcheon, incise carving at wrist on right side, left side with raised carved scrolls, a large raised carved scroll to rear of cheekpiece, engraved brass patch box with bird finial, typical Beyer beveled brass trigger guard, reconverted barrel and lock **3,500.00**

U.S. Model 1803, Harpers Ferry Armory, later production, c1814–20, 54 caliber, single shot, muzzleloader, 33″ part octagon and part round 36″ barrel, blade front sight, open rear sight, lock with integral forged iron flashpan with fence at rear, brass mountings, walnut half stock of 30½″ with small cheekrest, brass patchbox on right side of butt (Flayderman 9A-114) .. **2,750.00**

U.S. Model 1808, Thomas French, Canton, MA, Contract Musket, Harpers Ferry pattern, tail of lock stamped "CANTON/1810," below the pan with the eagle and "US" over "FRENCH" (well struck with no trace of "T."), barrel stamped "US/V" with sunken eagle head CT proof (Flayderman 9A-131) **1,000.00**

U.S. Model 1819, Hall, breech loading, second production type, Harpers Ferry Armory, John Hall's patents, 52 caliber, single shot, 32⅝″ round barrel, three barrel bands, breechblock deeply stamped "J. H. HALL/H.FERRY/1836" (Flayderman (A-249) **900.00**

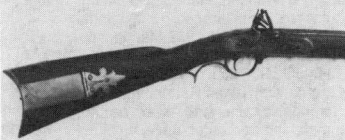

Pennsylvania Long Rifle, 55½″ l, Peter Moll, Hellertown, Warranted No. 58, artificially striped stock, c1830, $2,000.00.

PERCUSSION LONG ARMS

Note: Conversion of flintlock long arms to percussion was common practice. Most English, French, and U.S. military flintlock model long arms listed in the previous section can be found in percussion. Values for these percussion converted long arms are from 40 to 60% of the flintlock values previously noted.

English, 577 Rifled Musket, 39¼″ barrel fitted with folding leaf long range sight, lockplate stamped with crown and "1863/TOWER," walnut full stock with brass forend cap, trigger guard, and butt plate, orig nipple protector, complete with correct style English bayonet, excellent to mint condition . **1,200.00**

Kentucky Rifle, swivel breech, 51″ overall, deeply rifled 38 caliber octagonal barrels, sgd "JOHN . SHULER/LIVERPOOL. PA" on both top flats, one side of the barrel group a flat piece of steel, the other with four brass ramrod pipes, tiger stripped butt stock with engraved brass sideplate, light engraved brass trigger guard with double set triggers, engraved brass patchbox and toe plate, lightly engraved German silver escutcheon at wrist, 2″ inlay on left side, back action lock sgd "N. ASHMORE," old ramrod probably not orig **1,000.00**

Merrill, James H., Baltimore, MD, c1862–65, Serial No. 8100, 54 caliber, breechloader with action identical to carbine, 33″ round barrel, stamped "J. H. MERRILL BALTO./PAT. JULY 1858/APL. 9 MAY 21–28–61" forward of hammer, brass mountings and patchbox, full walnut stock, lug on right side of barrel at muzzle end for attaching saber type bayonet, complete and orig throughout, barrel with 95% of orig glossy brown finish (Flayderman 9B-077) **3,600.00**

U.S. Model 1842, Springfield Armory, c1844-1855, 69 caliber, single shot, muzzleloader, 42″ round barrel, three barrel bands, lockplate stamped with American eagle motif above "US" forward of hammer, stamped vertically behind hammer "Springfield/1852," inspector initial cartouche stamped on left side of stock, steel ramrod with trumpet head, bayonet lug on bottom of barrel at muzzle, walnut stock with comb (Flayderman 9A-291) **650.00**

Model 1863, Rifle Musket, Type II (a.k.a. Model 1864), Springfield Armory, c1864–65, 58 caliber, single shot, muzzleloader, 40″ round barrel, three barrel bands, lock stamped with eagle motif to right of hammer, "U.S./ SPRINGFIELD" beneath nipple bolster, "1864" at angle at rear section of lock, single leaf rear sight, walnut stock (Flayderman 9A-341) 800.00

RIFLES

BSA Model 12, 22 long rifle, single shot, 29" blued barrel, Martini-type action, match sights, checkered walnut straight grip stock and forearm 200.00

Harrington & Richardson Reising 60, semi-automatic, 45 caliber, blued 18¼" barrel, open rear sight, blade front sight, 12-shot detachable box, painted wooden one-piece semi-pistol grip stock and forearm 350.00

Marlin Model 100S Tom Mix Special, 22 short, long, long rifle, single shot, 24" round barrel, hooded front sight, peep rear sight, plain pistol grip stock and forearm 90.00

Military, United States

Model 1903, Springfield, caliber 30-06, 24" barrel, bolt action, repeating, manual thumb safety at rear of bolt, 5 shot box magazine, blade front sight, leaf with aperture, notched battle rear sight, plain one-piece stock and forearm, wood hand guard over barrel, cleaning rod-type bayonet 200.00

M1 Carbine, caliber 30, semi-automatic, gas operated, 18" barrel, 30 shot magazine, blade front sight with protective ears, flip-down rear sight, one-piece wood stock and forearm, wood hand guard on top of barrel 325.00

Remington No. 4S Boy Scout Model, 22 short, single shot, 28" medium round barrel, No. 4 rolling-block action, visible hammer, blade front sight, open "v" notch rear sight adjustable for elevation, musket-style, oiled walnut, one-piece full-length stock and forearm with steel buttplate 275.00

SHOTGUNS

Bernardelli Holland, 12 gauge, double barrel, 32" barrel, top lever break-open, hammerless, double trigger, automatic rejector, blued, straight stock 1,500.00

Fox Sterlingworth, 16 gauge, double barrel, 26" barrel, full & full choke, top lever break-open, hammerless, double trigger, blued, checkered walnut pistol grip stock and forearm 350.00

Ithaca Victory, 12 gauge, single barrel, 34" barrel, full choke, ventilated rib, top lever break-open, hammerless, blued, checkered pistol grip stock and forearm, standard grade 850.00

Savage Model 720, 12 gauge, 4-shot tubular, 30" cylinder bore, full choke, Browning patent, semi-automatic, hammerless, blued, checkered walnut pistol grip stock and forearm, plain receiver 175.00

Stevens, Model No. 970, 12 gauge, single shot, round barrel with octagon breech, 32" long, top lever break-open, hammerless, automatic shell ejector, automatic safety, blued, case hardened frame, checkered walnut pistol grip stock and forearm 65.00

COMMEMORATIVE PIECES AND REPLICAS

Note: Starting in 1985 Richard A. Bourne Co. began offering modern commemorative pieces for resale. The results are the beginning of establishing a true market value for these items. In 1988 Bourne sold a number of replica weapons. Again, the results represent an initial look at the resale potential of these weapons.

Pistol

Browning, 1878-1978 Centennial Set, Browning HP 9mm pistol, Serial Number 1878D-1353, chrome plated with gilt trigger, orig wood case 525.00

Colt, Buntline Commemorative Set, Serial Number NB1 690, 45 caliber, 12" barrel, nickel plated, Rampart Colt hard rubber grips, orig walnut display case with glass partition, plaque, 6 nickel plated dummy bullets, orig shipping carton, full documentation 600.00

Colt, Pocket Navy, replica, Serial Number 50545, 5½" barrel, orig carton, factory tag 200.00

Smith & Wesson, Ranger Commemorative Set, Model 19-3, Serial Number TR6124, .357 Magnum revolver, 4" barrel with "TEXAS RANGERS" stamping, right side of frame with Texas Ranger seal, orig wooden case with seal on lid, matching numbered knife 400.00

Rifle

Browing, Bi-Centennial Commemorative Rifle, Model 78, Serial Number 1776-0484, single shot, caliber 45-70, 24" octagonal barrel, orig alderwood case, matching number engraved knife and metal, orig carton, full documentation **950.00**

Churchill, "One Of One Hundred" Rifle, Churchill Gunmakers Ltd. for Interarms as part of their "One Of One Thousand" series to commemorate Interarms's 20th Anniversary, Serial Number 5, caliber 30-06, Mauser type action, 23¾" barrel, the action, floor plate, trigger guard, rear of barrel, and sighting ramp all specially scroll and game scene engraved, orig leather trunk, full documentation **2,600.00**

Churchill, "One Of One Thousand" Rifle, Churchill Gunmakers Ltd for Interarms, Serial Number 45, caliber .375 H&H, 26½" barrel, orig carton, full documentation **1,200.00**

Kentucky Rifle, replica, 38 caliber rifled octagonal browned barrel, 38" barrel, 53½" overall, fitted with peep front sight and windage adjustable rear sight, silver plated lock with simple engraved dec, grained full stock with silver and German silver inlays, openwork patchbox, sgd on wood inside patchbox "STOCK AND HARDWARE/BY LADOW JOHNSON/TOLEDO OHIO NOV 1954" **1,100.00**

Weatherby, 1976 Bi-Centennial, Mark V bolt action rifle, Serial Number B-0889, caliber 7mm Magnum, engraved floor plate, fancy stock with inlaid gilt "1976 BI-CENTENNIAL," never mounted with sights, orig carton **550.00**

Winchester, Bicentennial 76 Model 1894 carbine, Serial Number USA 04296, caliber 30-30, orig carton, full documentation **250.00**

FIREHOUSE COLLECTIBLES

History: The volunteer fire company has played a vital role in the protection and social growth of many towns and rural areas. Paid professional firemen usually are found only in large metropolitan areas. Each fire company prided itself on equipment and uniforms. Conventions and parades gave the fire companies a chance to show off their equipment. These events produced a wealth of firehouse related memorabilia.

Reference: Mary Jane and James Piatti, *Firehouse Collectibles,* The Engine House, 1979.

Museums: Insurance Company of North America (INA) Museum, Philadelphia, PA; Oklahoma State Fireman's Association Museum, Oklahoma City, OK; San Francisco Fire Dept. Memorial Museum, San Francisco, CA.

Additional Listings: See *Warman's Americana & Collectibles* for more examples.

Advertising
Booklet, "Footprints of Assurance," copyright by The Home Insurance Co., fire marks, 1st edition, Beck Engraving Co., 1953 .... **35.00**

Sign, 16 x 28", wood, Republic Underwriters of Dallas **125.00**

Watch Fob, Franklin Fire Insurance, brass, bust of Benjamin Franklin, fire pumper, emb on front **30.00**

Alarm Box, 16¾" h, cast iron, architectural form, pediment, raised letters "Fire Alarm Telegraph Station," alligatored red paint, polished brass numbers **85.00**

Axe, parade type, brass blade, black handle **150.00**

Badge, 2", shield shape, "Advance H. L. & E. Co. 1, Bellmore," Cairns & Bros, NY, c1880 .... **24.00**

Bell, 10", Edwards, 1872, D.C. transformer **25.00**

Belt, parade type, felt cov leather, "Dublin, No. 1," c1910 .... **60.00**

Book, *Fire Dept, Haverhill, MA, Complete History, 1897*, hardcover, 148 pgs **75.00**

Bucket, leather, painted dec
12½", green ground, scene of flaming house, fireman in foreground, scrolling frame, "No. 2, City Fire Society, Benjn. Dodd" written on white bands, handle detached, 1822 .... **9,350.00**

18", front painted with scene of town consumed in flames, fire fighters running through streets, shield shaped reserve inscribed "William Lovejoy" in white, medium blue ground, bowknot inscribed banner "Enterprise Fire-Club, 1810," blue painted tooled rim, leather encased rope swing handle, front yellow ground, back coral red ground ... **14,850.00**

Coat, parade type, tan, navy blue trim and piping, two rows of silver buttons **65.00**

Extinguisher
Badger's Pony, 1¼ gal, copper and brass **90.00**

Chemical, brass canister **80.00**

First Aid Kit, "Detroit Fire Dept," c1923 **60.00**

Gong, 16 x 9½", Gamewell, wall model, 6" brass bell, oak case **475.00**

Hat, ceremonial, parade, top hat style, hp, pressed felt
6" h, central oval reserve with Thomas Jefferson portrait medal-

lion, laurel wreaths, scrolled banner inscribed "Jefferson Hook & Ladder Company" in gilt letters, company insignia, hook, ladder, and pump on back, owner's initials "J.H." in shield, black ground, underbrim painted red, three paper int. labels **7,425.00**

6¾" h, front portrait medallion of General Lafayette, gilt leaf scrolling frame, sapphire blue banner inscribed "Lafayette Hose Company" in gilt letters, back with initials "F.A.," top with owner's initials "P.V." red ground, underbrim painted blue-green, c1840 ...... **5,500.00**

7" h, top painted with "At The Forge" after John Neagle, vignette framed by volutes inscribed "Mechanic Fire Compy" in gilt letters, reverse painted with wood fire hydrant flanked by initials "F" and "A," top painted with two lovers in landscape, owner's initials "J.M.W.," red ground, underbrim painted dark green **11,000.00**

Helmet, leather, black, gold eagle, red and white dec, made by Cairns & Brothers, NY, size 7¼", $175.00.

Helmet
Beaver holder, white, sewn seams . **300.00**
Leather, high eagle, black, front piece reads "Eureka Hose 14" **225.00**
Lantern, Dietz, clear glass, Fitzall National USA, globe, 1914 .... **95.00**
Photo
5 x 7", fireman wearing dress uniform, large parade ribbon from "Junior Fire Co of Reading, PA" **6.00**
11 x 8¼", firehouse, horse drawn steamers, Pittsburgh, PA, 1907 .. **3.00**
Postcard, Central Fire Station, Glens Falls, NY, multicolored, c1915 ..... **3.00**
Poster, litho, Newburg Fire Department,

1897, uniformed firemen, entwined hose, Centennial - Convention, Hudson River Firemans Assoc **200.00**
Ribbon, Good Will Steam Fire Eng. Co., East York, PA, Sesquicentennial, 1899, red, white, blue, and gold ... **50.00**
Trumpet, presentation
19", Britannia metal, engraving, including steamer, marked "Simpson Hall Miller Co., Wallingford, CT" .. **785.00**
20", silverplated, New York City, 1908 **1,250.00**

FIREPLACE EQUIPMENT

History: The fireplace was a gathering point in the colonial home for heat, meals, and social interaction. It maintained its dominant position until the introduction of central heating in the mid-19th century.

Because of the continued popularity of the fireplace, accessories still are manufactured, usually in an early American motif.

Reproduction Alert: Modern blacksmiths are reproducing many old iron implements.

Additional Listings: Brass and Iron.

Andirons, pr
16¼", wrought iron, serpent standard, open jaws, flicking tongue, splayed legs, pad feet, 19th C **4,125.00**
16½", brass, ball finial, turned standard, spurred arch legs, shod slipper feet, turned log stops, early 19th C **450.00**
18", brass and wrought iron, urn finial, beaded molding, rect plinth base, spur support, ball feet, c1795 ... **2,000.00**
19½", cast iron, figural, baseball batter holding bat over shoulder and baseball pitcher, 1900 uniform, minor repaint **6,600.00**

Fire Box, 14 x 20 x 22", cast iron, ornate handles and feet, $150.00.

25¾", wrought iron, skewer support, knob finial, arched legs, penny feet, 18th C **1,500.00**

Bellows

16", orig yellow paint, red, green, and black dec, brass nozzle **75.00**

17½", orig yellow paint, red, green, brown, and black stencil, fruits and foliage, brass nozzle **200.00**

18", painted and dec wood, turtle back, stenciled fruit compote, orig worn green ground, releathered sides, brass nozzle **170.00**

Clock Jack, 13", meat roasting rack, clockwork mechanism, brass, porcelain nameplate, bell, France **750.00**

Coal Shovel, 46¾", wrought iron, ram's horn finial **50.00**

Crane, 31", wrought iron, 18th C **110.00**

Ember Tongs, 14", wrought iron, punched penny ends **225.00**

Fender

32" l, brass and wrought iron, brass top rail, four ball finials on mesh grill **300.00**

42" l, brass, three panels, stylized swans and turned spindles, flame finials, 20th C **225.00**

48" l, 29¾" h, wrought iron, low rect, tall cutouts of polo players, early 20th C **750.00**

Fire Back, cast iron

19½" w, 24" h man on horse, inscription, "1794," Pennsylvania **1,650.00**

22½" h, arched molded crest and frame, three tulips, flowerhead and "1794," Pennsylvania **3,400.00**

30" w, 23" h, scrolling foliage, rect panel, pressed swags, Pennsylvania **775.00**

Fire Dogs, 12¾", ornate brass, floral scroll on cast bases, cherub heads, ball finial, 19th C **125.00**

Hearth Broom, 29¾" l, smoke grained white paint, red and bronze stenciling **375.00**

Kettle Shelf, 14", wrought iron, cast iron top, old black paint **65.00**

Screen, 29" w, 43" h, Louis XVI, French, tulipwood, serpentine cresting, fabric lined panel, hinged wooden writing surface, trestle supports, late 18th C **600.00**

Spider, copper, 3 wrought iron legs, shaped handles, marked "C.F.L." .. **85.00**

Spit, wrought iron, 8 hooks, long pan at bottom **375.00**

Toaster, 13 x 16", wrought iron, fancy iron work **400.00**

Tools, 26½", wrought iron, shovel and tongs, early 19th C **360.00**

Trivet

9 x 14", brass and wrought iron, pierced top, foliate motifs, raised

frontal scroll feet, rear penny feet, George III **550.00**

10½", iron and brass, reticulated top, turned wooden handle **75.00**

Warming Stand, 15 x 10½ x 28½", tin, domed top, molded door, brass ring handles, cabriole legs, penny feet, gold stencil, black ground **1,200.00**

FISCHER J.
BUDAPEST.

FISCHER CHINA

History: In 1893 Moritz Fischer founded his factory in Herend, Hungary, a center of porcelain production from the 1790s.

Confusion exists about Fischer china because of its resemblance to the wares of Meissen, Sevres, and Oriental export. It often was bought and sold as the product of these firms. Forged marks of other potteries are found on Herend pieces. The mark "MF," often joined, is the mark of Moritz Fischer's pottery.

Fischer's Herend is hard paste ware with luminosity and exquisite decoration. Pieces are designated by pattern names, the best known being Chantilly Fruit, Rothschild Bird, Chinese Bouquet, Victoria Butterfly, and Parsley.

Fischer also made figural birds and animal groups, Magyar figures (individually and in groups), and Herend eagles poised for flight.

Reference: Susan and Al Bagdade, *Warman's English & Continental Pottery & Porcelain, 1st Edition,* Warman Publishing Co., Inc., 1987.

Vase, 13¾" h, cornucopia body, pierced rim, painted floral motif, four feet with fish scale dec, stamped and imp 1913 mark, orig paper label, $275.00.

Bowl, 11 x 10″, reticulated, figural butterfly, marked **225.00**
Cache Pot, 5″, handled, Rothschild Bird pattern **160.00**
Charger, 13″, multicolored enamel floral dec, gold trim **325.00**
Egg Cup, gold trim **125.00**
Ewer
  7½″, enameled floral dec **200.00**
  16″, multicolored enamel floral dec, reticulated **300.00**
Jar, 7″, hexagon, multicolored enamel floral relief, reticulated, rose finial . . **275.00**
Nappy, 4½″, triangular, Victoria Butterfly pattern, gold trim **125.00**
Plate
  7½″, luncheon, Chantilly Fruit pattern **90.00**
  10½″, dinner, Parsley pattern **115.00**
Sauce Boat, underplate, and matching china ladle, Victoria Butterfly pattern, 3 pcs **250.00**
Tureen, cov, 8½″, handled, Chantilly Fruit pattern, natural molded fruit finial **300.00**
Urn, 12″, blue floral dec, reticulated, shield mark **325.00**
Vase
  4½″, raised panels, enameled floral dec **100.00**
  8″, gold handles, blue flowers and green leaves, reticulated, shield mark **230.00**
  8½″, barrel, reticulated **350.00**
  10½″, reticulated, flowers, pink, blue, green, and white **200.00**
  12″, bulbous, extended neck, cobalt blue reticulated handle, ochre, multicolored flowers, gold accents, deep rose sides **375.00**

FITZHUGH

History: Fitzhugh, one of the most recognized Chinese Export porcelain patterns, was named for the Fitzhugh family for whom the first dinner service was made. The peak period of production was from 1780 to 1850.

Fitzhugh features an oval center medallion or monogram surrounded by four groups of flowers or emblems. The border is similar to that on Nanking china. Occasional border variations are found. Butterfly and honeycomb are among the rarest.

Blue is the common color. Color is a key factor in pricing with rarity in ascending order of orange, green, sepia, mulberry, yellow, black, and gold. Combinations of colors are scarce.

Reference: Sandra Andacht, *Oriental Antiques & Art: An Identification And Value Guide,* Wallace-Homestead, 1987.

Reproduction Alert: Spode Porcelain Company, England, and Vista Alegre, Portugal, currently are producing copies of the Fitzhugh pattern. Oriental copies also are available.

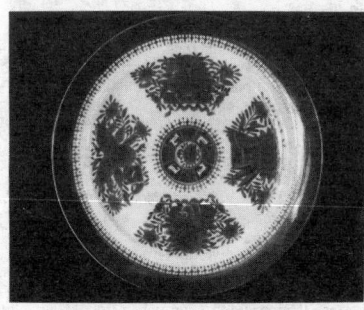

Plate, 9⅝″ d, orange, $300.00.

Basket, 7⅝″ l, oval 9¼″ stand, shades of orange, gilding in center, floral sprig in trellis diaper, beast medallion edged in spearheads and dumbbells, surrounded by four clusters of flowers and precious objects, pierced rim, gilt edge, metal grape cluster and loop replacement handles, c1820 . . . . . . **2,325.00**
Hot Water Dish, 10⅝″ d, underglaze blue, center pine cone and beast medallion, four clusters of flowers and precious objects in trellis diaper border, spearhead and dumbbell border, blue spouts, c1840 . . . . **400.00**
Plate
  7⅞″, dessert, orange, center floral sprig medallion, border of butterflies, diaper, and scalework panels, key fret and floral sprigs on gilt edged rim, c1820, pr **350.00**
  9¾″, dinner, orange, floral sprig in medallion of beasts and trellis diaperwork, edged in spearheads and dumbbells, four clusters of flowers and precious objects, set of six, minor chips and restoration, c1810 . **2,475.00**
Platter and Strainer, 15⅞″ l, oval, orange, deep platter, pierced strainer, gilt edged central aperture, three rows of smaller holes, floral sprig in medallion of beasts and trellis diaperwork, edged in spearheads and dumbbells, four clusters of flowers and precious objects, c1810 . . . . . . **2,750.00**
Salt, 4″ l, oval, underglaze blue, center pine cone and beast medallion, spearhead and dumbbell border, ruffled rim, Mared pattern border, feathered edge, fluted sides, four clusters

of flowers and precious objects, c1820, pr **1,430.00**

Soup Tureen, 13⅞" l, cov, 16⅛" platter, oval, orange, floral sprig in medallion of beasts and trellis diaperwork, edged in spearheads and dumbbells, four clusters of flowers and precious objects, foot and cavetto of platter with cell diaper border, border of diaper and scalework panels, butterflies, floral sprigs, and fret motifs on gilt-edged rims, re-gilt entwined strap handles, re-gilt flowerhead knob, c1810 .... **5,000.00**

FLASKS

History: A flask is a container for liquids, usually having a narrow neck. Early American glass companies frequently formed them in molds which left a relief design on the front and/or back. Historical flasks with a portrait, building, scene, or name are the most desired.

A chestnut is hand blown, small, and has a flattened bulbous body. The pitkin has a blown globular body with vertical ribs with a spiral rib overlay. Teardrop flasks are generally fiddle shaped and have a scroll or geometric design.

Dimensions can differ for the same flask because of variations in the molding process. Color is important, with scarcer colors demanding more money. Aqua and amber are the most common colors. Bottles with "sickness," an opalescent scaling which eliminates clarity, are worth much less.

Reference: George L. and Helen McKearin, *American Glass*, Crown Publishers, 1941 and 1948.

Chestnut
4¼", golden amber, vertical rib, pontil **200.00**

7" h, one half pint, eagle on one side, cornucopia on other, aqua, Keene, McKearin G2-18, $350.00.

4⅞", pale green, 10 diamond over flutes, pontil **425.00**
5", golden amber, swirled to left, pontil **200.00**
8¼", deep yellow green, applied flat string ring, large pontil, sheared mouth **125.00**
Coin Spot, 5¾", golden yellow, sheared, pontil **450.00**
Gemel, 11⅛" clear, pink and white looping, sheared mouth, applied white collar, polished pontil **100.00**
Historical
  Baltimore Liberty & Union, aqua, pt, McKearin GVI-003 .... **250.00**
  Byron & Scott, yellow olive, ½ pt, McKearin GI-114 .... **125.00**
  Eagle and drafted man, deep aqua, pt, Zanesville, McKearin GII-140 . **225.00**
  George Washington, aqua, 7", pt, McKearin GI-010 .... **210.00**
  Grant & Eagle, aqua, yellow amber striation, pt, McKearin GI-079a .. **250.00**
  Jenny Ling & Lyre, aqua, qt, McKearin GI-110 .... **700.00**
  Lowell Railroad and eagle, deep golden amber, ½ pt, McKearin GV-010 .... **150.00**
  Masonic & Frigate, yellow green, pt, Kensington, McKearin GIV-034 .. **1,300.00**
  Monument, Capt Brag, olive green, ½ pt, McKearin GVI-001a **850.00**
  Taylor & Monument, pink amethystine, pt, McKearin GI-073 ...... **750.00**
  US Army, blue green, flower, iron pontil, qt, McKearin GXII-015 ...... **310.00**
Ovoid, 6½", yellow green, 2 part mold, sheared neck, pontil **70.00**
Pitkin
  4⅞", olive green, ribs swirled to left, pontil **180.00**
  5¼", golden amber **300.00**
  6¼", green, ribs swirled to right, pontil **160.00**
  7", light olive amber, vertically ribbed, pontil **340.00**
  8½", ribs swirled to right, one flat side **90.00**
Pumpkinseed
  Light amber, wide collar lip **25.00**
  Purple, clock face, webbing **25.00**
Teardrop, 7¾", Tulip, etched frost border, wreath reverse **145.00**

FLOW BLUE

History: Flow blue or flowing blue is the name applied to china of cobalt and white whose color, when fired in a kiln, produced a flowing or smudged effect. The blue varies in color from dark cobalt to a grayish or steel blue. The flow varies from very slight to a heavy blur where the pattern cannot be easily recognized. The blue color does not permeate through the china.

Flow blue was first produced around 1835 in the Staffordshire district of England by a large number of potters including Alcock, Davenport, J. Wedgwood, Grindley, New Wharf, Johnson Brothers, and many others. The early flow blue, 1830s to 1870s, was usually of the ironstone variety. The late patterns, 1880s to 1910s, and modern patterns, after 1910, usually were made of the more delicate semi-porcelain variety. Approximately 95% of the flow blue was made in England, with the remaining 5% made in Germany, Holland, France, and Belgium. A few patterns also were made in the United States by Mercer, Warwick, and Wheeling Pottery companies.

References: Mary F. Gaston, *The Collector's Encyclopedia Of Flow Blue China,* Collector Books, 1983; Petra Williams, *Flow Blue China— An Aid To Identification,* Fountain House East, 1981, revised edition; Petra Williams, *Flow Blue China II,* Fountain House East, 1981, revised edition; Petra Williams, *Flow Blue China and Mulberry Ware—Similarity and Value Guide,* Fountain House East, 1981, revised edition.

EARLY PATTERNS: c1825-1850

Bowl
Fairy Villas, John Maddock, c 1842, 9″	85.00
Gironde, W H Grindley, c1842, 5″	20.00

Coffeepot, cov, Lobelia, G Phillips,
c1845	275.00

Creamer
Amoy, Davenport, c1844	225.00
Columbia, Clementson & Young, c1846, 5¾″	120.00
Flora, Thomas Walker, c1845	165.00

Cup and Saucer, handleless
Indian Jar, Jacob and Thomas Furnival, c1843	75.00
Pelew, E Challinor, c1840	100.00
Scinde, J & G Alcock, c1840	90.00

Cup Plate
Indian Jar, Jacob and Thomas Furnival, c1843	75.00
Scinde, J & G Alcock, c1840	75.00

Dinner Service, Amoy, Davenport,
c1844, service for six, handleless cups and saucers, creamer, sugar, sauce dishes, 7¼″, 9¼″, and 10¼″ plates	2,400.00
Gravy, Amoy, Davenport, c1844	260.00

Honey Dish, Indian Jar, Jacob and
Thomas Furnival, c1843, 5″	65.00

Pitcher, milk
Indian Jar, Jacob and Thomas Furnival, c1843	225.00
Lobelia, G Phillips, c1845	150.00
Scinde, J & G Alcock, c1840	135.00

Plate
Amoy, Davenport, c1844	85.00
Candia, Cauldon, c1841	45.00

Early Pattern, Manilla, 9″ plate, Podmore Walker & Co, c1845, $90.00.

Columbia, Clementson & Young, c1846, 7½″	40.00
Fairy Villas, 9″, John Maddock, c1842	40.00
Flora, Thomas Walker, c1845, 9½″	85.00
Gironde, 10″, W H Grindley, c1842	55.00
Indian Jar, Jacob and Thomas Furnival, c1843, 7½″	40.00
Manilla, Podmore Walker, 9″, c1845	90.00
Pelew, E Challinor, c1840, 10″	85.00
Scinde, Walker, 7″, c1847	55.00

Platter
Indian Jar, Jacob and Thomas Furnival, c1843, 18 x 14″	300.00
Pelew, E Challinor, c1840, 13 x 10″	190.00
Scinde, J & G Alcock, c1840, 16″	460.00

Relish, Scinde, J & G Alcock, c1840,
shell shape	85.00

Sauce
Pelew, E Challinor, c1840	40.00
Scinde, J & G Alcock, c1840	42.00

Sauce Tureen, cov, attached underplate
Oregon, T J & J Mayer, c1845, 6″ ladle, 3 pcs	425.00
Scinde, J & G Alcock, c1840	375.00

Soup Plate, flanged
Gironde, W H Grindley, c1842, 9″	55.00
Pelew, E Challinor, c1840, 10½″	125.00

Sugar, cov
Flora, Thomas Walker, c1845	175.00
Lobelia, G Phillips, c1845	150.00
Scinde, J & G Alcock, c1840	175.00

Teapot, cov, Lobelia, G Phillips, c1845	200.00

Vegetable, cov
Manilla, Podmore Walker, c1845	400.00
Scinde, J & G Alcock, c1840, 11 x 9″	350.00

Waste Bowl, Scinde, J & G Alcock,
c1840, 9″	150.00

MIDDLE PATTERNS: c1850-1870

Charger, Tyrolean, Wm Ridgway & Co, c1850, 12¼″	125.00

Creamer
    Coburg, John Edwards, c1860 . . . .   **150.00**
    Lozere, Edward Challinor, c1850 . . .   **75.00**
Lustre Band, Elsmore & Forster, c1860   **50.00**
Gravy Boat, Delft, Minton, c1870 . . . .   **75.00**
Ladle, Delft, Minton, c1870, 10″ **75.00**
Match Holder, Carlton, Samuel Alcock,
    c1850, marked "Carlton Ware," gold
    trim, 3½ x 2″ **55.00**
Pitcher, Gothic, Jacob Furnival, c1850,
    6½″ **125.00**
Plate
    Formosa, Thomas, John and Joseph
      Mayer, c1850, 9½″ **80.00**
    Gotha, Joseph Heath, c1850, 9½″ . .   **32.00**
    Gothic, Jacob Furnival, c1850, 9″ . .   **40.00**
    Monmouth, New Wharf Pottery,
      c1870 . . . .   **38.00**
Platter
    Canton, Maddock, c1850, 14″ **100.00**
    Madras, Samuel Alcock & Co, c1845,
      13½″ **150.00**
Sauce, Lustre Band, Elsmore & Forster,
    c1860 . . . .   **20.00**
Soup Plate, Gothic, Jacob Furnival,
    c1850, rimmed **65.00**
Syllabub Cup, Hindustan, John Mad-
    dock, c1855 . . . .   **75.00**
Vegetable, cov
    Coburg, John Edwards, c1860, 10 x
      7″ **400.00**
    Lozere, Edward Challinor, c1850, 10
      x 8″ **150.00**
Waste Bowl, Morning Glory, unknown
    English maker, c1860 . . . .   **125.00**

**Late Pattern, Touraine, cup and saucer,
Stanley Pottery Co., c1898, $45.00.**

LATE PATTERNS: c1880-1900s

Biscuit Jar, Watteau, Doulton, 1896–
    1930, metal top **325.00**
Bone Dish
    Argyle, Johnson Bros, c1900 . . . . .   **50.00**

Devon, Alfred Meakin, c1907 . . . . .   **50.00**
Duchess, W H Grindley, c1891 . . . .   **50.00**
Marechal Niel, W H Grindley, c1895   **25.00**
Touraine, Henry Alcock, c1898 . . . .   **50.00**
Tulip, Johnson Bros, c1900 . . . . . .   **50.00**
Blue Danube, Johnson Bros, c1900   **50.00**
Bowl, Richmond, Burgess & Leigh,
    c1905, 8″ **28.00**
Butter, cov, drain, Renown, Arthur Wilk-
    ison, c1907, marked "Royal Stafford-
    shire" **75.00**
Butter Pat, Non Pariel, Alfred Meakin,
    c1907 . . . .   **30.00**
Creamer
    Manhattan, Henry Alcock, c1900 . . .   **110.00**
    Renown, Arthur Wilkison, c1907,
      marked "Royal Staffordshire" . . .   **50.00**
    Syrian, W. H. Grindley, 1891 . . . . . .   **145.00**
Cup and Saucer
    Manhattan, Henry Alcock, c1900 . . .   **55.00**
    Renown, Arthur Wilkison, c1907,
      marked "Royal Staffordshire" . . .   **35.00**
Gravy, stand, Renown, Arthur Wilkison,
    c1907, marked "Royal Staffordshire"   **75.00**
Pitcher, water, Arcadia, Enoch Plant,
    c1900 . . . .   **285.00**
Plate
    Asiatic Pheasant, John Meir & Son,
      c1865, 8¾″ **25.00**
    Claremont, Johnson Bros, c1891,
      8½″ **40.00**
    Lancaster, New Wharf Pottery, c1891,
      9″ **40.00**
    Non Pariel, Alfred Meakin, c1907,
      7½″ **30.00**
    Normandy, Johnson Bros, c1900, 10″   **65.00**
    Waldorf, New Wharf Pottery, c1892,
      9″ **50.00**
Platter
    Albany, Grindley, c1899, 14″ **130.00**
    Argyle, Grindley, c1896, 13″ **90.00**
    Marechal Niel, W H Grindley, c1895,
      18″ **125.00**
    Oxford, Ford & Sons, c1900, 12½″ .   **80.00**
Sauce Dish, Renown, Arthur Wilkison,
    c1907, marked "Royal Staffordshire"   **15.00**
Soup Plate, flanged
    Madras, Doulton, c1900, rimmed . . .   **50.00**
    Non Pariel, Alfred Meakin, c1907 . .   **75.00**
Sugar, cov, Renown, Arthur Wilkison,
    c1907, marked "Royal Staffordshire"   **50.00**
Syrup, Warwick Pansy, Warwick
    China Co, c1900, metal top **150.00**
Teapot, Manhattan, Henry Alcock,
    c1900 . . . .   **285.00**
Vase, Cavendish, Keeling & Co., c1910,
    hexagonal **425.00**
Vegetable Dish, cov
    Argyle, W H Grindley, c1896 . . . . . .   **200.00**
    Manhattan, Henry Alcock, c1900 . . .   **185.00**
    Normandy, Johnson Bros, 1900 . . .   **225.00**
    Touraine, 10″, Henry Alcock, c1898 .   **215.00**

Yeddo, Arthur Wilkinson, c1907 ... **335.00**
Waste Bowl, Renown, Arthur Wilkison,
c1907, marked "Royal Staffordshire" **45.00**

FOLK ART

History: The definition of what constitutes folk
art is still being vigorously debated among collectors, dealers, museum curators, and scholars.
Some want to confine folk art to non-academic,
hand made objects. Others are willing to include
manufactured material. In truth, the term is used
to cover objects ranging from crude drawings by
obviously untalented children to academically
trained artists' paintings of "common" people and
scenery.

The folk art market is subject to hype and ma-
nipulation. Neophyte collectors are encouraged to
read "Edie Clark's "What Really Is Folk Art?," in
the December 1986 *Yankee.* Clark's article provides a refreshingly honest look at the folk art
market.

Finally, the folk art market is extremely trendy
and fickle. What is hot today can become cool and
passe tomorrow. Collecting folk art is not for the
weak-of-heart or the cautious investor.

References: Kenneth L. Ames, *Beyond Necessity: Art In The Folk Tradition,* W. W. Norton, 1978;
Robert Bishop and Judith Rieter Weissman, *Folk
Art: The Knopf Collectors' Guides To American
Antiques,* Alfred A. Knopf, 1983; Henry Niemann
and Helaine Fendelman, *The Official Identification
and Price Guide To American Folk Art, First Edition,* House of Collectibles, 1988.

Museum: Museum of American Folk Art, New
York, NY; Abby Aldrich Rockefeller Folk Art Center, Williamsburg, VA.

Bucket, Fifth Wedding Anniversary,
painted, labeled "1888/Emma and
Nick/5th Anniversary," white ground . **250.00**
Cake Board, mahogany, American,
probably J. Conger, MA, c1800, 15½

**Toy, peddler's wagon, fully harnessed
horses with smoke grained dec, driver
with mustache, straw type hat, and
cloth costume, "Red Cross Liniment,"
and "London Tonic Pills, C. A. Price,
Ricmond, Me," written on side,
$2,000.00.**

x 27½", carved in relief with spread-
winged American eagle flanked by an
American Indian wearing a plumed
headdress, flowing cloak, quiver of
arrows on his back, holding American
flag mounted on standard with Phry-
gian cap, figure drawn in chariot
made from cornucopia filled with fruit
and sheaves of wheat, bunches of
grapes, other side with figure of Columbia wearing flowing robes, holding
aloft a laurel wreath and US shield,
inscribed "America," eagle grasping a
set of scales in beak, left scale with
small barrels and symbols of trade,
and right set with plow, rake, and a
pitchfork as symbols of agriculture, almond shaped reserve with borders
filled with luxuriant and exuberant
grapevines and clusters **8,800.00**
Carving
Pilot house finial, plum acorn, American, 19th C, 9" h, turned wood
form, weathered ochre, white and
yellow paint, suspended from iron
hanger **715.00**
Rooster and Hen, Wilhelm Schimmel,
Cumberland Valley, PA, 19th C,
carved and painted, yellow and
white with red and black, rooster 5"
h, hen 3½" h **2,250.00**
Sign, fruit filled cornucopia, Odd-Fel-
lows, American, 19th C, pine, 13" l,
robustly carved, turned, and fluted
horn with gilded band and tip,
painted pineapple, plums, berries,
pears, and other fruit and leafage,
red, green, and gold, age crack in
base **1,760.00**
Wall Plaque, Eagle, John Halley Bel-
lamy, Kittery Point, ME, c1880,
pine, 24" l, 9½" h, stylized figure of
spread-winged American eagle
with neck jutting forward and turned
left, eagle grasping banner on
carved black painted pole inscribed
"Du Vivmus Vivamus," eagle
grasping suppressed US shield
with fragmentary claw, diamond-
like carving on neck, incised wing
detailed feathering **7,750.00**
Cast Iron
Drummer Andirons, World War II, 20
x 27 x 15, attached by screw thread
to cast iron grate, presented to
"Red" Bird Massillon, Ohio, band
leader **750.00**
Owl, 24", pedestal, third quarter of
19th C, roof ornament used to
scare pigeons, found on house in
Marietta, PA **1,700.00**
Clock Case, poplar and pine, 24" h,

primitive carved, round center with drop flanked by draped American flags, eagle finial, two worn layers of paint with traces of color, some edge damage and age cracks, circular medallion missing from base, works missing, face replaced with paper drawing **400.00**

Fire Hat, Ceremonial Parade

Neversink Fire Company, c1850, pressed felt top hat, painted with legend "Neversink Fire Company" in gilt lettering on red banner with foliate ends, back painted with large gilt number "3," top with owner's initials "H.H.K.," interior with chalk inscription "H.H. Krouss," green ground, underbrim painted coral red, 6½" h **6,050.00**

Pennsylvania State Seal, c1850, pressed felt top hat, painted with impressive American eagle standing on gilded and beaded shield of state of PA, flanked by two white horses, banner trimmed in gilding, inscribed "Pennsylvania," motto below "Virtue, Liberty & Independence," deep blue ground, fragment of paper label, inscribed in 19th C hand, some dents in crown, 8¼" h **18,700.00**

Western Hose Company, probably Pennsylvania, dated 1836, pressed felt top hat, painted red, two broad scrolling banners on front inscribed in gilt lettering "Western Hose Company," back with ornately rendered date "1836," top with initials "JB" in gilt script, interior with chalk inscription, "Western Hose," 7" h . **7,150.00**

Gameboard, checkerboard, wooden, 15⅜ x 24", worn black and white paint **175.00**

Indian Clubs, pr, turned maple, American, c1870, 23½" h, smoothed and turned pins with black and gold bands, inscribed within "G. T. Lyons" in gold on a black scrolled ground . . **500.00**

Military Banner/Flag, Twigg's Rifleman, Th. Jeffreys, dated July 21, 1847, 27½ x 31", obverse with resplendent figure of a spread-winged eagle rendered in gilding with banner in its beak inscribed "E Pluribus Unum," US shield on its breast with thirteen stars, head turned dexter, feet grasping olive branch and five arrows, sgd "Th. Jeffrys," and inscription "Under this shalt thou Conquer," blue silk, reverse with inscription "Present to Young Rough & Ready, Capt. M. K. Taylor of the Twiggs Riflemen by his Baltimore Friends, July 21, 1847" . . **15,400.00**

Mill Weight, rooster, cast iron, 19th C, flattened body with traces of orig white and red paint, cast inscription "10 ft no. 2," 9" h, 17" l **1,210.00**

Sandstone, carved

Indian chief with war bonnet, seated, base initialed "C.E.," 13¾" h **200.00**

Sheep on base, good primitive detail with freestanding legs and tail, 8½" h, minor edge chips **450.00**

Sign

"Box Office," panel, c 1890, pine, 48¼ x 11⅜", red, black, gold, and yellow ornamental lettering enclosing urn, baseball and bat, and vase of flowers, white ground, sgd "Theo. I. Josephs, Soldier's Home" **16,000.00**

"Dr. Farley" Medicine Wagon Trade, probably New England, 19th C, 16¼ x 23½", planked rect form, applied flat red painted molding, painted with figure of Indian medicine man holding bunches of herbs in hands, figure wearing a brown cloak and feathered headdress with brown moccasins, landscape with feathery sponge-painted trees below inscription "Dr. FARLEY" in gilt outlined in black **2,750.00**

Teapot, Anniversary, tin, American, dated 1856 and 1866, 9½" h, 10" w, oval pot, hinged lid, angular spout and black painted earred and spurred handle, lid with sheet-tin figures of man in swallowtail coat holding lady's hand, figures posed under canopy, concave shoulders imp on one side with date "1856" and "1866" on other **8,250.00**

Wall Box, American, dated 1821, pine, 7 x 4½ x 16", back panel with molded edge and carved applique of sunburst rosette over clock-like hand rising from three-quarter circle, base comprising an open well, painted red with black and white highlights, left side with initials "IP 68," right side painted with date "1821" **2,310.00**

Wood carver's tour-de-force whimsey, two free carved baskets and an ear of corn, top link is connected with string but probably had wooden fastener at one time, dark patina with minor edge damage, 12" h **205.00**

FOOD BOTTLES

History: Food bottles were made in many sizes, shapes, and colors. Manufacturers tried to make an attractive bottle that would ship well and allow the purchaser to see the product, thus assuring him that the product was as good and as well made as home preserves.

Reference: Ralph & Terry Kovel, *The Kovels' Bottle Price List,* Crown Publishers, Inc, 1984, 7th ed.

Periodicals: *Antique Bottle and Glass Collector,* P.O. Box 187, East Greenville, PA 18041.

Additional Listings: See *Warman's Americana & Collectibles* for more milk bottle listings.

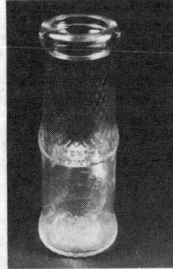

Milk Bottle, one half pint, "Miller's Dairy, Since 1892," $8.00.

Baking Powder, Eddy's, tin top	10.00
Butter, National, gal	240.00
Catsup, Pride Of The Farm, emb	10.00
Horseradish, Heinz Noble & Co, emb, 2 anchors and "Horseradish," horse head on lid, 5", 1873	275.00
Lemonade, G. Foster Clark & Co, Eiffel Tower, 2¾"	5.00
Milk	
Andrews Bros Pure Milk & Cream, Syracuse, NY, emb, ½ gal	50.00
Borden's Condensed Milk Co., emb eagle, qt	85.00
Curles Neck Dairy, emb, baby face .	15.00
Dean Dairy, maroon, pyro, pt	15.00
Dunmyer Dairy, qt	20.00
Murphy's Dairy, Neenah, emb, baby face neck, ½ pt	30.00
Old Homestead Products, crackle glass, cone shape, qt	50.00
Speedwell Farms, cow's head inside belt, pt	50.00
Mustard	
G.C. Giessen Mustard, NY, open pontil	35.00
Western Spice Mill, aqua, barrel shape	35.00
Olive Oil, Cooper Pure Olive Oil, Santa Barbara, CA, aqua, shoulder seal . .	7.00
Pepper Sauce	
C.L. Stickney, aqua, emb, panel sides	75.00
E.R. Durkee & Co., NY, emerald green, 7¾" h, patent Feb. 17, 1874	30.00
Pickle	
Bunker Hill, honey amber	25.00
Cathedral, Lockport, green, iron pontil, 7"	135.00
Davis, Wm, Boston, gherkins, six sided, metal label	325.00
Syrup	
Dr. Gunn's Onion Syrup	10.00
Howell's Cherry Julep, label	160.00
True Lemon Syrup, W. K. Lewis, Boston, aqua, qt	45.00
Vinegar, Whitehouse, jug, handle and spout, 10"	15.00

FOOD MOLDS

History: Food molds were used both commercially and in the home. For the most part, pewter ice cream molds and candy molds were used on a commercial basis; pottery and copper molds were used in homes. Today, both types are collected largely for decorative purposes.

Pewter ice cream molds were made primarily by two American companies: Eppelsheimer & Co. [molds marked E & Co., N.Y.] and Schall & Co. [molds marked S & Co.]. Both companies used a numbering system for their molds. The Krauss Co. bought out Schall & Co., removed the S & Co. from some, but not all the molds, and added more designs [marked K or Krauss]. The majority of pewter ice cream molds are individual serving molds. When used, one quart of ice cream would make eight to ten pieces. Scarcer, but still available, are banquet molds which used two to four pints of ice cream per example. European pewter molds [CC is a French mold mark] are available.

Chocolate mold makers are more difficult to determine. Unlike the pewter ice cream molds, maker's marks were not always on the mold or were covered by frames. Eppelsheimer & Co. of New York marked many of their molds, either with their name or with a design resembling a child's toy top with "Trade Mark" and "NY." Many chocolate molds were imported from Germany and Holland and were marked with the country of origin and, in some cases, the mold maker's name.

Reference: Judene Divone, *Chocolate Moulds: A History & Encyclopedia,* Oakton Hills Publications, 1987.

Additional Listings: Butter Prints.

CHOCOLATE MOLDS

Clamp Type, no hinge, two piece	
Cat, 8", marked "8230, Made in USA," Eppelsheimer "top" trademark	85.00
Clown, 9", marked "15262"	75.00
Donkey, 7", heavy wire clamps, marked "15919 Vormenfabriek, Tilburg, Holland"	35.00

Jack-O-Lantern, heavy wire clamp, unmarked	35.00
Rabbit, 3¼", marked "6626, 1, and 13"	20.00
Snowman with hat, 4"	45.00
Stocking, 8", marked "59 + 4271, Larrosh, Schw Gmund"	125.00
Teddy Bear, unusual clamps, marked "2644 + 11"	150.00
Frame or Book Type (Measurements based on single cavity size)	
Bird, 2¼ x 4¼", tin with copper	20.00
Christmas scene, 4½ x 8", unmarked	30.00
Easter Egg, 5 x 3", 2 cavities	25.00
Hearts, 6½ x 6", 2 cavities	60.00
Indian, 7½", copper	25.00
Lollipop, 8 x 10", eight rabbit cavities, unmarked	55.00
Pencil, 8½", two cavities, unmarked	30.00
Rabbit, 5 x 7½", pulling cart, landscape scene, sign reads "5 miles to go"	30.00
Sedan, 3 x 5", four door	10.00
Santa, 4½", unmarked	20.00
Turkey, 4½ x 3½", 2 cavities	50.00
Tray Type (Measurement is overall tray size)	
Chickens and rabbits, 11 x 17", six different rows, marked "2215.S"	95.00
Coin, "Rosemarie de Paris," 6 x 15", marked "Eppelsheimer & Co, NY, Feb 1944"	20.00
Hershey, bar, each section marked "Hershey"	20.00
Rooster, 12 x 10", 1 cavity	65.00

Cabbage, marked "S-162"	40.00
Christmas Fireplace, marked "E & Co, NY M1202"	75.00
Chrysanthemum, marked "313"	55.00
Eagle, marked "E-655"	90.00
Ear of Corn, marked "S & Co 270"	50.00
Football Player, marked "S-491"	55.00
Grape Leaf, marked "E-256"	40.00
Horn-of-Plenty, tin washed copper, marked "287"	25.00
Jockey and horse, marked "S-271"	68.00
King of Hearts, marked "E-920"	35.00
Lobster, marked "S-164"	58.00
Morning Glory, marked "S-239"	38.00
Owl, marked "S-175"	58.00
Pumpkin, marked "E-309"	25.00
Rose, cluster of 3, worn number	35.00
Sailboat, marked "S-553"	58.00
Santa	
Face wreathed in holly, badly worn number	40.00
Pulled by reindeer, added antler accessories	65.00
Strawberry, marked "503"	65.00
Tiger, 3 part, S-462	58.00
Turkey, marked "E & Co, NY," worn number	40.00
Uncle Sam, marked "S-407"	70.00

MISCELLANEOUS

Jelly, oval, rimmed tin, c1880	65.00
Pudding	
Cone, 8" h, 6¾" d, tin, spiral design	15.00
Star, 8" w, tin, five points	50.00

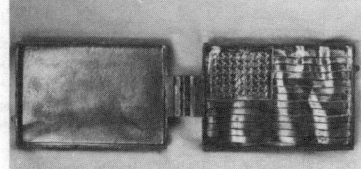

Ice Cream, flag, pewter, Krauss, NY, #282, $60.00.

ICE CREAM MOLDS

Banquet Size

Basket, French flared hinges, marked "Brevete, SGDG, Remarque Fabrique, CC"	200.00
Duck, marked "Krauss #44"	250.00
Log, 10"	175.00
Rooster, 11½"	400.00
Santa Claus, marked "E & Co #194"	350.00
Shell, marked "Krauss 36B"	200.00
Individual Size	
Battleship	35.00

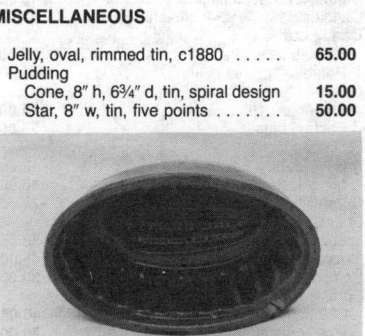

Pottery, 5³⁄₁₆ x 3⅜ x 2⅛", corn, $45.00.

POTTERY (Center Design Indicated)

Grape, ironstone, marked "Alcock"	65.00
Lion, ironstone	88.00
Rabbit, yellow ware, 8½"	200.00
Turk's Head, yellow ware, 9½, c1860	75.00

FOSTORIA GLASS   FOSTORIA

History: Fostoria Glass Co. began operations at Fostoria, Ohio, in 1887, and moved to Moundsville, West Virginia, its present location, in 1891. By 1925 Fostoria had five furnances and a variety of special shops. In 1924 a line of colored tableware was introduced. Fostoria was purchased by Lancaster Colony in 1983, and continues to operate under the Fostoria name.

Reference: Hazel M. Weatherman, *Fostoria, Its First Fifty Years*, published by author, c1972.

Collectors' Club: Fostoria Glass Society of America, P.O. Box 826, Moundsville, WV 26041.

Museum: Huntington Galleries, Huntington, WV.

Goblet, Vesper pattern, amber, $25.00.

Appetizer Set, 7 pc	200.00
Ashtray, Mayfair, red	17.50
Beer Mug, American	28.00
Bonbon, Colony, crystal, ftd	15.00
Bookends, pr, crystal	
Plume	60.00
Seahorses	120.00
Bowl	
6½", Fairfax, orchid	15.00
8", Pine, crystal, oval	35.00
13", Grape, orchid, oval flower frog	110.00
Butter, cov	
American	80.00
Jamestown, blue	50.00
Pioneer, green	48.00
Cake Salver, Heather, ftd	40.00
Candlesticks, Century, triple lite, pr	55.00
Candy, cov	
June, blue	225.00
Paradise, orchid	45.00
Celery	
American, 10"	18.00
Fairfax, blue	25.00
Champagne	
Buttercup	12.00
Minuet, crystal green-aqua base	10.00
Versailles, blue	28.00
Cheese & Cracker, 11"	
Baroque, crystal	50.00
June, pink	45.00
Compote, 6", Royal, green	30.00
Cordial	
Chintz, crystal	40.00
Pine, crystal	30.00
Vesper, green	45.00
Cream Soup, ftd, Fairfax, topaz	10.00
Creamer and Sugar	
Baroque, individual size, tray	40.00
Besty Ross, milk glass	22.00
Navarre, crystal	20.00
Vernon, green	45.00
Cruet, Century	32.50
Cup and Saucer, Fairfax, crystal	6.00
Demitasse Cup and Saucer, June, yellow	30.00
Epergne, Heirloom, pink, opal	100.00
Figure, mermaid	110.00
Goblet	
Corsage	18.00
Mother-of-Pearl	12.00
Willmere	15.00
Ice Bucket, tongs, Chintz, crystal	100.00
Ketchup Bottle, stopper, American	110.00
Lemon Dish, cov, American	28.00
Marmalade, cov, American	35.00
Mayonnaise, Holly, crystal, 3 pcs	50.00
Muffin Tray, Colony, handle	28.00
Mustard, cov, Baroque, azure, crystal spoon	75.00
Oyster Cocktail	
Colony	10.00
Holly	16.00
Pitcher	
Milk, Century	40.00
Water	
Corsage	200.00
June, crystal	200.00
Meadow Rose, crystal, 9½"	40.00
Trojan, topaz	225.00
Plate	
American, dinner	16.00
Chintz, salad, 6"	6.50
Royal Blue, dinner, 9¼"	28.00
Punch Set, Colony, crystal, bowl, 8 cups	700.00
Relish, Baroque, yellow, 7½ x 10", handle	20.00
Rose Bowl, American, 5"	25.00
Sherbet	
Corsage	12.00
Meadow Rose, 4½"	12.00
Toothpick, American	24.00
Torte Plate, American, oval	42.50
Tumbler, 5½", Versailles, blue	27.50
Vase, Baroque, yellow, 8"	50.00
Vegetable, American, oval, 2 part	24.00
Whipped Cream Pail, Versailles, pink	75.00
Whiskey Set, American, 8 pcs	200.00
Wine	
Chintz, crystal	24.00
Gadroon	18.00
Kasmir	26.00

Meadow Rose	**25.00**
Oriental	**12.00**
Trojan, topaz	**30.00**

FRAKTUR

History: Fraktur, the calligraphy associated with the Pennsylvania Germans, is named for the elaborate first letter found in many of the hand drawn examples. Throughout its history printed, partially printed-hand drawn, and fully hand drawn works existed side by side. Frakturs often were made by the school teachers or ministers living in rural areas of Pennsylvania, Maryland, and Virginia. Many artists are unknown.

Fraktur exists in several forms—geburts and taufschein (birth and baptismal certificates), vorschrift (writing example, often with alphabet), haus sagen (house blessing), bookplates and marks, rewards of merit, illuminated religious text, valentines, and drawings. Although collected for decoration, the key element in fraktur is the text.

Fraktur prices rise and fall along with the American folk art market. The key market place is Pennsylvania and the Middle Atlantic states.

References: Donald A. Shelley, *The Fraktur-Writings Or Illuminated Manuscripts Of The Pennsylvania Germans,* Pennsylvania German Society, 1961; Frederick S. Weiser and Howell J. Heaney (compilers), *The Pennsylvania German Fraktur Of The Free Library Of Philadelphia,* Pennsylvania German Society, 1976, two volumes.

Museum: The Free Library of Philadelphia, Philadelphia, PA.

HAND DRAWN

Anchor Artist, birth and baptismal, Centre County, 1843, 12 x 15¼", pen and ink and watercolor, maidens and architectural details, blue, red, brown, yellow, and black, creases, minor stains, short tears, frame 14½ x 18½"   **1,850.00**

Berks County Artist, birth and baptismal, Schuylkill County, PA, 1811, wove paper, pen and ink and watercolor, pair of parrots with striped necks, scalloped feathered bodies, herringbone tails, period painted frame 8⅛ x 12"   **4,500.00**

Blowsy (Flying) Angel Artist, birth and baptismal, Northampton County, PA, 1811, laid paper, 12½ x 15½", stylized flowers, birds, angels, red, yellow, olive green, and black, wear, tears, stains, and old repairs, frame 15¾ x 18¾"   **2,000.00**

Cross Legged Angel Artist, birth and baptismal certificate, Dauphin County, PA, c1807, 15½ x 13", all sides having panels with conventionalized plants and flowers, some emanating from urns, cross legged angel in center of top panel, text block with text in red and black, birth of Madalina Holstein   **1,500.00**

Flat Parrot Artist, birth and baptismal certificate, Berks Co., PA, c1810, 13¾ x 16½", central heart with text, dec include two mermaids, two parrots, two distlefinks, floral rosettes in top corners, and numerous flowers throughout, initials "I.T.W." at base of text, birth of Sarah Ohmacht   **4,000.00**

John Zinck, Lancaster County, 7⁵⁄₁₆ x 10⅛", birth and baptismal of John Kielhafner, 1834, artist sgd, $3,500.00.

Eyer, Johanna Adam, birth and baptismal, 1826, pen and ink and watercolor, pair of trumpeting red angels above apple tree with serpent, black painted ogee period frame 9 x 6½"   **9,350.00**

Lykens Valley Artist, Taufschein, baptismal record for Johann Frederick Lupold, June 6, 1789, 8¼ x 13¼", pen and ink and watercolor, framed   **2,500.00**

Portzline, Francis, birth and baptismal of Wilhelm Portzline, 1812, pen and ink and watercolor, pair of large parrots, other birds and hearts, graygreen, blue, yellow, red, and black, period frame 12½ x 15½"   **10,000.00**

Schmidt, Catarina, drawing, PA, c1824, wove paper, 11¾ x 13¾", pen and ink and watercolor, stylized urns of tulips and vining foliage, large birds in blue, green, yellow, and black, sgd in two places, dated in three places, frame 14 x 16"   **4,000.00**

Unknown Artist
 Birth and Baptismal
  Hanover Township, 1784, Adam

and Eve with apple, pen and ink and watercolor, period frame 7⅞ x 12½" **11,550.00**

York County, Manheim Township, dates 1794 and 1810, pen and ink and watercolor, pin pricked hearts, flowers, and pair of parrots, period frame 13¼ x 16" .. **1,760.00**

Bookplate, pen and ink and watercolor

1800, six birds perched in leafy vine, spiky flowers, red and yellow, period carved walnut frame 8 x 6" **3,000.00**

1812, Fronica Meuly, Lampeter Township, gentleman in top hat, red shallowtail coat, yellow vest, flowers, pair of green and yellow doves, frame 7½ x 12½" **6,875.00**

Drawing, PA, last quarter 18th C, two rows of eight soldiers, full dress, bayonetted rifles, halyards, banner, two soldiers playing the fife and drum, found on int. of blanket chest, now mounted on rice paper, period corner block frame 8½ x 14" **18,800.00**

Reward of Merit, bird in floral bush with one stylized tulip and one daisy above heart reserve reading "Das Hertze mein ist dir allein," signed "Anna/1827/Tier" in script on bottom, PA, 4¼ x 3¼" **350.00**

Valentine, pen and ink and watercolor

Cut out heart, inscription to Catherine Shimp..., frame 9¼ x 11¼" **850.00**

Folding, hearts, flowers, leaves, and trees, inscribed in center "Love to you my Friend This Ring is Round and Hath No End and So Is My...," drawn on both sides, frame 12½" sq, ... **2,475.00**

Vorschrift, Donigall Township, Lancaster County, PA, March the 8th 179-, laid paper, 8 x 13", pen and ink and watercolor, dec capital letters and flourish, green and brown, stains, fold line, damage from acid ink, frame 12¼ x 17¼" **400.00**

Young, Henry, Reverend

Birth and baptismal letter for Elizabeth Weaver, Centre County, 1854, pen and ink and watercolor, 11¾ x 7½", dark haired lady in floral printed dress, gentleman in black frock coat, green pants, holding bouquet of garden blossoms **4,125.00**

Birth letter for Daniel Brauflaeber, 1827, pen and ink and watercolor, four birds, two hearts, stars, and blossoms, red, yellow, blue, green, and rose, frame 11½ x 8" **6,000.00**

HAND DRAWN–PRINTED

Brechall, Martin, birth and baptismal, Bethlehem Township, Northampton County, PA, 1811, laid paper, 13 x 16", pen and ink and watercolor, stylized tulips and other flowers, red, blue, yellow, green, and black, minor wear, stains, and creases, frame 15¾ x 16¼" **3,600.00**

Krebs, Friederich, birth and baptismal, Northampton County, PA, 1806, laid paper, 12½ x 15½", pen and ink and watercolor, parrots, tulips, flowers, and hearts, red, yellow, green, brown, and black, printed label "F. Krebs," some fading, portions of one parrot restored, frame 14¼ x 17½" **800.00**

Otto, Heinrich, birth and baptismal, Lancaster Co., PA, 1774, 16½ x 13⅜", bird blocks on sides, hand drawn horizontal floral designs between text, birth of John Adam Bassler **1,500.00**

Pseudo-Otto Artist, birth and baptismal certificate, Frederick Co., MD, 1807, 16 x 13", reverse border block motif from Otto form, hand drawn floral motif between text, birth of Catherina Konig **1,500.00**

PRINTED

Adam and Eve, Ville, H. W., Lancaster **350.00**

Birth and Baptismal

Baumann, John, Ephrata **300.00**

Blumer & Busch, Allentown, PA, c1848, angels, birds, and eagle, minor creases, frame 14¼ x 17¼" **175.00**

Currier & Ives, New York **30.00**

Dreisbach, Bath **150.00**

Eagle Bookstore, Reading **60.00**

Ebner, Henrich, Allentown, PA, 1817, Lucerne County PA birth, artist sgd, minor wear, short tear, edge damage, frame 17 x 20" **200.00**

Kessler, Charles, Reading, PA, 1846 Berks County, PA birth, faded colors, frame 17½ x 20½" **75.00**

Lange, D. P., Hanover, PA, 1822, records 1813 birth in Bedfort County, PA, stains, tears, creased, frame 9¼ x 11¼" **150.00**

Lutz & Scheffer, Harrisburg **30.00**

Mentz, Georg W., Philadelphia **85.00**

Peters, G. S., Harrisburg **100.00**

Ritter, Johann, Reading, late form .. **60.00**

Sanno, Friederich, Carlisle **250.00**

Schnee, Joseph, Lebanon **300.00**

Haus Sagen (House Blessing)

Blumer & Bush, Allentown **150.00**

Ritter, Reading **100.00**

FRANKART

History: Arthur Von Frankenberg, artist and sculptor, founded Frankart, Inc., in New York City in the mid-1920s. Frankart, Inc., mass produced practical "art objects" in the Art Deco style into the 1930s. Pieces include aquariums, ashtrays, book-ends, flower vases, lamps, etc. Although Von Frankenberg used live female models as his subjects, his figures are characterized by their form and style rather than specific features. Nudes are the most collectible; caricatured animals and other human figures were also produced, no doubt, to increase sales.

With few exceptions, pieces were marked Frankart, Inc., with a patent number or "pat. appl. for."

Pieces were cast in a white metal composition in the following finishes: cream–a pale iridescent white; bronzoid–oxidized copper, silver, or gold; french–a medium brown with green in the crevices; gun metal–art iridescent gray; jap–a very dark brown, almost black, with green in the crevices; pearl green–pale iridescent green; and verde–a dull light green. Cream and bronzoid were used primarily in the 1930s.

Note: All pieces listed are all original in very good condition unless otherwise indicated.

Advisor: Walter Glenn.

Ashtray, chrome Scotty, black enamel base, marked "Frank Art Inc., Pat Appld For," $85.00.

Ashtray
9", ballerina dancing in center, 8" round onyx tray	275.00
13", pigeon, stylized, puffed out chest, holding 3" removable glass insert between spread wings	90.00

Bookends, pr
6", lions, seated, stylized chipped carved	80.00
7½", golfers in baggy pants	125.00
9½", Indian chief and squaw with papoose	175.00

Centerpiece Bowl, 15" d dish, 8½" peek-aboo nude flower frog	275.00
Clock, 10½", two nudes, rect glass case	975.00
Incense Burner, 5", female head on burner base, leaning back to blow smoke through her mouth	175.00

Lamp
7", two nudes, legs outstretched, sitting back to back, 5" sq crackle glass globe between them	425.00
9", two kneeling nudes, embracing 8" crackle glass globe	485.00
12", two nudes standing face to face, amber rods	825.00
13", two nudes, dancing back to back, geometric stacked base, 2½ x 11" crackle glass sq cylinder	525.00
23", two feminine figures, clad in pajamas and wide brimmed hats, strolling across base, silk shade .	390.00
Smoker's Set, 7", nude, seated and leaning back, geometric base, arms resting on removable glass cigarette box, 3" removable glass ashtray at feet, pr	285.00

Wall Plaque
6", seated nude, floral framework . .	275.00
7" sq, stylized horse head, ears back, rolling mane	125.00

FRANKOMA POTTERY

History: John N. Frank founded a ceramic art department at Oklahoma University in Norman and taught there for several years. In 1933 he established his own business and began making Oklahoma's first commercial pottery. Frankoma moved from Norman to Sapulpa, Oklahoma, in 1938.

A fire completely destroyed the new plant later the same year, but rebuilding began almost immediately. The company remained in Sapulpa and continued to grow. Frankoma is the only American pottery to be permanently exhibited at the International Ceramic Museum of Italy.

In September 1983 a disastrous fire struck once again, destroying 97% of Frankoma's facilities. The rebuilt Frankoma Pottery reopened on July 2, 1984. Production has been limited to 1983 production molds only. All other molds were lost in the fire.

Prior to 1954 all Frankoma pottery was made with a honey-tan colored clay from Ada, Oklahoma. Since 1954 Frankoma has used a brick red clay from Sapulpa. During the early 1970s the clay became lighter and is now pink in color.

There were a number of early marks. One most eagerly sought is the leopard pacing on the FRANKOMA name. Since the 1938 fire, all pieces have carried only the name FRANKOMA.

References: Phyllis and Tom Bess, *Frankoma Treasures,* published by authors, 1983; Susan N.

Cox, *Collectors Guide To Frankoma Pottery*, Book I, published by author, 1979, and Book II, published by author, 1982.

Additional Listings: See *Warman's Americana & Collectibles* for more examples.

Advisor: Phyllis Bess.

Ashtray
   Elephant, walking, trunk up, black
      glaze, 6½″ 30.00
   Texas, green, #459 . . . . 12.00
Bank
   Boot, Ada clay 10.00
   Elephant 6.00
Bookends, pr
   Clydesdale Horse, rearing, No. 431,
      8½″ 125.00
   Nude, seated, hair cascading over
      face, green, early clay, #425 . . . . 135.00
   Ocelot, walking, 7″
      Logo 250.00
      No logo 125.00
Bowl, 9 x 2½″, oval, Prairie Green,
   panther mark 45.00

Vase, 5½″, bulbous shape, green mottled glaze, cloud like design along incised line just above base, imp mark "Frankoma," $25.00.

Candlesticks, swirl pattern, double,
   glossy, 7″, pr 28.00
Cider Set, 8″ pitcher, 6 mugs, green and
   brown, 7 pcs 50.00
Compote, 8″, #105P 15.00
Cookie Jar, blue, mottled, Frankoma . . 50.00
Creamer, Wagon Wheel pattern, brown
   and cream glaze, 4½″ h 4.50
Cup and Saucer, brown and yellow,
   mottled 28.00
Figure
   Dreamer Girl, black glaze 125.00
   Fan Dancer, green and brown 100.00
   Indian Bowl Maker, bright orange
      glaze 85.00

Gravy Boat, Orbit dinnerware, 25
   ounce, #2S 20.00
Honey Pot, beehive, emb bee 15.00
Jewelry
   Bolo tie 20.00
   Earrings, pr
      Bowling ball and pin 18.00
      Tepee, orig card 25.00
   Pin, Cacti, orig cacti 45.00
   Tie Tac 20.00
Magazine Rack, Serva-Tray 45.00
Mask
   Afro Man 45.00
   Indian Chief, two feather headdress,
      Indian Maiden with headband, dark
      blue glaze, pr 75.00
   Tragedy, 9″, 1963 glaze, #118T . . . 20.00
Medallion
   Woman, 1⅞ x 1⅜″, white, pacing
      leopard logo 85.00
   World's Fair 25.00
Mug
   American Airlines, eagle, advertising 25.00
   Political
      1970, elephant, blue glaze 30.00
      1977, donkey, pink glaze 10.00
   War God, 20 oz 12.00
Pitcher
   Oklahoma Pond Juice 38.00
   #81, green 12.00
Planter
   Cactus, oblong, Ada clay 25.00
   Madonna of Grace 45.00
   Mallard, 9½″ 7.00
Plaque, buffalo mask 35.00
Plate
   Early Plainsman, 6½″ 3.50
   Easter, 1972, white, 6″ 12.00
   Madonna, bisque finish, 1977, 8½″ . 18.00
Platter, 10″, breakfast, Orbit dinnerware,
   #2QS 12.00
Salt and Pepper Shakers, pr
   Bulls, 1942 . . . . 45.00
   First National Bank of Tulsa 20.00
Sculpture
   Buffalo, 6½ x 3½″, #119 . . . . 225.00
   Coyote Pup, 7¾″, #105 . . . . 250.00
   Swan, brown, open tail, #229 . . . . . 20.00
Teapot, cov, 8 cup, #2T 35.00
Tumbler, bamboo 5.00
Vase
   Cockatoo, 8 x 5″, c1936 . . . . 75.00
   Flying Goose, 6″, pillow shape, #60B 15.00
   Ram's Head, 6″, Ada clay 20.00
Wall Pocket, Acorn, green, early clay,
   #190 . . . . 25.00

FRATERNAL ORGANIZATIONS

History: Benevolent and secret societies played an important part in American society from the late

18th to the mid-20th centuries. Initially the societies were organized to aid members and their families in times of distress or death.

They evolved from this purpose into important social clubs by the late 19th century. In the 1950s, with the arrival of civil rights, an attack occurred on the secretiveness and often discriminatory practices of these societies. The fraternal movement, with the exception of the Masonic organizations, suffered serious membership loss. Many local chapters closed and sold their lodge halls. This resulted in many fraternal items arriving in the antiques market.

Additional Listings: See *Warman's Americana & Collectibles* for more examples.

MASONIC

Ashtray, oval, copper, wreath design, symbol "F.A.M. February 21, 1907" symbol, matchbox holder center . . .	25.00
Box, 5″ w, 2″ h, brass, engraved Masonic symbol above "Work while it is day" inscription, moon and stars, slightly domed octagonal lid, conforming case and base, 19th C	70.00
Firing Glass, 3½″ h, copper wheel engraved Masonic square and compass, round base, trumpet bowl . . .	275.00
Goblet, 6″ h, 3½″ d, clear, engraved, early 19th C	185.00
Pin, 100th Anniversary, bronze, "Grand Lodge of Minnesota 1819–1919" . . .	20.00
Plate	
6″, Los Angeles, 1905, flowers dec .	40.00
8¼″ d, Toledo, 1906, polychrome center scene, fraternal symbols around scalloped rim, inscribed, 64th Annual Conclave of Toledo Commandery, 1906, Knowles, Taylor & Knowles	35.00
Pouch, 1¼ x 2½″, leather, black, snap top, gold Masonic symbol with "G" in center, includes silvered metal foldout razor	25.00
Stickpin, 14k gold, pearl setting	30.00
Teaspoon, SS, emb Chicago Temple scene bowl, Masonic symbols on handle	30.00
Tumbler, "Landmark Lodge No 127, Baltimore, 1866–1916," milk glass . .	40.00
Wine, 4⅜″ h, clear, knop stem, applied round base, pontil, arch, compass, square, moon, bell, and hourglass symbols within rect cartouche, reverse engraved "St Johns Lodge/No 281"	160.00

OTHERS

Benevolent & Protective Order of the Elks, B.P.O.E.	
Calendar Plate, 9½″, 1907	50.00

G. A. R., gavel, wood handle, emb metal thumb rest, ivory end, inscribed "W. F. Hutchinson, M. D. Comm. Arnold Park, NY, 1877-GAR-1876," $175.00.

Card Case, 1½ x 2″, SS, inscribed and dated 1913	95.00
Cigarette Case, brass, Elks emblem	20.00
Mug, purple, elk's head and clock, silver handle and trim	35.00
Paperweight, glass, round	15.00
Pitcher, 12″ h, china, purple shaded elk's head and clock emblems, white ground, National Art China, Trenton, NJ	95.00
Shaving Mug, gold on white, Elk emblem	40.00
Stein, 10″, pottery, hunter sprawled on ground, elk nearby, "We Are Brothers"	75.00
Eastern Star	
Compact, center emblem in lid	20.00
Cup and Saucer, emblem	10.00
Hatpin, SP	15.00
Plate, Indiana Grand Chapter, 1949 .	25.00
Independent Order of Odd Fellows, I.O.O.F.	
Cookie Mold, 5 x 6½″, oval, cast iron, 3 interlocking links and symbols, heart in hand	220.00
Dish, 5¾″, pink luster, c1840	65.00
Letter Opener, 4¾″, ivory color celluloid, black Denver convention 1908 inscription, bronc riding cowboy on reverse, Indiana Chapter, officers listed	25.00
Trivet, 8¼″ l, cast iron, insignia and heart in hand in laurel wreath . . .	25.00
Knights of Columbus	
Matchsafe, pocket, 1919	40.00
Sword, dress, detailed blade, scabbard, McLilley Co, Columbus, OH	45.00
Watch Fob, medallion type	35.00
Knights of Pythias, goblet, glass, clear, "1900, Rochester"	30.00
Shrine	
Chalice, glass, cranberry, 1908	60.00

Goblet, ruby flashed, St Paul, 1908 .	60.00
Hat, Fez, felt	20.00
Humidor, paneled clear glass, metal Art Nouveau style cov, various ornate emblems finial, Yaarab Temple, Atlanta	75.00
Plate, 10½", comic beat up Shriner center, camel border, desert and palms	55.00
Toothpick Holder, glass, clear, Pittsburgh and New Orleans, 1910 . . .	40.00
Woodsmen of the World, badge, memorial, Pioneer Camp No 1 W. O. W., Indianapolis, IN	10.00

FRUIT JARS

History: Fruit jars are canning jars used to preserve food. Thomas W. Dyott, one of Philadelphia's earliest and most innovative glass makers, was promoting his glass canning jars in 1829. John Landis Mason patented his screw-type canning jar on November 30, 1858. This date refers to the patent date, not the age of the jar. There are thousands of types of jars in many colors, types of closures, sizes, and embossings.

References: Alice M. Creswick, *The Red Book of Fruit Jars No. 5,* published by author, 1987; Bill Schroeder, *1000 Fruit Jars: Priced And Illustrated, Revised 5th Edition,* Collector Books, 1987.

AGWL, aqua, qt, handmade, wax seal	20.00
Air-Tight, amber, pt, handmade, zinc lid	50.00
American Fruit Jar, light green, qt, handmade, glass lid, wire bail	100.00
Anchor Hocking, clear, qt, machine made, glass lid, wire bail, anchor emb on side, H superimposed on anchor	5.00
Atlas Mason, aqua, qt, handmade, zinc lid	25.00
Ball	
Aqua, qt, handmade, glass lid,	

Drey Square Mason, clear, one half pint, emb name, zinc lid, $3.50.

ground top, emb in script "The Ball, Pat. Apl'd For"	45.00
Green, pt, handmade, zinc lid, ground lip, emb in script "Ball Mason's Patent 1858"	3.25
Banner, clear, qt, machine made, glass lid, wire bail, emb "Trade Mark Banner Warranted"	10.00
Blue Ribbon, clear, qt, glass lid, wire clip	7.50
Canadian King, clear, qt, machine made, glass lid, wide mouth	20.00
Clark Fruit Jar Co, blue, qt, handmade, glass lid emb "Clark Fruit Jar Cleveland"	48.00
Conserve, clear, qt, handmade, glass lid, wire bail	7.50
Dalbey's Fruit Jar, green, qt, handmade, metal lid, thumbscrews, emb "Dalbey's Fruit Jar, Pat Nov 16, 1858" . .	560.00
Doolittle, aqua, qt, handmade, glass lid, emb "Doolittle The Self Sealer" . . .	60.00
Double Safety, clear, pt, machine made, glass lid, wire bail	4.00
Eclipse, light green, qt, handmade, threaded glass lid, name emb on side	175.00
Economy, amber, pt, metal lid, spring clip	5.00
Empire, aqua, qt, handmade, stopper neck, name emb in arch	215.00
Favorite, aqua, pt, handmade, zinc lid, name emb in script	18.00
Flickinger, aqua, qt, handmade, glass lid, wire bail	18.00
Glassboro, aqua, qt, handmade, glass lid, screw band, emb "Glassboro Trade Mark Improved"	14.00
Good House Keepers, clear, 2 qt, machine made, zinc lid	2.00
H & S, aqua, qt, handmade, metal stopper, emb monogram	375.00
Hamilton, clear, qt, handmade, glass lid, metal clip	45.00
Hoosier, aqua, qt, handmade, threaded glass lid, emb "Hoosier Jar"	315.00
Independent, aqua, qt, handmade, glass screw lid	40.00
Kilner Jar, clear, pt, machine made, glass lid, screw band, emb "The Kilner Jar"	5.00
Mansfield, light green, pt, machine made, glass lid, screw band, emb "Mansfield Improved Mason"	15.00
Mason, green, qt, hand made, zinc lid, emb "S Mason's Patent 1858"	4.50
McDonald Perfect Seal, clear, pt, machine made, glass lid, wire bail, emb "McDonald Perfect Seal"	5.00
Ohio, clear, 2 qt, handmade, zinc lid, emb "Ohio Quality Mason"	12.00
Pansy, aqua, qt, handmade, 20 panels, emb "Pansy"	125.00

Pine Deluxe Jar, clear, pt, machine
made, glass lid, wire bail, emb 5.00
Regal, clear, qt, handmade, glass lid,
emb "Regal" in oval 3.00
Samco, clear, qt, zinc lid, emb in script
"SAMCO/SUPER JAR" 3.00
Star, aqua, qt, handmade, glass lid, zinc
band, star emb over name 75.00
Sure, aqua, qt, handmade, glass lid,
spring wire clip, emb 220.00
Tropical, clear, qt, machine made, zinc
lid, name emb in script 2.75
Weir, pottery jar, amber glass lid, lid emb
"The Weir/Patented March 1st, 1892" 10.00
Winslow Jar, aqua, qt, handmade, glass
lid, wire clip, emb 45.00
Worcester, aqua, qt, handmade, ta-
pered stopper, emb 85.00

FRY GLASS

History: The H.C. Fry Glass Co. of Rochester, Pennsylvania, began operating in 1901 and continued until 1933. Their first products were brilliant period cut glass. They later produced depression tablewares. In 1922 they patented heat resisting ovenware in an opalescent color. This "Pearl Oven Glass" was produced in a variety of oven and table pieces including casseroles, meat trays, pie and cake pans, etc. Most of these pieces are marked "Fry" with model numbers and sizes.

Fry's beautiful art line, Foval, was produced only in 1926-27. It is pearly opalescent, with jade green or delft blue trim. It is rarely signed, except for occasional silver overlay pieces marked "Rockwell." Foval is always evenly opalescent, never striped like Fenton's opalescent line.

Reproduction Alert: In the 1970s, reproductions of Foval were made in abundance in Murano, Italy. These pieces, including candlesticks, toothpicks, etc., have teal blue transparent trim.

Bouillon Cup and Saucer, two blue han-
dles, Foval 70.00
Casserole, cov, round, ovenware 25.00
Compote, 8¾" d, 6¾" h, pale blue loop-
ings, opal bowl, blue foot, Foval ... 175.00
Creamer, 4", yellow, pinched top, three
blue-green loops, applied deep blue
6" handle 150.00
Cruet, pedestal base, Foval 250.00
Cup and Saucer, Foval
Delft blue handle 70.00
Green handle 50.00
Goblet, fiery opal bowl, pink loopings,
Foval 85.00
Lemonade Tumbler, 6¼" h, Icicle pat-
tern, green handle 60.00
Pitcher, 6¼" d, 9¼" h, Diamond Optic,
chrome green, ground pontil 75.00

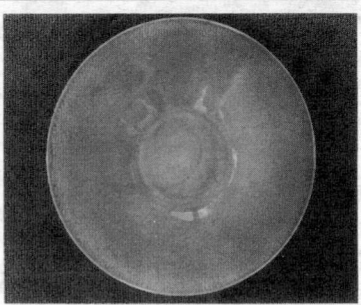

Saucer, Foval, $9.00.

Plate, 10½", grill, ovenware, marked
"Pearl Oven Ware" 30.00
Punch Cup, clear crackle finish cup,
deep blue handle 28.50
Tea Set, teapot, creamer, cov sugar,
two cups and saucers, ornate SS ov-
erlay on brilliant blue bands, smoky
blue-white opal ground, Delft blue
handles and finials, Foval 1,100.00
Toothpick, Delft blue handle, Foval ... 70.00
Vase, 12", opal, pink loopings 200.00
Water Set, tankard pitcher, six glasses,
Delft blue base and handles, 7 pcs . 265.00

FULPER POTTERY

History: The American Pottery Company of Flemington, New Jersey, made pottery jugs and housewares from the early 1800s. They made Fulper Art Pottery from approximately 1910 to 1930.

Their first line of art pottery was called Vasekraft. The shapes were primarily either rigid and controlled, being influenced by the arts and crafts movement, or of Chinese influence. Equal concern was given to the glazes which showed an incredible diversity.

Pieces made between 1910 and 1920 were of the best quality, because less emphasis was put on production output. Almost all pieces are molded.

Reference: Robert Blassberg, *Fulper Art Pottery: An Aesthetic Appreciation,* Art Lithographers, 1979.

Bookends, 8½", Ramses II, verte antique green glaze, paper label, pr .. 650.00
Bowl
  8½", rolled rim, green and gray streaks, glossy finish 85.00
  10", drip glaze finish, blue and yellow 80.00
Bucket, 5", green and brown glossy glaze, bail handle 65.00
Candlesticks, pr, Block, florals 45.00
Figure, 2¾ x 5½", frog, matte green, high gloss 45.00
Flower Frog, figural, nude, white glaze 100.00
Jar, 9", pedestal base, green shading to blue 400.00
Jardiniere, 4", brown, handles 100.00

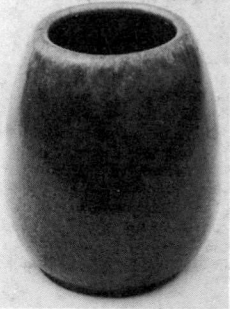

Vase, 3½" h, bulbous shape, mottled, red over green, apple skin motif, stamped mark, $50.00.

Lamp, perfume, figural
  Art Deco woman, orange glaze 160.00
  Parrot, blue, orange wing tips 465.00
Pitcher, 4", gray, brown, and blue high glaze 50.00
Platter, 13", emb fish swimming around int. rim, copper dust to green glaze . 375.00
Powder jar, figural Art Deco Egyptian woman on cov 250.00
Rose Bowl, 4¼", medium green, blue, and gunmetal gray streaks 400.00
Vase
  4", coiled, turquoise matte, sgd 35.00
  5½", bud, black mirror glaze 100.00
  7", three handles, high glaze, slate blue, green streaks, darker blue cascading crystals 165.00
  8", Rose Flambe, shaded to green at top, sgd 150.00
  8¼", bulbous, mirror brown glaze, gray-green and blue flambe shaded to rose matte glaze, raised mark, orig paper label 300.00

FURNITURE

History: Two major currents dominate the American furniture marketplace–furniture made in Great Britain and furniture made in the United States. American buyers continue to show a strong prejudice for objects manufactured in the United States. They will pay a premium for such pieces and accept them above technically superior and more aesthetic English examples.

Until the last half of the 19th century formal American styles were dictated by English examples and design books. Regional furniture, such as the Hudson River Valley [Dutch] and the Pennsylvania German styles, did develop. A less formal furniture, often designated as the "country" or vernacular style, developed throughout the 19th and early 20th centuries. These country pieces deviated from the accepted formal styles and have a genre charm that many collectors find irresistible.

America did contribute a number of unique decorative elements to English styles. The American Federal period is a reaction to the English Hepplewhite period. American designers created furniture which influenced, rather than reacted, to world taste in the Gothic Revival style, Arts and Craft Furniture, Art Deco, and Modern International movement.

FURNITURE STYLES [APPROX. DATES]

William and Mary	**1690–1730**
Queen Anne................	**1720–1760**
Chippendale	**1755–1790**
Federal [Hepplewhite]	**1790–1815**
Sheraton	**1790–1810**
Empire [Classical]...........	**1805–1830**
Victorian	
French Restauration........	**1830–1850**
Gothic Revival.............	**1840–1860**
Rococo Revival............	**1845–1870**
Elizabethan................	**1850–1915**
Louis XIV	**1850–1914**
Naturalistic	**1850–1914**
Renaissance Revival	**1850–1880**
Neo-Greek	**1855–1885**
Eastlake	**1870–1890**
Art Furniture................	**1880–1914**
Arts and Crafts	**1895–1915**
Art Nouveau	**1896–1914**
Art Deco..................	**1920–1945**
International Movement	**1940–Present**

In the 1986–87 auction season, a Philadelphia Chippendale wing chair sold for over two and one-half million dollars. Many other pieces broke the half million dollar barrier.

Country pieces, with the exception of Windsor chairs, seem to have stabilized and even dropped off slightly in value. The country-designer-look no longer enjoys the popularity it did during the American Bicentennial period.

Furniture is one of the few antiques fields where regional preferences are a factor in pricing. Victorian furniture is popular in New Orleans, and unpopular in New England. Oak is in demand in the Northwest, not so much in the Middle Atlantic states.

Prices vary considerably on furniture. Shop around. Furniture is plentiful unless you are after a truly rare example. Examine all pieces thoroughly. Too many furniture pieces are bought on impulse. Turn furniture upside down; take it apart. The amount of repairs and restoration to a piece has a strong influence on price. Make certain you know about all repairs and changes before buying.

Beware of the large number of reproductions. During the twenty-five years following the American Centennial of 1876, there was a great revival in copying furniture styles and manufacturing techniques of earlier eras. These centennial pieces now are over one hundred years old. They confuse many dealers and collectors.

The prices listed below are "average" prices. They are only a guide. High and low prices are given to show market range.

References: Joseph T. Butler, *Field Guide To American Furniture*, Facts on File Publications, 1985; Rachael Field, *Macdonald Guide To Buying Antique Furniture*, Macdonald & Co Publishers, Ltd, London, England, 1986; *Furniture Dealers' Reference Book, Zone 3, 1928-29*, reprint by Schiffer Publishing, Ltd., 1988; Phillipe Garner, *Twentieth-Century Furniture*, Van Nostrand Reinhold, 1980; Myrna Kaye, *Fake, Fraud, Or Genuine?: Identifying Authentic American Antique Furniture*, Little, Brown and Company, 1987; William C. Ketchum, Jr., *Furniture, Volume 2: Chests, Cupboards, Desks, & Other Pieces*, Knopf Collectors' Guides To American Antiques, Alfred A. Knopf, 1982; *Milo M. Naeve, Identifying American Furniture: A Pictorial Guide To Styles and Terms, Colonial to Contemporary*, American Association for State and Local History, 1981; Don & Carol Raycraft, *Collector's Guide To Country Furniture*, Collector Books, 1984; Marvin D. Schwartz, *Furniture: Volume 1: Chairs, Tables, Sofas & Beds*, Knopf Collector's Guides To American Antiques, Alfred A. Knopf, 1982; *Robert W. and Harriett Swedberg — American Oak Furniture, Style and Prices, Book II* (1984), Wallace-Homestead; *Country Furniture and Accessories with Prices, Book I* (1983), *Book II* (1984), Wallace-Homestead; *Country Pine Furniture*, Wallace-Homestead, 1983; *Furniture of the Depression Era*, Collector Books, 1987; *Victorian Furniture, Book I* (1976), *Book II* (1983), *Book III* (1985), Wallace-Homestead; *Wicker Furniture*, Wallace-Homestead, 1983; Lyndon C. Viel, *Antique Ethnic Furniture*, Wallace-Homestead, 1983.

There are hundreds of specialized books on individual furniture forms and styles. Two examples of note are: Monroe H. Fabian, *The Pennsylvania-German Decorated Chest*, Universe Books, 1978,

and Charles Santore, *The Windsor Style In America, 1730–1830, Vol. 1* (1981), *Vol. 2* (1987), Running Press.

Additional Listings: Arts and Craft Movement, Art Deco, Art Nouveau, Children's Nursery Items, Orientalia, Shaker Items, and Stickley.

BEDS

Art Deco, Jules Leleu, c1925, daybed, walnut, two high scrolling ends, rect plinth, tapering everted feet ending in scrolls, upholstered cushion and rolled pillows **4,000.00**

Arts and Crafts, Stickley, stained oak, head and footboard with thirteen wide slats, 58 x 82¼ x 44½" **2,000.00**

Chippendale
English, mahogany, molded canopy frame with carved detail, fluted posts, Marlborough feet, turned detail, swirled fluted urns, stop fluting upper posts, pale blue damask bed hangings and spread, ecru silk canopy liner, replacements, repairs, and minor damage, 54 x 72" mattress size, 94" h **4,000.00**

Massachusetts, c1760, mahogany and maple, four poster, straight sided upholstered canopy, simple headboard, fluted posts, ring at capital, rect block with brass rosettes, cabriole front legs, claw and ball feet, replaced hangings, 60 x 81 x 86" **15,000.00**

Empire, American
Birch, high poster, shaped headboard, turned, rope and acanthus carved posts, orig rope rails, arched canopy frame, 55 x 72 x 66¾" **1,350.00**

Mahogany
High Poster, c1835, acanthus, spiral, and pineapple carved posts, shaped headboard, 44½ x 77 x 96" **3,500.00**

Sleigh, c1840, scrolling headboard and footboard **800.00**

Tiger Maple, c1820–30, low poster, turned posts, paneled headboard, 49¾" l **1,650.00**

Empire Style, 20th C, mahogany, removable pineapple finials, turned and reeded posts, acanthus carving, minor edge damage, 50¾ x 74¼ x 60¾" mattress size **200.00**

Federal, American
Birch, tester, pencil head posts flanking shaped headboard, reeded and urn turned foot posts, turned and block feet, 46 x 72 x 79" **1,600.00**

Cherry, New England, c1805, carved

Bed, cherry, rope, pegs removed, $600.00.

and inlaid, four poster, fluted, tapered head and foot posts, shaped pine headboard, orig red stain, sq tapering diamond and checker inlaid legs, ebony inlaid spade feet, 76¾ x 54½ x 80" **12,750.00**

Mahogany, high poster, turned urn form posts, shaped headboard and footboard, 49 x 76 x 90" **1,800.00**

Maple, New England, late, c1820, four poster, tapered head posts, shaped pine headboard, reeded foot posts, ring turned molded canopy, turned feet, orig bed hangings, 80 x 82" **5,000.00**

Painted, c1800, low poster, turned head posts and foot posts, cyma shaped headboard and footboard, turned legs, painted blue, some restoration to paint, 47½ x 76" . . . **3,300.00**

Tiger Maple, late period, c1830, high poster, spiral and turned posts, shaped headboard and footboard, turned feet, 42 x 74 x 60" **800.00**

George III, c1800, carved and brass mounted walnut, four poster, circular tapered head posts, shaped mahogany headboard, reeded and acanthus carved foot posts, ring turned feet, castors, 65" w, 91½" h **10,000.00**

Louis XVI, c1785, mahogany, paneled head and footboards, stop fluted pillars, pomegranate finials, stamped "G Jacob," 77 x 45" **3,000.00**

Queen Anne, PA, early 19th C, turned and painted pine, low poster, head and foot posts with flattened ball finials, shaped head and footboards, tapered feet, orig rope rails, orig green paint, 48½ x 73¼" **3,000.00**

Sheraton, American, early 19th C, tester Cherry, turned posts and foot rail, shaped headboard, orig canopy . . **1,250.00**

Pine headboard, turned hardwood posts, reeded foot posts, orig rope rails, old dark brown finish, replaced canopy frame, minor edge damage posts, 47 x 72" mattress size, 58" h **2,600.00**

Victorian

Brass, c1900, straight top rail, curved corners, ring shaped capitals, cast iron side rails, 55 x 94 x 61" **1,000.00**

Cottage, c1890, bamboo style, maple and bird's eye maple **900.00**

Eastlake, American, walnut, applied carved plaque on headboard, roundels, carved pediment and finials, 53½ x 82 x 80" **1,200.00**

Elizabeth Revival, walnut, spool turned, child's, 25" w **400.00**

Renaissance Revival, c1875, walnut, arched cornice, molded headboard with scroll and foliate crest, inset burl walnut panel, 86½" h **1,000.00**

BENCHES

Chippendale Style, English, 19th C, mahogany, reupholstered brown leather top, cabriole legs, ball and claw feet, shell carved knee, old finish, 16 x 22" **350.00**

Cobbler's, pine and poplar, whittled legs, replaced leather seat and drawer, 28 x 60 x 19" **175.00**

Church Pew, oak, solid board back, plank seat, shaped ends, carved dec **250.00**

Deacon's, American, mid 19th C, chair leg base, old refinishing, 80¾" l . . . **400.00**

Decorated, polychrome stenciled flowers, foliage, and baskets of fruit, orig brown paint, yellow striping, some wear, touch up, and yellow strip repaint, 73" l **1,000.00**

Empire Style, country, painted and dec, flat crestrail, narrow cross rail continuing under turned arms, plank seat, turned legs, flat stretchers, old black paint, traces of yellow and gold striping, 82" l **550.00**

English, oak, wainscotte back, plank seat with brown velvet cushion, turned arm posts, carved apron, cabriole legs, repairs and replacements, 73¼" l **500.00**

Federal Style, PA, c1830, painted and dec, narrow rect crestrail with foliate devices, scrolled arms, plank seat, eight turned legs, flat front stretchers, painted yellow, black and green pinstriping, 76 x 32½" **2,800.00**

Settle, country

Chairback style, painted and dec, three chairbacks, turned spindles and legts, scrolled arms, worn brown repaint, free hand florals and foliage, yellow and white striping, 75½" **500.00**

Plank Seat, curved arms, spindle back with crest, simple trunings, refinished, replaced rungs, 96" l ... **375.00**

Wash, New England, late 18th C, pine, old natural finish, 75¾" l **400.00**

Water Bucket

Pine, painted, two tiers, oblong top, single board sides, cut-out feet, old worn white paint over blue, 54½ x 16 x 34½" **250.00**

Poplar, two tier, board and batten back, shaped sides, cut-out feet, mortised, worn green-gray paint, 39 x 13½ x 31½" **275.00**

Window

Federal, mahogany, sq end supports, three reeded columns, partially upholstered seat, reeded sq tapering legs, 44½ x 31½" **2,650.00**

George III, mahogany, rolled arms, rect padded seat cov in gold damask, straight blind fret carved legs, 33" l **3,750.00**

Work, pine, painted, sq nail construction, rect divided top, galleried sides, pull out drawer and tray on each side, tapering legs, 24 x 34 x 32" **350.00**

BENTWOOD

In 1856, Michael Thonet of Vienna perfected the process of bending wood using steam. Shortly after, Bentwood furniture became popular. Other manufacturers of Bentwood furniture were Jacob and Joseph Kohn; Philip Strobel and Son; Sheboygan Chair Co.; and Tidoute Chair Co. Bentwood furniture is still being produced today by the Thonet firm and others.

Box, dec, pine, two finger construction, laced construction lid, handle, sliding wooden bolt, carved scroll ears, orig red and black graining, green semicircular edging, name and 1848 in yellow script, 20½" l **500.00**

Chair

Austrian, side

Ash and beech, three balloon type overlapping loops, cane seat, carved side braces, tapered, flared, cylindrical legs **150.00**

Vienna Secession Style, c1910, back splat with three circular perforations, three slender spindles, painted black, set of 8 .... **4,250.00**

Josef Hoffman, side, three horizontal turned wood slat back, carved cornice, five turned wood vertical rods, solid seat, stencil dec on four straight legs, paper label, 36" h .. **225.00**

Thonet

Arm, c1935, lacquered, pine frame, upholstered back and continuous seat, 43" h **350.00**

*Side, cane seat **100.00**

Cradle, Thonet, c1904, suspended type, rect cradle, arched fronts, inverted U shaped bands, overhood crook, U shaped support, twin legs, 41" l, 43" h **275.00**

Hall Stand, Austrian, c1905, two bentwood sides supporting four shelves, carved umbrella recesses, 71¾" h .. **175.00**

Mirror, attributed to Koloman Moser, c1902, wall, rect beveled mirror plate, arched support surmounted by three pierced circles, bulbous pierced base on larger pierced oval, 41½" h **1,650.00**

Settee, J & J Kohn, elm and cane, three heart form back lobes, kidney shaped seat, scroll end arms, four cabriole legs, 55" l, 41" h, 20" d **400.00**

Table, Josef Hoffmann, c1905, circular top, wood spheres dec below rim, 21¼" h **300.00**

Washstand, Austrian, c1900, marble top, mirror back panel, inset pottery basin **900.00**

BLANKET CHESTS

Chippendale, New England, late 18th C, pine, country, lift top, single drawer, old refinish, orig hardware, 37½" w . **600.00**

Blanket Chest, camphor, dovetailed, brass hardware, 42½ x 21½ x 22", $275.00.

Country

American, early 19th C, pine, rect molded top, deep well, two long drawers, bracket feet, 39 x 18 x 37" **500.00**

Pennsylvania, 1787, pine, painted and dec, rect hinged top, well with till, two molded drawers, scroll-cut bracket feet, front and sides painted with stylized red and white tulips, brown ground, lower section painted red, restoration to feet and moldings, 50 x 22½ x 28¼″ **3,500.00**

Pennsylvania, Lebanon County, 1804, painted and dec pine, rect hinged lid, molded base, replaced ogee bracket feet, front painted with two arches centering flowers, inscription, brown grained ground, 50 x 22 x 24″ **3,300.00**

Pennsylvania, Lehigh County, c1810, painted and dec pine, rect top, till, front painted with eagle and shield, sides painted with hex signs, bracket feet, 51½ x 22¾ x 27½″ . **11,000.00**

Virginia Valley, walnut, dovetailed case and three drawers, shaped bracket feet, till with two dovetail drawers, old refinish, some damage, cracks, and repairs, 50¾ x 22½ x 29¼″ **2,100.00**

Decorated

Pine, black paint top edge molding, dovetailed, bracket feet, orig brown vinegar graining, "Christian Nisly 1819″ painted in white, repairs and replaced foot, worn paint, 51½ x 22¾ x 24½″ **700.00**

Pine, orig red paint, black brushed graining, sq corner post, paneled top sides, and ends, turned feet, replaced hinges, 35¾ x 22¾ x 24¾″ **225.00**

Pine, white panel front with red and white floral designs, polychrome floral dec lid and ends, orig blue paint, dovetailed lid, wrought iron strap hinges, bear trap lock, and end handles, missing till, age crack, minor damage and wear, 49¾ x 24½ x 22″ h **1,000.00**

Walnut, blue graining lid, nailed construction, cutout bracket feet, till with secret compartment, old dark paint, minor wear, replaced hinges and repairs, 33″ l **245.00**

BOOK CASES

Chippendale, Norwich, CT, cherry, bonnet top, fluted pilasters topped with Corinthian capitals, arched raised panel doors, broken arch cornice with carved rosettes, turned and flame twist finials, claw and elongated ball feet, band legs, ogee base with carved scrolls, four dovetailed overlapping drawers, slant top lid, fitted int., 40 x 19¾ x 84¼″ **62,500.00**

George I, walnut, double dome molded cornice, pair of arched and glazed doors, adjustable shelves, small drawers, lower portion with canted lid opening to form writing surface, stepped drawers and niches, two short and two long drawers, bracket feet, fielded panels of figured veneers, herringbone borders, 31 x 22 x 78″ **3,500.00**

George II

English, mid 18th C, mahogany, heavily molded cornice, dentil frieze, pair of parcel gilt, glazed, and mullioned doors, adjustable shelves, ploughed supports, cabinet base with two doors, bracket feet, 65 x 13 x 95½″ **7,000.00**

English, third quarter 18th C, mahogany, broken pediment cornice with dentil molding, pair of glazed and mullioned doors, adjustable shelves, lower portion of canted writing lid, fitted int. of drawers and valanced pigeonholes, center prospect door, proscenium flight of stairs, above two frieze and three full cockbeaded and graduated drawers, bracket feet, 42½ x 23 x 112″ **13,000.00**

London, mid 18th C, mahogany, breakfront, central portion surmounted by cornice with broken pediment, pair of glazed and hexagonally mullioned doors, flanked by pair of slightly recessed doors, patera and ribbon carved mullions, conforming base, four cabinet doors, bracket feet **34,000.00**

George II Style, 19th C, yewwood, molded cornice, arcaded frieze, four glazed doors with arched mullions, conforming projecting base of drawers and cabinets, bracket feet, 60½ x 19 x 77″ **18,000.00**

Mission Style, Skandia Furniture Co, Rockford, IL, birch type varnish finish, sectional, four graduated sections, hinged glass front, Viking trademark **575.00**

Regency, early 19th C

Mahogany, two sections, upper with break front, central pyramidal pediment with acroteria and twin cornices, four glazed doors, center pair mullioned, outer pair with brass grillwork, projecting lower section, tambour cov writing surface centered by cupboard doors and drawers, plinth, 84 x 21 x 98″ **25,000.00**

Mahogany and rosewood, rect outline with crescent facade, flat projecting cornice over plain frieze, four full glazed doors, shaped and slightly projecting cupboard base of four doors, 88 x 20 x 87″ **20,000.00**

BOXES

Apple, dovetailed, scalloped sides, cut
out handles, 10½ x 12¼″ **100.00**
Ballot, curly maple, 14″ l **400.00**
Bible, carved oak, English, late 18th C,
stylized carved medallions on top,
front, sides, and back, patented brass
hinges and locks, 14¾″ l **300.00**
Book, pine, lid and base moldings, orig
bat wing brass end handles, worn old
green paint, 18¼″ l **325.00**
Bride's, pine, polychrome floral dec,
German verses "Love me" and "I am
yours" on lid, orig blue paint, minor
wear, age cracks and damage, 16¾″
l **1,000.00**
Candle
Curly Walnut, dovetailed, curly poplar
sliding two board lid, end scratch
carved 1847, 16½″ l **225.00**
Fruitwood, hanging, dovetailed,
shaped back, conforming sliding
lid, 19½″ **600.00**
Pine, orig vinegar graining, brown
sponging on yellow ground, 11″ l . **85.00**
Poplar, dovetailed, raised panel lid
with beveled edges, 16½″ **75.00**
Deed, tole
Dome top, orig dark brown japanning,
red, yellow, and green floral dec,
6⅜″ l **135.00**
Orig black paint, white band, floral
dec in red, green, white, and black,
9½″ l **200.00**
Document
American, late 18th C, pine, flat top,
dovetailed, old brown paint, 14¾ x
8¾ x 10″ **150.00**
Pine, domed lid, orig hasp and lock,
orig red paint, 12¼″ l **135.00**
Election, black ball, cherry, dovetailed,
handle, 13″ l **50.00**
Hat, pine, triangular, applied diamond
shape dec, 9 x 20″ **160.00**
Knife
Adam Revival, late 19th C, mahogany, acorn finial, stepped lid, concentric tiers of cutlery rings, dished
socle and sq base, 27″ h, pr **4,250.00**
Country, mahogany, dovetailed,
scrolled edges, divider with handle,
old finish, minor damage and age
cracks, 9¼ x 15″ **135.00**
George III, c1795, inlaid mahogany,
shaped hinged lid, well pierced for
cutlery, int. lid with center inlaid
star, conforming base, 8¾ x 11½ x
14″, pr **2,750.00**
Hepplewhite, mahogany, edge inlay,
tooled brass escutcheon, 14¾″ h . **500.00**

Pantry, dec
Basswood, orig red and yellow flame
graining, orig brass bale, 12″ l . . . **150.00**
Poplar, brownish-red vinegar paint,
yellow ground, turned detail, 6¼″ h **575.00**
Pipe, pine, truncated, scalloped top,
spire like hanger, dovetailed drawer,
old brass pull, old alligatored finish,
6¾ x 4 x 21″ **1,300.00**
Puzzle, Tunbridge, English, c1850, end-
grain mosaic pattern, 2″ sq **100.00**
Salt, hanging
Pine
Scalloped ends and crest, two
compartments, replaced leather
hinges, worn red paint, minor
edge damage, 12 x 5 x 18″ . . . **500.00**
Spoon rack crest, painted, 12 x 6½
x 26½″ **1,500.00**
Poplar, chip carved and stamped de-
signs, relief carved crest, drawer,
refinished, 5½ x 8½ x 15¾″ **225.00**
Sewing, marquetry, geometric inlay,
slant top, maroon plush pincushion,
int. with till, secret compartment,
green paper lining, dec wrought iron
strap hinges, 10½ x 11¾ x 7¼″ . . . **175.00**
Spice, hanging
Chestnut, eight drawers, worn black
stenciled labels, late wire nail construction, 9¾ x 16½″ **140.00**
Pine, dovetailed, high carved crest,
heart shaped cut out, worn paint,
mouse hole in bottom corner
patched with tin, 13″ l **300.00**
Poplar, shaped crest, lift lid, 4 section
drawer, worn red finish, 7 x 7½ x
11½″ **175.00**
Storage, pine, Chippendale, c1780,
hinged lid, molded edge, false facade
of four small cock beaded drawers,
two working drawers, 31 x 18 x 27½″ **500.00**
Union, walnut, scratch carved dec of eagle in oval, American flags flying upside down, flowers, sgd "J. C. Wet-
tenmann, Union Box, 1874," replaced
hinges, 13″ l **175.00**
Writing, country, table top, pine, dove-
tailed case, old worn patina, replaced
hinges, minor age cracks, 25 x 16 x
7¾″ **50.00**

CABINETS

Apothecary, mahogany facade, pine,
dovetailed, 46 drawers, wood button
knobs, four base paneled doors, old
finish, gilt and black labels, new ply-
wood back, orig built-in, 73¾″ w,
50¼″ h **1,650.00**
Bar, Art Deco, attributed to Ray Hille,
c1930, bleached burl walnut, upright

rect center section, fluted doors, illuminated shelved int., mirrored peach glass, sliding shelf fitted with peach glass, two cupboard doors, two lower rect sections set with cupboard door and shelved int., scrolling U form support, rect plinth, 56¾ x 59¾" **1,550.00**

Bedside

Louis XV, mid 18th C, kingwood parquetry, oblong galleried top, dressing slide, cupboard, bombe case, slender cabriole legs, 17½ x 11½ x 32" **2,100.00**

Louis XVI, late 18th C, mahogany, rect white marble top, bronze gallery with three-quarter fret, conforming case, three full drawers, tapered turned fluted legs, basal shelf, 19 x 13½ x 28½" **1,100.00**

Cabinet, medicine, Humphrey's Veterinarian Specifics, oak, composition front, four shelves, 21 x 10 x 27½", $1,650.00.

China

Biedermeier, highly figured and burled olive wood veneer, ebonized trim, classical style details, architectural cornice, single glass door, two dovetailed drawers, refinished, 32 x 52 x 58" **600.00**

Victorian

Oak, hand carved gallery with 6 x 20" French beveled mirror, glass door and sides, 3 int. shelves, splayed feet, 30" w, 64" h **450.00**

Walnut, 62" h **375.00**

Country Store, dovetailed case, nine dovetailed drawers, orig blue paint, worn paper labels, orig brass pulls, 13 x 33½ x 25½" **1,500.00**

Curio, Louis XV Style, mahogany, brass ormolu trim **525.00**

Display

Empire, walnut, glass top cabinet on mahogany, rope leg table, 45 x 19¼ x 35⅞" **400.00**

Victorian, oak, two adjustable shelves, glass on four sides, full width door on front, 21¼ x 12¼ x 29" **225.00**

Filing, American, c1910, golden oak, plain vertical stack, five drawers, orig brass nameplates and pulls **400.00**

Kitchen, McDougall, Hoosier type, c1900, oak, two parts, three short cupboard doors with inset glass panels over pair of cupboard doors, white graniteware top, inset bread board, base with three graduated drawers, cupboard door, orig hardware and packing label, refinished . **500.00**

Liquor, George IV, English, c1830, mahogany, inlaid, brass banded corners, 18" w **420.00**

Medicine, Victorian, walnut, applied oak beading, hanging, corner, shaped gallery, mirror, single door, one int. shelf, 19 x 15 x 11" **125.00**

Music, Louis XV/XVI Transitional, bronze mounted, 38" h **375.00**

Serving, Neo-Classical, Germanic, early 19th C, rosewood, oblong white marble top in gilt bronze Greek key fretwork border, recessed shelf, conforming cabinet with full door mounted with Paris porcelain roundel of Roman riverscape, Neo-Egyptian term figures, turned legs, gilt bronze fretted borders, 24½ x 13 x 44½" **30,000.00**

Side

Baroque, Italian, walnut, rect molded hinged top, frieze writing drawer, paneled cupboard door, apron drawer, molded base, 25 x 13½ x 36" **2,400.00**

Empire, Classical Revival, attributed to Joseph Barry, Baltimore, c1820, mahogany and veneer, rect top, short drawer over cupboard door, beehive shaped panel flanked by caryatid columns, bulbous turned feet, 18" w, 44½" h, pr **7,700.00**

Spool, oak, four drawers, Dexter, 18¾ x 17⅛ x 16" **600.00**

Vitrine

Art Deco, c1930, shagreen and ivory, triangular cupboard, mirrored int., cov in green stained sharkskin, ivory bands, 58" h **4,500.00**

Louis XVI, gilt bronze mounts, ebonized legs, single door, 50" l **2,000.00**

CANDLE SHIELDS

George III, late 18th C, mahogany, adjustable needlework panel with landscape, 55½" **700.00**
Georgian Style, mahogany, oval needlework panel with still life of harvest fruit, tripod base, 59" h **800.00**
Regency, early 19th C, ebonized, painted chinoiserie figures, 57" h ... **375.00**
Victorian, Continental, 19th C, marquetry, floral needlework panel, 49" h .. **4375.00**

CANDLESTANDS

Centennial, Hepplewhite style, mahogany, elongated pentagonal top, old base repairs to tripod base **250.00**
Chippendale, Massachusetts, mahogany, turned column, spiral fluted urn, raised dish rim, tripod base with ribbed pad feet, 18" d, 27" h **9,000.00**
Federal, 19th C
  Country
    Birch, dish form top, turned urn form standard, cabriole legs, snake feet, 17 x 26½" **1,500.00**
    Painted, tilt top, circular top, turned standard, cabriole legs, snake feet, 19" d, 27" h **450.00**
    Lacquered, black, oval tilt top, urn form standard, arched supports, 13 x 23 x 28" **1,500.00**
    New England, c1805, mahogany, octagonal tilt top, fluted vase form standard, rounded down curving legs, rounded spade feet, restoration to cleats, 20½ x 15 x 30½" .. **6,650.00**
    New Hampshire, attributed to Dunlap Family, c1810, inlaid cherry, oval top with inlaid diamond motifs, tapered sq standards, line and diamond-inlaid down curving legs, blunt arrow feet, some repair to block, 18 x 13 x 29½" **2,750.00**
Federal Style, tip top
  Birch and maple, rect top, canted corners, birdcage support, vasiform standard, cabriole legs ending in club feet, 24 x 18 x 29" **300.00**
  Mahogany, oval top, vasiform standard, cabriole legs ending in club feet, 18 x 23 x 27" **1,900.00**
Hepplewhite, American, late 18th C
  Cherry, tilt top, elongated column, ring turned urn, spider legs with spade feet, 13 x 17½", 30¼" h **4,200.00**
  Curly Maple, tilt top, birdcage, refinished, braces under top replaced . **1,650.00**

CHAIRS

Art Deco
  Arm, Paul Frankl, c1925, black lacquer, continuous low back and arms formed of sq U form slats alternating with inset rect panels, upholstered sq seat, four straight rect legs, pink brocade upholstery, relacquered black, pr **2,310.00**
  Side, Paul Follott, c1912, carved walnut, open rounded back set with wide I form gridwork splat carved at top with flowers, buds and foliage, curved supports, rounded rect seat, shallow grooved apron, two tapering sq front legs with acanthus terminals, flattened ball feet, two tapering rect back legs **4,000.00**
  Slipper, lucite mounted, pale pink and blue print upholstery, matching footstool, pr **600.00**

Art Nouveau
  American, side, walnut, pressed leather seat, and back, flowing iris design, set of four **250.00**
  French, side, walnut, tall pierced foliate back, sq seat, sq legs, spade feet, 24" h, set of 4 .... **500.00**

Arts and Crafts, Mission Style
  Child's, armchair, Morris style, oak, adjustable back, orig cushions ... **225.00**
  Charles P. Lambert Co,
    Armchair, c1912, Morris style, oak, reclining oblong back, flattened arms, open sides, dark red leather cushions, orig label **1,430.00**
    Office, c1910, swivel, oak, upholstered leather back and seat, shaped curving open arms, branded label, 29 x 42" **500.00**
  Gustav Stickley, side, oak, sq back, nine vertical spindles, orig leather seat and tacks, Model No. 358, 39¾" h, pr **2,100.00**

Chippendale
  Boston-Salem area, MA, c1770, side, shaped crest above pierced vase form splat, slip seat, angular cabriole legs, claw and ball feet, orig pine corner blocks, some repair and chips, set of six **80,000.00**
  Massachusetts, c1780
    Armchair, wing, mahogany, shaped upholstered back, ogival wings, out scrolled arms, loose cushion seat, sq molded legs, H stretcher **10,250.00**
    Lolling, attributed to Joseph Short, Newburyport, c1780, mahogany, shaped upholstered back, shaped arms, scroll carved arm

supports, upholstered seat, sq molded legs, H stretcher **22,000.00**

Wing, c1790, carved mahogany, shaped crest, pierced vase form splat, shaped arms, scrolled handholds, slip seat, sq legs, pierced brackets, H stretcher . . **3,750.00**

New York, c1770, side, mahogany, shell and foliage carved cupid's bow crest, scrolling ears, pierced splat, slip seat, shell carved cabriole legs, claw and ball feet, pr . **3,400.00**

Philadelphia, c1780, walnut

Arm, rolled crest, pierced splat, scrolled arms, shaped supports, slip seat, Marlborough legs, H stretcher **3,250.00**

Side, acanthus carved shaped crest, Gothic strapwork splat, molded stiles, slip seat, beaded Marlborough legs, H stretcher . **1,500.00**

Side, cupid's bow crest continuing to scrolling ears, strapwork splat, slip seat, beaded Marlborough legs, H stretcher **1,250.00**

Colonial Style, side, mahogany, cupid's bow crest, pierced splat, slip seat, cabriole legs joined by box stretcher, set of 6 . . . . **650.00**

Empire

American, c1840, mahogany, armchair, shaped crest, scrolling arms, rush seat, sabre legs **500.00**

Baltimore, c1828–35, armchair, white paint and gilt, straight crest, scrolling sides, carved and padded arms, lotus terminals, palmette grips, sq slip seat, scrolled front legs, flaring rear legs, 24 x 20½ x 39″, pr **3,750.00**

Federal

American, attributed to Catskills, NY, side, curly maple, plain crestrail, pierced carved foliate stayrail, cane seat, ring turned legs, flaring feet, pr **600.00**

Boston, MA, c1800, side, inlaid mahogany, molded shield back, three molded splats, inlaid patera, upholstered seat, sq tapering legs, H stretcher **1,870.00**

Massachusetts, c1795, lolling, carved mahogany, upholstered back and seat, serpentine crest, shaped arms, molded arm supports, molded tapering legs **2,000.00**

New England, c1800, lolling, inlaid mahogany, serpentine upholstered crest, shaped arms, incised edges, line inlaid sq tapered legs, H stretcher **8,850.00**

NY, c1815, mahogany, sq molded

back surmounted by glyph carved tablet, four turned and reeded stiles, over upholstered seat, reeded straight tapered legs ending in spade feet, armchair and three side chairs **1,300.00**

Federal Style, mahogany, molded sq back with three rosette carved vertical splats, slip seat, straight tapered legs joined by H stretcher, two armchairs, six side chairs, set of 8 . . . . **2,200.00**

George I, early 18th C, library, mahogany, upholstered rect back, roll arms, and seat cov in floral gros point, cabriole legs anthemion carving at knees, pad feet **8,000.00**

George III, Provincial, mid 18th C

Arm, mahogany, shaped crest, pierced splat with Gothic quatrefoil ornaments, drop in seat, plain rails, straight tapered molded legs, H stretcher, pr **1,200.00**

Corner, Provincial, oak, shaped U form crest, baluster form supports, turned stiles, padded drop in seat, deeply shaped apron, straight legs **650.00**

Dining, mahogany, two armchairs, six side, shaped crest and leaf carved shoulders, pierced vase form splat, padded drop in seat, molded and gadrooned frame, cabriole legs, claw and ball feet, set of eight . . . **12,000.00**

Library, metamorphic, shaped crest, pierced baluster form splat, drop in seat lifting to form steps, pierced skirt **1,800.00**

George III Style, dining, ten side chairs, two armchairs, shaped molded crest, pierced vase form splat, padded seat, straight molded and blind fret carved legs, chamfered H stretcher, set of twelve **24,000.00**

Hepplewhite, armchair, Martha Washington style, mahogany frame, upholstered, line inlay, sq tapered legs, H stretcher **2,600.00**

Ladder Back, Delaware River Valley, c1760, armchair, turned and carved maple, rush seat, four serpentine graduated slats, shaped arms, turned legs, ball feet, frontal ball turned stretcher **3,500.00**

Louis XV, mid 18th C, side, walnut, arched cartouche form back, serpentine seat, recovered in orange roller emb mohair velvet, molded frame, carved summer flowers on crest and rail, cabriole legs, set of four **4,500.00**

Moravian, side, oak, shaped back, simple relief carving, plank seat, pencil post legs **100.00**

Queen Anne
  Boston, MA, c1740–60, walnut, side,
    shaped crest, carved center shell,
    vase form splat, balloon shaped
    seat, cabriole legs, pad feet joined
    by turned stretchers, rear stretcher
    replaced **11,000.00**
  Massachusetts, c1755, side, maple,
    yoke shaped crest, vase form splat
    and slip seat, arched skirt, cabriole
    legs, pad feet, turned stretchers .. **3,850.00**
  New York, c1720–50, side, turned
    maple and oak, back with turned
    finials, leather upholstered splat
    and seat, vase and block turned
    legs, turned frontal stretcher, vase
    form feet, paper label with inscrip-
    tion regarding orig owner **5,000.00**
  New York, c1740–60, side, maple,
    shaped crest, vase form splat, rush
    seat, tapered turned legs, pad feet **2,450.00**
  Philadelphia, c1750, side, walnut,
    shaped volute carved crest, center
    carved shell device, rounded stiles,
    vase form splat, balloon shaped
    slip seat, shell and volute carved
    cabriole legs, claw and ball feet, old
    repair to crest, inscribed Roman
    numeral I on inside of front seat rail
    and seat frame, back of crest fitted
    with 18th or 19th C wrought iron
    brace, part of a set made by Cap-
    tain Samuel Morris, Philadelphia . **74,250.00**
  Philadelphia, attributed to John Elliott,
    c1750, side, walnut, incised cupid
    bow's crestrail, scroll carved ears,
    center leaf and volute carved arch,
    solid vase form splat, slip seat,
    molded edge, shell carved apron,
    shell and volute carved cabriole
    legs, platform pad feet **8,525.00**

Queen Anne, transitional, mid 18th C,
    arm, fruitwood, bulb and wheel front
    stretcher, scrolled arms, replaced
    rush seat, pierced back splat, molded
    ears, Spanish foot, refinished **2,500.00**

Queen Anne Style, American, dining,
    yoke crest continuing to shaped
    stiles, urn form splat, balloon form slip
    seat, cabriole legs, claw and ball feet,
    set of 6 .... **1,400.00**

Regency
  Dining, c1810, klismos form, shaped
    crest, carved horizontal splat, slip
    seat, molded and spiral carved
    stiles, sabre legs, set of 6 ...... **7,000.00**
  Side, rosewood, English, 19th C,
    brass ornamentation, matched set
    of eight **4,750.00**

Sheraton
  Massachusetts or New Hampshire

coastal region, c1800, lolling, inlaid
    mahogany, as found good condition **5,750.00**
  Pennsylvania, country, early 19th C,
    plank seat, orig yellow-tan paint,
    black striping, set of five **375.00**

**Chair, Victorian, Renaissance Revival,
walnut, finger molded, nut carved
crest, upholstered, $450.00.**

Victorian
  Belter, John, side, rose and grape
    carved crests, upholstered back
    and seat, pr **4,500.00**
  Eastlake, armchair, walnut, uphol-
    stered seat and back **300.00**
  Elizabeth Revival
    Lady's, American, c1860, finger
      carved walnut frame, grape
      carved crest, fine upholstery ... **200.00**
    Side, Shaw Furniture Co, Cam-
      bridge, MA, early 20th C, walnut
      and laminated walnut, tall narrow
      back, open cut arched scroll cut
      crest, scroll and urn carved wide
      back, columnar turned stiles, up-
      holstered seat, trumpet turned
      front legs, scrolled front stretcher,
      labeled **350.00**
  Federal Revival, c1900, dining, six
    side chairs, two armchairs, mahog-
    any, flat crest, lyre form splat, curv-
    ing stiles, upholstered seats, sabre
    form front legs, set of eight **3,850.00**
  Gothic Revival, side, mahogany and
    mahogany veneer, slanting back,
    flat top rail with arcade of four
    pointed arches, straight sided up-
    holstered seat, scrolled knees and
    tapered feet, 33½" h **750.00**
  Renaissance Revival, c1870
    Armchair, child's, walnut, ebonized
      trim, arched crestrail, pierced urn
      form splat, arms with turned sup-
      ports, round tapered legs, toupie
      feet, 26½" h **450.00**

Side, walnut, pediment inscribed columnar stiles, upholstered back panel and seat, curved rails, trumpet shaped front columnar legs, round rear legs, 36½" h **250.00**

William and Mary, early 18th C, side, carved and turned, scroll carved crest, lozenge form caned back, turned stiles, caned seat, block and vase turned legs, bulbous front stretcher, block and ring turned H stretcher, pr **1,200.00**

Chair, Windsor, armchair, comb back, $3,000.00.

Windsor
Arm, American, c1800
Bow back, seven spindles, refinished **900.00**
Child's, sack back, bowed crest, five tapered spindles, elliptical seat, turned legs and stretchers, painted black over red **1,450.00**
Comb back, Wallace Nutting, curly maple, shaped pine seat, branded and paper label **1,800.00**
Side
Bow Back
New England, c1810, seven tapered spindles, plank seat, turned legs and stretchers, painted brown, set of 6 ..... **8,000.00**
New England, late 18th C, nine spindles, saddle seat, turned legs and stretchers, slightly cut down, old dark finish **450.00**
Tuck, Samuel J., c1795, nine spindles, saddle seat, old black finish **1,200.00**
Brace Back, Rhode Island, late 18th C, finely turned and widely splayed legs, old refinishing ... **1,100.00**

Fan Back
Wallace Nutting, orig label **725.00**
Pennsylvania, late 18th C, painted green, mounted on rockers **325.00**
Youth, American, c1850, three arrow splats, refinished **350.00**
Windsor Style, Colonial Furniture Co, Grand Rapids, MI, armchair, birch, maple finish, bow back, seven spindles, rush seat, 21 x 16 x 21½" **85.00**

CHESTS OF DRAWERS

Chippendale
American, cherry, rect top and case, five cockbeaded and graduated long drawers, canted and fluted sides, turned feet, 38 x 18 x 45" . **800.00**
Connecticut or New York, c1780, cherry, oblong top, molded edge, four graduated molded drawers, projecting gadrooned molding, claw and ball feet, 38½ x 18½ x 35" **9,350.00**
English
Cherry, dovetailed case, six graduated dovetailed drawers, beaded frames, molded cornice, ball and claw feet, replaced hardware and minor repair, old refinishing, 37¾" w, 53" h **2,100.00**
Oak, five dovetailed quarter sawed drawers, mahogany cross banding, applied edge beading, orig hardware, some edge damage and repair, 42⅜" w, 37¼" h ... **1,250.00**
New England, c1780, cherry, tall, molded cornice, six graduated molded drawers, restored bracket feet, 35¼ x 18 x 44" **5,000.00**
Pennsylvania, last quarter 18th C, walnut, four graduated drawers, bold ogee bracket base, refinished, orig hardware, 36" w **3,500.00**
Philadelphia, c1790, mahogany, bow front, oblong molded top of plum pudding mahogany, conforming case, four cockbeaded graduated long drawers, fluted quarter columns, molded base, raised ogee bracket feet, 45 x 22 x 37" **5,250.00**
Philadelphia, swell front, mahogany, ogee bracket base, fluted quarter columns, minor age separation in molding at top, replaced hardware, 41⅛" w **5,750.00**
Empire, American, c1830–40
Bird's Eye Maple, two parts, upper section with pair of half round shallow drawers over pair of cockbeaded short drawers, lower section with half round long drawer

overhanging three cockbeaded and graduated long drawers, half round columns, turned feet, 39 x 21 x 51" **700.00**

Cherry, country, rect top and case, one deep drawer overhanging three graduated long drawers, full columns, turned feet, 45 x 21 x 31" **350.00**

Cherry, high style, mahogany veneer facade, two tier step back top, scrolled crest, four dovetailed drawers, turned and rope carved column base with four dovetailed drawers, orig brasses, minor edge damage, veneer repair, old refinish, two top drawer replaced hardware, 44½ x 20 x 57¾" **1,400.00**

Cherry and curly maple, country, seven dovetailed drawers, tapered pilasters, turned feet, old worn finish, age cracks and minor damage, 43 x 22 x 51½" **550.00**

Curly maple, country, paneled ends, four dovetailed drawers, turned pilasters, refinished, replaced feet, 45¾ x 21 x 47" **850.00**

Mahogany, sleigh front, fine crotch grain mahogany facings and ripple molding, two small drawers over four graduated drawers, 40½" . . . **300.00**

Mahogany veneer, child's, sleigh front, back splash with two small drawers over four graduated drawers, orig wooden knobs and locks, 30" w **375.00**

Walnut, five overlapping dovetailed drawers, molded cornice, curly maple facings stiles and apron, refinished, repairs, and replaced hardware, 42¼" w, 41¾" h **1,000.00**

Federal
American, late 18th C, birch, four graduated drawers, old refinish, replaced hardware, 36½ x 17¾ x 41¾" **2,650.00**

Boston, MA, attributed to John and/or Thomas Seymour, c1805, inlaid mahogany, rect top, inlaid edge, four graduated line inlaid cockbeaded drawers, ivory keyholes, shaped and inlaid skirt, tapering legs, splayed inlaid feet, side brass carrying handles, 41½ x 21½ x 39" **28,600.00**

Country, early 19th C, cherry, rect top and case, four cockbeaded and graduated long drawers flanked by beaded stiles, turned legs, 42 x 20 x 42" **550.00**

English, c1830, mahogany, bow front, two cockbeaded short drawers, flanked by turned outset stiles, larger conforming case with four cockbeaded and graduated long

drawers flanked by rope turned stiles, turned legs, peg feet, 42 x 18 x 45" **1,200.00**

Mid-Atlantic states, c1815, walnut, bow front, oblong top, slightly bowed, four line and fan inlaid graduated drawers, bracket feet, 38 x 22 x 37" **2,200.00**

New England, country, cherry, rect top and case, two short drawers, three cockbeaded graduated long drawers, turned feet, 45 x 19 x 49" . . . **650.00**

New England, mahogany and satinwood, c1800, bow front, inlaid oblong top, conforming case with four tiger maple banded graduated long drawers with satinwood reserves, shaped skirt continuing to French bracket feet, 44 x 21 x 37" **6,500.00**

Federal Style, mahogany, rect top, two shallow drawers, one oval inlaid deep drawer, three cockbeaded and graduated long drawers, shaped skirt, bracket feet, 44 x 21 x 48" **425.00**

Chest of Drawers, Hepplewhite, c1800, walnut, figured walnut drawer fronts and scallop, dust panels between drawers, flared bracket feet, orig hardware and locks, 41½ x 35½ x 21½", $5,000.00.

Hepplewhite
American
Cherry, banded inlay top edge and around scrolled apron, five dovetailed drawers, four graduated with applied beaded edge, restoration, refinished, and replaced hardware, 43 x 17 x 42½" **850.00**

Walnut and veneer, walnut top and sides, four mahogany veneer dovetailed and cock beaded drawers with elongated oval inlays, French feet, inlaid ivory escutcheons, cross banded inlay top edge, orig brasses, 39½ x 21½ x 33½" **15,000.00**

Pennsylvania, curly walnut, dovetailed case, fluted quarter columns, eight dovetailed drawers, removable cornice with mahogany veneer band, French feet with scalloped apron, curly maple veneer band, refinished and replaced brasses, 39¾" w, 67¾" h **6,500.00**

Pennsylvania or Ohio, c1800

Cherry, tiger maple molding around top, four graduated drawers, orig hardware, 41½" **2,400.00**

Curly maple and walnut, four graduated drawers, orig oval brasses and escutcheons, 40" w **800.00**

Victorian, American, curly walnut, c1850, mahogany, scrolled splashboard, two drawer superstructure over recessed top, conforming case, four cockbeaded drawers, opalescent glass handles, shaped skirt, turned legs, 41 x 18 x 46" **850.00**

CHESTS, OTHER

See also Blanket Chests and Chests of Drawers

Bachelor's

Chippendale, English, mahogany, thumb molded top, five dovetailed drawers with applied edge beading, ogee feet, replaced back foot and hardware, 31½" w, 31¼" h **3,200.00**

George III, mahogany, oblong molded top, conforming case, cockbeaded drawers, molded base, bracket feet, pierced spandrels, 43¼ x 22½ x 38" **1,400.00**

Chest on Chest

Chippendale

English, 19th C, mahogany, eight dovetailed drawers, applied edge beading, dentil molded cornice, ogee feet, orig hardware, old finish, minor damage and repairs, 43" w, 70½" h **4,400.00**

New England, c1790, carved maple, two parts, molded cornice, five molded graduated drawers, base of four molded graduated long drawers, shaped bracket feet, 39½ x 19½ x 76" **8,250.00**

Georgian, walnut, dentil cornice molding, four tiers of graduated drawers, upper tier of three drawers, two drawer base, fluted quarter columns, ogee bracket feet, replaced brasses, minor restoration, 40 x 22 x 73½" **2,000.00**

Hepplewhite, PA, late 18th C, inlaid cherry, molded cornice, three small drawers over two drawers over three graduated drawers, two graduated drawers in low base, replaced brasses **4,300.00**

Commode

Art Deco, Clément Mère, c1925, rect inset top, rolled edge, one long drawer, central cupboard door opening to shelved int., six short drawers, int. lined with burled sycamore, gently curving apron, four Chinese inspired rect legs, cov in pressed leather, dyed all over pattern of circular stylized buds and blossoms, shades of rust, dark amber, mustard, brown, and gold, painted ivory circular handles, 37½ x 32⅞", pr **41,800.00**

Baroque, Austrian, c1725, walnut, oblong molded top with reverse serpentine front, conforming case, four full drawers, cross banded fielded panels, molded base, compressed bun feet, 49 x 26½ x 35" **2,750.00**

George III, English, c1790, inlaid burr walnut and burr yewwood, demilune, two doors with oval panels, 34 x 54 x 22" **10,000.00**

Highboy

Chippendale, CT, c1770, carved cherry, bonnet top, two parts, molded swan's neck crest, carved pinwheel terminals, three urn and spirally carved finials, three short drawers, lower section with four graduated drawers, scroll cut bracket feet, 38 x 20 x 85½" **35,000.00**

Chippendale Style, Philadelphia, mahogany, two parts, upper section with molded swan's neck pediment, rococo carved tympanum, five short drawers, three graduated long drawers flanked by fluted quarter columns, molded mid section, lower part with single full drawer, shell carved deep drawer flanked by short drawers, fluted quarter columns edged by carved skirt, acanthus carved cabriole legs, claw and ball feet, 45 x 20 x 84" **3,400.00**

Queen Anne, two parts

American, country, maple, five drawers, top with hidden molded cornice drawer, base with four overlapping dovetailed drawers, scrolled apron, cabriole legs, duck feet, old repairs and replacements, replaced legs and hardware, refinished, 36″ w, 68″ h **3,250.00**

Boston Area, MA, c1750, burl walnut veneer, flat top, upper section with projecting cornice, secret drawer, five drawers, lower section with mid molding above five cockbeaded drawers, shaped skirt, turned pendants, angular cabriole legs, pad feet, 40¼ x 22 x 69″ **18,000.00**

Delaware or Pennsylvania, c1750, carved and inlaid walnut, upper section with flat top, molded cornice, five short and three long molded graduated drawers, lower section with projecting mid molding, four short molded drawers, shaped skirt, center stellar and dot inlaid reserve, trifid feet, moldings restored, patches to case, 42 x 22½ x 74½″ **8,500.00**

New England, mid 18th C, cherry, upper section with molded flat top cornice, conforming case with two thumb molded short drawers, three graduated long drawers, lower section with single long drawer, three short drawers, cabriole legs, pad feet, 40 x 21 x 66″ **4,500.00**

New England, mid 18th C, maple, upper section with molded flat top cornice, conforming case, four thumb molded graduated long drawers, lower section with single fan carved deep drawer, shaped skirt, cabriole legs, pad feet, 38 x 19 x 64″ **5,000.00**

William and Mary, NY, c1720, flat top, turned and carved maple, two parts, upper section with molded cornice, two short, three long drawers, lower section with mid molding, three short drawers, shaped skirt, turned legs, shaped stretcher, ball feet, minor repairs to base, 38½ x 20½ x 77″ **9,600.00**

Lowboy
  Chippendale
    English, mahogany, molded edge top, three dovetailed drawers with applied edge beading, scalloped apron, sq legs with inside chamfer and molded edge, repairs and replacements, 16 x 31¾ x 28″ **1,200.00**
    Pennsylvania, probably Philadelphia, c1770, mahogany, rect top, five molded drawers, center drawer shell carved, fluted quarter columns, shaped skirt, acanthus carved cabriole legs, claw and ball feet, later casters, applied acanthus leaves missing, minor restoration, 34 x 24 x 30½″ **27,500.00**

Queen Anne
  Boston area, MA, c1755, walnut, rect top, thumb molded edge, notched corners, five molded drawers, center drawer carved with concave reserve, skirt with turned pendants, pad feet, slight restoration, 34 x 19¼ x 31″ ... **20,000.00**

Queen Anne, English, walnut, figured veneer, molded edge top with notched corners, scalloped apron, chamfered corners with fluting, three dovetailed drawers, cabriole legs, duck feet with pads, carved shells knees, repairs and replacements, 20 x 30 x 28″ **1,750.00**

William and Mary
  American, curly maple, two board top with thumb mold edge, three dovetailed drawers, scrolled apron, applied molding, turned legs, X stretcher, finial, ball feet, two apron drops missing, period replacement brasses and engraved escutcheons, 30¾ x 21¾ x 27¾″ **16,000.00**
  English, pine, walnut burl veneer, herringbone inlay top and around drawers, scalloped apron with turned drops and drawers with dovetailing, turned legs and cross stretcher, replaced legs stretchers and turned drops, minor repairs, 21¼ x 31¼ x 32″ .. **1,400.00**

CRADLES

Chippendale, birch, canted sides, scalloped headboard, turned posts and rails, refinished, 37½″ l **275.00**

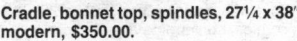

Cradle, bonnet top, spindles, 27¼ x 38″, modern, $350.00.

Country

Cherry, dovetailed, cut out heart ends, age cracks, refinished, 37½″ l **260.00**

Decorated, worn orig red and black graining, polychrome stenciled baskets of fruit, and white striping, hood, replaced rockers, 39″ l **175.00**

Pine, painted grain finish

Hooded, New England, c1840, arched hood, canted sides, shaped footboard, orig rosewood graining, gold stenciled dec, light blue int. **425.00**

Low, canted sides, sq corner posts, turned finials, shaped rockers, early 19th C, 40″ l **350.00**

Victorian, walnut, sausage turned spindles **260.00**

Windsor, NE, c1800–20, bamboo turned spindles, worn finish **800.00**

CUPBOARDS

Armoire

Art Nouveau, Louis Majorelle, c1900, carved walnut and fruitwood, upright rect form, crested top, carved apron with clusters of lilac blossoms and foliage, central cupboard door set with beveled glass mirror plate, flanked by two smaller conforming cupboard doors, one long and two short drawers, gilt-bronze leaf molded handles, four lug feet, 74½ x 96″ **8,250.00**

European Court Style, hardwood, carved top edge, paneled ends, applied moldings, carved figural pilasters with acanthus scrolls, two drawers and doors, old dark finish, repairs and restorations, replaced feet and early wrought iron lock, 51¼ x 20 x 44″ **750.00**

Victorian, Renaissance Revival, 19th C, handmade, oak, turned and carved detail, marquetry door panels, dovetailed drawers, mortised and pinned construction, marked "Made in England," 48½ x 20½ x 45¾″ **600.00**

Chifforobe, Art Deco Style, Tri-Bond Furniture, c1940, waterfall veneer, narrow center mirrored section, deep drawers on one side, cedar lined short wardrobe above drawers on other side **225.00**

Corner

Chippendale, late 18th C

Country, pine, two parts, upper section with molded and fretwork cornice, conforming case, single

Cupboard, wall, walnut, three shelves, three drawers over two doors, brass hardware, 52 × 18½ × 84″, $4,500.00.

glazed door, three fixed shelves, lower section with two paneled cupboard doors, molded base, bracket feet, 46 x 22 x 88″ **3,750.00**

Pennsylvania, c1780, inlaid walnut, two parts, upper section with projecting cornice over pair of arched glazed line inlaid doors, painted and shelved int., lower section with two cockbeaded drawers over pair of paneled cupboard doors, intersection line inlaid panels, minor restoration, 54 x 25½ x 80″ **5,775.00**

Federal, country

Cherry, New England, c1800, molded cornice, single glazed door over two short drawers, double paneled cupboard door, molded base, 48 x 19 x 88″ ... **2,200.00**

Walnut, country, early 19th C, molded cornice over conforming case, single glazed cupboard door, single drawer, pair of paneled cupboard doors, shaped skirt, bracket feet, 48 x 20 x 79″ **3,500.00**

Pine, country

New England, northern, late 18th or early 19th C, closed face, upper section with two glazed doors each with six glass lights, cupboard base with two paneled doors, old blue-green paint, 49½ x 22 x 74½″ **1,800.00**

Pennsylvania or New Jersey, c18th C, closed face, upper section with two arched glazed doors, three int. shelves, lower section with two paneled doors, two drawers, stepped molding, diagonal grooving, applied egg shaped ornamentation, later paint over orig pale yellow paint, 58½ x 28½ x 86½" **1,000.00**

Poplar, Gothic arch paned top doors with old wavy glass, cove molded cornice, paneled door base, cut out ogee type feet, old red repaint, replaced feet, 43" w, 82½" h **1,000.00**

Court, Federal, CT, c1815, inlaid cherry, projecting cornice over recessed cupboard section with two hinged doors, ebony inlaid columns, pair of hinged cupboard doors below, shelves, inset panel sides, bracket feet, 39½ x 21 x 57½" **16,500.00**

Hanging

Georgian, oak, c1800, molded cornice, conforming case, single paneled cupboard door, shell inlay, three fixed shelves, 40 x 21 x 45" **600.00**

Victorian, country, late 19th C

Cherry, projecting cornice, conforming case, single glazed cupboard door, shaped skirt, bracket feet, 28 x 13 x 33" **450.00**

Pine, corner, raised panel door, molded cornice, old refinishing, three holes, 32½ x 31½" **475.00**

Jelly

Pine, top and base edge molding, sq corner posts from feet, raised panel ends and doors, worn old blue, orig wrought iron butterfly type hinges, replaced shelves, wear and damage, 51" w, 60" h **450.00**

Poplar, country, low dovetailed gallery, paneled doors, two dovetailed drawers with ogee fronts, old red paint, simple cut out feet, some damage, 47 x 17½ x 52½" **550.00**

Linen Press, Hepplewhite, English, two pc, mahogany, double door top with oval inlaid panels and dentilated cornice, five pull out shelves int., base with applied edge beading, four dovetailed drawers, bracket feet, repairs, replaced hardware, and some cornice and molding damage, 46" w, 77½" h **8,750.00**

Pewter, American, late 18th, pine, three open shelves, scalloped details, shoe foot, old natural finish, 33¼ x 10½ x 45" **450.00**

Pie Safe

Butternut and poplar, country, dovetailed case, corner and base moldings, punched tin panels with star flower and bird dec, old worn green over red paint, orig cast iron latch, porcelain knob, removed batten, insect damage, 48½" w, 72" h **800.00**

Pine and poplar, two pc, double doors

with six glass panes, pie shelf, three dovetailed drawers and paneled doors in base, bracket feet, restoration and repairs, 56 x 19¼ x 84½" **2,600.00**

Wall

Country, early 19th C, walnut, step back, molded cornice above three fixed shallow shelves, breakfront base with four cockbeaded short drawers flanked by corner columns, pair of short drawers, pair of paneled doors, and pair of corner columns, bracket feet, 66 x 19 x 82" **4,000.00**

Pine and Poplar, two pc, top with paneled doors, rounded corners, bottom with three dovetailed drawers and two doors, carved foliage drawer pulls, refinished, replaced latches and cornice, 58¼ x 20 x 90" **1,000.00**

Poplar, two pc, top with pie shelf, double door with six panes glass, and arched top lights, molded cornice, base with paneled doors and three dovetailed drawers, replaced latches, old red traces, 56¾ x 19 x 85¼" **1,500.00**

Wardrobe

Arts and Crafts, Mission Style, Gustav Stickley, c1905, oak, flat rect top, two long paneled doors, two int. compartments, eight narrow drawers over two shelves, lower arched toe board, red decal mark, remnants of paper label, 33¼ x 59¾" **5,500.00**

Classical, NY, c1825, stenciled and gilt mahogany, two parts, upper section with removable cornice, arched frieze with stenciled fruit, lower section with two hinged doors, int. with two long drawers, free standing Ionic columns, eagle carved hairy paw feet, some restoration to gilding, 66 x 34 x 93" **8,000.00**

Victorian, country

Pine, dovetailed case, paneled doors, molded cornice, int. with orig shelf and carved pegs, scrolled dovetailed feet, refinished, minor repair and damage, 59" w, 78½" h **900.00**

Poplar, cherry finish, brushed graining, cove molded cornice, four panel door, flat base, one int. shelf, clothes hooks, 49¼ x 79½" **350.00**

DESKS

Art Nouveau, Carlo Bugatti, c1900, ebonized wood, carved, applied hammered copper and inlaid in Moorish taste, rect top, inset leather writing surface, small super-structure holding six short drawers inlaid in pewter with birds and bamboo, arched cubbyhole, arched and outward flaring front legs, trestle back supports, 24 x 19½ x 38" .. **6,600.00**

Arts and Crafts, designed by Otto Wager, executed by Gebruder Thonet, c1904–06, stained beechwood and aluminum, rect top, beige felt inset writing surface, back mounted with shelf, two short drawers in apron, round straight legs and side stretchers, front legs with alumunim studs, back panel with row of aluminum studs, 42½ x 26⅜ x 43" **22,000.00**

Chippendale
Butler's, mahogany, three dovetailed drawers with applied bead edge, fitted int. with dovetailed and concealed drawers, repairs, replaced feet, worn finish, replaced hardware, 43½" h **850.00**
English, 19th C, mahogany, tooled and gilded green leather top, nine dovetailed drawers, bracket feet, orig hardware, minor wear and repair, 59 x 30½ x 30¼" **1,900.00**

Chippendale Style
Colonial Desk Co, Rockford, IL, blister mahogany, slant front, fitted int. with valanced pigeonholes, two small drawers, flanking open center prospect, three drawers, shaped skirt, cabriole legs, eagle brasses, 37 x 20 x 43" **275.00**
Rockford Chair & Furniture Co, Rockford, IL, mahogany veneer and gumwood, slant front with floral dec oval inlay, four graduated drawers, eagle brasses, bracket feet, 38" w, 38" h **475.00**

Empire, butler's, American, c1835, cherry, rect top, conforming case, secretary drawer overhanging three cockbeaded graduated long drawers, spiral turned columns continuing to turned feet, 44 x 24 x 47" **850.00**

Federal
Lady's, late Federal, c1820, two parts, upper section with swan's neck pediment, pair of glazed cupboard doors, pair of short drawers, lower section with baize lined writing flap, two short and two long cockbeaded drawers, turned legs, 39 x 19 x 69" **950.00**
Partner's, early 19th C, mahogany, rect top, leather inset writing surface, conforming case, two sets of five cockbeaded drawers, eight turned legs with brass caps and casters, 60 x 42 x 32" **38,000.00**

Federal Style, lady's, mahogany, two parts, upper section with shaped pediment, urn form finials, inlaid frieze, two tracery glazed doors, eglomise panels of classical garden scene, lower section with writing flap, full drawer, two bottle drawers flanking knee well, reeded legs, turned feet, 36 x 19 x 82" **2,900.00**

George I, burl walnut, slant front, fitted int. with serpentine drawers and compartments, four graduated and cross banded drawers, bracket fee, 27¼ x 178½ x 38" **1,300.00**

George III Style, 19th C, mahogany, oblong top, inset tooled leather writing surface, conforming case, three frieze drawers, twin banks of three drawers, recessed center knee well, 58 x 24½ x 31" **1,500.00**

Governor Winthrop Style, Skandia Furniture Co, Rockford, IL, antique mahogany finish, slant front, fitted int. with pigeonholes and drawers, shell carved center door, automatic sliding lid supports, 37" w, 41" h **350.00**

Hepplewhite, butler's, curly maple, pullout desk with fitted drawers, five dovetailed drawers with cherry cross banding, sq tapered legs, reconstructed, refinished, and replaced hardware, 47¼ x 20 x 40¼" **1,700.00**

Queen Anne
Boston area, MA, c1760, carved mahogany, block front, slant, rect hinged lid, fitted int. with valanced pigeonholes over small drawers, center prospect drawer opening to two small drawers, document drawers flanking, four graduated long drawers, cockbeaded surrounds, molded base with shaped pendants, blocked bracket feet, 42 x 21 x 43½" **27,500.00**
English, table top type, burled walnut veneer, cross banding, dovetailed drawer with serpentine front, slant lid, fitted int., adjustable scrolled mirror with orig beveled glass, old replacement, replaced feet, 19¼ x 9½ x 34½" **1,400.00**

Schoolmaster
Pine, 19th C, hinged slant front writing surface, fitted int., straight tapered legs, 31 x 20 x 36" **175.00**
Country, early 19th C, grain painted, slant front, hinged, fitted well, molded mid section, conforming frieze with single thumb molded drawer, turned legs with H stretcher, 42 x 24 x 44" **3,400.00**

Sheraton, mahogany, pine and chestnut

secondary wood, top section with central door, four int. dovetailed drawers, tambour doors, fold down writing surface, base with three dovetailed drawers, applied edge bead, turned legs, ring turned posts, minor repairs, replaced brasses, 41 x 22 x 51" ... **800.00**

Dough Box, Lancaster, PA, grain painted, 31 x 15 x 33½", $300.00.

Desk, Wooton, walnut, burl walnut veneer, patented, $9,000.00.

√ictorian

Eastlake, walnut, burl veneer, lift top, incised lines, applied dec, 36 x 22 x 20" **375.00**

Wooten, walnut, detailed int. with files, cubby holes, drawers, and fall front **7,500.00**

Victorian Colonial Style, Stow-Davis, Grand Rapids, MI, oblong molded top, two banks of three drawers, center drawer, turned baluster feet, 60" l ... **350.00**

William and Mary, English, table top type, walnut veneer, line inlay, slant lid, fitted int., bracket feet, adjustable scrolled mirror with orig glass, old repairs and replacements, 16 x 8¾ x 27½" **1,000.00**

DOUGH TROUGHS

Decorated, pine, one board top, scrolled apron, splated base, turned legs, 25½ x 44¾ x 28¼' **500.00**

Maple, dovetailed, board and batten top, scalloped apron, rect legs, 35 x 22 x 30" **265.00**

Pine, early 19th C, one piece top, shaped ends, refinished, 19¾" **300.00**

Poplar

Corner post construction, mortised and pinned stiles, raised panels, lift lid, two section int., sliding bread

board and paddle, stripped, 38 x 25 x 36¼" **200.00**

Dovetailed, one board lid, splayed base, turned legs, red stain finish, age crack, some damage, added metal braces, 17¾ x 35 x 31½" .. **350.00**

Walnut, Louis XV, Provincial, mid 18th C, walnut, oblong molded top with serpentine front, canted dough box, conforming valanced skirt carved with flowering urn, turned supports and box stretcher, 40½ x 22 x 37" **2,100.00**

DRY SINKS

Butternut, two doors, one int. shelf, orig stippling and finish, 35 x 20 x 42" .. **450.00**

Curly Maple, rect well, work surface to right with short drawer, two poplar wood cupboard doors, short bracket feet, hardwood edge stripes, minor repairs, refinished, 55 x 34½" **2,200.00**

Grain Painted, New England, rect, tin lined well, rounded splashboard, two small drawers, two cupboard doors, int. shelves, bracket feet, brown and yellow pine graining, 49 x 38" **775.00**

Oak, zinc liner, two doors, 34 x 19 x 44" **500.00**

Pine and Poplar, country, paneled doors, traces of red and yellow paint, refinished, replaced drawer and wood pulls, 48½ x 20 x 37" **600.00**

Pine and Walnut, New England, rect galleried top, two cupboard doors, shelf, arched apron, 44 x 32¾" **725.00**

Poplar

Amish, Holmes County, OH, paneled doors, shaped skirt, two drawers, yellow paint, black graining over orig blue paint, 49" **2,000.00**

Country, old paint traces, reconstructed, 43½ x 19½ x 43" **385.00**

Frame, folk art style, assorted soft woods, 14 x 17", $125.00.

FRAMES

Brass
Floral scroll dec, 6½ x 4½"	85.00
Florentine styling, easel back, 8 x 14"	65.00

Curly Maple, cherry, butternut, 19½ x 15½ x 3" w, pr **250.00**

Empire, mahogany veneer, wide molding, 20 x 26" **50.00**

Folk Art, American, pine, one piece, carved, sunburst crest, 10½ x 17½" **125.00**

Mahogany, gold liner, 9 x 16" opening . **75.00**

Maple, bird's-eye veneer, gilded liner, 1⅞ x 13¾ x 16½" **100.00**

Pine, flat, block, corners with metal stars, 15 x 18" **75.00**

Poplar, beveled, orig red flame graining, 14½ x 16½" **135.00**

Shadow Box, Victorian
Circular, 21½"	100.00
Oval, 19¾ x 22¾"	100.00
Rect, walnut, double liner, 28 x 32"	115.00

Tramp Art, American, c1930, deeply layered and chip carved geometric top panel with heart in center, 47 x 40", pr **500.00**

HAT RACKS AND HALL TREES

Art Deco, French, c1925, wrought iron, rect, top set with shallow open hat shelf above octagonal mirror, shallow verde antico shelf on angled support wrought with straight bands and coils, two rect sections set with three coat hooks, outset rect umbrella stands, scrolls and imp geometric devices, 51¾ x 75" **12,100.00**

Horseshoe shape, wood, sq brass hooks, old black paint, silver trim, minor repair, 28 x 35" **185.00**

Jacobean Style, oak, paneled back with molded stile and rail construction, carved bands of stylized acanthus and marquetry birds and flowers, plank seat, turned legs joined by box stretcher, 58" l **1,400.00**

Umbrella Stand, cast iron, $125.00.

Victorian, solid brass, large beveled plate glass mirror supported by side posts with hooks, base of mirror supported by rect shelf with round legs joined at base by identical shelf, cast paw feet, brass scrolls, sunflower rosettes at mirror corners, foliate crest with cartouche, 38 x 12 x 81" **2,000.00**

Windsor, pine, bamboo turned, six knob like hooks, orig yellow varnish, black striping, 33¾" l **90.00**

ICE CREAM PARLOR FURNITURE

Chair
Arm, wood seat	125.00
Heart back, refinished	70.00
Spectacle, refinished	80.00

Stool
26½" h, refinished	50.00
30" h, 12" d seat, refinished	60.00

Table
27" sq, oak top	225.00
30" d, oak top	250.00

Table and 2 Chairs, child's, 18" d table, 9½" d chair seat, set **200.00**

Table and 4 Chairs, 30" d wood top table, 14" d chairs, replaced seats, refinished, set **500.00**

LOVE SEATS

Empire, French, c1810, mahogany and parcel gilt, upholstered, carved

sphinx heads, tapering supports, claw
feet **800.00**
Federal, New England, inlaid mahog-
any, removable rect crest, upholstered back, line inlaid curving arms,
upholstered seat, reeded legs, 51" l . **750.00**
George III, c1779, mahogany, adjusta-
ble armrests, sq, chamfered legs, up-
holstered, 57" l **3,300.00**
Oriental, c1900, carved hardwood,
dragon arms, 52" **700.00**
Regency, walnut, scrolling frame and
skirt, shell and acanthus carving, cabriole legs, tightly whorled feet, padded back, seat and arms in contem-
porary gros and petit point, 84" l . . . **3,750.00**
Venetian, rococo, 19th C, gilt carved
wood, floral brocade upholstered
cushion, carved frieze, cabriole legs,
24½ x 21½ x 15" **700.00**
Victorian, American, c1870–80, walnut,
three flower carved crests, good up-
holstery, 54" l **475.00**

MAGAZINE RACKS

Canterbury
George III
Mahogany, three bays, short turned
feet, castors, 23 x 17 x 20" . . . **450.00**
Pine, orig brown flame graining on
salmon ground, drawer in base,
castors, 15½ x 15½ x 17" **200.00**
Regency, early 19th C, mahogany,
four wells formed by skeletal frame,
full drawer, turned legs, brass castered feet, 18½ x 13½ x 18½" . . . **2,200.00**
Regency Style, Luce Furniture Co,
Grand Rapids, MI, mahogany type
finish, four wells, skeletal frame,
faux drawer with two pulls, turned
legs, brass castered feet **100.00**
Victorian, Eastlake, walnut, pierced
sides, turned posts, machine
carved, 13½ x 26" **125.00**
Mission
Roycroft, oak, c1910, carved em-
blem, 37" h **450.00**
Stickley, oak, c1910, rect decal "L. &
J. G. Stickley Bros" mark, 45" h . . **475.00**

MIRRORS

Art Deco
Cheval, German, ebonized, swivel
rect mirror, rounded edges, low sq
mount, artist sgd, 70" h **300.00**
Wall
28¼" h, circular glass mirror above
abstract bracket formed of overlapping circles in various tex-
tures, inset with semi-circular

Mirror, bureau, mixed woods, 13½ x 7½ x 21", $350.00.

wood band, inscribed "albert-
Cheuret," c1925, copy of Albert
Cheuret 1925 exhibition photo-
graph **10,000.00**
37 x 27", gilt wood, French, c1930,
frame closed at bottom and
sides, carved chevrons, stylized
sundials, and Chinese scrolls,
hung by gilt thread rope, tapering
rect beveled mirror plate **1,320.00**
52¼", wrought iron, rect, stepped
upper section flanked by cascading bands of coiling tendrils, top
and lower corners with beads,
French, c1925 . . . . **4,000.00**
Classical, c1830, gilt wood, projecting
cornice hung with acorns above two
rect mirrors, twisted colonettes, 34 x
60" **2,350.00**
Centennial, Queen Anne style, late 19th
C, mahogany faced, scalloped, shell
pediment, 32" h **200.00**
Chippendale, American, third quarter
18th C
Inlaid mahogany, wall, shaped crest
with over reserve of wingspread
eagle and shield, mirror plate over
shaped pendant, some restoration
to scrolls, 19½ x 38" **3,200.00**
Mahogany and gilt wood, wall, crest
with gilt wood phoenix, rect mirror
plate, shaped pendant, 19 x 35" . **3,000.00**
Mahogany veneer on pine, scroll dec,
gilded liner, carved and gilded side
draperies and crest ornaments,
beveled mirror, minor repairs and
veneer crack, 22¼ x 42" **600.00**
Empire, American
Gilt Wood, c1820, convex, eagle finial, carved gessoed and gilded
frame, foliage, acorns, and oak

leaves, discolored mirror glass, repairs, one leaf ornament replaced, 17½ x 32″ **2,500.00**

Gilt Wood, c1825–35, girandole, carved crest with center seahorse flanked by two eagles, circular frame, applied stars, gilt spherules, convex mirror, flanked by two candle arms over two entwined carved dolphins, 45″ h **21,000.00**

Gilt Wood, c1840, split baluster, eglomise panel of house by water, 20 x 40″ **175.00**

Gilt Wood, c1840, tabernacle, rect glass, molded cornucopia, flanked by split balusters, spherule hung broken cornice, 26 x 40″ **650.00**

Gilt Wood, c1850, rect glass, molded frame, anthemion dec straight balusters, rosette corners, 36 x 64″ . **950.00**

Mahogany, French, early 19th C, cheval, rect mirror plate, tilting framework, columnar supports, triangular cornice, plain frieze, curved supports, fitted ormolu laurel leaves, branches, rosettes, and acanthus leaves, 34½ x 76½″ . . . **3,300.00**

Federal

Cheval, Philadelphia, c1820, mahogany, rect mirror plate, ring turned framework, ball finials, applied brass roundels, turned traverse reeded down curving legs, brass animal paw feet and casters, 31 x 79″ **7,700.00**

Wall, c1810, gilt wood, molded spherule hung cornice, panel with diamond shaped reserves, rect mirror plate, 30½ x 46″ **2,860.00**

George II, mid 18th C, carved pine, mirrored plate in two sections, upper with flattened cartouche form and interlaced C and S scrolls, molded border ledges, lower part with similar ornaments and ruffled wave work, scrolling acanthus leaves and stalactites, 28 x 59″ **19,000.00**

Hepplewhite, English, mahogany, inlay and gilding, scroll dec, beveled glass, repairs, 20½ x 36¼″ **850.00**

Neo-Classical, early 19th C, overmantel, gilt wood

Rect glass surrounded by ten festooned gilt and polychrome eglomise panels, flanked by double reeded columns, acanthus carved ogee supports, spherule hung double broken cornice, 63 x 46″ **9,000.00**

Three beveled glass panels, surmounted by gilt eglomise panel with hilly landscapes, fluted half

round columns, spherule hung broken cornice, 63 x 28″ **3,800.00**

Queen Anne, mid 18th C

Mahogany frame, scrolled crest, two part glass, beveled and cut designs top, repairs and restoration, 18¼ x 33¼″ **750.00**

Walnut, English, two part beveled edge glass, discolored glass, 18¼ x 33½″ **950.00**

Walnut veneer on pine, ogee frame, gilded liner, relief carved and gilded foliage Prince of Wales feather crests, replaced mirror, 25½ x 51½″ **3,250.00**

Victorian

Dresser type, standing, cast iron frame, oval mirror opening, 11″ h . **100.00**

Pier, Renaissance Revival, walnut, baroque cartouche crest and scrolling foliage, baluster turned and reeded pilasters, white marble scalloped shelf, turned legs, c1860 . . **935.00**

Shaving, c1825, mahogany, rect plate in conforming frame, tapered stiles, oblong breakfront case, three short drawers, bun feet, 22½ x 8½ x 22″ **400.00**

ROCKERS

Arrow back, orig ink graining, scrolled arms, widely splayed back **160.00**

Art Deco, Louis Sognot, c1930, chromed metal, upholstered seat and back, 36″ h **1,200.00**

Arts and Crafts, Mission, Gustav Stickley, c1907, mahogany, nine spindle back, rush seat, 1″ red decal **725.00**

Boston, mid 19th C, maple, hinged writing arm **800.00**

Decorated, polychrome rose dec on crest and seat edge front, rabbit ear arrow back, orig medium green paint, gold and yellow striping, imp labels "J. Swint, Chair Maker," minor wear **100.00**

Ladder Back

Arm

Turned finials, five graduated slats, turned arm posts and front rungs, reeded and carved pinwheel design on arms and rockers, woven splint seat, worn red finish **1,450.00**

Turned posts and arms, turned finials, four slats, woven splint seat **250.00**

Child's, arm, turned finials, three slat back, sausage turnings, old red finish, replaced woven rope seat . . . **450.00**

Sewing, country, spindle back, old refinishing **75.00**

Sheraton, detail, old worn green repaint, gold striping, early replaced arms, edge damage, repaired crest **150.00**

Rocker, mixed woods, orig paint and stencil dec, c1900, $225.00.

Victorian, oak

Child's, pressed gallery, turned spindles, cane seat, 30" h 250.00

Molded grape and acorn crest, upholstered, open arms, 43" h 300.00

Quarter saw, hand carved back, upholstered spring seat, French legs 200.00

Windsor, c1850, grain painted, stencil dec, scrolled crest, tall spindle back, shaped seat, bamboo turned legs joined by box stretcher 350.00

Windsor Style, Colonial Furniture Co, Grand Rapids, MI, comb back, birch, mahogany finish, turned legs, 21 x 17 x 27½" h above seat 165.00

SECRETARIES

Art Deco, Rene Drouet, c1925, parchment, fall front, oval, top with inset door, leather lined writing surface, lighted, shelved int., two short drawers at top, bottom section with single cupboard door, shelved int., inset oval base, two ivory mounted keys, 29¼" w, 49½" h 8,000.00

Baroque, Italian, mid 18th C, walnut, cavetto molded cornice, canted lid, writing surface, fitted int., shaped case with frieze and three full drawers, scrolling angled corners, molded base, field cartouche form panels of oyster burl work, handed borders, 45 x 23 x 46½" 11,500.00

Chippendale, English, mahogany, top with geometric arrangement, carved mullions and classical entablature, carved gadrooned base, six dovetailed drawers with applied edge beading, slant top lid, fitted int., bracket feet, stenciled label "J. & H.

Jewells, Holborn," repairs, replaced feet, int. drawer, and hardware, 41¾ x 24 x 29½" 5,500.00

Classical, Philadelphia, c1820, gilt metal mounted satinwood, rosewood, and mahogany, flaring cornice above fall front, baize lined writing surface, int. with small drawers centering pigeonholes, exposed prospect section flanked by rosewood pilasters, pair of cupboard doors with free standing columns, carved animal paw feet, marble top missing, 38 x 21 x 63" . . 9,500.00

Empire

American, probably Boston, mahogany, molded rect top, conforming frieze with full drawer overhanging fall front writing surface, int. with shallow drawers, miniature Doric columns, mirrored back, over pair of paneled cupboard doors, flanked by freestanding Doric columns, 38 x 20 x 58" 4,000.00

English, mahogany, flame grain veneer, one dovetailed drawer and double door top, adjustable shelves, open base with one drawer with fitted writing desk, carved Ionic capitals columns, carved foliage design, paw feet, refinished, 37½ x 23 x 80" 2,300.00

European, oak, carved detail, fall front lid with fitted int., three dovetailed drawers, cornice drawer, pierced and carved crest, turned feet, refinished, 44 x 18 x 82½" . . 850.00

Federal

American, early 19th C, two parts, mahogany, upper section with cavetto molded cornice, pair of latticework glazed doors, lower section with butler's desk above three cockbeaded graduated long drawers, French bracket feet, top by association, 49 x 25 x 93" 1,600.00

American, early 19th C, two parts, mahogany and walnut, upper section with molded cornice, pair of latticework cupboard doors, two short inlaid drawers, lower section with slant front writing surface, fitted int., four graduated and inlaid long drawers, shaped skirt continuing to bracket feet, 37 x 19 x 68" 1,950.00

Portsmouth, NH, c1805, flamed birch inlaid mahogany, three sections, upper section with shaped pediment over center rect flamed birch panel surmounted by gilded wingspread eagle, two turned wood finials, middle section with pair of hinged glazed doors over pair of

Secretary, Hepplewhite, New England, tiger maple veneer and mahogany, $6,000.00.

tambour slides opening to fitted int. with valanced pigeonholes, two small drawers, center prospect door, lower section with hinged baize lined writing surface over four cockbeaded graduated drawers, slightly flaring bracket feet, 40 x 20 x 90″ **80,000.00**
Salem, MA, attributed to, c1815, two parts, carved mahogany, upper section with molded cornice, pair of glazed hinged mullioned doors, shelves int., two drawers, lower section with baize lined writing flap, three pull out slides, four drawers, center pair of cupboard doors, reeded turned feet, shaped crest missing, 41 x 24 x 76½″ **4,125.00**
George III, late 18th C, satinwood, two sections, upper section with shaped cornice, urn form acroteria enclosing clock and movement with enamel dial, gilt bezel, sprays of green and ochre laurel and bellflowers, above twin glazed and Gothic arched mullioned doors, projection lower section of frieze writing drawer, pair of cabinet doors, French bracket feet, rosewood cross banding, shell patera, 37½ x 22½ x 96″ **26,000.00**
Governor Winthrop Style, Colonial Desk Co, Rockford, IL, mahogany, broken arched pediment, center finial, pair of glazed, mullioned door, fluted columns, slant front, fitted int. with document sleeves, four small drawers, center prospect with acanthus carving flanked by columns, four graduated drawer base, eagle brasses, claw and ball feet, 41 x 21 x 87″ **600.00**

Sheraton Style, Luce Furniture, Grand Rapids, MI, veneered, broken pediment with fretwork, urn finial, pair of glazed arched mullioned doors, slant front with fitted int., over two small and two long drawers, tapered sq legs and feet **465.00**

Settee, American or English, late 17th or early 18th C, pine, oak, paneled front, sides, back, lift top seat, 30 x 19 x 27″, $600.00.

SETTEES

Art Deco, French, c1930, walnut, rect back, inset upholstered center, two partially upholstered scrolling arms, rect seat, wide U form support, four short legs, white muslin upholstery, 61″ l **3,300.00**
Chippendale Style, 20th C, mahogany, Neo-classical details, maroon silk with gold upholstering, 50″ l **670.00**
Classical, Boston, MA, c1815, mahogany, removable upholstered back, crest with two wheat carvings and center panel of cornucopia, scrolled arm supports, X-form slats, sunflower and acanthus carved seat rail, pair of stylized baskets, acanthus carved tapered feet, brass casters, some repairs, 84″ l **9,000.00**
Victorian, American, 19th C
Cast Iron, scrolled three section back, repainted, 45″ l **400.00**
Walnut, shield back, rose carved skirt **925.00**
Windsor
American, 1830–40
Country, spindle back, plank seat, refinished, 40″ l **800.00**
Step down, cradle, orig fence, old natural finish, 57½″ **450.00**

Pennsylvania, c1825, rect crest, twenty-four tapered and turned spindles, plank seat, turned legs and stretchers, crest painted with stylized fruit and leaf motifs, yellow, red, and black, green ground, feet reduced in height, 84" l **3,575.00**

SIDEBOARDS

Art Nouveau, Louis Majorelle, c1900, oak and mahogany, rect, bowed front, inset marble top, two long drawers, undulating brass pulls cast with sheaves of wheat, two cupboard doors with large applied brass sheaves of wheat and undulating leaves, molded apron, four lug feet, 65 x 39⅜" **5,000.00**

Empire

American, c1830, mahogany, oblong top, scrolling splashboard, conforming case, half round drawer flanked by two short drawers over pair of paneled cupboard doors, flanked by full columns, turned feet, 60 x 21 x 53" **500.00**

Country, pine, step back top with two curved front drawers, well shaped cut out crest, applied board base, paneled doors, two curved front drawers, refinished, 63 x 21 x 70" **225.00**

Sideboard, English, pine, three drawers, two cupboard doors base, 57 x 20 x 52½", $800.00.

Empire Style, mahogany, flame grained veneer, overhanging top with three dovetailed drawers, serpentine curve base, four conforming doors with Gothic arch panels, carved paw feet, freestanding columns with Ionic cap-

itals, age cracks and some edge damage, 65¼ x 23½ x 44⅜" **500.00**

Federal

Connecticut, c1805, inlaid mahogany, oblong top, serpentine front, three drawers over two pair of cupboard doors, sq tapering legs, 76 x 31 x 43" **11,000.00**

Country, mahogany, rect top, conforming case, two cockbeaded short drawers flanked by two arched panel cupboard doors, six turned legs, 46 x 23 x 41" **1,200.00**

New England, eastern, c1815, mahogany, inlaid, oblong top, line inlaid edge, three short drawers, pair of convex bottle drawers, center pair of hinged doors, reeded tapered legs, tapered feet, 67 x 24½ x 40¾" **10,000.00**

New England, eastern shore, c1805, mahogany, inlaid, oblong top, shaped front, conforming case, two pair of bowed drawers, cross banded center drawer, tambour slide, line, vine, and berry inlaid sq tapering legs, cross banded cuffs, 67½ x 25 x 40¾" **5,775.00**

Southern, c1800, mahogany, serpentine, oblong top, conforming case, single long drawer, pair of cupboard doors flanked by second pair of cupboard doors, straight tapered legs, banded cuffs, stringing dec, 72 x 26 x 38" **9,000.00**

George III, c1785, mahogany

Bow Front, oblong top, slightly bowed front, conforming recessed case, central frieze drawer, two bottle drawers, center well with carved spandrels, straight tapered molded legs, spade feet, 46½ x 22½ x 36" **3,250.00**

Breakfront, oblong cross banded top, bold serpentine facade, conforming case, two central frieze drawers, straight tapered legs, spade feet, highly figured veneer with cross banding and lining, 60 x 27 x 36" . **15,000.00**

Hepplewhite

English, early 20th C, mahogany, two level step top, inlay, bow front, five dovetailed drawers, sq tapered legs, spade feet, repairs, 87 x 25½ x 42" **3,300.00**

Pennsylvania, cherry, curly walnut inlays, diamonds around top, corner fans, oval patera ends, two dovetailed drawers, false drawer like side doors, orig brasses, refinished, veneer repairs, 68¼ x 21½ x 40" **7,500.00**

Victorian, Renaissance Revival
American

    Cherry, burled mahogany drawer fronts, burled arched panel doors   **350.00**

    Oak, quarter sawed, carved facade, three dovetailed drawers and two doors, old dark finish, minor wear, 65½ x 25 x 37" . . .   **400.00**

    English, oak, turned and carved legs, base shelf, marquetry apron, two dovetailed drawers, marked "Made in England," 24½ x 71½ x 39½"   **300.00**

SOFAS

Art Nouveau, Carlo Bugatti, c1900, ebonized wood, rect back and mechanical seat, slightly scrolling rect arms, parchment upholstery, painted swallows and leafy branches, hammered brass trim, four block form feet, 68⅜" l **1,650.00**

Chippendale, American, c1780, camel back, mahogany, upholstered arched back, out scrolled arms, sq molded legs and stretchers, restoration to stretchers, reduced in height, 81" l .   **3,575.00**

Chippendale Style, 20th C, camel back, upholstered ecru silk damask, down filled cushion, two throw pillows, carved Chinese fretwork legs, some wear, 86"l **1,200.00**

Empire

    American, NY, c1825, mahogany, cylindrical crest rail ending in acanthus carved scroll on right, continuing to cylindrical arm rail on left, acanthus carved terminal over columnar ormolu mounted arm support, fan shaped right arm carved with anthemion and acanthus leaves, resting on acanthus carved legs, melon gadrooned feet, 84" l .   **7,500.00**

Sofa, Federal, New York, 1785–1800, mahogany base, maple, beech, pine, and American gumwood, orig burlap on back, 98½" l, 39¼" h, 14½" h seat rail, $60,000.00.

English, mahogany frame

    Acanthus carved scrolls, arm facings, and winged paw feet, needs reupholstering, 94" l **500.00**

    Flame grain veneer, carved foliage, moss green striped velvet reupholstering, refinished, 79" l . . .   **300.00**

Federal

    Philadelphia, of the Haines-Connelly School, c1805, carved mahogany, reeded exposed crestrail continues to form reeded arm supports, upholstered seat, loose cushion, reeded edge flanked by flowerhead carved dies, acanthus carved and reeded tapering legs, brass casters, slight repair to crest, 81" l . . .   **6,200.00**

    Phyfe, Duncan, attributed to, c1800, drapery and thunderbolt carved crest, reeded arms with acanthus leaves on armrests, reeded seat rail and front legs, fine upholstery, 78¾" l **16,000.00**

Victorian, Rococo Revival, carved rosewood frame, vintage and floral detail, repairs, reupholstered in ecru damask, 77" l **1,300.00**

SPINNING WHEELS

Flax Wheel (Saxony), early, c18th C, mixed woods **125.00**

Wool Wheels (Walking)

    Oak, 44½" d wheel, turned legs, posts, spindles, bobbin reel missing **225.00**

    Oak, 45" d wheel, 60" h **275.00**

    Walnut, PA, mid 19th C **450.00**

STANDS

Basin, Federal, New England, c1820, corner, curly maple, shaped structure, circular top cut out, medial shelf with single cockbeaded hinged drawer, four circular turned legs, tapered feet, 23 x 18 x 40½" **2,000.00**

Bedside, Country, eastern VA, mahogany drop leaf top, mahogany veneer front, two dovetailed drawers, turned cherry legs, refinished, edge damage and repair, 15½ x 16¾ x 28" h **175.00**

Cellaret, George III, mid 18th C, mahogany, lozenge form, brass bands, twin loop carry handles, raked chamfered tapering legs, 24 x 17½ x 27½"   **7,500.00**

Desk, Louis Philippe, 19th C, figured walnut, rect, dished pen channel, two ink vials, carry handle, frieze drawer resting on angled stamped brass paw feet, 10½ x 8 x 5" **300.00**

Dumbwaiter, George III, late 18th C,

mahogany, three concentric tiers revolving on turned standard, tripod base, 23½″ d, 47″ h **600.00**

Etagere

Regency, late, early 19th C, six tiers, corner columnar supports, basal drawer, brass castered feet, 18 x 14 x 62″ **3,000.00**

William IV, c1840, mahogany, turned corner supports, reading stand, basal drawer, cupboard door, Pompeian legs, 20 x 14½ x 52″ **1,200.00**

Globe, Sheraton Style, mahogany, lighted globe included, marked "Edited 1938," 39″ h **500.00**

Lectern, Baroque Style, wooden, hand carved, 52″ h, 20th C **175.00**

Music, Regency, early 19th C, mahogany, rect cradled rest, two articulated candle arms adjusting on ratchet, bamboo turned standard, tripod base, 50½″ h **2,600.00**

Plate, George III, Provincial, late 18th C, mahogany, exaggerated D form cross section top, two section trough, fretted handle, pierced gallery, revolves, baluster form standard, down swept quatrepod base, 26″ h **2,400.00**

Portfolio, William IV, carved rosewood, folding mechanism, c1830–35 . . . . . **3,000.00**

Silver, George II, mahogany, rect top, pierced fretwork gallery, plain frieze, straight molded blind fret carved legs, joined to apron by pierced spandrels, upswept X form stretcher, gutta form feet, 34½ x 21 x 30″ **6,000.00**

Tool, blacksmith's, orig leather, top with four sections, small shelf base, refinished, 16 x 14 x 17½″ **175.00**

Urn, George II Style, mahogany, triangular galleried top above frieze of stalactites, three molded scrolling supports, tripod base, S curve legs, 10″ w, 44″ h, pr **6,500.00**

Wash

Hepplewhite

American, attributed to VA, corner, bow front, mahogany, gallery and cut out top with scalloped apron, bottom shelf with dovetailed drawer, sq tapering legs, outward flared feet, old finish, age cracks and repairs, 29½″ h **300.00**

Country, mahogany, cut out and dovetailed gallery top, bottom shelf with one dovetailed drawer, slender turned legs and posts, old finish, minor repairs, replaced brass lion end handle, 16½ x 15½ x 31″ **300.00**

Pine, brown vinegar graining, stenciled and freehand dec crest, one

Stand, wash, Victorian, walnut, shaped splat and back splash, 37½ x 18½ x 36½″, $250.00.

dovetailed drawer and gallery, turned feet and posts, orig yellow paint, gold and black striping, some wear, 29¾″ h **385.00**

Country, pine, one dovetailed drawer, sq tapered legs, old red paint, one drawer pull damaged, 19¾ x 24¾ x 29″ **225.00**

English, corner type, mahogany, inlay, dovetailed drawer and gallery, recovered matching mahogany top, repairs and some damage, 23¾″ w, 46¼″ h **325.00**

Regency, English, mahogany, turned rim and round shelf, age cracks, minor repair, 15½″ d, 30¼″ h **225.00**

Sheraton, American, country, walnut, mortised apron, turned legs, old dark finish, minor damage, 21¾ x 25½ x 27¾″ **215.00**

Victorian, American, c1825, painted, sq top, three quarter gallery, turned supports joined by medial platform with single full drawer, 19 x 16 x 39″ **400.00**

STEPS

Bed

Hepplewhite, English, mahogany, top door compartment, ebony inlay step risers, sq tapered legs, minor damage, 18 x 28 x 26¼″ **675.00**

Sheraton, English, mahogany, light hardwood veneer, contrasting cross banding, line inlay, turned feet and steps with red leather gilt tooling inset, gilt brass side handles, veneer damage and repair, 18 x 24½ x 28¾″ **925.00**

Library
  Georgian, Late, early 19th C, mahogany, 38″ h **2,600.00**
  Regency, English, early 19th C, quarter spiral, 45½″ **900.00**
  Victorian, oak, three steps **300.00**

STOOLS

Broom Maker's, splayed turned legs, mid shelf, wood and wrought iron clamps, worn gray paint, 36″ h . . . **200.00**
Foot
  Arts and Crafts, Mission style, oak, rect frame, narrow stretchers, upholstered insert, Stickley Bros metal tag, 18 x 12″ **200.00**
  Chippendale, English, 19th C, oval, mahogany, oval top, needlepoint floral scene and stag covering, cabriole legs, ball and claw feet, acanthus carved knees, wear and fading, marked "Made in England," 21 x 25″ **400.00**
  Empire, mahogany, sleigh form, 18″ l **200.00**
  Federal, MD or PA, c1810, mahogany, carved, rect rails, slip seat, reeded circular legs, tapered feet . **4,675.00**
  Mahogany, needlepoint cushions, floral spray, burgundy ground, pr . . **150.00**
  Jacobean, late 17th or early 18th C, walnut, rect padded top, turned legs and H stretcher **1,400.00**
  Louis XVI Style, gilt wood, rect padded top, water leaf tip molded frieze, patera carved dies, turned tapered fluted legs, pr **1,700.00**
  Regency, early 19th C, mahogany, oblong padded top, molded frieze, turned tapering scrolling legs carved at top with gilded acanthus leaves **9,000.00**
  Shaker, Mt Lebanon, NY, hardwood, sq top, cut corners, turned legs, two rungs, orig dark finish, 11½″ sq . . **250.00**
  Windsor, New England, c1800–15, oval scooped seat, splayed bamboo turned legs, H stretcher, stamped "M Cane," 10¾″ w seat, 11¼″ h **330.00**
  Windsor Style, upholstered floral oval top, splayed tapered legs, dark red paint over black, worn, 7 x 12″ . . . **30.00**
Harpsichord, Regency, English, early 19th C, walnut, adjustable, reupholstered seat **100.00**
Kitchen, Windsor, American, 19th C, tall, refinished, worn seat **65.00**
Milking, country, primitive, heart cut out handle, relief carving of cow, old dark finish, 18″ **285.00**

Piano, cast iron claw and ball feet, glass ball **125.00**

TABLES

Architect's, George II, mid 18th C, mahogany, rect top, conforming frieze with pull out writing drawers fitted with reading stand, straight tapered legs, modified block feet, 31½ x 20¾ x 31¾″ **1,000.00**
Banquet
  Federal Style, 20th C, flame mahogany, oval, string inlay, tapered legs, three leaves, 68 x 42 x 30″ **500.00**
  Hepplewhite, Hartford, CT, three part, mahogany, D shaped ends, molded tapered legs, refinished, 97½ x 39½ x 28¼″ **3,750.00**
Breakfast, Regency, early 19th C, rosewood, oblong top, calamander cross banding, paneled standard, four scrolls, incurvate plinth, shaped leaf carved legs, brass castered feet, 44½ x 65 x 28½″ **21,000.00**
Card
  Chippendale
    Boston, MA, c1765, carved mahogany, rect top, hinged leaf, single drawer frieze, ivory pull, cyma shaped skirt with center carved flower head pendant, angular cabriole legs, claw and ball feet, hinge damaged, patched to top, 32 x 15¾ x 28½″ **75,000.00**
    Rhode Island, c1780, mahogany, rect top, molded edge, hinged leaf, plain frieze, sq molded legs, pierced brackets, card drawer, 33 x 14¼ x 28½″ **7,750.00**
  Classical
    NY, c1820, brass inlaid, dec rosewood, oblong top, cross banded edge, hinged leaf swivels over well with marbleized paper lining, two tapered uprights, gilt anthemiums, dec medial stretcher, acanthus carved down curved legs, brass animal paw feet, casters, central mount on skirt missing, 36 x 18 x 29¼″ **11,000.00**
    NY, c1825, gilt mahogany, oblong top, hinged leaf, swivels above well with marbleized paper lining, plain frieze, four turned uprights, acanthus carved animal paw feet, casters, minor repair to veneer, 36 x 18 x 29½″ **2,450.00**
  Classical Style, Imperial Furniture Co, Grand Rapids, MI, Duncan Phyfe Style, mahogany veneer top and rails, solid mahogany lyre shaped

pedestal base, carved down swept legs, carved feet **300.00**

Empire, American

NY, c1820, School of Lannuier, rosewood, banded oblong top with rounded corners, hinged over conforming frieze, gilt highlighted lyre form support, shaped platform, gilt and ebonized acanthus carved paw feet and casters, 36 x 18 x 30" **62,500.00**

NY, c1830, mahogany, banded oblong top with rounded corners, hinged over ormolu mounted columnar standard, incurvate platform, gilt acanthus carved feet and casters, 36 x 18 x 31" **7,500.00**

Federal

American, c1795, satinwood inlaid mahogany, D shaped demi-lune, shaped leaf, patera-inlaid dies, molded sq tapering legs, 37½ x 18½ x 30" **2,750.00**

American, midwestern or southern, early 19th C, mahogany, fly leaf, foliate and gadroon carved base, four paw feet **850.00**

Late, c1820, mahogany, oblong top, conforming frieze with patera inlay, spiral turned legs, peg feet, 36 x 17 x 29" **1,000.00**

Massachusetts, Boston area, c1810, curly maple inlaid mahogany, oblong top, conforming shaped hinged leaf, frieze with center oval inlaid reserved, rect inlaid dies, Greek key banded border, ring turned and reeded tapering legs, tapered feet, repair to rear leg, 36 x 17¼ x 30" **3,350.00**

Massachusetts, from northeastern shore, c1815, flamed birch inlaid mahogany, oblong top, cross banded edge, conforming shaped hinged leaf, frieze with center oval inlaid reserve, rect inlaid dies flanking, ring turned reeded tapering legs, ball feet, repairs to front leg, 36½ x 18½ x 29" **2,000.00**

New York, c1800, mahogany, bow front top, string inlaid and paneled conforming frieze, five string inlaid straight tapered legs, banded cuffs, 36 x 18 x 29" . . . **1,900.00**

George III, late 18th C, mahogany, rect top cross banded in rosewood and satinwood, rounded corners, opens to leather lined playing surface, conforming frieze ornamented as fielded panels, straight tapered line inlaid legs, 36 x 18 x 29¼" **4,250.00**

Sheraton, American, c1800–10, inlaid mahogany, fluted legs **1,000.00**

Victorian, American, mid 19th C, cherry and walnut, rect hinged top, conforming frieze, single full drawer, block and ring turned legs, 37 x 21 x 29" **350.00**

Center, Empire Style, American, late 19th C, mahogany, circular top, ormolu mounted conforming frieze on three marble supports, incurvate medial platform, wing carved paw feet, 36 x 32" **1,500.00**

Console

Art Deco, French, c1925, veined black marble D shaped top, narrow wrought iron apron with wavy line between hammered borders, four scrolling supports with beaded centers, open D form base with medial band of tight scrolls, four hammered T form feet, 29⅞" h **3,500.00**

Georgian, pine, oblong green veined marble top, frieze of wave work, pendant pierced carved cartouche form skirt, straight tapered molded legs with bellflower carving, 43 x 21½ x 46½", one of pair later date, pr **21,000.00**

Louis XV, mid 18th C, gilt wood, oblong sepia and liver molded marble top, serpentine front, conforming frieze, pierced foliage, S shaped legs, pierced and shaped silhouette upswept stretcher, 44 x 22 x 33½" **8,500.00**

Dining

Chippendale Style, Rockford Furniture Co, Rockford, IL, rect top, rounded corners, corner inlays, five pairs of Sheraton type legs, 66" l . **175.00**

Federal

American, late, c1820, mahogany, rect, two deep drop leaves, modified ovolo corners, recessed frieze, ring turned legs, peg feet, 19 x 48 x 28" **350.00**

American, probably NY, c1805, mahogany, rect top, two hinged rect drop leaves, plain frieze, sq tapered legs, one leaf warped, 69½ x 48 x 29" **2,650.00**

New England, c1815, mahogany veneered cherry, two D shaped end sections, rect hinged leaf, plain frieze, ring turned and reeded tapering legs, button feet, 79 x 21½ x 29¼" **7,775.00**

Federal Style, mahogany, double pedestal, banded top, water leaf carved urn form standards, water leaf carved and reeded swept legs, brass paw feet, one leaf, 48 x 72 x 29" **3,250.00**

George III, mahogany, oblong top, three boards resting on twin pedestals, downswept quatrepods, club feet, two 26" leaves, 53 x 77 x 27½" **4,500.00**

Louis XVI, late 18th C, mahogany, extension, oval top, two drop leaves, recessed frieze, straight tapered legs of octagonal cross section, brass castered toe caps, four 19½" leaves, 62 x 55½ x 28" **8,250.00**

Victorian, American, mid 19th C, mahogany, drop leaf, rect molded top, deep drop leaves, conforming frieze, six turned legs, brass caps and casters, 22 x 48 x 29" **600.00**

Dressing

Empire, American, c1825, mahogany, oblong top, broken serpentine front, conforming case, three cockbeaded short drawers, spiral acanthus carved legs ending in peg feet, 36 x 20 x 30" **600.00**

Primitive, American, early 19th C, pine, scrolled side and back splashes, single drawer, simple turned legs, peg and hand wrought nail construction, refinished, 25¼" w **240.00**

Drop Leaf

Federal, mahogany, rect top, two deep leaves, recessed frieze, six straight tapered legs, 22 x 42 x 29" **1,300.00**

Victorian, American, c1850

Birch and cherry, rect top, two shallow drop leaves, recessed frieze, turned legs, 21 x 38 x 29" **350.00**

Cherry, rect top, two shallow drop leaves, conforming frieze, block and ring turned legs, 19 x 42 x 29" **400.00**

Victorian Style, American, mahogany, rect top, conforming frieze, turned legs, 21 x 42 x 30" **100.00**

Game

Arts and Crafts, Gustav Stickley, oak, orig leather top, mortise and tenon joints, X stretcher, sgd, 48¼" d, 30" h **5,000.00**

Chippendale, Philadelphia, c1780, mahogany, oblong top with outset corners, opens to baize lined playing surface, hollowed corner receptacles, conforming frieze with single cockbeaded short drawer, shell carved cabriole legs, claw and ball feet, 34 x 17 x 28½" **10,500.00**

Hutch, Queen Anne, American, early 18th C, pine and maple, hinged seat

Table, hutch, New England, 18th C, pine, oak shoes and cleats, oval, 46 x 66½ x 26½", $4,250.00.

lid replaced, old red paint, 49" d, 28½" h **3,500.00**

Library

Directorie, Anglais style, late 18th C, mahogany, oblong molded top inset with morocco writing surface, adjustable reading tablet, sham frieze of drawers, flight of steps, turned tapering legs, bronze ball feet, 41 x 25½ x 32" **38,000.00**

Federal, NY, c1815, brass inlaid mahogany, rect top, two clover shaped leaves, brass inlaid single drawer frieze, drop finials, drum carved standard, molded down curving legs, brass castered paw feet, one leg repaired, 45 x 36 x 29" **3,500.00**

Pembroke

Chippendale, American, late 18th C, rect top, two shallow drop leaves, recessed frieze with single full drawer, molded legs, pierced and arched X stretcher, 20½ x 36 x 27" **1,800.00**

Federal

American, c1800, mahogany, oblong top, bowed ends, two demilune drop leaves, rect frieze, single full drawer, straight tapered legs, 20 x 31 x 28" **950.00**

New York, c1800, inlaid mahogany, rect top, inlaid border, beveled edge, single drawer frieze, oval inlaid dies, line and bellflower inlaid tapering legs, cross banded cuffs, some veneer chips, 38½ x 29½ x 28½" **18,150.00**

Rhode Island, c1800, inlaid mahogany, oblong top, line inlaid border, two D shaped hinged leaves, single drawer frieze, bookend inlaid dies on line and icicle inlaid tapering legs, cross banded cuffs, minor repairs to inlay, 31 x 37¼ x 28" **12,000.00**

George III, third quarter 18th C, mahogany, oblong molded top, bowed ends, demi-lune drop leaves, conforming recessed frieze, full cockbeaded drawer within patera ornamented blocks, turned tapering fluted legs, brass castered feet, 19½ x 30 x 28" **6,250.00**

Pier

Classical, Philadelphia, c1820, gilt metal mounts, marble, rect white veined marble top, frieze with central dec of stenciled acanthus, columns with gilt metal capitals, ca. ved columns, mirror plate back, acanthus form gilded feet, 38¼ x 20 x 40¼" **6,875.00**

Neo-Classical, mahogany, rect marble top, conforming frieze, two caryatid mounted sq tapered columns, mirrored back flanked by pilasters, medial platform, gilt acanthus carved paw feet, 34 x 18 x 36" . . **17,000.00**

Sewing

Chinese Export, early 19th C, lacquer, lozenge form lidded box, bag slide, turned support, incurvate triangular base, paw feet, 18 x 13 x 30" . . . **1,200.00**

Federal

American, c1810, mahogany, astragal top hinged to conforming case, deep well, silk covering, flaring straight tapered legs, 24 x 13½ x 26½" **2,000.00**

Massachusetts, eastern, c1805, inlaid mahogany, oblong top, outset corners, two drawers, ring turned half columns, reeded and ring turned legs, tapered feet, lacks int. writing surface and sewing bag support, 20½ x 15½ x 29½" **2,860.00**

Regency, early 19th C, rosewood, rect top, D form drop leaves, nulling border, paneled frieze with full drawer and Vitruvian scroll form leaf brackets, tapering standard carved with shells and patera, scrolling water leaf carved legs, brass lion's paw feet, 19 x 18 x 28½" **8,250.00**

Side

Art Nouveau

Galle, marquetry, burlwood curved top, decorative stringing, inlaid columbine dec, three slender fluted triangular legs, inlaid sgd, 29" h **700.00**

Serrurier-Bovy, Gustave, c1900, walnut, shaped rect top, arched apron, four molded rect legs, stylized feather supports conjoined by straight stretchers, 35½ x 30" **2,250.00**

Chippendale, Newport, RI, c1780,

mahogany, carved, rect top, molded edge, molded short drawer, skirt with slightly projecting molding, sq stop fluted legs, 32½ x 22¼ x 27" **68,750.00**

Tavern

Country, New England, 18th C

Maple and pine, oval top, plain frieze, turned slightly swelled legs, button feet, top reset, minor repairs to tops of legs, 27¾ x 21¾ x 28" **2,750.00**

Pine, all orig, refinished, minor rest to rect top, 40 x 24¾ x 28" **450.00**

Queen Anne

American, 18th C, pine and maple, oval top, old natural finish, 37 x 23¾ x 25" **2,100.00**

New England, mid 18th C, maple, oval top painted green, natural finished legs, duck foot, three new braces under top, 34¼ x 27½ x 26¼" **3,500.00**

William and Mary Style, American, oval top, recessed frieze, turned splayed legs joined by box stretcher, 34 x 25 x 25" **675.00**

Table, tea, Philadelphia, c1780, walnut, birdcage support, carved knees, ball and claw feet, 24" d top, 27½" h, $3,250.00.

Tea

George II, mahogany, circular pie crust top tilting above fluted and acanthus leaf carved turned baluster, tripod base carved at knees with bellflowers, claw and ball feet, 29 x 29" **1,700.00**

Queen Anne, Boston area, MA, c1750, walnut, rect tray top, cymashaped projecting skirt, cabriole legs, pad feet, old repair to one leg, 27¾ x 18¾ x 27" **22,000.00**

Work

Empire

American, c1840, mahogany, sq top, shallow drop leaves, conforming frieze with two shallow drawers, columnar pedestal base, shaped medial platform, ball feet, 18 x 19 x 30″ **350.00**

Country, mid 19th C, birch, sq top, conforming frieze, single full drawer, block and ring turned legs, 17 x 17 x 29″ **225.00**

Federal

American, c1815, mahogany, oblong hinged top, adjustable baize lined writing surface, two drawers, turned standard, reeded down curving legs, brass animal paw feet, casters, pencil drawers missing, minor veneer repairs, 22 x 15½ x 33″ **2,250.00**

Country, cherry, sq top, outset corners, conforming frieze, two full drawers, turned stiles, turned legs, capped ball feet, 17½ x 16½ x 28½″ **675.00**

George III, late 18th C, penwork, lozenge form top, conforming case, two full drawers, straight tapered legs, basal stretcher, dec bands of honeysuckle, scrolling foliage, mythological animals, and draped urns, 18¼ x 13 x 27½″ **16,000.00**

Sheraton, American, early 19th C

Bird's Eye Maple, two drawers, turned legs, ball feet **1,450.00**

Tiger Maple, two drawers, turned legs, tapered feet **850.00**

TEA WAGONS

Black lacquer finish, raised Chinese figures in landscape, D drop leaves, turned legs, support, two wheels . . . **300.00**

Victorian, brass, glass **700.00**

Wicker, c1880, wrapped reed and rattan, close weave, removable glass top **450.00**

WAGON SEATS

Wagon seats cannot be classified with seats from a wagon. Early wagon seats were usually constructed with a double frame and a basketry-type seat. They served a dual purpose: in the house and in the family wagon for addition seating.

Country, board along back and sides above seats, trestle feet, board across front below seat, orig black, red, and gold paint, 34½″ l, 14″ h . . **525.00**

Ladder Back

Two slat back, turned stiles, splint seat, red paint, 35″ **565.00**

Three slat back, turned stiles, worn orig red paint with yellow striping, polychrome floral dec, painted scenes in ovals on top slats, replaced paper rush seat, 34¾″ l . . **370.00**

Pine, painted and dec, worn old dark gray paint, black, red, and yellow striping, 30″ l **125.00**

WICKER

Bench, window, scrolling arms, cane seat, scrolling on skirt, 34 x 18 x 29″ **300.00**

Book Case, ornate fan back, turned finials, 4 shelves, 19½ x 14 x 42″ . . . **225.00**

Cabinet, phonograph, Heywood Wakefield, hinged lid, door on front, int. with record storage, phonograph crank on side, 18 x 21 x 43″ **1,750.00**

Chair

Arm, rattan wrapped, close weave, geometric diamond shaped panel on back, upholstered seat **350.00**

Side, shaped woven crest, vase shaped ornate splat, pressed seat, 17½″ w, 39″ h **170.00**

Chaise Lounge, magazine holders on each side, curled up foot end, 33″ w, 54″ l **500.00**

Chest of Drawers, rattan wrapped, close weave, c1900, three drawers, 27 x 18 x 32″ **315.00**

Desk, kidney shape, built in letter holders, drawer, 36 x 19 x 29″ **330.00**

Etagere, rattan wrapped, fancy scroll work, 6 tiers, arch crest insert with oval mirror, X stretchers, cabriole legs, 69″ **1,000.00**

Ferner, cane and wicker, wrapped legs, 31″ h **235.00**

Highchair, natural color, wooden seat and foot rest **300.00**

Rocker

Platform, patent, rolled edge, high back, 25″ w, 47″ h **450.00**

Sewing, Art Deco, drawer, 33″ h . . . **150.00**

Settee, wood frame, cane seat, rect back, curved corners, basketweave pattern, 39 x 20 x 38″ **500.00**

Smoking Stand, brass tray, 28″ h **60.00**

Sofa, scrolling back with diamond design, upholstered seat, 65″ w, 37″ h . **275.00**

Stand, sewing, hickory, c1880, basketweave pattern, hinged top section on wooden frame, diamond dec woven on top, looped skirt, 15½ x 12¾ x 30½″ **175.00**

Stool, foot, oblong padded top, 14 x 10 x 9″ **80.00**

Table, wicker and ash, circular, basketweave pattern extending over edges
to arcaded skirt, 4 wicker cov legs,
iron caps on feet, 25″ d, 28″ h **125.00**
Towel Rack, wall mounted, oval beveled
mirror, 24 x 7 x 16″ **80.00**

YARN WINDERS

Floor Type, primitive, oak, mortised
frame, two reels, one stationary, one
adjustable, 51″ h **75.00**
Niddy Noddy, maple, mortised, 17¼″ l **80.00**
Spoke Type
4 spoke, curly maple, 27″ d, 35½″ h **125.00**
4 spoke, Shaker, Sabbathday Lake,
combination of hard and soft
woods, sq nail construction, geared
side counter needle, reel 26″, 32″ h **375.00**
6 spoke, walnut, turned legs, reel
spindles, chip carved details,
geared counter, old worn finish,
worn paper counter dial with name,
1845, 28½″ d, 41¾″ h **175.00**
Turned and chip carved detail, geared
counting mechanism, refinished, 30″
d, 40″ h reel **100.00**
Winding Reel, mahogany, two adjust-
able bobbins, quatrefoil base, 47½″
h **175.00**

GAME PLATES

History: Game plates, popular between 1870
and 1915, are specially decorated plates used to
serve fish and game. Sets originally included a
platter, serving plates, and a sauce or gravy boat.
Many sets have been divided. Today, individual
plates are used for wall hangings.

Reference: Susan and Al Bagdade, *Warman's
English & Continental Pottery & Porcelain, 1st Edition,* Warman Publishing Co., Inc., 1987.

BIRDS

Plate
9″
Duck, brown and yellow, artist sgd
"A Porter" **100.00**
Quail, artist sgd, marked "Lim-
oges" **50.00**
9¼″, prairie chicken in flight, artist sgd
"R K Beck" **55.00**
13″, pheasants and quail, cream and
green ground, artist sgd "Ch. Bar-
bois," pierced, facing pr **500.00**
13½″, quail, natural woodland setting,
gold rococo border, artist sgd,
marked "Limoges" **250.00**
Platter
12¾ x 10½″, pheasants, blue ground,
gold border, artist sgd "R K Beck" **65.00**

14″, pheasants, blue and white, Staffordshire, dated 1919, marked
"Barber & Kent" **60.00**
18½″, partridge, dark green border,
gold trim, artist sgd, marked "Theodore Haviland, Limoges" **275.00**

**Platter, 18½″ l, dark green border, gold
trim, partridge center, marked "Theodore Haviland, Limoges," artist sgd,
$275.00.**

20″, wild turkey, autumn sunset,
curled corners, printed eagle mark,
marked "Haviland & Co, Aug 10,
1880" **800.00**
Set
7 pcs, platter, six plates, artist sgd,
marked "Limoges" **700.00**
12 pcs, plates, realistic game birds,
tan and green wildflowers, cream
border, silver gilt, artist sgd "A
Pape, Sr," late 19th C **385.00**
13 pcs, platter, twelve plates, gold leaf
dec, French **900.00**
66 pcs, dinner service, hp birds, blue,
gray, and yellow grounds, marked
"Paul Mueller, Selb, Bavaria" **250.00**

DEER

Plate
13″, buck and doe standing in water,
forest scene, gold rim **120.00**
13¾″, hp, stag in woods, raised
enamel dec **200.00**

ELK

Plate
8¼″, two elk by forest brook, marked
"Dresden Semi-Porcelain" **35.00**
9″, natural colors, scalloped edge . . **40.00**

FISH

Plate
9"

Bass, artist sgd "Morley," marked "Lenox"	**60.00**
Lobster, claw formed rim, three claw form feet, surf and shell scene, printed eagle mark, marked "Haviland & Co, Aug 10, 1880"	**185.00**
10½", trout, cobalt border, marked "M Z Austria"	**65.00**

Platter

14", bass on lure, artist sgd "R K Beck"	**100.00**
16½", bass, water lilies, emb, artist sgd "Max," marked "Limoges"	**165.00**

Set

7 pcs, platter, six plates, artist sgd "R K Beck," marked "Buffalo Pottery"	**250.00**
9 pcs, 15 x 11½" platter, eight 8½" d plates, fish center, gold scalloped border, marked "M. Z. Austria"	**300.00**
10 pcs, platter, eight plates, sauce boat, marked "Austria"	**225.00**
11 pcs, platter, ten plates, artist sgd "Muville," marked "Limoges"	**550.00**
13 pcs, platter, twelve 8½" plates, marked "Austria, Imperial Crown China"	**265.00**

GAMES, 1840-1940

History: Mass production of board games did not take place until after the Civil War. Firms like McLoughlin Brothers, Milton Bradley, and Selchow and Righter were active in the 1860s, followed by Parker Brothers, who began in 1883. Parker Brothers bought out the rights to the W. & S. B. Ives Co., who had produced some very early games in the 1840s, including the "first" American board game, The Mansion of Happiness. All except McLoughlin Brothers are giants in the game industry today.

McLoughlin Brothers's games are a challenge to find. Not only does the company no longer exist [Milton Bradley bought them out in 1920], but the lithography on their games was the best of its era. Most board games are collected because of the bright, colorful lithography on their box covers. In addition to spectacular covers, the large McLoughlin games often had lead playing pieces and fancy block spinners, thus making them even more desirable.

Common games like Anagrams, Authors, Jackstraws, Lotto, Tiddledy Winks, and Peter Coddles do not command high prices, nor do the games of Flinch, Pit, and Rook, which still are being published.

Games, with the exception of the common ones

stated above, generally are rising in price. However, interesting to note is the fact that certain games dealing with good graphics on popular subject matter, e.g. trains, planes, baseball, Christmas and others, often bring higher prices because they are also sought by collectors in those particular fields.

Condition is everything when buying. Do not buy games that have been taped or that have price tags stickered on the face of their covers. Also, beware of buying games at outdoor flea markets where weather elements can cause fading and warping.

On September 17, 1988, Robert W. Skinner, Inc., auctioned the Game Preserve Museum collection, assembled by Lee and Rally Dennis. A record $4,600 was paid for McLoughlin Bros. "The Game of The Man In The Moon." A Charles B. Darrow "Monopoly," c1934, sold for $2,400. The sale was heavily lotted to the dismay of many collectors.

References: R. C. Bell, *The Board Game Book,* The Knapp Press, 1979; Lee Dennis, *Warman's Antique American Games, 1840-1940,* Warman Publishing Co., 1986; Brian Love, *Great Board Games, 1895–1935,* Macmillan Publishing Co., 1979; Brian Love, *Play The Game: Over 40 Games From The Golden Age Of Board Games,* Reed Books, 1978.

Collectors' Club: American Game Collectors Association, 4628 Barlow Dr., Bartlesville, OK 74006.

Museum: Washington Dolls' House and Toy Museum, Washington, D.C.

Additional Listings: See *Warman's Americana & Collectibles* for games from the post 1940 period.

Across the Yalu, Milton Bradley Co, boxed board game, c1905, 15 x 9", instructions on back of box cov, 13 pcs (12 colored wooden counters and spinner), multicolored litho board shows Yalu River in center with Russians on one bank and Japanese on the other, strategy game, unusual subject matter	**45.00**
Auto Race, Gorham Pressed Steel Corp, c1930, 10¾ x 22", multicolored litho metal board, 5 colored metal cars	**175.00**
Bagatelle, early push-type, 1⅛ x 9¹⁵⁄₁₆ x 19¼", wooden, multicolored litho pasted to face marking points, wooden stick with wooden block to push ball, one wooden and one clay ball, instructions pasted on back	**125.00**
Boston Game, The, Frederick J. Allen, educational cards, © 1905, 2⅞ x 4", 56 cards and instruction card, plain white backs, some card faces have photos of Boston historical sites	**25.00**

Fun At The Zoo, Parker Bros., 20 x 11″, wooden box, instructions on back of box cov, six colored wooden markers and spinner, multicolored litho board pictures, c1902, $225.00.

Brownie Portrait Cubes, McLoughlin Bros, © Palmer Cox, 1892, 5 x 13″, paper litho wooden blocks, six different Brownies **200.00**

Cargoes, No. 42, Selchow & Righter Co, boxed board game, c1935, 16½ x 9½″, instructions on back of box cov, 82 pcs (66 "cargo" cards, 10 "consignment" cards, 1 die, 4 metal steamships, and folding 3 face board), multicolored litho board shows map of world, designed by William Longyear **40.00**

Chiromagica, The, Educational Game, McLoughlin Bros, three circular cards with questions, orig box **250.00**

Crossing the Ocean, Parker Bros, boxed board game, © 1893, 14¾ x 8⅞,″ instructions on back of box cov, 4 colored wooden counters, multicolored litho board shows water surrounded by famous world ports, spinner affixed in lower right corner, track game **65.00**

Dewey at Manila, Chaffee & Selchow, card game, Starry Flag series, 1899, 6½ x 5″, 52 cards and instruction booklet, cards with pink and white back showing Dewey and ship Olympia **20.00**

Doctors and the Quack, Parker Bros, card game, c1887, 6½ x 4⅞″, numerous printed cards, no illus **22.00**

Excuse Me!, Parker Bros, card game, © 1923, 7½ x 4¾″, 124 printed pink and white cards and instruction sheet, no illus **10.00**

Flap Jacks, All-Fair boxed board game of skill, Alderman-Fairchild, © 1931, 15½ x 12½″, instructions on back of box cov, 10 pcs, all flap jacks, which are tossed into 5 numbered round holes on beige, blue, and red board **25.00**

Game of Balloon, R Bliss Manufacturing Co, c1889, 31 x 10½″, wooden standard and hoop, 2 hand tied racquets, 4 balloons, inflator, game counter, 4 score pins, instruction booklet, adv sheet, wooden dovetailed, hinged box **500.00**

Game of Cat, Chaffee & Selchow, c1900, 19½ x 10″, wooden box, instructions on back of box cov, spinner, 6 wooden counters, multicolored litho board pasted onto box bottom **200.00**

Game of Goose, Spear Works, 10 pcs, multicolored litho game board, 67 painted goose tokens, 2 wooden dice, wooden dice cup **150.00**

Game of Mail, Express or Accommodation, Milton Bradley, c1920, 22 x 14½″, wooden box, instructions on back of box cov, 5 pcs, multicolored litho board **300.00**

Game of Santa Claus and Steeplechase, McLoughlin Bros, wooden framed double-sided board, c1890, 14 x 14″, cardboard box of 20 implements (4 colored lead horses, 4 colored wooden tokens, 10 round wooden counters, metal spinner, and instruction sheet), both board sides multicolored litho: one shows horses around track, other simple track game, hole in center of board for spinner **95.00**

Game of Tortoise and the Hare, Russell Mfg Co, © 1927, 5⅞ x 9⅞″, 4 pcs (folded, multicolored litho paper board with directions insert, 2 round counters, 1 wooden die) **15.00**

Game of Walking the Tight Rope, #5125, McLoughlin bros, 1897, 11 × 9″, instructions on back of box cov, 2 wooden colored counters and spinner, multicolored litho board pasted on box bottom, shows clowns trying to bridge water and several falling in, track game **65.00**

Hop Scotch Tiddledy Winks, Parker Bros, game of skill, 1891, 10¼ x 6¾″, 25 pcs (1 cup, 20 winks, 2 felt pads, advertising sheet, instruction sheet), 1 felt is red and yellow with bull's-eye, other is hopscotch court **18.00**

Johnny Get Your Gun, Parker Bros, Inc, boxed board game, © 1928, 13½ x 11½″, instructions on back of box cov, 16 round colored wooden counters, multicolored litho board showing various animals in circles, spinner in center is in shape of rifle and made of wood and metal **35.00**

Lindy Hop-Off, Parker Bros, c1927, 14½ x 13⅜″, 25 pcs, 2 dice cups, 2 dice,

16 cards, 4 painted metal planes, instruction sheet, lift out folding multicolored litho board **375.00**

Little Boy Blue, Parker Bros, c1888, round box, 6" d, 6 pcs (wooden top, 2 white paper stars, 2 red paper stars, instruction booklet), board multicolored litho farm scene **25.00**

Little Cowboy Game, Parker Bros, c1895, 20½ x 10½", wooden box, instructions on back of box cov, 5 pcs, 4 round colored wooden counters, spinner, multicolored litho board with checkered oval track, cowboy and steer in center **325.00**

Magic Dots for Little Tots, artistic game, © 1907, 6 x 9⅝", 12 pcs (10 black and white perforated cards, 2 boxes of tiny cardboard dots to fill in the perforations to create colored picture) **20.00**

Master Rodbury and His Pupils, card game, 1844, W. & S. B. Ives Co, 2⅝ x 3¾", 18 cards and 1 instruction card, all cards hp, game invented by Anne Abbot **85.00**

Movie Inn, W.G. Young & Co, Inc, © 1917, 10⅞ x 7¼", multicolored litho board with 5 steel balls and instructions printed at bottom, a skill game invented by Willis G. Young **30.00**

Oriental Color Game, McLoughlin Bros, 1875, wooden box, 7½ x 4½", 56 pcs (54 multicolored litho cards, 1 litho double arrowed block spinner, and instruction booklet) **65.00**

Puss in the Corner, Parker Bros, © 1895, 7½" sq, instructions on back of cov, 13 pcs (12 wooden colored peg counters and spinner), multicolored litho board show one cat on each side, track game **35.00**

Ring My Nose, Milton Bradley Co, skill game, c1927, 8¼ x 12¼", 8 cardboard rings and metal screw for clown's nose, multicolored litho board show same picture of clown as on cov, target game **30.00**

Ring Toss or Quoits, Parker Bros, c1890, 7½" sq, instructions on back of box cov, 11 pcs (board for holding 5 wooden pegs, 5 cardboard hoops), skill game **25.00**

Santa Claus Puzzle Box, Milton Bradley Co, puzzle, c1926, 13 x 9", 3 puzzle pictures in black and white on back of box cov, contains 3 multicolored litho puzzles each with Christmas theme **95.00**

Siege of Havana, Parker Bros, c1898, 22½ x 16¼", wooden box, instructions on back of box cov, 9 pcs, multicolored litho board **475.00**

Steeple-Chase, unknown manufacturer, triangular trademark, c1890–95, 18 x 11½", directions on back of cov, 16 pcs, 6 numbered cards, 6 lead horses on stands, 3 dice, folding board, multicolored litho pictures **75.00**

Tally-Ho, Snow, Woodman & Co, c1880, 11¼" sq, 74 pcs (36 white wooden pegs, 36 black wooden pegs, lift out board, and instruction sheet), multicolored litho board with red star in center **45.00**

"White House," Thompson's Old Homestead Series, Thompson & Co., © 1905, 5½ x 3¾", 45 cards with instructions, card backs have green and white litho of White House **15.00**

Zippy Zeps Air Game, Alderman Fairchild Co., c1925, instructions on back of box cov, 31 pcs (25 cards, 5 colored metal zeppelins, and folding board), multicolored litho board, track game **75.00**

GAUDY DUTCH

History: Gaudy Dutch is an opaque, soft-paste ware made between 1790 and 1825 in England's Staffordshire district. Most pieces are unmarked; marks of various potters, including the impressed marks of Riley and Wood, have been found on pieces.

The pieces first were hand decorated in an underglaze blue, fired, and then received additional decoration over the glaze. Many pieces today have the over glaze decoration extensively worn. Gaudy Dutch found a ready market within the Pennsylvania German coummunity because it was inexpensive and intense with color. It had little appeal in England.

Reference: Eleanor and Edward Fox, *Gaudy Dutch,* published by author, 1970, out-of-print.

Reproduction Alert: Cup plates, bearing the impressed mark "CYBRIS," have been reproduced and are collectible in their own right. The Henry Ford Museum has issued pieces in the single rose pattern, although they are of porcelain and not soft-paste.

Butterfly
Bowl, 11"	**3,900.00**
Coffeepot, 11"	**3,750.00**
Cup and Saucer, handleless	**325.00**
Plate	
6½"	**650.00**
9¾"	**1,500.00**
Sugar	**900.00**
Teapot, 5", squat baluster form	**1,400.00**
Waste Bowl	**1,275.00**

Plate, 8″ d, Butterfly pattern, $975.00.

Carnation	
Bowl	
5½″ d	625.00
6¼″ d	450.00
Pitcher, 6″ h	510.00
Plate	
8″	575.00
9¾″	475.00
Tea Bowl and Saucer	495.00
Teapot	1,275.00
Toddy Plate	525.00
Waste Bowl	200.00
Dahlia	
Plate, 8″	775.00
Sugar	850.00
Tea Bowl and Saucer	700.00
Double Rose	
Bowl, 6¼″	400.00
Creamer	400.00
Gravy Boat	300.00
Plate	
7″	425.00
10″ d	370.00
Sugar, cov	775.00
Teapot	675.00
Toddy Plate, 4½″	150.00
Waste Bowl, 6½″ d, 3″ h	275.00
Dove	
Creamer	675.00
Plate, 10″	450.00
Waste Bowl	650.00
Flower Basket, Plate, 6½″ d	185.00
Grape	
Plate	
6″	390.00
7⅛″ d	225.00
Sugar, cov	450.00
Tea Bowl and Saucer	325.00
Toddy Plate, 5″	375.00
Oyster	
Bowl, 5½″	300.00
Coffeepot, 12″ h	550.00
Plate	
8¾″	425.00
9½″	400.00

Soup Plate, 8½″	450.00
Tea Bowl and Saucer	395.00
Toddy Plate, 5½″	425.00
Single Rose	
Bowl, 6″	275.00
Coffeepot, 10¾″, double gourd form	850.00
Cup and Saucer	75.00
Plate	
7″	410.00
8¼″	450.00
Quill Holder, cov	2,500.00
Sugar, cov	675.00
Toddy Plate, 5¼″	250.00
Sunflower	
Bowl, 6½″	425.00
Creamer	475.00
Tea Bowl and Saucer	775.00
Urn	
Creamer	325.00
Plate	
5″	450.00
8¼″	425.00
War Bonnet	
Bowl, cov	210.00
Coffeepot	3,900.00
Plate	
7″	475.00
8¼″ d	325.00
Teapot	975.00
Toddy Plate, 4½″	400.00
Zinnia	
Plate	
5¾″ d, marked "Riley"	175.00
9″	575.00

GAUDY IRONSTONE

History: Gaudy Ironstone was made in England around 1850. Most pieces are impressed "Ironstone" and bear a registry mark. Ironstone is an opaque, heavy body earthenware which contains large proportions of flint and slag. Gaudy Ironstone is decorated in patterns and colors similar to Gaudy Welsh.

Bowl and Pitcher Set	
Floral dec, green, blue, red, and black, red stick spatter band on pitcher, marked "Malkin & Co"	100.00
Rose dec, underglaze blue, red, and green enamel	275.00
Gold dec, 12″ h pitcher, 13½″ d bowl, orange and cobalt blue, scalloped, applied handle ends in fingers, marked "Stone China"	495.00
Coffeepot, 10″ h, strawberry	500.00
Pitcher	
8″ h, emb roses and flowers, blue underglaze, blue, red, and green enameling, some edge flakes	225.00

Soup Plate, 7⅝″ d, unmarked, $40.00.

9¼″ h, harlequin emb, red and green
    enamel and purple luster floral de-
    sign 150.00
Plate
    6¼″ d, morning glories and strawber-
        ries, underglaze blue, polychrome
        enamel and luster 50.00
    7⅞″ d, urn pattern 60.00
    8½″ d, strawberry pattern, red enamel
        wear 30.00
    9½″ d, urn pattern 135.00
    9⅜″ d, rose design, red, blue, green,
        and black 85.00
Platter
    10¾″ l, flowers and strawberries, un-
        derglaze blue, polychrome enamel
        and luster 150.00
    13½″ l, floral dec, underglaze blue
        strawberries, polychrome enamel,
        purple luster 200.00
Sugar, 8½″ h, cov, strawberry 400.00
Toddy Plate, 4¾″ d, urn pattern, under-
    glaze blue, polychrome enamel and
    luster 175.00

GAUDY WELSH

History: Gaudy Welsh is a translucent porcelain
that was originally made in the Swansea area of
England from 1830 to 1845. Although the designs
resemble Gaudy Dutch, the body texture and
weight differ. One of the characteristics is the gold
luster on top of the glaze.

In 1890, Allerton made a similar ware. These
wares are heavier opaque porcelain and usually
bear the export mark.

Reference: Howard Y. Williams, *Gaudy Welsh
China*, Wallace-Homestead, out-of-print.

Columbine
    Plate, 5½″ 40.00
    Tea Set, 17 pc, c1810 .... 475.00

Daisy and Chain
    Cream and Sugar 225.00
    Teapot 180.00
Dogwood
    Pitcher, 6″ h, English registry mark . 100.00
Flower Basket
    Bowl, 10½″ 175.00
    Mug, 4″ 65.00
    Plate
        7½″ 60.00
        8½″ sq 50.00
Grape
    Bowl, 5¼″ 40.00
    Child's Mug, 2⅜″ h 75.00
    Plate, 5¼″ 50.00
Morning Glory
    Compote, 10¼″ 235.00
    Creamer 85.00
    Platter, 11″ 75.00
    Teapot, cov, 5½″ 150.00

**Cup and Saucer, Shan Wa See pattern,
peppermint transfer, $65.00.**

Oyster
    Creamer, 3¾″ h, c1820 .... 80.00
    Cup and Saucer 50.00
    Jug, 5¾″ h, c1820 .... 200.00
    Mug
        3″ 60.00
        4⅛″ h, strap handle 110.00
    Pitcher, 3¼″ h 95.00
    Soup Plate, 10″ d, flange rim 75.00
Strawberry
    Mug, 4⅛″ h 125.00
    Plate, 8¼″ d 135.00
    Soup Plate, 9″ 100.00
Sunflower
    Pitcher, 5″ h, snake handle 150.00
Tulip
    Bowl, 6¼″ 40.00
    Cake Plate, 10″, molded handles .. 90.00
    Creamer, 5¼″ h 75.00
    Ewer, 4″ h 90.00
    Milk Pitcher 150.00
    Sugar, cov, 6¾″ h 100.00
    Teapot, 7¼″ h 140.00
Wagon Wheel
    Cup 50.00
    Plate
        5½″ d 30.00
        8¾″ d 75.00

GEISHA GIRL PORCELAIN

History: Geisha Girl porcelain is a Japanese export ware whose production commenced during the last quarter of the 19th century and continued heavily until WWII. The ware features kimono-clad Japanese ladies and children amidst Japanese gardens and temples. There are over 125 brightly colored scenes depicting the pre-modern Japanese lifestyle. Over 140 marks and almost 200 patterns and variations have been identified on pieces.

Geisha Girl ware may be totally hand painted, hand painted over a stenciled design, or occasionally decaled. The stenciled underlying design is usually red-orange, but also is found in brown, black, and green (rare).

All Geisha Girl items are bordered by one or a combination of blues, reds, greens, rhubarb, yellow, black, browns, or gold. The most common is red-orange. Borders may be wavy, scalloped, or banded and range from 1/16″ to 1/4″. The borders themselves often are further decorated with gold, white or yellow lacings, flowers, dots, or stripes. Some examples even display interior frames of butterflies or flowers.

Geisha Girl is found in many forms including tea, cocoa, lunch, and children's sets, dresser items, vases, serving dishes, etc. Large plates or platters, candlesticks, miniatures, and mugs are hardest to locate. Geisha Girl advertising items add to a collection.

Reference: Elyce Litts, *The Collectors Encyclopedia Of Geisha Girl Porcelain,* Collector Books, 1988.

Periodical: The Geisha Girl Porcelain Newsletter, P.O. Box 394, Morris Plains, NJ 07950.

Additional Listings: See *Warman's Americana & Collectibles* for more examples.

Reproduction Alert: Geisha Girl porcelain's popularity continued after WWII and it is being reproduced today. Chief reproduction characteristics are a red-orange border, very white and smooth porcelain, and sparse coloring and detail. Reproduced items include dresser, tea and sake sets, toothpick holders, small vases, table plates, and salt and pepper shakers.

Advisor: Elyce D. Litts.

Biscuit Jar, Gardening, ornate cobalt blue waved and circled border, ftd . .	40.00
Bon Bon Dish, 6″, chrysanthemum shape, Battledore pattern, olive green	22.00
Bowl	
8¾″, Inside The Teahouse, pale green, ftd	75.00
10″, Chinese Coin motif, ruffled, pierced handle	85.00
Calling Card Tray, 8 x 6″, Parasol F, free form, cobalt blue with gold	35.00
Child's Dishes	
Bowl, 2¼ x 1″, red, flower gathering	10.00

Demitasse Set, 15 pcs, pot, creamer and sugar, six cups and saucers, Parasol C	65.00
Butter Pat, cherry blossom shape reserve geisha, red line int. frame, flower and butterfly backdrop	10.00
Cracker Jar, Garden Bench E, wavy red with gold, mint green and gray geometric with gold	85.00
Creamer, 4″, Feeding The Carp, ribbed, hour glass shape, red with gold . . .	17.00
Cup and Saucer	
After Dinner	
Lady In Rickshaw B, ribbed cup, scalloped saucer, red	18.00
Pointing D, red	10.00
Tea, Garden Bench B, pedestal, lobed, scalloped saucer, red with gold	25.00
Dish, 8″, red with gold, reserve pattern, butterflies, chrysanthemums, and gold background	55.00
Egg Cup, child reaching for butterfly, red with gold	15.00

Salt, individual, marked "Nippon Hand Painted," $17.50.

Gravy Boat, drip plate, Rice Harvesters A, leaf shape, mint green, deep green, and red, gold border	25.00
Hair Receiver, Garden Bench B, red, maple leaf base	22.00
Humidor, Battledore pattern, blue scallop, gold line	70.00
Mustard Jar	
Circle Dance, red, gold lacing, spoon	25.00
Rendevous, apple green with gold .	30.00
Nappy, Temple A, underlying design, hand fluted edge, sea green border, handle	45.00
Plate	
6″, boy with scythe, cobalt blue with gold	10.00
6⅛″, Flag Day, red, yellow lacing . .	15.00

7⅜", Porch, cobalt blue with gold, fluted swirl, scalloped edge **15.00**

8½", children in boat, swirl, fluted, cobalt blue, gold lacing, scalloped edge **30.00**

Relish Dish, Picnic B, red-orange with gold, floret edge, reserves **25.00**

Salad Set, 7 pcs, master, six individual, red, gold buds **110.00**

Salt and Pepper Shakers, pr, 2", Garden Bench F, red-orange and gold top, cobalt shoulders **18.00**

Tea Set, 13 pcs, pot, sugar, creamer, five cups and saucers, Geisha In Sampan B, pink ground **50.00**

Tray, 5 x 5", heart shape, oversized irises, red **15.00**

Vase, 7", Processional, nishikide border, gold rim and handles **55.00**

GIRANDOLES AND MANTEL LUSTRES

History: A girandole is a highly elaborate branched candleholder, often featuring cut glass prisms surrounding the mountings. A mantel lustre is a glass vase with attached cut glass prisms.

Girandoles and mantel lustres usually are found in pairs. It is not uncommon for girandoles to be part of a large garniture set. Girandoles and mantel lustres achieved their greatest popularity in the last half of the 19th century both in the United States and Europe.

GIRANDOLES, pr

14¾", figural peg leg soldier and child, brass stem, cut glass prisms **125.00**

18", courting couple, brass relief, triple branch with prisms, marble base . . . **100.00**

18½", scrolled leaves, grape leaf bobeches, ornate casting, triangular base, 5 arms, 2 removable **300.00**

21" h, gilt metal, faceted glass, 3 light, Louis Philippe style **450.00**

24" h, cut glass, carved and gilded, draped white marble bases, Regency **5,500.00**

27", gilt metal, 3 tiered knopped baluster shaft, beaded drops and prisms entwining 4 candle arms, mounted and molded on glass, electrified **150.00**

MANTEL LUSTRES

11", black amethyst, 10 clear crystal prisms, clear knop stem **250.00**

13" h, gilt bronze and crystal, faceted collar, beaded molded and engine turned base, ball feet, George III, late 18th, early 19th C, pr **22,000.00**

Mantel Lustres, 12¼" h, cased glass, white ext., rose int., painted pink roses, green leaves, pr, $350.00.

14", ruby glass, enamel forget-me-not dec **425.00**

14½", pink cased, enamel painted flower swags with gilt scrolls, scalloped bulbous bowl, 2 rows clear prisms **275.00**

20" h, gilt bronze and cranberry glass, Napoleon III style, hurricane shades, pr **500.00**

24", ruby stained, enameled floral vines above fluted palmette panels, baluster shaft, clear prisms, hurricane shade, hexagonal base, electrified . **450.00**

GLASS, EARLY AMERICAN

History: Early American glass covers glass made in America from the colonial period through the mid-19th century. As such it includes the early pressed glass and lacy glass made between 1827 and 1840.

Major glass producing centers prior to 1850 were Massachusetts with the New England Glass Company and the Boston and Sandwich Glass Company, South Jersey, Pennsylvania with Stiegel's Manheim factory and Pittsburgh, and Ohio with Kent, Mantua, and Zanesville.

Early American glass was collected heavily during the 1920 to 1950 period. It has now regained some of its earlier popularity. Leading sources for the sale of early American glass are the mail auctions of David and Linda Arman and the auctions of Richard A. Bourne, Early Auction Company, Garth's, and Skinners.

References: William E. Covill, *Ink Bottles and Inkwells*, 1971; Lowell Inness, *Pittsburgh Glass: 1797–1891*, Houghton Mifflin Company, 1976; George and Helen McKearin, *American Glass*, Crown, 1975; George and Helen McKearin, *Two Hundred Years of American Blown Glass*, Doubleday and Company, 1950; Helen McKearin and

Kenneth Wilson, *American Bottles And Flasks*, Crown, 1978; Adeline Pepper, *Glass Gaffers of New Jersey*, Scribners, 1971; Jane S. Spillman, *American and European Pressed Glass*, Corning Museum of Glass, 1981; Kenneth Wilson, *New England Glass And Glassmaking*, Crowell, 1972.

Additional Listings: Blown Three Mold, Cup Plates, Flasks, Sandwich Glass, and Stiegel Type Glass.

Zanesville, flask, 6⅞″ w, 8¼″ h, brilliant amber, expanded vertical ribbing, 24 rib-mold, $1,250.00.

Amelung (New Bremen Glass)
Salt, 2½ x 2¾″, cobalt blue, pattern molded, checkered diamond, applied solid foot, ex-Guggenheim, Logan, and Gotjen collections ... 850.00
Wine, 6⅜″, clear, blown, applied dome foot, folded rim, hollow stem, small bubble in thick solid base of bowl, attributed to Amelung, ex-James and Eileen Courtney collection ... 250.00
Boston and Sandwich Glass Co, tumbler, 3¼″, Eye and Scale pattern, pillar flute motifs, listed as first pressed glass tumbler, 1827 ... 750.00
Ellenville, NY, creamer, 3¾″, brilliant yellow amber, blown, Jacob Relyea ... 500.00
Engraved
Goblet, 7″, clear, applied foot, hollow hourglass stem and bowl, copperwheel engraved ivy and B.D.C., attributed to NE Glass Co, ex-Philip Trier collection ... 100.00
Mug, clear
3¾″, handled, 24 wide ribs, applied strap handle with curl, copperwheel engraved tendrils, and letter P ... 125.00
5½″, applied foot and handle, Stiegel type copperwheel engraved tulip, ex-Philip Trier collection .. 125.00

Wine Funnel, 3⅜ x 5¾″, clear, engraved border of leaves and flowers, 8 cut flutes continue down stem ... 50.00
Keene, NH
Decanter, 7¼″, deep amber, pint, blown three mold, bubbles in neck, c1820 ... 350.00
Ink Bottle, 2⅜″, olive amber, octagonal ... 75.00
Kent, OH
Bottle, 7⅛″, aqua, tapered, 20 molded ribs, slightly swirled to the right, flanged lip, pontilled base ... 100.00
Smelling Salts Bottle, 3″, peacock blue, ovoid, 26 vertical molded ribs, sheared mouth and pontil ... 225.00
Lockport, NY
Salt, 3½″, bluish aqua brown, applied foot, knop stem, ex-James and Eileen Courtney collection ... 300.00
Tumbler, 3⅜ x 4⅛″, blue, free blown, cylindrical, plain lip, pontil, ex-McKearin, Abraham, and May collections ... 160.00
Mantua
Flask, 6″, blown chestnut, pale green, 16 swirled ribs ... 150.00
Pan
5¼″ x 1¾″ h, light green, blown, 15 diamond, folded rim, attributed to Mantua by Henry Hall White, ex-James and Eileen Courtney collection ... 1,950.00
6″ d, pale green, blown, 16 ribs, folded over rim ... 375.00
Toilet Bottle, 4½″ h, one-quarter pint, deep purple-amethyst, flared, flanged lip, pontiled base, ex-George McKearin and James Courtney collection ... 425.00
Marlboro Street Glassworks, Keene, NH
Flask, GIV-1, emb masonic emblem and American eagle, "IP" in oval, clear bluish-green, open pontil ... 250.00
Smelling Salts Bottle, 1⅞″ h, deep amethyst, flattened globular body, applied side quilling, sheared mouth, pontilled base, c1815–20, ex-collections George McKearin, Arthur Barris, David Hollander, and Marvin Engel ... 1,300.00
Midwestern
Bottle, globular, pale green
5¼″, 30 swirled ribs ... 225.00
6⅞″, 18 swirled ribs, minor sickness in base ... 100.00
Compote, 6 x 3⅞″, pressed Roman Rosette bowl, blown stem and base ... 150.00
Creamer and Sugar, 3½″, medium sapphire blue, blown, 17 swirled

ribs, drawn base, hollow foot, flared, folded rim, applied handle . **425.00**
- Flask, pitkin, olive green, half pint, 36 broken swirled ribs, five bubbles, c1790–1830 . . . . **200.00**
- Plate, 5″, eagle, ex-Howell Inness collection, 6 scallops damaged **575.00**

Mount Vernon Glassworks, New York, c1840
- Bowl, 5½ x 2⅜″, geometric, clear, gray tint **700.00**
- Decanter, clear, quart, GI-29, narrow flanged mouth, heavy int. haze . . **75.00**
- Pitcher, clear, GI-29, geometric, ribbed barrel design, large handle **1,100.00**

New England
- Compote, 7¼ x 4⅜″, clear, free blown, engraved with grapes and leaves, mounted on a serpentine three tiered pressed base, attributed to NE, slight stain under folded rim of bowl **65.00**
- Decanter, quart, clear, free blown, four rows of chain dec, orig mercurial stopper, made by Thomas Caines at South Boston or Phoenix Glass Works, light stains inside stopper **900.00**

New Geneva, PA
- Bottle, 5⅞″, chestnut, elongated and flattened, blue green, 16 vertical ribs, c1800–20 . . . . **175.00**
- Tumbler, 3⅛ x 4½″, yellow-green, plain sheared rim, large polished pontil **275.00**

New Jersey, South
- Bank, 10⅜″ h, clear, blown, applied rigaree and prunts, arch of four applied struts, applied chicken finial, solid ball stem attached to thick round base **1,200.00**
- Bottle, 7″, amethyst, triangular, heavy annealing marks, late 19th C **125.00**
- Cane, 32½″, clear, amber center, 4 applied opaque swirled ribs **125.00**
- Creamer, 4⅛″, cobalt blue, applied foot, handle, ring, and gadrooning, threaded lip, applied **575.00**
- Wine, 4⅜″, clear, smoky cast, thick applied base, iron pontil **75.00**

New York
- Bowl, 14 x 4¼″, aqua, folded rim, wear, star in flared rim **225.00**
- Compote, 6⅜ x 6¼″, free blown, clear, thick applied base, polished pontil **50.00**
- Vase, 4½ x 5½″, urn shape, yellow-green, rolled rim, large faint pontil **125.00**

Pittsburgh
- Bar Bottle, 10½″, medium amethyst, heavy applied lip, polished pontil . **650.00**
- Bowl, 4⅜ x 3⅞″, cobalt blue, clear foot, wide flaring rim, rough pontil **600.00**
- Candlestick
  - 10⅛″, clear, blown, wide foot, hollow pillar molded stem, bulbous socket, pewter insert **725.00**
  - 10¼″, clear, free blown, large hollow socket, heavy shaft, thick round base, white, amethyst red, and translucent blue green air twist ribbons in shaft **1,200.00**
- Celery Vase, 5¼ x 8¼″, clear, gadrooned base, copper wheel engraved swags, flowers, and leaves, flared mouth, solid wine glass stem, thick solid base **450.00**
- Compote
  - 8 x 7½″, clear, ftd, copper wheel engraving, swags, acorn-like tassels, solid knop stem, ex-Philip Trier collection **275.00**
  - 8¾ x 5¼″, cranberry cased bowl, clear solid knop stem, thick heavy base, c1850 . . . . **435.00**
- Creamer and Sugar, 3⅝″, clear, blown, blue applied rim, 12 panel bowl, flared foot, folded rim, applied handle **900.00**
- Lamp, 12¼″, clear, pressed base, blown hollow stem and font, wafers, cut foliage, panels, strawberry diamonds, and fans, pewter collar, minor chips on base **575.00**
- Pitcher, 9½″, clear, flint, Cleat pattern, applied handle and ring, ex-Philip Trier collection, minor wear and scratches **100.00**
- Powder Horn, 11¼″, blown, clear applied foot and 2 applied rings, red loopings, minor sickness **250.00**
- Sugar, 9⅞″, clear, applied domed foot with blue rim, blue looping on bowl and domed cov, clear finial, shallow flake on foot, ex-Philip Trier collection **1,150.00**
- Sweetmeat, 5¾ x 4⅝″, pillar molded, clear, ftd, flared folded rim, solid attached stem and base, 8 pronounced ribs, large pontil scar . . . **575.00**
- Tumbler, 3¼″
  - Clear, blown, cut flutes, strawberry point band, copperwheel engraving of flowers and seated greyhound **2,250.00**
  - Sapphire blue, 8 panel, ex-Lowell Inness collection **50.00**

Saratoga, compote, 4⅛ x 3¾″, amber, blown, one piece, hollow bulbous base and stem, flared bowl with folded in rim, very minor sickness and some residue in hollow foot, ex-James and Eileen Courtney collection **150.00**

South Boston
Bowl, 8 x 3⅜", clear, flint, applied
rings, ex-Philip Trier collection ... **75.00**
Pitcher, 7⅞", rings, applied handle . **200.00**
Unknown
Free Blown
Bowl, 4⅞ x 2⅞", puce, 16 vertical
ribs, broken swirl to right, ftd,
pontil, inward folded rim **250.00**
Decanter, quart, clear, 3 applied
pouring rings, pontil **50.00**
Hat, 9⅛", emerald green, slightly
rolled brim, pontil **125.00**
Jar
4½ x 6⅜", golden amber, cylindrical, wide flat folded rim, tubular pontil **300.00**
8", clear, 2 horizontal ribs, domed
dov, airtrip finial **150.00**
Pitcher, 8⅜", helmet shape, circular
foot, heavy horizontal mid rib,
fine applied handle, c1830 .... **400.00**
Vase, 12⅝", amethyst, trumpet, applied foot, hollow stem, folded
rim **200.00**
Pattern Molded
Bar Bottle, clear, Divided Diamond,
pint, heavy applied lip, polished
pontil **100.00**
Creamer, 5¼", cobalt blue, 16 vertical ribs, ftd, applied solid handle, curl ending, folded rim, attributed to Pittsburgh **400.00**
Goblet, 6⅜", canary, Ringed
Framed Ovals pattern **85.00**
Vase, 9¼", sapphire blue, Loop
pattern, gauffered rim, sq base,
ex-Arthur Reiter collection **850.00**
Whiskey Taster, 1⅞", clear, double
loop type pattern, polished base **25.00**
Wine, 4", clear, 12 panel pattern,
applied base, pontil **40.00**
Pillar Molded
Bar Bottle, 10⅛", clear, triangular,
8 heavy ribs, heavy applied lip
and pouring ring **100.00**
Celery Vase, 5⅛ x 8¾", clear, 12
swirled to right ribs, solid applied
stem, polished pontil **125.00**
Creamer, 6", clear, 8 ribs, solid
stem, thick applied base, solid
applied handle with curl, polished
pontil **200.00**
Decanter, 8½", clear, 8 blue ribs,
thick sloping lip and pouring ring,
polished pontil **1,200.00**
Salt, 2½ x 1¼", 12 wide ribs, pontil **65.00**
Sugar, 5⅜ x 4⅛", clear, 8 ribs,
folded rim, solid stem, thick applied base, polished pontil **200.00**

Zanesville
Bottle
4½", chestnut, pale green, blown,
24 vertical ribs, ex-James and Eileen Courtney collection, minor
ext. scratches **100.00**
5", chestnut, aqua, 24 vertical flattened ribs, pint, attributed to
Zanesville, OH, c1800–35 .... **75.00**
7⅜", globular, citron, blown, 24
swirled ribs, ex-James and Eileen Courtney collection, minor
traces of int. sickness **550.00**
Cruet, 6⅜", purple-blue, taper shape,
24 molded ribs, swirled to the left,
slightly flared, rolled lip **2,300.00**
Flask, GIV-32, emb Masonic arch and
farmer's arms, American eagle and
"Zanesville, Ohio J Shepard &
Co." reddish-amber, pint, open
pontil, c1820 .... **750.00**
Salt, 2½ x 3⅛", ftd, blue green, 24
vertical ribs, applied irregular solid
foot, pontil, ex-Ewing/Hoovler collection, slightly ground rim **1,200.00**
Scent Bottle, clear, 24 ribs, swirled to
the right, rolled over collar-pontil . **225.00**

GONDER POTTERY

History: Lawton Gonder established Gonder
Ceramic Arts, Inc., at Zanesville, Ohio, in 1941.
He gained experience while working for other factories in the area. Gonder experimented with
glazes, including Chinese crackle, gold crackle,
and flambe. Lamp bases were manufactured under the name Eglee at a second plant location.
Gonder pieces are clearly marked. The company ceased operation in 1957.

**Candleholders, 4¾" d, scalloped sides,
turquoise ext., pink coral int., marked
"E-14 Gonder," pr, $15.00.**

Bowl
2½ x 6", turquoise with brown int. .. **10.00**
4 x 9", ribbed, gray with pink int. **12.00**
7¾ x 7", blue and brown glossy glaze,
swirl, flower frog **20.00**

Cornucopia, 7″, turquoise and brown,
  marked "E5" 15.00
Ewer
  6″, gray, fluted 10.00
  12″, figural swan 30.00
Figure
  Horse, head, 13″ l, blue and green
    onyx glaze 40.00
  Panther, 18¼″ l, jade green 85.00
Tea Set, cov teapot, creamer, and cov
  sugar, brown mottled 25.00
Vase
  8½″, basket shape, pink flower motif   25.00
  9″, mottled turquoise and brown, pink
    int. 15.00
  12″, gray, marked "K-26" 12.00

GOOFUS GLASS

History: Goofus glass, also known as Mexican
Ware, Hooligan glass, and Pickle glass, is a
pressed glass with relief designs. The back or front
was painted. The designs are usually in red and
green with a metallic gold ground. It was popular
from 1890 to 1920 and was used as a premium at
carnivals.

It was produced by several companies: Cresent
Glass Company, Wellsburg, West Virginia; Impe-
rial Glass Corporation, Bellaire, Ohio; LaBelle
Glass Works, Bridgeport, Ohio; and Northwood
Glass Co., Indiana, Pennsylvania, Wheeling, West
Virginia, and Bridgeport, Ohio. Northwood marks
include "N," "N" in one circle, "N" in two circles,
and one or two circles without the "N."

Goofus glass lost its popularity when people
found the paint tarnished or scaled off after repeated washings and wear. No record of its manufacture has been found after 1920.

Reference: Carolyn McKinley, *Goofus Glass,*
Collector Books, 1984.

Additional Listings: See *Warman's Americana
& Collectibles* for more examples.

Bowl
  8¾″, fluted, beaded rim, relief
    molded, teardrops and red hearts   35.00
  9″, ruffled, relief molded, red roses .   20.00
  9½″, relief molded, red carnations . .   35.00
  11″, ruffled, relief molded, red cher-
    ries 25.00
Compote, 10¼″ d, relief molded, red
  fruits 65.00
Decanter, LeBelle Rose, orig stopper .   50.00
Dish, 7¼″, fluted, green, floral dec . . .   12.00
Plate
  6″, relief molded, red sunflower center   8.00
  8″, relief molded, red apples 15.00
Powder Jar, cov, 4½″ d, relief molded,
  white cabbage rose 20.00
Salt Shaker, Grape and Leaf, 2½ x 4″ .   18.00

**Vase, 7½″ h, Rose pattern, blown out
red roses, gold ground, $20.00.**

Syrup, relief molded, red roses, lattice
  work ground, orig top 45.00
Tray, 8¼ x 11″, chrysanthemum, bronze
  and red 35.00
Vase, relief molded
  Cabbage Rose, 7″ h, white 45.00
  Grapes, 8″ h, purple 20.00
  Parrot, 12″ h, red and blue bird,
    molded foliage 70.00
  Peacock, 10½″ h 75.00
  Statue of Liberty 100.00

MARK

W H GOSS

GOSS CHINA AND CRESTED WARE

History: In 1858 William H. Goss opened his
Henley factory and produced terra cotta ware. A
year later he moved to Stoke-on-Trent and added
Parian ware to his line. In 1883 Adolphus, William's son, expanded on his father's idea of decorating small ivory pots and vases, with the coat
of arms of schools, hospitals, colleges [especially
Oxford and Cambridge], and other motifs to appeal
to the souvenir seeking English "day-tripper." The
forms used were copied from ancient artifacts in
museums.

William died in 1906, his son in 1913. Following
business setbacks, the firm was sold in 1929 to
Geo. Jones & Sons Ltd., who had previously acquired Arcadian, Swan, and other firms that made
crested wares. As late as 1931 the Goss name
was still being used. In 1936–37 Cauldon Potteries

purchased the Goss assets. Production ceased in 1940. In 1954 Ridgeway and Adderley acquired all Goss assets [molds, patterns, designs, and right to use the Goss name and trademark].

From 1883 to 1931 pieces carry the mark of GOSHAWK, with W. H. Goss beneath, and "England" on later pieces. Many early examples carry an impressed "W. H. Goss," either with or without the printed mark.

Other manufacturers of crested ware in England were: Arcadian, Carlton China, Grafton China, Savoy China, Shelley, and Willow Art. Gemma in Germany also made crested wares.

Crests are of little value unless they match, e.g., Shakespeare's jug with Shakespeare's crest. Collectors tend to collect one form (vase, ewer, jug, etc.), one particular crest, or one type of object (boat, cat, dog, etc.). Price is determined not by crest, but size, condition, and bottom mark.

References: Sandy Andrews, *Crested China: The History of Heraldic Souvenir Ware,* Milestone Publications [England]; John Galpin, *A Handbook Of Goss China,* Milestone Publications; Nicholas Pine, *The 1984 Price Guide To Goss China,* Milestone Publications, 1984; Nicholas Pine and Sandy Andrews, *The 1984 Price Guide To Crested China* (including revisions to *Crested China*), Milestone Publications; Roland Ward, *The Price Guide To The Models Of W. H. Goss,* Antiques Collectors' Club.

Collectors' Clubs: The Goss Collectors Club, 3 Carr Hill Gardens, Barrowford, Nelson, Lancashire BB9 6PU; The Crested Circle, 26 Urswick Road, Dagenhem, Essex RM9 6EA.

Advisor: Mildred Fishman.

Mug, 3″ h, shield transfer "Rexet Nostra Jura-Great Yarmouth," marked "W. H. Goss," $24.00.

GOSS

Beer Bowl, dragon	25.00
Bottle, Swiss Vinegar, Wymondham	20.00
Bucket, Norwegian, Maldon	25.00
Building	
First and Last House	135.00
Huers House	200.00
Look Out House	140.00
Manx cottage	100.00
Shakespeare's house	100.00
St. Nicholas Chapel	200.00
Candle Snuffer, Aseroovy crest, white, 2¼″	50.00
Ewer	
Arundel, 4½″	20.00
Shrewsbury, 4″	20.00
Jug	
Assyrian Armour	20.00
Litchfield, Warwick	30.00
Shakespeare	30.00
Kettle, Hastings	20.00
Night Light, Robert Burns, 6″	150.00
Plate, 10″, Armoriai	25.00
Porringer, Deconport	35.00
Pot, Winchester, Lewes	30.00
Tray, 5″, crinkle	20.00
Urn, Falmouth	20.00
Vase	
Coronation Amphora	40.00
Doncaster, Seven Oaks	25.00
Pineapple, City of Edinburgh	30.00
Southwold	40.00
Winking Cat, 4″	25.00
Yorick's Skull	125.00

OTHER CRESTED WARE MANUFACTURERS

Arcadian	
Baby Chick, "Just Out," Cowes	15.00
Bathing Wagon, Stockbridge	30.00
Turtle, Infracombe	25.00
Warming Pan, Tesbury	30.00
Carlton	
Urn, Bourne	20.00
Vase	
Keswick	20.00
Mundesley-On-Sea	10.00
Clifton	
Elephant, Lewisham	20.00
Six sided container, Coventry	15.00
Florentine	
Suitcase, Frome	20.00
Tower, Blackpool	25.00
Gemma	
Coal Hod, Southport	20.00
Teapot, cov, Salesbury	30.00
Shelley	
Fish Basket, Fleetwood	30.00
Headlamp, Cockermouth Cycle Oil	45.00
Olive Jar, Sussex	25.00
Scent Bottle, Richmond Surry	25.00
Tea Caddy	
Abbey of Glastonbury	25.00
Florest Hova	25.00

Seashell, Saltburn-by-the-Sea **30.00**
Victoria, watering can, Matlock Bath . . **30.00**
Willow Art, urn, Tewkesbury **15.00**

GOUDA POTTERY   Zuid Holland

History: Gouda and the surrounding areas of Holland have been one of the principal Dutch pottery centers for centuries. Originally the potteries produced a simple utilitarian Delft type earthenware with a tin glaze and the famous clay smokers' pipes.

When the pipe making portion declined in the early 1900s, the Gouda potteries turned to art pottery. Influenced by the Art Nouveau and Art Deco movements, artists expressed themselves with free form and stylized designs in bold colors.

Reference: Susan and Al Bagdade, *Warman's English & Continental Pottery & Porcelain, 1st Edition,* Warman Publishing Co., Inc., 1987.

Reproduction Alert: With the Art Nouveau and Art Deco revivals of recent years, modern reproductions of Gouda pottery currently are on the market. They are difficult to distinguish from the originals.

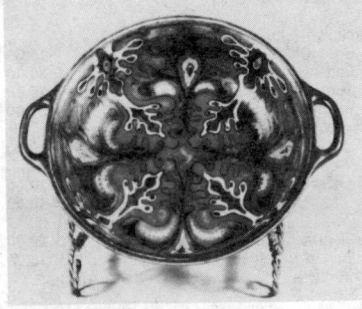

Bowl, 10¼" d, 2" h, two handles, multicolored, $150.00.

Ashtray, 4⅛" d, 1¼" h, green, cobalt, multicolored int., house mark, "Anne Royal" **40.00**
Basket, 6" d, 7¾" h, high matte glaze, floral dec **150.00**
Biscuit Jar, cov, 8", multicolored **130.00**
Bowl
  3" d, handles **32.00**

5½" d, 3½" h, Damascus mark **50.00**
Candlestick
  3¾", green, rust, cobalt, ochre, marked "Candis 1137" and house mark **50.00**
  4⅛" d, 7⅛" h, Spino pattern, yellow flowers, green leaves, black ground, satin finish, house mark, pr **150.00**
  6½" d, 3" h, circular, handle, matte green, yellow, blue, and cream dec, marked "0139 DAM II Holland," c1885 . . . . **100.00**
Charger, 12", multicolored flowers, rope border, black rim **150.00**
Compote, 7⅝", black ground, geometric design, multicolored scroll int. **165.00**
Dish, 8" d, 4" h, three sections, handle, brick, cream, blue, and gold dec, black ground, satin finish, crown mark and "Regina" **85.00**
Ewer, 9½", matte finish, Anjer house mark **125.00**
Humidor, 6" h, white high glaze, floral dec, Jilliana Gouda house mark . . . **250.00**
Incense Burner, 8" h, Roba, flowers and geometrics, green ground **100.00**
Inkwell, 8" w, attached pen tray, matte finish, blue, Purdah Gouda, orange and black house mark **200.00**
Jug, 10", orig stopper, multicolored dec, black matte ground **175.00**
Planter, 12" l, 7" w, 4" h, rect, Yssel pattern **150.00**
Plate, 10½", matte finish, multicolored dec **100.00**
Potpourri Jar, 4", high glaze, multicolored dec, black base **85.00**
Tobacco Jar, cov, 5", Verona pattern . . **80.00**
Tray, 10½", leaf dec, autumn colors . . **150.00**
Tumbler, 4⅜" h, 3⅝" d, multicolored flowers, green leaves, black ground, satin finish, marked "Nerf" and house mark **55.00**
Vase
  5¼", 6" w across handles, black matte finish, wide cobalt and multicolored band, Blareth house mark **60.00**
  7½", Effect pattern, stripes, black ground **45.00**
  8", multicolored flowers **48.00**
  11½", pitcher shape, extended bark neck, twig handle, scenic, windmill on obverse, lake on reverse, marked "Springer & Co/Elfangen, Germany," c1890 . . . . **150.00**

GRANITEWARE

History: Graniteware is the name commonly given to iron or steel kitchenware covered with enamel coating.

The first graniteware was made in Germany in the 1830s. Graniteware was not produced in the United States until the 1860s. At the start of World War I, when European manufacturers turned to the making of war weapons, American producers took over the market.

Colors commonly marketed were white and gray. Each company made their own special color, including shades of blue, green, brown, violet, cream, and red.

Older graniteware is heavier than new graniteware. Pieces with cast iron handles date from 1870 to 1890; wood handles date from 1900 to 1910. Other dating clues are seams, wood knobs, and tin lids.

References: Vernagene Vogelzang and Evelyn Welch, *Granite Ware, Collector's Guide With Prices,* Wallace-Homestead, 1981; Vernagene Vogelzang and Evelyn Welch, *Granite Ware, Book II,* Wallace-Homestead, 1987.

Collectors' Club: National Graniteware Society, 2818 Reamer Road, Center Point, IN 52213.

Reproduction Alert: Graniteware still is manufactured in many of the traditional forms and colors.

Additional Listings: See *Warman's Americana & Collectibles* for more examples.

Utensil Rack, 15¾″ w, 18″ h, four ladles, blue and white, $65.00.

Baby Bottle Warmer, gray and white speckled, electric	55.00
Bread Dough Pan, 16½″ d, 12″ h, perforated domed lid, ftd	35.00
Butter Churn, blue and white, swirl, orig lid	900.00
Candleholder, blue and white, marbleized	115.00
Casserole Dish, cov, cobalt blue and white, marbleized	45.00
Chamber Pot, cov, blue and white, marbleized	70.00

Coffeepot	
8″, medium blue	20.00
9″, cov, blue and white, marbleized, gooseneck spout	55.00
Colander	
Blue and white, marbleized, large	175.00
Orange, mottled, blue trim, ftd, handled	45.00
Cuspidor, gray, mottled, marked "Agate Ware"	20.00
Double Boiler, blue and white, 2 qt	15.00
Flask, gray, mottled	70.00
Funnel, mottled, blue gray	45.00
Grater, miniature, gray, mottled	125.00
Kettle, cov, 7″ h, 8½″ d, dark brown and white marbleized, wire bail handle	65.00
Ladle, 12″	10.00
Measure, pint, gray	25.00
Milk Can, gray, mottled, lid and bail, 1 gal	45.00
Milk Pan, gray, mottled, 11 x 2½″	20.00
Mug, 1″ h, 1″ d, cobalt blue and white marbleized	140.00
Muffin Pan, fluted, gray, mottled, 12 section	45.00
Pie Pan, 8¾″ d, Crysolite	25.00
Pitcher	
Blue and white	20.00
White, black trim	15.00
Pudding Mold, fluted edges	10.00
Roaster, 22 x 10″, cov	
Creamware	15.00
Blue and White	20.00
Sieve, gray, pan style	15.00
Soap Dish, 10″ h, sky blue, drain insert, ornate	50.00
Tea Kettle, blue and white enamel swirl pattern, stylized goose neck spout, 4 qts, handle	40.00
Tea Strainer, 3″, white, handle	10.00
Teapot, cov, blue, pewter trim, marked "Manning-Bowman"	45.00
Tray, 18″ d, red and white	35.00
Wash Basin, brown and white marbleized, two handles	55.00

GREENAWAY, KATE   K.G.

History: Kate Greenaway, or "K.G." as she initialed her famous drawings, was born in 1846 in London. Her father was a prominent wood engraver. Kate's natural talent for drawing soon was evident, and she began art classes at the age of 12. In 1868 she had her first public exhibition.

Her talents were used primarily in illustrating. She did cards for Marcus Ward, which are largely unsigned. China and pottery companies soon had her drawings of children appearing on many of their wares. By the 1880s she was one of the foremost children's book illustrators in England.

Reproduction Alert: Some Greenaway buttons have been reproduced in Europe and sold in the United States.

Advertising Trade Card, 2½ x 4⅝", $8.00.

Almanac, 1883, George Routledge & Sons	95.00
Biscuit Jar, cov, boy, pastel dec	150.00
Book	
Birthday Book For Children, 1st ed, 1880, George Routledge & Sons .	95.00
Language of Flowers, The, Kate Greenaway, illus, 1887, Frederick Warne & Co, Ltd	65.00
Pied Piper of Hamelin, The, Robert Browning, Kate Greenaway, illus, George Routledge & Sons	125.00
Bowl, amber daisy and button pattern, girl and dog on Reed and Barton SP holder	500.00
Bust, 5", girl with glasses, frilly bonnet, ribbons, lace	60.00
Children's Feeding Dish, cup, saucer, and 6" plate, 3 pcs	100.00
Figure	
7", girl holding pug dog, sgd	175.00
9½", children jumping rope, pr	600.00
Match Holder, girl helping little sister over log, place for matches and striker	85.00
Match Safe, SP, emb children	50.00
Mug, SS, "Bessie 1882"	60.00
Nodder, bisque, elderly couple, wearing eyeglasses, cloak, bonnet, and high hat	130.00
Picture Frame, 6 x 5", SS, two girls look out window, grandfather clock, blue velvet back, c1885	200.00
Plate, 9", children playing, with over- sized fruit, birds, and flowers	95.00
Print, 6 x 8", *Outdoor Tea Party*, fifteen girls, sgd	85.00

Salt and Pepper Shakers, pr, 4", boy and girl in long coats, girl with muff .	80.00
Sugar Shaker, boy in long coat, porce- lain	95.00
Tea Set	
3 pcs, floral motif, semi-porcelain . .	60.00
7 pcs, child's size, children and dachshund pulling tablecloth	150.00
Thimble Holder, girl holds SS thimble .	125.00
Tile	
6", sq "May"	75.00
"Pipe Thee High," small boy with horn, Wedgwood	75.00
Toothpick Holder, SP, ornate, girl, standing, marked "Tufts"	175.00
Vase, 6½", boy with school books . . .	90.00

GREENTOWN GLASS

History: The Indiana Tumbler and Goblet Co., Greentown, Indiana, produced its first clear, pressed glass table and bar wares in late 1894. Initial success led to a doubling of plant size in 1895 and other subsequent expansions, one in 1897 to allow for the manufacture of colored glass. In 1899 the firm joined the combine known as the National Glass Company.

In 1900, just before arriving in Greentown, Jacob Rosenthal developed an opaque brown glass, called "chocolate," which ranged in color from a dark, rich chocolate to a lighter "cream" coffee hue. Production of chocolate glass saved the financially pressed Indiana Tumbler and Goblet Works. The Cactus and Leaf Bracket patterns were made almost exclusively in chocolate glass. Other popular chocolate patterns are Austrian, Dewey, Shuttle, and Teardrop and Tassel. In 1902 National Glass Company bought Rosenthal's chocolate glass formula so other plants in the combine could use the color.

In 1902 Rosenthal developed the Golden Agate and Rose Agate colors. All work ceased on June 13, 1903, when a fire of suspicious origin destroyed the Indiana Tumbler and Goblet Company Works.

After the fire, other companies, e.g., McKee and Brothers, produced chocolate glass in the same pattern design used in Greentown. Later reproductions also have taken place, with Cactus among the most heavily copied pattern.

References: Brenda Measell and James Measell, *A Guide To Reproductions of Greentown Glass*, 2nd ed., The Printing Press, 1974; James Measell, *Greentown Glass, The Indiana Tumbler & Goblet Co.*, Grand Rapids Public Museum, 1979.

Collectors' Club: National Greentown Glass Association, 1807 West Madison, Kokomo, IN 56901. *N.G.G.A. Newsletter*, quarterly.

Museums: Greentown Glass Museum, Green-

town, IN; Grand Rapids Public Museum [Ruth Herrick Greentown Glass Collection], MI.

Additional Listings: Holly Amber and Pattern
Glass.

**Butter Dish, cov, Geneva pattern, choc-
olate glass, tripod feet, $425.00.**

Animal Dish, cov, cat, hamper base, red agate	350.00
Berry Set, Leaf & Bracket, chocolate, 7 pcs	235.00
Bowl	
Pattern No. 11, 6¼", blue, gold trim	125.00
Six Fluted, chocolate	150.00
Butter Dish , cov	
Daisy, milk glass	70.00
Leaf & Bracket, chocolate	175.00
Creamer	
Cactus, chocolate	110.00
Indian Head, nile green	475.00
Indoor Drinking Scene, 5½", choco-late	185.00
Compote, jelly, Cactus, chocolate	100.00
Cordial	
Overall Lattice	35.00
Shuttle	35.00
Cruet	
Chrysanthemum Leaf, chocolate	850.00
Geneva, chocolate	1,000.00
Leaf & Bracket, chocolate	65.00
Wild Rose & Bowknot, chocolate	300.00
Dolphin, cov, dish, chocolate	
Beaded edge	225.00
Sawtooth edge	185.00
Dresser Tray, Wild Rose and Bowknot	310.00
Goblet	
Beehive	60.00
Diamond Prisms	65.00
Lemonade Tumbler, Cactus, chocolate	75.00
Mug, 6½", Troubador, milk glass, cov	60.00
Nappy, Leaf & Bracket, chocolate, tri-angular	50.00
Pitcher, water, Ruffled Eye, chocolate	500.00

Plate, Serenade, chocolate	160.00
Relish, Leaf & Bracket, chocolate, 8"	70.00
Sauce	
Leaf Bracket, chocolate	25.00
Six Fluted, chocolate	225.00
Water Lily and Cattail, chocolate	90.00
Wild Rose and Bowknot, chocolate	75.00
Spooner, Wild Rose and Bowknot, chocolate	135.00
Stein, Serenade, clear	25.00
Syrup, Cord Drapery, chocolate	225.00
Tray	
Dewey, serpentine, canary yellow	60.00
Venetian, 4 x 5", chocolate	275.00
Tumbler	
Cactus, chocolate	55.00
Cord Drapery, chocolate	225.00
Geneva, chocolate	95.00
Icicle, chocolate	125.00
Wine	
Cord Drapery	75.00
Shuttle, clear	12.00

GRUEBY POTTERY

History: William Grueby was active in the ceramic industry for several years before he developed his own method of producing matte glazed
pottery and founded the Grueby Faience Company
in Boston, Massachusetts, in 1897.

The art pottery was hand thrown in natural
shapes, hand molded, and hand tooled. A variety
of colored glazes, singly or in combinations, were
produced with green being the most prominent. In
1908 the firm was divided into the Grueby Pottery
Company and the Grueby Faience and Tile Co.,
the latter making art pottery until bankruptcy forced
closure shortly after 1908.

References: Paul Evans, *Art Pottery of the
United States, 2nd Edition,* Feingold & Lewis Pub-
lishing Corp., 1987; Ralph and Terry Kovel, *The
Kovels' Collector's Guide to American Art Pottery,*
Crown Publishers, Inc., 1974.

Bowl, 3", green, turned in rim	100.00
Fireplace Mantel, frieze of eight tiles, 48" l	13,200.00
Lamp Base, 12 x 8", bulbous, pedestal base, green leaves and buds, orig brass oil fixtures	1,200.00

Paperweight, 4″, circular lozenge, emb three color Egyptian Scarab, blue ground **200.00**

Tile, 4⅛″ sq, graceful white swan swimming, blue sky, brown hills, green water **575.00**

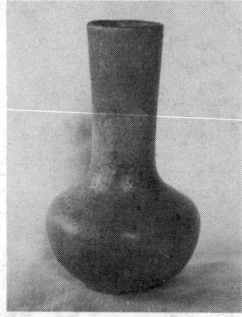

Vase, 6″, bulbous body, tapered neck, oatmeal glaze, marked, $275.00.

Vase
5¼″, ovoid, five molded broad leaves, matte cucumber green glaze, artist sgd **500.00**
6 x 4¾″, cylindrical, swollen base, modeled stylized lotus leaves, rich green matte glaze, imp mark, incised "MS" (Marie Seaman), green glaze sq **600.00**
10″, melon shape, molded broad angular leaves, long slender stems, small yellow buds, matte green glaze, artist sgd **4,400.00**

HAIR ORNAMENTS

History: Hair ornaments, one of the first accessories developed by primitive man, were used to remove tangles and keep hair out of one's face. Remnants of early combs have been found in many archeological excavations.

As fashion styles changed through the centuries, hair ornaments kept pace through design and use changes. Hair combs and other hair ornaments are made in a wide variety of materials, e.g., precious metals, ivory, tortoise shell, plastics, and wood.

Combs were first made in America during the Revolution when imports from England were restricted. Early American combs were made of horn and treasured as valued toiletry articles.

Reference: Evelyn Haetig, *Antique Combs and Purses,* Gallery Graphics Press, 1983.

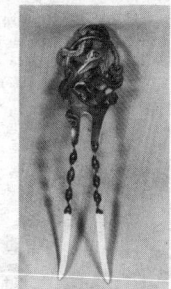

Comb, 4″ l, sterling silver serpent, two prongs, $45.00.

Back Comb
Bakelite, coral and gold wash filigree, Victorian, c1890 .... **250.00**
Celluloid, Spanish, Art Nouveau, c1910 .... **85.00**
Imitation goldstone, green stone, Victorian, c1900 .... **135.00**
Comb
Celluloid, Art Nouveau, French, c1900 .... **35.00**
Sterling, French, Victorian, c1860 .. **225.00**
Hairclip, rhinestone dec, c1930, pr ... **15.00**
Hairpin
Amber, Art Deco, c1925 .... **45.00**
Tortoise, sterling filigree, English, Victorian, c1890 .... **65.00**
Ornament
Celluloid
French, Art Nouveau, c1910 .... **55.00**
Victorian, c1900 .... **35.00**
Tortoise, Art Nouveau, c1910 ..... **65.00**
Side Comb, celluloid, Victorian, c1890 **25.00**

HALL CHINA COMPANY

History: Robert Hall founded the Hall China Company in 1903 in East Liverpool, Ohio. He died in 1904 and was succeeded by his son, Robert Taggart Hall. After years of experimentation, Robert T. Hall developed a leadless glaze in 1911, opening the way for production of glazed household products.

The Hall China Company made many types of kitchenware, refrigerator sets, and dinnerware in a wide variety of patterns. Some patterns were exclusive, such as Heather Rose for Sears.

One of the most popular patterns was Autumn Leaf, an exclusive premium designed in 1933 for the Jewel Tea Company by Arden Richards. Still a Jewel Tea property, Autumn Leaf has not been listed in catalogs since 1978 but, is produced on a replacement basis with the date stamped on the back.

References: Jo Cunningham, *The Autumn Leaf Story*, Haf-A-Productions, 1976; Harvey Duke, *Superior Quality Hall China*, published by author, 1977; Harvey Duke, *Hall 2*, published by author, 1985; Margaret and Kenn Whitmyer, *The Collector's Guide To Hall China*, Collector Books, 1985.

Additional Listings: See *Warman's Americana & Collectibles* for more examples plus a separate section on Autumn Leaf.

MISCELLANEOUS

Bean Pot, cov, New England, Chinese Red	40.00
Bowl, Radiance, Chinese Red, 14″	16.00
Coffee Server, Flare-Ware, brass warmer, 15 cup	25.00
Irish Coffee Mug, Chinese Red	8.00
Pretzel Jar, Morning Glory	55.00
Vase, bud, yellow	5.00
Water Server, Nora Daffodil	10.00

PATTERNS

Autumn Leaf. Premium for Jewel Tea Co. Produced from 1933 until 1978.

Bowl, berry	4.00
Casserole, cov, ind, 4″	18.00
Coffee Pot, 8″	24.00
Cream Soup	15.00
Custard Cup	4.00
Iced Tea, frosted	12.50
Jug, ball, #3	15.00
Mustard, 3 pc	40.00
Pitcher, 6″	12.00
Plate	
5½″, bread and butter	3.00
6″, salad	3.50
Platter, 9″	10.00
Souffle, large	12.00
Vegetable, oval	14.00
Warmer, round	105.00

Heather Rose. Produced during the 1940s.

Bowl, 6″, cereal	4.00
Creamer and Sugar	12.00
Cup and Saucer	4.00
Gravy Boat	10.00
Plate, 10″, dinner	5.00
Tureen, cov	18.00

Orange Poppy. Premium for Great American Tea Co. Produced from 1933 through 1950s.

Baker, fluted	12.00
Casserole, cov, oval	30.00
Creamer and Sugar	24.00
Cup and Saucer	7.00
Jug, 6½″	15.00
Plate, 9″	7.50
Salt and Pepper, handled, pr	18.00
Water Server, green	20.00

Rose Parade. Kitchenware line introduced in the 1940s.

Baker	18.00
Bowl, salad	15.00
Casserole, cov, tab handle	30.00
Creamer and Sugar	20.00
Salt and Pepper, sani-grid, pr	20.00
Teapot, 32 oz	25.00

Springtime. Premium for Standard Tea Co. Limited production.

Bowl, 10″, oval	8.50
Cake Plate	15.00
Creamer and Sugar	15.00
Cup and Saucer	8.50
Gravy	10.00
Pie Baker	15.00
Plate	
6¼″, bread and butter	4.00
9″, dinner	8.00
Platter, 13″	12.50
Soup Plate	5.25
Teapot, cov, 6 cup	40.00

Teapot, inverted spout, gray, gold floral trim, $8.00.

TEAPOTS

Airflow, turquoise, gold dec	30.00
Boston, green, gold dec	24.00
Disraeli, pink, gold dec	25.00
Globe, inverted spout, lemon	60.00
Nautilus, 6 cup, yellow	75.00
New York, brown, gold dec	20.00
Philadelphia, green, gold dec	28.00
Windshield, maroon, 6 cup, gold flowers	20.00

HAMPSHIRE POTTERY

History: In 1871 James S. Taft founded the Hampshire Pottery Company in Keene, New Hampshire. Production began with redwares and stonewares, followed by majolica decorated wares in 1879. A semi-porcelain, with the recognizable matte glazes plus the Royal Worcester glaze, was introduced in 1883.

Until World War I the factory made an extensive line of utilitarian and art wares including souvenir items. After the war the firm resumed operations, but only made hotel dinnerware and tiles. The company dissolved in 1923.

Reference: Joan Pappas and A. Harold Kendall, *Hampshire Pottery Manufactured by J. S. Taft & Company, Keene, New Hampshire,* published by author, 1971.

Vase, 3 x 6″, squatty, green matte glaze, $65.00.

Bowl
  3″, cobalt blue, crisp molded leaves, marked 85.00
  9⅞ x 2⅞″, bulb, dark matte green, yellow buds, light green leaves, glossy lime green int., unglazed bisque liner, marked 100.00
Chocolate Pot, 9½″, dark green glaze, raised leaf dec 100.00
Ewer
  8¼″, striated matte green, fancy looped handle 30.00
  11¼″, feathered blue glaze, wavy blue over gray 70.00
Mug, 7″, dark green glaze shading to red, relief border top and bottom . . .   50.00
Pitcher
  4½″, tan, high glaze, marked "Hampshire Pottery" 50.00
  8″, striated matte green, molded leaves 50.00
  9¾″, matte green, molded leaves . .   50.00
Umbrella Stand, 7 x 17⅝″, deep matte green, high relief trailing ivy, textured ground 65.00

Vase
  3¼″, textured lava like brown glaze .   85.00
  5½″, molded leaf dec, green matte glaze, two handles, pedestal base   100.00
  6½″, textured and feathery taupe-brown glaze, marked 75.00
  9 x 15½″, six emb long and wide pointed leaves alternating with six buds, matte green finish, paper label "Hampshire Ware, 1871" 600.00
  9½″, green leaves, yellow ground, marked 100.00
  12½″, beige, taupe runs, marked . . .   160.00

HAND PAINTED CHINA

History: Hand painting on china began in the Victorian era and remained popular through the 1920s. It was considered an accomplished art form for women in the upper and upper middle class households. It developed first in England, but spread rapidly to the Continent and America.

China factories in Europe, America, and the Orient made the blanks. Belleek, Haviland, Limoges, and Rosenthal are among the European firms. American firms include A. H. Hews Co., Cambridge, Massachusetts; Willetts Mfg. Co., Trenton, New Jersey; and Knowles, Taylor and Knowles, East Liverpool, Ohio. Nippon blanks from Japan were used heavily during the early 20th century.

The quality and design of the blank is a key factor in pricing. Some blanks were very elaborate. Many pieces were signed and dated by the artist.

Aesthetics is critical. Value is added to a piece when a decorator goes beyond the standard forms and creates a unique and pleasing design.

Bowl, 9″, sq, flowers, pink and blue dec   40.00
Cake Plate, 10½″, open handles, pastel

Compote, 8⅞″ d, 5½″ h, artist sgd, 1907, $125.00.

ground, deep purple blackberries and
foliage **48.00**
Candlestick, 5¾", pink roses, shaded
yellow and blue ground, gold trim . . **28.00**
Celery Tray, 11 x 6", scrolled rim, pastel
ground, small rust berry dec, artist
sgd, Limoges blank, dated 1899 . . . **60.00**
Cheese Dish, 6¼ x 9", cov, pink floral
sprays, green leaves, pale blue
shaded to white, gold trim, applied
handles **100.00**
Cider Set, pitcher, six handled mugs,
blackberries and foliage on pitcher,
different fruit on each mug, pastel
blue and green ground, 7 pcs **170.00**
Compote, 9⅞ x 5¼", multicolored flow-
ers, romantic landscape, matching pr **200.00**
Cruet, blue and white flowers, matching
stopper **65.00**
Cup, yellow, 1½" figural butterfly on
handle **20.00**
Dresser Tray, 11 x 16", center spray of
multicolored flowers, gold flower
wreath, white ground, pink border,
sgd **80.00**
Hatpin Holder, 6", roses, gold trim, black
ground **48.00**
Jewelry, brooch, tropical scene **20.00**
Pitcher, 6", leaves, gold handle and trim,
Limoges blank **90.00**
Plate, 11", scalloped gold trim border,
pastel yellow single rose, green foliage, artist sgd, Haviland blank, 1901 **65.00**
Platter, 9½ x 14", oval, peasants gathering hay and loading it onto horse
drawn wagon, unmarked Faience
blank **65.00**
Ring Tree, scalloped edge, pink flowers,
T.V. Limoges, France blank **38.00**
Shaving Mug, lady dressed in brown
and white, white plumes and red rib-
bon on hat **65.00**
Sweetmeat, 9" d, reticulated rim, low
pedestal base, deep purple blackberry dec, artist sgd, Haviland blank,
1901 . . . . **60.00**
Toothpick Holder, 2¼ x 2", shaded pink
to blue, pink flowers, gold trim **25.00**
Vase
4¾", floral and gold dec, artist sgd,
Bavarian blank **20.00**
7½", bud, daffodils, Rosenthal blank **45.00**
9½", orange poppies, green leaves,
gold outline and rim **65.00**

HATPINS AND HATPIN HOLDERS

History: When the vogue for oversized hats developed around 1850, hatpins became popular.

Designers used a variety of materials to decorate
the pin ends, including china, crystal, enamel, gem
stones, precious metals, and shells. Decorative
subjects ranged from commemorative designs to
insects.

Hatpin holders are porcelain containers which
set on a dresser to hold these pins. The holders
were produced by major manufacturers, among
which were Meissen, Nippon, R. S. Germany, R.
S. Prussia, and Wedgwood.

Reference: Lillian Baker, *Handbook for Hatpins
& Hatpin Holders,* Collector Books, 1983.

Collector's Club: International Club for Collectors of Hatpins and Hatpin Holders, 15237 Cha-
nera Avenue, Gardena, CA, 90249.

Museum: Los Angeles Art Museum, Costume
Dept., Los Angeles, CA

HATPINS

Art Deco, 1¼" round, ceramic porcelain,
painted, Eye of Horis motif, bezel
mount, brass button type sleeve,
c1920 . . . . **40.00**
Art Nouveau, half clam shell shape, de-
tailed woman in center, marked "ster-
ling front," 7¾" steel pin, c1905 . . . . **75.00**
Brass
Lacy openwork, 10½" l, large rhinestones on dome top **30.00**
Owl, figural **35.00**
Carnival Glass, figural, flying bat, black,
silver luster **32.00**
Crystal, hand cut, blown teardrop shape
inside, attached to 10½" brass pin . . **125.00**
China, pink relief molded flowers **35.00**
Cloisonne, Japanese, foil back, marked
in Japanese script **75.00**
German Silver, beetle, 1½ x 1¼", green
enameled wings and body, red eyes **60.00**
Ivory, 1⅛" elephant, hand carved **90.00**
Jet Glass, 3¼", cut and faceted, riveted
to wire frame, japanned pin shank . . **175.00**
Mosaic, brass button sleeve type me-
tallic mounting, gold wire trim, 8"
brass pin, stamped "GS," c1875 . . . **60.00**
Mother-of-Pearl, 2" d **15.00**
Peacock Eye Glass
Oval head, 7½" steel pin **40.00**
Three sided leaf motif, gilded brass,
peacock eye set atop **75.00**
Porcelain, hp, heavy gold overlay, 7½"
gilt pin, baroque sleeved dec, Victo-
rian motif, c1890 . . . . **90.00**
Rhinestones, 12¼" l, triangular frame,
filigree border, Austria **135.00**
Sterling Silver, ¾" d, figural, cherub . . **50.00**

HATPIN HOLDERS

Bisque, lavender, Art Nouveau style . . **175.00**
China
Austrian, hp rose dec, gold top **55.00**

Hatpin Holder, 5″ h, black ground, blue flowers, gold trim, marked "R. S. Germany," $32.50.

Belleek, hp "E" and floral dec, Willets	**65.00**
Limoges, gold emb border, cream ground	**30.00**
Royal Bayreuth, 4½″ h, Art Nouveau Lady, saucer base, blue mark	**450.00**
Royal Doulton, 6″ h, figural, Sam Weller, earth tone colors, Dickensware	**110.00**
R.S. Prussia, 4¾″ h, roses, luster finish, scalloped base	**235.00**
Schafer & Vater, pink, lady with fan	**225.00**
Nippon, 4″ h, hp pink roses, gold trim	**45.00**
Glass	
Carnival	
Butterfly and Berry pattern, blue, Fenton	**700.00**
Grape and Cable pattern, marigold, Northwood	**150.00**
Chocolate, 7⅞″ h, ftd, c1905	**295.00**
Pottery, 5″ h, hp rooster dec, "Keep Me on the Dressing Table," ftd, Torquay	**85.00**
Silver, 5½″ h, 16 pin holes, etched and engraved, unmarked, c1880	**120.00**

![H&C° L] ![H &C° L FRANCE]

HAVILAND CHINA

History: In 1842, American china importer David Haviland moved to Limoges, France, where he began manufacturing and decorating china specifically for the US market. Haviland is synonymous with fine, white, translucent porcelain although early hand painted patterns were generally larger and darker colored on heavier whiteware blanks than are later ones.

David revolutionized French china factories by both manufacturing the whiteware blank and decorating it at the same site. In addition, Haviland and Company pioneered the use of decals in decorating china.

David's sons, Charles Edward and Theodore split the company in 1892. Theodore opened an American division in 1936 which continues until today. In 1941 Theodore bought out Charles Edward's heirs and recombined both companies under the original name H and Co. The Haviland family sold its interests in 1981.

Charles Field Haviland, cousin of Charles Edward and Theodore, worked for, and then ran, the Casseaux Works after his marriage in 1857 until 1882. Items continued to carry his name as decorator mark until 1941.

Haviland patterns were not consistently named until after 1926. Pattern identification is difficult because of the similarity found in the over 66,000 patterns that have been made. Numbers assigned by Arlene Schleiger and illustrated in her books have become the identification standard for matching.

References: Mary Frank Gaston, *Haviland Collectibles & Art Objects*, Collector Books, 1984; Arlene Schleiger, *Two Hundred Patterns of Haviland China, Books I-V*, published by author, 1950–1977; Serry Wood, *Haviland-Limoges, China Classics II*, Century House, 1951; Harriet Young, *Grandmother's Haviland*, Wallace-Homestead, 1970.

Advisor: Peg Harrison.

Boullion Cup and Saucer, gold trim, emb fleur-de-lis, marked "G. D. A. France, G. B. Field Haviland, Limoges," $30.00.

Bouillon Cup and Saucer, small green flowers and leaves	**25.00**
Bowl	
5″, fruit, pink flowers, blue ribbon	**9.50**
5½″, fruit, Greek key design, black and yellow	**12.00**

7½", soup, apple blossom design,
scalloped edge **14.00**
Butter Dish
  2 pc, gold and white scalloped edge
    with bow forming handle **40.00**
  3 pc, Silver Anniversary pattern . . . **55.00**
Butter Pat, pansy-ragged robin, 1891
  mark **10.00**
Cake Plate, 10", blue flower spray, gold
  handles **40.00**
Coffeepot
  Blue and pink roses, individual **65.00**
  White and gold, rope handle, 1885
    mark **195.00**
Compote
  7" d, 3½" h, blue and pink flowers,
    smooth edges **40.00**
  9" d, 2¾" h, blue and pink flowers,
    gold scalloped **55.00**
Cream Soup and Saucer, Autumn Leaf
  pattern **25.00**
Creamer and Sugar, yellow floral spray,
  medium size **50.00**
Cup and Saucer
  Coffee, Moss Rose, 1885 mark **37.50**
  4 o'clock, pink flowers, green scroll . **25.00**
  Tea, pink roses, blue ribbon **35.00**
Demitasse Cup and Saucer, small
  green and red flowered border **25.00**
Dinner Set
  Service for 8, pale lavender and gold
    floral spray, scalloped edge, 63 pcs **895.00**
  Service for 12, gold scalloped edge,
    62 pcs **1,000.00**
Gravy Boat
  Oval, green and gold geometric de-
    sign, cov, attached tray **45.00**
  Round, gold band, attached tray . . . **35.00**
Plate
  6", biscuit, cobalt border design with
    deep pink flowers **10.00**
  7½", bread and butter, Clover pattern **16.00**
  8½", salad, pink flowers, green scroll,
    border pattern **14.00**
  9", luncheon, rose flowered border,
    cream edge **14.00**
  9¾", dinner, pink and yellow roses,
    scalloped edge **18.00**
  Oyster, blue and pink flowers, shell
    edge indentations **45.00**
Pitcher
  7", milk, gold and white **45.00**
  9", water, pink flowers **75.00**
Platter
  12", gold trim, smooth edge **35.00**
  16", blue flowers, gold scalloped edge **55.00**
  22", turquoise flowers around gold
    scalloped edge **65.00**
Ramekin and Saucer, green geometric
  design, gold edge **25.00**
Relish, white, scattered pink flowers,
  scalloped **30.00**

Soup Plate, 9½", small pink and blue
  flowers **18.00**
Vegetable Dish
  Oval, gold scalloped edge, cov **55.00**
  Round, pink apple blossoms, heavy
    gold handles **50.00**

HEISEY GLASS (H)

History: The A. H. Heisey Glass Co. began producing glasswares in April, 1896, in Newark, Ohio. Heisey was not a newcomer to the field, having been associated with the craft since his youth. Many blown and molded patterns were produced in crystal, colored, milk (opalescent), and Ivorina Verde (custard) glass. Decorative techniques of cutting, etching, and silver deposit were employed. Glass figurines were introduced in 1933 and continued until 1957 when the factory ceased production. All Heisey glass is notable for its clarity. Not all Heisey glassware is marked with the familiar "H" within a diamond.

References: Neila Bredehoft, *The Collector's Encyclopedia of Heisey Glass, 1925–1938,* Collector Books, 1986; Mary Louise Burns, *Heisey's Glassware of Distinction,* 2nd edition, published by author, 1983; Lyle Conder, *Collector's Guide To Heisey's Glassware for Your Table,* L-W Books, 1984; Tom Felt and Bob O'Grady, *Heisey Candlesticks, Candelabra, and Lamps,* Heisey Collectors of America, Inc, 1984; Sandra Stoudt, *Heisey On Parade,* Wallace-Homestead, 1985.

Collectors' Club: Heisey Collectors of America, P. O. Box 27, Newark, OH, 43055. *Heisey News* monthly.

Museum: National Heisey Glass Museum, Newark, OH.

Reproduction Alert: Some Heisey molds were sold to Imperial Glass of Bellaire, Ohio, and certain items were reissued. These pieces may be mistaken for the original Heisey. Some of the reproductions were produced in colors which were never made by Heisey and have become collectible in their own right.

Examples include: the Colt family in Crystal, Carmel Slag, Ultra Blue, and Horizon Blue: the mallard with wings up in Carmel Slag; Whirlpool (Provincial) in crystal and colors; and, Waverly, 7" oval footed compote in Carmel Slag.

Animal
  Asiatic Pheasant, sgd **240.00**
  Cygnet, sgd **125.00**
  Fighting Rooster **125.00**
  Goose, wings ½ **60.00**
  Goose, wings down **300.00**
  Mallard, wings ½ **140.00**
  Plug Horse **65.00**
  Pony, sitting **100.00**
  Ring Neck Pheasant **145.00**

Scottie	90.00
Sparrow	60.00

Ashtray

Crystolite, coaster, zircon, sgd	65.00
Empress, Sahara	75.00
Horsehead	45.00
Kohinoor, zircon, sgd	85.00
Basket, 7½", Lariat	75.00
Beer Mug, club drinking scene, 16 oz	125.00
Bitters Bottle, Puritan, paper label	40.00
Bookends, fish, pr	140.00

Bowl

Beaded Panel & Sunburst, 8", ftd	85.00
Empress, 10", oval, moongleam, sgd	50.00
Fish, figural	300.00
Hawthorne, 10"	85.00
Kalonyal, 9", ftd, sgd	225.00
Lodestar, 4", dawn, sgd	37.50
Pineapple & Fan, 8"	35.00
Rose, 12", etched, flared, crimped	50.00
Box, cov, 4¾", puff, Crystolite, sgd	48.00

Butter, cov

Locket on Chain	195.00
Orchid	125.00
Plantation, round, sgd	75.00
Victorian	40.00

Powder Box, 5″ d, Crystolite, $48.00.

Candle Block

Lariat, single	9.50
Ridgeleigh, pr	30.00

Candlesticks, pr

New Era, 2 lights	90.00
Orchid, mercury	55.00
Plantation, 3 lights	165.00
Thumbprint & Panel, 2 lights, moongleam	175.00

Champagne

Narrow Flute, 5 oz, sgd	12.00
Shasta, George IV cutting	28.00
Wabash, 6 oz, Mayflower etch, orig saucer	25.00
Cigarette Box, Puritan, horse head	45.00

Cigarette Holder

Crystolite, ftd	18.00
Ridgeleigh, sq	10.00
Cigarette Lighter, Crystolite	9.50

Cocktail

Aqua Caliente, Sahara, sgd	20.00
Banded Flute	11.00
Goose stem	175.00
Rooster	45.00

Cologne

Crystolite, 4 oz	65.00
Fairacre, 1 oz, flamingo	125.00

Compote

Albermarle, 7", Old Colony Plate etch, Sahara, ftd	65.00
Empress, 7", oval, crystal	35.00
Plantation, 8½"	38.00
Trojan, 7", flamingo	60.00

Creamer and Sugar

Empress, Sahara	50.00
Lariat, etched	25.00
Octagon, sgd	30.00
Orchid, ind size, sgd	85.00
Pleat & Panel, flamingo, sgd	65.00
Queen Ann, ind size, flamingo	45.00
Ridgeleigh, ind size, sgd	30.00
Waverly, Narcissus cut, sgd	50.00

Cruet

Greek Key, crystal, 2 oz	80.00
Pineapple and Gold Fan, green	175.00
Twist, 2½ oz	65.00
Cup and Saucer, Queen Ann, Orchid etch	40.00

Demitasse Cup and Saucer

Polo Player, etched, aqua	45.00
Yeoman, sgd	30.00

Goblet

Kimberly, 10 oz, Courtship cutting	40.00
Old Dominion, 8 oz, Trojan etch	22.00
Symphone, Danish Princess cut	32.50
Twist, 9 oz, flamingo, etched	25.00
Tyrolean, Orchid etch	28.00
Hair Receiver, Fan, sq, SS top	70.00

Ice Tub

Octagon, moongleam	85.00
Ridgeleigh, sgd	55.00
Twist, moongleam, sgd	85.00

Iced Tea

Cabachon, amber, crystal bowl	65.00
Pied Piper etch	12.00

Jelly Compote

Coarse Rib, 5", low ftd, moongleam, sgd	47.50
Greek Key, 5", low ftd, sgd	45.00
Orchid Etch, 7", ftd	60.00
Lemon Server, cov, Empress, 6", oval	30.00
Marmalade Jar, Puritan, mushroom stopper	40.00

Mayonnaise

Orchid etch, 3 pcs	100.00
Plantation, crystal, ftd, 3 pcs	75.00

Mustard, cov
Coarse Rib, flashed, sgd	50.00
Narrow Flute, sgd	32.50
Queen Anne, cov, paddle	35.00
Victorian	30.00
Whirlpool, sgd	38.00
Nappy, Twist, 4", flamingo	12.00

Nut Dish, individual
Empress, alexandrite	85.00
Lariat, sgd	12.00
Narrow Flute, silver dec	22.50

Oyster Cocktail
Kohinoor	8.00
Shasta, George IV cutting, 4"	22.00
Parfait, Old Sandwich	30.00

Pitcher, water
Crystolite, silver overlay	80.00
Lodestar, Dawn	90.00
Swan, crystal	350.00

Plate
Beehive, 4", flamingo	15.00
Grape, 10½", cut dec, divided	225.00
Empress, 7", sq, tangerine, sgd	200.00
Old Sandwich, 6", moongleam, sgd	15.00
Orchid, 10½"	65.00
Platter, Lariat, silverplated ship dec	50.00

Punch Set, Puritan, 13" ftd bowl, twelve
cups	200.00

Relish
Orchid, 11", 3 part	60.00
Queen Ann, 7", 3 part, floral & leaf cut	28.00
Rose Bowl, Pillows, ftd	100.00

Salt and Pepper Shakers, pr
Plantation	45.00
Ridgeleigh	45.00

Sandwich Plate, Yoeman, 10½", han-
dle, 1" gold overlay and enamel dec	45.00

Sherbet
Ipswich	12.00
Orchid etch	30.00
Rose etch	30.00
Wabash, Frontenac etch, hawthorne, low, sgd	24.00

Soda Glass
Polo Player, etched, 8 oz	35.00
Shasta, George IV cutting, 6 oz, ftd	22.00
Winchester, 18 oz	155.00
Spooner, Peerless, gold trim	40.00

Toothpick
Fandango	115.00
Prince of Wales Plume, sgd	135.00

Tumbler
Banded Flute	19.00
Old Sandwich, crystal	4.00
Prison Stripe, sgd	75.00
Victorian, barrel, sgd	25.00
Winged Scroll, custard	48.00

Vase
Empress, 9", moongleam	135.00
Punty & Diamond Point, 10"	40.00
Rooster, figural	70.00

Warwick, 7"	20.00

Wine
Park Lane	25.00
Saxony, Sahara	30.00
Symphone, Minuet etch	45.00
Victorian, sgd	20.00
Wabash, wide optic, sgd	12.00

HOLLY AMBER

History: Holly Amber, originally called Golden Agate, was produced by the Indiana Tumbler and Goblet Works of the National Glass Co., Greentown, Indiana. Jacob Rosenthal created the color in 1902. Holly Amber is a gold colored glass with a marbleized onyx color on raised parts.

A new pattern, Holly [No. 450], was designed by Frank Jackson for Golden Agate. Between January 1903 and June 1903, more than 35 items were made in this pattern; the factory was destroyed by fire in June.

References: Brenda Measell and James Measell, *A Guide To Reproductions of Greentown Glass*, 2nd ed., The Printing Press, 1974; James Measell, *Greentown Glass, The Indiana Tumbler & Goblet Co.*, Grand Rapids Public Museum, 1979.

Collectors' Club: National Greentown Glass Association, P. O. Box 508037, Cicero, IL 60650. *N.G.G.A. Newsletter*, quarterly.

Museums: Greentown Glass Museum, Greentown, IN; Grand Rapids Public Museum [Ruth Herrick Greentown Glass Collection], MI.

Additional Listing: Greentown Glass.

Compote, 7⅜" d, 6¾" h, $850.00.

Bowl
7½ x 4½ x 2", oval	360.00
8"	450.00
Butter Dish, cov, 7¼ x 6¼"	1,200.00
Compote, cov, 8½ x 12"	1,800.00
Creamer, 4½"	600.00

Cruet, 6½" h	2,100.00
Mug, 4½" h, handled	535.00
Nappy	375.00
Sauce Dish	225.00
Spooner	425.00
Sugar, open	425.00
Syrup, 5¾" h, SP hinged lid	2,000.00
Tray, water, round	600.00
Tumbler	385.00
Vase, 6"	425.00

HORN

History: For centuries horns from animals have been used for various items, e.g., drinking cups, spoons, powder horns, and small dishes. Some pieces of horn have designs scratched in them. Around 1880 furniture made from the horns of Texas longhorn steers was popular in Texas and the southwestern United States.

Additional Listings: Firearm Accessories.

Tablespoon, tapered handle, $17.50.

Beaker
3¼, name incised at lip, pattern of dots	40.00
6½", scratch carved compass star	50.00
Box, cov, 2¾", brass hinges	30.00
Cup, 3 x 5", scratch carved hunting scenes, applied handle	75.00

Furniture
Chair, arm, cowhide cov seat and back, longhorn top splat, U shaped back connected by smaller horns, twelve horns form legs and base, pr	2,000.00
Foot Stool, velvet upholstered seat, horn legs	150.00
Ladle, scratch carved reindeer in bowl	100.00
Offering Box, 7¼ x 3½ x 2", hanging type, slant top, arched back	40.00

Snuff Box, 1¾", wood plug, ring handle	48.00
Tumbler, 2½" h	20.00
Wall Hanging, 72" l, Texas longhorn steer, mounted in bound leather, wood base	125.00

HULL POTTERY

History: In 1905 Addis E. Hull purchased the Acme Pottery Company, Crooksville, Ohio. In 1917 the A. E. Hull Pottery Company began making a line of art pottery, novelties, stoneware, and kitchenware, later including the famous Little Red Riding Hood line. Most items had a matte finish with shades of pink and blue or brown predominating.

After a disasterous flood and fire in 1950, J. Brandon Hull reopened the factory in 1952 as the Hull Pottery Company. New, more modern style molds, mostly with glossy finish, were produced. The company currently produces pieces, e.g. the Regal and Floraline lines, for sale to florists.

Hull pottery molds and patterns are easily identified. Pre-1950 vases are marked "Hull USA" or "Hull Art USA" on the bottom. Many also retain their paper labels. Post-1950 pieces are marked "Hull" in large script or "HULL" in block letters.

Each pattern has a distinctive number, e.g., Wildflower with a "W" and number, Waterlily with an "L" and number, Poppy with 600 numbers, Orchid with 300 numbers, etc. Early stone pieces have an H.

References: Brenda Roberts, *The Collectors Encyclopedia Of Hull Pottery,* Collector Books, 1980.

Additional Listings: See *Warman's Americana & Collectibles* for more examples.

Advisor: Joan Hull.

Pitcher, 4¾" h, pink shaded to blue ground, yellow and red flowers, marked "Hull, USA, 14-43/4," $18.00.

PRE-1950 (MATTE)

Bowknot
Bowl, B-18, 5¾"	12.00
Candleholder, B-17, 3½", pr	15.00
Ewer, B-1, 5½", green to blue	40.00
Jardiniere, B-15, 5¾", green to blue	45.00
Teapot, B-20, 6"	30.00
Vase, B-8, 8½"	50.00

Calla Lily
Cornucopia, 570/33, 8", turquoise and cream	50.00
Vase, 560/33, 13"	70.00

Dogwood
Bowl, 521, 7", cream	35.00
Jardiniere, 516, 4¾", blue to pink, orig label	25.00
Vase, 516, 4¾", turquoise to cream .	25.00

Iris
Ewer, 13"	150.00
Jardiniere, 413, 5½", blue to pink . .	35.00
Vase, bud, 410, 7½", peach	40.00

Little Red Riding Hood
Bank, 7"	250.00
Cookie Jar, folded basket, 13"	75.00
Creamer, imp "Pat Des-No 135889"	10.00
Mustard, spoon, 5¼"	150.00
Pitcher, open head, 8"	150.00
Salt and Pepper, pr, imp "Pat Des-No 135889"	15.00

Magnolia
Basket, 10, 10½"	35.00
Candleholder, 27, 4", blue to pink, pr	35.00
Creamer and Sugar, 24 and 25, 3¾", brown to yellow, set	65.00
Lamp Base, 12½"	150.00
Pitcher, H-3, 5½"	12.50
Teapot, H-20, 6½"	30.00
Vase, 2, 8½", blue to pink	40.00

Mardi Gras/Granada
Basket, 65, 8"	40.00
Planter, 204, 6"	30.00
Vase, 216, 9"	45.00

Novelty
Bank, Piggy, emb florals, 14"	40.00
Casserole, Cinderella, 7½"	25.00
Shaving Mug, Old Spice, 3"	25.00

Orchid
Bookends, 316, 7", pr	400.00
Bowl, 314, 13"	75.00
Candy Dish, cov, 158	15.00
Vase, 308, 4¼"	25.00

Poppy
Basket, 601, 12"	7.50
Bowl, 608, 4¾"	5.00
Ewer, 610, 4¾"	50.00
Wall Pocket, 609, 9"	75.00

Rosella
Cornucopia, R-13, 8½"	35.00
Creamer and Sugar, R-4, 5½"	60.00
Wall Pocket, R-10, 6½"	30.00

Tulip
Vase, 100-33	
6½"	12.00
10"	18.00

Wildflower
Creamer, 73, 4¾", Sugar, 74, 4¾", and Teapot, 72, 8", set	400.00
Pitcher, W-2, 5½"	10.00
Vase, W-15-10½, 10½"	40.00

Woodland
Basket, W-9	45.00
Console Bowl, W-29	20.00
Cornucopia, W-10, 11"	35.00
Flowerpot and attached saucer, 5¾"	50.00

POST-1950

Blossom Flite
Basket, T-8, 8¼"	40.00
Cornucopia, T-6, 10¼", pink and charcoal	35.00
Planter, T-12, 10½", pink and charcoal	50.00

Butterfly
Ashtray, 7"	25.00
Basket, T-2	10.00
Bonbon, 6½"	25.00
Honey Jug, T-1	15.00
Pitcher, 8¾"	35.00
Teapot, T-14	15.00

Capri
Pitcher, 6¼"	25.00
Urn, 9"	30.00

Continental
Console Bowl, 51	10.00
Vase, strawberry design, imp "Hull USA 46"	15.00

Ebb Tide
Console Bowl, E-12	12.00
Creamer, E-15	7.50
Sugar, cov, E-16	7.50
Vase, E-6, fish	12.00

Imperial
Madonna, F-7, 7"	25.00
Planter, F-475, praying hands, 6" . .	25.00

Royal
Basket, W-9, 8¾"	25.00
Vase, 10¾"	25.00
Window Box, 82, 12½"	30.00

Serenade
Ashtray, S-23	15.00
Cookie Jar, imp "Hull USA O-18" . .	20.00
Sugar, cov, S-19	7.50
Planter, S-4	15.00

Tuscany
Candy Dish, 9, 8½"	25.00
Ewer, 13, 12"	50.00
Leaf Dish, 19, 13"	30.00

Woodland, glossy glaze
Candleholder, pr, W-30	12.00
Console Bowl, W-29	15.00
Jardiniere, W-7, 5½"	75.00
Pitcher Vase, W-6, 6½"	10.00

1935 1950

1957 ©by W. Goebel W. Germany 1964

Goebel Goebel

1972 1979

HUMMEL ITEMS

History: Hummel items are the original creations of Berta Hummel, born in 1909 in Massing, Bavaria, Germany. At age 18, she was enrolled in the Academy of Fine Arts in Munich to further her mastery of drawing and the palette. Berta entered the Convent of Siessen and became Sister Maria Inconnentia in 1934. In this Franciscan cloister, she continued drawing and painting images of her childhood friends.

In 1935 W. Goebel Co. in Rodental, Germany, began reproducing Sister Berta's sketches into 3 dimensional bisque figurines. The Schmid Brothers of Randolph, Massachusetts, introduced the figurines to America and became Goebel's U.S. distributor.

In 1967 Goebel began distributing Hummel items in the U.S. A controversy developed between the two companies involving the Hummel family and the convent. Law suits and countersuits ensued. The German courts finally effected a compromise. The convent held legal rights to all works produced by Sister Berta from 1934 until her death in 1946 and licensed Goebel to reproduce these works. Schmid was to deal directly with the Hummel family for permission to reproduce any preconvent art.

All authentic Hummels bear both the signature, M.I. Hummel, and a Goebel trademark. Various trademarks were used to identify the year of production. The Crown Mark (CM) was used in 1935, Full Bee (FB) 1940–1959; Small Stylized Bee (SSB) 1960–1972; Large Stylized Bee (LSB) 1960–1963; Three Line Mark (3L) 1964–1972; Last Bee Mark (LB) 1972–1980, Missing Bee Mark (MB) 1979–Present.

References: John F. Hotchkiss, *Hummel Art II*, Wallace-Homestead, 1981; Carl F. Luckey, *Hummel Figurines and Plates, 7th Edition*, Books Americana, 1984; Lawrence L. Wonsch, *Hummel Copycats With Values*, Wallace-Homestead, 1987.

Collectors' Clubs: Goebel Collectors' Club, 105 White Plains Road, Tarrytown, NY 10591. Insight quarterly newsletter; Hummel Collectors Club, 1261 University Drive, Yardley, PA 19067.

Additional Listings: See *Warman's Americana & Collectibles* for more examples.

Ashtray

Boy with bird, #166, FB, 6¼ x 3¼" .		120.00
Joyful, , #33, FB, 6 x 3½"		150.00
Let's Sing, #114, CM, 3½ x 6¾" . . .		300.00

Bookends, pr

Farm Boy and Goose Girl, #60/A & B, CM, 6"		800.00
Strolling Along, #5, CM		275.00

Candleholder

Herald Angels, #37, SB, 4"		125.00
Silent Night, #54, FB, 5½ x 4¾" . . .		250.00
Watchful Angel, #194, FB, 6½"		400.00

Candy Box

Chick Girl, #III/57, SB, 5¼"		225.00
Happy Pastime, #III/69, 3L, 6"		115.00
Joyful, #III/53, 3L, 6¼"		110.00
Singing Lesson, #III/63, CM, 5¼" . .		500.00

Dealer Plaque, #187, FB 800.00

Figure, 5¼" h, Postman, #119, marked "Goebel, W. Germany," $85.00.

Figurine

A Fair Measure, #345, LB	82.00
Angelic Song, #144, FB	105.00
Be Patient, #197/2/0, FB	125.00
Bird Watcher, #300, LB	65.00
Busy Student, #367	50.00
Celestial Musician, #188	80.00
Chicken Licken, #385, 3L	100.00
Close Harmony, #336	90.00
Confidentially, #314, LB	70.00
Coquette, #179, SB	105.00
Cow, #214-K, LB	45.00
Crossroads, #331, LB	130.00
Donkey, #214-J, LB	30.00
Drummer, #240, FB	90.00
Easter Time, #384, LB	85.00
Farewell, #65, LB	80.00
Feathered Friends, #344	80.00
Flower Madonna, color, #10/1, FB .	300.00
Flower Madonna, white, #10/1, FB .	125.00
Flower Vendor, #381	75.00
Girl With Sheet Music, #389, LB . . .	25.00
Going to Grandma's, #51/1, SM, 6"	300.00
Good Shepherd, #42/1, FB, 7½" . . .	2,000.00

Goose Girl, #47/3/0, LB 80.00
Happy Birthday, #176/0, FB, 5½" . . 200.00
Happy Pastime, #69 . . . . 45.00
Latest News, #184, LB 135.00
Letter to Santa, #340 . . . . 110.00
Little Bookkeeper, #306, LB 70.00
Little Fiddler, #4, LB 50.00
Little Pharmacist, #332, 3L 90.00
Little Thrifty, #188, LB 132.00
Mail's Here, #126, LB 300.00
Merry Wanderer, #11/0, FB 175.00
Mountaineer, #315, 3L 90.00
On Secret Path, #386, LB 75.00
Out of Danger, #56/B, FB, 6¼" 2,500.00
Playmates, #58/0, FM, 2" 150.00
School Girls, #177/I, SM, 7½" 800.00
She Loves Me, She Loves Me Not,
  #174, FM, 4¼" 200.00
Shepherd Boy, #2146, 3L 50.00
Singing Lesson, #63, LB 65.00
Sister, #98, CM, 4¾" 300.00
Smart Little Sister, #346, 3L 90.00
Stargazer, #132, LB 110.00
Street Singer, #131, LB 45.00
The Run-A-Way, #327, LB 80.00
Which Hand, #258, LB 45.00
Font
Angel with bird, #167, FB, 4¼ x 3¼" 50.00
Devotion, #147, SB, 5 x 3" 35.00
Guardian Angel, #248, 3L, 2¼ x 5½" 40.00
Holy Family, #246, SB, 3 x 4" 60.00
Seated Angel, #167, FB, 3¼ x 4¼" 70.00
White Angel, #75, SB, 3½ x 1¾" . . 30.00
Worship, #84, SB, 4¾ x 2¾" 45.00
Music Box, Little Band, with candle,
  #388M, 3L 250.00
Nativity Set
12 pcs, #214 A-O, current 700.00
16 pcs, #260, A-R, wood stable, cur-
  rent 2,875.00
Plaque
Ba-Bee Rings, #30 A-B, CM, 5" d, pr 400.00
Flirting Butterfly, #139, CM, 2½" . . . 250.00
Mail Coach, #140, LB, 4½ x 6¼" . . 130.00
Merry Wanderer, #92, FB, 4¾ x 5⅛" 185.00
Swaying Lullaby, #165, CM, 5¼ x
  4½" 850.00
Vacation Time, #125, CM, 5¼ x 4⅜" 550.00

IMARI

History: Imari derives its name from a Japanese
port city. Although Imari ware was manufactured
in the 17th century, the wares most commonly
encountered are those made between 1770 and
1900.

Early Imari was decorated simply, quite unlike
the later heavily decorated brocade pattern commonly associated with Imari. Most of the decorative patterns are an underglaze blue and overglaze
"seal wax" red supported by turquoise and yellow.

The Chinese copied Imari ware. Important differences of the Japanese type include grayer clay,
thicker glaze, runny and darker blue, and deep red
opaque hues.

The pattern and colors of Imari inspired many
English and European potteries, such as Derby
and Meissen, to adopt a similar style of decoration
for their wares.

Reference: Sandra Andacht, *Oriental Antiques
& Art: An Identification And Value Guide,* Wallace-
Homestead, 1987.

Reproduction Alert: Reproductions abound,
and many manufacturers continue to produce
pieces in the traditional style.

**Vase, 9½" h, blue dec of birds flying
over water, blue top border, white
ground, $140.00.**

Bowl
6½" d, blue, scalloped top, Tree pat-
  tern 125.00
7⅜" d, 3" h, polychrome enameling . 40.00
11" d, 3¾" h, polychrome, scalloped
  rim 300.00
12½" d, 4" h, blue and white 110.00
14" d, center painted flower bouquet,
  panels of flowers on everted rim,
  18th C 850.00
Cache Pot, 9½", sq, blue and white,
  birds flying over water, chamfered
  corners, scroll and floral border, ftd . 175.00
Charger
14½" d, gilt, underglaze blue, and colored enamel painted, central floral
  medallion, dark blue ground, gilt
  leafy scrolls, foliate edge, impressed "Yamatoku" 450.00
16⅜" d, blue and white, floral 225.00
18½" d, 3" h, blue and white, scal-
  loped rim 350.00
Chop Plate, 11¾" d, polychrome
  enamel 25.00
Cup, 3½" d, blue iris, gold outline, 1860 35.00

Dish

3¼", sq, eight white impressed mums, 1860 . . . . **30.00**

5½" d, blue, red, and gold, mums and butterflies panels **90.00**

Hibachi, 15¼" d, 11" h, blue and white, hand dec pine and bamboo medallions, shoreline scenes, reserved brown berries, floral transfer pattern rim and base, 1880 . . . . **750.00**

Jar, 24¾", cov, baluster shape, phoenix birds in flight and blossoming peony branches rising from open fence, lappet borders, blue bud knop, Chinese, Kangxi Period **3,750.00**

Plate

4¾" d, blue, red, green, and gold, pinwheel pattern, 1860 . . . . **120.00**

8½" d, dark blue, dark red, green, and gold, two multicolored dragon medallions, squirrel and melon vine panels, 1830 . . . . **175.00**

11", sq, blue and white, hp shoreline scene **140.00**

16" d, deep blue, red, and orange, peony center, three panels of mums on trellis, 1860 . . . . **1,000.00**

Platter, 10½ x 12", rect, hp shoreline scene, trees, and flowers, diapering **130.00**

Sake Cup, 2¼" d, 1½" h, scenic view of flowers, medallions, red-gold **40.00**

Tray, 6½" l, blue shoreline scene, gold accents, 1870 . . . . **60.00**

Urn, winged dragon and fantasy animals design, blue and underglaze red **375.00**

Vase

9½" h, blue birds flying over water on white ground, blue dec top **140.00**

18⅛" h, baluster form, red and blue, gold accents, tree peonies and flinches dec, flared rim, base and shoulder band dec, late 19th C, Japan **400.00**

IMPERIAL GLASS

History: Imperial Glass Co., Bellaire, Ohio, was organized in 1901. Its primary product was pattern (pressed) glass. Soon other lines were added including carnival glass, NUART, NUCUT, and NEAR CUT. In 1916 the company introduced "Free-Hand," a lustred art glass line, and "Imperial Jewels," an iridescent stretch glass that carried the Imperial cross trademark. In the 1930s the company was reorganized into the Imperial Glass Corporation and continues to produce a great variety of wares.

Imperial recently has acquired the molds and equipment of several other glass companies–Central, Cambridge and Heisey. Many of the "retired" molds of these companies are once again in use. The resulting reissues are marked to distinguish them from the originals.

Reference: Margaret and Douglas Archer, *Imperial Glass,* Collector Books, 1978.

Collectors' Club: National Imperial Glass Collectors Society, Box 534, Bellaire, OH 43906.

Additional Listings: See Carnival Glass, Pattern Glass, and *Warman's Americana & Collectibles* for more examples of Candlewick.

Vase, 6" h, blue body, white opalescent webbing and leaves, $235.00.

ENGRAVED OR HAND CUT

Bowl

6½", flower and leaf, molded star base **20.00**

9½", 3 sprays with flowers, molded star base **30.00**

Celery Vase, 3 side stars, cut star base **25.00**

Pitcher, 6", daisies, molded star base . **40.00**

Tumbler, buzz star dec **18.00**

JEWELS

Bowl, 9 x 4", irid amber **75.00**

Compote, 7½", irid teal blue **50.00**

Creamer, amethyst, pearl, and green luster **65.00**

Plate, 8", irid pale green **45.00**

Vase, 8", flared rim, irid silver, mulberry ground **120.00**

LUSTERED (FREE HAND)

Candlesticks, pr, 10¾", cobalt, white vine and leaf dec	325.00
Lamp Shade, 5", Art Nouveau, irid ivory, gold, and green feather pattern, colored threading, sgd	175.00
Rose Bowl, 6", irid orange, white floral cutting	65.00
Vase	
5", flared, blue and gold, textured irid finish	115.00
7", allover swirls, blue and white, white int.	150.00
8", irid red, ruffled trumpet top, irid brown stretched throat, verre de soie foot	230.00
10", blue and ruby irid, leaves and veins dec, cobalt blue foot	175.00
11", irid emerald green, imbedded white hearts and vines, orange luster throat, label	300.00

NUART

Lamp Shade	
Crystal, frosted int., cluster electric type, flower etching	25.00
Pearl ruby, fan and star etching	35.00

NUCUT

Bowl	
7½", berry	20.00
10¾", salad	32.00
Compote, 5½"	22.00
Creamer	12.00
Fern Dish, 8"	35.00
Nappy, 6", heart shape	20.00
Tumbler	15.00

PRESSED

Animal Dish, cov, milk glass, rabbit on nest, 4½"	25.00
Bowl	
8", blue, Empress, sq	22.00
9", milk glass, Roses pattern	12.50
Candlesticks, dolphin, blue, pr	28.00
Cheese Dish, Candlewick	0.00
Cologne Bottle, milk glass, blue, Hobnail, ruffled, stopper, pr	24.00
Compote, cov, red slag, satin, Herringbone pattern	15.00
Creamer, ftd, caramel slag	18.00
Cruet, Fancy Colonial, pink	30.00
Cup and Saucer, milk glass, grapes	5.00
Figure	
Bulldog	30.00
Scotty	45.00
Tiger, jade green	15.00
Goblet, 5½", Tradition, crystal	10.00

Jar, Cape Cod, peanut butter, lid, handle	65.00
Mug, red slag, robin	16.00
Pitcher, red slag, Windmill, pint	40.00
Plate, 7½", pink, Fancy Colonial	9.00
Rose Bowl, amber opal, oval, Lace Edge	25.00
Sherbet, ruby, Mt Vernon	5.00
Sugar, cov, Lace Edge, green opal	18.00
Swan, 4¾", amethyst	18.00
Toothpick, ivory, orig label	12.00

INDIAN ARTIFACTS, AMERICAN

History: During the historic period there were approximately 350 tribes of Indians, grouped into the following regions: Eskimo, Northeast and Woodland, Northwest Coast, Plains, and West and Southwest.

American Indian artifacts are quite popular. Currently the market is in a period of stability following a rapid increase of prices during the 1970s.

References: John W. Barry, *American Indian Pottery, 2nd Edition,* Books Americana, 1984; Lar Hothem, *Arrowheads & Projectile Points,* Collector Books, 1983; Lar Hothem, *North American Indian Artifacts, 3rd Edition,* Books Americana, 1984; *North American Indian Points,* Books Americana, 1984; Noel D. Justice, *Stone Age Spear And Arrow Points Of the Midcontinental and Eastern United States,* Indiana University Press, 1987; Sarah and William Turnbaugh, *Indian Baskets,* Schiffer Publishing, 1986.

Periodical: American Indian Basketry Magazine, P.O. Box 66124, Portland, OR 97266.

Note: American Indian artifacts listed below are objects made on the North American continent during the pre-historic and historic periods.

ESKIMO

Basket, trinket, 4¾ x 4¼", cylindrical, bands of color silk dec, finely woven, knop finial on lid, Aleut	1,000.00
Figure, 4" h, hunter, black stone, carved, incised detail	85.00
Knife, 13" l, antler, inscribed reindeer figures and geometric design, missing leather binding	25.00
Pants, 32" l, leather and baby reindeer fur, red velvet and felt trim, drawstring waist	20.00
Pipe, 10", ivory, engraved, 19th C	600.00

NORTHEAST AND WOODLANDS

Bowl, ceremonial, wood, carved masks at each end, False Face Society, Seneca, 19th C	6,000.00
Moccasins, child's, velvet cuff, beaded vamp, Iroquois	25.00

Pouch, 3½ x 4", black velvet, multico-
lored beads **60.00**
War Club, round, tin and feather dangle,
wood handle, 20th C, Iroquois **25.00**

NORTHWEST COAST

Basket, 16 x 25", imbricated design,
stitches missing **180.00**
Belt, 40¼" l, buffalo hide, 2 crosses,
brass and silver tacks form band, Nez
Perce **360.00**
Dish, 6¾" l, 2" h, stone paint, carved
frog, mounted on acrylic base **600.00**
Knife, fighting, ivory, carved, iron blade,
Tlingit **3,900.00**
Pipe, ceremonial, argilite, carved goat
head, thunderbird, and 3 human
faces, metal bowl, incised lid, mid
19th C, Haida **3,300.00**
Totem Pole, 56" h, 44" wing span, po-
lychrome paint **4,100.00**

PLAINS

Awl Case, 1½" w, 11" l, beaded, dark
blue, white ground, dentallium shell,
brass button closure, tin cone dan-
gles **125.00**
Basket, swing handle, Winnebago . . . **65.00**
Cradle Board, 21" l, deerskin cov board,
floral beading, fully clothed doll,
Blackfoot **650.00**
Doll, rag, 7½" h, horsehair hair, beaded
features, painted and fringed cloth
outfit **95.00**
Hammer, 8½" l, stone, rawhide cov
head and handle **185.00**
Headdress, 18" l, dyed feathers tipped
with red, loom beaded head band,
leather base **50.00**
Moccasins, 9½" l, yellow, red, and blue
beaded diamond, green ground,
Sioux **145.00**
Quirt, 31" l, blue, red and white heart,
gold translucent and multicolor bead
wrapping, dyed red horsehair end,
Sioux **45.00**
Quiver, 24" l, 40" l, bow case buckskin,
pierced geometric design, red stroud
trim, six steel tipped arrows, broken
strap **1,050.00**
Pouch
6" l, blue, red, yellow and white
beads, tin cone dangles **55.00**
9" l, smoked elkhide, yellow, white,
red, and blue beads, Sioux **85.00**
Rattle, 15½" l, multistripe, silver scratch
design, horsehair crest, string tassel,
silver base, beaded handle, Arapaho **100.00**
Skull Cracker, 36" l, blue and yellow
beaded design, sinew sewn, handle
attachments **675.00**

Water Jug, 9⅝", Cochiti Pueblo, New
Mexico, earthtones, c1910, $175.00.

WEST AND SOUTHWEST

Baking Basket, 11" d, 1¾" h, wire, Pa-
pago **65.00**
Basket
10" d, 5½" h, deep sloping sides, martynia and willow design, Pima . . . **140.00**
3½ x 7", 4" h, ovoid, black martynia
and willow fret design, Pima **100.00**
Blanket, 50 x 80", wool, multicolor design, gray ground, Chimayo **75.00**
Bracelet
Navaho, ⅜ x ½", SS and turquoise,
five stone sets **75.00**
Zuni, 1" w, SS, turquoise and coral
chip inlay **25.00**
Bowl, 9¾" d, 4" h, basketry, black mar-
tynia and yucca, Papago **65.00**
Cradle Board, 36" l, wood frame and
slats, cloth shade, c1930 . . . . **190.00**
Cup, 2¼" h, creamy orange slip, umber
band, artist sgd, Hopi **75.00**
Jacket, ladies, 32" l, blue wool, multicolor geometric design back, satin
bound seams, Chimayo **25.00**
Jar
8½" d, 8" h, curvilinear design, ochre
on buff, red ochre bottom, umber
step design above shoulder, early
1900s, Acoma **475.00**
6¼" d, 4½" h, pottery, umber geo-
metric design, red ochre bottom,
flat shoulder **150.00**
Kachina Doll, 9", maiden, polychrome
cape and dress, braided yarn hair . . **900.00**
Rug
36 x 57", dark brown and natural serrated design, varicolored red
ground **275.00**

39 x 55", wool, red, tan, dark brown, and natural, serrated design, corner fringe, Navaho **325.00**

INDIAN TREE PATTERN

History: The Indian Tree pattern is a popular pattern of porcelain made from the last half of the 19th century until the present. The pattern consisting of an Oriental crooked tree branch, landscape, exotic flowers, and foliage is found in predominately greens, pinks, blues, and oranges on a white ground. Several English potteries, including Burgess and Leigh, Coalport, and Maddock, made wares with the Indian Tree pattern.

Reference: Susan and Al Bagdade, *Warman's English & Continental Pottery & Porcelain, 1st Edition,* Warman Publishing Co., Inc., 1987.

Cup and Saucer, marked "Maddock, England," $25.00.

Berry Bowl, 5" dishes, marked "Maddox"	**20.00**
Bouillon Cup and Saucer, marked "Maddock, England"	**25.00**
Bowl	
7¼", handled	**15.00**
10 x 5½", fruit, ftd, scalloped, marked "Copeland and Spode"	**135.00**
Cake Plate, 10½", marked "Coalport" .	**30.00**
Chocolate Set, chocolate pot, six cups and saucers, marked "Copeland and Spode," 14 pcs	**180.00**
Compote, 8", ftd, marked "Coalport" . .	**60.00**
Cup and Saucer, marked "Coalport" . .	**25.00**
Egg Cup, marked "Coalport"	**12.00**
Pitcher, 6", marked "Maddox & Sons" .	**40.00**
Plate, 8", fluted, marked "Coalport" . .	**15.00**
Platter	
11 x 14¼", oval, marked "Maddock, England"	**65.00**
18½", marked "Spode"	**100.00**

Salt and Pepper Shakers, beehive shape, pr	**50.00**
Sauce Boat, 8", matching underplate, marked "Coalport," 2 pcs	**100.00**
Soup Plate, 9", marked "Maddock, England"	**20.00**
Sugar, cov, marked "Minton"	**50.00**
Tea Set, teapot, creamer, sugar, six cups and saucers, six 7" plates, marked "Coalport," 23 pcs	**300.00**
Vegetable Dish, cov, 11½", marked "Coalport"	**20.00**

INK BOTTLES

History: Ink was sold in glass or pottery bottles in the early 1700s in England. Retailers mixed their own formula and bottled it. The commercial production of ink did not begin in England until the late 18th century and in America until the early 19th century.

Initially, ink was supplied in pint or quart bottles, often of poor manufacture, from which smaller bottles could be filled. By the mid-19th century when writing implements were improved, emphasis was placed on making an "untippable" bottle. Shapes ranging from umbrella style to turtles were tried. Since ink bottles were displayed, shaped or molded bottles became popular.

The advent of the fountain pen relegated the ink bottle to the back drawer. Bottles lost their decorative design and became merely functionable items.

References: Ralph & Terry Kovel, *The Kovels' Bottle Price List,* 7th edition, Crown Publishers, 1984; Carlo & Dot Sellari, *The Illustrated Price Guide To Antique Bottles,* Country Beautiful Corp., 1975.

Periodicals: *Antique Bottle and Glass Collector,* P.O. Box 187, East Greenville, PA 18041.

Additional Listings: See *Warman's Americana & Collectibles* for more examples.

Aqua, 3" h, applied lip and collar, c1880, $10.00.

Butlers Ink, Cincinnati, aqua, twelve
sided, 2¾" **110.00**
Centennial Ink, dome lid, 1876 ...... **45.00**
Central Dome Ink, light olive green,
eight sided, open pontil, rolled lip .. **50.00**
Clam shape, cobalt **125.00**
William A. Davis, Boston, aqua, emb,
round, 7⅞" **15.00**
Farley's, amber, 3¾" **350.00**
Funnel shape, aqua, ribbed **70.00**
Harrison's Columbian, aqua, 1¾" **100.00**
Hohenthal Brothers & Co, olive green,
pour spout, 7⅛" **350.00**
Igloo Ink, cobalt, dome shape **150.00**
J. & I.E.M., igloo shape, golden amber,
1⅝" **80.00**
Keller's Ink, gray, bulbous, flared lip .. **20.00**
L.H. Thomas Co., Chicago, aqua **20.00**
Massachusetts Standard Record Ink,
clear **10.00**
Nicholas & Hall, clear, 2⅞" **10.00**
S.C. Stafford's Ink, cobalt, pour spout,
5", Made in USA **25.00**
Tetrapledal Ink, cobalt, faceted, ground
top, patent 1883 .... **25.00**
Thomas Master Ink, aqua **15.00**
Turtle shape, aqua, 2 x 4" **85.00**
Underwood's Ink, cobalt **15.00**
Water's Indelible Ink, aqua, round, 1⅝" **55.00**

INKWELLS

History: The majority of the commonly found inkwells were produced in the United States and Europe from the early 1800s to the 1930s. The most popular materials were glass and pottery because these substances resisted the corrosive effects of ink.

Inkwells were a sign of the office or a wealthy individual. The common man tended to dip his ink directly from the bottle. The period from 1870 to 1920 represented a "golden age," when inkwells in elaborate designs were produced.

References: William E. Covill, Jr., *Inkbottles and Inkwells,* William S. Sullwold Publishing, 1971; Betty and Ted Rivera, *Inkstands and Inkwells: A Collector's Guide,* 2nd edition, Crown Publishers, Inc., 1973.

Collectors' Club: Society of Inkwell Collectors, 5136 Thomas Avenue, Minneapolis, MN 55410.

Additional Listings: See *Warman's Americana & Collectibles* for more examples.

CERAMIC

Bisque, owl's head, glass eyes, ornate,
colorful **195.00**
Limoges, floral dec, 1850–60 .... **60.00**
Newcomb
3¼", rooster motif dec, high glaze, lid,
Marie LeBlanc, 1907 .... **1,500.00**
4¼" h, incised floral dec, high glaze,
lid, Henrietta Bailey, 1906 ...... **1,100.00**
Porcelain, Oriental design, removable
well, lid **85.00**
Redware, 3½" h, 3½" d, ruffled edge,
incised chain dec, matching cov with
applied pheasant form handle, mid
19th C **350.00**
Rockingham, 2¼" h, 3" d, paneled, emb
acanthus leaves **135.00**
Staffordshire
3", head, old lady, 1840 .... **195.00**
4⅝" h, salmon and gray enameling,
gilt trim, stag and doe, pr **250.00**
Wedgwood, 2¼" d, 1¾" h, basalt, vertical engraved sides, center surrounded by three small openings, imp
"B" on base, 18th C **135.00**

English, 3¾ x 6 x 9¾", oak, mahogany int., crystal wells, green stoppers, brass fittings, button feet, $140.00.

GLASS

Amber, 1¾" h, 2½" d, drum shape, flat
collar, plain base with large pontil .. **95.00**
Aqua, 2⅛" h, 1¾" domed, eight paneled
well, umbrella type, rolled lip, tubular
pontil, emb N. J. Simmonns/Mass .. **150.00**
Art Glass, feather design, irid blue and
purple **225.00**
Blown Three Mold, 2⅝" d, 2" h, olive
amber, GII-18 .... **125.00**
Clear, 3⅝" h, pressed, Columbian Exposition building, dome lift-off lid ... **200.00**
Cobalt Blue, 2¹/₁₆" h, 2⅛" d, cylindrical
well, inwardly folded lip, pontilled
base, emb Harrison's/Columbian/Ink **400.00**
Cranberry, 4" d, daisy form hinged pewter lid **225.00**
Cut Glass, 2¾" h, 2½" sq, royal blue,
matching lift-off lid **145.00**
Loetz type, 3" sq, irid amber, web pattern, hinged brass lid **230.00**

METAL

Brass
Lady, nude, Art Nouveau style **60.00**
Modeled Egyptian bust, hinged lid, glass insert **60.00**
Bronze
4¼" h, Spanish pattern, dore finish, orig glass insert, sgd "Tiffany Studios 1883" **550.00**
5¼" l, figural, dog **275.00**
Bronze and Enamel, urn form, stand, c1880 . . . . **325.00**
Cast Iron, double well, storks on sides, relief molded **50.00**
Pewter, 3½" d, 2⅛" h, ceramic insert, hinged lid **85.00**
Silver, 4¾" l, casket style, two wells, English **120.00**

MISCELLANEOUS

Onyx, 3½" h, green cylindrical, floral repousse dec, silver mounted, 1900 . . **190.00**
Stoneware, 3½" d, 1¾" h, drum shape, gray salt glaze, cobalt blue top **175.00**
Wood, maple, cobalt blue glass liner . . **15.00**

IRONS

History: Ironing devices have been used for many centuries, with the earliest references dating from 1100. Irons from the Medieval, Renaissance, and early industrial era can be found in Europe, but are rare. Fine brass engraved irons and hand wrought irons dominated the period prior to 1850. After 1850 irons began a series of rapid evolutionary changes.

Between 1850 and 1910 irons were heated in four ways: 1) a hot metal slug was inserted into the body, 2) a burning solid, e.g., coal or charcoal, was placed in the body, 3) a liquid or gas, e.g., alcohol, gasoline, or natural gas, was fed from an external tank and burned in the body, and 4) conduction heating, usually drawing heat from a stove top.

Electric irons have not yet found favor among iron collectors.

References: Esther S. Berney, *A Collectors Guide To Pressing Irons And Trivets,* Crown Publishers, Inc., 1977; A. H. Glissman, *The Evolution Of The Sad Iron,* published by author, 1970; Brian Jewell, *Smoothing Irons, A History And Collector's Guide,* Wallace-Homestead, 1977.

Collectors' Clubs: Friends of Ancient Smoothing Irons, Box 215, Carlsbad, CA 92008; Midwest Sad Iron Collectors Club, 500 Adventureland Drive, Altoon, IA 50009.

Museums: Henry Ford Museum, Dearborn, MI; Shelburne Museum, Shelburne, VT; Sturbridge Village, Sturbridge, MA.

Additional Listings: See *Warman's Americana & Collectibles* for more examples.
Advisors: David and Sue Irons.

Slug, brass, Danish, $125.00.

Box, 5" l, brass, rear hinged door, wrought iron handles screwed to body, Danish **140.00**
Charcoal, Acme, removable lid, rear single vent, patented Louis Margalis, Ravenna, Ohio, March, 1910 . . . . . **80.00**
Fluter
Champion Lightening Needle Plaiter, tin, pleated, 7¼ x 13½" **40.00**
The Best, hand, cast base and handle **50.00**
Goffering, brass, wrought iron slug, single barrel, Queen Anne feet, 4½" l, English **400.00**
Liquid Fuel
Alcohol, 18 holes on each side of body, saw grip handle, rear tank, German **100.00**
Gasoline, "Akron Lamp & Mfg Co, Ohio," rear cylindrical tank **40.00**
Miniatures
"Enterprise Star," cast, open hole in handle, 2½" **40.00**
Sad, removable handle, 4" l, Potts, Enterprise or others **65.00**
Swan, trivet, orig paint, 1¾–3" **150.00**
"The Pearl," wood grip, 4" l **85.00**
Speciality
Cap, "Kenrick Co," both ends pointed, 4–5", English **60.00**
Hat brim, "Tolliker," wood, 4–5" **50.00**
Polishing, convex bottom, Sidons, England **85.00**
Sleeve, "Ober Mfg Co, Chagrin Falls, Ohio," 8 x 2¾" **50.00**
Smoothing board, painted horse handle, carved dec, 30" l, Scandinavian **750.00**
Velvet, makes floral dec on ladies hats, brass convex top, concave bottom, leaf design **90.00**

IRONWARE

History: Iron, a metallic element that occurs abundantly in combined forms, has been known for centuries. Items made from iron range from the utilitarian to the decorative. Early hand-forged ironwares are of considerable interest to Americana collectors.

Reference: Kathryn McNerney, *Antique Iron*, Collector Books, 1984; Herbert, Peter, and Nancy Schiffer, *Antique Iron*, Schiffer Publishing Ltd., 1979.

Additional Listings: Banks, Boot Jacks, Doorstops, Fireplace Equipment, Food Molds, Irons, Kitchen Collectibles, Lamps, and Tools.

Andirons, 18″ h, simple tooling, curved feet, spit rests, pyramidal finials ... 100.00
Apple Peeler, 10″ l, wrought, pitted ... 100.00
Bench, cast, fern, orig paint, mid 19th C 1,100.00
Boot Scraper, cast, figural, dachshund, painted dark green, 21″ l 260.00
Can Opener, 6½″ l, cow shape 55.00
Candle Snuffers, scissor shaped, hand forged, 18th C 45.00
Candlestand, 54″ h, double, brass ball finial, faceted brass stop, three penny feet, twisted standard, spring tension adjustment 1,500.00

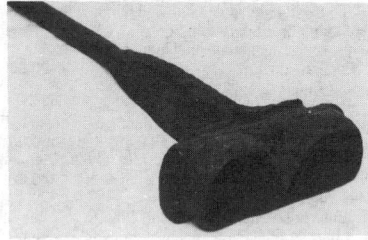

Branding Iron, initial "B," early, $35.00.

Candlestick, 6¼″ h, brass push up, worn tin plate 95.00
Cook Pot, 14¼″ h, cast, three legs, twisted wrought iron handle 75.00
Cookie Mold, cast, basket of flowers, 3½ x 5½″, 1800s 150.00
Cornbread Pan, cast, dec handles, twelve loaves, c1840 .... 40.00
Cornstick Pan, five ears 30.00
Cuspidor, 6½″ h, cast, top hat shape, gold repaint, marked "Bott Bro's, Columbus, O, Billard (sic) and Pool Tables" 155.00
Dough Scraper, 4¾″ w, wrought, shaped blade 55.00

Foot Scraper, 14″ h, cast, set in marble block 80.00
Foot Stool, 7½″ h, cast, old gold paint, dark red plush cov top 75.00
Fork, 31½″ l, wrought, incised scallops around flat handle, stamped initials "EN" 175.00
Jardiniere, cast, pierced scrolling handles, American, mid 19th C 275.00
Kettle Lifter, 16″ h, wrought 185.00
Match Holder, 8¾″ l, cast, black and bronze repaint 25.00
Matchsafe, cast, 8½″ h, two game bird pockets, rabbit, painted, hanging ... 130.00
Meat Hook, wrought
　Five hook, 17½″, twisted detail 65.00
　Six hook, 15″ d, 20″ h, ring with bale 190.00
Mortar and pestle, 7¼″ n, cast 30.00
Muffin Pan
　Eight section, fruit shapes, 7½ x 15″, marked "Cast in U.S.A." 40.00
　Twelve section, flower shapes, fluted 40.00
Nutcracker, dated 1914 .... 25.00
Planter, cast, nine arms, 19th C 150.00
Plate, 9⅝″ d, cast, pitted surface 100.00
Sewing Machine, 12″ l, 9″ h, cast, black paint, polychrome floral and gilt dec, steel foot plate labeled "Wilson Sewing Ma's Manf'g Co Cleveland, Ohio, Ketchum patent April 28, 1863″ 275.00
Shooting Gallery Figure
　Elephant, 9″ l, worn orange paint, pitted 100.00
　Indian in canoe, 9″ l, worn white paint 200.00
　Quail, 4¼″ h, worn white paint 50.00
Stationary Broiler, 15½ x 15½″, wrought, decorative detail 150.00
Strap Hinges, wrought, pr
　34½″ l, penny ends 80.00
　41″ l, bird head ends, curved beaks 140.00
　45″ l, stylized tulip ends 170.00
Sugar Nippers, 8½″ l, wrought 100.00
Tea Kettle, black, slide lid 50.00
Toaster, wrought
　16″ l, scrolled and twisted detail, swivel end 200.00
　18″ l, wrought, simple detail 175.00
Torchiere, wrought
　Four socket, 59½″ h, late 19th C ... 170.00
　Three socket, 56″ h, early 20th C .. 150.00
Trivet
　Oak leaf, 8½″ l, cast, 3 ftd, stem handle, early 1800s 85.00
　Pinwheel and heart design, cast, round, 7″ d, early repair 30.00
　Scroll design, 9¼″ l, wrought, wood handle, brass ferrule 30.00
Tree Holder, 11 x 11″, cast, emb trunk and root design, green paint, bronze highlights 75.00
Urn, cast, scrolled handles, American, mid 19th C 350.00

Warming Pan, pierced lid, orig turned
    wood handle, late 18th or early 19th
    C **250.00**
Windmill Weight, cast, horse **150.00**

IVORY

History: Ivory, a yellowish-white organic material, comes from the teeth or tusks of animals and
lends itself well to carving. It has been used for
centuries by many cultures for artistic and utilitarian items.

Ivory from elephants shows a reticulated crisscross pattern in a cross section. Hippopotamus
teeth, walrus tusks, whale teeth, narwhal tusks,
and boars tusks also are ivory sources. Vegetable
ivory, bone, stag horn, and plastic are ivory sub-
stitutes which often confuse collectors.

Note: Dealers and collectors should be familiar
with The Endangered Species Act of 1973,
amended in 1978, which limits the importation and
sale of antique ivory and tortoise shell items.

Box, 12", two hinged compartments,
    claw feet, cov **200.00**
Brush Pot, 6", shepherd boy resting on
    water buffalo in bamboo forest scene,
    dec picked out in black, carved wood
    base, Chinese, late 18th C **825.00**

Pendant, 2¼" l, carved rose, $175.00.

Candle Holder, 5", carved, relief flowers
    around neck, 11 layer mystery ball
    with Greek key base **200.00**
Cane Handle, crocodile, 7", fighting ti-
    ger **75.00**
Card Case, carved scene, French,
    c1880 .... **225.00**
Cigarette Holder, cat chasing ball **95.00**
Clothespins, 2¾" l, turned, set of 4,
    early to mid 19th C **225.00**
Fan
    Reticulated geometric design, mid
      19th C **40.00**

    Segmented, polychrome, French
      court scene, early 19th C **100.00**
Figurine
    Mice, 13¼", pushing egg, mahogany
      base **325.00**
    Woman, 6¼", nude, standing in gar-
      den **210.00**
Flask, 5" h, farmers, immortals, and
    landscape scene, scrolling foliage
    motif, 1800s, pr **625.00**
Frame
    1⅜ x 1½", easel type, engraved drag-
      ons, back closure **90.00**
    1⅞ x 2½", rect shape, mid 19th C .. **70.00**
Glove Stretcher, 9½" **50.00**
Incense Burner
    5" h, pierced, rings on handles, Foo
      dog cov **220.00**
    29" h, dragon panels, pierced work
      pagoda top, dragon fish handles . **5,000.00**
Letter Opener, 11" l, coiling snake ... **185.00**
Mask, 10" h, carved, king and queen . **1,250.00**
Match Box, 6" h, hanging, tin back, early
    to mid 19th C **350.00**
Match Safe, double sided, 1887 ..... **110.00**
Mirror, 10¾", hand held, young angel
    figure, carved, c1890 .... **1,100.00**
Napkin Ring, carved, dragon, black
    eyes **50.00**
Needle Case, carved, screw top cylin-
    der **95.00**
Pen Holder, 4", cylindrical, carved, three
    monkeys, wood base, ftd **125.00**
Pin, 1", water color dec, lady and man's
    hands joined before fountain,
    perched white doves, inscription
    "Friendship the Fountain of Love,"
    tooled gold metal case **3,300.00**
Pin Cushion, 8½" l, ebony screw-on
    clamp ornamented with mother-of-
    pearl **550.00**
Pipe, 14" l, chicken, rock, and floral mo-
    tif, stained, inscribed, 1800s **250.00**
Plaque, 4¼ x 6", relief molded, Venus
    and goat attended by a putto and two
    satyrs, lapis lazuli ground, framed,
    19th C **550.00**
Ruler, 6", folding, brass fittings **35.00**
Snuff Bottle, 8" h, relief, garden scene,
    painted **200.00**
Sword, 25" l, figural motif, scroll work,
    carrying loops **800.00**
Table Screen, 7" h, deeply carved and
    undercut on one side, reverse etched
    landscape scene, black pigment ... **1,430.00**
Tankard, 16¼", Alexander The Great In
    Battle **5,500.00**
Teapot, 5½", scenic panels, Greek key
    fret cov with flower finial, ftd wood
    base **225.00**
Thimble, carved, flowers and leaves,
    1880s **55.00**

Tray, 7⅝" l, carved pierced relief, Phoenix bird biting tasseled musical emblem, feathers form contours, traces of red and blue pigment, 18th C . . . **1,430.00**

Vase
  8", birds, picking berries **175.00**
  12¼" h, cylindrical form, carved exotic birds, peonies, chrysanthemums, and roses sprouting from jagged rocks **2,750.00**

JACK-IN-THE-PULPIT VASES

History: Jack-in-the-Pulpit glass vases, made in the trumpet form, were in vogue during the late 19th and early 20th centuries. The vases were made in a wide variety of patterns, colors, and sizes.

Additional Listings: See specific glass categories.

Pink and light green, transparent, ruffled, pontil mark, $140.00.

4½", opaque jade green, ruffled, emb ribbed base, enameled small white flowers, gold trim **75.00**
5⅜", opalescent, flower petal top, pink and yellow stripes **85.00**
5¾", spangle, white ext., pink int., ruffled rim, clear edging, mica flecks . . **120.00**
6½", gold luster, pinched body, Loetz . **175.00**
6¾", Mt Washington
  Burmese, trumpet **300.00**
  Satin, pale violet blue, pink ruffled rim **275.00**
7⅛", orange, sponged black dec, marked "Czechoslovakia" **48.00**
7¼"
  Rubina Verde, ruffled **135.00**
  Spatter, green, peach, yellow and white spatter at top, green DQ pattern body **55.00**
7½", silver overlay, ruffled, shaded purple **100.00**

10", cranberry, applied crystal rigaree and feet **200.00**
10¼", stretch, irid purple, Imperial . . . **90.00**
12½", trumpet, satin, white, lavender and white flowers, green leaves, ruffled rim, Mt Washington **325.00**
13¼", IVT, amberina **300.00**
15¾", cased, blue, white int., ruffled, applied crystal spiral trim, clear foot with scalloped shell trim **210.00**

JADE

History: Jade is the generic name for two distinct minerals, nephrite and jadeite. Nephrite, an amphibole mineral from Central Asia and used in pre-18th century pieces, has a waxy surface and ranges in hues from white to almost a black green. Jadeite, a pyroxene mineral found in Burma and used from 1700 to the present, has a glassy appearance and comes in various shades of white, green, yellow-brown, and violet.

Jade cannot be carved because of its hardness. Shapes are achieved through sawing and grinding with wet abrasives, such as quartz, crushed garnets, and carborundum.

Prior to 1800 few pieces are signed or dated. Stylistic considerations are used for dating. The Ch'ien Lung period (1736–95) is considered the "golden age" of Jade.

Reference: Sandra Andacht, *Oriental Antiques & Art: An Identification And Value Guide,* Wallace-Homestead, 1987.

Museum: Avery Brundage Collection, de Young Museum, San Francisco, CA.

Pendant, burial tomb type, $110.00.

Basket, 13" h, green and yellow, floral chain, 1900s **4,000.00**
Belt Buckle, 5⅜" l, brown and white, high relief carved and pierced, *chilong* confronting dragon head terminal **660.00**

Bottle, green, carved, floral motif, two
   handles **210.00**
Bowl
   5½" d, spinach green, tapered ev-
     erted rim, raised on ring foot,
     evenly flecked darker inclusions,
     white mottling toward bottom, pr . **935.00**
   10¼" w, white, high relief carved
     peonies and chrysanthemums int.,
     two reticulated bat form handles,
     relief band, amber flecking and fis-
     suring **7,150.00**
Box, 2⅝" w, cov, rect form, carved, chrysanthemums medallion surrounded
   by stylized lotus flower band, base
   with matching band, dark green
   stone, black flecking, pale inclusions **770.00**
Brush Pot, 4¾" h, cylindrical form,
   deeply carved and undercut, mountain landscape scene, dark green
   stone with black flecking, natural fis-
   suring **4,070.00**
Button, 2" w, moth shape, floral motif,
   c1900 .... **70.00**
Chime, musical, 19" w, six sided, angular form, two gilt painted dragons,
   dark stone with lighter mottling, white
   fissures, black and brown pigment
   traces, Qianlong, 1738 .... **8,250.00**
Cuspidor, 2½ x 5½", green **195.00**
Dish, 4¾ x 3¹/₁₆", white, scalloped, chrysanthemum center, China **500.00**
Figurine
   Buddha, 3" **130.00**
   Duck, 2" w, swimming, c1800 ..... **125.00**
   Pheasant, 5", China **75.00**
Hair Pin, 4" w, yellowish green, c1900 **250.00**
Hat Ornament, 15¾" l, hollowed icy
   white and bright green cylinder, pea-
   cock and black barbed feather on one
   end, pierced loop on other, 19th C . **1,100.00**
Mirror, 9 x 5", white, silver mounts,
   c1900 .... **1,000.00**
Pendant, 2¾" h, openwork, dragon de-
   sign **120.00**
Pomegranate, 2½" l, stem and leaves,
   c1900 .... **30.00**
Snuff Bottle, 2" h, ovoid form, low relief
   carved birds and flowers, pale green,
   white mottling **935.00**
Urn, 8" h, pale moss green, Chinese,
   1900s **4,200.00**
Vase
   3⅜" h, brown and white, tree section
     form, low relief carved, peacock
     perched on branch, rim ground, fis-
     sure, 17th C **1,100.00**
   5¾" h, white, carved, reticulated
     morning glory, incised leaf grooves,
     softly polished **2,310.00**
   9⅝" h, carved, openwork fret handles,
     white with milky flecks and pale

amber patches, matching cov, Qianlong mark and period **13,200.00**
10" h, green, trumpet shape **345.00**

JAPANESE AND CHINESE CERAMICS

History: The Chinese pottery tradition has existed for thousands of years. By the sixteenth century, Chinese ceramic wares were being exported
to India, Persia, and Egypt. The Ming dynasty
(1368-1643) saw the strong development of
glazed earthenwares and shapes. During the
Ch'ing dynasty, the Ch'ien Lung period (1736-95)
marked the golden age of interchange with the
west.

Trade between China and the west began in the
sixteenth century when the Portuguese established Macao. The Dutch entered the trade early
in the seventeenth century. With the establishment
of the English East India Company, all of Europe
was seeking Chinese-made pottery and porcelain.
Styles, shapes, and colors were developed to suit
Western tastes. The tradition continued until the
late nineteenth century.

Like the Chinese, the Japanese spent centuries
developing their ceramic arts. Each region established its own forms, designs, and glazes. Individual artists added to the uniqueness.

Japanese ceramics began to be exported to the
west in the mid-19th century. Their beauty quickly
made them a favorite of the patrician class.

The ceramic tradition continues into the 20th
century. Modern artists enjoy equal fame with older
counterparts.

Reference: Sandra Andacht, *Oriental Antiques
& Art: An Identification And Value Guide,* Wallace-
Homestead, 1987.

Periodical: *The Orientalia Journal,* P. O. Box
94P, Little Neck, NY 11363.

Additional Listings: Canton, Fitzhugh, Imari,
Kutani, Nanking, Rose Medallion, and Satsuma.

CHINESE

Bowl, 4½", blue and white, dragon,
   flaming pearls and rockwork, Daoguang **650.00**
Box, cov, 5½" d, white ware, circular,
   molded vertical ribbed sides, blossoming peony, molded double ring
   cov, Yuan, early Ming Dynasty **575.00**
Charger, 16", three rabbits, mountains,
   pines, and landscapes **385.00**
Figure
   7¼" l, puppy, gray pottery, high curled
     tail, broad compact body, blunt
     face, painted eyes, Han Dynasty **565.00**
   26" h, horse, unglazed pottery, head
     turned slightly left, mouth open,
     long mane, docked and bounded

tail, molded foliate tassels and saddle, front right foreleg raised, traces of red and black pigment, Tang Dynasty **10,000.00**

Plate, 11", blue and white, peonies in vase, floor screen, late Kangxi **250.00**

Rice Bowl, 4", blue and white, tea time scene in garden, penciled, Kangxi . . **450.00**

Shrine, 15¼" h, Blanc de Chine, jeweled seated Guanyin, galleried double lotus pedestal base, frame shaped nimbus molded with flowering lotus, 4 character studio mark, 19th C **450.00**

Tea Bowl, 5 " d, steep sides, lipped rim, grainy buff ring foot, light black streaked to chocolate brown to dark brown glaze, Henan, Song Dynasty . **600.00**

Vase, 5½", compressed ovoid, slightly flaring string cut foot, short out turned rim, straw glaze, Tang Dynasty **825.00**

CHINESE EXPORT

Barber Bowl, 11⅞", oval, armorial, iron-red, gold, turquoise, and rose, arms of Yaldwyn impaling Soame, grisaille cell diaper border, gilt flower heads, three iron-red edged gilt floral sprays on rim, c1735 . . . . **1,450.00**

Bowl

11 x 4½", multicolored masonic dec, gilt trim **600.00**

12", armorial, ext. front painted gold, brown, grisaille, brown, and iron red arms of Society of Caulkers, figures, and mottos, reverse iron-red and gold monogram "JEL" within blue and gold flowering boughs, gold husk-edged foliate border, int. painted blue and gold, central floral spray, floral vine and dot border, c1795 . . . . **1,500.00**

Charger, 14⅝", mythological, seated goddess Juno, Jupiter as eagle, Italianate walled town in background, gold, iron-red, and black flowering and fruiting vines border, c1745 . . . **2,900.00**

Coffeepot, 9¼", lighthouse shape, four panels of figures alternating with famille rose panels, orig lid, late 18th C **1,500.00**

Jardiniere, 15⅞", lobed body, thin maroon wave bands, clusters of flowers and fruit beneath foliate scroll and floral swag borders, blue Greek key border on footrim, c1785 . . . . **4,000.00**

Mug

4⅜", eagle perched on rocks, gilt stars, small foliate sprigs, brown monochrome, iron-red and blue band, entwined strap handle, iron-red floral terminals, American market, c1800 . . . . **800.00**

5⅜", armorial, front painted black, iron-red, gold, white, and rose, arms of Fitler of Norfolk, iron-red, blue, and gold rocaillerie above rose banderole with motto, handle flanked by goat's head crest above gilt initials "JF," gilt chain rim border, c1760 . . . . **1,325.00**

Plate

9", peonies and asters, pink petal tipped rim, c1740, pr **750.00**

9¹/₁₆", armorial, reticulated, center painted "Hope" wearing yellow robe, pink drapery, seated on brown rock, green plants, holding gray anchor, and leaning on salmon colored shield, arms of Ker, blue, gold, and iron-red arms of Martin, gold wavy husk chain, iron-red and gold paterae and anchor/cable devices, c1790 . . . . **1,000.00**

9⅞", central medallion of landscape, house, river, and two figures, sepia, gold, and black, double border dec, late 18th C **200.00**

Platter

11⅞", oval, armorial, iron-red, blue, and gold center arms of Montgomerie quartering Eglinton, purple flowered green boughs, blue and rose costumed Hope crest surmounted by "Garde Bien," gilt husk, foliage, and paterae garland, underglaze blue cell diaper band, Fitzhugh type butterfly border, worn gilding, c1785, pr **2,250.00**

16⅜", armorial, scalloped, grisaille, oxidized silver, coat of arms of Thomas Sanders, blue helmet, gold border of diaper panels between panels of lovebirds and wreaths, c1745, pr **2,750.00**

Soup Plate, 9", mahout wearing purple shirt, green pants, gray red elephant saddle, four gilt rose floral sprigs, for Indian market, c1780 . . . . **1,225.00**

Soup Tureen, cov, 12¾", circular, famille rose enamels of peonies and demi-chrysanthemums, grisaille, and gilding, shaded pink lotus bud finial . . . **1,350.00**

Tea Bowl, 4¼", ext. front painted brown monochrome, gilt edged oval of man holding walking stick, standing with four running dogs in field before Mount Vernon, reverse with shadow of initials "JMH," gold foliage scroll band rim, int. rim of gold, salmon, and iron-red Fitzhugh type butterfly border, floral spray, and fretwork beneath panels of diaper and scalework, c1802–05 . . . . **850.00**

Wine Cooler, 8″, armorial, arms of Saint-Saens of Burgundy, garland of pink roses, 3 character Chinese inscription, iron-red rim, c1770 .... **1,100.00**

Tea Bowl, 4¾″, hand modeled, irregular straight sides, small recessed ring foot, central well of flower head, peach glaze, double crackle pattern, Raku **150.00**
Teapot, 5½ x 5″, gray ware, polycolor, seven gods of wisdom, glazed and unglazed, Banko **410.00**
Vase
  7″, two monkeys separated by dragon costume, red ground, crackled glaze top, Sumida Guma **325.00**
  12″, heavily potted, hexagonal, short flaring neck, creamy ash glaze, green flashes, Sansho, Shigaraki, late 18th C **500.00**

Japanese Export, Jar, cov, 8″ h, two figures with glazed clothing on base, green marbleized glaze flowing from lid on to top of jar, unglazed base, figural finial, marked "Sumida," sgd "Inoue Ryosai," $350.00.

JASPERWARE

History: Jasperware is a hard, unglazed porcelain with a colored ground, varying from the most common blues and greens to lavender, yellow, red, or black. The white designs are applied in relief and often reflect a classical motif. Jasperware was first produced at Wedgwood's Etruria Works in 1775. Josiah Wedgwood described it as "a fine Terra Cotta of great beauty and delicacy proper for cameos."

Many other English potters, in addition to Wedgwood, produced jasperware. Two of the leaders were Adams and Copeland and Spode. Several continental potters, e.g., Heubach, also produced the ware.

Reference: Susan and Al Bagdade, *Warman's English & Continental Pottery & Porcelain, 1st Edition*, Warman Publishing Co., Inc., 1987.

Reproduction Alert: Jasperware still is made today, especially by Wedgwood.

Note: This category includes all pieces of jasperware which were made by companies other than Wedgwood. Wedgwood jasperware is found in the Wedgwood listing.

JAPANESE

Bottle, 10″, globular, blue and white stylized floral motif, elongated neck, thick ring foot, 18th C **140.00**
Bowl, monkey group, c1900, Banko .. **200.00**
Charger, 21″, three carp swimming near a bank of peony and plum branches, Arita, Meiji period **350.00**
Creamer, 4½″, seated figure, extended mouth forms spout, hair braid forms handle, black robe, blue garment, unglazed face, Sumida Guma **150.00**
Cup, 2⅛″ h, four petal edge reserves continuous band of abstract characters int., Kakiemon, 19th C **175.00**
Dish, fish shaped, cat at side, Banko . **70.00**
Incense Burner, 3½″, Shishi form, green glaze, Oribe **375.00**
Nodder, 3″, Fukesukesan, c1900 .... **300.00**
Plate, 7¾″, zodiac, scalloped edge, twelve animals in circular medallions, four variant stylized diaper ground, blossoming prunus blossoms on ext., chocolate rim, Arita, 19th C **225.00**
Steamer, cov, 7½″, deep cylindrical container, applied handle and lug, creamy heavily crackled underglaze blue, one side with stylized crab, other with calligraphy, cov sgd "kitai, Bizen," late 18th C, fitted box **750.00**

Cheese Dish, tan and white, marked "Adams," c1820, $400.00.

Biscuit Jar, 6 x 6″, bulbous, white relief hunting scene, dark blue ground, SP cover, rim, and handle, marked "Adams, England" 135.00

Bookends, pr, 5 x 4 x 4″, white relief cameos, columns and sphinx, blue ground, imp mark 85.00

Bowl, 7″, white relief classical figures, dark blue ground 225.00

Box, cov
  3⅞ x 2½ x 2⅛″, white relief winged lady, flowers, garlands and cherubs, blue ground, marked "Germany" 60.00
  5″, oval, white relief cherub and nymph, blue ground, marked "Schafer & Vater, Germany" 40.00

Chamberstick, black and white, snuffer 265.00

Clock, 9⅛″ h, white relief cherubs, foliage and flowers, sage green ground, clock not working 150.00

Coffeepot, 10″, white relief classical figures, green ground 185.00

Creamer, blue, Kewpie, sgd 165.00

Cup and Saucer, white relief classical figures, formal foliage and engine turning, blue ground, marked "Turner, England," c1800 .... 175.00

Hair Brush, lady's, white relief lady and cupid, lavender ground, brass rim and handle 100.0

Hair Receiver, 3⅜ x 3½″, white relief classical ladies and flowers, cupids on lid, blue ground, marked "Germany" 65.00

Jardiniere, 7½″, white relief of Columbus landing, light blue ground, marked "Copeland" 175.00

Jug, 8″, white relief fox hunting scene, green ground, c1820 .... 175.00

Match Box, cov
  Blue and white 85.00
  Lilac Dip 115.00

Perfume Bottle, blue and white, hallmarked SS top 275.00

Pin Dish, white Indian Chief dec, holding bow and arrow, green ground, marked "Heubach" 65.00

Plaque
  5½″, white relief of two children climbing on heron, two children in water, lilies of the valley border, green ground, marked "Germany" 70.00
  6½ x 5″, white relief Indian Chief, green, marked "Germany" 200.00

Salt Shaker, white relief classical figures, dark blue ground 60.00

Sugar, cov, 6″, two handles, white relief sacrifice scene, swan finial, blue ground, marked "Adams," c1800 ... 1,150.00

Urn, 8″ h, white relief hunting scene, cobalt blue ground, marked "Adams, Tunstall, England" 200.00

Vase, 7¾″, two green topiary tree handles, white relief of Art Nouveau woman's face, flowing hair, two white swans, lilac ground, marked "A Radford Pottery, Ohio" 850.00

JEWEL BOXES

History: The evolution of jewelry was paralleled by the development of boxes in which to store it. Jewel box design followed the fashion trends dictated by furniture styles. Many jewel boxes are lined.

Bronze, 8 x 6¼ x 5″, emb village scenes, four small feet, French, $250.00.

3½ x 5″, Bohemian, amber, etched animals, birds, and trees, key 350.00

3⅞ x 1¾″, jasperware, crimson and white, classical figures on lid, white raised cherubs around sides, marked "Wedgwood," c1920 .... 500.00

4½ x 5½″, sapphire blue, Mary Gregory dec of boy and girl, brass mounts and handles 600.00

4¾″, green, multicolored enamel flowers and butterfly, brass beaded ball feet and handles, Moser 750.00

5″ d, ball shape, cobalt blue, Mary Gregory dec of two children and fence, brass mounts and ball feet 425.00

5″ l x 5″ h, oblong, cranberry, enamel birds and floral dec, brass mounts and handles, key, Moser 1,400.00

5¾ x 5″, cranberry, gold enamel floral dec, brass mounts and ring, key ... 425.00

6″ h, round, cranberry, lid with enamel white slate roof, turret, and doves, blue enamel flowers, brass ring handles, and ball feet 400.00

7" d, round, frosted and clear light blue
glass, delicate enamel floral dec,
brass colored ormolu feet **300.00**

8 x 3", ormolu raised design collar, mottled
green, pink, and white flowers,
blue and beige leaves, pink silk lining,
hinged lid, c1904, Wavecrest **675.00**

9 x 4½" h, oblong, pink porcelain inserts,
enameled flowers, musical instruments,
brass beaded mounts, velvet
lined, engraved "Maison Boisser"   **450.00**

JEWELRY

History: Jewelry has been a part of every culture.
It was a way of displaying wealth, power, or
love of beauty. In the current antique marketplace,
it is easiest to find jewelry dating between 1800 to
1950.

Jewelry items were treasured and handed down
as heirlooms from generation to generation. In the
United States, antique jewelry is defined by law,
specifically U. S. Customs laws, as "heirloom/estate"
jewelry, i.e., at least twenty-five years old,
property acquired new, used, or through inheritance,
is used for old jewelry that does not meet
the "antique" definition.

The jewelry found in this listing fits either the
antique or "heirloom/estate" definition. The list
contains no new reproduction pieces. The jewelry
is made of metals and gemstones proven to endure
over time. Inexpensive and mass produced
costume jewelry is covered in *Warman's Americana
& Collectibles*.

Several major auction houses, especially Christie's,
Doyle's, Phillips, and Sotheby's in New York
City, hold specialized jewelry auctions several
times each year.

Note: The first step in determing the value of a
piece of old jewelry is to correctly identify the metal
and gemstones. Take into account the current
value of the metal and gemstones plus the piece's
age, identifying marks, quality, condition, construction,
etc.

References: Lillian Baker, *100 Years of Collectible
Jewelry,* Collector Books, 1986; Vivienne
Becker, *Antique and 20th Century Jewelry,* Van
Nostrand Reinhold; Rose L. Goldemberg, *Antique
Jewelry: A Practical And Passionate Guide,*
Crown Publishers, Inc., 1976; Arthur Guy Kaplan,
*The Official Price Guide To Antique Jewelry, Fifth
Edition,* House of Collectibles, 1985; Dorothy T.
Rainwater, *American Jewelry Manufacturers,*
Schiffer Publishing Ltd., 1988.

Periodical: *Collectors Clocks & Jewelry,* Schiffer
Publishing Ltd., 1469 Morstein Road, West
Chester, PA 19380.

Advisor: Elaine J. Luartes.

Dates:

Georgian	**1714–1837**
Victorian	**1837–1865**
Edwardian	**1885–1910**
Art Nouveau	**1880–1920**
Arts and Crafts	**1895–1915**
Art Deco	**1920–1930**
Art Retro	**1940–1950**

**Pin, 1½" l, Art Nouveau, Sterling silver,
woman with flowing hair, $90.00.**

Bar Pin

Art Deco, platinum, arrow head terminals,
2 fancy shaped and 8 scissor
cut amethysts, bordered by numerous
small diamonds, marked
"Spaulding & Co," c1920 . . . .   **4,400.00**

Art Nouveau, platinum, shaped bar,
studded with small demantoid garnets
and rose cut diamonds,
carved jade fruit terminals, rose cut
diamond caps, calibre cut sapphire
bands **2,325.00**

Arts and Crafts

Brass, etched, leaf design, 1⅞ x ⅜"   **65.00**

Sterling Silver, wrought flower,
bead, and leaf design, center baroque
pearl, Brandt Metal Crafters
. . . .   **125.00**

Edwardian, platinum and gold bar,
central old mine 1.25 ct diamond,
flanked by eight old mine diamonds
(approx 2.75 cts), c1900 . . . .   **3,850.00**

Bracelet

Art Deco

Bangle, platinum mounting, hinged,
flattened central panel set with
row of 9 emerald beads, studded
front and back with collet set old
European cut diamonds, black
onyx sections, single cut diamond
borders, c1925 . . . .   **33,000.00**

Double strand, 68 sapphire beads
studded with small French cut
diamonds, platinum spacers,
shaped links with French cut and
old European diamonds, c1930   **10,000.00**

Art Retro
Gold, 18K, modified tank style, curved polished gold links, single cabochon sapphire on clasp, (approx 90 dwts), Cartier **9,350.00**
Gold, double snake link, stylized buckle form slap set with 9 oval rubies, bands of small round diamonds, sgd "BB&B" (Bailey, Banks & Biddle), c1940 . . . . . . **3,575.00**

Arts and Crafts, SS
Cuff, center sq bezel cut green chrysoprase cabochon, pierced, smooth surface, Art Metal Shop mark **250.00**
Linked, bezel set round green malachite cabochons, detailed and intricate links, Kalo Shop **1,200.00**
Edwardian, bangle, matte gold, center oval shaped carved panel tinted blue, two Grecian figures with fruit filled vase, chased rose spray and C scroll borders, palmette motif sides, back lyre shaped links with traces of green enamel, rose cut and old mine diamonds, fitted leather box stamped "Hancocks & Co, London" **4,675.00**
Victorian
Enameled, 5 graduated oval lakeside scenes, textured gold scrolled borders, matching batons, scene titled on back, orig filled case, Swiss, c1850 . . . . . **2,700.00**
Mosaic, gold, 6 oval shaped micro mosaics of classical Italian scenes, black onyx frames, gold collets, polished gold rod spacers **2,420.00**

Brooch
Art Deco
Platinum, mansion shape, numer-

Beads, jade, 30″ l, $300.00.

ous baguette and single cut diamonds, Cartier, c1920 . . . . **10,000.00**
Platinum, oblong shaped mounting with stylized circular motifs, center .90 ct diamond, row of 10 baguette diamonds, 90 round diamonds (approx 8.70 cts), c1930 **6,600.00**
Platinum, red enameled Oriental design openwork plaque, applied black onyx cylinders, small old European and single cut diamonds, Cartier, c1930 . . . . **10,000.00**
Rock Crystal, carved elongated octagonal, platinum jackets designed s stylized plumes set with 20 old European cut diamonds, (approx 3.60 cts), numerous rose cut diamonds **6,650.00**

Art Nouveau
Gold, head of woman, diamond coronet, pear shaped diamond earrings, flanked by two peacocks with diamond set crowns, enameled blue and green feathers, claw holding old European cut diamond suspending diamond and pearl pendant, 2 button pearls on side, reverse lightly engraved **8,250.00**
Gold, two peacocks back to back, center oval shaped cabochon coral, tail feathers studded with small round sapphires, demantoid garnets, and diamonds, coral drop **7,150.00**
Platinum, oval, openwork, stylized floral pattern, honeycomb motif, 4 old European cut diamonds (approx 2.40 cts), 87 smaller old European cut diamonds (approx 5 cts) **7,750.00**

Art Retro
Gold, 14K, swallow in flight, 14 rose cut rubies, single cabochon ruby eye, small round demantoid garnets, numerous old European cut and single cut diamonds, c1940 **7,150.00**
Gold, 18K, flower girl, polished gold, full skirted dress, wide brimmed hat, holding flower filled basket over one arm, bundle of flowers in other, studded with small round rubies and sapphires, sgd "J. Lacloche, Paris, Regd. 9965" **2,310.00**

Arts and Crafts, SS, pansy, Kalo Shop, 1⅝ x 1¼″ **450.00**

Edwardian
Gold, cockatoo perched on branch, several old mine diamonds, small ruby eye, 3 golden pearls (approx 4.0 mm) on branch . . . **3,350.00**

Platinum, circular lacework motif, center 8.7 mm button pearl, several old mine and single cut diamonds, c1900 . . . . **3,850.00**

Edwardian Style, white and yellow gold, stylized shield and circle motif, 2 round diamonds (approx 2.00 cts), 126 small round diamonds (approx 3.50 cts), French calibre cut emeralds **6,160.00**

Georgian, silver and gold, en tremblant, leaf and berry motif, numerous old mine and rose cut diamonds, button pearl berries **3,575.00**

Victorian, 14K gold, stylized bow knot, 10 emerald cut and pear shaped emeralds, 7 old mine diamonds (approx 2.90 cts), borders of old mine, French cut, and single cut diamonds, Russian, St Petersburg, c1860 . . . . **33,000.00**

Victorian, late, platinum and gold, circular frame of interlocking plumes, numerous rose cut diamonds, center hexagon aquamarine (40 cts) . **11,550.00**

Pin, 2¼" w, Victorian, 14K gold, amethyst and seed pearls, moon motif, c1890, $300.00.

Buckle, Arts and Crafts
Belt, hammered silver, sgd "Gaylord," 2⅛ x 1⅜" **45.00**
Shoe, SS, smoothly planished, rect, fine raised edge, back engraved "M.L.M.," 2 x 1¼" **175.00**

Chain
Art Nouveau, Sautoir, latticework, small natural pearls (approx 3.5 mm) platinum and gold spacer bars, shield shaped plaque with numerous old European cut diamonds, 35" l **6,000.00**
Arts and Crafts, SS, wide hand wrought hammered links **80.00**
Edwardian, numerous oval shaped citrines, buff tops, faceted bottoms, yellow, orange, and madeira, small fancy shaped gold figure eight link and beadwork lozenges, 62" l, c1900 . . . . **4,450.00**

Chatelaine, Arts and Crafts, SS, 3 pierced elements on each side, center oval cabochons of dark lapis lazuli, Kalo Shop **1,500.00**

Choker-Necklace, Art Nouveau, 15K polished gold, 8 oval shaped opals in openwork frames, interlocking borders, circular spacer links, 13" l **3,000.00**

Clip
Art Deco, platinum, shield shape, cluster of carved sapphires, emeralds, and rubies, bordered by 40 old European cut and baguette diamonds, (approx 3.0 cts), sgd "Van Cleef & Arpels," c1935 . . . . **16,500.00**
Art Retro
Gold, 14K, polished, scrolling drapes, borders of calibre cut rubies and round diamonds, pr . . **4,125.00**
Gold, yellow and pink, stylized triangles, two rect tourmalines, bands of sq cut tourmalines and round diamonds, sgd BBB (Bailey, Banks & Biddle), c1940, pr . **5,500.00**

Compact, Art Retro, 18K gold, rect, polished gold studded with diamond stars, applied ballerina, rose cut diamond face, sapphire hemmed skirt, int. with fitted mirror and powder compartment, thumbpiece with calibre cut rubies, sgd "Van Cleef & Arpels, NY," c1945 . . . . **3,850.00**

Cuff Links, Arts and Crafts, SS
Lozenge shape, polished silver rim, niello int., pierced with 2 round holes, Allen Adler **65.00**
Mask shape, one Comedy, other Tragedy, openwork, Allen Adler . . **100.00**

Earrings
Art Deco, platinum mounting, small 4.mm natural pearl, graduated flexible fringe, collet set old European cut diamonds, drop shaped simulated pearls, single cut diamonds, leather box stamped Marzo, Paris, c1920 . . . . **2,310.00**
Art Retro, polished gold, scroll form clip, bands of sq cut rubies within sq cut diamond borders, French, c1940 . . . . **6,000.00**
Edwardian, chandelier design, flexible earring mounted with pear shaped mixed cut sapphire (approx 10.0 cts) and diamonds (approx 4.0 cts) set collet fringe, orig S. J. Philips, London case, c1900 . . . . **8,500.00**

Lavaliere
Art Nouveau, cluster of hanging flowers and fruit, diamond and green plique-a-jour enamel dec, marquise and brilliant set loop, platinum link chain set with pearls, marquise diamond clasp, c1900, attributed to Philippe Wolfers **1,300.00**

Arts and Crafts
    Gold, 14K, scrolled gold wire, bezel
    cut coral, teardrop coral pendant,
    Lebolt **675.00**
    Sterling Silver, shaded peacock
    blue enamel, Liberty style,
    Charles Horner **325.00**
Locket, Victorian, gold, oval, brown and
  white hardstone cameo, classical female head, half pearl border, c1890 **950.00**
Muff Chain, Victorian, gold, collet set,
  16 oval mixed cut sapphires (approx
  25.0 cts), scrolled links **1,500.00**
Necklace
  Art Retro, 18K gold, flexible, stylized
  flowerheads, blossoms centered
  with 125 round diamonds (approx
  6.20 cts), sgd "Cartier, Paris," 16" l **17,600.00**
  Victorian, gold, snake chain, sus-
  pending fringe of gold amphorae
  pendants, 5 oval shaped carbuncle
  garnets with rope twist frames, 3
  carbuncles as clasp, 18" l, c1860 . **4,675.00**
Pendant, Arts and Crafts, SS
  Cross, 2⅞" l, center sq faceted amethyst, 9½" l chain, Kalo Shop **600.00**
  Leaf detail at top overlaps bezel holding large oval polished black onyx,
  SS chain, Art Metal Shop mark . . **500.00**
Ring
  Art Deco, platinum band, gypsy set
  old European cut diamond (approx
  1.60 cts), rows of calibre cut black
  onyx **4,675.00**
  Art Nouveau, platinum, sq shaped 1.0
  ct old mine diamond, framed by cal-
  ibre cut sapphires **3,850.00**
  Art Retro
    Bombé gold mounting, five rows
    oval shaped rubies, c1940 . . . **3,100.00**
    Dome, 18K gold, round rubies, two
    florets with round sapphire pet-
    als, diamond centers, c1900 . . **4,125.00**
  Arts and Crafts, SS, applied flowers
  on sides, leaves overlapping bezel
  with large lapis lazuli cabochon, Art
  Metal Shop mark **250.00**
  Edwardian
    Platinum, 1.50 cts old mine dia-
    mond encircled by ten old mine
    diamonds, (approx .75 cts) **2,550.00**
    Platinum and 18K gold, oval
    shaped demantoid garnet (ap-
    prox 1.5 cts), 12 old mine dia-
    monds, marked "L. E. B. & B." . **4,450.00**
  Victorian, platinum, ribbed shank and
  bezels, two floral scrolls, small brilliant, 2 rose cut diamonds, c1900 **1,300.00**
Scarf Pin, Arts and Crafts, SS, rounded
  up center with bezel set amazonite
  cabochon, rect piercings, Kalo Shop,
  2½" l **235.00**

Stick Pin, Arts and Crafts, SS
  Asymmetric pierced ground, long
  piece of honey-brown jasper, attributed to Carence Crafters **150.00**
  Gold washed, silver bezel around
  large blister pearl, overlapping at
  upper left in delicate scalloped de-
  sign **125.00**
Suite
  Victorian, cruciform pendant, matching earrings, gold, detachable 17" l
  pendant with scroll shaped links, 20
  lapis lazuli intaglios, engraved with
  stylized ancient writing, clasp with
  blue chalcedony, matching earrings
  with four lapis and black stone intaglios, fitted leather box labeled
  "Au Vase D'Or Chauffert, Joaillier
  Jigoutier, Palais Royal No. 165" . . **5,500.00**
Watch Fob, Arts and Crafts, German silver, 3¼" l, geometric piercings, bezel
  set light green-blue fiery cabochon
  (similar to opal), black leather stripe
  with brass hook, Forest Craft Guild . **200.00**

JUDAICA

History: Throughout history, Jews have expressed themselves artistically in both the religious
and secular spheres. Most Jewish art objects were
created as part of the concept of "Hiddur Mitzva,"
i.e., adornment of implements involved in perform-
ing rituals both in the synagogue and home.

For almost 2,000 years, since the destruction of
the Jerusalem Temple in 70 A.D., Jews have lived
in many lands. The widely differing environments
gave traditional Jewish life and art a multifaceted
character. Unlike Greek, Byzantine, or Roman art
which have definite territorial and historical boundaries, Jewish art is found throughout Europe, the
Middle East, North Africa, and other areas.

Ceremonial objects incorporated not only liturg-
ical appurtenances, but also ethnographic artifacts
such as amulets and ritual costumes. The style of
each ceremonial object responded to the artistic
and cultural milieu in which it was created. Although diverse stylistically, ceremonial objects,
whether for Sabbath, holidays, or the life cycle,
still possess a unity of purpose.

Judaica has been crafted in all media, though
silver is the most collectible. Sotheby's, Christie's,
and Swann's hold several Judaica auctions in the
United States, England, Amsterdam, and Israel.

References: Abraham Kanof, *Jewish Ceremo-
nial Art*, Harry N. Abrams, n.d.; Cecil Roth, *Jewish
Art - An Illustrated History*, Graphic Society of New
York, 1971; *Jewish Art and Civilization*, Geoffrey
Wigoder, (ed.), Chartwell Books, 1972.

Museums: B'nai B'rith Klutznick Museum,
Washington, DC; H.U.C., Skirball Museum, Los
Angeles, CA; Jewish Museum, New York, NY; Ju-

dah L. Magnes Museum, Berkeley, CA; Maurice Spertus Museum of Judaica, Chicago, IL; National Museum of American Jewish History, Philadelphia, PA; Yeshiva University Museum, New York, NY.

Advisor: Arthur M. Feldman.

Beaker Cup, Russian silver	
2″, incised "shtetel scenes" dec, c1870	225.00
2½″, incised "shtetel scenes" dec, c1870	250.00
3⅞″, etched grapevines, 19th C	125.00
Candelabra, 15″ h, five light, baluster stem, pierced and chased lions amidst foliage upper section, domed circular base, on Polish, mid 19th C	300.00
Candlesticks, pr	
9″, brass, bulbous, chased, sq base, Polish, sgd "Warsaw," 19th C	400.00
12½″, brass, bulbous, sq base, Polish, sgd "Warsaw," 19th C	475.00
14½″, SS, detachable bobeches, Russian, hallmarked, 19th C	2,400.00
Etrog Container	
4 x 7″, box, octagonal, olivewood, hinged lid, attached carved etrog on top, Palestine, c1940	550.00
34½ x 5″, German silver, band of repousse bead dec at base and lid, mid 19th C	750.00
Lamp	
Hanukah, 10 x 10″, Polish silvered brass, Baroque foliage design on back plate, surmounted by repousse crown, two rampant lions on either side of menorah, sgd "Warsaw," mid 19th C	1,200.00
Sabbath/Hanukah, 9 x 10″, Bezalel silver, Yemenite filigree work, sgd "Bezalel, Jerusalem," 20th C	3,200.00
Mezuzah, 5½ x 1½″, replicated Chagall lithograph, 24 karat gold plated over bronze, 20th C	600.00
Mezuzah Case, 3½ x 5″, American silver, sgd "L. Wolpert," 20th C	550.00
Noisemaker, Purim, ivory, incised "Hamen" and "Esther," German, 19th C	900.00
Prayer Shawl Bag, 10 x 8″, velvet and silver thread, Moroccan, early 20th C	250.00
Rosewater Spice Container, 11½″, Middle Eastern silver, rounded bulbous container, incised foliage dec, long tapering top, ftd base	325.00
Seder Plate, 12 x 10″, ceramic, luster finish, Hebrew calligraphy in recessed compartments, Czechoslovakian, c1920	1,500.00
Seder Tray, 12″, pewter, Hebrew inscriptions, German, dated 1811	1,200.00
Shofar, 10″, molded rams horn, German, 19th C	100.00
Spice Tower, 10″, German silver, steeple form, molded circular base, repousse motifs, triple tier filigree rounded upper section, surmounted by flag, hallmarked	1,500.00
Torah Finials, pr	
14″, German silver and gilt, sgd "Posen" at base	3,000.00
15″, tiered, Moroccan style, stylized Menorah dec, French hallmarks, Moroccan, 19th C	6,000.00
Torah Pointer	
8″, Moroccan silver, incised dec, early 20th C	700.00
9″, Wood, Polish, 20th C	300.00
12″, Russian silver, filigree handle, 19th C	1,200.00
Wine Cup	
5¾″	
American silver, tulip form, stemmed, presentation inscription, dated 1866	475.00
English silver, tulip form, stemmed, incised floral dec, dated 1912	375.00
6″, Irish silver, stemmed, Hebrew inscription, dated 1973	550.00
12″, cov, German silver, stemmed, Hebrew inscription of blessing over wine, late 19th C	4,800.00

JUGTOWN POTTERY

History: In 1920 Jacques and Julianna Busbee left their cosmopolitan environs and returned to North Carolina to revive the state's dying craft of pottery making. Jugtown Pottery, a colorful and somewhat off-beat operation, was located in Moore County, miles away from any large city and accessible only "if mud permits."

Ben Owens, a talented young potter, turned the wares. Jacques Busbee did most of the designing and glazing. Julianna handled promotion.

Utilitarian and decorative items were produced. Although many colorful glazes were used, orange predominated. A Chinese blue glaze that ranged from light blue to deep turquoise was a prized glaze reserved for the very finest pieces.

Jacques Busbee died in 1947. Julianna, with the help of Owens, ran the pottery until 1958 when it was closed. After long legal battles, the pottery was reopened in 1960. It now is owned by Country Roads, Inc., a non-profit organization. The pottery still is operating and using the old mark.

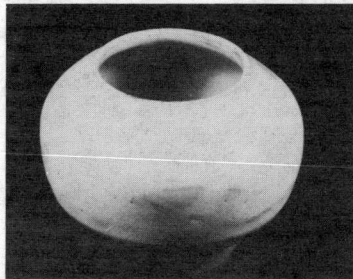

Bowl, 2½" opening, 4" h, gray and brown, c1922–47, $25.00.

Bean Pot, cov, orange, late	35.00
Bowl	
7 x 4½", frothy white over olive green flambe glaze	220.00
10⅝ x 4½", Chinese blue glaze, honey brown stain, marked	175.00
Candlesticks, 7", orange glaze, pr ...	50.00
Creamer, orange glaze, small	40.00
Jar, 10½", ovoid, four pinched strap handles, brown-olive green glaze, marked "Jugtown Ware"	45.00
Pitcher, 6½", incised dec	55.00
Plate, 6", orange glaze	25.00
Pot, 4", orange glaze, marked	50.00
Soup Tureen, cov, 7", orange glaze ..	28.00
Sugar, cov, Chinese blue	120.00
Teapot, cov, 6½", Chinese blue glaze .	80.00
Vase	
7½", turquoise ground, red-purple dec	80.00
8", Chinese blue, emb handles	210.00
13½", urn, emb twisted rope dec, four small handles, cobalt blue	175.00

KPM

K.P.M

History: The mark, KPM, has been used separately and in conjunction with other symbols by many German porcelain manufacturers, among whom are the Köknigliche Porzellan Manufactur in Meissen, 1720s; Köknigliche Porzellan Manufactur in Berlin, 1832–1847; and Krister Porzellan Manufactur in Waldenburg, mid-19th century.

Collectors now use the term "KPM" to refer to the high quality porcelain produced in the Berlin area in the 18th and 19th centuries.

Reference: Susan and Al Bagdade, *Warman's English & Continental Pottery & Porcelain, 1st Edition,* Warman Publishing Co., Inc., 1987.

Bowl, 11 x 13 x 3¼", leaf shape, molded petal edge, applied gold branch handle, int. scene of bird hovering over nest, multicolored flowers, ferns, and leaves, shaded light blue and pink ground, gold trim	650.00
Candelabra, 2 light, white, girl in tree, c1887	250.00
Cup and Saucer, ftd, pink floral medallions, gold enamel, cobalt blue ground	650.00
Figure, 2 seated children with birds, books, and flute at feet, blue and red KPM mark, 19th C	330.00
Jug, 4½", figural, court jester, sitting, pours from mouth, hat stopper, gold detailing, c1830	345.00

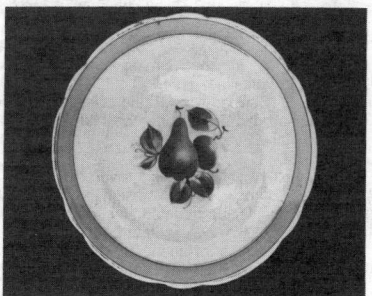

Plate, 8¼" d, pink band, multicolored pear and pium, gold trim, $37.50.

Painting on Porcelain	
Gypsy maiden playing mandolin, artist sgd, 11½ x 7⅞", c1900	4,125.00
Portrait, La Belle Chocolatiere, after Jean Etienne Liotard, 6 x 4"	350.00
Queen Louise, descending staircase, flowing white gown, ermine lined deep blue velvet robe, artist sgd "A Schnizel," after Richter, 16 x 10¼", c1900	5,500.00
Plaque	
Marquerite from Faust, large rose-bush, hp, artist sgd	950.00
Monk wearing brown robe, holding stack of dishes, gazes at 2 butterflies before open window, framed, marked, 11¼ x 8⅞"	1,650.00
Plate, 9½", armorial, reticulated gilt border, center mask head, crown, falcon, and rampant lion, heraldic arms ...	250.00

Tea Set, teapot, creamer, sugar, tray,
two plates, cups, and saucers, sgd
"KPM, King's Porcelain, Berlin" **650.00**
Vase, 6", Napoleon portrait, sgd "Wag-
ner" **625.00**

KAUFFMANN, ANGELICA

History: Marie Angelique Catherine Kauffmann
was a Swiss artist who lived from 1741 until 1807.
Her paintings were copied by many artists who
hand decorated porcelain during the 19th century.
The majority of the paintings are neo-classical in
style.
Reference: Susan and Al Bagdade, *Warman's
English & Continental Pottery & Porcelain, 1st Edition,* Warman Publishing Co., Inc., 1987.

**Plate, 9⅞″ d, three classical figures,
green scalloped design, white ground,
gold filigree, Austria beehive mark,
sgd, $85.00.**

Biscuit Jar, 5″ d, 7″ h, scenic panel with
three ladies and gentleman, pastels,
alternating green and maroon panels,
gold trim, SP rim, cov, and handle . . **145.00**
Bowl, 10″ sq, 3 maidens and cupid,
cranberry and gold border, Austria,
beehive mark **75.00**
Condensed Milk Can Holder, cov,
matching underplate, classical
maiden, green ground, gold tracery . **85.00**
Cup and Saucer, classical scene, royal
blue ground, beehive mark **100.00**
Demitasse Cup and Saucer, ftd, classical ladies scene, fruit on gold band,
beehive mark **55.00**
Demitasse Service, demitasse pot, six
cups and saucers, tray, classical
scenes, sgd, 14 pcs **950.00**
Marmalade Jar, cov, scene of Three
Graces **60.00**

Plate
6¼″, flowers, gold trim sgd **60.00**
8″, 3 maidens and cupid, gold trim,
beehive mark **60.00**
10″, scenic, 4 classical maidens with
cupid, beehive mark **150.00**
10½″, 2 ladies, green border, gold
trim **70.00**
Tobacco Jar, 7½″, dark green muted
with orange and yellow, SP rim and
lid **300.00**
Vase, 20″, classical scene, four maid-
ens, cobalt blue ground, sgd **400.00**

KEW BLAS

History: Amory and Francis Houghton established the Union Glass Company, Somerville, Massachusetts, in 1851. The company went bankrupt
in 1860, but was reorganized. Between 1870 and
1885 the Union Glass Company made pressed
glass and blanks for cut glass.
Art glass production began in 1893 under the
direction of William S. Blake and Julian de Cor-
dova. Two styles were introduced. A Venetian style
consisted of graceful shapes in colored glass, often flecked with gold. An iridescent glass, labeled
Kew Blas, was made in plain and decorated forms.
The pieces are close in design and form to Quezel
products, but lack the subtlety of Tiffany items.
The company ceased production in 1924.

**Tumbler, 3¾″ h, gold int., ribbed, Union
Glass Co, c1890–1924, $235.00.**

Bowl, 8½″, ruffled edge, blue int., dark
green ext., sgd **800.00**
Candlestick, 8½″, twisted stem, irid
gold, pr **725.00**
Compote, 7″, twisted stem, ribbed cup,
irid gold, pink highlights **375.00**

Decanter, 14″, green-gold irid, spherical long stemmed stopper, sgd	**275.00**
Goblet, 6″, irid gold, knob stem	**350.00**
Jack-In-The-Puplit Vase, 8¾″, irid gold	**750.00**
Pitcher, 5″, King Tut, white, green, and gold, blue handle, irid blue lining, sgd	**1,900.00**
Plate, 6″, irid gold, sgd	**180.00**
Rose Bowl, 3½″, green and gold hooked dec, butterscotch ground, gold lining, sgd	**525.00**
Salt, open, irid gold	**225.00**
Tumbler, 4″, pinched sides, gold luster, sgd	**235.00**

Vase

2¾ x 5½″, green and gold pulled design, gold int.	**750.00**
4¾″, bud, baluster, irid peach, dark peach feathering	**375.00**
5″, irid peach ground, dark peach feathers, gold int., sgd	**485.00**
6″, irid apricot, gold pulled feathers, tooled prunts	**825.00**
7½″, bell form, ruffled rim, irid gold, pulled feathers	**385.00**

KITCHEN COLLECTIBLES

History: The kitchen was a central focal point in a family's environment until the 1960s. Many early kitchen utensils were handmade and prized by their owners. Next came a period of utilitarian products made of tin and other metals. When the housewife no longer wished to work in a sterile environment, color was added through enamel and plastic and design served both an aesthetic and functional purpose.

The advent of home electricity changed the type and style of kitchen products. Many items went through fads. The high technology field already has made inroads into the kitchen, and another revolution seems at hand.

References: Jane H. Celehar, *Kitchens and Gadgets*, 1920 to 1950, Wallace-Homestead, 1982; Linda Campbell Franklin, *300 Hundred Years of Kitchen Collectibles, Second Edition,*, Books Americana, 1982; Glydon Shirley, *The Miracle in Grandmother's Kitchen*, published by author, 1983.

Periodical: Kitchen Collectibles News, Box 383, Murray Hill Station, New York, NY 10016.

Additional Listings: Baskets, Brass, Butter Prints, Copper, Fruit Jars, Food Molds, Graniteware, Ironware, Tinware, and Woodenware. See *Warman's Americana & Collectibles* for more examples including electrical appliances.

Apple Peeler, marked "Reading Hardware, 1878"	**45.00**
Biscuit Beater, wood, marked "Richardi & Bechtold"	**20.00**

Apple Peeler, cast iron and brass, patent marks, "Made only by the Reading Hardware Co, Reading, PA," $45.00.

Can Opener, steel blade, double foot, japanned iron handle, Sprague	**10.00**
Coffee Grinder, cast iron and wood, ornate emb top, two sliding panels, bottom drawer	**55.00**
Coffeepot, 8½″ h, enameled, pit bottom, tin cov	**30.00**
Colander, 10½″, aluminum, three cornered, daisy punches on sides	**15.00**
Cookie Board, 20 x 24½″, soft scrubbed finish	**150.00**
Corn Popper, metal, ventilated wire cov, handle, marked "Perfection"	**15.00**
Dough Box, 18 x 34″, dovetailed, splayed turned legs, two board top, refinished pine	**375.00**
Drying Rack, 42½″ w, 55½″ h, wood, dowel rod shelves, wheels	**75.00**
Egg Fryer, cast iron, handled, c1890 . .	**40.00**
Food Chopper, double tang, tin blades, emb "NRS & Co, Groton, NY Patd May 2, 93, No 20"	**35.00**
Funnel, enameled, seamless, handled, 1 pt, marked "Peerless"	**15.00**
Grater, 9″, tin, strap handle	**20.00**
Griddle, cast iron, marked "Griswold No. 7"	**35.00**
Ice Cream Freezer, wood, stave construction, marked "White Mountain Jr"	**250.00**
Ladle, 22″ l, copper bowl, wrought iron rat tail handle, hanging hook, c1800	**150.00**
Lemon Squeezer, cast iron, glass insert, 1882, marked "Kings"	**20.00**
Meat Cleaver, marked "Keen Kutter" .	**40.00**
Meat Tenderizer, gray stoneware, cobalt blue trim, sq wood handle	**450.00**
Muffin Pan, round cups, open handles, dated April 5, 1856	**150.00**
Pastry Wheel, 6⅜″ l, wood, relief carved floral handle, end serrated stamp . .	**175.00**
Potato Baker, lift out grill, tipping ring, 3 pcs	**50.00**

Potato Masher, wood, marked "Richardi
  & Bechtold" 10.00
Pumpkin Chopper, hand crank, dated
  1869 .... 350.00
Rolling Pin, 15" l, blown glass, amethyst 75.00
Salt Box, wood, bent rim, varnished .. 50.00
Sausage Stuffer, 4 qt, marked "Enter-
  prise" 45.00
Skillet, cast iron, lid, marked "Griswold
  No 10" 35.00
Skimmer, 8" d, tin, round strap handle 45.00
Spice Cabinet, wood, 8 drawers, la-
  beled 100.00
Strainer, 6½" l, tin, painted 20.00
Stove Plate, 5" d, emb, wild turkey and
  tree design 15.00
Tea Strainer, tin, ornate leaf design,
  1800s 10.00
Teakettle, 14" d, wrought handle, sliding
  lid, emb "Wood Bishop & Co, Bangor,
  ME," c1800 .... 100.00
Waffle Iron, cast iron, bail handle,
  marked "Griswold No 7," dated 1908 75.00
Water Pail, cedar wood, brass bound,
  handle 35.00

KUTANI

History: In the mid 1600s Kutani originated in
the Kaga province of Japan. Kutani comes in a
variety of color patterns, one of the most popular
being Ao Kutani, a green glaze with colors such
as green, yellow, and purple enclosed in a black
outline. Wares made since the 1870s for export
are enameled in a wide variety of colors and styles.
  Reference: Sandra Andacht, *Oriental Antiques
& Art: An Identification And Value Guide,* Wallace-
Homestead, 1987.

Berry Set, master bowl, six small bowls,
  multicolored enamel floral dec, red
  border, 7 pcs 165.00

Bowl, 7½" d, three men in red, $175.00.

Bottle, cov, red ground, gold dec, figures
  in garden, boy playing flute finial ... 900.00
Bowl
  4⅜", sq, polychrome, gold flowers,
    unglazed foot, sgd gold seal form 300.00
  7", One Thousand Faces, red dec,
    white ground 100.00
  7½", orange-red and green glaze,
    gold highlights, unglazed rim and
    foot, sgd "Dai Ni-pon Ku-tani tsu-
    kuru" 150.00
  9¾", flared, central reserve of young
    scholar, chrysanthemum blossoms
    in brocade bands, 6 character
    mark, pr 100.00
Charger, 14", figural landscape, multicolored, gilt border 225.00
Chocolate Pot, 8½", red, orange and
  gold, reserve panels of peonies and
  birds and people in gardens with
  peonies, Japanese 125.00
Creamer and Sugar, cov, 5 x 5¼" creamer, 7½ x 7" sugar, ftd, burnt orange
  ground, hp scenes, gold tracery, bamboo handles, sgd Oriental character,
  19th C 250.00
Cup and Saucer, people, flowers, trees,
  and clouds, gilt trim, late 30.00
Dish, 7½", octagonal, five children playing in garden 200.00
Ewer, 8¼", duck on floral base, key fret
  band, green, yellow, aubergine, and
  blue enamel 150.00
Figure, 11", man, standing, holding
  scroll and peach 175.00
Ginger Jar, cov, 5", blue, green, and car-
  mine enamel dec, fu dog finial 100.00
Hair Receiver, heart shape, One Thousand Faces, green glaze, sgd "Ao
  Kutani" 90.00
Sake Cup, 1⅞", floriform rim, short ring
  foot, enamel and gilt dec, patterned
  rim band, gilt scrolling flower and trellis dec 100.00
Teapot, 5½", bulbous, panels of garden
  scene 125.00
Tray, gilt river scene and boat, red
  ground 150.00
Umbrella Stand, 28", multicolored butterflies, flowers, foliage, and medallions 500.00
Vase
  9½", pear shaped, recessed ring foot,
    enamel and gilt dec, peach shaped
    reserves, brocade diamond and
    scrolling tendril ground 150.00
  10", double gourd shape, birds and
    flowers, gold, orange, 1875 ..... 175.00
  11¾", cylindrical, high shoulder, fierce
    dragon, green and turquoise on
    yellow and aubergine ground, sgd
    "Fuku," pr 275.00

13″, multicolored peacocks on rocks, peony blossoms, gilt trim, marked **250.00**

LALIQUE

A.LALIQUE

LALIQUE

History: Rene Lalique (1860–1945) first gained prominence as a jewelry designer. Around 1900 he began experimenting with molded glass brooches and pendants, often embellishing them with semiprecious stones. By 1905 he was devoting himself exclusively to the manufacture of glass articles.

In 1908 Lalique began designing packaging for the French cosmetic houses. He also produced many objects, especially vases, bowls, and figurines, in the Art Noveau style in the 1910s. The full scope of Lalique's genius was seen at the 1925 Paris International Exhibition of Decorative Arts. He later moved to the Art Deco form.

The mark "R. LALIQUE FRANCE" in block letters is found on pressed articles, tableware, vases, paperweights, and mascots. The script signature, with or without "France," is found on hand blown objects. Occasionally a design number is included. The word "France" in any form indicates a piece made after 1926.

The post–1945 mark is "Lalique France" without the "R," but there are exceptions to this rule.

Reference: Katherine Morrison McClinton, *Introduction to Lalique Glass*, Wallace-Homestead, 1978.

Reproduction Alert: Much faking of the Lalique signature occurs, the most common being the addition of an "R" to the post–1945 mark.

Ashtray, 6″ d, frosted intaglio curved fish, clear intaglio bubbles, script sgd "Lalique, France" **200.00**
Bowl
2½ x 4½″, clear and frosted, center stylized cherry tree medallion, sgd **75.00**
8″, swirl pattern, "R. Lalique" **275.00**
9½″, frosted running greyhound design, sgd **125.00**
13″, bubble, R. Lalique **375.00**
Box, cov
6⅝″ d, amber, six molded sparrow cov **715.00**
7″ d, molded, tinged with opalescence, molded signature "R. Lalique," c1925 . . . . **600.00**
Brooch, 3½″, oval, molded grasshoppers, blades of grass, frosted, clear blue, gilt metal backing, c1910 . . . . **1,000.00**
Centerpiece
8¼″ h, "The Three Graces," cherubs

clad by single vine, raised on D-shape base, script signature "Lalique, France" **420.00**
10″ h, molded, cherub dec, stamped "R. Lalique" **1,800.00**
Centerpiece Bowl
10″ d, Nemours, molded flower head with black glass center point ext., script signature "Lalique France" . **185.00**
14″ d, molded long leaves underneath to rim, script signature "Lalique France" **260.00**
Champagne Bucket, 7¼″ h, clear and frosted, cylindrical, molded vertical panels of birds in tree branches divided by raised plain vertical panels, 1930s, etched "R. Lalique France" . **500.00**

Vase, 3½″ h, lion's face, modern, script sgd, $50.00.

Chandelier, Coquilles shell design, orig glass ceiling mount, four suspension cords, molded and etched sgd **1,500.00**
Clock, Naiades, blue wash **2,250.00**
Decanter, 9¼″ h, clear and frosted, baluster body, circular foot, molded rooster stopper, two matching cordials, stenciled signature **650.00**
Dish, 14½″ d, opalescent, molded mermaid surrounded by swirling bubbles, three ftd, molded "R. Lalique," incised "France" and "No. 376" **2,100.00**
Figure, frosted
5″, Moquer, sparrow **375.00**
5⅛″ h, Naiade, seated mermaid . . . **1,540.00**
Hood Ornament, clear and frosted
5″ h, nude male archer **1,650.00**
6⅛″ h, falcon **1,450.00**
Jar, 4¼″ h, brown patinated, molded "R. Lalique," incised "R. Lalique France" **350.00**
Paperweight, 2¼ x 3¼″, rounded top, intaglio frosted nude, mermaid tail, acid etched script "Lalique, France" **300.00**
Perfume, 4″, heart shaped, Farouche, Ricci, sgd, red plush box **300.00**

Perfume Bottle, heart shape, 6″, Nina
  Ricci 200.00
Place Card Holder, molded, inscribed
  "R. Lalique France," set of twelve . .   600.00
Plaque, 1¾ x 1¼″, frosted, rect, molded
  female water sprite springing from
  water fountain, molded "LALIQUE" .   240.00
Stemware, clear glass foot and conical
  bowl, swelled cylindrical stem,
  molded overlapping leaves, four
  wines, four cordials, set of eight . . .   320.00
Tumbler, 5¾″ h, 3″ d, Jaffa pattern, amber, sixteen frosted, serrated V-
  shaped indented columns, incised
  "R. Lalique France" 250.00
Vase
  4¾″ h, Grenade, spherical, molded
    serrated arches, amber, clear and
    frosted 1,650.00
  5″, molded, irid, sgd "Lalique Paris"   450.00
  5¼″ h, birds, sgd "France" 300.00
  5½″ h, opal glass, molded swimming
    carp, c1925 . . . .   750.00
  6½″ h, Gui, molded, mistletoe berries
    and leaves, frosted 345.00
  8¾″, frosted, tulips in relief, SS de-
    posit 125.00
  12″ h, bird dec, ovoid form 850.00

LAMP SHADES

History: Lamp shades were made to diffuse the
harsh light produced by early gas lighting fixtures.
These early shades were made by popular Art
Nouveau manufacturers including Durand, Quezal, Steuben, Tiffany, and others. Many shades
are not marked.

References: Dr. Larry Freeman, *New Lights on
Old Lamps*, American Life Foundation, 1984; Jo
Ann Thomas, *Early Twentieth Century Lighting
Fixtures*, Collector Books, 1980.

Blue frosted glass, ribbed, emb florals,
2″ d fitter ring, $15.00.

Burmese, 8¾″ d, gas, birds, butterflies,
  and flowers dec 250.00
Cameo Glass, 2¼″ gaslight fitter ring,
  powder blue, white maidenhair fern
  sprays and border, English, pr 1,500.00
Cased, yellow, gold enameled trim, miniature lamp, SI-386 . . . .   365.00
Custard, 2″, nutmeg stain 35.00
Duncan & Miller, Diamond Edge 32.00
Durand
  3½″, candle, gold irid 120.00
  8″
    King Tut, orange irid, opal int. . . .   265.00
    Lily, gold threads, opal ground . . .   225.00
Fostoria
  5″, gold, green leaves and vines,
    white lustre ground 125.00
  5½″, opal, gold pulled dec, gold int. .   115.00
Handel, hanging dome type
  20½″, radiating geometric tiles, mot-
    tled ivory, reddish pink shading to
    mottled green, ochre, green, and
    turquoise winged motifs, ruby red
    lotus buds, imp "Handel," c1905 .   1,760.00
  23″, red flowers around multicolored
    border, sgd 1,200.00
Imperial-Nuart
  Crystal, electric, cluster type, frosted
    int., flower etching, No. 0553/31 . .   25.00
  Frosted, Pattern No. 591/6 . . . .   18.00
  Pearl Ruby, etched, Pattern No. 5913/
    103, fan, star dec 35.00
  Pressed, 4″ gas fitter collar, cut crys-
    tal, Pattern No. 46C 35.00
Lalique, hanging dome type
  12″, amber, shallow, molded shells,
    sgd 550.00
  14″, crystal, frosted, block panels,
    molded leaves, sgd 675.00
Leaded, hanging dome type
  17½″, Art Nouveau, stylized green flo-
    ral motif, c1925 . . . .   365.00
  24″, pink floral border 1,250.00
  24½″, caramel field, red poinsettias,
    green leaves 1,200.00
  27″, wild rose border, Duffner & Kim-
    berly, NY 3,500.00
Luster Art
  2¼″, calcite, threading 100.00
  4¼ x 4⅛″, white ext., gold irid int.,
    2¼″ fitter, sgd, set of four 300.00
  5″, double hooked blue pulled feather,
    gold border, opal, gold irid int., acid
    etched sgd 385.00
Northwood, 8¼″, light pink, etched flow-
  ers, frosted, ruffled 100.00
Opalescent, 9″ h, Hobbs Coin Dot pat-
  tern, clear, 5″ fitter 175.00
Pairpoint, candle lamp type
  Cut and frosted amethyst glass 125.00
  Multicolored floral puffy type 250.00

Quezal

3¾", Zipper, gold, opal **175.00**
4 x 5", sq, fluted, irid gold, sgd, 2¼"
  fitter, pr **150.00**
4½", gold irid, ten ribbed sides, sgd . **100.00**
4½", lily, white calcite ext., gold irid
  int., sgd **125.00**
4⅞", gold irid, feather dec, sgd **135.00**
5¾", blue feather, white ground, gold
  int. **225.00**

Steuben

4", green drape, wide gold border,
  pearly white calcite ground, silver
  aurene int., sgd **185.00**
5 x 4", pulled gold aurene feathers,
  green outline, calcite ground, gold
  int., marked, numbered #799 . . . **135.00**
5½", drag loop, brown aurene, calcite
  ground, gold int. **175.00**
5½", green, purple, gold irid, opal
  ground, fish net pattern, gold irid
  int. **175.00**

Tiffany

3½", candle, ruffled, Favrile **300.00**
16", dome, leaded, striated oxblood
  red, rose, violet, and blue woodbine
  leaves, striated blue, green, and
  opal ground, imp "Tiffany Studios,
  New York" **15,400.00**
29", Favrile, floral bouquet, multico-
  lored flowers, metal beaded edge,
  imp "Tiffany Studios, New York" . **28,600.00**

Webb, 4 x 6¾", satin, overlay, double
  cut white to chartreuse, leaf dec . . . **250.00**

LAMPS AND LIGHTING

History: Lighting devices have evolved from
simple stone age oil lamps to the popular electrified models of today. Aim Argand patented the first
oil lamp in 1784. Around 1850 kerosene became
a popular lamp burning fluid, replacing whale oil
and other fluids. In 1879 Thomas A. Edison invented the electric light bulb, causing fluid lamps
to lose favor and creating a new field for lamp
manufacturers to develop. Companies like Tiffany
and Handel developed skills in the manufacture of
electric lamps, having their decorators produce
beautiful aesthetic bases and shades.

References: J. W. Courter, *Aladdin, The Magic
Name in Lamps*, Wallace-Homestead, 6th Printing,
1980; J. W. Courter, *Collectors Manual & Price
Guide Nine, 1983*, published by author, 1982; Rob-
ert De Falco, Carole Goldman Hibel, John Hibel,
Handel Lamps, H & D Press, Inc., 1986; Dr. Larry
Freeman, *New Light on Old Lamps*, American Life
Foundation, 1984; Joanne C. Grant, *The Painted
Lamps of Handel*, published by author, 1978; Jo
Ann Thomas, *Early Twentieth Century Lighting
Fixtures*, Collector Books, 1980; Catherine M. V.
Thuro, *Oil Lamps*, Wallace-Homestead, 1976;

Catherine M. V. Thuro, *Oil Lamps II*, Thorncliffe
House, Inc., 1983.

Collectors' Club: Aladdin Knights, R.D. #1,
Simpson, IL 62985, *The Mystic Light of the Aladdin Knights*, (bi-monthly); Historical Lighting Society of Canada, P.O. Box 561, Postal Station R,
Toronto, ON M4G 4E1. *The Illuminator.*

Museum: Winchester Center Kerosene Lamp
Museum, Winchester Center, CT.

Additional Listings: See specific makers and
Pattern Glass.

**Early American, 5" l, 1¾" h, tin, fat lamp,
tavern type, $125.00.**

AMERICAN, EARLY

Betty

9½", tin, crimped edged stand, wire
  pick and chain **175.00**
52½", wooden stand, pr of wrought
  iron lamps, twisted hangers, sgd
  "H. & R. Boker" **275.00**
Crusie, wrought iron, 10½", double han-
  ger **175.00**
Kettle, 10", iron, trunnion, sliding reser-
  voir cov, hanger, PA, early 19th C . . **425.00**
Loom, wrought iron, hanging, adjusta-
  ble trammel, brass candle socket, ad-
  justs from 30 to 42½" **300.00**
Peg, 4½", tin, petticoat, whale oil burner,
  orig brown japanning **100.00**

BOUDOIR

Aladdin, 7", kneeling Arab woman . . . **115.00**
Gone-With-The-Wind, 13" h, 6" shade,
  white milk glass, emb plumes, yellow
  ground, green scroll highlights, #2
  kerosene burner **215.00**
Pairpoint, 14½" h, 8" d puffy frosted reverse painted shade, Apple Blossom
  pattern, baluster shaped silver finish
  metal base **1,100.00**

CHANDELIERS

Brandt, Edgar, 37"d, drum form wrought
  iron standard, six circular frosted
  glass shades cast with stepped lines
  and stylized flowers, imp "E Brandt,"
  c1925 . . . . **2,750.00**

Daum Nancy, 21¾" d, inverted conical ceiling cap, undulated cylindrical standard, two inverted conical shades, pendant teardrop finial, pale yellow glass with internal gold colored foil, etched radiating and scalloped dec, inscribed "Daum Nancy France," c1925 . . . . **6,750.00**

Tiffany, 29" d, sharp conical shade, all-over full blown blossoms and buds, mottled pastel yellow, dusty rose, pink striated apricot and opal, emerald and olive green leaves, opal ground of shaded green and sienna, beaded edge, imp "Tiffany Studios, New York," c1899–1920 . . . . **22,000.00**

DESK

Art Nouveau, painted glass shade, patinated metal, mounted with two buffalo **125.00**

Emeralite, cased green shade, brass base and adjustable stem **300.00**

Handel
18" l, 6½" d shade, roll top desk type, dome leaded rect green slag glass shade, heavy bronze base, ribbed arm on large inverted cylindrical petal base, shade and base sgd "Handel" **1,750.00**
26½" h, hexagonal acid etched yellow to orange shade, green leaves border, reverse painted, patinated metal swivel base, shade marked "Handel" **1,200.00**

Tiffany, c1899–1920
13½", nautilus shell form Favrile glass shade, striated emerald green and opal tiles, two bronze arms, cast dolphins standard, base imp "Tiffany Studios, New York" **10,000.00**
14" h, Favrile turtleback tile shade, bronze U shaped support, short standard, circular base with green glass cabochons, five ball feet, base imp "Tiffany Studios, New York, 28632," c1899–1920 . . . . . . **4,000.00**
15" h, Favrile linenfold shade, gilt bronze, counterbalance **4,000.00**

FLOOR

Brandt, Edgar, 78" h, flaring mottled apple green, tangerine, golden yellow, and coffee glass shade, raised bronze standard in form of giant coiling cobra on inverted woven basket, imp "E. Brandt," c1925 . . . . **38,500.00**

Duffner and Kimberly, 22" d shade, 64" h, cylindrical brass base, foliate motif, domed pink and white shade, amber poppies and green leaves border, scalloped border **4,000.00**

Handel, 57" h, 10" d shade, domical chipped, sand finished shade, int. painted with two multicolored parrots, heart shaped copper-bronze frame, tulip shaped socket, circular stepped footed base, shade sgd "Handel 6953 F.L.," (Florence Lewis) **8,250.00**

FLUID

Argand
14", heavy cast metal, brass dec, orig burner, sgd "J. B. Jones & Co, Boston Warranted," one orig chimney and cut etched shade, pr **1,200.00**
16", double, heavy cast brass/bronze, orig burners and shade holders . . **400.00**

Boston and Sandwich Glass Co, 8¾", clear, flint, Cable pattern, brass collar and burner, hexagonal base, pr **250.00**

Fibre Ware, papier mache, 10", turned maple stem, orig canvas lapel stamped "Fibre Ware Co, Portland, Maine," c1875 . . . . **150.00**

Hobbs, Quad Loop font, clear glass, mounted on blue alabaster Atterbury swan base, sgd "Patd Sept 29 1868" and "Nov 16 1869" **625.00**

New England Glass Co, 9½" h, globular cut, etched font, blown knob stem, octagonal pressed base, pewter collar **350.00**

Ripley & Co, 14⅝", clambroth and blue, brass collar, kerosene burner, clear chimney, base marked, patent dates **250.00**

HANGING

14", library, cranberry hobnail shade, drop-in brass font and frame, clear and cranberry cut prisms, white milk glass hanging matchholder, brass plated ceiling hook **1,150.00**

18 x 21½", wall mounted, three arm, cast iron, plain clear glass fonts, floral dec acid cut ruffled shades, gold and black frame dec **385.00**

27", double, angle, emb brass, clear glass elbows, milk glass shades . . . **425.00**

39", hall, Victorian, cranberry bull's eye shade, brass frame, smokebell **250.00**

STUDENT

German, 21", nickel plated brass, 7" old slant side white milk glass shade, height adjustment knob marked "German Student Lamp Co," burner marked "C. A. Kleeman Patented Mar 10 1863, Reissued Dec 30 1873 F. A. Hinrichs, New York" **325.00**

Student, 20¼″ h, single, pewter and brass, hp milk glass font, orig white cased glass shade, new chimney, patent June 4, 1870, electrified, $450.00.

Handel, 24½″ h, patinated metal base, sq foot, scrolled corners, central cylindrical stem, two curved arms, cream and red pond lily shade, base imp "Handel" **1,350.00**

Manhattan, 20½″, nickel plated brass, green cased shade, electrified **450.00**

Tiffany, 29¾″, double, bronze standard, central bulging cylindrical oil canister, green damascene shades, base imp "Tiffany Studios, New York" **8,000.00**

TABLE

Astral, 23″ h, brass, 6″ cut and frosted shade set in modified ring, fourteen 7″ speer prisms, substitute P & A Victor burner **425.00**

Banquet, 26″ h, 7″ frosted shade, heavily emb brass font, marble stem, brass plated foot **200.00**

Cameo, 15″ d domical shade of yellow glass overlaid in brown, cut stag in wooded landscape, sgd "Arsall" in cameo, black patinated peasant couple on base, figural base cast from model by Bruno Zach, base inscribed "Zach Austria" **3,000.00**

Gone-With-The-Wind

24½″ h, 9½″ ball shade, red satin glass, cherub pattern shade, kerosene burner, brass base, minor flakes **800.00**

25″ h, 12″ Tam O'Shanter shade, white milk glass, pink and green ground, mermaids, waves, and seagulls scene, beaded fringe, electrified **500.00**

30″ h, 12″ d shade, milk glass, gold ground, shepherd with sheep

scene on ball shaped shade, girl with flock on ewer shaped base, electrified **1,000.00**

Handel

22″ h, 18″ d shade, domical chipped, lightly sand finished shade, theroma obverse int. painting of sunset forest scene, red-orange sky, deep green foliage, bronze finish metal base with relief trees and leaves, raised root design base, base sgd "Handel" **2,150.00**

23½″ h, 18″ d shade, domical chipped, lightly sand finished shade, Birdcage dec, int. painted, black border of multicolored flowers and exotic bluebirds **2,500.00**

24″ h, 18″ d shade, domical chipped, sand finished shade

Treasure Island scene, int. painted with moonlit purple and blue scene of sailing ship near island, bronze metal inverted floriform stem base, six bracket feet ...**13,750.00**

Yellowstone National Park scene, ext. and int. shade painted with mountain landscape and two waterfalls, known as large brass finish metal base, broad Art Nouveau baluster stylized tree trunk form, molded with petals and low relief, sgd "W.R." (William Runge), numbered 6211 .....**21,000.00**

Pairpoint, 20″ h, 15″ d reverse painted domed shade, landscape scene of houses, trees, open fields, and blue skies, patinated metal conical base, painted "H Fisher, The Pairpoint Corp" **1,600.00**

Tiffany, c1899–1920

21″ h, 16″ d domical shade, allover pattern of black-eyed susans, pumpkin and mustard petals, deep brown centers, striated mint green leaves, striated green ground, three arm bronze support, cylindrical standard, applied coilings, cushion form circular base, four petal form feet, bronze finial, shade and base imp "Tiffany Studios, New york," c1899–1920 ......**26,500.00**

24″ h, 18½″ d shallow domical shade, allover pattern of dogwood branches and leaves, striated rose and pink, medium green and rose striated and fractured leaves, striated chocolate and deep ochre scrolling branches, sky and pale aquamarine ground, bronze urn form oil lamp base and finial, shade and base imp "Tiffany Studios, New York" **41,800.00**

LANTERNS

History: A lantern is an enclosed, portable light source, hand carried or attached to a bracket or pole to illuminate an area. Many lanterns can be used both indoors and outdoors and have a protected flame. Fuels used in early lanterns included candles, kerosene, whale oil, coal oil, and later gasoline, natural gas, and batteries.

Tole, 12½" h, four glass panels, painted black, attributed to New York State, mid 19th C, $100.00.

Barn, 15", 4 panel, pierced tin cone, wire bail, Dietz 150.00
Battery Operated, 8", tin, marked "Supreme," Embury Mfg Co, Warsaw, NY 35.00
Bicycle
  5¼", new silver paint, marked "Joseph Lucas Ltd, Patented Birmingham, Planet #33" 25.00
  6", nickel plated, marked "Hawthorne Mfg Co, Old Sol Pat. U.S.A." 48.00
  7", nickel plate over brass, marked "Solar-The Badger Brass Mfg Co, Kenosha, Wis, U.S.A.," last patent Feb 4, 1896 . . . . 65.00
Buggy, blue japanned finish, marked "Dominion Tubular Lamp Co, Square Lift No. 0," patent July 12, 1888 . . . 60.00
Candle, 9½", tin, four candles, frosted glass pane on back 175.00
Carriage, 26½" h, brass, Victorian, early 19th C, pr 1,000.00
Coleman No. 242, brass, nickel plated font, green porcelain top, clear globe 30.00
Dietz
  16", No. 1 Climax, tin, glass door, two glass sides, orig blue japanned paint, replacement metal kerosene font 50.00
  22", Station #60, wire bail and hanging hook, flat wick burner, clear

globe, painted black, white reflector int., cone shape 200.00
22¼", #2, sq, tubular, stenciled, reflector, electrified brass font, bail and back hanger 160.00
Hall, 7" d shade, cylindrical, cranberry glass 150.00
Hand, 6¾", tin, bull's eye lens, orig whale oil burner 50.00
House, 18½", Diamond, three corner shape, turret top, rear hanger, tin back, two glass front sides, iron candle socket 225.00
Kerosene, 20½", tin, emb brass label "Tubular Square Lamp," patent dates 1867, 1878, black paint, orig burner 100.00
Miner, tin, marked "Gateshead on Tyne," Patterson Lames, Ltd 50.00
Onion shaped globe, 11½", clear glass globe, tin base and top wire bail, brass cap, fancy vent and cut-outs, kerosene font 270.00
Pierced Tin, 12", New England Glass Co, patent Oct 24, 1854 . . . . 175.00
Railroad
  2 x 9½", pullman, nickle plated brass, glass chimney, marked "P.L.M.," chimney marked "SNCF" over "SA," spring fed candle 100.00
  11½", band handled twin tube, natural tin, brass cap 85.00
  13", tin fixed globe, wick burner with guards, tin arm ring, new black paint 75.00
  16½", switch, Adlake, four sides with wire bails, two red, two blue-green lenses, pr 175.00
Ship, 13", Dietz, orig red lens, wire bail, two tie down loops, orig black paint . 75.00
Skater's, 7½", Diamond, all brass, convex flat wick, marked "Patent Mar 1854, Lantern Pat 1866 and 1868," brass chain and finger ring 175.00
Telephone Co, 12", Dietz, marked "Bell System," red globe 125.00
Whale Oil, 11", tin, clear blown globe, patent 125.00

LEEDS CHINA

History: The Leeds Pottery in Yorkshire, England, began production about 1758. Among its products was creamware that was competitive with that of Wedgwood. The initial factory closed in 1820, but various subsequent owners continued until 1880. They made exceptional cream colored ware, either plain, salt-glazed, or painted with colored enamels, and glazed and unglazed redware.

Early wares are unmarked. Later pieces bear marks of "Leeds Pottery," sometimes followed by "Hartley-Green and Co." or the letters "LP". Reproductions also have these marks.

Reference: Susan and Al Bagdade, *Warman's English & Continental Pottery & Porcelain, 1st Edition,* Warman Publishing Co., Inc., 1987.

Leaf shaped dish, 4¾" d, blue Oriental dec, white ground, $150.00.

Bowl, ftd, oval, reticulated	175.00
Charger, 15½", five color urn, floral spray, blue feathered edge	450.00
Chestnut Bowl, cov, reticulated band on bowl, twisted rope handles, 1790–1800	775.00
Creamer, 3⅜" h, brown, yellow dec . .	125.00
Cup and Saucer, five color, floral and crosshatched dec	100.00
Cup Plate, 3¾", gaudy blue floral dec .	230.00

Jug
4½", baluster body, transfer printed in underglaze blue, iron-red, yellow, green, and brown enameled scene of hunter and two hounds, silver resist border, blue floral garland, c1815 . . . . 275.00
8¾", mask, figures of men and women, molded bead work borders, handle with floral terminals, enameled in iron-red, yellow, green, brown, and black, gilded, c1775 . . . . 575.00
Loving Cup, 4⅞" h, 2 handles ending in leaf terminals, three color dec, flowers, inscribed "Robert Hill 1791" . . . 400.00
Plate
7⅛", green molded feather edge, four color Gaudy dec 300.00
7¼", eagle dec, underglaze blue, brown, yellow, and green 240.00

8¾", creamware, scalloped blue border, blue flowers and leaves 120.00
9½", underglaze blue, Chinese landscape dec, c1780 . . . . 465.00
Platter
9¾ x 8", creamware, pierced basket loop border 150.00
16½", creamware, blue feather edge 165.00
Snuff Box, 2¾" d, cov, waisted cylindrical box, iron-red, puce, yellow, and green painted floral sprays, floral wreath enclosing inscription "When This You See, Remember Me, W.G. 1779," and "A Pinch Of This Deserv's a Kiss" 585.00
Sugar, cov, multicolored dec, shell handles, button finial 250.00
Teapot
5", octagonal, white with emb feathers, c1780 . . . . 415.00
7¼", Gaudy, blue, white floral dec, repairs to spout, lid 250.00
Toddy Plate, 5½",, peafowl in tree, five color dec 265.00

LENOX CHINA

History: In 1889 Jonathan Cox and Walter Scott Lenox established The Ceramic Art Co. at Trenton, New Jersey. By 1906 Lenox formed his own company, Lenox, Inc. Using potters lured from Belleek, Lenox began making an American version of this famous ware.

Older Lenox china has two marks: a green wreath and a pallette. The pallette mark appears on blanks supplied to amateurs who hand painted china as a hobby. The Lenox Company still exists and currently uses a gold stamped mark.

Reference: Mary Frank Gaston, *American Belleek,* Collector Books, 1984.

Additional Listings: Belleek.

Bowl, 5½", Durgin SS ftd holder	125.00
Box, cov	
4 x 5", hp, pink floral dec	50.00
7" l, green, gold trim, finial	100.00
Bust, 9", girl, glazed white, sgd	225.00
Cake Set, 10½" low pedestal plate, six 7½" plates, Mimosa pattern, green wreath mark, 7 pcs	175.00
Candleholder, insert, pewter handled holder	48.00
Coaster, 3" d, cobalt blue, SS overlay, gold washed	75.00
Compote, 7 x 5", fluted edge, light blue stem, white bowl, green wreath mark	60.00

Salt, 3″ l, 2″ h, swan, light coral, green mark, $27.50.

Creamer, 4″, creamy white, silver rim, SS pedestal base, green mark	25.00
Decanter Set, decanter, orig stopper, five shot glasses, ivory, gold trim, green mark, 6 pcs	110.00
Demitasse Cup and Saucer, hp, bird on branch, artist sgd	60.00
Desk Set, pink ribbons, green ivy, yellow rope, gold dec, green mark, 1896, 7 pcs	1,150.00
Figure	
Bird, 7″, on pedestal, open back, pink Floradora, 9½″	95.00
	125.00
Penguin, three colors, green wreath mark	180.00
Swan, 3″, pink	50.00
Loving Cup, two handles, "Sons of St Patrick," John Barry dec	175.00
Mug, cobalt blue, SS overlay bands	65.00
Plate, figural, fish shape, green mark	55.00
Powder Box, cov, rose	95.00
Salt, individual, hp	12.00
Salt and Pepper Shakers, pr, 5½″, multicolored, hand and cigar, gold wreath mark	45.00
Shoe, ornate dec, flowers, gilt trim	125.00
Teapot, 3½ x 3¾″, brown glaze, SS overlay, green wreath, unicorn mark	150.00
Toby Mug, William Penn	150.00
Tray, 14″, flower chain, hp, handled, palette mark	135.00
Vase, 8¼″, cornucopia, coral, gold dec, pedestal base, green wreath mark, pr	250.00

LIBBEY GLASS

History: In 1888 Edward Libbey established the Libbey Glass Company in Toledo, Ohio, after the closing of the New England Glass Works of W. L. Libbey and Son in East Cambridge, Massachusetts. The new Libbey company produced quality cut glass for the "Brilliant Period."

In 1930 Libbey's interest in art glass production was renewed. A. Douglas Nash was employed as a designer in 1931.

The factory continues production today as Libbey Glass Co.

Reference: Carl U. Fauster, *Libbey Glass Since 1818-Pictorial History & Collector's Guide,* Len Beach Press, 1979.

Additional Listings: Amberina Glass and Cut Glass.

Vase, 7⅞″ h, amberina, flared rim, scalloped edges, vertically ribbed baluster body, pedestal base, sgd, $1,000.00.

Bowl	
7″ d, amberina, ruffled flared rim, sgd	350.00
8″ d, Maize	100.00
Champagne, 6½″ h, twisted stem, thin green concentric circles	125.00
Compote, 7″ h, Zipper pattern, turquoise, twisted stem	275.00
Cordial, clear	
Concord pattern	45.00
Embassy pattern, 6¾″ h	75.00
Goblet, 7″ h, clear bowl, opal cat silhouette in stem, sgd	125.00
Pitcher, 8¾″ h, Maize, amber irid, blue husks, applied strap handle, Joseph Locke patent	585.00
Salt Shaker, Maize, creamy opaque, yellow husks, orig top	85.00
Sherbet, 5″ d, 5″ h, amberina, sgd, 1917	365.00
Sugar, 2¾″ h, cov, Optic Rib, pale blue opal, satin finish, gold enamel "World's Fair 1893"	150.00
Wine, 7″ h, clear bowl, black bear silhouette in stem	175.00

LIMITED EDITION COLLECTOR PLATES

History: Bing and Grondahl made the first collector plate in 1895. Royal Copenhagen issued their first Christmas plate in 1908.

In the late 1960s and early 1970s, several potteries, glass factories, mints, and artists began issuing plates commemorating people, animals, events, etc. Christmas plates were supplemented by Mother's Day plates, Easter plates, etc. A sense of speculation swept the field, fostered in part by flamboyant ads in newspapers and flashy direct mail promotions.

Collectors often favor the first plate issued in a series above all others. Condition is a prime factor. Having the original box also increases price.

Limited edition collector plates, more than any other object in this guide, should be collected for design and pleasure and only secondarily for rise in value.

References: Bradford Exchange, Ltd., *The Bradford Book of Collector's Plates,* Charles Winthrope & Sons, 1983; Diane Carnevale, exec. ed., *Collectibles Market Guide & Price Index To Limited Edition Plates, Figurines, Bells, Graphics, Steins, and Dolls, Fifth Edition,* Schiffer Publishing, 1988; Gene Ehlert, *The Official Price Guide To Collector Plates, Fifth Edition,* House of Collectibles, 1988.

Periodicals: Collector Editions, Collector Communications Corp, 170 Fifth Ave, New York, NY 10010; collectors Mart, WEB Publications, Inc. 15100 W. Kellogg, Wichita, KS 67235; Plate World Publication of Bradford Exchange, 9200 N. Maryland Ave., Niles, IL 60648.

Collectors' Club: International Plate collectors Guild, P. O. Box 487, Artesia, CA 90701.

Museum: Bradford Museum, Niles, IL.

Additional Listings: See *Warman's Americana & Collectibles* for more examples of collector places plus many other limited edition collectibles.

AMERICAN ROSE SOCIETY (United States)

1975, Oregold	140.00
1976, America	135.00
1977, Double Delight	112.00
1978, Color Magic	100.00
1979, Friendship	85.00
1980, Love	80.00
1981, White Lightnin	75.00
1982, Brandy	65.00
1983, Sun Flare	50.00
1984, Olympiad	50.00
1985, Peace	48.00

BAREUTHER (Germany)

Christmas Plates, Hans Mueller artist, 8″ d

1967 Stiftskirche, FE	100.00
1968 Kapplkirche	35.00
1970 Chapel in Oberndorf	18.00
1972 Christmas in Munich	20.00
1974 Church In The Black Forest . .	20.00
1976 Chapel in the Hills	25.00

1978 Mittenwald	30.00
1980 Miltenberg	38.00
1982 Bad Wimpfen	40.00
1984 Zeil on the River Main	42.50
1986 Christmas in Forchhe	42.50

Father's Day Series, Hans Mueller artist, 8″ d

1969 Castle Neuschwanstein	48.00
1970 Castle Pfalz	15.00
1972 Castle Hohenschwangau	30.00
1974 Wurzburg Castle	45.00
1976 Castle Hohenzollern	25.00
1978 Castle Falkenstein	30.00
1980 Castle Cochum	35.00
1982 Castle Zwingenberg	40.00
1984 Castle Neuenstein	42.50

Mother's Day

1969 Mother & Children	75.00
1970 Mother & Children	30.00
1972 Mother & Children	22.00
1974 Musical Children	35.00
1976 Rocking The Cradle	28.00
1978 Blind Man's Bluff	28.00
1980 The First Cherries	35.00
1982 Suppertime	40.00
1984 Village Children	42.50

BERLIN (Germany)

Christmas Plates, various artists, 7¾″ d

1970 Christmas In Bernkastel	130.00
1972 Christmas In Michelstadt	50.00
1974 Christmas In Bremen	25.00
1976 Christmas Eve In Augsburg . .	30.00
1978 Christmas Market At The Berlin Cathedral	55.00
1980 Christmas Eve in Mittenberg . .	55.00
1982 Christmas Eve In Wasserburg .	55.00
1984 Christmas in Ramsau	50.00
1986 Christmas Eve in Gelnhaus . .	65.00

BING AND GRONDAHL (Denmark)

Christmas Plates, various artists, 7″ d

1895 Behind The Frozen Window . .	3,600.00
1896 New Moon Over Snow Covered Trees	1,475.00
1897 Christmas Meal Of The Sparrows	1,100.00
1898 Christmas Roses And Christmas Star	600.00
1899 The Crows Enjoying Christmas	900.00
1900 Church Bells Chiming In Christmas	800.00
1901 The Three Wise Men From The East	485.00
1902 Interior Of A Gothic Church . .	285.00
1903 Happy Expectation of Children	150.00
1904 View of Copenhagen From Frederiksberg Hill	125.00

1905 Anxiety Of The Coming Christmas Night	130.00
1906 Sleighing To Church On Christmas Eve	95.00
1907 The Little Match Girl	125.00
1908 St. Petri Church of Copenhagen	85.00
1909 Happiness Over The Yule Tree	100.00
1910 The Old Organist	90.00
1911 First It Was Sung By Angels To Shepherds In The Fields	80.00
1912 Going To Church On Christmas Eve	80.00
1913 Bringing Home The Yule Tree	85.00
1914 Royal Castle of Amalienborg, Copenhagen	75.00
1915 Chained Dog Getting Double Meal On Christmas Eve	120.00
1916 Christmas Prayer of the Sparrows	85.00
1917 Arrival Of The Christmas Boat	75.00
1918 Fishing Boat Returning Home For Christmas	85.00
1919 Outside The Lighted Window	80.00
1920 Hare In The Snow	75.00
1921 Pigeons In The Castle Court	55.00
1922 Star Of Bethlehem	60.00
1923 Royal Hunting Castle, The Hermitage	55.00
1924 Lighthouse In Danish Waters	65.00
1925 The Child's Christmas	70.00
1926 Churchgoers On Christmas Day	65.00
1927 Skating Couple	110.00
1928 Eskimo Looking At Village Church In Greenland	60.00
1929 Fox Outside Farm On Christmas Eve	75.00
1930 Yule Tree In Town Hall Square Of Copenhagen	85.00
1932 Lifeboat At Work	90.00
1934 Church Bell In Tower	75.00
1936 Royal Guard Outside Amalienborg Castle In Copenhagen	70.00
1938 Lighting The Candles	110.00
1940 Delivering Christmas Letters	170.00
1942 Danish Farm On Christmas Night	150.00
1944 Sorgenfri Castle	120.00
1946 Commemoration Cross In Honor Of Danish Sailors Who Lost Their Lives In World War II	85.00
1948 Watchman, Sculpture Of Town Hall, Copenhagen	80.00
1950 Kronborg Castle At Elsinore	150.00
1952 Old Copenhagen Canals At Wintertime With Thorvaldsen Museum In Background	85.00
1954 Birthplace Of Hans Christian Andersen, With Snowman	100.00
1956 Christmas In Copenhagen	140.00
1958 Santa Claus	100.00
1960 Danish Village Church	180.00
1962 Winter Night	80.00

1964 The Fir Tree And Hare	50.00
1966 Home For Christmas	50.00
1968 Christmas In Church	45.00
1970 Pheasants In The Snow At Christmas	20.00
1972 Christmas In Greenland	20.00
1974 Christmas In The Village	20.00
1976 Christmas Welcome	25.00
1978 A Christmas Tale	30.00
1980 Christmas In The Woods	42.00
1982 The Christmas Tree	55.00
1984 Christmas Letter	55.00
1986 Silent Night, Holy Night	55.00

Jubilee, various artists

1915 Frozen Window	225.00
1920 Church Bells	65.00
1925 Dog Outside Window	285.00
1930 The Old Organist	225.00
1935 Little Match Girl	900.00
1940 Three Wise Men	1,950.00
1945 Amalienborg Castle	150.00
1950 Eskimos	175.00
1955 Dybbol Mill	200.00
1960 Kronborg Castle	100.00
1965 Churchgoers	40.00
1970 Amalienborg Castle	35.00
1975 Horses Enjoying Meal	50.00
1980 Yule Tree	60.00
1985 Lifeboat at Work	65.00

HAVILAND & PARLON (France)

Christmas Series, various artists, 10″ d

1972 Madonna And Child, Raphael, FE	80.00
1973 Madonnina, Feruzzi	100.00
1975 Madonna And Child, Murillo	45.00
1977 Madonna And Child, Bellini	40.00
1979 Madonna Of The Eucharist, Botticelli	125.00

Lady And The Unicorn Series, artist unknown, 10″ d

1977 To My Only Desire, FE	60.00
1979 Sound	50.00
1981 Scent	60.00

Tapestry Series, artist unknown, 10″ d

1971 The Unicorn In Captivity	145.00
1973 Chase Of The Unicorn	120.00
1975 The Unicorn Surrounded	75.00

LALIQUE (France)

Annual Series, lead crystal, Marie-Claude Lalique, artist, 8½″ d

1965 Deux Oiseaux (Two Birds), FE	800.00
1967 Ballet de Poisson (Fish Ballet)	200.00
1969 Papillon (Butterfly)	80.00
1971 Hibou (Owl)	60.00
1973 Petit Geai (Jayling)	60.00
1975 Due de Poisson (Fish Duet)	75.00

Left: Bing and Grondahl, Christmas, 1928, $60.00; right, Haviland and Parlon, Tapestry Series, 1974, $120.00.

LENOX (United States)

Boehm Bird Series, Edward Marshall Boehm, artist, 10½" d

1970 Wood Thrush, FE	225.00
1971 Goldfinch	65.00
1973 Meadowlark	60.00
1975 American Redstart	50.00
1977 Robins	55.00
1979 Golden-Crowned Kinglets	65.00
1981 Eastern Phoebes	100.00

Boehm Woodland Wildlife Series, Edward Marshall Boehm, artist, 10½" d

1973 Raccoons, FE	80.00
1975 Cottontail Rabbits	60.00
1977 Beaver	60.00
1979 Squirrels	75.00
1981 Martens	100.00

LLARDO (Spain)

Christmas, 8" d, undisclosed artists

1971 Caroling	30.00
1972 Carolers	35.00
1974 Carolers	75.00
1976 Christ Child	50.00
1978 Caroling Child	50.00

Mother's Day, undisclosed artists

1971 Kiss of the Child	75.00
1972 Birds & Chicks	30.00
1974 Nursing Mother	135.00
1976 Vigil	50.00
1978 New Arrival	55.00

RECO INTERNATIONAL (United States)

Christmas Series, Royale, various artists

1969 Christmas Fair, FE	125.00
1970 Vigil Mass	100.00
1971 Christmas Night	50.00
1972 Elks	40.00

1973 Christmas Down	35.00
1974 Village Christmas	60.00
1975 Feeding Time	35.00
1976 Seaport Christmas	30.00
1977 Sledding	30.00

REED & BARTON (United States)

Audubon Series, various artists

1970 Pine Siskin, FE	175.00
1971 Red-Shouldered Hawk	75.00
1972 Stilt Sandpiper	70.00
1973 Red Cardinal	70.00
1974 Boreal Chickadee	60.00
1975 Yellow Breasted Chat	60.00
1976 Bay-Breasted Warbler	60.00
1977 Purple Finsh	65.00

ROSENTHAL (Germany)

Christmas Plates, various artists, 8½" d

1910 Winter Peace	550.00
1911 The Three Wise Men	325.00
1912 Shooting Stars	250.00
1913 Christmas Lights	235.00
1914 Christmas Song	350.00
1915 Walking To Church	180.00
1916 Christmas During War	235.00
1918 Peace On Earth	210.00
1920 The Manger In Bethlehem	325.00
1922 Advent Branch	200.00
1924 Deer In The Woods	200.00
1926 Christmas In The Mountains	175.00
1928 Chalet Christmas	175.00
1930 Group Of Deer Under The Pines	225.00
1932 Christ Child	195.00
1934 Christmas Peace	200.00
1936 Nurnberg Angel	185.00
1938 Christmas In The Alps	190.00
1940 Marinen Church in Danzig	250.00
1942 Marianburg Castle	300.00
1944 Wood Scape	275.00

1946 Christmas In An Alpine Valley .	**250.00**
1948 Message To The Shepherds .	**875.00**
1950 Christmas In The Forest	**185.00**
1952 Christmas In The Alps	**190.00**
1954 Christmas Eve	**185.00**
1956 Christmas In The Alps	**190.00**
1958 Christmas Eve	**190.00**
1960 Christmas In Small Village . . .	**195.00**
1962 Christmas Eve	**185.00**
1964 Christmas Market In Nurnberg	**225.00**
1966 Christmas In Ulm	**250.00**
1968 Christmas In Bremen	**195.00**
1970 Christmas In Cologne	**165.00**
1972 Christmas Celebration In Franconia	**90.00**
1974 Christmas In Wurzburg	**100.00**

ROYAL COPENHAGEN

Christmas Plates, various artists, 6″ d 1908, 1909, 1910; 7″ 1911 to present

1908 Madonna And Child	**1,775.00**
1909 Danish Landscape	**150.00**
1910 The Magi	**120.00**
1911 Danish Landscape	**135.00**
1912 Elderly Couple By Christmas Tree	**120.00**
1913 Spire Of Frederik's Church, Copenhagen	**125.00**
1914 Sparrows In Tree At Church Of The Holy Spirit, Copenhagen	**100.00**
1915 Danish Landscape	**150.00**
1916 Shepherd In The Field On Christmas Night	**85.00**
1917 Tower Of Our Savior's Church, Copenhagen	**90.00**
1918 Sheep and Shepherds	**80.00**
1919 In The Park	**80.00**
1920 Mary With The Child Jesus . .	**75.00**
1921 Aabenraa Marketplace	**75.00**
1922 Three Singing Angels	**70.00**
1923 Danish Landscape	**70.00**
1924 Christmas Star Over The Sea And Sailing Ship	**100.00**
1925 Street Scene From Christianshavn, Copenhagen	**85.00**
1926 View of Christmas Canal, Copenhagen	**75.00**
1927 Ship's Boy At The Tiller On Christmas Night	**140.00**
1928 Vicar's Family On Way To Church	**75.00**
1929 Grundtvig Church, Copenhagen	**100.00**
1930 Fishing Boats On The Way To The Harbor	**80.00**
1932 Frederiksberg Gardens With Statue Of Frederik VI	**90.00**
1934 The Hermitage Castle	**115.00**
1936 Roskilde Cathedral	**130.00**
1938 Round Church In Osterlars On Bornholm	**200.00**

1940 The Good Shepherd	**300.00**
1942 Bell Tower of Old Church In Jutland	**300.00**
1944 Typical Danish Winter Scene .	**160.00**
1946 Zealand Village Church	**150.00**
1948 Nodebo Church At Christmastime	**150.00**
1950 Boeslunde Church, Zealand . .	**175.00**
1952 Christmas In The Forest	**120.00**
1954 Amalienborg Palace, Copenhagen	**150.00**
1956 Rosenborg Castle, Copenhagen	**160.00**
1958 Sunshine Over Greenland . . .	**140.00**
1960 The Stag	**140.00**
1962 The Little Mermaid At Wintertime	**200.00**
1964 Fetching The Christmas Tree .	**75.00**
1966 Blackbird At Christmastime . . .	**55.00**
1968 The Last Umiak	**40.00**
1970 Christmas Rose And Cat	**95.00**
1972 In The Desert	**85.00**
1974 Winter Twilight	**80.00**
1976 Danish Watermill	**80.00**
1978 Greenland Scenery	**80.00**
1980 Bringing Home The Christmas Tree	**65.00**
1982 Waiting For Christmas	**65.00**
1984 Jingle Bells	**60.00**
1986 Wait for Me	**55.00**

Mother's Day Plates, various artists, 6¼″ d

1971 American Mother	**125.00**
1972 Oriental Mother	**60.00**
1974 Greenland Mother	**55.00**
1976 Mermaids	**50.00**
1978 Mother And Child	**25.00**
1980 An Outing With Mother	**35.00**
1982 The Children's Hour	**45.00**

ROYAL DOULTON (Great Britain)

Beswick Christmas Series, various artists, earthenware in hand-cast bas-relief, 8″ sq

1972 Christmas In England, FE . . .	**40.00**
1974 Christmas In Bulgaria	**40.00**
1976 Christmas In Holland	**45.00**
1978 Christmas In America	**45.00**

Mother And Child Series, Edna Hibel artist, 8¼″ d

1973 Colette And Child, FE	**450.00**
1974 Sayuri And Child	**150.00**
1976 Marilyn And Child	**120.00**
1978 Kathleen And Child	**95.00**

Valentine's Day Series, artists unknown, 8¼″ d

1976 Victorian Boy And Girl	**60.00**
1978 If I Loved You	**40.00**
1980 On A Swing	**40.00**
1982 From My Heart	**40.00**
1984 Love In Bloom	**40.00**

WEDGWOOD (Great Britain)

Christmas Series, jasper stoneware, 8″ d

1969 Windsor Castle, FE	225.00
1971 Piccadilly Circus, London	40.00
1973 The Tower Of London	45.00
1975 Tower Bridge	40.00
1977 Westminster Abbey	48.00
1979 Buckingham Palace	55.00
1981 Marble Arch	75.00
1983 All Souls, Langham Palace	80.00
1985 The Tate Gallery	80.00
1987 Guildhall	80.00

Mother's Day, jasper stoneware, 6½″ d

1971 Sportive Love, FE	25.00
1973 The Baptism Of Achilles	20.00
1975 Mother And Child	35.00
1977 Leisure Time	30.00
1979 Deer and Fawn	35.00
1981 Mare And Foal	50.00
1983 Cupid And Butterfly	55.00
1985 Cupids and Doves	55.00
1987 Anemones	55.00

LIMOGES

History: Limoges porcelain has been produced in Limoges, France, for over a century by numerous factories other than the famed Haviland. One of the most frequently encountered marks is "T. & V. Limoges" which is the ware made by Tressman and Vought. Other identifiable Limoges marks are A. L. (A. Lanternier), J. P. L (J. Pouyat, Limoges), M. R. (M. Reddon), Elite and Coronet.

References: Susan and Al Bagdade, *Warman's English & Continental Pottery & Porcelain, 1st Edition,* Warman Publishing Co., Inc., 1987; Mary Frank Gaston, *The Collector's Encyclopedia Of Limoges Porcelain,* Collector Books, 1980.

Additional Listings: Haviland China.

Basket, 8″ l, yellow ground, crows and cherries dec, artist sgd "G Remy"	85.00
Biscuit Jar, cov, multicolored flowers, artist sgd	60.00
Chocolate Pot	
9½″, melon ribbed, burgundy and gold top and handle, pink and yellow floral dec	175.00
10½″, rose dec, gilt handle, top, bottom, and under spout, marked "H T & V Limoges, France"	175.00
Celery Dish, 6½ x 13½″, gold scalloped border, green and gray floral border, pink floral center, green mark "GDA/France"	40.00
Demitasse Cups and Saucers, floral dec, marked green and red "Theo Haviland, Limoges," set of 6	85.00

Dish, 13 x 4″, three sections, shaded pink, lavender and white floral dec, irregular gold edge and handle	140.00
Game Plate	
9″, set, different multicolored game bird in natural habitat in center, scalloped lacy gold and floral border, artist sgd "L Straus," set of 6	450.00
10″, boars in snow, artist sgd "Max Duck Pradet"	90.00
13½″, quail, natural woodland setting, gold rococo border, artist sgd	250.00
15″, fish, hp, artist sgd	145.00
Hair Receiver, hp, bluebirds, gold trim, three small feet	100.00
Lamp Base, 8″ h, pink roses, gray and tan ground, marked "Cincinnati"	175.00
Mug, 6″, burgundy and green, grapes, leaves, and vines, arched female figure handle	145.00
Nappy, 10″, handle, maple leaf shape, large pink roses, marked "Elite, Limoges, France"	55.00
Pitcher	
5½″, hp, dancing couple on both sides, gold trim, dated 1890	200.00
8½″, milk, white, rope and anchor handle	55.00
12″, tankard, emb handle and base, hp, three color grape cluster dec, marked "T & V"	150.00
13½″, tankard, hp, cavalier dec	450.00
14¾″, tankard, gooseberries, artist sgd "Le Roy, H W Guerin, Limoges, France"	275.00
15″, tankard, hp, large grapes and leaves, stylized hearts border, sgd "Xmas 1898 to Ernst Marie," marked "WG & Co"	300.00

Platter, 16½ x 9″, pink flowers, white ground, dated January, 1911, marked "T & V Limoges, Depose," $75.00.

Plaque, pierced for hanging	
5″ d, round, portrait of young woman, ebonized frame	400.00
10″, hp, black and yellow humming-	

bird, heavy gold rococo border, blue ground, white water lilies, fish in water, artist sgd **150.00**

11″, hp, grapes and watermelon, gold scalloped border, artist sgd **125.00**

12½″, Rococo gold borders, fishermen, one in rowboat, one on shore, pastel ground, marked, pr **500.00**

13⅜″, Rococo gold borders, rose brown and sepia, one titled "Ibis," other "Spatule," artist sgd, marked "Birds of North Africa," pr **425.00**

Plate

7″, hp, pink and white chrysanthemums, green and yellow ground, scalloped gold trim, artist sgd . . . **85.00**

8½″, hp, raspberries and leaves, gold scalloped rim, artist sgd **40.00**

9″, fisherman on riverbank, formal black framed gold border, 1878 . . **40.00**

9¼″, hp, kitten and butterfly, artist sgd "Coronet" **45.00**

Portrait Plate

American Indian, hp, artist sgd "Coronet" **65.00**

Queen Louise, 8″, gold trim, marked "Elite, Limoges, France" **45.00**

Punch Bowl, 9½″ d, 4½″ h, three colored grapes, foliage, pink int., pink and yellow ext., scalloped, gold trim, marked "TV" **185.00**

Relish Dish, hp, wild roses, gold handle, 3 pcs **50.00**

Sardine Set, 5½ x 4½″ cov box, 10 x 9″ tray, swimming fish, starfish, shells, and seaweed, pink and blue, "TV," 3 pcs **235.00**

Tray, 9 x 13″, hp, scalloped border, roses, green mark "J/L France" . . . **75.00**

Vase

6½″, bulbous, large pink, yellow, and purple mums, wide reticulated gold band, sgd "J/L France" **150.00**

10¼ x 9″, ovoid, two deer at forest edge **175.00**

24″, silver ground, enameled raspberries and leaves, magenta to rose and green, sgd "Sarlande/Limoges," c1900 . . . . **750.00**

LINENS

History: The term linen now has become a generic designation for household dressings for table, bed, or bath, whether made of linen, cotton, lace, or other fabrics.

Linen, as a table cover, is mentioned in the Bible and other writings of an early age. We see "borde cloths" in early drawings and paintings with their creases pressed in sharply. It was a sign of wealth and social standing to present such elegance.

During the period before the general use of forks when fingers were the accepted means of dining, napkins were important. They usually were rectangular and large in size. In the early 18th century, napkins lost their popularity. The fork had become the tool of the upper classes who apparently wished to show off their new found expertise in the use of the fork. After diners did much damage to tablecloths, finicky hostesses decided that the napkin was a necessity. It soon reappeared on the table.

The Victorian era gave us the greatest variety of household linens. The lady of the house had time to sit and sew a fine seam. Sewing became a social activity. Afternoon callers brought their handwork with them when they came to gossip and take tea. Every young girl was expected to fill her hope chest with fine examples of her prowess. In the late 19th century these ladies made some very beautiful "white work," using white embroidery of delicate stitchery, lace insertions, and ruffles on white fabrics. These pieces are highly sought after today.

The 20th century saw a decline in that type of fine stitchery. The social pace quickened. Household linens of that period show more bright colors in the embroidery, the designs become more lighthearted and frivolous, and inexpensive machine made lace was used. Kitchen towels were decorated with animals or pots and pans. Vanity sets dominated the bedroom; the Bridge craze put emphasis on tablecloths and napkin sets. To fill the desire for less expensive lace cloths and bedspreads, women of the Depression started crocheting. Many examples of this craft are available.

With the advent of World War II, more women went to work. The last remanence of fine stitchery quickly diminished. Technological advances in production and fibers lessened the interest in hand made linens.

Collecting And Use Tips: Most old linens are fragile, some are age stained from being stored improperly for years. Unless you have a secret for removing these stains without damaging the fabric, look for those items in very good or better condition.

Linens which are not used frequently are best stored unpressed, rolled Boy Scout style, and tucked away in an old pillowcase out of bright light. Be sure the linens and pillowcases have been rinsed several times to remove all residue of detergent.

For laundered pieces which are used often, wrap in acid free white tissue or muslin folders. If the tissue is not acid free, it will cause the folded edges to discolor. If possible, store on rollers to prevent creasing. Creased areas become weak and disintegrate in laundering. Acid-free wrapping material can be purchased from Talas, 104 Fifth Avenue, New York, NY 10011.

References: Virginia Churchill Bath, *Lace*, Henry Regnery Co., 1974; Lois Markrich and

Heinz Edgar Kiewe, Victorian Fancywork, Henry Regnery Co., 1974; *McCall's Needlework Treasury*, Random House, 1963; Francis M. Montgomery, *Textiles In America, 1650–1870*, W. W. Norton & C. (A Winterthur/Barra Book); Patricia Esterbrook Roberts, *Table Settings. Entertaining And Etiquette. A History And Guide*, Viking Press, 1967.

Collectors' Club: International Old Lacers, Box 1029, West Minster, CO 80030. Dues: $8.00.

Museums: Metropolitan Museum of Art, New York, NY; Museum of Early Southern Decorative Arts (MESDA) Winston-Salem, NC; Museum Of Fine Arts, Boston, MA; Rockwood Museum, Wilmington, DE; Shelburne Museum, Shelburne, VT; Smithsonian Institution, Washington, D.C.

Advisor: Alda Horner.

Antimacassar Set
    Filet crochet, nautical motif, ship center, anchors on arm pcs, c1930 .. **18.50**
    Linen, white, satin stitch monogram center, scalloped edges, c1890 .. **35.00**
Bedspread
    Appliqued, baby, cotton, white, animals and flowers, pastel shades, bound and backed blue print cotton **45.00**
    Battenberg, white, allover design, double size, c1890–1900 .... **375.00**
    Crocheted, white cotton, overall floral motif pattern, double size, instructions designed and furnished by Grace Coolidge (Mrs. Calvin Coolidge) **750.00**
    Muslin, bleached, two green bower peacock design, motif bolster end, twin size, 1930s kit **85.00**
    Rayon satin, pink, plain top, ruffled fall, double size, c1940 .... **45.00**
Blanket Cover, seersucker, white, machine bound, double size, c1935 ... **18.00**
Bolster Cover, pr
    Button back, linen, white, small tuck edge ruffles, heavy satin stitch floral design center **95.00**
    Throw type, cotton, white, lace edges ruffles around sides, center of one red embroidery "Sweet," other "Dreams," Pennsylvania, c1880–90 .... **85.00**
Bridge Set
    34 x 34"
        Linen, damask, pale pink, chrysanthemum pattern, four matching napkins **25.00**
        Organdy, light yellow, linen appliqued flowers outer edge, hemstitched around appliques and border, four matching napkins .. **50.00**
    35 x 35", linen, white, rose motif filet crocheted inserts on corners, cro-

cheted edge, four matching napkins **35.00**
Curtain Panel, pr, 36" w, 108" l, white net, overall floral design, machine tambour stitch, scalloped edges, pocket top, c1920 .... **85.00**
Doily
    28" d, Battenberg lace, white linen center, c1900 .... **45.00**
    25" d, two hand tatted rows of medallions, white linen center, c1920 . **35.00**
    24" d, linen, white, heavy padded satin-stitch butterflies and flowers, machine made Cluny lace border, c1900 .... **25.00**
    Set, six 15" d and 12" d, machine filet lace, cream, c1940 .... **40.00**
Dresser Scarf
    Alencon lace, 14" w, 48" l, floral and medallion designs, ecru, machine made, c1930 .... **40.00**
    Chantilly lace, 15" w, 40" l, white, floral design, machine made **15.00**
Handkerchief
    Chantilly Lace, 14 x 14", black center, 4" white organdy border, c1920 .. **35.00**
    Cotton, white, bright colored printed flowers, set of 3, c1935 .... **10.00**
    Linen, 12 x 12", white, Apenzell embroidery and drawn work, c1920 . **20.00**
    Swiss embroidery, 12½ x 12½", white, delicate lace border, maple framed under glass, early 20th C . **65.00**
Napkins
    Cocktail
        6" sq, linen, white, crocheted edge and one corner motif, set of 6 . **15.00**
        6 x 8", linen, lavender and green, bunch of grapes form, handmade, set of 6 .... **30.00**
    Dinner
        24" sq, linen, white, hand monogram "G" and hemstitched edges, set of 12 .... **55.00**
        24" sq, linen, double damask, white, chrysanthemum pattern, hand rolled edges, set of 6 .... **25.00**
        28 x 29", linen, damask, white, satin stripe design, satin stitch "E" center, hand rolled edges, set of 8 .... **80.00**
    Luncheon, 15" sq, Madeira, linen, white, pale blue embroidery and cut work corner, set of 8 .... **45.00**
Pillow Case
    Boudoir, 15" d, floral motif machine tape lace, pink satin backing, c1920 .... **25.00**
    Pair
        Linen, white, satin stitch monogram, hem stitched, c1900 .... **45.00**
        Muslin, white, embroidered girl with

full skirt and flowers, crocheted
edge, made from stamped kit,
c1930 .... **18.50**
Percale, French blue, satin stitch
"L," wide white crocheted border,
c1935–40 .... **22.50**
Place Mat, child's high chair tray, embroidered brown dog diving from
board, crocheted edge, made from
stamped kit, c1935 .... **12.00**
Sheet
Linen, hand turned hem top and bottom, double size, c1920 .... **25.00**
Muslin, white, 3″ w filet crochet rose
motif insert, double size, c1920 .. **15.00**

**Tea Cloth, 54″ sq, center of white linen
with hemstitched border, surrounded
by intricate hand crochet of flowers
and mesh design, all white, c1900,
$125.00.**

Table Cloth
18″ w, 112″ l, runner, French net, hand
embroidered flowers, pointe lace
flower inserts, c1900 .... **175.00**
53 x 72″, linen, hand loomed, seamed
center, woven heavy corded design, hand turned ends, one corner
embroidered in red cross-stitch
"D.F" and "1870" **45.00**
54 x 54″, tea cloth, linen, natural, Bat-
tenberg lace center motif and corners, four matching napkins, set . **45.00**
54 x 56″, luncheon, cotton, white, colorful linen flower appliques, crochet
edges, six matching napkins,
c1930-35, set **35.00**
68 x 86″, allover machine made lace,
natural, sq motif designs with floral
centers, merrow edges **45.00**
68 x 98″, dinner, linen, natural, cut
work and embroidered floral and
leaf pattern center and border, 8
matching napkins, set **195.00**
72″ d, rayon, double damask, yellow,

floral design, machine turned
edges, four napkins, set **15.00**
72 x 98″, linen, double damask, chrysanthemum pattern, hand turned
hem, 20th C **85.00**
72 x 101″, Chinese rice cloth, white,
four sections hemstitched together,
drawn work and embroidered floral
design, deep borders **65.00**
144 x 86″, banquet size, Pointe de
Venise, ecru, allover cupids, urns
and floral spray design, 12 linen
napkins with lace border and corner motif, handmade in China, orig
wrapping, unused, c1935–40, set . **1,200.00**
Tête-A-Tête Set, 1 mat, 2 matching
napkins, linen, light blue, two corners
with embroidered pink roses and
vines, c1940 .... **25.00**
Towel, linen
Damask
16 x 38″, red woven grape leaves
and vines border, fringe on each
end, c1900 .... **25.00**
Pair, woven cobalt blue floral design border, hem stitched, c1900 **65.00**
Hand loomed, 18″ w, 36″ l, each end
with crocheted lace, finely stitched
side hems, dated and sgd in black
ink "1830" **65.00**
Hand tatted edges and one end
c1930 .... **15.00**
Woven, red and blue Oriental design
and fringe on each end, c1920 .. **18.00**
Vanity Set, 3 pcs, muslin, white, embroidered cross-stitch floral design,
white machine made Cluny type lace
border, c1920–30 .... **22.50**

LITHOPHANES

History: Lithophanes are highly translucent porcelain panels with impressed designs. The design
is formed by the difference in thickness of the
plaque. Thin parts transmit an abundance of light
while thicker parts represent shadows.

Lithophanes were first made by the Royal Berlin
Porcelain Works in 1828. Other factories in Germany, France, and England later produced them.
The majority of lithophanes on the market today
were made between 1850 and 1900.

Collectors' Club: Lithophane Collectors Club,
2032 Robinwood Avenue, Toledo, OH 43620. *Lithophane Collectors Club Bulletin* (bimonthly).

Museum: Blair Museum of Lithophanes and
Carved Waxes, Toledo, OH.

Candle Shield, 9″, bronze collar, rococo
frame, two country boys on grass,
goat and castle in background **250.00**

Plaque, 4¼ x 5¼", classical woman in garden, imp "1308/52," c1860, $125.00.

Cup and Saucer, nude lady, moriage and dragon dec	45.00
Fairy Lamp, lady leaning from tower window, two panels, rural romantic scene	1,200.00
Lamp, 23½", double student type, four scenes, brass base, marked "Germany"	1,850.00

Lamp Shade
8" d, five panels, people in different poses, pressed metal frame	525.00
10" d, 5¼" h, five panels, childhood scenes, emb brass frame, marked "PPM"	550.00
13" d, seven panels, European and American scenic views, panel of woman carrying mousetrap upstairs, copper frame	700.00

Panel
KK, 8 x 16", General Zachary Taylor, holding telescope in left arm, men fighting battle in background, wreath, eagle, and two flags above, leaded frame, ruby flashed	675.00

PPM
4½ x 5¼", hunters in forest, marked	100.00
6½ x 8", elderly lady teaching girl to knit, lead mounted edge	150.00
PR Sickle, 4⅛ x 5", cupid and girl fishing	150.00
Unknown Maker, 6½ x 8", Christ holding orb with cross, incised "Inri/Die"	185.00
Portrait, oval, 7⅛ x 5¾", Samuel Colt, sitting at table, revolver in right hand, pair of dividers in left hand, unmounted	875.00
Stein, half liter, dancing couple, transfer of deer	100.00
Tea Set, teapot, creamer, cov sugar, six cups and saucers	150.00

Tea Warmer, 6 x 6", four panels	
Romantic, Sheffield SS holder, orig burner, 6 x 6"	275.00
Scenic, pierced top, metal frame, molded ftd base, Germany	165.00
Wall Lamp, brass frame, 2½" h conical four panel shade, woodland scenes, electrified	300.00

LIVERPOOL CHINA

History: Liverpool is the name given to products made at several potteries in Liverpool, England, between 1750 and 1840. Among the early potters who made tin enameled earthenwares, were Seth and James Pennington and Richard Chaffers.

By the 1780s tin glazed earthenware gave way to cream colored wares decorated with cobalt, enamel colors, and blue or black transfers.

The Liverpool glaze is characterized by bubbles and most often there is clouding under the foot rims. By 1800 about 80 potteries were working in the town producing not only creamware, but soft paste, soapstone, and bone porcelain.

Reference: Susan and Al Bagdade, *Warman's English & Continental Pottery & Porcelain, 1st Edition,* Warman Publishing Co., Inc., 1987.

Mug, 4½" h, marine transfer titled "Mariner's," $400.00.

Bowl, 8¼" d, underglaze blue scene of houses on wooded river islands, overglaze iron-red, green, and gilding, sgd "Philip Christian," c1770	825.00
Dish, 13½", blue and white dec, two fighting cocks, flowering tree, fenced garden, scrolling flowering branches border, c1760	625.00

Jug
7⅛", creamware, transfer printed, one side printed in black with green and yellow enameled sailing vessel, flying red, white, and blue American flag, green sea, reverse with oval portrait of George Washington, flanked by Justice and Liberty, border of stars and banderoles inscribed with names of first fifteen states, c1810, minor restoration to spout and foot rim **1,000.00**

10⁹⁄₁₆", creamware, transfer printed, one side with black printed oval map of thirteen colonies flanked by General Washington on left, figures of Liberty, Wisdom, and Justice on right, reverse with patriotic rhyme among trophies, American eagle under handle, Hope leaning on anchor beneath wreath inscribed "Jonathon and Mary Eldridge" under spout, floral garland printed and painted in black on rim, c1800 ... **1,225.00**

Mug
3½", creamware, polychrome transfer, west view of iron bridge over the Wear, marked "Phillips & Co Sunderland," c1813 .... **100.00**

5½", black transfer, polychrome transfer, farmer's arms, "God Speed the Plough" and "Peace and Plenty" **175.00**

Pickle Dish, leaf shape, finely molded veined int., short stem handle, underglaze blue central floral sprig, floral vine rim border, c1760 .... **575.00**

Pitcher
9⅜", polychrome transfer of tavern scene, winter scene beneath spout, amusing poems, c1790–1800 ... **400.00**

10¾", polychrome transfer, Washington standing on British lion, ribbon reading "By Virtue and Valour...The Foundation Of A Great Empire," black lettering, American ship at sea, medallion beneath spout "J. Tuttle" **675.00**

Plate, 9½", black transfer, British war sloop, full rigging and flags **100.00**

Soup Plate, 10", black transfer, British ship firing cannon **115.00**

Tea Caddy, creamware, 3¾", rect, painted chinoiserie, inky blue dec .. **245.00**

Tile, 5", black transfer, white ground, animals and birds **100.00**

LOETZ

History: Loetz is a type of iridescent art glass made in Austria by J. Loetz Witwe in the late

1890s. Loetz was a contemporary of L. C. Tiffany and worked in the Tiffany factory before establishing his own operation; therefore, much of the wares are similar in appearance to Tiffany. Some pieces are signed "Loetz," "Loetz, Austria," or "Austria." The Loetz factory also produced ware with fine cameos on cased glass.

Vase, 9¾" h, flared tricorn top, tapered cylindrical body, honeycomb concave depressions, irid pink, acid cut sgd "Loetz, Austria," $140.00

Bowl
3½", lemon yellow ruffled lip, navy blue lower section, deep green scrolling, pink-amber irid oil spots, inscribed "Loetz-Austria," c1900 . **1,450.00**

9 x 5½", pinched, rainbow shading, Damascene swirl pattern, oil spots **465.00**

Bride's Basket, amber, silver-blue irid oil spots, metal holder **350.00**

Cuspidor, 5 x 4½", melon ribbed, dimples, irid green, polished pontil **125.00**

Inkwell, 4½" h, narrow melon ribbing, hinged lid **425.00**

Jack-In-The-Pulpit Vase
6½", pinched body, gold luster **175.00**

8½", pinched, gold irid body, heavy teardrop SS overlay, jack-in-the-pulpit top extending to handle ... **4,000.00**

Rose Bowl, 4", irid gold, rose to lavender, pink oil spots, silver overlay ... **475.00**

Sweetmeat Jar, cov, wavy textured amber, irid pink and green, brass bail, pewter raspberry finial **275.00**

Vase
4", orange, silver irid waves, gold threading, silver overlay, floral pattern **285.00**

4½", dimples, irid gold and blue, gold lava dec **475.00**

6½", green, blue irid threading, dimpled sides, graceful top **650.00**

7½", amphora shape, red int., silver-blue irid concentric waves, sgd "Loetz, Austria" **1,000.00**
9½", flower form, irid dark blue, random crisscross threading **450.00**
9⅞", baluster, spreading foot, pale green, irid gold-green, silver-blue undulating waves, sgd "Loetz, Austria", c1900 .... **675.00**
10¼", irid red and blue, serpent encircling body **450.00**
10½", gold, enamel and painted iris dec, three ormolu feet **200.00**
10½" h, 9½" d, ovoid, mottled blue and yellow underglaze, cobalt blue and white flowers and trailing vines, sgd "Loetz-Austria" **475.00**
10¾", red, irid wheat sheave pattern, orig metal frame **975.00**
13", goose neck, blue and green, oil spot dec **875.00**
15", drape molded body, ruffled top, green, ornate bronze frame **250.00**

LOTUS WARE CHINA

History: Knowles, Taylor and Knowles Co., East Liverpool, Ohio, made a translucent, thinly potted china between 1891 and 1898. It compared favorably to Belleek. It first was marked "KTK." After being exhibited at the 1893 Columbian Exposition in Chicago, Col. John T. Taylor, company president, changed the marking to Lotus Ware, because the body resembled the petals of the lotus blossom.

Blanks also were sold to amateurs who hand painted them. Most artist-signed pieces fit this category.

Biscuit Jar, 7 x 6", multicolored, emb blackberry branches, sgd KTK **675.00**
Bowl
  5", pastel flowers, gold leaves, stems, beaded rim and feet **485.00**
  6", creamware, blue transfer print of landscape **125.00**
Candy Dish, 7½ x 5½", seaweed dec, coral feet **285.00**
Chocolate Pot, sunflowers, hp **375.00**
Creamer, 3⅞", floral dec, pale green neck, gold striping **90.00**
Cup and Saucer, coffee, blue flowers . **70.00**
Ewer, 10" h, floral sprays, garlands of raised blue forget-me-nots **700.00**
Pitcher
  6½", cream, gold dec **385.00**

Vase, 8″ h, green foliage, blue flowers, gold insect and trim, white ground, $600.00.

7½", pansy dec **365.00**
11", white, multicolored flowers, green leaves, gold trim **400.00**
Rose Bowl, 5 x 4½", white, gold flowers, leaves and branches, KTK **375.00**
Sugar, cov, white, hp flowers **175.00**
Syrup, cream, hp flowers, brass top and spout, KTK **325.00**
Tea Set, teapot, creamer, and sugar, gold leaf design, 3 pcs **600.00**
Vase, 6½", olive green, applied flowers and leaves in light green and white, pr **1,500.00**

LUSTER WARE

History: Lustering on a piece of pottery creates a metallic, sometimes iridescent, appearance. Josiah Wedgwood experimented with the technique in the 1790s. Between 1805 and 1840 luster earthenware pieces were created in England by makers such as Adams, Bailey and Batkin, Copeland and Garrett, Wedgwood, and Enoch Wood.

Luster decorations often were used in conjunction with enamels and transfers. Transfers used for luster decoration covered a wide range of public and domestic subjects. They frequently were accompanied by pious or sentimental doggerel as well as the humors of everyday life.

Copper luster was created by the addition of a copper compound to the glaze. It was very popular in America during the 19th century and experienced a collecting vogue from the 1920s to the 1950s. Today it has a limited market. The market stagnation can partially be attributed to the large number of reproductions, especially creamers and the "polka" jug, which fool many new buyers. Reproductions are heavier in appearance and weight than the earlier pieces.

Pink luster was made by using a gold mixture.

Silver luster was first covered completely with a thin coating of a "steel luster" mixture, containing a small quantity of platinum oxide. An additional coating of platinum, worked in water, was applied before firing.

Sunderland is a coarse type of cream colored eathenware with a marbled or spotted pink luster decoration which shades from pink to purple. A solution of gold compound applied to the white body developed the many shades of pink.

The development of electroplating in 1840 created a sharp decline in the demands for metalsurfaced earthenware.

Reference: Susan and Al Bagdade, *Warman's English & Continental Pottery & Porcelain, 1st Edition,* Warman Publishing Co., Inc., 1987.

Additional Listings: English Softpaste.

Copper Luster, 6⅜″ d bowl, blue band, applied multicolored pastoral and floral dec, pedestal base, $100.00.

COPPER

Bowl
5¾″, emb, green band	**60.00**
6″ d, blue band, copper luster body .	**25.00**

Creamer
4⅛″ h, red transfer in robin's-egg blue band, wide sections of copper luster	**30.00**
4½″, General Lafayette and surrender of Cornwallis commemoration transfer, canary luster band	**150.00**
Crocus Pot, 7½″, enameled blue, green, and white floral dec	**175.00**
Cup, 5″ h, enameled satyr-mask body, scroll handle, copper luster trim, frog figural inside	**95.00**
Cup and Saucer, stylized flower dec, highlighted copper luster	**55.00**
Goblet, 4¾″, floral band, worn purple luster	**55.00**
Jug, 5⅝″, woman and 2 children transfer, canary luster band	**200.00**
Mug, 3⅜″, floral dec, purple luster resist	**65.00**

Pitcher
4½″, youth and maiden in forest transfer, white bands, red enamel and purple luster	**50.00**
6½″, white, blue, and yellow florals, copper luster body, marked "Allerton"	**75.00**
7½″ h, relief deer dec, emb scroll around mouth	**40.00**
Puzzle Jug, 8⅞″, ironstone, dancers and clowns transfer, lion and unicorn mark, Elsmore and Forster	**100.00**
Shaving Mug, 4″, blue with copper diagonal stripes, pink inner rim	**55.00**
Tankard, 6 x 6¼″, cov, House pattern, pink luster band, copper luster body	**150.00**
Teapot, cov, floral enamels, copper luster body	**75.00**
Tumbler, 2⅝″, blue floral band	**35.00**
Waste Bowl, relief figures, blue band, ftd	**40.00**

Pink Luster, 8½″ d plate, House pattern, $50.00.

PINK

Bowl, 6½″, House pattern	**90.00**
Container, 2″ h, 2¾″ d, pink splash luster	**40.00**
Cup and Saucer, orange-red Cadmus, American Eagle, and Fulton's steamboat transfer, pink luster rim	**95.00**
Mug, child's, 2½″ h, 2⅝″ d, red man and woman transfer, pink luster bands . .	**45.00**
Pepper Pot, 4½″	**85.00**

Pitcher
4¾″ h, emb scenes, emb flowers band around collar, pink luster . . .	**185.00**
5″ h, hunting scene transfer highlighted applied enamel, mustard ground, pink luster bands	**190.00**
5⅝″ h, deep relief hunting scenes, pink luster and green enamel . . .	**55.00**

Plaque, 9¼ x 8″, polychrome "Retribution Steamer" titled transfer, pink border **125.00**
Plate
  7⅝″, king's rose, pink luster emb weave pattern border, set of 4 ... **210.00**
  7⅞″, lime green and castle dec wickered rim, openwork lattice border . **270.00**
Punch Bowl, 12 x 5″, hunting scenes . **675.00**
Sugar, black transfer, pink luster border **60.00**
Tea Bowl and Saucer, white ground, pink florals, leaves, and trim **75.00**
Vase, 4¼″, floral sprays, oval panel with butterfly, wigglework border, Leeds, 1810, pr **250.00**

Silver Luster, 3½″ d handless cup and 5½″ d saucer, $65.00.

SILVER

Bowl, 8⅜″ d, all-over leaf design **45.00**
Coffeepot, 11″, cov, urn shape, ribbed bead dec, pedestal base, button finial **250.00**
Creamer, 5¾″ h, garland design around top, pedestal base, silver luster body **85.00**
Jug, 4½″, round medallion of Peace as young girl, silver luster border **360.00**
Mug, child's, 2″, brown transfer, boys flying kite, silver luster rim, inscribed "For a favorite" **230.00**
Pitcher, mulberry transfer scene, silver luster body **165.00**
Salt Shaker
  4″, bulbous, beaded dec, pedestal foot **80.00**
  4¾″, man standing, drinking glass of ale **40.00**
Tea Set, 5½″ ribbed body teapot, creamer and sugar, 3 pcs **175.00**
Teapot, 6″, cov, ribbed design, ftd **120.00**

SUNDERLAND

Bowl, 8½ x 4″, Mariner's Arms and West View of Cast Iron Bridge transfer .. **125.00**

Cake Plate, 10″, pink, mottled **145.00**
Cup and Saucer, pink splash luster int., copper luster ext. **50.00**
Demitasse Cup and Saucer, House pattern, pink luster **45.00**
Figure, 8⅝″, lady holding sheaf of wheat **230.00**
Humidor, cov, Parliament building transfer, pewter lock **200.00**
Mug, 3″ h, House pattern, pink luster . **85.00**
Mustard Pot, cov, 3½″ h, cylindrical form, molded base, applied ribbed double twist handle, all-over pink splash luster dec **100.00**
Pitcher
  7⅜″ h, polychrome "Wear Bridge" transfer under spout, verse on one side, pink splash luster **350.00**
  8¾″ h, bas-relief strawberry and vine dec, pink luster trim, Georgian handle, 1810–30 .... **325.00**
Plaque, 8 x 7⅛″, "Prepare/To Meet Thy God," angel blowing trumpet transfer, white center, pink border **100.00**
Plate
  7¾″ d, Shepherd Boy transfer scene, pink luster border **65.00**
  9½ x 8⅜″, polychrome "An East View of the New Bridge, Sunderland" titled scene, white center, brown highlights, pink border **175.00**
Plate, 9″, Babes in Woods **125.00**
Platter, 7½ x 8½″, Adam Clark transfer **200.00**
Sugar, 8″ h, cov, octagonal, mottled, pink, pear finial, handled **60.00**
Tea Set, boat shape cov teapot, creamer and cov sugar, 2 cake plates, waste bowl and stand, dark pink luster foliate forms on white ground, pink luster borders, early 19th C, 27 pcs . **440.00**
Toothpick Holder, mottled, pink, enameled white daises, canary luster base band and leaves **65.00**
Waste Bowl, pink splash **55.00**

LUTZ TYPE GLASS

History: Lutz type glass is an art glass attributed to Nicholas Lutz. He made this type of glass while at the Boston and Sandwich Glass Co. from 1869 until 1888. Since Lutz type glass was popular, copied by many capable glass makers, and unsigned, it is nearly impossible to distinguish genuine Lutz products.

Lutz is believed to have made two distinct types of glass, striped and threaded glass. This style often is confused with a similar style Venetian glass. The striped glass was made by using threaded glass rods in the Venetian manner. Threaded glass was blown and decorated by winding threads of glass around the piece.

Bowl, 6" d, fluted edge, pink and gold threaded design, clear ground, broken pontil, $125.00.

Barber Bottle, 8", threaded latticino, opaque stripes **190.00**
Compote, 7" h, lavender, pink, and opalescent swirls, entwined serpent stem   **250.00**
Lemonade, 5½", cranberry, threaded, clear applied handle, engraved dec .   **120.00**
Plate, 6¼", goldstone, threaded, rose center shading into amber body, ruffled **90.00**
Tumbler, ftd, 3" h, gold and white latticino, threaded, six applied strawberries **85.00**
Whimsey, 6⅜" h, tiny "Frozen Charlotte" doll in clear glass tube, bulbous finial, knob stem and clear foot dec with latticino rings **300.00**

MAASTRICHT WARE

History: Maastricht, Holland, is where Petrus Regout founded the De Sphinx pottery, in 1836. The firm specialized in transfer printed earthenwares. Other factories also were established in the area, many employing English workmen and their techniques. Maastricht china was exported to the United States in competition with English products.

Reference: Susan and Al Bagdade, *Warman's English & Continental Pottery & Porcelain, 1st Edition,* Warman Publishing Co., Inc., 1987.

Bowl
7¼", Oriental scene **18.00**
8", Pajong pattern, black and tan transfer, white ground **35.00**

9½", blue and white florals, wreaths, and medallions, marked "Maastricht-Holland" **20.00**
Charger, 14½", blue and white, children skating, cottages, windmill, marked "J Sonnerville, Maastricht" **65.00**
Cup and Saucer, handleless, deep saucer, flow blue, pale blue ground, tulip, feather inside cup, marked "Maastricht-Pegout, Holland" **25.00**

Bowl, 6⅛" d, 3⅛" h, Honc pattern, marked "Maastricht, Petrus Regoulec Co., Made in Holland," $65.00.

Plate
8", Abbey pattern, blue and white . .   **20.00**
8¼", Indian Traffic pattern, blue, native on horseback selling fruit . . .   **35.00**
9", Willow pattern, pink **18.00**
9½", game bird, deep rust edge . . .   **30.00**
Tureen, cov, matching ladle, white . . .   **45.00**
Waste Bowl, 4", Pompeia pattern, flow blue, c1875 . . . .   **45.00**

MAJOLICA

History: Majolica, an opaque, tin glazed pottery, has been produced by many countries for centuries. It originally took its name from the Spanish Island of Majorca, where figuline (a potter's clay) is found. Today majolica denotes a type of pottery which was made during the last half of the 19th century in Europe and America.

Majolica frequently depicted elements in nature: leaves, flowers, birds, and fish. Human figures were rare. Designs were painted on the soft clay body using vitreous colors and fired under a clear lead glaze to impart the rich color and brilliance characteristic of majolica.

Among English majolica manufacturers who marked their works were: Wedgwood, George Jones, Holdcraft, and Minton. Most of their pieces can be identified through the English Registry mark and/or the potter-designer's mark. Sarreguemines in France and Villeroy and Boch in Baden, Germany, produced majolica that compared favorably with the finer English majolica. Most Continental pieces had an incised number on the base.

Although 600 plus American potteries produced majolica between 1850 and 1900, only a handful chose to identify their wares. Among these manufacturers were George Morely, Edwin Bennett, the Chesapeake Pottery Company, the New Milford-Wannoppee Pottery Company, and the firm of Griffen, Smith, and Hill. The others hoped their unmarked pieces would be taken for English examples.

References: Susan and Al Bagdade, *Warman's English & Continental Pottery & Porcelain, 1st Edition,* Warman Publishing Co., Inc., 1987; Mariann K. Marks, *Majolica Pottery: An Identification And Value Guide,* Collector Books, 1983; M. Charles Rebert, *American Majolica 1850–1900,* Wallace-Homestead, 1981.

Syrup, 8″ h, mottled blue ground, yellow and brown sunflower and leaves, twig handle, pewter top, marked "Etruscan Majolica," $225.00.

Bottle, figural, stork, 16″, rumpled top hat stopper, 4″ beak with spectacles, umbrella under arm, English 825.00
Bowl
  2¾″ d, 3¼″ h, raised basket design, green shading to brown 45.00
  9¾″, Classical series, putti riding lion center, laced leafy vines border, sepia tones, Etruscan 75.00
  10½″, ftd, cauliflower, Wedgwood . .   235.00
Bread Plate, Oak Leaf with Acorns, 12¼″ l 110.00
Butter Pat, Begonia Leaf, Etruscan . . .   20.00
Centerpiece, 22″ l, 14″ w, 10″ h, oval, 2″ flower form feet, cobalt body, multicolored dec, 2″ lady's heads on ends, flower garlands on sides, Holdcroft, English 985.00

Cheese Dish, 10 x 8″, fern and flowers, stippled blue ground, glazed pink int., twig handle, marked "George Jones," English 785.00
Cheese Dome, lily, swan finial, Etruscan   1,350.00
Compote, 10″ d, 7″ h, water lily molded bowl, 6″ figural crane base, American   275.00
Dish
  10¼ x 7 x 5¾″, cov, brown basketweave base, molded fruit and flower on lid, strap circle handle . .   100.00
  11¼″ d, 1¼″ h, wide molded rim, variegated light green-blue scrolls and flowers, variegated olive center, scene of gnomes and leaves, bird in flight 115.00
Match Holder, 4 x 5″, Janus type double classical heads, striker side, marked "Wedgwood," registry marks 165.00
Oyster Plate 45.00
Paperweight, 3 x 4″, brown owl, pebbled ivory ground, pink stars and flowers, marked "Mayer" 110.00
Pitcher
  4″, Corn pattern, lavender int. 65.00
  4½″, Hawthorne pattern, mottled colors, Etruscan 125.00
  5″, Birds in Nest 100.00
  5½″, Basketweave pattern, pink flowers, green leaves, brown ground, gold top dec 75.00
  8″, Owl, figural, unmarked Morley . .   165.00
  11″, Owl, figural, yellow and black eyes, gray and green feathers . . .   215.00
  12½″, light blue ground, multicolored raised flowers and leaves, floral medallion, openwork diamond design, English 125.00
Plate
  6½″, Grape Cluster, marked "Germany" 20.00
  7″, Rose pattern, Etruscan 70.00
  8″
    Floral and Three Leaf pattern . . .   45.00
    Shell and Seaweed pattern, albino   65.00
  9″
    Bamboo and Basketweave pattern, Banks & Thorley, England 60.00
    Begonia Leaf, Etruscan 100.00
  10½″, Blackberry and Basketweave .   75.00
Platter
  10″, Doghouse 65.00
  11″, Wild Rose and Rope, aqua ground, cobalt center 110.00
  12″, Sunflower, twig handles, English   85.00
Sardine Box, cov, 7½ x 6½ x 5″, Cobalt and Seaweed pattern, two fish finial   325.00
Sauce Dish, Begonia Leaf 35.00
Statue, 20″ h, American slave boy, holding 4 x 9″ wicker tobacco tray, 5″ floppy straw hat, detailed face, intaglio eyes, striped trousers 1,625.00

Spooner, Bird and Fan **100.00**
Teapot
  Figural, Sailor, third leg forms spout,
    coil of rope handle, blonde hair and
    beard, 8 x 10", English **545.00**
  Shell and Seaweed, albino, Etruscan **350.00**
Tureen, cov, 8½" l, molded bands of
  green foliage, pale lavender ground,
  yellow rim, naturally molded cov of
  seaweed and fish, England, c1870 . **770.00**
Vase
  5½", double openwork handles, iris
    dec, molded base **40.00**
  10½", molded iris flowers, brown and
    yellow ground **150.00**
Water Set, Pineapple, 9½" h pitcher,
  four matching tumblers, 5 pcs **250.00**

MAPS

History: Maps provide one of the best ways to
study the growth of a country or region. From the
16th to the early 20th century, maps were both
informative and decorative. Engravers provided ornamental detailing which often took the form of
bird's eye views, city maps and ornate calligraphy
and scrolling. Many maps were hand colored to
enhance their beauty.

Maps generally were published in plate books.
Many of the maps available today result from these
books being cut apart and sheets sold separately.

In the last quarter of the 19th century, representatives from firms in Philadelphia, Chicago, and
elsewhere traveled the United States preparing
county atlases, often with a sheet for each township and a sheet for each major city or town. Although mass produced, they are eagerly sought
by collectors. Individual sheets sell for $25 to $75.
The atlases themselves can usually be purchased
in the $200 to $400 range. Individual sheets should
be viewed solely as decorative and not as investment material.

Africa, "Map of Tripoli & Tunis," 1816,
  Colburn, 10 x 16", few minor folds . . **25.00**
Canada, "British America," London/
  New York, Tallis, 1851, engraved,
  outline color, 12¾ x 9½" **75.00**
Celestial, "The Stars in 6 Maps on the
  Gnomonic Projection," revised by
  Rev. W. R. Dawes, London, 1851, So-
  ciety for the Diffusion of Useful Knowl-
  edge, hand colored, 13½ x 17" **75.00**
Mexico, "Mexico or New Spain in which
  the Motions of Cortes may be traced,"
  London, W Stratchan & T Cadell,
  1795, engraving, 11⅜ x 15¼" **200.00**
North America, "North America...," Lon-
  don, R Wilkinson, 1808, 8¾ x 11¼",
  engraved, full orig color **50.00**
North and South America, "A General

and Particular Description of Amer-
  ica...," London, H Moll, c1727, 7¼ x
  6¾" image size **130.00**
United States
  "A Map of Proposed Chesapeake-
    Delaware Canal Routes," Philadel-
    phia, American Philosophical So-
    ciety, 1771, J Smithers after W
    Thomas Fisher, engraving, 12⅝ x
    17" **950.00**
  "Missouri Territory formerly Louisi-
    ana," Philadelphia, Matthew Carey,
    1814, orig outline color, 11¾ x 14",
    from *General Atlas* **650.00**
  Florida, US Dept of War, Topograph-
    ical Study of Florida, Washington,
    DC, 1891, 16⅜ x 27¼", chromolith-
    ograph in 3 colors **65.00**
  Georgia, "A New and Accurate Map
    of the Province of Georgia in North
    America," London, J Hinton, 1779,
    engraving, 12¾ x 10¾", published
    in *The Univeral Magazine* **300.00**
  Montana, "Great Falls, Montana,"
    Chicago, Rand McNally & Co,
    c1895, red and black, 26½ x 37½",
    issued by Great Falls Water Power
    and Townsite Company **575.00**
  Nevada, "Map of the State of Ne-
    vada," October 2, 1866, 19 x 26¼",
    from the *Landmark Atlas of the
    General Land Office* **400.00**
  New England, "The Counties of
    Barnstable, Dukes, and Nan-
    tucket," published by Henry E. Wail-
    ing, 1858, fair condition **250.00**
  New Mexico, "Official Map of New
    Mexico, Prepared under the direc-
    tion of the Bureau of Immigration,"
    1890, black and white, 25¼ x 31½" **600.00**
  Pennsylvania
    Map of Carlisle, 1867, dowels for
      hanging at top and bottom, ads
      in corners, lists of merchants in
      lower and upper right quadrants,
      36 x 44", browned **45.00**
    "Plan of Philadelphia," German,
      early 19th C, lithograph, 8⅛ x
      9½", German version of Birch
      plan **400.00**
  Utah, "Map of the Territory of Utah,"
    October 2, 1866, 18 x 25", from the
    *Landmark Atlas of the General
    Land Office* **450.00**
  "United States of America," engraved
    by Samuel Harrison, Philadelphia,
    Murray D. Fairman & Co, copyright
    July, 1818, tinting and color out-
    lines, 16¼ x 19½" **500.00**
West Indies, "A Map of the West Indies
  and Middle Continent of America...,"
  London, Thomas Kitchin after John

Blair, c1750, hand colored engraving,
16½ x 22½″ **450.00**

MARBLEHEAD POTTERY

History: This hand thrown pottery had its beginning in 1905 as a therapeutic program introduced by Dr. J. Hall for the patients confined to a sanitarium located in Marblehead, Massachusetts. In 1916 production was removed from the hospital to another site. The factory continued under the directorship of Arthur E. Baggs until it closed in 1936.

Most pieces found today are glazed with a smooth, porous, even finish in a single color. The most desirable pieces are decorated with conventionalized design in one or more subordinate colors.

Vase, 8″ h, 4″ w, tapered cylindrical shape, blue matte glaze, sgd, $200.00.

Bowl, 8 x 4″, plum, semi-matte finish . **85.00**
Chamberstick, 4″ h, rose matte glaze . **50.00**
Pitcher, 8¼ x 6″, bulging cylindrical form, angular handle, incised scenic band, dark brown trees, sage green ground, robin's egg blue int., incised ship mark and "AB" **850.00**
Urn, 4½ x 6¾″, bulging cylindrical form, wide mouth, sharply painted design, thin brown branches, green leaves, large yellow pomegranates, brown linear border, soft black outlines, grainy gray ground, dec by Hanna Tutt, die stamped mark **2,700.00**
Vase
3½ x 5¾″, cylindrical, bulging base,

four stylized trees, top form rim border, deep olive green, pea green matte ground **1,500.00**
4¼ x 3¼″, ochre bulbous base tapering upward to flared rim, stylized brown and olive green stem and leaf dec, stylized yellow roses, die stamped galleon mark **575.00**
5½ x 7½″, tapering, cylindrical form, incised clusters of deep blue wisteria blossoms, fine textured medium blue ground, die stamped mark **1,000.00**
12 x 9½″, bulbous, four broad, flat buttresses ending at collar rim, dark green geometric designs gently incised on medium-dark green ground, die stamped mark, orig paper label **6,600.00**

MARY GREGORY TYPE GLASS

History: The use of enameled decoration on glass, an inexpensive imitation of cameo glass, developed in Bohemia in the late 19th century. The Boston and Sandwich Glass Co. copied this process in the late 1880s.

Mary Gregory (1856–1908) was employed for two years at the Boston and Sandwich Glass Co. factory when the enameled decorated glass was being manufactured. Some collectors argue that Gregory was inspired to paint her white enamel figures on glass by the work of Kate Greenaway and a desire to imitate pate-sur-pate. However, evidence for these assertions is very weak. Further, a question can be raised whether or not Mary Gregory even decorated glass as part of her job at Sandwich.

The result is that "Mary Gregory Type" is a better term to describe this glass. Collectors should recognize that most examples are either European or modern reproductions.

Atomizer, 5¼″ h, 2½″ d, cranberry, old bulb with tassel, white enamel young girl **225.00**
Box, 4⅛″ h, 3⅝″ d, cov, hinged, round, olive-amber, girl with scarf, brass feet and rings on sides **300.00**
Cookie Jar, 7½″ h, 4½″ d, cranberry, young girl sitting on fence, emb plated lid, rim, and handle **450.00**
Cruet, ribbed, green, young girl carrying flowers, clear applied handle and stopper **75.00**
Decanter, cranberry, flat sides, boy and girl playing **300.00**
Jewel Box, cov
5″ d, blue, young girl with basket . . . **325.00**
5½″ d, 5″ h, round, cranberry, young

Pitcher, 10″ h, sapphire blue ground, white enamel young child, $325.00.

girl blowing bubbles, ftd ormolu base	**275.00**
6″ d, amber, two children playing . . .	**300.00**
Match Holder, 2¼″ h, 2¼″ d, cranberry, barrel shape, young boy	**85.00**
Paperweight, honey amber	**90.00**
Patch Box, cov, hinged, round	
1¼″ h, 1⅞″ d, cobalt blue, young girl with hat	**175.00**
1¾″ h, 2⅜″ d, lime green, round, young girl	**165.00**
Perfume, 4¾″ h, bulbous, sapphire blue, white enameled littled girl holding branch, all-over tiny silver snowflakes	**165.00**
Pin Tray, 4½ x 2″, oval, cranberry, little girl holding flower	**100.00**
Pitcher, 7½″ h, 5″ d, glass, lime green, round mouth, girl holding balloon, clear reeded applied handle	**200.00**
Stein	
5½″ h, cranberry, young boy dec, pewter lid with pink glass insert . .	**225.00**
6½″, sapphire blue, IVT, boy in pink suit, pewter lid with clear insert . .	**300.00**
Tumbler	
2½″ h, 1¾″ d, cranberry, facing pr, boy on one, girl on other	**100.00**
3″ h, 1¾″ d, young boy	**50.00**
Vase	
2⅛″ h, 2½″ d, cranberry, young girl with watering can	**100.00**
4″ h, 3½″ d, cranberry, bulbous shape, small neck, young girl . . .	**145.00**
4″ h, 5½″ l, oblong, sapphire blue, two girls picking flowers, ormolu base	**125.00**
6″ h, 2¼″ d, orange, young boy	**115.00**
6¼″ h, 2″ d, cylinder shape, bulbous base, cranberry, facing pr, boy on one, girl on other, pr	**225.00**
7½″ h, 3⅜″ d, cobalt blue, facing pr, little girls, pedestal foot, pr	**225.00**

7½″, blue, facing pr, children, pr . . .	**445.00**
7¾″ h, 2⅝″ d, pink overlay, white lining, ruffled top, young girl with butterfly	**150.00**
8¼″ h, 3⅞″ d, cranberry, young boy with cane	**200.00**
8⅝″, shaded pink satin overlay, white lining, young girl with hat sitting on rock, two butterflies in flight	**375.00**
9½″	
Cobalt blue, flat sided, white cherubs and flowers, gold centers, ormolu mounts, pr	**325.00**
Cranberry, young girl with rope of flowers	**125.00**
10″ h, 4½″ d, golden amber, young girl reaching for butterfly	**250.00**
10¾″ h, 4⅞″ d, black amethyst, facing pr, boy on one, girl on other, pr . .	**450.00**
12⅜″, electric blue, facing children, scalloped tops, pr	**550.00**
14″, cylindrical, pigeon blood, full figured Victorian women, ormolu base, matching pr	**1,250.00**
Whiskey Glass, 2¼″ h, 2⅛″ d, cranberry, bulbous, little girl	**85.00**
Wine Bottle	
7⅛″ h, 3⅛″ d, cranberry, young boy, orig clear bubble stopper	**195.00**
10″ h, 3″ d, cranberry, young girl, clear bubble stopper	**195.00**

MATCH HOLDERS

History: After 1850 the friction match achieved popular usage. The early matches were packaged and sold in sliding cardboard boxes. To facilitate storage and to eliminate the clumsiness of using the box, match holders were developed.

The first examples were cast iron or tin, the latter often having advertising on them. A patent for a wall hanging match holder was issued in 1849. By 1880 match holders also were being made from glass and china. Match holders lost popularity in the late 1930s and 1940s with the advent of gas and electric heat and ranges.

Advertising	
American Brewing Co., stoneware, salt glazed, striker on bottom	**65.00**
American Steel Fence	**75.00**
Barker Brand Clothing Collar, silvered brass, emb dog holding a man's collar, hinged lid, early 1900s . . .	**60.00**
C. E. Hiltz, emb, dimensional, litho, tin	**550.00**
Hood Rubber Company, boot shape, black, rubber, removable top, "Compliments of Hood Rubber Company/Boston, USA," c1800s, unused	**150.00**

La Confesion Cuban Cigar, gentleman holding cigar, dark blue metal finish on tin, hinged lid **75.00**
Old Judson **125.00**
Schlitz Beer, litho, cardboard **325.00**
The Fashion Clothing Store, silvered metal, 1902 calendar on reverse . **75.00**
Art Deco, nasturtium pattern, orange and yellow flowers, spattered brown, 4¾" d, 6⅛" h **140.00**
Brass, pig, figural, pocket type **110.00**
Cast Iron
    Double pouch, old paint, 4½ x 8" . . **85.00**
    Hunting scene, Germany **60.00**
    Open scrollwork, dated 1867 . . . . . **55.00**

Advertising, 3⅜ x 5", Old Judson, J. C. Stevens, Kansas City, MO, $125.00.

Glass
  Amber
    Oaken Bucket, 2⅝" d, 2⅝" h, orig wire handle **20.00**
    Witches kettle, wire bail **40.00**
  Apple Green, Indian head **40.00**
  Clear, Jumbo **40.00**
  Custard, Winged Scroll pattern, Heisey **100.00**
  Light Blue, Indian head **50.00**
  Milk Glass, Indian, orig gold dec, 3¼" h **175.00**
  Opaque, white
    Hand and fan **20.00**
    Indian head **50.00**
Pottery, cannon, Niloak **35.00**
Royal Bayreuth
  Cavalier musicians dec, hanging type **395.00**
  Devil and Cards, hanging type **195.00**
  Girl and dog dec **200.00**
  Poppy, red, hanging type **110.00**
Silver Plate, man riding horse, pocket type **85.00**

MATCH SAFES

History: Match safes are small containers used to safely carry matches in one's pocket. They were first used in the 1850s. Match safes are often figural with a hinged lid and striking surface.

Reference: Audrey G. Sullivan, *A History of Match Safes In The United States,* published by author, 1978.

Note: While not all match safes have a striking surface, this is one test, besides size, to distinguish a match safe from a calling card case.

1⅜" d, Sterling silver, billard scene, English, $275.00.

Advertising
  American Steam Packing Co., silvered brass, black and white cello, Indian head on one side, early 1900s **70.00**
  Anheuser-Busch, SP, eagle, 2¾" l, c1900 . . . . **40.00**
  Bamberger's Shoe Store, silvered brass, black wand white horse illus on one side, "Mens Shoe Annex" on other, early 1900s **50.00**
  Fairy Soap, metal **10.00**
  Fan Tan Cigars, silvered brass, black and white illus on one side, 1902 calendar on reverse **60.00**
  Fleischmann's Restaurant/Bakery, silvered brass and cello, early 1900s **60.00**
  Monitor Works, blue and white design, Monitor iron warship, "Use Monitor" on reverse, early 1900s . **75.00**
  Number Five Cigar, brass, engraved floral pattern, lid **75.00**
  Pabst, Milwaukee, brass **30.00**
  Rochester Composite Brick Co, sil-

vered brass, black and white brick, company address on reverse, early 1900s **70.00**
Brass, Art Nouveau style, raised relief lady in pearl panel on one side, raised hunting dog and rider's crop on other, late 1890s, early 1900s **75.00**
Cast Iron, hanging
　Bacchus Head, figural, open pocket, grapes and leaves back plate ... **85.00**
　Monks Head, cathedral spires on reverse **85.00**
Glass
　Amber, boot shape, hanging **20.00**
　Clear
　　3¹⁵⁄₁₆″ h, American shield form, marked "America and 1492/1892" **140.00**
　　4½″ h, Miss Liberty's head, hanging **80.00**
　Dark Blue, southern **70.00**
　Milk Glass, 3⅞″ h, blue, mottled, flag shield form, hanging, marked "America and 1492/1892" **175.00**
　Souvenir, Mount Vernon, silvered brass, Washington's Mansion and Tomb photos **45.00**
Sterling Silver
　Blue enameled center, "Y" and "99" on one side, engraved "PRB" initials on reverse, floral nouveau design **65.00**
　Enameled, "VR" and British flag, 1897 Jubilee **95.00**
Tin, hanging, open crimped shell red pocket, painted, triangular green back, asphaltum center striking surface, 2 x 3 x 5½″ **65.00**

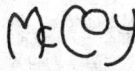

McCOY POTTERY

History: The J. W. McCoy Pottery Co. was established in Roseville, Ohio, in September, 1899. The early McCoy Co. produced both stoneware and some art pottery lines, including Rosewood. In October, 1911, three potteries merged creating the Brush-McCoy Pottery Co. This company continued to produce the original McCoy lines and added several new art lines. Much early pottery is not marked.

In 1910, Nelson McCoy and his father, J. W. McCoy, founded the Nelson McCoy Sanitary Stoneware Co. In 1925, the McCoy family sold their interest in the Brush-McCoy Pottery Co. and started to expand and improve the Nelson McCoy Co. The new company produced stoneware, earthenware specialities, and artware. Most of the pottery marked McCoy was made by the Nelson McCoy Co.

Reference: Sharon and Bob Huxford, *The Collectors Encyclopedia of McCoy Pottery,* Collector Books, 1980.

Additional Listings: *See Warman's Americana & Collectibles* for more examples.

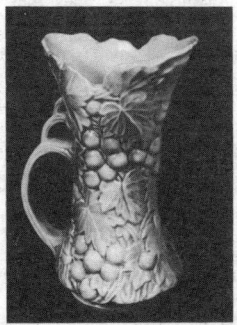

Pitcher, 9″ h, pale tinted green leaves and grapes, cream ground, marked "Loy-Nel," $35.00.

Basket, green, basketweave **24.00**
Birdbath, 27″ h, Greystone finish **65.00**
Bowl, Amaryllis pattern, pastel **20.00**
Cookie Jar
　Animal Crackers **30.00**
　Old Woman's Shoe **60.00**
　Tepee **75.00**
Cuspidor, 3½″ h, lady's, mottled yellow and brown Rockingham glaze, Nurock, 1916 .... **20.00**
Ewer, 10″, emb grapes and leaves, dark brown glaze, marked "Rosewood, McCoy," c1905 .... **185.00**
Jardiniere, 11¾ x 9″, hp, tulip dec, marked "Loy-Nel-Art" **160.00**
Jug, 5″, onyx glaze, rust, beige, and dark brown **32.00**
Mug
　Buccaneer and parrot, emb, green glaze, marked "Nelson McCoy Sanitary Stoneware Co," c1926 .. **15.00**
　Corn pattern, pale yellow kernels, green husk, c1910 .... **60.00**
　Little Red Riding Hood, marked "Brush-McCoy" **38.00**
Pitcher, 9½″ h, emb reserve of grapes and leaves, green and brown wood grain ground, c1920 .... **48.00**
Planter, figural
　Carriage with parasol, c1955 ..... **38.00**
　Duck with umbrella **35.00**
　Spinning Wheel **24.00**
Pretzel Jar, cov, emb buccaneer and parrot, green glaze, marked "Nelson

McCoy Sanitary Stoneware Co,"
c1920 .... **70.00**
Punch Bowl, pedestal base, emb
grapes and leaves, dark brown glaze,
marked "Olympia J W McCoy" **375.00**
Teapot, Parchment and Pine pattern . **18.00**
Tureen, El Rancho Bar-B-Que pattern,
sombrero cov, c1960 .... **50.00**
Urn, 6", onyx glaze, marked "Nelson-
McCoy" **32.00**
Vase
10", Springwood pattern, pink glaze,
1961 .... **20.00**
13", hp, wild roses dec, artist sgd,
marked "Loy-Nel-Art" **325.00**
14½", brown glaze, yellow flowers,
marked "Loy-Nel Art" **75.00**
Wall Pocket, mailbox shape, emb "Letters," green glaze **15.00**

McKEE GLASS

History: The McKee Glass Co. was established
in 1843 in Pittsburgh, Pennsylvania. In 1852 they
opened a factory to produce pattern glass. In 1888
the factory was relocated to Jeannette, Pennsylvania, and began to produce many types of glass
kitchenwares, including several patterns of
Depression Glass. The factory continued until
1951 when it was sold to the Thatcher Manufacturing Co.

McKee named its colors Chalaine Blue, Custard,
Seville Yellow, and Skokie Green. McKee glass
may also be found with painted patterns, e.g., dots
and ships. A few items were decaled. Many of the
canisters and shakers were lettered in black to
show the purpose they were intended for.

References: Gene Florence, *Kitchen Glassware of the Depression Years, 3rd edition*, Collector Books, 1988; Lowell Innes and Jane Shadel
Spillman, *M'Kee Victorian Glass*, Dover Publications, 1981.

Additional Listings: See *Warman's Americana
& Collectibles* for more examples.

Bowl, 4¾", Art Deco, black, ftd **15.00**
Box, cov, round, vaseline, sparrow finial **100.00**
Butter, lid, white, 1 lb **35.00**
Candy Dish, cov, 8½" h, black, Art Nou-
veau **90.00**
Cheese Dish, cov, Laurel, French Ivory **36.00**
Clock, amber, marked "Tambour Art" . **350.00**
Drawer Pull, Chalaine blue, medium
size, pr **25.00**
Egg Cup, French Ivory **5.00**
Goblet, Gothic, flint **37.50**
Lamp, 11", boudoir, Danse de Lumiere,
green satin finish, pr **450.00**
Punch Set, punch bowl, base, twelve
cups, milk glass, relief grape dec,
plastic ladle, orig box, 15 pc **85.00**

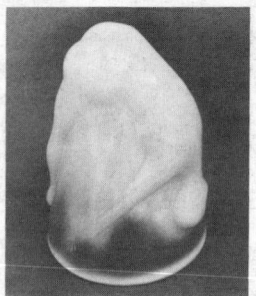

Tumbler, 3¼" h, "Bottoms-Up," caramel
opalescent, marked "Patent No.
77726," $60.00.

Reamer, lemon, custard **30.00**
Salt and Pepper Shakers, pr, 3", ribbed,
green **25.00**
Straw Holder Jar, SP top **75.00**
Vase
8½", nude, Chalaine blue, hp clothes **225.00**
Whiskey, Bottoms Up, caramel glass,
coaster **65.00**
Wren House, green **60.00**

MEDICAL AND APOTHECARY ITEMS

History: Medicine and medical instruments are
well documented for the modern period. Some
instruments are virtually unchanged since their invention. Others have changed drastically.

The concept of sterlization phased out decorative handles. Early handles of instruments were
often carved and can be found in mother-of-pearl,
ebony, and ivory. Today's sleekly designed instruments are not as desirable to collectors.

Apothecary items include items commonly found
in an apothecary and pertain to the items used to
store or prepare medications.

References: Bill Carter, Bernard Butterworth,
Joseph Carter, and John Carter, *Dental Collectibles & Antiques*, Dental Folklore Books of K.C.,
1984; Don Fredgant, *Medical, Dental & Pharmaceutical Collectibles*, Books Americana, 1981;
Keith Wilbur, *Antique Medical Instruments*, Schiffer Publishing, 1987.

Museums: National Museum of History and
Technology, Smithsonian Institution, Washington,
DC; Waring Historical Library, Medical University
of South Carolina, Charleston, SC.

APOTHECARY

Advertising Poster, Dr Meyers Foot
Soap, 1920, 38 x 25" **120.00**

Alcohol Burner, 2½", brass sterlizer .. **40.00**
Apothecary Jar
  11" h, Roseville, Twain series,
    marked "Rozart" **215.00**
  12½" h, frosted flower and pleat dec,
    amber stained flowers, teardrop
    shape, pleated pedestal base and
    cov, ball finial **300.00**

**Apothecary Jar, 8" h, emerald green,
ground stopper, recessed label, $40.00.**

Label Dispenser, McCourt Label Cabinet Co, oak and brass, holds 48 labels **85.00**
Leech Jar, carrying, hand blown glass,
  c1850 .... **60.00**
Measure, wooden, turned, 2 cups attached by stem **110.00**
Sign, Brickmore's Gall Cure, cardboard
  30 x 50" **85.00**

DENTAL

Cabinet, 36" d, mahogany finish, 32
  drawers, cupboard base, fan carving
  on door, ball and claw feet, 20th C . **1,000.00**
Chair, oak, early **165.00**
Drill, Electro Dental Mfg Co, patent Nov
  3, 1903, foot control patent Sept 9,
  1911 .... **60.00**
Instruments, ebony handles, c1860, set
  of 6 .... **160.00**
Tooth Display, 834 teeth mounted in
  carrying case, Trubyte Dentist Supply
  Co., NY **125.00**
Tooth Extractor **85.00**

MEDICAL

Amputation Bow Saw, ebony handle .. **120.00**
Bleeder, brass, twelve blades, spring
  loaded, orig case **200.00**
Book, "A Textbook of Practical Gyne-
  cology," Gilliam, 1913 .... **18.00**

Doctor's Bag, leather, bottles in side
  compartment, c1865 .... **100.00**
Ear Trumpet, tortoise shell, telescopic,
  T Hawksley, Ltd, London, c1870 ... **235.00**
Ether Mask, brass, English, c1900 ... **60.00**
Machine
  Cardiograph, electric, portable, c1930 **100.00**
  Master Violet Ray, No. 11 .... **40.00**
  Shock treatment, "Branston Standard
    Electrode," hand held, orig box .. **185.00**
Stethoscope, monaural, SS, ivory ear
  pc, English, c1875 .... **125.00**
Surgical Knife, SS, Gorham **60.00**
Urologist's "Kystoskop," c1910, orig box **75.00**

OPTICAL

Cornea Grafting Set, 12 instruments,
  ivory handles, velvet lined case, J
  Weiss & Sons, London, c1870 .... **160.00**
Eye Cup
  Green glass **10.00**
  Milk glass **15.00**
Opthalmoscope, patent 1924 .... **45.00**
Optometrist Lens Set, 30 lens, velvet
  lined case **35.00**

MEDICINE BOTTLES

History: The local apothecary and his book of
formulas played a major role in early America. In
1796 the first patent for a medicine was issued by
the United States Patent Office. Anyone could apply for a patent. As long as the dosage was not
poisonous, the patent was granted.

Patent medicines were advertized in newspapers and magazines and sold through the general
store and by "medicine" shows. In 1907 the Pure
Food and Drug Act, requiring an accurate description of contents of medicine on the label, put an
end to the patent medicine industry. Not all medicines were patented.

Most medicines were sold in distinctive bottles,
often with the name of the medicine and location
in relief. Many early bottles were made in the glass
manufacturing area of southern New Jersey. Later
companies in western Pennsylvania and Ohio
manufactured bottles.

References: Joseph K. Baldwin, *A Collector's
Guide To Patent And Proprietary Medicine Bottles
Of The Nineteenth Century*, Thomas Nelson, Inc.,
1973; Ralph & Terry Kovel, *The Kovels' Bottle
Price List, 7th ed.*, Crown Publishers, 1984; Carlo
& Dot Sellari, *The Illustrated Price Guide To An-
tique Bottles*, Country Beautiful Corp., 1975.

Periodicals: *Antique Bottle and Glass Collector*, P.O. Box 187, East Greenville, PA 18041.

Abbott Bros, Chicago, Rheumatic Remedy, amber, 6½" **12.00**
Alden's Catarrah Cure **25.00**

Dr. J. Pettit, Canker Balsam, 3⅛ x 1″, aqua, open pontil, hand tooled rolled lip, $20.00.

Arabian Tonic Blood Purifier, Stuart Howell, NY, aqua	25.00
Arthur's Renovating Syrup, pontil, blue green	160.00
Braddock's Pulmonary Cough Mixture, Hartford, CT, aqua	100.00
Brant's Indian Purifying Extract, rect, aqua	130.00
Carrington Croup Syrup	40.00
Chadwick's Compound Vegetable Liniment, rect, applied lip, open pontil, aqua	75.00
Corbin's German Drops, pontil, aqua	180.00
Curtin & Perkin's Cramp and Pain Killer, round, aqua	42.50
Dodd's Fever Cure	18.00
Empire Company's Nervine Balsam & Indian Remedy	8.00
Flagg's Good Samaritan Immediate Relief, Cincinnati, pontil, aqua	75.00
Gibb's Bone Liniment, octagonal, open pontil, olive green	600.00
Grove's Tasteless Chill Tonic, aqua	10.00
Hagan's Magnolia Balm, rect, milk glass, 5″	7.50
Hefferan's French Cold & Throat Remedy, clear	28.00
Hobensack's Medicated Worm Syrup, Philadelphia, rect, indented panels, aqua	50.00
Lake's Indian Specific, rect, deeply beveled corners, aqua	300.00
Mrs Allen's World Hair Restorer, amethyst	160.00
Nelson Baker & Co, amber, 9″	4.00
Oxien Pills, The Giant Oxien Co, Augusta, ME, clear, 2″	3.00
Pettit's Canker Balsam	20.00
Reed & Carnich, Jersey City, Peptenzyne, cobalt, 8½″	12.00

Royal Foot Wash, Eaton Drug Co, Atlanta	6.00
Well's Throat Balsam	15.00

MERCURY GLASS

History: Mercury glass is a light bodied, double walled glass that was "silvered" by applying a solution of silver nitrate to the inside of the object through a hole in the base of the formed object.

F. Hale Thomas, London, patented the method in 1849. In 1855 the New England Glass Co. filed a patent for the same type of process. Other American glass makers soon followed. The glass reached the height of its popularity in the early 20th century.

Salt, 1¾″ d, 1¼″h, silver, three applied clear feet, $32.50.

Bowl, 4¾″, enameled floral design, gold int.	50.00
Candlesticks, pr	
4 x 9½″	80.00
11″, enameled floral dec	115.00
Candy Dish, 4¼ x 8¼″, pedestal base, clear glass domed cov	30.00
Carafe, 5½″ d, 12″ h, mushroom stopper, dated 1909	50.00
Compote	
5¾ x 2¾″, shallow, etched birds and leaves	45.00
6½ x 7″, enameled white floral dec, gold int.	65.00
Creamer	
6½″, grapevine dec, etched, applied clear handle	125.00
6¾″, etched grape vine pattern, applied clear handle, Sandwich Glass Co	115.00
Curtain Tiebacks, 3″ d, etched grape pattern, pewter shanks, pr	50.00
Darner, umbrella shape, enameled floral dec, brass trim	60.00
Pitcher, 6″, etched ferns	135.00
Rolling Pin	60.00

Salt, 3", urn shape, ftd	**35.00**
Shaving Mug, fern dec	**40.00**
Sweetmeat Dish, 4" d, 7½" h, clear glass cov, pedestal base	**40.00**
Toothpick, white enameled floral dec, gold int.	**40.00**
Tumbler, 4½" h	**20.00**

Urn

12", gold int., floral and foliage dec .	**150.00**
13", baluster shape, marked "Harnish & Co, London"	**250.00**

Vase

7", ball shape, blue	**35.00**
12", ribbed, green, enameled floral dec, birds, pr	**125.00**

METTLACH

History: In 1809 Jean Francis Boch established a pottery at Mettlach in Germany's Moselle Valley. His father had started a pottery at Septfontaines in 1767. Nicholas Villeroy began his pottery career at Wallerfanger in 1789.

In 1841 these three factories merged. They pioneered in underglaze printing on earthenware, using transfers from copper plates, and in using coal fired kilns. Other factories were developed at Dresden, Wadgassen, and Danischburg.

The castle and Mercury emblems are the two chief marks. Secondary marks are known. The base also contains a shape mark and usually a decor mark. Pieces are found in relief, etched, prints under the glaze, and cameo.

Prices are for print under glaze unless otherwise specified.

References: Susan and Al Bagdade, *Warman's English & Continental Pottery & Porcelain, 1st Edition,* Warman Publishing Co., Inc., 1987; Gary Kirsner, *The Mettlach Book, Second Edition,* published by author, 1987, R. H. Mohr, *Mettlach Steins, Ninth Edition,* published by author, 1982.

Additional Listings: Villeroy & Boch.

Advisor: Ron Fox.

Beaker

2327/1173, ¼ L, dwarf holds goblet .	**100.00**
2327/1290C, ¼ L, Bavarian crest . .	**75.00**
2842/1175, ¼ L, old dwarf, cane at feet, broken wine goblet	**85.00**
3883/553, ¼ L, German man, leaning on rifle	**70.00**

Butter Dish, 18" d, cov, shamrock and rect dec, castle mark	**125.00**

Cigar Holder, figural boy, basket on back, peaked hat	**240.00**

Coaster

1032, 4¾", set of 4	**400.00**
2820, etched, college boy holding stein	**190.00**

Pitcher, wine, 13", 3 L, six tan relief friezes, center blue band of Merry Dancing People, marked "V & B, Mettlach"	**450.00**

Plaque

1044/263, 17¾", knights, maiden, and swan	**435.00**
1044/354, 14" d, Oriental woman in boat, watching sunset	**200.00**
1607, 11", etched, ladies representing summer and fall, sgd "Warth, 1893"	**500.00**
2148, 16¼", Snow White holding large bowl, sgd "H. Schlitt"	**1,400.00**
2621, 7", cavalier pouring wine	**175.00**
2749, 20", etched, church at end of winding road	**1,080.00**
2875, 17½" d, cameo, blue-green, white classical woman and man depicting industry	**745.00**

Plate, 3096, octagonal, Art Deco design, burnt gold, cream, and royal blue	**65.00**

Pokal

396, 17", relief, crown top, pedestal base, four scenes, German text . .	**450.00**
2058, 21", monkeys among branches, monkey on lid	**750.00**

Punch Bowl

1 qt, dwarfs carry pole, with grapes, from shoulders, lid lift is bottle held by sleeping dwarf	**375.00**
8 qt, 488, underplate and cov, relief grapes, lid shows cherubs, sqeezing juice from grapes into mouths	**1,000.00**

Stein, #2090II/10/94, matte finish, $700.00.

Stein

284, ½ L, hand enameled, fraternal crest, inscribed lid **100.00**

1526, ½ L, Eisenbahn Regt, Berlin, 1899–1901, roster, locomotive scene **280.00**

1530, ½ L, etched, man in brown robe and cap, smoking pipe, sgd "R. Buch '86" **375.00**

1642, ½ L, Warth, pewter **450.00**

2001A, ½ L, 4¼" d, 5¾ h, book type, titled "The Lawyer," etched pottery lids, owl on pewter thumbpiece, blue, tan, and brown **550.00**

2001C, ½ L, 4¼" d, 5¾ h, book type, titled "The Scholar," etched pottery lids, owl on pewter thumbpiece, blue, tan, and brown **550.00**

2180/955, 5 L, drinking scene, sgd "Heinrich Schlitt" **1,300.00**

2194, 3 L, relief, black whale story, alligator handle, turtle on lid **750.00**

2631, 2.5 L, cameo, boar hunt scene, Stahl **1,400.00**

2691, 2.75 L, inlay, man with guitar in cellar **1,100.00**

2790/6147, ½ L, bearded man **380.00**

2900, ½ L, etched **375.00**

2950, ½ L, cameo, Bavarian shield, relief lid **400.00**

2958, 3 L, etched, bowling scene, sgd "F.Q." **600.00**

3144, ½ L, etched, carved clock in wreath above shield, couple on each side, sgd "F. Quidenus" ... **600.00**

½ L, early relief, acorns, leaves, and branches **185.00**

Vase

1537, 5¾ x 14", etched four season panels with cherubs, pink lining .. **350.00**

1591, 9" **175.00**

1808, 10" **90.00**

1870, 14", blue ground, geometric dec, elephant handles, castle mark **345.00**

2414, 16¾", handled, oak leaves, brown acorns, green leaves, gray ground, pr **450.00**

MILITARIA

History: Wars always have been part of history. Until the mid-19th century, soldiers often had to fill their own needs, including weapons. Even in the 20th century a soldier's uniform and some of his gear are viewed as his personal property, even though issued by a military agency.

Conquering armed forces made a habit of acquiring souvenirs from their vanquished foes. They brought their own uniforms and accessories home as badges of triumph and service.

Saving militaria may be one of the oldest collecting traditions. Militaria collectors tend to have their own special shows and view themselves outside the normal antiques channels. However, they haunt small indoor shows and flea markets in hopes of finding additional materials.

Reproduction Alert: Pay special attention to Civil War and Nazi material.

Collectors' Clubs: Association of American Military Uniform Collectors, 446 Berkshire Rd, Elyria, OH 44035; Company of Military Historicans, North Main Street, Westbrook, CT 06498; Imperial German Military Collectors Association, Box 38, Keyport, NJ 07735.

Additional Listings: Firearms and Swords. See World War I and World War II in *Warman's Americana & Collectibles* for more examples.

WAR OF 1812

Hat, leather, attached brass eagle, metallic rope twists **600.00**

Powder Horn, 24" l, cannon, "Sacketts Harbor, May 12, 1813," naval battle scene, 3 large ships, several smaller ones **1,000.00**

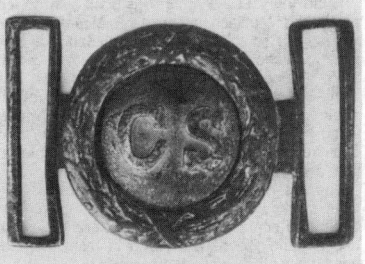

Civil War, belt buckle, Confederate, two pieces, $450.00.

CIVIL WAR

Advertising Button, Union-Confederacy handshake, blue and gray uniformed arms, Bailey & Co **25.00**

Bed, camp, wood, folding, trestle type legs, heavy linen, identification marks **300.00**

Belt Buckle, oval **45.00**

Blanket, coarse mixed tan wool, brown stripe, U.S. woven in center **500.00**

Bugle, copper and brass, standard issue, pitched in key of C, manufacturer's mark **285.00**

Bullet Mold, two cavity, 36 caliber **15.00**

Button, officer, Alabama Volunteer

Corps, 2 pcs, marked "A.V.C." between eagle wings 135.00

Canteen, wood, drum shape, carved name and regiment of Confederate soldier 1,100.00

Cartridge Box Plate, oval, marked "US," dug Charleston, SC 30.00

Chair, camp, folding, carpet seat 65.00

Document Box, 6 x 9 x 3½", painted scene, steam paddle boat, fort on hill, banner reads "April, 1863, USS Benton, Porters Flagship, Bald Head" .. 500.00

Hat, Naval type, straw 200.00

Knapsack, black waterproof canvas, 13 x 14" 75.00

Knife, Bowie, Louisiana state seal on handle 350.00

Saddle, Confederate, C.S. saddle shield 500.00

Shell, Parrott, Confederate, copper fuse plug 65.00

Soap Box, Army, hard rubber, Morning Exercise, razor with eagle, mirror .. 100.00

Stirrups, artillery, brass, marked "U.S." on base 40.00

Tintype, full length, unidentified Federal Cavalry man, gear, sword, and carbine 375.00

Uniform, frock coat
Confederate, double breasted, butternut color, lindsey-woolsey fabric .. 5,000.00
Federal, enlisted infantry, blue piping on collar and cuffs, 9 button front, maker and inspector marks in sleeve 1,900.00

Utensils, knife, spoon, fork, marked "Richards Patent of July 23, 1861," 2 pcs, ... 100.00

Whiskey Glass, 3", "Bumper to the Flag" 85.00

INDIAN WARS

Belt Buckle, brass
Eagle, large, inscribed E. Pluribus Unum, trace silver on back, tongue bar attached 65.00
US emb on front, marked "Anson Mills, patent 1881" 45.00

Powder Horn, 13" w, Jos Colton, Roxbury, 1764, map of Hudson River area, river scene 1,000.00

Scabbard, 18" l, blued metal, for 43/70 Springfield bayonet, state of MA, brass device 15.00

Textile, 23", multicolored print, Sitting Bull, Black Hawk, Osceola 100.00

FRANCO-PRUSSIAN WAR

Helmet, spiked, officer's silver garde star, black eagle on breast of heraldic eagle, plain spike, gilt, chin strap, rosettes, silk lining 1,500.00

Medal, French, veteran, black and green ribbon, 1870–71 .... 18.00

SPANISH-AMERICAN WAR

Ax, 11" blade, pike head, silver inlay in 13" handle 25.00

Flag, Cuban, red, white, and blue, heavy glazed muslin 250.00

Sleigh, blanket, 60" sq, horsehair, Dewey in center, laurel wreaths ... 200.00

Spoon, 3½ x 2½ x 16", pine, carved cannons, soldier with gun, initials, "July 8, 1899" 400.00

WORLD WAR I

Book, *Regimental History Of The 316 Infantry* 20.00

Buckle, US Balloon Corps, emb hot air balloon 25.00

Compass, marked "Made in France" . 30.00

Dog Tag Stamping Kit, orig wooden box, complete 95.00

$87 Field Phone, Western Electric, 1903, re-wired, working, pr 285.00

Flare Pistol, French, marked "Modele 1918" 125.00

Gun Sling, soft leather, 1917, for 03 Springfield 25.00

Map Case, leather, strap, 9 orig tour maps of France 35.00

Medallion, 2½", bronze, soldier crossing battlefield, reverse marked "1917 France 1919," 79th Division map ... 50.00

Medic Canteen, German, cup, marked "H.S.D. Argonne Nov 1," screw top, wood cov, leather harness, 1914 ... 35.00

Swagger Stick, 19", walnut, US Infantry officer 25.00

Trench Flashlight and Note Pad, German, black tin container, orig pad and pencil 40.00

Trench Knife, Austrian, scabbard, leather carrying thong 50.00

Tunic and Trousers, gabardine, pinback, Air Corps and US discs 60.00

Watch Fob, Fed Seal Officer, United States of America 7.50

WORLD WAR II

Armband, Japan, military police, red lettering, white cotton 35.00

Belt and Buckle, German Luftwaffe, silver wash on brass, 1942 .... 35.00

Flag, New Zealand PT boat, printed on blue cotton 35.00

Goggles, flyer's, Japanese, boxed, gray fur lined cups, yellow lenses 15.00

Map, escape, 20 x 24", black and white, Royal Air Force, north Italy **25.00**

Medal, Order of the Rising Sun, 7th Class, Japan, red and green enameling on presentation case, lapel ribbon **60.00**

Parade Hat, Italian Black Fascist, long tassel, orig hat badge **50.00**

Pilot's Wings, breast badge, snap on back **25.00**

Tunic, Marine Corps, dress blue, brass buttons, red piped shoulder boards . **25.00**

Whistle, 5", German, red bakelite over wood **20.00**

Wound Badge, German, silver, orig box, unissued **55.00**

KOREA

Jacket, Sargeant's OD, Ike style, pile lined cap with ear flaps **15.00**

Lead Soldiers, 1", models of American Army of Korean War period, flag bearer, trooper with tommy gun, rifleman, set of 18 . . . . **15.00**

Photo Album, 11 x 15", inscribed "Soul Patrol, Co B 2nd BN 23rd Inf, APW," 2nd Division insignia, photos of troops, guard duty, USO **25.00**

VIETNAM

Beret, black, S. Vietnam Special Forces, silvered device on plaque, sword and wreath, maker's tag **40.00**

Flag, Viet Cong, 16 x 23", gold star, squad level **30.00**

Helmet, Navy, patrol pilot's, lining, earphones, chin strap, white fiberglass body, decal on gold visor, dated 8-65 **20.00**

Knife, Marine, "Personal Release Gravity," multicolored dragon, marked "Saigon" **25.00**

U.S. Service Medal, bronze battle star, on ribbon **10.00**

MILK GLASS

History: Opaque white glass attained its greatest popularity at the end of the 19th century. American glass manufacturers made opaque white tablewares as a substitute for costly European china and glass. Other opaque colors, e.g., blue and green, were made. As the Edwardian era began, milk glass expanded into the novelty field.

The surge of popularity in milk glass subsided after World War I. However, milk glass continues to be made in the 20th century. Some modern products are reissues and reproductions of early forms. This presents a significant problem for collectors, although it is partially obviated by patent dates or company markings on the originals and by the telltale signs of age.

Collectors favor milk glass from the pre-World War I era, especially animal covered dishes. The most prolific manufacturers of these animal covers were Atterbury, Challinor-Taylor, Flaccus, and McKee.

References: E. McCamley Belknap, *Milk Glass*, Crown Publishers, 1949, out-of-print; Regis F. and Mary F. Ferson, *Yesterday's Milk Glass Today*, privately printed, 1981; Regis F. and Mary F. Ferson, *Today's Prices For Yesterday's Milk Glass*, privately printed, 1985; S. T. Millard, *Opaque Glass*, Wallace-Homestead, 1975, 4th edition.

Periodical: *Opaque News*, P. O. Box 402, Northfield, MN 55057.

Collectors' Club: National Milk Glass Collectors Society, 1203 South 12th St, Springfield, IL 62703.

Museum: Houston Antique Museum, Chattanooga, TN.

Notes: There are many so-called McKee animal covered dishes. Caution must be exercised in evaluating pieces because some authentic covers were not signed. Further, many factories have made, and many still are making, split rib bases with McKee-like animal covers or with different animal covers. There also is disagreement among collectors on the issue of flared vs. unflared bases. The prices for McKee pieces as given are for authentic items with either the cover or base signed.

Pieces are cross referenced to the Ferson's and Belknap's books by the (F —-) or (B —-) marking at the end of a listing.

Advisors: Regis and Mary Ferson.

Animal Dish, cov, 5⅜" w at base, reclining cat, ribbed base, "3" imp on inside of base, $60.00.

Animal Dish, cov
Dolphin, 7½" l, fish finial, Kemple reproduction (F214) **65.00**
Mother Eagle, adult bird spreads

wings over three chicks, Westmoreland reproduction (F126) ... 65.00

Rooster, 5½" l, opaque blue glass,
wide ribbed base, condiment container, Westmoreland Specialty Co.
(F11) 55.00

Bird House, 5¼" d, "Wren's Honeymoon Hut," marked "Mfg by McKee
& Co., Pat Appl'd For" on rim, green
roof, white sides, metal base (F223) 60.00

Bonbon, scoop shape, Eagle Glass Co.,
1899 (F597) 22.00

Bottle, 4¾" l, figural, potato, brown
paint, emb "World's Fair, 1893,"
threaded opening, (F494) 75.00

Bowl, 8" d
Arch Border, alternating wide curved
arches and interlocking narrow
pointed arches, Challinor, Taylor
(B100a) 30.00
King's Crown, figural, basketweave
pattern on slanted sides, vertical
bar pattern on base and eight triangular points forming crown
(B108b) 45.00

Butter Dish, cov, rect, Oval Medallion,
convex vertical edge resting on concave supports, spherical finial (F244) 50.00

Candlestick, figural
3⅜", clown, bust rises from wide
curved neck ruff (F129, W15c) ... 65.00
9½", crucifix, heavy base, thin cross-
bar (B29b) 25.00

Cologne Bottle, 11" h, Ray pattern, (also
known as Beaded Circle and Feather)
Dithridge & Co, c1890–1910 (F590) 40.00

Compote
7¾" d, Swimming Swans, pair of facing swans on water, row of cubes 50.00
8" d, round, Scroll, heavily emb pattern, alternating left and right
curved scrolls, Challinor, Taylor
(B127b) 75.00

Condiment Container, 4¼" d, kettle
drum cannon, Civil War type, stack of
shot resting on low base, crown top
or Fluted and Crown pattern, Westmoreland Specialty Co. (F559) 60.00

Fruit Immerser, 1½" h, scalloped circular disc, small pedestal, used for
home canning, four patent dates on
base, latest July 20, 1886 (F334) .. 15.00

Pickle Dish, 9¾" l, figural, fish, realisti-
cally marked, base imp "Patented
June 4, 1872," (F332b) 18.00

Pitcher, 8½", Windmill, fisherman in
boat on lake in center panel, windmill
scene in side oval panels, Imperial
(B87) 50.00

Plate
7¼", wide patriotic border, crossed
flags, four eagles, four clumps of

thirteen stars, full face cameo of
Taft, campaign item, 1908 (F564) 65.00
7½", Contrary Mule, mule pulling
back on rein, Westmoreland (B
271, row 5a) 30.00
9¼", Jefferson Davis, backward "C"
border, souvenir of Civil War Centennial, bust faces left, L. E. Smith
Glass Co. (F554) 45.00

Platter, 13¾", figural, fish, scales, gills,
fins, Atterbury, patent date June 4,
1872 (F337c) 50.00

Sugar, open
Casque, figural, armor type helmet,
English (B212) 42.00
Sunflower, row of paneled sunflowers
above row of paneled lilies of the
valley (B82b) 52.00

MILLEFIORI

History: Millefiori (thousand flowers) is an ornamental glass composed of bundles of colored
glass rods fused to become canes. The canes
were pulled while still ductile to the desired length,
sliced, arranged in a pattern and again fused together. The Egyptians developed this technique in
the first century B. C.; it was revived in the 1880s.

Reproduction Alert: Millefiori items, such as
paperweights, cruets, toothpicks, etc., are being
made by many modern companies.

**Vase, 5½" h, purple bands, white oval
lines, white bands, red flowers, yellow
centers, $150.00.**

Bowl, 2", pink, green, and white canes,
applied handles **35.00**
Cruet, faceted stopper, frosted handle . **70.00**
Goblet, 7½", clear stem and base **175.00**
Ink well, 4½" h, stopper, sgd "Paul Ysart" **175.00**
Lamp, 14" h, boudoir, 19th C, pr **200.00**

Paperweight

Baccarat

Concentric, 2″ d, star dust canes within two circles, salmon, white, and green **75.00**

Patterned, 3½″ d, large red and white central cane, garland of green and white star dust canes, two dark blue trefoil garland canes, white and red star dust canes **240.00**

Scrambled, 3¼″ d, colored canes, clustered with entwined threads **90.00**

Clichy, 1½″ d, concentric, central pink cane in blue, yellow, and white shades circles, five large pink and white roses outer garland alternating with green and pink pairs of canes **120.00**

New England, 3″ d, eight colored center clustered canes, outer band of canes, white entwined threads . . . **75.00**

Pitcher, 4⅞″ **55.00**

Sugar, cov, 3½ x 4″, cobalt blue, white flowers **110.00**

Tie Tack, green, multicolored canes . . **125.00**

Toothpick Holder, ruffled top, c1890 . . **145.00**

Vase

8″, all-over design, handled **195.00**

11″, bulbous, yellow and green, red dots **110.00**

MINIATURE LAMPS

History: Miniature oil and kerosene lamps, often called "night lamps," are diminutive replicas of larger lamps. Simple and utilitarian in design, miniature lamps found a place in the parlor (as "courting" lamps), hallway, children's rooms, and sickrooms.

Miniature lamps are found in many glass types from amberina to satin glass. Miniature lamps measure 2½ to 12 inches in height with the principal parts being the base, collar, burner, chimney, and shade. In 1877 both L. J. Atwood and L. H. Olmsted patented burners for miniature lamps. Their burners made the lamps into a popular household accessory.

Study a lamp carefully to make certain all parts are original; married pieces are common. Reproductions abound.

References: Ann Gilbert McDonald, *Evolution of the Night Lamp,* Wallace-Homestead, 1979; Frank R. & Ruth E. Smith, *Miniature Lamps,* Schiffer Publishing Ltd., 1981, 6th printing; Ruth E. Smith, *Miniature Lamps - II,* Schiffer Publishing Ltd., 1982; John F. Solverson, *Those Fascinating Little Lamps,* Antique Publications, 1988; John F. Solverson (comp.), *"Those Fascinating Little Lamps"/Miniature Lamps,* (includes prices for

Smith numbers) *Value Guide,* Antique Publications, 1988.

Note: The numbers given below refer to the figure numbers found in the Smith books.

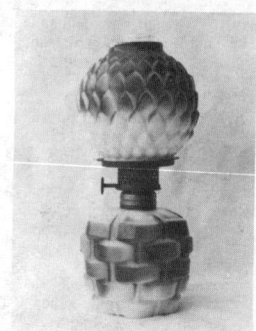

Smith 276, Pineapple In A Basket pattern, milk glass, green highlights, $330.00.

I-Figure III, Artichoke pattern, red, nutmeg burner **550.00**

I-Figure VIII, cameo, white maidenhair fern and butterflies, citron ground . . **5,400.00**

I-30, green glass, tin holder, acorn burner **115.00**

I-40, Spanish Lace, cranberry, applied handle, hornet burner **315.00**

I-50, log cabin, hornet burner, opaline . **725.00**

I-54, custard, emb brass band, iron ring handle, nutmeg burner **100.00**

I-86, double student lamp, brass, white bristol shades **435.00**

I-106, clear, block font and base, nutmeg burner missing **75.00**

I-121, acorn shape, emb acorn cap base, mercury glass, acorn burner . **115.00**

I-125, Christmas type, milk glass, acorn burner **125.00**

I-143, Lincoln Drape, frosted amber, acorn burner **125.00**

I-144, Westmoreland, clear, acorn burner **125.00**

I-166, Greek Key, acorn burner **80.00**

I-203, Plume pattern, white, opaque, gilt dec, nutmeg burner, 8¼″ h **115.00**

I-217, Brady's Night Lamp, satin glass, Consolidated Lamp and Glass Co., c1894, nutmeg burner **430.00**

I-221, emb floral dec, blue milk glass, horner burner **400.00**

I-231, Drape pattern, red satin, nutmeg burner, 8⅝″ h **275.00**

I-250, Diana, milk glass, painted dec, nutmeg burner **100.00**

I-276, Pineapple in a Basket, green milk glass, nutmeg burner **330.00**

I-286, Cosmos, 9″ h, electrified **75.00**

I-368, Spatter glass, molded beaded rib pattern, hornet burner **400.00**

I-390, melon ribbed, cased glass, yellow, glossy finish, nutmeg burner . . .   **500.00**

I-403, Beaded Drape, opal, ruby thumbprint, nutmeg burner **185.00**

I-439, Amberina glass, hornet burner .   **515.00**

I-482, Daisy and Cube pattern, vaseline, nutmeg burner **355.00**

I-508, Spanish Lace, nutmeg burner . .   **350.00**

I-610, Burmese, Webb, brown and green foliage, red berries **4,000.00**

II-Figure VII, rainbow satin, Kosmos Brenner burner, 10½″ h **2,700.00**

II-Figure XVIII, overshot, frosted, house scene, 5½″ **750.00**

II-Figure XXIX, SS pedestal base, emb scene, swirled emb ribbed rose shade, 13½″ h **700.00**

II-20, blue shade, Aladdin type **265.00**

II-28, Glow Lamp, milk glass, melon ribbed **150.00**

II-49, Little Banner **85.00**

II-82, Block pattern, 6½″ h, milk glass, matching globe **100.00**

II-95, clear, emb ribs, applied handle .   **55.00**

II-161, emb Prism pattern, Atterbury . .   **125.00**

II-165, clear, fine ribbing, acorn burner, patent collar **100.00**

II-184, Swirl, orig reflector **45.00**

II-331, bisque, cherub and butterfly . . .   **350.00**

II-368, milk glass, blue bands, pink flowers, green leaves, Dietz Night Light burner **460.00**

II-385, boudoir, brass base, fluted stem, brass cut design shade, pink silk and mica lining, beaded fringe **100.00**

II-393, peg, brass saucer, applied handle, milk glass font, nutmeg burner .   **70.00**

II-421, banquet, three tiers, milk glass, brass pedestal base **550.00**

II-428, Burmese shade and chimney, SS sq pedestal ribbed base, Hinks & Son burner **925.00**

II-452, Bristol glass, black wrought iron pedestal holder **325.00**

II-483, clear, light blue stain, enameled tulips and leaves, gold trim **425.00**

II-488, amber, applied handle **75.00**

MINIATURES

History: There are three sizes of miniatures: doll house scale (ranging from½ to 1″), sample size, and child's size. Since most earlier material is in museums or extremely expensive, the most common examples are 20th century.

Many mediums were used for miniatures: silver, copper, tin, wood, glass, and ivory. Even books were printed in miniature. Prices are broad ranged, depending on scarcity and quality of workmanship.

The collecting of miniatures dates back to the 18th century. It remains one of the world's leading hobbies.

References: Lillian Baker, *Creative and Collectible Miniatures*, Collector Books, 1984; Flora Gill Jacobs, *Dolls Houses in America: Historic Preservation in Miniature*, Charles Scribner's Sons, 1974; Flora Gill Jacobs, *History of Dolls Houses*, Charles Scribner's Sons; Constance Eileen King, *Dolls and Dolls Houses*, Hamlyn; Eva Stille, *Doll Kitchens, 1800–1980,* Schiffer Publishing, Ltd., 1988; Von Wilckens, *Mansions in Miniature*, Tuttle.

Periodicals: Miniature Collector, Collector Communications Corp., 170 Fifth Ave, New York, NY 10010; Nutshell News, Clifton House, Clifton, VA 22024.

Collectors' Clubs: International Guild Miniature Artisans, P.O. Box 842, Summit, NJ 07901. Newsletter (biannual); National Association of Miniature Enthusiasts, 123 N. Lemon St., Fullerton, CA 92632. *Miniature Gazette* (quarterly).

Museums: Kansas City Doll House Museum, Kansas City, MO; Margaret Woodbury Strong Museum, Rochester, NY; Mildred Mahoney Jubilee Doll House Museum, Fort Erie, Canada; Toy Museum of Atlanta, Atlanta, GA; Washington Dolls House and Toy Museum, Washington, DC.

Additional Listings: See Doll House Furnishings in *Warman's Americana & Collectibles* for more examples.

Sofa, 6¼″ l, cast iron, painted green, $125.00.

DOLL HOUSE SIZE

Armoire, oak, golden finish, 1″ scale, c1900 . . . .   **100.00**

Bathroom Set, Tootsietoy, metal, c1920, 8 pcs **90.00**

Bed

Maple, honey finish, scalloped head
and footboard, c1900, 6¼" **100.00**
Chair, 5½", carved wood, scrolled back
and arms, blue velvet upholstery, pr **50.00**
Chest, 11", walnut, Victorian, step back
top, hinged doors with Gothic shaped
arches, inset mirrors, two drawer
base, curved Federal style feet **50.00**
China Cabinet, oak, golden finish, mir-
rored door, c1890 . . . . **130.00**
Desk, Biedermeier, marble top, stencil
dec, black ground, c1860 . . . . **350.00**

Dining Room

Maple, Art Nouveau style, 4½ x 3½"
rect extension table, 2 leaves, 4
matching scrolled back chairs,
black leather seats and backs . . . **100.00**
Walnut, Eastlake style, c1868 . . . . . **140.00**
Dressing Table, maple, rect table,
carved legs, scrolled apron, white
marble top, mirrored cupboard, drawers, silver knobs, marbleized litho pa-
per on back, 6 x 4" **150.00**
Living Room Suite, metal, 4 pcs, love-
seat, recliner chair, two side chairs,
pink velvet upholstery, marked "The
Fairy Furniture Set, Always Ask For
Cooke's Indestructable Toys," orig
wood box **75.00**
Piano, upright, tin, brown painted
ground, gilt trim, scrolled crest, emb
back, scrolled swivel candle arms,
hinged keyboard cov, 3 legged stool
with painted red seat, 19th C, 3¼ x
3½" **80.00**
Settee, maple, Gothic style, 3 paneled
carved back, curved arms, wicker
seat, 6" l **75.00**
Sofa, Regency, black walnut, green vel-
vet upholstery, needlepoint and velvet
pillows, 1840 styling, 9½" **200.00**
Stove, tin, rect, painted red brick dec,
brass plated feet and door, 6 utensils,
German, 19th C, 7" **300.00**
Table, 5", carved wood, painted scene
on top **50.00**
Washstand, maple, honey finish, marble
top, c1900, 3¾ x 1½ x 4¼" **130.00**

ACCESSORIES

Baby Buggy, 4", metal, scrolled, four
wheels **75.00**
Basket, 3 x 1½", metal, moveable han-
dle **45.00**
Bathtub, 5½", tin, tall legs, lower shelf,
lavender, gold stripes, small matching
pail, gold faucet, marked "Made in
Germany" **60.00**
Bench, park type, metal **5.00**
Bird Cage, brass, parrot, 2⅛" **125.00**

**Book, 1³⁄₁₆ × ⅝ × 1⅜", white agate, en-
graved "Ella" on front, flower on back,
$35.00.**

Book

Alphabet, Kate Greenaway type, 2⅜
x 2¼ x 1" **100.00**
Dictionary, English, metal case, 1⅛ x
1¾", c1880 . . . . **150.00**
Candlesticks, brass, c1900, 1", pr **40.00**
Cat, bronze, Vienna **60.00**
Chamber Pot, yellow ware, white band,
applied handle, 2⅛" **30.00**
Christmas Tree, undecorated **20.00**

Clock

Mantle, tin, rect base, 4 paw feet,
scrolled framework, gilt circular
clock frame, asphaltum paint to im-
itate wood, 19th C, 5" **275.00**
Wall, regulator type, oak, golden finish, pendulum, c1880, 2", ... **150.00**
Coffee Grinder, wood base, iron fittings **85.00**
Compote, SS, filigree, lacy cutwork
bowl, ribbed pedestal, marked "Ger-
many," 19th C, 1½" d **40.00**
Dinner Service, porcelain, white, gilt
stripes and leaves, 2" goose neck coffeepot, creamer, sugar, spooner,
gravy boat, relish, cups, plates, and
saucers, orig box marked "Tea Set
Dejeuner", 19th C **100.00**
Dresser Set, hp, china, 15 pcs **25.00**
Fireplace, Victorian, filigree metal, orig
tools **90.00**
Goblet, silver, Meyers, 20th C, ½" . . . **60.00**
Kerosene Stove, cast metal **5.00**
Lamp, banquet, gilt metal, urn shaped
emb base, circular blown glass
shade, 4" **200.00**
Medicine Chest, gilt metal, rect, hinged
front door, shaped crest rail, one shelf
int., glass medicine type bottles, 19th
C, 2½ x 1½" **100.00**
Mirror, brass, ormolu, turned columns
support oval mirror, 19th C, 1 x 2" . . **100.00**
Mortar and Pestle, brass, flaring cylin-
der, 2" **50.00**
Sewing Kit, cardboard box, swinging
brass handle, ornate brass hinge,

patterned blue silk covering, pale blue silk quilted int., ivory thimble, darning egg, crochet hook, 2 scissors, hinge marked "Paris" **325.00**

Sewing Machine, tin, painted, c1920, 4" **45.00**

Stove, 12 x 7½ x 8", cast iron, six lift up burners, wood holder on side, sq doors, green, gray top, pink molded doors, one tin pan, cast iron pot ... **60.00**

Tea Set
  Enamel, Vienna, 8 pcs on tray, c1870 **3,000.00**
  Silver, cov teapot, creamer and sugar, Birmingham hallmark, 1906, 1¼" h, 3 pcs **140.00**

Towel Rack, Victorian, wooden **35.00**

Vase, Jasperware, trunk shaped, Art Nouveau dec, 1½" **25.00**

SAMPLE SIZE

Bucket, staves, metal bands, wire bail handle, 4½ x 5½" **145.00**

Chair
  Mahogany, Chippendale style, Centennial, modified lyre back, upholstered slip seat, cabriole legs, ball and claw feet, ornately carved stretcher, English, c1880, 11 x 25" **300.00**
  Walnut, four scroll shaped graduated back slats, acorn finials, scrolled arms, ball feet, rush seat, American, c1800, 6 x 14" **250.00**

Chest, Victorian, chestnut, three drawers, wooden knobs, scrolled base, carved mirror frame, two candle shelves, natural finish, ebony colored trim, American, c1865, 7 x 24" **275.00**

Desk, Hepplewhite, walnut and cherry, dovetailed, slant front, three drawers with inlay, pigeonholes, leather writing surface, scrolled legs, brass knobs, 7 x 5 x 10" **400.00**

Punch Bowl Set, blue irid stretch glass, six cups **275.00**

Rocker, Victorian, maple, bamboo styled turnings, acorn finials, brass tips, carpet upholstery, American, c1880, 26" **200.00**

Settee, painted and carved wood, shaped back of 3 arched crests above vase form splats, scrolled arms, plank seat, ring turned legs and stretchers, polychrome paint, brown ground, yellow and brown flowers, PA, c1845, 23" l **2,000.00**

Wardrobe, Empire, mahogany, single hinged door, arched mirror front, single brass drawer, wooden knobs, brass mounted keyholes, American, c1840, 9 x 13" **575.00**

Washstand, Hepplewhite, walnut, rect, finely turned pencil point bracketed

mirror, 2 drawers, inlay shelf, towel bar, New York, c1852, 9 x 5½ x 14" **800.00**

CHILD SIZE

Bedroom Suite, mahogany, brass pulls, 27 x 12" bed, scalloped head, foot, and side boards, cloth mattress and pillow, red and white spread, 15 x 13" man's desser with three large drawers and two small, 15 x 20" lady's dresser, two large drawers, three small, attached mirror, 12½ x 18" wardrobe, two doors, lower drawer . **700.00**

Blanket Chest, sponge painted pine, molded rect hinged lid, till, paneled front and sides, sponged brown and red over ochre, figures of prancing horses and geometric patterns, turned bun feet, Lancaster, PA, c1840, 25¼ x 12¾ x 13½" .... **1,350.00.**

Bureau, 28" h, Renaissance Revival, walnut type, dovetailed drawers, inlaid pearl button keyholes, quarter turned posts as corners, pivoting mirror **200.00**

Chair, 22" h, Windsor, fan back, labeled "Stickley" **575.00**

Dressing Table, 8 x 15", metal, painted white, wooden table top, floral design cotton and lace ruffle, celluloid box, mirror, comb, and brush **375.00**

Fainting Couch, 17 x 8", carved wood frame, brown imitation leather upholstery, turned legs **525.00**

Herb Drying Rack, wood, 7 x 6" **75.00**

Trunk, dome top, wood covered paper, separate tray, locks, matched set of 4 **175.00**

Wash Stand, 15" w, 19½" h, veneered wood, marble top, turned legs and towel racks, small round attached mirror, china wash bowl and pitcher, two oblong boxes, white and pink with floral dec **1,700.00**

MINTON CHINA

History: In 1793 Thomas Minton and others formed a partnership and built a small pottery at Stoke-on-Trent, Staffordshire, England. Production began in 1798 with blue printed earthenware, mostly in the Willow pattern. In 1798 cream colored earthenware and bone china were introduced.

A wide range of styles and wares was produced. Minton introduced porcelain figures in 1826, Parian wares in 1846, encaustic tiles in the late 1840s, and Majolica wares in 1850. Many famous designers and artists in the English pottery industry worked for Minton.

Many early pieces are unmarked or have a Sevres type marking. The "ermine" mark was used in the early 19th century. Date codes can be found on tableware and Majolica. Between 1873 and 1911 a small globe signed Minton with a crown on top was used.

In 1883 the modern company was formed and called Mintons Limited. The "s" was dropped in 1968. Minton still produces bone china tablewares and some ornamental pieces.

Reference: Susan and Al Bagdade, *Warman's English & Continental Pottery & Porcelain, 1st Edition,* Warman Publishing Co., Inc., 1987.

Tile, 8″ sq, Night and Day, blue scene, yellow sun, imp mark on back, $65.00.

Bowl
| 11″, flowerheads, leaves and scrolls in red, gilt trim, green ground, c1805 | 1,100.00 |
| 12½″, floral reserves, cobalt ground, gold trim, c1810 | 1,400.00 |

Breakfast Set, plate with attached toast rack, salt and pepper shakers, Dejeuneu, green mark 150.00
Bulb Planter, 2 x 2⅜ x 10¾″, majolica, emb brown fence, green leaves, turquoise lining, marked 125.00
Candlestick, 9″, majolica, figural, three monkeys, mustard green, yellow glaze 225.00
Centerpiece, 11″ l, pate-sur-pate, cartouches with putti, ivory and gilt reserves, brown ground, imp and printed factory marks, dec by H Hollins, c1872 .... 1,400.00

Compote, 8½ x 3″, white, red roses, marked 100.00
Cup and Saucer, ribbon swags, rose, c1805 .... 100.00
Demitasse Cup and Saucer, Indian Tree pattern, imp mark 35.00
Dinner Service, service for eight, Shaftesbury pattern, multicolored floral design, white ground, green enamel rims, 44 pcs 850.00
Dresser Set, 12 x 9″ tray, cov box, ring tree, gold and green flowers, white ground 200.00
Egg Cup, 3″, floral dec 25.00
Ewer, 8½″, turquoise, raised putti holding swags leading to Neptune seated under spout, mermaid handle, marked, c1868 .... 600.00
Figure
| Ariadne on Panther, 1864, 16″ .... | 600.00 |
| Sea Breezes, ivory and bronze on porcelain, 9″ .... | 200.00 |

Jug, 6¼″, applied hops and vine dec, 1848 .... 250.00
Marmalade jar, butterflies, blue ground, c1920 .... 35.00
Oyster Plate, emb fish, white ground . 50.00
Plate
| 10¼″, pate-sur-pate, blue border, white classical scenes, sgd "Birks" | 150.00 |
| 10½″, pate-sur-pate, three classical scenes in blue panels, sgd "AB" . | 125.00 |

Tile, 6″ sq
| King Henry .... | 65.00 |
| Taming of the Shrew .... | 65.00 |

Vase
4″, pink flowers and birds, blue X mark, c1810	120.00
5½″, bulbous, handled, green, white cameo	90.00
7½″, bud, flower dec	125.00
11″, burnt amber, pink, and blue flowers, marked, c1875	150.00

Vegetable Dish, cov, handled, floral dec 55.00
Wash Bowl and Pitcher, amethyst, ruby, and yellow floral dec 150.00

MOCHA

History: Mocha decoration usually is found on utilitarian creamware and stoneware pieces and is produced through a simple chemical action. A color pigment of brown, blue, green, or black is made acidic by an infusion of tobacco or hops. When the acidic colorant is applied in blobs to an alkaline ground, it reacts by spreading in feathery, seaplant-like designs. This type of decoration usually is supplemented with bands of light colored slip.

Types of decoration vary greatly, from those done in a combination of motifs, such as "Cat's

Eye" and "Earthworm," to a plain pink mug decorated with green ribbed bands. Most forms of mocha are hollow, e.g., mugs, jugs, bowls, and shakers.

English potters made the vast majority of the pieces. Marked pieces are extremely rare. Collectors group the ware into three chronological periods: 1780–1820, 1820–1840, and 1840–1880.

Reference: Susan and Al Bagdade, *Warman's English & Continental Pottery & Porcelain, 1st Edition,* Warman Publishing Co., Inc., 1987.

Jug, Seaweed pattern, brown, ochre, and green, c1780, $500.00.

Bowl
4¾ x 2¾", wide blue band, narrow pin stripe band	45.00
8¾ x 4", Earthworm and Cat's Eye pattern, brown and green-gray bands, black stripes, stained and cracked	200.00
Creamer, 3¾", white, black stripes, wide blue bands	150.00
Cup and Saucer, marbleized, black and white geometric border, emb white ribbed band	425.00
Miniature, chamber pot, 2", yellow, brown stripe, blue seaweed, white slip band	60.00

Mug
2⅞", ovoid, orange band, brown stripe, seaweed, leaf handle	175.00
3⅛", brown and white, black stripe, earthworm dec	225.00
3⅝", white, green, dark brown bands and dashes, leaf handle	185.00
5", brown band, black and blue stripes and seaweed, initialed, dated	150.00
6⅞", brown and green bands, narrow white striping, emb ribs, applied handle	300.00

Pepper Pot
4½", brown band, black twig dec, black and green stripes, c1820	225.00
4⅜", pear shape, white, brown and yellow-ochre stripes, chocolate brown dome top	135.00

Pitcher
6", barrel shape, tan bands, emb blue, green, and black stripes	450.00
7", chocolate brown band with white dec, blue, orange and brown stripes, emb leaf handle	350.00
8½", cov, Earthworm pattern, blue band, dark brown striping, crazing and stains	475.00
9¾", white slip band, blue feathered seaweed, yellowware ground, East Liverpool, OH	450.00

Salt, 3", white, blue bands, gray-green stripes	40.00

Salt and Pepper
Blue and white, black stripes, pr	140.00
Blue and white dec, pr	85.00

Shaker
3¼", emb checkerboard dec, brown, orange, and green	425.00
4¼", black and white wavy lines on blue, dome top	175.00
4⅝", blue and white, yellow wavy lines, dark blue dome top	200.00
4⅝", blue bands, emb black, white and blue stripes, earthworm and cat's eye dec in brown, white, and black	450.00

Stein, 7⅞", domed pewter lid, Earthworm pattern, blue ground, upper and lower bands of dark brown, name in script, dated 1854	550.00
Tureen, cov, 8½ x 7", emb rim, green, dark brown stripes, gray-green band, earthworm dec, ring handles	1,225.00

Waste Bowl
4⅝ x 2⅔", emb green rim, blue band, black stripes	120.00
7⅝ x 3⅞", tan bands, black stripes, seaweed	100.00

MONART GLASS

History: Monart glass is a heavy, simple shaped art glass in which colored enamels are suspended in the glass during the glass making process. This technique was originally develped by the Ysart family in Spain in 1923. John Moncrief, a Scottish glassmaker, discovered the glass while vacationing in Spain, recognized the beauty and potential market, and began production in his Perth glassworks in 1924.

The name "Monart" is derived from the surnames Moncrief and Ysart. Two types of Monart were manufactured: a "commercial" line which incorporated colored enamels and a touch of adventurine in crystal, and the "art" line in which the suspended enamels formed designs such as feathers or scrolls. Monart glass, in most instances, is not marked. The factory used paper labels.

Rose Bowl, 4¼" d, 3¾" h, acid etched, enameled purple violets, gold stems, gold dec, pinched sides, $135.00.

Vase
5½", deep green, raised enamel dec, sgd	145.00
7", cameo, oak leaves, textured green acorns, silver and gold dec, sgd	350.00
9", cylindrical, pansies, purple frosted ground	450.00
10¾", enameled blue and white iris, green leaves, gilt scroll rim	200.00
12½", cylindrical, cameo, lavender and gold flowers, leaves, frosted textured ground	450.00
13½", trumpet, enameled butterflies and dragonflies, silver and gold dec, sgd H	375.00
13¾", gilt chrysanthemum dec	225.00

Vase, 8½" h, green rim shaded to clear to brown, green pedestal, $60.00.

Basket, 4", mottled orange and green	90.00
Bowl	
9", Adventurine, blue, mottled brown, and goldstone, pebbled	135.00
10½ x 4¾", white, gray crackle, yellow and green flecks, oxblood red base and rim	150.00
Candlestick, 3", mottled blue shading to lavender, pr	75.00
Urn, 7", clear, yellow lacy inclusions and bubbles	85.00
Vase	
8½", goldstone shading to clear, Scottish Cluthra	150.00
14", bulbous, tapered, extended neck, flared rim, blue shaded to pink, gold highlights, Cluthra	625.00

MONT JOYE GLASS

History: Mont Joye is a type of glass produced by Saint-Hilaire, Touvier, de Varreaux & Company at their glassworks in Pantin, France. Most pieces were lightly acid etched to give them a frosted appearance and decorated with enameled floral decorations. All pieces listed are frosted, unless otherwise noted.

Bowl, 3¾", enameled floral dec, sgd	250.00
Pitcher, cameo, crystal green and gold, brass spout and handle, removable cov, artist sgd "Cristalle Rie Depantin"	485.00

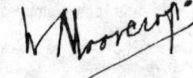

MOORCROFT

History: William Moorcroft was first employed as a potter by James Macintyre & Co., Ltd. of Burslem in 1897. He established the Moorcroft pottery in 1913. The company initially used an impressed mark, "Moorcroft, Burslem;" a signature mark, "W. Moorcroft," followed.

The majority of the art pottery wares were hand thrown, resulting in a great variation among similarly styled pieces. Color and marks are keys to determining age.

Walker, William's son, continued the business upon his father's death and made the same style wares. Modern pieces are marked simply "Moorcroft" with export pieces also marked "Made in England."

Reference: Susan and Al Bagdade, *Warman's English & Continental Pottery & Porcelain, 1st Edition,* Warman Publishing Co., Inc., 1987.

Vase, 12½″ h, $325.00.

Ashtray, 5¼″, triangular, cobalt blue, anemone center, orig paper label . .	50.00
Bowl	
4⅛″ d, fruit and leaves dec	65.00
8½″ d, Florian ware, yellow and green poppies, blue ground, printed mark, sgd "W Moorcroft, des," c1898 . .	675.00
Bulb Bowl, 6½ x 2¼″, dark blue and green ground, white and purple Narcissus, "Potter to the Queen" mark .	130.00
Candlesticks, pr, 6½″, Flambe, trees motif	475.00
Compote, 7½ x 5½″, Cornflower, mottled green ground, marked "W Moorcroft"	500.00
Ginger Jar, 7″, marked "Walter Moorcroft, 1960"	100.00
Goblet, 3¾ x 5¾″, multicolored panels, white ground, gilt trim, sgd "MacIntyre"	525.00
Jardiniere, 7″ h, cylindrical, ftd, pink and purple poppies, blue ground, imp and painted marks, pr	275.00
Lamp Base, 11″ h, Flambe Feather & Grapes, factory drilled	450.00
Match Holder, 2¾″ h″, pink thistle flowers, mottled green ground, coat of arms, Macintyre mark, green painted initials "WM," printed "Redley Hall," c1897	325.00
Plate, 10″, Reeds at Sunset, 1987 . . .	50.00
Vase	
3½″, pansies, script sgd	275.00
6¼″, bulb, pink and purple poppies, blue ground, imp and painted marks	125.00
8¾″, waisted cylindrical, brilliant red glaze, blossoming prunus, incised signature "W Moorcroft"	750.00
9″, baluster, lavender poppies shoulder dec, pale blue ground, imp	

Royal mark, 1930, blue painted signature, "W Moorcroft"	275.00
12¾″, bulbous, slim trumpet neck, mauve pomegranates, purple berries, olive leaves, dark blue ground, imp Burslem mark, 1916, painted green signature "W Moorcroft" . .	700.00
14½″, Wisteria, mottled green top, yellow, purple, pink, and red wisteria blossoms, green leaves, deep blue base, sgd "W Moorcroft," 1920, incised "Moorcroft, Burslem, England, #693"	2,250.00

MORIAGE, JAPANESE

History: Moriage refers to applied clay (slip) relief motifs and decorations used on certain classes of Japanese pottery and porcelain.

This decorating was done by three methods: 1), handrolling and shaping, which was applied by hand to the biscuit in one or more layers; the design and effect required determined thickness and shape, 2), tubing, or slip trailing, which applied decoration from a tube, like decorating a cake, and 3), hakeme, which is reducing the slip to a liquid and decorating a cake, and 3), hakeme, which is reducing the slip to a liquid and decorating the object with a brush. Color was applied either before or after the process.

Vase, 6″ h, 7″ d, shallow bulbous body, two handles, Lotus pattern, pink and green dec, yellow and brown ground, $140.00.

Biscuit Jar, 7¼″, lacy slip work	300.00
Bowl	
6″, pink and green on lavender, floral medallions, raised dots, ftd	100.00
7½″, green, floral center, intricate white slip work, scalloped edge, ftd	145.00
Creamer and Sugar, beading, gray dragon	80.00

Ewer, 7", lacy dec, floral on green
ground 85.00
Hatpin Holder, 4¾", green beading, red
flowers 60.00
Incense Burner, 3", gray, slip dragon,
finial, gold fu dog handles 25.00
Mug, 5½", pink roses, lacy slip work .. 85.00
Pitcher, 6", pink on white, floral, green
slip netting 85.00
Plate, 7½", blue and white, slip dragon,
set of 6 .... 85.00
Tea Set, 27 pcs, dragon dec, brown,
green, and white, raised star mark 250.00
Vase
7½", white on dark green, floral medallion, handled 200.00
10½", pink and orange on rose, floral
cartouch 225.00
11½", multicolored, slip flowers and
fronds, marble ground, Nippon ... 175.00
Wine Decanter, 7¾", wheat dec 275.00

Vase, 10"h, pinched top, clear green glass, enamel floral dec, $200.00.

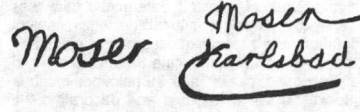

MOSER GLASS

History: Ludwig Moser (1833–1916) founded
his polishing and engraving workshop in 1857 in
Karlsbad (Karlovy Vary), Czechoslovakia. He employed many famous glass designers, e.g., Johann
Hoffmann, Josef Urban, and Rudolf Miller. In 1900
Moser and his sons, Rudolf and Gustav, incorporated Ludwig Moser & Söhne.

Moser art glass included clear pieces with inserted blobs of colored glass, cut colored glass
with classical scenes, cameo glass, and intaglio
cut. Many inexpensive enameled pieces also were
made.

In 1922 Leo and Richard Moser bought Meyr's
Neffe, their biggest Bohemian rival in art glass.
Moser executed many pieces for the Wiener Work-
startte in the 1920s. The Moser glass factory continues to produce new items.

Reference: Mural K. Charon and John Mareska,
*Ludvik Moser, King of Glass: A Treasure Chest of
Photographs And History,* published by author,
1984.

Basket, 8" d, 5" h, cobalt blue, applied
insects, gold metal frame 1,750.00
Beverage Set, 10¼" h hinged pitcher,
six 4⅛" tumblers, amber, multicolored
floral dec, gold trim, button prunts,
amber handle, pewter mounts, paper
label on pitcher 1,000.00
Bowl, 7¼ x 5⅝", pink opalescent, multicolored enameled oak leaves, applied lustered glass acorns, sgd ... 1,100.00
Box, 4½ x 4⅜", hinged cov, applied amber salamander, enameled flowers
and green foliage, three applied amber salamander feet, gold trim 575.00
Champagne, 8½" h, cranberry, multicolored flower dec 135.00
Compote, 8¼" d, 4" h, 4¼" d hollow
base, pale amber, electric blue rigaree, twelve multicolored leaves,
brown branches, gold leaves, red and
white cherries 845.00
Cordial, cranberry, heavy gold dec, applied opaque white snake on stem 90.00
Cruet
8", cranberry, heavy gold and multicolored enamel dec, gold handle
and stopper 900.00
8½", flat sided, green to clear, heavy
gold leaves, handle and stopper . 775.00
Demitasse Cup and Saucer, cranberry,
enamel birds and flower dec 300.00
Dresser Box, 5" d, 6½" h, cranberry ... 175.00
Ewer, 2½" d, 5¾" h, shaded amethyst
to clear, enameled pink and white
flowers, gold trim, small applied amethyst jewels 225.00
Goblet, cranberry, heavy gold dec, set
of 6 .... 400.00
Jewel Box
4¾" h, green, sq, heavy multicolored
enameled flowers and butterfly,
brass beaded ball feet and handles 750.00
5" l, 5" h, cranberry, oblong, enamel
birds and floral dec, brass mounts
and handles, key 1,400.00
5½" h, cranberry, heavy gold dec,
multicolored enamel leaves and
berries 700.00

Juice Glass, pink opal, jeweled and
enamel dec 65.00
Perfume Bottle, 2 x 4¾", amberina, blue
enameled florals, gray panels with
green applied jewels, gold neck band
with applied jewels, amber cut stop-
per, sgd 275.00
Pitcher
3", blue, gold flowers 325.00
4½", cranberry, sq mouth 225.00
8¼" h, 5⅞" d, ftd, amber, multicolored
pastel enameled flowers, leaves,
and bird in flight, gold outlines, sapphire blue handle and trim, eight
sapphire blue prunts, four sapphire
blue feet 275.00
Vase
3½", emerald green, enameled multicolored oak leaves, two applied
acorns, gold trim 165.00
8"
Blue, flared top, enamel floral dec,
clear ball stem with air-traps . . . 75.00
Cameo, burgundy over frosted amber ground, intaglio cut to clear
amber 1,100.00
Clear to green, intaglio cut flowers,
gold dec 300.00
10½", baluster, ribbed, greenish opal
to clear, enameled red and yellow
poppies, gold leaves and branches 325.00
12", amber body, applied deep blue
drip technique at top, enameled, hp
flowers, wheat, butterfly, blue ped-
estal foot 585.00
15", green, enamel figures in court-
yard, dated 1895, printed "Guten-
bergund-Wein" on base 1,450.00

MOSS ROSE PATTERN CHINA

History: Several English potteries manufactured china with a Moss Rose pattern in the mid-
1800s. Knowles, Taylor and Knowles, an American firm, began production of a Moss Rose pattern
in the 1880s.

The moss rose was a common garden flower
grown in English gardens. When American consumers tired of English china with oriental themes,
they purchased the Moss Rose pattern as a substitute.

Brush Holder, Shaw 100.00
Butter Pat, Meakin, set of 6
Round 90.00
Square 115.00
Cake Plate, ftd, Haviland 70.00
Creamer 40.00
Cup and Saucer, Haviland & Co, Lim-
oges 20.00
Gravy Boat and Underplate 75.00

Cup, 3¼" d, 2⅞" h, $15.00.

Plate
7", gold trim, Haviland 15.00
8", KTK 30.00
10" 40.00
Platter
12 x 18", rect 50.00
13½", Haviland 35.00
Shaving Mug, Maddock 30.00
Spittoon 135.00
Spooner, Meakin 60.00
Sugar, cov 50.00
Syrup, 8½", pewter top, KTK, c1872 . . 165.00
Teapot, 8½", bulbous, Meakin 75.00
Vegetable Dish, cov, Edward Bros, Eng-
land 95.00
Waste Bowl, cov, bamboo handle, Grin-
dley 335.00

MOUNT WASHINGTON GLASS COMPANY

History: In 1837 Deming Jarves, founder of the
Boston and Sandwich Glass Company, established for George D. Jarves, his son, the Mount
Washington Glass Company in Boston, Massachusetts. In the following years the leadership and
the name of the company changed several times
as George Jarves formed different associations.

In the 1860s the company was owned and operated by Timothy Howe and William L. Libbey. In
1869 Libbey bought a new factory in New Bedford,
Massachusetts. The Mount Washington Glass
Company began operating again there under its
original name. Henry Libbey became associated
with the company early in 1871. He resigned in
1874 during the general depression, and the glass
works was closed. William Libbey had resigned in
1872 to work for the New England Glass Company.

The Mount Washington Glass Company opened
again in the fall of 1874 under the presidency of
A. H. Seabury and the management of Frederick
S. Shirley. In 1894 the glass works became a part
of the Pairpoint Manufacturing Company.

Throughout its history the Mount Washington Glass Company made a great variety of glass including: pressed glass, blown glass and art glass, lava glass, Napoli, cameo, cut glass, Albertine, and Verona.

References: George C. Avila, *The Pairpoint Glass Story*, Reynolds-DeWalt Printing, Inc., 1968; Leonard E. Padgett, *Pairpoint Glass*, Wallace-Homestead, 1979; John A. Shuman III, *The Collector's Encyclopedia of American Art Glass*, Collector Books, 1988.

Museum: The New Bedford Glass Museum, New Bedford, MA.

Additional Listings: Burmese, Crown Milano, Peachblow, and Royal Flemish.

Biscuit Jar, 6″ d, 4″ h, orange and peach dec, yellow ground, silverplated lid marked "Pairpoint 3932," base marked "3932/222," $325.00.

Biscuit Jar, 6½ x 9¼″, melon ribbed, shaded blue ground, hp gold daisies, SP lid, handle and rim 1,200.00

Bowl
  3½″, melon shape, hp, pansy dec, gold dotted border, white ground . 215.00
  10½″ d, blue satin int., chrysanthemums and leaves ext., ruffled 200.00

Bride's Basket, 11″ pink ext. peachblow bowl, gold stylized flowers dec, ornate SP holder with aquatic marine motif, marked "Pairpoint Mfg Co" 800.00

Compote, 6¼″ d, 10″ h, Napoli, crystal clear body, pastel green chrysanthemum leaves on heavy wafer base, solid stem, ending with golden yellow blossoms on flared bowl 585.00

Condiment Set, mustard and spoon, matching salt and pepper shakers, satin, white, opaque, fluted, floral dec, 3 pc 225.00

Creamer, tomato shape, hp, floral and leaf dec, light green to white ground, SP handle and spout 265.00

Cruet, lusterless white, tiny blue blossoms and autumn leaves, gold detail

stripes, hollow mushroom-shaped stopper 1,250.00

Flower Frog, mushroom shape, lusterless white, leaf and foliage dec 125.00

Jack-in-the-Pulpit Vase, 13½″ h, trumpet, satin, white, lavender and white flowers, green leaves, ruffled rim ... 325.00

Jar, cov, 4¼″ d, opaque white, DQ, ivy dec, SP top, turtle finial, imp "M. W." 325.00

Mustard, cov, ribbed barrel, pink floral dec, white ground, SP cov and bail handle 85.00

Pickle Castor, deep cranberry satin, Optic Diamond and IVT pattern insert, gold spider chrysanthemum dec, ftd Simpson Hall frame, ornate engraved cover, orig silver 600.00

Potpourri Jar, wooden pail form, glossy finish, pansy dec, SP cov and bail handle, sgd "MW" 165.00

Rose Bowl, 3″, scalloped rim, lusterless white, hp Shasta daisy dec 75.00

Salt Shaker
  Acorn shape, swirled, floral dec, orig pewter top 130.00
  Chicken, hp, enameled red, purple, and blue floral dec, pink ground, orig paper label, "Pat. Applied For Mt. W.G. Co.," c1890 .... 525.00
  Cockleshell, hp, yellow violets, white opaque ground, orig top, c1890 .. 325.00
  Egg shape
    Burmese, floral dec, orig top 110.00
    Shaded pink to white ground, hp, daisy dec, orig top 75.00
  Fig, hp, purple floral dec, orig tops, matched pr 300.00
  Melon ribbed, floral dec 150.00

Sugar Shaker
  Egg shape, 3¼ x 4″, frosted clear glass, pastel pansies dec, metal top with prongs 585.00
  Melon ribbed, 3¾″ d, berries and leaves dec, SP top 275.00
  Tomato, blue and white enamel floral dec, yellow and peach ground, cast butterfly and floral top 215.00

Sweetmeat Jar, holly and berry dec, light green to white shaded ground, SP cov, sgd "MW" 325.00

Syrup, 4″ h, enamel floral dec, SP hinged lid 235.00

Toothpick, melon ribbed base, straight neck, violet dec, blue dotted top ... 120.00

Tumbler, 3½″, Verona pattern, hp, iris, flowing green leaves, heavy gold trim 75.00

Vase
  3¾″, lava, classic shape, two curled handles, shiny jet black body, inlaid blue, green, and pink chips, gold trim 1,750.00
  7¼″, rose bud and green leaf dec,

gold dotted top, gold trim, dark yellow shaded to white ground **325.00**
10¼", lava, jet black body, multicolored chips **1,750.00**

MULBERRY CHINA

History: Mulberry china, made primarily in the Staffordshire district of England between 1830 and 1850, is porcelain whose transfer pattern is the color of mulberry juice. The potters that manufactured flow blue also made Mulberry china; the ware often has a flowing effect similar to flow blue.

References: Susan and Al Bagdade, *Warman's English & Continental Pottery & Porcelain, 1st Edition*, Warman Publishing Co., Inc., 1987; Petra Williams, *Flow Blue China and Mulberry Ware-Similarity and Value Guide*, Fountain House East, Revised Edition, 1981.

Plate, 9¾" d, Tavoy pattern, T. Walker, c1845, $45.00.

Bowl
  Japan **35.00**
  Rhone, Thomas Furnival, 10¼", fruit, handles, ftd **42.00**
Butter Dish, cov, Coburg, John Edwards **120.00**
Coffeepot, cov, Singanese **75.00**
Creamer, Pelew, E Challinor, 5" **80.00**
Cup and Saucer, handleless
  Carrara, unknown maker **50.00**
  Corean, Podmore and Walker **60.00**
  Cyprus, Davenport **65.00**
  Marble, A Shaw **30.00**
  Pelew, E Challinor **45.00**
  Washington Vase, Podmore and Walker **60.00**
Pitcher, Schenectady On The Mohawk, unknown maker, 8" **150.00**
Plate
  Castle Scenery, unknown maker, 10½" **40.00**
  Cyprus, Davenport, 10½" **50.00**
  Jeddo, Adams and Son, 10½" **45.00**
  Neva, unknown maker **40.00**
  Pelew, E Challinor **40.00**
  Venus, Podmore and Walker **38.00**
  Washington Vase, Podmore and Walker, 9¾" **48.00**
Platter
  Cyprus, Davenport, 13½ x 10¼", c1850 . . . . **100.00**
  Tonquin, J Heath & Co, 12½ x 9½" . **125.00**
Shaving Mug, Washington Vase, Podmore and Walker **90.00**
Soup Plate, Peru, unknown maker, 10¾" **40.00**
Sugar, cov, Udina, J Clementson **80.00**
Teapot, cov, Jeddo, Adams **140.00**
Wash Bowl and Pitcher Set
  Cyprus, Davenport, pitcher, bowl, toothbrush holder, and cov soap dish with drain **675.00**
  Washington Vase, Podmore and Walker, pitcher, bowl, toothbrush holder, shaving mug, and cov soap dish **725.00**

MUSIC BOXES

History: Music boxes were invented in Switzerland around 1825. They cover a broad field of automatic musical instruments from a small box to a huge circus calliope.

A cylinder box consists of a comb with teeth which vibrate when stricking a pin in the cylinder and producing music from light tunes to opera and overtures.

The first disc music box was invented by Paul Lochmann of Leipzig, Germany, in 1886. It used an interchangeable steel disc with pierced holes bent to a point which hit the star-wheel as the disc revolved, and thus produced the tune. Discs were easily stamped out of metal, allowing a single music box to play an endless variety of tunes. It reached the height of its popularity from 1890 to 1910. The phonograph replaced it.

Music boxes also were put into many items, e.g., clocks, sewing and jewelry boxes, steins, plates, toys, perfume bottles, and furniture.

References: H. A. V. Bulleid, *Cylinder Musical Box Design and Repair*, Almar Press, 1987.

Collectors' Club: Musical Box Society, International, Rt. 3, Box 205, Morgantown, IN, 46160.

Museums: Bellms Cars and Music of Yesterday, Sarasota, FL; Lockwood Matthews Mansion, Norwalk, CT.

Additional Listings: See *Warman's Americana & Collectibles* for more examples.

CYLINDER-TYPE

2⅜" cylinder, 2 tune, burled wood case, comb marked "C P & C," 60 teeth . . **225.00**

17 x 11 x 9¼″, inlaid walnut case, 6″ cylinder, butterfly dec, extra drawer, Swiss, $800.00.

9″ cylinder, 4 tunes, Nicole Freres, plain fruitwood case, key wind, Geneva, c1840 . . . . **1,950.00**

11″ cylinder, 30 tunes, lever wind, inlaid walnut and simulated rosewwood case, zither attachment, marked "#1735," Switzerland, c1900 . . . . . **880.00**

11⅞″ cylinder, 2 tunes, brass bedplate, 103 teeth, keywind **3,000.00**

13″ cylinder, three cylinders, 8 tunes, inlaid lid, drawer in bottom, 92 teeth **3,200.00**

13½″ cylinder, 8 tunes, Sumbleme Harmonee, rosewood case, foliate marquetry on lid, lever movement, c1885 **450.00**

15″ cylinder, five cylinders, nine bells, wood block, drum, and replaced dancing doll, double spring barrel, orig tune sheet **5,800.00**

17″ cylinder, 24 tunes, burl walnut case, brass monogrammed plates, separate box holds 4 rolls, Switzerland . . **3,000.00**

19⅝″ cylinder, 18 tunes, Grand Format, rosewood case, inlaid colored wood and enameled musical trophies, rosewood, boxwood, and kingwood veneered lid, 3 prs brass case washers, orig tune card **6,000.00**

21″ cylinder, 12 tunes, walnut and floral marquetry case, hidden bell, drum, and castanet, spring movement, Switzerland, c1870 . . . . **1,550.00**

22″ cylinder, interchangeable, 7 cylinders, spirally pinned helecoidal, continuous play, 10 bells, fully restored, Made by Paillard Vaucher Fils **22,500.00**

DISC-TYPE

6½″ disc, 15 discs, walnut case, ratchet wound, single comb, trade decal, Germany, c1900 . . . . **250.00**

9½″ disc, 7 discs, Stella, Grand, table model, stained mahogany case, coffered lid, c1900 . . . . **1,600.00**

13⅝″ disc, Symphonion, Style 30A Deluxe, walnut case, double comb, inlaid lid, brass end handles, restored, German **3,250.00**

14½″ discs, 12 discs, Polyphon, walnut case, double comb with 12 bells, sepia litho inlaid lid, crank handle, bracket feet, restored, Germany, c1900 . . . . **5,200.00**

15½″ disc, Polyphon, floral marquetry lid, egg and dart dec case, peripheral movement, 1½ comb, Germany, c1900 . . . . **1,350.00**

17¼″ disc, Stella, table model, mahogany case, drawer **4,200.00**

19″ disc, 10 discs, Symphonion, Penny In Slot, rounded arched pediment, walnut case, split baluster moldings . **3,000.00**

24½″ disc, 24 discs, Polyphon, external operator's lever, base and gallery . . **11,500.00**

MISCELLANEOUS

Album, 2 tunes, brass fittings, and dec design, period photographs **225.00**

Automation, Singing Bird, 11⅝″, gilt metal, feathered bird on perch, domed cage, garland emb base, marked "France," 19th C **225.00**

Barrel Piano, 15″, child's, 4 tunes, children litho dec, red lacquer case, marked "Verbena" **125.00**

Carved Wood
　Fruit Dish, plays "Jean Arendet," musical movement, Germany **90.00**
　Swiss Chalet, 8¼ x 11″, 2 German tunes, orig paper label, lists names of tunes **125.00**

Clock and Singing Bird, combination, clock on left, bird on right in cage, Made in West Germany **225.00**

Coin Operated, 27″, 15 discs, double combs, oak, orchestral, Regina **10,800.00**

Organ, Paillard, St. Crorix, 10 Chinese tunes, 11 keys, 17 tooth comb, inlaid musical trophies, rosewood lid and box **2,900.00**

Organette
　Ariston, 22 cardboard discs, orig condition **550.00**
　Automatic, medlodista, 13 x 36 x 12″, stencil dec, G W Bates & Co, Boston, Mass **2,500.00**
　Mechanical Orguimette Co, 5 rolls, stained floor cabinet, roll storage drawer, musical boudoir **375.00**

Pianolin, 12 rolls, 44 pipes, violin and flute, oak, orig, North Tonawanda . . **10,000.00**

Roller Organ

Gem, stencils, five cobs, needs restoring **350.00**

Mascotte, 2½" rolls, 4 rolls, walnut case, Gately Mfg Co **250.00**

MUSICAL INSTRUMENTS

History: From the first beat of the prehistoric drum to the very latest in electronic music makers, musical instruments have provided popular modes of communication and relaxation.

The most popular antique instruments are violins, flutes, oboes, and other instruments associated with the classical music period of 1650 to 1900. Many of the modern instruments, such as trumpets, guitars, drums, etc., have value on the "used," rather than antique market.

The collecting of musical instruments is in its infancy. The field is growing very rapidly. Investors and speculators have played a role since the 1930s, especially in early string instruments. Sotheby's and Christie's hold annual auctions of fine musical instruments.

References: Tom and Mary Anne Evans, *Guitars: From the Renaissance To Rock; The Official Price Guide To Music Collectibles, Sixth Edition,* House of Collectibles, 1986.

Collectors' Club: Fretted Instrument Guild of America, 2344 South Oakley Avenue, Chicago, IL 60608.

Drum, $85.00.

Banjo, American

Gibson, 5 string, resonator, case ... **100.00**

Hutchins, 5 string, maple neck, abalone shell pattern peghead and fingerboard, steel rod inlaid underneath fingerboard **350.00**

Bassoon

Buffet-Crampon, Paris, 20th C **1,900.00**

Heckel, Biebrich, 20th C **1,600.00**

Cello

American, ebony fingerboard and tailpiece, solid ebony trimmings **650.00**

German, Sigfried Finkel, ivory frog and adjuster, pearl dots, octagonal stick mounted with gold and ivory **1,750.00**

Cornet

Concertone, 16½" l, brass, nickel silver mouthpiece, pearl buttons, one water key, c1920 .... **150.00**

Leaders' B-Flat, brass, polished, double water key, c1905–10 .... **275.00**

Cymbal, American, leather handles, c1900

10" **90.00**

13" **160.00**

Drum

Acme, Professional, c1900

Bass, 26" d **225.00**

Snare, 16" d **200.00**

Italian, bass, wood mountings, 18th C **1,000.00**

Fife, Crosby Model, ebony, c1900 .... **125.00**

Flute

American, 8 key, c1920 .... **125.00**

Flemish, walnut, 18th C **2,250.00**

Meyer, 10 key, c1900 .... **300.00**

Flute Harmonica, nickel plated frame, 10 key, two basses and bell **20.00**

Guitar

American, The Seroco, standard size, c1900 .... **325.00**

Italian, 38", five course, lavish ivory dec, arched back, by Matteo Sellas, Venice, c1920–40 .... **12,000.00**

Harp, English, polished walnut, late 18th C **1,250.00**

Mandolin

Concertone, spruce top, birch back and sides, basswood neck, black and white inlay around hole, ebonized fingerboard, tortoise celluloid guard plate, c1920 .... **75.00**

The Royal, 11 rosewood ribs, inlaid white holly, inlaid guard plate, early 1900 .... **450.00**

Melodeon, walnut, turtle back, applied fruit, flowers, and foliage, Victorian scrolled base, 51½" l, 36½" w, 33" h **2,400.00**

Organ

Prescott Bros, cabinet, walnut case, two sets of reeds, five stops, c1867 **450.00**

Williams Organ Co, Epworth, oak case, back grill, two and three-fifths ranks of reeds and octave coupler, 13 stops, c1890 .... **575.00**

Piano

Baby Grand, Hallet and Davis, 5'2" . **4,750.00**

Grand, Emerson Oak, new strings and hammer **6,000.00**

Spinet, John Player, London, walnut body, oak trestle stand, 5' 1½", inscribed "Johannes Player, Londini fecit," undated, 17th C **25,000.00**

Upright, Baldwin, rebuilt, early 1900 **600.00**

Piccolo, Atlas, cast metal, c1900 .... **55.00**

Saxophone
Dupont
Alto-Solo, polished brass, bell up-
right **170.00**
B-Flat Tenor, burnished nickel plate **250.00**
Marceau E-Flat Alto, SP, satin finish **175.00**
Tambourine, Albanian, silver jingles,
third quarter 19th C **100.00**
Trombone, Dupont
B-Flat
Baritone Valve, triple SP, satin fin-
ish **800.00**
Tenor Slide, burnished nickel plate **450.00**
E-Flat Alto Slide, polished brass . . . **650.00**
Trumpet, Concertone, nickel plated . . **200.00**
Tuba
Marceau E-Flat Bass, polished brass **275.00**
Sousaphone, B-Flat, brass, lacquer
bore **2,500.00**
Ukulele, mahogany body, brass peds,
block inlay around hole **60.00**
Violin
Amati, Jerome, Cremona, 1649–1740 **30,000.00**
Casini, A, Modena, 1630–1710 . . . . **7,000.00**
Pazzini, Giovanni, Brescia, Florence,
1630–66 . . . . **8,500.00**
Tanegian, Carlo, Milan, 1725–31 . . . **4,250.00**
Zither, Autoharp, 23 strings, five bars . **40.00**

MUSIC RELATED

Advertising, Poster, 47 x 33", Holton
Band Instrument, "Neil O'Brien Min-
strels," playing brass instruments in
uniform, oak frame **400.00**
Book
A Musical Grammar, J W Callcott,
London, 1806 . . . . **125.00**
Harmonia Festi, John, Alcock, oblong
folio, 59 pp, privately printed, Lich-
field, 1791 . . . . **175.00**
The Story of British Music, Crowest,
F, London, 1896 . . . . **30.00**
Guitar Case, wood, one half lined, lock,
handle, and hooks, American, c1890 **30.00**
Music Stand, French, bronze, tapered
neck, last quarter 18th C **3,000.00**
Sheet Music
Bye Lo, words and music, Ray Per-
kins, 1919 copyright **3.00**
Nelly Bly, 4th edition, black and white
lettering cov, Stephen Foster, Firth,
Pond & Co, 1850 copyright **10.00**
Tintype, 5 x 3½", man holding minstrel
banjo, c1860 . . . . **85.00**

MUSTACHE CUPS AND SAUCERS

History: Mustache cups and saucers were popular in the late Victorian era, 1880–1900. They
were made by many companies in porcelain and
silver plate. The cups have a ledge across the top
of the bowl of the cup to protect a gentleman's
mustache from becoming soiled while drinking.

Reference: Susan and Al Bagdade, *Warman's
English & Continental Pottery & Porcelain, 1st Edition,* Warman Publishing Co., Inc., 1987.

**Porcelain, "Think of Me," green trim,
gold lines, incised "Germany," $35.00.**

PORCELAIN

Floral dec
Blue flowers, gold trim, pink scroll,
marked "Haviland" **125.00**
Inscribed "A Present" in gold, Ger-
many **50.00**
Forget-Me-Not dec, inscribed "From a
Friend," bamboo handle **40.00**
Lilac and floral dec, white ground **40.00**
Lily-of-the-valley and violets dec, Ger-
many **45.00**
Mother and child, portrait, gold accents,
green Tetau mark **40.00**
Roses, pink and yellow, green leaves,
Germany **25.00**
Sponge dec
Colonial couple, gold trim, ftd, large **90.00**
Portrait medallion, kettle shape, gold
trim, ftd **65.00**
Wedding Band pattern, gold dec, white
ground **65.00**

SILVER PLATED

Left handed, engraved **165.00**
Relief scroll work center band, mono-
gram, Gorham, 1896 . . . . **15.00**

NAILSEA TYPE GLASS

History: Nailsea type glass is characterized by
swirls and loopings, usually white, on a clear or
colored ground. One of the first areas where this
glass was made was Nailsea, England, 1788–

1873, hence the name. Several other glass houses, including American factories, made this type of glass.

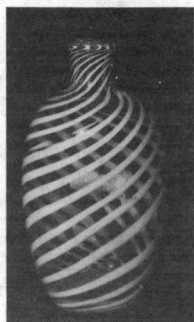

Flask, 7½″ h, white loopings, clear ground, orig stopper, $100.00.

Bell, 13″ h, clear, white looping, solid clear handle, beehive type finial, missing clapper 80.00
Bowl, 7⅝″ d, sapphire blue, opaque white looping, applied clear trim, feet and handles 175.00
Egg Cup, 4⅝″ h, opaque white, pink looping, hollow stem 150.00
Epergne, 15½″, green, white looping . 275.00
Flask, 6½″ l, white, pink looping 160.00
Flip, 8¼″ h, 6¼″ d, light green, milky green looping, plain sheared mouth, pontil 150.00
Lamp, 13″, white, crystal looping, double wick burner, ruffled shade with cranberry threading 1,000.00
Pitcher
   6¾″ h, aqua, opalescent looping, applied strap handle, crimped foot, 19th C 325.00
   9½″ h, deep greenish-aqua, white looping, applied solid curled end handle and base, sheared mouth, ftd 600.00
Rolling Pin
   17″ l, cylindrical, clear, pink and white looping, knop ends, America, late 19th C 155.00
   19″ l, pale violet, white looping, sheared ends with pontil 155.00
Rose bowl, 4″ d, egg shape, frosted blue, white opaque looping, 8 crimp top 175.00
Salt, clear, blue looping, ftd 60.00
Sugar Shaker, 5″, pear shape, blue, white looping, ftd, orig top 100.00

Vase
   8″ h, cylindrical, clear, white looping, flaring mouth and base, plain sheared rim and pontil 140.00
   9½″ h, 5″ d, light green, white looping, double ogee form, folded rim, applied solid stem and base, tubular pontil 275.00
Witch Ball, 7¾″ d, clear, white looping, matching 14⅞″ stand 750.00

NANKING

History: Nanking is a type of Chinese porcelain made in Canton, China, from the early 1800s into the 20th century for export to America and England. It often is confused with the Canton pattern.

Three elements help distinguish Nanking from Canton. Nanking has a spear and post border, as opposed to the scalloped line style of Canton. The blues may tend to be darker on the Nanking ware. Second, in the water's edge or Willow pattern, Canton usually has no figures. Nanking features a standing figure with open umbrella on the bridge. Finally, Nanking wares often are embellished with gold.

Green and orange variations of Nanking survive, although scarce.

Reference: Sandra Andacht, *Oriental Antiques & Art: An Identification And Value Guide,* Wallace-Homestead, 1987.

Reproduction Alert: Copies of Nanking ware currently are being produced in China. They are of inferior quality and decorated in lighter rather than the darker blues.

Platter, 11½ x 14½″, $400.00.

Bowl, 15″, oval, flat octagonal rim, c1800 . . . . 750.00
Chocolate Pot, 9″ h, pear shape, Buddhistic lion finial 750.00
Cup and Saucer, loop handle 50.00

Dish, 6" l, blue and white, leaf shape,
twig handle **225.00**
Flagon, 11½" h, orange peel glaze,
Buddhistic lion finial **2,000.00**
Gravy Boat, 7½" l, blue and white, gilt
trim, twisted handle **275.00**
Jug, cov, 9½", fu dog finial **285.00**
Lamp, wedding, 6¼ x 8¼", overall floral
dec, blue and white, vertical reticula-
tion **450.00**
Mug, 6⅛", water edge scene **350.00**
Plate, 9½", water edge scene, c1780–
1800 . . . . **375.00**
Platter
12", gold dec, irregular border, early
19th C **375.00**
17", dart border **500.00**
Tea Caddy, 5" h, blue and white, gilt trim **750.00**
Teapot, 5¼", gold dec, globular **350.00**
Vegetable Tureen, 9⅜", cov, rect, underglaze blue, Blue Willow pattern,
gilt rim and pine cone finial, trellis dia-
per border **250.00**

NAPKIN RINGS, FIGURAL

History: Gracious home dining during the Victorian era meant each household member had
their personal napkin ring. Figural napkin rings
were first patented in 1869. The remainder of the
19th century saw most plating companies, e.g.,
Cromwell, Eureka, Meriden, Reed and Barton,
etc., manufacturing figural rings, many copying
with slight variations the designs of other companies.

Values are determined today by the subject matter of the ring, the quality of the workmanship, and
the condition.

Reference: Victor K. Schnadig, *American Victorian Figural Napkin Rings,* Wallace Homestead,
1971, out-of-print.

Reproduction Alert: Quality reproductions do
exist.

Additional Listings: See *Warman's Americana
& Collectibles* for a listing of non-figural napkin
rings.

Advisors: Paul and Paula Brenner.

Baseball Player, standing next to ring,
bat on shoulder, rect base **235.00**
Bird, perched on top of ring, long tail,
elaborately scrolled base, Apollo Sil-
ver Plate Co, #141 . . . . **130.00**
Boy, standing behind ring, rect base,
Simpson, Hall, Miller Co **165.00**
Cat, standing beside ring, full figure, Eu-
reka Silver Plate Co **175.00**
Cherub
Four in "Atlas" pose, holding ring
above heads **120.00**

Monkey, oval base, marked "Derby Silver Co, #828," $275.00.

Pair, wings support elaborate chased
oval ring, Wilcox Silver Plate Co . **150.00**
Pulling cart, movable wheels **225.00**
Chick, standing guard over ring, oval
base, ball feet, portion of orig label,
Meriden, #222 . . . . **200.00**
Dog
Pulling cart, cherub riding on top of
ring, movable wheels **250.00**
Egyptian Figures, standing on both
sides of ring, elongated legs, bud
vase **190.00**
Fox
Sitting, oval ring on back, rect base . **160.00**
Standing on one side of ring, bunch
of grapes on other, vintage dec, or-
nate base **195.00**
Greenaway, Kate
Boy, pushing ring **175.00**
Girl with muff on one side, playful dog
on other **215.00**
Horse
Prancing, ring on back, sq base, ball
feet **175.00**
Pulling cart, movable wheels **225.00**
Lady, leaning toward child, heavily
draped attire, marked "Babcock" . . . **260.00**
Little Red Riding Hood, holding basket,
marked "Reed & Barton" **225.00**
Lily pad, finger grip handle supports
pedestal ring, shaped base **135.00**
Lion, standing, leaning against ring, rect
base **175.00**
Owl, perched on leaf shaped base, Van
Bergh Co, #99 . . . . **160.00**
Squirrel
Sitting, balanced on acorn pile, front
paws on ring, Simpson, Hall, Miller
Co **160.00**
Standing on branch, munching on
nut, tail draped over top of ring . . **140.00**
Turtle Doves, spread wings support
ring, Middletown Plate, #74 . . . . . . **130.00**

NASH GLASS

History: Nash glass is a type of art glass attributed to Arthur John Nash and his sons, Leslie H. and A. Douglass. Arthur John Nash, originally employed by Webb in Stourbridge, England, came to America and was employed in 1889 by Tiffany Furnaces at its Corona, Long Island, plant.

While managing the plant for Tiffany, Nash designed and produced iridescent glass. In 1928 A. Douglas Nash purchased the physical facilities of Tiffany Furnaces. The firm, A. Douglas Nash Corporation, remained in operation until 1931.

Vase, 9½″ h, green and gold irid body, clear irid base, unsigned, $275.00.

Bowl
  3½″ h, amber irid, shallow, ftd, inscribed "Nash 515" **200.00**
  15½″, Chintz, amber, blue, and green opal, turned down rim **300.00**
Candlesticks, pr, 5″ h, Chintz pattern, blood red, silver design **750.00**
Cordial, 4″ h, Chintz pattern, blue and green **55.00**
Creamer, 4¼″ h, clear, pale orchid and green design, clear handle **300.00**
Finger Bowl, matching underplate, 4¾″ d, opal rays, cranberry rim, sgd **175.00**
Goblet, 6½″ h, Chintz pattern, blue and green **60.00**
Perfume, 7⅞″ h, rays of blue and lilac, pale blue foot, orig pointed amber stopper with silvery blue irid **700.00**
Vase
  4¾″, pedestal, bluish gold, inscribed "Nash 644" **300.00**
  6½″, bulbous, feathery blue strokes, bubbly lime green streaks, sgd . . **400.00**
  12″, trumpet shape, vertical orange and yellow stripes, inscribed "Nash 62AA" **415.00**

NAUTICAL ITEMS

History: The seas that surround us have fascinated man since time began. The artifacts of sailors have been collected and treasured for years. Because of their environment, merchant and naval items, whether factory or handmade, must be of quality construction and long lasting. Many of these items are aesthetically designed as well.

Richard Bourne, Hyannis, Massachusetts, and Chuck DeLuca, York, Maine, regularly hold auctions of marine items.

References: Alan P. Major, *Maritime Antiques,* A. S. Barnes & Co., 1981; Jean Randier, *Nautical Antiques,* Doubleday and Co., 1977.

Periodical: *Nautical Brass etc.,* Box 744, Montrose, CA 91020.

Museums: Burgess Mariner's Museum, Newport News, VA; Museum of Science and Industry, Chicago, IL; Mystic Seaport Museum, Mystic, CT; National Maritime Museum, San Francisco, CA.

Advisor: Bill Wheeler.

Account Book, supply and sail making bills to ships, 1858–1862 . . . . **100.00**
Anchor Light, ship's, 22″ h, copper, H Henriksen, Bergen, Norway **100.00**
Bag, sailor's, macrame, 19th C **90.00**
Barometer, brass, mounting board with Swiss thermometer, gimbal, orig carrying case, marked "Made by F Darton & Co Ltd, London" **900.00**
Basket, lightship, 11″ d, circular, swing handle, Nantucket, 19th C **850.00**
Bell Clock, ship's, 6¼″ d, with strike, Seth Thomas, patented November 4, 1879 . . . . **650.00**
Billy Club, sailor's, 17½″ l, turned hardwood, whale ivory and baleen inlays, inlaid initials "C R S", mid 19th C . . **350.00**
Binnacle, 44″ h, brass, orig Sperry compass, compensating ball, mahogany base **800.00**
Binoculars, 15½″ l, leather wrapped, French **225.00**
Block, ship's, 10″ l, brass, star on each side, mounted, Made by Agnall & Loud, Boston **700.00**
Book Stand, 18″ l, scrimshaw, mahogany, two whale's teeth engraved with whale ship mounted on base, late 19th C, early 20th C **1,000.00**
Cane, captain's, 36⅝″ l, wood and baleen, inlaid ivory rings, faceted knob, 19th C **225.00**
Chest, 37″ l, pine, old green paint, American, 19th C **150.00**
Compass, dry card, 9¼ x 9½ pasteboard box, 19th C **125.00**
Depth Gauge, Riggs & Brother, Philadelphia, orig label, cased, marked "Dobbie's Patent Depth Gauge" . . . **225.00**

Ditty Box
Baleen, 5¾" l, oval, red, green, yellow, and blue mottled dec top, nine finger, early 19th C **225.00**
Whalebone, 10¼" d, mahogany top and bottom, swing handle, mid 19th C **1,800.00**
Figurehead, ship's, 60" h, full figure woman, carved, Maine, mid 19th C . **19,500.00**
Fishing Lure, 5" l, bone, handmade, sand eel form, 19th C **150.00**
Foghorn, brass, double action bellows, foot operated, marked "Made by Siebe Gorman & Co Ltd, Surrey, England," 19th C **200.00**
Harpoon Gun, 36" l, iron, percussion . **500.00**
Harpoon Head, 3⅛" l, whale ivory, incised designs, Savoonga, St Lawrence Island **100.00**
Heliograph, Mark V, brass, naval and military signaling device **500.00**
Hourglass, 7¼" h, 18th C **250.00**

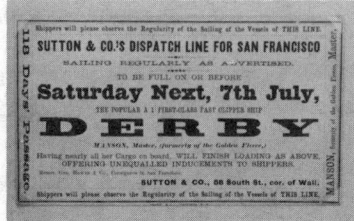

Clipper Ship Card, 6⅜ x 3⁹⁄₁₆", Derby, Sutton & Co's Dispatch Line for San Francisco, blue lettering, white ground, printed by Nesbit & Co., Printers, NY, $300.00.

Knife
Diver's, marked "Bomar Corp, Pittsburgh, PA" **200.00**
Folding, 5½", whalebone handles, "Quality" on blade **175.00**
Log Book Stamp, fruitwood, carved ship, mid 19th C **250.00**
Model
Scale
Black Ball Line Ship, 50" l, full sail, oak case **2,500.00**
Schooner, Dancing Feather, 33½" l, cased **3,500.00**
Warship, English, World War I, 20" l, cased **500.00**
Whaleship, Charles W Morgan, 30" l, natural finish hull, copper sheathed bottom, brass framed case, mahogany inlaid base ... **3,000.00**

Shadowbox, steamer, 32 x 7 x 15", 2 stacks, properly rigged masts, oil on canvas ground **500.00**
Mooring Buoy, 21" d, old red paint, orig 12 foot anchor chain, 19th C **250.00**
Mug, 3½" h, luster, two transfers entitled "The Sailor's Farewell" and "The Sailor's Return," Sunderland **200.00**
Oar, 17", whaleboat, steering, 19th C . **200.00**
Oar Locks, 8" l, bronze, pr **50.00**
Octant, Spencer, Browning & Rust, London, case labeled "F W Lincoln, Boston **650.00**
Painting
Hunter, F. Leo, (American, 20th C), Glory of Seas, 24 x 37", oil on canvas, clipper ship with sail set, gray-green water, pastel highlights, blue sky, molded gold frame, sgd "F L Hunter/1927" **800.00**
Jacobsen, Antonio, (American, 1850–1921), Steamship "Western Land", 30 x 50", oil on canvas, orig frame, sgd "A Jacobsen/1904" **5,000.00**
Wilkinson, Norman, (British, 19th/20th C), S. S. Eagle, 11 x 15½", watercolor, paddle wheel ship, flying pennants from bow to stern, unframed, sgd "Norman Wilkinson/10" **150.00**
Woodcock, Hartwell L., (American, 1853–1929), Bahamian Shipping Boats at Anchor, 13 x 19¾", watercolor, fishing boats group anchored in shallow water, land in distance with white lighthouse, framed and matted, sgd "Hart L Woodcock 1908" **1,600.00**
Powder Flask, copper, anchor, marked "Adams/1846" and "U.S.N." **210.00**
Powder Keg, 12" d, 13" h, copper, lidded, used on warships **225.00**
Quadrant, brass arm, cased, marked "Made by Brown of Bristol," English, late 18th C **800.00**
Rudder Steering Guide, orig ropework, early 19th C **100.00**
Scribe, 13¼" l, fruitwood, whalebone, and copper, brass thumb screw, adjustable, mid 19th C **375.00**
Sewing box, 13¾ x 8 x 9", three masted American sailing ship front panel, sides decorated with landscapes, militia parading in field with buildings and lighthouse top, four drawers inside, early 19th C **3,250.00**
Sextant, ebony, cased, Blachford & Co London label **550.00**
Sign, 18½" l, whale shape, Johah's Dance Hall adv, Hyannis, MA, c1920 **350.00**
Speaking Trumpet, captain's 16" l, brass, red paint inside **275.00**

20" l, engraved "L W Merrill," dated . **425.00**
Spyglass, brass, single draw, ropework cov, early 19th C **200.00**
Station Pointer, brass, cased, sgd "Coxe & Coombes/Davenport & Plymouth" **150.00**
Stern Board, 83", pine, black and gold, carved eagle **1,600.00**
Stove, 23½" l, cast iron, Tyson Furnace, raised ship designs on sides and end **225.00**
Telegraph, ship's, 44" h, brass **900.00**
Telescope, 25½" l, 3 draw, mahogany tube, Ramsden, London **175.00**
Travel Desk, 18¼ x 15 x 35", camphor wood, brass bound, fitted custom ebonized base, tambour lid, Chinese, 19th C **1,050.00**
Valentine, sailor's, 8½", double, "To My Love," 19th C **1,700.00**
Weathervane, 44½" l, 4 masted schooner, wood, orig paint **900.00**
Wheel, 48", *Ship Rousseau*, mahogany and oak **1,000.00**

NAZI ITEMS

History: The National Socialist Party came to power in the 1920s during a period of severe economic depression in Germany. Under the leadership of Adolf Hitler, the party assumed first political control and then social control over Germany. National socialism dominated all aspects of German life. World War II was launched in 1939 to achieve a military conquest of Europe. The Nazi era ended in 1945 when Germany surrendered at the end of World War II.

References: John M. Kaduck, *World War II German Collectibles,* published by author, 1978, 1983 price update; *The Official Price Guide To Military Collectibles,* Fifth Edition, House of Collectibles, 1985; Sydney B. Vernon, *Vernon's Collectors' Guide To Orders, Medals, and Decorations (With Valuations),* published by author, 1986.

Periodicals: *Military Collectors News,* P. O. Box 7582, Tulsa, OK, 74105; *The MX Exchange,* P. O. Box 3, Torrington, CT 06790.

Additional Listings: See *Warman's Americana & Collectibles* for more examples.

Armband, Hitler Youth, red and white, swastika, cotton **20.00**
Backpack, Army, horsehair, leather straps, maker's mark, 1936 .... **40.00**
Badge, General Assault, silver, c1940 . **30.00**
Banner, center swastika, 29 x 70" **65.00**
Bayonnet, single, etched **125.00**
Belt Buckle, DAF Labor Front, swastika in wheel **20.00**
Book
  Mein Kampf , by A. Hitler, 1933, 407 pgs, orig dust cov **15.00**

Schlag Auf Schlag Battle for Poland, German text, uniform and airplane photos **20.00**
Boots, leather, felt wool tops, Russian front style, reinforcement straps ... **30.00**
Breast Badge, Luftwaffe, pilot's, observer's, gold wreath, silver eagle holds swastika, orig blue case **250.00**
Brooch, large floral swastika, rect back, gilt, 1936 .... **15.00**
Car Pennant, 1936 Berlin Olympics, eternal flame, olympic symbol and date, tie ropes **75.00**
Currency, concentration camp, Flossenburg **65.00**
Dagger, Army officer, orange handle, silvered fittings, full eagle's breast, scabbard **140.00**
Dagger Holder, SS, black leather, buckle cross strap, RZM/SS mark **85.00**
Desk Plaque, Imperial German Hunting Assoc, stag head, crown, inscribed medal, marble base **90.00**
Document, Army "Kriegs-Chronik," service award **40.00**
First Aid Case, German Red Cross, leather, 1935, orig contents **20.00**

Close Combat Badge, silver, 50 Engagements, $100.00.

Flag
  Army, Regimental Battle, 84 x 144", double sided, eagle, swastika, tricolor **75.00**
  Parade, NSDAP, 45½" l, hp black swastika on white, double sided, c1920 .... **30.00**
Flag Pole Top, "Wird Waffe," bakelite spearhead and oak leaves, cross guard dated 1940, iron cross dated 1939 .... **40.00**
Funeral Sash, SS, fabric and paper, silver lettering, white fringe, large silver SS Runes **125.00**
Hat
  Panzer Officer, black wool, silver piping, silver eagle, two silver buttons on ear flaps, maker mark **300.00**

R.R. Supervisor, red wool, black velvet band, two gold eagles, rosettes, black visor, orig maker label **200.00**

SS, rabbit fur, quilted int., black ties at ear flaps, olive green wool body, RZM/SS, skull and eagle devices . **265.00**

Medal, German Red Cross, 1937, black enameled eagle and red cross, red and white ribbon **80.00**

Mittens, wool, Luftwaffe, gray wool, blue gray lining, leather tags, pr **15.00**

Pennant

Parade, 22 x 38″, triangular, sewn on swastika on both sides, District No. 16-246 .... **85.00**

Podium, NSDAP, white border and bottom fringe, large swastika **35.00**

Photo Album, 1942–43, official "Reichs - Autobahnen," 21 photos **85.00**

Pillowcase, 15 x 18″, NSDAP eagle and swastika, inscribed "Deutschland Erwacht" **50.00**

Plaque

6 x 8″, bronze, Hitler's profile, dark brown patina **175.00**

6¾ x 9″, Ex-Pres Von Hindenburg, copper plate, facial view, civilian dress **25.00**

Plate

7½″, white porcelain, DAF insignia . **12.00**

9″, green and white porcelain, green Luftwaffe eagle, Unit #O-H-2 .... **18.00**

Print

8 x 11″, Luftwaffe crew, preparing bomber for strike, marked "Berlin, 1940" **15.00**

8 x 11½″, Rescue at Sea, bomber crew rescued by pontoon plane, German, sgd, 1941 .... **15.00**

Ring, crossed swords, helmet, and swastika, silver **50.00**

Shirt, brown, S.A., black collar tabs, black piping, eagle buttons, c1933 . **125.00**

Snowsuit, mountain troops, white jacket, white painted buttons, attached hood, trousers, Gebirgsjager sleeve patch, 1943 .... **200.00**

Soup Bowl, NSDAP, 9″, large black eagle on bottom, 1938 .... **15.00**

Sword, police, scabbard **145.00**

Table Lamp, 16″ h, gold leaf, plaster, eagle, marbleized base, from Munich party headquarters **70.00**

Wall Streamer, 43 x 7″, NSDAP, two pc silk, light orange on red field, brass pole **35.00**

NETSUKES

History: The traditional Japanese kimono has no pockets. Daily necessities such as money, tobacco supplies, etc., were carried in leather pouches or *inros* which hung from a cord with a netsuke toggle. Netsuke comes from "ne" (to root) and "tsuke" (to fasten).

Netsukes originated in the 14th century and initially were associated with the middle class. By the mid-18th century all levels of Japanese society used them. Some of the most famous artists, e.g., Shuzan and Yamada Hojitsu, worked in the netsuke form.

Netsukes average 1 to 2 inches and are made from wood, ivory, bone, ceramics, metal, horn, nutshells, etc. The subject matter is broad based, but always portrayed in a lighthearted, humorous manner. A netsuke must have no sharp edges and balance so it hangs correctly on the sash.

Value depends on artist, region, material, and skill of craftsmanship. Western collectors favor *katabori*, pieces which represent an identifiable object.

Reference: Sandra Andacht, *Oriental Antiques & Art: An Identification And Value Guide,* Wallace-Homestead, 1987.

Collectors' Club: Netsuke Kenkyukai Society, Box 11248, Torrance, CA 90510.

Reproduction Alert: Recent reproductions are on the market. Many are carved from African ivory.

Carved ivory, 19th C, $125.00.

Acrobat, ivory, legs over head **150.00**

Angel, ivory, bending backwards, Ryo . **1,600.00**

Badger, ivory, c1900 .... **150.00**

Bird, ivory, holding prey, Hong Kong .. **120.00**

Boy, ivory, carved, standing behind sake cask, stained **90.00**

Cockerel, ivory, unsigned, c1800 .... **1,300.00**

Crane, ivory, seated looking over shoulder **45.00**

Daikoku, 2″ h, ivory, wearing robe belted below belly, mallet raised in right hand above rice sack, stained, sgd **110.00**

Dragon, 2″, ivory, coiled tail, sgd **50.00**

Dutchman, 3½″, carved, standing in short tunic with drawn saber, early 19th C **195.00**

Eagle with fish, ivory, c1900 .... **300.00**

Foo Dog, corozo nut, head tilted **75.00**
Game Hen **60.00**
Geisha, ivory, kneeling, white and red . **150.00**
Man, ivory, holding raised knife, un-
signed **200.00**
Mermaid, ivory, leaning on hand, Mei-
zan **475.00**
Monkey, wood, eating fruit, Masami,
c1900 .... **400.00**
Mother and Child, ivory **420.00**
Mouse, ivory
1¼" h **65.00**
2¼" h, pair **110.00**
Owl, ivory, jewel eyes **125.00**
Skull, 2", ivory, coiling snake, frog in
back, Meiji Period **660.00**
Sparrow, wood, stylized, flying **250.00**
Squirrel, ivory, laying on side, Baisho,
c1900 .... **160.00**
Tiger, ivory, baby under paw, c1900 .. **150.00**

NEWCOMB POTTERY

History: William and Ellsworth Woodward, two brothers, were the founders of a series of businesses which eventually merged into the Newcomb pottery effort. In 1885 Ellsworth Woodward, a proponent of vocational training for women, organized a school from which emerged the Ladies Decorative Art League. In 1886 the brothers founded the New Orleans Art Pottery Company with the ladies of the league serving as decorators. The first two potters were Joseph Meyer and George Ohr. The pottery closed in 1891.

William Woodward was on the faculty at Tulane. Ellsworth taught fine arts at the Sophie Newcomb College, a women's school which eventually merged with Tulane. In 1895 Newcomb College developed a pottery course in which the wares could be sold. Some of the equipment came from the old New Orleans Art Pottery.

Mary G. Sheerer joined the staff to teach decoration. In 1910 Paul E. Cox solved many of the technical problems connected with making pottery in a southern environment. Other leading figures were Sadie Irvine, Professor Lota Lee Troy, and Kathrine Choi. Pottery was made until the early 1950s.

Students painted a quality art pottery with a distinctive high glaze. Designs have a decidedly southern flavor, e.g., myrtle, jasmine, sugar cane, moss, cypress, dogwood, and magnolia motifs. Later matte glazed pieces usually are decorated with carved back floral designs. Pieces depicting murky, bayou scenes are most desirable.

References: Suzanne Ormond and Mary E. Irvine, *Louisiana's Art Nouveau: The Crafts Of The Newcomb Style*, Pelican Publishing Company, 1976; Jessie Poesch, *Newcomb Pottery: An Enterprise for Southern Women*, Schiffer Publishing, Ltd, 1984.

Collectors' Club: American Art Pottery Association, P.O. Box 714, Silver Spring, MD 20901.

Museum: Newcomb College, Tulane University, New Orleans, LA.

Vase, 6⅛" h, Louisiana Swamp scene, tree with Spanish moss, blue tones, shaded dark to light, matte glaze, $1,200.00.

Bowl, 5½" d, carved flowers on shoulder, four colors, sgd "Henrietta Bailey" **650.00**
Candlestick, 9¾", blue ground, pink
dogwood, artist sgd "Sadie Irvine,"
potter's mark "JM," paper label **625.00**
Flower Frog, 1⅝ x 4", nine holes, blue
and pink, artist sgd "Sadie Irvine" .. **185.00**
Pitcher, 7½", high glaze, deeply incised
yellow rosebuds, green leaves, light
blue and dark blue banded ground,
mottled medium to dark blue flared
base, Henrietta Bailey dec, imp "Q,"
1908 .... **2,400.00**
Vase
3", compressed spherical, matte pale
blue and yellow flowers, slender
green leaves, painted "NC" mark . **500.00**
4½", twelve carved daffodils, four
colors, sgd "AM" **725.00**
6", cylindrical baluster form, matte
green, blue landscape dec, imp
"NC 237," Joseph Meyer monogram **800.00**
7", clusters of small light blue flowers,
long green leaves, medium blue
ground, Alma Mason, imp "JM,"
"236" and "B" in circle **1,200.00**

8¼", baluster, carved clusters of light blue daffodils, long green stems, medium blue ground, artist Sadie Irvine, imp "JM," "250" and "JE8" — 900.00

8½", baluster, stepped neck, wide collar rim, carved pale blue grapes, thick green vine, blue-green ground, artist Sadie Irvine, marked "SI" in blue ink, imp "JM," "194" and "B" in circle — 750.00

NILOAK POTTERY, MISSION WARE

History: Niloak Pottery was made near Benton, Arkansas. Charles Dean Hyten experimented with native clay, trying to preserve its natural colors. By 1911 he perfected Mission Ware, a marbleized pottery in which the cream and brown colors predominate. The pieces were marked Niloak (kaolin spelled backwards).

After a devastating fire, the pottery was rebuilt and named Eagle Pottery. This factory included the space to add a novelty pottery line which was introduced in 1929. This line usually was marked Hywood-Niloak, until 1934 when the name Hywood was dropped from the mark. Mr. Hyten left the pottery in 1941. In 1946 operations ceased.

Additional Listings: See *Warman's Americana & Collectibles* for more examples, especially the novelty pieces.

Note: Prices listed below are for Mission Ware pieces.

Ashtray, 1½ x 4", swirl — 25.00
Bowl
  5 x 2" — 45.00
  10½ x 4" — 72.00

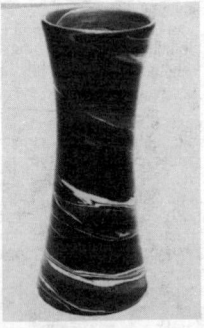

Vase, 9⅞" h, waisted, $150.00.

Clock, 4 x 5" — 175.00
Mug, 4 x 3" — 45.00
Pitcher, 10", strap handle — 125.00
Umbrella Stand, 22" — 350.00
Vase
  4", cylindrical — 40.00
  5" — 45.00
  6", cone, ftd — 55.00
  8", bud — 65.00
  11¾" h, 8" d, rolled rim, brown, blue, and cream, imp mark, orig blue label — 125.00
  14", hour glass shape — 175.00
Wall Pocket, dark red and brown glaze — 115.00

NIPPON CHINA, 1891-1921

History: Nippon, Japanese hand painted porcelain, was made for export between 1891 and 1921. In 1891, when the McKinley tariff act proclaimed that all items of foreign manufacture be stamped with their country of origin. Japan chose to use "Nippon." In 1921 the United States decided the word "Nippon" no longer was acceptable and required that all Japanese wares be marked with "Japan." The Nippon era ended.

There are over 220 recorded Nippon backstamps or marks. The three most popular are the wreath, maple leaf, and rising sun marks. Wares with variations of all three marks are being reproduced today. A knowledgeable collector can easily spot the reproductions by the mark variances.

The majority of the marks are found in three different colors: green, blue, and magenta. Colors indicate the quality of the porcelain used: green for first grade porcelain, blue for second grade, and magenta for third grade. Marks were applied by two methods, decal stickers under glaze and imprinting directly on the porcelain.

References: Gene Loendorf, *Nippon Hand Painted China*, McGrew Color Graphics, 1975; Joan Van Patten, *The Collector's Encyclopedia Of Nippon Porcelain, Series One*, Collector Books, 1979; Joan Van Patten, *The Collector's Encyclopedia Of Nippon Porcelain, Series Two*, Collector Books, 1982; Joan Van Patten, *The Collector's Encyclopedia Of Nippon Porcelain, Series Three*, Collector Books, 1986.

Collectors' Clubs: Great Lakes Nippon Collectors Club, Rt 2, Box 81, Peotone, IL 60468; International Nippon Collectors Club, Rt 2, Box 81, Peotone, IL 60468; Long Island Nippon Collectors Club, P. O. Box 88, Jericho, NY 11753; New England Nippon Collectors Club, 22 Mill Pond, North Andover, MA 01845.

Additional Listings: See *Warman's Americana & Collectibles*.

Advisor: Kathy Wojciechowski.

Ashtray, 5½", moriage dragon, slate gray ground, Royal Moriage mark — 175.00

Asparagus Set, 12 x 7½" tray, six
matching 7½" plates, green M mark   **350.00**
Basket
   4", pale blue tiny flowers outlined in
gold, gold handle, Rising Sun mark   **50.00**
   6 x 9 x 5", hp int., dogwood blossoms,
gold trim **45.00**
   7", cobalt ground, gold trim, portrait
medallion **225.00**
Berry Set, large master bowl, seven
matching small bowls, large traced
pink and blue flowers, green leaves,
fancy scalloped edges, Shinzo Nip-
pon mark **100.00**
Biscuit Jar, cov, English fox hunt scene   **300.00**
Bowl
   5¼", hp, scene on int. of bowl, trees
and rowboat by lake, blue and gold
trim, pedestal base, three gold
legs, two pcs, green M in wreath
mark **250.00**
   7", woodland scene, scalloped rim,
blue maple leaf mark **175.00**
   8½", crimped edge, pierced handles,
woodland stream scene, green M
in wreath mark **90.00**
   9", handles, hp int., yellow and purple
flowers **65.00**
   10"d, 2½" h, deep red ground, yellow
and pink flowers, all over gold dot,
scalloped edge, Royal Kinran mark   **75.00**

**Vase, 9¼" h, tapered cylinder, high
glaze, floral dec, pink, lavender, yellow,
green leaves, gold trim, $150.00.**

Cake Set, 10¾" d master plate with
pierced handles, five small serving
plates, swans swimming in lake, cobalt, heavy gold trim, maple leaf mark,
6 pcs **350.00**
Calling Card Tray, 7½", cobalt, pink and
red roses, gold trim, green M in
wreath mark **125.00**

Candlestick, 8", woman walking dog on
leash, purple and black, gold tracings   **115.00**
Candy Dish, 7", ftd, large red roses with
gold tracings, cobalt and gold trim,
wreath mark **75.00**
Celery Dish, gold beaded **30.00**
Celery Set, 13½" master celery dish, six
salts, hp stalk of celery in center,
wreath mark **175.00**
Child's Feeding Dish, 8", child playing
with dog, Rising Sun mark **85.00**
Chocolate Set, 10" chocolate pot, four
cups and saucers, beige ground, scenic palm trees and mountains,
beaded, China E-OH mark, 10 pcs .   **100.00**
Cigarette Box, 4½", farm scene on cov,
floral dec on base, wreath mark . . .   **225.00**
Compote, 7¾", floral center, Wedgwood
style border, three griffins base **450.00**
Condensed Milk Container, 6", tiny pink
and white roses, white beaded scrolling, mauve shaded ground, RC mark   **140.00**
Cup and Saucer, cottage and forest
scene, bisque, Shinzo mark **40.00**
Ewer
   9", ftd, moriage bird in flight and flowers, Hand Painted Nippon mark . .   **250.00**
   10¾", Halloween scene, tapestry,
maple leaf mark **700.00**
Ferner, 8¼", ftd, two handles, lake
shore scene, cobalt blue, gold crisscross trim, green M in wreath mark .   **325.00**
Hair Receiver, ftd, hp, pink flowers, gold
banding, Rising Sun mark **30.00**
Hatpin Holder, 5", gold scrolled design,
portrait of young lady in oval medallion, attached underplate, blue maple
leaf mark **185.00**
Humidor
   5¼", scenic, sgd **175.00**
   6", Indian chief on horseback, blown
out dec, tortoise shell ground,
green M in wreath mark **950.00**
   7", jockey on race horse, moriage
dec, green M in wreath mark **475.00**
   7¼", crouching lion, blown out dec,
green M in wreath mark **850.00**
Inkwell, 4 x 4", bisque, bird design,
beaded, colorful **150.00**
Jam Jar, 5½" h, matching 6⅛" under-
plate, cream ground, pink apple blossoms, green leaves, cobalt borders,
gold trim, green M in wreath mark . .   **70.00**
Lemonade Set, pitcher and five 3"
mugs, hp, sunset with sailboat **185.00**
Mayonnaise Set, ftd bowl, underplate,
ladle, cream ground, orange poppies
outlined in gold, RC mark, 3 pcs . . .   **75.00**
Mug, 5½", moriage dragon, gray
ground, artist sgd, green M in wreath
mark **125.00**
Napkin Ring, holly berries dec **35.00**

Nappy, 6¼", shaded pink roses, gold
dec, beaded, blue TS mark **125.00**
Pin Tray, relief molded flowers, earth
tones, bisque finish **45.00**
Pitcher, 11", pagoda and bridge, yellow
ground, enamel flowers, gold rim,
base, and handle, blue maple leaf
mark **250.00**
Plaque
7¾", bust of Indian chief, full headdress, moriage border, beading,
blue enameled flowers with red
jeweled center, pierced for hanging,
sgd **275.00**
8¾", mountain and lake scene, blue
and purple flower border, green M
in wreath mark **125.00**
10"
Fox Hunt, green M in wreath mark **175.00**
Indian on galloping horse, blown
out dec, green M in wreath mark **850.00**
11¼", Egyptian scene, people in sailboat, orange, brown, and lavender,
green M in wreath mark **125.00**
Plate
9", heavy red florals, wreath mark . . **75.00**
9½", hp, pink, castle, yellow trees and
water, green M in wreath mark . . . **95.00**
Powder Box, cov, 3¾", ftd, hp, small
pink flowers, blue Rising Sun mark . **35.00**
Punch Bowl, 10", cobalt and floral dec,
ftd stand, green maple leaf mark, 2
pcs **450.00**
Ring Tree, shallow dish base, gold
band, purple violets, gold trim, maple
leaf mark **75.00**
Stamp Box, geometric black stripes, int.
tray with two compartments, wreath
mark **90.00**
Stein, 7", Galle scene with brown mor-
iage trees, pale orange ground, white
enamel flowers, maple leaf mark . . . **400.00**
Sugar Shaker
4¼", cobalt, flower dec, matching cov,
blue maple leaf mark **150.00**
5", bisque, boat scene, cobalt, gold
handle **55.00**
Tankard, 10", pink floral panels, cobalt,
yellow, and green moriage **325.00**
Tea Strainer, 6", single handle, cobalt,
flowers, heavy gold rim, blue maple
leaf mark **100.00**
Tea Tile, 5½", Dutch windmill scene,
green M in wreath mark **40.00**
Teapot, butterflies **48.00**
Toast Rack, sections for 3 slices of
toast, white ground, gold raised
bunches of grapes and grape leaves,
Spoke mark **125.00**
Toothpick Holder, three handles, hp,
pyramids and palm tree scene, green
M in wreath mark **40.00**

Tray, 12 x 9", bisque, water scene,
heavy gold trim **100.00**
Urn, 18", portrait, heavy gold trim **850.00**
Vase
5", double handles, inlet and island
scene, delicate trees, all over gold
scrolling, jeweled medallions, cobalt blue bands, blue maple leaf
mark **120.00**
7", acorns and leaves, blown out dec,
blue maple leaf mark **450.00**
7¼", portrait, lady in pastel colors,
cream ground, all over gold designs and flowers, back panel of
red and pink roses, maple leaf
mark **195.00**
7¾", matte finish, cream ground,
peach and yellow roses, green
leaves, green M in wreath mark . . **100.00**
9", Art Nouveau style, orange pop-
pies, blue maple leaf mark **135.00**
11½", Art Nouveau style, woodland
scene, stylized dec, ram's head
handles **325.00**
12", cowboy on horse, desert back-
ground, gold handles, Imperial Nip-
pon blue mark **375.00**
12½", cream ground, crisscross gold
bands, purple and gold fruit, gold
handles, Royal Nishike mark **125.00**
13", handled, black border with gold
phoenix bird, green M in wreath
mark **235.00**
Whiskey Jug, 8", lake with trees scene,
sq shaped handle, blue maple leaf
mark **375.00**

NODDERS

History: Nodders are figurines with heads and/
or arms attached to the body with wires to enable
them to move. They are made in a variety of materials - bisque, celluloid, papier mache, porcelain,
and wood.

Most nodders date from the late 19th century
with Germany being the principal source of supply.
Among the American made nodders, those of Disney and cartoon characters are most eagerly
sought.

Black woman, seated, holds removable
watermelon, gray hair, head nods,
salt shaker type **50.00**
Boy, black, bisque, sitting, red turban,
gold cane, Germany **50.00**
Cat, black, composition, 5" **55.00**
Charlie Brown, composition, molded
black base, name on front, 5½", Lego
copyright sticker on bottom, mid
1960s **30.00**

Bisque, 3¼″ h, Chinaman, seated, blue robe, yellow and red trim, unmarked, $150.00.

Couple

Chinese, standing, 15″, French, pr	1,250.00
Victorian, blue costumes, wire glasses, gilt highlights, pr	225.00
Dog, Boxer, composition, brown flocking, gold paint, 7″ l	25.00
Donkey, celluloid, 3″	30.00
Elephant, composition, head and tail nod, 12″	125.00
Goose, celluloid, Germany, US Zone	30.00
Indian, male and female, drum base, salt shaker type, pr	20.00
Indian Princess, bisque, pale blue robe, gold trim, 3¾″	120.00
Jester, bisque, holding pipe, peach, white, and gold, 3½″	70.00
Juggler, seated man and woman playing drums, woman wearing gold and pink robe, pr	250.00
Little Orphan Annie, bisque, Germany	100.00
Man, comical, wood and composition, polychrome paint, top hat, 7½″	35.00
Monkey, celluloid, joined arms and legs, 6½″	65.00
Oriental Lady, robe dec, 15″	100.00
Oriental Man, bisque, holding knife and sheath, dressed in blue and white, skull cap, 5¾″	75.00
Pig, Oriental dressed standing upright, 5″	120.00
Rabbit, papier mache, glass eyes, 7″	65.00

NORITAKE CHINA

History: Morimura Brothers founded Noritake China in 1904 in Nagoya, Japan. They made high quality chinaware for export to the United States and also produced a line of china blanks for hand painting. In 1910 the company perfected a technique for the production of high quality dinnerware and introduced streamlined production.

During the 1920s Larkin Company, Buffalo, New York, was a prime distributor of Noritake China. Larkin offered Azalea, Briarcliff, Linden, Modjeska, Savory, Sheridan, and Tree In The Meadow patterns as part of their premium line.

The factory was heavily damaged during World War II; production was reduced. Between 1946 and 1948 the company sold their china under the "Rose China" mark, since the quality of production did not match the earlier Noritake China. An 1948 expansion saw the resumption of quality production and the use of the Noritake name once again.

There are close to 100 different marks for Noritake, the careful study of which can determine the date of production. Most pieces are marked "Noritake" and have a wreath, "M," "N," or "Nippon." The use of the letter "N" was registered in 1953.

References: Aimee Neff Alden and Marian Kinney Richardson, *Early Noritake China: An Identification And Value Guide To Tableware Patterns*, Wallace-Homestead, 1987; Joan Van Patten, *Collector's Encyclopedia of Noritake*, Collector Books, 1984.

Additional Listings: See *Warman's Americana & Collectibles* for price listings of the Azalea pattern.

Ashtray

Cat, 3 x 4¾″, figural, luster	110.00
Dog, individual	50.00
Horsehead	55.00

Bowl

5½″, swan on lake scene	20.00
6½″, sq, stylized scene	35.00
7½″, Art Deco, blue luster band, orange scenic center	20.00
8″, blown out chestnuts, blue and white	90.00
8½″, sq, 2 handles, bird dec	40.00
11″, blue and gold luster, molded ram's head handles	125.00
Bread Plate, 7 x 12″, ear of corn dec	50.00
Cake Plate, gold flowers and garland	60.00
Candy Dish, 15″ d, orange and pearl luster, black trim, green mark	35.00
Celery Tray, stylized blue flowers, yellow and blue butterflies	25.00
Chambersticks, 4½″ d, 3½″ h, tan luster ground, blue roses, black handles and trim, ftd base, sgd, pr	75.00
Chocolate Set, cov chocolate pot, six cups and saucers, white and cobalt dec, marked	250.00
Compote, blue, gold, and white, all-over fruit dec, 2 pc	175.00
Creamer and Sugar, irid blue, butterfly and orange flower	20.00
Cup and Saucer, Bahama pattern	20.00
Demitasse Set, cov demitasse pot, creamer, cov sugar, five cups and	

saucers, and 12" tray, yellow, white center band, multicolored hp delicate flowers outlined in black, black handles **400.00**

Dresser Set, white, cobalt blue and gold dec, marked, 8 pcs **130.00**

Figure, 11", Art Deco ladies, light green, gold Dore bases, sgd, pr **450.00**

Flower Frog, figural, cockatoo **75.00**

Humidor, 5¾", Art Deco, black and white owls, yellow eyes, black, white, and red dec **165.00**

Match Holder, figural
Bear **100.00**
Beehive, striker, gold luster **45.00**

Mayonnaise, cov, underplate, yellow and pink flowers, green foliage, red and gold border **25.00**

Bowl, 7¾" d, 2⅛" h, chestnuts, brown, orange, and yellow dec, three small looped feet, $100.00.

Mint Dish, 7", open handle, hp, blue and yellow flowers, copper-brown twining leaves **35.00**

Napkin Ring, Art Deco, man and woman, pr **100.00**

Nappy, raised gold **15.00**

Nut Bowl, gold, gray figural squirrel .. **85.00**

Nut Set, molded peanut bowl, 6 small peanut shaped dishes, 7 pc **125.00**

Plaque, scenic **70.00**

Potpourri Jar, 6", pierced cov, blue and white, red and yellow rosebud finial . **75.00**

Powder Jar, Art Deco, hp, irid white center, red, blue, and black daisies, irid blue border **70.00**

Salt, figural, butterfly **30.00**

Sandwich Server, 8", pearlized center, fruit dec, bird finial **160.00**

Spooner, figural birds on handles **75.00**

Sugar Shaker, 6½", scenic **30.00**

Tray, 7½", Dresdena, handles **15.00**

Vase
5¼", tree trunk, bird **165.00**

9½", scenic, multicolored, hp, green mark **100.00**

10", Art Nouveau landscape, handles **200.00**

11½", baluster, two gold handles, light and dark blue floral design, blue and yellow Phoenix Bird, green wreath mark **175.00**

Wall Pocket, Art Deco sailing ship scene, red mark **60.00**

NORITAKE: TREE IN THE MEADOW PATTERN

History: Tree In The Meadow is one of the most popular patterns of Noritake china. Since the design is hand painted, there are numerous variations of the scene. The basic scene features a large tree (usually in the foreground), a meandering stream or lake, and a peasant cottage in the distance. Principal colors are muted tones of brown and yellow.

The pattern is found with a variety of backstamps and appears to have been imported into the United States beginning in the early 1920s. The Larkin Company distributed this pattern through its catalog sales in the 1920–1930 period.

Reference: Joan Van Patten, *Collector's Encyclopedia of Noritake,* Collector Books, 1984.

Hair Receiver, 3⅛" d, 2¼" h, blue "Made in Japan" mark, $35.00.

Ashtray, hp, green M in wreath mark . **50.00**

Bowl, 7" **25.00**

Bread Tray **45.00**

Butter Dish, cov, insert **65.00**

Cake Plate, 10" **40.00**

Celery Dish, 12" **35.00**

Coffeepot, cov **185.00**

Compote **100.00**

Condiment Set **40.00**

Creamer and Sugar, cov **50.00**

Cup and Saucer **18.00**

Demitasse Pot, cov	160.00
Humidor, cov	375.00
Lemon Dish, 5½", handle	25.00
Mayonnaise, underplate and spoon	30.00
Nappy	15.00
Plate	
6½"	10.00
8½"	15.00
Platter, 10"	85.00
Salt and Pepper Shakers, pr	30.00
Shaving Mug	100.00
Sugar Shaker	30.00
Syrup	50.00
Teapot, cov	100.00
Toothpick, 2½"	55.00
Vase, 5¾", fan shape	115.00
Vegetable Dish, 9¼", oval	30.00
Waffle Set	65.00

NORTH DAKOTA SCHOOL OF MINES

History: The North Dakota School of Mines was established in 1890. Earle J. Babcock, an instructor in chemistry, was impressed with the high purity of North Dakota potter's clay. In 1898 Babcock received funds to develop his finds. He tried to interest commercial potteries in North Dakota clay, but had limited success.

In 1910 Babcock persuaded the school to establish a Ceramics Department. Margaret Cable, who studied under Charles Binns and Frederick H. Rhead, was appointed head. She remained until her retirement in 1949.

Decorative emphasis was placed on native themes, e.g., flowers and animals. Art Nouveau, Art Deco, and fairly plain pieces were made.

The pottery is marked in cobalt blue underglaze with "University of North Dakota/Grand Forks, N.D./Made at School of Mines/N.D. Clay" in a circle. Some earlier pieces only are marked "U.N.D." or "U.N.D./Grand Forks, N.D." Most pieces are numbered (they can be dated with University records) and signed by both the instructor and student. Cable signed pieces are most desirable.

Reference: *University Of North Dakota Pottery, The Cable Years*, Knight Publishing Company, 1977.

Ashtray, KEM design, seal 1930	145.00
Bowl, 4½", bison design, brown, sgd "Cable"	175.00
Figure	
Donkey, pale gray glaze	65.00
Horse, blue matte	75.00
Paperweight, prairie rose, brown	125.00
Pitcher, thick red glaze over green	60.00
Tumbler, 3 x 5¼", cylindrical, green, marked "University of North Dakota, Grand Forks, ND, Made of School of Mines ND Clay"	45.00

Vase, 4" h, 4½" d, squatty bulbous shape, shaded white to light green ground, impressed circular decoration separated by impressed leaf shape decoration, stamp mark, $175.00.

Vase	
3¾", medium green, glossy, marked "H"	50.00
4 x 4½", shaded white to light green ground, imp circular and foliage dec, stamped mark, inscribed "95A Huck"	175.00
6½ x 4", squat, cut back panel dec, ox pulling cov wagon, green, brown ground, circular ink mark, incised "JH"	400.00

OCCUPIED JAPAN

History: At the end of World War II, the Japanese economy was devastated. To secure needed hard currency, the Japanese pottery industry produced thousands of figurines and other knickknacks for export. From the beginning of the American occupation until April 28, 1952, these objects were marked "Japan," "Made in Japan," "Occupied Japan," and "Made in Occupied Japan." Only pieces marked with the last two designations are of strong interest to Occupied Japan collectors. The first two marks also were used at other time periods.

The variety of products is endless—ashtrays, dinnerware, lamps, planters, souvenir items, toys, vases, etc. Initially it was the figurines which attracted the largest number of collectors; today many collectors focus on non-figurine material.

References: Gene Florence, *The Collector's Encyclopedia Of Occupied Japan Collectibles*, Collector Books, 1976, 1982 edition; Gene Florence, *The Collector's Encyclopedia Of Occupied Japan Collectibles*, 2nd series, Collector Books, 1979, 1982 revision.

Collectors' Club: Occupied Japan Collectors

Club, 18309 Faysmith Avenue, Torrance, CA 90504.

Additional Listings: See *Warman's Americana & Collectibles* for more examples.

Bisque
Ashtray, nodder, black man smoking cigar	85.00
Corncupia, 7 x 8″, chariot, rearing horse, and two cherubs, multicolored beading, gold trim, unglazed	75.00
Demitasse Cup and Saucer, imitation Royal Vienna	20.00
Dish, Dutch girls on seesaw	28.00
Doll, 3″	10.00

Figures, couple, 5½″ h, man with tan coat, blue vest, and brown pants, lady with yellow skirt, blue bustle, and rose blouse, pr, $25.00.

Figure
Angel with flute	5.00
Bride and groom, pink bouquet . .	25.00
Frog, seated, holding lily pad	48.00
Lady, large, elegant, with dove . . .	50.00
Walking Bear, orig box	75.00
Flower Frog, 6″, figural, girl with bird on shoulder, pastel highlights, gold trim	45.00
Lamp base, Colonial couple, oval, painted details	30.00
Match Holder, 7 x 4½″, colonial couple, each holding basket, striker on side	40.00
Planter, duck, 6″	25.00
Toothpick Holder, young woman leaning against wall	20.00
Wall Pocket, 4 x 2¾ x 1½″, colonial woman on balcony	25.00

Celluloid
Baby Rattle, roly-poly clown	15.00
Doll, 12″, white dress	30.00
Tape Measure, pink pig	15.00
Toy, waltzing couple, orig box and key	65.00

Lacquerware, salad bowl, serving fork and spoon	20.00

Metal
Ashtray, round, devil's face, emb floral rim	15.00
Butter Dish, cov, glass liner	10.00
Cigarette Box, cov, dog head on red ground	10.00
Pencil Sharpener, figural bulldog head	10.00
Puzzle, 15 pcs, box, instructions . . .	45.00
Silent Butler, sq, metal handle	10.00

Paper
Fan	8.00
Umbrella, 3″ d	13.00
Papier Mache, tray, 8¼ x 5″, hp, roses, marked "Alcohol Proof/SS/Made in Occupied Japan"	18.00

Porcelain
Candy Dish, black ground, green glaze, double metal handle, pink flowers	15.00
Creamer, 3¼″, bird on bamboo plant, colored flowers, brown and gold border	10.00
Dish, leaf shape, curled, veined, green, marked "Chuba"	13.00
Salt and Pepper	
Frogs and tray, 3 pcs	13.00
Windmills, moving blades	25.00
Shelf Sitter, boy holding hat, blue pants, yellow coat	10.00
Tea Set, teapot, creamer, and sugar, figural tomato, 5 pcs	30.00
Toothpick Holder, little girl pushing baby carriage	5.00
Vase, bud, Kutani type, ftd, portrait of lady	8.00
Textile, four pc sheet set, two sheets, two pillow cases, double bed size, embroidered label	38.00

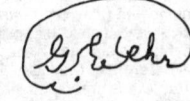

G.E.OHR, BILOXI.

OHR POTTERY

History: Ohr pottery was produced by George E. Ohr in Biloxi, Mississippi. There is some discrepancy as to when he actually established his pottery. Some suggest 1878, but Ohr's autobiography indicates 1883. In 1884 Ohr exhibited 600 pieces of his work, indicating that he had been working for some time.

Ohr's techniques included twisting, crushing, folding, denting, and crinkling thin walled clay into odd, grotesque, and sometimes graceful forms. Much of his early work is signed with an impressed stamp of his name and location in block letters. His later work, often marked with the flowing script designation "G E Ohr," was usually left unglazed.

In 1906, Ohr closed the pottery and stored over 6,000 pieces as his legacy to his family. He hoped it would be purchased by the U.S. Government, which never happened. The entire collection remained in storage until it was rediscovered in 1972.

Today Ohr is recognized as one of the leading potters in the American Art Pottery movement. Some greedy individuals have taken the later unglazed pieces and covered them with poor quality glazes, in hopes of making them more valuable. These pieces, usually with the flowing script mark, do not have "stilt marks" on the bottom.

Bank, 2¾" h, 5½" diagonally folded clay, unglazed, imp "G. E. OHR/BILOXI, MISS," $200.00.

Bank, 3⅛ x 2¼", potato, orange-brown, sgd 350.00
Basket, hanging, 6½" h, coiled int. . . . 360.00
Bowl, 4", bulbous, splotches of black and dark metallic brown, sand and gray ground, die stamped mark 175.00
Creamer, 4", free form, pinched and pulled neck, cut out handle, mauve glaze, green spots, incised "G. E. Ohr" 1,200.00
Figure, 9½ x 5½", conch shell, wide opening, rows of articulated spikes, orange brown and green sponged high glazed finish, incised "Geo E OHR," imp "G.E.OHR Biloxi" 2,500.00
Goblet, 6¾" h, straight cylindrical bowl, flared foot, bisque finish, incised lines, incised script mark 115.00
Inkwell, figural
2½ x 4", log cabin, green glaze, stamped "Geo E Ohr, Biloxi, Miss" 350.00
4½ x 3½", bulldog head, reglazed brown, imp "A Biloxi Welcome," lines of poetry, and "GE Ohr, Biloxi, Miss" 500.00
Mug, 5" h, cylindrical, bulbous waist,

high glaze brown surface, inscribed "G. E. Ohr" 300.00
Pitcher
3¾", squatty, deep carved pleats on indented middle band, ear shaped handle, bisque finish, incised sgd . 300.00
5½", ruffled opening, undulating handle, rose matte glaze, high gloss emerald green dripping, yellow high glaze int., obscured script on body, incised script "G.E.Ohr" . . . 1,400.00
Puzzle Mug, 5¼", rabbit head handle, metallic orange-brown glaze, gunmetal splotches, sgd 225.00
Vase
3 x 4¼", hour glass shape, wide flaring pinched neck, gunmetal to dark green high glaze, imp "Biloxi" . . . 1,400.00
4½", bulbous, large dimples, medium to spinach green glaze, sponged dark blue-green overglaze, diestamped "GEOHR Biloxi, Miss" . . 425.00

OLD IVORY
84

OLD IVORY CHINA

History: Old Ivory derives its name from the background color of the china. It was made in Silesia, Germany, during the second half of the 19th century. Marked pieces usually have a pattern number (pattern names are not common) and the crown Silesia mark.

Reference: Susan and Al Bagdade, *Warman's English & Continental Pottery & Porcelain, 1st Edition*, Warman Publishing Co., Inc., 1987.

Berry Bowl, #22, 10" 75.00
Berry Set
#11, 5 pcs 135.00
#73, 5 pcs 140.00
#82, 7 pcs 300.00

Relish Dish, 6¾" l, #15, $45.00.

Biscuit Jar, cov, #16 .... **175.00**
Bowl
  #16, 9½" **55.00**
  #84, 6", tab handle **60.00**
Cake Plate
  #22, 10" **75.00**
  #121 .... **100.00**
Celery Tray, No. 78, 9¼" l **62.00**
Chocolate Pot, #15 .... **275.00**
Chocolate Set, #73, marked "Silesia,"
  13 pcs **700.00**
Cup and Saucer
  #15 .... **45.00**
  #202 .... **35.00**
Plate
  #16, 7½" **25.00**
  #75, 6" **15.00**
  #VIII, 8", floral dec **50.00**
  #XI, 6" **15.00**
Platter, #22, 11½", holly dec **100.00**
Sugar, cov, #84 .... **50.00**
Toothpick, #75 .... **85.00**

OLD PARIS CHINA

History: Old Paris china is fine quality porcelain made by various French factories located in and about Paris during the 18th and 19th centuries. Some pieces were marked, but the majority was not. Characteristics of this type of china include fine porcelain, beautiful decorations and gilding. Favorite colors were dark maroon, deep cobalt blue, and a deep green.

Reference: Susan and Al Bagdade, *Warman's English & Continental Pottery & Porcelain, 1st Edition,* Warman Publishing Co., Inc., 1987.

Additional Listing: Continental China and Porcelain (General).

Basket, reticulated, white and gold
  dec,1825–30 .... **1,300.00**

Plate, 8⅛" d, pale blue-gray border, multicolored center with boy and girl, $50.00.

Cake Stand, Honore style, green border, 1840–50 .... **175.00**
Coffeepot, reserve landscape scene,
  beaded band, gilt ground **400.00**
Cologne Bottle, rect, stopper, green
  ground, 1840–60 .... **550.00**
Dessert Service, cov coffeepot, cov
  sugar, creamer, eight cups and saucers, eight fruit plates, serving plate,
  and waste bowl, floral, c1850–60 .. **150.00**
Fruit Bowl, reticulated, ftd, c1820 .... **80.00**
Inkstand, floral, orig inkwell and sander,
  1850–60 .... **650.00**
Plate
  9¼" d, flower basket center, gilt line
    and borders, ochre ground, c1830,
    pr **220.00**
  9⅜" d, greyhound, rabbit, figures on
    horses scene center, diamond and
    leaf design, gilt border, c1830 ... **130.00**
Presentation Cup, inscribed "Aus Dank-
  bar Keit," c1815 .... **50.00**
Sauce Tureen, cov, floral dec, ftd, c1850 **150.00**
Soup Plate, gold anhd white dec, set of
  12, 1865–70 .... **225.00**
Tureen, cov, pomegranate finials, c1850 **140.00**
Urn, cov, 14½" h, painted hunting
  scenes, molded acanthus and palmette scrolled double handle, gilt border, sq plinth base, pr **1,000.00**
Vase
  12¼" h, painted, flared, c1855–65 .. **175.00**
  13¼" h, floral, two handles, 1850–60 **1,300.00**
  15¼" h, embellished snail, c1860 .. **700.00**

OLD SLEEPY EYE

History: Sleepy Eye, a Sioux Indian chief who reportedly had a droopy eye, gave his name to Sleepy Eye, Minnesota, and one of its leading flour mills. In the early 1900s Old Sleepy Eye Flour offered four Flemish gray heavy stoneware premiums, decorated in cobalt blue: a straight-sided butter crock, curved salt bowl, stein, and vase. The premiums were made by Weir Pottery Company, later to become Monmouth Pottery Company, and finally to emerge as the present-day Western Stoneware Company of Monmouth, Illinois.

Additional pottery and stoneware pieces were issued. Forms included five sizes of pitchers (4, 5½, 6½, 8, and 9 inches), mugs, steins, sugar bowls, and tea tiles (hot plates). Most were cobalt blue on white, but other glaze hues, such as browns, golds, and greens, were used.

Old Sleepy Eye also issued many other items, including bakers' caps, lithographed barrel covers, beanies, fans, multicolored pillow tops, postcards, trade cards, etc. Production of Old Sleepy Eye stoneware ended in 1937.

In 1952 Western Stoneware Company made a 22 and 40 ounce stein in chestnut brown glaze with a redesigned Indianhead. From 1961 to 1972 gift editions, dated and signed with a Maple Leaf mark, were made for the Board of Directors and others within the company. Beginning in 1973, Western Stoneware Company issued an annual limited edition stein, marked and dated, for collectors.

Reference: Elinor Meugnoit, *Old Sleepy Eye*, published by author, 1979.

Collectors' Club: Old Sleepy Eye Collectors Club, Box 12, Monmouth, IL 61462. *Sleepy Eye Newsletter* (bimonthly).

Reproduction Alert: Blue and white pitchers, crazed, weighted, and often with a stamp or the word "Ironstone" are the most copied. The stein and salt bowl also have been made. Many reproductions come from Taiwan.

A line of fakes, new items which never existed, includes an advertising pocket mirror with miniature flour barrel label, small glass plates, fruit jars, toothpick holders, glass and pottery miniature pitchers, and salt and pepper shakers. One mill item has been made, a sack marked as though it were old but of a size that could not possibly hold the amount of flour indicated.

MILL ITEMS

Button, pinback, "Old Sleepy Eye For Me," chief bust portrait	150.00
Cookbook	
"Sleepy Eye Flour Mills/Cookbook," chief bust portrait, sq shape	250.00
"Sleepy Eye Milling Co," chief portrait, bread loaf shape	125.00
Demitasse Spoon, roses in bowl	135.00
Dough Scraper, wood handle with "Sleepy Eye Flour," tin blade	250.00
Label, barrel, "Hummer Flour," two hummingbirds around flowers, lithograph, round, 196 lbs	250.00
Letter Opener, bronze, Indian head on handle, marked "Sleepy Eye Milling co, Sleepy Eye, Minn"	750.00
Sheet Music, "Sleepy Eye," lyrics by Mark Hawkins, music by Hall Parks	200.00
Teaspoon, SP, Indian on handle, Unity	85.00
Trade Cards, framed, set of 10	1,500.00

OLD SLEEPY EYE CLUB CONVENTION ITEMS

Barrel, 1982	55.00
Membership pin, 1977	50.00
Mug, 1976	210.00
Pitcher, 1983	90.00

POTTERY AND STONEWARE

Mug, 4¼", blue bands	170.00
Pitcher	
4", blue and white	150.00

Vase, 9", blue and gray bullrush dec, $250.00.

5¼", blue on yellow, Indian head on handle	700.00
9", blue and white	230.00
Stein	
7¾"	
Blue on white, 1907–37	260.00
Brown on white	825.00
Director's, blue on white, 1968 to 1973	175.00
Sugar Bowl, 4" h, cobalt blue on white, 1906–37	360.00
Tea Tile, cobalt blue and white	1,000.00
Vase, blue on white	170.00

ONION MEISSEN

History: The blue onion or bulb pattern is of Chinese origin and depicts peaches and pomegranates, not onions. It was first made in the 18th century by Meissen, hence the name Onion Meissen.

Factories in Europe, Japan, and elsewhere copied the pattern. Many still have the pattern in production, including the Meissen factory now located in East Germany.

Note: Prices given are for pieces produced between 1870 and 1930. Many pieces are marked with a company's logo; after 1891 the country of origin is indicated on imported pieces. Early Meissen examples bring a high premium.

Bowl
9" w, sq slotted corners, gold edge, pre 1900	275.00
11 x 2½", round, gold edge, pre 1900	165.00

Soup Plate, 9¾″ d, scalloped edge, marked "Meissen," with a star, late, $45.00.

Box, cov, 4 x 4¼″, round, rose finial . .	70.00
Candlesticks, 7″, pr	75.00
Creamer and Sugar, gold edge, c1900, 3 pcs	175.00
Cup and Saucer, 2 pcs	65.00
Demitasse Cup and Saucer, gold edge, c1900, set of 7	55.00
Dinner Service, service for six, plus serving dishes, candlesticks, coffeepot, and teapot, 65 pcs	3,000.00
Dish, 7¾″ l, oval, marked	70.00
Funnel	50.00
Fruit Knives, set of 6	75.00
Meat Pounder, large	75.00
Melon Mold, handled	30.00
Mustard Pot, 4¾″, ladle and underplate	50.00
Pie Crust Crimper, wooden handle . . .	25.00
Plate	
5½″, marked	12.00
8½″, marked	25.00
9″, leaf shape	75.00
9¾″, marked	40.00
10″	75.00
14″	80.00
Platter	
12″, oval, marked	65.00
15 x 10″	75.00
17″, marked	225.00
21″ l, oval, mid 19th C	425.00
Pot de Creme	45.00
Salt and Pepper	40.00
Scoop, 9″ l	35.00
Serving Dish, butterfly shape, two sections, handle in center	225.00
Skimmer, reticulated, curved shape . .	60.00
Soup Tureen, marked	170.00
Tea Strainer, wooden handle	20.00
Teapot, 10″, mid 20th C	325.00
Tile	35.00
Tray, 15 x 9″, rect, flat, mid 20th C . . .	165.00

Vase, 6½″, bud	65.00
Vegetable, cov, 10″, sq	125.00

OPALESCENT GLASS

History: Opalescent glass is a clear or colored glass with milky white decorations which show a fiery or opalescent quality when held to light. The effect was achieved by applying bone ash chemicals to designated areas while a piece was still hot and then refiring it at tremendous heat.

There are three basic categories of opalescent glass: (1) Blown (or mold blown) patterns, e.g., Daisy & Fern and Spanish Lace; (2) Novelties, pressed glass patterns made in limited pieces which often included unusual shapes such as Corn or Trough; and (3) Pattern (pressed) glass.

Opalescent glass was produced in England in the 1870s. Northwood began the American production in 1897 at its Indiana, Pennsylvania, plant. Jefferson, National Glass, Hobbs, and Fenton soon followed.

Reference: William Heacock, *Encyclopedia of Victorian Colored Pattern Glass, Book II, Opalescent Glass from A to Z, Second Edition,* Antique Publications, 1977; William Heacock and William Gamble, *Encyclopedia of Victorian Colored Pattern Glass, Book 9, Cranberry Opalescent from A to Z,* Antique Publications, 1987.

Additional Listings: See Pattern Glass for pressed opalescent patterns.

Bowl, 9″ d, Spanish Lace, ruffled, flared rim, vaseline, $60.00.

BLOWN

Bowl, Poinsettia, clear, ruffled, ftd	55.00
Bride's Basket, Bubble Lattice, cranberry	150.00
Butter Dish, cov, Chyrsanthemum Base Swirl, cranberry	275.00
Castor Set, Opalescent Stripe, four bottles, cranberry opal cruet	250.00

Celery Vase
  Daffodil, blue **60.00**
  Reverse Swirl, canary yellow **35.00**
  Swirl, blue **75.00**
Cruet
  Hobbs Hobnail, cranberry, orig stop-
    per **300.00**
  Polka Dot, cranberry, orig stopper .. **300.00**
  Ribbed Opal Lattice, cranberry, orig
    stopper **245.00**
  Seaweed, blue, orig stopper **125.00**
  Spanish Lace, canary yellow, orig
    stopper **160.00**
  Stripe, blue, 6¾" h, applied blue han-
    dle, cut faceted blue stopper ... **125.00**
Finger Bowl, Chrysanthemum Base
  Swirl, cranberry **40.00**
Miniature Lamp, Snowflake, cranberry,
  Smith #186 .... **850.00**
Mustard Jar, Reverse Swirl, cranberry . **60.00**
Pitcher
  Lemonade, Hobbs Hobnail, vaseline **245.00**
  Water
    Buttons and Braids, cranberry ... **300.00**
    Paneled Sprig, cranberry **200.00**
    Poinsettia, blue, tankard, bulbous
      base **160.00**
    Seaweed, cranberry **275.00**
Punch Cup, Chrysanthemum Base
  Swirl, cranberry **35.00**
Rose Bowl, Swirl, canary yellow **40.00**
Salt Shaker
  Daisy and Fern, swirl, cranberry, orig
    top, Northwood **85.00**
  Diagonal Stripe, rubina, threaded
    opal stripes, orig lid **65.00**
Spooner, Reverse Swirl, blue **70.00**
Sugar, cov, Seaweed, cranberry **200.00**

Sugar Shaker
  Bubble Lattice, rubina **250.00**
  Inverted Fern, cranberry **200.00**
  Opal Lattice, cranberry **200.00**
  Paneled Sprig, cranberry **175.00**
  Ring Neck Coinspot, cranberry, orig
    top **120.00**
  Spanish Lace, blue, orig top **140.00**

Syrup
  Daisy and Fern, cranberry **240.00**
  Reverse Swirl, blue **150.00**
  Spanish Lace, vaseline, orig spring lid **325.00**
  Windows, blue **175.00**
Toothpick Holder
  Polka Dot, cranberry **75.00**
  Ribbed Lattice, blue **95.00**
  Swirl, cranberry **90.00**
Tumbler
  Button and Braids, blue **35.00**
  Daisy and Fern, cranberry **32.50**
  Paneled Sprig, cranberry **45.00**
  Poinsettia, cranberry **40.00**
  Stars and Stripes, cranberry **65.00**

Water Bottle, Reverse Swirl, cranberry
  opal, satin, 7" h **150.00**
Water Set, pitcher and six tumblers
  Polka Dot, cranberry **400.00**
  Spanish Lace, green **500.00**

NOVELTIES

Barber Bottle
  Polka Dot, blue **110.00**
  Stars and Stripes, blue **150.00**
  Swirl Stripe, cranberry, bulbous ... **145.00**
Basket, blue, oblong shape, indented
  hobs, clear thorn handle, c1920, 7 x
  6" **125.00**
Bowl, blue, shallow scalloped edge,
  strawberries and flowers pattern, 9⅝"
  d **75.00**
Bride's Bowl, blue, hobnail, ruffled top,
  10" d, 4½" h **55.00**
Curtain Tiebacks, pewter posts, pr ... **85.00**
Ewer, Striped Opal, vaseline, flattened
  bulbous shape, pink applied flowers,
  amber applied leaves and handle .. **140.00**
Plate, Wishbone and Drape, green ... **20.00**
Vase
  Aurora Borealis, blue **40.00**
  Piasa Bird, blue **50.00**
  Tree Trunk, green, 10¾" **35.00**

OPALINE GLASS

History: Opaline glass was a popular mid to late 19th century European glass. The glass has a certain amount of translucency and often is found decorated in enamel designs and trimmed in gold.

Mug, 4" h, white ground, cobalt blue trim, French, $100.00.

Basket
  6", white, gold trim, blue snake encir-
    cles handle, shiny ext., satin int. . **180.00**
  8 x 8", ftd, French green **45.00**

Bowl

3½", hat, fluted top, deep blue, white
  enamel dec **70.00**
8 x 4", yellow **75.00**
9", cov, ftd, enamel floral dec **60.00**

Box, cov

4", French green, hinged lid, gilt metal
  mountings **60.00**
6½", blue, floral enamel, tulip finial . **50.00**

Cologne Bottle, green, enamel
  beading, gilt scrolls, matching stopper **80.00**

Creamer, green, Wheat and Rushes
  pattern **42.00**

Cruet, 7", pink, tulip shaped stopper, applied opaque handle **200.00**

Epergne, three trumpet vases, blue .. **200.00**

Finger Bowl and Underplate, blue **70.00**

Goblet

5", white **25.00**
7", blue **35.00**

Inkwell, 3", Louis XVI, gilt bronze
  mountings, broken column shape,
  periwinkle blue shaft and leaf tip
  molded base **200.00**

Mug, Bird and Wheat pattern **40.00**

Perfume Bottle

4⅜", gold bronze filigree overlay collar and hinged cap, French, pr ... **200.00**
8½", pink, pr **300.00**

Pickle Castor, cov, green insert, SP ormolu frame, c1880 .... **175.00**

Pitcher, 7", hp, cherubs, artist sgd,
  stamped 1873 Paris Exposition **275.00**

Plate, 9¾", white scalloped edge, gilt
  trim **30.00**

Ring Tree, pale pink **75.00**

Rose Bowl, 3" d, hp **42.00**

Soap Dish, cov, blue, hp, floral dec ... **75.00**

Tumbler, 4½", white, 18th C equestrian
  figure, gilt trim **40.00**

Vase

5½", globular, slender neck, pink and
  yellow flowers, green leaves **100.00**
6¾", mauve, gold trim, French, pr .. **170.00**
9", bulbous, slender neck, dark green
  enameled floral dec, mint green
  ground, pr **125.00**
9½", bulbous, hp, peacock and flowers, beaded pedestal base, gold
  trim **175.00**

ORIENTAL RUGS

History: The history of oriental rugs or carpets
dates back to 3,000 B.C.; but, it was in the 16th
century that they became prevalent. The rugs originated in the regions of Central Asia, Iran (Persia),
Caucasus, and Anatolia. Early rugs can be classified into basic categories: Iranian, Caucasian,
Turkoman, Turkish, and Chinese. Later India, Pak-
istan, and Iraq produced rugs in the oriental style.

The pattern name is derived from the tribe which
produced the rug, e.g., Iran is the source for Ha-
madan, Herez, Sarouk, Tabriz, and others.

When evaluating an oriental rug, age, design,
color, weave, knots per square inch, and condition
determine the final value. Silk rugs and prayer rugs
bring higher prices.

References: Murray Island, *Oriental Rugs,
Third Edition,* New York Graphic Society; Linda
Kline, *Beginner's Guide To Oriental Rugs,* Ross
Books, 1980; Ivan C. Neff and Carol V. Maggs,
Dictionary of Oriental Rugs, Van Nostrand Rein-
hold Company, 1979.

Reproduction Alert: Beware! There are repainted rugs on the market.

Afshar, 6' 11" x 4' 11", ivory field, allover
  pattern of stylized palmettes, navy
  blue, rust, and gold, navy blue primary border of cartouches and running dog guard borders, c1930 .... **1,800.00**

Aubusson, 6' 11" x 5' 11", medium blue
  ground, ivory stepped medallion with
  floral spray and salmon floral arrangements, ivory primary border of
  floral design, four guard borders,
  backed, c1900 .... **6,000.00**

Baktiari, bag, 3' 10" x 3' 3", mixed techniques, Soumac woven ground, horizontal rows of stylized animals and
  geometric devices, pile woven skirt of
  latchhook octagons, early 20th C .. **450.00**

Bessarabian, 8' 5" x 6', allover pattern
  of multicolored hexagons and
  stepped medallions, beige primary
  border with florals, repairs, c1890 .. **5,000.00**

Caucasian

5' x 3', white ground, dark blue border,
  19th C **2,250.00**
8' x 5', red ground, figures, blue border, 20th C **4,500.00**
9' 8" x 4', blue ground, red, brown
  foliage, floral border, 19th C **3,500.00**

Chinese, 19' 3" x 10' 2", navy blue
  ground, center dragon and floral
  spray medallion, medium blue border
  of dragons, clouds, and Chinese symbols, c1920 .... **4,000.00**

Daghestan, 6' 3" x 3' 2", ivory ground,
  allover pattern of multicolored shield
  devices and serrated leaves, ivory
  primary border of hexagons, pair of
  chocolate dec guard borders, c1875 **21,000.00**

Gorovan, 7' 6" x 11' 6", room size ... **2,200.00**

Heriz, 12' 7" x 22' 9", white field, pole
  medallion, stepped dark blue spandrels and flowers, stylized cedar each
  corner, dark blue primary border, blue
  and red guard borders **20,000.00**

Karaja, 4' x 12' 10", runner **1,600.00**

Kashan, 4' 8" x 3' 5", prayer, silk, gold
  ground, asymmetrical design, trees of

Heriz, 100″ × 133″, midnight blue waterbug palmette and vine border, red field, large angular medallion anchored in fan palmettes, extending to stylized flowers and leaves, ivory and red spandrels, $3,750.00.

life, various flowers and birds, center scalloped cartouche, suspended lamp, two similar cartouches at top, navy blue primary border with ivory cartouches of animals and structures, pair of narrow dec guards, 1,200 knots per sq inch, c1920 . . . . **35,000.00**

Kazak

    5′ 1″ x 4′, prayer rug, tomato red ground, ivory lozenge with green and red latchwork medallion leading to prayer niche, ivory primary border of octagons and two reciprocal trefoil guard borders, minor crease wear **3,000.00**

    7′ 7″ x 4′ 4″, brick-red ground, three stepped medallions, medium blue and chocolate, latchhook diamonds, geometric devices, and birds surrounded by brown primary border of reciprocal "E" design, reciprocal trefoil border, three barberpole guard borders, Armenian weaver's inscription and date, early 20th C **4,000.00**

Kilim

    2′ 3″ x 4′ 6″, aqua, white, and tan, wear **35.00**

    4′ 8″ x 6′ 5″, yellow, green and salmon, wear **90.00**

Kirman

    5′ x 8″, bound edges, wear, sgd . . . **500.00**

    9′ 6″ x 13′ 9″, rose ground, floral design **2,700.00**

Kuba, runner, 10′ 2″ x 4′ 1″, gold ground, allover pattern of stylized floral design, ivory primary border of slant leaf and wine glass pattern, three dec guard borders, wear and repair along selvedges, late 19th C **5,000.00**

Ladrik, prayer rug, 5′ 5″ x 3′ 4″, brickred ground, hooked ivory prayer niche with stylized floral devices, brick-red panel of tulips, teal blue primary border of stylized lilies and rosettes, two meandering vine guard borders, wear, loss to guard borders and repairs, c1800 . . . . **3,800.00**

Mahal Wagireh, 4′ 10″ x 4′ 4″, brick-red ground, sparsely scattered pattern of vines and flowers, medium blue, gold, and green, gold meandering vine border, c1900 . . . . **1,200.00**

Northwest Persian, runner, 12′ 1″ x 3′ 8″, rust ground, stylized vines, palmettes, animals, and human figures, chocolate primary border of serrated leaves and rosettes, two narrow dec guard borders, early 20th C **2,000.00**

Ottoman, 5′ x 3′ 1″, prayer rug, silk and metal thread embroidery, cream ground, stylized palmettes and floral sprays, oblong panel of flowering vines, primary border of red and blue flowers, pair of boxed flower guard borders, backed, early 19th C **1,500.00**

Sarouk, 7′ x 4′ 8″, midnight blue ground, claret scalloped center medallion, various floral sprays, brick-red spandrels surrounded by midnight blue primary border of palmettes, two pairs of narrow dec guard borders, c1920 **2,000.00**

Serabend, 4′ 7″ x 6′ 5″, madder rose field of small boteh, blue corners, green primary border **750.00**

Tabriz

    4′ 6″ x 7′ 3″, tree with birds, replaced fringe **1,850.00**

    8′ 2″ x 10′ 8″, ivory ground, central trees, flowers, birds, leopards, monkeys, and other animal designs, seven borders **5,500.00**

    8′ 9″ x 11′ 10″, ivory field, repeating arabesques of red and blue vine and floral designs, wine red border, sgd **6,500.00**

Ziegler Mahal, 15′ 8″ x 12′ 4″, ivory ground, allover pattern of meandering vines and palmettes, rust primary border of palmettes and rosettes, pair of narrow dec guard borders, c1890 . . **13,000.00**

ORIENTALIA

History: Orientalia is a term used to apply to objects made in the Orient, which encompasses the Far East, Asia, China, and Japan. The diversity of cultures produced a variety of objects and styles.

Reference: Sandra Andacht, *Oriental Antiques & Art: An Identification And Value Guide*, Wallace-Homestead, 1987; John Esten (editor), *Blue and White China*, Little, Brown, and Company, 1987.

Periodical: *The Orientalia Journal, P. O. Box 94, Little Neck, NY 11363. Bimonthly newsletter.*

Additional Listings: Canton, Celadon, Cloisonne, Fitzhugh, Nanking, Netsukes, Rose Medallion, Japanese Prints, and other categories.

Basket, Japanese, ovoid body, vertical ribs, short everted rim, flared base, two ring handles, woven, sgd "Chinkusei," 8½" h **350.00**

Bird Cage, Japanese, lacquer and bamboo, rounded rect form, stylized gold waves, black ground, sculpted cabriole legs, 15" h, 13 x 9½" **3,200.00**

Biscuit Bowl, Chinese, Kangxi period and mark, three enameled yellow, aubergine, and pale green flower bouquets ext., divided by butterflies, engraved pair dragons chasing flaming pearl, 6" d **935.00**

Bowl
 Chinese, Junyao, Yuan Dynasty, conical sides, robin's egg blue mottled glaze, shades of purple edge, light brown rim, buff foot, 4¼" d **450.00**
 Japanese
  Arita, landscape, blue and white, 10" **100.00**
  Kutani, 19th C, hp, all-over bird and floral motif, sgd, 12" d **300.00**
 Korean, Koryo Dynasty, imp floral motif, double line border, molded celadon, 7" **300.00**

Brush Pot, Chinese, Kangxi period, Famille Verte, cylindrical, painted scholar and attendants, terrace and mountain scene, 5¼" h **1,800.00**

Carrying Case, Japanese, 19th C, brown and gilt, flower roundels dec, brown ground, 19 x 13 x 20½" **2,750.00**

Censer, Chinese, Ming Dynasty, gilt bronze, bulbous, five quatrefoil shaped floral reserved lobes, floral and leaf handles, reticulated cov with floral sprig handle, stippled ground, 4¼" h **800.00**

Charger, Imari, center bird and palm tree dec, 15¾" d **55.00**

Chest, Chinese, 19th C, rect, cloisonne mounts inlaid in mother-of-pearl, carnelian, and jade, front opening reveals five drawers, 9 x 18 x 14" . . . **3,000.00**

Clothing
 Kimono, Japanese, stitched bats and waves, blue, green, and orange, black ground, 61" **250.00**
 Jacket, Chinese, silk
  Coral, 19th C, counted stitch dec

on gauze, pavilion and landscapes scenes, embroidered white silk sleeve borders with figures, and garden setting, 34½" . **825.00**

 Turquoise, 19th/20th C, embroidered exotic birds, butterflies, and seasonal flowers, cloud collar dec, 38" **440.00**

Robe, Chinese, 19th C, silk, apricot, embroidered peonies and butterflies, Peking knot, white silk sleeve bands, 47" l **495.00**

Dish
 Chinese, Kangxi, blue and white, figures and garden setting dec, surrounded by diaper band, floral sprigs medallions, sprigs rim, 8½" d **385.00**

 Japanese, Kakiemon, 18th/19th C, scattered pinecone and needle dec ext., deer biting maple branch int. in blue, green, red, yellow, and black enamels, 8⅜" d **950.00**

Document Box, Chinese, vellum painted black, gilded flowers, 7" h, 13 x 3" . . **100.00**

Fan, Japanese, peacocks motif, gilt lacquer, tasseled cords, guard sticks, 9¼" **600.00**

Figure
 Ascetic, Chinese, 17th/18th C, gilt bronze, seated, wearing long string of beads, wearing long flowing robe with incised floral dec hem, deep set eyes, 16½" h **6,600.00**

 Bodhisattva, Japanese, Northern Qi/Sui Dynasty, 6th C, raised worn left hand, right hand holding rosary, diaphanous robe overlaid with ribbon-tied sashes, serene face, flame shaped nimbus, lotus pedestal, rect base, pigment traces, 11½" h, extensive restoration **1,450.00**

 Elephant, Japanese, 19th/20th C, bronze, ivory tusks, sgd, 12½" l . . . **400.00**

 Guanyin, Chinese, lacquered wood, twin chignon and crown, sculpted robes, mounted as lamp, 22" h . . **2,500.00**

 Tiger, Japanese, bronze, head turned to right, outstretched tail, mid stride, name cartouche, 19" l **385.00**

 Wen Ti, Chinese, Ming Dynasty, seated, animal resting by feet, black and brown features, hair, robes, and armor, 8¼" h **300.00**

Funerary Jar, Chinese, ovoid body, bands of sprigged figures around the shoulder, repeated around lid, finial, spotty green glaze, 20" h **500.00**

Furniture
 Altar coffer, Chinese, Huanghuali, rect top, mitered frame floating panel, two drawers with paktong

plate and bail handle, recessed panel above rect apron with flange brackets, cylindrical legs, 32 x 21½ x 46½" **6,875.00**

Basin Stand, Chinese, 16/17th C, six hinged legs, joined by upper and lower stretcher, 26¼" h **880.00**

Bench, Chinese, Hongmu, rect top, split cylindrical rod seat, legs joined by stretcher, 15½ x 12¼ x 32½" . **1,870.00**

Cabinet

Chinese, 17th C, black lacquer and hardstone, rect case, flowering branches and birds scene mounted doors, inlaid in quartz, serpentine, malachite and mother-of-pearl, dec hardstone paneled sides, two fitted drawers and shelve int., 55 x 16½ x 33¼" **3,300.00**

Korean, late 19th C, elmwood, 4 doors with stringing border, figured front, pierced brass mounts, 32¼" h **850.00**

Chair, Chinese, Huali, arm, rect splat with carved cloud scroll medallion, horseshoe back, cane seat, beaded apron **660.00**

Jewelry Cabinet, Japanese, 19th C, lacquer, front rickshaw scene, birds on sides, center doors, top and bottom drawers **650.00**

Screen, Chinese

Eight-fold, 18th C, brown coromandel lacquer, warrior scene beside pavilion, exotic birds border, reverse with numerous birds and plants, 82¾" h **12,650.00**

Eleven-fold, 19th C, hardwood, rect panels with mountainous village landscape scenes, picked out kingfisher feathers in various tones, confronting dragons top panel border, flowers below, 47½" h **9,900.00**

Settee, Chinese, Hongmu, 19th C, rect spindle back with three circular entwined dragons medallions, solid panel seat, cylindrical legs, box stretcher, 35" w **4,675.00**

Stool, Chinese, Huanghuali, 17th/18th C, rect top, cane seat, legs with hoof feet, joined by high box stretcher and transverse brace, retains some orig lacquer, 17¼ x 17½" **770.00**

Table

Chinese, coffee, rect top, five inset porcelain panels, painted with landscape, figural, and garden scenes, famille-rose colors, incurving legs **2,860.00**

Japanese, low, lacquer, cinnabar,

rect top, carved swirling waves with florals and leaves, keyfret pattern band, rounded notched corners, cabriole legs, carved shaped apron, 23 x 16½ x 8" .. **600.00**

Work Table, Chinese, c1830, black lacquer, landscape, figural, and floral design dec, oval paneled doors, swan neck pediment above, removable hinged writing box, cabriole legs with claw feet, fitted drawers and doors int., 59 x 25 x 24¼" **4,125.00**

Ginger Jar, 6½" h, red and green, circular lid, internal seal, $65.00.

Ginger Jar, 19th C, porcelain, blue and white, all-over floral motif, carved teak domical lid, 14" h **250.00**

Jar, Chinese, Kangxi period, Famille Verte, ovoid form, underglaze blue and enamels dec, children and ladies, garden and palace scene, pierced wood lid, jade inset, 8" h **6,000.00**

Libation Cup, 18th C, carved rhinoceros horn, ruyi fungus and bamboo stalks and leaves, light honey color, 3⅝" h **1,800.00**

Mask, Japanese, "No," demon, painted black and red **80.00**

Roof Tile, Chinese, Ming Dynasty, pottery, scholar wearing turquoise robe, aubergine borders, holds open book, glazed, 14" h **990.00**

Tea Caddy, Japanese, pottery, silver dragon and phoenix overlay, red ground **100.00**

Temple Gong, Japanese, deep bowl form, inscribed and dated 1684, fitted Chinese rosewood stand, iris dec, 14" **300.00**

Textile, Chinese

Cushion Cover, satin stitched center, scrolling lotus and swooping bats, pairs of dragons on sides, yellow,

green, blue, and coral, metallic
thread detailing, 59¾ x 50" **2,860.00**
Scroll, Qianlong, silk, embroidered,
satin stitch, bird and flowering prunus tree, some blossoms sewn with
seed pearls, peach, white, ream,
blue, and green, framed, 35 x 17½" **1,650.00**
Tray, Chinese, 19th C, marble and huali,
fret border, 15" w **1,045.00**
Tripod Censer, Chinese, late Ming dynasty, Guan type, cylindrical body, tab
feet cov with lavender-gray glaze,
crackle, 4" d **450.00**
Trunk, Japanese, 19th C, rect, raised
gold and brown lacquer, 3 friends,
pine, bamboo, and flowering prunus
designs, brown ground, black lacquer
int., 13½ x 23 x 16" **7,500.00**
Urn, Japanese, Jomon period, conical
body, buff clay, imp rope dec, three
twisted peak grooved rim, four vertical
carved grooves, 15" h **800.00**
Vase
Chinese
Peacock blue, ovoid body, slightly
flaring neck, cov with turquoise
glaze, mounted as lamp, 30" h . **850.00**
Powder blue, 19th C, peacocks
amid rock and flowering plants
dec, gilt, mounted as lamp, 32" h **1,100.00**
Japanese, 19th C, thousand face motif dec, two foo dog mounted handles, 18" h **300.00**
Wash Basin, Japanese, circular body,
lacquer, central horizontal rib, straight
sided, scrolling leafy tendril dec ext.,
3 supports, 19" d **500.00**

OVERSHOT GLASS

History: Overshot glass was developed in the
mid-1800s. A gather of molten glass was rolled
over the marver upon which had been placed
crushed glass to produce overshot glass. The
piece then was blown into the desired shape. The
finished effect was a glass that was frosted or iced
in appearance.

Early pieces mainly were made in clear. As the
demand for colored glass increased, color was
added to the base piece and occasionally to the
crushed glass.

Pieces of overshot generally are attributed to
the Boston and Sandwich Glass Co., although
many other companies also made it as it grew in
popularity.

Basket
4⅞" d, 5⅜" h, amethyst shading to
clear, emb melon ribs, ruffled, applied clear twisted handle **115.00**

**Bowl, 6" d, amberina, hexagonal,
$85.00.**

6" d, 7½" h, orange shaded to vaseline, octagonal, emb nubs on sides,
applied vaseline handle **200.00**
Cruet, rubena, applied clear reeded
handle, clear faceted cut stopper .. **175.00**
Fairy Lamp, 3" d, 4½" h, figural, crown
shape, clear marked "Clarke" base,
made for Queen Victoria's 1887 Jubilee
Cranberry **200.00**
Royal blue **185.00**
Pitcher
7" h, light blue, applied red-amber
handle **100.00**
7¼" h, 4¾" d, ice blue, bulbous, round
mouth, blue applied handle **135.00**
7¾", peachblow color, applied clear
handle, attributed to Mt Washington **200.00**
11¼" h, 5⅛" d, cranberry, ice bladder,
clear spun rope applied handle .. **375.00**
Rose Bowl, 3¾", rubena, applied flowers and pale green leaves **125.00**
Sugar Shaker, pink **100.00**

OWENS POTTERY

History: J. B. Owens began making pottery in
1885 near Roseville, Ohio. In 1891 he built a plant
in Zanesville and in 1897 began producing art
pottery. Not much art pottery was produced by
Owens after 1907, when most of their production
centered on tiles.

Owens Pottery, employing many of the same
artists and designs of its two crosstown rivals,

Roseville and Weller, can appear very similar to that of its competitors (i.e. Utopian—brown glaze; Lotus—light glaze; Aqua Verde—green glaze, etc.).

There were a few techniques used exclusively at Owens. These included Red Flame ware (slip decoration under a high red glaze) and Mission (over-glaze, slip decorations in mineral colors) depicting Spanish Mission scenes. Other specialities included Opalesce (semi-gloss designs in lustred gold and orange) and Coralene (small beads affixed to the surface of the decorated vases).

References: Paul Evans, *Art Pottery of the United States, 2nd Edition,* Feingold & Lewis Publishing Corp., 1987; Ralph and Terry Kovel, *The Kovels' Collector's Guide to American Art Pottery,* Crown Publishers, Inc., 1974.

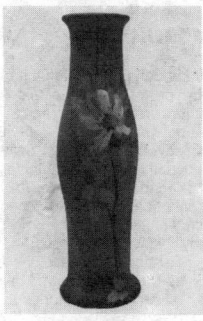

Vase, 13½″, Utopian, matte, $300.00.

Ewer, 7 x 6½″, early standard glaze, Art Nouveau sterling silver overlay, cluster of yellow leaves and blackberries, brown ground, incised "1773," die stamped "O"	900.00
Jardiniere	
9 x 7½″, orange tulips, brown glaze .	120.00
24″, matching pedestal base, Utopian, matte, tulips, ruffled	310.00
Lamp, 13½″, red flowers, gold dec, gold bands at top and base, black high glaze, Sudanese	250.00
Plaque, 17 x 11¼″, cloisonne dec, landscape with stucco cottage, aubergine and pink accents, brown roof, green trees, golden-yellow road, cobalt blue pond, contemporary golden oak frame	1,100.00
Umbrella Stand, 20½″, large brown iris dec, brown and green leaves, matte finish	250.00
Vase	
8¼″, dark brown, woman's face, red	

roses, marked "Owens/Henri Deaux"	325.00
9″, matte green, floral design band, four small feet	115.00
10½″, brown glaze, berries	75.00
10½ x 4″, Utopian, ovoid, wild rose .	200.00

PAIRPOINT

History: The Pairpoint Manufacturing Co. was organized in 1880 as a silverplating firm in New Bedford, Massachusetts. The company merged with Mount Washington Glass Co. in 1894 and became the Pairpoint Corporation. The new company produced speciality glass items, often accented with metal frames.

Pairpoint Corp. was sold in 1938 and Robert Gunderson became manager. He operated it as the Gunderson Glass Works until his death in 1952. From 1952 until the plant closed in 1956, operations were maintained under the name Gunderson-Pairpoint. Robert Bryden reopened the glass manufacturing business in 1970, moving it back to the New Bedford area.

References: Leonard E. Padgett, *Pairpoint Glass,* Wallace-Homestead, 1979; John A. Shumann III, *The Collector's Encyclopedia of American Art Glass,* Collector Books, 1988.

Additional Listings: See *Warman's Americana & Collectibles* for listings of modern Pairpoint Cup Plates.

Basket, 11 x 9 x 6″, intaglio grapes, cherries, and peaches	165.00
Biscuit Jar, 7 x 6″, hp daisy dec, apricot bulbous base, sgd and numbered	300.00
Bowl, 11 x 3½″, SP, leaf shape, figural squirrel, gold wash int.	175.00
Box, hinged cov, 7¼″, scalloped oval, cream, heavy gold dec, sgd	425.00
Cake Basket, SP, figural leaves and branches, raised fruit, ftd, emb	85.00
Candlesticks, pr, 11½″, amber, crystal bubble ball stems, bell shaped base	175.00
Candy Dish, 6″, Auroria, engraved grapes, bubble ball finial	160.00
Cigarette Holder, 7½″, figural cupid, crystal holder, floral etching	75.00
Cocktail, Rouge Flambe, low, pr	135.00
Cologne Bottle	
5¾″, globular stopper, regular air traps	50.00
7″, green body, clear foot, faceted paperweight stopper	200.00
7½″, medium opaque blue, white flowers, faceted paperweight stopper	225.00
Compote	
6 x 6″, crystal, etched leaf and floral dec	100.00

Urn, 15½" h, **Garden of Allah scene, five figures, two camels on obverse, three flamingoes on reverse, Limoges blank decorated at Pairpoint, attributed to Albert Steffin, $6,000.00.**

6½ x 6¼", Nottingham pattern	**125.00**
8½", amber, raspberries and leaves	**100.00**
Console Set, 14" bowl, 12" candlesticks, light green, bubble ball stems, cut and etched Vintage dec	**350.00**
Cordial, 3¾", etched Vintage pattern, honeycomb dec, amber	**25.00**
Cup and Saucer, SP, bright cut floral, sgd	**50.00**
Dresser Box, SP, blown out roses, tennis racquet	**50.00**
Handkerchief Box, intaglio flowers, hinged lid	**325.00**
Inkwell, 2¾" d, crystal, hinged lid	**45.00**
Jewel Box, 4½ x 3½", ftd, painted porcelain, insert on cov, silk lining, marked	**250.00**
Lamp, table, 19½" h, 15" reverse painted frosted shade, New Bedford waterfront, whaling ships at sunset, turned wooden base, brass trim, sgd "H. Fisher"	**1,800.00**
Napkin Ring, flower, leaves, domed base	**50.00**
Paperweight, 4½", green engraved candlestick base, clear bubble ball .	**45.00**
Perfume Bottle, 6", octagonal, ribbed stopper	**80.00**
Platter, 12 x 8½", white ground, two flying mallard ducks in blue, gray, white, and gold highlights, blazing gold sun, gold tracery, cobalt blue border, sgd "Frank Guba, Limoges, Pairpoint"	**485.00**
Punch Cup, Carnaria pattern, engraved grapes	**38.50**
Sherbet, Rouge Flambe, low, pr	**100.00**
Syrup Pitcher, 6½", floral etching, SP feet and lid	**65.0⌐**

Toothpick Holder, SP, figural, bear standing by barrel	**100.00**
Tureen, 8 x 5¾ x 6½", cov, egg shell ground, chrysanthemums and foliage, raised gold, fish finial, sgd "Pairpoint Limoges 2502/50"	**485.00**
Vase	
8⅝", bud, irid amber, SP holder, sgd	**275.00**
10", apple green, applied handles, orig label	**100.00**
11", green luster, engraved vintage, ten prisms, clear bubble ball	**135.00**
12", opaque white, oval landscape, fruit blossoms and snowbirds dec	**500.00**
Wine, red bowl, black glass base	**75.00**
Wine Coaster, SP, pierced, Sheffield type dec	**40.00**

PAPERWEIGHTS

History: Although paperweights had their origin in ancient Egypt, it was in the mid-19th century that this art form reached its zenith. The classic period for paperweights was 1845–55 in France where the Clichy, Baccarat, and Saint Louis factories produced the finest examples of this art. Other weights made in England, Italy, and Bohemia during this period rarely matched the quality of the French weights.

In the early 1850s New England Glass Co. in Cambridge, Massachusetts, and the Boston and Sandwich Glass Co. in Sandwich, Massachusetts, became the first American factories to make paperweights.

Popularity peaked during the classic period and faded toward the end of the 19th century. Paperweights were rediscovered nearly a century later in the mid-1900s. Contemporary weights still are made by Baccarat, Saint Louis, Perthshire, and by many studio craftsmen in the U.S. and Europe.

References: Paul Hollister, Jr., *The Encyclopedia of Glass Paperweights,* Paperweight Press, 1969; Leo Kaplan, *Paperweights,* published by author, 1985; George N. Kulles, *Identifying Antique Paperweights-Lampwork,* Paperweight Press, 1987; James Mackay, *Glass Paperweights,* Facts on File, 1973; Edith Mannoni, *Classic French Paperweights,* Paperweight Press, 1984; L. H. Selman Ltd, *Collector's Paperweights: Price Guide and Catalogue,* Paperweight Press, 1986.

Additional Listings: See *Warman's Americana & Collectibles* for examples of advertising paperweights.

ANTIQUE

American, fly, 2" d, life size, moves, octagonal	**150.00**
Baccarat	
Clematis, double, deep red, honey-	

comb cane stamens, green leaves and stem, white lace ground, green and white millefiori cane border .. **3,600.00**

Faceted, 3″ d, 100 year telephone commemorative, sgd, dated 1976, numbered "32" **175.00**

Garland, 2⅞″, blue, white, and red cane garland, white and green cane central circle, coral and green star center **600.00**

Interlacing canes, 3¼″ d, blue, red, yellow, and white, white latticinio ground, sgd, dated 1976, numbered "13" **175.00**

Millefiori, 3⅛″, patterned, eleven butterfly silhouette canes, twelve blue, white, and red crow's foot canes, corrugated florets row, seven shamrock silhouettes row, upset muslin ground **1,800.00**

Triple cut, 3″ d, six facets, mushroom shape concentric canes, light blue to white to clear overlay **50.00**

Bohemian, millefiori, multicolored center canes, deep blue and white spoke ground **750.00**

Clichy

Chequer, 2½″, faceted, blue and white latticinio canes, six windows, two roses and cane rows **1,000.00**

Concentric setup canes, 1¾″ d, pink, white, green, red, and blue **200.00**

Floral, 2¾″, brilliant colored floral canes, mottled emerald green and white ground **7,250.00**

Trefoil, seven pastry mold and red and white millefiori canes, deep turquoise ground **2,650.00**

Commemorative type

Union Glass Company, Remember the Maine, 2⅝″ d, white ship, orange, blue, white, yellow, and pink ground **100.00**

Unknown maker

Abe Lincoln, 4½ x 3″, rect, frosted bust **25.00**

Columbus, 4½″ l, 3½″ w, rect, standing, holding globe, reverse gold painted figure and fluted sides outline **210.00**

General John J Pershing, 1917, 3⅞″ d, circular, bust, reverse painted gold **160.00**

Independence Hall, 4¾ x 3¼″, oval, clear and frosted **60.00**

The Grand Army of the Republic, 2½″ d, white and clear **35.00**

28th National G A R Encampment Pittsburgh Sept 1894, 3″ d, clear, frosted and acid etched ground **100.00**

English, 6¼″, mantel ornament, multicolored **75.00**

Millville, umbrella, 3¼″ d, red, white, blue, and green, ftd **100.00**

Mt. Washington, Poinsettia, 3½″ d, pink, green leaves, multicolored swirled mound **200.00**

New England Glass Company

Miniature, 1¾″, pale pink petaled flower with white stripes, green leaves and stem **875.00**

Mixed Fruit, 2⅞″, three apples alternating with four cherries, white latticinio swirl ground **375.00**

Pear, 2¼″, natural color, clear base . **300.00**

Sandwich

Broken cane

2½″ d, abstract position **450.00**

2⅝″, bits and pieces of canes ... **200.00**

Poinsettia, 2½″, jeweled, pink, green leaves and stem **1,750.00**

Val St Lambert, cut star design, ruby flash overlay, flowers and vines sides **350.00**

Whitefriars, English

Bottle, ink, 5¾″ h, c1850s **150.00**

Canes, concentric setup

3⅛″, white, green, blue, and pink . **125.00**

3¼″, pink, lavender, blue, and yellow **150.00**

Rings, 3⅞″, concentric, pastel, c1850s **75.00**

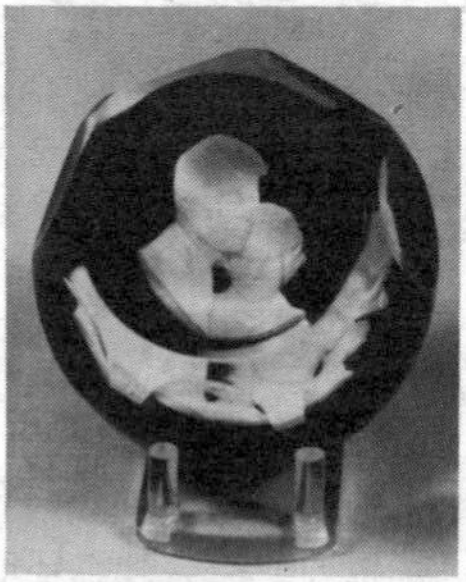

Modern, Cristal D'Albert, Jack and Jackie, emerald ground, paper label, $175.00.

MODERN

Ayotte, Rick

Robin, 1⅞″ d, perched on flowering dogwood **125.00**

Thrasher, 2⅛″ d, brown, perched on Cherokee rose **225.00**

Banford, Ray

Multifaceted, 2¾″ rose, white, and green **325.00**

Rose, 3¼″ d, pink, buds, green foliage **350.00**

Kaziun, Charles
  Pedestal
    1¾" h, 1³⁄₁₆" d, red flower, green
      leaves, gold shot green ground   350.00
    1¾" h, 1¼" d, lavender flower,
      green leaves, gold shot green
      ground 275.00
    1⅞" h, 1¼" d, yellow flower, green
      leaves, gold shot lavender
      ground 275.00
  Perthshire
    Square, 3" d, blue, red, green, yellow,
      and white, arranged as cross, sgd,
      dated 1979 . . . .   75.00
    Sunflower, 3" d, green, white, orange,
      and yellow, sgd dated 1979 . . . . .   75.00
  Saint Louis, faceted, 3" d, gold King Tut,
    blue ground, sgd base with cane,
    dated 1979 . . . .   100.00
  Smith, Gordon, clematis, 3⅛" d, red . .   250.00
  Stankard, Paul
    Bee, 3" d, landing on white flowering
      plant, pale blue ground, numbered
      "B632 1981" 1,200.00
    Faceted, 2¼" d, blue flowers, multiple
      buds, leaves, and stem, opaque
      white ground, numbered "1973/
      A329" 300.00
    Flower, 3¼" d, pink and white, green
      stems and leaves, sgd "Botanical
      Study A130 1980" 1,750.00
    Jack-in-the-pulpit, 3" d, seeds and
      root formation, pale lavender
      ground, numbered "A007 1983" . .   550.00
    Pond Lily, 3⅛" d , pinkish-white and
      yellow, six pads, cobalt blue
      ground, numbered "B711 1982" . .   700.00
    Slipper, 3½" d, pr, lady's, pink, two
      leaves and root formation, num-
      bered "2/75 B912 1983" 850.00
    Tapered, 4⅜" h, rect, pink flowering
      plant, ground and root formation
      sgd "Stankard #16 '81," inscribed
      "Ethel Noyes collection" 2,300.00
  Whittemore, Francis
    Bottle, perfume, 4¾" h, red rose in
      base and stopper, sgd 175.00
    Calla Lily, 2³⁄₁₆" d, white, ruby ground   200.00
    Flower, 2½", five blue petals, bud,
      and leaves, three stems, mottled
      pink ground, sgd 150.00
    Pedestal
      1⅞" d, 2½" h, horizontal pink rose,
        green leaves 175.00
      2½" h, yellow rose and leaves, sgd   150.00
    Slipper, 2³⁄₁₆" d, pr, ladies, yellow, fo-
      liage, emerald green ground 250.00
  Ysart, Paul
    Butterfly, 2⅞" d, pink, white, yellow,
      blue, and orange 500.00
  Ziegler & Phelps, Bridgeton Studios,
    tropical fish, 3" d 75.00

PAPIER MACHE

History: Papier Mache is made from a mixture
of wood pulp, glue, resin, and fine sand which is
subject to great pressure and then dried. The finished product is tough, durable, and heat resistant.
Various finishing treatments are used, such as
enameling, japanning, lacquering, mother-of-pearl
inlaying, and painting.

During the Victorian era Papier Mache articles
such as boxes, trays, and tables were in high fashion. Papier Mache also found use in the production
of banks, candy containers, masks, toys, and other
children's articles.

Roly Poly, left 6½" h, right 6¼" h, German, each, $150.00.

Bank, 6", Mickey Mouse, standing be-
  side chest 75.00
Bread Tray, 14¼" l, cartouche shape,
  blood red, floral spray and butterfly,
  cavetto and shaped border, gilt edge,
  black under surface, England, c1820   500.00
Candy Container
  Chick, nodding head 30.00
  Witch, 5" 100.00
Cup, 2½" h, floral dec, gold ground, red
  band top, black on base, made in
  USSR 40.00
Document Box, polychrome and gilt,
  English, 1850–60 . . . .   120.00
Fan, Troubadour scene, decoupaged
  and painted, reticulated, tassels, mid
  19th C 120.00
Figure
  12" h, winged cherub, gilt paint,
    c1900 . . . .   100.00
  32", workman in overalls, carrying
    lunch pail 700.00
  36", Poll Parrot, movable head 950.00
  48", Nipper dog 750.00
Lantern, 10½" w, owl, wings extended   185.00
Mask, 13½", man, hair, full beard 65.00
Music Stand, adjustable, inlaid mother-
  of-pearl, English, 1850–60 . . . .   200.00

Nodder, 3¾" h, turkey, male and female, orig black paint, polychrome trim, pewter feet, pr **100.00**

Pip-squeak

Cat, 3¾" h, black, wearing cloth suit, marked "Japan" **55.00**

Rooster, 6" h, orig polychrome paint   **145.00**

Snuff Box, round, yellow and brown transfer, Dr. Syntax The Shooting Pony **130.00**

Toy

Pull, 15½" l, tiger, painted cloth cov, glass eyes, cast iron wheel feet, repainted mouth, worn fur trim, teeth missing **90.00**

Squeak, 8½" h, round, wire cage, three birds **225.00**

Tray, 12 x 10", rect, grape dec, handled   **150.00**

Whistle, 5½" l, rooster, white, red trim .   **35.00**

PARIAN WARE

History: Parian ware is a creamy white, translucent, marble-like porcelain. It originated in England in 1842 and was first known as "Statuary Porcelain." Minton and Copeland have been credited with its development. Wedgwood also made it. In America, parian ware was manufactured by Chistopher Fenton in Bennington, Vermont.

At first parian ware was used only for figures and figural groups. By the 1850's it became so popular a vast range of wares were manufactured.

Bust, 6½" h, John Bright (English Orator, Statesman, Quaker, 1811–1889), by Robinson Leadbetter, $100.00.

Box, cov, oval, blue and white, lions in relief **45.00**

Bust

Apollo, 7", German **75.00**

Lord Zetland, marked "#23, Reg. 11th Dec/1868, Wedgwood," 21" .   **950.00**

Queen Victoria, marked "Robinson and Leadbetter" **350.00**

Compote, 10¼ x 10½", satyr and child holding large shell on shoulders, 3 rim chips **40.00**

Creamer, water lily dec **50.00**

Cup and Saucer, 4 x 3½", lily pond design, imp mark, c1865 . . . .   **85.00**

Dish, 8½" d, shallow, ftd, scalloped rim, deep relief, marked "Dale Hall Pottery, Longport Prize Medal, 1851" . .   **90.00**

Ewer, 10", twisted handle, mottled flowers and grapes **100.00**

Figure

Bather, 15¾", nude, holding object in hand, drapery at side, turtle beneath drapery, oval base **150.00**

Dancing girls, 10½", trio holding hands, gilded garlands, 7½" plinth   **135.00**

Medici Venus, 17" h, marked "Minton, 1851" **275.00**

Merry Wives of Windsor, marked "Sitzendorf" **350.00**

Nude, 12", standing, one hand on pillar beside her, chignon hairdo, round base **115.00**

Jar, cov, underplate, 7½" d, blue and white, stylized floral design, marked "S. Alcock," c1830 . . . .   **120.00**

Jug

7⅝", bark and vines, lavender, white int., dated 1847 . . . .   **140.00**

9¾", hinged pewter top, deep blue, emb white figures, women representing commerce, music, art, and science, English reg mark 1862 . .   **165.00**

Night Light, 5¾", figural, cottage, marked "W.H. Goss," c1893 . . . . . .   **200.00**

Pin Box, 3⅝" h, girl with hen and chicks   **75.00**

Pitcher, 7" and 7¾", polychrome scene on each side, raised cartouche, "Justice Watching over Repose of World" and "Justice Bringing Plenty and Industry", pr **100.00**

Platter, 13", basketweave, wheat sheaf handles **125.00**

Statue, 13" h, nude on swing, wood carved swing **725.00**

Sugar, 4¼", bellflower dec, ribbed ground, pedestal base **60.00**

Sugar Shaker, figural, owl **50.00**

Vase, 8", figural, hand, white **75.00**

Wall Figure, dove, Bennington **50.00**

PATE-DE-VERRE

History: Pate-de-Verre can be translated simply as glass paste. It is manufactured by grinding lead glass into a powder or crystal form, making it into a paste by adding a 2 or 3% solution of sodium silicate, molding, firing, and carving. The Egyptians discovered the process as early as 1500 B.C.

In the late 19th century, the process was rediscovered by a group of French glassmakers. Amalric Walter, Henri Cros, Georges Despret, and the Daum brothers were leading manufacturers.

Contemporary sculptors are creating a second renaissance, lead by the technical research of Jacques Daum.

Clock, 4½" sq, stylized leaf dec, orange and black, G. Argy Rousseau, clock labeled J. E. Caldwell & Co, metal back, $2,500.00.

Ashtray, 7", oval, yellow and brown central medallion of classical maiden, clear shading to blue and purple, sgd "Gabriel Argy-Rousseau" **350.00**
Bowl, 3½ x 2½", shallow, solid half sphere base, garland of blackberries and raspberries encircle bowl, translucent beige ground, sgd "G Argy-Rousseau" **700.00**
Box, cov, 3", leaf and berry motif, grasshopper finial, sgd "Walter," early 20th C **560.00**
Clock, 4½", sq, stars within pentagon and tapered sheafs motif, orange and black, sgd "G Argy-Rousseau," clock marked "J E Caldwell" **2,500.00**
Figure
  3¾", Pan, modeled by Henri Mercier, seated, playing pipes, deep lemon yellow and lime green, sgd "A Walter/Nancy and H. Mercier," c1925 . **1,650.00**
  5½", female satyr, modeled by Jean-Bernard Descomps, nude female figure, grassy ground, flesh tone, emerald green, and ochre, sgd "A Walter Nancy and JD," c1920 . . . **2,650.00**
  7¾", cloaked tangra figure, shaded seaform green and turquoise, sgd "A WALTER NANCY," c1920 . . . . **2,250.00**
Inkwell, 3½", lime green sides, sapphire blue and cinnamon streaked, low relief molding, olive green and deep amber maple leaves and pine

boughs, snail on circular cast cov, sgd "A Walter, Nancy and Berge Sc" . . . **1,200.00**
Lamp, 15⅜" h, 8" domical shade, bulbing cylindrical base, gray glass streaked with midnight blue and turquoise, shaded molded in low and medium relief with band of roundels enclosing sylized flowers, black, purple, and emerald green, base molded with conforming band, medial belt of tragic and comedic masks, raised flattened wrought iron base, four ball feet, sgd "G Argy-Rousseau," c1930 **55,000.00**
Pendant, 2 x 3", Art Nouveau, orig silk cord and tassel, sgd "A Rousseau" . **900.00**
Vase, 5¾", bulbous, waisted lower body, molded medium relief, two bands of upright lappets, wave edges, shades of magenta, tomato red, and black, gray mottled ground, sgd "G Argy-Rousseau, France," c1925 . . . . **5,000.00**

PATE-SUR-PATE

History: Pate-sur-Pate, paste on paste, is a 19th century porcelain form featuring relief designs achieved by painting successive layers of thin pottery paste one on top of the other.

About 1880 Marc Solon and other Sevres artists, inspired by a Chinese celadon vase in the Ceramic Museum at Sevres, experimented with this process of porcelain decoration. Solon migrated to England at the outbreak of the Franco-Prussian War and worked at Minton, where he perfected the pate-sur-pate process.

Bowl, 7 x 3½", mermaids, green and white irid, marked "Heubach" **365.00**
Box, cov, 2¼ x 5½", triangular, blue,

Plaque, 4" d, blue ground, white figures, young couple courting beneath trees, pastoral setting, marked "F. M./Limoges/France," wood frame, $325.00.

white nude seated on stream bank,
gold trim, sgd "Gol" in design, base
marked "F.M. Barbotine/Limoges,
France" **1,500.00**
Centerpiece, 11" l, pate-sur-pate, cartouches with putti, ivory and gilt reserves, brown ground, imp and
printed Minton factory marks, dec by
H Hollins, c1872 .... **1,400.00**
Chocolate Pot, gold star design, pearlized, scalloped base **135.00**
Cup, green, gold dragonflies, white
leaves **80.00**
Plaque
4 x 7", white dec, cobalt blue ground,
nymph and waves, marked "Limoges," 1900 .... **400.00**
10¼ x 6¼", girl, flowing gown, basket
of flowers **275.00**
Plate
9½", birds and branches, turquoise,
sgd "D Leroy, Minton" **450.00**
10½", pate-sur-pate, three classical
scenes in blue panels, sgd "AB,
Minton" **125.00**
Urn, 10", slate blue, white floral dec .. **475.00**
Vase
5", round, white blossoms, celadon,
gold feet and trim, marked "Minton"
7½" **325.00**
Pink, cherub and floral design on
front panel, tools, flowers and
hat, brown ground on back
panel, gold ring handles, gold
dec at base, red Minton mark .. **275.00**
White cupids, cobalt blue, gold trim
8½" **160.00**
Pilgrim style, two handles, celadon,
portrait of Eros and Venus, pate-
sur-pate trim at neck and base,
sgd "L. Solon, Minton" **475.00**
Tapered, flat shoulder, shallow circular neck, deep blue celadon
ground, front scene, classical
maiden releasing cupid from
basket, back, empty cage with
birds on branch, sgd "L. Solon,
Minton" **525.00**
8¾", five color, two cherubs over sea,
gilt trim, marked "Meissen" **1,000.00**
Wall Pocket, 9", maiden and cupid,
white figures, dark green ground ... **600.00**

PATTERN GLASS

History: Pattern glass is clear or colored glass
pressed into one of hundreds of patterns. Deming
Jarves of the Boston and Sandwich Glass Co.
invented the first successful pressing machine in
1828. By the 1860s glass pressing machinery had
been improved, and mass production of good

quality matched tableware sets began. The idea
of a matched glassware table service (including
goblets, tumblers, creamers, sugars, compotes,
cruets, etc.) quickly caught on in America. Many
pattern glass table services had numerous accessory pieces among which were banana stands,
molasses cans, water bottles, etc.

Early pattern glass (flint) was made with a lead
formula, giving it a ringing quality. During the Civil
War lead became too valuable to be used in glass
manufacturing. In 1864 Hobbs, Bruckunier & Co.,
West Virginia, developed a soda lime (non-flint)
formula. Pattern glass also was produced in
colors, milk glass, opalescent glass, slag glass,
and custard glass.

The hundreds of companies which produced
pattern glass have involved histories of development, expansions, personnel problems, material
and supply demands, fires, and mergers. In 1899
the National Glass Co. was formed as a combine
of nineteen glass companies in Pennsylvania,
Ohio, Indiana, West Virginia, and Maryland. U. S.
Glass, another consortium, was founded in 1891.
These combines resulted as attempts to save
small companies by pooling talents, resources,
and patterns. Because of this pooling, the same
pattern can be attributed to several companies.

Sometimes the pattern name of a piece was
changed from one company to the next to reflect
current fashion trends. U. S. Glass created the
States series by issuing patterns named for a particular state. Several of these patterns were new
issues, others were former patterns renamed.

References: Richard Carter Barret, *Popular
American Ruby Stained Pattern Glass,* Forward's
Color Productions, Inc., 1968; Bob H. Batty, *A
Complete Guide to Pressed Glass,* Pelican Pub-
lishing Co., Inc., 1978; E. M. Belnap, *Milk Glass,*
Crown Publishers, Inc., 1949; Regis F. and Mary
F. Ferson, *Yesterday's Milk Glass Today,* privately
printed, 1981; William Heacock, *Toothpick Hold-
ers from A to Z, Book 1, Encyclopedia of Victorian
Colored Pattern Glass,* Antique Publications,
1981; William Heacock, *Opalescent Glass from A
to Z, Book 2,* Antique Publications, 1981; William
Heacock, *Syrups, Sugar Shakers & Cruets, Book
3,* Antique Publications, 1981; William Heacock,
Custard Glass From A to Z, Book 4, Antique Pub-
lications, 1980; William Heacock, *U. S. Glass
From A to Z, Book 5,* Antique Publications, Inc.
1980; William Heacock, *Oil Cruets From A to Z,
Book 6,* Antique Publications, 1981; William Hea-
cock, *Ruby Stained Glass From A To Z, Book 7*
Antique Publications, Inc., 1986; William Heacock,
More Ruby Stained Glass, Book 8, Antique Pub-
lications, 1987; William Heacock and William
Gamble, *Cranberry Opalescent From A to Z, Book
9* Antique Publications, 1987; William Heacock,
Old Pattern Glass, Antique Publications, 1981;
William Heacock, *1000 Toothpick Holders: A Col-
lector's Guide,* Antique Publications, 1977, William
Heacock, *Rare and Unlisted Toothpick Holders,*

Antique Publications, 1984; William Heacock, *Collecting Glass, Research, Reprint and Reviews,* Volumes I, II, and III, Antique Publications; William Heacock and Fred Bickenheuser, *Glass from A to Z,* Antique Publications, 1981.

Minnie Watson Kamm, *Pattern Glass Pitchers, Books 1 through 8,* privately printed, 1970, 4th printing; Ruth Webb Lee, *Early American Pressed Glass,* Lee Publications, 1966, 36th edition; Ruth Webb Lee, *Victorian Glass,* Lee Publications, 1944, 13th edition; Bessie M. Lindsey, *American Historical Glass,* Charles E. Tuttle Co., 1967; Robert Irwin Lucas, *Tarentum Pattern Glass,* privately printed, 1981; Mollie H. McCain, *Pattern Glass Primer,* Lamplighter Books, 1979; Mollie H. McCain, *The Collector's Encyclopedia of Pattern Glass,* Collector Books, 1982 (Prices revised 1988); George P. and Helen McKearin, *American Glass,* Crown Publishers, 1941; James Measell, *Greentown Glass,* Grand Rapids Public Museum Association, 1979; James Measell and Don E. Smith, *Findlay Glass: The Glass Tableware Manufacturers, 1886-1902,* Antique Publications, Inc, 1986; Alice Hulett Metz, *LEarly American Pattern Glass,* privately printed, 1958; Alice Hulett Metz, *Much More Early American Pattern Glass,* privately printed, 1965.

Dori Miles, *Wallace-Homestead Price Guide To Pattern Glass, 11th Edition,* Wallace-Homestead, 1986; S. T. Millard, *Goblets I,* privately printed, 1938, reprinted Wallace- Homestead, 1975; S. T. Millard, *Goblets II,* privately printed, 1940, reprinted Wallace-Homestead, 1975; Arthur G. Peterson, *Glass Salt Shakers: 1,000 Patterns,* Wallace-Homestead, 1970; John A. Shuman III, *The Collector's Encyclopedia of American Art Glass,* Collector Books, 1988; Jane Shadel Spillman, *American and European Pressed Glass in the Corning Museum of Glass,* Corning Museum of Glass, 1981; Jane Shadel Spillman, *The Knopf Collectors Guides to American Antiques, Glass Volumes 1 and 2,* Alfred A. Knopf, Inc., 1982, 1983; Doris and Peter Unitt, *American and Canadian Goblets,* Clock House, 1970; Doris and Peter Unitt, *Treasury of Canadian Glass,* Clock House, 1969, 2nd edition; Peter Unitt and Anne Worrall, *Canadian Handbook, Pressed Glass Tableware,* Clock House Productions, 1983; Dina von Zweck, *The Woman's Day Dictionary of Glass,* The Main Street Press, 1983.

Museums: Corning Museum of Glass, Corning, NY. National Museum of Man, Ottawa, Ontario, Canada.

Periodical: *Glass Collector's Digest,* Richardson Printing Corp., P. O. Box 663, Marietta, OH 45750.

Additional Listings: Bread Plates, Children's Toy Dishes, Cruets, Custard Glass, Milk Glass, Sugar Shakers, Toothpicks, and specific companies.

Abbreviations:
ah—applied handle
GUTDODB—Give Us This Day Our Daily Bread
hs—high standard
ls—low standard
ns—new stopper
os—original stopper

We continue to be fortunate in assembling a panel of prestigious pattern glass dealers to serve as advisors in reviewing the pattern glass listings found in this edition. Their dedication is symbolic of those dealers and collectors who view price guides as useful market tools and contribute their expertise and time to make them better.

Research in pattern glass is continuing. As in the past, we have tried to present patterns with correct names, histories, and pieces. Catagories have been changed to reflect the most current thinking of all patterns alphabetically. Colored, opalescent, and clear patterns now are included in one listing, avoiding duplication of patterns and colors.

Pattern glass has been widely reproduced. We have listed some known reproductions in the pattern introductions, others are marked with an asterisk in the listings. These markings are given only as a guide and clue to the collector that some reproductions may exist in a given pattern.

Advisors: John and Alice Ahlfeld, Mike Anderton, Jerry R. Baker, William Jenks, and Darryl K. Reilly.

ABERDEEN

Non-flint, maker unknown, c1870.

	Clear		Clear
Butter, cov	45.00	Goblet	25.00
Compote		Pitcher, water	60.00
Cov.	42.50	Sauce, flat	15.00
Open	25.00	Sugar	
Creamer	40.00	Cov.	40.00
Egg Cup	30.00	Open	20.00

ACTRESS (Theatrical)

Made by LaBelle Glass Co., Bridgeport, Ohio, and Crystal Glass Co., c1870. All clear 20% less. Some items have been reproduced in clear and color by Imperial Glass Co.

	Clear and Frosted		Clear and Frosted
Bowl		Creamer	75.00
6", ftd	50.00	Dresser Tray	60.00
7", ftd	50.00	Goblet, Kate Claxton (2	
9½", ftd	85.00	portraits)	90.00
8", Miss Neilson	80.00	Marmalade Jar, cov	125.00
Bread Plate		Mug, HMS Pinafore	50.00
7 x 12", HMS Pinafore	90.00	Pickle Dish, Love's Request	
9 x 13", Miss Neilson,		is Pickles	50.00
motto	70.00	Pickle Relish, different ac-	
Butter, cov	90.00	tresses	
Cake Stand, 10"	145.00	4½ x 7"	40.00
Candlesticks, pr	250.00	5 x 8"	40.00
Celery Vase		5½ x 9"	40.00
Actress Head	125.00	Pitcher	
HMS Pinafore, pedestal	140.00	Milk, 6½", HMS Pinafore,	
Cheese Dish, cov, The Lone		Fanny Davenport and	
Fisherman on cov, Two		Miss Neilson	275.00
Dromios on base	250.00	Water, 9", Romeo & Ju-	
Compote		liet,balcony scene	250.00
Cov, hs, 8" d	225.00	Salt, master	70.00
Cov, hs, 10" d	250.00	Salt Shaker, orig pewter top	40.00
Cov, hs, 12" d	300.00	Sauce	
Open, hs, 10" d	90.00	Flat	18.00
Open, hs, 12" d	120.00	Footed	20.00
Open, ls, 5" d	45.00	Spooner	65.00
Open, ls, 6" d	50.00	Sugar, cov	90.00
Open, ls, 7" d	65.00		

ADONIS (Pleat and Tuck, Washboard)

Pattern made by McKee Bros. of Pittsburgh, Pennsylvania in 1897.

	Canary	Clear	Deep Blue
Bowl, 5", berry	15.00	12.00	20.00
Butter, cov	70.00	60.00	80.00
Cake Plate, 11"	25.00	18.00	32.00
Cake Stand, 10½"	45.00	30.00	50.00
Celery Vase	35.00	30.00	40.00
Compote,			
Cov, hs	65.00	50.00	75.00
Open, hs, 8"	45.00	40.00	50.00
Open, jelly, 4½"	28.00	18.00	32.00
Creamer	28.00	22.50	32.00
Pitcher, water	55.00	45.00	60.00
Plate, 10"	25.00	18.00	32.00
Relish	18.00	15.00	20.00
Salt and Pepper pr	40.00	35.00	45.00
Sauce, flat, 4"	10.00	8.50	12.00
Spooner	35.00	30.00	38.00
Sugar, cov	40.00	35.00	45.00
Syrup	150.00	50.00	150.00
Tumbler	22.00	16.00	24.00

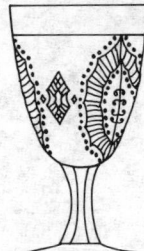

AEGIS (Bead & Bar Medallion, Swiss)

Non-flint pattern made by McKee and Brothers of Pittsburgh, Pennsylvania, in the 1880's. Shards have also been found at the site of the Burlington Glass Works, Hamilton, Ontario.

	Clear		Clear
Bowl, oval.	15.00	Pickle, 5 x 7"	15.00
Butter, cov	35.00	Pitcher, water	55.00
Compote		Salt	15.00
Cov, hs	40.00	Sauce	
Open, hs	25.00	Flat	7.50
Creamer	30.00	Footed	10.00
Egg Cup	25.00	Spooner	15.00
Goblet	30.00	Sugar, cov	35.00

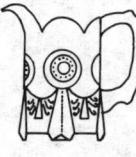

ALABAMA (Beaded Bull's Eye and Drape)

Made by U. S. Glass Co., c1898. One of the States patterns. Also found in green (rare).

	Clear	Ruby Stained		Clear	Ruby Stained
Bowl, berry, master .	30.00	—	Nappy	25.00	—
Butter, cov	60.00	175.00	Pitcher, water	65.00	—
Castor Set, 4 bottles,			Relish	15.00	35.00
glass frame	125.00	—	Salt & Pepper	65.00	—
Celery Vase	35.00	—	Spooner	30.00	—
Compote, open, 5",			Sugar, cov	48.00	—
jelly	65.00	—	Syrup	125.00	250.00
Creamer	45.00	60.00	Toothpick	60.00	150.00
Cruet, os	65.00	—	Tray, water, 10½" . .	40.00	—
Dish, rect	20.00	—	Tumbler	45.00	—
Honey Dish, cov . . .	60.00	—			

ALASKA (Lion's Leg)

Non-flint opalescent made by Northwood Glass Co. from 1897 to 1910. Forms are square except cruet, tumblers, salt and pepper shakers. Some pieces are found with enamel decoration. Sauces can be found in clear ($30.00); the creamer ($110.00) and spooner ($95.00) are known in clear blue.

	Clear Emerald Green	Blue Opal	Vaseline Opal	White Opal
Banana Boat	100.00	275.00	250.00	75.00
Bowl, berry, ftd	55.00	115.00	95.00	45.00
Butter, cov	150.00	280.00	275.00	150.00
Celery Tray	—	130.00	110.00	85.00
Creamer	42.50	85.00	80.00	40.00
Cruet	225.00	250.00	230.00	135.00
Pitcher, water	65.00	385.00	375.00	175.00
Salt Shaker, dec . . .		60.00	55.00	45.00
Sauce	42.50	45.00	35.00	25.00
Spooner	55.00	65.00	55.00	50.00
Sugar, cov	65.00	150.00	130.00	100.00
Tumbler	40.00	75.00	65.00	55.00

ALL-OVER DIAMOND (Diamond Splendor, Diamond Block #3)

Made by George Duncan and Sons, Pittsburgh, Pennsylvania, c1891 and continued by U.S. Glass Co. It was occasionally trimmed with gold, and had at least 65 pieces in the pattern. Biscuit jars are found in three sizes; bowls are both crimped and non-crimped; and nappies are also found crimped and non-crimped in fifteen sizes. Also made in ruby stained.

	Clear		Clear
Biscuit Jar, cov	60.00	Ice Tub, handles	35.00
Bitters Bottle	30.00	Lamp, Banquet, tall stem	140.00
Bowl		Nappy	
7″	20.00	4″	15.00
11″	35.00	9″	35.00
Cake Stand	35.00	Plate	
Candelabrum, very ornate, 4		6″	15.00
arms with lusters	175.00	7″	15.00
Celery Tray, crimped or		Pickle Dish, long	15.00
straight	20.00	Pitcher, water, bulbous, 6	
Claret Jug	50.00	sizes	45–60.00
Compote, cov	40.00	Punch Bowl	50.00
Condensed Milk Jar, cov	25.00	Salt Shaker	20.00
Cordial	35.00	Spooner	20.00
Creamer	20.00	Sugar	
Cruet, patterned stopper		Cov	35.00
1 oz	50.00	Open	18.00
2 oz	45.00	Syrup	55.00
4 oz	45.00	Tray	
6 oz	25.00	Ice Cream	30.00
Decanter		Water	30.00
Pint	45.00	Wine	30.00
Quart	45.00	Tumbler	15.00
Egg Cup	20.00	Water Bottle	35.00
Goblet	25.00	Wine	20.00

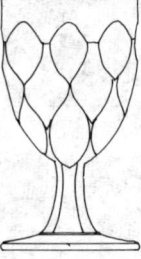

ALMOND THUMBPRINT (Pointed Thumbprint, Finger Print)

An early flint glass pattern with variants in flint and non-flint. Pattern has been attributed to Bryce, Bakewell, and U. S. Glass. Sometimes found in milk glass.

	Flint	Non-Flint		Flint	Non-Flint
Butter, cov	80.00	40.00	Decanter	70.00	—
Celery Vase	50.00	25.00	Egg Cup	45.00	25.00
Champagne	60.00	35.00	Goblet	28.00	12.00
Compote			Salt		
Cov, hs, 4¾″, jelly	60.00	40.00	Flat, large	25.00	15.00
Cov, hs, 10″	80.00	45.00	Ftd, cov	45.00	25.00
Cov, ls, 4¾″	55.00	30.00	Ftd, open	25.00	10.00
Cov, ls, 7″	45.00	25.00	Spooner	20.00	15.00
Open, hs, 10½″	65.00	—	Sugar, cov	60.00	40.00
Cordial	40.00	30.00	Sweetmeat Jar, cov	65.00	45.00
Creamer	65.00	40.00	Tumbler	45.00	20.00
Cruet, ftd, os	55.00	—	Wine	30.00	12.00

AMAZON (Sawtooth Band)

Non-flint; made by Bryce Brothers, Pittsburgh, Pennsylvania, late 1870s–1880 and also by the U. S. Glass Co., c1890. Mostly found in clear, either etched or plain. Heacock notes pieces in amber, blue, vaseline, and ruby stained. Over 65 pieces made in this pattern, including a toy set. Add 200% for color, e.g., pedestalled amber cruet with maltese cross stopper ($165.00) and pedestalled blue cruet with hand and bar stopper ($200.00). An amethyst cruet with a hand-bar stopper ($275.00) also is known.

	Etched	Plain		Etched	Plain
Banana Stand	95.00	65.00	Cordial	40.00	25.00
Bowl			Creamer	30.00	28.00
4", scalloped	—	10.00	Cruet, os	50.00	45.00
4½", scalloped . . .	—	10.00	Egg Cup	—	14.00
5", scalloped	—	15.00	Goblet		
6", scalloped	—	25.00	4½"	28.00	—
6½", cov, oval . . .	—	50.00	5"	25.00	—
7", scalloped	—	20.00	6"	30.00	—
8", scalloped	—	25.00	Pitcher, water	60.00	55.00
9", cov	30.00	25.00	Relish	28.00	25.00
Butter, cov	65.00	50.00	Salt & Pepper, pr . . .	50.00	40.00
Cake Stand			Salt		
Large	—	50.00	Individual	—	15.00
Small	—	40.00	Master	—	18.00
Celery Vase	35.00	30.00	Sauce, ftd	10.00	10.00
Champagne	—	35.00	Spooner	25.00	20.00
Claret	35.00	25.00	Sugar, cov	55.00	45.00
Compote			Syrup	50.00	42.50
Cov, hs. 7"	—	65.00	Tumbler	25.00	20.00
Open, 4½", jelly . .	45.00	35.00	Wine	25.00	20.00
Open, hs, 9½",					
sawtooth edge .	—	45.00			

ANTHEMION (Albany)

Non-flint made by Model Flint Glass Co., Findlay, Ohio, c1890–1900, and by Albany Glass Co. Also found in amber and blue.

	Clear		Clear
Bowl, 7", sq, turned-in edge .	20.00	Pitcher, water	50.00
Butter, cov	65.00	Plate, 10"	20.00
Cake Plate, 9½"	35.00	Sauce	10.00
Cake Stand	40.00	Spooner	25.00
Celery Vase	35.00	Sugar, cov	35.00
Creamer	30.00	Tumbler	25.00
Marmalade Jar, cov	40.00		

APOLLO

Non-flint, first made by Adams and Co., Pittsburgh, Pennsylvania, c1870, and later by U. S. Glass Co., c1891. Frosted increases price 20%. Also found in ruby stained and engraved.

	Clear			Clear
Bowl		Cruet		65.00
4″	10.00	Egg Cup.		30.00
5″	10.00	Goblet		35.00
6″	12.00	Lamp, 10″.		90.00
7″	15.00	Pickle Dish		15.00
8″	20.00	Pitcher, water		65.00
Butter, cov	55.00	Salt		20.00
Cake Stand		Salt Shaker.		25.00
8″	35.00	Sauce		
9″	40.00	Flat.		10.00
10″	50.00	Ftd, 5″.		12.00
Celery Tray, rect	20.00	Spooner		25.00
Celery Vase	25.00	Sugar, cov		40.00
Compote		Sugar Shaker		45.00
Cov, hs	65.00	Syrup		110.00
Open, hs	35.00	Tray, water		45.00
Open, ls, 7″	25.00	Tumbler		30.00
Creamer.	35.00	Wine		35.00

ARCHED FLEUR-DE-LIS (Late Fleur-De-Lis)

Made by Bryce, Higbee and Co., in 1897–1898. Also gilded.

	Clear	Ruby Stained		Clear	Ruby Stained
Banana Stand. . . .	35.00	150.00	Relish, 8″	15.00	—
Bowl, 9″, oval	18.00	—	Salt Shaker.	16.00	45.00
Butter, cov	40.00	135.00	Sauce	8.00	20.00
Cake Stand	35.00	—	Spooner, double-		
Compote, jelly, cov .	18.00	—	handled.	20.00	65.00
Creamer.	30.00	60.00	Sugar, cov, double		
Dish, shallow, 7″ . .	12.50	25.00	handled.	35.00	100.00
Mug, 3¼″	—	35.00	Toothpick	30.00	300.00
Olive, handled.	15.00	—	Tumbler	15.00	45.00
Pitcher, water	125.00	300.00	Vase, 10″	35.00	75.00
Plate, 7″, sq	12.00	45.00	Wine	25.00	65.00

ARCHED OVALS

Made by U. S. Glass Co., c1908. Found in gilt, ruby stained, green, and rarely in cobalt blue. Popular pattern for souvenir wares.

	Clear	Cobalt	Green	Ruby Stained
Bowl, berry	12.50	—	18.00	—
Bowl, cov, 7″	40.00	—	—	—
Butter, cov	45.00	—	50.00	80.00
Cake Stand	35.00	—	—	—
Celery Vase	15.00	40.00	20.00	—
Compote				
Cov, hs, 8″, belled	42.00	—	—	—
Open, hs, 8″	30.00	—	—	—
Open, hs, 9″	35.00	—	—	—
Creamer.				
Ind	20.00	—	—	—
Regular.	30.00	—	—	25.00

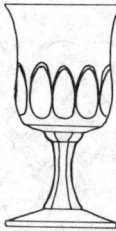

	Clear	Cobalt	Green	Ruby Stained
Cruet	35.00	—	45.00	—
Goblet	20.00	—	30.00	35.00
Mug	18.00	30.00	20.00	25.00
Pitcher, water	30.00	—	40.00	—
Plate, 9″	20.00	—	25.00	—
Punch Cup	8.00	—	—	—
Relish, oval, 9″	20.00	—	—	—
Salt & Pepper, pr. . .	45.00	—	50.00	—
Sauce	7.50	—	—	—
Saucer	—	—	—	30.00
Syrup	35.00	—	—	—
Spooner	20.00	—	25.00	35.00
Sugar, cov	35.00	—	40.00	—
Toothpick	18.00	50.00	25.00	35.00
Tumbler	12.00	25.00	18.00	30.00
Wine	25.00	—	30.00	32.00

ARGUS

Flint, thumbprint type pattern made by Bakewell Pears & Co. in Pittsburgh, Pennsylvania, in the early 1870s. Copiously reproduced, some by Fostoria with raised "HFM" trademark for Henry Ford Museum.

	Clear		Clear
Ale Glass	75.00	Lamp, ftd	75.00
Bitters Bottle	60.00	Mug, ah	65.00
Bowl, 5½″	50.00	Pitcher, water, ah	250.00
Butter, cov	85.00	Salt, master, open	20.00
Celery Vase	80.00	Spooner	48.50
Champagne	65.00	Sugar, cov	65.00
Creamer, applied handle . . .	70.00	Tumbler, bar	65.00
Decanter, qt	70.00	Whiskey, applied handle . . .	75.00
Egg Cup	20.00	Wine	45.00
Goblet	35.00		

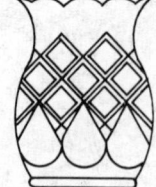

ART (Job's Tears)

Non-flint produced by Adams and Co., Pittsburgh, Pennsylvania, in the 1870s. Reissued by U. S. Glass Co. in the early 1890s. A milk glass covered compote is known.

	Clear	Ruby Stained		Clear	Ruby Stained
Banana Stand	95.00	195.00	Cake Stand		
Biscuit Jar	135.00	195.00	9″	55.00	—
Bowl			10¼″	65.00	—
6″ d, 3¼″ h, ftd . .	30.00	—	Celery Vase	30.00	65.00
7″, low, collar			Compote		
base	30.00	—	Cov, hs, 7″	55.00	185.00
8″, berry, one end			Open, hs, 9″, flar-		
pointed	50.00	55.00	ed scalloped		
Butter, cov	60.00	100.00	edge	50.00	—

	Clear	Ruby Stained		Clear	Ruby Stained
Open, hs, 9½" d,			Pitcher		
9"h	60.00	—	Milk.	90.00	150.00
Open, hs, 10" . . .	65.00	—	Water, 2½ qt	85.00	—
Creamer			Plate, 10"	35.00	—
Hotel, large, round			Relish.	21.00	65.00
shape	45.00	55.00	Sauce		
Regular.	55.00	60.00	Flat, round, 4" . .	15.00	—
Cruet, os	125.00	225.00	Pointed end.	18.50	—
Goblet	58.00	—	Spooner	25.00	55.00
Mug	35.00	—	Sugar, cov	45.00	85.00
			Tumbler	45.00	—
			Vinegar Jug, 3 pt. . .	75.00	—

ASHBURTON

A popular pattern produced by Boston and Sandwich Glass Co. and McKee Brothers from the 1850s to the late 1870s with many variations. Originally made in flint by New England Glass Co. and others and later in non-flint. Prices are for flint. Also reported is an amber handled whiskey mug and a scarce emerald green wine glass ($200.00). Some items known in fiery opalescent.

	Clear		Clear
Ale Glass, 5".	85.00	Honey Dish.	15.00
Bar Bottle		* Jug, qt	90.00
Pint.	38.00	Lamp	75.00
Quart	75.00	* Lemonade Glass.	55.00
Bitters Bottle.	55.00	Mug, 7"	110.00
Bowl, 6½".	75.00	Pitcher, water	450.00
Carafe	175.00	Plate, 6⅝"	75.00
Celery Vase, scalloped top. .	110.00	Sauce	15.00
Champagne, cut	75.00	Spooner	40.00
Claret, 5¼" h	50.00	* Sugar, cov	90.00
Compote, open, ls, 7½". . . .	65.00	Toddy Jar, cov	300.00
Cordial, 4¼" h.	75.00	Tumbler	
Creamer, ah	195.00	Bar	75.00
Decanter, qt, cut and		Water	75.00
pressed, os	250.00	Whiskey	60.00
Egg Cup		Whiskey, ah	100.00
Double	95.00	Water Bottle, tumble up	95.00
Single	30.00	* Wine	
Flip Glass, handled	125.00	Cut	65.00
* Goblet	37.00	Pressed	40.00

ATLANTA (Square Lion, Clear Lion Head)

Produced by Fostoria Glass Co., Moundsville, West Virginia, c1895. Pieces are usually square in shape. Also found in milk glass, ruby and amber stain.

	Clear	Frosted		Clear	Frosted
Bowl			Celery Vase	45.00	75.00
7", scallop rim . . .	60.00	—	Compote		
8", low collar			Cov, hs, 7".	90.00	125.00
base	55.00	—	Cov, hs, 8" d, 9½"h	110.00	150.00
Butter, cov	60.00	110.00	Open, hs, 5", jelly.	55.00	—
Cake Stand, 10" . . .	95.00	—	Creamer.	50.00	65.00

	Clear	Frosted		Clear	Frosted
Cruet	125.00	—	Salt		
Goblet	50.00	60.00	Individual	30.00	—
Marmalade Jar	65.00	85.00	Master	50.00	70.00
Pitcher, water	125.00	—	Sauce, 4″	22.00	—
Relish, oval	35.00	—	Spooner	50.00	—
Salt & Pepper, pr.	90.00	—	Sugar, cov	65.00	—
			Toothpick	55.00	60.00
			Tumbler	35.00	—
			Wine	40.00	—

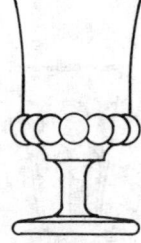

ATLAS

Non-flint glass pattern occasionally ruby stained and etched. Made by Adams and Co., U. S. Glass Co. in 1891, and Bryce Brothers, Mt. Pleasant, Pennsylvania, in 1889.

	Clear	Ruby Stained		Clear	Ruby Stained
Bowl, 9″	20.00	—	Salt		
Butter, cov, regular	45.00	75.00	Master	20.00	—
Cake Stand			Individual	20.00	—
8″	35.00	—	Sauce		
9″	40.00	95.00	Flat	10.00	—
Celery Vase	28.00	—	Footed	15.00	20.00
Champagne, 5½″ h	40.00	—	Spooner	30.00	35.00
Compote			Sugar		
Cov, hs, 8″	65.00	—	Cov	38.00	65.00
Cov, hs, 5″, jelly	50.00	65.00	Open	20.00	—
Open, ls, 7″	40.00	—	Syrup (molasses		
Creamer			can)	65.00	—
Table, ah	30.00	55.00	Toothpick	20.00	45.00
Tankard	25.00	—	Tray, water	75.00	—
Goblet	40.00	55.00	Tumbler	28.00	—
Marmalade Jar	45.00	—	Whiskey	20.00	45.00
Pitcher, water	45.00	—	Wine	25.00	—
Salt & Pepper, pr.	20.00	—			

AURORA (Diamond Horseshoe)

Made in 1888 by the Brilliant Glass Works, which only existed for a short time. Taken over by the Greensburg Glass Co. who continued the pattern. Also found etched.

	Clear	Ruby Stained		Clear	Ruby Stained
Bread Plate, 10″, round, large star in center	30.00	35.00	Relish Scoop, handle	10.00	25.00
Butter, cov	45.00	90.00	Salt & Pepper, pr.	45.00	80.00
Cake Stand	35.00	85.00	Sauce, flat	8.00	18.00
Celery Vase	30.00	40.00	Spooner	25.00	48.00
Compote, cov, hs	65.00	110.00	Sugar, cov	45.00	65.00
Creamer	35.00	50.00	Tray, water	45.00	60.00
Goblet	30.00	45.00	Tray, wine	35.00	60.00
Mug, handle	50.00	65.00	Tumbler	25.00	45.00
Olive, oval	18.00	35.00	Waste Bowl	30.00	45.00
Pitcher, water	40.00	100.00	Wine	20.00	40.00
			Wine Decanter, os	75.00	150.00

AUSTRIAN (Finecut Medallion)

Made by Indiana Tumbler and Goblet Co., Greentown, Indiana, 1897. Experimental pieces were made in cobalt blue, nile green, and opaque colors.

	Amber	Canary	Clear	Emerald Green
Bowl				
8″, round	—	150.00	55.00	—
8¼″, rect	—	145.00	50.00	—
Butter, cov	185.00	300.00	90.00	—
Compote, open, ls . .	—	150.00	75.00	—
Cordial	145.00	150.00	50.00	150.00
Creamer	120.00	125.00	40.00	120.00
Goblet	—	150.00	40.00	—
Nappy, cov	—	135.00	55.00	—
Pitcher, water	—	350.00	100.00	—
Plate, 10″	—	—	40.00	—
Punch Cup	150.00	150.00	18.00	125.00
Rose Bowl	—	150.00	50.00	—
Sauce, 4⅝″ d	—	50.00	20.00	—
Spooner	—	100.00	40.00	—
Sugar, cov	—	175.00	45.00	—
Tumbler	175.00	85.00	25.00	—
Wine	175.00	150.00	30.00	150.00

AZTEC

Made by McKee Glass Co., 1900 to 1910. Late imitation cut pattern, often marked "PRES-CUT" in circle in base; about 75 items in pattern.

	Clear		Clear
Bon Bon, ftd, 7″	15.00	Goblet	35.00
Bowl, berry	15.00	Pitcher, ah, ½ gal	35.00
Butter, cov	40.00	Plate	20.00
Cake Plate, trilobed	20.00	Punch Bowl, stand, and 12	
Cake Stand	30.00	handled cups	125.00
Carafe, water	40.00	Punch Cup	8.00
Celery Tray	15.00	Relish	15.00
Celery Vase	18.00	Salt & Pepper, pr	35.00
Champagne	25.00	Sauce	10.00
Compote, open	30.00	Soda Fountain Accessories	
Condensed Milk Jar	18.00	Crushed Fruit Jar	55.00
Cordial	20.00	Straw holder, glass lid . . .	65.00
Cracker Jar, cov	50.00	Spooner	15.00
Creamer		Sugar, cov	25.00
Individual	15.00	Syrup	50.00
Regular	25.00	Toothpick	18.50
Cruet	35.00	Tumbler	
Crushed Fruit Bowl, cov,8½″	75.00	Iced Tea	22.00
Cup	8.00	Water	20.00
Decanter, cut stopper	32.50	Whiskey	12.00
Finger Bowl, underplate	20.00	Wine	25.00

BALL AND SWIRL

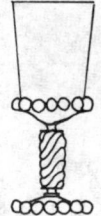

Made by McKee Glass Co, Jeanette, PA, 1894.

	Clear		Clear
Butter, cov	35.00	Pitcher, water	40.00
Cake Stand	35.00	Sauce, ftd	12.50
Compote, open, hs	30.00	Spooner	20.00
Creamer	24.00	Sugar, open	22.50
Goblet	20.00	Syrup	40.00
Mug		Tumbler	15.00
Large	18.00	Wine	28.00
Small	12.00		

BALTIMORE PEAR (Gipsy)

Non-flint, originally made by Adams and Company, Pittsburgh, Pennsylvania, in 1874. Also made by U. S. Glass Company in 1890s. There are 18 different size compotes. Given as premiums by different manufacturers and organizations. Heavily reproduced. Reproduced in cobalt blue.

	Clear		Clear
Bowl		* Pitcher	
6"	30.00	Milk	65.00
9"	40.00	Water	95.00
Bread Plate, 12½"	70.00	Plate	
* Butter, cov	75.00	8½"	30.00
* Cake Stand, 9"	50.00	10"	40.00
* Celery Vase	50.00	Relish	25.00
Compote		* Sauce	
Cov, hs, 7"	80.00	Flat	15.00
Cov, ls, 8½"	45.00	Footed	20.00
Open, hs	30.00	Spooner	42.50
Open, jelly	28.50	* Sugar	
* Creamer	30.00	Cov	50.00
* Goblet	35.00	Open	30.00
Pickle	18.50	Tray, 10½"	35.00

BANDED PORTLAND (Virginia #1, Maiden's Blush)

States pattern, originally named Virginia, by Portland Glass Co. Painted and fired green, yellow, blue, and possibly pink; ruby stained, and rose-flashed (which Lee notes is Maiden's Blush referring to the color, rather than the pattern, as Metz lists it). Double flashed refers to color above and below the band, single flashed refers to color above or below band only.

	Clear	Color Flashed	Maiden's Blush Pink
Bowl, 9"	30.00	—	40.00
Butter, cov	50.00	165.00	85.00
Cake Stand	55.00	—	—
Candlesticks, pr	95.00	—	—
Carafe	80.00	—	90.00
Celery Tray	25.00	—	—
Celery Vase	35.00	—	45.00

	Clear	Color Flashed	Maiden's Blush Pink
Cologne Bottle	45.00	65.00	85.00
Compote			
Cov, hs, 7″.	95.00	—	—
Cov, jelly, 6″.	40.00	65.00	—
Creamer			
Individual, oval. . .	25.00	35.00	38.00
Regular, 6 oz. . . .	35.00	45.00	50.00
Cruet, os	60.00	90.00	125.00
Decanter, handled. .	50.00	—	—
Dresser Tray.	50.00	—	—
Goblet	35.00	55.00	65.00
Lamp			
Flat.	45.00	—	—
Tall.	50.00	—	—
Nappy	15.00	55.00	65.00
Olive	18.00	—	—
Pin Tray	16.00	—	25.00
Pitcher, water,			
tankard	75.00	90.00	250.00
Pomade Jar, cov . . .	35.00	45.00	—
Punch Bowl, hs. . . .	110.00	—	300.00
Punch Cup	20.00	—	30.00
Relish			
6½″.	25.00	30.00	20.00
8¼″.	20.00	35.00	—
Ring Holder, gold rim and post, scarce.	80.00	—	—
Salt & Pepper, pr. . .	45.00	75.00	75.00
Sardine Box	55.00	—	—
Sauce, round, flat, 4 or 4½″	12.00	—	20.00
Spooner.	28.00	—	45.00
Sugar			
Cov, large	45.00	75.00	75.00
Open, individual, oval	20.00	—	35.00
Sugar Shaker, orig top	45.00	—	85.00
Syrup	50.00	—	135.00
Toothpick	35.00	45.00	40.00
Tumbler	25.00	—	45.00
Vase			
6″	20.00	—	38.00
9″	35.00	—	50.00
Wine	35.00	—	75.00

BARBERRY (Berry)

Non-flint made by McKee Glass Co. and the Boston and Sandwich Glass Co. in the 1860s and 1880s. 6″ plates are found in amber, canary, pale green, and pale blue; they are considered scarce. Also alleged to have been made at Iowa City. Pattern comes in "9 berry bunch" and "12 berry bunch" varieties.

	Clear		Clear
Bowl		Cup Plate	15.00
6″, oval	20.00	Egg Cup	20.00
7″, oval	25.00	Goblet	23.00
8″, oval	28.00	Pickle	10.00
8″, round, flat	30.00	Pitcher, water, appliedhandle	100.00
9″, oval	32.00	Plate, 6″	20.00
Butter		Salt, master, ftd	25.00
Cov	50.00	Sauce	
Cov, flange, pattern on		Flat	10.00
edge	100.00	Footed	15.00
Cake Stand	150.00	Spooner, ftd	30.00
Celery Vase	40.00	Sugar	
Compote		Cov	45.00
Cov, hs, 8″, shell finial	75.00	Open, buttermilk type	30.00
Cov, ls, 8″, shell finial	55.00	Syrup	150.00
Open, hs, 8″	35.00	Tumbler, ftd	25.00
Creamer	30.00	Wine	30.00

BARLEY

Non-flint, originally made by Campbell, Jones and Co., c1882, in clear; possibly by others in varied quality. Add 100% for color which is hard to find.

	Clear		Clear
Bowl		Pitcher, water	
8″, berry	15.00	Applied handle	95.00
10″, oval	20.00	Pressed handle	45.00
Bread Tray	30.00	Plate, 6″	35.00
Butter, cov	42.50	Platter, 13″ l, 8″ w	30.00
Cake Stand		Relish	
8″	25.00	Flat, 8″ l, 6″ w	18.00
10″	30.00	Wheelbarrow, 8″, pewter	
Celery Vase	25.00	wheels	60.00
Compote		Salt, master, wheelbarrow,	
Cov, hs, 6″	45.00	pewter wheels	75.00
Cov, hs, 8½″	60.00	Sauce	
Open, hs, 8½″	35.00	Flat	9.00
Cordial	50.00	Footed	12.00
Creamer	30.00	Spooner	20.00
Goblet	28.00	Sugar, cov	35.00
Honey, ftd, 3½″	8.00	Vegetable Dish, oval	15.00
Marmalade Jar	55.00	Wine	30.00
Pickle Castor, SP frame and			
tongs	90.00		

BASKETWEAVE

Non-flint, c1880. Some covered pieces have a stippled cat's head finial.

	Amber or Canary	Apple Green	Blue	Clear	Vaseline
Bowl	22.00	—	25.00	18.00	—
Bread Plate, handled, 11″	—	—	25.00	10.00	—

	Amber or Canary	Apple Green	Blue	Clear	Vaseline
Butter, cov	35.00	60.00	40.00	30.00	40.00
Compote, cov, 7". . .	—	—	—	35.00	—
Cordial	25.00	40.00	28.00	20.00	30.00
Creamer.	30.00	50.00	35.00	28.00	36.00
Cup & Saucer.	35.00	60.00	35.00	30.00	38.00
Dish, oval	12.00	20.00	15.00	10.00	16.00
Egg Cup.	18.00	30.00	20.00	15.00	25.00
* Goblet	28.00	50.00	35.00	20.00	30.00
Mug	25.00	40.00	25.00	15.00	30.00
Pickle.	18.00	30.00	20.00	15.00	22.00
Pitcher					
Milk.	40.00	60.00	45.00	35.00	50.00
* Water	60.00	75.00	80.00	45.00	65.00
Plate, 11", handled .	25.00	38.00	25.00	20.00	30.00
Sauce	10.00	10.00	12.00	8.00	12.00
Spooner	30.00	36.00	30.00	20.00	30.00
Sugar, cov	35.00	60.00	35.00	30.00	40.00
Syrup	50.00	75.00	50.00	45.00	55.00
* Tray, water, scenic center	35.00	45.00	40.00	30.00	55.00
Tumbler, ftd	18.00	30.00	20.00	15.00	20.00
Waste Bowl.	20.00	36.00	25.00	18.00	25.00
Wine	30.00	50.00	30.00	25.00	30.00

BEADED ACORN MEDALLION (Beaded Acorn)

Made by the Boston Silver Glass Co., East Cambridge, Massachusetts, c1869.

	Clear		Clear
Butter, cov, acorn finial.	65.00	Plate, 6"	30.00
Champagne	65.00	Relish.	15.00
Compote, cov, hs	50.00	Salt, master	28.00
Creamer.	40.00	Sauce, flat	15.00
Egg Cup.	20.00	Spooner	25.00
Goblet	25.00	Sugar, cov	45.00
Pitcher, water	90.00	Wine	40.00

BEADED BAND

Attributed to Burlington Glass Co., Hamilton, Ontario, Canada, c1884. Limited production and scarce pattern. May have been made in light amber and other colors.

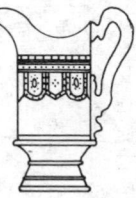

	Clear		Clear
Butter, cov	35.00	Relish	
Cake Stand, 7⅝"	25.00	Double	30.00
Compote, cov		Single	15.00
hs, 8"	55.00	Sauce, ftd.	10.00
ls, 9"	50.00	Spooner	25.00
Creamer.	28.50	Sugar, cov	40.00
Goblet	28.00	Syrup	85.00
Pickle, cov	45.00	Wine	25.00
Pitcher, water, applied strap handle.	100.00		

BEADED GRAPE MEDALLION

Non-flint made by Boston Silver Glass Co., Cambridge, Massachusetts, c1868. Also found in flint; add 40%.

	Clear		Clear
Bowl, 7″	25.00	Honey Dish, 3½″	10.00
Butter, cov, acorn finial	50.00	Pitcher, water, ah	125.00
Cake Stand, 11″	150.00	Plate, 6″	30.00
Celery Vase	50.00	Relish	
Castor Set, 4 bottles	110.00	Cov	140.00
Compote		Open, mkd "Mould Pat'd	
Cov, collared base	80.00	May 11, 1868	40.00
Cov, hs	75.00	Salt	
Open, hs, 8″	35.00	Individual, flat	20.00
Creamer, applied handle	45.00	Master, ftd	20.00
Egg Cup	25.00	Spooner	30.00
Goblet		Sugar, cov, acorn finial	60.00
Buttermilk	30.00	Vegetable, cov, ftd	75.00
Lady's	30.00	Wine	55.00

BEADED MIRROR (Beaded Medallion)

Flint pattern made by Boston Silver-Glass Co, Sandwich, Massachusetts, patented May 11, 1869. Finials are acorn shaped. Also found in non-flint. Values are about the same.

	Clear		Clear
Butter, cov	40.00	Goblet	25.00
Castor Bottle		Pitcher, water	85.00
Mustard	15.00	Plate, 6″	20.00
Oil	25.00	Relish	18.50
Set, 5 pcs, metal frame	100.00	Salt, ftd	18.00
Celery	35.00	Sauce, flat	8.00
Compote, cov, hs	50.00	Spooner	25.00
Creamer	42.00	Sugar, cov	45.00
Egg Cup	18.50		

BEADED SWIRL (Swirled Column)

Made by George Duncan & Sons, c1890. The dual names are for the two forms of the pattern. Beaded Swirl stands on flat bases and is solid in shape. Swirled Column stands on scrolled (sometimes gilded) feet, and the shape tapered towards the base. Some pieces trimmed in gold and also in milk white.

	Clear	Emerald Green		Clear	Emerald Green
Bowl			Compote		
Berry, 7″	12.00	20.00	Cov, hs	42.00	52.00
Flat	18.00	25.00	Open, hs	38.00	45.00
Footed, oval	18.00	24.00	Creamer		
Footed, round	18.00	24.00	Flat	25.00	35.00
Butter, cov	35.00	45.00	Footed	30.00	40.00
Cake Stand	35.00	45.00	Dish	12.00	18.00
Celery Vase	30.00	55.00	Egg Cup	14.00	15.00

	Clear	Emerald Green		Clear	Emerald Green
Goblet	35.00	40.00	Sugar, cov		
Mug	10.00	12.00	Flat	35.00	45.00
Pitcher, water	40.00	85.00	Sugar Shaker	35.00	60.00
Sauce			Footed	35.00	45.00
Flat	8.00	12.00	Syrup	48.00	100.00
Footed	10.00	14.00	Tumbler	20.00	30.00
Spooner			Wine	28.00	35.00
Flat	25.00	40.00			
Footed	30.00	45.00			

BEADED TULIP (Andes)

Non-flint made by McKee Brothers, Pittsburgh, Pennsylvania, c1894.

	Clear	Emerald Green		Clear	Emerald Green
Bowl, 9½", oval	20.00	—	Relish	20.00	—
Butter, cov	50.00	125.00	Sauce		
Cake Stand	50.00	—	Flat, leaf shape edges	10.00	—
Compote, cov, hs	55.00	—	Footed	12.00	—
Creamer	35.00	75.00	Spooner	30.00	—
Goblet	35.00	—	Sugar, cov	45.00	80.00
Marmalade Jar	40.00	—	Tray		
Pickle, oval	18.00	—	Water	50.00	—
Pitcher			Wine	50.00	—
Milk	30.00	65.00	Wine	30.00	—
Water	65.00	—			
Plate, 6"	25.00	—			

BEATTY HONEYCOMB (Beatty Waffle)

Non-flint made by Beatty Glass Co., Tiffin, Ohio, c1888. Reproduced by Fenton Glass in green opalescent (basket, rose bowl, and vases) and milk glass.

	Blue Opal	White Opal		Blue Opal	White Opal
Bowl, berry	100.00	50.00	Pitcher, water	200.00	150.00
Butter, cov	120.00	90.00	Salt & Pepper, pr.	65.00	45.00
Celery Vase	85.00	45.00	Sauce	20.00	20.00
Creamer			Spooner	40.00	30.00
Individual	35.00	20.00	Sugar, cov		
Regular	30.00	25.00	Individual	65.00	55.00
Cruet, os	250.00	150.00	Regular	70.00	65.00
Mug	35.00	25.00	Toothpick	50.00	45.00
Mustard	60.00	45.00	Tumbler	50.00	40.00

BEATTY RIB (Ribbed Opal)

Non-flint made by Beatty and Sons Glass Co., Tiffin, Ohio, c1888. May have been made in vaseline opalescent.

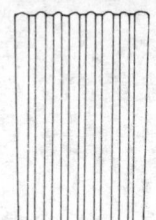

	Blue Opal	Clear Opal		Blue Opal	Clear Opal
Bowl, berry			Pitcher, water	150.00	120.00
Rect	60.00	55.00	Relish.	25.00	15.00
Round.	65.00	50.00	Salt, individual	30.00	25.00
Butter, cov	100.00	75.00	Salt & Pepper, pr. .	150.00	100.00
Celery Vase	65.00	50.00	Sauce		
Cracker Jar, cov . . .	300.00	150.00	Rect	30.00	15.00
Creamer			Round.	30.00	15.00
Individual.	30.00	20.00	Spooner	45.00	35.00
Regular.	60.00	35.00	Sugar		
Dish, oblong, 4⅞ x			Individual.	30.00	25.00
⅝".	25.00	15.00	Regular, cov	60.00	40.00
Finger Bowl	45.00	30.00	Toothpick, 2⅞"	45.00	35.00
Matchholder, 1¹⁵⁄₁₆".	50.00	45.00	Tumbler	45.00	35.00

BEAUTIFUL LADY

Made by Bryce, Higbee and Co. in 1905.

	Clear		Clear
Banana stand, hs	30.00	Goblet	35.00
Bowl		Pitcher, water	45.00
8", low collared base	15.00	Plate	
9", flat.	18.00	7", sq	15.00
Bread Plate	15.00	8"	15.00
Cake Plate, 9".	25.00	9"	25.00
Cake Stand, hs.	35.00	11"	25.00
Compote		Salt and Pepper	40.00
Cov, hs	35.00	Spooner	15.00
Open, hs.	25.00	Sugar, cov	25.00
Open, jelly.	15.00	Tumbler	12.00
Creamer.	25.00	Vase, 6½".	15.00
Cruet	30.00	Wine	20.00

BELLFLOWER

A fine flint glass pattern first made in the 1830s and attributed to Boston and Sandwich. Later produced by McKee Glass Co. and other firms for many years. There are many variations of this pattern - single vine and double vine, fine and coarse rib, knob and plain stems, and rayed and plain bases. Type and quality must be considered when evaluating. Very rare in color. Prices are for high quality flint. Reproductions have been made by the Metropolitan Museum of Art. Abbreviations: DV - double vine; SV - single vine; FR - fine rib; CR - coarse rib.

	Clear		Clear
Bowl		SV-FR, knob stem, rayed	
6" d, 1¾" h, SV	75.00	base, barrel shape. . .	100.00
8", all types	75.00	Compote	
Butter, cov, SV-FR.	100.00	Cov, hs, 8" d, SV-FR	375.00
Castor Set, 5 bottle, pewter		Cov, ls, 7" d, SV	200.00
stand	225.00	Cov, ls, 8" d, SV	225.00
Celery Vase, SV-FR	175.00	Open, hs, 8", SV	225.00
Champagne		Open, ls, 7", DV-FR, scal-	
DV-FR, cut bellflowers . . .	250.00	loped top	100.00

	Clear		Clear
Open, ls, 7", SV	100.00	Milk, DV, pint	175.00
Open, ls, 8", SV	100.00	Milk, SV-CR, quart	175.00
Open, ls, 9", SV-CR	125.00	Water, DV-CR	350.00
Cordial, SV-FR, knob stem,		* Water, SV-FR	250.00
rayed base, barrel shape	115.00	Plate, 6", SV-FR	125.00
Creamer, DV-FR	135.00	Salt, master	
Decanter		SV-FR, ftd	65.00
Pint, SV-FR, bar top	90.00	DV-FR	20.00
Quart		Sauce, flat, SV-FR	15.00
DV-FR, orig patterned		Spooner	
stopper	275.00	DV	45.00
SV-FR, bar top	185.00	SV-FR	35.00
Dish, SV-FR, 8", round, flat,		Sugar	
scalloped top	65.00	Cov, DV	100.00
Egg Cup		Cov, SV-CR	95.00
CR	35.00	Open, DV-CR	45.00
SV-FR	40.00	Sweetmeat, cov, hs, 6", SV	300.00
Goblet		Syrup, ah	
DV-FR, cut bellflowers	230.00	Ftd, 10 sides	750.00
SV-CR, barrel shape	45.00	SV-FR	550.00
SV-CR, straight sides	40.00	Tumbler	
SV-FR, knob stem, barrel		DV-CR	95.00
shape	55.00	SV-FR, ftd	90.00
* SV-FR, plain stem, rayed		* SV-FR, cut bellflowers	250.00
base, barrel shape	30.00	Whiskey, 3½", SV-FR	135.00
Hat, SV-FR, made from tum-		Wine	
bler mold, rare	350.00	DV-FR, cut bellflowers,	
Honey Dish, SV-FR, 3"	35.00	barrel shape	250.00
Lamp, whale oil, SV-FR,		SV-FR, knob stem, rayed	
brass stem, marble base	175.00	base, barrel shape	90.00
Mug, SV-FR	250.00	SV-FR, plain stem, rayed	
Pitcher		base, straight sides	75.00
Milk, DV-FR	500.00		

BETHLEHEM STAR (Star Burst; Bright Star)

Made by Indiana Glass Co., Dunkirk, IN, c1907.

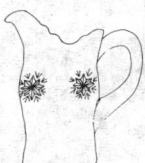

	Clear		Clear
Butter, cov	35.00	Goblet	30.00
Celery Vase	25.00	Pitcher, water	55.00
Compote		Relish	15.00
Cov, hs, 8"	55.00	Sauce, flat	10.00
Cov, hs, 4½"	45.00	Spooner	25.00
Creamer	30.00	Sugar, cov	40.00
Cruet, os	35.00	Wine	25.00

BIGLER

Flint, made by Boston and Sandwich Glass Co. and by other early factories. A scarce pattern in which goblets are most common and vary in height, shape and flare. Rare in color.

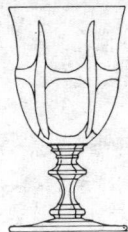

	Clear			Clear
Ale Glass	65.00	Goblet		
Bar Bottle, qt	80.00	Regular		45.00
Bowl, 10″ d	40.00	Short Stem		50.00
Butter, cov	125.00	Lamp, whale oil, monument		
Celery Vase	100.00	base		155.00
Champagne	75.00	Mug, applied handle		60.00
Compote, 7″	40.00	Plate, 6″		32.00
Cordial	50.00	Salt, master		20.00
Creamer	75.00	Tumbler, water		55.00
Cup Plate	30.00	Whiskey, handled		100.00
Egg Cup, double	50.00	Wine		45.00

BIRD AND STRAWBERRY (Bluebird)

Non-flint, c1890. Made by Beatty and Indiana Glass Co., Dunkirk, IN. Pieces occasionally highlighted by the coloring of birds blue, strawberries pink, and leaves green, plus the addition of gilding.

	Clear	Colors		Clear	Colors
Bowl			Cup	25.00	—
5″	25.00	45.00	Goblet	100.00	350.00 +
9½″	45.00	85.00	Nappy	40.00	—
10½″	55.00	95.00	Pitcher, water	225.00	350.00
Butter, cov	100.00	200.00	Plate, 12″	125.00	—
Cake Stand	65.00	125.00	Punch Cup	20.00	—
Celery Vase	45.00	—	Relish	20.00	—
Compote			Spooner	45.00	100.00
Cov, hs	125.00	200.00	Sugar, cov	65.00	125.00
Open, ls, ruffled	65.00	125.00	Tumbler	45.00	75.00
Jelly, cov, hs	150.00	—	Wine	50.00	—
Creamer	55.00	135.00			

BLEEDING HEART

Non-flint, originally made by King & Son, Pittsburgh, PA, c1870, and by U. S. Glass Co., c1898. Also found in milk glass. Goblets are found in six variations. Note: A goblet with a tin lid, containing a condiment (mustard, jelly, or baking powder) was made. It is of inferior quality compared to the original goblet.

	Clear		Clear
Bowl		Cov, ls, 7½″	60.00
7¼″, oval	30.00	Cov, ls, 8″	75.00
8″	35.00	Open, ls, 8½″	30.00
9¼″, oval, cov	65.00	Creamer, applied handle	65.00
Butter, cov	85.00	Creamer, molded handle	35.00
Cake Stand		Dish, cov, 7″	55.00
9″	60.00	Egg Cup	45.00
10″	85.00	Egg Rack, cov, 3 eggs	350.00 +
11″	90.00	Goblet, knob stem	35.00
Dessert slots	125.00	Honey Dish	15.00
Compote		Mug, 3¼″	40.00
Cov, hs, 8″	75.00	Pickle, 8¾″ l, 5″ w, pear	
Cov, hs, 9″	95.00	shape	35.00
Cov, ls, 7″	60.00	Pitcher, water, ah	150.00

	Clear			Clear
Plate	75.00	Sauce, flat		10.00
Platter, oval	65.00	Spooner		30.00
Relish, oval, 5½ x 3⅝"	35.00	Sugar, cov		60.00
Salt, master, ftd	45.00	Tumbler, ftd		90.00
Salt, oval, flat	20.00	Wine		150.00+

BLOCK AND FAN

Non-flint made by Richard and Hartley Glass Co., Tarentum, PA, late 1880s.
Continued by U. S. Glass Co. after 1891.

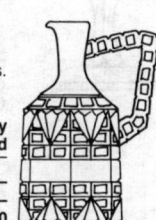

	Clear	Ruby Stained		Clear	Ruby Stained
Biscuit Jar, cov	65.00	150.00	Dish, large, rect.	25.00	—
Bowl			Finger Bowl	55.00	—
4", flat	15.00	—	Goblet	45.00	85.00
8", flat	25.00	—	Ice Tub	45.00	50.00
8", ftd	20.00	—	Orange Bowl	50.00	—
9½"	30.00	—	Pickle Dish	20.00	—
10 x 6", rect	50.00	—	Pitcher		
Butter, cov	50.00	85.00	Milk	35.00	—
Cake Stand			Water	45.00	125.00
9"	35.00	—	Plate		
10"	42.00	—	6"	20.00	—
Carafe	40.00	95.00	10"	22.00	—
Celery Tray	30.00	—	Relish, rect	25.00	—
Celery Vase	35.00	75.00	Rose Bowl	25.00	—
Compote			Salt & Pepper	30.00	—
Open, hs, 8"	40.00	165.00	Sauce		
Open, ls, 4"	10.00	—	Flat, 5	8.00	—
Open, ls, 7"	25.00	—	Ftd, 3¾"	12.00	25.00
Open, ls, 8"	30.00	—	Spooner	25.00	—
Condiment Set, salt,			Sugar, cov	50.00	—
pepper & cruet on			Sugar Shaker	40.00	—
tray	75.00	—	Syrup	65.00	95.00
Creamer			Tray, Ice Cream,		
Individual	—	35.00	rect	75.00	—
Regular	25.00	45.00	Tumbler	30.00	—
Large	30.00	100.00	Waste Bowl	30.00	—
Small	35.00	75.00	Wine	45.00	65.00
Cruet, os	40.00	—			

BOUQUET

(Narcissus Spray) Made by Indiana Glass Company, c1918. Flowers and leaves
are found with cranberry or amethyst flashing. Prices are for clear, flashed pieces
would be approximately 20% higher.

	Clear		Clear
Bowl, berry		Pitcher, water	40.00
6", ind	12.00	Sauce	5.00
8", master	18.00	Spooner	20.00
Butter, cov	40.00	Sugar, cov	35.00
Cake Plate	28.00	Tumbler	18.00
Creamer	25.00	Water Tray	45.00
Nappy	15.00		

BOW TIE

Non-flint made by Thompson Glass Co., Uniontown, PA, c1889.

	Clear			Clear
Bowl			Pitcher	
7"	32.50		Milk	
8"	40.00		5½"	45.00
10¼ d, 5" h	65.00		8"	80.00
Butter, cov	65.00		9"	90.00
Butter Pat	25.00		Water	75.00
Cake Stand, large, 9" d	60.00		Punch Bowl	100.00
Compote, open			Relish, rect	30.00
hs, 5½"	60.00		Salt	
hs, 9¼"	65.00		Individual	20.00
ls, 6½"	45.00		Master	40.00
ls, 8"	55.00		Salt Shaker	65.00
Creamer	65.00		Sauce, flat	18.00
Goblet	65.00		Spooner	35.00
Honey, cov	55.00		Sugar, cov	55.00
Marmalade Jar	75.00		Tumbler	50.00
Orange Bowl, ftd, hs, 10"	75.00			

BROKEN COLUMN (Irish Column, Notched Rib, Rattan)

Made in Findlay, Ohio, c1891, by Columbia Glass Co., c1892, and later made by U. S. Glass Co. May also have been made at Portland, ME. Notches may be ruby stained. A cobalt blue cup is known. The square covered compote has been reproduced. Some items have been reproduced for the Metropolitan Museum of Art. Some items are reproduced by the Smithsonian Institution with a raised "SI" trademark.

	Clear	Ruby Stained		Clear	Ruby Stained
Banana Stand	110.00	—	Cov, hs, 10"	110.00	350.00
Basket, ah,12" h, 15"			Open, hs, 7" d	—	150.00
l	125.00	—	Open, hs, 8" d	75.00	175.00
Biscuit Jar	85.00	165.00	Open, ls, 5" d, 6"		
4", berry	—	20.00	h, flared	65.00	135.00
6", berry	20.00	45.00	Creamer	42.50	125.00
8"	35.00	—	Cruet, os	85.00	150.00
9"	40.00	—	Decanter	95.00	—
Bread Plate	60.00	125.00	Finger Bowl	30.00	—
Butter, cov	85.00	175.00	* Goblet	48.00	100.00
Cake Stand			Marmalade Jar	85.00	—
9"	70.00	225.00	Pickle Castor, sp		
10"	80.00	245.00	frame	150.00	400.00
Carafe, water	65.00	150.00	Pitcher, water	90.00	215.00
Celery Tray, oval	35.00	—	Plate		
Celery Vase	50.00	135.00	4"	—	20.00
Champagne	100.00	—	5"	35.00	—
Claret	75.00	—	7½"	40.00	95.00
Compote			Relish		
Cov, hs, 5¼" d,			Oval, 7½ x 4"	20.00	—
10¼" h	90.00	200.00	Oval, 11 x 5"	22.00	—
Cov, hs, 7" d,			Rect, 7½ x 5"	25.00	—
12"h	85.00	—	Salt Shaker	45.00	65.00

	Clear	Ruby Stained		Clear	Ruby Stained
* Sauce, flat	15.00	30.00	Syrup	130.00	400.00
* Spooner	35.00	85.00	Tumbler	45.00	55.00
Sugar, cov	75.00	140.00	Vegetable, cov	90.00	—
Sugar Shaker	85.00	200.00	Wine	75.00	125.00

BUCKLE

Flint and non-flint pattern. Sandwich Glass Co. in Massachusetts is attributed to the flint production. The non-flint production was made by Gillinder and Sons in Philadelphia, PA, in the late 1870s.

	Flint	Non-Flint		Flint	Non-Flint
Bowl			Creamer, ah	110.00	40.00
8", berry, orig had			Egg Cup	35.00	28.00
wire basket			Goblet	40.00	30.00
frame	60.00	50.00	Pickle	40.00	15.00
10"	60.00	50.00	Pitcher, water, ah	500.00	85.00
Butter, cov	65.00	60.00	Salt, flat, oval	30.00	15.00
Cake Stand, 9¾"	—	30.00	Salt, footed	24.00	18.00
Compote			Sauce, flat	10.00	8.00
Cov, hs, 6" d	95.00	40.00	Spooner	40.00	35.00
Open, hs, 8½",			Sugar, cov	75.00	55.00
fluted	45.00	40.00	Tumbler	55.00	30.00
Open, ls	40.00	35.00	Wine	90.00	45.00

BUCKLE WITH STAR (Orient)

Non-flint made by Bryce, Walker and Co. in 1875, U. S. Glass Co. in 1891. Finials are shaped like Maltese crosses.

	Clear		Clear
Bowl		Relish	15.00
6", cov	25.00	Salt, master, ftd	20.00
7", oval	15.00	Sauce	
8", oval	15.00	Flat	8.00
9", oval	15.00	Footed	10.00
10", oval	18.00	Spooner	25.00
Butter, cov	50.00	Sugar	
Cake Stand	30.00	Cov	45.00
Celery Vase	30.00	Open	25.00
Compote		Syrup	
Cov, hs, 7"	60.00	Applied handle, pewter or	
Open, hs, 9½"	30.00	Brittania top, man's head	
Creamer	35.00	finial	80.00
Goblet	30.00	Molded handle, plain tin	
Mug	60.00	top	60.00
Mustard, cov	75.00	Tumbler	55.00
Pickle	15.00	Wine	35.00
Pitcher, water, appliedhandle	70.00		

BUDDED IVY

Non-flint, c1870. Contemporary of Stippled Ivy. Pieces have applied handles and ivy leaf finials.

	Clear		Clear
Butter, cov	45.00	Relish	15.00
Compote		Salt, ftd	25.00
Cov, hs	60.00	Sauce, ftd	7.50
Cov, ls	45.00	Spooner	24.00
Open, hs	25.00	Sugar	
Creamer	30.00	Covered	45.00
Egg Cup	30.00	Open	25.00
Goblet	27.50	Syrup	85.00
Pitcher, water	50.00	Wine	35.00

BULL'S EYE

Flint made by the New England Glass Co. in the 1850s. Also found in colors and milk glass, which doubles the price.

	Clear		Clear
Bitters Bottle	80.00	Goblet	65.00
Butter, cov	150.00	Lamp	100.00
Carafe	45.00	Mug, 3½", applied handle	110.00
Castor Bottle	35.00	Pitcher, water	285.00
Celery Vase	85.00	Relish, oval	25.00
Champagne	95.00	Salt	
Cologne Bottle	85.00	Individual	38.50
Cordial	75.00	Master, ftd	100.00
Creamer	125.00	Spooner	40.00
Cruet	85.00	Sugar, cov	125.00
Decanter, qt, bar lip	120.00	Tumbler	85.00
Egg Cup		Water Bottle, tumble up	100.00
Cov	165.00	Whiskey	70.00
Open	48.00	Wine	50.00

BULL'S EYE AND DAISY

Made by U. S. Glass Co., 1909. Also made with amethyst, blue, green, and pink stains in eyes. Prices close to ruby stained pieces.

	Clear	Emerald Green	Ruby Stained
Bowl	12.00	16.00	25.00
Butter, cov	25.00	28.00	90.00
Celery Vase	18.00	25.00	40.00
Creamer	25.00	28.00	50.00
Decanter	—	110.00	—
Goblet	25.00	28.00	50.00
Pitcher, water	35.00	40.00	95.00
Salt Shaker	20.00	20.00	35.00
Sauce	7.00	10.00	20.00
Spooner	20.00	25.00	40.00
Sugar, open	22.00	30.00	45.00
Tumbler	14.00	16.00	35.00
Wine	24.00	32.50	42.50

BULL'S EYE AND FAN (Daisies in Oval Panels)

Made by U.S. Glass, c1910. Also made in blue; prices same as emerald green.

	Amethyst Stain	Clear	Emerald Green	Pink Stain	Sapphire Blue Stain
Bowl					
5″, pinched ends .	—	—	18.00	—	—
8″, berry	—	15.00	20.00	—	30.00
Butter, cov	—	45.00	65.00	—	—
Cake Stand	—	25.00	—	—	—
Creamer					
Individual.	—	14.00	—	—	—
Regular.	—	25.00	30.00	—	35.00
Custard Cup	—	10.00	—	—	—
Goblet	25.00	24.00	45.00	25.00	45.00
Lemonade Mug. 5″ .	—	20.00	—	—	—
Pitcher					
Lemonade, ftd . . .	—	55.00	—	—	—
Water, tankard . . .	55.00	40.00	100.00	50.00	100.00
Relish.	20.00	18.00	35.00	20.00	35.00
Sauce	25.00	16.00	20.00	25.00	30.00
Spooner	25.00	21.50	45.00	25.00	45.00
Sugar, cov	40.00	35.00	60.00	30.00	35.00
Toothpick . . , ...	—	35.00	45.00	65.00	—
Tumbler	55.00	15.00	45.00	40.00	35.00
Wine	22.00	20.00	40.00	40.00	25.00

BULL'S EYE WITH DIAMOND POINT (Union)

Made in flint by New England Glass Co., c1869.

	Clear		Clear
Butter, cov	250.00	Salt, master, cov	100.00
Celery Vase	150.00	Sauce	20.00
Champagne	145.00	Spill	75.00
Cologne Bottle, os.	90.00	Spooner	125.00
Creamer.	200.00	Sugar, cov	175.00
Cruet, os	80.00	Syrup	175.00
Decanter, qt, os.	200.00	Tumbler	145.00
Egg Cup.	90.00	Tumble-Up	165.00
Goblet	110.00	Whiskey	150.00
Honey Dish, flat	25.00	Wine	135.00
Lamp, finger, applied handle	150.00		
Pitcher, water, 10¼″, tankard	275.00		

BULL'S EYE WITH FLEUR-DE-LIS

Flint, c1850.

	Clear		Clear
Ale Glass	250.00	Bowl, fruit.	85.00
Bar Bottle, qt	110.00	Butter, cov	175.00

	Clear		Clear
Celery Vase	85.00	Pitcher, water	400.00
Creamer	250.00	Salt, master	55.00
Egg Cup	50.00	Spooner	50.00
Goblet	85.00	Sugar, cov	115.00
Lamp, marble base	175.00	Wine	90.00
Mug, handle	100.00		

BUTTERFLY & FAN (Grace, Japanese)

Non-flint pattern made by Duncan, Pittsburgh, PA, c1880.

	Clear		Clear
Bread Plate	80.00	Creamer, ftd	45.00
Butter, cov		Goblet	50.00
Flat	100.00	Marmalade Jar	75.00
Footed	75.00	Sauce, ftd	15.00
Celery Vase	75.00	Spooner	30.00
Compote		Sugar, ftd	
Cov, hs, 8" d	95.00	Covered	65.00
Cov, hs, 7" d	95.00	Open	30.00
Open, hs	30.00		

BUTTON ARCHES

Non-flint, made by Duncan and Miller Glass Co. in 1885. Pieces have frosted band. Some pieces, known as "Koral," usually souvenir type, are also seen in clambroth, trimmed in gold. The toothpick holder comes in both a smooth scallop and beaded scallop variety. They have the same value. In the early 1970s souvenir ruby stained pieces, including a goblet and table set, were reproduced.

	Clambroth	Clear	Ruby Stained
Bowl, 8"	—	20.00	50.00
Butter, cov	—	48.00	100.00
Cake Stand, 9"	—	35.00	180.00
Compote, jelly	—	48.00	50.00
Creamer	25.00	20.00	45.00
Cruet, os	—	55.00	175.00
* Goblet	40.00	25.00	40.00
Mug	30.00	25.00	30.00
Mustard, cov, underplate	—	—	100.00
Pitcher			
Milk	—	35.00	80.00
Water, tankard	—	75.00	125.00
Plate, 7"	—	10.00	25.00
Punch Cup	—	15.00	25.00
Salt, ind	—	15.00	—
Salt Shaker, three types	—	15.00	30.00
Sauce, flat	—	12.50	22.00
Spooner	—	25.00	40.00
Sugar, cov	—	35.00	75.00
Syrup	—	—	175.00
Toothpick	30.00	24.00	35.00
Tumbler	20.00	24.00	35.00
Wine	25.00	15.00	35.00

BUTTON BAND (Umbilicated Hobnail, Wyandotte)

Non-flint made by Ripley and Co. in 1880s and U. S. Glass Co. in 1890s. Can often be found engraved, priced the same.

	Clear		Clear
Bowl, 10″	30.00	Goblet	40.00
Butter, cov	45.00	Pitcher	
Cake Stand, 10″	60.00	Milk	40.00
Castor Set, 5 bottles in glass		Water, tankard	50.00
stand	135.00	Spooner	20.00
Compote		Sugar, cov	30.00
Cov, hs, 9″	95.00	Tray, water	40.00
Open, ls	45.00	Tumbler	20.00
Cordial	25.00	Wine	35.00
Creamer	30.00		

CABBAGE ROSE

Non-flint made by Central Glass Co, Wheeling, WV, c1870. Reproduced in colors.

	Clear		Clear
Basket, handled, 12″	100.00	Cov, ls, 8½″	110.00
Bitters Bottle, 6½″ h	125.00	Open, hs, 7½″	75.00
Bowl, Oval		Open, hs, 9½″	100.00
7½″	32.50	Creamer, applied handle	55.00
8½″	38.00	Egg Cup	35.00
9½″	40.00	* Goblet	35.00
Bowl, Round		Mug	60.00
6″	25.00	Pitcher	
7½″, cov	65.00	Milk	150.00
7½″, open	35.00	Water	125.00
Butter, cov	60.00	Relish, 8½″ l, 5″ w, rose-filled	
Cake Stand		horn of plenty center	38.00
11″	40.00	Salt, master, ftd	25.00
12½″	50.00	Sauces, six sizes	10–20.00
Celery Vase	48.00	Spooner	25.00
Champagne	50.00	Sugar	
Compote		Cov	55.00
Cov, hs, 7½″	110.00	Open, buttermilk type	40.00
Cov, hs, 8½″	120.00	Tumbler	40.00
Cov, ls, 6″	95.00	Wine	40.00
Cov, ls, 7½″	100.00		

CABLE

Flint, c1850. Made by Boston and Sandwich Glass Co. to commemorate the laying of Atlantic Cable. Also found with amber stained panels and in opaque colors (rare).

	Clear		Clear
Bowl		Champagne	250.00
8″, ftd	45.00	Compote, open	
9″	70.00	hs, 5½″	65.00
Butter, cov	100.00	ls, 7″	50.00
Cake Stand, 9″	55.00	ls, 9″	55.00
Celery Vase	75.00	ls, 11″	75.00

	Clear		Clear
Creamer	400.00	Pitcher, water, rare	500.00
Decanter, qt, ground stopper	225.00	Plate, 6″	75.00
Egg Cup		Salt, ind, flat	35.00
Cov	225.00	Salt, master, cov	45.00
Open	60.00	Sauce, flat	20.00
Goblet	70.00	Spooner	40.00
Honey Dish	15.00	Sugar, cov	120.00
Lamp, 8¾″		Syrup	175.00
Glass Base	135.00	Tumbler, ftd	175.00
Marble Base	100.00	Wine	175.00

CACTUS

Non-flint made by Indiana Tumbler and Goblet Co. c1895. Made in clear and chocolate. Pattern made in opalescent vaseline by Fenton Art Glass in 1950.
Additional Listings: Greentown Glass (chocolate pieces).

	Clear		Clear
Bowl		Pitcher, water	175.00
7¼″ d	50.00	Plate, 7½″	80.00
8¼″	70.00	Sauce	
Butter, cov	125.00	Flat, 5¼″	32.50
Cake stand	165.00	Footed	45.00
Celery Vase	80.00	Spooner	50.00
Compote, cov, hs, 8¼″	125.00	Sugar, cov	80.00
Creamer, cov	80.00	Syrup	65.00
Cruet, os	100.00	*Toothpick	50.00
Mug	50.00	Tumbler	45.00
Nappy	50.00	Vase, 6″	60.00

CALIFORNIA (Beaded Grape)

Non-flint made by U. S. Glass Co., Pittsburgh, PA, c1890. Also with gold trim. Many pieces reproduced.

	Clear	Emerald Green		Clear	Emerald Green
Bowl			Cruet, orig swirled		
5½″, sq	15.00	20.00	stopper	65.00	115.00
5½ x 8″	—	30.00	* Goblet	35.00	50.00
6″ sq	—	25.00	Olive, handle	20.00	35.00
7½″, sq	25.00	35.00	Pickle	20.00	30.00
8″, round	28.00	30.00	Pitcher		
Bread Plate, 10¼ x			Milk	75.00	—
7¼″	25.00	45.00	Water	85.00	120.00
Butter, cov	65.00	100.00	* Plate, 8¼″, sq	28.00	40.00
Cake Stand, 9″	65.00	85.00	Salt & Pepper	45.00	65.00
Celery Tray	30.00	45.00	* Sauce, 4″	15.00	18.00
Celery Vase	45.00	65.00	Spooner	30.00	45.00
* Compote			Sugar, cov	45.00	55.00
Cov, hs, 6½″	65.00	95.00	Sugar Shaker	75.00	85.00
Open, hs, 5″, sq	55.00	75.00	Toothpick	35.00	65.00
Open, hs, 7″	45.00	80.00	* Tumbler	32.50	45.00
Open, hs, jelly	55.00	75.00	* Wine	35.00	65.00
Creamer	40.00	50.00			

CANADIAN

Non-flint, made by Burlington Glass Works, Hamilton, Ontario, Canada, c1870.

	Clear		Clear
Bowl, 7″ d, 4½″ h, ftd	60.00	Goblet	45.00
Bread Plate, 10″	45.00	Mug, small	40.00
Butter, cov	85.00	Pitcher	
Cake Stand, 9¼″	95.00	Milk	90.00
Celery Vase	65.00	Water	125.00
Compote		Plate, 6″, handles	30.00
Cov, hs, 6″	50.00	Sauce	
Cov, hs, 7″	95.00	Flat	15.00
Cov, hs, 8″	110.00	Footed	18.00
Cov, ls, 6″	50.00	Spooner	45.00
Open, ls, 7″	35.00	Sugar, cov	90.00
Creamer	65.00	Wine	40.00

CANE

Non-flint made by Gillinder Glass Co. and McKee Glass Co., c1885. Goblets and toddy plates with inverted "buttons" known.

	Amber	Apple Green	Blue	Clear	Vaseline
Bowl, 9½″, oval	15.00	—	—	—	—
Butter, cov	45.00	60.00	75.00	40.00	60.00
Celery Vase	38.00	40.00	50.00	32.50	40.00
Compote, open, ls, 5¾″	28.00	30.00	35.00	25.00	35.00
Cordial	—	—	—	25.00	—
Creamer	35.00	40.00	50.00	25.00	30.00
Finger Bowl	20.00	30.00	35.00	15.00	30.00
Goblet	28.50	40.00	35.00	20.00	35.00
Honey Dish	—	—	—	15.00	—
Match holder, kettle	18.00	—	35.00	30.00	35.00
Pickle	25.00	20.00	25.00	15.00	20.00
Pitcher, milk	60.00	55.00	65.00	40.00	55.00
Pitcher, water	60.00	75.00	65.00	40.00	55.00
Plate, toddy, 4½″	20.00	25.00	30.00	14.00	18.00
Salt & Pepper	60.00	50.00	80.00	30.00	70.00
Sauce, flat	—	9.50	—	7.00	—
Slipper	30.00	—	25.00	15.00	30.00
Spooner	42.00	35.00	30.00	20.00	30.00
Sugar, cov	45.00	45.00	45.00	25.00	45.00
Tray, water	35.00	35.00	45.00	30.00	40.00
Tumbler	24.00	30.00	35.00	20.00	25.00
Waste Bowl, 7½″	35.00	30.00	35.00	20.00	30.00
Wine	35.00	40.00	35.00	20.00	35.00

CANE HORSESHOE (Paragon)

Made by U. S. Glass Co., 1909. Prices are for pieces with gold trim.

	Clear		Clear
Bowl, 8″	15.00	Cake Stand	30.00
Butter, cov	25.00	Celery Tray	20.00

	Clear		Clear
Celery Vase	25.00	Pitcher, water	40.00
Compote		Relish	15.00
Cov, hs	45.00	Sauce	10.00
Open, hs	35.00	Spooner	20.00
Open, ls	35.00	Sugar, cov	30.00
Creamer	30.00	Syrup	35.00
Cruet, os	30.00	Tumbler	15.00
Goblet	20.00	Wine	20.00

CAPE COD

Non-flint, attributed to Boston and Sandwich Glass Co., c1870.

	Clear		Clear
Bowl, 6″, handled	30.00	Marmalade Jar, cov	65.00
Bread Plate	45.00	Pitcher	
Butter, cov	65.00	Milk	65.00
Celery Vase	45.00	Water	85.00
Compote		Plate	
Cov, hs, 6″ d	50.00	5″, handles	30.00
Cov, hs, 8″	100.00	10″	45.00
Cov, hs, 12″	175.00	Platter, open handles	45.00
Cov, ls, 6″	50.00	Sauce, ftd	15.00
Open, hs, 7″	50.00	Spooner	35.00
Creamer	45.00	Sugar, cov	55.00
Decanter	160.00	Wine	35.00
Goblet	45.00		

CARDINAL

Non-flint, c1875, attributed to Ohio Flint Glass Co., Lancaster, OH. There were two butter dishes made, one in the regular pattern and one with three birds in the base - labeled in script Red Bird (cardinal), Pewit, and Titmouse. The latter is less common. Goblet and creamer reproduced.

	Clear		Clear
Butter, cov		Pitcher, water	150.00
Regular	65.00	Sauce	
Three birds in base	100.00	Flat, 4″	12.00
Cake Stand	75.00	Footed, 4½″ or 5½″	20.00
* Creamer	35.00	Spooner	35.00
* Goblet	30.00	Sugar	
Honey Dish, 3½″		Cov	65.00
Cov	45.00	Open	35.00
Open	20.00		

CAROLINA (Inverness)

Made by Bryce Brothers and later by U. S. Glass Co., as part of the States series, c1903. Ruby stained pieces often are souvenir marked. Some clear pieces found with gilt or purple stain.

	Clear	Ruby Stained		Clear	Ruby Stained
Bowl, berry	15.00	—	Pitcher, milk	45.00	—
Butter, cov	50.00	—	Plate, 7½"	12.00	—
Cake Stand	35.00	—	Relish	12.00	—
Compote			Salt Shaker	15.00	35.00
Open, hs, 8", beaded	50.00	—	Sauce		
Open, hs, 9½"	20.00	—	Flat	8.00	—
Open, jelly	10.00	—	Footed	10.00	—
Creamer	20.00	—	Spooner	20.00	—
Goblet	25.00	45.00	Sugar, cov	25.00	—
Mug	30.00	35.00	Tumbler	15.00	—
			Wine	20.00	35.00

CATHEDRAL (Orion)

Non-flint pattern made by Bryce Bros., Pittsburgh, PA., in the 1880s and by U. S. Glass Co. in 1891. Also found in ruby stained, add 50% to clear prices.

	Amber	Amethyst	Blue	Clear	Vaseline
Bowl, berry, 8"	35.00	50.00	40.00	25.00	40.00
Butter, cov	60.00	110.00	62.00	45.00	60.00
Cake Stand	50.00	75.00	60.00	40.00	68.00
Celery Vase	35.00	60.00	40.00	30.00	38.00
Compote					
Cov, hs, 8"	80.00	125.00	100.00	70.00	90.00
Open, hs, 9½"	50.00	85.00	65.00	40.00	—
Open, ls, 7"	45.00	80.00	35.00	25.00	48.00
Open, jelly	—	—	—	25.00	
Creamer					
Flat, sq	50.00	82.00	—	35.00	48.00
Tall	45.00	80.00	50.00	30.00	45.00
Cruet, os	80.00	—	—	45.00	—
Goblet	48.00	70.00	50.00	30.00	55.00
Lamp, 12¾" h	—	—	185.00	—	—
Pitcher, water	75.00	110.00	75.00	60.00	100.00
Relish, fish shape	40.00	50.00	50.00	—	45.00
Salt, boat shape	15.00	30.00	20.00	10.00	20.00
Sauce					
Flat	16.00	30.00	20.00	12.00	16.00
Footed	18.00	35.00	22.00	15.00	20.00
Spooner	40.00	65.00	50.00	35.00	45.00
Sugar, cov	70.00	100.00	60.00	50.00	60.00
Tumbler	32.50	40.00	35.00	25.00	40.00
Wine	40.00	60.00	55.00	28.00	50.00

CHAIN WITH STAR

Non-flint, made by Portland Glass Co, Portland, ME, and U. S. Glass Co., c1890.

	Clear		Clear
Bread Plate, 11", handles	30.00	Compote	
Butter, cov	35.00	Cov, hs	55.00
Cake Stand		Cov, ls	45.00
8¾"	30.00	Open, hs	30.00
10½"	35.00	Open, ls	30.00

	Clear			Clear
Creamer	25.00	Sauce		
Goblet	25.00	Flat		10.00
Pickle, oval	10.00	Footed		12.00
Pitcher, water	50.00	Spooner		20.00
Plate, 7"	25.00	Sugar, cov		35.00
Relish	10.00	Syrup		45.00
Salt Shaker	25.00	Wine		20.00

CHAMPION (Greentown #11)

Made by McKee Bros. and Indiana Tumbler and Goblet Co., 1894–1917. Pieces are often found with gold trim.

	Amber Stained	Clear	Emerald Green	Ruby Stained
Bowl, sq or round				
Berry, master	55.00	—	—	65.00
Berry, individual	—	—	—	20.00
Butter, cov	100.00	45.00	—	100.00
Cake Stand	100.00	35.00	—	90.00
Celery Vase	—	—	—	100.00
Compote				
Cov	—	55.00	—	—
Open, fluted top	150.00	40.00	—	225.00
Creamer	—	25.00	—	60.00
Cruet, os	150.00	30.00	—	195.00
Cup	—	—	—	25.00
Goblet	65.00	25.00	—	65.00
Ice Bucket	125.00	40.00	—	—
Marmalade Jar	—	25.00	—	—
Pickle Dish, 8"	—	15.00	—	—
Pitcher, water	150.00	70.00	—	175.00
Plate, 8" or 10"	—	25.00	—	—
Rose Bowl	—	25.00	45.00	—
Salt Dip	—	10.00	—	65.00
Salt Shaker	35.00	15.00	—	35.00
Spooner	40.00	20.00	—	45.00
Sugar, cov	75.00	40.00	—	85.00
Syrup	150.00	75.00	—	—
Toothpick	65.00	20.00	40.00	70.00
Tray, water	—	45.00	—	—
Tumbler	40.00	15.00	—	45.00
Wine	—	20.00	—	—

CHANDELIER (Crown Jewel)

Non-flint, O'Hara Glass Co., Pittsburgh, PA, c1880, continued by U. S. Glass Co. Also attributed to Canadian manufacturer. Sauce bowls made in amber, $35.00.

	Etched	Plain		Etched	Plain
Banana Stand	—	100.00	Celery Vase	40.00	40.00
Bowl, 8" d, 3¼" h	35.00	37.50	Compote		
Butter, cov	85.00	65.00	Cov, hs	80.00	75.00
Cake Stand, 10"	85.00	65.00	Open, hs, 9½"	70.00	68.00

	Etched	Plain		Etched	Plain
Creamer	60.00	45.00	Sauce, flat	—	16.50
Finger Bowl	40.00	30.00	Sponge Dish	—	30.00
Goblet	50.00	75.00	Spooner	38.00	35.00
Inkwell, dated hard			Sugar, cov	75.00	85.00
rubber top	—	85.00	Sugar Shaker	125.00	110.00
Pitcher, water	115.00	135.00	Tray, water	70.00	50.00
Salt, Master	—	40.00	Tumbler	45.00	35.00
Salt & Pepper	75.00	65.00	Violet Bowl	—	40.00

CHECKERBOARD (Bridal Rosette)

Made by Westmoreland Glass Co., early 1900s. Reproduced since the 1950s in milk glass and in recent years with pink stain. The Cambridge "Ribbon" pattern, usually marked Nearcut, is similar.

	Clear		Clear
Bowl, 9", shallow	20.00	Plate	
Butter, cov	35.00	7"	22.00
Celery Tray	15.00	10"	25.00
Celery Vase	30.00	Punch Cup	5.00
Compote, open, ls, 8"	25.00	Salt and Pepper	40.00
Creamer	25.00	Sauce, flat	8.00
Cruet, os	40.00	Spooner	24.00
Cup	10.00	Sugar, cov	35.00
Goblet	30.00	Tumbler	
Honey, cov, sq, pedestal	45.00	Iced Tea	15.00
Pitcher		Water	18.00
Milk	40.00	Wine	12.00
Water	35.00		

CLASSIC

Clear and frosted non-flint produced by Gillinder and Sons, Philadelphia, PA, in the late 1870s. Pieces with log feet instead of a flat or collared base are worth more.

	Clear		Clear
Bowl, 7", cov, log feet	125.00	Plate	
Butter, cov, log feet	200.00	Jas G. Blaine	185.00
Celery Vase		Pres. Cleveland	180.00
Collared	100.00	Thomas H. Hendricks	170.00
Log feet	125.00	John A. Logan	225.00
Compote		Warrior	160.00
Cov, 6½", collared	150.00	Sauce	
Cov, 6½", log feet	250.00	Flat	25.00
Cov, 7½"d, log feet	225.00	Log Feet	30.00
Cov, 8½", collared	175.00	Spooner	
Cov, 12½", collared	325.00	Collared	95.00
Open, 7¾", log feet	100.00	Log feet	125.00
Creamer	125.00	Sugar, cov	
Goblet	250.00	Collared	150.00
Marmalade Jar, cov	350.00	Log feet	175.00
Pitcher, water		Sweetmeat Jar	175.00
Collared	200.00		
Log feet	250.00		

CLASSIC MEDALLION (Cameo #1)

A pattern of 1870–1880, maker unknown.

	Clear		Clear
Bowl		Open, 7"d, 3¾"h	30.00
6¾", ftd	38.00	Creamer	35.00
8", straight sides	30.00	Pitcher, water	80.00
Butter, cov	40.00	Sauce, ftd	15.00
Celery Vase	30.00	Spooner	25.00
Compote		Sugar, cov	40.00
Cov, hs	50.00		

CLEAR DIAGONAL BAND

Non-flint, c1880. Also has been found in light amber.

	Clear		Clear
Bread Plate, Eureka	28.00	Marmalade Jar	35.00
Butter, cov	40.00	Pitcher, water	40.00
Cake Stand	40.00	Plate	15.00
Celery Vase	20.00	Relish, oval	8.00
Compote		Salt & Pepper	30.00
Cov, hs	45.00	Sauce, flat	7.50
Cov, ls	30.00	Spooner	20.00
Creamer	25.00	Sugar, cov	40.00
Dish, oval	10.00	Wine	20.00
Goblet	15.00		

CLEMATIS

Non-flint made in the late 1870s.

	Clear		Clear
Butter, cov	40.00	Sauce, flat	10.00
Creamer	35.00	Spooner	25.00
Goblet	30.00	Sugar, cov	45.00
Lamp, 12", iron base	50.00		

COLORADO (Lacy Medallion)

Non-flint States pattern made by U. S. Glass Co. in 1898. Made in amethyst stained, ruby stained, and opaque white with enamel floral trim, all of which are scarce. Some pieces found with ornate silver frames or feet. Purists consider these two are separate patterns, with the Lacy Medallion restricted to souvenir pieces. Reproductions have been made.

	Blue	Clear	Green
Banana Stand	45.00	25.00	40.00
Bowl			
6"	35.00	20.00	30.00
7½", ftd	40.00	25.00	35.00
8½", ftd	65.00	45.00	60.00

	Blue	Clear	Green
Butter, cov	200.00	60.00	125.00
Cake Stand	70.00	55.00	65.00
Celery Vase	65.00	35.00	48.00
Compote			
Open, ls, 6"	45.00	20.00	42.00
Open, ls, 9¼" . . .	95.00	35.00	65.00
Creamer			
Individual.	45.00	24.00	40.00
Regular.	95.00	45.00	70.00
Mug	40.00	20.00	30.00
Nappy	40.00	18.00	35.00
Pitcher			
Milk.	145.00	—	100.00
Water	375.00	125.00	185.00
Plate			
6"	50.00	18.00	45.00
8"	65.00	20.00	60.00
Punch Cup	30.00	20.00	25.00
Salt Shaker.	65.00	30.00	40.00
Sauce, ruffled	35.00	15.00	25.00
Sherbet	50.00	25.00	45.00
Spooner	75.00	40.00	60.00
Sugar			
Cov, regular.	80.00	65.00	75.00
Open, individual . .	35.00	24.00	30.00
Toothpick	60.00	30.00	45.00
Tray, Calling Card . .	45.00	25.00	35.00
Tumbler	35.00	18.00	30.00
Vase, 12"	85.00	35.00	60.00
Violet Bowl	60.00	—	—
Wine	—	25.00	40.00

COMET

Flint made by Boston and Sandwich Glass Co in the late 1840s and early 1850s.

	Clear		Clear
Butter, cov	200.00	Pitcher, water	500.00
Compote, open, ls	140.00	Spooner	85.00
Creamer.	175.00	Tumbler	110.00
Goblet	125.00	Whiskey	110.00
Mug	135.00		

CONNECTICUT

Non-flint. One of the States patterns made by U. S. Glass Co., c1900. Found in plain and engraved. Two varieties of ruby stained toothpicks ($90.00) have been identified.

	Clear		Clear
Biscuit Jar	25.00	Butter, cov	35.00
Bowl		Cake Stand	40.00
4"	10.00	Celery Tray.	20.00
8"	15.00	Celery Vase	25.00

	Clear		Clear
Compote		Relish.	12.00
Cov, hs	40.00	Salt & Pepper	35.00
Open, hs, 7"	25.00	Spooner	25.00
Creamer	28.00	Sugar, cov	35.00
Dish, 8", oblong.	20.00	Sugar Shaker	35.00
Lamp, enamel dec.	85.00	Toothpick	40.00
Lemonade, handled.	20.00	Tumbler, water	15.00
Pitcher, water	40.00	Wine	35.00

CORD AND TASSEL

Non-flint, made by La Belle Glass C., Bridgeport, OH, and patented by Andrew Baggs in 1872. Also made by Central Glass Co. and other companies. Heavily reproduced.

	Clear		Clear
Bowl, oval.	20.00	* Goblet	35.00
Butter, cov	65.00	Lamp, ah, pedestal	100.00
Cake Stand, 10"	65.00	Mug, ah	55.00
Castor Bottle.	25.00	Mustard Jar, cov	45.00
Celery Vase	35.00	Pitcher, water, ah	95.00
Compote		Salt & Pepper	45.00
Cov, hs,.	90.00	Sauce	10.00
Open, ls	35.00	Spooner	25.00
Cordial	40.00	Sugar, cov	55.00
Creamer.	25.00	Syrup.	125.00
Egg Cup.	35.00	Tumbler, water	45.00
Dish, oval, vegetable.	25.00	* Wine	35.00

CORD DRAPERY

Made by National Glass Co., Greentown, IN, from 1899 to 1903; later by Indiana Glass at Dunkirk, IN, after 1907.

	Amber	Blue	Clear	Emerald Green
Bowl, 7½"	25.00	25.00	20.00	30.00
Butter, cov	75.00	75.00	60.00	150.00
Cake Stand	50.00	55.00	45.00	75.00
Compote				
Open, 6"	45.00	60.00	48.00	85.00
Open, 7"	75.00	75.00	60.00	95.00
Open, jelly.	—	55.00	45.00	—
Creamer.	45.00	50.00	40.00	60.00
Cruet, os	265.00	100.00	90.00	125.00
Cup	18.00	18.00	15.00	25.00
Goblet	50.00	50.00	55.00	65.00
Jelly, cov	85.00	95.00	65.00	115.00
Pickle, 9¼", oval . . .	40.00	—	25.00	—
Pitcher, water	175.00	175.00	60.00	175.00
Plate	35.00	40.00	25.00	40.00
Relish.	25.00	25.00	22.00	30.00
Sauce, flat	15.00	15.00	10.00	15.00
Spooner	40.00	40.00	35.00	45.00

	Amber	Blue	Clear	Emerald Green
Sugar, cov	125.00	60.00	45.00	75.00
Syrup	295.00	—	90.00	—
Sweetmeat, cov, 6½"d, 5¼" h	165.00	—	—	—
Toothpick	500.00	500.00	80.00	500.00
Tumbler	30.00	30.00	32.00	45.00
Wine	45.00	45.00	40.00	60.00

CORDOVA

Non-flint made by the O'Hara Glass Co., Pittsburgh, Pa. It was exhibited for the first time at the Pittsburgh Glass Show, December 16, 1890. Toothpick has been found in ruby stained, valued at $35.00.

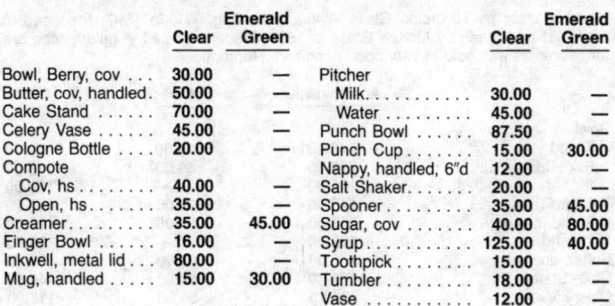

	Clear	Emerald Green		Clear	Emerald Green
Bowl, Berry, cov . . .	30.00	—	Pitcher		
Butter, cov, handled .	50.00	—	Milk	30.00	—
Cake Stand	70.00	—	Water	45.00	—
Celery Vase	45.00	—	Punch Bowl	87.50	—
Cologne Bottle	20.00	—	Punch Cup	15.00	30.00
Compote			Nappy, handled, 6"d	12.00	—
Cov, hs	40.00	—	Salt Shaker	20.00	—
Open, hs	35.00	—	Spooner	35.00	45.00
Creamer	35.00	45.00	Sugar, cov	40.00	80.00
Finger Bowl	16.00	—	Syrup	125.00	40.00
Inkwell, metal lid . . .	80.00	—	Toothpick	15.00	—
Mug, handled	15.00	30.00	Tumbler	18.00	—
			Vase	12.00	—

COTTAGE (Dinner Bell)

Non-flint made by Adams and Co., Pittsburgh, PA, in the late 1870s and U. S. Glass Co. in the 1890s. Known to have been made in emerald green, amber, light blue, and amethyst. Add 50% for amber, 75% for other colors.

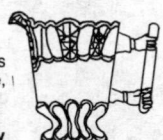

	Clear	Ruby Stained		Clear	Ruby Stained
Banana Stand	55.00	—	Cov, hs 7"	65.00	—
Bowl			Cov, hs hs, 8" . . .	60.00	—
7 ½, oval	15.00	—	Cov, hs, 8¼"	80.00	—
9½, oval	20.00	—	Open, hs, 8¼"d . .	65.00	—
Butter, cov			Jelly	35.00	45.00
Flat	45.00	—	Creamer	25.00	50.00
Footed	45.00	—	Cruet, os	55.00	—
Cake Stand			Cup and Saucer . . .	35.00	—
9"	40.00	—	Dish, oval, deep . . .	20.00	—
10"	45.00	—	Finger Bowl	18.00	—
Celery Vase	35.00	—	Goblet	25.00	—
Champagne	65.00	75.00	Pitcher		
Compote			Milk	28.00	—
Cov, hs 6"	60.00	—	Water	50.00	—

	Clear	Ruby Stained		Clear	Ruby Stained
Plate			Saucer	15.00	40.00
5"	5.00	—	Spooner	20.00	—
6"	18.00	—	Sugar, cov	45.00	—
7"	15.00	—	Syrup	85.00	—
8"	15.00	—	Tray, water	35.00	—
9"	20.00	—	Tumbler	25.00	—
Relish	10.00	—	Waste Bowl	20.00	—
Salt Shaker	35.00	—	Wine	35.00	—

CROESUS

Made in clear by Riverside Glass Works, Wheeling, WV, in 1897. Produced in amethyst and green by McKee Glass in 1899. Pieces trimmed in gold; prices are for examples with gold in very good condition. Reproduced.

	Amethyst	Clear	Green
Bowl			
4", ftd	45.00	10.00	30.00
6¼", ftd	200.00	65.00	115.00
8", flat	165.00	—	120.00
8", ftd	115.00	25.00	115.00
8", ftd, cov	145.00	35.00	115.00
10", ftd	165.00	—	120.00
* Butter, cov	175.00	85.00	165.00
Cake Stand, 10"	175.00	40.00	140.00
Celery Vase	275.00	55.00	115.00
Compote			
Cov, hs, 5"	115.00	28.00	115.00
Cov, hs, 6"	115.00	28.00	115.00
Cov, hs, 7"	135.00	30.00	125.00
Open, hs, 5"	65.00	18.00	60.00
Open, hs, 6"	75.00	18.00	60.00
Open, hs, 7"	80.00	20.00	75.00
Compote, jelly	225.00	20.00	185.00
Condiment Set (cruet, salt & pepper on small tray)	225.00	185.00	185.00
Creamer			
Individual	100.00	—	185.00
Regular	150.00	55.00	65.00
Cruet, os	325.00	135.00	185.00
Pitcher, water	350.00	80.00	235.00
Plate, 8", ftd	75.00	20.00	65.00
Relish, boat shaped	70.00	30.00	60.00
Salt & Pepper	135.00	40.00	125.00
Sauce			
Flat	40.00	15.00	32.00
Footed	45.00	18.00	40.00
Spooner	80.00	60.00	70.00
Sugar, cov	175.00	85.00	125.00
*Toothpick	100.00	25.00	85.00
Tray, condiment	75.00	25.00	30.00
*Tumbler	65.00	20.00	40.00

CRYSTAL WEDDING

Non-flint made by Adams Glass Co., Pittsburgh, PA, in the late 1880s and U. S. Glass Co. in 1891. Also found in frosted, amber stained, and cobalt blue (rare). Heavily reproduced in clear, ruby stained, and milk with enamel trim.

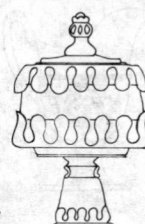

	Clear	Ruby Stained		Clear	Ruby Stained
Banana Stand	85.00	—	Pitcher		
4½", ind berry	15.00	—	Milk, round	110.00	—
6", sq, cov	65.00	—	Milk, sq	125.00	—
7", sq, cov	75.00	—	Water, round	110.00	195.00
8", sq, master			Water, sq	165.00	—
berry	50.00	—	Plate, 10"	25.00	40.00
8", sq, cov	60.00	—	Relish	20.00	—
Butter, cov	50.00	125.00	Salt		
Cake Plate, sq	45.00	85.00	Individual	20.00	—
Cake Stand, 10"	60.00	—	Master	35.00	—
Celery Vase	45.00	75.00	Salt Shaker	50.00	—
Champagne	65.00	—	Sauce	15.00	20.00
Compote			Spooner	30.00	60.00
Cov, hs, 7 x 13"	100.00	—	Sugar, cov	70.00	85.00
Open, hs, 7", sq.	60.00	—	Syrup	150.00	200.00
Open, ls, 5", sq	50.00	—	Toothpick	50.00	—
Creamer	50.00	75.00	Tumbler	35.00	45.00
Cruet	85.00	—	Vase		
Goblet	55.00	85.00	Footed, twisted	25.00	—
Nappy, handle	25.00	—	Swung	25.00	—
Pickle	25.00	—	Wine	45.00	—

CUPID AND VENUS

Non-flint made by Richards and Hartley Glass Co., Tarentum, PA, in the late 1870s. Also made in vaseline, rare.

	Amber	Clear		Amber	Clear
Bowl			Cruet, os	—	135.00
8", cov, ftd	—	28.00	Goblet	—	65.00
9", oval	—	32.00	Marmalade Jar, cov	—	65.00
Bread Plate	75.00	40.00	Mug		
Butter, cov	—	55.00	Miniature	—	40.00
Cake Plate	—	45.00	Medium, 2½"	—	35.00
Cake Stand	—	60.00	Large, 3½"	—	40.00
Celery Vase	—	40.00	Pitcher		
Champagne	—	90.00	Milk	190.00	75.00
Compote			Water	215.00	65.00
Cov, hs, 8"	—	80.00	Plate, 10", round	75.00	40.00
Cov, ls, 7"	—	65.00	Sauce		
Cov, ls, 9"	—	95.00	Flat	—	10.00
Open, ls, 8½",			Footed, 3½", 4"		
scalloped	135.00	35.00	and 4½"	—	15.00
Open, hs, 9¼"	—	45.00	Spooner	—	35.00
Cordial, 3½"	—	75.00	Sugar, cov	—	65.00
Creamer	—	36.50	Wine, 3¾"	—	85.00

CURRANT

Non-flint, made by Campbell, Jones and Co., and patented in 1871.

	Clear		Clear
Bowl, 7", vegetable	18.00	Pitcher	
Butter, cov	75.00	Milk, ah	125.00
Cake Stand		Water, ah.	85.00
9¼".	60.00	Plate, oval	
11".	85.00	5" x 7".	25.00
Celery Vase	4500	6" x 9".	30.00
Compote		Salt, ftd	30.00
Cov, hs, 8".	65.00	Sauce, ftd, 4"	12.00
Cov, hs, 9".	135.00	Spooner	25.00
Cov, hs, 12".	195.00	Sugar	
Cov, ls, 8".	45.00	Cov.	55.00
Cordial	45.00	Open, buttermilk type	30.00
Creamer, ah	45.00	Tumbler, ftd	30.00
Egg Cup.	25.00	Wine	25.00
Goblet	30.00		

CURRIER AND IVES

Non-flint made by Bellaire Glass Co. in Findlay, OH, in 1890. Known to have been made in colors, but rarely found. A decanter is known in ruby stained.

	Clear		Clear
Bowl, oval, 10", canoe		Water	70.00
shaped	30.00	Plate, 10"	20.00
Butter, cov	50.00	Relish.	18.00
Compote		Salt Shaker.	30.00
Cov, hs, 7½"	95.00	Sauce, oval	12.00
Open, hs, 7½", scalloped .	50.00	Spooner	30.00
Creamer.	30.00	Sugar, cov	45.00
Cup and saucer	30.00	Syrup	75.00
Dish, oval, boat shaped, 8" .	27.50	Tray	
Goblet, knob stem	30.00	Water, Balky Mule	65.00
Lamp, 9½", hs	75.00	Wine, Balky Mule.	50.00
Pitcher		Water Bottle, 12" h, os.	55.00
Milk.	60.00	Wine, 3¼".	18.00

CURTAIN (Sultan)

Clear non-flint pattern made by Bryce Brothers, Pittsburgh, Pennsylvania, late 1870s.

	Clear		Clear
Bowl		Castor Set, salt, pepper, and	
7½".	30.00	mustard, stand.	115.00
8"	45.00	Celery Tray.	30.00
Butter, cov	55.00	Celery Vase	30.00
Cake Stand		Compote, open, hs, 10". . . .	45.00
8".	40.00	Creamer.	25.00
9½".	45.00	Cruet, os	45.00

	Clear		Clear
Finger Bowl	30.00	Sauce, 4¾"	8.00
Goblet	30.00	Spooner	25.00
Mug	25.00	Sugar	
Pickle	10.00	Covered	38.00
Pitcher, water	75.00	Open	20.00
Plate, 7", sq	20.00	Tray, water	35.00
Salt Shaker	25.00	Tumbler	20.00

CURTAIN TIE BACK

Clear non-flint pattern made in the mid 1880s.

	Clear		Clear
Bowl, 7½", sq	18.00	Salt & Pepper, pr.	35.00
Bread Plate	35.00	Sauce	
Butter, cov	40.00	Flat	12.00
Celery Vase	36.00	Footed	14.00
Compote, cov, hs	40.00	Spooner	30.00
Creamer	28.00	Sugar	
Goblet		Covered	32.00
Fancy base	30.00	Open	18.00
Flat base	20.00	Tray, water	30.00
Pickle	12.00	Tumbler	18.00
Pitcher, water	45.00	Wine	20.00
Relish	12.00		

CUT LOG (Cat's Eye and Block, Ethol)

Non-flint, made by Greensburg Glass Co., 1888. Also reported in camphor glass, but rare.

	Clear		Clear
Biscuit Jar	95.00	Goblet	45.00
Bowl, 10", deep, ftd,		Mug, large	45.00
scalloped	40.00	Mustard Jar	35.00
Butter, cov	65.00	Olive Dish	20.00
Cake Stand		Pitcher, water, ah	75.00
9"	45.00	Relish	25.00
10"	55.00	Salt & Pepper, pr.	60.00
Celery Tray	20.00	Salt, master	85.00
Celery Vase	40.00	Sauce	
Compote		Flat	20.00
Cov, hs, 7¼"	85.00	Footed	25.00
Cov, hs, 12½"	90.00	Spooner	35.00
Cov, jelly, 6¼"	45.00	Sugar	
Open, hs, 8"	55.00	Cov, regular	55.00
Open, hs, 10"	70.00	Cov, ind.	30.00
Creamer		Open, ind	20.00
Individual	15.00	Tumbler	45.00
Regular, 5"	40.00	Wine	30.00
Cruet, os	50.00		

DAHLIA

Non-flint, made by Portland Glass Co, Portland, ME, c1865, and Canton Glass Co., c1880. Also attributed to a Canadian manufacturer.

	Amber	Apple Green	Blue	Clear	Vaseline
Bowl	30.00	25.00	25.00	18.00	30.00
Bread Plate	55.00	50.00	50.00	45.00	55.00
Butter, cov	80.00	70.00	70.00	40.00	80.00
Cake Plate	60.00	45.00	45.00	24.00	60.00
Cake Stand, 9"	72.50	50.00	50.00	25.00	72.50
Champagne	80.00	65.00	65.00	55.00	80.00
Compote					
Cov, hs, 7"	100.00	85.00	85.00	55.00	80.00
Open, hs, 8"	60.00	45.00	45.00	30.00	60.00
Cordial	55.00	50.00	50.00	35.00	55.00
Creamer	40.00	35.00	35.00	25.00	40.00
Egg Cup					
Double	80.00	65.00	65.00	50.00	80.00
Single	55.00	40.00	40.00	25.00	55.00
Goblet	65.00	55.00	55.00	35.00	65.00
Mug					
Large	55.00	55.00	55.00	35.00	55.00
Small	50.00	45.00	40.00	30.00	50.00
Pickle	35.00	30.00	30.00	20.00	35.00
Pitcher					
Milk	70.00	55.00	55.00	40.00	70.00
Water	100.00	90.00	90.00	55.00	90.00
Water, applied handle	—	—	—	125.00	—
Plate					
7"	45.00	40.00	40.00	20.00	45.00
9", handles	35.00	45.00	50.00	18.00	50.00
Platter	50.00	45.00	45.00	30.00	50.00
Relish, 9½" l	20.00	20.00	20.00	15.00	25.00
Salt, ind, ftd	35.00	30.00	30.00	5.00	35.00
Sauce					
Flat	15.00	12.00	15.00	10.00	15.00
Footed	20.00	15.00	15.00	10.00	20.00
Spooner	50.00	45.00	50.00	35.00	50.00
Sugar, cov	75.00	60.00	60.00	40.00	75.00
Syrup	75.00	—	—	55.00	—
Wine	45.00	40.00	45.00	25.00	45.00

DAISY AND BUTTON

Non-flint pattern made in the 1870s by several companies in many different forms. In continuous production since inception. Also found in amberina, amber stain, and ruby stained.

	Amber	Apple Green	Blue	Clear	Vaseline
Bowl, triangular	40.00	45.00	45.00	25.00	65.00
Bread Plate, 13" . . .	35.00	60.00	35.00	20.00	40.00
Butter Chip	10.00	24.00	15.00	8.00	25.00
Butter, cov					
Round	70.00	90.00	70.00	65.00	95.00
Square	110.00	115.00	110.00	100.00	120.00

	Amber	Apple Green	Blue	Clear	Vaseline
Butter Pat	30.00	40.00	35.00	25.00	35.00
Canoe					
4"	12.00	24.00	15.00	10.00	24.00
8½"	30.00	35.00	30.00	25.00	35.00
12"	60.00	35.00	28.00	20.00	40.00
14"	30.00	40.00	35.00	25.00	40.00
Castor Set					
4 bottle, glass std.	90.00	85.00	95.00	80.00	75.00
5 bottle, metal std	105.00	100.00	110.00	100.00	95.00
Celery Vase	45.00	50.00	40.00	30.00	48.00
Compote					
Cov, hs, 6"	35.00	50.00	45.00	25.00	50.00
Open, hs, 8"	75.00	65.00	60.00	40.00	65.00
Creamer	35.00	40.00	40.00	18.00	35.00
Cruet, os	100.00	60.00	55.00	45.00	60.00
Egg Cup	20.00	30.00	25.00	15.00	30.00
Finger Bowl	30.00	50.00	35.00	30.00	42.00
Goblet	40.00	50.00	40.00	25.00	40.00
Hat, 2½"	30.00	35.00	40.00	20.00	40.00
Ice Tub	—	—	—	—	75.00
Inkwell	40.00	50.00	45.00	30.00	45.00
Parfait	25.00	35.00	30.00	20.00	35.00
Pickle Castor	125.00	90.00	150.00	75.00	150.00
Pitcher, water					
Bulbous, reed					
handle	125.00	95.00	90.00	75.00	90.00
Tankard	62.00	65.00	62.00	60.00	65.00
Plate					
5", leaf shape . . .	20.00	24.00	16.00	18.00	25.00
6", round	10.00	22.00	15.00	6.50	24.00
7", square	24.00	35.00	25.00	15.00	35.00
Punch Bowl, stand .	90.00	100.00	95.00	85.00	100.00
Salt & Pepper	30.00	40.00	30.00	20.00	35.00
Sauce, 4"	18.00	25.00	18.00	15.00	25.00
Slipper					
5"	45.00	48.00	50.00	45.00	50.00
11½"	40.00	50.00	30.00	35.00	50.00
Spooner	40.00	40.00	45.00	35.00	45.00
Sugar, cov	45.00	50.00	45.00	35.00	50.00
Syrup	45.00	50.00	45.00	30.00	45.00
Toothpick					
Round	40.00	55.00	25.00	40.00	45.00
Urn	20.00	25.00	20.00	10.00	35.00
Tray	65.00	65.00	60.00	35.00	60.00
Tumbler	18.00	30.00	35.00	15.00	25.00
Vase, wall pocket . .	125.00	—	—	—	—
Wine	15.00	25.00	20.00	10.00	45.00

DAISY AND BUTTON WITH CROSSBARS (Mikado)

Non-flint pattern made by Richards and Hartley, Tarentum, PA, c1888.

	Amber	Blue	Clear	Vaseline
Bowl				
6"	26.00	30.00	20.00	28.00
9"	40.00	40.00	25.00	35.00

	Amber	Blue	Clear	Vaseline
Bread Plate	30.00	45.00	25.00	35.00
Butter, cov				
Flat...........	55.00	55.00	45.00	55.00
Footed	—	75.00	25.00	60.00
Celery Vase	36.00	40.00	30.00	50.00
Compote				
Cov, hs, 8"......	55.00	65.00	45.00	55.00
Open, hs, 8"	45.00	50.00	30.00	45.00
Open, ls, 7"	30.00	—	—	—
Creamer				
Individual.......	25.00	30.00	18.00	30.00
Regular........	42.50	45.00	35.00	40.00
Cruet, os	75.00	55.00	35.00	100.00
Goblet	40.00	40.00	25.00	40.00
Mug, 3"h.........	15.00	18.00	12.50	20.00
Pitcher				
Milk...........	45.00	50.00	35.00	50.00
Water	85.00	70.00	45.00	65.00
Salt & Pepper.....	40.00	45.00	30.00	40.00
Sauce				
Flat...........	15.00	18.00	10.00	15.00
Footed	18.00	25.00	15.00	24.00
Spooner.........	35.00	35.00	25.00	35.00
Sugar, cov				
Individual.......	25.00	35.00	10.00	25.00
Regular........	50.00	60.00	25.00	55.00
Syrup...........	90.00	110.00	35.00	90.00
Toothpick........	40.00	40.00	28.00	35.00
Tumbler	20.00	25.00	18.00	25.00
Wine	30.00	35.00	25.00	30.00

DAISY AND BUTTON WITH NARCISSUS (Daisy and Button with Clear Lily)

Non-flint made in late 1890s. Later made by Indiana Glass Co. Dunkirk, IN, into 1920s. Sometimes found with flowers flashed with cranberry flashing and pieces trimmed in gold. Many pieces have been reproduced.

	Clear	Flashed Color		Clear	Flashed Color
Bowl, 6" w, 9¼" l, oval, ftd........	45.00	—	Salt Shaker.......	18.00	—
Butter, cov	50.00	—	Sauce		
Celery Vase	20.00	—	Flat...........	10.00	—
Compote, open, ls..	35.00	—	Footed, 4"......	15.00	—
Creamer.........	25.00	—	Spooner	30.00	—
Decanter, os	40.00	62.50	Sugar, cov	38.00	42.50
Goblet	25.00	—	Tray, water or wine,		
Pitcher, water	50.00	70.00	10"...........	30.00	40.00
Punch Cup	10.00	18.00	Tumbler	18.00	20.00
			Wine	22.00	25.00

DAISY AND BUTTON WITH V ORNAMENT (Van Dyke)

Made by A. J. Beatty & Co., 1886–1887.

	Amber	Blue	Clear	Vaseline
Bowl				
9″	35.00	42.00	45.00	55.00
10″	40.00	45.00	40.00	45.00
Butter, cov	85.00	80.00	65.00	90.00
Celery Vase	50.00	55.00	30.00	55.00
Creamer.	30.00	50.00	30.00	50.00
Finger Bowl	28.50	45.00	22.50	55.00
Goblet	35.00	45.00	25.00	50.00
Mug	20.00	30.00	20.00	35.00
Pickle Castor	120.00	120.00	85.00	100.00
Pitcher, water	65.00	90.00	48.00	60.00
Punch Cup	12.00	20.00	12.50	25.00
Sauce, flat	20.00	20.00	12.00	30.00
Spooner.	40.00	38.50	35.00	45.00
Sugar, cov	60.00	50.00	40.00	75.00
Toothpick	32.50	40.00	28.50	35.00
Tray, water	55.00	65.00	35.00	55.00
Tumbler	25.00	28.00	15.00	35.00

DAKOTA (Baby Thumbprint, Thumbprint Band)

Non-flint made by Ripley and Co., Pittsburgh, PA, in the late 1880s and early 1890s. Later reissued by U. S. Glass Co. as one of the States patterns. Prices listed are for etched fern and berry pattern; also found with fern and no berry, and oak leaf etching, and scarcer grape etching. Other etchings known include fish, swan, peacock, bird and insect, bird and flowers, ivy and berry, stag, spider and insect in web, buzzard on dead tree, and crane catching fish. Sometimes ruby stained with or without souvenir markings. There is a four piece table set available in a "hotel" variant, prices are about 20% more than the regular type.

	Clear Etched	Clear Plain	Ruby Stained
Basket, 10 x 2″, metal bail	150.00	90.00	165.00
Bottle, 5½″	45.00	35.00	—
Bowl, berry	45.00	30.00	—
Butter, cov	65.00	60.00	125.00
Cake Cover, 8″	300.00	200.00	—
Cake Stand			
9½″.	58.00	35.00	—
10½″.	65.00	45.00	—
Celery Tray.	35.00	25.00	—
Celery Vase	40.00	30.00	—
Compote			
Cov, hs, 5″	60.00	—	—
Cov, hs, 7″	65.00	—	—
Cov, hs, 8″	75.00	—	—
Cov, hs, 9″	75.00	—	—
Cov, hs, 12″	95.00	75.00	—
Cov, 6″, jelly	65.00	50.00	—
Open, hs, 7″	55.00	40.00	—
Open, hs, 10″ . . .	75.00	60.00	—
Condiment Tray, metal handles . . .	—	75.00	—
Creamer.	50.00	28.50	65.00
Cruet	75.00	55.00	—
Goblet	35.00	28.00	75.00

	Clear Etched	Clear Plain	Ruby Stained
Pitcher			
Milk.	100.00	80.00	200.00
Tankard	125.00	95.00	225.00
Water	95.00	75.00	190.00
Plate, 10″	85.00	—	—
Salt Shaker.	65.00	50.00	125.00
Sauce			
Flat.	20.00	18.00	—
Footed	25.00	20.00	—
Spooner	30.00	25.00	65.00
Sugar, cov	65.00	55.00	85.00
Tray, water	100.00	75.00	—
Tumbler	35.00	30.00	40.00
Waste Bowl.	75.00	45.00	—
Wine	40.00	20.00	45.00

DART

Clear non-flint pattern made in Ohio in the 1880s.

	Clear		Clear
Bowl.	12.00	Goblet	24.00
Butter, cov	25.00	Pitcher, water	35.00
Compote		Sauce, ftd.	12.50
Cov, hs, 8½″ d, 12½″ h. . .	60.00	Spooner	20.00
Open, jelly.	18.00	Sugar, cov	35.00
Creamer.	25.00	Tumbler	15.00

DEER AND DOG

Non-flint pattern made in the c1870s. Pattern identified by frosted dog finial. Found in both etched and non-etched styles.

	Clear		Clear
Butter, cov	125.00	Mug.	40.00
Celery Vase	75.00	Pitcher, water, ah	150.00
Compote, cov, 7″, ls, non-		Sauce, ftd.	20.00
etched.	100.00	Spooner	60.00
Creamer.	75.00	Sugar, cov	125.00
Goblet	65.00	Wine	45.00
Marmalade Jar, cov	100.00		

DEER AND PINE TREE (Deer and Doe)

Non-flint pattern, made by Belmont Glass Co., and McKee Glass Co. 1883. Souvenir mugs with gilt found in clear and olive green. Also made in canary (vaseline). The goblet has been reproduced.

	Amber	Apple Green	Blue	Clear
Bread Plate	90.00	90.00	100.00	75.00
Butter, cov	125.00	110.00	115.00	95.00
Cake Stand	—	—	—	75.00
Celery Vase	—	—	—	50.00
Compote				
Cov, hs, 8″, sq . . .	—	—	—	25.00
Open, hs, 7″	—	—	—	45.00
Open, hs, 9″	—	—	—	55.00
Creamer	95.00	85.00	90.00	65.00
Finger Bowl	—	—	—	55.00
* Goblet	—	—	—	55.00
Marmalade Jar	—	—	—	75.00
Mug	40.00	45.00	50.00	40.00
Pickle	—	—	—	24.00
Pitcher				
Milk	—	—	—	70.00
Water	125.00	110.00	115.00	100.00
Platter, 8 x 13″	—	—	80.00	60.00
Sauce				
Flat	—	—	—	20.00
Footed	—	—	—	28.00
Spooner	—	—	—	40.00
Covered	—	—	—	85.00
Open	—	—	—	25.00
Tray, water	100.00	—	90.00	100.00

DELAWARE (Four Petal Flower)

Non-flint pattern made by U. S. Glass Co. c1899. Also found in amethyst (scarce), clear with rose trim, custard, and milk glass. Prices are for pieces with perfect gold trim.

	Clear	Green With Gold	Rose With Gold
Banana Bowl	50.00	55.00	65.00
Bowl			
8″	30.00	35.00	50.00
9″	25.00	60.00	58.00
Bride's Basket, SP frame	—	115.00	165.00
Butter, cov	60.00	125.00	145.00
Claret Jug, tankard shape	110.00	195.00	200.00
Celery Vase, flat . . .	75.00	90.00	95.00
Creamer	45.00	65.00	70.00
Cruet, os	90.00	200.00	250.00
Finger Bowl	25.00	50.00	45.00
Lamp Shade, round .	—	—	75.00
Pin Tray	30.00	55.00	65.00
Pitcher, water	50.00	150.00	125.00
Pomade Box, jeweled	—	200.00	350.00
Puff Box, bulbous, jeweled	—	175.00	315.00
Punch Cup	18.00	30.00	35.00
Sauce, 5½″, boat . .	15.00	35.00	30.00

	Clear	Green With Gold	Rose With Gold
Spooner	45.00	60.00	55.00
Sugar, cov	65.00	85.00	100.00
Toothpick	50.00	90.00	150.00
Tumbler	20.00	45.00	48.50
Vase			
6″	—	45.00	70.00
8″	—	55.00	75.00
9½″	—	80.00	85.00

DEWDROP IN POINTS

Non-flint made by Brilliant Glass Works, Brilliant, OH, in the late 1870s and Greensburg Glass Co, Greensburg, PA, after 1889.

	Clear		Clear
Bread Plate	25.00	Pitcher, water	35.00
Butter, cov	40.00	Plate, 12″	20.00
Cake Stand	40.00	Platter, 9 x 11¾″	25.00
Compote		Sauce	
Cov, hs	75.00	Flat	10.00
Open, hs	25.00	Footed	15.00
Open, ls	22.50	Spooner	20.00
Creamer	30.00	Sugar, cov	40.00
Goblet	25.00	Wine	25.00
Pickle	15.00		

DEWDROP WITH STAR

Non-flint made by Campbell, Jones and Co., Pittsburgh, PA, in 1877. There was no goblet made in this pattern. This pattern has been reproduced in color.

	Clear		Clear
Bowl		Honey, underplate	75.00
6″	8.00	Lamp, patented 1876	85.00
7″	20.00	Pitcher, water, ah	125.00
9″, ftd	24.00	*Plate	
Bread Plate, sheaf of wheat		5″	12.00
center	35.00	7″	15.00
Butter, cov, dome lid	50.00	9″	20.00
Cake Stand	40.00	Relish	15.00
Celery Vase	40.00	*Salt, ftd	20.00
Cheese Dish, cov, dome lid	110.00	Sauce	
Compote		Flat	10.00
Cov, hs, dome lid	75.00	Footed	12.00
Cov, ls, 5″	60.00	Spooner	35.00
Open, hs	45.00	Sugar, cov, domed lid	50.00
Creamer, ah	35.00		

DEWEY (Flower Flange)

Made by Indiana Tumbler & Goblet Co., Greentown, IN, 1894. Later by U. S. Glass Co. until 1904. Some experimental colors were made including a nile green opaque mug ($75.00).

	Amber	Caramel	Clear	Green	Vaseline
Bowl, 8", ftd	65.00	175.00	50.00	65.00	70.00
Butter, cov	75.00	160.00	45.00	65.00	95.00
Creamer	45.00	150.00	30.00	50.00	55.00
Cruet, os	125.00	180.00	75.00	145.00	125.00
Mug	55.00	155.00	35.00	55.00	58.00
Parfait	35.00	—	—	—	—
Pitcher, water	90.00	175.00	55.00	175.00	175.00
Plate, 7½", ftd	35.00	130.00	30.00	40.00	65.00
Relish	42.00	145.00	20.00	42.00	45.00
Sauce, flat	25.00	—	5.00	25.00	30.00
Spooner	40.00	130.00	25.00	40.00	50.00
Sugar, cov					
Individual	45.00	—	25.00	45.00	65.00
Regular	50.00	150.00	35.00	55.00	75.00
Tumbler	55.00	150.00	40.00	45.00	65.00

DIAGONAL BAND

Made in c1875-1885, maker unknown.

	Amber	Apple Green	Clear
Bread Plate	30.00	35.00	24.00
Butter, cov	60.00	80.00	35.00
Cake Stand	40.00	55.00	30.00
Celery Vase	45.00	50.00	25.00
Compote			
Cov, hs, 7"	65.00	80.00	55.00
Cov, ls, 8"	62.50	70.00	45.00
Open, hs, 7½" . . .	45.00	50.00	20.00
Creamer	40.00	50.00	30.00
Goblet	30.00	45.00	28.00
Pitcher			
Milk	50.00	—	32.00
Water	65.00	95.00	40.00
Plate, 6"	—	—	12.50
Relish, 6⅞" oval . . .	14.00	18.00	10.00
Sauce			
Flat	—	—	6.00
Footed	—	15.00	12.50
Spooner	24.00	40.00	20.00
Sugar			
Cov	40.00	50.00	30.00
Open	22.00	28.00	15.00
Wine	35.00	45.00	20.00

DIAMOND POINT

Flint, originally made by Boston and Sandwich Glass Co., in the 1830-1840 period, and by the New England Glass Co. Many other companies manufactured this pattern throughout the 19th century.

	Flint	Non-Flint		Flint	Non-Flint
Bowl			Goblet	45.00	35.00
7″, cov	60.00	20.00	Honey	15.00	—
8″, cov	60.00	20.00	Mustard, Brittania		
8″, open	45.00	15.00	cov	25.00	—
Butter, cov	95.00	50.00	Pitcher		
Cake Stand, 14″ ..	185.00	—	Pint...........	160.00	—
Candlesticks, pr ...	145.00	—	Quart	275.00	—
Celery Vase	68.00	30.00	Plate		
Champagne	85.00	—	6″	30.00	—
Claret..........	90.00	—	8″	50.00	—
Compote			Salt, master, cov ..	75.00	—
Cov, hs, 8″......	135.00	—	Salt & Pepper ...	45.00	—
Open, hs 10½″,			Sauce, flat	14.00	—
flared.........	100.00	—	Spillholder	45.00	—
Open, hs, 11″,			Spooner	40.00	25.00
scalloped rim ..	110.00	—	Sugar, cov	65.00	—
Open, ls, 7½″ ...	50.00	40.00	Syrup	150.00	—
Cordial	165.00	—	Tumbler, bar.....	65.00	35.00
Creamer, ah	115.00	—	Whiskey, ah	70.00	—
Decanter, qt, os. ...	165.00	—	Wine	75.00	30.00
Egg Cup.........	40.00	20.00			

DIAMOND QUILTED

Non-flint, c1880. Heavily reproduced.

	Amber	Amethyst	Blue	Clear	Vaseline
Bowl					
6″	10.00	20.00	—	—	—
7″	18.00	—	—	—	25.00
Butter, cov	50.00	100.00	100.00	40.00	75.00
Celery Vase	35.00	60.00	50.00	40.00	40.00
Champagne	—	36.00	—	21.00	38.00
Compote					
Cov, hs, 8″......	140.00	120.00	120.00	45.00	90.00
Open, ls, 9″.....	—	—	—	15.00	35.00
Creamer.........	45.00	40.00	70.00	25.00	55.00
*Goblet	40.00	40.00	40.00	30.00	35.00
Mug	—	30.00	40.00	—	—
Pitcher, water	75.00	85.00	80.00	50.00	75.00
Sauce					
Flat...........	12.00	—	16.50	8.00	18.00
Footed	16.00	18.00	18.00	12.00	22.00
Spooner.........	35.00	40.00	40.00	30.00	50.00
Sugar, cov	50.00	75.00	55.00	40.00	60.00
Tray...........	55.00	70.00	75.00	30.00	65.00
*Tumbler	45.00	40.00	40.00	25.00	32.50
Vase, 9″.........	—	—	—	48.00	—
* Wine	20.00	40.00	35.00	15.00	20.00

DIAMOND SPEARHEAD

Made by Northwood-Dugan Glass Co., Indiana, PA, around 1900. No cruet reported. A cake stand has been found, but it was not listed in early catalogues. Also made in canary opalescent, prices same as blue opalescent. A cake stand, 10″, $65.00, and a carafe, $180.00 are known in canary opalescent.

	Clear	Cobalt Blue Opal	Green Opal	Sapphire Blue Opal	White Opal
Bowl, berry	20.00	—	40.00	40.00	35.00
Butter, cov	40.00	150.00	85.00	75.00	—
Carafe	—	—	180.00	—	—
Celery Vase	20.00	—	45.00	40.00	35.00
Compote					
Cov, hs	—	—	35.00	30.00	32.00
Cov, ls, jelly	—	—	60.00	50.00	—
Creamer.	20.00	70.00	35.00	30.00	32.00
Cup and Saucer . . .	—	—	60.00	60.00	—
Goblet	—	—	90.00	90.00	—
Mug	20.00	—	55.00	50.00	—
Pitcher, water	50.00	200.00	85.00	75.00	—
Plate, 10"	—	—	80.00	—	—
Relish.	—	—	25.00	20.00	—
Sauce	—	—	15.00	10.00	—
Spooner	20.00	—	50.00	40.00	—
Sugar, cov	30.00	—	50.00	45.00	—
Syrup	—	230.00	75.00	65.00	—
Toothpick	—	125.00	85.00	90.00	—

DIAMOND THUMBPRINT

Flint, attributed to Boston and Sandwich Glass Co., and other factories from 1840 to 1850s. Compotes are being reproduced for Sandwich Glass Museum.

	Clear		Clear
Bitters Bottle, orig pewter pourer, applied lip, polished pontil	475.00	Decanter	
		Pint, ns	175.00
		Quart, os	225.00
Butter, cov	200.00	Finger Bowl	100.00
Celery Vase, scalloped top. .	185.00	* Goblet	350.00
Champagne	265.00	Honey Dish.	25.00
Compote		Pitcher, water	650.00
Cov, hs, 8"	150.00	Sauce, flat	25.00
Open, ls, scalloped, 8" . . .	50.00	* Spooner	85.00
Cordial	300.00	Sugar, cov	150.00
Creamer.	225.00	Tumbler, bar	125.00
		Whiskey, applied handle . . .	300.00
		Wine	250.00

DRAPERY (Lace)

Non-flint made by Doyle and Co., Pittsburgh, PA, in the 1870s. Reportedly made by Sandwich Glass Co. at an earlier period. Pieces with fine stippling have applied handles; pieces with coarse stippling have pressed handles.

	Clear		Clear
Butter, cov	45.00	Pitcher, water, ah	85.00
Buttermilk	30.00	Plate, 6"	30.00
Compote, ls	55.00	Sauce, flat	10.00
Creamer, applied handle . . .	35.00	Spooner	40.00
Egg Cup.	25.00	Sugar, cov	40.00
Goblet	35.00	Tumbler	28.00

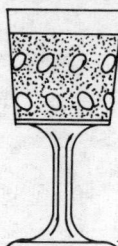

EGG IN SAND (Bean)

Non-flint, c1880. Has been reported in colors, but rare.

	Clear		Clear
Bread Plate, octagonal	25.00	Salt and Pepper	65.00
Butter, cov	48.00	Sauce	12.00
Compote, cov, jelly	45.00	Spooner, flat rim	28.00
Creamer.	30.00	Sugar, cov	35.00
Dish, swan center	40.00	Tray, water	40.00
Goblet	35.00	Tumbler	30.00
Pitcher, water	45.00	Wine	35.00
Relish.	12.00		

EGYPTIAN

Non-flint, attributed to Boston and Sandwich Glass Co., c1870.

	Clear		Clear
Bowl, 8½".	50.00	Goblet	45.00
Bread Plate		Honey	14.00
Cleopatra	40.00	Pickle, oval	20.00
Mormon Temple.	300.00	Pitcher, water	185.00
Butter, cov	85.00	Plate, 12", handles,	
Celery Vase	75.00	Pyramids.	75.00
Compote		Relish.	20.00
Cov, hs, 7", Sphinx base. .	250.00	Sauce, ftd, 4½".	15.00
Open, hs, 7½", Sphinx		Spooner	40.00
base.	75.00	Sugar, cov	70.00
Creamer.	50.00		

EMPRESS

Made by Riverside Glass Works, Wellsburg, WV, c1898. Also found in amethyst (rare). Clear and emerald green pieces trimmed in gold; prices are for pieces with gold in very good condition.

	Clear	Emerald Green		Clear	Emerald Green
Bowl, 8½".	—	45.00	Pitcher, water	65.00	150.00
Breakfast Set, ind creamer and			Salt Shaker.	30.00	50.00
			Spooner	30.00	45.00
sugar	40.00	—	Sugar, cov	45.00	125.00
Butter, cov	50.00	100.00	Sugar Shaker	55.00	110.00
Celery Vase	55.00	—	Syrup.	60.00	275.00
Creamer.	35.00	75.00	Toothpick	—	150.00
Cruet	50.00	135.00	Tumbler	32.50	55.00
Oil Lamp, atypical . .	60.00	—			

ESTHER (Tooth and Claw)

Non-flint made by Riverside Glass Works, Wellsburg, WV, c1896. The green has gold trim. Also found in ruby stained and amber stained with enamel decoration.

	Clear	Green	Ruby Stained
Bowl, 8″	35.00	50.00	—
Butter, cov	65.00	100.00	150.00
Cake Stand, 10½″ . .	60.00	80.00	—
Celery Vase	40.00	90.00	—
Compote, jelly, hs . .	—	75.00	
Cracker Jar.	—	—	200.00
Creamer.	45.00	70.00	75.00
Cruet, os	45.00	245.00	—
Goblet	40.00	95.00	75.00
Pitcher, water	65.00	165.00	250.00
Plate, 10″	—	60.00	—
Relish.	20.00	25.00	40.00
Salt & Pepper	50.00	100.00	—
Spooner	35.00	50.00	60.00
Sugar, cov	55.00	70.00	100.00
Syrup	—	175.00	—
Toothpick	45.00	75.00	—
Tumbler	25.00	48.50	55.00
Wine	35.00	—	—

EUREKA

Flint made by Mckee & Bros in Pittsburgh, PA, in the late 1860s. Pieces have applied handles and bud finials. Made in flint and non-flint.

	Clear		Clear
Bowl		Creamer.	45.00
6″, round	25.00	Egg Cup.	30.00
7″, oval	30.00	Goblet	28.00
8″, oval	40.00	Pitcher, water	95.00
Butter, cov	60.00	Salt, ftd	30.00
Champagne	30.00	Sauce, flat	12.50
Compote		Spooner	40.00
Cov, hs	85.00	Sugar, cov	50.00
Open, hs.	50.00	Tumbler, ftd	25.00
Cordial	40.00	Wine	25.00

EXCELSIOR

Flint made by several firms, including Sandwich and McKee, from 1850s-1860s. Quality and design vary. Prices are for high quality flint.

	Clear		Clear
Bar Bottle	50.00	Open, hs	85.00
Bowl, 10″, open.	125.00	Cordial	40.00
Bitters bottle	75.00	Creamer.	85.00
Butter, cov	100.00	Egg Cup	
Candlestick.	125.00	Double	55.00
Celery Vase, scalloped top. .	75.00	Single	40.00
Champagne	60.00	Goblet, Maltese Cross	50.00
Claret.	45.00	Lamp, hand	95.00
Compote		Mug	30.00
Cov, ls	125.00	Pickle Jar, cov.	45.00

	Clear		Clear
Pitcher, water	350.00	Syrup	110.00
Salt, master	30.00	Tumbler, bar	50.00
Spillholder	75.00	Whiskey, Maltese Cross	65.00
Spooner	60.00	Wine	45.00
Sugar, cov	85.00		

EYEWINKER

Non-flint made in Findlay, OH, in 1889. Reportedly made by Dalzell, Gilmore and Leighton Glass Co., who were organized in 1883 in West Virginia, moved to Findlay in 1888. Made only in clear glass; colors have been reproduced. A goblet and toothpick were not originally made in this pattern.

	Clear		Clear
Banana Stand, hs	135.00	Cruet	65.00
Bowl		Lamp, Kerosene	125.00
6½"	25.00	Nappy, folded sides, 7¼"	30.00
9", cov	75.00	Pitcher, water	95.00
* Butter, cov	70.00	Plate	
Cake Stand, 8"	55.00	7"	30.00
Celery Vase	45.00	9", sq, upturned sides	65.00
Compote		10", upturned sides	85.00
Cov, hs, 6½"	60.00	Salt Shaker	35.00
Cov, hs, 9½"	90.00	Spooner	35.00
Open, 7¼", with fluted		Sauce	15.00
edge	65.00	Sugar, cov	55.00
Open, 4½", jelly	45.00	Syrup, pewter top	125.00
Creamer	65.00	Tumbler	35.00

FEATHER (Doric)

Non-flint made in Indiana in 1896 and by McKee Glass. Later the pattern was reissued with variations and quality differences. Also found in amber stain (rare).

	Clear	Emerald Green		Clear	Emerald Green
Banana Boat, ftd	75.00	175.00	Celery Vase	35.00	85.00
Bowl, oval			Champagne	65.00	—
8½"	25.00	—	Compote		
9¼"	18.00	75.00	Cov, hs, 8½"	125.00	250.00
Bowl, round			Cov, ls, 4¼",		
4"	15.00	—	jelly	40.00	100.00
4½"	15.00	—	Cov, ls, 8¼"	150.00	—
6"	20.00	—	Open, ls, 4"	15.00	—
7"	25.00	75.00	Open, ls, 6"	20.00	—
8"	30.00	85.00	Open, ls, 7"	30.00	—
Bowl, sq			Open, ls, 8"	35.00	—
4½"	15.00	—	Cordial	125.00	—
8"	30.00	—	Creamer	40.00	85.00
Butter, cov	65.00	130.00	Cruet, os	45.00	250.00
Cake Plate	30.00	—	Dishes, nest of 3: 7",		
Cake Stand			8", and 9"	40.00	—
8"	40.00	125.00	Goblet	58.00	150.00
9½"	50.00	125.00	Honey Dish	15.00	—
11"	70.00	175.00	Marmalade Jar	100.00	

	Clear	Emerald Green		Clear	Emerald Green
Pickle Castor	145.00	—	Spooner	25.00	60.00
Pitcher			Sugar, cov	45.00	80.00
Milk	50.00	165.00	Syrup	125.00	300.00
Water	75.00	250.00	Toothpick	65.00	150.00
Plate, 10″	35.00	—	Tumbler	45.00	85.00
Relish	18.00	—	Wine		
Salt Shaker, pr	35.00	70.00	Scalloped border	40.00	—
Sauce	12.00	—	Straight border	25.00	—

FESTOON

Non-flint, 1890-1894. No goblet or wine was made in this pattern.

	Clear		Clear
Bowl		Plate, 7, 8, 9″	30.00
7 x 4½″, rect	25.00	Relish, 9 x 5½″	40.00
8″, Berry	25.00	Sauce, flat	7.50
9″, rect	30.00	Spooner	35.00
Butter, cov	38.00	Sugar	
Cake Stand, 10″	40.00	Cov	45.00
Compote, open, hs	65.00	Open	20.00
Creamer	38.00	Tray, water, 10″	35.00
Marmalade Jar, cov	60.00	Tumbler	22.00
Pickle Castor, cov	110.00	Waste Bowl	30.00
Pitcher, water	65.00		

FINECUT

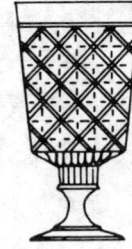

Non-flint made by Bryce Bros., Pittsburgh, PA, c1879, and by U. S. Glass Co. in 1891.

	Amber	Blue	Clear	Vaseline
Bowl, 8¼″	15.00	20.00	12.00	15.00
Bread Plate	50.00	60.00	25.00	50.00
Butter, cov	55.00	75.00	45.00	60.00
Cake Stand	—	—	30.00	—
Celery Tray	—	45.00	25.00	40.00
Celery Vase, SP holder	—	—	—	115.00
Creamer	35.00	40.00	20.00	75.00
Goblet	45.00	55.00	22.00	42.00
Pitcher, water	95.00	95.00	50.00	75.00
Plate				
6″	—	20.00	8.00	—
7″	25.00	40.00	15.00	20.00
10″	30.00	50.00	21.00	45.00
Relish	35.00	40.00	18.00	35.00
Sauce, flat	14.00	15.00	10.00	14.00
Spooner	30.00	45.00	18.00	40.00
Sugar				
Covered	45.00	55.00	35.00	45.00
Open	40.00	45.00	25.00	40.00
Tray, water	50.00	55.00	25.00	50.00
Tumbler	—	—	18.00	28.00
Wine	—	—	24.00	30.00

FINECUT AND BLOCK

Made by King Glass Co., Crystal Glass Co. in c1890, and by McKee Glass Co. c1894. Also attributed to Portland Glass Co. Made in clear, solid colors of amber, blue, and yellow (all comparable in price), and in clear with color blocks.

	Clear	Solid Colored Pieces	Colored Block: Amber	Colored Block: Blue	Colored Block: Yellow or Pink
Bowl, 9″	35.00	—			
Butter, cov					
Flat	65.00	—	—	—	—
Footed	75.00	165.00	—	—	—
Cake Stand					
Large	40.00	—	—	—	—
Small	35.00	—	—	—	—
Celery Tray	30.00	45.00	50.00	45.00	60.00
Compote					
Cov, ls	35.00	—	—	—	—
Open, ls, 8½″	30.00	—	45.00	40.00	45.00
Open jelly	18.00	50.00	75.00	75.00	75.00
Cordial	—	—	—	65.00	—
Creamer	45.00	65.00	70.00	60.00	70.00
Goblet					
Buttermilk	30.00	—	—	55.00	85.00
Lady's	45.00	—	—	50.00	—
Regular	32.00	65.00	60.00	65.00	60.00
Pitcher					
Milk	45.00	85.00	95.00	95.00	125.00
Water	45.00	85.00	95.00	95.00	125.00
Plate, 5¾″	12.50	—	—	—	—
Punch Cup	12.00	—	—	20.00	—
Relish, rect	12.00	—	55.00	50.00	55.00
Salt, individual	12.00	—	—	—	—
Salt, master	—	—	35.00	—	—
Sauce					
Flat	10.00	16.00	16.00	12.00	16.00
Footed	12.00	18.50	18.00	14.50	—
Spooner	30.00	45.00	55.00	65.00	50.00
Sugar, cov	45.00	—	120.00	130.00	120.00
Tray					
Ice Cream	55.00	—	—	—	—
Water	60.00	—	—	—	—
Tumbler	20.00	50.00	50.00	45.00	45.00
Wine	30.00	—	45.00	45.00	45.00

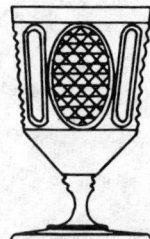

FINECUT AND PANEL

Non-flint pattern made by many Pittsburgh factories in the 1880s. Reissued in the early 1890s by U. S. Glass Co. An aqua wine is known.

	Amber	Blue	Clear	Vaseline
Bowl				
7″	28.00	35.00	15.00	25.00
8″, oval	55.00	—	18.00	30.00
Bread Plate	50.00	45.00	30.00	—
Butter, cov	45.00	75.00	40.00	60.00

	Amber	Blue	Clear	Vaseline
Cake Stand, 10″ . . .	50.00	55.00	30.00	50.00
Compote				
Cov, hs	125.00	135.00	50.00	130.00
Open, hs	65.00	65.00	35.00	60.00
Creamer	35.00	50.00	25.00	40.00
Goblet	40.00	48.00	20.00	30.00
Pitcher				
Milk	65.00	—	—	50.00
Water	85.00	85.00	40.00	45.00
Plate, 7¼″	25.00	30.00	15.00	25.00
Platter	30.00	50.00	25.00	30.00
Relish	20.00	30.00	16.00	18.00
Sauce, ftd	14.00	25.00	8.00	15.00
Spooner	35.00	45.00	20.00	30.00
Sugar, cov	37.50	42.50	30.00	32.50
Tray, water	60.00	55.00	50.00	60.00
Tumbler	25.00	30.00	20.00	38.00
Waste Bowl	30.00	35.00	20.00	35.00
Wine	30.00	35.00	20.00	35.00

FINE RIB

Flint made by New England Glass Co. in the 1860s. Later made in non-flint, which has limited collecting interest and priced at approximately one third the value of flint.

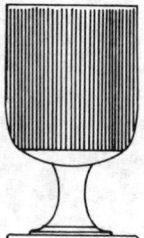

	Clear Flint		Clear Flint
Bitters Bottle	65.00	Lamp	150.00
Bowl, 7″, cov	85.00	Mug	45.00
Butter, cov	75.00	Pitcher, ah	
Castor Set	200.00	Milk	250.00
Celery Vase	50.00	Water	350.00
Champagne	65.00	Plate, 6″ or 7″	20.00
Compote		Salt	
Cov, hs, 8″	65.00	Cov, ftd	85.00
Open, hs, 7¾″	50.00	Individual	35.00
Open, ls, 9″	60.00	Spooner	65.00
Cordial	85.00	Sugar, cov	75.00
Creamer, applied handle . . .	125.00	Tumbler, bar	85.00
Decanter, quart bar lip	75.00	Tumble-up	125.00
Egg Cup	48.00	Whiskey, handled	75.00
* Goblet	60.00	Wine	45.00
* Honey Dish, 3½″d	16.00		

FISHSCALE (Coral)

Non-flint made by Bryce Brothers, Pittsburgh, PA, in the mid-1880s and by U. S. Glass Co. in 1891.

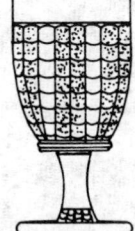

	Clear		Clear
Bowl		Butter, cov	45.00
Cov, 7″	45.00	Cake Plate	55.00
Cov, 9½″	55.00	Cake Stand	
Open, 8″	20.00	9″	30.00
Bread Plate	28.00	10½″	35.00

	Clear		Clear
Celery Vase	30.00	Plate	
Compote		7", round	20.00
Cov, hs, 8"	85.00	9", square	20.00
Open, hs, 8"	30.00	Relish	15.00
Open, hs, 9"	40.00	Salt Shaker	55.00
Open, jelly	18.00	Sauce	
Creamer	30.00	Flat	7.50
Goblet	27.00	Footed	15.00
Lamp, Finger	75.00	Spooner	25.00
Mug, large	35.00	Sugar, cov	50.00
Pitcher		Tray, condiment, rect	35.00
Milk	35.00	Tumbler	65.00
Water	55.00	Waste Bowl	25.00

FLAMINGO HABITAT

Maker unknown, etched pattern.

	Clear		Clear
Bowl, 10", oval	40.00	Open, 6"	40.00
Celery Vase	45.00	Creamer	40.00
Champagne	45.00	Goblet	30.00
Cheese Dish, blown, folded		Sauce, ftd	15.00
rim, dome lid	95.00	Spooner	25.00
Compote		Sugar, cov	50.00
Cov, 4½"	75.00	Tumbler	30.00
Cov, 6½"	95.00	Wine	42.00
Open, 5", jelly	35.00		

FLEUR-DE-LIS AND DRAPE (Fleur-de-Lis and Tassel)

Non-flint made by U. S. Glass Co., c1892. Clear and emerald green pieces often trimmed with gilt. Also made in milk glass (rare).

	Clear	Emerald Green		Clear	Emerald Green
Bowl	15.00	30.00	Cup	20.00	30.00
Butter, cov	45.00	55.00	Cup and Saucer	25.00	35.00
Cake Stand	35.00	55.00	Goblet	35.00	45.00
Claret	35.00	50.00	Honey Dish, cov	40.00	55.00
Compote			Mustard Jar, cov	35.00	50.00
Cov, ls			Pitcher		
5"	30.00	40.00	Milk	40.00	60.00
6"	35.00	40.00	Water	50.00	65.00
7"	35.00	45.00	Plate, 8"	24.00	35.00
8"	45.00	60.00	Salt Shaker	20.00	35.00
Open, hs			Spooner	25.00	40.00
5"	25.00	30.00	Sugar, cov	30.00	55.00
6"	25.00	30.00	Syrup, metal top	50.00	125.00
7"	30.00	35.00	Tumbler	20.00	30.00
8"	30.00	40.00	Waste Bowl	30.00	40.00
Creamer	25.00	40.00	Water Tray, 11½"	24.00	50.00
Cruet, os	45.00	85.00	Wine	25.00	45.00

FLORIDA (Emerald Green Herringbone, Paneled Herringbone)

Non-flint made by U. S. Glass Co., late 1880s-1890s. One of States patterns. Reproduced in green and other colors.

	Clear	Emerald Green		Clear	Emerald Green
Bowl			Pitcher, water	50.00	75.00
7¾".	20.00	25.00	Plate		
9".	20.00	25.00	7½".	10.00	18.00
Butter, cov	40.00	55.00	9¼".	15.00	28.00
Cake Stand			Relish		
Large	60.00	68.00	6", sq	10.00	15.00
Small	28.00	38.00	8½", sq	15.00	22.00
Celery Vase	30.00	35.00	Salt Shaker.	25.00	50.00
Compote, open, hs,			Sauce	8.00	15.00
6½", sq	—	40.00	Spooner	20.00	35.00
Creamer.	30.00	45.00	Sugar		
Cruet, os	40.00	115.00	Cov.	32.00	50.00
* Goblet	25.00	40.00	Open	18.00	25.00
Mustard Pot, attach-			Syrup	60.00	175.00
ed underplate, cov	25.00	45.00	Tumbler	20.00	30.00
Nappy	15.00	25.00	Wine	25.00	50.00

FLOWER POT

(Potted Plant) Non-flint pattern made in the 1880s. There are occasional pieces found in amber and vaseline.

	Clear		Clear
Bread Plate	45.00	Pitcher	
Butter, cov	50.00	Milk.	40.00
Cake Stand, 10½".	48.00	Water	55.00
Compote		Salt Shaker.	20.00
Cov, 7"	45.00	Sauce, ftd.	8.50
Open, 7¼".	20.00	Spooner	25.00
Creamer.	30.00	Sugar, cov	40.00
Goblet	35.00		

FLUTE

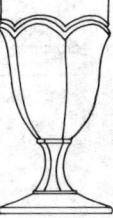

More than 15 Flute variants were produced in flint and non-flint glass from the 1850s through the 1880s. Some of the flint variants are Beaded Flute, Bessimer Flute, New England Flute, etc., all with comparable prices. Prices listed are for flint.

	Clear		Clear
Ale Glass	50.00	Creamer.	45.00
Bitters Bottle.	75.00	Decanter, bar lip	100.00
Butter, cov, ls	60.00	Egg Cup	
Candlestick, 4"	50.00	Double	50.00
Claret.	45.00	Single	40.00
Compote		Goblet	25.00
Open, ls, 8½"	40.00	Honey	18.00
Open, ls, 9½"	45.00	Lamp	75.00

	Clear		Clear
Mug	35.00	Tumbler	15.00
Pitcher, water	75.00	Whiskey, handled	30.00
Sauce, flat	18.00	Wine	25.00
Sugar, cov	50.00		

FRANCES WARE

Made by Hobbs, Brockunier & Co., Wheeling, West Virginia, c1880. A clear frosted hobnail or swirl pattern glass with amber stained top rims. It may be pressed or mold blown. Swirl pieces are noted, otherwise they are hobnail.

	Clear	Frosted/ Amber Stain		Clear	Frosted/ Amber Stain
Bowl, 7½"	50.00	75.00	Sauce, 4", sq	18.00	32.00
Box, 5¼", round, cov	45.00	65.00	Spooner	45.00	60.00
Butter, cov	80.00	110.00	Sugar, cov	60.00	85.00
Creamer	50.00	85.00	Sugar Shaker, swirl	65.00	125.00
Finger Bowl, 4"	40.00	50.00	Syrup, swirl	85.00	165.00
Mustard, cov, swirl	—	135.00	Toothpick	75.00	95.00
Pitcher			Tray		
8½"	90.00	150.00	Leaf shape, 12"	75.00	125.00
11"	150.00	185.00	Rect, rounded edges, 14 x		
Salt Shaker			9½"	110.00	150.00
Hobnail	50.00	65.00	Water, oval	—	150.00
Swirl	30.00	65.00	Tumbler	35.00	45.00

FROSTED CIRCLE

Produced by Bryce Bros., Pittsburgh, Pennsylvania, from 1876 to c1885. Later by U. S. Glass Co. in the late 1890s. Reproduced.

	Clear Circle	Frosted Circle		Clear Circle	Frosted Circle
Bowl, cov			* Goblet	35.00	45.00
7"	20.00	25.00	Juice	15.00	25.00
8"	25.00	30.00	Pitcher, water	55.00	85.00
Butter, cov	55.00	65.00	Plate		
Cake Stand			4"	10.00	22.00
8"	30.00	35.00	9"	22.00	25.00
9½"	40.00	50.00	Punch Cup	15.00	20.00
Champagne	35.00	65.00	Salt Shaker	25.00	35.00
Compote			Sauce	8.50	12.00
Cov, 7", hs	30.00	65.00	Spooner	35.00	40.00
Cov, 8", hs	45.00	75.00	* Sugar, cov	42.50	50.00
* Open, 7", hs	20.00	30.00	Sugar Shaker	40.00	65.00
* Open, 10", hs	45.00	55.00	Syrup	95.00	145.00
Creamer	30.00	60.00	Tumbler	25.00	35.00
Cruet, os	45.00	65.00	Wine	35.00	45.00
Cup and Saucer	25.00	40.00			

FROSTED LEAF

Flint pattern made c1850. Later production attributed to Portland Glass Co in 1863 and 1874.

	Clear		Clear
Butter, cov	135.00	Lamp, oil	500.00
Celery Vase	145.00	Pitcher, water	400.00
Champagne	160.00	Salt, ind	50.00
Compote, cov	250.00	Sauce, flat	28.00
Creamer	300.00	Spooner	85.00
Decanter, os, qt.	250.00	Sugar, cov	175.00
Egg Cup	100.00	Tumbler	150.00
Goblet	75.00		

FROSTED STORK

Non-flint made by Crystal Glass Co, Bridgeport, OH, c1880. Now reproduced. Details of the stork's activities differ from scene to scene on the same piece.

	Clear		Clear
Bowl, 9″	50.00	Platter, 11½ x 8″	
Bread Plate, oval	50.00	101 border	70.00
Butter, cov	85.00	Scenic border	68.00
Creamer	45.00	Relish	45.00
Finger Bowl	50.00	Sauce, flat	20.00
* Goblet	70.00	Spooner	40.00
Jam Jar, cov	100.00	Sugar, cov	95.00
Pickle, cov, stork finial	125.00	Tray, water	100.00
Pitcher, water	200.00	Waste Bowl	50.00

GALLOWAY

Non-flint made by U. S. Glass Co., 1904. Clear glass with and without gold trim; also known with rose stain and ruby stain.

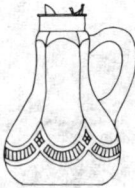

	Clear w/ Gold	Rose Stained		Clear w/gold	Rose Stained
Basket, no gold	75.00	—	Cruet	45.00	—
Bowl			Egg Cup	25.00	—
6½″	25.00	—	Finger Bowl	40.00	—
8½″, oval	25.00	—	Goblet	65.00	—
8½″, round	25.00	—	Lemonade	35.00	—
9¾″	35.00	50.00	Mug	38.00	50.00
11″ d, 3″ h	45.00	—	Nappy, tricorn	—	50.00
Butter, cov	65.00	125.00	Olive, 6″	20.00	30.00
Cake Stand	60.00	90.00	Pitcher		
Carafe, water	55.00	85.00	Milk	40.00	—
Celery Vase	35.00	75.00	Tankard	75.00	—
Champagne	45.00	—	Water, ice lip	65.00	175.00
Compote			Plate, 8″, round	40.00	65.00
Open, hs, 4¼″	30.00	—	Punch Bowl	160.00	—
Open, hs, 10″,			Punch Bowl Plate,		
scalloped	85.00	—	20″	65.00	—
Creamer	30.00	50.00	Punch Cup	10.00	15.00

	Clear w/ Gold	Rose Stained		Clear w/ Gold	Rose Stained
Relish.	20.00	30.00	Sugar, cov	55.00	75.00
Rose Bowl	25.00	—	Sugar Shaker	40.00	—
Salt Dip	25.00	—	Syrup.	65.00	—
Salt & Pepper, pr. . .	35.00	—	Toothpick	30.00	55.00
Sauce			Tumbler	25.00	—
Flat.	10.00	—	Vase; swung.	30.00	—
Footed	12.00	—	Waste Bowl.	38.00	—
Sherbet	25.00	—	Water Bottle	40.00	—
Spooner	30.00	80.00	Wine	45.00	—

GARFIELD DRAPE

Non-flint pattern issued in 1881 by Adams & Co., Pittsburgh, Pennsylvania, after the assassination of President Garfield.

	Clear		Clear
Bread Plate		Honey Dish.	15.00
Memorial, portrait of		Goblet	40.00
Garfield	65.00	Pitcher	
"We Mourn Our Nation's		Milk.	70.00
Loss", portrait	75.00	Water, ah.	75.00
Butter, cov	60.00	Water, strap.	100.00
Cake Stand, 9½".	75.00	Relish, oval.	15.00
Celery Vase	40.00	Sauce	
Compote		Flat.	8.50
Cov, hs, 8".	100.00	Footed	12.00
Cov, ls, 6"	60.00	Spooner	30.00
Open, hs, 8½"	40.00	Sugar, cov	60.00
Creamer.	45.00	Tumbler	35.00

GEORGIA (Peacock Feather)

Probably Richards and Hartley, but reissued by several glass companies, including U. S. Glass Co. in 1902 as part of their States series. Rare in blue. (Chamber lamp, pedestal base, $275.00). No goblet known in pattern.

	Clear		Clear
Bowl, 8"	20.00	Lamp	
Butter, cov	45.00	Chamber, pedestal.	65.00
Cake Stand, 11"	40.00	Hand, oil, 7"	80.00
Compote		Pitcher, water	70.00
Cov, hs, 8".	50.00	Plate, 5¼".	18.00
Open, hs, 7"	30.00	Relish.	10.00
Open, jelly.	20.00	Salt Shaker.	70.00
Condiment Set, tray, oil cruet,		Sauce	12.50
salt and pepper	75.00	Spooner	35.00
Creamer.	35.00	Sugar, cov	45.00
Cruet, os	55.00	Syrup, metal lid.	55.00
Decanter	70.00	Tumbler	25.00

GIANT BULL'S EYE (Bull's Eye and Spearhead)

Made by Bellaire Glass Co., Findlay, Ohio, and continued by U. S. Glass Co. after 1891.

	Clear		Clear
Bowl, 8″	25.00	Decanter, os	50.00
Brandy bottle, os, tall,		Goblet	35.00
narrow	55.00	Lamp, handled	125.00
Butter, cov	45.00	Pitcher, water	75.00
Cake Stand	30.00	Relish.	15.00
Cheese Dish, cov	45.00	Tray, wine, 7¼″	45.00
Claret Jug, tankard shape . .	60.00	Tumbler	30.00
Compote, cov	75.00	Vase	35.00
Creamer.	30.00	Wine	30.00
Cruet, os	60.00		

GOOSEBERRY

Non-flint of the 1880s. Made by Boston and Sandwich Glass Co. and others in clear and milk glass. Reproduced in milk glass.

	Clear	Milk Glass		Clear	Milk Glass
Butter, cov	50.00	60.00	Mug	35.00	40.00
Compote			Pitcher, water, ah . .	165.00	100.00
Cov, hs, 6″.	45.00	65.00	Sauce	10.00	15.00
Cov, hs, 7″.	55.00	75.00	Spooner	25.00	30.00
Cov, hs, 8″.	65.00	90.00	Sugar, Cov	45.00	55.00
Creamer.	30.00	50.00	Syrup, ah	75.00	90.00
Goblet	35.00	45.00	Tumbler	35.00	40.00

GOTHIC

Flint made by Boston and Sandwich Glass Co., c1860s.

	Clear		Clear
Bowl, 7″	70.00	Creamer.	35.00
Butter, cov	85.00	Egg Cup.	50.00
Castor Set	100.00	Goblet	65.00
Celery Vase	85.00	Sauce, flat	18.00
Champagne	125.00	Spooner	40.00
Compote		Sugar, cov	85.00
Cov, hs, 8″.	110.00	Tumbler	95.00
Open, ls, 7″	65.00	Wine	95.00

GRAND (Diamond Medallion)

Non-flint, made by Bryce, Higbee and Co. 1885. Stemware comes in plain and ringed stems.

	Clear		Clear
Bowl, 6", cov.	30.00	Creamer	25.00
Bread Plate, 10"	25.00	Goblet	30.00
Butter, cov		Pitcher, water	40.00
Flat	35.00	Plate, 10"	25.00
Footed	45.00	Relish, 7½", oval	10.00
Cake Stand		Salt Shaker	30.00
8"	30.00	Sauce	
10"	35.00	Flat	7.50
Celery Vase, pedestal	25.00	Footed	10.00
Compote		Spooner	20.00
Cov, hs, 5½"	60.00	Sugar, cov	35.00
Cov, hs, 7½"	75.00	Syrup, metal top	90.00
Open, hs, 9"	65.00	Waste Bowl, collared	30.00
Cordial	50.00	Wine	25.00

GRAPE AND FESTOON WITH STIPPLED LEAF

Non-flint pattern made by Doyle & Company, Pittsburgh, PA, in the early 1870s.

	Clear		Clear
Bowl	15.00	Pitcher	
Butter, cov	50.00	Milk, ah	65.00
Celery Vase	40.00	Water, ah	85.00
Compote		Plate, 6"	18.00
Cov, hs, 8"	115.00	Relish	12.50
Open, ls, 8"	75.00	Salt, ftd	24.00
Creamer, ah	45.00	Sauce, flat, 4"	12.00
Egg Cup	20.00	Spooner	35.00
Goblet	35.00	Sugar, cov	50.00
Lamp, oil, 7½"	65.00	Wine	45.00
Mug	20.00		

GRASSHOPPER (Long Spear)

Maker unknown; over 40 pieces documented. Pieces without the grasshopper bring 40–50% less. Creamer and sugar known in vaseline and blue. Goblet is modern.

	Amber	Clear		Amber	Clear
Bowl			Pitcher, water	125.00	75.00
Covered	55.00	35.00	Plate		
Open, ftd	—	25.00	8½", ftd	—	25.00
Butter, cov	90.00	65.00	9", ftd	—	20.00
Celery Vase	90.00	80.00	10½", ftd	—	25.00
Compote			Salt Dip	—	40.00
Cov, hs, 7"	—	50.00	Salt Shaker	—	35.00
Cov, hs, 8½"	—	65.00	Sauce		
Creamer	60.00	40.00	Flat	—	10.00
Marmalade Jar, cov,			Footed	—	15.00
insert	—	125.00	Spooner	75.00	65.00
Pickle	—	20.00	Sugar, cov	80.00	70.00

HAIRPIN (Sandwich Loop)

Flint pattern made in the Sandwich factory c1850. Finials are acorn shaped, handles are applied.

	Clear		Clear
Celery Vase	40.00	Salt, cov, ftd	85.00
Champagne	50.00	Sauce, flat	15.00
Compote, cov hs	225.00	Spooner	40.00
Creamer, ah	55.00	Sugar, cov	95.00
Decanter, os, qt.	65.00	Tumbler	30.00
Egg Cup	30.00	Whiskey, handled	45.00
Goblet	40.00	Wine	35.00

HALLEY'S COMET (Etruria)

Clear non-flint pattern made by Model Flint Glass Co, c1880. The tail of the comet forms continuous loops. A ruby stained wine is known.

	Clear		Clear
Bowl		Cruet, os	60.00
4", cov, 3 ftd	40.00	Goblet	30.00
8"	25.00	Pitcher, water	85.00
9"	28.00	Punch Cup	35.00
Butter, cov	80.00	Relish.	25.00
Cake Stand	75.00	Salt & Pepper, pr.	45.00
Celery Vase	30.00	Spooner	35.00
Compote		Sugar, cov	65.00
Cov, hs, 10".	60.00	Syrup	50.00
Open, hs, 8"	40.00	Tumbler	25.00
Creamer.	35.00	Wine	25.00

HAND (Pennsylvania #2)

Made by O'Hara Glass Co., Pittsburgh, Pennsylvania, c1880. Covered pieces have a hand holding bar finial, hence the name.

	Clear		Clear
Bowl		Goblet	42.50
9"	20.00	Marmalade Jar, cov	50.00
10"	38.00	Pickle.	20.00
Butter, cov	75.00	Pitcher, water	75.00
Cake Stand	55.00	Sauce	
Celery Vase	42.50	Flat.	8.00
Compote		Footed	15.00
Cov, hs, 7".	60.00	Spooner	30.00
Cov, hs, 8".	95.00	Sugar, cov	75.00
Open, hs, 7¾"	45.00	Syrup.	45.00
Open, ls, 9"	20.00	Tumbler	75.00
Cordial, 3½"	75.00	Wine	50.00
Creamer.	40.00		

HANOVER (Block With Stars #2, Blockhouse)

Originally made by Richards and Hartley, of Tarentum, Pennsylvania, in 1888 and possibly earlier. Made in many pieces. Also made in blue.

	Clear	Dark Amber		Clear	Dark Amber
Bowl, 10″, berry....	20.00	40.00	Ketchup Bottles, pr .	50.00	75.00
Bread Plate, 10″ ...	20.00	30.00	Mug		
Butter, cov	40.00	80.00	Large	22.00	48.00
Cake Stand, 10″ ...	42.00	62.00	Small	18.00	40.00
Celery Vase	27.00	38.00	Pitcher, water	50.00	85.00
Cheese Dish, cov,			Plate		
10″	50.00	95.00	4″............	25.00	40.00
Compote			6″............	25.00	40.00
Cov, hs	45.00	90.00	10″...........	18.00	45.00
Open, hs.......	40.00	—	Puff Box, glass lid ..	45.00	—
Open, ls	40.00	45.00	Sauce, ftd........	10.00	15.00
Creamer.........	30.00	45.00	Spooner	25.00	37.00
Cruet, os	20.00	—	Sugar, cov	45.00	55.00
Goblet	25.00	55.00	Tumbler	25.00	30.00

HARTLEY (Paneled Diamond Cut With Fan)

Non-flint pattern made by Richards and Hartley in 1880s, and by U. S. Glass Co in 1891. Trilobed form has either plain or engraved panels. Twenty-three pieces documented.

	Amber	Blue & Vaseline	Clear
Bowl, berry			
7″, ftd	30.00	35.00	15.00
9″............	30.00	35.00	15.00
Bread Plate, trilobed	30.00	40.00	20.00
Butter, cov	50.00	60.00	40.00
Cake Stand, 10″ ...	45.00	50.00	40.00
Celery Vase	30.00	40.00	25.00
Compote			
Cov, ls, 7¾″.....	65.00	75.00	45.00
Open, 7″ and 8″..	30.00	40.00	18.00
Creamer.........	30.00	35.00	20.00
Dish, centerpiece ..	40.00	45.00	20.00
Goblet	35.00	40.00	25.00
Pitcher			
Milk, qt	80.00	85.00	75.00
Water, ½ gal	90.00	90.00	85.00
Plate	45.00	50.00	30.00
Relish...........	18.00	20.00	15.00
Spooner	28.00	30.00	18.00
Sugar, cov	40.00	50.00	30.00
Tumbler	30.00	35.00	20.00
Wine	40.00	45.00	20.00

HEART WITH THUMBPRINT (Bull's Eye in Heart)

Non-flint, made by Tarentum Glass Co. 1898. Some emerald green pieces have gold trim. Made experimentally in custard, blue custard, opaque nile green and cobalt. Some pieces are found with ruby stain. (Creamer $175.00)

	Clear	Emerald Green
Banana Boat......	75.00	—
Barber Bottle	100.00	—
Bowl		
7" sq.........	35.00	—
9"...........	42.00	—
9½" sq	35.00	—
10" scalloped....	35.00	—
Butter, cov	125.00	175.00
Cake Stand, 9" ...	125.00	—
Carafe, water	100.00	—
Card Tray.......	20.00	—
Celery Vase	65.00	—
Compote		
Open, hs, 7½", scalloped.....	150.00	—
Open, hs, 8½"...	100.00	—
Cordial, 3" h	125.00	—
Creamer		
Ind	22.50	45.00
Regular........	60.00	110.00
Cruet	75.00	—
Finger Bowl	45.00	—
Goblet	58.00	150.00
Hair Receiver, metal lid...........	65.00	—
Ice Bucket	60.00	—
Lamp		
Finger........	65.00	115.00

	Clear	Emerald Green
Oil, 8"	50.00	160.00
Mustard, SP cov ...	95.00	100.00
Nappy, turned up edges	32.50	65.00
Pitcher, water	90.00	—
Plate		
6"	25.00	75.00
10"	35.00	—
Powder Jar, SP cov.	65.00	—
Punch Cup.......	22.00	45.00
Rose Bowl		
Large	60.00	—
Small	30.00	—
Salt & Pepper.....	95.00	—
Sauce, 5"........	18.00	35.00
Spooner........	50.00	—
Sugar		
Ind	25.00	35.00
Regular, cov	85.00	90.00
Syrup.........	95.00	—
Tray, 8¼" l, 4¼" w..	35.00	—
Tumbler	60.00	—
Vase		
6"............	35.00	65.00
10"	60.00	—
Wine	45.00	—

HICKMAN (La Clede)

Non-flint pattern made by McKee Glass Co., Pittsburgh, Pennsylvania, c1897. Also made in ruby stain (rare).

	Clear	Emerald Green
Banana Stand, ftd ..	65.00	—
Bon bon, 9", sq....	15.00	—
Bottle, Pepper.....	25.00	—
Bowl		
Round, or with scalloped top		
4"	12.00	—
4½"	12.00	—
5"	14.00	—
6"	15.00	—
7"	15.00	—
8"	18.00	—
Square, 7"......	15.00	18.00
Butter, cov	35.00	58.00
8½"...........	30.00	—
9½"...........	32.50	—
Celery Vase	28.00	—
Champagne	25.00	—
Cologne Bottle, faceted stopper	30.00	—

	Clear	Emerald Green
Compote		
Cov, hs, 7"......	55.00	—
Open, hs, 8"	45.00	—
Open, ls, 4½", jelly	40.00	45.00
Condiment Set, handled tray, cruet, pepper bottle, open salt.......	85.00	—
Cordial.........	24.00	—
Creamer........	25.00	35.00
Cruet, os	45.00	—
Cup, Custard	12.00	—
Dish, 4" sq	16.00	—
Goblet	35.00	50.00
Ice Bucket	60.00	—
Lemonade	12.00	—
Mustard Jar, underplate, cov	45.00	—
Nappy, 5"	10.00	—

	Clear	Emerald Green		Clear	Emerald Green
Olive, 4", handle . . .	10.00	20.00	Salt Shaker, single		
Pickle	15.00	20.00	Round, long cut		
Pitcher, water	55.00	—	neck	15.00	—
Plate, 9¼".	15.00	—	Round, squat. . . .	20.00	30.00
Punch Bowl	175.00	375.00	Square	20.00	—
Punch Cup	10.00	15.00	Spooner	27.00	—
Punch Glass, ftd . . .	30.00	—	Sugar, cov	42.00	50.00
Relish.	18.00	15.00	Sugar Shaker	45.00	—
Rose Bowl	25.00	—	Toothpick	45.00	75.00
Salt, individual, flat,			Tumbler	30.00	—
sloping sides	10.00		Vase, 10¼".	12.00	45.00
			Wine	30.00	—

HIDALGO (Frosted Waffle)

Non-flint made by Adams and Co., Pittsburgh, Pennsylvania, in the early 1880s and U S Glass Co in 1891. This pattern comes etched and clear, and also with part of pattern frosted. Add 20% for frosted. Rare in color.

	Amber Stained	Clear		Amber Stained	Clear
Bowl, 10", sq	35.00	20.00	Pitcher		
Bread Plate, cupped,			Milk.	—	40.00
sq, 10"	75.00	60.00	Water	—	45.00
Butter, cov	—	50.00	Plate, 10"	—	35.00
Celery Vase	35.00	20.00	Salt, master, sq. . . .	—	25.00
Compote			Salt & Pepper	—	40.00
Cov, hs, 7½"	85.00	65.00	Sauce, handled. . . .	—	10.00
Cov, ls, 6"	—	50.00	Spooner	—	20.00
Open, hs, 10" . . .	—	45.00	Sugar, cov	—	48.00
Open, hs, 11" . . .	—	50.00	Sugar Shaker	—	45.00
Cruet	—	65.00	Syrup.	—	60.00
Cup and Saucer . . .	—	40.00	Tray, water	—	55.00
Goblet	40.00	20.00	Tumbler	—	25.00
Nappy, handled, sq .	—	18.00	Waste Bowl.	—	25.00
Pickle, boat shaped.	18.00	12.00			

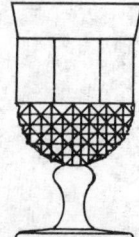

HINOTO (Diamond Point With Panels)

Flint made by Boston and Sandwich Co in the late 1850s.

	Clear		Clear
Butter, cov	85.00	Salt	35.00
Celery Vase	65.00	Spooner	35.00
Champagne	60.00	Sugar, cov	75.00
Cologne Bottle, os.	48.00	Tumbler	45.00
Creamer.	75.00	Whiskey	50.00
Egg Cup.	35.00	Wine	60.00
Goblet	60.00		

HOBNAIL, OPALESCENT

Made by several companies with variations in forms of pieces, c1880–1900. Pieces are found round in shape, with frilled tops, pieces on three feet, pieces on four feet, square in shape or octagonal in shape. Highly reproduced. Fenton Glass still makes this pattern.

	Blue Opal	Opal	Vaseline Opal	White Opal
Bar Bottle	—	150.00	—	—
Butter, cov				
Flat	100.00	110.00	105.00	85.00
Four Feet	110.00	115.00	110.00	90.00
* Celery Vase	85.00	120.00	100.00	65.00
* Creamer				
Flat	95.00	115.00	110.00	85.00
Four Feet	100.00	120.00	115.00	95.00
Cruet, os	—	350.00	125.00	50.00
Mug	35.00	55.00	50.00	30.00
Pitcher, water	100.00	275.00	120.00	95.00
Sauce, flat	25.00	35.00	30.00	20.00
Spooner				
Flat	25.00	40.00	30.00	20.00
Four Feet	35.00	40.00	30.00	25.00
Sugar, cov				
Flat	40.00	60.00	55.00	30.00
Four Feet	45.00	65.00	60.00	35.00
*Sugar, open	20.00	25.00	15.00	—
Syrup	85.00	200.00	165.00	75.00
Toothpick	30.00	50.00	50.00	30.00
Tray, water, 11½" . .	35.00	40.00	30.00	—
Tumbler	40.00	65.00	50.00	30.00
*Wine	24.00	28.00	17.50	—

HOLLY

Non-flint made by Boston and Sandwich Glass Co., late 1860s, early 1870s.

	Clear		Clear
Butter, cov	150.00	Salt	
Cake Stand, 11"	125.00	Flat, oval	65.00
Celery Vase	60.00	Ftd	60.00
Compote, cov, hs	165.00	Sauce, flat	20.00
Creamer, applied handle . . .	125.00	Spooner	60.00
Egg Cup	65.00	Sugar, cov	125.00
Goblet	100.00	Tumbler	125.00
Pitcher, water ah	225.00	Wine	125.00

HONEYCOMB

A popular pattern made in flint and non-flint glass by numerous firms, c1850–1900, resulting in many minor pattern variations. Rare in color.

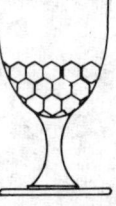

	Flint	Non-Flint		Flint	Non-Flint
Ale Glass	50.00	25.00	pat'd May 11,		
Barber Bottle	45.00	25.00	1869," acorn fi-		
7¼", oval, base			nial on cov	90.00	40.00
mkd "Mould			10"	—	40.00

	Flint	Non-Flint		Flint	Non-flint
Butter, cov	65.00	45.00	Lemonade	40.00	20.00
Cake Stand	55.00	35.00	Mug, half pint	25.00	15.00
Castor Bottle	25.00	18.00	Pitcher, water, ah	100.00	60.00
Celery Vase	45.00	20.00	Plate, 6″	—	12.50
Champagne	65.00	—	Pomade Jar, cov	48.00	20.00
Claret	35.00	—	Relish	30.00	—
Compote, cov, hs			Salt, master, cov,		
6½″ x 8½″h	100.00	50.00	ftd	35.00	40.00
9¼ x 11½″h	110.00	65.00	Salt & Pepper	—	40.00
Compote, open, hs			Sauce	12.00	7.50
7 x 5″h	35.00	25.00	Spillholder	24.00	—
7 x 7″h	60.00	40.00	Spooner	35.00	15.00
7½″, scalloped			Sugar, cov		
top	40.00	—	Frosted rosebud		
8 x 6¼″h	65.00	—	finial	—	50.00
11 x 8″h	135.00	—	Regular	75.00	45.00
Compote, open, ls,			Tumbler		
7½″, scalloped	40.00	—	Bar	35.00	—
Cordial, 3½″	25.00	—	Flat	—	12.50
Creamer, ah	35.00	20.00	Footed	—	15.00
Decanter			Lemonade	40.00	—
Pint	55.00	18.50	Vase		
Quart, os	70.00	65.00	7½″	45.00	—
Egg Cup	18.00	20.00	10½″	75.00	—
Finger Bowl	48.00	—	Whiskey, handled	125.00	—
Goblet	25.00	15.00	Wine	35.00	15.00
Honey, cov	—	25.00			
Lamp					
All Glass	—	45.00			
Marble base	—	40.00			

HORN OF PLENTY

A fine flint glass pattern reputed to have been first made by Boston and Sandwich Glass Co. in the 1850s. Later made in flint and non-flint by other firms.

	Clear Flint		Clear Flint
Bowl, 8½″	145.00	Cordial	150.00
Butter, cov		Creamer, applied handle	
Conventional finial	125.00	5½″h	235.00
Shape of Acorn	130.00	7″h	175.00
Butter Pat	20.00	Decanter	
Cake Stand	350.00	Pint	150.00
Celery Vase	150.00	Quart, os	100.00
Champagne	115.00	Egg Cup	45.00
Compote		* Goblet	60.00
Cov, hs, 6¼″	175.00	* Lamp	200.00
Open, hs, 7″	125.00	Mug, small, applied handle	150.00
Open, hs, 8″	115.00	Pepper Sauce Bottle, pewter	
Open, hs, 9¼″	200.00	top	200.00
Open, hs, 10½″	140.00	Pitcher, water	575.00
Open, ls, 8″	55.00	Plate, 6″	100.00
Open, ls, 9″	85.00	Relish, 7″ l, 5″ w	45.00

	Clear Flint		Clear Flint
Salt, master, oval, flat	75.00	Tumbler	
Sauce		Bar	85.00
4½"	20.00	Water	75.00
5¼"	25.00	Whiskey	
Spillholder	65.00	Applied handle	235.00
Spooner	45.00	Shot glass, 3"	100.00
Sugar, cov	125.00	Wine	125.00

HORSESHOE (Good Luck, Prayer Rug)

Non-flint made by Adams & Co. and others in the 1880s.

	Clear		Clear
Bowl, cov, oval		Goblet	
7"	150.00	Knob Stem	40.00
8"	195.00	Plain Stem	38.00
Bread Plate, 14 x 10"		Marmalade Jar, cov	110.00
Double horseshoe		Pitcher	
handles	65.00	Milk	110.00
Single horseshoe handles .	40.00	Water	75.00
Butter, cov	85.00	Plate	
Cake Plate	40.00	7"	45.00
Cake Stand		10"	48.00
9"	70.00	Relish, 5 x 7"	20.00
10"	80.00	Salt	
Celery Vase, knob stem	40.00	Individual, horseshoe	
Cheese, cov, woman		shape	20.00
churning	275.00	Master, horseshoe shape	100.00
Compote		Sauce	
Cov, hs, 7", horseshoe		Flat	10.00
finial	65.00	Footed	15.00
Cov, hs, 8 x 12¼"	125.00	Spooner	35.00
Cov, hs, 11"	135.00	Sugar, cov	65.00
Creamer, 6½"	95.00	Vegetable Dish, oblong	35.00
Doughnut Stand	75.00	Wine	175.00
Finger Bowl	80.00		

HUBER

(Straight Huber) Flint pattern made by Boston and Sandwich Glass Co, Sandwich, MA, and Bakewell, Pears and Co, Pittsburgh, PA, in the 1860s. Also found in non-flint, values would be 35% of prices shown.

	Clear		Clear
Ale Glass	20.00	Claret	55.00
Bitters Bottle	50.00	Compote	
Bowl		Cov, hs, 8"	100.00
6"	40.00	Cov, hs, 10"	100.00
7", cov	70.00	Cov, ls, 8"	100.00
Butter, cov	85.00	Open, 7"	60.00
Celery	65.00	Open, 8", engraved	75.00
Champagne	45.00	Cordial	50.00

	Clear		Clear
Creamer	80.00	Pitcher, water	150.00
Decanter		Plate, 7½"	30.00
Bar Lip, pt	70.00	Salt, ftd	25.00
Bar Lip, qt	75.00	Sauce, flat	15.00
Stopper, pt	85.00	Spooner	35.00
Stopper, qt	85.00	Sugar, cov	70.00
Egg Cup		Tumbler	
Handle	40.00	Jelly	25.00
Regular	30.00	Water	25.00
Goblet	40.00	Whiskey	35.00
Lemonade	25.00	Wine	40.00
Mug	35.00		

HUMMINGBIRD (Flying Robin)

Non-flint, c1880. A clear water pitcher is known in a mold variant.

	Amber	Blue	Canary	Clear
Butter, cov	110.00	110.00	85.00	60.00
Celery Vase	90.00	90.00	65.00	45.00
Compote, hs, open	95.00	95.00	65.00	48.00
Creamer	75.00	75.00	60.00	40.00
Goblet	55.00	70.00	50.00	35.00
Pitcher				
Milk	65.00	95.00	—	50.00
Water	125.00	150.00	100.00	85.00
Sauce, ftd	25.00	30.00	30.00	18.00
Spooner	40.00	75.00	45.00	30.00
Sugar, cov	100.00	100.00	65.00	55.00
Tray, water	150.00	120.00	80.00	60.00
Tumbler, bar	75.00	75.00	45.00	30.00
Waste Bowl, 5¼"	—	—	—	35.00
Wine	—	—	—	65.00

ILLINOIS

Non-flint. One of the States patterns made by U. S. Glass Co., c1897. Most forms are square. A few items are known in ruby stained, including a salt, $50.00, and a lidless straw holder with the stain in the inside, $95.00.

	Clear	Emerald Green		Clear	Emerald Green
Basket, applied handle, 11½"	100.00	—	Cruet	55.00	—
Bowl, 8"	35.00	—	Marmalade Jar	135.00	—
Butter, cov	60.00	—	Olive	12.00	—
Candlesticks, pr	80.00	—	Pitcher, milk, round, SP rim	175.00	—
Celery Tray, 11"	40.00	—	Pitcher, water		
Cheese, cov	50.00	—	Square	65.00	—
Creamer			Tankard, round, SP rim	75.00	135.00
Ind	30.00	—	Plate, 7", sq	25.00	—
Regular	40.00	—			

	Clear	Emerald Green		Clear	Emerald Green
Relish			Sugar		
7½" x 4"	18.00	—	Ind	30.00	—
8½ x 3"	18.00	—	Regular, cov	55.00	—
Salt			Sugar Shaker	65.00	—
Ind	15.00	—	Syrup, pewter top . .	95.00	—
Master	25.00	—	Toothpick		
Salt and Pepper, pr	35.00	—	Adv emb in base .	45.00	—
Sauce	15.00	—	Plain	30.00	—
Spooner	35.00	—	Tray, 12 x 8", turned		
Straw Holder, glass			up sides	50.00	—
cov	175.00	400.00	Tumbler	25.00	40.00
			Vase, 6", sq	35.00	45.00

INTAGLIO (Flower Spray with Scroll)

Made by Northwood Co., Indiana, Pennsylvania, c1899. Also reported in custard trimmed in green and gold. Creamers in blue opalescent were used as premiums in 1901 by Arbuckle Coffee.

	Blue Opal	Custard	Vaseline Opal	White Opal
Bowl, berry	50.00	50.00	60.00	45.00
Butter, cov	165.00	175.00	170.00	150.00
Compote, jelly	45.00	100.00	60.00	35.00
Creamer	60.00	100.00	50.00	40.00
Cruet, os	100.00	250.00	110.00	95.00
Pitcher, water	200.00	—	225.00	125.00
Sauce	35.00	90.00	42.00	25.00
Spooner	75.00	115.00	80.00	50.00
Sugar, cov	150.00	100.00	100.00	85.00
Tumbler	50.00	70.00	58.00	45.00
Wine	—	—	—	20.00

INVERTED FAN AND FEATHER

Made by Northwood Co., Wheeling, West Virginia, c1900. Also known in carnival and canary opalescent. See Pink Slag.

	Blue Opal	Clear Opal	Custard	Green With Gold
Bowl, berry				
Individual	40.00	—	40.00	—
Master	125.00	100.00	225.00	110.00
Butter, cov	275.00	195.00	245.00	200.00
Compote, jelly	200.00	195.00	175.00	195.00
Creamer	80.00	65.00	175.00	85.00
Cruet	200.00	195.00	575.00	195.00
Pitcher, water	325.00	200.00	500.00	215.00
Rose Bowl, ftd	150.00	—	—	—
Salt Shaker, single .	—	—	95.00	—
Spooner	100.00	75.00	100.00	75.00
*Sugar, cov	145.00	95.00	125.00	100.00
*Tumbler	80.00	25.00	80.00	35.00

INVERTED FERN

Flint, c1860. Attributed to Boston and Sandwich Glass Co. Goblets reproduced in color.

	Clear		Clear
Butter, cov	95.00	Pitcher, water	250.00
Champagne	125.00	Salt, master, ftd.	35.00
Compote, open, hs, 8"	55.00	Sauce, flat	10.00
Creamer, applied handle	125.00	Spooner	40.00
Egg Cup	30.00	Sugar, cov	75.00
Goblet, rayed base	45.00	Tumbler	95.00
Honey Dish	15.50	Wine	60.00
Plate, 6"	100.00		

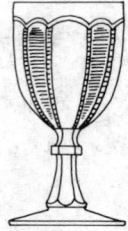

IOWA (Paneled Zipper)

Non-flint made by U. S. Glass Co. c1902. Part of the States pattern series. Available in clear glass with gold trim (add 20%) and ruby or cranberry stained. Also found in amber (goblet $65.00), green, canary, and blue. Add 50% to 100% for color and amber stained.

	Clear		Clear
Bowl, berry	12.00	Olive	18.00
Bread Plate, motto	80.00	Pitcher, water	50.00
Butter, cov	40.00	Punch Cup	18.00
Cake Stand	35.00	Salt Shaker, single	24.00
Carafe	35.00	Sauce, 4½"	6.50
Compote, cov, 8"	40.00	Spooner	30.00
Corn Liquor Jug, os	60.00	Sugar, cov	35.00
Creamer	30.00	Table Set, 4 pc	125.00
Cruet, os	30.00	Toothpick	22.00
Cup	18.00	Tumbler	25.00
Goblet	28.00	Wine	30.00
Lamp	125.00		

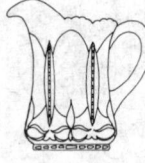

IRIS WITH MEANDER (Iris)

Made by Jefferson Glass Co., Steubenville, Ohio, c1903. Available in gold trim in clear, apple green, amethyst (toothpick $50.00; water pitcher $115.00), and blue. Also found in amber, opalescent (rare) and green opalescent (usually found in berry sets and toothpicks).

	Blue Opal	Canary Opal	White Opal
Bowl, berry	95.00	80.00	50.00
Butter, cov	310.00	195.00	125.00
Compote, jelly, 5"	85.00	75.00	50.00
Creamer	145.00	100.00	60.00
Cruet, os	200.00	150.00	100.00
Pickle	30.00	30.00	20.00
Pitcher, water	225.00	200.00	125.00
Plate, 7"	50.00	60.00	35.00
Salt & Pepper	100.00	100.00	85.00
Sauce	30.00	30.00	30.00

	Blue Opal	Canary Opal	White Opal
Spooner	75.00	65.00	50.00
Sugar, cov	150.00	100.00	80.00
*Toothpick	85.00	60.00	50.00
Tumbler	60.00	45.00	30.00
Vase, 11″	60.00	35.00	25.00

IVY IN SNOW (Ivy in Snow-Red Leaves, Forrest Ware)

Non-flint pattern made by Co-operative Flint Glass Co., Beaver Falls, Pennsylvania, in the 1880s. Phoenix Glass of Monaco, Pennsylvainia, also produced this pattern from 1937 to 1942 and was called Forrest Ware. Ivy In Snow-Red Leaves is the name used for pieces where the leaves are ruby stained. Some pieces have a ruby stained band. Also known in amber stained. Widely reproduced pattern.

	Clear	Ruby Stained		Clear	Ruby Stained
Bowl			Pitcher		
7″	20.00	—	Milk	—	200.00
8 x 5½″	30.00	—	Water	55.00	—
Butter, cov	55.00	—	Plate		
Cake Stand, 8″	45.00	—	6″	20.00	—
Celery Vase	25.00	75.00	7″	25.00	—
Compote			10″	30.00	—
Cov, hs, 8″	75.00	—	Relish	18.00	—
Open, jelly	30.00	—	Spooner	35.00	60.00
Creamer			Sugar		
Regular	28.00	75.00	Covered	50.00	75.00
Tankard	35.00	135.00	Open	35.00	50.00
Finger Bowl	25.00	—	Syrup	70.00	275.00
Goblet	32.00	65.00	Tumbler	25.00	45.00
Marmalade Jar	35.00	—	Wine	32.00	55.00
Mug	25.00	40.00			

JACOB'S LADDER (Maltese)

Non-flint made by Portland Glass Co, Portland, ME, and Bryce Bros, Pittsburgh, PA, in 1876, and U. S. Glass Co in 1891. A few pieces found in amber, yellow, blue, pale blue, and pale green.

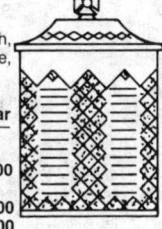

	Clear		Clear
Bowl		Cologne Bottle, Maltese	
6″ x 8¾″	15.00	cross stopper, ftd	85.00
6¾″ x 9¾″	20.00	Compote	
7½″ x 10¾″	20.00	Cov, hs, 6″	60.00
9″, berry, ornate SP holder,		Cov, hs 7½″	60.00
ftd	125.00	Cov, hs, 9½″	125.00
Butter, cov	65.00	Cov, hs, 13½ x 9″	75.00
Cake Stand		Open, hs, 7½″	35.00
8″ or 9″	50.00	Open, hs, 8½″, scalloped	30.00
11″ or 12″	60.00	Open, hs, 9½″, scalloped	38.00
Castor Bottle	18.00	Open, hs, 10″	40.00
Castor Set, 4 bottles	100.00	Creamer	35.00
Celery Vase	35.00	Cruet, os, ftd	85.00

	Clear		Clear
Goblet	50.00	Footed, 4"	12.00
Honey, 3½"	12.00	Spooner	30.00
Marmalade Jar	75.00	Sugar	
Mug	100.00	Cov.	55.00
Pitcher, water	150.00	Open	20.00
Plate, 6¼"	20.00	Syrup	
Relish		Knight's Head finial	125.00
7¾ x 5½"	15.00	Plain top	70.00
9½ x 5½"	15.00	Tumbler, bar	75.00
Salt, master, ftd.	20.00	Wine	32.50
Sauce			
Flat, 4", and 5"	8.00		

JERSEY SWIRL (Swirl)

Non-flint pattern made by Windsor Glass Co., Pittsburgh, Pennsylvania, c1887. Heavily reproduced in color. The clear goblet also reproduced.

	Amber	Blue	Canary	Clear
Bowl, 9¼"	55.00	55.00	45.00	35.00
Butter, cov	55.00	55.00	50.00	40.00
Cake Stand, 9"	75.00	70.00	45.00	30.00
* Celery Vase	42.00	42.00	35.00	30.00
* Compote, hs, 8" . . .	50.00	50.00	45.00	35.00
Creamer	45.00	45.00	40.00	30.00
Cruet, os	—	—	—	25.00
* Goblet				
Buttermilk	40.00	40.00	35.00	30.00
Water	40.00	40.00	35.00	30.00
Marmalade Jar	—	—	—	50.00
Pickle Castor, SP				
frame and lid	—	—	—	125.00
Pitcher, water	50.00	50.00	45.00	35.00
Plate, round				
6"	25.00	25.00	20.00	18.00
8"	30.00	30.00	25.00	20.00
10"	38.00	38.00	35.00	30.00
Salt, Ind	20.00	20.00	18.00	15.00
Sauce, 4½", flat . . .	20.00	20.00	15.00	10.00
Spooner	30.00	30.00	25.00	20.00
Sugar, cov	40.00	40.00	35.00	30.00
Tumbler	30.00	30.00	25.00	20.00
Wine	50.00	50.00	40.00	18.00

JUMBO

A non-flint novelty pattern made by Canton Glass Co., Canton, Ohio, in the 1870s and by Aetna Glass in 1883. The unique motif was used to commemorate P. T. Barnum's famous elephant, "Jumbo."

	Clear		Clear
Butter, cov		holder with bottles	550.00
Oblong, plain Jumbo	250.00	Compote	
Round, Barnum's head. . .	325.00	Cov, 7"	400.00
Castor Set, elephant's head		Cov, 8"	500.00

	Clear			Clear
Cov, 10″	750.00		Spoon Rack	350.00
Cov, 12″	800.00		Spooner, Barnum's head	100.00
Creamer, plain Jumbo	225.00		Sugar, cov, Barnum's head	400.00
Goblet	350.00		Toothpick, box on back	125.00

KANSAS (Jewel With Dewdrop)

Non-flint originally produced by Co-Operative Flint Glass Co., Beaver Falls, Pennsylvania. Later produced as part of the States pattern series by U. S. Glass Co. in 1901. Also known with jewels stained in pink or gold. Mugs have been reproduced in vaseline, amber, and blue.

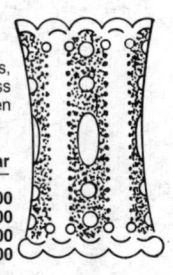

	Clear			Clear
Banana Stand	90.00		Open, ls, 6½″	45.00
Bowl			Creamer	40.00
7″, oval	35.00		Goblet	55.00
8½″	45.00		Mug, regular	45.00
Bread Plate, ODB	45.00		Pitcher	
Butter, cov	65.00		Milk	50.00
Cake Plate	45.00		Water	60.00
Cake Stand			Relish, 8½″, oval	20.00
7⅝″	45.00		Salt Shaker	50.00
9″	50.00		Sauce, flat, 4″	15.00
10″	85.00		Sugar, cov	65.00
Celery Vase	45.00		Syrup	125.00
Compote			Toothpick	50.00
Cov, hs, 7″	80.00		Tumbler	40.00
Cov, hs, 8″	125.00		Whiskey	15.00
Open, hs, 6½″, jelly	50.00		Wine	65.00
Open, hs, 9½″	60.00			

KENTUCKY

Non-flint made by U. S. Glass Co., c1897, as part of the States pattern series. The goblet is found in ruby stained ($50.00). A footed, square sauce ($30.00) is known in cobalt blue with gold. A toothpick holder is also known in ruby stained, $150.00.

	Clear	Emerald Green		Clear	Emerald Green
Butter, cov	50.00	—	Punch Cup	10.00	15.00
Cake Stand, 9½″	40.00	—	Salt & Pepper	50.00	—
Creamer	25.00	—	Sauce, ftd, sq	8.00	12.00
Cruet, os	45.00	—	Spooner	35.00	—
Cup	10.00	20.00	Sugar, cov	30.00	—
Goblet	20.00	50.00	Toothpick, sq	35.00	85.00
Nappy	10.00	15.00	Tumbler	20.00	30.00
Pitcher, water	55.00	—	Wine	28.00	38.00
Plate, 7″, sq	15.00	—			

KING'S CROWN (Ruby Thumbprint; X.L.C.R.)

Known as Ruby Thumbprint when pieces are ruby stained. A non-flint pattern made by Adams and Co., Pittsburgh, Pennsylvania, in the 1890s and later. Made in clear and with the thumbprints stained amethyst, gold, green, and yellow, and in clear with etching and trimmed in gold. It became very popular after 1891 as ruby stained souvenir ware. Cobalt blue pieces reported as very rare. Approximately 87 pieces documented. NOTE: Pattern has been copiously reproduced for the gift-trade market. New pieces are easily distinguished: in the case of Ruby Thumbprint, the color is a very pale pinkish red; green and blue pieces have an off-color. Reproduced in milk glass. Available in amethyst stained in goblet ($30.00) and wine ($10.00) and in green stained in goblet ($25.00) and wine ($15.00). Add 30% for engraved pieces.

	Clear	Ruby Stained		Clear	Ruby Stained
Banana Stand, ftd . .	85.00	135.00	Creamer		
Bowl			Ind	25.00	35.00
9¼", pointed	35.00	90.00	Regular	50.00	65.00
10", scalloped . . .	45.00	95.00	Cup & Saucer	55.00	70.00
Butter, cov	50.00	90.00	Honey, cov, sq	—	175.00
Cake Stand			Goblet	30.00	45.00
9"	65.00	125.00	Lamp, oil, 10"	135.00	—
10"	75.00	125.00	Mustard, cov	48.00	75.00
Castor Bottle	45.00	70.00	Pickle, lobed	18.00	40.00
Castor Set, glass			Pitcher		
stand, 4 bottles . .	175.00	325.00	Milk, tankard	75.00	100.00
Celery Vase	40.00	60.00	Water, bulbous . . .	95.00	225.00
Claret	35.00	50.00	Water, tankard . . .	110.00	200.00
Compote			Plate, 7"	20.00	—
Cov, hs, 6"	85.00	—	Punch Bowl, ftd	275.00	—
Cov, hs, 7"	45.00	195.00	Punch Cup	25.00	—
Cov, hs, 8"	55.00	245.00	Salt, master, sq	25.00	60.00
Cov, ls, 12"	90.00	225.00	Salt, ind, oblong . . .	16.00	30.00
Open, hs, 5½" . . .	55.00	65.00	Salt & Pepper	40.00	70.00
Open, hs, 7½" . . .	45.00	—	Sauce, 4"	15.00	20.00
Open, hs, 8¼" . . .	75.00	95.00	Spooner	45.00	50.00
Open, ls, 5¼" . . .	30.00	45.00	Sugar, cov	50.00	85.00
Open, ls, 9"	40.00	—	Toothpick	24.00	38.00
Cordial	48.00	—	Tumbler	18.00	38.00
			Wine	25.00	40.00

KING'S #500

Made by King Glass Co. of Pittsburgh, Pennsylvania in 1899. It was made in clear, frosted, and a rich, deep blue, known as Dewey Blue, both trimmed in gold. Continued by U. S. Glass Co. in 1891 and made in a great number of pieces. A clear goblet with frosted stem ($50.00) is known. Also known in dark green and a ruby stained sugar is reported ($95.00).

	Clear w/Gold	Dewey Blue w/Gold		Clear w/Gold	Dewey Blue w/Gold
Bowl			9"	14.00	45.00
7"	10.00	30.00	Butter, cov	50.00	125.00
8"	12.00	35.00	Cake Stand	40.00	60.00

	Clear w/Gold	Dewey Blue w/Gold		Clear w/Gold	Dewey Blue w/Gold
Celery Vase	20.00	—	Lamp		
Compote			Hand.	45.00	—
Covered	45.00	—	Stand	65.00	—
Open	30.00	—	Pitcher, water	55.00	200.00
Creamer.	30.00	50.00	Relish.	20.00	30.00
Cruet	45.00	175.00	Rose Bowl	20.00	45.00
Cup	15.00	15.00	Salt Shaker, single .	15.00	40.00
Decanter, locking			Sauce	15.00	35.00
top	100.00	—	Spooner.	30.00	70.00
			Sugar, cov	45.00	75.00
			Syrup.	55.00	225.00
			Tumbler	20.00	30.00

KLONDIKE (Amberette, English Hobnail Cross)

This pattern reported to have been made originally by A. J. Beatty And Co., c1885. It was also made by Hobbs, Brockunier Co., and Dalzell, Gilmore and Leighton Co. Made in colors other than clear and amber stained, which are the original colors. Made to commemmorate the Alaskan Gold Rush. The frosted panels depict snow; the amber bands, gold. Found clear and frosted, with or without scrolls, depending on the maker. Prices are listed for frosted; clear prices would be approximately 20% of those shown.

	Frosted Amber Stain		Frosted Amber Stain
Bowl, berry, 8".	175.00	Salt Shaker, single	100.00
Butter, cov	300.00	Sauce, flat	75.00
Cake Stand, 8", sq	500.00	Spooner.	175.00
Celery Tray.	200.00	Sugar, cov	250.00
Celery Vase	225.00	Syrup, pewter lid.	650.00
Condiment Set, cruet and		Toothpick	400.00
shaker on tray	1,000.00	Tray, 5½", sq	200.00
Creamer.	250.00	Tumbler	100.00
Cruet, os	550.00	Vase, trumpet shape	
Goblet	400.00	8"	275.00
Pitcher, water	575.00	10"	265.00
Punch Cup	100.00	Wine	300.00

KOKOMO (Bar and Diamond, R and H Swirl Band)

Made in clear glass by Richards & Hartley, Tarentum, Pennsylvania in the late 1880s to 1891. Found in ruby stained and etched. About 54 pieces manufactured.

	Clear	Ruby Stained		Clear	Ruby Stained
Bowl, 8½", ftd	24.00	—	Open, hs, 6"	25.00	—
Bread Tray	30.00	45.00	Open, hs, 7"	30.00	—
Butter, cov	35.00	—	Open, hs, 8"	35.00	—
Cake Stand	45.00	165.00	Open, ls, 7½" . . .	20.00	—
Celery Vase	15.00	45.00	Condiment Set, ob-		
Compote			long tray, shakers,		
Cov, hs, 7½"	35.00	165.00	cruet.	80.00	195.00
Open, hs, 5"	20.00	—	Creamer, ah	35.00	50.00

	Clear	Ruby Stained		Clear	Ruby Stained
Cruet	35.00	—	Sauce, ftd, 5"	8.00	10.00
Decanter, 9¾", wine	55.00	95.00	Spooner	25.00	45.00
Finger Bowl	25.00	35.00	Sugar, cov	45.00	65.00
Goblet	20.00	45.00	Sugar Shaker	35.00	75.00
Lamp, hand, atypical—has no diamonds.	50.00	100.00	Syrup	45.00	130.00
			Tray, water	35.00	90.00
			Tumbler	20.00	35.00
Pitcher, water, tankard	55.00	95.00	Wine	20.00	35.00
Salt & Pepper in holder	45.00	—			

LEAF AND DART (Pride)

Made by Boston and Sandwich Glass Co., Sandwich, Massachusetts, and Richards and Hartley Flint Glass, Pittsburgh, Pennsylvania, c1860. Shards have been found at Burlington Glass Works, Hamilton, Ontario.

	Clear		Clear
Bowl, 8¼", ftd	25.00	Salt, master, ftd	
Butter, cov	85.00	Cov.	65.00
Celery Vase	30.00	Open	30.00
Creamer, ah	40.00	Sauce, 4", flat	8.50
Cruet, pedestal, ah	100.00	Spooner	35.00
Egg Cup.	20.00	Sugar, cov	45.00
Goblet	30.00	Syrup	80.00
Honey Dish.	5.00	Tumbler, ftd	25.00
Pitcher, water, ah	80.00	Wine	35.00
Relish.	15.00		

LIBERTY BELL (Centennial)

Made by Gillinder and Co., Philadelphia, Pennsylvania for the Centennial Exposition, 1876. Some items also made in milk glass. Reproduced. Some reproductions bear the year "1976" and "200 Years" instead of the original inscriptions.

	Clear		Clear
Bowl, 8", ftd	100.00	Plate	
Bread Plate, 13⅜ x 9½"		6", dated	75.00
Clear, no signatures	85.00	8"	55.00
Milk glass, sgd John Hancock	200.00	10"	80.00
		Platter, 13 × 8", twig handles,	
Butter, cov	110.00	13 states	65.00
Creamer		Relish, oval.	45.00
Applied handle.	85.00	Salt Dip, ind, oval	35.00
Reed handle	100.00	Salt Shaker.	95.00
Goblet	30.00	Sauce, ftd	25.00
Mug, snake handle	335.00	Spooner	45.00
Pickle.	45.00	Sugar, cov	90.00
Pitcher, water, ah	400.00		

LILY OF THE VALLEY

Non-flint pattern made by Boston & Sandwich, Sandwich, Massachusetts, in the 1870s. Shards have also been found at Burlington Glass Works, Hamilton, Ontario. Lily of the Valley on Legs is a name frequently given to those pieces having three tall legs. Legged pieces include a covered butter, covered sugar, creamer and spooner. Add 25% for this type.

	Clear		Clear
Butter, cov	70.00	Water	135.00
Cake Stand	65.00	Relish	15.00
Celery Tray	40.00	Salt, master	
Celery Vase	48.00	Cov.	125.00
Compote		Open	50.00
Cov, hs, 8½"	85.00	Sauce, flat	12.00
Open, hs	50.00	Spooner	35.00
Creamer, applied handle	70.00	Sugar	
Cruet, os	80.00	Covered	75.00
Egg Cup	40.00	Open, buttermilk type	50.00
Goblet	40.00	Tumbler	
Honey	12.00	Flat	50.00
Nappy, 4"	20.00	Footed	65.00
Pickle, scoop shape	20.00	Vegetable Dish, oval	30.00
Pitcher		Wine	100.00
Milk	95.00		

LINCOLN DRAPE WITH TASSEL

Flint pattern made originally by Boston & Sandwich Glass Co., probably continued by other companies, c1865. Commemorative of Lincoln's death. Items without tassels are valued at 20% less. Some very rare pieces in cobalt blue are 200% more.

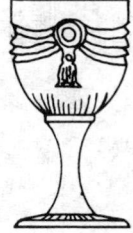

	Clear		Clear
Butter, cov	100.00	Honey	20.00
Celery Vase	90.00	Lamp, marble base	125.00
Compote		Pitcher, water, ah	350.00
Cov, hs, 8½"	150.00	Plate, 6"	80.00
Open, hs, 7½"	75.00	Salt, master, ftd	125.00
Open, ls, 6"	65.00	Sauce, 4"	20.00
Creamer, ah	125.00	Spill	50.00
Egg Cup	40.00	Spooner	75.00
Goblet		Sugar, cov	115.00
Lady's	165.00	Syrup, ah	175.00
Water	150.00	Wine	135.00

LION

Made by Gillinder and Sons, Philadelphia, Pennsylvania, in 1876. Available in clear (20% less). Many reproductions.

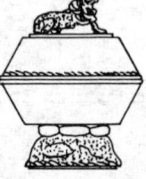

	Frosted		Frosted
Bowl, oblong		lion handles, GUTDODB.	125.00
6½ x 4¼"	55.00	Butter, cov	
8 x 5"	50.00	Lion's head finial	90.00
Bread Plate, 12" including		Rampant finial	125.00

	Frosted		Frosted
Cake Stand	85.00	Marmalade Jar, rampant finial	85.00
Celery Vase	85.00	Paperweight, lion head	125.00
Champagne	175.00	Pitcher	
Cheese, cov, rampant lion finial	400.00	Milk	375.00
Compote		Water	250.00
Cov, hs, 7", rampant finial	150.00	Relish, lion handles	38.00
* Cov, hs, 9", rampant finial, oval, collared base	150.00	Salt, master, rect lid	250.00
		* Sauce, 4", ftd	25.00
Cov, 9", hs	185.00	* Spooner	70.00
Open, ls, 8"	75.00	Sugar, cov	
Cordial	175.00	Lion head finial	85.00
* Creamer	65.00	Rampant finial	95.00
Egg Cup, 3½" h	65.00	Syrup, orig top	350.00
* Goblet	70.00	Wine	185.00
Lamp	350.00		

LOG CABIN

Non-flint made by Central Glass Co. Wheeling, West Virginia, c1875. Also available in color, but rare. Creamer, spooner, and covered sugar reproduced in clear and cobalt blue.

	Clear		Clear
Bowl, cov, 8 x 5¼ x 3⅝"	225.00	Pitcher, water	300.00
Butter, cov	250.00	Sauce, flat	75.00
Compote, hs, 10½"	275.00	* Spooner	120.00
* Creamer	115.00	* Sugar, cov	250.00
Marmalade Jar, cov	275.00		

LOOP (Seneca Loop)

Flint, c1850s–1860s; later in non-flint. Made by several firms. Sandwich produced fiery opalescent pieces. Yuma Loop is a contemporary with comparable values.

	Flint	Non-Flint		Flint	Non-Flint
Bowl, 9"	50.00	25.00	Goblet	21.00	18.00
Butter, cov	60.00	40.00	Pitcher, water, ah	170.00	60.00
Cake Stand	100.00	—	Salt, master, ftd	25.00	18.00
Celery Vase	65.00	20.00	Spooner	30.00	24.00
Champagne	45.00	24.00	Sugar, cov	70.00	30.00
Compote			Syrup	95.00	—
Cov, hs, 9½"	135.00	—	Tumbler		
Open, hs, 9"	115.00	40.00	Footed	25.00	15.00
Cordial, 2¾" h	40.00	20.00	Water	40.00	20.00
Creamer, ah	70.00	35.00	Wine	30.00	12.00
Egg Cup	30.00	20.00			

LOOP AND DART

Clear and stippled non-flint pattern of the late 1860s and early 1870s. Made by Boston & Sandwich, Sandwich, Massachusetts, and Richards & Hartley, Tarentum, Pennsylvania. Pattern related to Loop and Dart with Diamond Ornament and Loop and Dart with Round Ornament. Flint add 25%.

	Clear		Clear
Bowl, 9", oval	25.00	Pitcher, water	75.00
Butter, cov	45.00	Plate, 6"	35.00
Cake Stand, 10"	40.00	Relish.	18.00
Celery Vase	35.00	Salt, master	50.00
Compote		Sauce	5.00
Cov, hs, 8"	85.00	Spooner	30.00
Cov, ls, 8"	65.00	Sugar, cov	50.00
Creamer.	38.00	Tumbler	
Cruet, os	75.00	Footed	30.00
Egg Cup.	25.00	Water	25.00
Goblet	30.00	Wine	40.00
Lamp, oil	85.00		

LOOP AND DART WITH DIAMOND ORNAMENT

Clear and stippled non-flint pattern of the late 1860s and early 1870s. Made by Boston & Sandwich, and Richards & Hartley. Pattern related to Loop and Dart and Loop and Dart with Round Ornament. Flint add 25%.

	Clear		Clear
Bowl, 9", oval	20.00	Spooner	25.00
Butter, cov	45.00	Sugar	
Celery Vase	30.00	Covered	40.00
Creamer.	35.00	Open	20.00
Egg Cup.	24.00	Tumbler	
Goblet	32.00	Footed	35.00
Relish.	15.00	Water	40.00
Salt, master	18.00	Wine	35.00
Sauce, flat	4.50		

LOOP AND DART WITH ROUND ORNAMENT

Clear and stippled non-flint pattern of the late 1860s and early 1870s. Made by Boston & Sandwich, and Richards & Hartley, also attributed to Portland Glass Co, Portland, ME. Pattern related to Loop and Dart and Loop and Dart with Diamond Ornaments. Flint add 25%.

	Clear		Clear
Bowl, 9", oval	28.00	Water	32.00
Butter, cov	80.00	Pitcher, water	90.00
Butter Pat.	15.00	Plate, 6"	35.00
Celery Vase	35.00	Relish.	15.00
Champagne	80.00	Salt, master	28.00
Compote		Sauce, flat	8.00
Cov, hs, 8".	85.00	Spooner	26.00
Cov, ls, 8"	65.00	Sugar, cov	60.00
Open, hs, 8"	45.00	Tumbler	
Creamer.	35.00	Footed	30.00
Egg Cup.	30.00	Water	35.00
Goblet		Wine	35.00
Buttermilk	35.00		

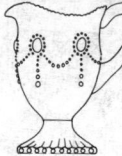

LOOP AND JEWEL (Jewel and Festoon; Venus)

Non-flint made by Beatty Glass and National Glass Co. then continued by Indiana Glass Co. Made until 1915. About 40 pieces known. A few rare pieces available in milk white.

	Clear		Clear
Bowl, 8″	15.00	Relish, 8″	22.00
Butter, cov	55.00	Salt & Pepper	32.00
Compote, 6½″	20.00	Sauce, flat, 4″	5.00
Creamer	25.00	Sherbet	45.00
Dish, 5″ sq	15.00	Spooner	25.00
Goblet	18.00	Sugar, cov	40.00
Pickle, 8″, rect.	18.00	Syrup	55.00
Pitcher, water	45.00	Vase, 8¾″	40.00
Plate, sq.	15.00	Wine	30.00

LOUISIANA (Sharp Oval and Diamond, Granby)

Made by Bryce Bros., Pittsburgh, Pennsylvania in 1870s, continued later (about 1892) by U. S. Glass Co. as one of the States patterns. Also available with gold and also comes frosted.

	Clear		Clear
Bowl, 9″, berry	20.00	Mug, handled, gold top	25.00
Butter, cov	70.00	Nappy, 4″, cov.	30.00
Cake Stand	45.00	Pitcher, water	65.00
Celery Vase	30.00	Relish.	15.00
Compote		Spooner	25.00
Cov, hs, 8″	50.00	Sugar, cov	45.00
Open, hs, 5″, jelly	40.00	Tumbler	22.00
Creamer.	32.50	Wine	35.00
Goblet	30.00		
Matchholder, attached saucer.	30.00		

MAGNET AND GRAPE (Magnet and Grape with Stippled Leaf)

Flint first made by Boston and Sandwich Glass Co., c1860. Later non-flint versions have grape leaf in either clear or stippled. Reproduced by Metropolitan Museum, New York with frosted leaf.

	Flint Frosted Leaf	Non-Flint Stippled or Clear Leaf		Flint Frosted Leaf	Non-Flint Stippled or Clear Leaf
Bowl, cov, 8″	—	75.00	Open, hs, 7½″	110.00	65.00
Butter, cov	185.00	40.00	Cordial, 4″	125.00	—
Celery Vase	165.00	25.00	* Creamer	175.00	40.00
Champagne	135.00	45.00	Decanter, os		
Compote			Pint	150.00	75.00
Cov, hs, 4½″	125.00	—	Quart	200.00	85.00

	Flint Frosted Leaf	Non-Flint Stippled or Clear Leaf		Flint Frosted Leaf	Non-Flint Stippled or Clear Leaf
Egg Cup	90.00	25.00	Salt, ftd	60.00	25.00
* Goblet			Sauce, 4"	24.00	8.00
American Shield. .	300.00	—	Spill	65.00	—
Low Stem	75.00	—	Spooner	95.00	30.00
Regular stem. . . .	70.00	30.00	* Sugar, cov, ...	145.00	80.00
Pitcher			Syrup	125.00	55.00
Milk, ah.	—	75.00	* Tumbler, water	110.00	30.00
Water, ah.	350.00	75.00	Whiskey	140.00	25.00
Relish, oval.	35.00	15.00	* Wine	90.00	50.00

MAINE (Paneled Stippled Flower)

Non-flint made by U. S. Glass Co., Pittsburgh, Pennsylvania c1890. Researchers dispute if goblet was made originally. Sometimes found with enamel trim or overall turquoise stain.

	Clear	Emerald Green		Clear	Emerald Green
Bowl, 8"	30.00	40.00	Mug	35.00	—
Bread Plate, oval, 10			Pitcher		
× 7¾"	30.00	—	Milk.	—	85.00
Butter, cov	48.00	—	Water	50.00	125.00
Cake Stand	40.00	60.00	Relish.	15.00	—
Compote,			Salt Shaker, single .	30.00	—
Cov, jelly	—	65.00	Sauce	15.00	—
Open, hs, 7"	20.00	30.00	Sugar, cov	45.00	75.00
Open, ls, 8"	38.00	55.00	Syrup	75.00	225.00
Open, ls, 9"	30.00	35.00	Tumbler	20.00	45.00
Creamer	30.00	—	Wine	50.00	75.00

MANHATTAN

Non-flint with gold, made by U. S. Glass Co., c1902. A depression glass pattern also has the "Manhattan" name. A table sized creamer and covered sugar are known in true ruby stained, and a goblet in known in old marigold carnival glass. Heavily reproduced.

	Clear	Rose Stained		Clear	Rose Stained
Biscuit Jar, cov	60.00	85.00	Cheese, cov, 8⅜" d.	—	115.00
Bowl			Compote, cov, hs,		
6"	18.00	—	9½"	45.00	—
8¼", scalloped. . .	20.00	—	Creamer		
9½"	22.00	—	Individual.	20.00	—
10"	22.00	—	Regular.	30.00	60.00
12½"	25.00	—	Cruet		
Butter, cov	55.00	—	Large	65.00	115.00
Cake Stand, 10" . . .	40.00	50.00	Small	50.00	—
Carafe, water	40.00	65.00	* Goblet	25.00	—
Celery Vase	25.00	—	Ice Bucket	—	65.00

	Clear	Rose Stained		Clear	Rose Stained
Olive, Gainsborough	30.00	—	Straw Holder, cov ..	65.00	—
Pitcher, water, tank-			Sugar		
ard, ½ gal	60.00	—	Individual, open ..	12.00	—
Plate			Regular, cov	40.00	65.00
6″	6.50	30.00	Syrup.	48.00	175.00
8″	15.00	—	Toothpick	30.00	—
10¾″.	20.00	—	Tumblers		
Punch Bowl	125.00	—	Ice Tea	30.00	—
Punch Cup	10.00	—	Water	20.00	—
Relish, 6″	12.00	—	Vase, 6″	18.00	—
Salt Shaker, single .	20.00	35.00	Violet Bowl	20.00	—
Sauce	14.00	20.00	Water Bottle	40.00	—
Spooner	20.00	—	Wine	20.00	—

MAPLE LEAF

Non-flint pattern made by Gillinder & Sons, c1850. Heavily reproduced in clear and colors.

	Amber	Blue	Canary/ Vaseline	Clear	Frosted
Bowl					
5½″, oval.	—	—	45.00	25.00	—
6″, ftd	45.00	60.00	50.00	35.00	40.00
Bread Plate	65.00	85.00	75.00	75.00	85.00
Butter, cov	75.00	80.00	75.00	65.00	70.00
Cake Stand, 11″ . . .	60.00	65.00	60.00	45.00	50.00
Celery	45.00	50.00	45.00	35 .00	40.00
Compote					
Cov, hs, 9″.	65.00	90.00	65.00	85.00	100.00
Jelly	50.00	60.00	50.00	40.00	45.00
Creamer.	65.00	65.00	68.00	5 0.00	55.00
Goblet	85.00	100.00	95.00	65.00	90.00
Pitcher					
Milk.	80.00	95.00	85.00	65.00	75.00
Water	85.00	100.00	90.00	75.00	80.00
Platter, 10½″.	45.00	50.00	50.00	40.00	45.00
Relish.	18.00	22.00	18.00	12.00	15.00
Sauce					
5″	14.50	18.00	15.00	10.00	12.00
6″, ftd	28.00	30.00	28.00	15.00	20.00
Spooner.	60.00	75.00	60.00	40.00	45.00
Sugar, cov	50.00	100.00	80.00	65.00	75.00
Tumbler	40.00	45.00	40.00	35.00	45.00

MARDI GRAS (Duncan and Miller #42, Paneled English Hobnail with Prisms)

Made by Duncan and Miller Glass Co., c1898. Available in gold trim and ruby stained.

	Clear	Ruby Stained		Clear	Ruby Stained
Bowl, 8″, berry	18.00	—	Butter, cov	65.00	145.00

	Clear	Ruby Stained		Clear	Ruby Stained
Cake Stand, 10"	65.00	—	Water	75.00	200.00
Celery Tray, curled			Plate, 6"	6.00	—
edges	25.00	—	Punch Cup	10.00	—
Champagne, saucer	32.00	—	Relish	12.50	—
Claret	35.00	—	Sherry, flared or		
Compote			straight	20.00	—
Cov, hs	55.00	—	Spooner	25.00	—
Open, jelly, 4½"	30.00	55.00	Sugar, cov	35.00	65.00
Cordial	35.00	—	Syrup, metal lid	65.00	—
Creamer			Toothpick	35.00	125.00
Ind, oval	20.00	—	Tumbler		
Regular	35.00	60.00	Bar	25.00	—
Finger Bowl	20.00	—	Champagne	20.00	—
Goblet	35.00	—	Water	30.00	40.00
Lamp Shade	35.00	—	Vase, trumpet shape,		
Pitcher			3 sizes	20.00	—
Milk	50.00	—	Wine	30.00	65.00

MARYLAND (Inverted Loop and Fan; Loop and Diamond)

Made originally by Bryce Brothers, Pittsburgh, Pennsylvania. Continued by U. S. Glass Co. as one of their States patterns.

	Clear w/gold	Ruby Stained		Clear w/gold	Ruby Stained
Banana Dish	30.00	—	Olive, handled	12.00	—
Bowl, berry	15.00	—	Pitcher		
Bread Plate	25.00	—	Milk	40.00	—
Butter, cov	65.00	—	Water	50.00	100.00
Cake Stand, 8"	40.00	—	Plate, 7", round	25.00	—
Celery Tray	20.00	—	Relish, oval	18.00	—
Celery Vase	25.00	—	Salt Shaker, single	30.00	—
Compote			Sauce, flat	14.00	20.00
Cov, hs	65.00	100.00	Spooner	30.00	—
Open, hs, 7½"	40.00	—	Sugar, cov	45.00	60.00
Open, jelly	25.00	—	Toothpick	85.00	150.00
Creamer	30.00	55.00	Tumbler	25.00	50.00
Goblet	30.00	48.00	Wine	40.00	75.00

MASCOTTE (Minor Block)

Non-flint made by Ripley and Co., Pittsburgh, Pennsylvania, in the 1870s. Reissued by U. S. Glass Co. in 1898. The butter dish shown on Plate 77 of Ruth Webb Lee's *Victorian Glass* is said to go with this pattern. It has a horseshoe finial and was named for the famous "Maude S," "Queen of the Turf" trotting horse during the 1880s. Apothecary jar and pyramid jars made by Tiffin Glass Co. in the 1950s.

	Clear	Etched		Clear	Etched
Bowl			Cov, 8"	—	50.00
Cov, 5"	—	35.00	Cov, 9"	—	55.00
Cov, 6"	—	35.00	Open 9"	35.00	40.00
Cov, 7"	—	45.00	Butter Pat	8.00	12.00

	Clear	Etched		Clear	Etched
Butter, cov			Pitcher, water	55.00	65.00
"Maude S"	100.00	—	Plate, turned in		
Regular	50.00	65.00	sides	38.00	—
Cake Basket, handle.	80.00	65.00	Pyramid Jar, 7" d,		
Celery Vase	35.00	40.00	one fits into other		
Cheese, cov	70.00	80.00	and forms tall jar-		
Compote			type container with		
Cov, hs, 5"	—	40.00	lid, three sizes		
Cov, hs, 6"	—	45.00	with flat sepa-		
Cov, hs, 7"	—	55.00	rators	40.00	—
Cov, hs, 8"	75.00	85.00	Salt Dip	25.00	—
Cov, hs, 9"	—	90.00	Salt Shaker, single .	25.00	25.00
Open, hs, 5"	—	25.00	Sauce		
Open, hs, 6"	—	25.00	Flat	8.00	15.00
Open, hs, 7"	—	30.00	Footed	12.00	16.00
Open, hs, 8"	—	35.00	Spooner	30.00	35.00
Open, hs, 9"	—	35.00	Sugar, cov	40.00	45.00
Open, ls, 8"	30.00	45.00	Tray, water	40.00	55.00
Creamer	30.00	45.00	Tumbler	20.00	35.00
Goblet	40.00	45.00	Wine	25.00	30.00

MASSACHUSETTS (Geneva #2, M2-131)

Made in 1880s, maker unknown, and continued in 1898 by U. S. Glass Co. as one of the States series. The vase ($45.00) and wine ($45.00) are known in emerald green. Some pieces reported in cobalt blue and marigold carnival glass. Reproduced in clear and colors.

	Clear		Clear
Bar Bottle, metal shot glass		Pitcher, water	75.00
for cover	75.00	Plate, 8"	32.00
Basket, 4½", ah	50.00	Punch Cup	15.00
Bowl		Relish, 8½"	25.00
6", sq	17.50	Rum Jug	90.00
9", sq	20.00	Spooner	22.00
* Butter, cov	75.00	Sugar, cov	40.00
Celery Tray	28.00	Toothpick	40.00
Cologne Bottle, os.	37.50	Tumbler	
Compote, open	35.00	Champagne or Juice	25.00
Cordial	55.00	Water	30.00
Creamer	28.00	Whiskey (shot)	15.00
Cruet, os		Vase	
Regular	40.00	6½", trumpet	25.00
2 oz	55.00	7"	25.00
Goblet	45.00	9", trumpet	35.00
Mug	24.00	Wine	40.00
Olive	8.50		

MEDALLION (Hearts & Spades, Spades)

Non-flint, c1880. A reproduction butter dish may be found with an "IG" trademark.

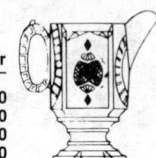

	Amber and Canary	Apple Green and Blue	Clear
*Butter, cov	40.00	50.00	35.00
Cake Stand, 9¼". . .	45.00	55.00	25.00
Celery Vase	30.00	40.00	20.00
Compote, cov, hs . .	50.00	60.00	40.00
Creamer.	40.00	45.00	30.00
Cruet	—	—	20.00
Egg Cup.	25.00	40.00	20.00
Goblet	35.00	45.00	20.00
Pickle.	20.00	25.00	15.00
Pitcher, water	55.00	65.00	45.00
Sauce			
Flat.	12.00	15.00	10.00
Footed	14.00	20.00	12.00
Spooner	28.00	40.00	20.00
Sugar, cov	40.00	50.00	25.00
Tumbler	25.00	35.00	15.00
Wine	30.00	40.00	20.00

MEDALLION SUNBURST

Made by Bryce, Higbee & Co of Bridgeport, Pennsylvania, c1905.

	Clear		Clear
Bowl		Pitcher	
8¼", sq	28.00	Milk.	45.00
9¼", round	30.00	Water	50.00
Butter, cov	50.00	Plate, 7¼".	25.00
Butter Pat.	5.00	Punch Cup	15.00
Cake Stand		Relish.	12.00
9¼".	65.00	Salt Dip	10.00
10½".	70.00	Salt & Pepper, pr.	35.00
Celery Vase	24.00	Sauce, flat	10.00
Compote, open, hs, 8".	25.00	Spooner	20.00
Creamer.	25.00	Sugar, cov	30.00
Cruet, os	20.00	Toothpick	25.00
Goblet	24.00	Tumbler	20.00
Mug, 3¼"	18.00	Vase, 9½".	32.50
		Wine	30.00

MELROSE

Non-flint pattern made by Greensburg Glass Co., Greensburg, Pennsylvania, in 1887 in clear, etched, and ruby stained. Add 20% for etching.

	Clear		Clear
Bowl, berry	20.00	Compote	
Butter, cov	45.00	Cov, hs, 8".	90.00
Cake Plate	30.00	Open, hs, 7"	25.00
Cake Stand	32.00	Open, jelly.	18.00
Celery Vase	25.00	Creamer.	25.00

	Clear			Clear
Goblet	20.00	Spooner		30.00
Pitcher, water	45.00	Sugar, cov		35.00
Plate, 8″	10.00	Tray, water 11½″		45.00
Salt, individual	6.00	Tumbler		15.00
Salt Shaker	15.00	Waste Bowl		20.00
Sauce, flat	8.00	Wine		20.00

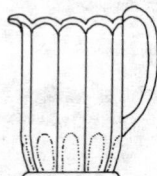

MICHIGAN (Loop & Pillar)

Non-flint made by U. S. Glass Co., c1893. One of the States pattern series. The 10¼″ bowl ($42.00) and punch cup ($12.00) are found with yellow or blue stain. Also found with painted carnations. Other colors include "Sunrise," gold, and ruby stained.

	Clear	Rose Stained		Clear	Rose Stained
Bowl			Olive, two handles	—	35.00
7½″	15.00	—	Pickle	12.00	20.00
9″	35.00	60.00	Pitcher		
10¼″	35.00	62.00	8″	50.00	—
Butter, cov	60.00	110.00	12″	70.00	150.00
Celery Vase	35.00	85.00	Punch Bowl, 8″	50.00	—
Compote			Punch Cup	8.00	—
Jelly, 4½″	25.00	—	Relish	20.00	—
Open, hs, 9¼″	65.00	—	Salt Shaker, single, 3		
Creamer			types	20.00	30.00
Ind, 602 tankard	20.00	65.00	Sauce	10.00	15.00
Regular	30.00	50.00	Sherbet, cup,		
Cruet, os	60.00	175.00	handled	7.00	15.00
Crushed Fruit Bowl	75.00	—	Spooner	40.00	50.00
Finger Bowl	15.00	—	Sugar, cov	50.00	65.00
Goblet	35.00	55.00	Syrup	75.00	—
Honey Dish	10.00	—	Toothpick	45.00	100.00
Lemonade Mug	20.00	35.00	Tumbler	30.00	40.00
Nappy, Gainsbor-			Vase, bud	35.00	35.00
ough handle	35.00	—	Wine	35.00	50.00

MINERVA

Non-flint made in the United States and probably in Canada in the 1870s. There are two forms.

	Clear		Clear
Bowl		10½″	120.00
Footed	40.00	13″	145.00
Rectangular		Compote	
7″	25.00	Cov, hs, 7″	90.00
8 x 5″	30.00	Cov, ls, 8″	85.00
9″	45.00	Open, hs, 10″	60.00
Bread Plate	65.00	Open, hs, octagonal ftd	95.00
Butter, cov	85.00	Creamer	50.00
Cake Stand		Goblet	75.00
8″	95.00	Marmalade Jar, cov	150.00
9 x 6½″	100.00	Pickle	30.00

	Clear		Clear
Pitcher		Sauce	
Milk.	75.00	Flat.	15.00
Water	165.00	Footed, 4″	20.00
Plate		Spooner	55.00
8″	55.00	Sugar	
10″, handled	60.00	Cov.	65.00
Platter, oval, 13″	65.00	Open	35.00

MINNESOTA

Non-flint made by U. S. Glass Co., late 1890s. One of the States patterns. A two-piece flower frog has been found in emerald green ($46.00).

	Clear	Ruby Stained		Clear	Ruby Stained
Basket	65.00	—	Mug	25.00	—
Biscuit Jar, cov	55.00	150.00	Olive	15.00	25.00
Bowl, 8½″, flared	30.00	—	Pitcher, water, tank-		
Butter, cov	55.00	—	ard	85.00	200.00
Carafe	35.00	—	Plate		
Celery Tray, 13″	25.00	—	5″, turned up		
Compote			edges	25.00	—
Open, hs, 10″,			7⅜″ d	15.00	—
flared	60.00	—	Relish	20.00	—
Open, ls, 9″, sq	55.00	—	Sauce, boat shape	15.00	35.00
Creamer			Spooner	25.00	—
Individual	20.00	—	Sugar, cov	40.00	—
Regular	30.00	—	Syrup	55.00	—
Cruet	35.00	—	Toothpick, 3 handles	35.00	—
Cup	18.00	—	Tumbler	18.00	—
Goblet	28.00	50.00	Wine	40.00	—
Hair Receiver	30.00				

MISSOURI (Palm and Scroll)

Non-flint made by U. S. Glass Co. c1899, one of the States pattern series. Also made in amethyst and canary.

	Clear	Emerald Green		Clear	Emerald Green
Bowl, berry, 8″	15.00	35.00	Pitcher		
Butter, cov	45.00	65.00	Milk	40.00	85.00
Cake Stand, 9″	50.00	—	Water	75.00	85.00
Celery Vase	30.00	—	Salt Shaker, single	25.00	40.00
Cordial	35.00	—	Sauce, flat, 4″	14.00	16.00
Creamer	25.00	40.00	Spooner	25.00	48.00
Cruet	55.00	125.00	Sugar, cov	50.00	65.00
Dish, cov 6″	65.00	—	Syrup	65.00	—
Doughnut stand, 6″	40.00	—	Tumbler	20.00	38.00
Goblet	50.00	60.00	Wine	38.00	50.00
Mug	35.00	45.00			
Pickle Dish, rectan-					
gular	18.00	27.50			

MOON AND STAR (Palace)

Non-flint and frosted (add 30%). First made by Adams & Co., Pittsburgh, Pennsylvania, in 1874 and later by several manufacturers, including Pioneer Glass who probably decorated ruby stained examples. Six different compotes documented. Also found with frosted highlights. Heavily reproduced in clear and color.

	Clear		Clear
Bowl		Cruet	125.00
6"	25.00	Egg Cup.	35.00
8", Berry	30.00	Goblet	45.00
12½", Round	42.00	Lamp	140.00
Bread Plate, rect.	45.00	Pickle, oval	20.00
Butter, cov	65.00	Pitcher, water, ah	175.00
Cake Stand, 10"	50.00	Relish.	20.00
Carafe	40.00	Salt, ind	10.00
Celery Vase	35.00	Salt & Pepper, pr.	70.00
Champagne	40.00	Sauce	
Claret.	47.50	Flat.	8.00
Compote		Footed	12.00
Cov, hs, 8".	75.00	Spooner	45.00
Cov, hs, 10".	68.00	Sugar, cov	65.00
Cov, ls, 6½"	55.00	Syrup	150.00
Cov, ls, 10"	68.00	Tray, water	65.00
Open, hs, 9"	40.00	Tumbler, ftd	60.00
Open, ls, 7½"	25.00	Wine	50.00
Creamer, ah	55.00		

NAILHEAD (Gem)

Non-flint, made by Bryce, Higbee, and Co., in 1880s. Also found in ruby stained (goblet at $30.00, pitcher at $65.00).

	Clear		Clear
Bowl, 6"	15.00	Creamer.	25.00
Butter, cov	40.00	Goblet	25.00
Cake Stand		Pitcher, water	35.00
9½"	30.00	Plate	
10½"	35.00	Round, 9"	20.00
Celery	30.00	Square, 7"	15.00
Compote		Sauce, flat	10.00
Cov, 8", hs.	45.00	Spooner	24.00
Cov, ls, 7"	45.00	Sugar, cov	40.00
Open, hs, 6½"	25.00	Tumbler	35.00
Open, 9½", hs	40.00	Wine	15.00

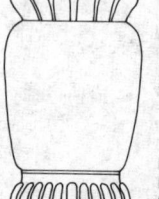

NEVADA

Non-flint made by U. S. Glass Co. as a States Pattern. Pieces are sometimes partly frosted and have enamel decoration. Add 20% for frosted.

	Clear		Clear
Biscuit Jar	45.00	Celery	27.50
Butter, cov	68.00	Compote, cov, 8", hs	45.00
Cake Stand, 10"	35.00	Creamer.	32.00

	Clear			Clear
Cruet	35.00	Salt Shaker, single, two		
Cup, custard	12.00	types		15.00
Pickle, oval	10.00	Sauce		10.00
Pitcher, water, tankard, ½		Spooner		35.00
gal	40.00	Sugar, cov		35.00
Salt		Syrup, tin top		45.00
Ind	8.00	Toothpick		38.00
Master	14.00	Tumbler		15.00

NEW ENGLAND PINEAPPLE

Flint made by Boston and Sandwich Glass Co. in early 1860s. Rare in color. The goblet has been reproduced in clear and color.

	Flint	Non-Flint		Flint	Non-Flint
Bowl, 8", scalloped	85.00	—	Pitcher, water	350.00	—
Cake Stand	115.00	—	Plate, 6"	90.00	—
Castor Bottle	50.00	—	Salt		
Castor Set, 4 bottles,			Ind	24.00	—
complete	300.00	—	Master	45.00	40.00
Champagne	175.00	—	Sauce		
Cov, hs, 5"	150.00	—	Flat	15.00	10.00
Cov, hs, 8"	175.00	—	Footed	28.00	—
Open, hs, 7"	90.00	—	Spillholder	60.00	—
Open, hs, 8½"	125.00	—	Spooner	50.00	35.00
Creamer, applied			Sugar, cov	125.00	55.00
handle, 2 sizes	185.00	70.00	Sweetmeat, cov	225.00	—
Decanter, qt, os	225.00	—	Tumbler		
Egg Cup	50.00	35.00	Bar	125.00	—
Lady's	100.00	—	Water	85.00	—
Regular	65.00	—	Whiskey, handled	145.00	—
Mug	95.00	—	* Wine	150.00	—

NEW HAMPSHIRE (Bent Buckle, Modiste)

Non-flint made by U. S. Glass Co. in the States Pattern series. There is a large ruby mug ($50.00), 5½" bowl ($25.00), syrup ($48.00), toothpick ($40.00), and tumbler ($40.00). A vase is known in green stain ($30.00).

	Clear w/gold	Rose Stained		Clear w/gold	Rose Stained
Bowl			Goblet	25.00	50.00
Flared, 8½"	15.00	25.00	Mug, large	15.00	45.00
Round, 8½"	18.00	30.00	Pitcher, water, tank-		
Square, 8½"	25.00	35.00	ard	70.00	90.00
Butter, cov	45.00	70.00	Relish	18.00	—
Cake Stand, 8¼"	30.00	—	Sugar		
Carafe	60.00	—	Cov	45.00	60.00
Celery Vase	35.00	50.00	Ind, open	20.00	25.00
Compote, open	38.00	42.00	Syrup	75.00	—
Creamer			Toothpick	25.00	40.00
Ind	20.00	30.00	Tumbler	18.00	32.00
Regular	30.00	45.00	Vase	20.00	35.00
Cruet	55.00	135.00	Wine	28.00	50.00

NEW JERSEY (Loops and Drops)

Non-flint made by U. S. Glass Co. in States Pattern Series. Items with perfect gold are worth more than those with worn gold. An emerald green 11″ vase is known, value $75.00.

	Clear w/gold	Ruby Stained		Clear w/gold	Ruby Stained
Bowl			Water		
8″, flared	25.00	50.00	Applied handle .	80.00	210.00
9″	32.50	65.00	Pressed handle	50.00	185.00
10″, oval	30.00	—	Plate		
Bread Plate	30.00	—	Flat	12.00	—
Flat	75.00	100.00	Footed	22.00	—
Footed	125.00	—	12″	30.00	—
Cake Stand, 8″ . . .	65.00	—	Salt & Pepper		
Celery Tray, rectan-			Hotel	50.00	—
gular	25.00	—	Small	35.00	55.00
Compote			Sauce	14.00	30.00
Cov, hs, 5″, jelly . .	45.00	55.00	Spooner	27.00	75.00
Cov, hs, 8″	75.00	—	Sugar, cov	60.00	80.00
Open, hs, 6¾″ . . .	30.00	—	Sweetmeat, 8″, open,		
Open, hs, 8″	60.00	—	ftd	40.00	—
Creamer	35.00	60.00	Syrup, no gold	90.00	—
Cruet	50.00	—	Toothpick	55.00	225.00
Goblet	40.00	—	Tumbler	28.00	45.00
Olive, pointed,			Wine, straight or		
flared	18.00	—	flared	42.00	65.00
Pickle, rect	15.00	—			
Pitcher					
Milk, ah	75.00	—			

O'HARA DIAMOND (Sawtooth and Star)

Non-flint, made by O'Hara Glass Co. in 1928 and by U. S. Glass Co. in 1898.

	Clear	Ruby Stained		Clear	Ruby Stained
Bowl, berry			Lamp, Oil	50.00	—
Individual	—	25.00	Pitcher, water,		
Master	25.00	75.00	tankard	—	165.00
Butter, cov, ruffled			Plate		
base	45.00	125.00	7″	20.00	—
Compote			8″	30.00	—
Cov, hs	40.00	185.00	10″	40.00	—
Open, hs, jelly . . .	48.00	145.00	Salt, master	15.00	35.00
Condiment Set, pr			Salt Shaker	—	35.00
salt and pepper,			Spooner	20.00	55.00
sugar shaker, tray	—	250.00	Sugar, cov	35.00	90.00
Creamer	30.00	60.00	Sugar Shaker	55.00	150.00
Cruet	55.00	150.00	Syrup	55.00	200.00
Cup and Saucer . . .	40.00	60.00	Tumbler	30.00	45.00
Goblet	25.00	50.00			

ONE HUNDRED ONE

Non-flint made by the Bellaire Goblet Co., Findlay, Ohio, in the late 1870s.

	Clear		Clear
Bread Plate, 101 border, Farm implement center, 11"	75.00	Pitcher, water, ah	120.00
Butter, cov	40.00	Plate	
Cake Stand, 9"	65.00	6"	15.00
Celery Vase	50.00	7"	20.00
Compote		8"	20.00
Cov, hs, 7"	60.00	Relish	15.00
Cov, ls	60.00	Sauce	
Creamer	45.00	Flat	10.00
Goblet	48.00	Footed	15.00
Lamp, hand, oil, 10"	80.00	Spooner	25.00
		Sugar, cov	45.00
		Wine	60.00

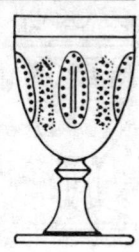

OPEN ROSE

Non-flint, c1870. Attributed to Boston and Sandwich Glass Co.

	Clear		Clear
Bowl, oval, 9" x 6"	25.00	Regular	28.00
Butter, cov	55.00	Pitcher, water, ah	165.00
Compote		Relish	15.00
Cov, hs, 8"	60.00	Salt, ind, ftd	30.00
Cov, hs, 9"	60.00	Sauce	10.00
Open, ls, 7½"	35.00	Spooner	40.00
Creamer	40.00	Sugar	
Egg Cup	25.00	Cov	50.00
Goblet		Open	30.00
Lady's	30.00	Tumbler	50.00

OREGON #1 (Beaded Loop)

Non-flint. First made in the 1880s. Reissued in 1907 as one of the States series. Reproduced in clear and color by Imperial.

	Clear		Clear
Bowl		Mug	35.00
7"	15.00	Pickle Dish, boat shape	15.00
8"	15.00	Pitcher	
9", berry, cov	25.00	Milk	40.00
Bread Plate	35.00	Water	60.00
Butter, cov	35.00	Relish	15.00
English	65.00	Salt, master	18.00
Flanged	50.00	Sauce	
Flat	40.00	Flat, 3½ to 4"	10.00
Cake Stand	35.00	Footed, 3½"	15.00
Carafe, water	35.00	Spooner	
Celery Vase	30.00	Flat	24.00
Compote		Footed	26.00
Open, hs, 8"	50.00	Sugar, cov	
Open, ls, 9"	40.00	Flat	25.00
Creamer		Footed	30.00
Flat	30.00	Syrup	55.00
Footed	35.00	Toothpick	35.00
Cruet	45.00	Tumbler	25.00
Goblet	35.00	Wine	40.00
Honey Dish	10.00		

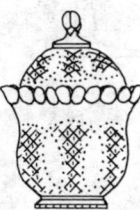

PALMETTE

Non-flint, late 1870s. Syrup known in milk glass.

	Clear		Clear
Bowl		Cup Plate	45.00
8"	25.00	Egg Cup	35.00
9"	15.00	Goblet	35.00
Bread Plate, handled, 9"	30.00	Lamp, 8½", all glass	80.00
Butter Dish, cov	65.00	Pickle, scoop shape	18.00
Butter Pat	20.00	Pitcher, water, ah	110.00
Cake Stand	60.00	Relish	18.00
Castor Bottle	20.00	Salt, master, ftd	22.00
Castor Set, 5 bottles	125.00	Salt Shaker	55.00
Celery Vase	40.00	Sauce, flat, 6"	10.00
Champagne	85.00	Shaker, saloon, oversize	60.00
Compote		Spooner	35.00
Cov, hs, 7"	65.00	Sugar, cov	55.00
Cov, hs, 8½"	75.00	Syrup, ah	100.00
Cov, hs, 9¾"	85.00	Tumbler	
Open, ls, 5½"	25.00	Bar	60.00
Open, ls, 7"	30.00	Water, ftd	40.00
Creamer, ah	50.00	Wine	90.00

PANELED FORGET-ME-NOT (Regal)

Non-flint, made by Bryce Bros., Pittsburgh, Pennsylvania, c1870. Made in limited production in amethyst and green.

	Amber	Blue	Clear
Bread Plate	—	—	25.00
Butter, cov	45.00	60.00	30.00
Cake Stand, 10"	70.00	90.00	45.00
Celery Vase	45.00	70.00	36.00
Compote			
Cov, hs, 7"	—	—	65.00
Cov, hs, 8"	80.00	100.00	68.00
Open, hs, 8½", scalloped rim	—	—	55.00
Open, hs, 10"	—	—	40.00
Creamer	45.00	60.00	35.00
Cruet, os	—	—	45.00
Goblet	50.00	65.00	32.00
Marmalade Jar, cov.	60.00	80.00	40.00
Pickle, boat shape	25.00	35.00	15.00
Pitcher			
Milk	—	—	50.00
Water	90.00	110.00	75.00
Relish, scoop shape	—	—	65.00
Salt & Pepper, pr.	—	—	65.00
Sauce, ftd	18.00	25.00	15.00
Spooner	40.00	50.00	25.00
Sugar, cov	60.00	80.00	40.00
Wine	55.00	70.00	55.00

PANELED "44" (Athenia, Reverse "44")

Non-flint made by U. S. Glass Co., c1912. Most pieces bear intertwined U. S. Glass Co. mark in base. Forms include pedestals and handles. Comes trimmed in gold and untarnishable platinum. Lemonade set (six piece set $150.00), goblet, and covered butter ($95.00) in rose or green staining. Some pieces in plain blue.

	Clear w/ platinum		Clear w/ platinum
Bon Bon, trifid ftd, cov	35.00	Olive, flat, handless	30.00
Bowl, 8″, flat	50.00	Pitcher, water	
Butter, cov, flat	55.00	Flat, bulbous, ½ gal	90.00
Candlestick, 7″	50.00	Footed, tankard	95.00
Cruet	65.00	Salt & Pepper, pr.	75.00
Creamer		Sugar, cov, flat, handled. . . .	60.00
Flat.	45.00	Sugar, powdered, flat, no	
Footed	55.00	handles	55.00
Finger Bowl	30.00	Toothpick	45.00
Goblet	45.00	Tumbler, water	30.00
Lemonade Set, pitcher, 6		Vase, loving cup shape	40.00
tumblers	200.00	Wine	50.00

PANELED THISTLE (Delta)

Non-flint made by J. P. Higbee Glass Co., Bridgeville, Pennsylvania, in the early 1900s. The Higbee Glass Co. often used a bee as a trademark. This pattern has been heavily reproduced with a similar mark. Occasionally found with gilt. A covered sugar in ruby stained is known.

	Clear		Clear
Basket, small size	50.00	Water	70.00
Bowl		Plate	
8″, bee mark	25.00	7″	20.00
9″, bee mark	30.00	10″, bee mark	30.00
Bread Plate	40.00	Punch Cup, bee mark	25.00
Butter, cov, ...	60.00	Relish, bee mark.	15.00
Cake Stand, 9″	35.00	Rose Bowl, 5″	50.00
Celery Tray.	20.00	Salt, ind	20.00
Celery Vase	30.00	Sauce	
Champagne, bee mark	35.00	Flared, bee mark	14.00
Compote		Footed	20.00
Open, hs, 8″	30.00	Spooner	25.00
Open, hs, 9″	35.00	Sugar, cov	45.00
Open, ls, 5″, jelly	30.00	Toothpick, bee mark	45.00
Creamer, bee mark	40.00	Tumbler	25.00
Cruet, os	50.00	Vase	
Doughnut Stand, 6″.	25.00	5″	25.00
Goblet	35.00	9¼″	25.00
Honey, cov, sq, bee mark. . .	75.00	Wine, bee mark.	30.00
Pitcher			
Milk.	60.00		

PAVONIA (Pineapple Stem)

Non-flint made by Ripley and Co. in 1885 and by U. S. Glass Co. in 1891. This pattern comes plain and etched.

	Clear	Ruby Stained		Clear	Ruby Stained
Bowl, 9″	20.00	—	Cake Stand, large,		
Butter, cov, flat	75.00	125.00	etched.	55.00	—

	Clear	Ruby Stained		Clear	Ruby Stained
Celery Vase, etched	45.00	75.00	Plate, 6½″, etched..	17.50	—
Compote			Salt		
Cov, hs, 6″......	45.00	—	Ind	15.00	50.00
Cov, hs, 8″......	55.00	—	Master	28.00	50.00
Open, jelly, etched.	38.00	—	Salt Shaker.......	25.00	—
Creamer, etched ...	48.00	65.00	Sauce, ftd, 3½″ or		
Cup and Saucer ...	35.00	—	4″............	15.00	—
Finger Bowl, ruffled			Spooner, pedestal..	45.00	50.00
underplate......	48.00	110.00	Sugar, cov, flat	55.00	75.00
Goblet, etched	35.00	60.00	Tray, water, etched .	75.00	—
Mug............	—	50.00	Tumbler, etched		
Pitcher			bellflowers......	30.00	38.00
Lemonade......	125.00	135.00	Wine, etched	35.00	40.00
Water	75.00	125.00			

PENNSYLVANIA (Balder)

Non-flint issued by U. S. Glass Co., 1898. Also known in ruby stained. A ruffled jelly compote documented in orange carnival.

	Clear w/gold	Emerald Green		Clear w/gold	Emerald Green
Biscuit Jar, cov	65.00	100.00	Goblet	20.00	—
Bowl			Juice Tumbler.....	12.00	10.00
8″, berry	25.00	35.00	Pitcher, water	60.00	—
8″, sq	20.00	40.00	Punch Bowl	175.00	—
Butter, cov	55.00	85.00	Punch Cup	10.00	—
Carafe	45.00	—	Salt Shaker.......	10.00	—
Celery Vase	45.00	—	Sauce	10.00	—
Compote, hs, ruffled,			Shot Glass	18.00	—
jelly...........	50.00	—	Spooner.........	24.00	35.00
Creamer			Sugar, cov	40.00	55.00
Ind	18.00	35.00	Syrup	50.00	—
Regular........	22.00	50.00	Toothpick	35.00	90.00
Cruet, os	41.00	—	Tumbler	28.00	40.00
Decanter, handle,			Whiskey	15.00	—
os............	100.00	—	Wine	15.00	40.00

PICKET

Non-flint made by the King Glass Co., Pittsburgh, Pennsylvania in the 1870s. Pattern has five different size compotes. Toothpick holders are known in apple green, vaseline, and purple slag.

	Clear		Clear
Bowl, 9½″, sq	30.00	Open, hs, 6″	30.00
Bread Plate	70.00	Open, hs, 7″, sq........	35.00
Butter, cov	45.00	Open, hs, 8″	35.00
Celery Vase	40.00	Open, hs, 10″, sq.......	70.00
Compote		Open, ls, 7″...........	50.00
Cov, hs, 6″...........	65.00	Creamer............	40.00
Cov, hs, 8″...........	100.00	Goblet	30.00
Cov, ls, 8″	125.00	Pitcher, water	75.00

	Clear			Clear
Salt		Spooner		30.00
Ind	10.00	Sugar, cov		45.00
Master	35.00	Toothpick		35.00
Sauce		Tray, water		50.00
Flat	15.00	Waste Bowl		30.00
Footed	20.00	Wine		50.00

PINEAPPLE AND FAN #1 (Heisey's #1255)

Made by A. H. Heisey and Co., Newark, Ohio, c1897, before the Heisey trademark was used. Came in about 70 pieces. Pieces often trimmed in gold. Also known in custard and ruby stained (toothpick at $125.00).

	Clear	Emerald Green		Clear	Emerald Green
Banana Stand	20.00	—	Goblet	15.00	—
Biscuit Jar, cov	55.00	150.00	Mug	30.00	45.00
Bowl, 5½"	12.00	30.00	Pitcher, water	60.00	225.00
Butter, cov	50.00	175.00	Rose Bowl	35.00	75.00
Cake Stand	45.00	75.00	Salt, ind	25.00	—
Celery Tray, flat	25.00	—	Salt Shaker	20.00	—
Compote			Spooner	30.00	65.00
Open, hs, 8"	30.00	225.00	Sugar, cov		
Open, jelly, 5"	32.00	—	Individual	25.00	50.00
Creamer			Regular	45.00	125.00
Individual	25.00	50.00	Syrup	60.00	250.00
Regular	35.00	95.00	Toothpick	75.00	150.00
Cruet	60.00	295.00	Tumbler	25.00	60.00
Custard Cup	12.00	30.00	Vase, 10", trumpet	25.00	45.00

PORTLAND

Non-flint pattern made by several companies c1880–1900. An oval pintray in ruby souvenir ($20.00) is known, and a flat sauce ($25.00).

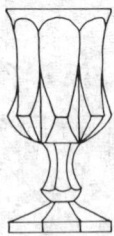

	Clear w/gold		Clear w/gold
Basket, handled	85.00	Lamp base, 9"	75.00
Biscuit Jar	50.00	Pitcher, water, straight sides	55.00
Bowl		Pomade Jar, SP top	30.00
Berry	20.00	Puff Box, glass lid	35.00
Small, flat, cov	30.00	Punch Bowl, 13⅝", ftd	150.00
Butter, cov	50.00	Punch Cup	15.00
Cake Stand, 10½"	45.00	Relish	15.00
Carafe, water	45.00	Salt Shaker	16.00
Celery Tray	25.00	Sauce	8.00
Compote		Spooner	35.00
Cov, hs, 6"	60.00	Sugar, cov	45.00
Open, hs, 8¼"	40.00	Sugar Shaker	40.00
Open, hs, 9½"	45.00	Syrup	50.00
Open, ls, 7"	45.00	Toothpick	25.00
Creamer	30.00	Tumbler	20.00
Cruet, os	48.00	Vase	25.00
Decanter, qt, handled	50.00	Water Bottle	40.00
Goblet	35.00	Wine	30.00

PRIMROSE

Non-flint made by Canton Glass Co., Canton, Ohio, c1880. Also made in milk glass. Apple green is scarce.

	Amber and Yellow	Blue and Green	Clear
Bowl, 8″	32.00	35.00	24.00
Butter, cov	50.00	60.00	35.00
Cake Stand, 10″ . . .	50.00	65.00	40.00
Celery Vase	35.00	40.00	25.00
Compote, cov, ls, 6″	40.00	45.00	30.00
Creamer.	35.00	48.00	30.00
Egg Cup.	30.00	35.00	20.00
Goblet			
Knob Stem	40.00	45.00	30.00
Plain Stem	35.00	40.00	25.00
Lamp, finger	—	—	195.00
Pickle.	18.00	20.00	14.00
Pitcher			
Milk.	45.00	55.00	35.00
Water	55.00	50.00	48.00
Plate			
4½″.	15.00	20.00	12.00
9″, handled	30.00	35.00	20.00
Platter, 12 x 8″	35.00	45.00	30.00
Relish.	18.00	20.00	14.00
Sauce, ftd.	18.00	25.00	15.00
Spooner.	25.00	30.00	20.00
Sugar, cov	40.00	55.00	35.00
Tray, water	50.00	60.00	35.00
Waste Bowl.	32.00	35.00	28.00
Wine	40.00	45.00	28.00

PRINCESS FEATHER (Rochelle)

Non-flint made by Bakewell, Pears & Co. in the late 1870s. Occasional pieces made in flint. Later by U. S. Glass Co. in the 1890s. Also made in milk glass. A rare blue opaque tumbler has been reported.

	Clear		Clear
Bowl		Goblet	40.00
7″, cov, pedestal	35.00	Pitcher, water	65.00
7″, oval	20.00	Plate	
8″, oval	25.00	6″.	30.00
9″, oval	30.00	7″.	35.00
Butter, cov	50.00	8″.	40.00
Cake Plate, handled	35.00	9″.	45.00
Celery Vase	40.00	Relish.	20.00
Compote		Sauce	8.00
Cov, hs, 7″.	50.00	Spooner.	30.00
Cov, hs, 8″.	50.00	Sugar	
Open, ls, 8″.	35.00	Cov.	55.00
Creamer, ah	55.00	Open	25.00
Dish, oval	20.00	Wine	45.00
Egg Cup.	40.00		

PRISCILLA #1 (Findlay)

Non-flint made by Dalzell, Gilmore & Leighton, Findlay, Ohio, in the late 1890s and continued by National Glass Co. Fenton reproduced pattern in clear, colors, and opalescent in 1951. Also introduced many forms different from the original such as 12½" plate, goblet, wine, 6" handled bonbon, and sugar and creamer.

	Clear		Clear
Banana Stand	80.00	Doughnut Stand	60.00
Biscuit Jar	145.00	Goblet	40.00
Bowl		Mug	20.00
8½"	18.00	Pitcher, water	
10¼", straight sides	50.00	Bulbous	90.00
Butter, cov	68.00	Tankard	85.00
Cake Stand, 9½"	60.00	Plate	25.00
Celery Vase	55.00	Sauce	8.00
Compote		Spooner	30.00
Cov, hs, 9"	75.00	Sugar, open	20.00
Open, hs, 7"	45.00	Syrup	90.00
Open, hs, 10", scalloped	60.00	Toothpick	40.00
Creamer	25.00	Tumbler	25.00
Cruet, os	65.00	Wine	35.00

PRISM WITH DIAMOND POINTS

Flint made by Bryce Brothers and also attributed to Boston and Sandwich Glass Co. A flint milk glass spooner is known.

	Clear		Clear
Butter, cov	65.00	Pitcher, water	100.00
Compote, cov, hs, 6"	90.00	Salt, master, cov	30.00
Creamer	75.00	Spooner	45.00
Egg Cup		Sugar, cov	50.00
Double	55.00	Tumbler	40.00
Single	25.00	Wine	50.00
Goblet	45.00		

QUARTERED BLOCK (Duncan & Miller #24)

Made by Duncan & Miller Co. c1903.

	Clear	Ruby Stained		Clear	Ruby Stained
Bowl	25.00	60.00	Spooner	20.00	45.00
Butter, cov	45.00	125.00	Sugar, cov	40.00	45.00
Celery Vase	30.00	—	Syrup	50.00	—
Compote, open, hs	35.00	—	Toothpick	30.00	85.00
Creamer	30.00	55.00	Tumbler	20.00	40.00
Goblet	38.00	—	Vase	15.00	—
Lamp	75.00	—	Water Bottle	35.00	—
Pitcher, water	45.00	150.00	Wine	30.00	—
Sauce	7.50	—			

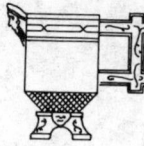

QUEEN ANNE (Bearded Man)

Non-flint made by LaBelle Glass Co., Bridgeport, Ohio, c1879. Finials are Maltese cross. At least 28 pieces documented. A table set and water pitcher are known in amber.

	Clear		Clear
Bowl, cov		Egg Cup	45.00
8″, oval	45.00	Pitcher	
9″, oval	55.00	Milk	45.00
Bread Plate	50.00	Water	80.00
Butter, cov	65.00	Spooner	40.00
Celery Vase	35.00	Sugar, cov	55.00
Compote, cov, ls, 9″	75.00	Syrup	90.00
Creamer	38.00		

QUESTION MARK (Oval Loop)

Made by Richards and Hartley in 1895 and later by U. S. Glass Co., 1891. An 1888 catalog lists 32 pieces. Scarce in ruby stained.

	Clear		Clear
Bowl		Cordial	20.00
4″, round, ftd	15.00	Creamer	30.00
7″, oblong	18.00	Goblet	20.00
7″, round, ftd	20.00	Nappy, ftd	20.00
8″, oblong	25.00	Pitcher	
8″, round, ftd	25.00	Milk, bulbous	40.00
9″, oblong	30.00	Milk, tankard	40.00
10″, oblong	25.00	Water, bulbous	45.00
Butter, cov	30.00	Water, tankard	45.00
Candlestick, chamber, finger		Salt Shaker	15.00
loop	45.00	Sauce, 4″, collared	10.00
Celery Vase	28.00	Spooner	20.00
Compote		Sugar Shaker	35.00
Cov, hs, 7″	50.00	Sugar, cov	25.00
Cov, hs, 8″	65.00	Tumbler	15.00
Open, hs, 7″	25.00	Wine	20.00
Open, ls	15.00		

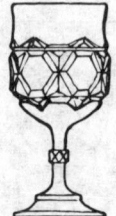

RED BLOCK (Late Block)

Non-flint with red stain made by Doyle and Co.; later made by five companies plus U. S. Glass Co. in 1892. Prices for clear 50% less.

	Ruby Stained		Ruby Stained
Bowl, 8″	75.00	Pitcher, water, 8″ h	175.00
Butter, cov	110.00	Rose Bowl	75.00
Celery Vase, 6½″	85.00	Sauce, flat, 4½″	20.00
Creamer		Salt Dip, ind	50.00
Individual	45.00	Salt Shaker, single	60.00
Regular	70.00	Spooner	45.00
Decanter, 12″, os, variant	175.00	Sugar, cov	75.00
*Goblet	45.00	Tumbler	35.00
Mug	40.00	*Wine	35.00

REVERSE TORPEDO (Bull's Eye Band, Bull's Eye with Diamond Point #2, Pointed Bull's Eye)

Made by Dalzell, Gilmore & Leighton Glass Co., Findlay, Ohio, c18881890. Also attributed to Canadian factories. Sometimes found with etching.

	Clear		Clear
Banana Stand, 9¾"	135.00	Open, hs, 7"	65.00
Biscuit Jar, cov	165.00	Open, hs, 8⅜" d	45.00
Bowl		Open, hs, jelly	50.00
8½", shallow	30.00	Open, ls, 9¼", ruffled	
9", fruit, pie crust rim	68.00	edge	90.00
10½", pie crust rim	75.00	Goblet	85.00
Butter, cov	75.00	Honey Dish, sq	145.00
Cake Stand	85.00	Pitcher, water, tankard,	
Celery Vase	55.00	10¼"	150.00
Compote		Sauce, flat, 3¾"	24.00
Cov, hs, 7"	80.00	Spooner	30.00
Cov, hs, 10"	125.00	Sugar, cov	85.00
Cov, hs, 6"	80.00	Syrup	165.00
Open, hs, 10½" d, V shape		Tumbler	35.00
bowl	90.00		

RIBBED IVY

Flint, late 1850s. Attributed to Boston and Sandwich Glass Co.

	Clear		Clear
Bowl, 6"	15.00	Salt, master	
Butter, cov	100.00	Cov	115.00
Castor Bottle	35.00	Open, scalloped rim	40.00
Celery Vase	350.00	Sauce	12.00
Champagne	100.00	Spooner	40.00
Compote		Sugar, cov	80.00
Cov, hs, 6", jelly	125.00	Sweetmeat, cov, on stand	165.00
Open, hs, 9", scalloped		Tumbler	
edge	85.00	Bar	75.00
Creamer	125.00	Water	75.00
Decanter, quart, os	150.00	Whiskey	
Egg Cup	30.00	Handled	100.00
Goblet	45.00	Plain	70.00
Hat	385.00	Wine	100.00
Pitcher, water, ah	150.00		

RIBBON

Non-flint, usually frosted, made by Bakewell, Pears, Pittsburgh, Pennsylvania, in the late 1860s. It has been erroneously called "Frosted Ribbon" at times, which can be confusing. Other Ribbon patterns are Clear Ribbon, Frosted Ribbon, Double Ribbon, Fluted Ribbon, and Grated Ribbon. Compotes have been reproduced in clear and color by Fostoria for the Henry Ford Museum gift shop, and are usually sgd "HFM."

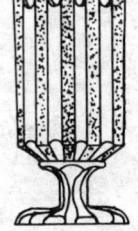

	Frosted		Frosted
Butter, cov	70.00	Celery Vase	40.00
Cake Stand, 8½"	40.00	Cheese, cov	85.00

	Frosted		Frosted
Cologne Bottle, os	65.00	Salt Shaker	40.00
Compote		Sauce	
Cov, hs, 8″	75.00	Footed	18.00
Cov, ls, 7″	45.00	Tab-handled	18.00
Open, hs, 10½″, SP, Dolphin stand	275.00	Spooner	35.00
		Sugar, cov	65.00
Open, ls, 7″	35.00	Tray, water, 15″	100.00
Creamer	30.00	Waste Bowl	35.00
*Goblet	35.00	Wine	125.00
Pitcher, water	75.00		
Platter, 9″ x 13″, oblong, cut corners	62.50		

RIBBON CANDY (Bryce)

Non-flint, made by Bryce Brothers, Pittsburgh, Pennsylvania, 1880s. Reissued by U. S. Glass Co. in 1890s. Bowls come in a variety of sizes: open or with lids; flat or with a low collared foot. Also known in emerald green.

	Clear		Clear
Bowl		Open, ls, 8″	25.00
3½″, round	10.00	Cordial	45.00
4″, round	10.00	Creamer	25.00
8″, oval	25.00	Cruet, os	65.00
8″, round	25.00	Cup and Saucer	40.00
Butter, cov		Goblet	65.00
Flat	50.00	Honey, cov, sq	75.00
Footed	55.00	Lamp, oil	75.00
Cake Stand		Pitcher	
8″	30.00	Milk	45.00
10½″	45.00	Water	75.00
Claret	40.00	Plate	
Compote		6″	18.00
Cov, ls, 5″	30.00	8″	25.00
Cov, ls, 6″	30.00	9½″	30.00
Cov, ls, 7″	40.00	11″	35.00
Cov, ls, 8″	40.00	Relish	16.00
Open, hs, 5″	20.00	Salt Shaker	35.00
Open, hs, 6″	25.00	Sauce	
Open, hs, 7″	30.00	Flat, 4″	10.00
Open, hs, 8″	35.00	Footed, 4″	12.00
Open, ls, 3″	12.00	Spooner	25.00
Open, ls, 4″	12.00	Sugar, cov	40.00
Open, ls, 5″	12.00	Syrup	90.00
Open, ls, 6″	15.00	Tumbler	25.00
Open, ls, 7″	20.00	Wine	45.00

RISING SUN (Sunshine)

Made by Ripley and Co., then continued by U. S. Glass Co. in 1908 at Glassport, Pennsylvania. Also found in carnival and scarce in ruby stained. A sugar cube dispenser in a silver plated holder was made for the Alaska-Yukon Pacific Exposition in 1909 ($150.00).

	Clear w/gold	Rose or Green Decorated		Clear w/gold	Rose or Green Decorated
Bowl, berry	12.00	—	Pitcher, water	95.00	—
Butter, cov	32.50	45.00	Relish	15.00	—
Cake Plate, 10½"	22.50	—	Sauce, flat	8.00	—
Cake Stand	35.00	—	Spooner	18.00	—
Celery Vase	25.00	30.00	Sugar, cov		
Compote			Regular or Hotel, three-handled	40.00	—
Cov, hs	45.00	—	Tall, ftd, no handle	35.00	—
Open, hs	30.00	35.00	Toothpick, triple-handled	18.00	35.00
Creamer			Tumbler	15.00	25.00
Regular or Hotel	25.00	—	Whiskey (shot)	12.00	16.00
Tall, ftd	22.50	—	Wine	25.00	30.00
Cruet, os	40.00	—			
Dish, ruffled edge	15.00	—			
Goblet	20.00	25.00			

ROMAN KEY (Frosted Roman Key)

Flint glass pattern of the 1860s made Union Glass Co. and by others in several variants. Available in clear but not as popular. Sometimes erroneously called "Greek Key."

	Flint Frosted		Flint Frosted
Bowl		Egg Cup	45.00
8"	45.00	Goblet	50.00
10"	50.00	Pitcher, water	225.00
Butter, cov	80.00	Plate, 6"	28.00
Celery Vase, ftd	80.00	Salt, ftd	45.00
Champagne	80.00	Sauce, 4"	18.00
Compote		Spooner	45.00
Open, hs, 8", cable rim	60.00	Sugar, cov	85.00
Open, ls, 7"	95.00	Tumbler, bar	45.00
Creamer, applied handle	125.00	Wine	85.00
Decanter, os	160.00		

ROMAN ROSETTE

Non-flint made by Bryce, Walker and Co. 18751885. Reissued by U. S. Glass Co. in 1892 and 1898. Attributed to Portland Glass Co. Also seen with English registry mark. Also known in amber stained.

	Clear	Ruby Stained		Clear	Ruby Stained
Bowl			Compote		
6"	12.00	—	Cov, hs, 4½", jelly	50.00	—
8½"	22.00	50.00	Cov, hs, 6"	65.00	—
Bread Plate	30.00	75.00	Creamer	32.00	45.00
Butter, cov	50.00	125.00	Cordial	50.00	—
Cake Stand, 9"	45.00	—	*Goblet	40.00	—
Celery Vase	30.00	95.00	Lemonade Mug	35.00	—

	Clear	Ruby Stained		Clear	Ruby Stained
Mug	35.00	—	Sauce	15.00	20.00
Pitcher			Spooner	25.00	45.00
Milk.	45.00	150.00	Sugar, cov	45.00	95.00
Water	50.00	140.00	Syrup.	65.00	125.00
Plate, 7½".	35.00	65.00	Wine	35.00	55.00
Relish, oval, 9"	20.00	40.00			
Salt & Pepper, glass tray	55.00	100.00			

ROSE-IN-SNOW

Non-flint made by Bryce Bros., Pittsburgh, Pennsylvania in the square form, c1880. Also made in the more common round form by Ohio Flint Glass Co. and after 1891 by U. S. Glass Co.

	Amber and Canary	Blue	Clear
Butter, cov			
Round.	50.00	125.00	45.00
Square	60.00	150.00	50.00
Cake Stand, 9"	—	—	90.00
Compote			
Cov, hs, 8"	125.00	175.00	80.00
Cov, ls, 7"	100.00	150.00	75.00
Open, ls, 5¾" . . .	40.00	120.00	35.00
Creamer			
Round.	60.00	100.00	45.00
Square	65.00	120.00	45.00
* Goblet	40.00	75.00	35.00
* Mug, "In Fond Remembrance" . .	45.00	110.00	32.00
* Pickle Dish			
Double, 8½" x 7" .	45.00	110.00	100.00
Single, oval, handles at end. . . .	25.00	95.00	20.00
Pitcher, water, ah . .	175.00	200.00	125.00
Plate			
5"	—	—	35.00
6"	20.00	80.00	18.00
7"	22.00	82.00	20.00
Platter, oval.	—	—	125.00
Sauce			
Flat.	15.00	20.00	12.00
Footed	8.00	48.00	18.00
Spooner			
Round.	30.00	80.00	25.00
Square	38.50	100.00	35.00
Sugar, cov			
Round.	55.00	120.00	50.00
Square	48.00	140.00	45.00
Tumbler, bar	55.00	100.00	50.00

ROSETTE (Magic)

Non-flint made by Bryce Bros., Pittsburgh, Pennsylvania, in the late 1870s. Continued by the U. S. Glass Co. Later made in Ohio in 1898.

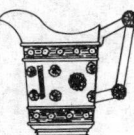

	Clear		Clear
Bowl, 7¼", cov	30.00	Pickle	12.00
Bread Plate, 9", handles	25.00	Pitcher	
Butter, cov	35.00	Milk, qt	50.00
Cake Stand		Water, ½ gal	65.00
7"	24.00	Plate, 7"	12.00
10"	26.00	Relish, fish shape	15.00
11"	35.00	Salt Shaker	25.00
Celery, 8"	20.00	Sauce, flat, handled	8.00
Compote		Spooner	25.00
Cov, hs, 6"	40.00	Sugar, cov	35.00
Cov, hs, 8"	70.00	Sugar Shaker	35.00
Cov, hs, 11½"	50.00	Tray, 10¼"	35.00
Open, hs, 7"	30.00	Tumbler, 5"	16.00
Open, hs, 4½", jelly	25.00	Waste Bowl	25.00
Creamer	25.00	Wine	20.00
Goblet	30.00		

ROYAL IVY ("New" Jewel)

Non-flint made by Northwood Glass Co. in 1889. Made in cased spatter, clear and frosted rainbow cracquelle, clear with amber, stained ivy, and clambroth opaline. These last mentioned were experimental pieces, not made in sets.

	Clear Frosted	Rubena Clear	Rubena Frosted
Bowl, berry, small	20.00	30.00	45.00
Butter, cov	100.00	175.00	275.00
Creamer, ah	60.00	150.00	200.00
Cruet	90.00	225.00	325.00
Marmalade Jar, SP cov	125.00	—	—
Miniature Lamp	—	—	350.00
Pickle Castor, SP frame	125.00	—	375.00
Pitcher, water, ah	110.00	175.00	275.00
Rose Bowl	55.00	70.00	85.00
Spooner	45.00	70.00	95.00
Sugar, cov	150.00	165.00	180.00
Sugar Shaker	65.00	135.00	150.00
Syrup	120.00	225.00	300.00
Toothpick	50.00	90.00	125.00
Tumbler	35.00	50.00	60.00

ROYAL OAK (Acorn)

Non-flint made by Northwood Glass Co., Martins Ferry, Ohio, c1899. In early 1900s, it was made in opaque, white with colored tops and colored acorns and leaves. Milk-white pieces are rare.

	Clear Frosted	Rubena Clear	Rubena Frosted
Butter, cov	150.00	150.00	200.00
Creamer	75.00	125.00	150.00
Cruet, os	150.00	425.00	480.00

	Clear Frosted	Rubena Clear	Rubena Frosted
Mustard Jar, cov . . .	90.00	—	—
Pickle Castor	100.00	150.00	225.00
Pitcher, water	100.00	350.00	350.00
Salt Shaker, single .	40.00	45.00	65.00
Spooner	50.00	75.00	100.00
Sugar, cov, acorn finial	85.00	150.00	180.00
Sugar Shaker	75.00	135.00	165.00
Syrup	135.00	—	—
Tumbler	40.00	65.00	85.00

SAWTOOTH (Mitre Diamond)

An early clear flint-glass pattern made in the late 1850s by the New England Glass Co., Boston and Sandwich Glass Co., and others. Later made in non-flint by Bryce Brothers and U. S. Glass Co. Also known in milk glass and clear deep blue.

	Flint	Non-Flint		Flint	Non-Flint
Butter, cov	75.00	45.00	Plain Stem	—	20.00
Cake Stand, 10″ . . .	85.00	55.00	Pitcher, water		
Celery Vase, 10″ . . .	60.00	30.00	Applied handle. . .	125.00	95.00
Champagne	55.00	30.00	Pressed handle . .	—	55.00
Compote			Plate, 6½″.	45.00	30.00
Cov, hs, 9½″	85.00	48.00	Pomade Jar, cov . . .	50.00	35.00
Open, ls, 8″, sawtooth edge	50.00	30.00	Salt		
Cordial	30.00	65.00	Cov, ftd	65.00	40.00
Creamer			Open, smooth edge	25.00	20.00
Applied handle. . .	75.00	40.00	Spooner	65.00	25.00
Pressed handle . .	—	30.00	Sugar, cov	65.00	35.00
Cruet, acorn stopper	100.00	—	Tumbler, bar	50.00	25.00
Egg Cup	45.00	25.00	Wine, knob stem . . .	35.00	25.00
Knob Stem	45.00	25.00			

SCALLOPED DIAMOND POINT (Late Diamond Point Band, Panel with Diamond Point, Diamond Point With Flute)

Non-flint pattern. Not to be confused with early flint Diamond Point. Made by Central Glass Co., Wheeling, West Virginia. Also made by U. S. Glass Co. after 1891. A wine ($75.00) is known in electric blue, and in amber ($50.00).

	Clear		Clear
Bowl, oval, 9″	20.00	Goblet	30.00
Butter Dish, cov	35.00	Mustard Jar, cov	30.00
Cake Stand		Pickle Dish, oval	20.00
8″	30.00	Pickle Jar, cov.	45.00
12″	60.00	Plate	
Cheese Dish, cov, 8″	50.00	5″	12.00
Compote		9″	20.00
Cov, hs, 8″.	75.00	Sauce, ftd, 4″	10.00
Open, hs, 7″ d	40.00	Spooner	25.00
Cov, 5″, jelly	35.00	Sugar, cov	35.00
Creamer	60.00	Wine	35.00

SCALLOPED TAPE (Jewel Band)

Non-flint, c1880. Maker unknown. Occasionally found in amber, blue, canary, and light green.

	Clear		Clear
Bread Plate, oval, "Bread Is The Staff of Life"	45.00	Pitcher	
Butter, cov	35.00	Milk	35.00
Cake Stand	35.00	Water	50.00
Celery Vase	35.00	Plate, 6"	15.00
Compote		Sauce	
Cov, hs, 8"	55.00	Flat, 4"	8.50
Open, hs	40.00	Ftd	12.00
Creamer	30.00	Spooner	20.00
Dish, rect, cov, 8"	45.00	Sugar, cov	35.00
Egg Cup	25.00	Tray, 6 x 7"	25.00
Goblet	30.00	Wine	25.00

SCROLL (Stippled Scroll)

Non-flint, made by Duncan Glass Co., c1870s. Also made in milk glass. Some items reproduced by Imperial.

	Clear		Clear
Butter, cov	50.00	Master	25.00
Celery	30.00	Sauce	10.00
Compote		Spooner	30.00
Cov, hs	65.00	Sugar	
Open, hs	35.00	Cov	45.00
Creamer, ah	40.00	Open, buttermilk	30.00
Goblet	35.00	Tumbler, ftd	25.00
Pitcher, water, ah	75.00	Wine	30.00
Salt, ftd			
Individual	20.00		

SCROLL WITH FLOWERS

Non-flint. Attributed to Central Glass Co. in the 1870s and Canton Glass Co. Occasionally found in amber, apple green, and blue.

	Clear		Clear
Butter, cov	40.00	Pickle, handled	18.00
Cake Plate, 10½", handled	25.00	Pitcher, water	45.00
Compote, cov	45.00	Plate, double-handled, 10½"	40.00
Cordial	35.00	Sauce, double-handled	10.00
Creamer	40.00	Spooner	28.50
Egg Cup, handled	18.00	Sugar, cov	45.00
Goblet	25.00	Wine	30.00
Mustard Jar, cov	50.00		

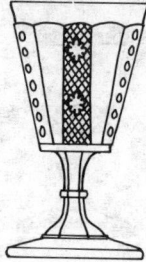

SEDAN (Paneled Star and Button)

Clear non-flint pattern made in the 1870s.

	Clear		Clear
Bowl	20.00	Relish	10.00
Butter, cov	38.50	Salt Shaker	20.00
Celery Tray	18.00	Sauce, flat	5.00
Celery Vase	25.00	Spooner	18.00
Compote		Sugar	
Cov, hs, 8½"	35.00	Covered	35.00
Open, hs	20.00	Open	15.00
Creamer	24.00	Tumbler	20.00
Goblet	20.00	Wine	18.00
Pitcher, water	35.00		

SHRINE (Jewel with Moon and Star)

Non-flint made by Beatty & Indiana Glass Co., Dunkirk, Indiana, c. late 1880s.

	Clear		Clear
Bowl		Pitcher, water	
4"	15.00	Normal Size	50.00
6½"	25.00	Jumbo Size	100.00
9½"	30.00	Platter	40.00
Butter, cov	50.00	Relish	15.00
Cake Stand, 8½"	40.00	Salt Shaker	30.00
Celery	45.00	Sauce	25.00
Creamer	40.00	Spooner	30.00
Goblet	45.00	Sugar, cov	50.00
Pickle	20.00	Tumbler	
		Lemonade	36.00
		Water	35.00

SHUTTLE (Hearts of Loch Haven)

Made by Indiana Tumbler and Goblet Co., Greentown, Indiana, between 1894 and 1903. Some items reproduced.

	Clear	Caramel		Clear	Caramel
Bowl, berry	25.00	—	Mug	25.00	95.00
Butter, cov	50.00	150.00	Pitcher, water	50.00	—
Celery Vase	30.00	—	Spooner	20.00	—
Cordial	32.00	—	Sugar, cov	40.00	—
Creamer	30.00	—	Tumbler	25.00	80.00
Cruet, os	75.00	—	Wine	20.00	50.00

SKILTON (Oregon #2)

Made by Richards & Hartley of Tarentum, Pennsylvania in 1888 and by U. S. Glass after 1891. This is not one of the U. S. Glass States pattern series and should not be confused with Beaded Loop, which is Oregon #1, named by U. S. Glass Co. It is better known as Skilton (named by Millard) to avoid confusion with Beaded Loop.

	Clear	Ruby Stained
Bowl		
4", round	10.00	—
5", round	15.00	—
6", round	20.00	—
7", rect	20.00	—
8", rect	25.00	—
9", rect	30.00	—
Butter, cov	45.00	110.00
Cake Stand	35.00	—
Celery Vase	35.00	95.00
Compote		
Cov, hs, 7"	45.00	—
Cov, hs, 8"	45.00	—
Open, ls, 4"	10.00	—
Open, ls, 7"	25.00	—
Open, ls, 8"	30.00	75.00

	Clear	Ruby Stained
Creamer	30.00	55.00
Dish, oblong, sq	25.00	—
Goblet	35.00	50.00
Olive, handled	20.00	—
Pickle	15.00	—
Pitcher		
Milk	45.00	125.00
Water	50.00	125.00
Salt & Pepper, pr	45.00	—
Sauce, ftd	12.00	20.00
Spooner, flat	25.00	55.00
Sugar, cov	35.00	85.00
Tray, water	45.00	—
Tumbler	25.00	40.00
Wine	30.00	45.00

SNAIL (Compact, Idaho, Double Snail)

Non-flint made by George Duncan & Sons, Pittsburgh, Pennsylvania, c1880, and by U. S. Glass Co. in the States Pattern series. Ruby stained pieces date after 1891. Add 30% for engraved pieces.

	Clear	Ruby Stained
Banana Stand	145.00	225.00
Basket, cake or fruit		
9"	85.00	—
10"	95.00	—
4"	20.00	90.00
4½"	20.00	—
7", cov	60.00	45.00
7", oval	28.00	45.00
7", round	28.00	45.00
8", cov	60.00	45.00
8", oval	28.00	45.00
8", round	28.00	45.00
9", oval	30.00	—
9", round	30.00	—
10"	35.00	45.00
Butter, cov	75.00	160.00
Cake Stand		
9"	75.00	—
10"	85.00	—
Celery Vase	35.00	85.00
Cheese, cov	95.00	—
Compote		
Cov, hs, 6"	50.00	—
Cov, hs, 7"	50.00	100.00
Cov, hs, 8"	80.00	135.00
Cov, hs, 10"	125.00	—
Open, hs, 6"	30.00	—
Open, hs, 7"	45.00	—

	Clear	Ruby Stained
Open, hs, 8"	35.00	—
Open, hs, 9", twisted stem, scalloped	75.00	—
Creamer	65.00	75.00
Cup, Custard	30.00	—
Cruet, os	100.00	275.00
Finger Bowl	50.00	—
Goblet	65.00	95.00
Marmalade, cov	—	125.00
Pitcher		
Milk, tankard	100.00	—
Water, bulbous	125.00	—
Water, tankard	135.00	250.00
Plate		
5"	35.00	—
6"	35.00	—
7"	40.00	—
Punch Cup	35.00	—
Relish, 7", oval	25.00	—
Rose Bowl		
3"	50.00	—
5"	45.00	—
6"	45.00	—
7"	50.00	—
Salt		
Ind	35.00	—
Master	35.00	75.00

	Clear	Ruby Stained		Clear	Ruby Stained
Salt Shaker			Sugar Shaker	85.00	200.00
Bulbous	65.00	90.00	Syrup	125.00	225.00
Straight sides	60.00	90.00	Tumbler	55.00	65.00
Sauce	—	45.00	Vase	50.00	—
Spooner	35.00	75.00	Violet Bowl, 3″	50.00	—
Sugar			Wine	65.00	—
Ind, cov	50.00	—			
Regular, cov	60.00	100.00			

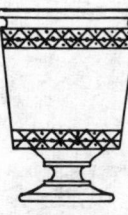

SPIREA BAND

Non-flint made by Bryce, Higbee & Co., Pittsburgh, Pennsylvania, c1885.

	Amber	Blue	Clear	Vaseline
Bowl, 8″	25.00	40.00	22.00	30.00
Butter, cov	50.00	55.00	35.00	45.00
Cake Stand, 11″	45.00	55.00	40.00	45.00
Celery Vase	40.00	50.00	25.00	40.00
Compote, cov, hs, 7″	44.00	65.00	40.00	44.00
Cordial	38.00	42.00	20.00	38.00
Creamer	37.50	44.00	35.00	35.00
Goblet	25.00	30.00	20.00	35.00
Pitcher, water	65.00	80.00	35.00	60.00
Platter, 10½″	32.00	42.00	20.00	32.00
Relish	30.00	35.00	18.00	30.00
Sauce				
Flat	10.00	12.00	5.00	9.00
Ftd	15.00	18.00	8.00	14.00
Spooner	30.00	35.00	20.00	35.00
Sugar, open	32.00	40.00	25.00	32.00
Tumbler	24.00	35.00	20.00	30.00
Wine	30.00	35.00	20.00	30.00

SPRIG

Non-flint made by Bryce, Higbee & Co., Pittsburgh, Pennsylvania, mid-1880s.

	Clear		Clear
Bowl, 10″, scalloped	45.00	Pitcher, water	50.00
Bread Plate	40.00	Relish	12.00
Butter, cov	65.00	Salt, master	55.00
Cake Stand, 8″	35.00	Sauce	
Celery Vase	40.00	Flat	12.00
Compote		Ftd	15.00
Cov, hs	60.00	Spooner	25.00
Open, hs	45.00	Sugar, cov	40.00
Creamer	30.00	Wine	45.00
Goblet	35.00		

STAR ROSETTED

Non-flint made by McKee Brothers, Pittsburgh, PA, c1875.

	Clear		Clear
Bread Plate	40.00	Goblet	25.00
Butter, cov	48.00	Pickle	14.00
Compote		Pitcher, water	50.00
Cov, hs, 8½"	60.00	Plate, 7"	20.00
Cov, jelly	55.00	Relish, 9"	14.00
Cov, sweetmeat	55.00	Sauce	
Open, hs, 6½"	18.00	Flat	7.00
Open, hs, 7½"	20.00	Footed	12.00
Open, hs, 8½"	35.00	Spooner	25.00
Creamer	35.00	Sugar, cov	48.00

STARS AND STRIPES (Brilliant)

Made by Jenkins Glass Co., Kokomo, Indiana, in 1899. Appeared in 1899 Montgomery Ward catalog as "Brilliant."

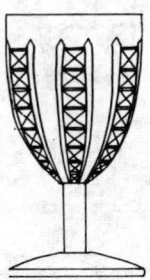

	Clear		Clear
Bowl, berry	15.00	Pitcher, water	40.00
Butter, cov	20.00	Salt Shaker	15.00
Celery Vase	15.00	Sauce	6.00
Cordial	15.00	Spooner	15.00
Creamer	18.00	Sugar, cov	20.00
Cruet Set	35.00	Tumbler	15.00
Cup, sherbert, handled	8.00	Wine	15.00
Goblet	20.00		

STATES, THE (Cane and Star Medallion)

Non-flint made by the U. S. Glass Co. in 1908. Also found in emerald green; add 50%.

	Clear w/ gold		Clear w/ gold
Bowl		Punch Cup	10.00
7", round, 3 handles	30.00	Relish, diamond shape	35.00
9¼", round	30.00	Salt & Pepper	40.00
Butter, cov	65.00	Sauce, flat, 4", tub shape	15.00
Celery Tray	20.00	Spooner	25.00
Cocktail	25.00	Sugar	
Compote		Covered	40.00
Open, hs, 7"	35.00	Open, ind	15.00
Open, hs, 9"	50.00	Open, table	20.00
Creamer		Syrup	65.00
Ind, oval	18.00	Toothpick, flat, rectangular,	
Regular, round	30.00	curled lip	45.00
Goblet	32.00	Tray, 7¼" l, 5½" w	18.00
Pitcher, water	45.00	Tumbler	22.00
Plate, 10"	35.00	Wine	27.00
Punch Bowl, 13" d	75.00		

STIPPLED CHAIN

Clear non-flint pattern made by Gillinder and Sons, Philadelphia, Pennsylvania, c1870.

	Clear		Clear
Bowl	15.00	Pitcher, water	65.00
Butter, cov	50.00	Relish	10.00
Cake Stand	45.00	Salt, ftd	20.00
Celery Vase	40.00	Sauce, flat	10.00
Creamer	35.00	Spooner	25.00
Egg Cup	20.00	Sugar, cov	40.00
Goblet	20.00	Tumbler	20.00
Pickle	15.00		

STIPPLED DOUBLE LOOP

Clear and stippled non-flint pattern of the 1880s.

	Clear		Clear
Butter, cov	50.00	Salt Shaker	20.00
Cake Stand	40.00	Spooner	20.00
Celery Vase	40.00	Sugar, cov	25.00
Creamer	35.00	Tumbler	30.00
Goblet	60.00	Wine	25.00
Pitcher, water	55.00		

STIPPLED GRAPE AND FESTOON

Non-flint made by Doyle and Co, Pittsburgh, PA, c1870. Pieces have applied handles and acorn finials.

	Clear		Clear
Butter, cov		Pickle	30.00
Flange	60.00	Pitcher	
Regular	45.00	Milk	75.00
Celery Vase	45.00	Water	90.00
Compote		Relish	30.00
Cov, hs, 8"	45.00	Sauce, flat	12.00
Cov, ls, 8"	35.00	Spooner	30.00
Cov, ls, 9"	55.00	Sugar	
Open, ls	35.00	Cov	60.00
Creamer	50.00	Open	40.00
Egg Cup	35.00	Wine	45.00
Goblet	32.50		

STRAWBERRY AND CURRANT (Multiple Fruits)

One of a non-flint series of fruit patterns which has become known as Multiple Fruits (Cherry and Fig, Loganberry and Grape, Blackberry and Grape, and Cornucopia with Sprig of Cherries). They were made by Dalzell, Gilmore, and Leighton in Findlay, Ohio. A Loganberry and Grape jelly goblet, with "U" shaped bowl; is of inferior quality and not part of the pattern.

There are matching pieces in all forms, although whether or not all forms were made in all four patterns is not known. Reproduction goblets and other items are found in clear, opalescent, and colors.

	Clear		Clear
Butter, cov	50.00	Pitcher	
Celery Vase	35.00	Milk	40.00
Cheese, cov	50.00	Water	50.00
Compote		Sauce, ftd	10.00
Cov, hs, 8″ d	70.00	Spooner	30.00
Open, hs	35.00	Sugar, cov	40.00
Creamer	40.00	Syrup	80.00
* Goblet	35.00	Tumbler	25.00
Mug	35.00		

STRIGIL

Non-flint pattern made in the 1880s by Tarentum Glass Co, Tarentum, PA. May be gilded.

	Clear		Clear
Bowl, 8″	20.00	Pitcher	
Butter, cov	35.00	Milk	30.00
Celery Tray	15.00	Water	35.00
Celery Vase	25.00	Punch Cup	10.00
Creamer	15.00	Sauce, flat	5.00
Cruet, os	25.00	Spooner	18.00
Egg Cup	20.00	Sugar, cov	32.00
Goblet	40.00	Tumbler	18.00
		Wine	25.00

SWAG WITH BRACKETS

Made by Jefferson Glass Co., Steubenville, Ohio, c1904. Also found in non-opalescent, gold trimmed, amethyst, blue, and vaseline.

	Blue and Canary Opal	Green Opal	White Opal
Butter, cov	175.00	150.00	100.00
Compote, Jelly	45.00	55.00	30.00
Creamer	80.00	75.00	55.00
Cruet, os	150.00	110.00	—
Pitcher, water	250.00	200.00	130.00
Salt Shaker, single	50.00	40.00	35.00
Spooner	75.00	65.00	40.00
Sugar, cov	150.00	85.00	50.00
* Toothpick	125.00	85.00	40.00
Tumbler	65.00	50.00	35.00

TEARDROP AND TASSEL (Sampson)

Non-flint made by the Indiana Tumbler & Goblet Co., Greentown, Indiana, c1890, to celebrate Admiral Sampson's victory in the Spanish-American War.

	Clear	Cobalt Blue	Emerald Green	Nile Green Opaque
Bowl, 7½"	40.00	55.00	50.00	75.00
Butter, cov	55.00	95.00	155.00	325.00
Celery Vase	40.00	—	—	—
Compote				
Cov, hs, 7"	75.00	90.00	80.00	125.00
Cov, jelly	65.00	—	—	—
Open, ls, 5"	20.00	—	—	—
Open, ls, 8"	30.00	45.00	35.00	65.00
Creamer	45.00	100.00	45.00	90.00
Goblet	110.00	125.00	175.00	95.00
Pickle	20.00	55.00	40.00	55.00
Pitcher, water	50.00	150.00	150.00	900.00
Salt Shaker, single .	50.00	75.00	60.00	70.00
Sauce	15.00	20.00	—	—
Spooner	30.00	45.00	35.00	65.00
Sugar, cov	60.00	135.00	70.00	90.00
Tumbler	40.00	50.00	45.00	65.00
Wine	65.00	80.00	70.00	110.00

TENNESSEE (Jewel and Crescent; Jeweled Rosette)

Made by King Glass Co., Pittsburgh, Pennsylvania, and continued by U. S. Glass Co., in 1899, as part of the States series.

	Clear	Colored Jewels		Clear	Colored Jewels
Bowl, berry	20.00	30.00	Creamer	25.00	—
Bread Plate	40.00	75.00	Goblet	40.00	—
Butter, cov	55.00	—	Mug	35.00	—
Cake Stand			Pitcher		
9½"	35.00	—	Milk	55.00	—
10½"	45.00	—	Water	65.00	—
Celery Vase	35.00	—	Relish	20.00	—
Compote			Spooner	35.00	—
Cov, 5", jelly	40.00	55.00	Sugar, cov	45.00	—
Open, hs, 8"	45.00	—	Syrup	90.00	—
Open, hs, 9"	45.00	—	Toothpick	80.00	50.00
Open, hs, 10"	45.00	—	Tumbler	35.00	—
Open, ls, 7"	35.00	—	Wine	65.00	85.00

TEXAS (Loop with Stippled Panels)

Non-flint made by U. S. Glass Co., c1900, in the States Pattern series. Occasionally pieces found in ruby stained. Reproduced in solid colors.

	Clear w/gold	Rose Stained		Clear w/gold	Rose Stained
Bowl			9", scalloped	35.00	50.00
7"	20.00	40.00	Butter, cov	75.00	125.00

	Clear w/gold	Rose Stained		Clear w/gold	Rose Stained
Cake Stand, 9½"...	60.00	80.00	Plate, 9".........	35.00	60.00
Celery Tray.......	30.00	—	Sauce		
Celery Vase	40.00	—	Flat...........	12.00	15.00
Compote			Footed	15.00	—
Cov, hs, 6".....	60.00	—	Spooner.........	35.00	—
Cov, hs, 8".....	75.00	—	Sugar		
Open, hs, 5"	40.00	—	Individual, cov ...	45.00	—
Creamer			Regular, cov	65.00	—
Individual.......	20.00	—	Toothpick........	25.00	95.00
Regular........	40.00	—	Tumbler	25.00	—
Cruet, os	60.00	165.00	Vase		
Goblet	85.00	95.00	6½"...........	25.00	—
Pickle, 8½".......	25.00	—	9"............	35.00	—
Pitcher, water	75.00	—	Wine	50.00	100.00

TEXAS BULL'S EYE (Filley, Bull's Eye Variant)

Originated by Bryce Bros., Pittsburgh, Pennsylvania, and continued by Findlay Glass, Findlay, Ohio. Also made in Canada. Originally made in semi-flint (no bell tone, but some lead content).

	Clear		Clear
Butter, cov	55.00	Sugar	
Creamer...............	35.00	Cov.................	45.00
Egg Cup..............	30.00	Open	40.00
Goblet...............	30.00	Tumbler	50.00
Pitcher, water	55.00	Wine	25.00
Spooner...............	25.00		

THISTLE (Early Thistle)

Non-flint, made by Bryce, Walker & Co. in 1872.

	Clear		Clear
Bowl, 8"	30.00	Relish................	25.00
Butter, cov	55.00	Salt, ftd	35.00
Cake Stand, large	75.00	Sauce, flat	12.00
Compote		Spooner..............	35.00
Cov, hs	85.00	Sugar	
Cov, ls	50.00	Cov.................	65.00
Cordial..............	60.00	Open, buttermilk type....	40.00
Creamer, ah	65.00	Syrup................	100.00
Egg Cup..............	40.00	Tumbler	40.00
Goblet	45.00	Wine	50.00
Pitcher, water, ah	100.00		

THOUSAND EYE

The original pattern was non-flint made by Adams Glass Co, Tarentum, PA, 1875, and by Richards and Hartley, 1888. (Their Pattern No. 103). It was made in two forms: Adams with a three knob stem finial, and Richards and Hartley with a plain

stem with a scalloped bottom. Several glass companies made variations of the original pattern and reproductions were made as late as 1981. Crystal Opalescent was produced by Richards and Hartley only in the original pattern. (Opalescent celery vase $70.00; open compote, 8″, $115.00; 6″ creamer, $85.00; ¼ gallon water pitcher, $140.00; ½ gallon water pitcher, $180.00; 4″ footed sauce, $40.00; spooner, $60.00; and 5″ covered sugar, $80.00). Covered compotes are rare and would command 40% more than open compotes. A 2″ mug in blue is known.

	Amber	Apple Green	Blue	Clear	Vaseline
ABC Plate, 6″, clock center	50.00	55.00	52.00	45.00	52.00
Bowl, large, carriage shape	—	—	85.00	—	85.00
Butter, cov					
6¼″.	65.00	75.00	70.00	45.00	90.00
7½″.	65.00	75.00	70.00	45.00	90.00
Cake Stand					
10″	50.00	78.00	55.00	30.00	84.00
11″	50.00	78.00	55.00	30.00	84.00
Celery, hat shape . .	50.00	65.00	60.00	35.00	55.00
Celery Vase, 7″	50.00	60.00	52.00	45.00	55.00
Christmas Light	27.00	45.00	35.00	25.00	40.00
Cologne Bottle	25.00	45.00	35.00	20.00	45.00
Compote, cov, ls, 8″, sq.	—	100.00	100.00	—	—
Compote, open					
6″	35.00	40.00	38.00	25.00	38.00
7″	38.00	44.00	40.00	30.00	40.00
8″, round	40.00	50.00	44.00	35.00	48.00
8″, sq, hs.	39.00	50.00	48.00	38.00	55.00
9″	48.00	56.00	52.00	40.00	52.00
10″	55.00	65.00	60.00	45.00	60.00
Cordial	35.00	52.00	40.00	25.00	58.00
Creamer					
4″	32.00	40.00	36.00	25.00	38.00
6″	38.00	75.00	55.00	35.00	72.00
Creamer & Sugar Set	—	—	—	100.00	—
*Cruet, 6″.	40.00	58.00	47.00	35.00	60.00
Egg Cup.	65.00	85.00	70.00	45.00	90.00
*Goblet	37.00	42.00	38.00	35.00	45.00
Honey Dish, cov, 6 × 7¼″.	85.00	95.00	90.00	70.00	92.00
Inkwell	45.00	—	75.00	35.00	80.00
Jelly Glass	20.00	25.00	22.00	15.00	23.00
Lamp, Kerosene					
hs, 12″	120.00	150.00	130.00	100.00	140.00
hs, 15″	125.00	155.00	135.00	110.00	150.00
ls, handled	110.00	115.00	110.00	90.00	120.00
Mug					
2½″.	23.00	30.00	25.00	20.00	32.00
3½″.	23.00	30.00	25.00	20.00	32.00
Nappy					
5″	34.00	—	39.00	30.00	45.00
6″	39.00	—	44.00	35.00	52.00
8″	45.00	—	50.00	42.00	60.00
Pickle.	25.00	30.00	27.00	20.00	29.00
Pitcher					
Milk, cov, 7″	85.00	110.00	105.00	70.00	105.00
Water, ¼ gal	70.00	85.00	80.00	55.00	80.00

	Amber	Apple Green	Blue	Clear	Vaseline
Water, ½ gal	80.00	92.00	84.00	65.00	85.00
Water, 1 gal.....	90.00	100.00	95.00	85.00	95.00
*Plate, sq, folded corners					
6"	24.00	28.00	26.00	20.00	26.00
8"	26.00	30.00	28.00	22.00	30.00
10"	34.00	50.00	36.00	25.00	34.00
Platter					
8 × 11", oblong..	40.00	48.00	42.00	38.00	45.00
11", oval	75.00	80.00	55.00	40.00	75.00
Salt Shaker, pr					
Banded........	60.00	66.00	62.00	58.00	62.00
Plain..........	50.00	60.00	55.00	40.00	56.00
Salt, ind	80.00	95.00	90.00	50.00	90.00
Salt, open, carriage shape	—	—	—	50.00	—
Sauce					
Flat, 4"	10.00	22.00	12.00	8.00	15.00
Footed, 4"	12.00	25.00	15.00	10.00	20.00
Spooner.........	32.00	48.00	40.00	27.00	45.00
*String Holder	35.00	60.00	45.00	29.00	40.00
Sugar, cov, 5"	52.00	70.00	54.00	45.00	55.00
Syrup, pewter top ..	80.00	100.00	70.00	55.00	70.00
Toothpick					
Hat...........	35.00	52.00	58.00	30.00	45.00
Plain..........	35.00	50.00	55.00	25.00	40.00
Thimble........	55.00	—	—	—	—
Tray, water					
12½", round	64.00	78.00	65.00	55.00	60.00
14", oval	65.00	80.00	75.00	60.00	74.00
*Tumbler	26.00	62.00	34.00	21.00	30.00
*Wine	35.00	50.00	40.00	20.00	40.00

THREE-FACE

Non-flint made by George E. Duncan & Son, Pittsburgh, Pennsylvania, c1872. Designed by John E. Miller, a designer with Duncan, who later became a member of the firm. Companies in the Pittsburgh area produced many patterns in expectation of the 1876 Philadelphia Centennial Exposition. It has been heavily reproduced.

	Clear		Clear
Biscuit Jar, cov	300.00	Cov, hs, 8"..........	175.00
Butter, cov	140.00	Cov, hs, 9"..........	190.00
Cake Stand		Cov, hs, 10".	225.00
9"	165.00	Cov, ls, 6"	160.00
10"	170.00	Cov, ls, 4"	150.00
11"	175.00	Open, hs, 7"	75.00
Celery Vase		Open, hs, 8"	75.00
Plain...............	95.00	Open, hs, 9"	135.00
Scalloped	95.00	Open, ls, 6"..........	75.00
Champagne		Open, jelly, paneled "Huber" top.	85.00
Hollow stem...........	250.00	Creamer...............	135.00
Saucer type...........	150.00	Goblet	85.00
Claret................	100.00	Lamp, Oil	150.00
Compote		Marmalade Jar	200.00
Cov, hs, 7".	165.00		

	Clear		Clear
Pitcher, water	350.00	Spooner	80.00
Salt Dip	35.00	Sugar, cov	110.00
Salt & Pepper	75.00	Wine	100.00
Sauce, ftd	25.00		

THREE PANEL

Non-flint made by Richards & Hartley Co., Tarentum, Pennsylvania, c1888, and by U. S. Glass Co. in 1891.

	Amber	Blue	Clear	Vaseline
Bowl				
7"	25.00	40.00	20.00	45.00
8½"	25.00	40.00	20.00	45.00
10"	40.00	50.00	35.00	48.00
Butter, cov	45.00	50.00	40.00	50.00
Celery Vase, ruffled top	55.00	65.00	35.00	55.00
Compote, open, ls, 7"	35.00	55.00	25.00	40.00
Creamer	40.00	45.00	38.00	40.00
Cruet	250.00	—	—	—
Goblet	32.00	40.00	28.00	38.00
Mug	35.00	45.00	25.00	35.00
Pitcher, water	100.00	125.00	40.00	110.00
Sauce, ftd	20.00	12.00	10.00	18.00
Spooner	40.00	45.00	30.00	42.00
Sugar, cov	55.00	60.00	48.00	70.00
Tumbler	35.00	40.00	20.00	30.00

THUMBPRINT, EARLY (Argus, Giant Baby Thumbprint)

Flint originally produced by Bakewell, Pears and Co, Pittsburgh, PA, c1850-60. Made by several factories in various forms. Reproduced in color by Fenton.

	Clear		Clear
Ale Glass	40.00	Creamer	60.00
Banana Boat	150.00	Decanter, qt, os	
Berry Set, 7 pcs	195.00	Pattern base	125.00
Bitters Bottle	140.00	Plain base	85.00
Bowl, 6"	35.00	Egg Cup	40.00
Cake Stand	50.00	Goblet	50.00
Celery Vase		Honey Dish	10.00
Patterned base	100.00	Plate, 8"	50.00
Plain base	90.00	Salt, master, ftd	35.00
Champagne	100.00	Spooner	45.00
Claret	70.00	Sugar, cov	65.00
Compote		Tumbler	43.00
* Cov, 4"	80.00	Wine	75.00
* Cov, ls, 7"	100.00		
Open, 8", scalloped top, flared	125.00		

TOKYO

Made by Jefferson Glass Co., Steubenville, Ohio, c1905. Also found in clear, blue, and apple green—all with gold trim. Some reproductions made by and signed Fenton.

	Blue Opal	Green Opal	White Opal
Bowl, berry	55.00	45.00	35.00
Butter, cov	135.00	100.00	70.00
Compote, jelly	40.00	45.00	35.00
Creamer	80.00	60.00	50.00
Cruet	185.00	140.00	90.00
Dish, 6½"	40.00	45.00	40.00
Pitcher, water	185.00	150.00	100.00
Salt Shaker, single .	50.00	40.00	30.00
Sauce	30.00	25.00	20.00
Spooner	45.00	40.00	30.00
Sugar, cov	95.00	75.00	60.00
Toothpick	110.00	80.00	50.00
Tumbler	50.00	45.00	35.00
Vase	60.00	60.00	45.00

TORPEDO (Pigmy)

Non-flint made by Thompson Glass Co., Uniontown, Pennsylvania, c1889. A black amethyst master salt ($150.00) also known.

	Clear	Ruby Stained
Banana Stand	75.00	—
Bowl		
Cov, 7" d, 7¼" h. .	65.00	—
Cov, 8"	40.00	—
Open, 4"	—	20.00
Open, 7"	18.00	—
Open, 8"	20.00	—
Open, 9"	20.00	45.00
Open, 9½", flared rim.	38.00	—
Butter, cov	85.00	—
Cake Stand, 10" . . .	85.00	—
Celery Vase, scalloped top.	42.00	—
Compote		
Cov, hs, 13¾" . . .	165.00	—
Cov, hs, 4", jelly. .	65.00	—
Open, hs, 8½" . . .	48.00	—
Open, jelly	48.00	—
Creamer	50.00	—
Cruet, os, ah.	80.00	—
Cup and Saucer . . .	65.00	—
Decanter, os, 8" . . .	85.00	—
Finger Bowl	55.00	—
Goblet	50.00	85.00
Lamp		
3", handled	75.00	—
8", plain base, pattern on bowl . . .	85.00	—

	Clear	Ruby Stained
Marmalade Jar, cov.	55.00	—
Pickle Castor, sp holder	125.00	—
Pitcher		
Milk, 8½"	75.00	150.00
Water, 10½"	85.00	175.00
Punch Cup	25.00	—
Salt		
Ind	20.00	—
Master	30.00	—
Salt Shaker, single, 2 types	50.00	—
Sauce, 4½", collared base	15.00	—
Spooner, scalloped top	45.00	—
Sugar		
Cov.	65.00	—
Open	30.00	—
Syrup	95.00	175.00
Tray, water		
10", round	85.00	—
11¾", clover shaped	75.00	—
Tumbler	40.00	50.00
Wine	90.00	—

TRUNCATED CUBE (Thompson's #77)

Non-flint made by Thompson Glass Co., Uniontown, Pennsylvania, c1892. Also found with engraving.

	Clear	Ruby Stained		Clear	Ruby Stained
Bowl			Pitcher, water, tank-		
4", berry	—	15.00	ard	50.00	110.00
8"	—	40.00	Spooner	30.00	50.00
Butter, cov	50.00	90.00	Salt Shaker, single	15.00	30.00
Celery Vase	40.00	55.00	Sugar, cov	30.00	70.00
Creamer			Syrup	40.00	100.00
Ind	20.00	35.00	Toothpick	30.00	40.00
Regular	35.00	75.00	Tumbler	22.50	35.00
Decanter, os, 12" h	60.00	150.00	Wine	25.00	40.00
Goblet	30.00	50.00			

TULIP WITH SAWTOOTH

Originally made in flint glass by Bryce Bros., Pittsburgh, Pennsylvania, c1860. Later made in non-flint.

	Flint	Non-Flint		Flint	Non-Flint
Bottle, bar	70.00	—	Decanter, os		
Bottle, pint	—	45.00	Handle	150.00	—
Butter, cov	125.00	82.00	No handle	—	45.00
Celery Vase	85.00	24.00	Egg Cup	40.00	—
Champagne	75.00	35.00	Goblet	65.00	30.00
Compote			Mug	80.00	—
Cov, hs, 6"	90.00	—	Pitcher, water	150.00	—
Cov, hs, 8½"	95.00	—	Plate, 6"	60.00	—
Cov, ls, 8½"	85.00	—	Pomade Jar	45.00	—
Open, hs, 8"	—	60.00	Salt, master, plain		
Open, ls, 9"	60.00	—	edge	28.00	15.00
Creamer	85.00	—	Spooner	35.00	—
Cruet			Sugar, cov	95.00	—
Applied handle	60.00	—	Tumbler		
Pressed handle	—	40.00	Bar	85.00	28.00
			Footed	50.00	—
			* Wine	60.00	20.00

TWO PANEL

Non-flint in oval forms made by Richards and Hartley Glass Co., Tarentum, Pennsylvania, 1880–1886, and by U. S. Glass Co. in 1891.

	Amber	Apple Green	Blue	Clear	Vaseline
Bowl					
5½"	35.00	40.00	40.00	15.00	25.00
8"	35.00	40.00	40.00	20.00	35.00
10 x 8½ x 3"	—	50.00	—	—	—
Butter, cov	50.00	55.00	55.00	30.00	40.00

	Amber	Apple Green	Blue	Clear	Vaseline
Celery Vase	45.00	50.00	50.00	25.00	40.00
Compote, cov hs,					
6½", oval	55.00	—	—	35.00	75.00
7⅜ x 9 x 12¾" . . .	—	100.00	—	—	—
8"	85.00	85.00	95.00	35.00	95.00
10 x 8½ x 3"	—	100.00	—	—	—
Creamer	40.00	45.00	45.00	20.00	35.00
* Goblet	30.00	35.00	45.00	28.00	40.00
Lamp, high standard	85.00	125.00	100.00	45.00	115.00
Mug, 2 sizes	30.00	35.00	40.00	20.00	30.00
Pitcher, water	60.00	60.00	65.00	35.00	50.00
Platter	25.00	—	—	—	—
Salt					
Ind	18.00	15.00	18.00	5.00	15.00
Master	20.00	25.00	20.00	10.00	12.00
Salt Shaker	40.00	45.00	40.00	25.00	30.00
Sauce					
Flat, oval	10.00	12.00	10.00	8.00	10.00
Footed	12.00	14.00	15.00	10.00	12.00
Spooner	45.00	50.00	45.00	25.00	35.00
Sugar, cov	50.00	55.00	55.00	30.00	40.00
Tray, water	50.00	55.00	55.00	45.00	50.00
Tumbler	35.00	42.50	35.00	15.00	40.00
Waste Bowl	40.00	45.00	40.00	20.00	30.00
*Wine	40.00	45.00	40.00	20.00	30.00

U. S. COIN

Non-flint frosted, clear, and gilted pattern made by U. S. Glass Co. in 1892 for three or four months. Production was stopped by U. S. Treasury because real coins, dated as early as 1878, were used in the molds. 1892 coin date is the most common.

	Clear	Frosted
Bowl		
6"	170.00	220.00
9"	215.00	325.00
Bread Plate	175.00	325.00
Butter, cov, dollars and halves	250.00	450.00
Cake Stand, 10" . . .	225.00	400.00
Celery		
Tray	200.00	—
Vase, quarters . . .	135.00	350.00
Champagne	—	400.00
Compote		
Cov, hs, 7"	300.00	500.00
Cov, hs, 8", quarters and dimes .	—	415.00
Open, hs, 7", quarters and dimes .	200.00	300.00
Open, hs, 7", quarters and halves .	225.00	350.00
Open, 8⅜ d, 6½" h	—	240.00
Creamer	350.00	500.00

	Clear	Frosted
Cruet, os	375.00	500.00
Epergne	—	1,000.00
Goblet	250.00	400.00
Goblet, dimes	—	550.00
Lamp		
Round font	275.00	450.00
Square font	300.00	—
Mug, handled	185.00	300.00
Pickle	200.00	—
Pitcher, water, dollars	400.00	800.00
Sauce, ftd, 4", quarters	100.00	185.00
Spooner, quarters . .	225.00	325.00
Sugar, cov	225.00	350.00
Syrup, dated pewter lid	—	525.00
* Toothpick	180.00	275.00
Tray, water, 8", rect .	275.00	—
Tumbler	135.00	235.00
Waste Bowl	225.00	—
Wine	225.00	375.00

U. S. SHERATON (Greek Key)

Made by U. S. Glass Co in 1912. This pattern was made only in clear, but can be found trimmed with gold or platinum. Some pieces are marked with the intertwined U. S. Glass trademark

	Clear		Clear
Bon Bon, 6″, ftd	15.00	Squat, medium	30.00
Bowl		Tankard	35.00
6″, ftd, sq	15.00	Plate, sq	
8″, flat	12.00	4½″	8.00
8″, ftd, sq	14.00	9″	12.00
Bureau Tray	30.00	Pomade Jar	14.00
Butter, cov	35.00	Puff Box	14.00
Celery Tray	30.00	Punch Bowl, cov, 14″	90.00
Compote		Ring Tree	25.00
Open, 4″, jelly	12.00	Salt Shaker	
Open, 6″	14.00	Squat	12.00
Creamer		Tall	15.00
After dinner, tall, sq ft	12.00	Salt, ind	14.00
Berry, bulbous, sq ft	15.00	Sardine Box	35.00
Large	18.00	Spooner	
Cruet, os	25.00	Handled	15.00
Finger Bowl, underplate	24.00	Tray	12.00
Goblet	18.00	Sugar, cov	
Lamp, miniature	50.00	Individual	15.00
Marmalade Jar	30.00	Regular	20.00
Mug	15.00	Sundae Dish	8.50
Mustard Jar, cov	25.00	Syrup, glass lid	35.00
Pickle	10.00	Tumbler	
Pin Tray	9.00	Iced Tea	12.00
Pitcher, water		Water	10.00
One half gallon	30.00		

UTAH (Frost Flower, Twinkle Star)

Non-flint made by U. S. Glass Co. in 1901 in the States Pattern series. Add 25% for frosting.

	Clear		Clear
Bowl		Creamer	30.00
Cov, 6″	20.00	Goblet	25.00
Open, 8″	18.00	Pickle	12.00
Butter, cov	35.00	Pitcher, water	48.00
Cake Plate, 9″	20.00	Salt & Pepper, pr	40.00
Cake Stand		Salt & Pepper, in holder	45.00
8″	20.00	Sauce, 4″	9.00
10″	30.00	Spooner	15.00
Celery Vase	20.00	Sugar, cov	35.00
Compote		Tumbler	15.00
Cov, ls, 6″, jelly	25.00	Wine	45.00
Open, ls, 6″, jelly	18.00		

VALENCIA WAFFLE (Block and Star #1)

Made by Adams & Co., c1885–1895; continued by U. S. Glass after 1891.

	Amber	Apple Green	Blue	Clear	Vaseline
Bowl, berry	15.00	25.00	20.00	12.00	15.00
Bread Plate	30.00	—	30.00	25.00	35.00
Butter, cov	55.00	65.00	45.00	40.00	42.50
Cake Stand, 10″ . . .	60.00	40.00	45.00	38.00	40.00
Celery Vase	40.00	40.00	45.00	30.00	40.00
Castor set, complete	60.00	—	65.00	50.00	60.00
Compote					
Cov, hs, 7″ d	60.00	75.00	75.00	50.00	70.00
Cov, ls	40.00	50.00	65.00	30.00	40.00
Creamer.	35.00	—	45.00	30.00	32.50
Dish	20.00	—	25.00	10.00	20.00
Goblet	40.00	—	40.00	30.00	35.00
Pitcher					
Milk.	40.00	50.00	45.00	35.00	40.00
Water	65.00	50.00	50.00	40.00	45.00
Relish or Pickle. . . .	20.00	20.00	25.00	15.00	20.00
Salt Dip	35.00	—	—	—	—
Sauce, ftd, 4″, sq. . .	12.00	—	18.00	10.00	15.00
Spooner	30.00	—	35.00	20.00	35.00
Sugar, cov	40.00	—	50.00	35.00	45.00
Syrup	95.00	80.00	95.00	—	—
Tray, 10½ x 8″	—	35.00	—	—	—
Tumbler	25.00	—	30.00	18.00	25.00

VERMONT (Honeycomb with Flower Rim; Inverted Thumbprint with Daisy Band)

Non-flint made by U. S. Glass Co., 1899–1903. Also made in custard (usually decorated), chocolate, caramel, and novelty slag, milk glass, and blue. Toothpick has been reproduced in clear and opaque colors.

	Clear w/gold	Green w/gold		Clear w/gold	Green w/gold
Basket, handle	30.00	45.00	Pitcher, water	50.00	115.00
Bowl, berry	25.00	45.00	Sauce	15.00	25.00
Butter, cov	40.00	75.00	Spooner	25.00	75.00
Celery Tray.	30.00	35.00	Sugar, cov	35.00	80.00
Creamer.	30.00	55.00	*Toothpick	35.00	60.00
Goblet	40.00	60.00	Tumbler	20.00	40.00

VIKING (Bearded Head)

Non-flint, made by Hobbs, Brockunier, and Co. in 1876 as their centennial pattern. No tumbler or goblet originally made.

	Clear		Clear
Apothecary Jar, cov.	45.00	Celery Vase	45.00
Bowl		Compote	
Cov, 8″, oval	55.00	Cov, hs, 9″.	95.00
Cov, 9″, oval	65.00	Cov, ls, 8″, oval	75.00
Bread Plate	70.00	Open, hs.	60.00
Butter, cov	75.00	Creamer, 2 types.	50.00

	Clear		Clear
Cup, ftd	35.00	Relish	25.00
Egg Cup	40.00	Salt, master	40.00
Marmalade Jar	90.00	Sauce	15.00
Mug, applied handle	50.00	Spooner	35.00
Pitcher, water	110.00	Sugar, cov	65.00

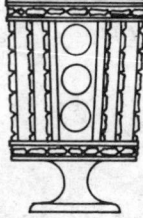

WAFFLE AND THUMBPRINT

Flint made by the New England Glass Co. and Boston & Sandwich Glass Co., c1850. Later by Bryce, Walker & Co., Pittsburgh, Pennsylvania.

	Clear		Clear
Bowl, 5 x 7"	30.00	Lamp	
Butter, cov	95.00	9½"	115.00
Celery Vase	105.00	11", whale oil	175.00
Champagne	90.00	Pitcher, water	400.00
Claret	110.00	Salt, master	45.00
Compote, cov, hs	150.00	Spooner	45.00
Creamer	125.00	Sugar, cov	125.00
Decanter, os		Sweetmeat, cov, hs, 6"	150.00
Pint	100.00	Tumbler	
Quart	145.00	Flip Glass	125.00
Egg Cup	45.00	Water, ftd	75.00
Goblet, knob stem	65.00	Whiskey	95.00
		Wine	65.00

WASHINGTON (Early)

Flint made by New England Glass Co., c1869.

	Clear		Clear
Ale Glass	125.00	Egg Cup	75.00
Bowl, 6 x 9", oval	45.00	Goblet	115.00
Bottle, bitters	85.00	Honey Dish, 3½"	30.00
Butter, cov	175.00	Lamp	145.00
Celery Vase	95.00	Pitcher, water	375.00
Champagne	125.00	Plate, 6"	60.00
Compote		Salt, master	55.00
Cov, hs, 6"	125.00	Sauce	25.00
Cov, hs, 10"	175.00	Spooner	65.00
Cordial	150.00	Sugar, cov	125.00
Creamer	200.00	Tumbler	85.00
Decanter, os	150.00	Wine	125.00

WASHINGTON CENTENNIAL (Chain with Diamonds)

Non-flint made by Gillinder & Co., Philadelphia, Pennsylvania, for centennial celebration.

	Clear		Clear
Bread Plates		"George Washington"	90.00
"Carpenter's Hall"	100.00	"Independence Hall"	100.00

	Clear		Clear
Butter, cov	80.00	Pitcher, ah	
Cake Stand		Milk	85.00
8½"	45.00	Water	100.00
10"	65.00	Relish, claw handle, dated	48.00
Celery Vase	40.00	Salt, master, oval, flat	35.00
Champagne	65.00	Sauce, flat	12.00
Compote		Spooner	35.00
Cov, hs, 9"	75.00	Sugar, cov	70.00
Open, hs, 8"	45.00	Syrup, metal lid	150.00
Creamer, ah	90.00	Tumbler	45.00
Egg Cup	45.00	Wine	50.00
Goblet	45.00		

WEDDING RING (Double Wedding Ring)

Flint, c1860; non-flint, c1870s. Toothpick, frequently seen in muddy purple, not originally made. Reproduced in various colors.

	Flint		Flint
Butter, cov	100.00	Pitcher, water	185.00
Celery Vase	80.00	Relish	60.00
Champagne	95.00	Sauce	30.00
Cordial	85.00	Spooner	80.00
Creamer	85.00	Sugar, cov	100.00
Decanter, os	125.00	Tumbler	85.00
Goblet	65.00	Wine	90.00

WESTWARD HO! (Pioneer)

Non-flint, usually frosted, made by Gillinder & Sons, Philadelphia, Pennsylvania, late 1870s. Molds made by Jacobus who also made Classic. Has been reproduced.

	Clear		Clear
Bread Plate	175.00	Marmalade Jar, cov	175.00
Butter, cov	185.00	Mug	
Celery Vase	125.00	2"	225.00
Compote		3½"	150.00
Cov, hs, 5"	225.00	Pitcher, water	200.00
Cov, hs, 9"	235.00	Sauce, ftd, 4½"	35.00
Cov, ls, 5"	150.00	Spooner	85.00
Open, hs, 8"	125.00	Sugar, cov	175.00
Creamer	95.00	Wine	200.00
Goblet	80.00		

WHEAT AND BARLEY (Duquesne)

Non-flint made by Bryce Bros., Pittsburgh, Pennsylvania, in the late 1870s. Later made by U. S. Glass Co., 1891.

	Amber	Blue	Clear	Vaseline
Bowl, 8", cov	35.00	40.00	25.00	35.00
Butter, cov	45.00	60.00	35.00	55.00

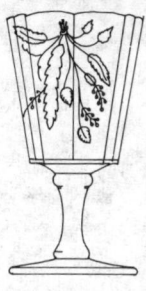

	Amber	Blue	Clear	Vaseline
Cake Stand				
8"	30.00	45.00	20.00	30.00
10"	40.00	50.00	30.00	40.00
Compote				
Cov, hs, 7"	45.00	55.00	40.00	45.00
Cov, hs, 8"	50.00	55.00	45.00	50.00
Open, hs, jelly	32.50	40.00	30.00	35.00
Creamer	30.00	40.00	28.00	35.00
Goblet	35.00	47.50	25.00	40.00
Mug	30.00	40.00	20.00	35.00
Pitcher				
Milk	60.00	75.00	30.00	75.00
Water	80.00	85.00	45.00	85.00
Plate				
7"	20.00	30.00	15.00	25.00
9", closed handles	25.00	35.00	20.00	40.00
Salt & Pepper	45.00	55.00	35.00	45.00
Sauce				
Flat, handle	12.00	15.00	10.00	15.00
Footed	15.00	15.00	10.00	15.00
Spooner	30.00	40.00	24.00	30.00
Sugar, cov	40.00	50.00	35.00	40.00
Syrup	175.00	195.00	45.00	—
Tumbler	38.50	35.00	18.00	30.00

WILDFLOWER

Non-flint made by Adams & Co., Pittsburgh, Pennsylvania, c1874, and by U. S. Glass Co., c1898. This pattern has been heavily reproduced.

	Amber	Apple Green	Blue	Clear	Vaseline
Bowl, 8", sq	25.00	35.00	35.00	18.00	25.00
Butter, cov					
Collared base	40.00	50.00	50.00	35.00	45.00
Flat	35.00	45.00	45.00	30.00	40.00
Cake Stand, 10½"	50.00	80.00	75.00	45.00	50.00
Champagne	40.00	55.00	50.00	32.00	45.00
Celery Vase	55.00	60.00	55.00	35.00	55.00
Compote					
Cov, hs, 8", oblong	80.00	85.00	85.00	50.00	75.00
Cov, ls, 7"	—	—	70.00	—	—
Open, hs	80.00	—	—	—	—
Creamer	32.50	50.00	35.00	40.00	45.00
* Goblet	30.00	40.00	40.00	25.00	40.00
Pitcher, water	55.00	75.00	50.00	40.00	65.00
Plate, 10", sq	30.00	30.00	45.00	25.00	30.00
Platter					
10", oblong	40.00	45.00	40.00	30.00	30.00
11 x 8", deep scalloped edges	—	—	45.00	—	—
Relish	20.00	22.00	20.00	18.00	20.00
* Salt, turtle	45.00	50.00	50.00	30.00	40.00
Salt Shaker	25.00	55.00	35.00	20.00	45.00
Sauce, ftd, 4", round	17.50	18.00	18.00	15.00	17.50

	Amber	Apple Green	Blue	Clear	Vaseline
Spooner	30.00	35.00	30.00	20.00	40.00
Sugar, cov	45.00	45.00	50.00	30.00	45.00
Syrup	125.00	150.00	140.00	65.00	150.00
Tray, water, oval	50.00	60.00	60.00	40.00	55.00
Tumbler	40.00	35.00	35.00	25.00	35.00
Wine	45.00	45.00	45.00	25.00	45.00

WILLOW OAK (Wreath)

Non-flint made by Bryce Bros. Pittsburgh, Pennsylvania, c1880, and by U. S. Glass Company in 1891.

	Amber	Blue	Canary	Clear
Bowl, 8″	25.00	40.00	48.00	20.00
Butter, cov	55.00	65.00	80.00	40.00
Cake Stand, 8½″	60.00	65.00	70.00	45.00
Celery Vase	45.00	60.00	75.00	35.00
Compote				
Cov, hs, 7½″	50.00	65.00	80.00	40.00
Open, 7″	30.00	40.00	48.00	25.00
Creamer	40.00	50.00	60.00	35.00
Goblet	40.00	50.00	60.00	35.00
Mug	35.00	45.00	54.00	30.00
Pitcher				
Milk	50.00	60.00	72.00	45.00
Water	55.00	60.00	72.00	50.00
Plate				
7″	35.00	45.00	54.00	30.00
9″, closed handles	32.50	35.00	42.00	30.00
Salt Shaker	25.00	40.00	55.00	20.00
Sauce				
Flat, handle, sq	15.00	20.00	24.00	10.00
Footed, 4″	20.00	25.00	30.00	15.00
Spooner	35.00	40.00	48.00	30.00
Sugar, cov	68.50	70.00	75.00	40.00
Tray, water, 10½″	35.00	50.00	60.00	30.00
Tumbler	30.00	35.00	45.00	25.00
Waste Bowl	35.00	40.00	40.00	30.00

WISCONSIN (Beaded Dewdrop)

Non-flint made in Pittsburgh, Pennsylvania, in the 1880s. Later made by U. S. Glass Co. in Indiana, 1903. One of States patterns. Toothpick reproduced in colors.

	Clear		Clear
Banana Stand	75.00	Butter, flat flange	75.00
Bowl		Cake Stand	
4½ x 6½″	28.00	8½″	45.00
6″, oval, handled, cov	40.00	9½″	55.00
7″, round	30.00	Celery Tray	45.00
8″, oblong, preserve	35.00	Celery Vase	45.00

	Clear			Clear
Compote			Pitcher	
Cov, hs, 6″	45.00		Milk	55.00
Cov, hs, 7″	55.00		Water	70.00
Cov, hs, 8″	65.00		Plate, 6¾″	25.00
Open, hs, 9½″	35.00		Punch Cup	12.00
Open, hs, 10½″	35.00		Relish	25.00
Open, jelly	20.00		Salt Shaker, single	30.00
Condiment Set, SP, horse-			Spooner	30.00
radish on tray	100.00		Sugar, cov	55.00
Creamer	50.00		Sugar Shaker	90.00
Cruet, os	80.00		Sweetmeat, 5″, ftd, cov	35.00
Cup & Saucer	50.00		Syrup	110.00
Goblet	50.00		*Toothpick	55.00
Marmalade Jar, straight			Tumbler	40.00
sides, glass lid	125.00		Wine	75.00
Mug	35.00			

WYOMING (Enigma)

Made by U. S. Glass Co., in the States Pattern series, 1903.

	Clear			Clear
Bowl, 8″	15.00		Goblet	65.00
Butter, cov	50.00		Mug	40.00
Cake Plate	55.00		Pitcher, water	75.00
Cake Stand	70.00		Relish	12.00
Compote, cov, hs, 8″ d.	85.00		Spooner	30.00
Creamer			Sugar, cov	45.00
Covered	50.00		Syrup, small	35.00
Open	35.00		Wine	85.00

X-RAY

Non-flint made by Riverside Glass Works, Wellsburg, West Virginia, 1896 to 1898. Prices are for pieces with gold trim. A toothpick holder is known in amethyst ($125.00). Also, a toothpick holder with marigold iridescence is known ($35.00).

	Clear	Emerald Green			Clear	Emerald Green
Bowl, berry, 8″, beaded rim	25.00	45.00		Goblet	20.00	35.00
Butter, cov	40.00	75.00		Pitcher, water	40.00	75.00
Celery Vase	—	50.00		Salt & Pepper, pr.	25.00	45.00
Compote				Sauce, flat	8.00	15.00
Cov, hs	40.00	65.00		Spooner	25.00	40.00
Jelly	—	40.00		Sugar		
Creamer				Cov, regular	35.00	45.00
Individual	15.00	30.00		Open, individual	18.00	30.00
Regular	30.00	60.00		Syrup	—	265.00
Cruet	—	140.00		Toothpick	30.00	60.00
Cruet Set, 4 leaf clo-				Tumbler	12.00	25.00
ver tray	125.00	350.00				

YALE (Crow-foot, Turkey Track)

Non-flint made by McKee and Brothers Glass Co., Jeannette, Pennsylvania, patented, 1887.

	Clear		Clear
Butter, cov	45.00	Pitcher, water	50.00
Bowl, berry, 10½"	20.00	Relish, oval	10.00
Cake Stand	55.00	Salt Shaker, single	30.00
Celery Vase	35.00	Sauce, flat	10.00
Compote		Spooner	20.00
Cov, hs	48.00	Sugar, cov	35.00
Open, scalloped rim	25.00	Syrup	65.00
Creamer	30.00	Tumbler	20.00
Goblet	30.00		

ZIPPER (Cobb)

Non-flint made by Richards & Hartley, Tarentum, Pennsylvania, c1880.

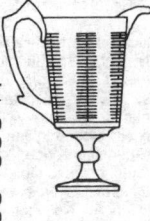

	Clear		Clear
Bowl, 7"	15.00	Pitcher, water, ½ gal	40.00
Butter, cov	40.00	Relish, 10"	15.00
Celery Vase	25.00	Salt Dip	5.00
Cheese, cov	55.00	Sauce	
Compote, cov, ls, 8"	45.00	Flat	5.00
Creamer	35.00	Footed	10.00
Cruet, os	42.00	Spooner	25.00
Goblet	20.00	Sugar, cov	35.00

ZIPPERED BLOCK (Cryptic, Nova Scotia Ribbon & Star, Duncan #90)

Non-flint made by George A. Duncan & Sons, Pittsburgh, Pennsylvania, in the late 1870s and later by U. S. Glass. Also made in Canada. Comes frosted and frosted with cut stars. Add 20% for frosting.

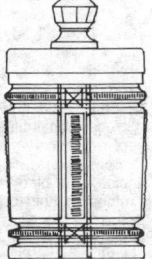

	Clear	Ruby Stained		Clear	Ruby Stained
Butter, cov	75.00	150.00	Pitcher, water	125.00	185.00
Celery	40.00	—	Salt Shaker	50.00	80.00
Compote, cov, hs	125.00	—	Sauce	15.00	25.00
Creamer	45.00	100.00	Spooner	30.00	60.00
Goblet	40.00	60.00	Sugar, cov	60.00	115.00
Lamp	85.00	—	Tumbler	30.00	45.00
Pickle, oblong	25.00	40.00			

S.E.G.

PAUL REVERE POTTERY

History: Paul Revere Pottery, Boston, Massachusetts, was an outgrowth of a club known as "The Saturday Evening Girls." The S.E.G. was a group of young female immigrants who met on Saturday nights for reading and crafts such as ceramics.

Regular production began in 1908. The name Paul Revere was adopted because the pottery was located near the Old North Church. In 1915 the firm moved to Brighton, Massachusetts. Known as the "Bowl Shop," the pottery grew steadily. In spite of popular acceptance and technical advancements, the pottery required continual subsidies. It finally closed in January, 1942.

Items produced ranged from plain and decorated vases to tableware to illustrated tiles. Many decorated wares were incised and glazed either in an Art Nouveau matte finish or an ocasional high glaze.

In addition to the impressed mark, paper "Bowl Shop" labels were used prior to 1915. Pieces also can be found dated with P.R.P. or S.E.G. painted on the base.

References: Paul Evans, *Art Pottery of the United States, Second Edition,* Feingold & Lewis Publishing Corp, 1987; Ralph and Terry Kovel, *The Kovels' Collector's Guide to American Art Pottery,* Crown Publishers, Inc., 1974.

Bowl, 7½ x 3″, ftd, stylized band of yellow blossoms, brown ground, black outlines, white glazed edge, yellow ground, marked "S.E.G."	375.00
Calendar Holder, 3¼ x 3″, self standing, glossy cobalt blue, incised landscape of green cedar trees, brown trunks, green grass, blue river, green hills, blue sky, black outlines, two brass studs to hold paper calendar, artist sgd, 1916	200.00
Charger, 11½″, white, blue band, hen and chick motif, marked "S.E.G." . .	200.00
Egg Cup, 1½″, gray, dark blue band, crouching rabbits and swimming ducks	75.00

Vase, 6½″ h, mustard yellow, marked "PR" on horse, $60.00.

Mug, 5 x 6″, three deeply incised brown Viking ships, green sails, blue and white water, cream sky, marine blue bands, black outlines, marked "S.E.G." and "5-17"	1,500.00
Paperweight, 2½″, hexagonal, bright yellow, incised chocolate brown sailing ship, sgd "Sara Galner, 1915" . .	140.00
Tile, 5¼″ sq, deeply incised beige fox standing under tree, light green ground, sgd "FR, 1910"	375.00
Trivet, 5¼″ sq, olive green geometric border, black outline, green matte center, corner feet, sgd "S. E. G.," "R. B.," and "G6.6.11"	275.00
Vase, 5 x 4″, squat, oviform, inward curving rim, large opening, band dec with stylized yellow tulips, light green leaves, brown ground, black outlines, white rim, yellow ground, marked "S.E.G"	350.00
Wall Pocket, 6″, mottled blue glaze, orig paper label	75.00

PEACHBLOW

History: Peachblow, an art glass which derives its name from a fine Chinese glazed porcelain, resembles a peach or crushed strawberries in color. Three American glass manufacturers and two English firms produced peachblow glass in the late 1880s. A fourth American firm renewed the process in the 1950s. The glass from each firm has its own identifying characteristics.

Hobbs, Brockunier & Co., Wheeling peachblow: Opalescent glass, plated or cased with a transparent amber glass; shading from yellow at the base to a deep red at top; glossy or satin finish.

Mt. Washington "Peach Blow": A homogeneous glass, shading from a pale gray-blue to a soft rose color. Pieces may be enhanced with glass appliques, enameling, and gilting.

New England Glass Works, New England peachblow [advertised as "Wild Rose," but called "Peach Blow" at the plant]: Translucent, shading from rose to white; acid or glossy finish. Some pieces enameled and gilted.

Thomas Webb & Sons and Stevens and Williams, England: Around 1888 these two firms made a peachblow style art glass marked "Peach Blow" or "Peach Bloom." A cased glass, shading from yellow to red. Occasionally found with cameotype designs in relief.

Gunderson Glass Co.: About 1950 produced peachblow type art glass to order; shades from an opaque faint tint of pink, which is almost white, to a deep rose.

Reference: John A. Shuman III, *The Collector's Encyclopedia of American Glass*, Collector Books, 1988.

Note: All pieces listed below are satin finish unless otherwise noted.

GUNDERSON

Bowl, 4¾", shading from soft blue to pink	80.00
Compote, 6" d, 5⅛" h	225.00
Decanter, 12", applied shell handle, orig stopper, acid finish	750.00
Vase, 8½", classic shape, sq base, applied serpentine handles	150.00

MT. WASHINGTON

Creamer, 3", ribbed, applied handle	350.00
Cruet, 5½" h, cylindrical ribbed body, blackberry vine dec, orig white faceted molded stopper with blue-gray tint, two small foot flakes on base	985.00
Darner, inscribed "World's Fair–1893," acid finish	165.00
Pitcher, 7¾", overshot, applied clear handle	275.00
Sugar, cov, orig paper label	1,750.00
Vase	
4", World's Fair, 1893" and gold leaf dec, pontil	200.00
8¼", lily	2,450.00

NEW ENGLAND

Bowl, 5½", ruffled rim	375.00
Celery Vase	875.00
Creamer and Sugar, ribbed, white handles	1,100.00
Finger Bowl, 5¼ x 2½"	335.00
Pitcher, 6¼", crimped top, applied handle	1,285.00
Punch Cup, 2¾" h, intense crimson blush, white reeded handle	385.00
Rose Bowl, 3⅞" d	450.00
Spooner, 4⅝" h	385.00

New England, 2¼" h, toothpick, $400.00.

Sweetmeat Jar, acid finish, SP cov, peach knob, SP handled frame sgd "Pairpoint Mfg Co., Quadruple Plate," c1900	300.00
Sugar, ribbed	300.00
Toothpick Holder, 2¼" h, tricorn	400.00
Tumbler, 3⅝"	350.00
Vase	
4", sq top, two applied opaque white fluted handles	700.00
6¼", ball shaped base, long slender neck, acid finish	575.00
8", lily, 3" deep crimson top	645.00
11¾", lily, acid finish	800.00
18½", trumpet	675.00

WEBB

Bowl, 4⅝ x 5", clear rigaree around top, applied clear branches, leaves, and flowers, three applied clear feet, creamy white lining, acid finish	400.00
Finger Bowl, 5 x 2¼", crimped top, applied clear rigaree, creamy white lining, acid finish	175.00
Ginger Jar, cov, enameled blue and white blossoms, white and brown leaves, sgd	400.00
Rose Bowl, 4" d, molded shell dec	385.00
Scent Bottle, 2¾" d, enameled blue, white, and yellow forget-me-nots, green leaves, creamy white lining, acid finish, hallmarked SS screw on dome top	650.00
Vase	
10½", heavy gold prunus flowers, leaves, butterfly and flying duck, acid finish	400.00
10½ x 5" d, cream lining, deep rose to pink, gold branches and prunus blossoms, butterfly in flight, acid finish, facing pr	1,250.00

WHEELING

Claret, 9" h, amber twisted handles, faceted stoppers, acid finish, SS mounts, pr **2,800.00**
Cruet
  6½", mahogany top shading to cherry red to cream base, white int., trefoil top **1,285.00**
  7½", bulbous, yellow shading to deep red, opaque white int., yellow ribbed handle, matching cut stopper **375.00**
Finger Bowl, 4¾ x 2½", cased, yellow shading to deep red, opaque white int. **400.00**
Mustard Pot, 3", orig top **600.00**
Pitcher, 6¼" d, 7½" h, wide fuchsia shoulderband, clear amber handle . **985.00**
Punch Cup, 3⅝" h **300.00**
Salt Shaker, 2¾" h, orig top **325.00**
Toothpick Holder, 2¼" h, cylindrical top, squatty bulbous base **1,850.00**
Vase
  7", cylindrical, flared, ruffled top, narrow amber border, Drape pattern . **650.00**
  7½" h, Morgan, acid finish **750.00**

Bowl
  4⅜" d, flared rim, ring foot, purple, pr **220.00**
  6", cobalt, two etched lotus reserves, diaper border **150.00**
  7" d, 3" h, blue overlay flowers, butterfly, and foliage, white ground, teakwood stand **250.00**
Cup and Saucer, blue overlay dragons and clouds, white ground, SS saucer **185.00**
Jar, 5¾", cov, urn shape, cobalt, geometric pattern **600.00**
Snuff Bottle, 3¼ x 2½", blue overlay, cameo cut flowers and birds **200.00**
Vase
  8⅞", baluster, royal blue overlay people and insect, white ground, 20th C, pr **450.00**
  9", bulbous, cameo, flaring top, red cut to white, Peking duck and lotus flowers, double ring neck, pr **550.00**
  10", baluster, yellow overlay monkey and pine tree, white ground, early 20th C, pr **300.00**
  11", baluster, waisted neck, continuous landscape, bearded sage seated on grassy slope **2,250.00**
  12", yellow overlay fish, white ground **375.00**

PEKING GLASS

History: Peking glass is a type of cameo glass of Chinese origin. Its production began in the 1700s and continued well into the 19th century. The background color of Peking glass may be a delicate shade of yellow, green, or white. One style of white background is so delicate and transparent that it often is referred to as the "snowflake" ground. The overlay colors include a rich garnet red, deep blue, and emerald green.

PELOTON

History: Wilhelm Kralik of Bohemia patented Peloton art glass in 1880. Later it also was patented later in America and England.

Peloton glass is found with both transparent and opaque grounds with opaque being more common. Opaque colored glass filaments (strings) are applied by dipping or rolling the hot glass. Generally, the filaments (threads) are pink, blue, yellow, and white (rainbow colors) or a single color. Items also may have a satin finish and enamel decorations.

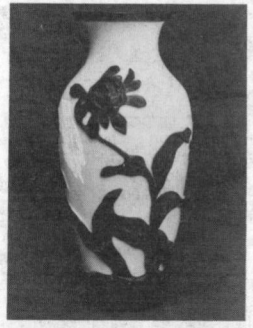

Vase, 8" h, red floral pattern, white ground, $225.00.

Tumbler, 3¾" h, yellow, pink, red, light blue, and white strings, clear ground, $125.00.

Biscuit Jar
   4½ x 6¾", melon ribbed, multicolored
     strings, light blue ground, cased,
     white lining, satin finish, SP rim,
     cov, and bail handle **600.00**
   5¾" d, 5¼" h, melon ribbed, multico-
     lored strings, cased, white lining,
     SP top **550.00**
Bowl, boat shaped, rainbow strings . .   **325.00**
Cruet, 6", amber body, multicolored
   strings **350.00**
Pitcher
   7", multicolored strings, amber
     ground **300.00**
   11", multicolored strings, amber
     ground, clear applied reeded han-
     dle **545.00**
Plate
   6¼", ruffled, pink, blue, yellow, and
     white strings, clear ground **100.00**
   7¾", blue strings, clear ground,
     enamel floral dec **100.00**
Rose Bowl, 3½" d, ribbed, multicolored
   strings, opaque white ground, applied
   crystal shell feet **300.00**
Sweetmeat Jar, 5¼" d, pink, yellow,
   white, and blue strings, robin's egg
   blue ground, cased, white lining, SP
   rim, cov, and handle **585.00**
Vase, 4¼ x 4¾", tricorn folded top, multicolored strings, white cased ground   **300.00**

PERFUME, COLOGNE, AND SCENT BOTTLES

History: Decorative bottles to hold scents have been made in various shapes and sizes. They reached a "golden age" during the second half of the 19th century.

An atomizer is a perfume bottle with a spray mechanism. Cologne bottles usually are larger and have stoppers which also may be used as applicators. A perfume bottle has a stopper that often is elongated and designed as an applicator.

Scent bottles are small bottles used to hold a scent or smelling salts. A vinaigrette is an ornamental box or bottle with a perforated top used to hold aromatic vinegars or smelling salts. Fashionable women of the late 18th and 19th centuries carried them in purses or slipped them into gloves in case of a sudden fainting spell.

Reference: Hazel Martin, *A Collection Of Figural Perfume & Scent Bottles,* published by author, 1982; Jacquelyne Jones-North, *Commercial Perfume Bottles,* Schiffer Publishing, 1987; Jacquelyne North, *Perfume, Cologne, and Scent Bottles,* Schiffer Publishing, 1987; Jean Sloan, *Perfume and Scent Bottle Collecting With Prices,* Wallace-Homestead, 1986.

Atomizer, 5½" h, cranberry opalescent striped base, $85.00.

ATOMIZERS

Baccarat, etched florals, chrome top,
   sgd **80.00**
Cambridge Glass, 6¼", gold stippled,
   opaque jade, silk lined box **135.00**
DeVilbiss, gold overlay, irid, round tray,
   lidded box **245.00**
Imperial, Candlewick, DeVilbiss **35.00**

COLOGNES

Bohemian, tall, ftd, green, floradora,
   orig stopper **125.00**
Cameo, French, 2¼" d, 5¼" h, corset
   shape, orchid maple leaves and seed
   pods cut to greenish frosted ground,
   French hallmarks on SS collar and
   repousse top **300.00**
Cranberry, 7½", allover enameled dec,
   white, blue, and yellow flowers, green
   leaves, outlined in gold, clear ball
   stopper **200.00**
Crystal, 8¼", swirled, large single air
   bubble in steeple shaped stopper . .   **60.00**
Early American, 4½" h, deep purple-
   amethyst, flared, flanged lip, pontil
   base, attributed to Mantua, OH **425.00**
Moser, miniature, multicolored florals
   and blue beetle, allover branching
   gold filigree design, stopper, orig label   **265.00**
Spatter, cased, 8½" h, 1¾" d, cylindrical,
   applied handle, gold "Rickensecker's
   Sweet Clover Cologne, NY", orig
   brass ring handled stopper reads
   "Rickensecker's" **250.00**
Webb, 6", bulbous, satin, deep amber
   shading to yellow to deep red at base,
   SS screw top **300.00**

PERFUMES

Baccarat, Rose Teinte, 1½" d, 4¼" h,
   swirl **65.00**

California Perfume Co, 3¼" h, violet sachet, clear glass, half full, violet paper label, 1912 . . . . **125.00**

Cranberry
2¾" d, 5½" h, cut glass, cranberry, beveled, clear cut faceted bubble stopper **110.00**
3⅜" l, ¾" oval, attached chains and ring, lacy filigree openwork ormolu, gilt collar, engraved, hinged lid, inner stopper, finger ring **235.00**
6¼" h , cranberry, ten cut panels, repousse silver cap ends, one hinged, one screws off **225.00**

Cut Glass
2¼" d, 5½" h, heart shape, clear, cut flowers on front and back, clear cut faceted stopper **75.00**
3" d, 6" h, green cut to clear, prism and mirror cut, clear cut faceted stopper **135.00**

Czechoslovakian, cut glass, green, fancy cut, dauber **65.00**
German, porcelain, floral dec **40.00**
Lalique, 4", heart shape, Farouche, Ricci, sgd, red plush box **300.00**
Mary Gregory, 4¾" h, bulbous, sapphire blue, white enamel little girl holding branch, allover tiny silver snowflakes **165.00**
Moser, 4½" l, lay down, cranberry, white overlay, gold holly leaves and thistles, unsigned **235.00**
Opaline, 8½", pink, cream, and gold fleur-de-lis, matching dec stopper . . **150.00**
Spatter Glass, cranberry, leaf mold, bulbous, orig stopper **100.00**
Staffordshire, 2¾ x 2¾ x 2¾", pillow, hp, garlands, gold dec, corner tassels, pr **200.00**
Wave Crest, winged cherub with blue ribbons, raised dotted pink and white flowers, blue butterfly **345.00**

SCENTS

Burmese, 2½" d, 3½" h, acid finish, gold leaves and berries, hallmarked SS screw on dome cap **700.00**
Early American
1⅞" h, deep amethyst, flattened globular body, applied quilling down sides, sheared mouth and pontil, attributed to Marlboro Street Glassworks, Keene, NH, c1815–20 . . . **1,300.00**
3" h, ovoid, peacock blue, pattern molded, twenty-six vertical rib pattern, sheared mouth and pontil, attributed to Kent, OH **250.00**
3⅝" h, medium amethyst, applied amethyst quilled ribbons down each side, sheared mouth and pontil, 18th C **1,500.00**

Mont Joye, 2¾" d, Narcissus pattern . **125.00**
Northwood, 1⅛" d, 1¾" h, pull-up design, eight horizontal bands, alternating stripes of rust, chartreuse, and white, SS cap **385.00**
Paperweight, 3½" d, 5½" h, red rose with dark green leaves paperweight in clear 1½" d ball stopper, clear glass body, sgd "Kaziun" **1,250.00**

Vinaigrette, 1" h, stein shape, silver, enameled, marked "Gruss a München," $500.00.

VINAIGRETTES

Cobalt Blue, 2¼", corset shape, heavy gold enameling, tiny gold flowers, green leaves **165.00**
Cranberry, 2¼ x 1", rect, cut all around, enameled tiny pink roses, green leaves, gold dec hinged lid, stopper, finger chain **165.00**
Gold, 18K, yellow **375.00**
Sterling Silver, 2 x 1½", engraved scrolling, scene on top, hinged lid, pierced gold inner lid, Birmingham 1849, maker Nathaniel Mills **275.00**

PETERS AND REED POTTERY

History: J. D. Peters and Adam Reed founded their pottery company in South Zanesville, Ohio, in 1900. Common flowerpots, jardinieres, and cooking wares comprised their early major output. Occasionally art pottery was attempted, but it was not until 1912 that their Moss Aztec line was introduced and widely accepted. Other art wares included Chromal, Landsun, Montene, Pereco, and Persian.

Peters retired in 1921 and Reed changed the name of the firm to Zane Pottery Company. Marked pieces of Peters and Reed Pottery are unknown.

Jug, 4½″ d, 4″ h, high glaze, applied gold lion's head and grapevines, dark brown glaze, unsigned, $60.00.

Bowl
4 x 2″, Moss Aztec, dragonfly dec . .	20.00
9½″, lotus and buds relief, matte green, rust highlights	60.00

Bookends, 5″, Pereco, stylized dec, matte green glaze, pr . . . . | 30.00

Candlesticks, pr, Black Mirror pattern . | 18.00

Jug
5½″, brown high glaze, leaf sprig dec, lion head	50.00
8″, mottled blue, traces of tan and blue drip	15.00

Mug, 5¾″, high glaze, floral sprigs . . . | 35.00

Nursing Feeder, grape and leaf garland dec around spout, glossy brown glaze | 28.00

Pitcher, 6½″, tankard, Moss Aztec, artist sgd . . . . | 45.00

Tankard Set, 17″ brown high glaze tankard, grape sprig dec, 4 matching mugs, 5 pcs . . . . | 250.00

Vase
3½″, Zane Ware, squat, blues and browns	15.00
6″, Zane Ware, slender, browns	15.00
6½″, Zane Ware, squat, browns, drip effect	25.00
7¾″, blackberry dec	45.00
8″, Zane Ware, slender, blues	18.00
9¾″, Moss Aztec, pine cone dec . . .	60.00
10″, brown glaze, wreath	40.00
12″, Landsun, blue glaze	90.00

Wall Pocket
7¾″, Pereco, Egyptian dec	75.00
9″, Moss Aztec, Art Nouveau figural nude	150.00

PEWTER

History: Pewter is a metal alloy, consisting mostly of tin with small amounts of lead, copper, antimony, and bismuth added to improve forma-

bility and hardness. The metal can be cast, formed around a mold, spun, easily cut, and soldered to form a wide variety of utilitarian articles.

Pewter ware was known to the ancient Chinese, Egyptians, and Romans. English pewter supplied the major portion of the needs of the American colonies for nearly 150 years before the American Revolution. The Revolution ended the embargo on raw tin and allowed the small American pewter industry to flourish. This period lasted until the Civil War.

The listing concentrates on the American and English pewter forms most often encountered by the collector.

Reference: Donald L. Fennimore, *The Knopf Collectors' Guides to American Antiques, Silver & Pewter,* Alfred A. Knopf, Inc., 1984.

Collectors' Club: Pewter Collector's Club of America, 15 Indian Trail, Woodbridge, CT 06515.

Basin, 8″ d, deep, Richard Austin, $450.00.

Baptismal Bowl, Dixon & Smith, English, 1811–22, gadrooned rim . . . . | 285.00

Basin
Austin, Nathaniel, Charlestown, MA, 1763–1800, 9⅛″	550.00
Barns, Blakslee, Philadelphia, PA, 1812–17, 10⅜″	400.00
Boardman, Thomas D., Hartford, CT, c1820, 8″ d	300.00
Danforth, Samuel, Hartford, CT, c1800, very faint mark, 6⅝″ d . . .	400.00
Edgar, Curtis & Co., English export, 1793–1801, 7¾″	265.00
Ellis, Samuel, London, 18th C, 9⅛″ .	200.00

Jones, Gershom, Providence, RI, late 18th C
6″ d, clear touch, normal wear . . .	550.00
8″ d, faint touch, normal pitting and wear	175.00

Lee, Richard, Springfield, VT, 1795–1815
5¾″ d	300.00

5¹⁵⁄₁₆" d, very minor imperfections **400.00**
Piggott, Francis, London, c1736–60,
period engraving on base, initials
"FK," 9⅛" d **150.00**
Stafford, Spencer, Albany, NY, c1820,
7¾" d **300.00**
Beaker
Unmarked, American, polished, mi-
nor denting, 5⅜" h **175.00**
Woodbury, J. B., Beverly, MA, and
Philadelphia, PA, 1830–38, handle,
good mark, 3" **400.00**
Yale, Hiram, Wallingford, CT, 1822–
31, cast dec handle, 2¾" h **150.00**
Bedpan, Thomas Danforth Boardman,
Hartford, CT, c1820, 10½" l, triple
touch marks **400.00**
Bowl, unmarked American, 6" d, ftd .. **250.00**
Candlestick
Calder, William, Providence, RI,
1817–56, minor pitting on base, 10"
h **325.00**
Dunham, Rufus, Westbrook, ME,
c1840, straight line touch, 6" h, pr **900.00**
Gleason, Roswell, Dorchester, MA,
c1840, 6½" h **250.00**
Homan & Co., Cincinnati, OH, 1847–
90, 10" h, pr **450.00**
Hopper, Henry, NY, straight line touch,
10" h **275.00**
Ostrander & Norris, New York City,
1848–50, saucer base, resoldered,
4" h **150.00**
Smith & Co., Boston, MA, mid 19th
C, curved line touch, 6⅛" h **150.00**
Unmarked, attributed to J. A. & H. H.
Graves, Middletown, CT, c1850,
9¾" h, pr **350.00**
Wildes, Thomas, Philadelphia, PA
and New York City, 1829–40,
straight line touch, complete with
bobeche, 10" h **200.00**
Castor Set
Smith, Eben, Beverly, MA, 1813–56,
four clear bottles **375.00**
Trask, Israel, Beverly, MA, 1807–56,
5 clear Sandwich Glass "Gothic
Arch" pattern bottles, three with
orig pewter tops, 9½" h **250.00**
Chamberstick, Meriden Britannia Co.,
1850, saucer base, gadroon molding,
4¼" h **225.00**
Charger
Badger, Thomas, Boston, MA, 15" d **800.00**
Eadem, Semper, Boston, MA, 12⅛" d **600.00**
Hamlin, Samuel, Hartford, CT and
Providence, RI, late 18th C, 13½"
d **750.00**
Leapidge, Thomas, London, 1673–
1725, 15" d **200.00**
Nicholas, O., triple reed rim, 20¼" d **700.00**
Pierce, Samuel, Springfield, MA,

11¼", pitting, knife marks, dent in
rim **210.00**
Unidentified Maker, French, late 18th
C, 14¾" d **250.00**
Coffeepot, cov
Bailey, Timothy, and James H Putnam, Malden, MA, 1830–35, 11",
clear touch **350.00**
Boardman, Thomas Danforth, Hartford, CT, 1805–50, 11", baluster
shape, Boardman and Hart touch
marks, New York address, "X"
quality mark **475.00**
Dunham, Rufus, Westbrook, MA,
c1840, straight line touch, 12" h .. **400.00**
Gleason, Roswell, Dorchester, MA,
c1840, pear shape, 12" h **450.00**
Griswold, Ashbill, Meriden, CT, 10½",
pyriform **350.00**
Porter, Freeman, Westbrook, MA,
c1840, lighthouse shape, circular
touch, 10½" h **350.00**
Smith, Eben, Beverly, MA, 1814–56,
lighthouse shape, line mark **575.00**
Communion Flagon
Boardman, Thomas Danforth, Hartford, CT, 11" **1,800.00**
Kirchen, Georg, German, 1763,
hinged cov, oval finial, heart motifs
dec **725.00**
Smith, Eben, Beverly, MA, 1814–56,
10½", lighthouse shape, straight
line touch **425.00**
Creamer, Joseph, Henry, English export, London, 1740–85, 3 small feet,
marked "HJ" **2,500.00**
Cup, Birch & Villers, England, 1775–
1820, double handles **325.00**
Dish, deep
Boardman, Thomas, Hartford, CT,
1805–50, single reed, mark struck
twice, 9¼" **600.00**
Calder, William, Providence, RI,
c1830, 10⅜" d **450.00**
Hamlin, Samuel, Hartford, CT, late
18th C, normal wear **600.00**
Roos, Sven Bengtsson, Goteborg,
Sweden, 1768–1802, hammered
surface, 13" **250.00**
Egg Cup, unmarked, American, 2⁹⁄₁₆" . **50.00**
Flagon
Carter, A., Channel Island Guernsey
type, 1730–70, two lion marks,
"CM" and London marks, 10¼" h **975.00**
Preaux, N. cylindrical shape, flat cov **875.00**
Funnel, unmarked, American, ring han-
ger, 4⅜" d, 6⅜" l **125.00**
Inkwell, unmarked, American, 5 quills,
6⅞" d **150.00**
Ladle
Danforth, Josiah, Middletown, CT,
13¼" **600.00**

Stedman, Simeon, Hartford, CT, 1818–25, birch handle **350.00**

Unmarked, American, 13¾″, engraved handle **225.00**

Yates, John, Birmingham, England, c1835, minor pitting bowl int., 13½″ l **80.00**

Lamp, 6″ h, double font, handle, Morey & Smith, Boston, $350.00.

Lamp
Camphene
Ostrander & Noyes, New York City, 1848–50, resoldered handle, saucer base, 8½″ **400.00**

Porter, Freeman, Westbrook, ME, 1835–1860, orig divirgent camphene burner, 5½″ h **250.00**

Unmarked, New England, c1840, 7½″ h **250.00**

Chamber
Capen & Molineaux, New York City and Dorcester, MA, 1844–54, marked "3", pr **325.00**

Gleason, Roswell, Dorchester, MA, c1845, saucer base, lemon font, orig whale oil burner, 4½″ h ... **325.00**

Tauton Britannia Mfg Co., Taunton, MA, 1830–35, marked "T.B.M Co/24," 3¾″ h, pr **650.00**

Gimbal
Capen & Molineaux, New York City and Dorcester, MA, 1844–54, 5¾″ h **300.00**

Dunham & Sons, Portland, ME, 1861–82, arched touch, 4½″ ... **600.00**

Grease, Continental, 18th or early 19th C, 9″ h **150.00**

Spout, Continental, 19th C, orig pickwick and hinged lid, 11″ h **170.00**

Whale Oil
Endicott & Sumner, New York City,

1946–51, orig camphene burner and caps, 4⅞″ h **300.00**

Gleason, Roswell, Dorchester, MA, c1845, orig whale oil burner, 9″ h **500.00**

Smith & Co., orig double drop whale oil burner, 5⅝″ h **375.00**

Trask, Israel, Beverly, MA, c1840, 6¼″ h **400.00**

Measure, English
Graduated set of 9, from ¼ pint to 1 quart, bellied **600.00**

One Half Pint, Channel Island Jersey type, 1750–1800 .... **375.00**

Mug
Pint, unmarked, American, attributed to Boston, MA, c1840, slight pitting, 4⅝″ h **250.00**

Pint, unmarked, English, pouring spout, unidentified touch, monogrammed "RCW," 5¼″ h **100.00**

Quart, Whitmore, Jacob, Middletown, CT, 1758–90, fair mark **1,750.00**

Pitcher
Boardman, Thomas Danforth, Hartford, CT, 1805–50, 10″ h **925.00**

Dunham, Rufus, Westbrook, ME, c1845, two quart size, cider type, 6½″ h **350.00**

Gleason, Roswell, Dorchester, MA, 1822–71, cov, 9″ h **650.00**

Richardson, George, Sr, Boston, MA, 1818–28, cov, 10″h **750.00**

Unmarked, American, pigeon breasted, reverse "C" handle, removable lid, 5½″ h **300.00**

Plate
Badger, Thomas, Boston, MA, c1790, Boston scroll mark, 7⅞″ d **250.00**

Compton, Thomas, English export, 1802–17, single reed, 7⅝″ **150.00**

Danforth, Thomas, II, Middletown, CT, 1755–82, single reed, 8″ **650.00**

Jones, Gershom, Providence, RI, 1774–1908, single reed, 8⅜″ **550.00**

Jupe, John, London, 1737–75, smooth brim, 9¼″ d, set of 4 .... **300.00**

Kilbourn, Samuel, Baltimore, MD, 1814–39, single reed, 8¾″ d **425.00**

Love, Philadelphia, PA, late 18th–early 19th C, single reed, 7¾″ ... **450.00**

Swanson, Thomas, c1770, Ellis and Swanson marks, 7⅞″ d, pr **150.00**

Unmarked, American, 7⅝″ d **75.00**

Whitmore, Jacob, Middletown, CT, c1770, 8″ d **250.00**

Porringer
Boardman, Thomas D. and Sherman Boardman, c1810–30, Hartford, CT 4″ d, old English handle **600.00**

5″ d, keyhole type crown handle, triangular bracket **325.00**

Unmarked
Attributed to Danforth or Boardman, CT, c1830, old English style handle, 3¼" d **175.00**
Attributed to David Melville, Newport, RI, c1780–90, Rhode Island flowered handle initialed "FGW," 5" d **150.00**
Salt, Boyd, Parks, Philadelphia, PA, 1795–1819, ftd, beaded rim and base **950.00**
Soap Box, unmarked, American, 4⅜", circular, hinged lid **125.00**
Soup Plate, Swanson, Thomas, English export, 1753–83, Samuel Ellis hallmarks, single reed, 8⅜" **175.00**
Sugar Bowl, cov
Boyd, Parks, attributed to, Philadelphia, PA, 1795–1819, beaded lid, rim, and foot **7,500.00**
Richardson, George, Boston and Cranston, RI, 1818–45, fine condition **3,000.00**
Spoon, William Bradford, New York City, 1719–85, 6⅝" l, round bowl **1,600.00**
Syrup, unmarked, American, miniature lighthouse coffeepot shape, 5½" h, lid poorly resoldered to hinge **225.00**

PHOENIX BIRD CHINA

History: Phoenix Bird pattern is a blue and white china exported from Japan during the 1920s to 1940s. A limited amount was made during the "Occupied Japan" period.

Initially it was available at Woolworth's 5 & 10, through two wholesale catalog companies, or by selling subscriptions to needlecraft magazines. Myott Son & Co., England, also produced this pattern under the name "Satsuma," c1936. These earthenware items were for export only.

Once known as "Blue Howo Bird China," the Phoenix Bird pattern is the most sought after of seven similar patterns in the Hō-ō bird series. Other patterns are: Flying Turkey (head faces forward with heart-like border); Howo (only pattern with name on base); and, Twin Phoenix (border pattern only, center white). The Howo and Twin Phoenix patterns are by Noritake and are occasionally marked "Noritake." Flying Dragon (bird-like), an earlier pattern, comes in green and white as well as the traditional blue and white and is marked with six oriental characters. A variation of Phoenix Bird pattern has a heart-like border and is called Hō-ō.

Phoenix Bird pattern has over 500 different shapes and sizes. Also varying is the quality found in the execution of design, shades of blue, and shape of the ware itself. All these factors must be considered in pricing. The maker's mark tends to add value; over 90 marks have been cataloged.

Post 1970 pieces were produced in limited shapes with precise detail, but are on a milk white ground and usually don't have a maker's mark. When a mark does appear on a modern piece, it appears stamped in place.

Reference: Joan Collett Oates, *Phoenix Bird Chinaware*, privately printed, *Book One*, 1984, *Book Two (A Through M)*, 1985, *Book Three (N through Z and Post 1970)*, 1986.

Collectors' Club: Phoenix Bird Collectors of America, 5912 Kingsfield Drive, West Bloomfield, MI 48233. *Phoenix Bird Discoveries*.

Additional Listings: See *Warman's Americana & Collectibles* for more examples.

Advisor: Joan Oates.

Tea Set, child's, #2, $75.00.

Bowl, 10", fruit	45.00
Butter Pat	8.00
Cake Tray, cut out handles	40.00
Cup, Irish coffee	30.00
Dish, 8⅞" d	30.00
Hot Water Pot, cov	35.00
Jar, cov, bath salts	35.00
Matchbox Holder, Ho-O, stand	75.00
Nut Cup, three feet	15.00
Pie Plate, 6¾" d, plain edge	10.00
Plate	
Chop, 11¼"	55.00
Luncheon, 8½", marked "Nippon" ..	22.00
Platter	
13½ x 9", scalloped	45.00
15 x 10¾", plain edge	60.00
Reamer, pitcher base	55.00
Rice Bowl, #2-A, 4½" d, 2" h	8.00
Rice Tureen, #1, "S" style handles, 6½" h	80.00
Salt Shaker, #1, six sided, flat top ...	15.00
Sauce Boat, #3, 3½" h	30.00
Sherbet, Ho-O	20.00
Soap Dish, 7½"	25.00
Sugar, #32, dainty cov and handle, 3½" h, 3¼" d	18.00
Syrup, #12, Ho-O	20.00
Tankard, water, 6½" h	75.00
Tea Plate, #1, 7¼" l, 6¼" w, cup cut-out, unglazed	20.00
Teapot, #11-B	45.00
Tile, 6"	25.00

PHOENIX GLASS

History: Phoenix Glass Company, Beaver, Pennsylvania, was established in 1880. Known primarily for commercial glassware, the firm also produced a molded, sculptured, cameo-type line from the 1930s until the 1950s.

Vase, 6¾" h, 7" w, light blue, Lalique-type mold, $135.00.

Ashtray, triangular, Praying Mantis ...	40.00
Bowl	
8", boat shape, sculptured green lemons and foliage, white ground ...	75.00
14", sculptured diving nudes, three colors	190.00
Box, cov, 7¼ x 4¾", oval, scalloped, sculptured fruits and leaves, white ground	75.00
Cigarette Box, cov, 4½ x 3½", sculptured white flowers, blue ground ...	60.00
Creamer and Sugar, Catalonia pattern, yellow	40.00
Lamp, table	
6½", sculptured lavender peonies, white ground	80.00
11", sculptured yellow ferns and foliage, gray ground	120.00
15", Bluebell pattern, pr	210.00
23", Bluebell pattern, pr	165.00
Planter, 3¼ x 8½", sculptured green lion, white ground	50.00
Plate	
8¼", dancing nudes, yellow	50.00
8½", kumquats, green	40.00
Vase	
5", sculptured white pine cones, green ground, paper label	55.00
6¼", sculptured pink peonies, green leaves, white ground	80.00
8½", sculptured white dancing nudes, light green ground	130.00
9", pillow shape, sculptured deep blue fish, white ground	200.00
10"	
Madonna	125.00
Wild Rose, white pearlized russet	125.00
10½"	
Daises, white sculptured flowers, light brown ground, orig paper sticker	130.00
Dogwood, sculptured flowers, yellow, green, brown, and white ..	100.00

PHONOGRAPH RECORDS

History: With the advent of the more sophisticated recording materials, such as 33⅓ RPM long playing records, 8-track tapes, cassettes, and compact discs, earlier phonograph records became collectors' items. Most have little value. The higher priced examples are rare (limited production) recordings. Condition is critical.

References: L. R. Docks, *1915-1965 American Premium Record Guide, 3rd Edition,*, Books Americana, 1986; Jerry Osborne and Bruce Hamilton, *Soundtracks & Original Cast Albums Price Guide*, O'Sullivan Woodside & Co., 1981; Jerry Osborne and Bruce Hamilton, *Record Albums Price Guide*, O'Sullivan Woodside & Co., 4th Edition, 1982; Peter A. Soderbergh, *Dr. Records Original 78 RPM Price Guide*, Wallace-Homestead, 1983; Peter A. Soderbergh, *Olde Records Price Guide*, 1900–1947, Wallace-Homestead, 1980.

Periodical: *Goldmine*, 700 E. State Street, Iola, WI 54990.

Additional Listings: See "Records" in *Warman's Americana & Collectibles* for those recordings in price range from: $5.00 to $25.00.

Note: Most records, especially popular recordings, have a value of less than $3.00 per disc. *The records listed here are classic recordings of their type and in demand by collectors.*

Andrews Sisters, Bei Mir Bist Du Schoen, Decca 1562	5.00
Louis Armstrong	
I Ain't Got Nobody, Okeh 8756	15.00
Oriental Strut, Okeh 8299	40.00
When It's Sleepy Time Down South, Okeh 41504	15.00
Fred Astaire, Hang on to Me, Columbia 3970	10.00
Mildred Bailey, (with Casa Loma), You Call It Madness, Brunswick 6184 ..	10.00
Count Basie, One O'Clock Jump, Decca 1363	8.00
Bix Beiderbecke, Davenport Blues, Gennett 5654	25.00
Bunny Berigan, Let Yourself Go, Vocalion 3178	10.00

Eubie Blake, It Looks Like Love, Crown
3105 .... 10.00
Cab Calloway, You Gotta Ho-De-Ho,
Banner 32945 .... 8.00
Hoagy Carmichael, Georgia on My
Mind, Victor 23013 .... 20.00
Jack Crawford & His Orchestra, For My
Baby, Champion 15404 .... 15.00
Johnny Dodds, Weary Blues, Vocalion
15632 .... 60.00
Dorsey Brothers Orchestra, The Spell
of the Blues, Okeh 41181 .... 25.00
Duke Ellington
Red Hot Band, Vocalion 1153 .... 75.00
Trombone Blues, Pathe 36333 .... 40.00
Jim Europe, Broadway Hit Medley,
Pathe 22082 .... 35.00
Jan Garber, Puttin On the Ritz, Colum-
bia 2115D 10.00
Benny Goodman, Slow But Sure, Mel-
otone 12205 .... 15.00
Fletcher Henderson
Chattanooga, Ajax 17017 .... 25.00
Chime Blues, Black Swan 2116 ... 45.00
Feeling the Way I Do, Banner 1364 . 10.00
Hightower's Nighthawks, Squeeze Me,
Black Patti 8045 .... 200.00
Earl Hines, Stowaway, Quality Real
Special R-7038 .... 100.00
Billie Holiday, Me, Myself and I, Vocalion
3593 .... 10.00
Jimmy Joy & His Orchestra, Wild Jazz,
Okeh 40420 .... 30.00
Guy Lombardo, You Are Too Beautiful,
Brunswick 6500 .... 10.00
Wingy Mannone, Trying to Stop My
Crying, Vocalion 15797 .... 40.00
Glenn Miller, Moonlight Bay, Decca
1239 .... 10.00
New Orleans Rhythm Kings, Clarinet
Marmalade, Gennett 5220 .... 100.00
King Oliver, Zulus Ball, Gennett 5275 . 300.00
Gil Rodin & His Orchestra, If I Could Be
with You, Crown 3016 .... 20.00
Noble Sissle, Crazy Blues, Edison
50754 .... 10.00
Frankie Trumbauer & His Orchestra,
Blue River, Okeh 40879 .... 25.00
Thomas "Fats" Waller, Savannah
Blues, Victor 20776 .... 25.00
Lawrence Welk, Shanghai Honeymoon,
Gennett 20341 .... 30.00
Clarence Williams, New Orleans Hop
Scop Blues, Okeh 4975 .... 75.00

PHONOGRAPHS

History: Early phonographs were commonly
called "talking machines." Thomas A. Edison invented the first successful phonograph in 1877.
Other manufacturers followed with their variations.

Collectors' Club: Antique Phonograph Collectors Club, 502 E. 17th Street, Brooklyn, NY 11226.
The Antique Phonograph Monthly (10 issues).

**Edison, Amberola Model 30, 11 x 14¼
x 12½", four minute cylinder, built in
horn, hand crank, oak case, $325.00.**

Apollo, floor model, disc, fruitwood
case, record storage, European
maker 385.00
Berliner, trademark, Gramophone 1,600.00
Brunswick Parisiane, collapsible card-
board horn 400.00
Busy Bee, cylinder model, open works 300.00
Columbia
AQ Graphophone, key wind, tin horn,
six cylinder records, 1886 ...... 225.00
Grafanola Baby Regent 400.00
Edison
Amberola X, recorder attachment,
orig box, 1913–14 .... 525.00
Diamond Disc Model No S19 ..... 150.00
Fireside Model, 9¾" w, bentwood cov,
oak case, cygnet horn 950.00
Garrard, snakeskin horn hand crafted,
1920 .... 1,250.00
Harmony, oak case, painted morning
glory horn 400.00
Haywood Wakefield, wicker 1,750.00
Junophone, table model, oak case,
metal woodgrain finish horn 250.00
Kalamazoo Duplex 1,350.00
McDonald Graphophone, open works,
oak base 800.00
Pathe Actuelle, table model, gold morn-
ing glory dec horn, case with corner
dec 450.00
Regina Reginaphone Disc Musical Box
and Phonograph, oak case, MOP in-
lay, five 15½" discs, c1904 .... 2,000.00
Victor
Model 1050, includes record changer 450.00

V, oak case, corner columns, 26"
black ribbed horn **1,250.00**
Victrola, Model VI, table type, oak . . . **150.00**
Zonophone
Champion, table model, oak case,
ribbed brass horn **750.00**
Type A, table model, oak case, corner
columns, beveled glass sides,
black metal horn with brass bell . . **1,500.00**

PICKARD CHINA

History: The Pickard China Company was
founded by Wilder Pickard in Chicago, Illinois, in
1897. Originally the company imported European
china blanks, principally from the Havilands at Limoges, which they then hand painted. The firm pres-
ently is located in Antioch, Illinois.

Bowl, 9⅞", pierced handle, hp, gooseberries and leaves, gilt edge dec, art-
ist sgd **125.00**
Box, cov, 2¾ x 5¾", stylized gold, black
and ivory flowers **90.00**

**Pitcher, 8", black panels, gold top, artist
sgd "Hessler," marked "Handpainted
China/W/Pickard/A," $200.00.**

Candlesticks, pr, 3 x 4½", etched gold **40.00**
Celery Tray, 13½ x 6¼", gold band,
grape dec, creamy ground, sgd
"Challinor" **85.00**
Chocolate Pot, 11½", white MOP
ground, orchids and leaves dec . . . **155.00**
Coffee Set, coffeepot, creamer, and

sugar, Bird of Paradise dec, colorful,
Art Nouveau, c1910, 3 pcs **275.00**
Compote, 10", blackberry dec, gold trim,
artist sgd **145.00**
Creamer and Sugar, cov
Art Deco, green clover and geometric
dec, gold trim, 1915 . . . . **50.00**
Large roses, brown ground, gold trim,
sgd "LeRoy" **90.00**
Demitasse Pot, poinsettia dec, dated
1910, artist sgd, marked "Pickard" . **200.00**
Dinner Service, 52 pcs, service for six,
plus serving pcs, heavy gold border,
c1925, marked "Pickard, Rosenthal" **5,200.00**
Dish
8", pierced, handled, scenic garden
wall, rich colors **225.00**
13¼", pierced handles, four floral
groups, green center, gilded floral
design, gold edge, artist sgd **95.00**
Ewer, 6½", bulbous, tricorn, deep sea
green matte ground, gold blueberries
and leaves, heavy gold spout, handle,
and neck, gold swirls, artist sgd "Cou-
fall," 1905 mark **325.00**
Hatpin Holder, violets **60.00**
Jam Jar, cov, cream ground, orange
water lilies, green lily pads, gold outlined, scalloped gold rim, slot for
spoon, artist sgd "Tolpin," 1898 mark **165.00**
Jug, 7½", stopper, Indian corn dec, artist
sgd, circle mark **265.00**
Mustard Jar, oval, cov, attached under-
plate, hp, Art Deco design, green and
gold, marked "Pickard" **35.00**
Pitcher, 7¼", cream ground, green and
yellow shading, grapes, green and
brown leaves, heavy gold trim, c1905 **200.00**
Plate
7¾", irid floral dec, gold and red tra-
cery, artist sgd **55.00**
8½", seashells by water's edge, gold,
MOP border **60.00**
Powder Box, 4" cov, hp, roses, sgd
"A.K. France," and "Wall" **125.00**
Salt and Pepper Shakers, pr, gold band
with pink and blue floral clusters,
MOP ground, c1910 . . . . **45.00**
Tea Set, 11" round tray, dolphin head
spouted teapot, tankard shape creamer and cov sugar, MOP rainbow
ground, pink, rose, and turquoise tulips, heavy gold, allover tracery, artist
sgd, 1898 mark **650.00**
Tray, 15½" l, scenic, pierced handle,
gold rim, artist sgd "Gasper" **150.00**
Vase
6½", stylized lavender flowers, trailing
leaves, cream ground, gold trim . . **148.00**
7¾", cylindrical, scenic, moon, lake,
pine trees, leaf mark **245.00**
8", phoenix birds, gold dots, royal

blue, narrow black and white stripe on top, royal blue stripe on bottom, 1910 mark, artist sgd "Coufall" .. **235.00**
9", large gold chrysanthemums, green leaves, shaded multicolored ground, gold trim, artist sgd, 1898 mark **300.00**
10", hp, tree scene, sgd "E. Challinor" **225.00**
11", cylindrical, hp, maiden, partially clad, long red hair, butterfly in hand, white ground, artist sgd "M" **235.00**
17½", cylindrical, wide mouth, arched scroll handles, large bright red poinsettias, artist sgd, c1905 .... **650.00**
Vegetable, cov, Cinderella pattern **50.00**
Wine Set, decanter, orig stopper, eight wines, tray, black ground, gold grapes, sgd "Hess" **625.00**

PICKLE CASTORS

History: A pickle castor is a table accessory used to serve pickles. It generally consists of a silver plated frame fitted with a glass insert, matching silver plated lid, and matching tongs. Pickle castors were very popular during the Victorian era. Inserts are found in pattern glass and colored art glass.

11¾" h, clear acid etched insert with floral and bird medallion, octagonal, silver plated, matching tongs, marked "Meriden Co. 182," $200.00.

Amethyst, applied floral dec, SP frame and lid **275.00**
Blue, Daisy and Button pattern insert, SP frame, glass lid **200.00**
Cranberry
  Coin Spot, enamel dec, SP holder . **225.00**
  Inverted Thumbprint, double, gold floral and scroll enamel dec, ornate

ftd Wilcox frame and cov, braided handle, resilvered **600.00**
Ribbed, twelve ribs, eight columns of enameled flowers and blue dots, ornate SP frame and tongs, marked "B Meriden Co., Quadruple Plate" **345.00**
Mt Washington, deep satin cranberry Optic Diamond and IVT pattern insert, gold spider chrysanthemum dec, ftd Simpson Hall frame, ornate engraved cov, orig silver **600.00**
Opalescent, Daisy and Fern, blue, apple blossom mold, ornate ftd SP frame, orig tongs **250.00**
Pigeon Blood, Bulging Loop pattern, 8", SP ftd frame, marked "Empire Mfg Co" **285.00**
Rubena, Ribbed Optic pattern, hp enamel white daisies sprays, blue forget-me-nots, gold leaves, ftd base, ornate SP lid, bail, and side trim, marked "Colonial Silver Plate Co., Portland, ME" **400.00**

PIGEON BLOOD GLASS

History: Pigeon blood refers to the deep orangish-red colored glass ware produced around the turn of the century. Do not confuse it with the many other red glass wares of that period. Pigeon blood has a very definite orange glow.

Biscuit Jar, 8½" h to top of finial, ribbed, silverplated fittings, $275.00.

Biscuit Jar, Beaded Drapery pattern, ornate SP rim, cov, and handle **185.00**
Bowl, 9", c1880 .... **150.00**
Bride's Basket, 9½" d, enamel floral dec, SP holder **200.00**
Creamer, Torquay pattern, SP rim and handle **115.00**

Cruet, IVT, orig stopper	225.00
Pickle Castor, 8", SP holder marked "Empire Mfg Co., Quadruple Plate"	250.00
Pitcher	
IVT, clear applied handle	250.00
Torquay pattern	320.00
Salt and Pepper Shakers, pr	
Bulging Loops pattern, orig tops	110.00
Decorated, squatty, raised fleur-de-lis and white enameled flowers	150.00
Sugar Shaker, Bulging Loops pattern, orig top	220.00
Syrup, Scroll and Net pattern, satin finish, applied frosted handle, orig top	575.00
Table Set, cov butter, creamer, spooner, cov sugar, Torquay pattern, orig SP rims and lids	575.00
Vase, 10½", enameled flowers	175.00

PINK SLAG

History: True pink slag is found only in the molded Inverted Fan and Feather pattern. Quality pieces shade from pink at the top to white at the bottom.

Reproduction Alert: Recently pieces of pink slag, made from molds of the now defunct Cambridge Glass Company, have been found in the Inverted Strawberry and Inverted Thistle pattern. This is not considered "true" pink slag and brings only a fraction of the Inverted Fan and Feather pattern prices.

Tumbler, 3⅞" h, Inverted Fan and Feather, $450.00.

Berry Bowl, master, 9", ftd	500.00
Butter, cov	650.00
Compote, jelly	375.00
Creamer	450.00
Cruet, 6½" h, orig stopper	1,300.00
Marmalade Jar, cov	875.00
Pitcher, water	775.00
Punch Cup, 2½" h, ftd	275.00

Spooner	350.00
Sugar, cov	550.00
Toothpick	400.00
Tumbler	425.00

PIPES

History: The history of pipe making dates as early as 1575. Almost all types of natural and man-made materials, some which retained smoke and some that did not, were used to make pipes. Among the materials were amber, base metals, clay, cloisonn, glass, horn, ivory, jade, meerschaum, parian, porcelain, pottery, precious metals, precious stones, semi-precious stones, assorted woods, *inter alia*. Chronologically the four most popular materials and their generally accepted introduction dates are: c1575, clay; c1700, woods; c1710, porcelain; and, c1725, meerschaum.

National pipe styles exist around the globe, wherever tobacco smoking is custom or habit. Pipes reflect a broad range of themes and messages, e.g., figurals, important personages, commemoration of historical events, mythological characters, erotica and pornographica, the bucolic, the bizarre, the grotesque, and the graceful.

Pipe collecting began in the mid-1880s; William Bragge, F.S.A., Birmingham, England, was an early collector. Although firmly established through the efforts of free-lance writers, auction houses, and museums (but not the tobacco industry), the collecting of antique pipes is an amorphous, maligned, and misunderstood hobby. It is amorphous because there are no defined collecting bounds; maligned because it is conceived as an extension of pipe smoking, now socially unacceptable [many pipe collectors are avid non-smokers]; and, misunderstood because of its association with the "collectibles" field.

References: R. Fresco-Corbu, *European Pipes*, Lutterworth Press, 1982; E. Ramazzotti and B. Mamy, *Pipes et Fumeurs des Pipes. Un Art, des Collections, Sous le Vent*, 1981; Benjamin Rapaport, *A Complete Guide To Collecting Antique Pipes*, Schiffer Publishing, 1979.

Collectors' Club: Pipe Collectors International, Inc., P. O. Box 22085, 6172 Airways Boulevard, Chattanooga, TN 37422. *Pipe Smoker.*

Museums: Museum of Tobacco Art and History, Nashville, TN; National Tobacco-Textile Museum, Danville, VA; U.S. Tobacco Museum, Greenwich, CT.

PIPES

Briar, 11", carved bearded man bowl, horn stem	150.00
Burl, 3½" l, carved fist bowl, sapling stem	85.00

Carved Meerschaum bowl, Lopoldo Weiss, Genoa, orig case, $350.00.

Clay
4¼″, blue and white bowl, brown stem, Ohio	150.00
6½″, sailor smoking pipe, c1800	500.00
Ivory, angel with wings, amber stem	150.00

Meerschaum, carved
4¼ x 2¼″, mountain goat bowl, amber stem	85.00
4½″, lady's leg with garter, orig case	100.00
5½″ l, sultan head with jeweled turban bowl, amber stem	95.00
6″ l, Art Nouveau lady bowl, golden amber stem	75.00
7″, American shield, red stem	45.00
7½″, running dog bowl with SP trim, turned wood and pearl stem	35.00
12″ l, two Indians with rifles and hunting dog bowl, orig case	900.00
13″ l, ivory bowl and carved stag segment	35.00

Opium, 21″, hand carved poppy above brass bowl, Chinese	125.00

Porcelain
6″ l, hand holding dog bowl, orig stem	125.00
19″, , twig stem, brass fittings, Bavarian	50.00
26″, hp, stags in woods, Germany	90.00

Scrimshaw, 4½″, whale ivory and baleen, Azorean	250.00
Silver bowl and bit, 12½″ l, enameled dec, Chinese	120.00
Spatter Glass, 7″ l, oval bowl	75.00
Sterling Silver, boatswain, macrame cord	25.00

Wood
Curved bowl, silver trim, 6″ l	25.00
Hand holding bowl, carved	75.00

TAMPS

Bone, 2¾″ l, horn shape, silver trim	25.00

Brass
2⅛″, hand holds clay pipe	20.00
3¼″ h, turned wood handle	15.00
Napoleon figure, 1840	125.00
Glass, blue and white, Bristol, 1860	50.00
Ivory, leg, steel rivets, c1800	175.00
Sterling Silver, 2¼″, pick and folding spoon, marked "Tiffany & Co"	20.00

POCKET KNIVES

History: Alcas, Case, Colonial, Ka-Bar, Queen, and Schrade are the best of the modern pocket knife manufacturers, with top positions enjoyed by Case and Ka-Bar. Knives by Remington and Winchester, firms no longer in production, are eagerly sought.

Form is a critical collecting element. The most desirable forms are folding hunters (1 and 2 blades), trappers, peanuts, Barlows, elephant toes, canoes, Texas toothpicks, Coke bottles, gun stocks, and Daddy Barlows. The decorative aspect also heavily influences prices. Values are for pocket knives in mint condition.

References: James F. Parker, *The Official Price Guide to Collector Pocket Knives, 9th Edition*, House of Collectibles, 1987; Jim Sargent, *Sargent's American Premium Guide To Pocket Knives: Identification and Values*, Books Americana, 1986; Ron Stewart and Roy Ritchie, *The Standard Knife Collector's Guide*, Collector Books, 1986.

Periodical: *Knife World*, P. O. Box 3395, Knoxville, TN 37917.

Collectors' Clubs: American Blade Collectors, P.O. Box 22007, Chattanooga, TN 37422; Canadian Knife Collectors Club, 3141 Jessuca Court, Mississauga, ON L5C1X7; The National Knife Collectors Association, 7201 Shallowford Road, Chattanooga, TN 37421.

Museum: National Knife Museum, Chattanooga, TN.

Additional Listings: See *Warman's Americana & Collectibles* for more examples.

CASE

Case uses a numbering code for its knives. The first number (1–9) is the handle material; the second number (1–5) designates the number of blades; the third and fourth number (0–99) is the knife pattern. Stage (5), pearl (8 or 9), and bone (6) are most sought in handle materials. The most desirable patterns are 5165—folding hunters, 6185—doctors, 6445—scout, muskrat—marked muskrat with no number, and 6254—trappers.

In the Case XX series a symbol and dot code is used to designate a year.
1920–40
1139, banana	150.00
5111½ blade, lock	600.00
53131, canoe	1,000.00
5452	300.00

6245, dog groomer	200.00
6261	120.00
8265	1,000.00

1940–65

4200, melon taster, serrated blade	150.00
42507, "Office Knife" on handle	100.00
5265	200.00
61093	175.00
62009, Barlow	100.00
6214, with shield	65.00
640045R, scout	25.00
Muskrat	90.00

1965–70, XX series

32095, fisherman's	100.00
5254	85.00
5172, bulldog	150.00
6111½	100.00
6143, Daddy Barlow	40.00
92042	100.00

1970–80 (number of dots indicates year)

2137, sod buster	25.00
52131, canoe	100.00
5375, stag	70.00
6246R, rigger	45.00
P13755, stag, Kentucky Bicentennial	50.00

KA-BAR (Union Cutlery Co., Olean, NY)

The company was founded by Wallace Brown at Tidioute, PA in 1892. It was relocated in Olean, NY, in 1912. The products have many stampings including Union [inside shield], U-R Co. Tidioute [variations], Union Cutlery Co. Olean, NY, Alcut Olean, NY, Keenwell, Olean, NY, and Ka-Bar. The larger knives with a profile of a dog's head on the handle are most desirable. Pattern numbers rarely appear on a knife prior to the 1940's.

1154, leg knife	150.00
21107, Grizzly	2,000.00
2217, rigger	70.00
61161, composition handle	125.00
6191, knife, fork, spoon	625.00
6250, elephant toe	300.00
6260 KF	100.00
Cigar Cutter	150.00

KEEN KUTTER (Simons Hardware, St. Louis, MO)

K0643, pearl	75.00
K1771¾, Daddy Barlow	150.00
K1898¾, toothpick	100.00
K8464¼, Kattle	50.00

REMINGTON, last made in 1940

R1128, bullet	1,100.00
R1273, bullet	1,500.00
R1535, florist	80.00
32373, cattle	250.00

R273, Texas Jack	190.00
3335, scout, red, white, and blue	285.00
4235, red, white, and blue	200.00
Bullet, authorized reproduction	60.00

WINCHESTER

1050, Texas toothpick	300.00
1701, Barlow	100.00
1920, hunter	1,100.00
2070, office knife	75.00
2380, doctor's	350.00
3022, whittler	250.00
3376	250.00

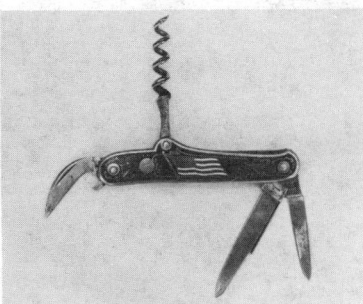

Kastor, champagne knife, cloisonne flag, $125.00.

OTHER MANUFACTURERS

Elephant Toe	
Cattaraugus Cutlery Co.	300.00
New York Knife Co.	350.00
Folding Hunter	
Baker, U.S.A.	100.00
Bower, Atlanta, GA	85.00
Cattaraugus Cutlery Co.	350.00
Marbles Arms Co.	350.00
New York Knife Co.	500.00
C. Platts & Sons, Eldred, PA	100.00
Queen Cutlery Co., Titusville, PA	100.00
Schrade Walden, Walden, NY	150.00
Union Razor Co., Titusville, PA	100.00
Valley Forge Cutlery Co., NJ	200.00
Western States Cutlery Co., Boulder, CO, buffalo skull mark	300.00
George Wosterholm & Son Cutlery Co., General Taylor	1,500.00

POISON BOTTLES

History: Poison bottles were designed to warn and prevent accidental intake or misuse of their poisonous substances, especially in the dark. Poison bottles generally were made of colored glass, embossed with "Poison" or a skull and crossbones, and sometimes were coffin-shaped.

John H. B. Howell of Newton, New Jersey, designed the first safety closure in 1866. The idea did not become popular until the 1930s when bottle designs became simpler and the user had to read the label to identify the contents.

References: Ralph and Terry Kovel, *The Kovels' Bottle Price List, 7th Edition,* Crown Publishers, Inc., 1984; Carlo & Dot Sellari, *The Illustrated Price Guide to Antique Bottles,* Country Beautiful Corp., 1975.

Periodicals: *Antique Bottle and Glass Collector,* P.O. Box 187, East Greenville, PA 18041.

4⅛" h, green-brown, side embossed "Not To Be Taken," bottom embossed "Cash/Boots Chemist," $12.50.

A.B.M., Tinct Iodine, amber, emb, skull
  and crossbones, stopper 10.00
Carbolic Acid, cobalt blue 25.00
Chester A. Baker, Boston, cobalt 45.00
Crandall Pharmacal Co., Brooklyn, NY,
  triangular shape, emb, 3" h 20.00
Coffin, cobalt blue, label 50.00
Dead Shot Sure Death To All Insects,
  Scranton, PA 10.00
Dicks Ant Destroyer, Finlay Dicks & Co,
  New Orleans 30.00
Dr. Detwiler, Ph.C. Druggist, yellow amber, emb, ribbed corners 20.00
Grasselli Arsenate of Lead, "Poison"
  emb on shoulder 50.00
Leavin's English Vermin Destroyer,
  aqua, oval, open pontil, 9" 175.00
Millings, R. C., Bed Bug Poison, Charleston, SC, clear, side shoulder strap, 6½" 20.00
Mulford, cobalt blue, skull and crossbones 15.00

Norwich, IGA, cobalt, 8" 75.00
Owl Drug Co, cobalt blue, carbolic acid
  label 65.00
The Oriental Embalming Fluid Poison,
  The Egyptian Chemical Co., Boston,
  MA, sq, emb, 9" h 40.00
Triloids, cobalt, three sided, 3½" 10.00
Wyeth, cobalt blue 10.00

POLITICAL ITEMS

History: Since 1800 the American presidency always has been a contest between two or more candidates. Initially souvenirs were issued to celebrate victories. Items issued during a campaign to show support for a candidate were actively being distributed in the William Henry Harrison election of 1840.

Campaign items cover a wide variety of materials—buttons, bandannas, tokens, pins, etc. The only limiting factor has been the promoter's imagination. The advent of television campaigning has reduced the emphasis on individual items. Modern campaigns do not seem to have the variety of materials which were issued earlier.

References: Herbert Collins, *Threads of History,* Smithsonian Institution Press, 1979; Theodore L. Hake, *Encyclopedia of Political Buttons, United States, 1896–1972,* Americana & Collectibles Press, 1985; Theodore L. Hake, *Political Buttons, Book II, 1920–1976,* Americana & Collectibles Press, 1977; Theodore L. Hake, *Political Buttons, Book III, 1789–1916,* Americana & Collectibles Press, 1978; Edmund B. Sullivan, *American Political Badges and Medalets, 1789–1892,* Quarterman Publications, Inc., 1981. (Note: Theodore L. Hake issued a revised set of prices for his three books in 1984.)

Collectors' Club: American Political Items Collectors, P.O. Box 340339, San Antonio, TX 78234.

Museum: Smithsonian Museum, Washington, D.C.

Note: The abbreviation "h/s" is used to identify a head and shoulder photo or etching of a person.

Additional Listings: See *Warman's Americana & Collectibles* for more examples.

Advisor: Theodore L. Hake.

Badge, 1¾ x 3½", Republican National
  Convention/1952 Chicago Press inscription, brass, white ribbon 25.00
Ballot, sample, Harrison-Morton, 1888,
  Maryland Republican ticket, blacksmith hand and hammer 12.00
Bandanna
  Cleveland-Stevenson,1892, 19 x 22",
    jugate, "Our Choice," red, white,
    and black, shields with engraved
    portraits, crossed flags and shield
    above, banner beneath, star border   150.00

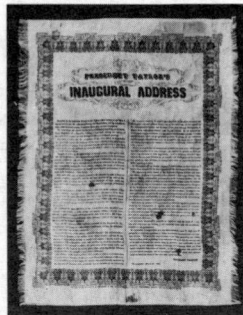

Broadside, 14 x 17¼", silk, President Taylor's Inaugural Address, March 5, 1849, printed by J Murphy & Co, Baltimore, MD, light green border, frayed on edges, soiled, $350.00.

Wilson, 1912, 17" sq, photo center, surrounded by state seals, corners with eagles, multicolored **100.00**

Bank, 2 x 3 x 4½", Roosevelt, metal, white, three dimensional, bronze finish, slotted hinged door trap base, key included, c1930 . . . . **50.00**

Banner, 6½ x 7", Roosevelt, fabric, red, white, and blue, yellow cord hanger, wood rod top, inscribed "To Keep The Nation Firm Give Him Another Term", 1940 . . . . **25.00**

Bookmark, Willkie, 7" l, jugate, aluminum, portraits on front, paragraph on back **50.00**

Button, Roosevelt, red, white, and blue, $5.00.

Button
Bryan, 1896, ⅞", silver ground, black letters, inscribed "I Never Use Gold-Do You?" **20.00**

Cox, 1920, 1¼", silhouette photo center, black and white, block letter border "Peace/Progress/Prosperity/For President" **200.00**

Dewey-Bricker, 1944, 1", jugate, silhouette portrait, sweeping arch names above, red, white, and blue . . . **30.00**

Harding, 1920, ⅞", center photo, black, blue, and white, white border with block letters, "For President/Warren G Harding" **8.00**

Kennedy, 6", color portrait, blue, white, and orange rim, inscribed "Man Of The Sixties/Inauguration Day January 20, 1961" **20.00**

McKinley, 1900, 1¾", portrait, rosy cheeks, bright gold ground **20.00**

Taft, 1910, 1½", jugate, Taft and William II portraits, white sepia, yellow, green, and red tinting, inscribed "Sixth Annual German Day, Aug 8, 1910-Compliments Of The DuBois Art Studio" **100.00**

Wilson-Marshall, 1916, ⅞", jugate, black and white portraits, red, white, and blue ground **25.00**

Clicker, Parker, 1904, 1¼", celluloid, multicolored, "For President Alton B Parker" **50.00**

Cigarette Box, Nixon, cardboard, red, white, and blue lid, inscribed "Campaign '72/I Want To Make It Perfectly Clear, I'm For Nixon/King Size Filter Cigarettes," unopened **25.00**

Cigarette Lighter, 1½ x 2¾ x ½", "Franklin D Roosevelt Our President" slogan and portrait, chromium plated, silver lines, c1930 . . . . **75.00**

Coaster, 3" d, Willkie, tin litho, blue and white portrait, eight raised metal star designs, raised dark red rim **15.00**

Cup, 4" h, waxed paper, red, white, and blue, "Eisenhower For President" and He'll "Never Win Unless Your Register And vote" slogans **10.00**

Cup Plate, Harrison, Fort Megis, 3½", log cabin center, "Tippecanoe/W H Harrison," meandering floral vine border **50.00**

Fan, Wilson, 1912, 8", heart shape, Washington, Lincoln, and Wilson portraits, multicolored, red, white, and blue star border, stick **25.00**

Glass, 5½" h, United States/Russian Summit Meeting, black building illus, white lettering "L B Johnson and A N Kosygin/Summit Meeting/Hollybush/Glassboro State College/Glassboro, NJ/June 23 and June 25/1967 on back" **12.00**

Invitation, Truman Inaugural Gala, emb

gold symbol, includes envelope, ticket ordering card, and return envelope . **40.00**

Handkerchief, 22 x 24¾", Harrison-Morton, 1888, white cotton, blue, red, and dark brown print, penciled numbers . **150.00**

Knife, pocket type, Wilson 1916 campaign, obverse bust portrait, reverse Uncle Sam **45.00**

License Plate

Landon, 8¾ x 6", white block letters, "Landon/Barrows/White," green ground **30.00**

Smith, 4 x 6", tin, oval, red, white, and blue, "Al Smith for President" ... **40.00**

Match Book Cover, Eisenhower-Nixon, 1952, Ike silhouette front, Nixon on back, red, white, and blue **4.00**

Match Safe, 2½" h, Cleveland 1888 campaign, brass, bust figural **150.00**

Medal

Taylor, 1848, 1⅝", front portrait, details on reverse, white metal **35.00**

Woodrow Wilson, 3" d, bronze, 1917 **45.00**

Paperweight, 3 x 3 x 1", clear glass, sepia photo, inscribed "G A R Washington, DC, October 6-11, 1902/President Theo Roosevelt" **75.00**

Pencil, mechanical

Johnson, 5¾", "Compliments of Lyndon B Johnson Your United States Senator," red white, and blue, top black and white photo and signature under plastic **20.00**

Roosevelt, Franklin D., 3½" l, blue portrait with "Roosevelt And Humanity" on one, black portrait and "Win With Willkie" on other, white pearlized finish, stars on blue ground top, red stripe bottom, pr . **40.00**

Pencil Cover, LBJ initials, 1964, 8", die-cut felt, red western hat **5.00**

Pennant, Kennedy-Johnson, 1960, banner with names across center, red, white, and blue **12.00**

Pin

Herbert Hoover 1932, 1", brass, raised detailed portrait, gold finish, made by "Medallic Art Co, NY" .. **10.00**

Stevenson For President, 1½", plastic, white, raised red lettering **15.00**

Pipe, Taft, clay, white, black and white enamel paint on eyes and mustache, blue paint tie, stem marked with name, serial number and maker's inscription "Gambier A Paris" **75.00**

Pitcher, 6" h, china, color portrait, Kennedy, White House, and family, gold trimmed top edge and handle, c1961 **15.00**

Plate

Dewey, 1949, 6½", china, white, blue Dewey illus, "New York State Fair/

Chamber of Commerce Farm Dinner/ Syracuse 1949" **10.00**

Taft-Sherman, 1908, 9¾", jugate, blue and white, seven Washington DC scenes border, marked "Rowland & Marsellus" **60.00**

Playing Card, deck, Mondale-Ferraro illus, blue on silver, inscribed "Fair Play Will Prevail/Minnesota AFL-CIO", sealed orig cellophane **8.00**

Pocket Watch, 2" d, Carter-Mondale, silver case, black and white photos and numbers, yellow circle border **40.00**

Postage Stamp Case, 2 x 3", McKinley Inauguration, silvered brass, front "President McKinley March 4, 1901" inscription around McKinley, Washington Monument, and the White House, reverse Capitol scene and "Postage Stamps" **75.00**

Postcard

Eisenhower, 1952, multicolored Ike in Cadillac convertible photo, Margaret Truman Launderette background **15.00**

McKinley, 1900, three quarter portrait in costume, "Sir Knight Wm McKinley, black and white **20.00**

Poster

McCarthy 1968 Campaign, "Peace," sgd "Ben Shahn" **90.00**

McGovern, 14 x 22", red, white, and blue, flag design **10.00**

Rockefeller, 22 x 28", black and white, governor campaign, c1960 ..... **10.00**

Program, 8½ x 11", Truman Inauguration 1949, 72 pgs, black and white photos **30.00**

Puzzle, Richard Nixon, 500 pcs, 15 x 22" finished, picture on each side, orig box with same picture each side, copyright 1970, The Puzzle Factory . **10.00**

Ribbon

John C Fremont, 1856 Campaign, blue, bust portrait **175.00**

Lincoln Birth Centennial, Lincoln/Clinton, IA/1809–1909, 2¼ x 6", silk, black, sepia cello portrait button center, gold inscription **10.00**

Ring, Ike, plastic, dark green, white scroll design **15.00**

Salt and Pepper Shaker, china, figure, John F Kennedy salt, rocking chair pepper, brown detailing **30.00**

Sheet Music, *Answer Mr. Wilson's Call*, 4 pgs, patriotic cov **15.00**

Stereo Cards, McKinley-Hobart, 1901, floral funeral scene, sepia portraits, inked dates of death on back ·..... **3.00**

Stickpin

Bryan, 1900, paper photo, black and white, brass frame, orig luster ... **25.00**

Parker, 1904, sepia portrait, brass . . **10.00**
Sticker, window, Willkie-McNary, 3 x 5″,
   blue and white, orange stars **10.00**
Tab
   Bryan, 1900, cardboard, red, white,
     and blue bow design portrait center,
     inscribed "For President William J
     Bryan" **10.00**
   Hoover, 1928, ¾″, litho, red, white,
     and blue **5.00**
Textile, 20 x 26″, shield shape, cotton,
   printed eagle, crossed flags, and
   Washington and Harrison busts with
   1789 and 1889 dates of death, woven
   black linen backing **115.00**
Token
   Grant Monument Souvenir, 1890, ½″,
     brass, "Let's Have Peace," slogan,
     Lord's Prayer back, monument . . **5.00**
   Harrison, 1840, 1⅛″, brass, date of
     birth and portrait front, log cabin
     back **10.00**
Toothpick Holder, Roosevelt-Fairbanks
   1904 campaign, custard glass, trans-
   fer **125.00**
Watch Fob
   Bryan-Kern, enamel/brass, red,
     white, and blue, spread winged ea-
     gle center, 1908 . . . . **35.00**
   Our Next President William H Taft,
     metal, white, some silver gilt finish
     remains **25.00**

POMONA GLASS

History: Pomona glass, produced only by the New England Glass Works and named for the Roman goddess of fruit and trees, was patented in 1885 by Joseph Locke. It is a delicate lead, blown art glass which has a pale, soft beige ground and a top one inch band of honey amber.

There are two distinct types of backgrounds. First ground, made only from late 1884 to June 1886, was produced by fine cuttings through a wax coating followed by an acid bath. Second ground was made by rolling the piece in acid resisting particles and acid etching. Second ground was made in Cambridge until 1888 and until the early 1900s in Toledo where Libbey moved the firm after purchasing New England Glass works. Both methods produced a soft frosted appearance, with fine curlicue lines more visible on first ground pieces. Designs are used on some pieces, which were etched and then stained in color. The most familiar design is blue cornflowers.

Do not confuse Pomona with "Midwestern Pomona," a pressed glass with a frosted body and amber band.

Reference: Joseph and Jane Locke, *Locke Art Glass: A Guide For Collectors,* Dover Publications, 1987.

Punch Cup, 2⅛″ d, 2⅜″ h, Cornflower, second grind, $80.00.

Cruet, 7¼″ h, pansy and butterfly dec,
   2nd grind, amber irid stopper **465.00**
Lemonade Glass
   DQ, 5¾″ h, clear handle and rim, 1st
     grind **165.00**
   Rivulet dec, 2nd grind **185.00**
Pitcher
   4½″ h, IVT, sq top, 1st grind **350.00**
   6¾″ h, IVT, bluebird and flowers . . . **100.00**
   7″ h, red and jade green stained mai-
     denhair fern, 1st grind **185.00**
Toothpick Holder, swirled amber stripes,
   tri-corner rim **350.00**
Tray, 12½ x 7½″, blue stained cornflow-
   ers, 2nd grind **400.00**
Tumbler
   Acorn and Oak Leaves, blue and am-
     ber **25.00**
   Blueberries, blue stained berries, 2nd
     grind **165.00**
   Cornflower
     1st grind **85.00**
     2nd grind **80.00**
Vase, 6¼″ h, ovoid, amber stained
   flared rim, wafer base, 1st grind . . . **285.00**
Water Set, pitcher, eight tumblers,
   stained, blue cornflowers, amber rim,
   1st grind, 9 pcs **950.00**
Wine, 4⅝″ h, DQ, applied clear stem
   and foot, 2nd grind **90.00**

PORTRAIT WARE

History: Plates, vases, and other articles with portraits on them were popular in the second half of the 19th century. Although male subjects, such as Napoleon or Louis XVI, were used, the ware usually depicted a beautiful woman, often unidentified.

A large number of English and Continental China manufacturers made portrait ware. Because most ware was hand painted, an artist's signature often is found.

Additional Listings: KPM and Royal Vienna.

Compote, 9½", portrait dec in bowl, cobalt blue ground, gold dec, two handles **165.00**

Cup and Saucer, 5 x 7", three small round portraits of men and women dressed in 18th C attire in int., large center portrait of Louis XVI on saucer, dark rose, teal blue, and gold, marked "N" with crown, artist sgd **100.00**

Dresser Tray, 12" l, two portrait medallions, four floral medallions, gold design, white ground, marked "Nippon" **225.00**

Jewel Box, 10½ x 5", blown-out florals, ribbons on cov, center multicolored portrait of seated woman, 18th C attire, beige ground, gold highlights, marked "Mt Washington" **950.00**

Plaque, pierced for hanging
  9¾", cavalier, hp, artist sgd, marked "Coronet" **165.00**
  10", Lund, hp, artist sgd "F Tenner," beehive mark **350.00**
  10¼", bust of beautiful lady, green ground, gold rococo border, artist sgd, marked "Coronet" **165.00**

Veiled woman, white robe and hat, holding fan, marked "Volkstadt" **75.00**
10"
  American Indian, hp, artist sgd "Coronet" **65.00**
  Queen Louise, beehive mark **110.00**
11¾", five portraits of Louis XV, Marie Theresa, and Marie Antoinette, gold trim, blue ground, pierced for hanging **140.00**
17", woman, jade green border, gold trim, marked "Victoria, Austria" .. **150.00**

Shaving Mug, woman, dressed in brown and white, white plumes and red ribbon on hat **65.00**

Tile, lady wearing large hat, round ... **42.50**

Vase
  6", tapestry, three classical ladies, marked "Germany" **165.00**
  10", blonde lady, daisies in hair, multicolored flowers, gold scroll handles **250.00**
  14", titled lady, burgundy ground, heavy gold trim **300.00**

Plate, 8½" d, lady with dark hair, gray scarf, shaded ochre rim, marked "TVL, Franzant Mehlem," $50.00.

Plate
  6½", young woman, lacy gold border, marked "R. S. Malmaison" **30.00**
  8", Queen Louise, gold trim, marked "Elite, Limoges, France" **45.00**
  8½", medallions of Josephine, Maria de Medici, and Duchess de Bourgogne, floral medallions, scalloped gilt edge **65.00**
  9½"
    Amicitia, brunette woman, gold trim, blue underglaze beehive mark **175.00**

POSTERS

History: The poster was an extremely effective and critical means of mass communication, especially in the period before 1920. Enormous quantities were produced, helped in part by the propaganda role posters played in World War I.

Print runs of two million were not unknown. Posters were not meant to be saved. Once they served their purpose, they tended to be destroyed. The paradox of high production and low survival is one of the fascinating aspects of poster history.

The posters of the late 19th century and early 20th century represent the pinnacle of American lithography printing. The advertising posters of firms such as Strobridge or Courier are true classics. Philadelphia was one center for the poster industry.

Europe pioneered in posters with high artistic and aesthetic content. Many major artists of the 20th century designed posters. Poster art still plays a key role throughout Europe today.

References: John Barnicoat, *A Concise History of Posters*, Harry Abrams, Inc., 1976; George Theofiles, *American Posters of World War I: A Price and Collector's Guide*, Dafram House Publishers, Inc.; Walton Rawls, *Wake Up, America!: World War I and The American Poster*, Abbeville Press, 1988; Stephen Rebello and Richard Allen, *Reel Art: Great Posters From The Golden Age of The Silver Screen*, Abbeville Press, 1988.

Additional Listings: See *Warman's Americana & Collectibles* for more examples.

Advisor: George Theofiles.

ADVERTISING

"Cars Love Shell," 48 x 33, amusing image, yellow, red, blue, black, and orange, bright green ground, American 90.00

"Cognac J. Dupont & Co," Champenois, 24 x 35", beautiful woman wearing flowered hat and flowing attire, holding glass of cognac, Art Nouveau border 475.00

"Hauswaldt's Chocolade," 19 x 31", c1905, cup of hot chocolate, smiling girl's face, red and orange, green Art Nouveau border 200.00

"Plow Boy Tobacco," 40 x 18", c1900, litho on cloth, Plow Boy package . . . 125.00

"Styleplus Clothes," 1919, 28 x 18", gentleman hailing cab in styleplus clothes 70.00

"Take Some Home - Independent Brewing Co. Of Pittsburgh," Maynard Williamson, 21 x 11", c1910, old fashioned beer bottle, car card 90.00

"Wilhelm Moser Restaurant," Ludwig Hohlwein, 36 x 49", 1909, still life, seafood, champagnes, liqueurs, and fruits, deep burgundy border 1,200.00

"Wings Cigarettes," 24 x 11", blue, green, yellow, brown, and red 50.00

CIRCUS, SHOWS, AND ACTS

"Biller Bros 3 Ring Wild Animal Circus," 28 x 42", attacking tiger, red, black, orange, blue, and green, stark white ground 80.00

"Blackstone and His Big Magical Revue," 28 x 22", Baltimore stage performance 50.00

"Clyde Beatty Circus," Roland Butler, 28 x 21", red, yellow, blue, and black . . 75.00

"Downie Bros, Big 3-Ring Circus/ Leaps," Erie, 27 x 41", c1925, litho, performers leaping over elephants, horses, and camels 125.00

Hagenbeck-Wallace, "Trained Wild Animal Circus/The Great Angelu Troupe," 41 x 28", c1935, troupe engaged in acrobatic marvels 175.00

Ringling Bros and Barnum & Bailey, Bill Bailey, "World's Largest Menagerie," 24 x 28, c1944, charging rhino, emerging from yellow-green jungle landscape, affixed orig date sheet . . 75.00

MOVIE

One Sheet, Silent
  "Broken Chains," 1923, Coleen Moore, 22 x 14" 60.00
  "Dawn of Revenge," 1922, Richard C.

Travers, 41 x 27", stone litho, red, yellow, brown, and black, black on blue ground 225.00

"Madame Sans Gene," 1922, Gloria Swanson, 11 x 14", color portrait, Paramount 175.00

"The Black Pirate," 1926, Douglas Fairbanks, 22 x 28", three color tinted action scenes 1,200.00

One Sheet, 27 x 41"
  "Border Badmen," 1945, Buster Crabbe 45.00
  "Boy Of The Streets," 1937, Jackie Cooper, portrait, red, yellow, blue, green, and brown 100.00
  "Five Bad Men," c1930, Noah Berry, Continental Litho 125.00
  "Hidden Danger," Johnny Mack Brown, 1948, Brown portrait with gun in hand, small Raymond Hatton and Max Terhune images ... 50.00
  "High Noon," 1956, Gary Cooper, Cooper and Grace Kelly sepia tone image on white paper 60.00
  "Of Mice And Men," 1939, Betty Field, pin-up, Hal Roach Studios, United Artists 200.00
  "Phantom Stallion," 1954, Rex Allan, Allan and Koko portrait, Slim Pickens vignette 50.00
  "Riders Of The Dawn," c1935, Jack Randall, Monogram Pictures 125.00
  "The Daltons Ride Again," 1945, Lon Chaney, Noah Beery, Jr, Universal 40.00
  "The Showdown," 1940, William Boyd, Hopalong tied to wagon wheel, gunmen shadows approach, Paramount 100.00
  "The Bronze Venus," c1943, Lena Horne, Morgan Litho 135.00
  "Where The Buffalo Roam," c1935, Tex Ritter, Monogram Pictures ... 125.00

Three Sheets
  "Charlie Chan In The Feathered Serpent," 41 x 81", c1944, Roland Winters, Keye Luke, and two Oriental stars, Monogram Pictures . . 150.00
  "Cuentema Tu Vida," (Spanish title for Spellbound), 40 x 80", 1945, Ingrid Bergman embracing Gregory Peck as he holds straight razor, deep black ground, "United Artists 900.00

THEATRICAL

"A Square Man," Strobridge, c1893, 30 x 40", man holding tablet before group of men, exploding cave background 150.00

"Fantasies of 1929," Larry Benner, 28 x 20", vaudeville dancer, chorus line dances behind her 75.00

"Felix Ferry," 1931, 40 x 26", black and white tuxedoed singer, some foxing . **200.00**

"O'Reilly's Party," c1893, Murray & Murray, 22 x 28", two restrained men in party scene, double portrait insert upper right **125.00**

"Peck's Bad Boy," 29 x 14", boy posed impishly before Perkins & Co grocery emporium **100.00**

"Rosemarie," 40 x 90", British WW2 production litho, Canadian Mountie, Western Canadian setting **200.00**

"Three Penny Opera," Paul Davis, 82 x 41", printed on two panels **300.00**

"Uncle Tom's Cabin," T. D. Middaugh's Original New Orleans, 28 x 21", Eliza and black faced Topsy portraits, flower bouquet, red, blue, pink, green, yellow, and brown **175.00**

TRANSPORTATION

"Braniff International Airways," 29 x 26", map showing cities served by Braniff, two continents **75.00**

"Clement Cycles and Automobiles, Paris," F. Bombled, 49 x 36", c1914, French army officers, riding in Clement motorcar **325.00**

"Olympic Rubber Co," Louis Raemaekers, 28 x 38", c1910, man in tuxedo, holding new slender tire in air **900.00**

"Renault," 1925, 63 x 46", car racing across dirt country roads, cloud of dust, red, yellow, blue, green, and black, open reserve bottom **500.00**

"Snow Trains/Boston and Maine RR," C. Neuwelt, c1935, 29 x 21", blue, brown, red, tan, and black, stylized air brush design, close-up laughing lady headed for ski slopes **100.00**

"The Greyhound Lines," Walt Brownson, 20 x 20", c1938, streamlined bus, passing Southern plantation . . **150.00**

WORLD WAR I

"A Wonderful Opportunity For You/United States Navy," 38 x 20", prewar recruiting design, orange, yellow, gray, blue, and black **150.00**

"Every Girl Pulling For Victory," Edward Penfield, 28 x 22", red, white, and blue, woman wearing sailor blouse, pulling oars on boat "Victory" **125.00**

"Follow The Flag For Freedom, The Navy Strikes Now," James Daugherty, 14 x 22", stylized Columbia pointing sword to multicolored horizon affront flag, sailor looks on **125.00**

"I Summon You To Comradeship In The Red Cross," Harrison Fisher, 39 x 29",

girl draped in American flag, shimmering US capitol ground **140.00**

"Men Wanted For The Army," 40 x 30", 1910 . . . . **50.00**

"Voiteg Preissig," 36 x 25", young soldier wielding axe and rifle, green landscape, red bolts of lightning, black clouds **175.00**

WORLD WAR II

"Americans Suffer When Careless Talk Kills!," 20 x 14", viewer of woman crushing Western Union telegram to breast, forlornly staring elderly couple look on **40.00**

"Care Is Costly," Adolph Treidler, 26 x 18", bandaged soldier sends message "Buy War Bonds & Stamps" . . **60.00**

"Every Mother's Son Is Counting On You," 40 x 20, Navy life scenes photo **50.00**

"Keep 'Em Rolling," 40 x 30", gun crew montage, red, white, and blue field . **70.00**

"Loose Talk Can Cost Lives," C. C. Beall, 15 x 20", pair beer drinking factory workers, smiling Hitler background **75.00**

"My Girl's A Wow/Woman Ordnance Worker," Adolph Treidler, 40 x 28", smiling soldier shares photo of his girl **80.00**

"Remember Dec. 7th!," 28 x 22", tattered American flag, raised at half mast, flame and smoke background **120.00**

"Save Waste Fats For Explosives," W. H. D. Koerner, 22 x 15", unusual design **50.00**

POT LIDS

History: Pot lids are the lids from pots or small containers which originally held ointments, pomades, or soap. Although a complete set of pot and lid is desirable to some collectors, lids are the most collectible. The lids frequently were decorated with multicolored underglaze transfers of rural and domestic scenes, portraits, florals, and landmarks.

The majority of the containers with lids were made between 1845–1920 by F. & R. Pratt, Fenton, Staffordshire, England. In 1920, F. & R. Pratt merged with Cauldon Ltd. Several lids were reissued by the firm using the original copper engraving plates. They were used for decoration and never served as actual lids. Reissues by Kirkhams Pottery, England, generally have two holes for hanging and often are marked as reissues. Cauldon, Coalport, and Wedgwood were other firms making reissues.

References: Susan and Al Bagdade, *Warman's English & Continental Pottery & Porcelain, 1st Edi-*

tion, Warman Publishing Co., Inc., 1987; A. Ball, *The Price Guide to Pot-Lids And Other Underglaze Multicolor Prints On Ware,* Antique Collectors' Club, 1980; Barbara and Sonny Jackson, *American Pot Lids,* published by authors, 1987.

Note: Sizes are given for actual pot lids; size of any framing not included.

Baby and Dog	50.00
Battle Of The Nile, Pratt, ebonized oak frame, 4″	250.00
Bellevue Tavern, Pratt, 4¾″	150.00
Church Of The Holy Trinity, Stratford on Avon, 4¾″	450.00
Cries of London	45.00
Dr Johnson, 4⅛″	375.00
Enthusiast, The	145.00
French Street Scene, Fenton, 4⅛″	80.00
Garibaldi	105.00
Good Dog, circular ebonized frame, gilt liner, 5″	250.00

Pratt, 4″ d, Walmer Castle, $200.00.

Lady with Guitar	125.00
Landing the Fare	185.00
Late Prince Consort, The, Fenton, circular mahogany stained frame, 4⅛″	125.00
L'Exposition Universelle De 1867	40.00
Letter From the Diggings, A, Fenton, circular mahogany frame, 4″	200.00
Lobster Sauce, Pratt	275.00
Pair, A	155.00
Peace	50.00
Pegwell Bay, Fenton, 4¼″	200.00
Philadelphia Exhibition 1876, framed, 4¼″	400.00
Pretty Kettle Of Fish, third variety, Fenton, circular mahogany frame, 4″	150.00
Race, A	175.00
Residence of Anne Hathaway	120.00
Revenge, registry marks	155.00
Royal Harbour, Rumsgate	75.00
Ruined Temple, The	35.00
Second Appeal, The, Fenton, 4⅛″	100.00

Seven Ages of Man, The, framed, 4⅛″	225.00
Shrimpers, The, Fenton, 4⅛	50.00
Skewbald Horse, The	110.00
Sportsman, The	85.00
Strasberg, marbleized surround, matching jar	200.00
Tam O'Shanter, Fenton, circular mahogany frame, 4″	150.00
Thames Embankment, framed, 3¾″	300.00
Times, The, Fenton, circular mahogany frame, 4″	100.00
Truant, The	65.00
Uncle Toby	30.00
Village Wedding, The	80.00
Walmer Castle Kent, with sentry, marked "Tatnell & Son Manufacturers Pegwell Bay Near Ramsgate," framed, 4½″	200.00
Wimbledon 1860	165.00
Wolf and Lamb	100.00

PRATT

PRATT
FENTON

PRATT WARE

History: The earliest Pratt earthenware was made in the late 18th century by William Pratt, Lane Delph, Staffordshire, England. In 1810–1818, Felix and Robert Pratt, William's sons, established their own firm, F. & R. Pratt, in Fenton in the Staffordshire district. Potters in Yorkshire, Liverpool, Sunderland, Tyneside, and Scotland copied the ware.

The wares consisted of relief molded jugs, commercial pots and tablewares with transfer decoration, commemorative pieces, and figure and animal groups.

Much of the early ware is unmarked. The mid-19th century wares bear several different marks in conjunction with the name Pratt, including "& Co."

References: Susan and Al Bagdade, *Warman's English & Continental Pottery & Porcelain, 1st Edition,* Warman Publishing Co., Inc., 1987; John and Griselda Lewis, *Pratt Ware 1780–1840,* Antique Collectors' Club, 1984.

Additional Listing: Pot Lids

Bouquet Holder, 6¾″, cornucopia, 2 children standing on either side, blue, green, brown, and ochre, c1790	500.00
Cottage, 3½″, small white bricks, doors and window outlined in blue, panes and roof in yellow, c1820	275.00
Creamer, 4¾″, raised dec of children at play, heart shaped cartouche, underglaze blue, green, and brown	175.00

Plate, 8½″ d, Philadelphia Public Building, blue ground, $125.00.

Figure, 8″, Flora, c1790 . . . . 200.00
Inkwell, 1¾″, figural, dog on footstool,
  c1800 . . . . 400.00
Jar, cov, lid dec
  4″, round, Shakespeare's Birthplace
    Stratford-on-Avon pearl dot border 200.00
  4¾″, oblong, The Stone Jetty, sgd
    "Fenton" 150.00
Miniature, cradle, sleeping child, yellow
  and dark blue 350.00
Mug, 5¼″, frog 130.00
Pipe, 10″, coiled snake, yellow and
  brown dec, blue dots, c1780 . . . . . . 1,200.00
Pitcher
  6¼″, naval heroes, Captains Hardy
    and Nelson, brown, blue, black,
    and ochre, c1797 . . . . 350.00
  9⅛″, drinking scene, polychrome,
    emb 200.00
Plaque, 13″, Christ in the Wheat Field,
  multicolored, turned out rim, sgd "J
  Austin," c1851 . . . . 100.00
Plate
  8½″, Philadelphia Exhibition 1876 . . 125.00
  9″, Haddon Hall, classic figures, bor-
    der, sgd "Fenton, England" 75.00
Pot Lids, see POT LIDS
Sauce Boat, 7 x 4½″, fox head body,
  swan head, neck, and wings as handle, brown, green, blue, and ochre,
  c1770 . . . . 1,200.00
Tea Bowl and Saucer, 5¼ x 2⅜″, pea-
  fowl perched on leafy branch, blue,
  yellow, green, and ochre 275.00
Tea Caddy, 4½″, relief of comedians,
  three color, lid missing 150.00
Teapot, 10 x 5¼″, relief dec of drapes
  and tassels, leaves and husks, gray-
  green, olive green, and ochre, c1790 400.00
Toby Jug, 3½″, Englishman, multico-
  lored 100.00

PRINTS

History: Prints serve many purposes. They can be a reproduction of an artist's paintings, drawings, or designs. Prints themselves often are an original art form. Finally, prints can be developed for mass appeal as opposed to aesthetic statement. Much of the production of Currier & Ives fits this latter category. Currier & Ives concentrated on genre, urban, patriotic, and nostalgia scenes.

Prints are beginning to attract a wide following. This is partially because prices have not matched the rapid rise in oil and other paintings.

References: Frederic A. Conningham and Colin Simkin, *Currier & Ives Prints, Revised Edition*, Crown Publishers, Inc., 1970; Michael Ivankovich, *A Price Guide to Wallace Nutting Pictures*, Cheetah Prints, 1984; Denis C. Jackson, *The Price & Identification Guide to J. C. Leyendecker & F. X. Leyendecker*, published by author, 1983; Carl F. Luckey, *Collector Prints Old and New*, Books Americana, 1982; Craig McClain, *Currier & Ives: An Illustrated Value Guide*, Wallace-Homestead, 1987; Wallace Nutting, *The Wallace Nutting Expansible Catalog* (reprint of 1915 catalog), Diamond Press, 1987; Ruth M. Pollard, *The Official Price Guide To Collector Prints, 7th Edition*, House Of Collectibles, 1986.

Collectors' Clubs: American Historical Print Collectors Society, Inc., 25 West 43rd St., Suite 711, New York, NY 10036. *Imprint*; Prang-Mark Society, Century House, Old Irelandville, Watkins Glen, NY 14891. *Prang-Mark Society Newsletter*.

Reproduction Alert: Reproductions are a problem, especially Currier & Ives prints. Check the dimensions before buying any print.

Ackermann, Arthur, & Sons, Inc, NY,
  Whaling in American Waters, hand
  colored litho, foam on waves highlighted in white oil paint, medium folio,
  orig label 250.00
Albee, Grace Thurston Arnold, Ameri-
  can, Nayatt, etching, sgd in pencil
  across lower margin "ED 35, Nayatt,
  Grace A Albee, N.A./1954," full margins, 6¼ x 7½″, good condition mat
  and frame 275.00
Arms, John Taylor, The Sarah Jane,
  etching and drypoint, sgd in pencil,
  numbered 62/78, titled, 1920, 10½ x
  7⅛″ 850.00
Audubon, John J., American, 1785–
  1851
  American Avocet, #318, published by
    Robert Havell, London, Whitman
    watermarked paper, 1826–38, 29½
    x 25¼″ 1,600.00
  American Crow, #225, published by
    Bien, late 1850s, foxed, trimmed . 100.00
  American Robin, #142, published by
    J T Bowen, 1840–71, 11 x 7″ . . . 325.00

Bonaparte's Flycatcher, #72, published by Bien, late 1850s, unevenly toned, 26 x 19" **700.00**

Brown Finch, #187, published by J T Bowen, 1840–71, 11 x 7" **75.00**

Carolina Wren, #78, published by Robert Havell, London, Whitman watermarked paper, 1826–38, foxed, 38 x 25¼" **100.00**

Common Mockingbird, #138, published by Bien, late 1850s, 39 x 26" **2,500.00**

Mallard Duck, #385, published by J T Bowen, 1840–71, 11 x 7" **425.00**

Pigeon Hawk, #104, published by Robert Havell, London, Whitman watermarked paper, 1826–38 26 x 20½" **1,200.00**

Redwing Starling, #216, published by Bien, late 1850s, 39 x 26" **1,250.00**

Savannah Bunting, #160, published by J T Bowen, 1840–71, 11 x 7" . **175.00**

Virginia Rail, #205, published by Robert Havell, London, Whitman watermarked paper, 1826–38 . . . **2,600.00**

Whip-Poor-Will, #42, published by J T Bowen, 1840–71, 11 x 7" **250.00**

Yellow Billed Cuckoo, #275, published by Bien, late 1850s, 39 x 26" **1,750.00**

Bartlett, William Henry

Schuylkill Water Works, hand colored litho, 6 x 8" **50.00**

View from Mt Holyoke, hand colored litho, 6 x 8" **50.00**

Baskin, Leonard, Conrad, woodcut, pencil sgd lower right, numbered 26/90, oval, 4½ x 3½" **125.00**

Beal, Reynolds, American 1867–1951

Cape Cod, etching, sgd and dated in pencil lower left "Reynolds Beal/1915," full margins, 7¾ x 9¾", good condition mat and frame **300.00**

Gloucester, etching, sgd and dated in pencil lower left "Reynolds Beal/1929," full margins, 6⅛ x 10", good condition mat and frame **200.00**

North Truro-Cape Cod, etching, sgd and dated in pencil lower left "Reynolds Beal/1915," full margins, 7¾ x 9¾", good condition mat and frame **400.00**

Benson, Frank Weston, American, 1862–1951

Evening Flight, 1927, litho, artist's proof, label on reverse "Arthur H. Harlow & Co., Inc., NY," sgd in pencil lower left, title on reverse, full margins, 7¾ x 9¾", matted and framed **700.00**

In Dropping Flight, 1926, etching, trial proof (one of four), label on reverse "Arthur H Harlow and Co., Inc, NY," sgd in pencil lower left "Frank W

Benson," titled on reverse, full margins, 10¾ x 13½", good condtion mat and frame **1,300.00**

The Alarm, 1917, etching, artist's proof, label on reverse "Arthur H Harlow and Co., Inc, NY," sgd in pencil lower left "Frank W Benson," titled on reverse, full margins, 7¾ x 9¾", good condtion mat and frame **900.00**

Biddle, George, American, 1885–1973, Three Graces, etching, pencil sgd, dated 1926 lower right, 13 x 9½" . . . **100.00**

Birch, William Russell, American, 1755–1834, High Street from the Country Marketplace, Philadelphia - Procession of the Death of George Washington, engraving, 8¼ x 11" **200.00**

Burr, George Elbert, American, 1859–1939, The Mirage, drypoint, sgd in pencil, numbered 31/40, wove paper, 6¾ x 9¾ **300.00**

Calder, Alexander, American, 1898–1976, Crescent and Moon, litho, pencil sgd lower right, numbered 62/90, 22½ x 17¾" **400.00**

Chagall, Marc, Solomon, sgd in pencil, color litho, numbered 34/75, 1956, cream wove, full sheet printed to edges, 14 x 10¼" **1,400.00**

Currier & Ives, American, c1860

A Staunch Pointer, litho, paper toned, slightly foxed, good margins, small folio, orig frame **450.00**

American Homestead Autumn, litho, paper toned, two small tears upper center, good margins, small folio, period Victorian frame **350.00**

American Homestead Spring, litho, slightly foxed, good margins, small folio, period Victorian frame **300.00**

American Homestead Summer, litho, slightly foxed, good margins, small folio, period Victorian frame **275.00**

American Homestead Winter, litho, paper toned, good margins, small folio, period Victorian frame **700.00**

Camping Out, Some of the Right Sort, litho, not full margins, large folio, old fruitwood frame **1,500.00**

Fruit Piece, litho, full margins, small folio, orig frame **175.00**

Lake George, NY, litho, deeply toned, foxed, good margins, small folio, natural finish orig frame **100.00**

My Boyhood's Home, litho, full margins, small folio, period Victorian frame **325.00**

On A Point, litho, evenly toned and faced, full margins, water mark in upper left margin, small folio **600.00**

Polk, James K., litho, paper toned, evenly faded, small folio, orig frame **75.00**

Stratford on Avon, litho, excellent margins, good color, some foxing, small folio, orig frame **75.00**

The Fall of Richmond, Va. on the Night of April 2nd, 1865, litho, paper toned and lightly foxed, good margins, small folio, period Victorian frame **235.00**

The Life of a Fireman, hand colored litho, 17 x 25¾" **1,500.00**

Durer, Albrecht

St. Christopher, engraving 1521, inscribed in ink on reverse, collection stamp, good impression, trimmed, 4⅝ x 2⅞", framed **1,600.00**

Torch Dance At Augsburg, The, woodcut, c1516, good impression, first state, thin laid paper, trimmed to borderline, 9 x 9¾" **2,300.00**

Virgin On A Crescent With Crown Of Stars And Scepter, The, engraving, 1516, fair impression, laid paper, thread margins, 4¼ x 3" **400.00**

Eby, Kerr, American, 1889–1946, Christmas Trees, etching, sgd in pencil, white wove paper, full margins, 9¼ x 12¾" **600.00**

Eldred, Lemuel D., American, 1848–1921

Fishing Village, etching, sgd in etching and in pencil lower right "L D Eldred," minor wrinkles, full margins, 4 x 6½", matted and framed **375.00**

Hauling Nets, etching, sgd in etching and in pencil lower right "L D Eldred," minor wrinkles, full margins, 4¼ x 6½", matted and framed **400.00**

Low Tide, etching, sgd in etching lower right, sgd in pencil in margin lower right, paper toned to woody brown, full margins, 4⅛ x 6¾", good mat and frame **475.00**

Ship Under Sail, etching, printed by H I Jenkins, sgd in etching lower left "L D Eldred," sgd in pencil by printer lower right, paper toned, full margins, 6½ x 12", framed **575.00**

Endicott & Co, NY, 1859, publisher, Sperm Whaling No. 1 - The Chase, created from drawings by Albert Van Best and Robert Swain Gifford with corrections by Benjamin Russell, large folio, litho, orig gold leaf frame **1,200.00**

Fox, R Atkinson, Canadian, 1860–1935

Approaching Storm **55.00**

Poppies **40.00**

Spirit of Youth **65.00**

Friedlander, Johnny, Abstract Figures Reclining, litho, pencil sgd lower right, numbered 75/100, 23 x 31" **275.00**

Gallagher, Sears, American, 1869–1955, Afternoon Respite, etching, sgd

in etching lower left with cojoined monogram, full name sgd in pencil in lower left, full margins, 5¾ x 8¾", good condition mat and frame **325.00**

Gifford, Robert Swain, American, 1840–1905

Hunting, etching, sgd and dated in etching, "R Swain Gifford/79," full margins, 4¼ x 7¾", matted, unframed **200.00**

Mideastern Village, etching, sgd and dated in etching "R Swain Gifford/1891," large water stain upper left into etching, water stain bottom margin, full margins, 4⅜ x 7¼", framed **140.00**

Mouth of the Apponagansett River, etching, sgd and dated in etching lower left "R Swain Gifford/1883," sgd in pencil lower right, full margins, 7¾ x 11", matted and framed **850.00**

Windblown Trees, etching, sgd and dated in etching "R Swain Gifford/1868," sgd below etching "Drawn and etched by R Swain Gifford," full margins, 4¾ x 7", good condition mat and frame **300.00**

Grant, Gordon Hope, American, 1875–1962

Sun and Shadow, litho, published by Associated American Artists, NY, title on label on back, sgd in pencil lower right, 9 x 12", matted and framed **325.00**

The Sand Dune, litho, sgd in pencil lower right, full margins, 9 x 11¾", matted and framed **100.00**

Gutmann, Bessie Pease

An Anxious Moment, litho, hand colored, 18½ x 16", orig mat and frame **45.00**

Nitey-nite, litho, hand colored, 12 x 21" **25.00**

The New Love, litho, hand colored, 15 x 11", orig frame **40.00**

Wedding March, litho, hand colored, 16 x 21", orig frame **85.00**

Homer, Winslow, Union Pond, Williamsburgh, Long Island, 26¾ x 16⅞", c1862, litho by Thomas & Eno **3,500.00**

Icart, Louis, French, US copyrights after 1920

Apple Girl, litho, fourteen colors, 1928, double matted, gold frame . **400.00**

Blancherus, litho, sgd in pencil, blindstamp, 1921, 20 x 15½" **857.00**

In The Nest, litho, sgd in pencil, framed **950.00**

Japanese Garden, litho, sgd in pencil, good condition mat and frame . . . **1,000.00**

Laughing, litho, sgd in pencil, blindstamp, framed **1,100.00**

Paris Flowers, litho, sgd in pencil, framed **1,200.00**

Speed II, litho, sgd in pencil, published by Icart Society NY, annotated **2,250.00**

Kellog

Battle of Champion Hills, MS, May 16, 1863, litho **120.00**

Double Fishing, litho, small folio ... **150.00**

Rural Sweets, litho **60.00**

Thomas Wildey, Father of the Order of Oddfellows, litho **48.00**

Kinney, Troy, American, 1870–1938

Arcadia, etching, sgd and presentation in lower left, foxed, full margins, 6½ x 7½", fair condition mat and frame **40.00**

The Serenade, etching, sgd and presentation in lower margin, full margins, 6¼ x 7½", fair condition mat and frame **25.00**

Kurz and Allison, American, 1833–1903

Battle of Antietam, Sept 17 1862, litho, large folio **200.00**

Battle of Lexington, litho, black and white, medium folio, slightly foxed **35.00**

Columbus Returns to Barcelona, litho, color, large folio **150.00**

Flags of the Union, 1898, litho, color, large folio **165.00**

Storming Stony Point, litho, black and white, medium folio **35.00**

Washington Entering Trenton, litho, black and white, medium folio ... **50.00**

Levine, Jack, Gangster's Funeral, etching, pencil sgd lower right, numbered 101/120, 19½ x 25½" **250.00**

Mason, Roy Martell, American, 1886–1972, Guides, etching, sgd, titled with presentation in pencil in lower margin, full margins, 9 x 3¾", good condition mat, unframed **200.00**

McKenney and Hall, American

John Ridge, Cherokee Chief, Greenough, 1836, litho, 14 x 20" **125.00**

Mon Chonsia, Kansas Chief, Rice and Clark, 1843, litho, 14 x 20" .. **200.00**

Waa Pa Shaw, Sioux Chief, Biddle, 1836, litho, 14 x 20" **175.00**

Moskowitz, Ira, American, Newburgh Ferry, published by Public Works of Art Project, NY, litho, sgd in pencil lower right, full margins, 7¾ x 11¾", unframed **100.00**

Nutting, Wallace, American, 1862–1941

Bit of Gossip, litho, 16" **100.00**

Garden Steps, Mrs Nutting's Floral Arrangements, litho, 8 x 10" **65.00**

Going Forth of Betty, litho, 6 x 9½" . **120.00**

Hollyhock Cottage, litho, 11 x 13" .. **35.00**

Old Drawing Room, litho, 13" **100.00**

Stitch in Time, MA, litho, 8 x 10" ... **85.00**

Maxfield Parrish, Garden of Allah, 15 × 30", $300.00

Woodland Cathedral, VT, litho, 8 x 10" **50.00**

Parrish, Maxfield, American, 1870–1966

Garden of Opportunity, litho, 1925, 25 x 24", triptych **250.00**

Jason and the Talking Oak, litho, 1908, 11 x 9" **60.00**

The Broadmoor Hotel, litho, 1915, 8 x 7" **65.00**

Valley of Enchantment, 1946, litho, medium folio **60.00**

Platt, Charles Adams, American, 1861–1933, Fish House Interiors, etching, sgd and dated upper left in etching, sgd in pencil lower right, titled in margin, 4¾ x 7¾", good condition mat and frame **300.00**

Plowman, George Taylor, View of Boston and Boston Harbor, etching, sgd in pencil lower center, toned, full margins, 8½ x 11⅛", poor condition mat and frame **275.00**

Prang, Louis

Battle of Fort Hudson, litho, published by Prang's American Litho Co ... **175.00**

Carnations and Mignonette, litho, color, 1885, 7½ x 10¾" **20.00**

Pansies, litho, color, 1885, 7½ x 10½" **18.00**

Sheriden's Ride, litho, published by Prang's American Litho Co **150.00**

Rogets, Robert Bruce, American, Off In A Calm, litho, sgd in pencil lower right, titled left, full margins, 8 x 10¾", matted and framed **75.00**

Soyer, Raphael, Four Female Nudes, litho, artist's proof, pencil sgd, 22 x 16" **175.00**

Taber, Charles & Co, New Bedford, MA

Private Signals Of The Whaling Vessels Belonging To The Port Of New Bedford, 1857, litho, large folio, orig oak frame **4,500.00**

Sperm Whaling No. 2, The Conflict, from painting by J Cole, printed by Prang & Mayers Lithography, Boston, MA, 1858, litho, large folio, orig gold leafed frame **3,600.00**

Toulouse-Lautrec, de, Henri, L'Argent 1893, litho, sgd in litho upper left "T-L" in circle, full margins, 14⅛ x 10⅞", framed **650.00**

Unknown Publisher, The Trotting Mare "American Girl," litho, small folio, modern frame and matting **200.00**

Walker, W B, Death of Admiral Lord Nelson, mezzotint, published for Knot Co, London, Jan 20, 1806, 9⅞ x 13½", Hogarth type frame **575.00**

Wengenroth, Stow, American, 1906–1978, Quiet Day, Wellfleet, MA, March 1939, litho, full margins, 6⅛ x 10½" **225.00**

Whistler, James Abbott McNeill, American, 1834–1903
Billingsgate, 1859, etching, trimmed margins, 6 x 8⅞" **425.00**
Little Salute, etching, 2nd state, laid paper, 3¼ x 8⅓, framed **550.00**

Woodbury, Charles Herbert, American, 1864–1940, Tide Rips, Portsmouth, etching, full margins, 9 x 10¾", matted and framed **250.00**

Zorn, Anders, Against the Current, etching, sgd in pencil, 1919, 4½ x 6⅜" . **275.00**

PRINTS-JAPANESE

History: Buying Japanese woodblock prints requires attention to detail and skilled knowledge of the subject. The quality of the impression (good, moderate, or weak), the color, and condition are critical. Various states and strikes of the same print cause the price to fluctuate. Knowing the proper publisher and censor's seals are helpful in identifying an original print.

Most prints were recopied and issued in popular versions. These represent the vast majority of the prints found in the marketplace. These popular versions should be viewed solely as decorative since they have little value.

A novice buyer should seek expert advice before buying. Talk with a specialized dealer, museum curator, or auction division head.

The listings below concentrate on details to show the depth of data needed for adequate pricing. Condition and impression are good, unless indicated otherwise.

O = Oban, 10 x 15"   C = Chuban,
t = tat-e,   7 x 10"
   large in width   H = Hosoban,
y = yoke-e,   5½ x 13"
   large in length   T = Triptyck

Reference: Sandra Andacht, *Oriental Antiques & Art: An Identification And Value Guide*, Wallace-Homestead, 1987.

Buncho, courtesan *Nishikigi* of the Kanaya standing before a *tokonoma* with a spray of plum blossoms in her hand, scroll on wall sgd *Ippitsusai* and seal *Mori uji*, minor fading, one set of three entitled *Wrestling Match or Battle of Flowers*, H **3,500.00**

Eisen
Imayo jibin sankumimai, high ranking courtesan, sgd *Keisai Eisen-ga,* with *kiwame* and publisher's seals, fair impression and color, center crease, fair state **175.00**
Ukiyo nijuyonko series, Yang Hsiang shown teasing cat, sgd *Keisai Eisen-ga,* with kiwame and publisher's seal, good impression, slight wrinkling, Ot **725.00**

Eizan, Kakemono-E, humorous tiger emerging from behing large stalk of bamboo, sgd *Kikugama Eizan hitsu,* good impression, fair color, good condition **375.00**

Gakutei, seated geisha playing the *biwa,* from *Hanazo bantsuki* series, sgd *Gakutei,* color slightly faded, C . **950.00**

Harunobo, courtesan showing the neck of her kamoro before a screen dec with farmers harvesting rice, entitled *Jin, Virtue,* from *The Five Cardinal Virtues* series, sgd *Suzuki Harunobo ga,*Ct **7,750.00**

Hiroshinge, figures walking across bridge, late strike, Oy, $125.00.

Hiroshige
Fishing boats at Tsuikudajima in Buyp Province, *Shokoku meisho* series, "Famous Places in Various Provinces," sgd *Hiroshiga ga,* published by Dansendo, *unchima-e* center fold, margins slightly soiled, backed **5,750.00**

Kanagawa-Dai no tei, hilltop view, from *Tokaido Gojusan-tsugi* series, sgd *Hiroshige-ga,* red gourd shaped seal with *kiwame* and *Takenouchi* seals, fair impression, good color, backed, left margin trimmed, Oy **125.00**

Mishima asagiri, "Morning Mist, Mishima," from *Toto meisho* series, "Famous Places of the Eastern Capital," sgd *Hiroshege ga,* with *Hoseido/Senkakudo,* publisher's seals, margins trimmed, slightly rubbed, and soiled, Oy **675.00**

Hiroshige II, Chuban Album, complete set of series *Edo meisho yonju hakkei/Forty-eight famous Sights of Edo,* each sgd *Hiroshige-ga,* some margins with *aratame/negetsu* (c1860) and publisher *Tsuta-ya Kichizo* seals, good states, laid down, Ct **1,350.00**

Hokuji, *omocha-e* with inset *okubi-e* portrait of *Ichimura Kakitsu* next to eight scappered depictions of various hair styles and hats, individual label cartouches, sgd *Shunkosai Hokushuga* with artist, carver, and publisher *Toshijura-ya Shinbei* seals, fair impression, Ot **325.00**

Hokusai

Aoyama enza matsu, "The cushion pine at Aoyama," from *Fugaku sanjurokkei* series, "Thirty-six views of Mt Fuji," sgd *Hokusai litsui hitsu,* slightly faded, center fold, Oy . . . **2,650.00**

Sinsho Suwa-ko, "Lake Suma in Shinano Province," from *Fugaku sanjurokkei* series, "Thirty-six views of Mt Fuji," sgd *Zen Hokusai litsui hitsu,* publisher's seal *Eijudo,* Oy **4,250.00**

Uki-e depicting the Oji Inari Shrine, sgd *Hokusai ga,* slightly faded and trimmed, Oy **300.00**

Kawase Hasui

Ebisu Harbor, Sado Island in Winter, *Tabi miyage dinishi* series, sgd *Hasui,* seated *kawase,* dated Taishi 10 (1921), *Watanabe* publisher's seal, Oy **1,200.00**

Okayamajo no Asahi/Dawn at Okayama Castle, dated Showa 30 (1955), misty view of castle, sgd *Hasui,* circular *Watanabe Shosaburo* seal, good impression, color, and state, Ot **350.00**

Kikumaro, courtesan seated by hibachi, surrounded by female attendants, blossoming prunus and sparrow, sgd *Kikumaro hitsu,* fair impression, poor color, stained, Ot **275.00**

Kunisada

Kakemono-e, high ranging courtesan walking in elaborate kimono, sgd *Kochoro Kunisada hitsu,* with *aratame/negetsu* seal, c1865, good impression, fair color, faded, toned, trimmed, backed **225.00**

Three bijin walking with long sword and flute under flowering cherry trees at night, sgd *Kochoro/Ichiyosai Toyokuni ga,* two *nanushi* and publisher seals, good impression, toned, backed, OtT **200.00**

Kotondo, Beauty in sudden shower, sgd *Genjin ga,,* dated Showa 4 (1929), numbered 84/200, published by Sakai-Kawaguchi, large Ot **1,000.00**

Kuniyoshi

Giyu hakken-den series, depicting *Inyuama Dosetsu,* sgd *Ichiyasi Kuniyoshi-ga,* two *naushi* and publisher seals, fair impression and color, faded, fair state, Ot **100.00**

Tanuki print showing four drunken badgers dancing and singing, illus text passage, sgd *Ichiyusai Kuniyoshi-giga,* and one *nanushi* and anonymous publisher's seal, fair impression and color, slightly faded, Ot **150.00**

Oda Kazuma, entitled *Matsue Ohashi/The Great Bridge of Matsue,* group of figures crossing bridge in snow storm, sgd *Kazuma hitsu,* red artist's seal, right margin with title and dated Taisho 13 (1924), very good impression and color, Oy **850.00**

Tori Kyonagi, from series *Hinagata wakana no hatsumoyo,* sgd *Kiyonaga ga,* fair impression and color, faded, rough margins, Ot **750.00**

Toyokuni I, three courtesans and their attendants strolling on busy street, sgd *Toyokuni-ga, kiwame* and *Iwatoya Kisaburo* publisher's seal, fair impression, pool color, faded, fair state, Ot **400.00**

Utamaro, one courtesan standing over another in front, sgd *Utamaro hitsu,* with *kiwame, negetsu,* (1806) and publisher's seals, fair impression, poor color, faded, wrinkled, Ot **300.00**

Utamaro II, Beauty, half length, holding up her baby who plays with ball, sgd *Utamaro hitsu, kiwame* seal, publisher's seal *Iwatoya Kisaburo,* and censor's seal of Kisabura, Ot **2,000.00**

Yakamura Koko (Toyonari), three quarter view of actor *Matsumoto Koshiro* as *Sekibei,* sgd *Koka-ga,* publisher's seal and blind printed date Taisho 8 (1919), good impression and color, Ot **900.00**

Yoshikawa Kampo, actor *Nakamura Ganjiro* as *Kamiya Jihei* (c1922), sgd, publisher *Sato Shotaro*, reverse with additional publisher cartouche, edition 51/200, good impression and color, foxed, slightly toned, Ot **375.00**

Yoshitoshi

Diptych Set, from series *Shinsen Azuma Nishiki-e*/*Newly Selected Edo Color Prints*, entitled *Tamiya Botaro no Hanashi*/*the Story of Tamiya Botaro*, sgd *Yoshitoshi*, one seal reading *Taiso*, left margin dated Meiji 19 (1886) and publisher *Tsunanshima Kamekichi* cartouche, good impression and colors, margins partially trimmed, Ot **650.00**

Triptych Set, entitled *Taiheiki 'Sengatake' honjun no zu*, showing samurai *Takuma Morimasa* bound in ropes held by warriors, sgd *Ikahaisai Yoshitoshi hutsu* with *aratame*/*negetsu* (c1867) and publisher *Tsunajima Kamekuchi* seals, fair impression and color, fair state, Ot **300.00**

PURPLE SLAG (MARBLE GLASS)

History: Challinor, Taylor & Co., Tarantum, Pennsylvania, c1870s–80s, was the largest producer of purple slag in the United States. Since the quality of pieces varies considerably, there is no doubt other American firms made it as well.

Purple slag also was made in England. English pieces are marked with British Registry marks.

Other color combinations, such as blue, green, or orange, were made, but are rarely found.

Additional Listings: Greentown Glass (chocolate slag) and Pink Slag.

Reproduction Alert: Purple slag has been heavily reproduced over the years and still is reproduced at present.

Salt, 5″ l, 2″ h, shoe shape, $135.00.

Bowl, 8″, Dart Bar pattern	48.00
Butter Dish, cov, cow finial	35.00
Cake Stand, plain	120.00
Celery Vase, fluted	80.00
Compote	
5″ d, Scroll with Acanthus pattern ..	40.00
5″ d, 4½″ h, Beaded Hearts pattern .	70.00
Creamer, Sunflower pattern	55.00
Jack-In-The-Pulpit Vase, 6″	30.00
Match Holder, 5″, dolphin head	65.00
Plate, 10″, lattice edge	75.00
Spooner, Scroll with Acanthus pattern .	60.00
Toothpick, Scroll with Acanthus pattern	115.00
Vase, 10″ h, 7″ mouth, wispy purple swirls, cloudy and clear body	100.00
Whiskey, 2½″ h, thimble shape	35.00

QUEZAL   Quezal

History: The Quezal Art Glass Decorating Company, named for the "quetzal," a bird with brilliant colored feathers, was organized in 1901 in Brooklyn, New York, by two disgruntled Tiffany workers, Martin Bach and Thomas Johnson. They soon hired two more Tiffany workers, Percy Britton and William Wiedebine.

The first products, unmarked, were exact Tiffany imitations. In 1902 the "Quezal" trademark was first used. Quezal pieces differ from Tiffany pieces in that they are more defined and the decorations more visible and brightly colored. No new techniques came from Quezal.

Johnson left in 1905. T. Conrad Vahlsing, Bach's son-in-law, joined the firm in 1918, but left with Paul Frank in 1920 to form Lustre Art Glass Company which copied Quezal pieces. Martin Bach died in 1924; and, by 1925 Quezal ceased operations.

Wares are signed "Quezal" on the base of vases and bowls and rims of shades. The acid-etched or engraved letters vary in size and may be found in amber, black, or gold. A printed label of a quetzal bird was used briefly in 1907.

Bowl	
7½″ d, gold, green swirls, sgd	475.00
12″ d, peacock blue, hammered silver base, marked "Oscar B Bach, NY"	500.00
Candlesticks, 7¾″, irid blue, sgd, pr ..	550.00
Candy Dish, 5¾ x 2¼″, irid gold, folded foot, sgd	285.00
Flower Bowl, 5″ d, 4″ h, feather design around shoulders, opal body	475.00
Lamp, 17″, table, gold vine dec, green leaves, sgd	1,350.00
Lamp Shade	
4½″ h, gold, Calcite ruffled rim, dec, sgd	150.00
5″, green feather dec, gold body, pr .	650.00
6″, Calcite ribbed ext., opal int., pr ..	475.00

Vase, 3″ h, four pinched dimples, gold irid, sgd, $400.00.

Nut Dish, 3″, gold irid, sgd	135.00
Salt, 2½″ d, gold luster, sgd	100.00
Vase	
4½″ h, gold irid flared top, opal bulbous base, gold and green swirls and zig-zag lines dec, sgd	850.00
6″ h, green feather design, white and light gold int., sgd	225.00
6⅞″ h, irid blue luster, sgd	350.00
8″ h, gold, bluish-green pulled swirls, sgd	600.00
8¼″, bluish-gold, three applied gold feet	375.00
9¼″, gold irid, random threading	425.00
10½″, opaque white, irid gold and orange dec	1,250.00
12¼″, bud, gold luster, sgd	175.00

QUILTS

History: Quilts have been passed down as family heirlooms for many generations. Each is an individual expression. The same pattern may have hundreds of variations in both color and design.

The advent of the sewing machine increased, not decreased the number of quilts which were made. Quilts still are being sewn today.

The key considerations for price are age, condition, aesthetic beauty, and design. Prices are now at a level position. The exception is the very finest examples which continue to bring record prices.

References: American Quilter's Society, *Gallery of American Quilts, 1849–1988,* Collector Books, 1988; Cathy Florence, *Collecting Quilts: Investments In America's Heritage,* Collector Books, 1985; William C. Ketchum, Jr., *The Knopf Collectors' Guides to American Antiques: Quilts,* Alfred A. Knopf, Inc., 1982; Rachel and Kenneth Pellman, *The World of Amish Quilts,* Good Books, 1984; Schnuppe von Gwinner, *The History of the Patchwork Quilt,* Schiffer Publishing Ltd, 1988.

Acorn and Wreath, appliqued, old chintz English print back, red print, green print ground, c1850, 82 x 106″	1,400.00
Amish, pieced	
Carpenter's wheel, teal green, maroon, and orangish-tan, maroon ground, sgd "Mrs. Jacob Schwartz," 80 x 94″	170.00
Nine Patch, plum, burgundy, brown, navy, and teal wool patches, olive green ground, tulip stitched green border, black binding, burgundy foot end corner blocks	600.00
Star, ecru, slate blue ground, 79 x 92½″	200.00
Bow ties and bobbins, pieced, purple and white optical design, 70 x 80″	375.00
Broderie Perse, pieced, appliqued, leafy chintz tree with pink, green, and yellow peacock perched in branches, and pink, blue, and yellow blossom cluster border central panel, mounted on white cotton ground, multiple outer borders in trapunto meandering vine and mustard yellow, pink, and green pieced bow-tie and block pattern, and pink, green, and beige floral chintz, diagonal line and tiny seed stitching, Brosus Family Hancock, Maryland, mid 19th C, 96″ sq	5,500.00

Birds and Flowers, pieced cotton, rings of flowers, four inward facing peafowl, center double headed bird, 86″ sq, presentation type, c1880, $1,100.00.

Clover Blossom, pieced, cotton, rose, light green, and off white, rose thread even quilting, wide rose border with cable quilting, three sides with 3″ w rose fringe, c1920, 68 x 79″	350.00
Dogwood, appliqued, realistic branches and flowers, medium green ground, spider web quilting between floral designs, 72 x 89″	135.00

Fleur-de-lis, appliqued, red and light
blue, pencil quilt pattern, 80″ sq ... **175.00**
Floral, appliqued, red, green, and yellow
calico and solid, white ground, birds,
cornucopia, urns, and floral border, 82
x 96″ **650.00**
Geometric design, pieced, two shades
goldenrod and white, 76″ sq **100.00**
Interlocking circles, pieced, red, white,
and blue segments, white ground, 64
x 84″ **400.00**
Irish Chain, pieced, blue and white, 67
x 78″ **100.00**
Liberty and Washington, pieced, appliqued and embroidered, red, green,
yellow, blue, brown, and white printed
and solid calico patches, figures with
spread winged American eagle
above, red and green blossom border, trimmed with red and yellow pos-
ies, white cotton ground, diagonal line
stitching, sgd "Eliza Conklin, Claver-
ack, 1849″, 76 x 92″ **15,400.00**
Log Cabin, (Straight Furrow), pieced,
turkey red, rose, dark maroon, and
dark indigo blue prints, hand applied
binding, diagonal quilting, un-
bleached muslin back, 64 x 82″ **325.00**
Love Apple, pieced, appliqued, red, yellow, pink, and green patches, green
pumpkin vine border, white cotton
ground, triple channel stitches, diamond square quilting, c1855, 84 x 88″ **2,475.00**

Mariner's Compass, appliqued, red,
green, and yellow, red and green
sash border, NY, c1890, 76 x 95½″ . **1,000.00**

Oak Leaves, appliqued, red and green
calico, four leaf medallions, white
ground, stylized meandering border,
92 x 94″ **500.00**

Pinwheel and Star, pieced, appliqued,
red, yellow and slate blue patches,
tulip plants with scalloped leaves border, white cotton ground, radiating
outline stitching, 19th C, 88 x 90″ .. **1,430.00**

Poppy, appliqued, red and green, black
embroidered detail, mid 20th C, 72 x
88″ **150.00**

Stars, pieced, green, pink, and white,
penciled quilt pattern, machine sewn
binding, 82″ sq **175.00**

Stylized flower, appliqued, red and blue,
meandering border, feather wreath
circles between flowers, machine
sewn flower stems and vines, 75 x
78″ **200.00**

Tea Rose and Brier, appliqued, brier
stitching, red and green, white
ground, blue binding, 82 x 75″ **300.00**

QUIMPER

History: Quimper faience, dating back to the
17th century, is named for Quimper, a French town
where numerous potteries were located. Several
mergers resulted in the evolution of two major
houses - the Jules Henriot and Hubaudire-Bousquet factories.

The peasant design first appeared in the 1860s,
and many variations exist. Florals and geometrics,
equally popular, also were produced in large quantities. During the 1920s the Hubaudire-Bousquet
factory introduced the Odetta line which utilized a
stone body and Art Deco decorations.

The two major houses merged in 1968, each
retaining its individual characteristics and marks.
The concern suffered from labor problems in the
1980s and recently was purchased by an American group.

Marks: The HR and HR Quimper marks are
found on Henriot pieces prior to 1922. The HenRoit
Quimper mark was used after 1922. The HB mark
covers a long span of time. The addition of numbers or dots and dashes refers to inventory numbers and are found on later pieces. Most marks
are in blue or black. Pieces ordered by department
stores, such as Macy's and Carson Pirie Scott,
carry the store mark along with the factory mark,
making them less desirable to collectors. A com-
prehensive list of marks is found in Bondhus's
book.

References: Susan and Al Bagdade, *Warman's
English & Continental Pottery & Porcelain, 1st Edi-
tion,* Warman Publishing Co., Inc., 1987; Sandra
V. Bondhus, *Quimper Pottery: A French Folk Art
Faience,* published by author, 1981; Millicent Mali,
Quimper Faience, Airon, Inc., 1979; Marjatta Ta-
buret, *La Faience de Quimper,* Editions Sous le
Vent, 1979, French text.

Museums: Musee des Faiences de Quimper,
Quimper, France; Victoria and Albert Museum,
French Ceramic Dept., London, England.

Advisors: Susan and Al Bagdade.

Ashtray, 7¼″ d, bust of male peasant in
center, three green sponged rests,
green, red, and yellow florals on ext.,
marked "Henriot Quimper, France" . **50.00**
Bone Dish, 9⅛″ l, scalloped border outlined in blue, red, and green florals,
male seated on rock on one, female
on other, marked "Henriot Quimper,
France," pr **280.00**
Bookends, 8¾″ h, figural, seated male,
playing bagpipe, female knitting,

brown base, sgd "C. Maillard," marked "Henriot Quimper," pr **575.00**

Bowl

5⅛", berry, frontal view of male peasant, int. and ext. floral bands, compressed handles, marked "Henriot Quimper, France" **75.00**

7⅛", scalloped rim outlined in blue, floral chain border, male peasant on one, female on other, marked "HB Quimper, France," pr **190.00**

7⅝", fish fins and tail outlined in red and green, head outlined in bowl, male peasant on int., Art Deco style, marked "HB Quimper" **50.00**

Compote, 9 x 4½", ftd, peacock, cobalt, orange, and green, white ground, marked "HB Quimper, Kenilworth Studios, France" **80.00**

Cup and Saucer

Heart shape, peasant and florals, marked "HB Quimper" **65.00**

Hexagonal, florals, yellow ground . . **40.00**

Platter, rect, marked "Henriot Quimper France," $95.00.

Ewer, 9½" h, frontal view of female peasant, red, blue, and green florals, orange dashes at base, marked "Henriot Quimper, France" **190.00**

Figure

5⅞", sailor, bending over holding coil of rope forming bowl, blue tunic, brown pants, Modern Movement, marked "HB Quimper" **185.00**

10", dancing peasant couple, Modern Movement colors, artist sgd, marked "Henriot Quimper, France" **250.00**

13½", pair of male bagpipers, dark blue-green trousers, one with blue jacket, other with green jacket, black hats, sgd "R Micheau-Verniz" on base, marked "Henriot Quimper," c1950 reissue **120.00**

18" h, 21" w, male peasant swinging two dancing females, black, gold trim, white coifs, sgd "R Micheau-Verniz," marked "Henriot Quimper" **500.00**

Fish Platter, 22" l, 12" w, center peasant courting scene, blue and green dec riche border, Brittany crest, scalloped rim, unmarked **935.00**

Ginger Jar, 16½", peacocks, cockatoos, and florals, soft blue ground, marked "HB Quimper" **770.00**

Gravy Boat, 6½" l, two tab handles, blue and red outline dashes, female peasant, two spouts, marked "M," "G," "HB Quimper" **125.00**

Jardiniere, 13" l, double bagpipe shape, blue emb bows at corners, scene of male and female peasant resting in meadow, stylized flowers on reverse, marked "HR Quimper" **1,980.00**

Liqueur Set, 6½" h bottle, 7¾" d tray, five drinking thimbles, red, green, and blue flowers, tan ground, marked "HB Quimper" **235.00**

Melonnier, 13½" handle to handle, two peasants playing musical instruments center scene, blue dec riche border, Brittany crest, green handles with emb shells, marked "Henriot Quimper, France" **500.00**

Menu Card Holder, 3½" h, figural, leaf, green leaves, dark blue ground, Brittany crest, split on top for card, marked "Quimper" **160.00**

Mirror Frame, 16" w, 18" h, dark blue Rouen-style dec, cartouche of male and female peasants on sides, Quimper crest on top, age crack, marked "PB Quimper" **2,100.00**

Mustard Jar, 3⅜ x 2¼", floral band between blue and orange bands, two vertical pierced tabs, male peasant on cov, marked "HB Quimper" **65.00**

Oyster Plate, 9¼", six outlined wells with red, green, and blue florals, separated by green crosshatching, female peasant in center condiment well, raised foot, marked "HB Quimper, France" **125.00**

Pitcher

8", figural, bust, female peasant, gold coif forms handle and spout, brown hair, cream ground, marked "HB Quimper" **190.00**

8¼", red and green florals, male peasant, straight sides, pedestal base, unmarked **150.00**

9", two tone blue florals in crosshatched top band, Celtic bands on base, marked "Porquier-Beau" . . **990.00**

Plaque

4½" d, frontal view of male peasant

on one, female on other, blue scalloped edge with streaks, small loops for hanging, marked "Henriot Quimper, France," pr 80.00

15″ w, 18″ h, octagonal, relief molded, tavern scene, soft blues, greens, and tans, marked "Doyeched" at top, "Quimerch" on base, marked "Porquier-Beau" 1,870.00

Plate

7″, slightly scalloped rim outlined in blue, male peasant, floral band border, marked "HB Quimper" 40.00

8¾″, sq, male peasant, red, blue, and yellow florals on border, ermine tails at corners, marked "Henriot Quimper, France" 135.00

9¾″, apricots with leaves, multicolored, indented rim, repaired, marked "Porquier-Beau" 600.00

10″, female peasant in center, scalloped edge outlined in blue, red, and green chain on border, sgd "HB Quimper" 140.00

Platter

10″, wavy rim outlined in blue, female peasant, red, blue, and green floral border, marked "HB Quimper, France" 150.00

12¼″, slightly wavy rim, male peasant, red, blue, and green floral border, marked "HB Quimper, France" 175.00

14½″, border divided into four panels, florals in large panels, four dots in small panels, male and female peasants, c1950, marked "HB Quimper, France" 215.00

Porringer, pierced for hanging

6½″ handle to handle, blue center rooster, blue rim and wing handles, marked "Henriot Quimper" 45.00

7″ handle to handle, male peasant in center, blue and yellow band border, tab handles, marked "Henriot Quimper, France" 45.00

Relish Dish, 9⅛″ sq, four compartments, frontal view of male and female peasants, multiple dot chains, yellow ground, marked "Henriot Quimper, Made In France" 125.00

Relish Tray, 6⅝″ l, 4⅛″ w, sq, clipped corners, male peasant, red, blue, and green floral border, black ermine tails at corners, pierced for hanging, paint flaking and chips, marked "Henriot Quimper, France" 55.00

Snuff Bottle, bagpipe shape, male peasant, artist sgd 315.00

Soup Plate, 9¾″ d, large dark blue open flower in center, blue and red hexagon, tan ground, marked "Henriot Quimper" 100.00

Strawberry Bowl, 8¾″ l, 7¾″ w, large and small basins separated by partition, wavy blue rim stripe, red and blue florals, male peasant on int., marked "HB Quimper, France" 150.00

Tea Service, 8½″ teapot, creamer, cov sugar, five cups and saucers, 16 x 11½″ tray, bagpipe shaped, bow finials, male and female peasant, dark blue and gold bands, marked "Henriot Quimper, France" 1,980.00

Vase

4¾″ h, bud, bust of male peasant, orange and rust dots and florals, tan ground, two blue open handles, sgd "Rennes," marked "Henriot Quimper, France" 125.00

5¼″, bulbous, male peasant on one, female on other, large open florals on reverse, orange accents, marked "Henriot Quimper, France," pr 260.00

23½″, reaper and seated peasant woman with child on front, green vertical dec riche bands, Quimper crest at neck, open florals on reverse, marked "HR Quimper" . . . 1,760.00

Vegetable Dish, cov, 12″ handle to handle, red and blue florals in baskets, scattered florals, blue sponged finial and open handles, inside rim chip, marked "Henriot Quimper, France" . 400.00

RADIOS

History: The radio was invented over 100 years ago. Marconi was the first to assemble and employ the transmission and reception instruments that permitted sending electric messages without the use of direct connections. Between 1905 and the end of World War I many technical advances were made to the "wireless," including the invention of the vacuum tube by DeForest. By 1920 technology progressed. Radios filled the entertainment needs of the average family.

Changes in design, style, and technology brought the radio from the black boxes of the 1920s to the styled furniture pieces and console models of the 1930s and 1940s, to midget models of the 1950s, and finally to the high-tech radios of the 1980s.

References: Philip Collins, *Radios: The Golden Age,* Chronicle Books, 1987; Alan Douglas, *Radio Manufacturers of the 1920's, Volume 1,* Vestal Press Ltd., 1988; Robert Grinder and George Fathauger, *Radio Collectors Directory And Price Guide,* Ironwood Publishing, 1986; David and Betty Johnson, *Antique Radios: Restoration and Price Guide,* Wallace-Homestead, 1982.

Periodical: *Radio Age,* 636 Cambridge Road, Augusta, GA 30909.

Collectors' Clubs: Antique Wireless Association, 17 Sheridan Street, Auburn, NY 13021; Antique Radio Club of America, 81 Steeplechase Road, Devon, PA 19333.

Museums: Antique Wireless Museum, East Bloomfield, NY; Caperton's Radio Museum, Louisville, KY; Muchow's Historical Radio Museum, Elgin, IL; Museum of Wonderful Miracles, Minneapolis, MN; New England Museum of Wireless and Steam, East Greenwich, RI; Voice of the Twenties, Orient, NY.

Additional Listings: See *Warman's Americana & Collectibles* for more examples.

RCA Victor, 11 x 7¼ x 7½", electric, white plastic case, $400.00.

Admiral, Super Airoscope, table model	65.00
Airline, beehive case, 1930s	70.00
Buckingham, Model 30, speaker inside	120.00
Champion, Cathedral model	170.00
Crosley	
Bandbox	60.00
Model 51, 1924	90.00
Emerson, U series model	40.00
Federal, crystal set, Buffalo, NY, patented 1917	200.00
Grebe, Model CR-9, 1921	525.00
Kennedy, Model 220, battery operated, 1921	300.00
Metro, Super 7, tubes, gold silk screen, 1926	125.00
RCA	
Model 140, 1934	120.00
Radiola 60, No 103 speaker, 9 tube, 1928	500.00
Sentinel, Model 76A, console, three band, 1937	70.00
Stewart Warner, 10 tube, tombstone case	200.00
Volta, crystal set	185.00

RAILROAD ITEMS

History: Railroad collectors have existed for decades. The merger of the rail systems and the end of passenger service made many objects available to private collections. The Pennsylvania Railroad sold its archives at public sale.

Railroad enthusiasts have organized into regional and local clubs. Join one if interested. Your local hobby store can probably point you to the right person. The best pieces pass between collectors and rarely enter the general market place.

References: Stanley L. Baker, *Railroad Collectibles: An Illustrated Value Guide, 3rd Edition,* Collector Books, 1985; Phil Bollhagen, *The Pictorial Value Guide to Railroad Playing Cards,* published by author, 1987; Arthur Dominy and Rudolph A. Morgenfruh, *Silver At Your Service,* published by authors, 1987; Richard Luckin, *Dining On Rails,* published by author, 1983, out-of-print.

Museums: Baltimore and Ohio Railroad, Baltimore, MD; Museum of Transportation, Boston, MA; New York Museum of Transportation, Albany, NY; California State Railroad Museum, Sacramento, CA.

Collectors' Clubs: Railroad Enthusiasts, 456 Main Street, West Townsend, MA 01474; Railroadiana Collectors Association, P.O. Box 365, St. Ignatius, MT 59865; Railway and Locomotive Historical Society, 3363 Riviera West Drive, Kelseyville, CA 95451.

Periodicals: Key, Lock and Lantern, P.O. Box 15, Spencerport, NY 14559; U.S. Rail News, P.O. Box 7007, Huntington Woods, MI 48070-7007.

Additional Listings: See *Warman's Americana & Collectibles* for more examples.

Advisor: Alan H. Altman.

Ashtray, Cotton Belt Route, 3½" d, copper, logo on bottom	20.00
Baggage And Brass Check	
C&NW, "C.&N.W.Ry. 633," time check, 1½ x 1¾", flat top, round bottom	17.50
GN, "G.N.Ry. 86," 1¼" d, key tag	10.00
SP, "794 SOU.PAC.R.R. to C.S.&C.C.RY," 1½ x 2", strap	40.00
Button, uniform	
ERIE, large silver dome, Scovill Mfg. Co., Waterbury, CT	6.00
ROCK ISLAND LINES, star center, Pettibone Bros, Cincinnati, OH	4.00
China	
Baker, oval, Reading, Stotesbury, 6¾ x 5½", Scammell (Lamberton) China, backstamp	225.00
Bouillion Cup, Southern Pacific, Prairie Mountain Wildflowers, 3¾", Syracuse China, backstamp	75.00
Bowl, Florida East Coast, Carolina, 5¾", Buffalo China, backstamp	85.00
Butter Pat, Atlantic Coast Line, Flora of the South, 3½", Buffalo China, backstamp	100.00
Cereal Bowl	
Baltimore and Ohio, Centenary,	

6¼", Shenango China, backstamp **38.00**
Union Pacific, Desert Flower, 6½", Syracuse China, backstamp ... **35.00**
Compote, footed, New York Central, Albany, 7¼", Shenango China, backstamp **275.00**
Creamer, New York, Chicago & St Louis, Fort Wayne, 3" h, side logo, Shenango China, no backstamp . **185.00**
Cup and Saucer, Wabash, Banner, both with top logo, Syracuse China, no backstamp **250.00**
Egg Cup, double, pedestal, Missouri-Kansas-Texas, Katy Ornaments, 4" h, Syracuse China, no backstamp **75.00**
Gravy Boat, Atchison, Topeka & Santa Fe, Mimbreno, Syracuse China, no backstamp **150.00**
Plates
4¾" square, tea, Chesapeake & Ohio, Silhouette, Martha & George dancing with hands up on top, Syracuse China, no backstamp **225.00**
6¼", Norfolk & Western, Syracuse China, no backstamp **75.00**
6½", Pennsylvania, Broadway, top logo, Scammell (Lamberton) China, backstamp **38.00**
9¾", dinner, Chicago, Milwaukee, St. Paul & Pacific, Galatea, Syracuse China, no backstamp ... **125.00**
9¾", Erie, Starucca, top logo, Walker China, no backstamp .. **195.00**
Platter, oval, Delaware & Hudson, Canterbury, 10¼ x 7", top logo, Syracuse China, no backstamp **225.00**
Sugar Packet Holder, Fred Harvey, Cactus Logo, side logo, Syracuse China, no backstamp **100.00**
Glassware
Cordial, Santa Fe, 4½" h, applied Santa Fe white script logo **50.00**
Goblet, Union Pacific, stemmed, 5½" h, 3½" d, etched "UNION PACIFIC" inside shield **15.00**
Highball, Lehigh Valley, 4½" h, maroon and white train and Northeastern map of U.S. marking route of LVRR **75.00**
Water, Delaware & Husdon, 4½" h, 2¼" d, applied D&H shield logo with "the D&H" inside the shield **20.00**
Wine, Canadian Pacific, stemmed, 4" h, 2" d, etched "CANADIAN PACIFIC" script logo on side, ornate facets surrounding glass **35.00**
Hat With Badge
Missouri Pacific, two silver bands running around, silver "MISSOURI PACIFIC LINES" buttons on each

side, cap badge is red Buzzsaw logo with "MISSOURI PACIFIC LINES" inside and "TRAINMAN" below **150.00**
New York Central, two gold bands running around, two gold NYC buttons, cap badge is "NEW YORK CENTRAL CONDUCTOR," badge has blue enamel oval logo with New York Central System inside . **85.00**
Penn Central, red PC logo cap badge, "STATION MASTER" below **60.00**
Head Rest, Pennsylvania, 15 x 18", brown PRR logo and electric train, tan ground **10.00**

Lamp, Stationmaster, PA RR, $30.00.

Lantern
Cumberland Valley Railroad, RR Signal Lamp & Lantern Co., New York, double horizontal wire guard, brass top bellbottom frame, manufacturer's name on top, snapoff bellbottom has patent date of Aug. 31, '75, frame marked on lid CVRR, globe is 5⅜" unmarked clear, has "SAFETY FIRST" cast below the Corning glass manufacturer mark **850.00**
Great Northern Railway, Adams & Westlake "The Adams," last patent date is Nov. 30, '97, double horizontal guard, twist-off pot and burner, globe is 5⅜" clear, unmarked, frame marked "G.N.Ry." . **150.**
Lantern Globes
New York Central & Hudson River, 5⅞", red cast flashed globe has "NYC & HRR" inside rectangular panel, extended base **300.00**
Rutland, 6", green etched "RUTLAND R.R. Co.," manufactured by "MAC-BETH No. 277 PEARL GLASS" .. **200.00**

Locks, Brass
  Boston & Maine Railroad, brass
    switch lock is marked up the back-
    side B&M RR LS S, manufactured
    by "SHERBURNE & CO./BOS-
    TON/MASS.", early style lock **125.00**
  Chesapeake & Ohio, six lever, round
    style, cast over front side C&O RY
    Co., hallmarked "MILLER LOCK
    CO." **285.00**
  Illinois Central Railroad, six lever,
    round style, cast over front side
    ICRR **185.00**
Pass
  Allegheny Valley Railroad, 1870s, lo-
    comotive **20.00**
  Missouri Pacific, 1920s **4.00**
Playing Cards, boxed double decks
  (Note: Numbers refer to Phil Bollhag-
  en's *The Pictorial Value Guide To
  Railroad Playing Cards*: 1987)
  Erie, train through logo, E18a (yellow
    diamond, blue ground) and
    E18b(blue diamond, yellow
    ground) **85.00**
  Louisville & Nashville, L62 (engine)
    and L63 (six scenes) **45.00**
  Norfolk & Western, N&W in circle,
    N40a (blue) and N40b (black) . . . **45.00**
  Pennsylvania, gold border, P25 (two
    trains and trestle) and P26 (two
    trains and cornfield) **75.00**
Police Badge, Northern Pacific, "RAIL-
  ROAD WATCHMAN, N.P.RY.," 2½",
  six pointed star, nickel plated, black
  letters, St. Paul Stamp Works **100.00**
Ruler, Soo Line, 12", tin, map and logo,
  red letters, white ground **6.50**
Silver Flatware
  Bouillion Spoon, Mo.Pac.Ry., bottom
    marked, Saxony, Gorham **50.00**
  Butter Knife, Boston & Maine RR, top
    marked, #165, Meridian **50.00**
  Cocktail Fork, C.&E.I., bottom
    marked, Modern, Reed & Barton . **35.00**
  Fork
    Reading, top marked, Kings, Inter-
      national Silver **25.00**
    Soo Line, top marked, Windsor,
      Reed & Barton **25.00**
  Fruit Knife, Lackawanna, top marked,
    Cromwell, International Silver . . . **20.00**
  Ice Teaspoon, NPR, top marked,
    Winthrop, Gorham **25.00**
  Knife, Southern, top marked, Carlton,
    Reed & Barton **20.00**
  Teaspoon
    Fred Harvey, bottom marked, Al-
      bany, International Silver **10.00**
    PRR (logo), top marked, Kings, In-
      ternational Silver **25.00**

Silver Holloware
  Butter Icer, Denver & Rio Grande
    Western, 3¼", International Silver,
    backstamped with name of railroad **85.00**
  Cheese Scoop, Western Pacific, 8¼"
    l, Belmont pattern, Reed & Barton,
    top mark reads "W.P.Ry." **95.00**
  Coffee Pot, California Zephyr, 10 oz,
    #05089, International Silver, back-
    stamped with name of railroad . . . **95.00**
  Creamer, hinged lid, Pennsylvania, ⅝
    pint, side logo is raised PRR key-
    stone, Gorham, backstamped with
    name of railroad **165.00**
  Ladle, New York Central, Century pat-
    tern, International Silver, back-
    stamped with name of railroad . . . **50.00**
  Mustard Pot, New York, New Haven
    & Hartford, 3¾" h, #0501, Wallace,
    backstamped with name of railroad **65.00**
  Sugar Bowl, lid, double-handled, At-
    lantic Coast Line, 10 oz, #05070C,
    side logo reads ACL, International
    Silver, backstamped with name of
    railroad **85.00**
  Sugar Tongs, Chesapeake & Ohio,
    5¼" l, Waverly pattern, top marked,
    Albert Pick, no backstamp **150.00**
  Teapot, Southern Pacific, 12 oz,
    #1400C, Reed & Barton, back-
    stamp "S.P.LINES" **135.00**
  Toothpick Holder, Great Northern,
    2¼" h, 2" w, #S004, side logo is
    incised GNR, MIBI Co., back-
    stamped with name of railroad . . . **175.00**
  Tureen, lid, double-handled, Chicago,
    Burlington & Quincy, 1 pint, #092-
    H, side logo is raised backwards
    BR, pagoda style top, Reed & Bar-
    ton, no backstamp **165.00**
Switch Keys, Brass
  MK&T RY, Slaymaker, football hall-
    mark **25.00**
  N.P.R.R., Fraim, keystone hallmark . **15.00**
  Santa Fe, A&W/SY, football hallmark **20.00**
Time Table, Union Pacific, 1945 . . . . . **8.00**
Ticket Punch, star pattern, unknown
  maker **7.50**

RAZORS

History: Razors date back several thousand
years. Early man used sharpened stones. The
Egyptians, Greeks, and Romans had metal razors.
  Razors made prior to 1800 generally were
crudely stamped WARRANTED or CAST STEEL,
with the maker's mark on the tang. Until 1870
almost all razors for the American market were
manufactured in Sheffield, England. Most blades
were wedge shaped; many were etched with slogans or scenes. Handles were made of natural

materials: various horns, tortoise shell, bone, ivory, stag, silver, and pearl. All razors were handmade.

After 1870 razors were machine made with hollow ground blades and synthetic handle materials. Razors of this period usually were manufactured in Germany (Solingen) or in American cutlery factories. Hundreds of molded celluloid handle patterns were produced.

Cutlery firms produced boxed sets of two, four, and seven razors. Complete and undamaged sets are very desirable. Most popular are the 7-Day sets with each razor etched with a day of the week.

The fancier the handle or more intricately etched the blade, the higher the price. Rarest handle materials are pearl, stag, sterling silver, pressed horn, and carved ivory. Rarest blades are those with scenes etched across the entire front. Value is increased by certain manufacturer's names, e.g., H. Boker, Case, M. Price, Joseph Rogers, Simmons Hardware, Will & Finck, Winchester, and George Wostenholm.

hgb = hollow ground blade
wb = wedge blade

Reference: Robert A. Doyle, *Straight Razor Collecting, An Illustrated Price Guide*, Collector Books, 1980, out-of-print.

Periodical: *Blade Magazine*, P.O. Box 22007, Chattanooga, TN 37422.

Additional Listings: See *Warman's Americana & Collectibles* for more examples.

Advisor: Robert A. Doyle.

Safety, 9½" l, Ideal Safety Razor, patent dates of Sept 21, 1868, June 12, 1900, and March 5, 1906, leather-like case, $20.00.

AMERICAN BLADES

American Knife Co, Plymouth Hollow, Conn, wb, stamped "A Real American," rounded black horn handle, c1860s 70.00
Challenge Cutlery Co, Bridgeport, Conn, blade etched "Rince," black peacock pattern 55.00
Levering Razor Co, NY, light gold blade with "Mail Pouch" tobacco adv and "Unrivalled, Fully Warranted," imitation ivory handle with fish scale pattern 40.00
Novelty Cutlery Co, Canton, OH, USA, rounded point blade, handle with cow, horse, train, and owner's name and address, front dated "1921," German Silver ends 80.00
John J. Saffa, St. Louis, scene of two gold colored camels and scroll on blade with "Silver Steel," ivory colored handle 25.00
Henry Sears & Sons, blade etched "Genuine German Concave," imitation ivory handle, orig box with adv . 18.00
Schumates Shuraco, blade etched with gold open razor and gentleman's head and "Shumate Registered Trade Mark," orange front and green back celluloid handle, MOP tang ... 65.00
Union Razor Cutlery Co, Union City, GA, banded tobacco pattern handle 40.00
Will & Fink, San Francisco, CA, hgb, ivory handle, German silver and brass pin tang 150.00

ENGLISH BLADES, SHEFFIELD

Etched "Ask For Wade & Butcher's Hollow Ground Razor," picked bone pattern handle 100.00
Wm Greaves & Sons Sheaf Works, wb, sq point, mottled horn handle, engraved inlaid escutcheon plate, c1820 .... 20.00
Turniss Cutler & Stacey Sheffield, unusual shaped point blade, tang stamped "For Use," two pressed intertwined snakes on mottled horn handle 615.00
Wade & Butcher, hgb, engraved and ornate escutcheon plate with two inlaid engraved star shaped metal dec, mottled horn handle, blade etched "The Celebrated Hollow Ground Razor," c1850 .... 65.00
George Wostenholm & Sons, Celebrated I*XL Razor Washington Works, wb, etched spread American eagle and "The Congress Razor," notched point, black horn handle with five sided pewter cap end, c1830s 100.00

GERMAN BLADES

Asco Cutlery Co, clean blade, burgundy and pink handle with beetle crawling on bark, oak leaves, and acorns ... 120.00
B. J. Eyre Germany, hgb, blade etched "Extra Hollow Ground" in gold, imitation ivory handle with light blue peacock feather pattern 75.00

H. & A. Cutlery Co, hgb, imitation ivory
handle, pearl tang 25.00
H. Boker & Co, etched blade with Amer-
ican Lines S.S. St. Louis Ship scene,
black celluloid handle 125.00
W. H. Morley & Co, blade etched "Real
Hollow Ground," imitation ivory handle with raised orange flower and rib-
bon dec 55.00
Westfield Mfg Co, hgb, checkered
raised shield on ivory handle 50.00

SWISS BLADES

Jacques Lecoultre, frameback, wafer
blade, tang stamped "M. M. & Co,"
engraved plated steel blade "William
Ernest Barnes December 30th 1869"   37.50
Joh Engstrom Eskilstuna, frameback,
wafer blade, tang with dates up to
1881, ivory handle 50.00

SETS OF RAZORS

7-Day Set, Oscars Special, hgb, ivory
handles, burgundy leather cov wood
case emb with "S. L. McBean," purple
velvet lined slotted int. 150.00
7-Day Set, A. J. Jordan Sheffield, Eng,
blades engraved with days of week,
tangs etched "Old Faithful," ivory
handles with pointed ends, oak case
with peeled perimeter and inlaid
brass escutcheon plate, purple lining   240.00
7-Day Set, Sheffield Steel Warranted,
rounded point hgb, imitation ivory
handles, tangs stamped "K" in a circle, leather cov wood case, burgundy
velvet lined slotted int. 130.00
7-Day Set, Taylor Eye-Witness Shef-
field, semi-wedge blades with engraved days on top, ivory handle,
leather cov wood case with German
silver escutcheon plate, blue lining
with gold adv, lock, and key 235.00

RED WING POTTERY

History: The Red Wing pottery category covers
several potteries from Red Wing, Minnesota. In
1868 David Hallem started Red Wing Stoneware
Co., the first pottery, with stoneware as its primary
proded Wing Union Stoneware Co.,
made stoneware until 1920 when it introduced a
pottery line which it continued until the 1940s. In
1936 the name was changed to Red Wing Potteries, Inc. During the 1930s it introduced several
popular lines of hand painted pattern dinnerware
which were distributed through department stores,
Sears, and gift stamp centers. Dinnerware declined in the 1950s, being replaced with hotel and
restaurant china in the early 1960s. The plant
closed in 1967.

References: David A. Newkirk, *A Guide To Red
Wing Markings,* Monticello Printing, 1979; Dolores
Simon, *Red Wing Pottery With Rumrill,* Collector
Books, 1980; Lyndon C. Viel, *The Clay Giants,
The Stoneware of Red Wing, Goodhue County,
Minnesota,* Book 2 (1980), Book 3 (1987), Wal-
lace-Homestead.

Additional Listings: See *Warman's Americana
& Collectibles* for more examples.

Vase, 8½", light blue glaze, imp mark,
$60.00.

Ashtray, Minnesota Twins World Series,
1965 . . . .   60.00
Butter Crock, white, blue adv, two
pounds, marked "Red Wing" 85.00
Casserole, cov, Saffron, small, stone-
ware 125.00
Clock, electric, Mammy shape 90.00
Cookie Jar
Dutch Girl, yellow and brown trim . .   48.00
Pineapple, dark blue 35.00
Crock, 5 gallon, elephant ear leaves,
#5, salt glaze 175.00
Custard Cup, spongeband 75.00
Figure, gopher on football 100.00
Flower Pot, 10", ribbons and berries,
Brushware 50.00
Jar, white, shield shaped adv, marked .   150.00

Jug
Advertising
"Aleda Vinegar - For Pickling and Table, Milwaukee Vinegar," brown glazed shoulder, white glazed base 85.00
"Henry Bosquet," one eighth pint . 100.00
Beehive, 5 gallon, white glaze
Birch leaves dec, pouring lip 250.00
Red Wing decal, large decal, oval "Red Wing Union Stoneware Co" mark 165.00
Shoulder, 2 gallon, brown and white, MN adv 100.00
Mixing Bowls, 6¾ and 9⅝" d, Saffron Ware, wide lip, fluted body, blue and brown marbleized type dec, yellow ground, stamped "Red Wing Saffron Ware" 200.00
Pitcher
6", Cherry Band pattern, blue and white stoneware 148.00
12" h, Bob White pattern 20.00
Sewer Tile, sample
Clay, marked "Red Wing Sewer Pipe" 35.00
Salt glaze, marked "Union Stoneware, Red Wing Minn" 125.00
Slop Jar, cov, blue stripe band, lily on front 135.00
Umbrella Stand, florals, Brushware ... 125.00
Vase
6", green glaze int., two handles ... 35.00
12D, green, yellow int., children on swings 60.00
12½", Bamboo pattern, green and yellow 45.00
Wall Pocket, Gardenia, ivory 35.00
Water Cooler, 3 gallon, white, stoneware, red wing, oval "Red Wing Union Stoneware" mark 350.00

REDWARE

History: The availability of clay, the same used to make bricks and roof tiles, accounted for the great production of red earthenware pottery in the American colonies. Redware pieces are mainly utilitarian—bowls, crocks, jugs, etc.

Lead glazed redware retained its reddish color, but a variety of colored glazes were obtained by the addition of metals to the basic glaze. Streaks and mottled splotches in redware items resulted from impurities in the clay and/or uneven firing temperatures.

"Slipware" is a term used to describe redwares decorated by the application of slip, a semi-liquid paste made of clay. Slipwares were made in England, Germany, and elsewhere in Europe for decades before becoming popular in the Pennsylvania German region and elsewhere in colonial America.

Bank
3⅝" h, tooled band, knob finial, unglazed, black stenciled label "Charity" 150.00
4¾" h, jug shape, red paint 65.00
6½" h, 5¾" d, beehive shape, peg finial, clear lead glaze, slight greenish tint 210.00
Basin, 18" d, tin glaze 60.00
Basket, 3¼" h, 6" d, hanging, red and white, yellow slip, green and brown glaze, notched rim pot and saucer, three pierced holes, restored 1,300.00
Bean Pot, 5⅝" h, dark brown glazed int., two rim chips 225.00
Bottle, 11¼" h, donut shape, amber glaze, brown flecks 125.00
Bowl
7¾" d, crimped edges, orange-red, unglazed purple-brown back 120.00
10½" d, 2" h, yellow slip dec 180.00
13¼" d, yellow slip dec with green and brown, glaze flakes 325.00
13½" d, Moravian slip, galleried rim, brown concentric rings with central stylized flowerhead dec, wavy line border, mustard yellow ground ... 260.00
Bucket, 20" h, pierced cylindrical body, strap handle 85.00
Bust, 13" h, young boy's head, brown glaze, late 19th 55.00

Cup, 3¾" d, 5" l including handle, 1⅞" h, green mottled glaze, Thomas Stahl, 1938, $70.00.

Charger
11⅜" d, coggled edge, four line yellow slip dec 1,050.00
12¼" d, coggled edge, yellow slip design, mottled brownish glaze 250.00
13¾", coggled edge, yellow slip combware dec 1,150.00
Colander, 9¾ x 7", clear glaze, brown flecks, orange-brown ground, rim handles, three applied feet 300.00

Creamer, 4" h, incised band, four vertical lines of black iridescent glaze .. **110.00**

Crock

4", glazed int., imp C link **75.00**

9" h, clear glaze, brown splotches, applied handles **175.00**

Cup, 4" d, greenish glaze, orange spots, yellow slip wavy lines **85.00**

Cuspidor

3⅛" h, 7½" d, red and white slip, green and brown sponged glaze under clear lead glaze, foot chips and wear **100.00**

5½" d, reddish-brown glaze, mottled dark brown, handle **75.00**

8¼" d, dark brown sponged stripes . **95.00**

Custard Cup, 2⅜", incised "TS Stahl, Sept 1, 1940" bottom **50.00**

Dish

6¾" d, yellow slip dec, coggled edge **130.00**

8¾" d, yellow slip dec, crimped edge, unglazed red back **150.00**

11½" l, yellow slip dec, figure eights within squiggle borders, 19th C .. **700.00**

Figure, 6½", parrot, mounted on perch, orange brown glaze, dark brown streaking, incised wing and feather detail **1,000.00**

Flask, 8", brown splotches, clear glaze, orange ground, New England **275.00**

Flower Pot

4⅞" h, 5⅞" d, unglazed, imp "John Bell/Waynesboro" **80.00**

5" h, 6⅛" d, red and white slip, brown sponged, clear lead glaze ext., attached undertray imp "John Bell/ Waynesboro" **190.00**

7⅝" h, 8⅛" d, white slip, applied brown slip and dabbed green glaze swag design dec, double roulette rim, attached ruffled undertray, imp "SOLOMON BELL" **425.00**

9½" h, 8" d, red and pale yellow slip, brown and green glazes, double scored rim, notched undertray attached undertray, chips and crazing **245.00**

Jar

5½" h, 5¼" d, brown sponge, clear lead glaze, stamped "John Bell...Waynesboro" on side, incised script "To Mifs Laura Wolfinger/ March/14/1876/J. W. B." **600.00**

6¼" h, white slip, brown, and tan marbleized glaze **200.00**

7¼" h, reddish glaze, yellow slip around lip **120.00**

8¼" h, tooled straight and wavy lines, greenish glaze, orange spots **140.00**

12½" h, baluster form, flaring rim, two applied handles, unglazed band of coggled dec ext., manganese flow-

ers and glaze int., imp "John W. Bell" **525.00**

13¼" h, 15" d, tooled stripe, dark int. glaze, applied handles **95.00**

Jug

8¾", ovoid, green and orange spotted glaze, handle, NH, ex McKearin collection **500.00**

10¾" h, dark brown glaze, ribbed strap handle, wide mouth **40.00**

Inkwell, 3½" h, 3½" d, incised chain dec, overall clear lead glaze, ruffled edge, applied pheasant handle cov, head of pheasant glued **350.00**

Loaf Pan, 16¼", coggled edge, fine line yellow slip dec, flakes and chip **1,250.00**

Milkpan, 10" d, yellow slip "1813" between double lines, wavy line border, black back **110.00**

Mold

7 x 3", Turk's head, mottled green and amber glaze, brown splotches .. **100.00**

8⅝" d, 2½" h, turk's head, brown sponging, clear glaze **65.00**

8¾" d, scalloped edge, medium to light brown glaze **100.00**

Mug, 4⅜" h, 4¼" d, brown sponging, clear lead glaze, top and bottom thumbnail grooves, imp "John Bell" . **550.00**

Pie Plate

3⅝" d, deep, stippled rust glaze, c1820 .... **110.00**

7⅜" d, intersecting wavy lines, yellow slip **135.00**

7½" d, coggled edge, three line yellow slip dec **100.00**

9¾" d, crimped edge, brown, glazed **110.00**

11" d, coggled edge, mustard yellow glaze **275.00**

Pitcher

4⅝", glaze, dark brown splotches, strap handle **345.00**

5" h, pinched spout, white slip, mottled brown glaze **65.00**

5¼" h, pinkish-brown glaze, darker brown mottled dec, incised band, lid **150.00**

6½" h, clear glaze, brown splotches, ribbed strap handle **145.00**

6⅝" h, reddish-brown glaze, dark brown splotches, formed handle . **450.00**

7½" h, red and white overall slip, brown spattered, clear lead glaze, bold handle **325.00**

Plate

8½", zigzag and parallel line yellow slip dec, reddish brown glaze, chips **225.00**

10¼", yellow slip dec, parallel zigzag lines and commas, reddish brown glaze, rim chip and roughage ... **325.00**

11⅛", zigzag yellow slip dec, reddish brown glaze, rim chips **425.00**

11¾", sgraffito, tulips and star type flowers radiating from urn, yellow glaze, green highlights **7,200.00**

Puzzle Jug, 8", yellow slip dec, John Howarth, 1871 .... **250.00**

Salt, 2⅛" h, 2½" d, manganese glaze, ftd, scuffing and small chip **170.00**

Tankard, 4½" h, brown glaze, pewter lid, engraved "G.F." **45.00**

Toddy Plate, 5⅝", yellow slip dec, green wavy line rim **500.00**

Vase

  3⅝", sgraffito, birds and flowers, tricolor, bulbous base, marked "DDR, June 5, 1828, PA" **1,500.00**

  4¼" h, dark greenish black glaze, bulbous base, triangular mouth **85.00**

Washbowl, 10⅝ x 5", brown-amber glaze int., attached soap dish **400.00**

RELIGIOUS ITEMS

History: Objects for the worshipping or expression of man's belief in a superhuman power are collected by many people for many reasons.

Icons are included since they are religious momentos, usually paintings with a brass encasement. Collecting icons dates from the earliest period of Christianity. Most available today were made in the late 19th century.

"The Holy Rosary," 17 x 26 x 3½", wood and plaster frame, chalkware figures, lithograph scroll, copyright 1912 by Koening, $185.00.

Bible, family, 1800-1900, published in US, center pages family data **35.00**

Collection Box, 24¾" l, walnut, carpet lining, old dark finish, pencil post handle **75.00**

Communion Flagon, 10½", lighthouse shape, pewter, marked "Eben Smith, Beverly, MA," c1815 .... **425.00**

Figure

  Madonna and Child, 13" h, porcelain,

standing on crescent moon, crown surmounted by cross, child held in left arm, Nymphenburg **240.00**

Saint, 12", bust, wood, youthful male, French, c1750 .... **600.00**

Font, 6", Holy Water, porcelain, gold rococo dec, white ground, Germany .. **150.00**

Hymnal, watercolor fraktur bookplate, leather bound, 1790 .... **350.00**

Icon, Russian

  5¼ x 4⅜", Kazan Mother of God, shaded enamel halos, silver filigree okhlad, Moscow, c1900 .... **1,320.00**

  14⅜ x 11⅝", The Holy Visage, stylized bust, surrounded by halo, rect painted panel, 17th C **825.00**

Needlework, 18¾ x 23", silk panel, Moses' rescue from bull rushes scene, watercolor faces and arms, oval eglomise glass and gilt frame . **200.00**

Painting

  Italian, Madonna, Child, and St. Catherine, 36¾ x 26½", oil on canvas, seated woman, baby in her lap, kneeling woman, forest landscape, titled frame, 1480–1528 .... **21,000.00**

  Spanish, Saint Judas Thaedo, Apostle, 25¼ x 19¾", oil on canvas, half figure, reading book, title across top, framed, 1618–82 .... **4,000.00**

Pew, oak, plank seat, solid board back, ends carved with simple design ... **250.00**

Reliquary, 7 x 5 x 20½", 64 ozs, German silver gilt, miniature skeletal altar type, with twelve niches, carved ivory figures of Madonna, child, apostles, and saints, frame with agates and semi precious stones, hallmarks of Gregor Nicholas Bierfreund, Nuremberg, c1766 .... **7,750.00**

Retalbo on tin

  Jesus, 7 x 9", praying, patina, several pierced spots, one for hanging ... **45.00**

  Virgin Mary, 13½ x 20", carrying wrapped and pierced heart, draping and details, tin frame separated from picture, hinged door missing **25.00**

Sampler, Ann Allsop, 9¾ x 12½", green, brown, white, rose, and blue silk stitches, group of figures in upper right titled Crucifixion, Adam and Eve figures, apple tree with coiling serpent, animals and leaves **1,430.00**

Shrine, 26", pine, hanging, painted, scroll crest, crosses **125.00**

REVERSE PAINTING ON GLASS

History: The earliest examples of reverse painting on glass were produced in the 13th century

Italy. By the 17th century the technique had spread to Central and Eastern Europe. It spread westward as the glass industry center moved to Germany in the late 17th century.

The Alsace and Black Forest region developed a unique portraiture style. The half and three-quarter portraits often were titled below the portrait. Women tend to have general names. Most males are of famous men.

The English used a mezzotint method, rather than free-style, to create their reverse paintings. Landscapes and allegorical figures were popular. The Chinese began working in the medium in the 17th century, eventually favoring marine and patriotic scenes.

Reverse painting was done in America. Most were by folk artists, unsigned, who favored portraits, patriotic and mourning scenes, floral compositions, landscapes, and buildings. Known American artists include Benjamin Greenleaf, A. Cranfield, and Rowley Jacobs.

In the late 19th century commercially produced reverse paintings, often decorated with mother-of-pearl, became popular. Themes included the Statue of Liberty, the capitol in Washington, D.C., and various world fairs and expositions.

PORTRAITS

7¾ x 10½", Sylvia, woman in red dress,
  blue ground, orig frame **100.00**
9½ x 11½", Mailanderin, woman with
  flowers in her hair, replaced frame,
  9½ x 11½" **135.00**
9½ x 12", Emilie, balloon sleeve dress,
  large collar **500.00**
10 x 8", woman wearing plumed hat,
  seated by column, orig frame **375.00**
12½ x 9½", fashionable lady, titled "Par-
  isien," 19th C **1,200.00**
14½ x 11½", George Washington and
  family, Chinese Export School, 19th
  C, molded wooden frame **3,600.00**
15¾ x 11½", man and woman in land-
  scape, Chinese Export School, late
  18th or early 19th C **2,750.00**

SCENES

10 x 6½", Battleship, *USS Maine* **60.00**
10 x 8", landscape, pink, gray, white,
  green, and brown, Chinese Export
  School **175.00**
10 x 14½", Summer-Winter, winter land-
  scape with woman in velvet coat,
  summer landscape with young
  woman in straw bonnet carrying sickle, sprays of wheat, Chinese Export
  School, 19th C, pr **800.00**
14¼ x 10¼", winter landscape, Currier
  and Ives type, inscribed American
  Farm Scene, orig frame **100.00**

Pastoral scene, 16 x 20⅛", sgd "L. Ray," wood and plaster gilt frame, $75.00.

20 x 27", Blarney Castle, forest scene,
  castle on right, touches of mica and
  abalone **125.00**
12¼ x 10" h, farmers in cove, parcel gilt
  frame, Continental, late 18th C, pr . .   **2,400.00**
27 x 18½", Adoration of the Magi, later
  carved giltwood frame, Italian **425.00**

RIDGWAY

History: Throughout the 19th century the Ridgway family, through a series of partnerships, held a position of importance in Shelton and Hanley, Staffordshire, England. The connection began with Job and George, two brothers, and Job's two sons, John and William. In 1830 John and William separated with John retaining the Cauldon Place factory and William the Bell Works. By 1862 the porcelain division of Cauldon was carried on by Coalport China Ltd. William and his heirs continued at the Bell Works and the Church [Hanley] and Bedford [Shelton] works until the end of the 19th century.

Many early pieces are unmarked. Later marks include the initials of the many partnerships.

References: Susan and Al Bagdade, *Warman's English & Continental Pottery & Porcelain, 1st Edition,* Warman Publishing Co., Inc., 1987; G. A. Godden, *The Illustrated Guide To Ridgway Porcelains,* Barrie & Jenkins, 1972.

Additional Listings: Staffordshire, Historical, and Staffordshire, Romantic.

Ashtray, 5 x 3½", Coaching Days, metal
  matchbox holder **50.00**
Beverage Set, 6½ x 12⅜" tankard
  pitcher, six 4¼ x 5" mugs, Coaching
  Days, caramel ground, black scene,
  silver luster top bands and handles .   **300.00**
Bowl
  6", Shakespeare **25.00**

9½", Coaching Days 60.00
Box, 5 x 4 x 2", Coaching Days, five
scenes 85.00
Cheese Dish, cov, light brown floral
transfer 65.00

Creamer and Sugar, white ground, gray dec, heavy gold trim, $85.00.

Chop Plate, 13½", Coaching Days, "In
A Snow Drift," brown, Nov 1905 ... 125.00
Coffeepot, cov, 7½", Coaching Days, silver luster 85.00
Compote, 3", pink chrysanthemums,
gold trim, pr 65.00
Cup Plate, Marmora 40.00
Mug, silver luster trim
4", Shakespeare 35.00
4⅝", Coaching Days, light gold, black
scenes 35.00
5", Coaching Days 40.00
Pitcher, Chester pattern, blue and white 45.00
Syrup, 6", pewter top, 1835 .... 150.00
Tankard, Coaching Days, silver luster
bands and handle
9½" 100.00
10⅛" 110.00
Tea Caddy, 4 x 5¾", round cov, Coaching Days, scenes on all sides 150.00
Tea Tile, 6" d, round, Coaching Days . 100.00
Tray
8¼", Bank of Savannah, handles .. 165.00
12½", Coaching Days, A Christmas
Visitor, green, June 1907 .... 120.00
Vase, 4⅞", Coaching Days, egg shape,
caramel ground, black scenes, silver
luster top band and handle 60.00

RING TREES

History: A ring tree is a small, generally saucer shaped object made of glass, porcelain, metal, or wood with a center post in the shape of a hand, branches, or cylinder for hanging or storing finger rings.

GLASS

Baccarat, 3" h, vaseline, swirl pattern . 50.00
Lalique, 5" h, 3¾" d, figural center, madonna, frosted, marked "R. Lalique,
France 288" 195.00
Opaline, 3¼" h, blue, hp orange and
gold dec, ftd 45.00
Val St. Lambert, 4¼" d, 3½" h, acid cut-
back orchid like flowers, acid etched
background, cut center column, sgd 175.00

METAL

Bronze, 5 x 3", figural, parrot 45.00
Figural, Open hand, metal saucer, engraved edge, marked "Wilcox" 50.00
Sterling Silver, ornate base, gadroon
edge 45.00

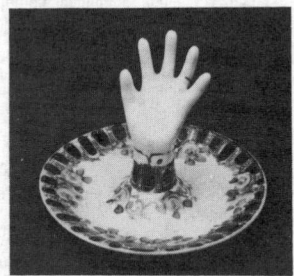

Porcelain, gold trim, maple leaf and handpainted mark, $47.50.

PORCELAIN

Jasperware, 3⅛" d, 3¼" h, deep blue,
white relief classical bust medallions 50.00
Limoges, hp pink flowers, scalloped
edge, marked "T & V" 40.00
Nippon
Figural, 3½", green wreath mark ... 30.00
Hand
Floral dec, gold ground 40.00
Ship scene, gold edge 60.00
Porcelain, hand and dish, hp rose dec,
gilting, marked "Hand Painted" and
maple leaf mark 47.00
R.S. Germany, blue forget-me-nots,
pastel ground, gold trim 60.00

POTTERY

Zsolnay, 3½", irid gold 75.00

ROCKINGHAM AND ROCKINGHAM BROWN GLAZED WARES

History: Rockingham ware can be divided into two categories. The first consists of the fine china and porcelain pieces made between 1826 and 1842 by the Rockingham Company of Swinton, Yorkshire, England, and its predecessor firms: Swinton, Bingley, Don, Leeds, and Brameld. The Bramelds developed the cadogan, a lidless teapot. Between 1826 and 1842 a quality soft paste body with a warm, silken feel was developed by the Bramelds. Elaborate specialty pieces were made. By 1830 the company employed 600 workers and listed 400 designs for dessert sets and 1,000 designs for tea and coffee services in their catalog. Unable to meet its payroll, the company closed in 1842.

The second category of Rockingham ware is pieces produced in the famous Rockingham brown glaze, which was intense and vivid purple-brown when fired. It had a dark, tortoise shell mottled appearance. The glaze was copied by many English and American potteries. American manufacturers who used Rockingham glaze include D. & J. Henderson of Jersey City, New Jersey, United States Pottery in Bennington, Vermont, potteries in East Liverpool, Ohio, and several potteries in Indiana and Illinois.

Reference: Susan and Al Bagdade, *Warman's English & Continental Pottery & Porcelain, 1st Edition,* Warman Publishing Co., Inc., 1987.

Additional Listings: Bennington and Bennington-Type.

Plate, 8¼″ d, blue and white transfer, romantic scene, imp "Brameld" mark, $85.00.

Bedpan, 16¾″ l	50.00
Bowl, 14″ d, 6½″ h, emb ext.	55.00
Container, 9″ d, 6″ l, flower pot shape, side handles	45.00
Figure	
Dog, 10″ h, seated, free standing front legs, hand tooling	175.00
Lions, 9½″ l, 6⅝″ h, rect bases, good detail and glaze, pr	400.00
Food Mold, 8½″ d, Turk's head, brown glaze, green flint enamel	75.00
Goblet, 5⅝″ h	525.00
Inkwell, 4¾″ l, lion	125.00
Jar, cov, 8½″ d, 8½″ h, emb designs	35.00
Miniature	
Bean Pot, 2¾″, lid	25.00
Cuspidor, 1⅝″ d	110.00
Jug, 1½″ h	10.00
Pitcher, 1⅞″ h, incised diamond and floral dec	60.00
Mixing Bowl, 16½″ d, 6⅝″ h, 1849 mark	2,600.00
Pitcher	
7¼″ h, detailed emb scenes of camel and elephant, imp mark "R Bew, Bilston"	45.00
7¾″ h, Paneled Grapevine pattern	1,050.00
9¼″ h, emb wreath with hanging game	25.00
12½″ h, hound handle, Vance Faience Pottery Co	600.00
Platter, 11½″ l	35.00
Teapot, 8¼″ h, emb design, portrait of lady	60.00
Toby	
9½″ h, coachman, period pewter and cork pouring stopper	450.00
Vase, 12″ h, stork	30.00
Wall Pocket, toby shape	365.00
Washboard, 11½ x 11″ panel, 23½ x 12⅜″ hardwood frame	200.00

ROCKWELL, NORMAN

History: Norman Rockwell (February 3, 1894–November, 1978) was a famous American artist. During the time he painted, from age 18 until his death, he created over 2,000 works.

His first professional efforts were illustrations for a children's book. He next worked for *Boy's Life,* the Boy Scout magazine. His most famous works were used by *Saturday Evening Post* for their cover illustrations.

Norman Rockwell painted everyday people in everyday situations, mixing a little humor with sentiment. His paintings and illustrations are treasured because of this sensitive approach. Rockwell painted people he knew and places with which he was familiar. New England landscapes are found in many of his illustrations.

References: Denis C. Jackson, *The Norman Rockwell Identification And Value Guide To: Mag-*

azines, Posters, Calendars, Books, 2nd Edition, published by author, 1985; Carl F. Lucky, *Norman Rockwell Art and Collectibles*, Books Americana, Inc., 1981; Mary Moline, *Norman Rockwell Collectibles, 5th Edition*, Rumbleseat Press, 1984.

Museums: Corner House, Stockbridge, MA; Norman Rockwell Museum, Northbrook, IL.

Reproduction Alert: Because of the popularity of his works, they have been reproduced on many objects. These new collectibles should not be confused with original artwork and illustrations. However, they do allow a collector more range in collecting interests and prices.

Additional Listings: See *Warman's Americana & Collectibles* for more examples.

HISTORIC

Advertising Blotter, Fisk Tires, 1924	**25.00**
Calendar, 1951, Four Seasons	**35.00**
Magazine Advertisement	
Listerine, black and white, Delineator 1929	**2.50**
Pratt & Lambert, black and white, Good Housekeeping, 1925	**6.50**
Magazine Cover	
Country Gentleman, August 25, 1917	**15.00**
Life, August 9, 1917	**25.00**
Saturday Evening Post, 1936, Springtime	**7.50**
Sheet Music, "I'm Sorry I Made You Cry"	**5.00**

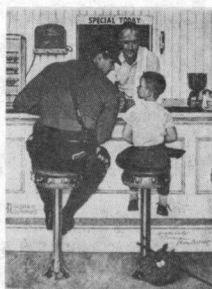

Print, 11 x 14", The Runaway, *Saturday Evening Post* cover, Sept 20, 1958, sgd by Rockwell, $350.00.

MODERN

Bell, Lincoln Mint, Downhill Daring, 1975	**80.00**
Coin	
Four Freedoms, Kennedy Mint, set of four	**175.00**

Four Seasons, Hamilton Mint, set of four	**100.00**
Figure	
Danbury Mint, Caught In The Act, 1980	**60.00**
Gorham, Four Seasons Series No. 2, Young Love, 4 pc set, 1973	**1,100.00**
Goebel Hemmelwerk, His First Smoke	**400.00**
Dave Grossman, No Swimming, 1973	**35.00**
Rockwell Museum	
Bedtime, 1979	**60.00**
First Prom, 1980	**90.00**
Ingot, Hamilton Mint, Four Freedoms, set of 5, silver, 1974	**250.00**
Plate	
Home For Christmas, Franklin Mint, 1975	**190.00**
Last Minute Changes, Lynell Studios, 1979	**30.00**
Toymaker, Rockwell Society, 1977	**195.00**
Print	
Circle Fine Arts, limited edition, sgd and numbered, titled "Children At The Window," 1976	**1,700.00**
Ettinger, Ltd, limited edition, sgd and numbered, titled "Football Hero," 1978	**2,300.00**
Stein, Music Lesson, 1982, Rockwell Museum	**125.00**
Thimble, Gorham, Tiny Tim, 1980	**20.00**
Tray, 11" d, The Country Postman, US Postal Credit Union, 1976	**18.00**

ROGERS & SIMILAR STATUARY

History: John Rogers, born in America in 1829, studied sculpturing in Europe and produced the first plaster-of-paris statue, "The Checker Players," in 1859. It was followed by "The Slave Auction" in 1860.

His works were popular parlor pieces of the Victorian era. He produced at least 80 different subjects and the total number of groups made from the originals is estimated to be over 100,000.

Casper Hennecke, one of Rogers' contemporaries, operated C. Hennecke & Company from 1881 until 1896 in Milwaukee, Wisconsin. His statuary often is confused with Rogers' work since both are very similiar.

It is difficult to find a statue in undamaged condition and with original paint. Use the following conversions: 10% minor flaking; 10% chips; 10–20% piece or pieces broken and reglued; 20% flaking; 50% repainting.

References: Paul and Meta Bieier, *John Rogers' Groups of Statuary*, published by author, 1971; Betty C. Haverly, *Hennecke's Florentine Statuary*, published by author, 1972; David H. Wallace, *John Rogers: The People's Sculptor*, Wesleyan Univ., 1976.

Hennecke's Florentine Statuary, First Love, 13½" h, $200.00.

ROGERS

Bath, 27", sgd	2,000.00
Charity Patient, 22", 1866	650.00
Courtship In Sleepy Hollow, 16½", 2/8/ 1870	750.00
Elder's Daughter, 21½", 1887	800.00
Favored Scholar, 21", 1873	425.00
First Ride, 18", 1888	750.00
Hide and Seek: Whoop!, 46", 1874	775.00
Is It So Nominated In The Bond?, 23", 1880	375.00
Private Theatricals, 24", 6/1/1871	700.00
Returned Volunteer, How The Fort Was Taken, 20", 1864	600.00
Rip Van Winkle On The Mountain, 21", 7/25/1871	500.00
School Examination, 20", 1867	500.00
We Boys, 17", head down, 1872	425.00
Weighing The baby, 21", 11/21/1876	550.00

ROGERS TYPE

Croquet Player, 18"	200.00
Evening Devotion, 21"	250.00
Family Cares, 13"	95.00
Lost & Found, 19"	100.00
Red Riding Hood, 11½"	350.00
Welcome, 32", alabaster	300.00

ROOKWOOD POTTERY

History: Mrs. Marie Longworth Nicholas Storer, Cincinnati, Ohio, founded Rookwood Pottery in 1880. The name of this outstanding American art pottery came from her family estate "Rookwood," named for the rooks (crows) which inhabited the wooded grounds.

There are five elements to the Rookwood marking system—the clay or body mark, the size mark, the decorator mark, the date mark, and the factory mark. Rookwood art pottery can best be dated from factory marks.

In 1880–1882 the factory mark was the name "Rookwood" incised or painted on the base. Between 1881 and 1886 the firm name, address, and year appeared in an oval frame. Beginning in 1886, the impressed "RP" monogram appeared and a flame-mark was added for each year until 1900. After 1900 a Roman numeral, indicating the last two digits of the year of production, was added at the bottom of the "RP" flame-mark monogram. This last mark is the one most often found on Rookwood pottery today.

Though the Rookwood pottery filed for bankruptcy in 1941, it was soon reorganized under new management. Efforts at maintaining the pottery proved futile, and it again was sold in 1956 and in 1959. The pottery was moved to Starkville, Mississippi, in conjunction with the Herschede Clock Co. It finally ceased operation in 1967.

Rookwood wares changed with the times. The variety is endless, in part because of the great variations in glazes and designs due to the creativity of the many talented artists.

References: Herbert Peck, *The Book of Rookwood Pottery*, Crown Publishers, Inc., 1968; Herbert Peck, *The Second Book of Rookwood Pottery*, published by author, 1985.

Collectors' Club: American Art Pottery Association, P.O. Box 714, Silver Spring, MD 20901.

Ashtray, 3", horse portrait, shades of brown, celadon green ground, artist sgd "Ora King, 1946"	100.00
Biscuit Jar, 6", cream gloss, relief fruits and flowers, c1943, sgd	175.00
Bookends, pr	
Elephant, celadon	145.00
Panthers, matte green glaze, 1939	175.00
Bowl	
5½ x 4", dark brown leaves, purple flowers, light green ground, artist sgd "CST, 1927"	150.00
8" d, 4¼" h, standard dark green glaze, gold and yellow palm leaves, cutouts between leaves, c1893, artist sgd "Harriet Strafer"	3,500.00
Candlesticks, mottled blue green glaze, matte, marked "#1635," 1921, pr	160.00
Console Set, blue matte finish, 11" d bowl supported by three figural elephants on 6¾" base, candlesticks 5¾" h figural elephants, trunks raised, sgd, 1929	400.00
Cup and Saucer, 3½", octagonal, din-	

nerware, blue sailing ships, white glaze **65.00**

Ewer, 5½ x 9″, white blossoms, green leaves, heavy slip relief against olive green bisque ground, tooled gilded neck, artist sgd "Grace Young, 1897" ... **250.00**

Figure, elephant, aventurine glaze, red, brown, and gold dust, c1937 ..... **220.00**

Figurine, Spanish Woman, 11″ h **285.00**

Honey Jug, 4¾", black and white swallow flying over bamboo stalks, tan sky, brown top and handle, gold accents, Limoges finish, artist sgd "Albert Valentien" **400.00**

Jar, cov, bulbous, William Hentschel
12 x 18½", raised squeezebag stylized leaves dec, olive-brown and dark blue matte glaze, pale blue and white ground, 1926 .... **1,500.00**
13 x 19″, raised squeezebag stylized leaves dec, olive-brown and dark blue ground, dark blue and white ground, 1926 .... **1,800.00**

Ashtray, Rook, reddish-brown glaze, $115.00.

Jug, 2⅝ x 4½", moss green, carved ferns and leaves **250.00**

Lamp, 23½", kerosene oil, yellow chrysanthemums, green leaves, brown ground, artist sgd "A. V. B." (Artus Van Briggle) **750.00**

Mug, 5″, black boy portrait, artist sgd, 1901 .... **2,200.00**

Paperweight, dog, ivory, artist sgd, 1934 **120.00**

Planter, Ambrosia, artist sgd "Louise Abel, 1926" **500.00**

Plaque
5¾ x 7½", titled "Birches," white birch trees, green spring foliage, violet-purple sky, artist sgd "Lenore Asbury, 1919," orig frame **750.00**
5¾ x 7¾", vellum, titled "Driveway,"

tree lined road with tracks, royal blue horizon, artist sgd "Fred Rothenbusch," orig frame and factory seal **700.00**
7¾ x 6″, vellum, titled "Northern Birches," birch trees, pale pink snow covered ground, artist sgd "Sara Sax," orig frame and factory seal **1,800.00**

Tile
Architectural, 8″ sq, two galleons, deep relief, four colors **400.00**
Tea, ivy and lavender flowers, ivory ground **120.00**

Vase
3¼", yellow jonquils, shiny green shading to brown ground, artist sgd "L. Van Briggle, 1901" **235.00**
5″, floral, wide silver bands, iris glaze, artist sgd "K. Shirayamadani," 1901 .... **4,000.00**
5 x 11″, vellum glaze, snowy landscape, dark blue trees, yellow horizon, artist sgd "S. E. Coyne" ... **900.00**
5½ x 10½", baluster, iris glaze, taupe, ochre, and white toadstools, black to pale peach to loden green ground, artist sgd "Carl Schmidt, 1908" **7,500.00**
5½ x 12½", bulbous, two handles, elongated cylindrical neck, flared rim, standard glaze, yellow dogwood blossoms, green and yellow leaves, burnt orange to yellow ground, artist sgd "Kataro Shirayamandani, 1890" **850.00**
5½ x 12¾", cylinder, modeled, deeply carved blood red and lime green poppy blossoms and pods, matte maroon and dark blue ground, 1907 .... **1,500.00**
5¾ x 10¾", bulbous, slightly flared rim, vellum, carnations dec, medium blue to celery green to pale pink ground, artist sgd "Edward Diers, 1928" **800.00**
6″, sea green, fish, artist sgd "E & H," 1905 .... **3,000.00**
6½" h, blue matte with lime green, flying geese band, marked "LA", c1908 .... **475.00**
8″, porcelain, wax resist type glaze, sgd **775.00**
9″, three birds in flight, standard glaze, artist sgd "CCL," 1906 ... **2,000.00**
12″, carved florals, artist sgd "K. Shirayamadani, 1929" **2,200.00**
22″, floor, bulbous, flared collared neck, slip-relief poppy blossoms and stems, chocolate to golden brown ground, artist sgd "Mary Nourse, 1902" **3,500.00**

ROSE BOWLS

History: A rose bowl, a decorative open bowl with a crimped, pinched, or petal top, held fragrant rose petals or potpourri which served as an air freshener in the late Victorian period. Practically every glass manufacturer made rose bowls in a variety of patterns and glass types, including fine art glass.

Additional Listings: See specific glass categories.

Opalescent Stripe, blue, $75.00.

3⅛ x 2⅞", gold prunus dec, shaded brown satin glass, gold butterfly, Webb	375.00
3¼", gold flowers and insects dec, brown ground, Webb	125.00
3⅞ x 3¼", rivulet pattern MOP, shaded chartreuse green, white int., eight crimp top, applied ruffled base	250.00
4½", swirled white, yellow and puce, blue int., Northwood	250.00
4⅜", gold flowers and insects, peachblow ground, Webb	350.00
4¾ x 8⅛", cream opaque, amber applied handle, leaves, and branches, pink applied flowers	200.00
5½ x 5½", emb ribbed DQ, MOP, shaded rose, white int., six crimp top, clear applied blue-green feet	375.00
5⅜ x 4", rose overlay satin glass, multicolored petit point enamel, gold trim, white int.	325.00
7¼ x 7½", DQ, MOP, satin, amberina shading, Webb	1,200.00

ROSE CANTON, ROSE MANDARIN, ROSE MEDALLION

History: The pink rose color has given its name to three related groups of Chinese export porcelain. Rose Mandarin was produced from the late 18th century to approximately 1840. Rose Canton began somewhat later extending through the first half of the 19th century. Rose Medallion originated in the early 19th century and was made through the early 20th century.

Rose Mandarin derives its name from the Mandarin figure(s) found in garden scenes with women and children. The women often feature gold decorations in their hair. Polychrome enamels and birds separate the scenes.

Rose Medallion has alternating panels of figures and birds and flowers. The elements are four in number, separated evenly around the center medallion. Peonies and foliage fill voids.

Rose Canton is similar to Rose Medallion except the figure panels are replaced by flowers. People are present only if the medallion partitions are absent. Some patterns have been named—Butterfly and Cabbage, Rooster, etc. The category actually is a catchall for all pink enamel ware not fitting into the first two groups.

Reference: Sandra Andacht, *Oriental Antiques & Art: An Identification And Value Guide*, Wallace-Homestead, 1987.

Reproduction Alert: Rose Medallion is still made, although the quality does not match the earlier examples.

ROSE CANTON

Bowl	
6¾ x 3½", rice	65.00
10", gold trim, scalloped	250.00
Box, 13", domed lid, octagonal, c1800	250.00
Brush Pot, 4¾", ladies in pavilion, reticulated, relief molded, gilt trim, c1850	300.00
Creamer, 4", double twisted handle, gilt trim	200.00
Demitasse Cup and Saucer, floral panels, c1860	50.00
Dish, 10½ x 9½", shell shape, gold trim, c1850	450.00
Jar, 3½ x 3⅜", barrel shape, c1850	200.00
Plate, 8½", floral, insects on border	85.00
Platter, 9", gold trim, c1800	200.00
Vase, 10½", medallions with flowers, butterflies, and birds, floral borders, mid 19th C	400.00

ROSE MANDARIN

Bowl, 9", Oriental figures, river landscape, floral panels, int. rim border, c1870	800.00
Brush Box, 4", oval	150.00
Mug, 5½", figures in court setting	250.00
Plate, 8⅛", set of 8	250.00
Punch Bowl, 13", two ribbon tied floral bouquets, smaller sprigs within four cartouches on ext., int. with central	

floral cluster, garlands, figures, black
band, c1780 .... **2,350.00**
Soup Plate, 8″ 100.00
Tea Set, cov teapot, cup, orig woven
basket, 4 pcs 175.00

**Rose Medallion, 8¼ x 9½″, covered
vegetable dish, nut finial, Mandarin
dec, c1775, $350.00.**

ROSE MEDALLION

Basket, 12″ d, reticulated sides, match-
ing underplate, late 19th C 450.00
Bouillon cup and saucer 45.00
Bowl, 10 x 4″, black outlined reserves,
19th C 225.00
Butter Pat, 3″ 35.00
Candlesticks, 8″, 1820–40, pr 700.00
Creamer, 4″, bulbous, late 19th C 75.00
Flask, 18¼″, bottle shape, cov, gold
knob, scenic center medallion with
court figures, floral dec, late 19th C . 300.00
Plate
8″, center with crest of Macartney &
Filgate 700.00
10″, gold trim 150.00
Sauce Boat, cov, 7½″, gold handles and
finial 400.00
Sugar, cov, 6″, late 19th C 100.00
Umbrella Stand, 24″, 19th C 725.00
Vase, 24″, slender ovoid, puckered
sides, ribbon and bow at neck to imitate cloth bag, applied fu dog handles, 19th C, pr 1,000.00
Vegetable Dish, cov, almond shape, letter "C" in gilded medallions on lid and
center of dish, orange glaze 465.00

MARKE

ROSENTHAL

History: Rosenthal Porcelain Manufactory be-
ation.

Reference: Susan and Al Bagdade, *Warman's
English & Continental Pottery & Porcelain, 1st Edition,* Warman Publishing Co., Inc., 1987.

Bonbon, 2½ x 5¼″, Winifred pattern,
pink Moss Rose dec, SS base 25.00
Bowl, 10¾″, pink, strawberries and
leaves, scalloped gold trim, scroll
handle, red glazed underside, artist
sgd 85.00
Cake Plate, 10″, multicolored roses, cobalt blue and gold border 50.00
Compote, 12″ d, ladies' heads, fruit and
flowers, gold trim, gold handles 100.00
Creamer and Sugar, gold trim, sgd
"Donatello" 36.00
Cup and Saucer, Maria pattern, heavy
silver overlay 60.00
Dresser Set, lavender flowers, gold trim,
3 pcs 75.00
Figure
3″, rabbit, dark brown 30.00
3¾ x 1¾″, butterfly 75.00
5½″, nude, kneeling, sgd "A Caas-
mann" 400.00
6½″, girl feeding fawn, artist sgd ... 165.00
7½″, springer spaniel, basket, 1932 . 175.00
11″, princess and frog 300.00
Fruit Bowl, 9″, grapes and leaves,
cream ground, gold handles 165.00
Fruit Set, 10″ bowl, six 8″ plates, blue,
green, yellow, and pink with pink
roses, gold dec, 7 pcs 385.00
Game Set, Fish, 9″ plates, fish swimming in water, scalloped gold rim, set
of 6 .... 175.00
Gravy Boat, Moss Rose, attached underplate 35.00
Nappy, brown nuts and flowers on gold
ground, ruffled rim 55.00

**Figurine, 10¼″ h, "Goldfish," artist sgd
"Heidenreich," $750.00.**

Nut Set, master bowl, six 3½" serving
  bowls, Pompadour pattern, cream
  ground, ornate gold scrolled rim, 7
  pcs **60.00**
Plate
  8½", hp, grapes and roses **40.00**
  10¼", hp, multicolored roses, cobalt
    blue and gold border, open handle,
    artist sgd **48.00**
Vase
  6", white, black cats **40.00**
  7", crackle, rust foliage, artist sgd
    "Stockmayer," 1946 .... **90.00**
  8", portrait, classical lady, crimson,
    green, and gold **150.00**
  9½", tulip shape, hp, pastel flowers,
    artist sgd **80.00**
  10", white **65.00**
  11¼", Victorian ladies, gold scroll
    frame on cobalt blue ground **410.00**

ROSEVILLE POTTERY

History: In the late 1880s a group of investors purchased the J. B. Owens Pottery in Roseville, Ohio, and made utilitarian stoneware items. In 1892 the firm was incorporated and joined by George F. Young who became general manager. Four generations of Youngs controlled Roseville until the early 1950s.

A series of acquisitions began: Midland Pottery of Roseville in 1898, Clark Stoneware Plant in Zanesville (formerly used by Peters and Reed), and Muskingum Stoneware (Mosaic Tile Company) in Zanesville. In 1898 the offices also moved from Roseville to Zanesville.

In 1900 Roseville introduced its art pottery—Rozane. Rozane became a trade name to cover a large series of lines. The art lines were made in limited amounts after 1919.

The success of Roseville depended on its commercial lines, first developed by John J. Herald and Frederick Rhead in the first decades of the 1900s. In 1918 Frank Ferrell became art director and developed over 80 lines of pottery. The economic depression of the 1930s brought more lines, including Pine Cone.

In the 1940s a series of high gloss glazes were tried to revive certain lines. In 1952 Raymor dinnerware was produced. None of these changes brought economic success. In November 1954 Roseville was bought by the Mosaic Tile Company.

References: Sharon and Bob Huxford, *The Collectors Encyclopedia Of Roseville Pottery*, Collector Books, 1976; Sharon and Bob Huxford, *The Collectors Encyclopedia Of Roseville Pottery, Second Series*, Collector Books, 1980.

Collectors' Club: American Art Pottery Association, P. O. Box 714, Silver Spring, MD 20901.

Additional Listings: See *Warman's Americana & Collectibles* for more examples.

Apothecary Jar, cov, 11", Twain series,
  marked "Rozart" **215.00**
Ashtray
  Creamware, "Smoke Al Rashid" ... **50.00**
  Pine Cone, 4", blue **85.00**
Basket
  Columbine, brown, 12½" **100.00**
  Dogwood, 6" **100.00**
  Rozane, green **145.00**
  Water Lily, 8" **75.00**
  Zephyr Lily, blue **75.00**
Bookends, pr, Snowberry, blue **110.00**
Bowl
  Monticello, 13", double handles, blue **100.00**
  Pine Cone, 6", brown, double handles **65.00**
  Rosecraft, orange and brown, 5 x 1½" **45.00**
  White Rose, marked "387-4" **40.00**
Candlesticks, pr
  Donatello, 6½", early stamp mark,
    orig sticker **275.00**
  Morning Glory, 4¾", green, orig
    sticker **250.00**
Children's Dishes
  Creamer, 3½", duck in top hat, untied
    shoes, green band, marked "Rv" . **60.00**
  Feeding Dish, 8", seated dog, gray
    band, sgd "Rv" **65.00**
Cider Set, Peony, green, 7½" pitcher,
  four mugs **325.00**
Compote
  Donatello, 4" **60.00**
  Velmoss Scroll, ftd **80.00**
Console Bowl, Blackberry, 13" **115.00**
Cup, Magnolia **38.00**
Ewer
  Bittersweet, 8" **48.00**
  Ming Tree, 10", turquoise **100.00**
Jardiniere
  Baneda, green, 6" **85.00**
  Blackberry, 4" **125.00**
  Carnelian, 6½ x 7" **65.00**
  Cherry Blossom
    4", brown **120.00**
    7" **90.00**
  Dahlrose, 6 x 8" **145.00**
  Donatello, 7" **100.00**
  Jonquil, 6" **110.00**
  Old Ivory, 10 x 7" **165.00**
  Pine Cone, green, 7" **55.00**
Lamp
  Orian, red **185.00**
  Sunflower **165.00**
Mug
  Creamware, Osman Temple, 1916 . **125.00**
  Rozane, cherries, 4" **150.00**

Planter, Pasadena, green, orig frame .	45.00
Tankard Set, Moose, pitcher and six mugs	275.00
Tea Set, Snowbery, blue	165.00
Umbrella Stand, Donatello, 21″	300.00

Urn

Florentine, 8 x 8½″	115.00
Monticello, 7½″, turquoise, crayon mark	125.00

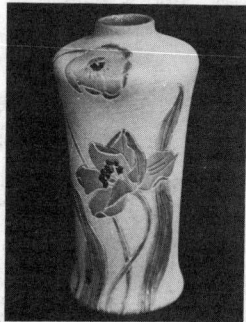

Vase, 6¼″ h, Woodland, Rozane Ware, $750.00.

Vase

Baneda, 6″, blue, handles	65.00
Blackberry, 6″, handles	150.00
Columbine, 14½″, blue, handles	175.00
Dahlrose, 12″, orig label	75.00
Ferrella, 6″, red	175.00
Fudji, 5½ x 8½″, squeeze-bag dec, high glaze, gold, turquoise, and midnight blue Alhambraesque design, bisque ground, emb "Rozanne Ware," artist sgd	900.00
Futura, 7½″, globular	225.00
Imperial II, 4½″, turquoise	85.00
Jonquil, mottled brown and green ground, white and yellow jonquils, green leaves	
4¾″ d, 4½″ h	60.00
5¼″ d, 6½″ h, orig silver label, c1931	70.00
Luffa, brown, 8″	100.00
Monticello, 5″	50.00
Orian, red, 7½″	125.00
Sunflower, 5¼″	70.00
White Rose, 4″	20.00
Windsor, 5″, blue, handles	75.00

Wall Pocket

Fuschia, rust and brown	200.00
Futura, 6¼ x 8¼″, brown ground, blue, yellow, green, and lavender panels, c1928	125.00
La Rosa, c1924	75.00

ROYAL BAYREUTH

History: In 1794 the Royal Bayreuth factory was founded in Tettau, Bavaria. Royal Bayreuth introduced their figural patterns in 1885. Designs of animals, people, fruits, and vegetables decorated a wide array of tablewares and inexpensive souvenir items.

Tapestry ware, rose and other patterns, were made in the late 19th century. The surface of the ware feels and looks like woven cloth. Tapestry ware was made by covering the porcelain with a piece of fabric tightly stretched over the surface, decorating the fabric, glazing the piece, and firing.

The Royal Bayreuth crest mark varied in design and color. Many wares were unmarked. It is difficult to verify the chronological years of production due to the lack of records.

Royal Bayreuth still manufactures dinnerware. It has not maintained production of earlier wares, particularly the figural items.

Reference: Susan and Al Bagdade, *Warman's English & Continental Pottery & Porcelain, 1st Edition,* Warman Publishing Co., Inc., 1987.

Additional Listings: Sunbonnet Babies.

Corinthian

Chamberstick, large, green, serpentine handle	115.00
Creamer, blue mark	90.00
Humidor, cov	200.00
Jardiniere, 8 x 6″	90.00
Pitcher, 5½″	55.00
Smoke Set, ashtray and holder	45.00
Toothpick, blue mark	75.00

Devil and Cards

Candy Dish	175.00
Creamer	125.00
Cup and Saucer	150.00
Dresser Tray	200.00
Match Holder, wall	250.00
Pitcher, devil handle, green mark, 4¾″	165.00
Salt, master	150.00

Grape Cluster

Demitasse Cup and Saucer, MOP, cerise shading	75.00
Marmalade, cov, green	150.00
Pitcher, white MOP, lavender, marked "Germany"	325.00
Sugar, cov	100.00

Lobster

Ashtray	50.00
Creamer	45.00
Pitcher, milk	100.00
Sauce	65.00

Miscellaneous Patterns

Ashtray, scenic, men fishing from rowboat, wishbone handle, gold trim	50.00
Biscuit Jar, cov, figural, strawberry, 6¼"	125.00
Cake Plate, 10½", open handles, pink and green cherries, blossoms and leaves, satin finish	45.00
Candleholder, figural, dog, 2½ x 4 x 4", black satin, orange trim, tail forms handle, blue mark	130.00
Candy Dish, oval, Bavarian women and horses	65.00
Chocolate Pot, cov, boy seated on log	250.00

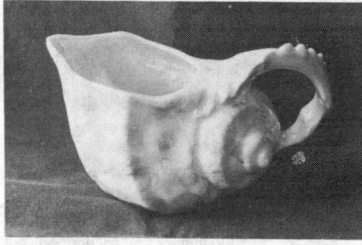

Creamer, 3¼" h, 5¼" w, Conch Shell pattern, white irid, $65.00.

Creamer, figural

Apple	75.00
Bellringer	235.00
Coachman	180.00
Elk, 4¼" h, 3½" d, brown and cream shades, blue mark	65.00
Frog, 3¾ x 5, green, yellow, and orange	100.00
Lemon	100.00
Oak Leaf	85.00
Parakeet	125.00
Parrot, green, blue mark	210.00
Robin	140.00
Rose	150.00
Stag, 4½", blue mark	85.00
Water Buffalo, red	130.00
Hatpin Holder, farmer holding reins of two horses, farmhouse in background, scalloped saucer base, blue mark	235.00
Match Holder, stork, enamel dec, green and yellow ground	250.00
Plate, 9", girl with basket of flowers, gold scrolled edge	400.00

Rose Bowl, 2⅞" h, girl and dog dec	65.00

Pitcher, water, figural

Apple	90.00
Cat, 2⅝ x 4¾", black satin, yellow eyes, orange mouth and nose	90.00
Oak Leaf, 6¾" h	160.00
Rooster, 5", blue satin, orange comb and trim	100.00
Relish Dish, 7½", poinsettia dec	135.00
Salt Shaker, ivory	25.00
String Holder, rooster, multicolored	225.00
Teapot, sheep scene, red ground	245.00
Toothpick, figural, clown, holder on back, blue mark	500.00
Tureen, figural, rose, cov and underplate	250.00

Vase

2⅜ x 3⅜", cows, two handles, green ground, hallmarked SS top rim, blue mark	40.00
2¾" h, 2½" d, ball shape, ftd, hunt scene, blue mark	45.00

Nursery Rhyme

Basket, girl and dog playing	200.00
Bell, Little Jack Horner, verse	225.00
Bowl, 9½", Goose Girl	135.00
Candlestick, Little Bo Peep, 4"	65.00
Child's Feeding Dish, Jack and the Beanstalk	85.00
Salt and Pepper Shakers, Little Boy Blue and Jack and Jill, pr	200.00

Poppy

Cake Plate, MOP, open handles	200.00
Creamer, red	90.00
Nut Dish, red	50.00
Salt Shaker	25.00

Sandbabies

Box, cov	80.00
Creamer	65.00
Inkwell, blue mark	400.00
Plate, 7½"	50.00

Snowbabies

Cereal Set, sledding	150.00
Inkwell	100.00
Plate, 6", babies playing	70.00

Sunbonnet Babies

Bell	350.00
Candlesticks, 4½" h, babies fishing, pr	325.00

Creamer

3½", babies ironing	185.00
4", babies cleaning, tankard	200.00
Cup and Saucer, babies sewing	145.00
Dish, babies sewing, diamond shape	150.00
Hatpin Holder	225.00
Mug, babies sewing	150.00
Nappy, babies cleaning	155.00
Pitcher, milk, fishing	300.00

Plate

5", babies ironing	145.00
6½", babies washing	120.00
7½", babies washing	125.00

Tomato
Biscuit Jar, cov 125.00
Box, cov, 3¾" d, 3¼" h, blue mark . 40.00
Cup and Saucer 85.00
Gravy Boat 50.00
Mustard, cov 55.00
Teaset, teapot, creamer, cov sugar . 180.00
Toothpick Holder, round, children play-
ing ring around the rosey, four raised
feet, two handles, blue mark 150.00

Tapestry, pitcher, 5", white ground, gold trim, $300.00.

ROSE TAPESTRY

Bowl, 11", pink roses, molded edge . . 750.00
Cake Plate, 9¾", pierced handles, blue
mark 235.00
Creamer, 4", three color roses, gold trim
on handle and rim 200.00
Dresser Tray, 8¼ x 11½", three color
roses 325.00
Hair Receiver, 4¾ x 2¾", pink roses . . 200.00
Hatpin Holder, green mark 300.00
Pin Dish, leaf shape, green mark 150.00
Planter, 2 gold handles 250.00
Plate, 7½", three color roses, scalloped,
gold rim 225.00
Ring Tree, pink, white roses 175.00
Slipper 375.00
Sugar, cov, pink and yellow 300.00
Teapot, cov 200.00
Toothbrush Holder, 2¼" d, 4¼" h, three
color roses, ftd 225.00
Toothpick, 4½", pink roses 475.00
Vase, 4", multicolored flowers and
leaves, blue mark 225.00

TAPESTRY, MISCELLANEOUS

Box, cov, 3½", hunt scene 120.00
Clock, Christmas cactus, blue mark . . 485.00

Creamer, tankard shape, girl with hat
and muff 100.00
Dresser Tray, Japanese chrysanthe-
mum dec, leaf shape 200.00
Humidor
Bell Ringer pattern 750.00
Scenic, cows in pasture 475.00
Match Holder, tavern scene, gold trim,
blue mark 225.00
Pin Dish, leaf shape, colonial couple . 150.00
Pitcher
4", hounds swimming with stag, blue
mark 160.00
6", women bathing by castle 425.00
Powder Dish, cov, 5½ x 3½", colonial
couple dancing 475.00
Stamp Box, colonial dec, undertray . . 80.00
Vase, 4", ovoid, scenic, deer, trees, gold
trim, blue mark 225.00

ROYAL BONN

History: In 1836 Franz Anton Mehlem founded
a Rhineland factory that produced earthenware
and porcelain, including household, decorative,
technical, and sanitary items. In 1890 the name
Royal was added to the mark. All items made after
1890 include the name "Royal Bonn." The firm
reproduced Hochst figures between 1887 and
1903. These figures, produced in both porcelain
and earthenware, were made from the original
molds from the defunct Prince-Electoral Mayence
Manufactory in Hochst. The factory was purchased
by Villeroy and Boch in 1921 and closed it in 1931.

Reference: Susan and Al Bagdade, *Warman's
English & Continental Pottery & Porcelain, 1st Edition,* Warman Publishing Co., Inc., 1987.

Biscuit Jar, 5¼" d, 7" h, beige ground,
pink and blue flowers, green leaves,
brass rim, cov, and handle 100.00
Bottle, 9", vine and flowers, brown mark 110.00
Bowl
8½", hp, floral dec, SP rim, sgd and
numbered 145.00
9½", cream, floral dec, metal rim,
c1760 . . . . 185.00
Celery Tray, floral dec 75.00
Cheese Dish, cov, pink floral design . . 95.00
Cup and Saucer, blue and white, wild
roses 30.00

Vase, 9¾″ d top, 10½″ h, multicolored, gold trim, marked "Bonn," $500.00.

Ewer, 12½″, hp bird, orchids, and dragonfly, encircling gold lizard handle . 175.00
Jam Jar, floral dec, beige ground, SP lid and bail 55.00
Mug, 4″, blackberries and flowers, shaded green ground 50.00
Teapot, 4½ x 9½″, cream, red, black and blue florals, gold gilding, marked "1755" 50.00
Vase
  5 x 8″, brown and yellow ground, gold and orange floral dec 100.00
  5½″, Victorian boy and girl sledding, shaded fuchsia ground 75.00
  7″, globular, Boucher scenes, blue transfers, 1850 .... 75.00
  8¾″, flared, white roses, shaded green ground 100.00
  11″, multicolored floral dec, sgd and numbered 115.00
  12″, bulbous, gold neck, multicolored goose flying into golden sun, green frogs 250.00
  13½″, portrait, Victorian lady, artist sgd 600.00
  16½″, cov, turquoise body, twin gild handles, circular molded base ... 225.00

threatened in 1779, the Danish king acquired ownership, appointing Mueller manager and adopting the name "Royal Copenhagen." The crown sold its interest in 1867; the company remains privately owned today.

Blue Fluted, Royal Copenhagen's most famous pattern, was created in 1780. It is of Chinese origin and comes in three styles: smooth edge, closed lace edge, and perforated lace edge (full lace). Many other factories copied it. Flora Danica, named for a famous botanical work was introduced in 1789 and remained exclusive to Royal Copenhagen. Botanical illustrations were done free hand; all edges and perforations were cut by hand.

Royal Copenhagen porcelain is marked with three wavy lines which signify ancient waterways and a crown, the latter added in 1889. Stoneware does not have the crown mark.

Reference: Susan and Al Bagdade, *Warman's English & Continental Pottery & Porcelain, 1st Edition,* Warman Publishing Co., Inc., 1987.

Additional Listings: Limited Edition Collectors' Plates.

Bouillon Cup and Saucer, Flora Danica pattern, botanical specimen within border, pink enamel and gilding, set of 12 .... 6,875.00
Bowl, 4½″, orange blossoms, green leaves 85.00
Box, egg shape, seagulls on cov 165.00
Dessert Plate, 10″, Flora Danica pattern, set of 6 .... 1,600.00

Figurine, 6⅞″ h, "Old Lake Oje," Mr. Sandman from Hans Christian Andersen, crown mark, numbered #1129, $500.00.

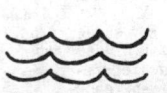

ROYAL COPENHAGEN

History: Franz Mueller established a porcelain factory at Copenhagen in 1775. When bankruptcy

Figure
  2¾″, mouse seated on nut, #511 .. 35.00
  3 x 5″, Satyre holding snake, sitting, #1712 .... 200.00

3 x 5½ x 6½", Satyre playing with
bear, #648 . . . .   **225.00**
3¾", three penguins, standing **190.00**
4½", Pekingese, tan and white, beg-
ging on haunches, #1776 . . . . . .   **135.00**
5¾", girl with doll, #3539 . . . .   **85.00**
6" Fawn, seated, c1930 . . . .   **150.00**
7½", boy, sitting on rocks whittling
stick, sgd on back of rocks, #905   **265.00**
7½ x 13½", European pheasant . . .   **150.00**
8", Pan, playing pipes, lizard at base,
#1020 . . . .   **235.00**
8½", Pan, sitting on column, holding
flute, rabbit at base **375.00**
Gravy Boat, underplate, white, blue
morning glories **50.00**
Jar, cov, 8½", reserves of farmers with
oxen, milkmaid finial **120.00**
Pitcher, 4", cobalt blue, floral dec **50.00**
Plate
7", commemorative, Frederick IX,
1947–72, blue and white **45.00**
8½", outdoor winter scene **45.00**
Platter, 17¼", oval, Flora Danica pat-
tern, marked and numbered **450.00**
Salt and Pepper, 2½", Fluted Lace pat-
tern, blue and white, pr **65.00**
Tea Set, Fluted Lace pattern, blue and
white, 5 pcs **275.00**
Tray, 6½", round, rose, fish swimming .   **125.00**
Urn, 18½", commemorative, horse and
rider, artist sgd "Gotfried Roti," c1900   **900.00**
Vase
4½", dogwood blossoms, #1584-271   **60.00**
7", mermaid on rocks, gazing into har-
bor **65.00**
7¾", floral and dragonfly dec, c1890   **150.00**
9", white rose, 1895 . . . .   **115.00**
15", bulbous, floral bouquet, blue
ground, artist sgd, 1925 . . . .   **330.00**
Wall Plaque, 13", young girl, artist sgd
"J Hedegaard" **200.00**

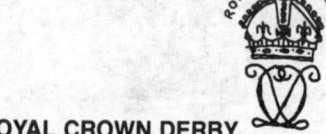

ROYAL CROWN DERBY

History: Derby Crown Porcelain Co., established in 1875 in Derby, England, had no connection with earlier Derby factories which operated in
the late 18th and early 19th centuries. In 1890 the
company was appointed "Manufacturers of Porcelain to Her Majesty" (Queen Victoria) and from
that date has been known as "Royal Crown
Derby."

Derby porcelains from 1878 to 1890 carry only
the standard crown printed mark. After 1891 the
mark carries the "Royal Crown Derby" wording;
and, in the 20th century "Made in England" and
"English Bone China" were added to the mark.

A majority of these porcelains, both tableware
and figures, were hand decorated. A variety of
printing processes were used for additional adornment. Today, Royal Crown Derby is a part of Royal
Doulton Tableware, Ltd.

Reference: Susan and Al Bagdade, *Warman's
English & Continental Pottery & Porcelain, 1st Edition,* Warman Publishing Co., Inc., 1987.

**Cup, saucer, and plate, Mikado pattern,
blue dec, white ground, marked
"XXVII," $35.00.**

Bowl, Chinoiserie dec, four small feet .   **125.00**
Creamer and Sugar, cov, Dublin shape,
Imari pattern **300.00**
Cup and Saucer, floral garlands, gold
trim, cream ground, c1820 . . . .   **115.00**
Demitasse Cup and Saucer, Imari pat-
tern **32.00**
Ewer, 7½", raised gold dec on reticu-
lated cobalt blue neck and handle,
enameled flowers on gold ground . .   **650.00**
Libation Cup, figural, hare head, early
19th C, pr **4,250.00**
Plate
6", Imari pattern **45.00**
7⅛", Pattern 2451 . . . .   **50.00**
9", Japanese pattern, blue, iron-red,
and gilt, set of 12 . . . .   **475.00**
Tea Set, teapot, creamer, cov sugar,
eight cups and saucers, white molded
swirled ground, gilt, sprigs of magenta and cobalt cornflowers, early
19th C **750.00**
Urn, cov, 5", yellow ground, leaves and
butterflies, molded mask handles,
1887 . . . .   **400.00**

Vase

   7", twin handles, wide mouth, gilt dec,
yellow grazed ground, slight resto-
ration on neck **500.00**

   10", pink ground, single hp blossom **425.00**

   11½" h, bulbous, heavy gold and
green dec, pedestal foot, slender
neck, flowers, marked **155.00**

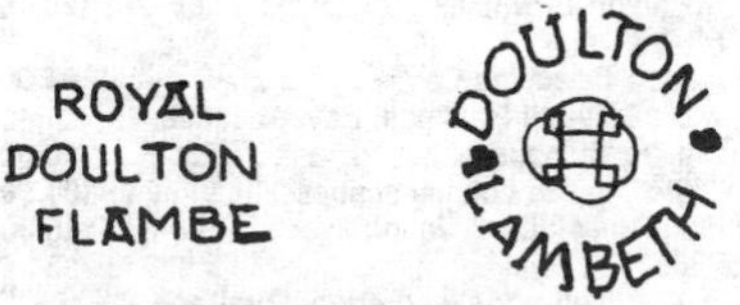

ROYAL DOULTON FLAMBE

ROYAL DOULTON

History: Doulton pottery began in 1815 under the direction of John Doulton at the Doulton & Watts pottery in Lambeth, England. Early output was limited to salt-glazed industrial stoneware. John Watts retired in 1854. The firm became Doulton and Company, and production was expanded to include hand decorated stoneware such as figurines, vases, dinnerware, and flasks. In 1872 the firm began marking their ware "Royal Doulton."

In 1878, John's son, Sir Henry Doulton, purchased Pinder Bourne & Co. in Burslem and the companies became Doulton & Co., Ltd. in 1882. Decorated porcelain was added to Doulton's earthenware production in 1884. The Royal Doulton mark was used on both wares.

Most Doulton figurines were produced at the Burslem plants from 1890 until 1978, when they were discontinued. A new line of Doulton figurines was introduced in 1979.

Beginning in 1913, an "HN" number was assigned to each new Doulton figurine design. The "HN" numbers refers to Harry Nixon, a Doulton artist. "HN" numbers were chronological until 1940, after which blocks of numbers were assigned to each modeler. From 1928 until 1954, a small number appeared to the right of the crown mark; this number added to 1927 gives the year of manufacture of the figurines.

Dickens ware, in earthenware and porcelain, was introduced in 1908. The ware was decorated with characters from Dickens' novels. The line was withdrawn in the 1940s, except for plates which continued until 1974.

Character jugs, a 20th century revival of early Toby models, were designed by Charles J. Noke for Doulton in the 1930s. They come in 4 major sizes and feature fictional characters from Dickens, Shakespeare and other English and American novelists, and historical heroes.

Doulton's Rouge Flambee (also Veined Sung) is a highly glazed, strong colored ware noted most for the fine modeling and exquisite colorings, es-

pecially in the animal items. The process used to produce the vibrant colors in this ware is a Doulton secret.

Production of stoneware at Lambeth ceased in 1956; production of porcelain continues today at Burslem.

References: Susan and Al Bagdade, *Warman's English & Continental Pottery & Porcelain, 1st Edition*, Warman Publishing Co., Inc., 1987; Ralph and Terry Kovel, *The Kovels' Illustrated Price Guide to Royal Doulton*, Crown, 1980; Jocelyn Lukins, *Collecting Royal Doulton Character & Toby Jugs*, Venta Books, 1985; Kevin Pearson, *The Character Jug Collectors Handbook, 3rd Edition*, Kevin Francis Publishing Ltd, 1986; Kevin Pearson, *The Doulton Figure Collectors Handbook*, Kevin Francis Publishing Ltd, 1986; Ruth M. Pollard, *The Official Price Guide To Royal Doulton, Fifth Edition*, House of Collectibles, 1986; Princess and Barry Weiss, *The Original Price Guide to Royal Doulton Discontinued Character Jugs, Sixth Edition*, Harmony Books, 1987.

Periodical: *Collecting Doulton*, BBR Publishing, 2, Strattford Avenue, Elsecar, Barnsley, S. Yorkes, S74 8AA, England.

Animal Mold

   Airedale, HN1023 . . . . **75.00**

   Cat, 5", sitting, white, #2539 . . . . . . **120.00**

   Chestnut mare and foal, #2522, 10 x
6½" **425.00**

   English Setter, HN1050 . . . . **85.00**

   Mountain Sheep, #2661 . . . . **175.00**

   White Tailed Deer, #2658 . . . . **350.00**

Ashtray, John Barleycorn **100.00**

Biscuit Jar, 6 x 7¾", cream ribbed
ground, band of turquoise, birds and
animals on band, SP top, rim, and
handle, marked "Doulton, Burslem
Pottery" **200.00**

Bowl, 8⅞ x 4¼", blue, brown geometric
borders, cows and horses grazing,
sgd "Hannah Barlow, 1885" **650.00**

Candlesticks, 10¼", floral, blue ground,
pr **150.00**

Character Jug, tiny, 1¼"

   Arry **175.00**

   Paddy **100.00**

   Sam Weller **100.00**

Character Jug, miniature, 2¼ to 2½"

   Captain Ahab **20.00**

   Fortune Teller **325.00**

   Toby Philpots **45.00**

   Turpin, Dick, horse **25.00**

Character Jug, small, 3½ to 4"

   Buzz Fuzz **100.00**

   Fortune Teller **300.00**

   Mikado **250.00**

   St. George **65.00**

Character Jug, large, 5¼ to 7"

   Captain Ahab **60.00**

   Drake **120.00**

Friar Tuck	365.00
Simple Simon	525.00
Whittington, Dick	375.00

Demitasse Cup and Saucer, 2 x 1½" cup, 3⅜" saucer, deep teal blue, lighter blue chrysanthemums, heavy gold trim, heavy gold lining in cup, imp mark, 1896 .... 100.00

Dickensware

Ashtray, Tony Weller	35.00
Bowl, 6", Bill Sykes	40.00
Coffeepot, 7¼", cov, Tony Weller	200.00
Fruit Bowl, 9⅜ x 2⅞", scalloped edge, marked "Mark Topley"	100.00
Jug, 6½", sq, Captain Cuttle	115.00
Pitcher, 3½" d, 7⅜" h, sq, Alfred Jingle	118.00
Plate, Sam Weller and M Packmack	65.00
Tray, 4 x 5⅜", Barnaby Rudge	50.00

Vase

6¾", Sydney Carton	130.00
7¾", handles, Alfred Jingle	150.00

Figurine, "This Little Pig, HN1793," red blanket, purple flowers, copyright 1938, $85.00.

Figure

A La Mode	170.00
Adrienne, #2304	145.00
Beat You To It	240.00
Bell O'Ball, #1997, c1950	275.00
Bedtime Story, #2059	175.00
Elegance, #2264	115.00
Fiona, #1933, 1941	700.00
Fleur, #2368	125.00
Good King Wenceslas, #2118	275.00
Prince Phillip, #2386	325.00
Royal Governor's Cook, #2233	325.00
Sunday Best, #2206	200.00
Votes for Women	200.00
Wardrobe Mistress, #2145	475.00

Flambe

Animal Mold

Cat	65.00
Elephant, #489A	115.00
Fish, 12½"	800.00

Bowl, 9¾ x 3", handled, Oriental style	225.00
Vase, 9", Veined Sung, bulbous	250.00
Jardiniere, 7½", cow, sgd "Hannah Barlow"	650.00
Jug, Sairey Gamp, small A mark	65.00

Mug

Beefeater	110.00
Captain Ahab	55.00
Gondolier	200.00
Parson Brown	120.00

Pitcher

5½", Coaching Days	85.00
6", Battle of Hastings, Bayeux tapestry, bulbous	90.00
6½", Italian country scenes	100.00
Plaque, 14", Long John Silver	125.00

Plate

9", ruffled and fluted edge, floral and fine border, gold tracery 100.00

Series Ware

Match Striker, 4⅜ x 3", Dutch People series, old Dutch man and woman on front, crying child at feet, hallmarked SS band around base ... 150.00

Pitcher, 4½", Arabian Nights series, Ali Baba 80.00

Plate

10", Automotive series, "A-Nerve-Tonic"	250.00
10⅜", Arrival of Unknown Princess, Arabian Nights series, multicolored, cream ground	120.00

Sugar, cov, handles, 3⅜ x 6⅛ x 4½", Dutch People series, old Dutch man and woman on front, crying child at feet, figural windmill knob, arly mark 100.00

Tray, 5 x 11", Robin Hood series	85.00
Tumbler, 4", Jackdaw of Rheims series	125.00

Vase

2 x 4 x 5½", flattened shape, Robin Hood series, Robin Hood slays Guy of Gisborne on front 100.00

5½", 2 handles, Gaffers series ... 85.00

Shakespeare Ware

Biscuit Jar, 5¼ x 7¼", Ophelia, SP top, rim, and handle 250.00

Jug, 4⅝" d, 6⅜" h, Portia	110.00
Tile, Much Ado About Nothing	60.00

Vase

3⅛" d, 11⅞" h, pastels, Romeo and Juliet, facing pr 425.00

3¾" d, 8½" h, Cardinal Wolsey, red dress, pastel ground, two handles 165.00

Stoneware

Biscuit Jar, 5" d, 6¾" h, cobalt blue borders, tan ground, emb blue flowers, brown leaves, hallmarked SS rim and handle, stoneware lid ... 175.00

Mug, 4⅜" d, 6" h, tan panels, emb off-

white figures of Victorian man and woman riding bicycles, soldier standing by bicycle, brown handle and edging, marked "Doulton Lambeth Stoneware" **275.00**
Toby, 6½", multicolored, marked "Double X stoneware, H. Simian, Doulton, Lambeth, England" **325.00**
Tankard, 6", Queen Elizabeth at Old Moreton Hall, c1920 .... **20.00**
Toby, seated
  4½", Sairey Gamp, #6263, c1950 .. **175.00**
  5½", Happy John, #6070, c1939 ... **45.00**
Vase
  7½", goat scene, sgd "Florence Barlow," c1878 .... **200.00**
  10", bulbous, cream ground, young man, purple and rose dec **135.00**
  12", urn shape, allover autumn maple leaf dec, incised veins, blue-green ground, cobalt blue int. and base, pr **450.00**
  16", bulbous, tapering neck, stylized floral reserve, blue ground, pr ... **360.00**

ROYAL DUX

History: Royal Dux porcelain was made in Dux, Bohemia (Czechoslovakia) by E. Eichler at the Duxer Porzellan-Manufaktur, established in 1860. Many items were exported to the United States. By the turn of the century Royal Dux figurines, vases, and accessories were captivating consumers, especially Art Nouveau designs.

A raised triangle with an acorn and the letter "E" plus Dux, Bohemia was used as a mark between 1900 and 1914.

Reference: Susan and Al Bagdade, *Warman's English & Continental Pottery & Porcelain, 1st Edition,* Warman Publishing Co., Inc., 1987.

Bust, Shakespeare, mask and dagger on base, pink triangle mark **325.00**
Calling Card Tray, 4", figural, frog standing on large open shell, beige, matte finish, pink triangle mark **115.00**
Candlestick, 13" h, figural, boy wearing knickers **160.00**
Centerpiece
  11 x 4¼ x 7¾", figural pair of nudes kneeling, central flared vase, creamy white, cobalt blue and gold trim **400.00**
  12 x 15 x 20", figural maidens and

Vase, 15½", woman with outstretched arms, rising from sea, $325.00.

two cherubs, holding up shell bowl, matte finish **875.00**
Compote, 20⅝", three dancing female figures, emb bowl and base, sgd ... **725.00**
Figure
  4 x 5½ x 9", Art Deco woman, blue irid satin gown, green trim and hat, satin flesh tones **275.00**
  6 x 9", dancing couple, cobalt blue coat, multicolored florals on cobalt dress, white ground, gold trim, pink triangle and paper label **150.00**
  8", woman, cobalt blue gown **135.00**
  8½", girl, nude, flower on knee and book **330.00**
  10", Cubist woman **150.00**
  12¾", woman holding blue glazed dress up at side, gold high heels, socle base, pink triangle mark ... **565.00**
  15", boy on donkey, pre World War I mark **400.00**
  16", peasant boy carrying basket on shoulder, rose breeches, tan boots and hat, green and gold, matte finish, pink triangle mark **450.00**
  16¼", Rebecca at the Well **550.00**
Pin Tray, figural, Art Nouveau maiden on wave **300.00**
Tobacco Jar, 8", figural, man's head, nightcap, smoking pipe **160.00**
Vase
  10", relief molded cyclamens **100.00**
  14", Art Nouveau, peach stylized flowers and leaves, gold tracery, yellow ground, base band of molded green foliage **225.00**

ROYAL FLEMISH

History: Royal Flemish was produced by the Mount Washington Glass Co., New Bedford, Massachusetts. The process was patented by Albert Steffin in 1894.

Royal Flemish has heavy raised gold enamel lines on frosted transparent glass that separates areas into sections, often colored in russet tones. It gives the appearance of stained glass windows with elaborate floral or coin medallions in the design.

Advisors: Clarence and Betty Maier.

Vase, 15¾" h, Guba Duck dec, attributed to Frank Guba, blazing sun of raised gold as background for lead mallard, ten other ducks encircle perimeter of vase, background of irregular panels of pastel tan and frosted clear, mauve and gold embellishments on upper 3" of crown like top, $5,950.00.

Biscuit Jar, 7½" h, irregular pastel mauve and tan panels, Roman motif medallions background, raised gold embellishments on neck and shoulders, gilt finish on emb collar, lid, and handle, sgd "P" in diamond logo . . . 1,850.00
Ewer, 12" h, gold and silver rampant lion and shield, raised gold borders, pastel blue cross with raised gold borders on reverse, applied twisted rope handle 3,250.00
Pitcher, 7¼" h, tan panels, five silver blossoms and foliage dec, clear glass handle 2,250.00
Rose Jar, 9" h, ball shape, roses dec, pastel blue and mauve panel background, ball shape lid, gold embellishments finial 2,750.00
Vase
5¾" h, 7¼" d, squatty shape, pastel pansy dec 1,850.00
7⅞" h, pink peonies dec, tan and frosted clear paneled background 950.00

ROYAL RUDOLSTADT

History: Johann Fredrich von Schwarzburg-Rudolstadt was the patron of a faience factory located in Rudolstadt, Thuringen, East Germany, from 1720 to c1790. The pottery's mark was a hayfork and later crossed two-prong hayforks in imitation of the Meissen mark.

In 1854 Ernst Bohne established a factory in Rudolstadt. His pieces are marked "EB."

The "Royal Rudolstadt" designation originated with wares imported by Lewis Straus and Sons (later Nathan Straus and Sons) of New York from the New York and Rudolstadt Pottery between 1887 and 1918. The factory's mark was a diamond enclosing the initials "RW" and which was surmounted by a crown. The factory manufactured several of the Rose O'Neill (Kewpie) items.

Reference: Susan and Al Bagdade, *Warman's English & Continental Pottery & Porcelain, 1st Edition,* Warman Publishing Co., Inc., 1987.

Plate, 8⅞" d, ivy motif, white ground, gold trim, marked "Germany/RW/Rudolstadt," $40.00.

Biscuit Jar, 8", corset shape, multicolored floral panels 140.00
Bonbon, handle, pink roses, white ground 50.00
Bowl, 8⅜", ftd, hp, poppies 65.00
Cake Plate, 10¼", hp, white flowers . . 48.00
Celery Dish, 13", handles, hp, yellow roses, gold trim, artist sgd 80.00
Child's Feeding Dish, 7¾" d, kewpies, sgd "Rose O'Neill" 235.00

Chocolate Set, cov chocolate pot, four cups and saucers, roses and ferns dec, gold trim, 9 pcs **100.00**

Creamer and Sugar, cov, purple pansies, cream ground, gold trim **75.00**

Dresser Tray, tray, hatpin holder, hair receiver, camellias, green leaves, pastels, gold trim, imp mark "Royal Rudolstadt Coronet B Prussia" **225.00**

Ewer

12", cobalt blue neck, allover gold enameling, hp, couple in garden, gold reticulated handle **215.00**

13¼", cream and light pink shell body, pebbled ground, brown worm type handle **175.00**

Figure, 5½", hunchback, brown hat, blue trousers, red cloak, floral vest, c1880, marked **125.00**

Hair Receiver, hp, pastel florals **45.00**

Inkwell, 6 x 3½", attached saucer, multicolored flowers, cream ground . . . **65.00**

Pitcher, 15½", jeweled, inlaid gold leaves **300.00**

Plate

8", eight kewpies playing, hp foliage border, marked **125.00**

8½", chickens and roosters **65.00**

9⅝", purple flowers, gold highlights . **60.00**

Relish, 13", bluebird dec **40.00**

Sweetmeat Jar, cov, 5½ x 8", pink florals, green and rust leaves, cream ground, SP holder, marked "Middletown" **135.00**

Tray, 12 x 8½", double pierced handles, daylily dec **70.00**

Urn, 25½", floral dec, imp mark **575.00**

Vase

9¼", florals, gold scroll handles, emb lip **120.00**

12", baluster, hp, pink roses, pastel ground, gold trim **75.00**

ROYAL VIENNA

History: Production of hard paste procelain in Vienna began in 1720 with Claude Innocentius du Paquier, a runaway employee of the Meissen factory. In 1744 Empress Maria Theresa brought the factory under royal patronage; subsequently the ware became known as Royal Vienna. The firm went through many administrative changes until it closed in 1864. The quality of its workmanship always was maintained.

Many other Austrian and German firms copied the Royal Vienna products, including the use of the "Beehive" mark. Many of the pieces on today's market are from these firms.

Reference: Susan and Al Bagdade, *Warman's English & Continental Pottery & Porcelain, 1st Edition,* Warman Publishing Co., Inc., 1987.

Plate, 10" d, red border, beehive mark, $300.00.

Box, 3 x 4¾", titled "Judgment of Paris," cupid on front panel **300.00**

Charger

13", classical scene, pseudo marks, gilt metal frame **600.00**

20½" d, titled "Columbus Triumphant Return," landing, party, Indians, and bounty, marked **1,400.00**

Compote

9", Psyche **135.00**

9½", 2 handles, portrait dec, cobalt blue ground, gold trim **150.00**

Cup and Saucer

Portrait of girl, overall blue jewels . . **300.00**

Warriors and girl on cup, raised gold and white dec, different scenes on saucer, pink, blue, and gold **390.00**

Ewer, 9 x 7", two ladies portraits, five cherubs, cobalt blue ground, gold trim **150.00**

Inkwell, mechanical, snail, Paris, 19th C **100.00**

Plate

9", two ladies and cupid in garden . . **100.00**

9½", two girls feeding birds in garden setting, multicolored intricate raised border, beehive mark **650.00**

9¾", Daphne & Apollo, beehive mark **400.00**

Portrait Plate

9", Lassitude, woman, titled, artist sgd "Wagner" **400.00**

10", Lund, titled, artist sgd "F Tenner," marked **350.00**

13", Musik, titled, blue beehive mark **350.00**

Stein, 6" h, seated monk with stein, cobalt blue ground, gold trim, artist sgd "Wagner" **900.00**

Tea Caddy, cov, 6¾", Apollo with book, maiden with flute, artist sgd "Kooller" **600.00**

Urn, cov
  9½", woman and cherub, red ground,
    gold trim, artist sgd, c1880 . . . . . **215.00**
  12", classical scene, cobalt ground,
    gold trim, artist sgd "Heer," pr . . . **900.00**
Vase
  7¾", two handles, maroon, ornate
    gold bands, flowers, and leaves,
    portrait of woman, artist sgd "Wag-
    ner," blue underglaze beehive mark **350.00**
  8", pillow form, red roses decal,
    shaded ground **90.00**
  9¼", cottage scene, blown out iris on
    body, blown out leaf as handle,
    green shading, red "Royal Vienna"
    mark **525.00**
  11½", bride and maid, wreath in hair,
    artist sgd "Wagner" **900.00**
  12", portrait, titled "Inspiration," ivory
    ground, ftd, artist sgd "Rissner" . . **825.00**

ROYAL WORCESTER

History: In 1751 the Worcester Porcelain Company, led by Dr. John Wall and William Davis, acquired the Bristol pottery of Benjamin Lund and moved it to Worcester. The first wares were painted blue under the glaze, followed closely by painting on the glaze in enamel colors. Among the most famous 18th century decorators were James Giles and Jefferys Hamet O'Neale. Transfer-print decoration was developed by the 1760s.

A series of partnerships took over upon Davis's death in 1783: Flight (1783–93), Flight & Barr (1793–1807), Barr, Flight & Barr (1807–13), and Flight, Barr & Barr (1813–40). In 1840 the factory was moved to Chamberlain & Co. in Diglis. Decorative wares were discontinued. In 1852 W. H. Kerr and R. W. Binns formed a new company and revived the ornamental wares.

In 1862 the firm became the Royal Worcester Porcelain Co. Among the key modelers of the late 19th century were James Hadley and his three sons and George Owen, expert at pierced clay pieces. Royal Worcester absorbed the Grainger factory in 1889 and the James Hadley factory in 1905. Modern designers include Dorothy Boughty and Doris Lindner.

References: Susan and Al Bagdade, *Warman's English & Continental Pottery & Porcelain, 1st Edition,* Warman Publishing Co., Inc., 1987; David, John, and Henry Sandon, *The Sandon Guide To Royal Worcester Figures, 1900–1970,* The Alderman Press, 1987.

Museum: Charles William Dyson Perrins Museum, Worcester, England.

Basket, 9⅝" l, blue and white, Pine
  Cone pattern, oval, center underglaze
  blue transfer print of fruit cluster and
  flowers, pierced basketwork sides,
  trellis diaper and leaf scroll border,
  twisted rope handles with blossom
  and foliage terminals, underglaze
  blue filled crescent mark, c1775 . . . **825.00**
Bough Pot, 7¹³/₁₆" d, blue and white,
  Garden Rose pattern, scalloped D
  shape, horizontally ribbed, large quatrefoil shaped aperture, small circular
  holes, scalloped and glazed back, underglaze blue transfer print of insects,
  sprays, and sprigs of roses, c1770 . **1,150.00**
Bowl, 4⁵/₁₆", Red Bull pattern, black
  transfer print ext., iron-red, green,
  blue, rose, and yellow enamel dec,
  black enamel line int. border, c1758 **575.00**
Box, 1⅞" h, three sided, hunt scene,
  sgd **65.00**
Cache Pot, 8" d, 7" h, circular, lug han-
  dles, Kakiemon style dec, Chamber-
  lain, pr **5,750.00**
Caudle Cup, cov, deep saucer, 5¾ x
  4¹⁵/₁₆", Old Japan Fan pattern, green
  and iron-red floral sprig finial, pseudo
  Chinese character marks within dou-
  ble underglaze blue circle,c1768 . . . **1,320.00**

**Vase, 8¾" h, reticulated top, gold trim
and handles, floral dec, cream ground,
$400.00.**

Creamer, 4⅛" l, blue and white, Early
  Creamboat Sprays pattern, hexagonal, palmette molded spout, scalloped edged rococo cartouche on
  sides, underglaze blue transfer
  printed floral sprig, int. with sprigs and
  sprays, underglaze blue hatched
  crescent mark, c1757 . . . . **715.00**
Figure
  6⅞", Irishman, beige satin finish, nat-
    ural colors, Countries of the World
    Series, c1891 . . . . **400.00**
  7⅛", Yankee, beige satin finish, nat-
    ural colors, Countries of the World
    Series, c1891 . . . . **400.00**

Garniture, three cov urns, each with pierced and plain lid, scenic reserve panels, apple green ground, gilding, Granger, early 19th C, 3 pcs **1,600.00**

Milk Jug
2¹⁵/₁₆" h, Valentine pattern, pear shaped body, rose, green, iron-red, blue, and yellow dec, purple diaper panel int., c1760 . . . . **1,650.00**

3⅛" h, c1772–75, pear shaped, Famille Rose palette, Chinese boy standing beside table, underglaze blue husks, tassels, arches, and dots border, repaired chip on spout **300.00**

Pitcher
10", tankard, gold ribbing around body, orange, gold, and blue florals, purple thistles and pinks, high relief gold branches, thread wrapped gold handle, purple mark, 1884 . . **275.00**

13½", Persian shape, reticulated neck, butterflies and bees, c1880 . **725.00**

Plate
7⅜", Fan Paneled Landscape pattern, powder blue ground, cobalt blue dec, center pagoda, four fan shaped panels with river vignettes alternating with four small roundels of floral sprigs, underglaze blue disguised "W" mark, c1775 . . . . **500.00**

8⅛", Imari pattern, two shades of underglaze blue, iron-red, green, yellow, purple, and gold, two phoenix birds in flight over vase, restored, c1765 . . . . **225.00**

8⅞", Sir Joshua Reynolds pattern, Kakiemon style palette, Chinese pheasant perched on rock, brown edged rim, incised crescent mark near footrim, c1770 . . . . **1,800.00**

Sauceboat, 5⅞" l, oval, blue and white, Sinking Boat Fisherman pattern, scallop shell molding, foliate sprays, strapwork border, pineapple motif on spout, workman's underglaze blue mark, c1754 . . . . **4,125.00**

Spoon Tray, 5⅞" l, King of Prussia pattern, hexagonal, fluted, black center transfer print, bust length portrait of Frederick the Great by Robert Hancock, banner inscribed "The King of Prussia," black enamel line border, anchor rebus of William Holdship, sgd "RH Worchester," c1757–60 . . . . . . **2,650.00**

Sweetmeat Dish, 6⁷/₁₆" w, Parrot pattern, Blind Earl raised dec, rose leaves sprays, two puce and green rosebuds, green and brown twig handle, center of rose peonies, gold grapes, brown pomegranates, and green leaves, gilt edge, c1768 . . . . **1,000.00**

Teabowl and Saucer, 2⅞" d, Old Japan

Fan pattern, underglaze blue branches with iron-red blossoms on underside of saucer, c1768 . . . . **250.00**

Teapot
5½", De Jeuner service, butterflies and flowing bamboo, raised feet, c1876 . . . . **800.00**

6¾", sq body, swan neck, ring handles, high relief flowing foliage, c1884 . . . . **675.00**

Vase, 7 x 9", cream gloss, gold and silver flowers, bird, and butterfly, burnished gold serpent handles, 1882 mark **475.00**

Wall Pocket, 11¾", blue and white, Cornucopia Daisy pattern, spirally molded cornucopia, scrolled rim, large daisies and peonies dec, pr, c1760 . . . . **2,500.00**

Wine Jug, 9¾" h, 6¼" d, bulbous, 3¼" d base, five multicolored florals, irid brown and gold handle and trim, funnel shape opening one side, long spout, purple mark, 1884 . . . . **325.00**

ROYCROFT

History: Elbert Hubbard, founder of the Roycrofters in East Aurora, New York, during the turn of the 19th and 20th centuries, was considered a genius in his day. He was an author, lecturer, manufacturer, salesman, and philosopher.

Hubbard established a campus which included a printing plant where he published "*The Philistine*," "*The Fra*," and "*The Roycrofter*." His most famous book was "*A Message to Garcia*," published in 1899. His "community" also included a furniture manufacturing plant, a metal shop, and a leather shop.

References: Nancy Hubbard Brady, *The Book of The Roycrofters*, House of Hubbard, 1977; Nancy Hubbard Brady, *Roycroft Handmade Furniture*, House of Hubbard, 1973; Charles F. Hamilton, *Roycroft Collectibles*, A. S. Barnes & Company, Inc., 1980; Paul McKenna, *A New Pricing Guide For Materials Produced by The Roycroft Printing Shop*, Tona Graphics, 2nd edition, 1982.

Additional Listing: Arts and Crafts Movement and Copper.

Bookends, pr, 4¼ x 3 x 5", copper on brass, overlapping graduated triangles, imp "Roycroft," orb mark **225.00**

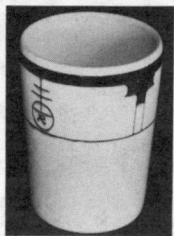

Tumbler, 4″ h, china, marked "Buffalo China," $25.00.

Candlesticks, pr, 12″, hammered copper, four strips form body and feet, riveted, circular bobeche, dark patina, die-stamped mark 1,400.00

Desk, 43 x 15 x 56¼″, drop front, recessed paneled sides, three drawers, full int. gallery, long strap hinges, oval iron hardware, orig dark brown finish, red tiger striping, marked "Roycroft" on backsplash 5,000.00

Lamp
  Desk, 16 x 7½″, hammered copper, helmet shade, cylindrical copper shaft, flared circular base, imp orb mark, rewired 550.00
  Table, 16 x 20″, hammered copper, conical shade of green-yellow triangular glass panels with pink and green rectangles, tall flaring base with two riveted bands and triangular handles, circular foot, orig brass wash, die-stamped mark .. 5,000.00

Vase, 3¼ x 6¼″, cylinder, pierced and applied nickel-silver band, orig dark brown patina 325.00

RUBENA GLASS

History: Rubena crystal is a transparent blown glass which shades from clear to red. It also is found as the background for frosted and overshot glass. It was made in the late 1800s by several glass companies, including Northwood and Hobbs, Brockunier & Co. of Wheeling, West Virginia.

Rubena was used for several patterns of pattern glass including Royal Ivy and Royal Oak.

Atomizer, 6¾″, incised floral dec 145.00
Basket, 3½ x 5½″, threaded dec, clear applied twisted handle 120.00
Biscuit Jar, 7 x 9″, melon ribbed body . 165.00
Celery, IVT, ruffled rim 75.00
Compote, 8¼″ d, Honeycomb pattern, low standard 60.00

Creamer, Medallion Sprig, clear applied handle 150.00
Cruet, IVT pattern, clear applied reeded handle, orig cut stopper 385.00
Finger Bowl, matching underplate 80.00
Lamp Shade, ruffled, etched floral dec . 85.00
Mustard Jar, Baby Thumbprint, enamel floral dec, SP lid 100.00
Perfume, 1¾ x 5⅝″, paneled, clear cut faceted stopper 80.00
Pitcher, 8½″, IVT 250.00
Punch Cup, clear applied handle 85.00
Spooner, Royal Oak, frosted 115.00
Syrup, threaded, Northwood 350.00

Vase, 6″ h, bud, enameled floral dec, $65.00.

Toothpick, 3¼″, polychrome enamel crane and leaves 65.00
Tumbler, IVT 40.00
Vase
  5″, coralene dec, gold trim 275.00
  6″, bud, enameled floral dec, diamond band 65.00

RUBENA VERDE GLASS

History: Rubena Verde, a transparent glass that shades from red in the upper section to yellow-green in the lower, was made by Hobbs, Brockunier & Co., Wheeling, West Virginia, in the late 1880s. It often is found in the inverted thumbprint (IVT) pattern, termed "Polka Dot" by Hobbs.

Bride's Basket, 12½″, cased, ruffled edge, multicolored dainty floral dec . 365.00
Bowl
  5½″, opal crimped top, rigaree trim, seven shell feet 100.00
  9½″, Hobnail pattern, crimped rim .. 175.00
Butter Dish, cov 400.00

Vase, 4" h, 2¼" d, webbed ext., $235.00.

Celery, 6¼", IVT	225.00
Creamer, 5", bulbous, amber applied handle	215.00
Epergne, 16" h, single center lily, applied rigaree, pr	500.00
Finger Bowl, matching underplate, IVT	65.00
Pitcher, 8", bulbous, sq mouth, Hobnail pattern, vaseline applied handle	265.00
Salt Shaker, 4¼" h, pewter top, enameled floral dec	185.00
Sweetmeat Dish, 5¾" d, 5¼" h, octagonal top, fine notch cutting around edge, vaseline shell trim rigaree applied at center, SP basket frame	145.00
Syrup, IVT, applied handle, pewter lid, marked "Pat. March 29, '83"	335.00
Tumbler, 4", Hobnail pattern	150.00

Vase

4", webbed dec	235.00
6½", cylindrical, Hobnail pattern	275.00
10", enameled florals, gold trim	165.00
12¼", cylindrical, ruffled rim, paneled, enameled white daisies, coral pink flowers, green foliage	185.00

Reference: William Heacock, *Encyclopedia of Victorian Colored Pattern Glass, Book 7: Ruby-Stained Glass From A to Z,* Antique Publications, Inc., 1986.

Bell, etched holly and berries, clear handle and clapper	75.00
Butter Dish, cov, 6½ x 5¾", Lancaster Fair, 1916, Button Arches pattern	150.00
Cordial, Syracuse Fair, 1905	38.00
Creamer, St Louis World's Fair, 1904, Star of David pattern, 3½"	125.00
Goblet, Glencoe, MN, gold trim	32.50

Mug

Gettysburg, PA	45.00
1900, etched leaf dec, Button Band pattern, 2½ x 3½"	25.00
Winona, July, 1910	38.00

Pitcher

Cedar Rapids, IA	42.00
Ocean City, NJ, 1912	40.00

Plate, St Louis World's Fair, 1904, Festival Hall, Cascade Gardens	45.00

Punch Cup

Lovie Briggs, 1904, Button Arches, 2½ x 2¾"	28.00
Paducah, VT, Button Arches, 2¾ x 2¼"	20.00
Salt Shaker, Center Lovell, ME	20.00

Toothpick

Bucyrus, OH, Beaded Swag	40.00
Naomi, Rib and Bead	60.00

Tumbler

Indiana, 1910, Diamond Peg	30.00
Scranton, PA, Mother	40.00

Wine

Asbury Park, NJ	36.00
Pan American Expo, 1901, Zipper Slash	40.00

RUBY STAINED GLASS, SOUVENIR TYPE

History: Ruby stained glass was produced in the late 1880s and 1890s by several glass manufacturers, primarily in the area of Pittsburgh, Pennsylvania.

Ruby stained items were made from pressed clear glass which was stained with a ruby red material. Pieces often were etched with the name of a person, place, date, or event and sold as souvenirs at fairs and expositions.

In many cases one company produced the pressed glass blanks; a second company stained and etched them. Many patterns were used, but the three most popular were Button Arches, Heart Band, and Thumbprint.

Tumbler, 3⅞" h, 2⅞" d, Button Arches pattern, etched "Carnival, July 29, 1904," reverse etched "J. M. Craig," $30.00.

RUSSIAN ITEMS

History: During the late 19th and early 20th centuries Russia contained skilled craftsmen in lacquer, silver, and enamel wares. Located mainly in Moscow during the Czarist era, 1880–1917, were a group of master craftsmen, led by Faberge, who created exquisite enamel pieces. Faberge also had an establishment in St. Petersburg and enjoyed the patronage of the Russian Imperial family and the royalty and nobility from throughout Europe.

Almost all enameling was done on silver. Pieces are signed by the artist and the government assayer.

The Russian Revolution in 1917 brought an abrupt end to the century of Russian craftsmanship. The modern Soviet government has exported some inferior enamel and lacquer work, usually lacking in artistic merit. Modern pieces are not collectible.

Advisors: Melvin and Barbara Alpern.

Box, enameled, green, turquoise, pink, amber, gold, and navy, made by Six Masters Artel, Moscow, 1900, $1,750.00.

ENAMELS

Beaker, 4¼″ h, plique a jour enamel on gilded silver, brilliant colored birds in garden, Ivan Khlebnikov, Moscow, 1900 . . . . **3,500.00**
Bowl, 5¼″ d, silver gilt, eight panel, enameled int. and ext., colorful peacocks and foliage, gilded stippled ground, florals on white ground, Maria Semyenova, Moscow, c1900 . . . . . . **4,125.00**
Box, gold wash, hinged lid, "84" mark, "Z.Z." maker's mark **400.00**
Charkahs, 2¼″ l, Pan Slavic enameling, fitted holly wood box, clover shape, stylized bird handles, A Lubavin, Moscow, 1895, pr **500.00**
Cigar box, 5″ l, silver, enameled tobacco leaf domed cover inscribed "Amer-

ican," paper tax band edge, engraved flower sides, presentation inscription gilt int. base, The Sixth Artel, Moscow, c1910 . . . . **6,050.00**
Cigarette Box, lacquered enamel **245.00**
Cigarette Case
  Gilded Silver, 5¼″ l, rectangular, en plein enamel scene of young girl in village by river, 11th Masters Artel, Moscow, 1900 . . . . **3,000.00**
  Silver, marked "sovereign head-91" . **300.00**
Condiment, Kovsh shape, "84" mark, "EP" maker's mark, enamel loss . . . **200.00**
Cup and Saucer, 4¾″ d saucer, silver, gilt, enameled, multicolored foliage in geometric borders, scroll handle, Nicholai Alexkseev, Moscow, 1892 . . . **1,430.00**
Kovsh, 5″ l, gilded silver, shaded enamel, pastel flowers, avocado ground, hook shape handle, Gustav Klingert, Moscow, 1900 . . . . **2,600.00**
Salt, 2¼″ d, open, gilded silver, shaded pastel flowers, 3 ball feet, Maria Semenova, Moscow, 1895 . . . . **800.00**
Shot Glass, gold wash, "84" mark, "AH" maker's mark **275.00**
Spoon
  Berry, 7¾″ l, shaded enamel pastel flowers on gilded silver, aurbergine ground, Pavel Ovchinnikov, Moscow, 1900 . . . . **900.00**
  Caviar, 7″ l, dark blue champleve enamel on gilded silver, Art Nouveau style, right angle bowl, Anton Kuzmichev, Moscow, 1900 . . . . . . **900.00**
  Demitasse, 4¼″ l, fig shape bowl, enameled stylized shaded flowers on gilded silver, Nikolai Alexkseev, Moscow, 1900, set of 6 . . . . **1,200.00**
Sugar Basket, 4½″ d, enameled panels of colorful flowering foliage on sky blue, Chinese red, sea green and cream ground, onion dome enameled aurbergine topped panels, swing handle, matching spoon with hook handle, Maria Semenova, Moscow, c1900 . . . . **2,420.00**
Sugar Shovel, 4½″ l, blue champleve enamel, cryillic monogram, Anton Kuzmechev, Moscow, 1890 . . . . **650.00**
Whiskey Glass, 1¼″ d, 1⅞″ h, silver, enameled multicolored geometric designs, marked "84" and initialed, Russia **355.00**

MISCELLANEOUS

Bowl, 8¼ x 3⅜″, ceramic, red, black, and gold, Oriental dec, marked **55.00**
Coin, gold, 10 rubles, 1899 . . . . **175.00**
Figure
  Man sitting on bench, holding con-

certina, bisque, 4¾ x 6¾", marked "Gardner" **450.00**
Yakut woman and dog **90.00**
Plate, 9½", ceramic, red and gold, Oriental dec, marked **45.00**
Samovar, 22½" h, brass plated, fluted tapering sides, service tray, 19th C . **100.00**
Teapot, 6 x 4½", porcelain, blue, rose, and lavender flowers, magenta floral medallions **140.00**
Tray, 9", brass, handled, hallmarked .. **90.00**

SILVER

Basket, 11⅜" d, overlaid napkin, c1889 **2,860.00**
Beaker, 2⅞ x 2½", gilded upper border and int., engraved strapwork, foliage, Kiev and Moscow, c1735–55, pr ... **600.00**
Bell, 4½", Imperial eagle, C Tegelston, 1839 .... **1,100.00**
Box, 2⅞" l, oval, gilt, shaded enamel, flowers, cream ground, hinged, 6th Masters Artel, Moscow, 1910 ..... **1,500.00**
Cigar Box, 8½", engraved tax bands, chased simulated wood grain, Ovchinnikov, Moscow, 1889 .... **4,625.00**
Cup and Saucer, 4¾", peasant man, bear, Faberge, 1894 .... **2,425.00**
Inkwell, 10¼", Bogaryr holding sword, marked, c1900 .... **3,850.00**
Mug, child's, Sterling, engraved scene, gold wash int., marked "84," 1891 .. **155.00**
Snuff Box, black enamel lid, dated 1873 **175.00**
Watch, emb Nicholas II likeness center, open face **250.00**

SABINO GLASS

History: Sabino glass, named for its creator Ernest Marius Sabino, originated in France in the 1920s and is an art glass which was produced in a wide range of decorative glassware: frosted, clear, opalescent, and colored glass. Both blown and pressed moldings were used. Hand sculpted wooden molds that were cast in iron were used and are still in use at the present time.

In 1960 the company introduced a line of figurines, one to eight inches high, plus other items in a fiery opalescent glass in the Art Deco style. Gold was added to the batch to attain the fiery glow. These pieces are the Sabino that is most commonly found today. Sabino is marked with the name in the mold, an etched signature, or both.

Ashtray
  Butterfly **80.00**
  Round **65.00**
  Swallow, large **45.00**
  Thistle **35.00**
Bird
  Feeding, small **20.00**

Turkey, 2" l, 2¼" h, molded signature, "Sabino, France," **$35.00.**

Nesting, small **20.00**
Shivering **40.00**
Chick, jumping **45.00**
Bowl
  Berry **50.00**
  Fish **50.00**
  Shell **45.00**
Box, Petalia **90.00**
Butterfly
  2¾", wings open **30.00**
  6" **185.00**
Dog
  Pekingese, small **20.00**
  Poodle, 1¾" **20.00**
  Scottie **65.00**
Elephant **25.00**
Perfume, dancers **100.00**
Scent Bottle, Pineapple, 5" **165.00**
Shell **55.00**
Snail, 3" **25.00**
Sparrow, small **45.00**
Statue
  Madonna, 5" **80.00**
  Woman, nude, long flowing hair, 6½" **125.00**
Vase
  7" h, 6" w, Art Deco, twelve different 3" to 5" female nudes filling baskets with flowers and fruits, jungle background, Cubist style, opalescent, molded "Sabino, France" **800.00**
  11" h, 7" w, six lobes, Art Deco geometrics, royal blue, satin finished, polished highlights, sgd **575.00**

C S SALOPIAN

SALOPIAN WARE

History: Salopian ware was made at Caughley Pot Works, Salop, Stropshire, England, in the 18th century by Thomas Turner. The ware is polychrome on transfer. One time classified as Polychrome Transfer, it retains the more popular name of Salopian. Wares are marked with an "S" or "Salopian" impressed or painted under the glaze. Much of it was sold through Turner's Salopian warehouse in London.

Plate, 8¾" d, octagonal, Oriental pattern, $175.00.

Bowl
  6½", polychrome, classical figures within ovals on brown transfer of florals, ochre, pink and green highlights 80.00
  11", Bird on Branch pattern, blue and white 400.00
Creamer and Sugar, man and woman having tea in garden, black and white transfer 450.00
Cup and Saucer
  Monochrome, brown flowers and leaves transfer, applied blue rim .. 15.00
  Polychrome, blue, yellow, ochre, and green flowers and leaves, tiny flake on saucer foot rim 90.00
Cup Plate, 4½", Deer pattern, polychrome dec 425.00
Mug, 4", Bird on Branch pattern 250.00
Pitcher
  5½", Oriental scene, blue, c1790 ... 400.00
  12½", Bird on Branch pattern, blue and white 850.00
Plate
  6", Deer, green, yellow, black, and white 200.00
  7¾", polychromed Creil scene of man, woman, and child, hut and church background, black transfer with applied yellow, blue, red, blue-green highlights 25.00
  8" d, fisherman and net transfer ... 85.00
  8½", Double Deer, green, yellow, black, and white 225.00
  8¾", octagonal, Oriental scene 175.00

Teapot
  4 x 8¼", boy carrying lamb, blue and white 465.00
  Birds and Flowers 500.00
  Milkmaid and Cow 450.00

SALT AND PEPPER SHAKERS

History: Collecting salt and pepper shakers, whether late 19th century glass forms or the contemporary figural and souvenir types, is becoming more and more popular. The supply and variety is practically unlimited; the price for most sets is within the budget of cost conscious, young collectors. Finally, their size offers an opportunity to assemble a large collection in a small amount of space.

One can specialize in types, forms, or makers. Great art glass artisans such as Joseph Locke and Nicholas Kopp, designed salt and pepper shakers in the normal course of their work. Arthur Goodwin Peterson is the leading research scholar in the field. His *Glass Salt Shakers: 1,000 Patterns* provide the reference numbers given below. Peterson made a beginning; there are hundreds, perhaps thousands of patterns still to be cataloged.

The clear colored and colored opaque sets command the highest prices, clear and white sets the lowest. Although some shakers, e.g., the tomato or fig, have a special patented top and need it to hold value, it is not detrimental to the price to replace the top of a shaker.

The figural and souvenir type is often looked down upon by collectors. Sentiment and whimsy are prime collecting motivations. The large variety and current low prices indicate a potential for long term price growth.

Generally older shakers are priced by the piece, figural and souvenir types by the set. The pricing method is indicated at each division. All shakers are assumed to have original tops unless noted. Identification numbers are from Peterson's book.

References: Gideon Bosker, *Great Shakes: Salt and Pepper For All Tastes*, Abbeville Press, 1986; Melva Davern, *The Collectors' Encyclopedia of Salt & Pepper Shakers: Figural And Novelty*, Collector Books, 1985; Helene Guarnaccia, *Salt & Pepper Shakers*, Collector Books, 1984; Helene Guarnaccia, *Salt & Pepper Shakers II: Identification & Values*, Collector Books, 1989; Mildred and Ralph Lechner, *The World of Salt Shakers*, Collector Books, 1976; Arthur G. Peterson, *Glass Salt Shakers: 1000 Patterns*, Wallace-Homestead, 1970.

Additional Listings: See *Warman's Americana & Collectibles* for more examples.

ART GLASS (PRICED INDIVIDUALLY)

Cord and Tassel, Double, round, glossy pink marbleized glass, orig tin top,

Double Cord and Tassel pattern, glossy pink marbleized base, orig top, made by Consolidated Lamp and Glass Co, $35.00.

Consolidated Lamp and Glass, 1894, 157-M	35.00
Egg, flat side, white satin finish, 2½", pewter top, made for Libbey, Columbian Exposition of 1893, 28-B	65.00
Erie Twist, white satin glass, hp, delicate pink flowers, shaded buff leaves, 2 pc pewter top, patent 1892, 28-H	100.00
Flower Band, 2½", large squatty base, raised flower band around base, pink cased glass, orig tin top, 29-G	50.00
Inverted Fan and Feather, pink slag, 31-O	250.00
Little Apple, 2½", small, round, satin finish, hp, pink and light yellow blossoms, shaded mint green to ivory, Mt. Washington, pewter top, 33-B	35.00
Peachblow, Wheeling, orig top	300.00
Quilted Phlox, 3½", pale green cased glass, orig tin top, Northwood, 36-H	45.00
Rubena, enameled dec, pewter top, 175-O	185.00
Satin, Raindrop, MOP, royal blue shading to pastel blue base	235.00
Spatter, vaseline and cranberry spatter, leaf mold, orig top	85.00

FIGURAL AND SOUVENIR TYPES (PRICED BY SET)

Bathing Beauties, flapper style bathing suits, one reclining, one sitting, hp, naturalistic colors, Germany	38.00
Billiken, white, opaque, and crystal, gilt, shape of Buddha, inscription on base "The God of things as they ought to be," patent 1908, tin top, 22-U	55.00
Binoculars, 2 pc set, matching stand	55.00
Dutch Boy and Girl, white metal figural top, clear base	85.00

Dogs, cast metal, 3", green paint, amber glass eyes	65.00
Farmer Pig, gold trim, marked "Shawnee"	25.00
Poppy, orange, green leaves, marked "Royal Bayreuth"	40.00
Twisted Dice, opaque white, black spots	100.00

OPALESCENT GLASS (PRICED INDIVIDUALLY)

Alaska, vaseline	55.00
Argonaut Shell, blue, 153-K	50.00
Beatty Honeycomb, white, 22-Q	24.00
Reverse Swirl, clear, white stripes	48.00
Swag with Brackets, canary, 174-J	50.00

OPAQUE GLASS (PRICED INDIVIDUALLY)

Beaded Dahlia, blue	24.00
Cathedral Panel	14.00
Clover Leaf, blue, 25-C	25.00
Cotton Bale, green, 25-W	30.00
Diamond Point and Leaf, blue, 27-K	60.00
Georgia Gem, custard, gold trim	30.00
Paneled Sprig, milk glass, green dec	32.00
Sunset, milk glass, 40-U	15.00

PATTERN GLASS (PRICED INDIVIDUALLY)

All-Over Diamond	20.00
Banded Portland, maiden's blush	35.00
Button Arches, ruby stained, 24-C	30.00
Cane, apple green, 156-H	25.00
Colorado, blue, 25-H	65.00
Dew and Raindrop, 158-O	20.00
Esther, pink, 28-I	50.00
Feather, 28-N	18.00
Grand	30.00
Heart with Thumbprint, gold trim, 30-P	48.00
Honeycomb, non-flint, 31-I	20.00
Maine, 33-M	30.00
Nevada	15.00
New Jersey, hotel size, 34-E	25.00
O'Hara Diamond, ruby stained	35.00
Pineapple and Fan #1, 168-Q	20.00
Priscilla #2, emerald green, 169-G	30.00
Question Mark	15.00
Red Block, 169-R	60.00
Ribbon Candy	35.00
Skilton	24.00
Stars and Stripes, 173-S	15.00
Thousand Eye, vaseline	30.00
Tepee	16.00
Wheat and Barley, blue	35.00
Willow Oak, canary	48.00

SALTGLAZED WARES

History: Saltglazed wares have a distinctive "pitted" surface texture, made by throwing salt into the hot kiln during the final firing process. The salt vapors produce sodium oxide and hydrochloric acid which react on the glaze.

Many Staffordshire potters produced large quantities of this type of ware during the 18th and 19th centuries. A relatively small quantity was produced in the United States. Saltglazed wares still are made today.

Reference: Susan and Al Bagdade, *Warman's English & Continental Pottery & Porcelain, 1st Edition,* Warman Publishing Co., Inc., 1987.

Pitcher, 9″ h, bamboo design, rope banding, gray, marked "Ridgway & Co, England," $125.00

Batter Jug, 11″ h, baluster shape, cylindrical rim, blue slip floral dec painted applied handles, impressed mark and No 2, highlights, tin cov, Cowen & Wilcox, Harrisburg, PA, 1870–90 ..... 1,870.00
Bottle, 9¼″, globular, applied foliage, c1755 .... 400.00
Crock, cobalt, holly dec, #2 .... 50.00
Dish, 10″, lobed, pierced, allover herringbone, basketweave, and diaper panels, c1760 .... 425.00
Flask, 7″, pig figural, reclining, cobalt blue eyes, inscribed "Fine Old Bourbon, in a Hop...Cairo Mounds, Chicago, St. Louis, Cincinnati," c1860 . 1,350.00
Jar
  12″ h, ovoid, everted rim, painted blue slip, cherry dec, impressed mark and number 3, blue highlights, Cowden & Wilcox, Harrisburg, PA, 1870–90 .... 410.00
  13¼″ h, baluster form, everted rim, two applied handles, impressed "Boston," 19th C 65.00
  16″ h, baluster shape, painted blue floral slip dec, impressed 5 and highlights, applied molded handles, PA, 19th C 240.00
Jug
  13¾″ h, tapered cylindrical, rounded

shoulders, blue painted slip floral dec, impressed mark and number 3, Cowden & Wilcox, Harrisburg, PA, 1870–90 .... 260.00
  14½″, cylindrical, sloping shoulders, blue painted cock and bull slip dec applied molded handle, impressed mark and 2, George A Satterlee and Michael Morey, New York Stoneware Co, 1861–85 .... 1,760.00
  17½″, ovoid, applied molded handle, painted blue slip number 3 and highlights, 19th C 175.00
Plate, 9½″, polychrome, central diaper and basketweave cartouche, pierced border, c1760 .... 725.00
Soup Plate, 9¼″, polychrome, flowers and vase, molded basketweave and diaper border, c1755 .... 475.00
Teapot, 7″, cov, trailing flowering branches, straight spout, crabstock handle and finial 450.00

SALTS, OPEN

History: When salt was first mined, the supply was limited and expensive. The necessity for a receptacle in which to serve the salt resulted in the first open salt, a crude, hand-carved, wooden trencher.

As time passed salt receptacles were refined in style and materials. In the 1500s both master and individual salts existed. By the 1700s firms such as Meissen, Waterford, and Wedgwood were making glass, china, and porcelain salts. Leading manufacturers in the 1800s included Libbey Glass Co., Mount Washington, New England Glass Company, Smith Bros., Vallerysthal, Wavecrest, Webb, and many outstanding silversmiths in England, France, and Germany.

Open salts were used as the only means of serving salt until the appearance of the shaker in the late 1800s. The ease of procuring salt from a shaker greatly reduced the use and need for the open salts.

References: William Heacock and Patricia Johnson, *5,000 Open Salts: A Collectors Guide,* Richardson Printing Corporation, 1982; L. W. and D. B. Neal, *Pressed Glass Dishes Of The Lacy Period 1825–1850,* published by the author, 1962; Allan B. and Helen B. Smith have authored and published ten books on open salts beginning with *One Thousand Individual Open Salts Illustrated* (1972) and ending with *1,334 Open Salts Illustrated: The Tenth Book* (1984). Daniel Snyder did the master salt sections in Volumes 8 and 9. In 1987 Mimi Rudnick compiled a revised price list for the ten Smith Books.

Note: The numbers in parenthesis refer to plate numbers in the Smith's publications.

CONDIMENT SETS WITH OPEN SALTS

China, boat shaped, inscribed "A Present from Cleethorpes" (461) 50.00
Porcelain, light pink with gold trim on leaf shaped holder, marked "Made in Bavaria" (388) 125.00
Silver Plated, 3 pcs, emb pattern around bowls, Oriental (461) 50.00

Individual, clear, Heisey, "H" in diamond mark, $22.50.

INDIVIDUALS

China
  Dresden Saxony, lily dec on one side (434) 45.00
  Majolica, flower shape, overlapping leaves, marked "No 35" (439) ... 60.00
  Unknown Maker, Viking ship, complete plique-a-jour in blue, red, and vaseline, very unusual (455) 1,000.00
Colored Glass
  Blue, stretch glass, unmarked (485) 70.00
  Cameo, Webb, red ground, white lacy dec around bowl, sgd, matching spoon (137) 600.00
  Cobalt Blue, pedestal, sgd "Steuben" (485) 225.00
  Cranberry, cut back to clear (446) .. 85.00
  Green, wide lacy border (378) 100.00
  Irid Gold, sgd "Quezal" (92) 200.00
  Lavender, pedestal, frosted (373) .. 75.00
  Ruby, blown, white lace trim (447) .. 95.00
Cut Glass
  Eight curved sides, polished cut bottom (470) 10.00
  Pedestal, unsgd, faceted base (118) 52.00
  Round, alternating zippered and starred panels (361) 25.00
  Triangular, Star and Diamond, sgd "Hawkes" (466) 65.00
  Tub, tab handles, Diamond and Fan (361) 55.00
Double Salts
  China
    Birds, gold rims, bug shown on inside bottom (460) 85.00

Meissen, floral dec inside and out, crossed swords and crown mark (460) 75.00
Glass
  Blue, silver frames, four ribbed paw feet (460) 80.00
  Milk Glass, turquoise, sgd "Vallerystahl" and "Made In France" (460) 35.00
  Vaseline, ten paneled, tall handle (460) 50.00
In Metal Frames
  Clear, ftd SS holder with four peacocks around outside, marked "Sterling" (411) 45.00
  Cobalt blue liner, basket, pierced ribbon handles, marked "E.P.N.S." (413) 35.00
Metal
  Copper, heavy, pedestal, deep maroon enamel (414) 25.00
  Sterling Silver, cov, handle, 3 feet, ornately dec bowl, hole in cov for spoon, marked "L.P.G." and "No 90" (353) 55.00
Pressed Glass
  Elliptical, round, rayed bottom (362) 18.00
  Heisey, octagonal paneled salt on sloping octagonal base, marked with Heisey "H" in diamond (475) 32.50
  Liberty Bell, clear, oval, 2¼" 20.00
  Thumbprint, pedestal, double round base, wide top rim, round thumbprints around bowl (362) 27.00
Wood, Sandalwood, spoon (233) 25.00

FIGURALS

Donkey, painted, pulling colorful painted cart (458) 27.50
Lafayette Boat, deep cobalt blue, emb "Lafayet, [sic] Sandwich, B & S Glass Co," c1830, several chips 725.00
Sleigh with Cupid driving reindeer, SS, made in Germany (352) 400.00

MASTERS

China
  Belleek, shell shaped (314) 40.00
  Gien, trencher type (317) 140.00
  Leeds, boat shaped, pedestal (313) 65.00
  Minton, ftd, #57957 (314) 47.50
  Unknown Maker, round, subtly ribbed, floral dec, gold and green border (384) 45.00
Colored Glass
  Amber, boat shaped, Wildflower pattern (317) 60.00
  Aventurine, narrow base (316) 55.00
  Cranberry, horizontal colored ribs (316) 65.00

Master, 2¾″ h, fiery opalescent, six panels, flared, $175.00.

End of Day, cased, scalloped, five clear shell feet (447)	**225.00**
Fiery Opalescent	
Blue, Gothic Arch and Heart pattern, Sandwich, c1840, 3⅞″ l . .	**285.00**
White, baskets of fruit and floral designs, emb on base "N. E. Glass Company Boston," 2⅞″ l	**275.00**
Olive-green, beaded scroll and scrolled leaf design, attributed to Mt Vernon NY Glassworks, 2⅞″ l, c1840	**1,200.00**
Cut Glass, round, diamond pattern on top of bowl, ribbed base (404)	**30.00**
Lacy	
Clear	
Gothic Arch (GA4a:410)	**130.00**
Horn of Plenty (329)	**60.00**
Oval Diamond on Pedestal (OP3:407)	**150.00**
Colored	
Basket of Flowers, opaque blue (BF1C:324)	**350.00**
Eagle, fiery milky opal, American eagle on all four corners, shield center, Sandwich Glassworks, c1840, 3″ l	**650.00**
Scrolled Heart, green, (SC7:324) .	**270.00**
Staghorn, cobalt blue (SN1:324) .	**225.00**
Metal	
Gold, pedestal, plain, marked "1880" (349)	**85.00**
Pewter, pedestal, cobalt blue liner (349)	**60.00**
Silver, sterling, ftd, rams' heads, Gorham (281)	**80.00**
Pressed Glass	
Electric (334)	**30.00**
Gear (335)	**25.00**
Hobnail, round (407)	**30.00**
Palmette (471)	**57.50**
Square Pillared (341)	**25.00**
Vintage (340)	**30.00**
Wildflower, turtle base (335)	**45.00**
Pressed Glass, Pedestal	
Barberry (344)	**33.00**
Eyewinker (346)	**80.00**
Hamilton (344)	**35.00**
Loop Design, French (331)	**85.00**
Paneled Diamond (331)	**45.00**
Sandwich, opaque light blue, scalloped foot, emb floral band, chips on upper rim, 2¹⁄₁₆″ h, c1840	**375.00**

SAMPLERS

History: Samplers served many purposes. For a young child they were a practice exercise and permanent reminder of stitches and patterns. For a young woman they demonstrated her skills in a "gentle" art and preserved key elements of family genealogy. For the mature woman they were a useful occupation and functioned as gifts or remembrances, e.g., mourning pieces.

Schools for young ladies of the early 19th century prided themselves on the needlework skills they taught. The Westtown School in Chester County, Pennsylvania, and the Young Ladies Seminary in Bethlehem, Pennsylvania, are two examples. These schools changed their teaching as styles changed. Berlin work was introduced by the mid-19th century.

Examples of samplers date back to the 1700s. The earliest ones were long and narrow, usually done only with the alphabet and numerals. Later examples were square. At the end of the 19th century, the shape tended to be rectangular.

The same motifs were used throughout the country. The name is a key element in determining the region. Samplers are assumed to be on linen unless otherwise indicated.

References: Glee Krueger, *A Gallery of American Samplers: The Theodore H. Kapnek Collection,* Bonanza Books, 1984 edition; Betty Ring, *American Needlework Treasures; Samplers and Silk Embroideries From The Collection of Betty Ring,* E. P. Dutton, 1987; Anne Sebba, *Samplers: Five Centuries of a Gentle Craft,* Thames and Hudson, 1979.

1721, Anne Chase, Rhode Island, wool, red, blue, green, and yellow silk stitches, pious verse alternating with wide bands of stylized flowers and birds, carnations and acorns border, lower band sgd "Anne Chase Made This Sampler In The Thirteenth Year of Her Age 1721," framed, 12¼ x 8¼″	**7,150.00**
1735, Mary Heaviside, homespun, precise small stitches, prim stylized flowers, alphabets and verse in tiny letters, Lord's Prayer and Apostles'	

Creed, "Mary Heaviside, her work aged 10 years 1735," lower right corner is soiled, small holes and wear, framed, 11 x 14¼" **1,200.00**

1768, Rebecca Leach, New England, alphabet, pastoral landscape with seated lady, lambs, birds, dogs, trees, and flowers, serpentine floral border, 17 x 14" **7,000.00**

1787, Mary Ann Redar, linen homespun, precise small stitches, "The Deity and Humanity of Christ...," multicolored floral border, lower band "Mary Ann Redar finished this sampler June the 30, 1787 in the fourteenth year of her age," small holes, gilt frame, 15 x 18" **600.00**

1797, Sarah Younge, homespun, poem titled "On Education," embroidered pastoral scene with house, trees, birds, green hills, dog and shepherd boy and girl, vining floral border, "Sarah Younge work September 1797," minor wear, small holes, 13½ x 15¾" **2,600.00**

1799, Ann Tindau, homespun, precise small stitches, intricate design, brown, olive, blue, red, white, and green, vining border, butterflies, birds, sheep, flowers, angels, scene with

Armstrong School, Lancaster, PA, 1801, birds, hearts, flowers, two women, large church, verse, and inscription "Ann Harbst a daughter of Henry and Elisabeth Harbst was born the 10th day of August in the Year of our Lord 1792 & made this sampler in the 9th year of her age in Mrs Armstrong's School AD1801," and "Ann Harbst is my name. Lancaster is my Habitation. Kings Street is my dwelling place & Christ is my salvation," 17½ x 18", framed, $11,250.00.

trees and tomb, royal couple, and verse, "Ann Tindau finished this work May the 10, 1799, aged eleven years," framed, 13¾ x 19" **1,000.00**

1803, Dorcas Shaw, five different styles of alphabet, numerals 1 through 13, four lines of verse, soft colored landscape with house, fence, and trees, border of vine and berries, "Dorcas Shaw, Portland, AET 14 1803," later oak frame, 21 x 16" **3,250.00**

1807, unidentified maker, finely woven homespun, precise small stitches, multicolored rows of alphabets, Bible verses, geometric floral borders, floral design with anchor and date "1807," minor stains, old beveled frame, 19¾ x 19½" **575.00**

1812, Ann Hootton, ship, flowers, landscape with house, trees, animals, basket of flowers, birds, etc., "Wrought by Ann Hootton Daughter of William and Hannah Hootton 1812," water stains, modern frame, 19 x 17" **3,700.00**

1813, Mary Ann Webster, Woodbury School, pious verse, landscape vignette with log cabin and pine tree, floral border, 15½ x 12" **800.00**

1814

Coleman, Sarah, homespun, well executed floral embroidery border, center rows of alphabets, numbers, verse, and "Sarah Coleman, 1814," framed, 13 x 14½" **2,200.00**

Davis, Hannah, Philadelphia, PA, loosely woven linen, green, rose, yellow, blue, white, and gold silk stitches, pious verse separated by bands of stylized flowers and bunches of grapes, lower border inscribed "Hannah Davis work in the 13th year 1814," silk ribboned border, framed, 19 x 16¼" **5,225.00**

1821, Mary Paul, Germantown, PA, eight lines of verse entitled "Mary's Wish," flowers, birds, insects, small landscape with dog and residence in center, modern frame, 25½ x 26" .. **5,250.00**

1827, Amey E Latham, alphabet and three different forms, house, trees, fence and crows in landscape at bottom, flowering plants and birds encircling signature "Amey E Latham, Aged 11, 1827," Victorian frame, 15¼ x 15¾" **700.00**

1829, Maria Bake, Pennington, NJ, six lines of verse titled "Extract," full basket of flowers, "Work'd by Marie Bake at Eliza A. Rue's School, Pennington NJ, Anno Domini 1829," gold leaf period frame, 16 x 17" **3,600.00**

1837, Elizabeth Turner, linen homespun, precise small stitches, stylized floral border, alphabets, numbers, and poem, green, gold, brown, and blue, "Elizabeth Turner finished this sample June 5 aged 11 years 1837," grained frame, 16¾ x 20¼" **2,100.00**

1842, indistinct name, ticking, multicolored stylized designs of people, ships, flowers, dogs, and birds, traces of black floss where alphabets and verse were located, dated "1842," scalloped finished edges, faded colors, minor stains, framed, 16½ x 20" **250.00**

1884, Ann Eliza Maude, needlepoint, memorial, multicolored flowers, tomb, cherubs, figures, weeping willows, "Ann Eliza Maude work May 18th 1884, age 14," minor stains, framed, 28½" sq **275.00**

SANDWICH GLASS

History: In 1818 Deming Jarves was listed in the Boston Directory as a glass factor. The same year he was appointed general manager of the newly formed New England Glass Company. In 1824 Jarves toured the glass-making factories in Pittsburgh, left New England Glass Company, and founded a glass factory in Sandwich.

Originally called the Sandwich Manufacturing Company, it was incorporated in April 1826 as the Boston & Sandwich Glass Company. From 1826 to 1858 Jarves served as general manager. The Boston & Sandwich Glass Company produced a wide variety and quality of wares. The factory used the free-blown, blown three-mold, and pressed glass manufacturing techniques. Clear and colored glass both were used.

Competition in the American glass industry in the mid-1850s forced a lowering of quality of the glass wares. Jarves left in 1858, founded the Cape Cod Glass Company, and tried to maintain the high quality of the earlier glass. At the Boston & Sandwich Glass Company emphasis was placed on mass production. The development of a lime glass (non-flint) led to lower costs for pressed glass. Some free-blown and blown-and-molded pieces, mostly in color, were made. Most of this Victorian era glass was enameled, painted, or acid etched.

By the 1880s the Boston & Sandwich Glass Company was operating at a loss. Labor difficulties finally resulted in the factory closing on January 1, 1888.

References: Raymond E. Barlow and Joan E. Kaiser, *The Glass Industry In Sandwich*, Vol. 3 and Vol. 4, distributed by Schiffer Publishing, Ltd.; George S. and Helen McKearin, *American Glass*, Crown Publishers, Inc., 1941 and 1948; Ruth Webb Lee, *Sandwich Glass. The History Of The Sandwich Glass Company*, Charles E. Tuttle, 1966; Ruth Webb Lee, *Sandwich Glass Handbook*, Charles E. Tuttle, 1966; L. W. and D. B. Neal, *Pressed Glass Dishes Of The Lacy Period 1825–1850*, published by author, 1962; Catherine M. V. Thuro, *Oil Lamps II: Glass Kerosene Lamps*, Wallace-Homestead, 1983.

Periodical: *The Sandwich Collector*, McCue Publications, P. O. Box 340, East Sandwich, MA 02537.

Museum: Sandwich Glass Museum, Sandwich, MA.

Additional Listings: Blown Three Mold and Cup Plates.

Bowl
7¼", Oak Leaf, clear, lacy	30.00
7½", Tulip and Acanthus, clear lacy .	30.00
Butter Dish, Horn of Plenty, clear, flint .	60.00
Candlestick, 9" h, columnar, opaque, powdery purple-blue, rough sandy finish	450.00
Champagne Glass, Sandwich Star, clear	300.00

Compote
6" d, 7½" h, cov, Sandwich Star, clear	175.00
6⅛" d, 7½" h, cov, Lincoln Drape . .	150.00
7¼" d, Plume, lacy, clear	175.00
8" d, 5¾" h, Diamond Thumbprint, clear, bowl tilts to one side	60.00
11⅛" d, 8½" h, Loop	150.00
Dish, 9½" d, quatrefoil, lacy, clear	200.00
Egg Cup, Horn of Plenty, flint, pr	65.00

Goblet
Bull's Eye and Fleur-De-Lis, clear . .	70.00
Comet, clear	70.00
Sandwich Star, clear	475.00

Lamp
9¾" h, Diamond Point and Bull's Eye, inverted pattern, clear	110.00
10" h, Vine	175.00
11" h	
Acanthus Leaf, opaque, jade green and white	400.00
Bull's Eye and Ellipse, clear, orig brass collar and camphene burner	150.00
Harp, clear, orig pewter collars and camphene burners, pr	425.00
Paperweight, 5 x 3¼ x 1⅛", book shape, vaseline, cut all-over, medallion on fruit, monogrammed "E.C.G."	300.00

Relish Dish
6¼" l, Sandwich Star, clear	50.00
8" l, oval, lacy, clear	60.00

Salt
Boat, blue, mottled, opaque	1,350.00
Eagle, opalescent	350.00
Gothic Arch, medium blue, opalescent	325.00
Hexagonal, ftd	
Cobalt blue	175.00

Salt, 3″ l, 2⅛″ h, lacy, clear, basket of flowers in center, Neal BF-16, $90.00.

Peacock blue	200.00
Scroll, bluish-white, opaque, beaded	100.00
Shell, lacy, clear, pedestal base	950.00
Sauce Dish	
Loop, cov, clear	75.00
Peacock Eye, 4¼″ d, sapphire blue, lacy, rim chips	160.00
Sword and Cross, 4½″ d, sapphire blue, lacy, rim chips	175.00
Spill Holder, Sandwich Star, opaque white	275.00
Spoon Holder, Loop pattern, clear, pr	150.00
Sugar, cov, Acanthus Leaf and Shield, lacy, clear, lid	300.00
Syrup, 6″ h, Star and Punty pattern, opaque white	65.00
Vase	
9½″ h, Bull's Eye and Diamond Point, clear	100.00
10¼″ h, Loop pattern, canary yellow, gauffered rim	350.00
Whiskey Taster	
Clear, lacy	175.00
Cobalt blue, nine paneled	120.00
Powder blue, paneled, translucent	140.00
Sapphire blue, hexagonal	110.00
Wine glass, Sandwich Star, clear	190.00

SARREGUEMINES
SARREGUEMINES CHINA

History: Sarreguemines ware is a faience porcelain, i.e., tin-glazed earthenware. The factory was established in Lorraine, France, in 1770, under the supervision of Utzcheider and Fabry. The factory was regarded as one of the three most prominent manufacturers of French Faience. Most of the wares found today were made in the 19th century. Later wares are impressed Sarreguemines and Germany due to a change of boundaries and location of the factory.

Reference: Susan and Al Bagdade, *Warman's English & Continental Pottery & Porcelain, 1st Edition*, Warman Publishing Co., Inc., 1987.

Animal Covered Dish, 5¾″, hen and chicks	115.00
Box, heart shape, floral dec, ormolu mount, c1760	100.00
Character Jug, 7½″, The Scotsman, red hair, blue and red hat	75.00
Creamer, 5″, row of ducks and frogs, flower border	50.00
Ewer, 10″, tan, gold butterflies and flowers	75.00
Figural Bottle, 9½″, man riding potato	100.00
Oyster Plate, set of 4	150.00
Pitcher, 8¼″, emb shoemaker scenes	150.00

Character Jug, Lawyer, marked "French Majolica," $125.00.

Plate	
7¾″, NY World's Fair, 1939	35.00
8½″, Majolica, strawberries and floral trim, aqua ground	70.00
9″, Majolica, asparagus, naturalistic colors	30.00
Rose Bowl, 4″ d, Majolica, multicolored floral dec	80.00
Tea Service, florals, ornate shapes, c1840, 14 pcs	500.00
Tobacco Jar, cov, relief masks, brown, yellow trim	75.00
Vase, 8½″, Majolica, gargoyles and lizards	125.00
Wall Shelf, 17″, bearded Norse god in relief, cobalt blue, brown, and green	850.00

SARSAPARILLA BOTTLES

History: Sarsaparilla refers to a number of tropical American, spiny, woody vines of the lily family whose roots are fragrant. An extract was obtained from these dried roots and used for medicinal purposes. The first appearance in bottle form dates from the 1840s. The earliest bottles were stoneware, later followed by glass.

Carbonated water often was added to sarsaparilla to make a soft drink or to make consuming it more pleasurable. For this reason, sarsaparilla and soda became synonymous even though they were two different entities.

References: Ralph & Terry Kovel, *The Kovels' Bottle Price List, 7th Edition,*, Crown Publishers, 1984; Carlo & Dot Sellari, *The Illustrated Price Guide to Antique Bottles.* Country Beautiful Corp., 1975.

Periodicals: *Antique Bottle and Glass Collector,* P.O. Box 187, East Greenville, PA, 18041.

Additional Listings: See *Warman's Americana & Collectibles* for a list of soda bottles.

A.H. Bull, Hartford, 7″	35.00
Brown's Sarsaparilla, aqua	10.00
Burr & Waters, pottery, gray salt glaze	100.00
Charles Joly Jamaica Sarsaparilla, Philadelphia, amber, 10″	15.00
Dalton's Sarsaparilla and Nerve Tonic, blue label	35.00
Dr. Pope's Sarsaparilla, rect, aqua, pontil	85.00
Dr. Townsend's, emerald green, iron pontil	130.00
Edward Wilder's Sarsaparilla & Potash, Louisville, KY, pt	40.00
Gooch's, blue	150.00
Hoods & Ayers	10.00
J.L. Kelley & Co, aqua, open pontil	265.00
Merchants, green, iron pontil	140.00
Recamier, amber	30.00
Sand's Genuine, rect, qt	85.00
Sawyers Eclipse, aqua	30.00
Wetherell's, aqua	40.00

SATIN GLASS

History: Satin glass, produced in the late 19th century, is an opaque art glass with a velvety matte (satin) finish, achieved through treatment with hydrofluoric acid. A large majority of the pieces were cased or had a white lining.

While working at the Phoenix Glass Company, Beaver, Pennsylvania, Joseph Webb perfected Mother-of-Pearl (MOP) satin glass in 1885. Similar to plain satin glass in respect to casing, MOP satin glass has a distinctive surface finish and an integral or indented design, the most common being diamond quilted (DQ).

The most common colors are yellow, rose, or blue. Rainbow coloring is considered choice. Satin glass, both plain and MOP, has been widely reproduced.

Additional Listings: Cruets, Fairy Lamps, Miniature Lamps, and Rose Bowls.

Bowl
6 x 5″, DQ, MOP, shaded blue, three frosted trunk vase feet	450.00

Biscuit Jar, 7¾″ h, handpainted enameled dec, silverplated rim, lid, and bail handle, $400.00.

8 x 4⅛″, DQ, MOP, rose pink, crimped top, applied clear feet, berry pontil, marked "Patent"	600.00
9⅜ x 11¾ x 7½″, shaded teal blue, small red cherries and green leaves, frosted edging, fluted, ormolu foot	450.00
Bride's Bowl	
9½″, MOP, blue, moire pattern, SP holder with strawberries and leaves applied to handle, marked "Simpson, Hall, Miller Co."	350.00
10½ x 3⅜ x 3⅜″, DQ, MOP, blue int., ruffled	350.00
Candlesticks, pr, 8¾″ h, yellow, brown roses, dark painted rims and bases	150.00
Creamer, 4½ x 3¼″, raindrop, MOP, blue, frosted blue reeded handle	225.00
Cruet	
5″ h, DQ, MOP, pink, thorn handle and stopper	575.00
7″ h, herringbone, MOP, pink, frosted handle and thorn stopper	375.00
Dresser Jar, cov, 3½″ h, yellow, gold flowers, red leaves	165.00
Ewer, 12½″, DQ, MOP, shaded rose, tricorn ruffled top, applied thorn handle	450.00
Plate, 6⅛″ d, DQ, MOP, rainbow, ruffled, cream satin back	400.00
Salt Shaker, MOP, raindrop, shading from royal blue top to pastel base	235.00
Toothpick Holder, 2½″ h, DQ, MOP, yellow	350.00
Tumbler	
Blue, Drapery pattern	50.00
Oyster white, flowers and insects dec	35.00
Vase	
4⅝ x 5⅜″, ribbed, MOP, rose red, dimpled sides	500.00
5⅞ x 6¼″, pulled feather, rosy brown	

feathers, blue ext., creamy yellow int., Northwood **1,250.00**
9″, pull-up type, butterscotch and white, frosted thorn handles, Northwood **385.00**
11⅛ x 6⅛″, Coinspot, MOP, shaded green, ruffled top, gold leaves, pink and lavender flowers **900.00**

SATSUMA

History: Satsuma, named for a war lord who brought skilled Korean potters to Japan in the early 1600s, was a hand-crafted Japanese faience glazed pottery. It is finely crackled, has a cream, yellow-cream, or gray-cream color, and is decorated with raised enamels in floral geometric and figural motifs.

Figural satsuma was made specifically for export in the 19th century. Later satsuma, referred to as satsuma-style ware, is Japanese porcelain also hand decorated in raised enamels. From 1912 to the present, satsuma-style ware has been mass produced. Much of the ware on today's market is of this later period.

References: Sandra Andacht, *Oriental Antiques & Art: An Identification And Value Guide*, Wallace-Homestead, 1987; Sandra Andacht, *Treasury of Satsuma*, Wallace-Homestead, 1981.

Beaker, gold, multicolored flowers, blue ground, 20th C **185.00**
Biscuit Jar, 6½ x 6″, orange, bamboo type handles, diaper border **100.00**
Bottle, 12 x 9″, bulbous, feudal lords, fluted top, allover diapers, ftd, 1885 . **275.00**
Bowl
4″, dragon and men, 1890 . . . . **100.00**
5″, lobed, wisteria ext., riverscape and wisteria dec int., sgd **80.00**
7″, landscape scene, seven sages, gold trim, black ext. **165.00**
Brush Pot, water plants dec, Kinkozan **120.00**
Button, set of 4, round, peony dec . . . **25.00**
Charger, 12⅞″ d, red and black flowers and birds, white ground, gold trim . . **120.00**

Tea Set, Thousand Flowers pattern, c1900, $200.00.

Creamer and Sugar, cov, floral pattern **350.00**
Cup and Saucer, flowers and butterflies, 1900 . . . . **45.00**
Dish, 9⅞″, Kannon, arhats, and dragon, int. dec, scalloped, gilt ground, c1900 **265.00**
Figure
3″, elephant, c1935 . . . . **30.00**
5″, crab, 1850s **750.00**
Figurine, 17½″ h, 19″ w, Manjushii sitting on lion, c1860 . . . . **2,750.00**
Incense Burner, 4″, ovoid squat, three arrow form molded flowerheads reserves, cream glaze, tripod feet, reticulated cov, Meiji period **150.00**
Jar, cov
3¾″ d, circular, lidded, black and gold signature, Japanese, 19th C **200.00**
5″, prunus branch with bird, diaper border neck band and handles . . **225.00**
Mug, 6½ x 4⅝″, scenery and gold pagoda, dull black finish, sgd with Oriental characters **50.00**
Pitcher, 4½″, warrior scene, gold scrolled handle, c1920 . . . . **230.00**
Plaque
9½″ d, waterfowl and pond scene, florals, foliage, and hanging wisteria, gold and red border, gold trim, Meiji period, c1900 . . . . **225.00**
9¾″, wisteria, peonies, and water fowls, 1900 . . . . **225.00**
Plate
6¾″, figure, landscape scene, 1890s **250.00**
9″, mother and children in garden, flowers and butterflies border, Japanese **290.00**
Tea Bowl, 5″, maple trees dec extend to int., marked "Yabu Meizan" **825.00**
Tea Caddy, cov, 5½″, blooming prunus tree, bird, brocade ground, handles . **175.00**
Teapot
Overall florals, family life scalloped reserves, gold ground, 3½″ h, Meiji period, c1900 . . . . **275.00**
Shishi motif, multicolored, cross, circle, and blue gosu, c1800 . . . . . . **700.00**
Tile, 3¾ x 5½″, women and children crossing bridge to crowded country inn, polychrome and gilt dec **300.00**
Tray, 7″ w, florals, relief cranes, c1800 **600.00**
Urn
14″ h, Geisha girl scene, bird handle, Awata Satsuma, c1920, pr **265.00**
50″, ladies in garden scene, temple, winged dragon handles **1,400.00**
Vase
4¾″ h, scenic design, wood base, orig velvet lined case, Meiji period, 1868–1912 . . . . **350.00**
6″, Buddhist saints and bijin reserves, waisted neck, ftd **220.00**
7″ h, blue shading to pink, butterflies

and flowers trailing over fence
scene 325.00
9½", pink and yellow on cobalt, floral,
gold outlines, 1890 .... 95.00
14¾" h, four figures and dragon, gilt,
dark ground 65.00
18" h, hp, urn shape, florals and two
green moriage hawks, tan, yellow,
and green ground 300.00
23" h, drilled and fitted as lamp 55.00
Warming Plate, 9¾", hot water compartment, polychrome, gold highlights, sgd red underglaze 175.00

SCALES

History: Prior to 1900 the simple balance scale commonly was used for measuring weights. Since then scales have become more sophisticated in design and more accurate. A variety of styles and types include beam, platform, postal, and pharmaceutical.

Collectors' Club: International Society of Antique Scale Collectors, 111 N. Canal St., Chicago, IL 60606.

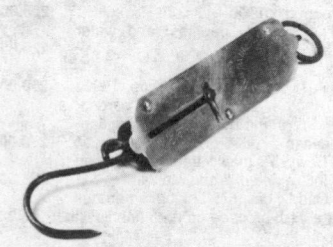

Balance, marked "Chatillion Improved, New York, Patent Dec 10, 1867," $60.00.

Balance
Brass, marble base, 21" h 40.00
Countertop type, walnut and brass,
carved hand-form support with
pedestal, Antico Verde marble
base, brass pans, 25½" h, Italy,
18th C 330.00
Fairbanks, 15½" l, 8¾" h, marked "Iz
8," 50% orig paint 50.00
Spring, Chatillons Spring Balance,
hanging type, brass face, 17 x 4½" 60.00
Candy
Anderson Computing Scale Co, 2 lb 250.00
Detecto Gram, cast iron, brass pan,
3 lb, 1930s 135.00
Enterprise Manufacturing Co., Phila,
PA, tin scoop, brass slide 135.00

National, decal, restored 350.00
Peerless Weighing Machine Co, NY,
lollipop type, "Honest Weight 1¢,"
68" h 635.00
Coin-operated Sidewalk Scale
Grapette Soda adv, 1 ¢ 2,200.00
O. D. Jennings, white, porcelain ... 1,000.00
Counter, The Computing Scale Co.,
Dayton, Ohio, USA pat 1885, emb,
orig 400.00
Egg, 8½ x 6½ x 3", aluminum weight
indicator, brass head screw, red
weighing arm 35.00
Feed, red and white checked top, blue
and cream bottom, metal pan, "Pur-
ina Feed Saver and Cow Culler" adv 70.00
Gold Coin, brass scale, fitted brass box,
orig weights, 8½" l 50.00
Pharmacy, oak case, beveled glass and
marble top, 1800s 295.00
Postal, "Hanson Bros. Scale Co.,"
c1925 .... 35.00
Steelyard, wrought iron, brass inlay and
fig shape weight, 32" l, pitted 25.00
Store
Country Store, brass and cast iron,
scarlet, red and gold pin striping,
red, white and blue shield, brass
pan and hardware, 10 14" x 12",
National 300.00
Grocery, tin, hanging, weighs to 30
lbs 45.00

SCHLEGELMILCH PORCELAINS

History: Erdmann Schlegelmilch founded his porcelain factory in Suhl in the Thuringia region in 1861. Reinhold, his brother, established a porcelain factory at Tillowitz in Upper Silesia in 1869. In the 1860s Prussia controlled Thuringia and Upper Silesia, both rich in the natural ingredients needed for porcelain.

By the late 19th century an active export business was conducted with the United States and Canada due to a large supply of porcelain at reasonable costs achieved through industrialization and cheap labor. Both brothers marked their pieces with the RSP mark, a designation honoring Rudolph Schlegelmilch, their father. Over 30 mark variations have been discovered.

The Suhl factory ceased production in 1920, unable to recover from the effects of World War I. The Tillowitz plant, located in an area of changing international boundaries, finally came under Polish socialist government control in 1956.

References: Susan and Al Bagdade, *Warman's English & Continental Pottery & Porcelain, 1st Edition,* Warman Publishing Co., Inc., 1987; Mary Frank Gaston, *The Collector's Encyclopedia Of R.S. Prussia and Other R.S. and E.S. Porcelain,* Collector Books, 1982; George W. Terrell, Jr.,

Collecting R.S. Prussia Identification and Values,
Books Americana, 1982; Clifford S. Schlegelmilch, *Handbook Of Erdmann And Reinhold Schlegelmilch, Prussia-Germany And Oscar Schlegelmilch, Germany, 3rd Edition*, published by author, 1973.

Reproduction Alert: Many "fake" Schlegelmilch pieces are appearing on the market. These reproductions have new decal marks, transfers, or recently hand painted animals on old, authentic R.S. Prussia pieces.

R. S. Germany, vases, pair, 11¼" h, floral dec, gold trim, blue ground, $450.00.

R. S. GERMANY

Ashtray, round, Nightwatch scene, brown ground	250.00
Berry Set, master and four serving bowls, roses, yellow, orange, and white, shaded brown to light green ground, blue mark	90.00
Biscuit Jar	
Poppies dec, gold trim	85.00
Roses dec, blue and cream	65.00
Bonbon Dish, center handle, white poppies, shaded green ground	35.00
Bone Dish, gray, gold band, blue mark	30.00
Bowl	
9", earth tones with allover white snowballs, single handle, steeple mark	115.00
10", three stylized blue orchids, gold	75.00
Bread Tray, 14", shaded white to green ground, yellow and white roses in basket, open handles, blue mark	140.00
Cake Set, orange and yellow roses, lacy gold trim, brown border, 6 pcs	110.00
Celery Tray, 12¼ x 5⅜", cream to light gray ground, pink roses, green leaves	50.00

Chocolate Pot	
5", child's, green and white floral dec, blue mark	120.00
10½", pale green, pink, yellow, and white roses, blue mark	150.00
Chocolate Set, chocolate pot, cov, five cups and saucers	
Carnations dec, gold trim, black mark	400.00
Cotton Plant dec, blue mark	450.00
Tulips, Art Deco style dec, paneled mold, white flowers, green ground	325.00
Creamer, corset shape, luster green, pink roses, four ftd	15.00
Cup, 2½", pearlized ground, hp, chrysanthemum florals	20.00
Demitasse Coffeepot, roses dec	75.00
Dresser Set, tray, powder jar, hair receiver, hatpin holder, violets dec	225.00
Dresser Tray, 11½", shaded green ground, red and pink roses	90.00
Hair Receiver, 3½", hp, violets	40.00
Hatpin Holder, hexagonal, molded feet, white, delicate floral dec	45.00
Inkwell, cov, lily of the valley dec	65.00
Marmalade Jar, cov, floral	20.00
Mustache Cup, peach dec, green leaves	55.00
Mustard Jar, cov and ladle, hp, rose dec	45.00
Nut Dish, floral, satin finish, set of 6	125.00
Pitcher, 5¾", milk, rose and chrysanthemums, blue mark	65.00
Plate, 9½", red and yellow roses, lily of the valley dec, gold trim, marked "E. S. Germany, Prov. Saxe"	30.00
Ramekin, satin finish, rose dec	30.00
Tidbit Tray, 6½" d, center handle, berries dec	15.00
Toothpick Holder, three gold handles	30.00
Vase	
3½", crowned cranes dec	800.00
6", double handles, Nightwatch scene, gold and red trim	400.00
6½", blue irid ground, gold tracings, emb mold, portrait of woman, long hair, wearing wreath of flowers, gold medallion, beading, and handles, marked "E S Germany, Royal Saxe"	165.00

R. S. POLAND

Bowl, 10½", satin finish, heart mold, poppies	230.00
Candlestick, 6", violets, lily of the valley dec, shiny finish	110.00
Hair Receiver, violet, lily of the valley dec	100.00
Planter, 6 x 7", floral dec	215.00
Powder Jar, violets, lily of the valley dec	90.00
Vase	
4½ x 8¾", cream ground, pink and white roses, gold band around top	

garlands of gold roses and leaves, marked "R. S. Poland" **165.00**
7½", swans, lake, woods scene around circumference **285.00**

R. S. Prussia, bowl, 11″ d, pink rose, green trim, $325.00.

R. S. PRUSSIA

Biscuit Jar, 6¾", Scallop and Fan mold, lavender and white flower, red mark **200.00**
Bowl
  6″, carnation mold, roses, ftd, red mark **150.00**
  7″, lettuce mold, dogwood and pine, red mark **200.00**
  9¼", five portrait medallions, cobalt blue and gold border, floral center **800.00**
  10″, iris mold, blue, aqua, yellow ... **150.00**
  10½", blown out, roses, satin finish . **185.00**
  12½", swan scene, scalloped mold, red mark **400.00**
Bun Dish, 12¼ x 6″, two large center pink roses, scalloped edge, red mark **85.00**
Bread Plate, 13½" l, gold beading, pink flowers on water, open handles, red mark **125.00**
Cake Plate
  10″, carnation mold, pink poppies, pearl border, open handles, red mark **165.00**
  10¾", handles, pink roses dec, raised white and green leaf dec, creamy yellow ground **200.00**
  11″, blown out leaves border, green shaded to creamy yellow, pink center roses, gold trim **200.00**
Celery, 12½"
  Cloverleaf mold **250.00**
  Dogwood blossoms, red mark ... **100.00**
  Swan scene, scalloped mold, red mark **400.00**
Chocolate Pot, cobalt blue, carnation mold **1,200.00**

Creamer and Sugar
  Pink and white dogwood, gold trim, green tint ground, mold marked #14 .... **80.00**
  Pink poppies, gold trim, pastel ground, ftd, sq base, red mark ... **130.00**
  Sheepherder, black swallows, flower finial, red mark **475.00**
Cup and Saucer, pedestal, floral, red mark **50.00**
Demitasse Cup and Saucer, carnation mold, cobalt blue, red mark **300.00**
Hair Receiver, 5 x 3″, round, blown out body, pink roses, gold trim, red mark **185.00**
Mustard Jar, white satin ground, pink floral dec, flower finial, red mark ... **125.00**
Nappy, bud festooned handle, sapphire blue, raised flowers, center floral, red steeple mark **75.00**
Nut Dish, deep burgundy rim, gold design, pink roses, light blue flowers, pedestal base, handles, underplate . **50.00**
Pitcher
  8 x 6½", lemonade, shaded green to cream ground, pink roses, red mark **300.00**
  10″, blown out iris, green shadow flowers, steeple mark **400.00**
  10½", tankard, poppies, blown out base, leaves and cherries, red mark **675.00**
  13½", tankard, stippled mold, large pink and red roses, red mark **765.00**
Plaque, 11¼", mill scene, green ground, lavender and yellow border **710.00**
Plate, 9½", iris mold, castle scene, pastels **600.00**
Powder Jar, stippled floral, red mark .. **100.00**
Relish, scattered flowers, undecorated jewels, red mark **50.00**
Shaving Mug, Hidden Image, lip, unmarked **250.00**
Spooner, floral, two handles, red mark **150.00**
Sugar Shaker, 4¾", luster finish, scalloped base, rose dec, red mark **235.00**
Tea Set, teapot, creamer, and cov sugar, ftd, cream, pink flowers and dec, gold beads, red mark **275.00**
Toothpick Holder, basket and roses .. **130.00**
Vase
  6¾", lavender violets, red mark **175.00**
  8½", lily mold, gold Greek Key dec on shaded pink border, floral dec center, gilt dec **150.00**

R. S. SUHL

Bowl, 10″, sheepherder scene, cottage, red mark **500.00**
Compote, 4½", ftd, creamy roses, gold stencil design, green mark **200.00**
Pitcher, 5½", white ground, red roses, unmarked **100.00**

R. S. Suhl, vase, Mill scene, $400.00.

Vase, 9½", Gibson Girl portrait, red
mark **800.00**

R. S. TILLOWITZ

Bowl, 10 x 6¼", oval, hp, pheasant hen
and cock, blue mark **275.00**
Marmalade Jar, floral, underplate **50.00**
Pitcher, lilies of the valley dec, matching
underplate **40.00**

**R. S. Tillowitz, cheese and cracker
dish, 8½" d, 2½" h, blue mark, "Germany" in green, $50.00.**

Plate
6", lilies of the valley dec, set of 5 . .   **30.00**
7", stylized butterfly border, gold rim
and handles, blue mark **45.00**
Tray, five sided, roses **25.00**
Vase, 7¼", owl dec **100.00**

Schneider

SCHNEIDER GLASS

History: Brothers Ernest and Charles Schneider, founded a glassworks at Epiney-sur-Seine, France, in 1913. Charles, the artistic designer, previously had worked for Daum and Galle.

Although Schneider art glass is best known, the firm also made table glass, stained glass, and lighting fixtures. The art glass exhibits simplicity of design; bubbles and streaking often are found in larger pieces. Other wares include cameo cut and hydrofluoric acid etched designs.

Schneider signed their pieces with a variety of script and block signatures, "Le Verre Francais," or "Charder." Robert, son of Charles, assumed art direction in 1948. Schneider moved to Loris in 1962.

**Dish, 13½" d, 5½" h, orange shaded to
dark blue, amethyst base with white
ribbing, sgd, etched "Schneider" on
top of base, $275.00.**

Bowl
4¼", mottled white and orange, sgd   **65.00**
9¼", flattened globular shape, clear,
mottled cream shading to magenta,
orange and deep purple splashes,
c1925 . . . .   **165.00**
Candlestick, 5½", paperweight base,
coral and pink double clematis **175.00**
Compote
8½" d, 5½" h, lavender shading to
deep blue rim, wrought iron base,
clusters of glass cherries **225.00**
12" d, 4" h, mottled amethyst bowl,
black base, and stem **400.00**
Pitcher, 6¼", mottled pink, dark maroon
handle, orig paper label, sgd **365.00**
Vase
5½", blue, black, and clear, cased orange int., blown into wrought iron
base, sgd, marked "France," c1925   **275.00**
7½", stylized lavender flowers, mottled milky white and orange
streaked ground, sgd "Charder" .   **375.00**
8½", mottled orange, purple, cream,
and yellow, sgd **285.00**
9", blood red, dripping at top **1,150.00**
10", bulbous, cylindrical neck, deep
lavender streaked with blue, two or-

ange handles on neck, inscribed
"Schneider/France" **400.00**
15″, red, blue dripping from top, pur-
ple base, sgd, pr **1,200.00**
17¼″, teardrop, wide flaring lip, mot-
tled periwinkle blue, cherry red
ground, sgd, c1925 . . . . **935.00**

SCHOENHUT TOYS

History: Albert Schoenhut, son of a toymaker, was born in Germany in 1849. In 1866 he ventured to America to work as a repairman of toy pianos for Wanamaker's, Philadelphia, Pennsylvania. Finding the glass sounding bars inadequate, he perfected a toy piano with metal sounding bars. His piano was an instant success, and the A. Schoenhut Company had its beginning.

From that point, toys seemed to flow out of the factory. Each of his six sons entered the business. The business prospered until 1934 when misfortune forced the company into bankruptcy. In 1935 Otto and George Schoenhut contracted to produce the Pinn Family Dolls.

At the same time, the Schoenhut Manufacturing Company was formed by two other Schoenhuts. Both companies operated under a partnership agreement that eventually led to O. Schoenhut, Inc., which continues today.

Some dates of interest: 1872-toy piano invented; 1903-Humpty and Dumpty and Circus patented; 1911–1924-wooden doll production; 1928–1934-composition dolls.

Reference: Richard O'Brien, *Collecting Toys, 4th Edition*, Books Americana, 1985.

Elephant, glass eyes, repainted trunk, $100.00.

Animal
Bear, brown, glass eyes, Style III . . **175.00**
Billy Goat, 9″ **75.00**
Buffalo, glass eyes **225.00**
Donkey, 10″, laughing **50.00**
Elephant, 7″ l, tin, 3 pcs **60.00**
Gazelle, glass eyes, c1910 . . . . **500.00**

Horse, 10″, Appaloosa **75.00**
Kangaroo, painted eyes, Style II . . . **300.00**
Leopard, glass eyes **225.00**
Poodle, painted eyes **120.00**
Reindeer **125.00**
Rhinoceros, jointed **90.00**
Building Toy, Little Village Builder, orig
box **75.00**
Circus
Accessory
Chair **20.00**
Platform **15.00**
Tent, side show **1,800.00**
Horse, jointed, circus rider saddle . . **70.00**
Humpty Dumpty Complete Set, per-
formers with glass eyes, accesso-
ries, tent with wood base, Humpty
Dumpty Circus box top, damaged **600.00**
Performer
Clown, 9″ h, wood **30.00**
Lion Tamer, wood head **170.00**
Man, 6″, carved wood head and body,
oversized ears and feet, wide grin,
orig cotton and felt costume **125.00**
Ringmaster **75.00**
Dirigible, 13″, orig box, c1929 . . . . . **75.00**
Doll
11″, bald head, decaled blue eyes,
closed mouth, jointed body, mod-
ernly made suit dressed **225.00**
11½″, decaled blue eyes, single
stroke brows, closed mouth, jointed
body, orig brown wig, redressed in
modern clothes, round stitches "C
HE Schoenhut" on head, oval
stitches, "Schoenhut Doll/ Pat Jan
17th 1911/USA" on body **450.00**
14″ h, baby, bald head, decaled blue
eyes, closed mouth, curved limb
body, knitted outfit dressed **275.00**
Farm Character
Goat, painted eyes **150.00**
Horse, 10″, painted eyes **150.00**
Milkmaid **75.00**
Piano
13 x 9″, baby grand, 12 keys **160.00**
19½ x 20 x 10″, upright, wood, stool,
18 keys **155.00**

SCIENTIFIC INSTRUMENTS

History: Chemists, doctors, geologists, navigators, and surveyors used precision instruments as tools of their trade. Such objects are well designed and beautifully crafted. The principal medium is brass. Fancy hardwood cases also are common.

Reference: Crystal Payton, *Scientific Collectibles Identification & Price Guide*, published by author, 1978; Anthony Turner, *Early Scientific Instruments, Europe 1400–1780*, Sotheby's Publications, 1987.

Microscope, Bausch & Lomb, three lens, turret, mechanical stage, orig clips, orig box, $300.00.

Barograph, brass and glass, cased, sgd "Short & Mason, London, England" . **500.00**

Barometer

Stick type, 38¼" h, pine, thermometer, sgd "C Wilder, Peterboro, New Hampshire, Woodruffs pat. June 5, 1860" **1,000.00**

Wheel type, 27" h, 11½" w, Louis XV style, gilt bronze, circular face, rams heads suspending garlands, plumes and tassels base, sgd "Couilleau Paris" **660.00**

Chondrometer, 12¼" l, 19th C, cased, sgd "De Grave, Short & Fanner" . . . **425.00**

Chronometer, cased, 19th C, sgd "Robert Roskell, Liverpool" **1,400.00**

Compass, 2" d, convex glass lens, hand colored engraved paper face, turned wood case **150.00**

Gyroscope, 10½" h, lacquered, accessories, late 19th C, base sgd "T. Cooke & Sons, York & London" . . . **600.00**

Hydrometer, Baume, orig box **80.00**

Micrometer, Starrett 4, orig case **45.00**

Octant, mid 18th C, sgd "I. Uring, London," incomplete **850.00**

Planisphere, Hammett's **175.00**

Quadrant, ebony, brass arm, sgd "Dollond of London" **600.00**

Slide Rule, wood and celluloid, case, marked "Keuffel & Esser," dated 1900 . . . . **35.00**

Telescope, 39" l, 65" h, brass, oak tripod base with turned legs, sgd "M Jaggli, Zurich" **200.00**

Thermometer, desk type, bronze and marble, vendome column form, Paris, c1900 . . . . **1,900.00**

SCRIMSHAW

History: Norman Flayderman defined scrimshaw as "the art of carving or otherwise fashioning useful or decorative articles as practiced primarily by whalemen, sailors, or others associated with nautical pursuits." Many collectors expand this to include the work of Eskimos and War of 1812 French POWs.

Collecting scrimshaw was popularized during the presidency of John F. Kennedy.

References: E. Norman Flayderman, *Scrimshaw, Scrimshanders, Whales And Whalemen,* N. Flayderman & Co., 1972, out-of-print; Richard C. Malley, *Graven By The Fishermen Themselves,* Mystic Seaport Museum, Inc., 1983.

Periodical: *Whalebone,* P. O. Box 2834, Fairfax, VA 22031.

Museums: Cold Spring Harbor Museum, Long Island, NY; Kendall Whaling Museum, Sharon, MA; Mystic Seaport Museum, Mystic, CT; National Maritime Museum, San Francisco, CA; Old Dartmouth Historical Society, New Bedford, MA; Whaling Museum, Nantucket, MA.

Reproduction Alert: The biggest problem in the field is fakes. A very hot needle will penetrate the common plastics used in reproductions. Ivory will not generate static electricity when rubbed, plastic will. Patina is not a good indicator; it has been faked with tea, tobacco juice, burying in raw rabbit hide, and other ingenious ways. Usually an old design will not be of consistant depth of cut as the ship rocked and tools dulled; however, skilled forgers have even copied this.

Advisor: Bill Wheeler.

Book, *Susan's Teeth and Much About Scrimshaw,* Everett U Crosby, published Nantucket Island, limited edition, 500 copies, 1955 . . . . **850.00**

Snuff Box, 3 x 1½", shaped oval, top diamond inscribed "R. N." (Royal Navy) and anchor, other side inscribed "Capt. N. C. Norten, dates of service on ends (1831 and 1841), fluting, highlighted with lampblack, $400.00.

Buggy Whip, 82" l, whale ivory and whalebone sections, baleen rings, two rope carvings, mid 19th C **2,000.00**

Butter Mold, 5⅛" h, circular, wood, carved rosette, whale ivory handle, early to mid 19th C **275.00**

Candle Stand, 15⅝" d, 29½" h, octagonal, geometric wood and whale ivory inlays, American, 19th C 1,500.00
Cane
- 31⅞" l, wood and whalebone, whale ivory and baleen rings, 19th C . . . 250.00
- 36" l, wood shaft, turned whale ivory knob, American, mid 19th C 130.00
- 36⅝" l, captain's, inlaid ivory, wood, and baleen rings, faceted knob, 19th C 225.00
- 37½" l, wood, whale ivory tip and knob, partially wound baleen and ropework, diamond shape wood inlays, 19th C 150.00

Cane Head, 9¾" l, whale ivory, baleen rings, mid 19th C 275.00
Chest, 20¾ x 9½ x 9", walnut or mahogany and pine, three inlaid abstract whalebone figures on front panel and initials "G W T," hinged top 500.00
Corset Busk, 13" l, engraved, basket of red flowers, "Josephs" under church with bell, weathervane, and clock, mid 19th C 200.00
Desk, 20¾ x 19 x 7½", table, island wood, whale ivory, abalone, and ebony inlays, slant lid, "Thomas D Carr 1850" on front 3,100.00
Eagle's Head, 5¾" l, engraved head and emblem on one side, sculptured on other, probably represents Civil War "Old Abe" eagle, 19th C 2,200.00
Foot Stool
- 10" l, panbone, four legs, inscribed "Mary Mace Fellows/March 8, 1851" on top 500.00
- 14" l, black walnut, fruitwood sides, wood and whalebone inlays, mid 19th C 700.00

Game Box, 18½", sq, wood, abalone shell, and whalebone inlays, chess ext., backgammon board int., mid 19th C 1,600.00
Hat Rack, 27⅞" l, oak board, mounted with five whale's teeth, 19th C 450.00
Hourglass, 5" d, 8¾" h, ebony, whale ivory feet and blocking, late 18th, early 19th C 800.00
Jagging Wheel
- 6" l, walrus ivory, handle with open cut hearts and clubs on one side, engraved leaves and berries on other side, American, 19th C 750.00
- 7⅜" l, whale ivory and ebony, unicorn, missing horn, American, 19th C . . 1,300.00

Jewel Box, 11¾" l, geometric and compass rose wood, whale ivory, and abalone inlays, mid 19th C 450.00
Knitting Needle, 14½" l, coconut wood, whale ivory tips, whale ivory finial dec with alternating exotic wood and whale ivory, 19th C, pr 650.00
Letter Opener, 7⅛" l, bone, dagger form, inlaid glass bead handle, mid 19th C 150.00
Mirror, 12¾" h, 8⅞" w, half column style, four diamond shape whalebone inlays, American, 1830–40 . . . . 500.00
Napkin Ring, whale ivory, turned inlaid bands of red wax, mid 19th C, pr . . 125.00
Ostrich Egg, engraved, sailor and sweetheart, eagle, flag, stars, and ship, orig ropework hanger 250.00
Panel, 3¼ x 5⅛", Mediterranean ruins, sea, boat, and mountains scene, mid 19th C 100.00
Pointer
- 19⅛", octagonal, whalebone, whale ivory and wood handle, mid 19th C 175.00
- 32⅝" l, whalebone, baleen separator, carved facet whale ivory knob . . . 150.00

Puzzle Box, 3" l, wood, whale ivory escutcheon and knob, made by sailor, mid 19th C 125.00
Rolling Pin
- 11½" l, four walrus ivory pcs, mid 19th C 750.00
- 16" l
  - Fruitwood, turned whale ivory knobs, mid 19th C 400.00
  - Hardwood, whale ivory knobs separated with baleen rings, whale ivory knobs, mid 19th C 450.00

Sewing Box
- 4½ w, inlaid whale and elephant ivory, fitted clamp, drawer, mid 19th C . . 275.00
- 8", sq, island wood, geometric wood inlays, inlaid whale ivory and abalone shell compass rose, diamonds and spandrel dec, mid 19th C . . . 600.00

Stand, 5⅜" h, bone and rose or tulip wood, engraved, mid 19th C 60.00
Swift
- 19" h, orig pink ribbon ties, 19th C . 1,900.00
- 19¼" h, double, old blue ribbon ties, 19th C 2,600.00
- 21" h, whale tooth engraved clamp, American ship, two arrow pierced hearts, and lyre flanked by American flags, early to mid 19th C . . . 2,750.00

Tool, 5⅛" l, whale ivory handle, fitted double blade with brass slide 200.00
Toy, 7¾" h, whale ivory and wood, polychrome dec, minstrel man doing balancing act, mid 19th C 2,100.00
Tray, 20" l, 12" w, wood, ivory and ebony inlaid in exotic woods, galleried rim, 19th C 700.00
Watch Fob, whale ivory, book form, engraved, colored Masonic symbols, mid 19th C 375.00

Whale Tooth

4⅛″, engraved, ship portrait *Hope*, sgd and dated "P81," Paul Vardiman 325.00

4⅜″, engraved, full length man portrait, sgd "G" lower left, William Gilkerson 675.00

5⅜″, engraved, lady portrait, sgd lower left, Frank Barcellos 400.00

7″ l, capture of whale scene, sgd lower right, DeMont 600.00

SEBASTIAN MINIATURES

History: Sebastians are hand painted, lightly glazed figurines of characters from literature and history. They range in size from 3 to 4 inches. Each figurine is made in limited numbers. Other series include children and scenes from family life.

Prescott W. Baston, the originator and designer of Sebastian figures, began production in 1938 in Marblehead, Massachusetts. Sebastian Studios are located in Hudson, Massachusetts. Prescott Baston died on May 25, 1984.

Each year a Sebastian Auction is held in Boxborough, Massachusetts, at the Sebastian Collector's Society meeting. Prices are determined from this source plus the work of the Sebastian Exchange Board which develops a price list that is the standard reference for the field.

Reference: Dr. Glenn S. Johnson, *The Sebastian Miniature Collection & A Guide To Identifying, Understanding, and Enjoying Sebastian Miniatures,* Lance Corp., 1982.

Collectors' Club: Sebastian Collector's Society, 321 Central Street, Hudson, MA 01749. *Sebastian Miniature Collectors Society News* (quarterly) and *The Sebastian Exchange.*

Abraham Lincoln, looking ahead, Marblehead label 100.00

The Skipper, 3¾″ h, copyright 1966, P. W. Baston, $25.00.

Aunt Betzy Trotwood, Marblehead label	50.00
Benjamin Franklin Printing Press	60.00
Christmas Morning	45.00
Cleopatra, version I, 1950–62	200.00
Corner Drug Store	50.00
Daniel Boone, 1940–45	140.00
Gathering Tulips	125.00
George Washington, cannon, sgd, 1947	85.00
In The Candy Store, (Necco Candy), 1947	165.00
James Monroe and Elizabeth Monroe, Marblehead mark, pr	200.00
John Smith and Pocahontas, orig Marblehead mark, pr	200.00
Jordon Marsh Observer	75.00
Lion, c1947	25.00
Little Mother	55.00
Mr. Beacon Hill	60.00
Paul Revere, Marblehead label	90.00
Pilgrims, Marblehead label, MIB	65.00
Santa Claus, 1980	80.00
Sidewalk Days, pr, MIB	120.00
Stagecoach	60.00
Uncle Sam, green label	45.00
Victorian Couple, Marblehead label ..	50.00
Williamsburg Lady	125.00

SEVRES

History: The principal patron of the French porcelain industry in early 18th century France was Jeanne Antonette Poisson, Marquise de Pompadour. She supported the Vincennes factory of Gilles and Robert Dubois and their successors in its attempt to make soft paste porcelain in the 1740s. In 1753 she moved the porcelain operations to Sevres near her home, Chateau de Bellevue.

The Sevres soft paste formula used sand from Fontainbleau, salt and saltpeter, soda of alicante, powdered alabaster, clay, and soap. Louis XV allowed the firm to use the "double L's." Many famous colors were developed, including a cobalt blue. The great scenic designs on the ware were painted by such famous decorators as Watteau, La Tour, and Boucher. In the 18th century Sevres porcelain was the world's foremost diplomatic gift.

In 1769 kaolin was discovered in France, and a hard paste formula developed. The baroque gave way to rococo, a style favored by Jeanne du Barry, Louis XV's next mistress. Louis XVI took little interest in Sevres. Many factories began to turn out counterfeit copies. In 1876 the factory was moved to St. Cloud and was eventually nationalized.

Reference: Susan and Al Bagdade, *Warman's English & Continental Pottery & Porcelain, 1st Edition,* Warman Publishing Co., Inc., 1987.

Ewer, 12″ h, pastel ground, metal handles, rim and base, artist initials, $300.00.

Bowl, 12½″ d, serving, scrolled reserve with exotic birds, apple green ground, gilt handles, blue L mark 475.00
Cache Pot, 9″ h, cylindrical, reserves of elegant figures in garden landscape, pink ground, gilt scroll borders, pr . . 950.00
Charger, 19″ d, Louis XVI center portrait, Marie Antoinette above, ladies of court around edge, blue and gold, names on back 1,150.00
Compote, 10⅝″ d, center portrait medallion of Louis XVI, gilt scroll and floral border, pink ground, two gilt lined flat handles 250.00
Cruet, 8½″ h, pale green, gold scrolls and florals dec, clear free form handle, ball shaped stopper with teardrop air-trap, orig paper label 435.00
Cup and Saucer, gilt and floral panels, apple green ground, set of 6 . . . . . . 365.00
Dessert Service, partial, three tier cake stand, two ftd bowls, four low compotes, bands of trailing fruit tree flowers, wrought gilt bands and roundels, imp blue mark, initialed by decorators and gilders, c1820 . . . . 1,500.00
Dresser Box, 5¾″, oval, portrait medallion of lady on cov, floral side dec, gold bronze mounts 300.00
Ecuelle, cov, and stand, blue roses and foliage, gilded leaves, intertwined handles on cup, sprig handle on cov, oval 7½″ stand, blue enameled inter-

twined L's crowned above letter R, c1770 . . . . 1,400.00
Pitcher and Bowl, rose water, pyriform lidded 9″ h pitcher, landscape reserve panels of cockerels and fruit filled baskets, trailing bands of summer flowers, 9″ d bowl with reserve panel of wild fowl and similar ornaments, gilt bands, c1793 . . . . 2,000.00
Plate
8″, embracing couple, garden setting, yellow dec, scalloped gold dec rim, artist sgd, marked "Chateau St Cloud" 85.00
9⁹⁄₁₆″, botanical, yellow, purple, rose, and green, two dahlia blossoms on one, spray of geranium and azaleas on other, gilt foliate vine, pale blue patterned rim, gilt florette trelliswork dec, botanical inscriptions on back, artist sgd, c1836, pr . . . 8,000.00
Portrait Plate, 9½″, Napoleon, white horse, battle scene, cobalt blue border with gold leaves, artist sgd 250.00
Teapot, 5½″, Louis VX, scrolling diagonal bands of gilt vermicelli alternating with bands of trailing roses, cobalt blue ground, underglaze blue intertwined L's centering K for year 1763 700.00
Urn, gilt bronze mounts
8¼″, red ground, multicolored floral reserve, handles, marked 325.00
26¼″, maiden in white gown, blue sash, pink drape, garlands, two cupids, reverse doves and cupid, waisted neck and pedestal dec with trophy panels, late 19th C 850.00
30″, cov, apple green ground, sgd "L. Demmer" 1,600.00
36″, nymph dec, sgd "Labarre" 3,200.00

SEWING ITEMS

History: As late as 50 years ago, a wide variety of sewing items were found in almost every home in America. Women of every economic and social status were skilled in sewing and dress making.

Even the most elegant ladies practiced the art of embroidery with the aid of jeweled gold and silver thimbles. Sewing birds, an interesting convenience item, were used to hold cloth (in the bird's beak) while sewing. Made of iron or brass, they could be attached to table or shelf with a screw-type fixture. Later models featured a pincushion.

References: Joyce Clement, *The Official Price Guide To Sewing Collectibles,* House of Collectibles, 1987; Victor Houart, *Sewing Accessories: An Illustrated History,* Souvenir Press (London), 1984; Gay Ann Rogers, *An Illustrated History of Needlework Tools,* John Murray (London), 1983; Estelle

Zalkin, *Zalkin's Handbook Of Thimbles & Sewing Implements, First Edition.* Warman Publishing Co., 1988.

Collectors' Club: Thimble Collectors International, P. O. Box 2311, Des Moines, IA 50310.

Periodical: *Thimbletter*, 93 Walnut hill Road, Highlands, MA 02161.

Museums: Fabric Hall, Historic Deerfield, Deerfield, MA; Museum of American History, Smithsonian Institution, Washington, D.C.; Shelburne Museum, Shelburne, VT.

Additional Listings: See *Warman's Americana & Collectibles* for more examples.

Sewing Box, 5¹/₁₆ x 4 x 1½", red leather, paper center medallion of girl in yellow dress, $25.00.

Bodkin
Sterling Silver, engraved, floral dec, hallmarked 25.00
Wood, 3¼", yew, burl box with inlaid edges, c1790 . . . . 130.00
Box
6 x 9", semicircular, marbleized oil cloth on cardboard, blue velvet int., blue ribbon trim, stamped label "Sabbath day Lake Shakers, Maine" 100.00
10⅞ x 7¾ x 3⅜", fruitwood, "Ship Louise Leaving Boston" entitled scene dec, painted shields on top and sides, painted imitation scrimshaw inlays, c19th C 650.00
11" l, mahogany, figured, dovetailed case, drawer, ivory eyelets per thread 100.00
Buttonhole Cutter, 3", iron, hand forged blade, handle, c1820 . . . . 65.00
Catalog
Renival Sewing Machine 15.00
Montgomery Ward Sewing Machines, early 1900s 40.00
Singer Sewing, 16 pgs, 1920s 8.00

Chatelaines
Leather, three straps connect to scissors and case, thimble holder, and pencil, English, c1900 . . . . 185.00
Sterling Silver, ring top, chains connect to note pad, thimble and thimble case, and buttonhook, English 500.00
Crochet Hooks, whale bone, carved, set of 3 . . . . 225.00
Darner, ebony 15.00
Darning Ball, blue, blown, white pulled loops, Nailsea 110.00
Embroidery Hoop, 6¼" d, walnut and cherry, table clamp, hand made, Shaker 120.00
Hem Gauge, heart and rose, relief design 25.00
Knitting Needle, bone, plain, pr 20.00
Needle and Pin Case
Ivory, book shape, fabric pages 95.00
Leather, 2 x 1⅞", black, emb gold, fabric embroidered pages holds pins 45.00
Pin Cushion
Black Girl, print fabric 30.00
Chicken, 4", spool base 45.00
Mama Mouse, pushing carriage . . . 15.00
Punch, ivory, 3⅛", turnings on top . . . 30.00
Seam Cutter, ivory, Buddha figure . . . 20.00
Sewing Bird
German Silver, 5½", one pincushion, emb bird and clamp 90.00
Iron, brass heart shaped thumb screw, 4½" h 110.00
Tin plated, velvet cushion, 4¾" h . . . 115.00
Sewing Case, 4½" l, oval, straw work, elaborate design, lavender and blue shades, early 19th C 100.00
Sewing Kit, Lydia Pinkham adv, tatting needle and thread, tape measure . . 45.00
Spool Cabinet, Richard Silk Co, 7½ x 15 x 14", wood and glass, gold and black lettering, three drawers, counter top display 85.00
Tape Measure, pig, celluloid, creamy ivory 22.00

SHAKER

History: The Shakers, so named because of a dance used in worship, are one of the oldest communal organizations in the United States. This religious group was founded by Mother Ann Lee who emigrated from England and established the first Shaker community near Albany, New York, in 1784. The Shakers reached their peak in 1850 with 6,000 members.

Shakers lived celibate and self-sufficient lives. Their philosophy stressed cleanliness, order, simplicity, and economy. Highly inventive and motivated, the Shakers created many utilitarian household forms and objects. Their furniture reflected a striving for quality and purity in design.

In the early 19th century, the Shakers produced many items for commercial purposes. Chairmaking and the packaged herb and seed business thrived. In every endeavor and enterprise, the members followed Mother Ann's advice: "Put your hands to work and give your heart to God."

References: Charles R. Muller and Timothy D. Rieman, *The Shaker Chair*, The Canal Press, 1984; Don and Carol Raycraft, *Shaker, A Collector's Source Book II*, Wallace-Homestead, 1985; June Sprigg and David Larkin, *Shaker Life, Work, and Art*, Stewart, Tabori & Chang, 1987.

Periodical: *The Shaker Messenger*, P.O. Box 45, Holland, MI 49423.

Swift, umbrella style, walnut, pine standard, $150.00.

Basket
6¼ x 12", cheese, maple and ash, red stain 550.00
6½ x 3¼", berry, wooden, Sabbathday Lake Community 150.00
12 x 28¾ x 18½", wool, ash splint, double wrapped rim and handles . 300.00
14½ x 13¼", ash, hickory handle, round top, sq base 200.00
Bonnet, dark brown palm and straw, black ribbons, 9" flounce, KY 375.00
Box
3⅛ x 7½", oval, four fingers, orig dark red stain, sgd and dated 1857 on lid 300.00
3¾ x 12 x 8¼", document, walnut, dovetailed lid, varnished, New Lebanon 350.00
4¼ x 7⅛ x 11⅛", oval, five fingers, maple and pine, ... 500.00
6", round, pine, orig blue paint, straight seam, copper tacks 125.00
7 x 22 x 9½", seed, pine, natural finish, stenciled, divided, Enfield ... 600.00
Brush, 14", dusting, worn gray paint .. 75.00
Bucket, 9½ x 10", lid, four laps, copper tacks, wooden pins and handle 200.00

Carrier, 4 x 6½ x 7⅛", butternut, dovetailed, hoop handle, Enfield 700.00
Cheese Drainer, 18 x 6", tin, pierced sides and bottom 325.00
Clothes Hanger, 46", Mount Lebanon . 90.00
Coffeepot, 11", tin, handle at right angle, Sabbathday Lake 250.00
Drying Rack, 54 x 31 x 15", pine, blue paint, three bars 500.00
Furniture
Bed, 23 x 66 x 32", pine, turned maple posts, wood wheels, Mount Lebanon 1,000.00
Bench, 72", meetinghouse, pine, red stain, Canterbury 850.00
Blanket Chest, 35 x 42 x 20", poplar, orig red stain, one drawer 3,000.00
Chair, ladder back, maple turned tapering stiles, bulbous finials, three graduated slates, tape seat, tilters 500.00
Chest, 41¼ x 18¼ x 51½", pine, five graduated drawers, turned wooden knob, tapered feet, Waterville, NY 12,800.00
Cradle, cherry, hood with coffered top, shaped sides, pierced hand holds, shaped rockers 800.00
Rocker
Child's, orig seat and back, "O" Model, refinished 1,200.00
Turned and black painted maple, lemon form finials on stiles, mushroom handholds, tape seat, marked "Shakers No. 5, Mt. Lebanon, NY," 19th C 750.00
Settee, 34 x 58", birch and pine, nineteen spindles, varnished, Enfield . 5,000.00
Table
90", pine top, trestle base 23,000.00
144", two board tiger maple top, old red paint on underside, tiger maple cleats, evenly spaced iron rivets 43,000.00
Glove Stretcher, 15", pr 275.00
Herb Chest, 15 x 24 x 9", pine, natural finish, nine drawers 400.00
Knife Tray, two section, tiger stripe maple 140.00
Medicine Bottle, clear glass, yellow label "Shaker's Extract of Poke Root, Mt. Lebanon, NY" 60.00
Mail Box, 20 x 24 x 11", pine, natural finish, hinged lid, Enfield 500.00
Pin Cushion, 6", maple, red velvet cushion, thimble holder, varnished 350.00
Rack, pegboard, pine and maple, holds 12 x 16¾" mirror, hardwood framed, orig red satin finish 435.00
Rug, 23½ x 33", sewn, brown, blue, green, aubergine, pink, and old wool shag 600.00
Scoop, 2½", apple butter, carved walnut, one piece 285.00

Seeder, 93", wood and sheet metal, hand carried	**75.00**
Seive, wood, plaid horsehair liner	**85.00**
Sewing Box, small, oct, poplar, paper label, Sabbathday Shakers, Maine	**145.00**
Sewing Basket, curved handles, curlique trim, pocket with strawberry	**185.00**
Shelf, hanging, 21 x 15", pine, rect superstructure above three shelves	**550.00**
Spice Chest, 7 x 13 x 6", poplar, nine drawers, walnut pulls, natural finish	**300.00**
Swift, umbrella style, walnut, pine standard	**150.00**

SHAVING MUGS

History: Shaving mugs hold the soap, brush, and hot water used to prepare a beard for shaving. They come in a variety of materials including tin, silver, glass, and pottery. One style is the scuttle, so called because of its "coal scuttle" shape, with separate compartments for water and soap.

Shaving mugs were popular between 1880 and 1925, the period of the great immigration to the United States. At first barber shops used a common mug for all customers. This led to an epidemic of a type of eczema, known as barber itch.

Laws were passed requiring each individual to have his own mug. Initially names and numbers were used. This did not work well for those who could not read. The occupational mug developed because illiterate workers could identify a picture of their trade or an emblem of its tools. Fraternal emblems also were used and were the most popular of the decorative forms. Immigrants especially liked the heraldry of the fraternal emblems since it reminded them of what they knew in Europe.

European porcelain blanks were decorated by American barber supply houses. Prices ranged from fifty cents for a gold name mug to two dollars and fifty cents for an elaborate occupational design. Most of the art work was done by German artists who had immigrated to America.

The invention of the safety razor by King C. Gillette, that was issued to three and one-half million servicemen during World War I, brought an end to the shaving mug era.

References: Susan and Al Bagdade, *Warman's English & Continental Pottery & Porcelain, 1st Edition,* Warman Publishing Co., Inc., 1987; Phillip L. Krumholz, *Value Guide For Barberiana & Shaving Collectibles,* published by author, 1988; Robert Blake Powell, *Occupational & Fraternal Shaving Mugs of The United States,* published by author, 1978.

Advisor: Edward W. Leach.

BARBER SHOP: FRATERNAL

American Legion, emblem star, name, gold trim	**400.00**

Mug, gray and white horses, green ground, gold trim, marked "Royal China International, H. L. Purnell Co." in gold, $225.00.

Ancient Order United Workmen, anchor shield, A.O.U.W. initials	**250.00**
Grand Army of the Republic, American spread eagle over cannon and American flag above star shape medal in center, pink and blue floral design with gold highlights on sides, marked "D & Co France"	**150.00**
Knights of Columbus, blue wrap, gold trim, black "F.D. Conner" with gold highlighting, red, white, and blue symbol with gold highlighting, gold raised enamel flowers, green stamped "Germany" on bottom	**40.00**
Knights of Pythias, F.C.B. on shield, suit of armor, crossed halberds	**125.00**
Oddfellows, "H.S. Evans" and three loops across center with "F.L.T" in gold, marked "Royal China International" on bottom	**45.00**
Patriotic Order Sons of America, shield, star, bust of Washington, P.O.S.A., gold scrollwork	**150.00**
United Mine Workers Of America, flowers around rim, bottom marked "C.T. Germany"	**50.00**
Woodman of the World, blue maple leaf, stump, axe, bird, logging tools	**150.00**

BARBER SHOP: OCCUPATIONAL

Artist, palette, brushes	**225.00**
Baker, putting bread in oven, dough box, work bench	**375.00**
Bartender, saloon scene, back bar, bottles, bartender, 2 customers	**350.00**
Baseball Player, player batting, catcher, 2 men in field	**750.00**
Blacksmith, horseshoe, flowers, and leaves, blue ribbon, bottom marked	

"MEW Barber Supply Utica, NY, V&D Austria" **200.00**
Brewery, T. Helb Brewery, buildings, horse, and wagon **700.00**
Butcher, skinning steer, other steer hanging on rack **450.00**
Carpenter, sawing board, house frame, pile of lumber **425.00**
Cigar Maker, hand holding cigar **300.00**
Cyclist, man riding bike on dirt road, wearing blue outfit, trees, grass, fence, and house **525.00**
Delivery Wagon, two horses pulling wagon full of watermelons, driver with whip, tan ground, gold scroll each side, "1256 H" on bottom **275.00**
Doctor, Dr. E.L. Woodford, gold dec, top and bottom bands, dane across center, marked "Limoges, France, 772" . **60.00**
Electrician, electric generator **275.00**
Farmer, 2 horses pulling plow, farm house **250.00**
Fireman
  Helmet, axes, ladder, and nozzles . . **400.00**
  Two horses pulling steam engine, driver **650.00**
Hardware Clerk, clerk showing customer saw, barrels, shelves, merchandise **450.00**
Hatmaker, derby, gold trim **275.00**
Moving and Hauling, two brown horses, pulling wagon, gold rim, dated 1924, bottom marked "Royal China International" **235.00**
Musician
  Kettle drum player, kettle drum **400.00**
  Piano player, upright piano **350.00**
Painter
  Bucket of paint, brushes **200.00**
  Painter on scaffold, painting building **500.00**
Pharmacist, yellow mortar and pestle, black highlighting, gold floral design on each side, name "W. F. Dodson," gold "4017" on bottom **175.00**
Photographer, taking picture of woman in chair **1,575.00**
Policeman, blue uniform, badge, and nightstick **675.00**
Restaurant, restaurant int., waiter and customers, yellow floor and ceiling, blue background hanging light fixtures, wall pictures **820.00**
Tinsmith, gray tools with orange, marked "7168, 303, TK, 50, Vienna Austria" on bottom **190.00**
Watchmaker, gold watch and chain . . . **275.00**

BARBER SHOP: OTHER

American Eagle, perched on American shield clutching arrows, gold trimmed banner in beak with name in black,

hp, dark blue wrap, white and rouge highlights, marked "V.D. Austria" . . . **125.00**
Elk Head, mountain background **60.00**
Liberty Bell, bell with crack, "1776" scroll on each side **200.00**
Man in black carriage, wearing derby and lap robe, brown trotting horse, green stamped "KPM Germany" on bottom **80.00**
Pennsylvania, Seal of, "Virtue, Liberty & Independence" **190.00**
Personalized
  Clyde Barr, winter scene, raised enamel highlights, marked "Koken St. Louis, The World's Our Field, and W.G. & Co, Limoges France" **65.00**
  H.C. Schmidt, hp, flowering lily scene, top and bottom gold bands, marked "Vienna, Austria" and red "2857" on bottom **30.00**
Railroad, locomotive and coal car dec **50.00**
Seashore scene, gold highlighted pyramid shape scene with two blue bands on sides, purple mountain background, c1885 . . . . **50.00**
Shield, compass, arm with hammer, and square, emb scroll on both sides . . . **85.00**
Sports
  Hunter, shooting bird, brown and white dog, sunset background, marked "Koken Barbers' Supply Co St. Louis, USA" **165.00**
  Target, rifles, powder horn, and flowers **200.00**
St. Bernard, pink rim, marked "Made in Germany" **30.00**

Scuttle, 3¾ x 6½", china, red and pink rose dec, white ground, gold trim, marked "Germany," $90.00.

SCUTTLES

Daisy pattern, ivory and brown **25.00**
Eagle holding arrow on flag shield . . . **75.00**

Floral Spray	40.00
Gambling, Lucky Spots, shows spread of aces, flowers on back	125.00
Horses in field	50.00
Silver Plate, emb trim, ornate handle with insert and brush	65.00

SHAWNEE POTTERY

History: The Shawnee Pottery Co. was founded in 1937 in Zanesville, Ohio. The company acquired a 650,000 square foot plant that formerly housed the American Encaustic Tiling Company and where it produced as many as 100,000 pieces of pottery per day until 1961, when the plant closed.

Shawnee limited its chief production to kitchenware, decorative art pottery, and dinnerware. Distribution was primarily through jobbers and chain-stores.

Shawnee can be marked "Shawnee," "Shawnee U.S.A." "USA #—," "Kenwood," or with character names, e.g., "Pat. Smiley," "Pat. Winnie," etc.

Reference: Mark Supnick, *Collecting Shawnee Pottery: A Pictorial Reference And Price Guide*, published by author, 1983.

Advisor: Mark Supnick.

Cookie Jar, 10″ h, Corn King pattern, marked "Shawnee USA 66," $80.00.

Ashtray, squirrel, marked "USA"	10.00
Candle Holder, 6½″, hand dec gold trim, pr	12.00
Cookie Jar	
Dutch Girl, marked "USA"	50.00
Lucky Elephant, gold trim and decals, marked "USA"	120.00
Mugsey, marked "USA"	75.00
Smiley Pig, gold trim, flower decal, flowers on bib, marked "USA"	130.00
Creamer, Corn King, No. 70	12.00
Cup and Saucer, corn, cup marked "90," saucer marked "91"	30.00

Darning Egg, figure	20.00
Planter	
Cockatiel, marked "Shawnee 523"	10.00
Fawn, gold trim, marked "USA 535"	14.00
Windmill, gold trim, marked "Shawnee 715"	22.00
Platter, 12″, corn, marked "Shawnee 96"	20.00
Relish Tray, corn, marked "Shawnee 79"	14.00
Salt and Pepper, Smiley Pig, red collar, pr	20.00
Sprinkler Bottle, Sprinkle Plenty, Chinese boy	16.00
Sugar, cov, corn pattern, white and green glaze	20.00
Teapot	
Granny Anne, gold trim and decals, marked "Granny Anne"	90.00
Rose	20.00
Two daises	20.00
Vase	
Bow Knot, marked "USA 819"	12.00
Cornucopia, 5″, green	10.00
Fan, 4¼″ h, yellow and green, blue flower, marked "USA"	8.00
Hand, marked "USA"	18.00
Vegetable Dish, 9″, corn, marked "Shawnee 95"	18.00

SILHOUETTES

History: Silhouettes (shades) are shadow profiles, produced by hollow cutting, mechanical tracing, or painting. They were popular in the 18th and 19th centuries.

The name came from Etienne de Silhouette, a French Minister of Finance, who tended to be tight with money and cut "shades" as a pastime. In America the Peale family was one of the leading silhouette makers. An impressed stamp marked "PEALE" or "Peale Museum" identifies their work.

Silhouette portraiture lost popularity with the introduction of daguerreotype prior to the Civil War. In the 1920s and 30s a brief revival occurred when tourists to Atlantic City and Paris had their profiles cut as souvenirs.

Reference: Blume J. Rifken, *Silhouettes in America, 1790–1840, A Collectors' Guide*, Pardigm Press, 1987.

Children	
4½ x 5″, girl, hollow cut, gilt highlights, red coral necklace, penciled lace ruffle, gilted black lacquered frame	375.00
4½ x 5¾″, girl and boy, cut, titled "Agnes and Lindsey," sgd "Auguste Edouart 1831"	450.00
Gentlemen	
2¾ x 4″, bust, hollow cut, inscribed "Joshua Baily, age 37, November 20, 1835"	475.00

Andrew Jackson, painted features, 10 x 6½", framed, $150.00.

4 x 4⅝", oval, pen and ink, black shadow box frame	120.00
6 x 4", Richard Channing Moore, 1762, full figure, holding cane, name on back, 18th C	175.00

Group
12 x 13⅜", facing pair, full length silhouette of seated lady and gentleman, watercolor highlights, minor paint flaking, rosewood veneer frames	800.00
12 x 14", two young girls and mother in parlor, litho ground, signed and dated in center, "Aug.n Edouart fecit, Brooklyn, Sept 20, 1843"	4,850.00
18¾ x 15½", two men and women, seated on chairs, pen, ink, and pencil room int., sgd "Aug Edouart, fecit 1840," bird's eye maple frame	600.00

Ladies
4 x 4⅜", young woman, hollow cut, black cloth backing, paper stained, gilt frame	130.00
4 x 4⅝", old woman wearing elaborate bonnet, ink on paper, gilt highlights, old gilt frame	125.00
4 x 4⅞", woman wearing lacy collar, pen and ink, orig black reeded frame	275.00
4½ x 5¼", old woman wearing bonnet, cut silhouette, worn gilt detail, sgd on back "cut with scissors by E Whittre," black lacquer frame, gilt brass trim	85.00
4⅝ x 3⅜", titled "Mrs. Sturdivant," green paper background, modern frame	100.00
5⅞ x 6⅝", young woman, hollow cut, paper with emb mark "Museum," (Peale Museum), black cloth backing, minor stains and creases, mahogany veneer frame	200.00

6 x 7", young woman, hollow cut, pencil, pen, and ink detail, black paper backing, eglomise glass mat, framed	200.00

SILVER

History: The natural beauty of silver lends itself to the designs of artists and craftsmen. It has been mined and worked into an endless variety of useful and decorative items. Pure silver is too soft to be fashioned into strong, durable, and serviceable utensils. Therefore, a way was found to give silver the required degree of hardness by adding alloys of copper and nickel.

Silversmithing in America goes back to the early 17th century in Boston and New York. It began in the early 18th century in Philadelphia. Boston was influenced by the English styles, New York by the Dutch.

References Frederick Bradbury, *Bradbury's Book of Hallmarks,* J. W. Northend, Ltd, 1987; Louise Bilden, *Marks Of American Silversmiths In the Ineson-Bissell Collection,* Univ. of VA Press, 1980; Rachael Feild, *Macdonald Guide To Buying Antique Silver and Sheffield Plate,* Macdonald & Co., 1988; Donald L. Fennimore, *Silver & Pewter,* Alfred A. Knopf, [Knopf Collector's Guides To American Antiques] 1984; Dorothy T. Rainwater, *Encyclopedia of American Silver Manufacturers, 3rd Edition;* Schiffer Publishing Ltd., 1986; Dorothy T. and H. Ivan Rainwater, *American Silverplate,* , Schiffer Publishing, Ltd., 1988; Peter Waldon, *The Price Guide To Antique Silver, 2nd Edition,* , Antique Collectors' Club, 1982 (price revision list 1988); Seymour B. Wyler, *The Book Of Old Silver, English, American, Foreign,* Crown Publishers, Inc., 1937 (available in reprint).

Periodical: *Silver,* P. O. Box 1243, Whittier, CA 90609.

Additional Listings: See Silver Flatware in *Warman's Americana & Collectibles* for more examples in this area.

American, Coin, teaspoon, 5½" l, G. Lenhart, York County, PA, $45.00.

AMERICAN, 1790–1840
Mostly Coin

Coin silver is slightly less pure than sterling silver. Coin silver has 900 parts silver to 100 parts alloy. Sterling silver has 925 parts silver. American silversmiths followed the coin standards. Coin silver also is called Pure Coin, Dollar, Standard, or Premium.

Adams, William, NY, c1838, knife tray, 16¼" l, elongated oval form, tapered sides and gadroon rim, marked on base "W ADAMS" and "NEW-YORK" in serrated rect, 24 ozs **5,500.00**

Anthony, Joseph, Jr, Philadelphia, PA, c1780–90, mug, 5⅝" h, baluster, leaf capped double scroll handle, contemporary engraved initials, later gilt int., drilled base, 16 ozs, 4 dwts **1,000.00**

Baldwin & Jones, Boston, c1815, coffeepot, 11¾" h, inverted pear shape with gadroon rim and girdle, engraved with monogram "L.M.B.," leaf capped scroll handle, domed cov with foliate finial, spreading base raised on four winged paw feet, marked on base "BALDWIN & JONES" in scroll shaped punch twice, 45 ozs, 6 dwts **900.00**

Brevoort, John, NY, mid 18th C, tankard, 7½" h, tapering cylinder, engraved coat of arms, molded rim and base, stepped flat top lid, crenelated edge, scrolled thumbpiece hinged to scrolling handle, 30 ozs **13,000.00**

Brigden, Zachariah, Boston, MA, c1760, sauce boat, 7⅜" l, bombé oval form, waved rim, leaf capped double scroll handle, three scroll supports, shell terminals, marked in script, 12 ozs, 10 dwts **12,100.00**

Burt, John, Boston, MA, c1720, porringer, 5⅛" d, pierced handle without arches, initialed, repairs to base, maker's mark on back of handle "IB" crowned in cartouche, 9 ozs **1,450.00**

Childs, George K., Philadelphia, PA, 1837, ladle, 3 ozs **125.00**

Edwards, John, Boston, c1730, pepper box, 3", cylindrical form with projecting molded borders and scroll handle, bun shaped cov pierced with concentric rows of dots, base engraved "IWR" and the weight "3 ozs," marked on body left of handle "IE" crowned above quatrefoil in shaped shield, 2 ozs, 16 dwts **6,325.00**

Forbes, Colin V. G., NY, c1820, preserve jar, cov, bombé vase shape, pedestal base, four leaf-headed paw feet, stamped foliage and floral borders, shoulder chased with similarly

dec band, scroll handle, domed hinged cov, bud finial, 10 ozs **1,775.00**

Henchman, Daniel, Boston, MA, c1750, sauce boat, 7⅜" l, shallow bombé oval form with waved rim, flying scroll handle raised on three hoof feet headed by oval bosses, the front foot scratched with initial "G," marked on base "Henchman" in rect, 11 ozs, 12 dwts **5,500.00**

Humphreys, Richard, Philadelphia, PA, 1775, cann, 5⅛", baluster form, engraved with contemporary foliate monogram "T.I.P.," leaf capped double scroll handle, molded spreading foot, base engraved with contemporary initials "E⋅M to TIP," marked on base "R Humphreys" italics in shaped punch, 13 ozs, 16 dwts **6,250.00**

Hurd, Jacob, Boston, MA, c1750, cann, 5", baluster form, molded rim and spreading base, scroll handle engraved with initals "T," the side later engraved with "N.H." in script within wreath, "E.C." in shaped roman letters, "H.P." in later initials in script and "S.W." in old English letters, above each other, presumably for the later owners of the cann, repairs to base, marked at rim left of handle "HURD" in rect, 11 ozs, 12 dwts **1,250.00**

Hyde & Goodrich, New Orleans, LA, c1840, salver, 12" l, rect, surface engraved with scrolling foliage and flowers, band of leaves and flowers applied to rim, four openwork shell and leafy scroll feet, 23 ozs **1,000.00**

Johnson, M. W., Albany, NY, 1815, sugar tongs, shell form nips, 1 oz . . **75.00**

Lansing, Jacob Gerritse, Albany, NY c1750, creamer, 4¼" h, baluster form, shaped rim, double scroll handle, three paw feet with shell terminals, base engraved with contemporary initials, marked twice on base, 5 ozs, 10 dwts **6,000.00**

Lansing, Jacob Jacobese and Abraham Schuyler, Albany, NY c1740, waiter, 5¾" d, molded piecrust rim, three scroll supports, engraved underneath, marked underneath IL&AS in cartouche shaped punch, 6 ozs, 6 dwts **5,500.00**

Lownes, Joseph, Philadelphia, PA, c1810, cann, 4⅜" h, tapered cylindrical form, chased hoops, angular scroll handle, engraved with contemporary presentation inscription, marked twice on base, 14 ozs, 10 dwts **3,000.00**

Mood, John and Peter, Charleston, SC, c1835, fish slice, 12⅛", fiddle pattern, engraved with initial "B," blade pierced with scrolls, 6 ozs **775.00**

Myers, Myer, NY, c1750–60, coffeepot, plain tapered cylindrical form, tuck-in base, molded foot, swan-neck spout with rococo cartouche, leaf cap, shell mounted upper handle terminal, domed cov, bud finial, wooden handle, marked in script on base, 38 ozs, 10 dwts **50,000.00**

Nichols, Basset, Providence, RI, 1815, sugar nips, etched floral dec, 1 oz . . **100.00**

Richardson, Joseph, Jr., Philadelphia, PA, 1777, sugar tongs, etched bell-flower dec, 1 oz **425.00**

Sayre, J, NY
  Coffeepot, 9⅞″ h, octagonal urn shape, bright cut, collar of half-stars and festoons, conforming urn finial, rect pedestal base, ball feet, marked on foot rim, c1805–10, 34 ozs, 10 dwts **1,550.00**
  Teapot, 10¾″ h, lobed urn form, grapevine collar, ovolo borders, eagle head handle, pedestal base, four ball feet, later initial, c1810, 37 ozs **1,320.00**

Simpkins, William, Boston, MA, c1730–40, porringer, 5″ d, bowed sides, domed center, pierced handle engraved with initials, bell motif, maker's mark double struck, 6 ozs, 5 dwts . . **1,450.00**

Tyler, Andrew, Boston, c1730, caster, 6½″ h, baluster form, pierced bayonet top, banded sphere finial, 6 ozs . . . **7,250.00**

Wilson, Robert, New York, NY, c1815, soup ladle, 14¾″, engraved oval medallion with pendant foliage on handle **400.00**

SILVER, AMERICAN, 1840–1920
Mostly Sterling

There are two possible sources for the origin of the word sterling. The first is that it is a corruption of the name Easterling. Easterlings were German silversmiths who came to England in the Middle Ages. The second is that it is named for the starling (little star) used to mark much of the early English silver.

Sterling silver has 925/1000 parts pure silver. Copper comprises most of the remaining alloy. American manufacturers began to switch to the sterling standard about the time of the Civil War.

Bailey, Banks And Biddle Co, tea tray, 30½″ l, shaped oval form, shell and gadroon border, applied fluted molded hand grips at ends, plain face centered with scrolled monogram, 164 ozs, 10 dwts **1,800.00**

Ball Black & Co, c1865, compote, 13¾″, shallow boat shaped bowl, chased grapevine collar, applied ram's heads,

forked loop handles with applied putto heads, classical medallions, and beads on stem, engraved strapwork border on foot **1,210.00**

Black, Starr & Frost, NY, c1910
  Cocktail Set, pitcher form shaker, twelve cups, two handled rect 23½″ tray, chased panels with shells and foliage, strapwork, borders of running leaves, 165 ozs **3,850.00**
  Tea and Coffee Set, teapot, coffeepot, creamer, waste bowl, cov sugar, kettle on lampstand, rect handled 31¼″ tray, baluster shape, chased swags of fruit, borders of lobes and beads, scroll handles capped by leaves and fruit swags, ivory finials with leafy calyx, monogrammed, 387 ozs, 10 dwts **8,250.00**

Chicago Silver Co.
  Bowl, ftd, 9½″ d, 3½″ h, fluted sides, flute lines on ext., 17 ozs **1,800.00**
  Napkin Ring, 3⅛″ l, ⅞″ w, central cartouche with flowerheads **50.00**

Sterling, American, tea set, total weight 317 troy ounces, marked "Shreve & Co, San Francisco," $4,500.00.

Cooper, Francis W., Amity Street, NY, c1850, flagon, cov, 13″ h, pear shaped, circular base, chased palm leaves, engraved inscription, scrolled handle, hinged cov, ropework thumbpiece, 18 ozs **600.00**

David, John, Jr., Philadelphia, PA, c1780, creamer, 5¼″ h, inverted pear shape, beaded rim, leaf capped scroll handle, engraved with later presentation inscription, 2 ozs **400.00**

Dominick & Haff, 20th C, tray, 13½″ d, circular, engraved border armorial, retailed by J. E. Caldwell & Co, 36 ozs **300.00**

Dupuy, Daniel, Philadelphia, PA, c1770, lemon punch strainer, 9″ l, pierced flowerhead in bowl, two foliage scroll handles, 9 ozs **715.00**

Durgin Co., Wm. B., Concord, NH
  Coffee Spoons, set of 6, 4¼″ l, en-

graved dec at end, engraved "1912" on back **125.00**

Soup Tureen and Cover, 14" l over handles, oval bombé form, gadrooned body, foot, rim, and domed cov, monogrammed, rod and ring handles, c1890, 48 ozs **1,000.00**

Gale & Hayden, NY, mid 19th C, pitcher, water, 14½" h, ewer shaped, double C scroll handle, chased acanthus leaves, engraved floral dec, molded socle base, 29 ozs **900.00**

Graff, Washbourne & Dunn, c1910, centerpiece, 22" l, boat shape, applied festoons pendant from ram's heads, ribbon-bows, paneled ground, applied urns on neck below fluted and beaded rim, scroll handles dec with husk pendants, pedestal foot chased with running laurel, monogrammed, 144 ozs, 10 dwts **5,000.00**

Gorham Mfg Co., Providence, RI

Bell, 4¾", lobed body, case and chased winged cherubs, flowers, shells, and ribbons, matted ground, theatrical masks at base, three classical female figures supporting globe form handle, monogrammed, c1890, 6 ozs **700.00**

Butter Dish, cov, pr, circular, waved rims, chased border of shells, rim foot, domed cov chased with swags dividing fluted shell pendants and panels of flowers, baluster finials, scrolled straps, beaded borders, bases engraved "S J Sorg," c1887, 38 ozs **2,200.00**

Flatware, 194 pcs, St Dunstan pattern, chased, initialed "R," fitted case, c1915, 250 ozs **7,000.00**

Hot Water Jug, 12¾" h, vase shaped body copied from George III design by Charles Wright, London, 1777, chased acanthus leaves, leaf and floral swags through rings, gadrooned neck rim, raffia handle, domed cov, pineapple finial, c1910, 30 ozs **900.00**

Tea and Coffee Set, teapot, coffeepot, creamer, waste bowl, cov sugar, kettle on lampstand, oval handled 30¼" tray, partly fluted vase shape, urn finials, borders of urns and paterae, ribbon tied swags of flowers, c1910–20, 298 ozs, 10 dwts **7,000.00**

Howard and Co, NY, c1900

Finger Bowl, 5" d, silver-gilt, cylindrical, rounded base, rim foot, wide rims case and pierced with flowers, scrolled foliage, and shell work, monogrammed, set of 12, 127 ozs **2,250.00**

Loving Cup, 8½" h, three handles, presentation inscription, 45 ozs . . **700.00**

International Silver Co, Meridian, CT

Tea and Coffee Set, teapot, coffeepot, creamer, waste bowl, cov sugar, kettle on lamp stand, oval handled 27½" l tray, vase shape, husk festoons, leaves and flowerheads on rims, monogrammed, c1920, 249 ozs, 10 dwts **4,450.00**

Kirk, S. and Son, Baltimore, 1880—90

Coffee and Tea Service, 6 pcs, teapot, coffeepot (7½" h), cov sugar bowl, creamer, and waste bowl, baluster form partly chased with flowers and foliage on matted grounds, matching two handle oval tea tray (26¾" l over handles), raised border chased with matching dec, surface with two bands of scrolling foliage, bases engraved with presentation inscriptions, 20th C, 170 ozs **5,750.00**

Creamer and Sugar, 8¾" h creamer, cov sugar, vase shape, chased flowers, matted ground, angular handle, ram's head terminals, 32 ozs, 10 dwts **600.00**

Kettle on Stand, 17¾" h, bombé pear form, emb with bands of lobes surrounded by chased scrolls on matted ground, lampstand with a pierced apron of cartouches and beading, c1860, 96 ozs excluding later plated lamp **1,900.00**

Salver, 14⅛" d, circular with overlapping leaf-tip rim, border chased with alternating sprays of flowers and pastoral scenes, surface with wide band of sunbursts, center engraved with monogram within a leafy circle, raised on four claw and ball feet, c1900, 34 ozs **900.00**

L'Hommedieu, J A, Mobile, AL, c1850, soup ladle, 12¼" l, fiddle pattern, terminal engraved with contemporary script initial, marked on back of stem, 6 ozs, 10 dwts **700.00**

Richardson, Joseph, Jr, c1790, 14⅜ " h coffeepot and 4¾" d waste bowl, beaded rims, urn form, pedestal foot, spool form cov with urn finial, wood scroll handle, bowl with beaded rim and pedestal foot, engraved monogram, 57 ozs **11,000.00**

Schultz, A. G. & Co, Baltimore, MD, c1910, tea set, 9¾" h teapot, creamer, cov sugar, and waste bowl, circular bodies, repousse, chased castles and bridges, hunter, hound, and hare near water mill scene, grape bunch finials, 92 ozs **2,250.00**

Swan, Robert, Worcester, MA and Philadelphia, PA, c1790
Goblet, 6⅜" h, beaded rims, flared foot, 6 ozs, 8 dwts **1,550.00**
Tea Set, partial, 11⅛" h teapot, 10" h sugar, urn form, beaded and galleried rim, pedestal foot, spool form cov, urn finials, engraved monogram, wood handle, 39 ozs **8,875.00**

Tiffany & Co, NY
Asparagus Dish, 12" l, pr, rect, undulating rims, applied scrolls, flowers, and shells at angles, matching pierced and engraved liners, four claw and ball feet, c1902–07, 78 ozs **4,000.00**
Candelabra, 16¾" h, pr, five lights, reeded tapered stem, central knop, applied with four branches, campana sconces, detachable nozzles, beaded and lobed base, four paw feet with shells and foliage, marked, c1900, 115 ozs **12,100.00**
Cann, 5¼" h, tapered cylindrical, three applied enameled naval pennants tied in clover leaf rope knot, inscribed, glass base, c1884 . . . . **1,450.00**
Pitcher, water, 7½" h, baluster form, hammered surface, molded strap handle, monogrammed, c1880, 22 ozs **2,250.00**
Plate, dinner, 9¾" d, set of twelve, circular, rims applied with oval beads surrounded by scrollwork, fluted border mounted with heart motifs, rim foot, bases initialed, c1902–7, 204 ozs **9,950.00**
Platter, 20½" l, oval, molded and gadrooned borders, c1907, 80 ozs . . **1,800.00**
Punch Bowl, 15" d, matching ladle, Chyrsanthemum pattern, circular bombé form, shaped overhanging rim, applied flowerheads and foliage, pedestal base on four panel feet with flowers, both pieces with script initial, c1890–1902, 106 ozs **15,400.00**
Tankard, 9¾" h, tapered sq form, high incurved waist, upper body modeled in form of stylized bird head, C scroll handle, wedge shaped thumbpiece, chased with spirals, scrolls, graduated beads, hammered ground, gilt int., marked on base "Tiffany & Co/6654 Makers 4163/Sterling-Silver/M/2315," c1880, 20 ozs **12,100.00**

Whiting, Frank, 20th C
Flower Bowl, 12⅜" l, shaped circular, border chased with flowers and foliage, monogrammed, two SP detachable liners, retailed by J. E. Caldwell & Co, 22 ozs **600.00**

Whiting Mfg Co, Providence, RI, centerpiece, basket form, pierced sides, graduated interlaced loop design, pierced rim band of running leaves and flowerheads, scrolled strap handles, pedestal foot, monogrammed, retailed by J J Sweeney, Jewelry, c1915, 49 ozs **2,250.00**

Wilson, R. & W., Philadelphia, PA, c1840
Bosun's Whistle, 5¾" l, curved tube, spherical terminal and plane panel, pendant ring, c1840 . . . . **1,650.00**
Flatware Service, partial, twelve dinner forks, eleven tablespoons, twelve teaspoons, 50 ozs **450.00**
Sugar Tongs, c1825 . . . . **100.00**

Woods & Co, Richard W., NY, racing cups, cov, pr, bell shaped, chased rococo ornaments, applied racing horses, reel-shaped cov chased with oak garlands, engraved Westchester racing inscriptions, won by Oedipus, c1950, 119 ozs, 10 dwts **2,350.00**

SILVER, CONTINENTAL

Continental silver does not have a strong following in the United States. The strong feeling of German silver cannot compete with the lightness of the English examples. In Canada, Russian silver finds a strong market.

Austrian, coffeepot, 9½" h, pyriform body, scrolling spout, 19th C, approx 19½ ozs **300.00**
Belgium, creamer, helmet form, berry dec scroll handle, 1780, 10 ozs **100.00**

Danish
Compote, 6½" h, inverted bell form oval bowl set on stiff leaf band on fluted domed base, all on four bun support, Aug. Thomsen, 1920, 16 ozs **425.00**
Creamer and Sugar, 3¾" h and 3¼" h, tulip shape, hammered surface, beaded foliate handles, Georg Jensen Silversmith, designed by Harald Nielsen, Copenhagen, 20th C **700.00**
Platter Spoon, 14¼", peened finish, beaded terminal, maker and pattern untraced, 5 ozs **80.00**

Dutch
Box, fish form, 833 fine silver, 5¼" l, hinged head with jeweled eyes, articulated body, fitted with clear glass flacon with stopper, 19th C, 1 oz, 10 dwts **250.00**
Snuff Box, 1⅞" l, cartouche shape, molded rim, cov engraved with cipher, hinged lid, Amsterdam, c1740 . . . . **1,150.00**

Spoon, 5⅝″ l, oval bowl, scrolled stem engraved with initials, lobate female bust terminal, monogram maker's mark AVC, Haarlem, 1645   **1,100.00**

French

Bowl, cov, 8½″ d stand, lobed circular form, gadroon, shell, and foliate borders, two handles, Charles-Nicholas Odiot, Paris, c1840, 29 ozs   **3,100.00**

Cake Basket, 14⅜″ l, rect, gadroon rim, border engraved with contemporary arms, wirework sides, pedestal base with gadroon borders, swing handle rising from leaves to fruit and flower high relief garland, detachable gilt-metal liner, marked on body and handle, Charles-Nicholas Odiot, Paris, 1819–38, 63 ozs **3,575.00**

Ewer, 9⅞″ h, Regency style, helmet form, molded borders, harp shaped handle, flat chased strapwork and shells, matted ground, trophy of dolphins, paddles, and shells, monogrammed, Teétard Frères, Paris, c1900, 37 ozs, 10 dwts **2,000.00**

German

Beaker

3¼″ h, tapered cylindrical form, engraved swags of fruit, narrow band of scrolling foliage, Leon Hardt Rothaer I, Hamburg, c1680, 3 ozs, 10 dwts **3,300.00**

3⅜″, slightly tapered, cylindrical form, band of matted dec, molded rim, base engraved with contemporary arms and initials, Johann Hoffler, Nuremberg, c1680, 15 dwts **2,100.00**

Box

3¾″ l, rect, Singing Bird, top chased with figures in landscape, hinged cov, brightly feathered mechanical bird, early 20th C **1,350.00**

5¼″, turquoise cabochon on lift lid, etched plume dec, scroll feet, 6 ozs **250.00**

Centerpiece, oval, beaded rim, ribbon bows, pierced sides, chased laurel swags, lion mask and laurel wreath pendant handles, four scroll foliate supports, gilt int., glass liner, late 19th C, 42 ozs **2,650.00**

Compote, 15″ h, pr, quatrefoil base, pastoral scenes and trophies, pierced diaper ground, matching bowl, female figural stem, cut glass festoon engraved bowl, late 19th C, 44 ozs, 10 dwts **2,650.00**

Snuff Box, 3⅛″ l, silver-gilt, cartouche shape, chased hunter and hound, fanciful rococo landscape, shell-

work chased sides, fitted int., Theodor Dassdorf, Augsburg, 1743 . . .   **4,300.00**

Spoon, 7⅝″ l, oval engraved bowl, initials within wreath below spreading foliage, tapered hexagonal stem, seal top terminal, engraved date 1690, Christian Menzel, Breslau .   **900.00**

Tankard, 9½″ h, parcel-gilt, barrel chased with scene of patriarch making offering to warrior, chased armorials beneath foliage mantle, foot and cov chased with band of scrolling tulips, forked thumbpiece and ball finial, maker's mark PMS in monogram, Hamburg, c1690, 38 ozs **8,850.00**

Tea Set, 5¾″ h teapot, creamer, and cov sugar, Louis XVI style, paneled pear shaped body, applied festoons, band of matted flutes, ram's masks spouts, tea plant finials, early 20th C, 31 ozs **2,000.00**

Vase, 17¾″, cov, pr, baluster form, chased swags of flowers, spiral flutes, dolphin form handles, applied putti and salamanders on shoulders, winged putti finials, late 19th C, 106 ozs **5,000.00**

Italian

Dessert Flatware, silver-gilt, twelve pistol handled knives, twelve two prong forks, fitted 18th C tooled leather box, 20th C **900.00**

Lamp, Sanctuary, 21″ h, baluster form, pierced and chased with floral reserves, borders of still leaves, hung by three chains from cherub heads, three matching smaller lamps, mid 19th C, 149 ozs **6,000.00**

Vase, 800 fine silver, 9¾″, paneled ovoid body, fluted collar and spreading circular base, applied leaf scroll and floral trophies at "corners" of shoulder, modern, 19 ozs **200.00**

Portuguese

Centerpiece, nine basket epergne with canopy, Chinoiserie dec, bells hung from top, pineapple finial, Georgian style, retailed by Shreve, Crump & Low Co, Boston, 414 ozs **18,700.00**

Ewer, 13¾″ h, helmet shape, partly fluted, engraved with contemporary arms, applied female mask within strapwork, raised female caryatid handle, detachable calyx chased with still leaves, strapwork, and shells, screw-on foot, modern base, unmarked, c1730, 54 ozs, 10 dwts   **2,875.00**

Tray, 833 fine silver, 24¾″ long excluding handle, shaped oval form, border of chased and emb scrolls, shells, and flowers, scroll form bracket handles, unknown maker, Oporto, c1886–1938, 128 ozs ... **800.00**

Spanish, soup tureen, cov, 21⅞" l, shaped oval bombé form, part chased rococo ornaments, foliate and floral handles, scroll supports with foliage, matching domed cov, floral spray finial, base stamped "Luis Sanz," 20th C, 208 ozs **6,600.00**

SILVER, ENGLISH

From the seventeenth century to the mid-19th century, English silversmiths set the styles which American silversmiths copied. The work from the period exhibits the highest degree of craftsmanship. Active collection of English silver takes place in the American antiques marketplace.

James I
Spoon, 6¾" l, seal top, terminal priced ER, William Bartlett, Exeter, c1610 **1,200.00**
Charles I
Spoon, Apostle, St Philip wearing St Espirit nimbus, terminal, maker's mark I. P., Exeter, c1635 .... **1,000.00**
Charles II
Caudle Cup, 4¾" d, slightly flared lip contained by "S" scroll cast handles with putti head terminals, above a band of chased acanthus, resting on a simple socle, maker's mark probably "IH" over fleur-de-lis, London, c1764–65, approx 8 ozs **800.00**
Queen Anne
Chocolate Pot, 9" h, tapering cylindrical form, stepped dome lid, scrolling spout, treen handle lacking, Henry Green, London, c1711, approx. 19 ozs **1,000.00**
Dessert Flatware, twelve dognose rattail spoons, twelve cannon handled knives with later silver blades, twelve two pronged cannon handled forks, engraved arms in scrolled cartouches headed and terminated in leaves, fitted fishskin case, London, c1705 .... **5,000.00**
Teaspoons, set of six, silver-gilt, plain dognose terminals, rattail bowls, fitted fishskin case, green velvet and silk lining, Thomas Spackman, London, 1706 .... **3,000.00**
George I
Bell, 4" h, table, molded borders, seated putto, maker's mark partly visible, possibly David Willaume, London, 1714 .... **4,675.00**
Waiter, 5¾" w, sq, raised rim incurved at angles above shaped bracket

feet, center engraved with contemporary architectural cartouche enclosing later arms, engraved border of strapwork enclosing leaves, diaper, and brickwork, David Willaume, London, 1725, 5 ozs **2,100.00**

George II
Beaker, 7⅜" h, Scandinavian style, tapered cylindrical, molded borders, engraved crest between ribbon timed crossed fronds, William Partis, Newcastle, 1749, 16 ozs .. **4,500.00**
Bowl, 7" d, molded rims, later chased flowers, foliage, scrolls and shellwork, engraved crest, repaired, Jonah Clifton, London, 1732, 16 ozs, 10 dwts **675.00**
Castor Set, 9¼" h, central cartouche shaped handle, front applied with rococo shield engraved contemporary arms, three baluster form castors, pierced cov, pair silver mounted bottles, cinquefoil stand, shell and scroll feet, Samuel Wood, London, 1747, 56 ozs, 10 dwts .. **5,225.00**
Coffeepot, 8¼", tapered cylindrical, tuck-in base, engraved contemporary arms in baroque cartouche, lobed and fluted swan neck spout, dome cov, urn finial, repair at arms, marked on base and cov, George Wickes, London, 1738, 17 ozs, 10 dwts **1,875.00**
Epergne, 22" l, 15½" h, center pierced with diaper and applied trailing flowers above apron cast and pierced with spread winged dragon, central basket with scrolled ends applied with Chinamen heads wearing straw hats and feathered collars, scroll openwork branches supporting shallow spiral ribbed dishes with openwork flower, scroll, and shell dec rims, baskets engraved with armorials in rococo cartouches, four multiple scroll feet with openwork terminals, scalework reserves, fully marked, William Cripps, London, 1755, mark of John Jacob as retailer, 194 ozs, 10 dwts **50,000.00**
Sauce Boat, 8" l, pr, fluted shell shape, engraved contemporary coat of arms in rococo cartouche, later crests, leaf capped double scroll handles, cast fluted pedestal base, shaped rims, Frederick Kandler, London, 1747, 42 ozs **8,525.00**
George III
Bacon Dish, 11" l, rect, beaded borders, matching handles, hot water base with cov spout, low domed

cov, bone pineapple finial, crested, Burrage Davenport, London, 1781, 25 ozs **1,320.00**

Beer Jug, 7¼", baluster form, faceted short spout rising from pear shaped motif, partly faceted scroll handle, engraved with later royal arms attributed to Edward, Duke of Windsor, circular foot rim, Ralph Richardson Chester, 1767, 25 ozs, 10 dwts **5,000.00**

Chamber Stick, snuffer, circular dish base, London, 1797, 7 ozs **200.00**

Cup, child's, 2¾" h, ribbed barrel form, loop handle, London, 1799, 2 ozs **125.00**

Dish Cross, 12" l, adjustable shell supports, engraved crest, William Plummer, London, c1770, 13 ozs . **1,870.00**

Entree Dish, cov, 15⅞" l, rect, gadroon, shell, and foliate border, dome cov with lobed border, finial of leaf and reeded arch rising from lion's head and paws, Sheffield plated warming stand with lobed borders, four paw supports, reeded and foliate handles by Matthew Boulton Plate Co, Paul Storr, London, 1811, 72 ozs **4,000.00**

Epergne, 12⅜" h, pierced stars and quatrefoils on basket and neck, detachable branches with beaded rims, neck engraved, pierced rococo apron, stand on four foliate scroll supports, Thomas Pitts, London, 1763, later branches with maker's mark MG, London, 1880, 76 ozs **5,000.00**

Mug, 7⅞" h, baluster, molded waistband, double scroll handle, later spout, maker's mark J*M, (Jacob Marsh or John Moore,) London, 1772, 32 ozs **1,550.00**

Salver, 8" d, gadrooned feather border, claw and ball feet, London, 1768, 13 ozs **500.00**

Sauce Tureen, 9½" l, cov, boat shape, gadroon border, engraved later crests and mottoes, harp scaled handles, pedestal base, domed cov with scroll and leaf ring finial over matted paterae, William Fountain, London, 1803, 56 ozs .. **5,500.00**

Server, flat, engraved heraldic crown, pierced blade, London, 1816, 5 ozs **150.00**

Sugar Tongs, etched bellflower dec, Hester Bateman, London, 1770, 1 oz **175.00**

Teaspoons, set of six, bright cut crown, "I love Liberty" and bird flying from cage on reverse of bowl, London, 1804, 3 ozs **325.00**

Vinaigrette, 1" l, rect, engraved scalework, oval reserve, gilt int., hinged grill pierced and engraved with flowers, John Shaw, Birmingham, 1795 .... **200.00**

George IV

Egg Codler, 13½" l, two handled circular stand, gadroon, shell, and foliate borders, paw feet with acanthus sprays, fitted central campana shaped bowl on lampstand, removable frame for six eggs, surrounded by six matching egg cups and salt cellar, six hourglass patterned egg spoons, salt spoon by Paul Storr, 1810, fully marked, John Edward Terry, London, 1829, 66 ozs . **3,300.00**

Plate, 9⅝", dinner, set of twelve, shaped gadroon rims, borders engraved with armorials, backs stamped "Garrards Panton Street, London," Robert Garrard & Bros, London, 1827, 234 ozs, 10 dwts .**17,600.00**

Salt Spoon, set of four, silver-gilt, George II style, double shell bowls, scalework stems entwined with serpents, female mask and leaf terminals, Edward Farrell, London, 1823, 3 ozs **700.00**

Tea Set, tea urn, creamer, sugar, melon form, repousse floral dec, shell form ftd supports, London, 1829, 87 ozs **1,800.00**

Tea Tray, 24¾" l, rect, serpentine inner border, gadroon rim, leaf framed double shells at intervals, scrolled acanthus handles, double shell feet, Philip Rundell, London, 1821, 130 ozs **5,225.00**

Vegetable Dish, 10¾" d, set of four, lobed and fluted circular form, shaped gadroon borders, conforming Sheffield plated cov, engraved crest and monogram, SS pepper shaped finials, Robert Garrard & Bros, London, 1826, 156 ozs **7,425.00**

Wine Coolers, 10¼" h, pr, campana form, lobed and fluted lower body, reeded handles, acanthus, gadroon, shell, and foliate rims, pedestal base, crests, detachable Sheffield plated liners, detachable rims missing, Matthew Boulton Plate Co, Birmingham, 1824, 157 ozs **16,000.00**

George V

Salver, 8" d, piecrust rim, pad feet, Sheffield, 1935, 11 ozs **200.00**

William IV

Hot Water Jug, 9½" h, ribbed baluster form, lower body chased in repeating flowerhead pattern, upper body chased with flowers on matted ground, shellwork foot and lip, leafy scroll handle, melon finial with maker's mark W.M., Benjamin Smith III, London, 1830, 34 ozs **3,650.00**

Shaving Set, pr of 5¾" l razors, chased on both sides with husk pendants on matted ground, engraved interlaced ciphers and crests, steel blades, strop in leather sheath, silver gilt handle with scrolled molded rim, cased with husks in rococo cartouche, Paul Storr, London, 1833 . . . . **2,750.00**

Soup Tureen, cov, 15" l, 12" h, ram's head and garland dec, mask head lion ring handles, hoofed feet, J Charles Edington, London, 1834, 136 ozs **6,000.00**

Victorian

Candelabra, 19⅛" h, pr, figures of Flora holding sprig in left hand, raised right hand holding three tendril wrapped branches with petal form sconces and drip pans, triform base cast at angles with foliate scrolls, monograms, Barnard, London, 1866 . . . . **9,350.00**

Centerpiece, 15½", silver-gilt, Egyptian style, rect, serpentine sides, paw feet, four lying sphinxes support cut glass bowl, palmette borders, Walker & Hall, Sheffield, 1900, 86 ozs **6,875.00**

Inkstand, 16¾" l, shaped oval, undulating scrolled rim with cartouches and shellwork at intervals, four coiled scroll supports, surface with kidney shaped wells, engraved arms, raised center mounted with seal box, taperstick, and detachable nozzle, two silver mounted cut glass bottles, R & S Garrard & Co, London, 1852, 67 ozs **4,675.00**

Knife Tray, 18" l, oblong, everted sides, gadroon rim, engraved armorials, maker's mark of James Garrard for R & S Garrard & Co, London, 1892, 52 ozs **4,450.00**

Plate, 9⅞", dinner, set of twelve, shaped gadrooned rims, borders engraved with crest, base stamped "Smith & Nicholson Duke St, Linn Inn Fields," Stephen Smith & William Nicholson, London, 1855, 286 ozs **11,000.00**

Tea Caddy, bombé sides applied at angles with lobes and acanthus, chased floral swags, shellwork base, hinged cov, Chinaman finial, John Edward Terry, London, 1944, 35 ozs **3,750.00**

Tea Set, teapot, 9¼" h coffeepot, creamer, two handled sugar, compressed circular form, reeded borders, gilt int., leaf capped scroll handles, hinged covs, flower spray finials, four anthemion and scrolled paneled feet, engraved shoulder crests, John James Keith, London, 1844, 67 ozs **3,000.00**

Edwardian

Cup, 14¾", cov, two handles, early George III style, pear shaped body, chased sloping sprays of flowers and scrolls, matching domed cov and foot, gadroon borders, engraved arms, London, 1902, retailed by Hancock & Co, 64 ozs . . **1,550.00**

Inkstand, 15⅛" l, early 18th C style, copy of inkstand by Anthony Nelme, London, 1718, rect, bowed ends, molded rim, four scroll feet, loose octagonal pen holder, diaper pierced candle sconce, two capstan shaped inkwells, removable cov glass inkwells, dated "26 April 1910," Britannia standard, Henry and Arthur Vander, London, retailed by Tessiers Ltd, 89 ozs, 10 dwts . **4,450.00**

SILVER, ENGLISH, SHEFFIELD

Sheffield Silver, or Old Sheffield Plate, was made by a fusion method of silver plating used from the mid-18th century until the mid-1880's when the silver electroplating process was introduced.

Sheffield plate was discovered in 1743 when Thomas Boulsover of Sheffield, England, accidentally fused silver and copper. The process consisted of sandwiching a heavy sheet of copper between two thin sheets of silver. The result was a plated sheet of silver which could be pressed or rolled to a desired thickness. All Sheffield plate articles were worked from these plated sheets.

Most of the silver plated items found today marked "Sheffield" are not early Sheffield plate. They are later wares made in Sheffield, England.

Argyle, 6⅜", cylindrical, beaded rim, raffia wrapped handle, shell terminal, faceted ovoid knob, c1830 . . . . **275.00**

Cake Basket, 14⅞" l, rect, flower dec gadroon rim, sides chased scrolls and berried foliage, interlaced ribbonwork handle, satyr masks terminals, four paw feet, c1820 . . . . **725.00**

Coffee Urn, two handled urn form, beaded rim, engraved crest and initial, bud finial, pedestal foot, four ball supports, c1780 . . . . **600.00**

Entree Dish, cov, pr

14⅜" l, shaped rect, acanthus

scrolled rims, shells and flower sprays at intervals, covs engraved twice with contemporary arms and continental coronet, detachable foliate finials, two handled warming base, J Dixon & Sons, c1840 ... **950.00**

16½″, rect, ends scrolled to form handles, applied acanthus leaves, gadroon borders, detachable reeded and foliate ring finials, engraved mitre crests, c1810 .... **2,310.00**

Fish Knives and Forks, twelve each, bright cut blade, bone handles, custom fitted case, 1899 .... **575.00**

Fruit Knives and Forks, six each, bright cut blade, ribbed pearl handles, custom fitted case, c1876 .... **715.00**

Hot Water Urn, 17⅜″, urn form, engraved band of scrolling foliage and flowers, scalloped rims, pedestal foot, four ball feet, lion mask and ring handles, applied roundel engraved with name and date, c1792 .... **600.00**

Sheffield, tray, 19¼″ d, scroll center, outer edge in relief, four feet, $500.00.

Muffineer, domical pierced lid, circular ftd base, custom case, 1839, 5 ozs . **60.00**

Salver, 24″ d, circular, pierced border, relief dec of flowers, foliage, and scrolls, center engraved armorials, flat chased band of rococo ornaments, matted ground, three panel feet, c1825 .... **2,350.00**

Sauce Tureen, cov, pr

7½″ l, rect, gadroon rims with foliage and flowers at angles, four foliate and floral headed ball supports, engraved arms on cov, detachable foliate ring handles, c1825 .... **900.00**

8¼″ l, oval bombé form, gadroon rims with flowerheads and leaves, acanthus handles, four paw feet with spreading acanthus, shaped rim cov, leafy scroll ring finial topped with shell, dense bed of leaves and flowerheads, c1820 .... **1,100.00**

Soup Tureen, cov, stand, 18″ l, circular bombé form, engraved armorials, reeded handles wrapped with grapevine, acanthus spray feet, molded rims with flowers, shells, and leaves, domed cov with silver heraldic finial by John Figg, London, 1842, detachable liner, Waterhouse, Hatfield & Co, c1835 .... **5,725.00**

Tea Tray

30½″, oval, ribbon tied reeded and foliate rim, flat chased surface, band of Louis XVI dec, center engraved cipher below crown, Odiot, Paris, c1850 .... **1,100.00**

31¾″ l, rect, undulating border, gadroon rim, leaf and double shells at intervals, matching handles, center large engraved owl crest, Matthew Boulton Plate Co, c1810 .... **3,325.00**

Tureen, cov, 14½″ l, twin snake form handles, claw and ball supports ... **1,200.00**

Venison Dish, cov, 24½″, oval, gadroon rim, hot water compartment with pierced central cov and spigot, domed cov, foliate ring handle, engraved crest, c1800 .... **2,425.00**

Wine Coolers, pr

7⅝″ h, fluted circular form, vine branch handles, applied spreading grapevine, four shell feet flanked by acanthus, egg and dart borders, detachable fluted rim and liners, J Watson & Son, c1830 .... **4,125.00**

8¾″ h, campana form, partly lobed and fluted, engraved on both sides with contemporary armorials, scrolls and grapevines borders, C scroll handles, detachable rims and liners, c1820 .... **2,750.00**

9⅛″ h, partly lobed campana form, matching pedestal foot, cornucopia handles, detachable rims and liners, c1810 .... **3,575.00**

SILVER, PLATED

Plated silver production by an electrolytic method is credited to G. R. and H. Elkington, England, in 1838.

In electroplating silver, the article is completely shaped and formed from a base metal and then coated with a thin layer of silver. In the late 19th century, the base metal was Britannia, an alloy of tin, copper, and antimony. Other bases are copper and brass. Today the base is nickel silver.

In 1847 the electroplating process was introduced in America by Rogers Bros., Hartford, Connecticut. By 1855 a number of firms were using the method to mass produce silver plated items in large quantities.

The quality of the plating is important. Extensive use or polishing can cause the base metal to show through. The prices for plated silver items are low, making it a popular item with younger collectors.

Biscuit Box, 6½″ h, oval, lift lid, ftd tray base	175.00
Candelabra, 23⅝″ h, pr, lobed and fluted baluster stems, serpentine branches, campana shaped sconces, detachable sconces, Elkington & Co, 1850	2,200.00
Candlesticks, pr, 10⅝″, tulip form sconces, detachable nozzles, foliate rims, baluster stem, shaped circular base, c1840	100.00
Centerpiece, 14¼″ h, partly draped female holding bird, standing on globe supported by three dolphins, shell base sprouting three branches to hold cut glass dishes, c1860	500.00

Plated, syrup pitcher, 7½″ h, floral relief and incised dec, marked "Samson, Hall, Miller & Co," Tiffany monogram, $75.00.

Collar Button Box, 2¼″ d, emb sides, figural collar button on lid with engraving " HERE'S YOUR COLLAR BUTTON," marked "Holman Silver Co.," four SS buttons inside	32.50
Condensed Milk Can Holder, cylindrical body, emb band at top and bottom, simple "C" handle, hole in lid for ladle, marked "Rogers & Bros."	50.00
Hot Water Kettle, stand and burner, 12¼″, oval, lobed sides, gadroon rims, foliage capped handles and spout, four scroll supports, Gorham Mfg Co, Providence, RI, 1900	250.00
Ladle, 11″, bright cut floral pattern on	

handle, engraved flowers inside bowl, Myrtle pattern, Pairpoint	65.00
Muffin Basket, 13″ l, oval, pierced ribbed sides, twin scrolled handles	75.00
Salver, 8″ d, George III style, shell scallop rim, scroll feet	80.00
Spoon Warmer, nautilus shaped holder, flip lid opening on top for storage of large serving spoons at table, shell rests on mound of simulated rocks, shell shape thumb rest at one end, English	175.00
Tea and Coffee Set with matching tray, Baroque pattern, coffeepot, teapot, cov sugar, and creamer, height of coffeepot 11″, length of two handled waiter 23¾″ excluding handles, Wallace	325.00
Tea Tray, 24¼″ l excluding handles, shaped oval tray with face hand engraved with scrolls and flowers, molded scroll and shell border, ftd, bracket handles, monogrammed, English	200.00
Tureen, ftd bowl with applied scrollwork terminals, satin bright cut finish, flowers, ferns, leaves, and scrolls around fancy monogram "E.M.M." on front, beaded edges, trimmed handles, marked "Homan Silverplate Company," small ladle marked "Benedict"	85.00
Warming Stand, shell form, two parts, branch form supports, Victorian	200.00

SILVER DEPOSIT GLASS

History: Silver deposit glass, consisting of a thin coating of silver actually deposited on the glass by an electrical process, was popular at the turn of the century. The process was simple. The glass and a piece of silver were placed in a solution. An electric current was introduced which caused the silver to decompose, pass through the solution, and remain on those parts of the glass on which a pattern had been outlined.

Bonbon, 7″, handle, ftd	50.00
Bowl, 5½″, vines and leaves dec, scalloped edge	40.00
Compote, 7″, floral dec	75.00
Cracker Jar, cov, 6½″ d, black, floral dec	65.00
Creamer and Sugar, floral dec	80.00
Decanter, 9″ h, emerald green, hollow stopper	55.00
Pitcher, 7¾″ green, large flowers and leaves, double horizontal ring foot	65.00
Serving Plate, 12½″ d, black amethyst, Art Nouveau lily dec, pierced handles	55.00
Toothpick, 2½″	40.00

Vase, 16″ h, green ground, c1920, $85.00.

Tumbler, 4⅝″, flared top	20.00
Wine Set, decanter, four glasses, green, 5 pcs	75.00

SILVER OVERLAY

History: Silver overlay is silver applied directly to a finished glass or porcelain object. The overlay is cut and decorated, usually by engraving, prior to being molded around the object.

Glass usually is of high quality, either crystal or colored. Lenox used silver overlay on some porcelain pieces. The majority of design motifs are from the Art Nouveau and Art Deco periods.

Perfume Bottle, 4½ x 2⅛″, floral scroll dec, matching stopper, $325.00.

Cruet, 9″, vine dec, cobalt blue	65.00
Decanter, 10″ h, pinched shape, white, orig stopper	75.00
Flask, 4¼″ h, 2¼″ w, clear with scrolls overlay, hinged SS top	140.00
Inkwell, 3 x 2¼″, triangular, green, marked "General Supply Co, Danielson, Conn, pat #879470"	325.00

Loving Cup, 3½″, cranberry glass, 3 handles	500.00
Perfume Bottle	
3½″ h, cranberry, orig stopper	210.00
4″ h, ball shape, cranberry, SS floral and scroll overlay, orig stopper . .	300.00
5″ h, bulbous, green, orig stopper . .	375.00
Pitcher, 9″, clear, wild ducks in marsh dec	50.00
Vase	
2⅝″ h, bulbous, amber, iridescent gold, pink, and blue-green highlights, cut foliate and scrolled design overlay, flared polished rim, marked "Sterling" near base	500.00
6″ h, trumpet shape top, cranberry, floral and scroll overlay	475.00
8″ h, trumpet shape, green, heavy floral overlay, name shield, marked .	275.00
Whiskey Bottle, 22¾″ h, clear, leaf and thistle overlay, SS corked stopper, sgd "Hawkes"	275.00

SILVER RESIST

History: Silver resist ware was first produced about 1805. It is similar to silver luster in respect to the silvering process and differs in that the pattern appears on the surface.

The outline of the pattern was drawn or stenciled on the ware's body. A glue or sugar-glycern adhesive was brushed over the part not to be lustered, causing it to "resist" the lustering solution which was applied and allowed to dry. The glue or adhesive was washed off. When fired in the kiln, the luster glaze covered the entire surface except for the pattern.

Bowl, 6″, floral border	60.00
Creamer, 3¼″, dark brown, flower each side, two handles	75.00
Cup and Saucer, overall floral pattern .	50.00

Cup and Saucer, 2½″ h cup, 5½″ d saucer, Greek key dec, $75.00.

Jug, 4¼" h, band of flowering foliage, Staffordshire, 19th C **85.00**

Mug, 3½", bird, flowers, line border, Leeds, c1815 .... **100.00**

Pitcher

  4⅜", black transfer, enameled iron-red, blue, yellow, black, brown, and green robin on oak branch, c1815 **385.00**

  4½", floral design, two white reserves with Oriental scenes **125.00**

  5", birds and foliage, Staffordshire, c1820 .... **200.00**

  5⅜", two hunters, one aiming rifle at bird, other seated on fallen tree, Staffordshire, c1815 .... **525.00**

  6¼", luster, canary ground, flowering dec, Staffordshire, c1810 .... **300.00**

Wine, 4½", purple-pink luster, feathering above graduated dots, cream foot and int., iron-red rim, pedestal, and foot, c1810 .... **350.00**

SMITH BROS. GLASS

History: After establishing a decorating department at the Mount Washington Glass Works in 1871, Alfred and Harry Smith struck out on their own in 1875. Their New Bedford, Massachusetts, firm soon became known worldwide for its fine opalescent decorated wares, similar in style to those of Mt. Washington.

Their glass often is marked on the base with a red shield enclosing a rampant lion and the word "Trademark."

Reproduction Alert: Beware of examples marked "Smith Bros."

Biscuit Jar, cov, 7¼" h, barrel shape, melon ribbed, enameled blue pansies and buds, cream ground **585.00**

Bowl, 5½", melon ribbed, beaded rim,

Vases, 4¾" h, pair, hand painted, gold rim, ground pontil, $90.00.

pale blue and violet pansies, cream ground, sgd **275.00**

Creamer and Sugar, blue pansy dec, SP mountings and cov, rampant lion mark **300.00**

Dresser Jar, cov

  3¼" d, melon ribbed, lavender and blue pansies, "Hail Happy Morn," sgd **125.00**

  5½" d, melon ribbed, multicolored pansy dec **300.00**

Ferner, 10", melon ribbed, glossy white, violets and leaves, orig metal insert, sgd **675.00**

Mustard Jar, 3¼", heron dec, SP top . **35.00**

Perfume, 5" h, emb flower cap, enameled floral dec, sgd **350.00**

Rose Bowl, 5½" d, wild roses dec, jeweled stamens, autumn colored leaves, rampant lion mark **250.00**

Syrup, 5" h, conical, gold prunus flowers, rampant lion mark, SP lid and handle **375.00**

Toothpick, ribbed, opaque white, blue dot rim, pastel floral dec **125.00**

Vase

  5 x 4", tricorn, pinched, shasta daisy dec, brown and gold, white dotted top **225.00**

  8¾", pillow shape, leafy vine, pink and blue clematis, raised gold borders **385.00**

SNOW BABIES

History: Snow babies, small bisque figurines spattered with glitter sand, were made originally in Germany and marketed in the early 1900s. There are several theories about their origin. One is that German doll makers copied the designs from the traditional Christmas candies. Another theory, the most accepted, is that they were made to honor Admiral Peary's daughter who was born in Greenland in 1893 and was called the "Snow Baby" by the Eskimos.

Reference: Ray and Eilene Early, *Snow Babies*, Collector Books, 1985.

Angel, 1¾", sitting, outstretched arms . **200.00**

Baby

  Holding baton **110.00**

  Holding hockey stick, 1½" **85.00**

  Kneeling on one knee, 1" **55.00**

  Laying on side, 1½" **90.00**

  Laying on tummy, 1" **60.00**

  Playing saxophone, marked "Germany" **75.00**

  Sitting

    On snow covered cardboard box, 2¼" **125.00**

    Outstretched arms and legs, 2¼" . **135.00**

Pair of babies, 2½" w, 1½" h, one sitting on sled, the other pulling, $100.00.

Skating, 2" h, red suit and hat, sgd "Germany"	30.00
Carolers, three standing in snow, lantern, 2¼", Germany	85.00
Figure	
Penguin, 4", Germany	70.00
Polar Bear, 2½", standing	125.00
Snow Girl, sitting upright on bisque sled, raised arms, 2¼"	100.00
Snow Pup on skies, marked	110.00

SNUFF BOTTLES

History: Tobacco usage spread from America to Europe to China during the 17th century. Europeans and Chinese preferred to grind the dried leaves into a powder and sniff it into their nostrils. The elegant Europeans carried their snuff in boxes and took a pinch with their finger tips. The Chinese upper class, because of their lengthy fingernails, found this inconvenient and devised a bottle with a fitted stopper and attached spoon.

In the Chinese manner, these utilitarian objects soon became objects d'art. Snuff bottles were fashioned from precious and semi-precious stones, glass, porcelain and pottery, wood, metals, and ivory. Glass and transparent stone bottles often were enhanced further with delicate hand paintings, some done on the interior of the bottle.

Reference: Sandra Andacht, *Oriental Antiques & Art, An Identification and Value Guide*, Wallace-Homestead, 1987.

Collectors' Club: International Chinese Snuff Bottle Society, 2601 North Charles Street, Baltimore, MD 21218.

Agate, round, translucent, brown, fishing motif, c1800	700.00
Amber, round, gold, brown streaks, c1800	425.00
Aquamarine, sq, stag motif, c1900	550.00
Chalcedony, round, flat sides, pink-gray, orange, streaks, tree and boat motif, mock handles	625.00

Cinnabar, 2⅞"	35.00
Cloisonne, 3", pear shape, blue background, red panels of flowers, butterfly	80.00
Crystal, sq, opaque, thin black lines, c1800	250.00
Enamel, white, plants and dragonfly motif, 1800s	425.00
Glass, octagonal, orange and yellow, c1700	900.00

Ivory, 2¼" h, man holding cup on obverse, five vertical lines of characters on reverse, 20th C, $150.00.

Ivory, hourglass shape, flat sides, trees, flowers, foliage, and bat motif, c1800	650.00
Jade, oval, rough texture, brown streaks	380.00
Jadeite, green Foo dogs, 1900s	1,100.00
Limestone, round, flat sides, c1800	350.00
Malachite, carved front, gourds, banded, c1900	140.00
Olive Amber, 5¾" h, 3⅛" w, rect, chamfered corners, flared mouth, turned lip, smooth base	110.00
Opal, 2" h, green and pink, fish and seaweed motif, 63 carats	300.00
Porcelain, 2⅞", polychrome enameling, jade lids, pr	50.00
Sage Green, 4¹/₁₆" h, 2⅜" w, sq, sloping shoulders, slightly flared mouth, tubular pontil	50.00
Silver, round, turquoise enamel, blue, floral motif, c1800	250.00
Tiger-eye, floral tree motif, c1800	325.00
Tortoise shell, gilt detail	450.00
Yi-Hsing, flat circular form, prunus blossom dec side, bamboo reverse, stopper	1,300.00

SOAPSTONE

History: The mineral steatite, known as soapstone because of its greasy feel, has been utilized for carved figural groups and other designs by the Chinese and others. Utilitarian pieces also were made. Soapstone pieces were very popular during the Victorian era.

Vase, 9½" w, 6¾" h, Chinese, four openings, red tones, c1900, $135.00.

Bookends, elephants, 1890	50.00
Box, 3 x 5", inlaid pearl, artist sgd	40.00
Cigarette Box, floral design, carved, China	.00
Figure	
Fisherman, 21", carved base	300.00
Monkeys, 5", green	50.00
Lady, 10⅛", tan and rust, mottled, c1900	65.00
Incense Burner, 8", black, 19th C	325.00
Inkwell, geometric carving on sides	140.00
Match Holder, elaborate carving	55.00
Paperweight, three monkeys	45.00
Teapot, 5" h	350.00
Toothpick Holder, monkey, carved	25.00
Urn, 7¼" d, 10¼" h, carved figures, buildings, florals, and trees, elephant head handles, wood stand	150.00
Vase	
7", carved, flowers and leaves, ftd	100.00
8" h, floral dec	70.00
13¾", relief carved flowers and bird, red carved base	55.00

SOUVENIR AND COMMEMORATIVE CHINA AND GLASS

History: Souvenir, commemorative, and historical china and glass includes those items produced to celebrate special events, places, and people.

Among the china plates, those by Rowland and Marcellus and Wedgwood are most eagerly sought. Rowland and Marcellus, Staffordshire, England, made a series of blue and white historic plates with a wide rolled edge depicting scenes beginning with the Philadelphia Centennial in 1876 and continuing to the 1939 New York's Fair. Wedgwood collaborated in 1910 with Jones, McDuffee and Stratton to produce a series of historic dessert-sized plates depicting scenes throughout the United States.

Many localities issued plates, mugs, glasses, etc., for anniversary celebrations or to honor a local historical event. These items seem to have greater value when sold in the region from which they originated.

Commemorative glass includes several patterns of pressed glass which celebrate persons or events. Historical glass includes campaign and memorial items.

References: Bessie M. Lindsey, *American Historical Glass*, Charles E. Tuttle Company, Inc., 1967; Frank Stefano, Jr., *Wedgwood Old Blue Historical Plates And Other Views Of The United States Produced For Jones, McDuffee & Stratton Co., Boston, Importer; A Check-List with Illustrations*, published by author, 1975.

Periodical: *Travel Collector*, P. O. Box 475, Marion, WI 54950-0475.

Collectors' Club: Souvenir China Collectors Society, Box 562, Great Barrington, MA 01230.

Additional Listings: Cup Plates, Pressed Glass, Political Items, and Staffordshire, Historical. Also see *Warman's Americana & Collectibles* for more examples.

Plate, 9⅞", blue, "Compliments of the Railway Post Office Clerks of the First Division Convention, 1904," imp and marked "Wedgwood," imp logo of postal clerks on back, $55.00.

CHINA

Bread Plate, frosted FDR center, 1904	155.00
Cup and Saucer	
Iowa State Capitol, white, gold trim	25.00
Waterfront Business Section, Seattle, WA, Nippon, SBN mark	40.00

Pitcher
General Andrew Jackson, 8", copper
luster, transfer 125.00
Washington Hotel, Seattle, 3½" 25.00
Plate
FDR, Hyde Park, 7" 15.00
Grant's Tomb, Riverside Drive on the
Hudson, 7½" d, blue, Wedgwood . 110.00
Panama Canal, Columbia, mermaid
and Triton 85.00
Saratoga, NY, 10½" d, dark blue,
rolled edges, vignette border, Row-
land and Marcellus 50.00
US Capitol, 9" 25.00
U. S. Grant, dessert, hp, tulip, camel-
lia center, valanced, buff band bor-
der 185.00
White House, 9" 25.00
Tray, George and Martha Washington
portrait, "Washington's Home, Mt Vernon, VA" center, 11 x 7½", sq corners,
enhanced enameling, gold trim, Germany 80.00

GLASS

ABC Plate, Centennial Exposition 1876,
6¾", clear, alphabet border 120.00
Bank
Independence Hall, 7¼" h, clear ... 70.00
New York 1940 World's Fair marked
on one side, other "Glass Center,"
3¼" h, sq, clear 35.00
Bread Plate
Eagle and Constitution, "Give Us This
Day" 100.00
Three Presidents, "In Remembr-
ance" 100.00
Creamer and Sugar, Vinton, IA, custard,
pr 70.00
Desk Stand, 6½" l, Memorial Hall form
inkwell, Philadelphia Exposition 1876,
clear 180.00
Dish, U.S. Grant, octagonal, "Patriot &
Soldier" 65.00
Frying Pan, Pan-American souvenir,
6⅞" l, milk glass, engraved on back
"Mrs. Annie Bitner" 120.00
Jar, 12½" h, 5" d, Statue of Liberty, clear,
worn gold dec, pr 120.00
Lamp, 9" h, Pan American Exposition
1901, Buffalo, NY, miniature, globular 100.00
Plate
William McKinley Commemoration,
7½", milk glass 140.00
Machinery Hall picture, marked "Co-
lumbian Exposition/Chicago 1893,"
11½" d, satin glass, white, Mt
Washington 350.00
US Battleship Maine, 7¼", milk glass,
orig dec 40.00
World's Fair 1893, Santa Maria, 6¼"

d, satin glass, white, Mt. Washing-
ton 300.00
Platter
American Flag, 9⅜ x 6¾", rect, clear,
48 stars 210.00
Bunker Hill, 13¼" l, oval, clear 50.00
Carpenters Hall, 12" l, clear 70.00
Independence Hall, 12" l, clear 50.00
Liberty Bell, 13½" l, oval, milk glass,
Hancock signature 280.00
Mug, child's, World's Fair 1893 ...... 90.00
Salt and Pepper Shaker, Columbian Ex-
position 1893, egg shape, raised let-
tering, Mt Washington, pr 150.00
Sugar and Creamer, Texas Centennial,
clear 50.00
Toothpick, Statue of Liberty, amber ... 45.00
Tray, 16" l, Niagara Falls, clear, frosted 275.00
Vase, 6⅛" h, The Administration Build-
ing/World's Fair Chicago 1893, trans-
fer, satin glass, pale yellow, bottom
marked "Austria" 175.00
Whiskey, Bumper to the Flag, 3" 85.00

SOUVENIR AND COMMEMORATIVE SPOONS

History: Souvenir and commemorative spoons
have been issued for hundreds of years. Early
American silversmiths engraved presentation
spoons to honor historical personages or mark key
events.

In 1881 Myron Kinsley patented a Niagara Falls
spoon; and, in 1884 Michael Gibney patented a
new flatware design. M. W. Galt, Washington, D.C.,
issued commemorative spoons for George and
Martha Washington in 1889. From these beginnings a collecting craze for souvenir and commemorative spoons developed in the late 19th and first
quarter of the 20th century.

References: Dorothy T. Rainwater and Donna
H. Fegler, *American Spoons, Souvenir and His-
torical,* Everybodys Press, Inc., 1977; Dorothy T.
Rainwater and Donna H. Fegler, *A Collector's
Guide To Spoons Around The World,* Everybodys
Press, Inc., 1976; *Sterling Silver, Silverplate, and
Souvenir Spoons With Prices,* L-W Inc., 1988.

Collectors' Club: American Spoon Collectors,
Box 260, Warrensburg, MO 64093. Dues: $12.50.

Additional Listings: See *Warman's Americana
& Collectibles* for more examples.

Apostles, set of 12 .... 400.00
Arms of New York City, Tiffany 95.00
Betsy Ross, house in bowl 50.00
Boston Tea Party 25.00
Cheyenne, Wyoming 20.00
Coney Island Skyline 50.00
Eddy, Mary Baker (founder of Church of
Christ, Scientist), full figure handle . 175.00

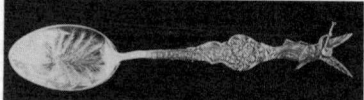

Teaspoon, Los Angeles, CA, embossed palm tree in bowl, Sterling silver, $30.00.

Fort Ticonderoga, 1775, Ethan Allen . .	30.00
Golden Gate Bridge, San Francisco . .	25.00
Grover Cleveland	40.00
Hot Springs, Ark, SS	45.00
Houston, TX, SS	35.00
Idaho, state seal handle	40.00
Jackson Monument	35.00
Kansas City, 1889, cupid handle	20.00
Lancaster, PA	20.00
Marquette, MI, Light House Point	60.00
Mayflower	20.00
Mt Tom Railway, Holyoke, MA	45.00
Niagara, 1891, SS	50.00
Norfolk, VA, crab handle	40.00
Pan American Exposition	35.00
Prudential Insurance Building	25.00
Roosevelt, Theodore, plain bowl, full figure on horseback handle	125.00
Santa Barbara, CA	35.00
Spain Coat of Arms, enameled	75.00
St Augustine	25.00
St Paul's Church, gold wash bowl, Tiffany	95.00
State Capitol, Helena, MT, SS	40.00
Statue of Liberty, Brooklyn Bridge, river, and boats bowl, figure atop handle .	235.00
Texas Centennial 1839–1936	60.00
United States Seal	125.00
US Indian Industrial School, Mt Pleasant, MI, Indian head handle	45.00
Washington's Inauguration	30.00
West Point Cadet	20.00
World's Fair, St Louis, 1904	50.00

SPANGLED GLASS

History: Spangled glass is a blown or blown molded variegated art glass, similar to spatter glass, with the addition of flakes of mica or metallic aventurine. Many pieces are cased with a white or clear layer of glass. Spangled glass was developed in the late 19th century and still is being manufactured.

Originally spangled glass was attributed only to the Vasa Murrhina Art Glass Company of Hartford, Connecticut, which distributed the glass for Dr. Flower of the Cape Cod Glassworks, Sandwich, Massachusetts. However, research has shown that many companies in Europe, England, and the United States made spangled glass, and attributing a piece to a specific source is very difficult.

Basket	
5" d, pink, mica flecks, white lining, applied clear twisted thorn handle	110.00
5½" d, pink, crimped edge, reeded thorn twisted handle	185.00
6", tortoise shell, clear thorn handle .	125.00
7½", light green, ribbon candy rim, clear brier form handle	100.00
8¾ x 10", crimped flared top, white ext. caramel int., melon-ribbed, gold mica flecks, fish scale handle	295.00
Berry Bowl, cased, cranberry, leaf mold pattern, Hobbs, c1890	40.00
Bride's Basket, 10", pink shaded to white, silver flecks, ruffled edge, shiny finish	75.00

Tumbler, 3¾" h, tortoise shell type mottling, large brown spots, traces of mica flakes, white ground, cased white int., $75.00.

Candlestick, 8", green and maroon, gold mica, white cased, pr	100.00
Creamer, 5¾", swirled, pigeon blood red, green, yellow, opaque white, and green aventurine, clear reeded handle	150.00
Cruet, bulbous, clear, profuse white mottling, applied handle, faceted stopper, silver mica flecks, Hobbs, Brockunier & Company	435.00
Ewer, 3½" d, 8⅜" h, apricot, white lining, mica flecks, applied thorn handle . .	125.00
Jack-in-the Pulpit Vase, 5¾" h, white ext., pink int., jack-in-pulpit shape, clear edging and mica flecks, ruffled rim	120.00
Pitcher, 6¾" h, cobalt blue, gold flakes, applied amber handle with flakes . .	225.00
Rose Bowl, 4¼" d, clear, white, light blue, pink, yellow, peach, orange, and maroon spatter, silver mica flecks, crimped top	245.00
Tumbler, red, silver mica flecks	90.00
Water Pitcher, cranberry spatter, gold mica flecks	265.00

Vase
  8½" h, flattened oval, applied cran-
    berry rigaree, copper aventurine
    flecks, scroll handles, c1880 .... **300.00**
  9¾" h, pink, white lining, mica flecks,
    applied vaseline loop handles, shell
    trim **100.00**

SPATTER GLASS

History: Spatter glass is a variegated blown or
blown molded art glass. It originally was called
"End-of-Day" glass, based on the assumption that
it was made from leftover batches of glass at the
end of the day. However, spatter glass was found
to be a standard production item for many glass
factories.

Spatter glass was developed at the end of the
19th century and still is being produced. It was
made in the United States and Europe.

Reproduction Alert: Many modern examples
come from Czechoslovakia.

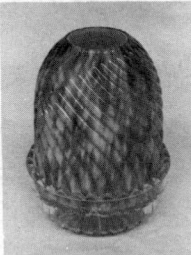

**Fairy Lamp, 4½" h, orange, red, and
yellow, white ground, clear base
stamped "Clarke," $150.00.**

Basket
  5 x 6½", ruffled oval top, emb swirls,
    peach and white spatter, clear ap-
    plied thorn handle **150.00**
  6 x 7¾ x 8½", overlay, pink, blue, and
    gold, white int., clear thorn handle
    and feet **175.00**
  8" h, tortoise shell, wide handle with
    gold prunt and prunus dec **185.00**
Candlestick, 7½", flared socket, twisted
    hourglass stem, domed ribbed base,
    yellow, red, and white spatter **35.00**
Cruet, red and white spatter, clear ap-
    plied handle, clear foot, clear ball
    stopper **85.00**
Darning Egg, red, yellow, and green,
    clear applied handle **125.00**
Jack-In-The-Pulpit Vase, 7¼", green,

  peach, yellow, and white spatter,
    green DQ body **60.00**
Jar, cov, 3¾ x 6½", maroon, white, yel-
    low, and green, white cased int., clear
    applied feet and finial **80.00**
Pitcher
  6½", bulbous, dark red spatter,
    opaque yellow ground, yellow lin-
    ing, clear applied reeded handle . **200.00**
  7⅞", bulbous, tricorn ruffled top, pink
    and white, clear applied reeded
    handle **175.00**
  9", pink and green spatter, white lining **150.00**
Rose Bowl, 3½" d, octagonal crimped
    top, rose, white cased int. **100.00**
Salt, 3¾ x 3 x 1½", maroon, yellow, and
    white spatter, white lining, clear ap-
    plied shell rim **50.00**
Tumble-Up, bottle and matching tum-
    bler, elongated thumbprint pattern,
    green, red, yellow, and pink, white
    cased int., clear applied leaf feet, 2
    pcs **300.090**
Tumbler, brown and yellow spatter ... **25.00**
Water Set, 6 x 7⅛" pitcher, four 2¾ x
    3¾" tumblers, pink, white, maroon,
    green, and yellow spatter, white int.,
    clear reeded handle **325.00**

SPATTERWARE

History: Spatterware is made of common earthenware, although occasionally creamware was
used. The earliest English examples were made
about 1780. The peak period of production was
1810–1840. Marked pieces are rare. Firms known
to have made spatterware are Adams, Barlow, and
Harvey and Cotton.

The amount of spatter decoration varies from
piece to piece. Some objects simply have decorated borders. These often are decorated with a
brush, requiring several hundred touches per
square inch to achieve the spatter effect. Other
pieces have the entire surface covered with spatter. Aesthetics of the final product is a key to value.

Collectors today focus on the patterns—Cannon, Castle, Fort, Peafowl, Rainbow, Rose, Thistle, Schoolhouse, etc. On flat ware the decoration
is in the center. On hollow pieces it occurs on both
sides.

Color of spatter is another price key. Blue and
red are most common. Green, purple, and brown
are in a middle group. Black and yellow are scarce.

Like any soft paste, spatterware was easily broken or chipped. Prices are for pieces in very good
to mint condition.

References: Susan and Al Bagdade, *Warman's English & Continental Pottery & Porcelain,
1st Edition,* Warman Publishing Co., Inc., 1987;
Carl and Ada Robacker, *Spatterware and Sponge,*
A. S. Barnes & Co., 1978.

Reproduction Alert: "Cybris" spatter is an increasing collectible ware made by Boleslow Cybris of Poland. The design utilizes the Adams type peafowl and was made in the 1940s. Many contemporary craftsmen also are reproducing spatterware.

Creamer, Thistle pattern, blue spatter, $375.00.

Bowl, 7½" d, yellow and red spatter, piecrust applied rim	200.00
Creamer, 5⅜", oct paneled form, abstract blue flower, blue, black, red, and brown spatter	325.00
Cup and Saucer, handleless	
Acorn, two shades of green and black, purple spatter	525.00
Christmas Ball, red and green spatter	500.00
Cornflowers, blue, green, and black, red and yellow rainbow spatter border	675.00
Plaid, blue, red, and green spatter	525.00
Rooster, red, blue, yellow, ochre, and black rooster, blue spatter	600.00
Rose, red, green, and black flower, blue spatter	200.00
Thistle, red and green flower, yellow spatter	650.00
Miniature	
Cup and Saucer, red spatter, marked "Staffordshire, England"	75.00
Sugar, Fort, blue spatter	350.00
Teabowl and Saucer, Tree pattern, black and green, blue spatter border	450.00
Pepper Pot, 4¾" h, pierced domed cov, Peafowl, blue, ochre, rose, and black peacock on branch, yellow spatter, marked "Staffordshire," c1840	1,200.00
Pitcher, 7¾", paneled body, Rose pattern, I red, blue, green, and black rose, white ground, blue spatter	300.00
Plate	
Castle, 8⅜", green spatter	250.00
Clover, 9½", green spatter, red blossoms, black trailing vines	375.00
Peafowl, 9½", red, green, yellowochre, and black peafowl, blue spatter, rim flakes	200.00
Rainbow, 8⅛", scalloped edge, red, blue, and green spatter, imp "Adams"	165.00
Schoolhouse, 7½", three color, green spatter	625.00
Star, 8½", red, blue, and green, blue spatter, imp "Stone China"	300.00
Thistle, 8⅝", yellow spatter	600.00
Saucer, 6" d, Star pattern, red, green, and blue star, blue spatter, imp "C," England, c1840	90.00
Soup Plate, 9½", Peafowl, red, blue, green, and black peafowl, red spatter, imp "Adams," minor stains	120.00
Sugar, cov, Thistle, red and green flower, yellow spatter, hairline	315.00
Toddy Plate, 5¼", Bull's Eye pattern, blue spatter	85.00
Waste Bowl, Christmas Ball, red and green, yellow spatter	250.00

SPONGEWARE

History: Spongeware is a specific type of decoration, not a type of pottery or glaze.

Spongeware decoration is found on many types of pottery bodies—ironstone, redware, stoneware, yellow ware, etc. It was made in both England and the United States. Marked pieces indicate a starting date of 1815, with manufacturing extending to the 1850s.

Decoration is varied. In some pieces the sponging is minimal with the white underglaze dominant. Other pieces appear to be sponged solidly on both sides. Pieces from 1840–1860 have sponging which appears in either a circular movement or a streaked horizontal technique.

Examples are found in blue and white, the most common colors. Other prevalent colors are browns, greens, ochres, and greenish-blue. The greenish-blue results from blue sponging which has been overglazed in a pale yellow. A red overglaze produces a black or navy color.

Other colors are blue and red (found on English creamware and American earthenware of the 1880s), gray, grayish-green, red, dark green on stark white, dark green on mellow yellow, and purple.

References: Susan and Al Bagdade, *Warman's English & Continental Pottery & Porcelain, 1st Edition*, Warman Publishing Co., Inc., 1987; Earl F. and Ada Robacker, *Spatterware and Sponge*, A. S. Barnes & Co., 1978.

Bean Pot, ochre, brown, and green	200.00

STAFFORDSHIRE ITEMS

Bowl
6¼", brown, blue, and white 65.00
7" d, tan and blue sponging, light gray
ground 35.00
Bowl and Pitcher Set, 11½ x 8½", blue
and olive green, blue bands, white
ground 350.00
Bread Plate, 10" l, blue sponging, double open handles 100.00
Cookie Jar, gold highlights, green,
brown, and ochre 300.00
Cup and Saucer, earthenware, blue
sponging, c1840 .... 130.00
Cuspidor, 7½", blue sponge dec and
bands, white ground 90.00

Jug, $125.00.

Custard Cup, blue sponging, white
ground 60.00
Jardiniere, 11 x 8¼", blue dec, gold
flecked green rim, white ground ... 100.00
Mixing Bowl, 12¼" d, blue sponging,
molded design, white ground 125.00
Mug, 4¼" h, brown sponging, yellow
ground 70.00
Pie Plate, 9" d, brown and green
sponge, cream ground 50.00
Pitcher
4½" h, adv, green and brown sponging, tan ground 60.00
5½" h, yellow ware, green and brown
sponging 70.00
8¾" h, tapered cylinder, blue sponged
bands, pinched spout, molded
strap, white ground 230.00
Plate
3⅛" d, blue sponging, white ground . 60.00
10¼" d, blue sponging, emb scalloped edge, white ground 175.00
Platter, 12 x 8", blue sponging, white
ground, Trenton, NJ, c1865 ...... 210.00
Salt and Pepper Shakers, hand thrown,
white, green and amber sponge, pr . 95.00
Slop Jar, blue and white 265.00
Toddy Plate, 4¾", blue and white,
marked "Burford Bros" 40.00

History: A wide variety of ornamental pottery
items originated in England's Staffordshire district,
beginning in the 17th century and extending to the
present. The height of production was from 1820
to 1890.

These naive pieces are considered folk art by
many collectors. Most items were not made carefully; some were even made and decorated by
children.

The types of objects are varied, e.g., animals,
cottages, and figurines (chimney ornaments). The
key to price is age and condition. The older the
piece, the higher the price is a general rule.

References: Susan and Al Bagdade, *Warman's
English & Continental Pottery & Porcelain, 1st Edition*, Warman Publishing Co., Inc., 1987; P. D. Gordon Pugh, *Staffordshire Portrait Figures Of The
Victorian Era*, Antique Collectors' Club Ltd.

Animal
Cat, 5", saltglaze, solid agate, seated
brown marbleized body, blue tinged
left haunch, incised eyebrows and
whiskers, brown eyes, cobalt blue
washed ears, some glaze crackling
and speckling, minor chips, c1745–
55 .... 1,350.00
Greyhound, 12", seated, hare at feet,
19th C, pr 225.00
Hen, 8", black and white, light brown
basketweave base 250.00
Poodle, 9½", standing, white, holding
a yellow fruit basket, oval base
edged in gilding, mid 19th C 300.00
Rabbit, 2⅛ x 3⅝", reclining, polychrome 125.00
Bank, 5", cottage, white snow on roof,
2 chimneys, black outline, c1885 .. 200.00
Box, 3⅝", rect, primrose ground, emb,
painted sprays of flowers, gilt metal
mounts 460.00
Chimney Ornament
6", two girls at dog house, one on
roof, other petting dog at door ... 100.00
16¼", blacksmith 175.00
Cream Bowl, 5⅜" d, reticulated cov, 6¼"
d stand, and 7⅛" l ladle, creamware,
circular, gray shaded green husk garland and floral sprig, green entwined
stem handles, green floral sprig finial,
stand with fluting, pierced rim painted
with green husks, conforming dec on
pierced ladle bowl, floral and leaf
sprig on shell and scroll molded terminal, c1790 .... 2,350.00
Figure
6⅜" and 7¹¹⁄₁₆", pr, pearlware, Walton
type, modeled as doe and stag,
white spotted iron-red coats, brown
hooves, antlers, green and brown

mottled tree, mound base with applied turquoise moss, white and blue scrollwork, ears restored, c1820 .... **1,100.00**

6¾″, Mansion House Dwarf, pearlware, Monsieur Le Grand, yellow hat, iron-red jacket with ochre dots, yellow breeches, green and ochre mound base, applied flowers, 1820 **200.00**

Inkwell, 4⅞″, man, black hat and breeches, green jacket, blue scarf, red shirt, holding fish, seated on tan mound, basket forms inkwell, mid 19th C **150.00**

Jug

5⅛″ h, saltglaze, pear shaped body, enameled rose, blue, yellow, green, brown, and black bird flying towards tree in fenced garden, yellow and blue floral sprigs under spout, green band and black scallop rim border, brown vine int. border, small hair cracks, c1760 .... **1,000.00**

6½″, canary yellow and silver luster, commemorative, transfer printed in iron-red, bust length portrait of Sir Francis Burdett, inscription below, obverse with additional inscription within foliage wreath, silver luster neck, iron-red line border on rim, handle and spout, c1810 .... **600.00**

Mug, child's, 2½″ h, saltglaze, enameled rose, blue, green, iron-red, and sepia insect crawling on thorny rose stem, reeded strap handle, iron-red trellis diaper rim band, blue and green foliate sprig on int., c1760 .... **2,000.00**

Pastille Burner, 4⅝″, house, yellow sides, gray windows, roofed ochre

Pastille Burner, 3½″ d, 5″ h, cottage, pink roof, green leaves, multicolored flowers, gilt trim white ground, c1850, $750.00.

door, olive green roof, two yellow chimneys with brown edging, green grassy mound base, c1790 ...... **675.00**

Plaque, 8¾ x 11¼″, Babes in the Woods, pearlware, two brown haired girls wearing cobalt blue jackets, blue and rose dotted skirts, sleeping, blue, rose, and green flowers, three green leafed brown trees, black edged chambered rect rim with border of brown birds perched on rose-fruited green grapevine, c1840 .... **800.00**

Plate, 8⅝″ d, pearlware, center painted with large spray of two yellow, blue, and brown pansies, blue, green, and brown leaves, scalloped rim, molded scalework and green leaves, c1840, set of 6 .... **1,000.00**

Sauceboat

5⅞″ l, pearlware, figural, fish and chicken, molded as body of chicken, brown comb, cobalt blue eyes, green spotted plumage, wing and tail feathers delineated in blue, brown glazed fish head at top of tail, open mouth forms spout, dimpled green molded base, c1790 .. **1,450.00**

7⅜″ l, figural, fish, molded scales, open mouth forms spout, fins, eyes, and rim heightened in green glaze, oval base with molded water weeds and waves, small chips **600.00**

Stirrup Cup

4⅝″, pearlware, hand form, clenched fist with rose fingernails, backed edged rose and blue striped cuff, c1845 .... **100.00**

5⅜″, ironstone, fox head, shaded iron-red and ochre mask, gray and black muzzle and eyes, green collar edged in black and white with gilt center square, c1810 .... **525.00**

Teapot, cov, spherical body

4″ h, saltglaze, enameled rose, turquoise, green, iron-red, yellow, and black bowknotted bouquet, pink, yellow, and iron-red demiflowerhead border within turquoise and yellow scallops, iron-red flowerhead finial, green crabstock handle, c1760 .... **1,870.00**

5″ h, creamware, purple, iron-red, yellow, green, blue, and black, two Chinoiserie figures, reverse with one figure waving string of husks, iron-red edged panel surrounded by purple foliate scrolls, ear shaped handle, iron-red landscape vignettes on cov, attributed to William Greatbatch, c1775 .... **2,550.00**

5¼″ h, saltglaze, iron-red, blue, yellow, green, and black floral bou-

quet, rose ground, crabstock han-
dle, c1760 . . . . **4,675.00**

STAFFORDSHIRE, HISTORICAL

History: The Staffordshire district of England is
the center of the English pottery industry. There
were eighty different potteries operating there in
1786, with the number increasing to 179 by 1802.
The district includes Burslem, Cobridge, Eturia,
Fenton, Foley, Hanley, Lane Delph, Lane End,
Longport, Shelton, Stoke, and Tunstall. Among the
many famous potters were Adams, Davenport,
Spode, Stevenson, Wedgwood, and Wood.

In historical Staffordshire the view is the most
critical element. American collectors pay much
less for non-American views. Dark blue pieces are
favored. Light views have lost popularity during
the past five years and, in many cases, have
dropped in value. Among the forms, soup tureens
have shown the highest price increases.

A recent development in historical Staffordshire
is the mail auctions of David Arman of Woodstock,
Connecticut, who is following a marketing trend
which he and other dealers have established for
a number of specific antiques categories.

References: David and Linda Arman, *Historical
Staffordshire: An Illustrated Check List,* published
by author, 1974, out-of-print; David and Linda Arman, *First Supplement, Historical Staffordshire:
An Illustrated Check List,* published by author,
1977, out-of-print; Susan and Al Bagdade, *Warman's English & Continental Pottery & Porcelain,
1st Edition,* Warman Publishing Co., Inc., 1987;
Ada Walker Camehl, *The Blue China Book,* Tudor
Publishing Co., 1946, (Dover, reprint); A.W. Coysh
and R. K. Henrywood, *The Dictionary Of Blue And
White Printed Pottery, 1780–1880,* Antique Collectors' Club, 1982; Ellouise Larsen, *American Historical Views On Staffordshire China,* 3rd Edition,
Dover Publications, 1975.

Notes: Prices are for proof examples. Adjust
prices by 20% for an unseen chip, a faint hairline,
or an unseen professional repair; by 35% for knife
marks through the glaze and a visible professional
repair; by 50% for worn glaze and major repairs.

The numbers in parenthesis refer to items in the
books by Linda and David Arman, which constitute
the most detailed list of American historical views
and their forms.

W.ADAMS&SONS   ADAMS

ADAMS

The Adams family has been associated with ceramics from the mid 17th century. In 1802 William
Adams of Stoke-upon-Trent produced American
views.

In 1819 a fourth William Adams, son of William
of Stoke, became a partner with his father and
was later joined by his three brothers. The firm
became William Adams & Sons. The father died
in 1829 and William, the eldest son, became manager.

The company operated four potteries at Stoke
and one at Tunstall. American views were produced at Tunstall in black, light blue, sepia, pink,
and green in the 1830–40 period. William Adams
died in 1865. All operations were moved to Tunstall. The firm continues today under the name of
Wm. Adams & Sons, Ltd.

**Adams, U. S. Views series, Lake
George, 13¼″ platter (448), $225.00.**

Hudson River Series
Fair Mount, 4″ cup plate, pink (459) .	**80.00**
Fort Edwards, Hudson River, 5¼″ plate, pink (460)	**60.00**
Log Cabin, medallions of Gen. Harrison on border, waste bowl, brown(458) .	**250.00**
U. S. Views, Catskill Mountain House, 10¼″ soup plate, light blue (445) . . .	**75.00**

CLEWS

From sketchy historical accounts that are available, James Clews took over the closed plant of
A. Stevenson in 1819. His brother Ralph entered
the business later. The firm continued until about
1836 when James Clews came to America to enter
the pottery business at Troy, Indiana. The venture
was a failure because of the lack of skilled workmen and the proper type of clay. He returned to
England but did not re-enter the pottery business.

Clews, States plate, 8¾″ d, (5) $225.00.

Cities Series, dark and medium blue
Baltimore, vegetable dish (17)	5,000.00
Philadelphia, 5½″ plate (26)	425.00
Quebec, 9″ plate (28)	225.00
Sandusky, 17″ platter, dark blue (B-29)	4,700.00

Doctor Syntax, dark blue
Doctor Syntax disputing his bill with landlady, 10″ plate (38)	225.00
Doctor Syntax mistakes a gentleman's house for an inn, 10″ soup (42)	150.00
Doctor Syntax with the dairy maid, 3⅞″ cup plate (46)	500.00
Doctor Syntax, advertisement for a wife, 16″ platter (64)	550.00
Don Quixote, repose in woods, 6″ plate (71)	150.00
Sancho Panza and the priest and barber, 7½″ plate (75)	150.00

Landing of Lafayette at Castle Garden, dark blue (1)
Pitcher, 8″	825.00
Plate, 5½″	250.00
Plate, 10″	275.00
Platter, 15″	650.00
Soup Plate, 9″	225.00
Vegetable Dish, 10″ square	900.00

Peace and Plenty dark blue, (A-34a)
Plate, 9″	250.00

Picturesque Views Series
Hudson, Hudson River
Soup Plate, 10½″, brown (107)	60.00
Near Hudson, Hudson River, brown, 7″ plate (113)	60.00

Peace and Plenty, dark blue (34)
Plate, 10″	225.00

Pittsfield Elm, dark blue (33)
Plate, 8″	225.00
Platter, 15″	600.00

States or American and Independence Series, dark blue
Building, Deer on Lawn, 10½″ soup plate (A-2)	500.00
Building, Sheep on Lawn, 8⅞″ plate (5)	225.00
Mansion, circular drive, vegetable dish (14)	800.00
Mansion, winding drive, 4⅞″ h creamer, unrecorded form	1,500.00
Three Story Mansion, 4½″ cup plate, three small rim roughages (7)	400.00
Two Story Building, curved drive, 8″ plate (9)	225.00

J.&J. JACKSON

J. & J. JACKSON

Job and John Jackson began operations at the Churchyard Works, Burslem, about 1830. The works formerly were owned by the Wedgwood family. The firm produced transfer scenes in a variety of colors, such as black, light blue, pink, sepia, green, maroon and mulberry. Over 40 different American views of Connecticut, Massachusetts, Pennsylvania, New York, and Ohio were issued. The firm is believed to have closed about 1844.

Job and John Jackson, Skenectady on the Mohawk River, 6½″ h pitcher (494), $125.00.

American Scenery Series, all colors
Deaf & Dumb Asylum, Phila, 7″ plate (471)	70.00
Fort Ticonderoga, New York, gravy tureen with cover (473)	250.00
State House, Boston, 10½″ plate (484)	60.00
View of the Canal, Little Falls, Mohawk River, 10½″ plate (490)	125.00

Miscellaneous
New York, Select Sketches series, 17″ platter (496)	400.00
Schenectady on Mohawk River, 8″ pitcher (494)	275.00

THOMAS MAYER

In 1829, Thomas Mayer and his brothers, John and Joshua, purchased Stubbs' Dale Hall Works of Burslem. They continued to produce a superior grade of ceramics.

Arms of the American States, dark blue
GA, 11¾" vegetable dish (500)	3,000.00
MA, 9½" platter (502)	3,500.00
MD, ftd scalloped rim punch bowl, 4⅞" h, 11½" d, unlisted form, brilliant, high glaze, soft blue, crisp transfer	8,700.00
NY	
9¾" plate	650.00
10" plate	600.00
Lafayette at Washington's Tomb, dark blue, sugar bowl (511)	700.00
Lafayette at Franklin's tomb, dark blue, waste bowl (512)	600.00

CHARLES MEIGH

Job Meigh began the Meigh pottery in the Old Hall Pottery, in 1780. Later his sons and grandsons entered the business. The firm's name is recorded as Job Meigh & Sons, 1823; J. Meigh & Sons, 1829; Charles Meigh, 1843.

The American Cities and Scenery series was produced by Charles Meigh between 1840 and 1850. The colors are light blue, brown, gray, and purple. Sometimes the colors appear in combination.

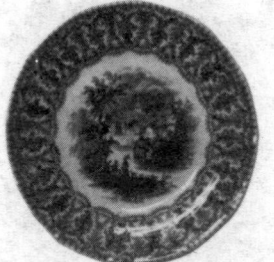

Meigh, American Cities and Scenery series, Village of Little Falls, 8¼" d plate (558), $60.00.

Albany, 13 ½, pitcher (544)	**1,225.00**
Ballston Springs, bowl (545)	**275.00**
Capitol at Washington, butter dish, cov (550)	**375.00**
New York (from Weehawken), compote, cov, round (553)	**300.00**
Utica, 7¼" plate	**75.00**
Yale College, New Haven, chamber pot, interior (560)	**250.00**

MELLOR, VENEABLES & CO.

Little information is recorded on Mellor, Veneables & Co. except that they were listed as potters in Burslem in 1843. Their Scenic Views series with the Arms of the States Border does include the arms for New Hampshire. This state is missing from the Mayer series. However, the view was known in England and collectors search for a Mayer example.

Arms of States, white body, light color transfers, eight states in varying combinations (529)
Cup Plate, 4"	100.00
Plate, 7½ to 10"	75.00
Waste Bowl	150.00
Scenic Views, Arms of States Border, light blue, pink, brown, purple	
Caldwell (Lake George,) 10½" plate (518)	60.00
View of Baltimore, 19½" platter (523)	275.00
View of New York From Weehawken, sauce dish (525)	45.00

J.W. R.

Stone China

W. RIDGWAY

J. & W. RIDGWAY AND WILLIAM RIDGWAY & CO.

John and William Ridgway, sons of Job Ridgway and nephews of George Ridgway who owned Bell Bank Works and Couldon Place Works, produced the popular Beauties of America series at the Couldon plant. The partnership between the two brothers was dissolved in 1830. John remained at Couldon.

William managed the Bell Bank works until 1854. Two additional series were produced based upon the etchings of Bartlett's American Scenery. The first series had various borders including narrow lace. The second series is known as Catskill Moss.

Beauties of America is in dark blue. The other series are found in the light transfer colors of light blue, pink, brown, black, and green.

J. W. Ridgway, Beauties of America series, Deaf and Dumb Asylum, Hartford, CT, 14¾″ l platter, medium blue, $700.00.

American Scenery
Columbia Bridge on the Susquehanna, Pitcher (281)	275.00
Peekskill Landing, Hudson River Vegetable Dish (287)	200.00

Beauties of America, dark blue
Almshouse, New York, 16″ platter (255)	600.00
City Hall, New York, 10″ plate, medium dark blue (A-260)	150.00
Court House, Boston, 10½″ platter, medium dark blue	1,100.00
Exchange, Baltimore, cup plate (264)	450.00
Exchange, Charleston, 8½″ gravy tureen undertray	600.00
Hospital, Boston, 12″ platter, medium dark blue	950.00
Library, Phila, 8″ plate (268)	175.00
Octagon Church, Boston, 10″ soup plate, medium dark blue (A-271) .	265.00
Pennsylvania Hospital, Philadelphia, 19″ platter, medium dark blue (B-272)	1,100.00

Catskill Moss
Kosciusko's Tomb, 10″ soup (305) .	70.00
Meredith, 9½″ plate (307)	60.00
President's House, tray (311)	100.00

Columbia Star, Harrison's Log Cabin
End View, soup (276)	90.00
Side View, plate, 10¼″, plowing, (277)	90.00
Sugar Bowl (277)	275.00

ROGERS

ROGERS

John Rogers and his brother George established a pottery near Longport in 1782. After George's death in 1815, John's son Spencer became a partner and the firm operated under the name of John Rogers & Sons. John died in 1816. His son continued the use of the name until he dissolved the pottery in 1842.

Boston Harbor, dark blue (441)
Cup and Saucer	600.00
Sugar Bowl	600.00

Boston State House, dark blue (442)
Plate, 10″	125.00
Platter, 14″	475.00

Zebra, medium dark blue
Basket, openwork, scalloped rim, emb handles, underglaze eagle and imp marks	575.00
Cup and Saucer	175.00

STEVENSON

As early as the 17th century the name Stevenson has been associated with the pottery industry. Andrew Stevenson of Cobridge introduced American scenes with the flower and scroll border. Ralph Stevenson, also of Cobridge, used a vine and leaf border on his dark blue historical views and a lace border on his series in light transfers.

The initials R. S. & W. indicate Ralph Stevenson and Williams are associated with the acorn and leaf border. It has been reported that Williams was Ralph's New York agent and the wares were produced by Ralph alone.

Ralph Stevenson, Vine Border series, Exchange, Charleston, vegetable dish, cover not shown (375), $1,200.00.

Acorn and Oak Leaves Border, dark blue

Baltimore Exchange, 5½″ plate (348)   750.00
Harvard College, 10″ soup (352) . . .   275.00
Octagon Church, Boston, 4½″ cup plate (356) 750.00
Park Theater, New York, 10″ plate (357) 175.00
St Paul's Church, New York, 6¼″ medium blue plate 800.00

Floral and Scroll Border, dark blue

City Hall, New York, 7″ plate (397) .   1,100.00
Columbia College, New York, 6½″ soup (398) 900.00
New York from Brooklyn Heights, 10¼″ medium blue plate 950.00
New York from Heights near Brooklyn, 16¼″ medium dark blue platter   1,600.00

Lace Border

Erie Canal at Buffalo, 10″ soup (386)   150.00

Lace Border

New Orleans
   Cup and Saucer (387) 100.00
   Teapot (387) 225.00

Vine Border

Almshouse, Boston, 14″ platter (365)   700.00
Capitol, Washington, 10″ soup (370)   400.00

STUBBS

In 1790 Stubbs established a pottery works at Burslem, England. He operated it until 1829 when he retired and sold the pottery to the Mayer brothers. He probably produced his American views about 1825. Many of his scenes were from Boston, New York, New Jersey and Philadelphia.

Rose Border, dark blue

City Hall, NY
   Pitcher, 6″ h (335) 375.00
   Sugar Bowl (336) 350.00
   Teapot (336) 500.00

Spread Eagle Border, dark blue

Church in the City of New York, 6⅛″ plate (322) 750.00
City Hall, New York, 6½″ plate, (A-323) 200.00

Jos. Stubbs, Spread Eagle border, Fair Mont near Philadelphia, 10″ d plate, $200.00.

Fair Mount Near Philadelphia, 10″ plate (A-324a) 200.00
Upper Ferry Bridge over the River Schuylkill (332)
Plate, 8¾″ 150.00

S. TAMS & CO.

The firm operated at Longton, England. The exact date of its beginning is not known, but believed to be about 1810–15. The company produced several dark blue American views. About 1830 the name became Tams, Anderson, and Tams.

Capitol at Harrisburg, PA, soup tureen, cov (513) 6,500.00
Capitol, Washington, wash bowl (514) .   1,500.00
Henry Clay . . . Star of West, plate (515A) 1,750.00
United States Hotel, Philadelphia, bowl, beaded rim (515) 2,000.00

WOOD

Enoch Wood, sometimes referred to as the Father of English Pottery, began operating a pottery at Fountain Place, Burslem, in 1783. A cousin Ralph Wood was associated with him. In 1790 James Caldwell became a partner and the firm was known as Wood and Caldwell. In 1819 Wood and his sons took full control.

Enoch died in 1840. His sons continued under the name of Enoch Wood & Sons. The American views were first made in the mid 1820s and continued through the 1840s.

It is reported that the pottery produced more signed historical views that any other Staffordshire firm. Many of the views attributed to unknown makers probably came from the Woods.

Marks vary, although always with the name Wood. The establishment was sold to Messrs. Pinder, Bourne & Hope in 1846.

Wood & Son, French views, La Grange, The Residence of the Marquis de Lafayette, 10¼″ plate, dark blue, $185.00.

Celtic China, light transfer colors
  Buffalo on Lake Erie, vegetable dish
    (236) 275.00
  Harvard College, 10″ plate (240) . . . 100.00
  Natural Bridge, VA, 9¼″ plate (244) . 75.00
  Pass in the Catskill Mountains, 7″
    plate (247) 75.00
  Trenton Falls, 8″ plate (251) 60.00
Floral Border, irregular, dark blue
  Commodore MacDonnough's Victory
    (154)
    Cream Pitcher, 3½″ h, barrel
      shaped 1,750.00
    Plate, 6½″ 350.00
    Plate, 9″ 375.00
  Erie Canal, View of the Aqueduct
    Bridge at Little Falls (158)
    Pitcher, 6 11½″ 1,250.00
    Soup Plate, 10¼″ 850.00
    Sugar Bowl 750.00
Shell Border, circular center, dark blue
  Baltimore and Ohio Railroad, 10⅛″
    soup plate (183) 700.00
  Chief Justice Marshall Troy, 8⅛″ plate
    (127) 450.00
  Chiswick on the Thames, gravy tureen, orig lid, undertray and ladle . 2,000.00
  City of Albany, 10¼″ plate (163) . . . 425.00
  Highlands, Hudson River, 5¾″ plate
    (167) 875.00

Mount Vernon, 7½″ plate (173) 500.00
Railroad, Baltimore and Ohio, level,
  10″ plate (183) 600.00
Union Line, 10″ plate (144) 575.00
Shell Border, irregular center, dark blue
  Commodore MacDonnough's Victory
    (130)
    Plate, 9″ 375.00
    Teapot 750.00
  Cowes Harbor, 6½″ plate (B-132) . . 215.00
  Eddistone Lighthouse, 8½″ open vegetable dish 700.00
  Union Line, 9¼″ plate (144) 375.00
  Wadsworth Tower, 4½″ pitcher (147) 550.00

UNKNOWN MAKERS

Anti-Slavery (608)
  Cup Plate, 4″, light blue 450.00
  Plate, 6″, light blue 200.00
Basket of Flowers, 4½″ cup plate, dark
  blue 100.00
Batahla, 11 x 8½″ oval bowl, dark blue 900.00
Erie Canal inscription
  Pitcher, 5¾″, dark blue (598) 1,400.00
  Plate, 10″ (597) 450.00
Maypole, 6¾″ pitcher, medium dark
  blue, floral border, village scene with
  livestock in foreground, people dancing 200.00

STAFFORDSHIRE, ROMANTIC

History: The Staffordshire district of England produced dinnerware with romantic scenes between 1830 and 1860. A large number of potters were involved and over 800 patterns have been identified.

The dinner services came in a variety of colors with light blue and pink perhaps the most popular. Usually the pattern is identified on the back of the piece. It was not uncommon for two potters to issue pieces with the same design. Therefore, check the pattern name as well as the maker's name.

It would be impossible to list all patterns. A representative selection follows. Some price ranges to keep in mind are: cups and saucers (handleless) $35–50; cup plates $40–75; plates, 9–10″, $10–50; platters $25–75.00.

Reference: Petra Williams, *Staffordshire: Romantic Transfer Patterns*, Fountain House East, 1978; Petra Williams, *Staffordshire II*, Fountain House East, 1986.

Arabesque, grayish blue, Edwards &
Son
  Creamer 50.00
  Gravy Boat 40.00
  Relish, small, oblong 25.00

Sugar Bowl, covered, Singanese pattern, J. Wedgwood, pink, $65.00.

Vegetable Dish, open	35.00
Waste Bowl	35.00

Balantyre, J Alcock
Bowl, 8"	40.00
Cup Plate, 12 sided	50.00
Creamer	50.00
Plate	
9½", 12 sided	25.00
10½", 12 sided	30.00
Relish, oblong, fluted ends	25.00
Teapot	150.00

Caledonia, William Adams, c1800–1864
Bowl	35.00
Creamer	50.00
Cup and Saucer	40.00
Plate	
7½", pink	55.00
8½", dark blue	125.00
10½", pink	70.00
Sugar Bowl	75.00

Cowslip, W Ridgway
Creamer	50.00
Cup and Saucer, handle	40.00
Custard Cup	25.00
Ladle, 15", design on bowl and handle	100.00
Relish, shell shaped	48.00

Etruscan Vase, blue and brown, Thomas, John, Joseph Mayer, c1843–55
Bowl, 7"	42.00
Plate, 10½"	50.00
Platter, 16 x 11½"	125.00
Relish, 5"	30.00
Saucer	25.00
Soup Plate, wide flange	60.00

Garden Scenery, pink, Mayer
Bowl, 4"	25.00
Cup and Saucer, handle	50.00
Cup Plate, 12 sided	30.00
Plate, 12 sided	45.00
Sauce	25.00

Soup Plate	45.00
Teapot	140.00
Vegetable, open	65.00

Ivanhoe, Podmore Walker & Co., 1834–1859
Bowl	32.50
Creamer	50.00
Plate, 12 sided	37.50
Sugar	70.00

Millenium, Ralph Stevenson & Son, 1832–1835
Bowl	30.00
Creamer	45.00
Cup and Saucer	32.50
Plate, 10½", red	45.00
Vegetable Bowl, open	75.00

Oriental, Ridgway, c1830–34
Creamer	65.00
Cup and Saucer, handleless	55.00
Cup Plate	50.00
Plate	48.00
Platter, 11½ x 7"	75.00
Tureen, cov, octagonal	125.00

Priory, Edward Challinor and Co., c1853–1862
Bowl	40.00
Creamer	55.00
Cup and Saucer, handleless	35.00
Plate, 9½", octagonal	50.00
Platter, 11½" x 17"	80.00
Soup Plate	55.00
Sugar, cov, handles	125.00
Teapot, pagoda shape	135.00
Toddy Plate, 5", light blue	30.00

Undina, black and blue, J Clementson, registered Jan 7, 1852
Plate	40.00
Relish, oval, shell shaped	45.00
Wash Bowl and Pitcher	250.00

STAINED AND/OR LEADED GLASS PANELS

History: American architects in the second half of the 19th century and the early 20th century used stained and leaded glass panels as a chief decorative element. Skilled glass craftsmen assembled the designs, the best known being Louis C. Tiffany.

The panels are held together with soft lead cames or copper wraps. When purchasing a panel, check the lead and have any repairs made to protect your investment.

Collectors' Club: Stained Glass Association of America, 1221 Locust St, Suite 405, St. Louis, MO 63103. *Stained Glass Magazine* (quarterly).

Leaded	
36 x 36", blue bunch of grapes, green leaves, blue scroll, opal red ribbon, amber ground, self frame of blue panes, orig wood frame	500.00

Panel, 14 x 33", multicolored, $275.00.

43 x 29", green, red, and blue, enameled waterfall, grassy hill, conifers, and blossoming bushes, opal blue glass sky, American, 20th C **1,000.00**

144 x 48", church, brilliant colored landscape, angel appearing to Mary, dedication and inscribed geometric panels, sgd "Tiffany" **4,500.00**

Stained

16½ x 14⅛", rect, mosaic, two opposing parrots, iridescent colors, exotic leafage ground, 1899–1920 **6,325.00**

22 x 32", two rose tulips, stem and leaves, cobalt blue-green reserve, yellow opaque ground, orig frame **165.00**

29 x 40", bird, berried branches, Frohe, 1890 .... **2,000.00**

39 x 24½", blue shield crest, yellow faceted circular center, surrounded by floral vines, flanked by elongated pointed panels, squared diamond motif, light pink reserve, orig frame **225.00**

STANGL POTTERY BIRDS

History: Stangl ceramic birds were produced from 1940 until the Stangl factory closed in 1972. The birds were produced at Stangl's Trenton plant and shipped to their Flemington, New Jersey, plant for hand painting.

During World War II the demand for these birds and Stangl pottery was so great that 40 to 60 decorators could not keep up with the demand. Orders were contracted out to private homes. These orders then were returned for firing and finishing. Colors used to decorate these birds varied according to the artist.

As many as ten different trademarks were used. Almost every bird is numbered; many are artist signed. However, the signatures are used only for dating purposes and add very little to the value of the birds.

Several birds were reissued between 1972 and 1977. These reissues are dated on the bottom and valued at approximately one half of the older birds.

References: Joan Dworkin and Martha Horman, *A Guide To Stangl Pottery Birds,* Willow Pond Books, Inc., 1973; Norma Rehl, *The Collectors Handbook of Stangl Pottery,* Democrat Press, 1982.

Additional Listings: See Stangl pottery in the American Dinnerware category in *Warman's Americana & Collectibles* for more examples.

Bluebird, #3276, blue and yellow, $65.00.

3274, Penguin, 5½" h	280.00
3400, Love Bird, 4" h	33.00
3401D, Double Wren	60.00
3402S, Oriole, 3¼" h	35.00
3405D, Double Cockatoo	70.00
3405S, Cockatoo	50.00
3443, Duck, flying, 9" h	225.00
3444, Cardinal, 6½"	55.00
34444, Cardinal, 6"	55.00
3448, Blue Headed Vireo	35.00
3454, Key West Quail Dove, 9' h	225.00
3484, Cockatoo, 11⅜" h	200.00
3491, Hen Pheasant, 6¼ x 11"	145.00
3492, Cock Pheasant, 6¼ x 11"	150.00
3581, Chickadees, 10" l	140.00
3582, Parakeets, pr, 7" h	110.00
3584, Cockatoo, sgd "Jacob"	125.00
3585, Rufous Hummingbird	35.00
3589, Indigo Bunting, 3¼" h	37.50
3598, Kentucky Warbler, 3" h	35.00
3635, Goldfinches group, 4 x 11½" ...	160.00
3715, Blue Jay, 10¼"	355.00
3746, Canary, facing right, rose flower, 6¼" h	130.00
3758, Magpie Jay	585.00
3813, Evening Grosbeak	75.00
3815, Western Blue Bird	136.00
3848, Golden-crowned Kinglet	50.00
3851, Red Breasted Nuthatch	58.00

STATUES

History: Beginning with primitive cultures, man produced statues in the shape of people and animals. During the Middle Ages most works were religious and symbolic in character and form. The Renaissance rediscovered the human and secular forms.

During the 18th and 19th centuries it was fashionable to have statues in the home. Many famous works were copied for popular consumption.

Statuette or figurine denotes smaller statues, one-fourth life size or smaller.

Reference: Anita Jacobsen (ed.), *Jacobsen's Painting and Bronze Price Guide,* published by author.

Additional Listings: Bronzes and Busts.

Woman, 13½″ h, marble, sq veined marble base, $200.00.

Bronze
16″ h, woman, parcel gilt, bare breasted, standing on leopard skin holding staff, mounted on revolving base **1,500.00**
17½″ h, dancer, swaying, dark brown patina, circular marble base, inscribed "Colinet," c1925 . . . . **770.00**
27½″ h, classical woman, standing, fastening her drapery, brown patina **990.00**
33¾″ h, Aurora, Art Nouveau style, holding scarf and diaphanous gown, standing in chariot, cupid and doves, Auguste Moreau, late 19th C **2,500.00**
35″ h, seated beauty, wearing wide brimmed summer hat, parasol in right hand, molded socle inscribe "L'ete," French, 19th C **6,050.00**
4′10″ h, rearing horse, resting on flared tail, pricked ears **3,500.00**
Bronze and Ivory
10¼″ h, Pierrot, cast, carved, polychrome, clown holding sword in left hand, right hand to heart, octagonal

black base, inscribed "Roland Paris" **1,900.00**
16⅛″ h, dancer, cast carved, polychrome, bare breasted, holding garland to chest wearing slit skirt, inscribed base mounted on brown onyx and black stone base, Samuel Lypchytz **2,700.00**
Cast Iron, 33½″, eagle, American, late 19th, early 20th C **1,200.00**
Ceramic, 24½″ h, owl, perched on oak branch, brown, green, and yellow painted, inscribed "Binali," impressed "Made in Italy **140.00**
Ivory
8⅜″ h, nun, carved, dressed in hood and draped gown, outstretched hands, gilt detail, carved and incised pedestal, wood base, Goa, 18th C **375.00**
23″ h, maiden, wearing ornate robe, holding flower basket in left hand, flowering branch in right, Chinese **1,650.00**
Limestone, 48″ h, Guanyin, Song style, standing, wearing flowing robe, holding flower in each hand, serene features, tiara, mounted on detachable lotus petal base **6,050.00**
Marble, 58″ h, Pan, standing, Carrara, 18th C **2,900.00**
Metal, 16½″ h, Indian, patina, sgd "Cornelius and Baker, Philadelphia," mid 19th C **800.00**
Porcelain, 14½″ h, gentleman, plumed hat, gilt lined cloak, molded base, Marseilles, late 18th C **275.00**
Wood
42″ h, Guanyin, holding lotus flower, dressed in multicolored robe, bare chest, standing on double lotus base, polychrome pigment highlights, c1900 . . . . **500.00**
7′ 10″ h, horse, carved, painted dappled pale brown and white, pricked ears, movable mouth, horsehair tail, metal rolling stand, c1880 . . . **4,400.00**

STEIFF

History: Margarete Steiff, GmbH, established in Germany in 1880, is known for very fine quality stuffed animals and dolls as well as other beautifully made collectible toys. It is still in business, and its products are highly respected.

The company's first products were wool-felt elephants made by Margaret Steiff. In a few years the elephant line was expanded to include a donkey, horse, pig, and camel.

By 1903 the company also was producing a jointed mohair Teddy Bear, whose production dramatically increased to over 970,000 units in 1907.

Margarete's nephews took over the company at this point. The bear's head became the symbol for its label, and the famous "Button in the Ear" round, metal trademark was added.

Newly designed animals were added: Molly and Bully, the dogs, and Fluffy, the cat. Pull toys and kites also were produced, as well as larger animals on which children could ride or play.

Become familiar with genuine Steiff products before purchasing an antique stuffed animal. Plush in old Steiff animals was mohair; trimmings usually were felt or velvet. Unscrupulous individuals have attached the familiar Steiff metal button to animals that are not Steiff.

References: Peggy and Alan Bialosky, *The Teddy Bear Catalog*, Workman Publishing, 1984, revised edition; Shirley Conway and Jean Wilson, *Steiff Teddy Bears, Dolls, and Toys With Prices*, Wallace-Homestead, 1984; Margaret Fox Mandel, *Teddy Bears And Steiff Animals*, Collector Books, 1984.

Collectors' Club: Hobby Center Toys Steiff Club, 7856 Hill Avenue, Holland, OH 43528.

Additional Listings: Teddy Bears. See Stuffed Toys in *Warman's Americana & Collectibles* for more examples.

Pull Toy, horse, 20″ h, c1900, $575.00.

Bat, 4½″ h, 8″ wingspan, gray mohair body, plastic wings, felt ears, chrome button, orig tags, 1950s 400.00
Bear, 27″ l, iron and rubber wheel base, pull string growl box, orig button in ear 400.00
Cat, 7″, plush cotton, green glass eyes, orig red rayon bow, c1930 .... 100.00
Dog
  Boxer, 10 x 10″, brown mohair, leather collar, button, US Zone Germany, sgd "H O Steiff" 120.00
  Pug, 14″, white and chocolate brown mohair, spoked cast iron wheels, c1910 .... 275.00
  St Bernard, 9″ l, 6″ h, pewter ear button, wood wheels 320.00

Elephant, 17½″, black button eyes, pull cord sound box, four wood wheels, c1920 .... 275.00
Fish, 11″ l, mohair, open felt mouth, large eyes 85.00
Lion, 15″, plush, gold, brown glass eyes, white mane, four brass wheels, c1950 350.00
Monkey, 13″, brown mohair, fully jointed, straw stuffed, open-close mouth 175.00
Owl, 5½″ h, mohair, jointed head, green eyes, felt feet and wing tips 75.00
Pigeon, 9″ h, plush white felt tail and wings 100.00
Rabbit, 12½″ l, felt, orig metal tab in ear, wood wheels marked "Steiff/Made in Germany" 600.00
Reindeer, 9″, tan mohair, felt antlers, sewn nose and mouth, glass eyes, raised button, 1950s 225.00
Teddy Bear, 18″ h, gold mohair, straw stuffed, shoebutton eyes, button in ear, c1915 .... 2,100.00

STEINS

History: A stein is a mug especially made to hold beer or ale, ranging in size from the smaller ³⁄₁₀ liters and ¼ liters to the larger 1, 1½, 2, 3, 4, and 5 liters, and in rare cases to 8 liters. (A liter is 1.05 liquid quarts.)

Master steins or pouring steins hold 3 to 5 liters and are called krugs. Most steins are fitted with a metal hinged lid with thumblift. The earthenware character-type steins usually are German in origin.

References: Susan and Al Bagdade, *Warman's English & Continental Pottery & Porcelain, 1st Edition*, Warman Publishing Co., Inc., 1987; Major John L. Hairell, Ret, *Regimental Steins*, published by author, 1984; Gary Kirsner and Jim Gruhl, *The Stein Book*, Glentiques, Ltd., 1984; Dr. Eugene Manusov, *Encyclopedia of Character Steins*, Wallace-Homestead, 1976; Eugene V. Manusov and Mike Wald, *Character Steins: A Collector's Guide*, Cornwall Books, 1987; Mike Wald, *HR Steins*, SCI Publications, 1980.

Collectors' Club: Stein Collectors International, P.O. Box 463, Kingston, NJ 08528. *Prosit* (quarterly).

Additional Listings: See Mettlach.
Advisor: Ron Fox

Bisque, ½ L, satin, Bohne 330.00
Glass
  Blown
    ½ L, ruby stained, cut 200.00
    2 L, white opaline body, blue handle 175.00
  Mold Blown, ½ L, amber prism lid .. 90.00
  Pressed
    Enamel florals, ruby prism lid 125.00
    Occupation, wagon driver, inlay .. 100.00

Skull, ½ liter, Edward Boehm & Sons, beige, white, brown, and black, impressed "9136/2," $600.00.

Faience
<pre>
¾ L, floral, pewter handle, Bayrueth
    factory 130.00
1 L
  Blue green, Crailsheim factory, mid
    18th C 525.00
  Floral, South German, Mid 18th C   300.00
</pre>
Mettlach
Etched
<pre>
  ½ L, club, # 2090, sgd "Schlitt" . .   525.00
  ³⁄₁₀ L, dwarf in nest, #2134 . . . . .   520.00
  1 L, carnivalist, #2778, sgd
    "Schlitt" 1,100.00
Etched and glazed, 1 L, David and
    Goliath, #2718 . . . . 2,750.00
Relief, 1 L, Imperial eagle, wearing
    blue max medal, #2204 . . . .   740.00
</pre>
Pewter
½ L, relief
<pre>
  Hunter and game 90.00
  Young girls 75.00
</pre>
Porcelain, ½ L
<pre>
17 Inft Regt Germersheim 1909–11,
    rear roster four maneuver scenes,
    repaired tang 240.00
21 Pioneer Regt Mainz 1907–09, rear
    roster, two bridge building scenes   390.00
138 Inft Regt Dieuze 1911–13, rear
    roster, four maneuver scenes . . .   500.00
</pre>
Pottery, ½ L
<pre>
Chinaman 300.00
Bowling Pin, three bowling scenes .   240.00
Football, college flags with "P" 230.00
3 Eisenbahn Regt Berlin-Hanau
    1909–11, rear roster, bridge and
    train scenes, locomotive finial,
    guard star on thumblift 1,050.00
</pre>
Stoneware
Relief
<pre>
  ½ L, hunter and game animals . .   250.00
  1 L, tavern scene 110.00
L B & C, ½ L, scotsman 440.00
Westerwald, ³⁄₁₀ L, cobalt, applied re-
    lief bird dec, c1700 . . . .   390.00
</pre>

STEUBEN GLASS

History: Frederick Carder, an Englishman, and Thomas G. Hawkes of Corning, New York, established the Steuben Glass Works in 1904. In 1918 the Corning Glass Co. purchased the Steuben Company. Carder remained with the firm and designed many of the pieces bearing the Steuben mark. Probably the most widely recognized wares are "Aurene," "Verre De Soie," and "Rosaline," but many other types were produced.

The firm continues operating, producing glass of exceptional quality.

References: Paul Gardner, *The Glass of Frederick Carder,* Crown Publishers, 1971; Paul Perrot, Paul Gardner, and James S. Plaut, *Steuben: Seventy Years Of American Glassmaking,* Praeger Publishers, 1974.

Museum: The Corning Museum of Glass, Corning, NY.

Vase, 7½" h, green swirl pattern, clear glass, scalloped and rolled edge, sgd, $200.00.

ACID CUT BACK

<pre>
Bowl, 6", green jade cut to lighter green
    jade 750.00
Lamp, table
  24" h, black iris and leaves, bubble
    textured ground, black band at top
    and base, orig Roycroft hardware   425.00
  33" h, green, clusters of grapes,
    leaves, and trailing vines, brass
    acanthus leaf base, Greek theatri-
    cal mask finial 400.00
</pre>

Vase
8″, green jade cut to alabaster, Matzu
   pattern **1,000.00**
10½″ h, 9″ d, blue Aurene, black vintage cutting, sgd **2,300.00**

ANIMALS

Cat, 8¼″, modeled by Donald Pollard,
   restored **175.00**

AURENE

AURENE

Bowl, 6″ d, blue, sgd **375.00**
Candlesticks, pr, 10″, bluish gold,
   twisted stem, sgd **925.00**
Compote, 6″ h, blue, sgd **700.00**
Goblet, twisted stem, gold **250.00**
Lamp Shade, ribbed, 5½″ h, 2″ fitter,
   gold, sgd, pr **200.00**
Lamp, table, 27″ h, 6″ gold melon ribbed
   body, ormolu mounts, black marble
   base **525.00**
Lemonade, 6½″, gold, handle, circular
   foot **150.00**
Perfume, melon ribbed, gold **200.00**
Plate, 8½″, gold **75.00**
Salt, gold, sgd "#2611" **175.00**
Vase
2½″, classical shape, gold **350.00**
5″, urn, gold, sgd **375.00**
6½″, blue, sgd **425.00**
8½″, fan, greenish gold, opal vine and
   heart dec, sgd **1,300.00**
10″, stick, gold, blue highlights, sgd
   and numbered **260.00**
10¼″, flared, ftd, blue, silver paper
   label **725.00**
15″, trumpet, gold, sgd "Aurene 3844" **700.00**

CALCITE

Bowl, 12″ d, gold **400.00**
Compote, 7¾″ d, 8″ h, gold **400.00**
Finger Bowl, ribbed, matching under-
   plate, gold **185.00**
Parfait, gold, matching underplate ... **125.00**
Sherbert and underplate, gold **140.00**
Vase, 8″ h, trumpet, gold **400.00**

CINTRA

Bowl, blue, applied orange Cintra rim,
   sgd **585.00**
Champagne, opal **150.00**

CLUTHRA

Chalice, green shaded to white, random
   trapped air bubbles **125.00**

Urn, 6½″, pink, handles, sgd **650.00**
Vase
6″, pink **900.00**
6¼″, white, sgd "K, 1968-6" **175.00**
8″, white, random trapped air bubbles, shape no. 2683 .... **900.00**
8¼, Pomona green, random trapped
   air bubbles **650.00**

JADE

Bowl, 9½ x 3½″, light blue **375.00**
Candleholder, 11¾″, alabaster trim,
   unsgd **210.00**
Compote, 6″ d, 3½″ h, green bowl, ala-
   baster stem and base **110.00**
Iced Tea Glass, 6″ h, translucent white
   handle **125.00**
Parfait, yellow, alabaster stem **40.00**
Sherbet and Underplate, alabaster stem **85.00**
Vase, 8 x 9¼″, cone shape, diagonally
   ribbed, #6171, sgd **200.00**
Wine, 7¼″, alabaster twist stem **100.00**

MISCELLANEOUS

Bowl, 8½″ d, clear, bell shaped, molded
   foliage base, circular foot, modeled
   by James McNaughton, numbered, pr **500.00**
Compote, Pomona Green, 7″ h, twisted
   hollow stems, applied glass prunts, pr **300.00**
Lamp Shade, 3⅞ x 3⅝″, irid gold, green,
   and white feather pattern, random
   threading, pr **175.00**
Plate, 8½″ d, topaz, sgd, set of 6 .... **210.00**
Salad Bowl, 11″ d, modeled by George
   Thompson **275.00**
Vase
7½ x 10″, cased, brilliant cobalt blue,
   c1920, sgd **160.00**
7½ x 12″, Selenium, red, diagonally
   ribbed body, pedestal foot **275.00**
8½″, Tyrian, green shading to bluish
   purple, gold Aurene leaves and
   trailing vines, hooked gold Aurene
   and opal dec around collar **10,000.00**
9 x 10″, beaker form, flaring rim, brilliant cobalt blue, c1920, sgd **150.00**

ORIENTAL POPPY

Dessert Plate, 8½″ d **150.00**
Vase, 4½″ h **1,200.00**

ROSALINE

Bouillon Cup and Saucer, alabaster
   handles **125.00**
Compote, 8″, alabaster stem and foot . **275.00**
Cup and Saucer, alabaster handle ... **150.00**
Goblet, 6″, flaring rim **125.00**

Lamp Base, Matsu-No-Ke dec, orig	
hardware	**350.00**
Sherbet and Underplate	**150.00**
Underplate, 6″ d, pink	**60.00**
Vase	
6″, trumpet, alabaster pedestal foot .	**165.00**
9″, bud, alabaster foot, sgd	**285.00**

VERRE DE SOIE

Bowl, 8″ d, green threading, DQ int. . .	**150.00**
Perfume, 4″ h, wisteria pointed stopper	**275.00**
Vase	
3⅛″, wide horizontal rim, abstract	
ruby threading	**100.00**
10″, cylindrical, ring base	**75.00**

STEVENGRAPHS

History: Thomas Stevens of Coventry, England, first manufactured woven silk designs in 1854. His first bookmark was produced in 1862, followed by the first Stevengraphs, perhaps in 1874, but definitely in 1879 at the York Exhibition. The first "portrait" Stevengraphs (of Disraeli and Gladstone) were produced in 1886, and the first postcards incorporating the silk woven panels in 1903. Stevens offered many other items with silk panels, including valentines, fans, pin cushions, needle cases, etc.

Stevengraphs are miniature silk pictures, matted in cardboard, and usually having a trade announcement, or "label," affixed to the reverse. Thomas Stevens' name appears on the mat of the early Stevengraphs directly under the silk panel. Many of the later "portraits" and the larger silks (produced initially for calendars) have no identification on the front of the mat other than the phrase "woven in pure silk" and have no label on the back. Other companies, notably W. H. Grant of Coventry, copied this technique. Their efforts should not be confused with Stevengraphs.

American collectors favor the Stevengraphs of American interest, such as "Signing of the Declaration of Independence," "Columbus Leaving Spain," "Landing of Columbus." Sports related Stevengraphs such as "The First Innings" (baseball), and "The First Set" (tennis) are also popular, as well as portraits of Buffalo Bill, President and Mrs. Cleveland, George Washington, and President Harrison.

The bookmarks are longer than they are wide, have mitred corners at the bottom, and are finished with a tassel. Originally, Stevens' name was woven into the fold-over at the top of the silk, but soon the identification was woven into the fold-under mitred corners. Almost every Stevens bookmark has such identification, except the ones woven at the World's Columbian Exposition in Chicago, 1892–93.

Postcards with very fancy embossing around the aperture in the mount almost always have Stevens' name printed on them. Embossed cards from the "Ships" and "Hands Across The Sea" series generally are not printed with Stevens' name. The most popular postcard series in the United States are "Ships" and "Hands Across the Sea," the latter incorporating two crossed flags and two hands shaking. Seventeen flag combinations have been found, but only seven are common. Stevens produced silks that were used in the "Alpha" Publishing Co. cards. Many times the silks were the top or bottom half of regular bookmarks.

References: Geoffrey A. Godden, *Stevengraphs and Other Victorian Silk Pictures*, Associated University Presses, Inc., 1971; Chris Radley, *The Woven Silk Postcard*, privately printed, 1978; Austin Sprake, *The Price Guide to Stevengraphs*, The Antique Collectors' Club, Baron Publishing, 1972.

Collectors' Club: Stevengraph Collectors' Association, 20B Curtis Ave, Camden, ME 04843. Newsletter (quarterly).

Museum: Coventry, England.

Note: Prices are based on pieces in mint or close to mint condition.

Advisor: John High.

BOOKMARK

A Wish	**40.00**
Apostle's Creed, The	**65.00**
Babes in the Wood	**70.00**
Dickens, Charles	**100.00**
Happy May Thy Birthday Be	**60.00**
Home Sweet Home	**135.00**
I Love Little Pussy, 1874	**75.00**
Merry Christmas And A Happy New	
Year, pointed on both ends	**100.00**
Morning Hymn - Awake My Soul	**75.00**
New Year's Auld Lang Syne	**70.00**
Prince of Wales anthem, 1863	**100.00**
Shakespeare, triple	**150.00**
To A Dear Friend	**50.00**

Postcard, Shakespeare and views of Stratford, $50.00.

STEVENGRAPH

Buffalo Bill, Nate Salsbury, Indian Chief, orig mat and frame, 8 x 7"	500.00
Death of Nelson	200.00
Declaration of Independence	350.00
Finish, The	150.00
For Life or Death, fire engine rushing to burning house, orig mat and frame .	325.00
Good Old Days, The	200.00
H. M. Stanley, famous explorer	300.00
Kaiser Wilhelm II	325.00
Landing of Columbus, The	350.00
Last Lap, The	250.00
Park In Coventry, 7 x 13"	150.00
President Cleveland	350.00
Water Jump, The	175.00

STEVENS AND WILLIAMS

History: In 1824 Joseph Silvers and Joseph Stevens leased the Moor Lane Glass House at "Briar Lea Hill" (Brierly Hill), England, from the Honey-borne family. In 1847 William Stevens and Samuel Cox Williams took over, giving the firm its present name. In 1870 the firm moved to its Stourbridge plant. In the 1880s the firm employed such renowned glass artisans as Frederick C. Carder, John Northwood, other Northwood family members, James Hill, and Joshua Hodgetts.

Stevens and Williams made cameo glass. Hodgets developed a more commercial version using thinner-walled blanks, acid etching, and the engraving wheel. Hodgetts, an amateur botantist, was noted for his brilliant floral designs.

Other glass products and designs manufactured by Stevens and Williams include intaglio ware, Peach Bloom (a form of peachblow), moss agate, threaded ware, "jewell" ware, tapestry ware, and Silveria. Stevens and Williams made glass pieces covering the full range of late Victorian fashion.

After WWI the firm concentrated on refining the production of lead crystal and achieving new glass colors. In 1932 Keith Murray came to Stevens and Williams as a designer. His work stressed the pure nature of the glass form. Murray stayed with Stevens and Williams until WWII and later followed a career in architecture.

Reference: R.S. Williams-Thomas. *The Crystal Years,* Stevens and Williams Limited, England, Boerum Hill Books, 1983.

Additional Listings: Cameo Glass.

Basket, 5" d, 9" h, creamy opaque, applied green and amber ruffled leaves,

Chalice, 9⅛" h, clear sapphire blue ground, enameled flowers motif, acid cut signature "S & W," $165.00.

applied amber feet and handle, rose pink lining	350.00
Bonbon, 5½" d, 2¾" h, flared, clear, threaded rose, c1890, unsgd	45.00
Bowl, 6¾" d, 3¼" h, pink, mother-of-pearl satin Swirl pattern, cream lining, box pleated top	495.00
Cruet, 6¼" h, Rosaline, alabaster handle	300.00
Pitcher, 10½" h, applied amber feet and rim, green handle form green leaves and yellow flower, cranberry overlay, blue int.	595.00
Plate, 4¾" d, ruffled shell shape, pink to green mother-of-pearl satin Swirl pattern, cream underside	175.00
Rose Bowl	
3¾" d, 3½" h, cranberry opalescent, satin finish, alternate plain panels alternated with raised emb beaded panels, upright box pleated top . .	175.00
6" d, creamy opaque, applied pin, amber, and gold florals and leaves, eight crimp top, sgd	165.00
Sweetmeat Jar	
5 x 3", shiny finish, brick-red peachblow, raised gold bamboo stalks dec, bamboo motif gold finish collar, cov, and bail handle	865.00
6" h, 3½" d, cov, cream, opaque, three applied amber and green leaves, pink lining, SP rim, lid and handle	195.00
Tumbler, 3¼" d, 3¾" h, amber glass, applied amber pear and apple, green leaves, amber branch	225.00
Vase	
3½", cameo, three geese and palm trees, clear amber on frosted amber ground, sgd	275.00

5" h, pull-up dec, ivory, blue, and sienna, Northwood's, marked "Patent" on base **775.00**

6", gourd neck, MOP, lavender and rose swirl **350.00**

7¼ x 4¼", cream opaque ext., pink int., three large colored applied leaves, amber applied rigaree ... **115.00**

8" h, egg shape, pink overlay, three applied amber feet, three opal applied flowers **375.00**

STICKLEYS

History: There were several Stickley brothers: Albert, Gustav, Leopold, George, and John George. Gustav often is credited with creating the Mission style, a variant of the Arts and Crafts style. Gustav headed Craftsman Furniture, a New York firm, much of whose actual production took place near Syracuse. A characteristic of Gustav's furniture is exposed tenon ends. Gustav published *The Craftsman*, a magazine supporting his anti-machine points of view.

Originally Leopold and Gustav worked together. In 1902 Leopold and John George formed the L. and J. G. Stickley Furniture Company. This firm made Mission style furniture and cherry and maple early American style pieces.

George and Albert organized the Stickley Brothers Company, located in Grand Rapids, Michigan.

Reference: David M. Cathers, *Furniture Of The American Arts and Crafts Movement*, New American Library, 1981.

Book, 11 x 8¼", *Craftsman Homes,* 1909, orig buckram cov **185.00**

Bookcase

32¾ x 25 x 25", revolving, four sides, top with four tenons extending as legs, X stretcher **1,300.00**

55 x 29¾ x 12", single door, sixteen glass panes, four keyed through tenons on sides, orig medium to dark brown finish **2,500.00**

Candlesticks, 11½" h, copper, tapering sectioned stems, circular cup, two pc bobeche, orig liners, dark patina, paper label, pr **600.00**

Catalog, The Work of L. & J. G. Stickley, Fayetteville, NY, 9½ x 7¼" **75.00**

Chair

Arm, 32½ x 29", Mission Oak, four horizontal back slats, five vertical side slats, red decal Gustav Stickley mark **500.00**

Side, 36" h, Mission Oak, two horizontal back slats, orig sq leather seat, straight legs, orig finish, marked "L. & J. G. Stickley for Onodaga Shops," c1904, pr **850.00**

Chest of Drawers, 64 x 42 x 22", two short over two long drawers, large faceted wooden pulls, chamfered sides, toe board with inverted "V", mirror supported by tapering posts, iron faceted hardware, orig dark brown finish, large red decal **4,000.00**

Cigar Box, 8½ x 10 x 7", hammered copper, four exaggerated flared feet, riveted, rect top, arched handle, orig dark brown patina, die stamped mark **2,800.00**

Inkwell, 2½" h, hammered copper, hinged cov, riveted, orig patina, marked "Gustav Stickley" **150.00**

Jardiniere, 12" h, hammered copper, ruffled top, two handles, marked "G. Stickley" **500.00**

Magazine Stand, 47 x 29¾ x 12", broad slat on each side, five shelves with short gallery, orig medium to dark brown finish **800.00**

Mirror, 40 x 23", hall, four heavy hammered copper hooks, top rail with inverted "V", two long curved corbels, medium to dark brown finish, "L. & J. G. Stickley" label **1,800.00**

Rocking Chair, 33¼ x 25¾ x 28", "V" back, orig medium brown finish, orig leather seat, branded mark **600.00**

Settee, 29 x 76 x 32", eight broad back slats, three end slats, paper label .. **8,500.00**

Table

30 x 36", lamp, circular, stacked stretchers, orig medium brown finish, small box decal mark **2,000.00**

30 x 54 x 31½", library, corbels under two drawers, medial shelf, iron hardware, orig medium to dark brown finish, paper label **1,300.00**

Wall Sconces, hammered copper, long rect backplates, scrolled ends with forked copper straps, circular bobeches, orig dark dark brown patina, pr **900.00**

STIEGEL TYPE GLASS

History: Baron Henry Stiegel founded America's first flint glass factory at Manheim, Pennsylvania, in the 1760s. Although clear glass was the most common color made, amethyst, blue (cobalt), and fiery opalescent are found. Products included bottles, creamers, flasks, flips, perfumes, salts, tumblers, and whiskeys. Prosperity was short lived. Stiegel's extravagant living forced the factory to close.

It is very difficult to identify a Stiegel-made item. As a result the term "Stiegel type" is used to identify glass made at that time period in the same shapes and colors.

Enamel decorated ware also is attributed to Stiegel. True Stiegel pieces are rare. An overwhelming majority is of European origin.

Reference: Frederick W. Hunter, *Stiegel Glass*, 1950, available in Dover reprint.

Reproduction Alert: Beware of modern reproductions, especially in enamel wares.

Mug, 6⅛" h, enameled, center shield with carpenter's and blacksmith's tools, floral dec on sides, "Das ihre bare Huff and Wassen/Schmidt Hand werck 1790," $375.00.

ENAMELED

Bride's Bottle, clear, blown
  5⅛", enameled flowering plants, faint chemical deposit **150.00**
  6¾", enameled flowering plants and man with shoulder yoke, orig pewter collar **175.00**
  7", enameled flowering plants and dancing man playing French horn, orig pewter collar **175.00**
Flip, clear, blown
  3½", enameled flowers, berries, and running rabbit **325.00**
  3⅞", enameled flower and running deer **150.00**
Mug, 3¾", clear, blown, multicolored enameled berries, applied strap handle **225.00**

ENGRAVED

Flip, clear, blown
  5", engraved drapery around rim, blown panel molded **200.00**
  5⅛", engraved urn of flowers **150.00**
  6½", engraved elaborate border dec   **200.00**
  7½", engraved rim and squiggle dec, matching lid, blown panel molded   **575.00**
  7⅞", engraved tulips, c1770 . . . . . .   **350.00**
Mug, 6⅜", clear, blown, large engraved tulip plant, applied strap handle **250.00**
Nursing Bottle, 3⅜", blown half-post

type, clear, pontil, engraved bow and leaf dec **175.00**
Whiskey Tumbler, 3⅛", clear, blown, engraved sunburst with two birds **575.00**

OTHER

Bowl, blown mold, 3 x 2⅛", Expanded DQ, deep cobalt blue, applied foot .   **1,150.00**
Creamer, blown mold
  3⅜", Expanded DQ, sapphire blue, applied foot, c1770 . . . .   **750.00**
  3¾", Expanded DQ, deep cobalt blue, applied handle **1,150.00**
Salt, blown mold, Expanded DQ, cobalt blue, ftd **750.00**
Scent Bottle, 2¾" l, swirled, deep cobalt blue **150.00**

STONEWARE

History: Made from dense kaolin clay and commonly salt-glazed, stonewares were hand-thrown and high-fired to produce a simple, bold vitreous pottery. Stoneware crocks, jugs, and jars were produced for storage and utility purposes. This use dictated shape and design—solid, thick-walled forms with heavy rims, necks, and handles with little or no embellishment. When decorated, the designs were simple: brushed cobalt oxide, incised, slip trailed, stamped, or tooled.

Stoneware has been made for centuries. Early American settlers imported stoneware items at first. As English and European potteries refined their earthenware, colonists began to produce their own wares. Two major North American traditions emerged based only on the location or type of clay. North Jersey and parts of New York comprise the first area; the second was eastern Pennsylvania spreading westward and into Maryland, Virginia, and West Virginia. These two distinct locations, style of decoration, and shape are discernible factors in classifying and dating early stoneware.

By the late 18th century, stoneware was manufactured in all sections of the country. During the 19th century, this vigorous industry flourished until glass "fruit jars" appeared and the widespread use of refrigeration. By 1910, commercial production of salt-glazed stoneware came to an end.

References: Georgeanna H. Greer, *American Stoneware: The Art and Craft of Utilitarian Potters*, Schiffer Publishing, Ltd., 1981; Don and Carol Raycraft, *Country Stoneware And Pottery*, Collector Books, 1985.

Bank, 3¼", cobalt blue polka designs, dots, and "E D," tooled bands with applied leaves and stars, coin slot with incised design, made for Edward Dunaway, Greensboro, PA druggist .   **3,000.00**
Batter Pail
  Cowden & Wilcox, Harrisburg, front and back dec, 1 gallon **1,400.00**

Nichols Sipe & Co, Williamsport, PA, three steeple flowers, replaced ears, 2 gallon **525.00**

Bottle, blue band, 1 qt, marked "Hyde Park" **50.00**

Bowl, Geo. W. Miller, Strasburg, Va 1, 10 x 5¾", brushed blue rim design, hairline in bottom, rim chips **250.00**

Butter Churn

J. Burger Jr, Rochester, NY, cobalt blue flower perched on leaf dec, blue "4," molded handles, orig wood top **1,700.00**

I. M. Mead & Co, Portage Co, Ohio, 22¾" h, ovoid, brushed cobalt blue flower, imp label **275.00**

M. C. Webster & Son, Hartford," 13½", cobalt dec on molded handles, orig oak plunger, lid missing **200.00**

Jug, 17½" h, 4 gallon, double bird on flower, J Norton & Co, c1859–61, $800.00.

Canning Jar

N. Clark & Co, Lyons, 9½", ovoid, imp label **75.00**

A. P. Donaghho, Parkersburg, WV, stencil, 2 qt **35.00**

Unknown Maker, three blue bands, 1 qt **95.00**

Cooler

C. Crolius Manufacturer, New York, 15" h, keg shape, emb bands, cobalt blue highlight **325.00**

Unknown Maker, 11½" l, 8½" h, barrel shape, cobalt blue foliage dec and incised horse on each side, blue highlights, four feet **750.00**

Crock

D. F. & L. C. Brown, Colchester, CT, stenciled eagle and shield, blue highlighted name, wood lid, 3 gallon **150.00**

John Burger, Rochester, blue flower dec and "3," molded handles, imp signature, lid, 2 gallon **400.00**

J. Fisher & Co, Lyons, NY, blue open flower dec and "2," molded handles, imp signature, 2 gallon **200.00**

N. Clark & Co, Lyons, cobalt flowering plant dec, blue "4," molded handles with blue ends, imp mark, 4 gallon **400.00**

N. Clark Jr, Athens, NY, cobalt dragonfly dec, double handles, imp signature encircling "5," 5 gallon . **1,300.00**

T. Harrington, Lyons, blue multiple flower dec and "2," molded handles, imp signature, 2 gallon **250.00**

S. Hart, Fulton, 12" h, cobalt blue slip double birds with polka dots and "5," imp label, crack in back **175.00**

O. L. & A. K. Ballard, Burlington, VT, 15" h, ovoid shape, grapevine and two bunches of grapes dec, molded handles, imp "3," 3 gallon **1,650.00**

S. L. Pewtress, New Haven, CT, 8", cobalt blue quill work bird on branch, imp label with cobalt blue highlights, rim chip **275.00**

D. L. Ratcliff & Co, Wheeling, WV, 5¾", cobalt blue stenciled label .. **125.00**

T. F. Reppert, Greensboro, PA, cobalt blue stenciled dec, 4 gallon **125.00**

U Kendall's Factory, Cini, OH, 13", cobalt blue splashes, molded handles, several rim chips, vertical crack **150.00**

Unknown Maker

10", brushed cobalt blue dec, pecking chicken, imp "3," edge chips **250.00**

12½", cobalt floral and leaves dec, molded handles, 2 gallon **325.00**

White's Utica, cobalt turkey dec, heavy molded rim, molded handles, 5 gallon **1,500.00**

F. T. Wright & Son Stoneware, Taunton, MA, blue bunch of grapes dec, molded handles, imp signature, 1 gallon **160.00**

Cup and Saucer, "Dan E Mercer" on cup, "Greensboro Silver Cornet Band" on saucer, gray, brown brushed dec, cup handle glued **3,100.00**

Figure, cat 14¼", gray body, running olive-amber glaze, primitive detail, Albany slip int. **1,200.00**

Flower Pot

Coggle wheel work, blue bands, 1 qt, attributed to Whites, Utica **60.00**

Three large dec around sides, stamped "4," attributed to Fort Edward **275.00**

Jar

C. Crolius Manufactured, Manhattan-Wells, NY," 7½", ovoid, imp swags, single flower, and label, blue highlights, applied blue handles **1,150.00**

Hamilton & Jones, Greensboro, PA, Star Pottery, 7⅛", brushed cobalt blue lines, stenciled label **325.00**

I. M. Mead, Mogadore, OH, 14¼" h, ovoid, brushed cobalt blue flower and "3" **375.00**

J. M. Pruden, Manufacturer, Elizabeth, NJ, 2, 11¾" h, cobalt blue slip stylized floral design, imp label, rim and handle chips **150.00**

F. Stetzenmeyer and G. Goetzman, 11¾" h, ovoid, cobalt blue slip laurel wreath and "2," imp label **225.00**

Unknown Maker
9½", brushed cobalt blue scene of three figures, tooled lines, lip chip, 1 gallon **1,300.00**
13¾", ovoid, brushed cobalt blue tulip dec, imp shoulder band and reeded handles, 3 gallon **725.00**
17¾" h, ovoid, cobalt blue quill work flourish **95.00**

Jug
Clark and Fox, 12", cobalt blue stylized bird and slip date 1835 .... **300.00**

N. Clark & Co, Lyons, ovoid shape, blue flower with leaves dec and "2," imp signature, 2 gallon **175.00**

W. H. Farrar & Co, Geddes, NY, cobalt tulip dec, 2 gallon **400.00**

J. Fisher, Lyons NY, cobalt dragonfly dec and "2," imp signature, 2 gallon **175.00**

James Hamilton & Co, Greensboro, PA, 14½", ovoid, stenciled cobalt blue tavern scene, three men, one falling backwards, and "2" **4,100.00**

L. S. Hubbard & Co...Buffalo, NY, 10½", cobalt name, gallon **200.00**

C. J. Merrill, 13", ovoid, cobalt blue splash, 2 gallon **210.00**

New York Stoneware Co, Fort Edward, NY, cobalt flying eagle carrying banner dec, faint crack, 2 gallon **2,750.00**

J. & F. Norton, Bennington, VT, cobalt blue "I. W. C." initials and squiggle dec beneath, repaired handle, 1 gallon **150.00**

H. Purdy, OH, 2, 14¼" h, ovoid, brushed cobalt blue flower, gray salt glaze with golden highlights .. **500.00**

Unknown Maker
10¾", cobalt blue floral dec, "one" written on back, molded handles, 1 gallon **400.00**
13¼", cobalt dec on ends of handles, small circular design on front, 3 gallon **150.00**

A. O. Whittemore, Havana, NY, 2,

11¾", brushed cobalt blue floral design, imp label **250.00**

Keg, six blue lines encircle key, pine frame, marked "A. A. Co Pat applied for," 2 gallon **175.00**

Meat Tenderizer
Gray, cobalt blue trim, serrated ends, 4⅜" **725.00**
Oak handle, patent Dec 25, 1877 .. **160.00**

Milk Bowl
Sipe & Sons, Williamsport, PA, cobalt blue flower, 1½ gallon **285.00**
Unknown Maker, 12½", cobalt blue three petal flowers, pouring spout **225.00**

Miniature, jug, 2⅝", ovoid, strap handle, inscribed "Mrs S. G. Hazard, Taunton, MA" on front, c1835 .... **500.00**

Mug, coggle wheel design, blue bands
Marked "MAX-AMS" on bottom **30.00**
Rochester Brew Co, Rochester, NY adv, marked "No. 20" on bottom .. **75.00**

Pitcher
9¾" h, cobalt thistles dec, deeply incised name and address, "Josephine Scull, Smithville, NJ," minor age wear **4,000.00**
Dark Blue, ½ pt **225.00**
Light Blue
1 pt **310.00**
1 qt **345.00**

Salt, 2⅝ x 1⅝", cobalt blue dec, two rim chips **500.00**

Shaving Mug, 4⅝", brushed cobalt blue floral design, rim hairline **2,400.00**

Spittoon, M. Woodruff, Cortland, cobalt dec, "2," rim chip **425.00**

Syrup Jug, E. & L. P. Norton, Bennington, VT, Albany slip, 2 gallon **40.00**

Water Cooler, lid, Cupid **600.00**

STONEWARE, BLUE AND WHITE

History: Blue and white stoneware refers to molded, salt glazed, domestic, utilitarian earthenware with a blue glaze produced in the late 19th and early 20th centuries. Earlier stoneware was usually handthrown and either undecorated, hand decorated in Spencerian script floral and other motifs, or stenciled. The stoneware of the blue and white period is molded with a design impressed, embossed, stenciled, or printed.

Although known as blue and white, the base color is generally grayish in tone. The blue cobalt glaze may coat the entire piece, appear as a series of bands, or accent the decorative elements.

All types of household products were available in blue and white stoneware. Bowls, crocks, jars, pitchers, mugs, and salts are just a few examples. The ware reached its height between 1870 and 1890. The advent of glass jars, tin containers, and chilled transportation brought its end. The last blue and white stoneware was manufactured in the 1920s.

Reference: Kathyrn McNerney, *Blue & White Stoneware,* Collector Books, 1981.

Collectors' Club: Blue & White Pottery Club, P. O. Box 297, Center Point, IA 52213.

Reproduction Alert: A vast majority of the blue and white stoneware found in antiques shops and flea markets is unmarked reproductions from Rushville Pottery, Rushville, OH.

Spittoon, 7½″ d top, 5″ h, emb bows and stippling, $80.00.

Bowl
7″, Wildflower, stencil design, blue rim, underglaze rickrack bands top and bottom	65.00
10½″ d, feathers, double ring	100.00

Butter Crock, 6½″ d, 5½″ h, Swastika emblem, snap-in bail 140.00
Butter Dish, cov, Apple Blossom 250.00
Canister, cov
Oatmeal	275.00
Raisins	235.00

Cookie Jar, 9″ h, Turkey Eye, diffused bands, acorn finial 140.00
Cooler, 17″ h, 15″ d, polar bear dec, brass nickel plated spigot, finial lid . 500.00
Creamer
Arc and Leaf, paneled, 4½″ h	70.00
Cow	30.00

Custard Cup, 4″ d, 3½″ h, blue and orange brush dec, wide blue band ... 65.00
Match Holder, 5½″ d, 5″ h, Duck 65.00
Mixing Bowl, 7½″ d, Flying Bird 175.00
Mug
Basketweave and Flower, 5″ h, bulbous, rolled rim, rope handle	60.00
Flying Bird	125.00

Pie Plate, 10½″ d, blue on blue, raised grooved base 100.00
Pitcher
Cattail	140.00
Dutch Farm, 9″	175.00

Garden Rose 265.00
Roaster
12″ d, 8½″ h, Wildflower	110.00
19″ l, 9″ h, diffused blues, applied handles, flat finial	150.00

Rolling Pin, Wildflower, 7″ 250.00
Salt Crock, Butterfly, hanging 100.00
Shaving Mug, Bowtie and Roses 75.00
Soap Dish, Beaded Medallion with Rose, emb lines 120.00
Soup Bowl, 6½″ d, brush dec 150.00
Teapot, 9″ h, 6½″ d, Swirl, double wire bail, wood hand grip, relief split balls, lid with finial 350.00
Tobacco Jar, 6½″ h, 5″ d, deep blue, berry scrolls, "Duke of Monmouth" on one side, "M.C.C. Co." on other, cork lid vent, mushroom finial, ornate, dated "1905" on base 200.00
Toothbrush Holder, Rose and Fishscales 50.00
Umbrella Stand, 24″ h, 10″ d 250.00
Washbowl and Pitcher, Rose and Fishscales 250.00

STRETCH GLASS

History: Stretch glass was produced by many glass manufacturers in the United States between the early 1900s and the 1920s. The most prominent makers were Cambridge, Fenton (who probably manufactured more stretch glass than any of the others), Imperial, Northwood, and Steuben. Stretch glass can be identified by its iridescent, onionskin-like effect. Look for mold marks. Imported pieces are blown and show a pontil mark.

Reference: Berry Wiggins, *Stretch Glass,*, Antique Publications, n.d.

Dish, 6½″ w, 3″ h, peacock, scalloped at corners, Imperial, marked, $125.00.

Bon Bon, Florentine green, dolphin handle, Fenton 45.00
Bowl
   7½", sq, orange, Imperial 50.00
   8¾", rolled in, paneled 20.00
   9½", Treebark, ftd 22.00
   9¾", orange, ftd 48.00
   10", round, blue, sq ftd base, Northwood 32.00
Candlestick, 8½", vaseline, pr 70.00
Candy Dish, 9½", cov, pink 30.00
Compote
   9½" d, 5½" h, vaseline, bark patterned stem, sgd "Northwood" ... 135.00
   9", white 32.00
Plate
   6", octagonal, vaseline 10.00
   8", 14 panel, amberina 40.00
Shade, white 35.00
Sherbet, liner, vaseline 20.00
Vase
   5", white irid, fluted top 325.00
   6", hp florals and leaves, rolled rim, clear ribbed int. 30.00
   7", fan shape, vaseline 25.00

STRING HOLDERS

History: The string holder developed as a utilitarian tool to assist the merchant or manufacturer who needed tangle-free string or twine to tie packages. The early holders were made of cast iron, some patents dating to the 1860s.

When the string holder moved to the household, lighter and more attractive forms developed, many made of chalkware. The string holder remained a key kitchen element until the early 1950s.

Cream colored cat, red ball of string, plaster, $30.00.

Advertising
   Buster Brown, 15" h, diecut figures, cast iron base, tin windmill top ... 550.00
   Jaxon Soap, cast iron 65.00
   Red Goose Shoes, tin, hanging type 200.00

   "Use Handy Box French Shoe Blacking," hanging type, patented 1881 335.00
Bronze, grapevine pattern, green glass, Tiffany Studios 325.00
Ceramic
   Cat 10.00
   Rooster, Royal Bayreuth 225.00
Cast Iron
   Beehive, 6" h, 8" base, dated "Apr. 1865" 50.00
   Dutch Girl, hanging type 20.00
   Sphere, 8¼" h, comical woman's head with opening in mouth for string, ftd, old red paint 175.00
Chalkware
   Apple, berries 20.00
   Chef, figural, black and white 40.00
   Court Jester 35.00
   Old lady, sitting in rocking chair, ... 25.00
Glass, 4¼" h, 4¼" d, clear, applied blue rim and finial 80.00
Wood, teapot, chef decal 25.00

SUGAR SHAKERS

History: Sugar shakers, sugar castors, or muffineers all served the same purpose: to "sugar" muffins, scones, or toast. They are larger than salt and pepper shakers, were produced in a variety of materials, and were in vogue in the late Victorian era.

CHINA

Meissen, 6½", baluster, hp, multicolored floral spray, ozier band, pierced cov edged in puce, c1750, chip on finial 450.00
Schlegelmilch, R S Prussia, 4¾", luster finish, rose dec, scalloped base, red mark 235.00
Smith Bros, 6", opaque white, floral dec, SP top 75.00
Wedgwood, blue, white classical figures 48.00

Leaf Umbrella, cased blue, Northwood, $225.00.

GLASS

Amberina, 5¼", DQ, MOP, pewter top .	650.00
Cranberry, Coin Spot, orig top	125.00
Crown Milano, ribbed, wild rose dec ..	475.00
Cut Glass, 3¾", Block and Fan, stars, rayed base, SS chased top and rim	175.00
Duncan Miller, Late Block, ruby stained, c1890	200.00
Findlay, 5", pale blue, ribbed top, floral design base	450.00
Libbey, Maize, amber leaf dec	85.00
Milk Glass, 5⅞", white, yellow bands, pastel flowers, nickel plated brass top	45.00
Mount Washington, 3¼ x 4", egg shape, frosted clear glass, pastel pansies dec, metal top with prongs	585.00
Opalescent, Reverse Swirl, cranberry, Buckeye Glass	200.00
Pattern Glass	
Banded Portland, maiden's blush, orig top	120.00
Pineapple and Fan	25.00
Royal Oak, frosted crystal, orig top .	65.00
Snail, ruby stained, orig top	200.00
Rubena, Royal Ivy, orig top	110.00
Satin, 3¼", Fleurette pattern, pink, squatty, brass top	125.00

SWANSEA

History: This superb pottery and porcelain was made at Swansea (Glamorganshire, Wales) as early as the 1760s with production continuing until 1870.

Marks on Swansea vary. The earliest marks were SWANSEA impressed under glaze and DILL-WAN under glaze after 1805. CAMBRIAN POT-TERY was stamped in red under glaze from 1803-1805. Many fine examples, including the Botanical series in pearlware, are not marked, but may have the botanical name stamped under glaze.

Fine examples of Swansea often may show imperfections, such as firing cracks. These pieces are considered mint because they left the factory in this condition.

Reference: Susan and Al Bagdade, *Warman's English & Continental Pottery & Porcelain, 1st Edition,* Warman Publishing Co., Inc., 1987.

Reproduction Alert: Swansea porcelain has been copied for many decades in Europe and England. Marks should be studied carefully.

Cup and Saucer, 3⅝" cup, 6" saucer, floral dec, c1815	120.00
Dessert Tray, 9½", hp, creamware, gilding, polychrome, under glaze mark Swansea, c1780	275.00
Dish, 11", botanical series, c1805	325.00

Cup and Saucer, 3⅝" d cup, 6" d saucer, c1815, $120.00.

Plate	
7¾", hp, creamware, flowers, reticulated, marked "Dillwyn," c1805 ..	190.00
8½", center floral, molded foliate scroll rim	230.00
Punch Bowl, earthenware, Oriental dec, marked "Cambrian Pottery," c1803 .	1,000.00
Serving Dish	
8", sq, sweetpeas, botanical, c1805 .	175.00
11½", oblong, lily, pink, botanical, c1805	350.00

SWORDS

History: The first swords in America came from Europe. The chief cities for sword manufacturing were Solingen in Germany, Klingenthal in France, and Hounslow and Shotley Bridge in England. Among the American importers of these foreign blades was "Horstmann" whose mark is found on many military weapons.

New England and Philadelphia were the early centers for American sword manufacturing. By the Franco-Prussian War, the Ames Manufacturing Company of Chicopee, Massachusetts, was exporting American swords to Europe.

Sword collectors concentrate on a variety of styles: commission vs. non-commission officers' swords, presentation swords, naval weapons, and swords from a specific military branch such as cavalry or infantry. The type of sword helped identify a person's military rank and, depending on how he had it customized, his personality as well.

Following the invention of repeating firearms in the mid-19th century, the sword lost its functional importance as a combat weapon and became a military dress accessory. Condition is a key criterion determining value.

Reference: Harold L. Peterson, *The American Sword 1775–1945,* Ray Riling Arms Books Co, 1965.

AMERICAN

Artillery, Foot, sword, 1832, 25", Roman type short sword, brass eagle pom-

Civil War, Naval officer, made by Tiffany, New York City, 29" blade, engraved eagle, $325.00.

mel, "Ames Mfg Co, Chicopee, MA," leather scabbard 350.00
Artillery, sword, Model 1833,"N.P. AMES," 1835, brass hilt inspected "JM," "H.K.C.," and "ORD," orig brass mounted black leather scabbard 500.00
Cavalry, saber, Contract of 1812-1813, Starr, 33¾" wide curved blade deeply stamped "P/HHP/N. STARR" at obverse ricasso, iron stirrup hilt, black leather cov grip, orig japanned steel scabbard, slight repair to scabbard . 350.00
Cavalry, saber, Contract of 1816, Starr, cast iron hilt, wood grip with leather, "N. Starr and U.S./P/LS," iron japanned scabbard 300.00
Cavalry, saber, Model 1860, light, 30¾", brass half basket hilt, wood grip with leather and brass wire, iron scabbard 200.00
Cavalry, Saber, Model 1860, Deluxe, 41" overall, 35" blade, 21" etched pattern on both sides, obverse with foliage, an American eagle, a trophy of arms, and scrolls with "Ames Mfg. Co./Chicopee/-Mass" at ricasso, reverse with scrolls, a trophy of arms and "US" in script letters, gilt brass hilt with sharkskin wrapped grip cast with light relief work at the top of the pommel and rear of knuckle guard, bright finished steel scabbard 3,250.00
Fraternal, Ames, regular, 29½" blade, etched for 19", obverse with profuse foliage, "Charles S. Tanner," and a standing knight in armor and "Ames Sword Co./Chicopee, Mass.," gilt brass hilt with anchor on the langet over "HOPE," fitted with black grip with gilt cross, orig black leather scabbard with engraved gilt brass mounts, the throat with "IN HOC SIGNO/VINCES" with a snake and cross 45.00
Infantry, Officer, 1820-50, 35" brass hilt and Indian head pommel, mother of pearl or ivory grip with brass wire, black etched with eagle and military motif, brass scabbard 650.00

Musician's Sword, Model 1840, stamped at obverse ricasso "U.S./1863/F.S.S.," reverse stamped "C. ROBY W CHELMSFORD.MS," orig issue scabbard 400.00
Naval, Cutlass, 1841, 26¼", brass hilt and grip, half basket, guard, "N. P. Ames/Springfield" and "U.S.N./1843/RC," leather scabbard 600.00

EUROPEAN

Continental, Cavalry, saber, 38", 32½" slightly curved blade, iron hilt with two branches stamped "G.A./III," wooden grips covered with black leather, iron scabbard 200.00
English
  Naval, Officer, 35¼", 30" single edged blade with rounded back, etched "PROSSER/Maker To The/Queen & Royal Family, London," and with naval themes, brass hilt with large gilt brass guard with crown and naval anchor, lion's head pommel, sharkskin over wood grip 200.00
  Officer, saber, 30⅜", curved single edged 25¼" blade, brass hilt cast in one piece with lion's head pommel, black leather scabbard with brass mounts 175.00
French, Officer, saber, 40½", 35¼" slightly curved blade, obverse engraved and gilt dec against blued ground and marked "Gendarmerie du Roi," reverse with military motifs and Sun King emblem, blade sgd "Coulaux Freres Klingenthal," gilted brass hilt with three branches with relief floral work, pommel emb fleur-de-lis, black leather and wire grip, steel scabbard with gilted brass carrying ring mounts 800.00
Halbert Head, 24½" head, 42½" overall including orig straps for attaching to pole, pole partially broken and cut off just beyond end of straps, blade marked with large deep anchor shape maker's stamp 425.00

TEA CADDIES

History: Tea once was a precious commodity. Special boxes or caddies were used as containers to accomodate different teas, including a special cup for blending.

Around 1700 silver caddies appeared in England. Other materials, such as Sheffield plate, tin, wood, china, and pottery, also were used. Some tea caddies became very ornate.

4⅛ x 4⅝ x 5", rosewood, dome top, inlaid fruitwood on corners, brass hinges, one int. compartment, $500.00.

German Silver, 5" h, repousse design, jar covers 75.00

Ivory, 7½ x 8½ x 5", Dutch baroque style, domed lid, Hereid finial, single well, engraved Renaissance scenes panels, scrolling foliage borders, one panel sgd "Sumnuriva Ooado," 19th C 5,500.00

Maple, 6 x 12 x 6", oblong top inlaid in ebony lining, twin well and mixing cylinder int., Regency 225.00

Maple and Sycamore, 8 x 13 x 7½", cavetto molded lid, incanted case, partitioned int., Regency, 19th C ... 300.00

Rosewood, 8 x 13 x 7", canted lid, twin caddies, mixing well, gadrooned base, fluted bun feet, ornamented partie boulle work 400.00

Tole, reverse painted glass sides, brass cap 345.00

Tortoise Shell, 5½ x 7 x 4½", lozenge form cross section, slightly domed lid, twin canisters, ball feet 550.00

Veneer, 4½", high figured and tiger striped, edge inlay, hinged lid, inner lid, refinished 50.00

Walnut, 6 x 9 x 5", Georgian, oblong molded top, bombe case, three partitioned wells, mid 18th C 650.00

TEA LEAF IRONSTONE CHINA

History: Tea Leaf Ironstone china flowed into America from England in great quantities in the 1860 to 1910 period and graced the tables of working class America. It traveled to California and Texas in wagons and by boat down the Mississippi River to Kentucky and Missouri. It was too plain for the rich homes; its simplicity and strength appealed to wives forced to watch pennies. Tea Leaf found its way into the kitchen of Lincoln's Springfield home; sailors ate from it aboard the *Star of India*, now moored in San Diego and still displaying Tea Leaf.

Tea Leaf was not manufactured exclusively by English potters in Staffordshire, contrary to popular opinion. Although there were more than 30 English potters producing Tea Leaf, at least 21 American potters helped satisfy the demand. However, American potters perpetuated the myth by using backstamps bearing the English coat-of-arms and the marking "Warrented." The American housewife favored imported ware to that made by Americans.

Anthony Shaw (1850–1900) first registered the pattern in 1856 as Luster Band and Sprig. Edward Walley (1845–56) already was decorating ironstone with luster trefoil leaf, a detached bud, and trailing green vine. Walley's products are designated Pre-Tea Leaf and are sought by eclectic collectors. Other early variants include "Morning Glory" and "Pepper" by Elsmore & Forster(Foster) (1853–57) and "Teaberry" by Clementson Bros. (1832–1916). Clover leaf, cinquefoil, and pinwheel all may be found in a collection specializing in early ware.

The most prolific Tea Leaf makers were Anthony Shaw and Alfred Meakin (1875–). Johnson Bros. (1883–), Henry Burgess (1864–92) and Arthur J. Wilkinson (1897–), all of whom shipped much of their ware to America and followed close behind Shaw and Meakin.

Although most of the English Tea Leaf is copper luster, Powell & Bishop (1868–78) and their successors, Bishop & Stonier (1891–1936), worked exclusively in gold luster. Beautiful examples of gold luster by H. Burgess still are being found. Mellor, Taylor & Co. (1880–1904) used gold luster on their children's tea sets.

J. & E. Mayer, Beaver Falls, Pennsylvania, were English potters who immigrated to America and produced a large amount of copper luster Tea Leaf. The majority of the American potters decorated with gold luster, with no brown underglaze like that found under the copper luster.

East Liverpool, Ohio, potters such as Cartwright Bros. (1864–1924), East End Pottery (1894–1909), Knowles, Taylor & Knowles (1870–1934), and others decorated only in gold luster. Since no underglazing was used with the gold, much of it has been washed away.

By the 1900s Tea Leaf's popularity had waned. The sturdy ironstone did not disappear. It was stored in barns and relegated to attics and basements. Much of it was disposed in dumps, where one enterprising collector has dug up some beautiful pieces.

A frequent myth about Tea Leaf is that pieces marked "Wedgwood" are THE Wedgwood, Josiah. This is not true! Dealers and collectors who perpetuate this myth should be confronted. Enoch Wedgwood was the only potter of that name to produce Tea Leaf. Enoch Wedgwood's product is beautiful with large showy leaves. He deserves full credit for his work.

Reference: Annise Doring Heaivilin, *Grandma's Tea Leaf Ironstone*, Wallace-Homestead, 1981.

Collectors' Club: Tea Leaf Club International, P. O. Box 904, Mount Prospect, IL 60056. *Tea Leaf Reading* (bimonthly).

Museums: Lincoln Home, Springfield, IL; Sherman Davidson House, Newark OH; Ox Barn Museum, Aurora, OR.

Reproduction Alert: There are reproductions that are collectible, and there are *reproductions!* Avoid the latter. Collectible reproductions were made by Cumbow China Decorating Co. of Abington, Virginia, from 1932 to 1980. Wm. Adams & Sons, an old English firm, made reproduction Tea Leaf from 1960 to 1972. Red Cliff, who decorated Hall China blanks with Tea Leaf and clearly marked them, worked in the late 1960s and early 1970s.

Ruth Sayer started making Tea Leaf reproductions in 1981. Although her early pieces were not marked, all of it now is marked with a leaf and the initials "RS" on the bottom. In 1968 Blakeney Pottery, a Staffordshire firm, manufactured a poor quality reproduction of Meakin's Bamboo pattern and marked it "Victoria." It was distributed through a Pennsylvania antiques reproduction outlet.

Advisor: Julie Rich.

Cup and Saucer, 2¼" d cup, 5¾" d saucer, $55.00.

Baker, 4 x 6", open, Alfred Meakin	40.00
Bowl	
7", sq, Meakin	30.00
9½", round, Meakin	70.00
Brush Holder, 5¼", scalloped rim, Alfred Meakin	200.00
Butter Dish, cov, orig insert, 3 pc	
4½ x 5½", H Burgess	125.00
5⅜", sq, Wedgwood	120.00
Butter Pat	
Round, Alfred Meakin	12.00
Square, Wedgwood	12.00
Casserole, 8 x 10', cov, nut finial, marked "Rd April 7, 1856"	150.00
Chamber Pot, lid, Meakin	150.00

Child's Tea Set, Elsmore & Forster, teapot, creamer, sugar, waste bowl, six handleless cups, saucers, and plates, bellflower finials	1,000.00
Coffeepot	
Elsmore & Forster variant	100.00
Meakin, 6¾"	75.00
Compote, 9" d, rim foot, Meakin	175.00
Creamer and Sugar	
Alfred Meakin	175.00
Mellor, Taylor & Co	225.00
Cup Plate, 3¼", unmarked	38.00
Cup and Saucer	
Elsmore & Forster, Pepper Leaf variant	60.00
Thomas Furnival & Sons, deep saucer	75.00
A Shaw, handleless	110.00
Gravy Boat, 5½ x 9½" tray, Mellor, Taylor & Co	80.00
Mug, emb, Lily of the Valley, A Shaw	140.00
Nappy, 4¼", scalloped edge, fluted sides, Mellor, Taylor & Co	25.00
Pitcher	
East End Pottery, American, 7", milk	100.00
John Edwards, 5¼", feather design on sides, bulbous top	130.00
Thomas Furnival & Sons, 6", cream, rooster head pattern	115.00
Plate	
7", W H Grindley & Co	12.00
8½", Clementson	18.00
9", Meakin	10.00
9¾", Davenport	25.00
10", underglaze, copper luster, emb rim, Powell & Bishop	16.00
Platter	
8½ x 12¼", oval, Mellor, Taylor & Co	40.00
9½ x 13½", molded handles, Thomas Furnival & Sons	55.00
11", oval	50.00
14 x 10", Alfred Meakin	30.00
Relish	
4½ x 7½", Wedgwood	30.00
8½ x 4¾", A Meakin, bamboo style	20.00
Sauce Boat, Peerless	60.00
Sauce Tureen, cov, underplate, and ladle, cable style, A Shaw	300.00
Saucer, deep, Alfred Meakin	12.00
Soap Dish, lid, drainer, Wilkinson, AJ	165.00
Soup Tureen, lid, ladle, Powell & Bishop	250.00
Spoon Rest, 5¼ x 8¾", mitten shape, cable style, Thomas Furnival & Sons	45.00
Sugar, cov, Meakin	45.00
Teapot	
W Adams, Empress shape, c1960	110.00
Alfred Meakin, 7⅝" h, squatty shape, emb leafy floral design	185.00
Vegetable Dish	
Covered, rect	
Meakin, 9"	50.00
Wedgwood	100.00

Open, Anthony Shaw, round	20.00

Washbowl and Pitcher

Davenport, 14″ d, pink and copper luster	575.00
Wilkinson, AJ	250.00

Waste Bowl

Alfred Meakin	55.00
Wilkinson, AJ, straight sides	45.00

TEDDY BEARS

History: Originally thought of as "Teddy's Bears," the name comes from President Theodore Roosevelt. These stuffed toys are believed to have originated in Germany and in the United States during the 1902–03 period.

Most of the earliest Teddy Bears had humps on their backs, elongated muzzles, and jointed limbs. The fabric used was usually mohair; the eyes were either glass with pin backs or black shoe buttons. The stuffing was generally excelsior. Kapok (for softer bears) and wood-wool (for firmer bears) also were used as stuffing materials.

Quality older bears often had elongated limbs, sometimes with curved arms, oversize feet, and felt paws. Noses and mouths were black and embroidered onto fabric.

The earliest Teddy Bears are believed to have been made by the original Ideal Toy Corporation in America and a German company, Margarete Steiff, GmbH. Bears made in the early 1900s by other companies can be difficult to identify because they had a strong similarity in appearance and because most tags or labels were lost through childhood play.

Teddy Bears are rapidly increasing as collectibles and their prices are increasing proportionately. As in other fields, desirability should depend upon appeal, quality, uniqueness, and condition. One modern bear already has been firmly accepted as a valuable collectible among its antique counterparts: the Steiff Teddy put out in 1980 for the company's 100th anniversary. This is a reproduction of that company's first Teddy and has a special box, signed certificate, and numbered ear tag. Eleven thousand of these were sold worldwide.

References: Peggy and Alan Bialosky, *The Teddy Bear Catalog*, Workman Publishing, 1984, revised edition; Shirley Conway and Jean Wilson, *Steiff Teddy Bears, Dolls, and Toys With Prices*, Wallace-Homestead, 1984; Margaret Fox Mandel, *Teddy Bears And Steiff Animals*, Collector Books, 1984; Ted Menten, *The Teddy Bear Lovers Catalog*, Delilah Communications, Ltd., 1983; Patricia N. Schoolmaker, *A Collector's History Of the Teddy Bear*, Hobby House Press, Inc., 1981; Helen Sieverling (comp.) and Albert C. Revi (ed.), *The Teddy Bear And Friends Price Guide*, Hobby House Press, Inc., 1983.

Periodicals: *The Teddy Bear And Friends*, Hobby House Press, Inc., 900 Frederick Street, Cumberland, MD 21502. Subscription: $9.95; *The Teddy Bear News*, P. O. Box 8361, Prairie Village, KS 66208. Subscription: $15.00.

Collectors' Clubs: Good Bears Of The World, P. O. Box 8236, Honolulu, HI 96815. *Bear Tracks* (quarterly); Teddy Bear Boosters Club, P. O. Box 520, Stanton, CA 90680; Teddy Bear Collectors Club, P. O. Box 601, Harbor City, CA 90710.

15″, Gund, mohair, gold, jointed, felt paws, $200.00.

BEARS

4¾″, mohair, jointed limbs, tail moves head up and down and side to side, c1950	300.00
7¼″ h, mohair, beige, fully jointed, glass eyes, tag and ear button	80.00
8¾″ h, mohair, fully jointed, shoe button eyes, yellow sweater, early 1900s . .	150.00
9½″, wool, brown, jointed limbs, swivel head, straw stuffed, shoe button eyes, black sewn nose and mouth, felt paws, c1900	175.00
11″, mohair, tan, wired limbs, blonde plush ears, snout, and feet, open mouth glass eyes, felt pads, Germany, c1930	50.00
12″ h, mohair, fully jointed, glass eyes, long nose, wearing indigo uniform trimmed with red tape, England, early 1900s	225.00
13″ h, Petsy, button and tag	120.00
15″ h, mohair, yellow, excelsior stuffed, fully jointed, shoe button eyes, long nose, felt paws, pink vest, c1918 . .	275.00
15½″, mohair, cinnamon, excelsior stuffed, black button eyes, long arms, modified hump, Steiff, c1906	950.00
16¼″ h, jointed limbs and neck, button in ear	125.00

17", plush, brown, molded muzzle, squeaker tail, cream paws and ears, Ideal **60.00**
19", yellow plush, swivel joints, glass eyes with pupils, wide apart ears, protruding snout, back hump, c1910 .. **500.00**
24½", jointed limbs and neck, button in ear **300.00**
30" h, plush, hinged arms and legs, cloth pads, wide apart ears, glass eyes, long snout, hump back, button on neck, inscribed, early 1900s **550.00**

BEAR RELATED ITEMS

Muff, 14" h, mohair, light gold, quilted lining, glass eyes, black sewn nose . **350.00**
Perfume Bottle, 3¾", mohair, jointed limbs, removable head, black button eyes, black sewn nose and mouth, glass bottle **200.00**
Tea Set, child's, doll size, teapot, creamer, sugar, three cups and saucers, bicycling bears dec, Bavarian china . **75.00**

TELEPHONES

History: The deregulation of the nation's telephone industry and increasing interest in antique telephones has led to increasing values for old telephones and equipment.

Lovers' telegraphs and other crude sound operated and unpatented telephones existed prior to Alexander Graham Bell's 1876 patent. However, it is generally accepted that Bell invented the telephone powered by electricity.

The most valuable antique telephones come from the pre-1895 period and must be marked, dated, or easily documented. Instruments also must be unaltered and have all major original parts. Telephones marked Charles Williams, Jr., a Boston manufacturer whose factory was the "birthplace" of the infant Bell Telephone Company, are among the most valued.

Post 1895 telephones have value if modified or converted to be compatible with today's modern phone network. Conversions should be done by an expert who will supply additional parts without removing any of the major components to accomplish conversion.

Refinishing also requires expert skills. Do not remove original circuitry. Restoring nickel and black baked enamel finishes is most desirous. Buffing original parts to expose the brass beneath will make it difficult to distinguish those parts from the many dated and old fashioned marked, solid brass fake parts and whole telephones which have been flooding the market for a decade. No mass produced telephone made in the United States prior to 1950 was offered with a shiny brass finish!

Reference: R.H. Knappen, *History And Identification Of Old Telephones*, 2 volumes, published by author, 1978; R.H. Knappen, *Old Telephones Price Guide And Picture-Index To History Of Old Telephones*, published by author, 1981.

Collectors' Club: Telephone Collectors International, P.O. Box 700165, San Antonio, TX 78270.

Advisor: Dan Golden.

Automatic, Dialing Telephones
  Couch, S.H., Autophone **250.00**
  Globe Automatic, wall model **950.00**
  Lorimer Automatic, all models **1,500.00**
  Monson Automatic, wall model **1,200.00**
  National Automatic, wall model **1,500.00**
  Ness Automatic, wall model **700.00**
  Select-O-Phone **200.00**
  Strowger Patent
    Automatic Electric, candlestick model **1,200.00**
    Pre-1898 models **2,500.00**
    Wall Model, large **1,500.00**
    Wall Model, small **650.00**
Double Box Telephones
  48" l, tandem, any manufacturer ... **550.00**
  49 to 60" l, tandem two boxes **750.00**
  60 to 70" l, tandem two boxes **1,200.00**
  71" and longer **1,500.00**
  Oak, plain, Stromberg-Carlson type, c1899 .... **350.00**
  Unusual in any way, any manufacturer **450.00**

Candlestick, no dial, Western Electric, Patent in USA Jan 26, 1915, $95.00.

Fiddleback Telephones
  Gillian, American Bell, Blake or Charles Williams transmitter **1,000.00**
  Vought Berger, Kellogg, Western Electric, Stromberg-Carlson, Dean, Diamond, etc **275.00**
Pay Phones
  Common 1950s style **195.00**

Gray Pay Station
  Desk Model, wood, slots for coins
    up to dollar, marked **3,000.00**
  Wall Phone, wood **2,500.00**
  Wall Phone, 72″ **3,000.00**
  1920s style (Known as Laurel &
    Hardy style) **400.00**
  Pay Box, cast iron, small, c1910 . . . **150.00**
Single Box Wall Telephones, wood
Picture Frame Front
  Cathedral Top, lightning arrestors
    at top 300–400.00
  1910–15 . . . . **225.00**
  Plain Front, 1915–20 . . . . **200.00**
  Unusual style 450–600.00
Stands
  Gossip Benches, approx **70.00**
  Ornate, carvings **600.00**
  Plain, 1920s style **150.00**
Switchboards
  Hotel Annunciators 50–400.00
  Mansion Annunciators, depending on
    size and ornateness 75–450.00
  Pre-1894, wall mount, marked Amer-
    ican Bell-Blake, Gillian, Edison, Na-
    tional Bell, or Charles Williams . . **2,000.00**
  Pre-1910, wall mount **500.00**
  Pre-1935
    Light Bulbs **250.00**
    Transmitter broom **400.00**
  1935 to present . . . . **Surplus Value**
Telephone Booths
  1890s, leaded glass **2,000–3,500.00**
  1910 to 1912, single door **2,000.00**
  1914 to 1940, folding door
    Oak **1,200.00**
    Walnut **1,100.00**
Triple Box
  American Bell, Edison, Blake, Ber-
    liner on transmitter **1,700.00**
  American Electric, Kokomo **1,200.00**
  Bell Telephone **1,200.00**
  Chicago **950.00**
  Elliott **1,200.00**
  Gilliand **2,000.00**
  Keystone **900.00**
  Mianus **900.00**
  Molecular **1,400.00**
  Note: If any of these sets are missing
    the 7″ long exposed terminal re-
    ceiver, subtract $150.00.
Upright Desk Stands (Candlestick
Phones)
  Hour Glass or Potbelly shape **750.00**
  Oil Can shape **500.00**
  Straight Pipe, regular style
    Dial type **185.00**
    No dial **95.00**
    With magneto box **160.00**
  Notes: Extremely unusual candlestick phones
made of wood or in an outrageous style may be
worth in excess of $1,000.00. all phones mass

produced from the WWI to 1950 were made in
black. The Western Electric model is now being
reproduced in solid shiny brass.

TEPLITZ CHINA

History: Around 1900 twenty-six ceramic manufacturers were located in Teplitz, a town in the
Bohemian province of Czechoslovakia. Other potteries were located in the nearby town of Turn.
Wares from these factories were molded, cast, and
hand decorated. Most are in the Art Nouveau and
Art Deco styles. Most pieces do not carry a specific
manufacturer's mark. They are simply marked
"Teplitz," "Turn-Teplitz," and "Turn."

Reference: Susan and Al Bagdade, *Warman's
English & Continental Pottery & Porcelain, 1st Edition,* Warman Publishing Co., Inc., 1987.

Bowl, 5½″, girl pulling rooster's tail,
  marked "Stellmacher" **55.00**
Candlestick, 5¼″, figural, woman wear-
  ing flowing gown, marked **140.00**
Compote, 6″, Art Nouveau woman, high
  relief florals, marked "Amphora-Te-
  plitz" **400.00**
Dish, 7½″, couple seated on bench,
  handled **175.00**
Ewer
  7¼″ h, 5″ d, lavender and pink florals,
    gold outlining, branches, and
    leaves, burnished gold trim **110.00**
  9″, variegated purple poppies, bulbs,
    gold dec, cream ground, molded
    flowers, applied handle, marked
    "RS & K" **80.00**
  10″, applied white florals, narrow
    white neck, cobalt blue ground,
    gold trim, ornate handle **140.00**
Figure, 18½″, young woman, elaborate
  dress, sgd **450.00**
Loving Cup, 15 x 9¾″, reticulated outer
  wall, turquoise, amber, opal, and cobalt blue jewels, gold scalloped rim,
  foot, and twisted branch handles . . . **325.00**
Pitcher, 9½″, green and pink, lily pad
  dec, c1895 . . . . **190.00**
Vase
  4¾″ h, Sunbonnet baby dec, green
    ground **135.00**
  5″, bud, multicolored geometric dec,
    relief rooster head medallion, han-
    dled **90.00**

Vase, 15″ h, amphora-type, base of handle sgd "G. Klint," marked "Crown Oak Ware Teplitz/Austria, B. B. 3903," $350.00.

7½″ h, poppy design, blue glaze, four handles, pr	150.00
8¼″, gray, incised cavalier, triangular crimped rim, three rolled under handles, marked "Stellmacher"	140.00
10″, applied grapes and vines, sgd	140.00
15″ h, bulbous base, cobalt and light blue flowers, gold outlining, cream ground, two gold trimmed loop handles	265.00
18½″, lavender poppies and green leaves, creamy ivory ground, gold trim, crown mark	200.00
Window Box, 4¾ x 5 x 14¼″, yellow, purple, and lavender iris, Egyptian form mark	225.00

TERRA COTTA WARE

History: Terra cotta is ware made of a hard, semi-fired ceramic clay. The color of the pottery ranges from a light orange-brown to a deep brownish red. It is usually unglazed, but some pieces can be found partially glazed or decorated with slip designs, incised, or carved. Examples include utilitarian objects as well as statuettes and large architectural pieces. Fine early Chinese terra cotta pieces recently have brought substantial prices.

Bust

12″, woman's head, orange and yellow hair	100.00
16½″, young woman, marble socle, Louis XVI style	500.00

Figure

African, holding knees	100.00
Girl, 15″ h, playing mandolin, c1870	275.00

Jar, cov, straight sides, disc base, enameled geometric band on shoulder and domed cov	60.00
Match Holder, 9¼″, figural, colonial seated man, tricorn hat, polychrome blue vest, white shirt, brown pants, holding bucket, c1800	450.00
Model, lions, recumbent, wavy mane, open mouth, rect plinth, 13 x 19″, pr	1,550.00
Nodder, monkey, 3¾″ h, pink vest, high glaze	150.00

Figurine, 4½″ h, boy leaning on fence, Italian, $50.00.

Stein, applied caneware iris, c1800	85.00
Tobacco Jar, 10″, figural, man in long tailed coat, white vest, skull cap	165.00
Vase, 13″, gourd shape, black relief dragon, two handles	85.00

TEXTILES

History: Textiles are cloth or fabric items, especially anything woven or knitted. Those that survive usually represent the best since these were the objects that were used carefully and stored by the housewife.

Textiles are collected for many reasons—to study fabrics, understand the elegance of an historical period, and for decorative and modern use. The renewed interest in clothing has sparked a revived interest in textiles of all forms.

Reference: William C. Ketchum, Jr., *The Knopf Collectors' Guides to American Antiques, Quilts,* Alfred A. Knopf, Inc., 1982; Betty Ring, *Needlework: An Historical Survey,* Main Street Press, 1984 (revised edition); Helene Von Rosenstiel, *American Rugs And Carpets: From The Seventeenth Century To Modern Times,* William Morrow And Company, 1978; Carleton L. Safford and Robert Bishop, *America's Quilts And Coverlets,* Bonanza Books, 1985.

Collectors' Club: Costume Society of America, 330 West 42nd Street, Suite 1702, New York, NY 10036.

Additional Listings: Clothing, Linens, Quilts, and Samplers.

Bedspread
    Lace, 88 x 115″, Battenburg **700.00**
    Silk, 74 x 86″, embroidered, blue and
       white and white doves and floral pattern,
       deep blue ground, braided blue and
       white 5″ fringe, c1920 .... **225.00**
Blanket
    Homespun, 72 x 94″, wool, gold, blue,
       and brown, red cross stitch initials
       SF (Samuel Fry, PA) **200.00**
    Wool, white, embroidered with large
       house, two trees, red leaves, floral
       sprays, perched bluebird, side
       meandering floral border, sgd
       "Phebe," PA, 19th C **600.00**
    Bolster Cover, 20 x 51″, homespun, blue
       and white, button closure, embroi-
       dered red initials JR **300.00**
    Collage, fabric, gray, ivory and black silk
       and silk threads, Quaker woman in
       bonnet and shawl, husband with hat,
       sgd "R P Bye," early 20th C, pr ... **350.00**

Coverlet, jacquard, J. Lutz, E. Hempfield Township, For Rebecca Hershey, 1839, 99 x 77 with 4½″ fringe, $750.00.

Coverlet
    Jacquard
       One piece, 80″, red, blue, moss
          green, and beige, stylized tulips,
          grapes and vine border, orig
          fringe **350.00**
       Two pieces, 80 x 99″, red, green,
          blue, and beige, six hex sign type
          designs surrounded by pome-
          granates and florals, circular de-
          vices and floral border **425.00**

    Two pieces, 68 x 92″, red, ivory,
       and red, bird, tree, and floral mo-
       tif, Bucks County, PA, 1838 ... **725.00**
    Overshot, 88 x 98″, 3 pc, intricate op-
       tical pattern, indigo blue, onion skin
       brown, and natural **400.00**
Family Record, 17 x 17¼″, pink, white,
    green, and beige silk threads, loosely
    woven linen ground, Andrews and
    Anniss family names worked on
    eared vase, sprouting blossoms, bud
    and leaf border, needlework, Ameri-
    can, 19th C, framed, some discolor-
    ation and stains **950.00**
Picture, embroidered
    10½ x 6½″, beadwork, urn form floral
       motif, silk ground, English, early
       19th C **100.00**
    13½ x 9½″, silk threads, waterworks
       enclosed in classical gazebo,
       young woman playing lute in fore-
       ground, green, yellow, and gold silk
       and chenille trees, black oval glass
       mat, early 19th C, framed **600.00**
    19 x 24″, attributed by Samuel Fol-
       well, Philadelphia, green, gold,
       beige, yellow, and pale pink silk
       threads, painted silk ground, young
       maiden seated on rock, leafy clump
       of trees, flock of sheep at right, man
       driving herd of sheep in back-
       ground, bottom inscribed "She-
       pherdess of the Alps," late 18th C,
       framed **1,575.00**
    20½ x 27″, Samuel Folwell, Philadel-
       phia, gold, green, yellow, and rose
       silk and silk chenille, painted silk
       ground, elegantly dressed young
       maiden leaning over pedestal in-
       scribed "Sacred to friendship," two
       doves perched on top, garland of
       roses, two large weeping willow
       trees, thatched roof cottage, young
       girl playing with lamb, black oval
       eglomise mat with gilt border and
       flowers, early 19th C, framed **5,225.00**
Pillow Case, 20 x 35″, homespun, white,
    pieced calico star, woven and tied
    fringe, embroidered name and date,
    Susanna Hoch, 1884, pr **500.00**
Pocket, lady's, bleached linen pouch,
    embroidered flowers and blossom
    stars, red, yellow, green, and blue
    wool threads, green, red, and white
    printed cotton trim, initials MF in red
    cotton thread, PA, late 18th C **1,900.00**
Rug
    Braided, 30 x 38½″, rag, horse on
       hooked pale orange center, blue,
       red, and white striped ground ... **175.00**
    Hooked
       23 x 35″, American eagle in flight,

holding arrows, stars in background **385.00**

23 x 43", floral medallion of multicolored blossoms, gray ground reserved on black ground, dated 1945 .... **75.00**

41½ x 51", red, brown, black, gray, and white fabric, large horse prancing before brick wall, garden of spring flowers, American, late 19th or early 20th C **3,250.00**

Penny, 35¼ x 53", wool and flannel, concentric coins of green, brown, magenta, lavender, red, yellowgold, and black, linen backing, red and black scalloped border **825.00**

Sewn, 24½ x 37", yarn, light and dark brown, light olive green, blue, red, rose, and gray wool, dog with white forehead, wagging pink tongue, crescent moon and stars, blossoming rose and buds in background, American, 19th C **5,775.00**

Show Towel

17 x 53", homespun, cut work and fringe, red and blue embroidery of stylized flowers and birds, sgd "Ann Snavley, 1838" **1,100.00**

17 x 61½", homespun, cut work panel, red and blue embroidery of stylized pots and flowers, sgd "Elizabeth Binkley is my name, Manheim Township is my dwelling place. The Rose is red, the leves (sic) is green" **375.00**

19¼ x 55", homespun, fringe and narrow cut work, red and blue embroidery, stylized stars, flowers, dog, birds, sgd "Maria Burkholder, 1846" **500.00**

Tapestry

Brussels, 108 x 142", silk details, Demeter borrowing girdle of Aphrodite, rocky grotto with waterfall, detailed landscape with volcano in distance, Brussels Brabant signature and shield at bottom center, 17th C **18,000.00**

Franco-Flemish, 80 x 84", figural, coronation of young king kneeling in foreground while bishop anoints head **2,250.00**

French, 28 x 36", petit point and tapestry panel, mythical race between Atlanta and Hippomenes with golden apples **650.00**

Therom, watercolor stenciled on velvet, woven gold basket, peaches, plums, grapes, and melon, American, c1830, orig frame and wood stretchers **6,000.00**

Wall Hanging

11¾" d, stumpwork, young couple, cottage, beehive, and spinning wheel, sailing ship, English, early 18th C, orig circular frame **300.00**

13½ x 17½", stumpwork, green, blue, yellow, and rose silk and wool threads, silk ground, raised work, courtier and lady, large manor house, large blossoms border, recumbent lion and stag, chenille trees, English, late 17th C, framed **825.00**

THIMBLES

History: Thimbles often are thought of as common household sewing tools. Many are. However, others are miniature works of art, souvenirs of places, people, and events, or gadgets (thimbles with expanded uses as attached threaders, cutters, or magnets).

There were many thimble manufacturers in the United States prior to 1930. Before we became a "throw-away" society, hand sewing was a never ending chore for the housewife. Garments were mended and altered. When they were beyond repair, pieces were salvaged to make a patchwork quilt. Thimble manufacturers tried to create a new thimble to convince the home sewer that "one was not enough."

By the early 1930s only one manufacturer of gold and silver thimbles remained in business in the United States, The Simons Brothers Company of Philadelphia, which was founded by George Washington Simons in 1839. Simons Brothers thimbles from the 1904 St. Louis World's Fair and the 1893 Columbian Exposition are prized acquisitions for any collector. The Liberty Bell thimble, in the shape of the bell, is one of the most novel.

Today, the company, owned by Nelson Keyser, continues to produce silver and gold thimbles. The Simons Brothers Company designed a special thimble for Nancy Reagan as a gift for diplomats wives who visit the White House. The thimble has a picture of the White House and the initials, "N.D.R."

Thimbles have been produced in a variety of materials: gold, silver, steel, aluminum, brass, china, glass, vegetable ivory, ivory, bone, celluloid, plastics, leather, hard rubber, and silk. Common metal thimbles usually are bought by the intended user, who makes sure the size is a comfortable fit. Precious metal thimbles often were received as gifts. Many of these do not show signs of wear from constant use. This may result from ill fit of the thimble or from it simply being too elegant for mundane work.

During the 20th century thimbles were used as advertising promotions. It is not unusual to find a thimble that says, "You'll Never Get Stuck Using Our Product" or a political promotion stating, "Sew It Up—Vote for John Doe for Senator."

References: Helmut Greif, *Talks About Thimbles*, Fingerhutmuseum Creglingen, Germany,

1983 (English edition available from Dine-American, Wilmington, DE); Edwin F. Holmes, *A History Of Thimbles,* Cornwall Books, 1985; Myrtle Lundquist, *The Book Of A Thousand Thimbles,* Wallace-Homestead, 1970; Myrtle Lundquist, *Thimble Americana,* Wallace-Homestead, 1981; Myrtle Lundquist, *Thimble Treasury,* Wallace-Homestead, 1975; John von Heille, *Thimble Collectors Encyclopedia,* Wallace-Homestead, 1986; Estelle Zalkin, *Zalkin's Handbook of Thimbles & Sewing Implements, First Edition,* Warman Publishing Co., 1988.

Periodical: *Thimbletter,* 93 Walnut Hill Road, Newton Highlands, MA 02161.

Collectors' Club: Thimble Collectors International, P. O. Box 2311, Des Moines, IA 50310.

Advisors: Estelle Zalkin.

Reproduction Alert: Reproductions can be made by restrikes from an original die or cast from a mold made from an antique thimble. Many reproductions are sold as such and priced accordingly. Among the reproduced thimbles are a pre-revolution Russian enamel thimble and the Salem Witch thimble (the repro has no cap, and the seam is visible).

Left: French, blue enameled band inscribed "Prefitez du Temps," seed pearl rim, $550.00; right: enamel dec on gold, Middle East origin, $350.00.

Brass
Christmas bells and holly on band	30.00
Love token message on band	25.00

Dorcas
Daisey pattern	50.00
Engraved band	60.00
Gold, marked "9 ct, Steel Lined"	300.00
Star pattern	50.00

Enamel
Dutch scenes, blue, German, made by Gabler	75.00
Floral dec bands, American, early 20th C	50.00
Russian, pre-revolution	1,000.00

Gold
Cupid, three diamonds on band, made by Simons Brothers Company	425.00
Dome cap, unmarked, 16th C	300.00
High relief dec, alternating diamonds and rubies on band, Continental	350.00
Relief birds on bands, American, late 19th C, early 20th C	125.00
Scenic bands, American, 20th C	100.00

Porcelain
Belleek, Ireland	35.00
Hand painted, American, late 19th, early 20th C	50.00
Royal Crown Derby, English, modern	30.00
Royal Worcester, birds, English, sgd "William Powell," c1940	250.00

Silver
Engraved bands, American	35.00
Filigree, scent bottle and tape, English, c1830	1,000.00
Hand chased, India, 19th C	125.00
Ornate bands, Continental, 20th C	30.00
Scalloped rim, English, 19th C	60.00

Souvenir and Commemorative
Atlantic City, NJ	75.00
Betsy Ross, Bicentennial, enamel on silver, transfer print, Holland	60.00
Bunker Hill	125.00
Columbian Exposition, 1893, buildings on band	275.00
Florence, Italy, cathedral, enamel on silver, transfer print, semi-precious stone cap	100.00
Golden Gate Exposition, San Francisco, 1939	225.00
Hot Springs, VA, Ketcham and McDougall	100.00
Liberty Bell	60.00
Louisiana Purchase Exposition, St Louis, MO, 1904, gold	550.00
Queen Elizabeth Coronation, 1952	135.00
Statue of Liberty, made by Simons Brothers Company	20.00
St. Peter's, Rome, SS, English	60.00
Westminster Cathedral, enamel on silver, transfer prints, English, modern	35.00

Tortoiseshell
Gold inlaid dec, cap, and lining	300.00
Gold medallion and cap, Piercy's Patent	1,300.00

THREADED GLASS

History: Threaded glass is glass decorated with applied threads of glass. Before the English invention of a glass threading machine in 1876, threads were applied by hand. After this invention, threaded glass was produced in quantity by practically every major glass factory.

Threaded glass was revived by the art glass manufacturers, such as Durand and Steuben, and continues to be made today.

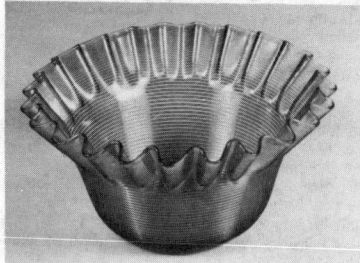

Finger Bowl, 5″ d, fluted edge, chartreuse, $65.00.

Atomizer, blue threads, red ground	**80.00**
Basket	
Cranberry, ruffled top, clear thorn handle	**150.00**
Rubena, 3½″ d, clear applied twisted handle	**120.00**
Bowl, white threads, clear ground, polished pontil	**30.00**
Cheese Dish, cov, 7½″, light blue opal threading on upper half of bell shaped dome, faceted knob	**115.00**
Epergne, 9½″ d, 15″ h, four orange to clear threaded vases, petal scalloped tops, clear branches, orange threaded base	**650.00**
Finger Bowl, 5″, fluted edge, chartreuse threads	**65.00**
Perfume, 5½″, blown, machine applied threads, Lutz type	**250.00**
Rose Bowl, 5 x 6¾″, cranberry threads, clear ground	**50.00**
Salt, 2¾ x 1½″, opaque white threads, cranberry ground, clear applied petal feet	**65.00**
Sugar Shaker, pink threads, clear ground	**75.00**
Syrup, 8″, pewter cov, handle, and base	**125.00**
Tumbler, 4¼″, aqua threads, clear ground	**200.00**
Vase	
5″, green threads, clear ground	**60.00**
6″, gold threads, irid blue ground	**300.00**
8½″, pink threads, clear ground	**125.00**

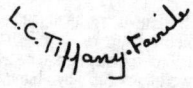

TIFFANY

History: Louis Comfort Tiffany (1849–1934) established a glass house in 1878 primarily to make stained glass windows. There he developed a unique type of colored iridescent glass called Favrile. His Favrile glass differed from other art glass in manufacture as it was a composition of colored glass worked together while hot. The essential characteristic is that ornamentation is found within the glass. Favrile was never further decorated. Different effects were achieved by varying the amount and position of colors which project movement in form and shape.

In 1890, in order to utilize surplus materials at the plant, Tiffany began to design and produce "small glass" such as iridescent glass lamp shades, vases, and stemware and tableware in the Art Nouveau manner.

Commercial production began in 1896. Most Tiffany wares are signed with the name L. C. Tiffany or the initials L.C.T. Some pieces also carry the word "Favrile" as well as a number. A number of other marks can be found, e.g., Tiffany Studios and Louis C. Tiffany Furnaces.

Louis Tiffany and the artists in his studio also are well known for the fine work in other areas—bronzes, pottery, jewelry, silver and enamels.

References: Victor Arwas, *Glass, Art Nouveau and Art Deco,* Rizzoli International Publications, Inc., 1977; *The Art Work of Louis C. Tiffany,* Apollo Books, 1987; Robert Koch, *Louis C. Tiffany, Rebel In Glass,* Crown Publishers, Inc., 1966; John A. Shuman III, *The Collector's Encyclopedia of American Art Glass,* Collector Books, 1988.

Note: All glass is of the Favrile type unless otherwise noted.

BRONZE

Alarm Clock, travel, 8 day, brown leather case	**150.00**
Candlestick, 14″ h, two arm, tapering cylindrical standard with two wide C-scroll arms, bulbous candle cups of green Favrile glass, center teardrop finial with snuffer and chain, irregular circular base, imp "Tiffany Studios/New York/10080," c1899	**2,750.00**
Desk Set, gilt-bronze, Venetian pattern, rocker blotter, letter rack, pen brush, matchstand, pen tray, letter opener, memo pad holder, cov double inkwell, four blotter corners	**2,750.00**
Lamp Base, 28¼″ h, Indian type, cylindrical standard, flattened circular base cast with geometric pattern of nail heads, green-brown patina, imp "Tiffany Studios/New York/539"	**4,000.00**
Ornament, 9¾″ l, bronze framework, Favrile glass, orig bronze chains, dragonfly, wings spread, wintergreen body, red cabochon eyes, striated green and opalescent filigreed wings, green, amber, and opalescent striated ground, c1899	**3,100.00**
Stamp Box, 4½″ l, gilt bronze, Favrile	

glass mosaic dec, rect, two amber irid scarab beetles on cov, gilt bronze legs and center orb, azure, silvery-blue irid, sea green, irid mustard, sienna, and amber brickwork patterned ground, int. cast with two stamp holders, imp "Tiffany Studios/New York," c1899 . . . . **16,500.00**

Vase, gold irid, two scrolling handles, circular base, sgd "1067-9673 L, L. C. Tiffany, Favrile," $775.00.

GLASS

Bowl
3½ x 2½", bluish gold, dec, sgd "L. C. T." **275.00**
10¼", irid blue, opal pastel, sgd "L. C. T. Favrile" **350.00**
12 x 3½", gold irid, stretched flared edge, intaglio cut butterfly, orig Tiffany foil label, sgd "Tiffany Favrile 1925" **1,115.00**
Candlesticks, pr, 4" h, irid blue, luster, pc of orig paper label, numbered and sgd "L. C. T. Favrile" **600.00**
Cologne, 5¾", mustard gold, abstract feather pattern on shoulder, orig stopper, sgd **650.00**
Compote, 3½" h, gold irid, hollow flared stem, sgd **200.00**
Cup and Saucer, gold, shell and rickrack dec, ornate handle **525.00**
Finger Bowl, matching underplate, gold irid **275.00**
Lamp Base, Favrile, vines and heart design, marked "L. C. Tiffany" **2,450.00**
Tile, 6" sq, irid blue, brass mounts, sgd "Louis C. Tiffany Furnaces Inc., Favrile 551" **125.00**
Vase
4¾", flower form, greenish blue pulled

feather, opal and gold stretch border, pedestal base, sgd "L. C. T. 5320B" **1,300.00**
10", trumpet, ribbed, gold, pedestal base, sgd "L. C. Tiffany," orig paper label **700.00**
10½", flower form, ruffled top, delicate stem, ribbed pedestal base, bluish gold, sgd "L. C. T." **1,550.00**

LAMPS

Candlestick, 17¼" h, gilt-bronze, flattened drip pan, urn form nozzle, standard cast with acanthus leaves, filigree conical shade with grapevine pattern over dusty rose glass liners, shade and base imp "Tiffany Studios/New York," c1920, pr **2,875.00**
Chandelier, 29" d, sharply conical shade, allover dec of full-blown blossoms and buds, mottled pastel golden yellow, dusty rose, pink, striated apricot and multicolored opal flowers, emerald and olive-green leaves, opal, shaded green, and sienna confetti glass ground, beaded edge, imp "Tiffany Studios/New York," c1899 . . . . **20,000.00**
Floor, 63" h, 22¼" d domical Favrile glass shade, striated and mottled golden yellow, ochre, and mustard tulip blossoms, emerald, olive, and spring green leaves, green and opal ground, cylindrical bronze standard ending in elongated petals on circular base, four petal form feet, bronze finial, shade imp "Tiffany Studios NY 1548," base imp "Tiffany Studios/New York/25390," and Tiffany Glass and Decorating Company monogram **44,000.00**
Piano, 11½" h, 6¾" d domical amber irid shade molded with two rows, pivoting on harp form gilt-bronze support, domed circular base, shade inscribed "L.C.T.," base imp "Tiffany Studios/New York/418," c1899 . . . . **4,000.00**
Table
25" h, 18" d Lemon Leaf shade, bronze turtle back base, sgd "Tiffany Studios, New York" **12,500.00**
26" h, 20" d shade, long stemmed green daffodils, sgd "Tiffany Studios, New York," bronze base . . . **19,000.00**

SILVER

Asparagus Dish, 13¾" l, rect, undulating sides, florence scroll rims, pierced cartouches topped by flower sprays, four leaf and paw feet, mono-

grammed, removable liner, c1891, 38 ozs, 10 dwts **1,900.00**
Centerpiece, 13¾" l, fluted fan shape, pierced formal foliage above cast band of chrysanthemums and leaves, four paw feet with acanthus foliage, c1902–07, 35 ozs, 10 dwts **2,000.00**
Nut Dish, shell shape, ftd
  2¾ x 2" **50.00**
  5 x 4½", monogrammed, ball feet .. **85.00**
Picture Frame, 4 x 5½" **150.00**
Scent Flask, 3⅜" l, Japanese style, flattened oval, chased and applied silver and copper, trailing wisteria, two applied gold butterflies, ladybug applied to screw on cap, c1873–91, 2 ozs .. **900.00**
Soup Ladle, Chrysanthemum pattern, 10¾" l, swirl fluted oval bowl, relief chrysanthemum leaves and bud on handle, monogrammed, c1880, 11 ozs **900.00**
Talcum Powder Shaker, 2", 2 pcs .. **65.00**
Tea and Coffee Set, partial, 12⅜" h teapot, hot water jug, creamer, waste bowl, kettle on lampstand, paneled bombé bodies, monograms, chased necks with strapwork enclosing husks and flowerheads, c1907, 119 ozs .. **1,600.00**
Tray, 11" d, circular, Chrysanthemum pattern, applied flowers and garland border, engraved center, c1891 .... **1,350.00**

TIFFIN GLASS

History: A. J. Beatty & Sons built a glass manufacturing plant in Tiffin, Ohio, in 1888. On January 1, 1892, the firm joined the U. S. Glass Co. and was known as factory "R". Quality and production at this factory were very high and resulted in fine depression era glass. Beginning in 1916 wares were marked with a paper label. From 1923 to 1936, Tiffin produced a line of black glassware, called Black Satin. The company discontinued operation in 1980.

References: Fred Bickenheuser, *Tiffin Glassmasters, Book I*, Glassmasters Publications, 1979; *Tiffin Glassmasters, Book II*, Glassmasters Publications, 1981; Fred W. Bickenheuser, *Tiffin Glassmasters, Book III*, Glassmasters Publications, 1985.

Bonbon, Fontaine, pink, 3 ftd **45.00**
Bouillon Cup and Saucer, Fontaine, green **60.00**
Bowl, June Night, crimped, 9½" **40.00**
Champagne
  Cherokee Rose **18.00**
  Flanders, pink **25.00**
  Fontaine, pink **30.00**
  June Night **14.00**

Lemonade Set, pitcher, four cups, green, threaded, black handle, $100.00

Claret
  Cherokee Rose **32.50**
  June Night **32.50**
Cocktail
  Fontaine, pink **18.00**
  La Fleur, yellow **24.00**
Cordial
  Flanders, pink **55.00**
  Persian Pheasant, crystal **55.00**
Creamer, Cerise, crystal, ftd **25.00**
Cup and Saucer
  Flanders, ftd **35.00**
  Rosalind, yellow **35.00**
Goblet
  Cerise, crystal, water **22.50**
  Cherokee Rose **24.00**
  June Night, gold trim **22.00**
Iced Tea Tumbler, Flanders, yellow .. **24.00**
Mayonnaise Set, June Night, 3 pcs .. **45.00**
Oyster Cocktail, Fontaine, pink **20.00**
Parfait
  Flying Nun, green **40.00**
  June Night **35.00**
Pitcher
  Flying Nun, green, cov **475.00**
  Fontaine, pink, ftd **300.00**
Plate
  Byzantine, dinner, crystal, 10½" .. **35.00**
  Empire Twilight, 8" **17.50**
  Flanders, dinner, crystal, 10½" **35.00**
  Rosalind, dinner, yellow, 10½" **35.00**
  Wisteria, pink, 8" **16.00**
Relish, Rambling Rose, crystal, 3 part **17.50**
Salad Bowl, June Night, 10" **42.00**
Salt and Pepper Shakers, pr, Cerise, crystal **75.00**
Sherry, Persian Pheasant **14.00**
Sugar, cov
  Cherokee Rose **16.00**
  Flying Nun, green **65.00**
  Rambling Rose **10.00**
Vase
  Cerise, bud, 10½" **25.00**
  Fuchsia, beaded, crystal, 11" **65.00**
Wine
  Fontaine, green **40.00**
  Persian Pheasant, crystal **35.00**

TILES

History: The use of decorated tiles peaked during the latter part of the 19th century. Over one hundred companies in England alone were producing tiles by 1880. By 1890 companies had opened in Belgium, France, Australia, Germany, and the United States.

Tiles were not limited to adorning fireplaces. Many were installed into furniture, such as washstands, hall stands, and folding screens. Since tiles were easily cleaned and, hence, hygienic, they readily were used on the floors and walls of entry halls, hospitals, butcher shops, or any place where sanitation was a concern. Many public buildings and subways also employed tiles to add interest and beauty.

Condition is an important fact in determining price. A cracked, badly scuffed and scratched, or heavily chipped tile has very little value. Slight chipping around the outer edges of a tile is, at times, considered acceptable by collectors, especially if these chips can be covered by a frame.

It is not uncommon for the highly glazed surface of some tiles to have become crazed. Crazing is not considered a deterent so long as it does not detract from the overall appearance of the tile.

References: J. & B. Austwick, *The Decorated Tile,* Pitman House Ltd., 1980; Susan and Al Bagdade, *Warman's English & Continental Pottery & Porcelain, 1st Edition,* Warman Publishing Co., Inc., 1987; Julian Barnard, *Victorian Ceramic Tiles,* N. Y. Graphic Society Ltd., 1972; Terence A. Lockett, *Collecting Victorian Tiles,* Antique Collectors Club, 1979; Hans Van Lemmen, *Tiles: A Collectors' Guide,* Seven Hills Books, 1985.

Collectors' Club: Tile & Architectural Ceramics Society, Ironbridge Gorge Museum, Ironbridge, Telford, Shropshire, England TF8 7AW.

Wedgwood, 3⅜ x 4¾″, King's Chapel, Boston, light brown, 1898 calendar on back marked "Jones, McDuffie & Stratton Co., Pottery Merchants, Boston, USA," $200.00.

American Encaustic Tile Co, Zanesville, OH
3″ sq, portrait of President Wm Mc-Kinley, blue glazed intaglio, 1896, biography pasted on back 120.00
4″ sq, Oriental junk, pagoda in background 25.00
6″ sq
  Fortune And The Boy, transfer printed, polychrome 75.00
  The Lion In Love, transfer printed, polychrome 85.00
18 x 6″, hunting dogs, high relief, sponged pale aqua and honey brown glossy glaze 250.00
Batchelder, 4″ sq
  Hunter and dog in woods, bas relief, reddish brown clay, high gloss light blue rubbed into background 80.00
  Landscape of trees, water, and bridge, deeply imp, red clay, light chalky blue brushed into recessed areas 75.00
Beaver Falls, 6″, large standing squirrel, incised and outlined in black, squirrel and border in medium blue, kelly green ground, marked 60.00
California Art, 5½″, scenic, relief, natural colors 18.00
Cambridge Art Tile Co, Covington, KY, 18 x 6″, classical female figures in sheer drapery, Night and Morning, pr 475.00
Claycraft, CA, 35 x 23½″ 24 tile frieze, articulated scene of dirt road winding towards stone bridge, grove of fir and maple trees, Cottswald type cottage, molded wooden frame 2,100.00
Corn Bros, 6″, Art Nouveau leaves, light green and white, dark green ground 45.00
Delft, 5″ sq, purple and white, scenes, five houses, single boat, set of six .. 270.00
William DeMorgan, 6″ sq, hedgehog, ruby luster glaze 400.00
Grueby
  4½″ sq, landscape, trees, stream and mountain, green, blue, yellow, and brown, orig condition, marked "Architectural" 600.00
  6 x 6¼″, white trotting horses, green grass, light blue sky, sgd "KC" on back 375.00
  8″ sq, mocha brown galleon, billowing white sails, choppy powder blue sea, medium blue sky, black wood frame, sgd "EH," partial black stamp 850.00
J. & J. G. Low, Chelsea, MA
  4″, bearded man, laurel wreath, green gloss 150.00
  6 x 5″, cupid on flying bird, olive gloss, 1883 .... 175.00
  6″ sq, boy reading book, high gloss

amber glaze, back sgd, artist sgd "Arthur Osborne," on front obscured by glaze, c1881 .... **200.00**
6 x 8", President Grant, emb, amber **125.00**
7 x 7¾", flowers, brown shaded to amber **40.00**
Minton China Works, 6" sq, transfer printed
Adam and Eve driven out of Eden, blue, cream ground **30.00**
Alfred, black on white, from "Early English History" series by J Moyr Smith **50.00**
Farmyard scene, sheep, brown on white, sgd "W Wise," 1879 ..... **80.00**
Hancock House, brown on white ... **30.00**
Interstate Industrial Expo, Chicago, 1880 .... **50.00**
Romeo and Juliet, sepia **30.00**
Moravian Pottery & Tile Works, Doylestown, PA
4" sq, Aladdin Lamp **40.00**
7¼ x 4", Knight in armor, on horseback, ochre and blue **60.00**
Mosaic Tile Co., Zanesville, OH
4" sq, German Shepherd dec, 4" sq **115.00**
6" sq,
Hercules, Walter Crane **100.00**
Little Bo Peep, blue, tan, and cream, Walter Crane **100.00**
Pardee
3½", Alice in Wonderland, rabbit, hexagonal **110.00**
4", houses and trees, matte glaze, brown and green, 1910 .... **225.00**
Pewabic Pottery, Detroit, MI
2¾" sq, bird of paradise, gray-taupe bird, cranberry red ground, high luster finish **60.00**
3" sq, Detroit Skyline, round, emb, brown on blue **70.00**
Richards, H., 6", Art Nouveau flower, tube lined, red and green, cream ground **75.00**
Robertson, Los Angeles, 8" sq, scenic, cloisonne dec, winding brown road through rolling green hills, fortress .. **1,300.00**
Trenton Tile Co., Trenton, NJ
4¼" sq, portrait of woman, brown glaze **60.00**
6"
Flower, tan glossy glaze **20.00**
Portrait of gentleman, classical, emb, amber, sgd "Issac Broome" **150.00**
U. S. Encaustic Tile Works, Indianapolis, IN
6" sq, girl with bundle of sticks, emb, amber **85.00**
18 x 6", Dawn, woman, emb, green glaze **175.00**

Unmarked
4¼" sq, flowers, high relief, glossy dark green **40.00**
6" sq, Victorian, water lily, shaded brown painted flowers, off white ground **50.00**
23½ x 23¾", architectural, sailing ship in relief, round top, sq base, brown and green, suspended from brass chain **100.00**
Wedgwood
6" sq
December, brown transfer of boy with mistletoe in hand approaching girl, imp "Josiah Wedgwood & Sons, England" **65.00**
Moth from Midsummer's Night Dream, blue transfer, white ground **100.00**
Red Riding Hood and wolf, black transfer, white ground, Crane design **110.00**
8", hunting dog and bird, brown transfer, white ground **100.00**
Wheatley, 4", good luck symbol **48.00**

TINWARE

History: Beginning in the 1700s many utilitarian household objects were made of tin. Tin is nontoxic, rust resistant, and fairly durable, so it can be used for storing food. It often was plated to iron to provide strength. Because it was cheap, tinware and tin plated wares were in the price range of most people.

An early center of tinware manufacture in the United States was Berlin, Connecticut. Almost every small town and hamlet had its own tinsmith, tinner, or whitesmith. Tinsmiths used patterns from which to make items. They cut out the pieces, hammered and shaped them, and soldered the parts. If a piece was used with heat, a copper bottom was added because of the low melting point of tin. The Industrial Revolution brought about machine made, mass produced tinware pieces. The hand made era ended by the late 19th century.

This category is a catchall for tin objects which do not fit into other categories in our book.

Additional Listings: Advertising, Kitchen Collectibles, Lanterns, Lamps and Lighting, and Tinware: Decorated.

Arm Chair, bowback Windsor style, white paint, gold trim **525.00**
Battle Axe, 21 x 12", whimsey **135.00**
Candle Tray, 9¼ x 19 x 12¾", rect, formed strap handle, holds 24 candles **650.00**
Candelabra, 12 x 7", three holders,

Dipper, 12½″ l handle, 6″ d bowl, $40.00.

mounted on scrolled arms in ascending order, pr	550.00
Centerpiece, 14½″, whimsey, tiered, traces of green paint	175.00
Chamberstick, 10½ x 9⅝″, whimsey	350.00
Coffee Grinder, tin, hanging, Parker	45.00
Cookie Cutter	
Father Christmas, sack on back	180.00
Flower Basket	40.00
Goose, flying	45.00
Heart and Hand	500.00
Horse, 6½″ l, large	140.00
Fan, 18¾ x 13¼″, whimsey, PA, c1850	725.00
Lamp	
Oil, 6¾″ h, saucer base, traces of gold and silver paint, Kinnear Patent	135.00
Skater, 6½″ h, clear pressed globe, marked "Perko Wonder Junior"	70.00
Lantern, 5¼″ h, octagonal, bail, Christmas light style, clear glass	50.00
Miniature, whimsey	
Cradle, 6½ x 10 x 6½″, crimped dec, sgd "A.A. Swinton, Jr"	1,050.00
Dresser, 8 x 5½ x 3″	220.00
Mistletoe Ball, 6¼″ d, hinged	450.00
Oyster Ladle	25.00
Quilt Pattern, 5½″ l, horse, pitted and rusted	20.00
Sconces, 15½ x 5½ x 4″, porch roof style, pr	675.00
Shaving Mug, 4½ x 5⅞″, whimsey	110.00
Spice Canisters and Carrier, 8½ x 8½ x 5¾″, crimp dec	250.00
Tree Holder, Santa, poinsettias	40.00
Wedding Bell, 9½ x 3⅝″, whimsey, marked patent date	125.00

TINWARE: DECORATED

History: Decorating sheet iron, tin, and tin coated sheet iron sheet dates back to the mid-18th century. The Welsh called the practice pontipool, the French To'le Peinte. In America the center for tin decorated ware in the late 1700s was Berlin, Connecticut.

Several styles of decorating techniques were used: painting, japanning, and stenciling. Designs were done by both professionals and itinerants. English and Oriental motifs strongly influenced both form and design.

A special type of decoration was the punch work on unpainted tin practiced by the Pennsylvania tinsmiths. Forms included coffeepots, spice boxes, and grease lamps.

Tray, 8½ x 12½″, yellow line, white bands with red flower and green leaves, chamfered corners with red ground and yellow lines, $250.00.

Basket, 10½ x 9″, crimp and curl dec	825.00
Cake Cover, 8 x 14″, applied flower dec, PA, c1880	1,200.00
Cache Pot, 12″, oval cross section, scalloped border, band of gilded stencil flowers and birds dec, Empire, 19th C	350.00
Candle Lantern, 12″ h, semi-circular, single punched design, hinged door, ring handle	125.00
Canteen, 5⅝″ h, punched star and circle design	95.00
Coffeepot, 11″ h, punched tulip dec	1,400.00
Food Grater, 14¼″ l, punched, wood frame, mortised and turned handle	85.00
Foot Warmer	
7½ x 8½″, punched heart and circle design, mortised frame, turned corner posts, old brown finish	200.00
8 x 9″, heart and circle design, mortised wood frame, turned posts	200.00
8½″ l, punched circles and diamonds, mortised wood frame, turned posts	125.00
9″ l, punched circles, hearts, and diamonds, mortised wood frame, turned posts, worn red finish, int. pan	225.00
Lantern, 16″ h, old yellow japanning, hinged door, added candle socket, reflector slot	115.00

Nutmeg Grater, 6" l, brown japanning, hand crank **175.00**

Painting, 13 x 70", landscape, blue frame **70.00**

Pie Safe, 40 x 32 x 20", punched, hanging, deer and "Bread" on front door panels, birds, rabbits, and date 1894 on side panels, trees and squirrels on back panel **1,000.00**

Pudding Mold, 4 x 6⅝ x 4¾", punched shell and heart dec **900.00**

Rattle, 12¼ x 7½ x 6¼", punched dec, inscribed "December 8, 1879, for good boys only" **350.00**

Silhouette, 8 x 6¼", woman, punched, showing hair comb and necklace, c1835 .... **200.00**

Tray, 10½ x 13½", rect, beaded and pierced border, figural panel of two ladies in garden, George III, late 18th C **500.00**

Urns, 13" h, black ground, acorn finial, lion mask handles, stenciled panel with peasants in farmyard, Neoclassical, early 19th C, pr **1,400.00**

TOBACCO CUTTERS

History: Before pre-packaging, tobacco was delivered to merchants in bulk form. Tobacco cutters were used to cut the tobacco into desired sizes.

17¼" l, Red Tin Tag, Lorillards Chew Climax Plug, brass cutting piece marked "Made by Penn Hardware Co., Reading, PA, $100.00.

Arrow-Cupples Co **40.00**
Battle Axe **175.00**
E.C. Simmons, Keen Cutter **150.00**
Griswold No. 3 .... **100.00**
Master Workman, orig label **95.00**
Paraflint, brass, dog, engraved sides . **230.00**
Pennsylvania Hardware Co, 1900 .... **45.00**
R.J. Reynolds Co, orig black japanned finish **85.00**
Spear Head, ornate **225.00**
Star Brand Tobacco, 1885 .... **50.00**
Unmarked
  Silver Plate, horse head, bridle and mane **90.00**
  Wood, guillotine, 10" h **90.00**

Wrought and cast iron, pitted, wood base **75.00**

TOBACCO JARS

History: A tobacco jar is a container for storing tobacco. Tobacco humidors were made of various materials and in many shapes, including figurals. The earliest jars date to the early 17th century. However, most examples in today's market were made in the late 19th or early 20th centuries.

Student, 4⅞" h, boy, blue cap, yellow band, light green bowtie, high glaze, #6597/71, $90.00.

Bisque
  Black man, wearing high pointed collar, Germany **200.00**
  Skull, sitting on book, wearing golfing cap **125.00**
Cut Glass
  8" **275.00**
  9" h, hobstars, strawberry diamond, fan, lid, cut knob **525.00**
Lead Crystal, brass lid **25.00**
Majolica
  Lady, pink turban, intaglio eyes, 4 x 5" **75.00**
  Monk, smiling, cigarette in mouth, pink and light blue, Germany **95.00**
Pottery
  5¼" h, black lady, bust, light blue headdress **110.00**
  5⅝" h, black man, bust, straw hat, gold earrings **130.00**
  12" h, ovoid, blue and white, embellished oval panel, blue foliate garlands, inscribed "N3" or "N12," brass cap, Dutch, pr **1,210.00**
  13" h, oviform, blue and white, floral and foliate scroll cartouche, urn

and stylized flower heads and leaves, inscribed "RAPPE," brass cov, Dutch **935.00**

Brown and tan, raised design, Copeland-late Spode **60.00**

Skull and cigarette dec, Ed Diers, 1898 .... **1,650.00**

Stoneware, blue floral dec, gray pebbled ground, Star of David lid, bail handle **210.00**

TOBY JUGS

History: A toby jug is a drinking vessel usually depicting a full-figured, robust, genial drinking man. They originated in England in the late 18th century. The term "Toby" probably related to the character Uncle Toby from *Tristam Shandy* by Laurence Sterne.

References: Susan and Al Bagdade, *Warman's English & Continental Pottery & Porcelain, 1st Edition,* Warman Publishing Co., Inc., 1987; Vic Schuler, *British Toby Jugs,* Kevin Francis Publishing Ltd. (London), 1986.

Additional Listings: Royal Doulton.

Reproduction Alert: Within the last 100 years or more, tobies have been reproduced copiously by many potteries in the United States and England.

5⅜" h, Old Staffo Toby, Shorter & Sons Ltd., Staffordshire, $40.00.

Bennington, Rockingham glaze, 11" h, coachman wearing tassels, 1849 mark **400.00**

Evans, 10¾", Napoleon, ironstone, multicolored enamel, marked "Napoleon Jug-patent applied for, Alfred E Evans, Philadelphia, PA" **375.00**

Graniteware, 10½", Napoleon, standing, yellow waistcoat, blue vest, marked "Made at Trenton, NJ" **400.00**

Leeds Type, 9¾", man, seated, blue and yellow mottled coat, yellow pants, brown hair, hat, and shoes, holding jug on left knee, pipe between legs, c1800 .... **850.00**

Pratt

9½" h, man seated, brown mottled coat, yellow vest, gray breeches, holding jug, late 18th C **550.00**

10" h, man seated, mottled coat, holding foam filled jug, led, c1800 ... **1,600.00**

Royal Doulton

4½", Cap'n Cuttle, seated, c1948 .. **165.00**

5½", Sir Winston Churchill **60.00**

7¼", Huntsman, c1910 .... **350.00**

9", Cliff Cornell, brown **375.00**

Staffordshire

4½", man, seated, green hair, cobalt blue, copper lustre trim, holding mug and snuff box **120.00**

9½", man, seated

Blue coat, yellow breeches, foaming jug on left knee, late 18th C **900.00**

Green coat, pink vest, yellow breeches, black hat, pipe and jug, early 19th C **300.00**

9¾", man, seated

Brown coat, yellow hat, holding jug and goblet in hands, 19th C ... **250.00**

Gray coat, yellow breeches, white hat, holding jug on left knee, late 18th C **700.00**

10¾" h, man seated, green coat, yellow breeches, holding foaming jug, late 18th C **550.00**

11¼" h, man seated, blue coat, yellow vest, green breeches, holding goblet and bottle, early 19th C **1,300.00**

11½" h, man, standing, blue coat, cannon, titled "Nelson" **250.00**

Wood, Ralph, 9½", man seated, green waistcoat, gray jacket, dark hat, one hand raised to mouth **900.00**

Yellow Ware, 9½" h, man standing, glazed yellowish-tan and dark brown splashes, Derbyshire, mid 19th C .. **100.00**

TOOLS

History: Before the advent of assembly line and mass production, practically everything required for living was handmade at home or by a local tradesman or craftsmen. The cooper, the blacksmith, the cabinet maker, and the carpenter all had their special tools.

Early examples of these hand tools are collected for their workmanship, ingenuity, place of manufacture, or design. Modern day craftsman often search out old hand tools for use to authentically recreate the manufacture of an object.

References: Ronald S. Barlow, *The Antique Tool Collector's Guide to Value*, Windmill Publishing Company, 1985, (1987 reprint with current prices); Kathryn McNerney, *Antique Tools, Our American Heritage*, Collector Books, 1979; R. A. Salaman, *Dictionary of Tools*, Charles Scribner's Sons, 1974.

Collectors' Club: Early American Industries Association, P. O. Box 2128, Empire State Plaza Station, Albany, NY 12220. *The Chronicle* (monthly).

Museum: Shelburne Museum, Shelburne, VT.

Drills, archaminan: (top,) 9¾" l, German, prior to World War II, $35.00; (bottom,) 7¾" h, ebonized, gentleman's style, $25.00.

Anvil, marked "Fisher, Trenton"	100.00
Axe, 7½ x 4½", Winchester	85.00
Brace, 11" l, hand forged iron, speckled ash burl grip, "C" scroll	100.00
Caliper, jeweler's, 3½" l, inlaid brass and copper circles, brass and copper rivet	85.00
Caulking Hammer, 13 x 13", shipwright's	50.00
Chisel, corner, two cutting edges, 18th C	75.00
Clamp, 24" l, miter jack, bird's eye maple, metal screw shaft	140.00
Drill, eggbeater type, brass	250.00
Jigsaw, mounted on wood base, marked "Shipman & Binder"	100.00

Level
Cherry, 24", sight insight stock, sq framed round inclinometer, marked "American Combined Level and Grade Finder, Manufactured by Edward Helb, Railroad, York Co, PA, US, July 12, 1904"	225.00
Rosewood, 22" l, brass trim, marked "Stratton Brothers, Greenfield, MA," patent dates 1872 and 1887	120.00
Mallet, 11¼" l, burl wood, stamped "S Coss"	50.00
Monkey Wrench, 21", Winchester	100.00
Mortise Gauge, oval head, ebony, brass face plate, solid brass rod stem	75.00

Plane
Bench type, carriage makers, Keen Kutter No. 10	165.00
Block type, Stanley No. 100½	55.00

Smoothing type, Sargent No. 407	110.00
Rule, 24" l, folding type, brass edge, Stanley No. 62	25.00

Saw
Buck, 15½", mortised wood frame	45.00
Fret, 13" l, 6" blade, brass trim, iron fittings, wood frame	75.00
Hand, Winchester No. 10	50.00

Screwdriver
Electrician's, insulated head, Stanley No. 45, marked "Hurwood"	8.00
Ratchet, round wood handle, Yankee No. 15	10.00
Scribe, hand forged iron, 6" carved wood handle, full bodied naked woman, hooked end	350.00
Square, Stanley No. 18	15.00
Vise, 38" h, bench type, harness maker's, leather strap, foot treadle	175.00
Woodgraining Set, three rollers, instruction book, Davis Co, 1904	25.00
Wrench, plier type hand lever, quick adjust crescent type, marked "Universal Wrench Co, Detroit-Windsor, patent 6-3-19"	25.00

TOOTHPICK HOLDERS

History: Toothpick holders, indispensible table accessories of the Victorian era, are small containers used to hold toothpicks.

They were made in a wide range of materials: china (bisque and porcelain), glass (art, blown, cut, opalescent, pattern, etc.), and metals, especially silver plate. Makers include both American and European firms.

Toothpick holders were used as souvenir items by applying decals or transfers. The same blank may contain several different location labels.

References: William Heacock, *Encyclopedia Of Victorian Colored Pattern Glass, Book I, Toothpick Holders From A To Z*, Antique Publications, 1981; William Heacock, *1,000 Toothpick Holders: A Collector's Guide*, Antique Publications, 1977; William Heacock, *Rare & Unlisted Toothpick Holders*, Antique Publications, 1984.

Collectors' Club: National Toothpick Collector's Society, P. O. Box 246, Sawyer, MI 49125.

Additional Listings: See *Warman's Americana & Collectibles* for more examples.

Advisor: Judy Knauer.

Art Glass
Burmese, florals, berries, and oak leave dec, hexagonal rim	350.00
Cameo, deep red etching fading to opaque ground, sgd "Legras"	160.00
Peachblow, yellow shading to deep red, white int., Hobbs, Brockunier & Co, Wheeling, WV, c1886, 2¼"	1,850.00

Phoenix Glass, odd angles shape,
light green 65.00
Pomona, amber ruffled rim, ftd fan
shape 400.00
Spatter, pillar ribbed pattern, cranberry, frosted 125.00
Tiffany, irid gold, squatty bulbous
body, loop handles, sgd on base "L.
C. T. Y2088," c1900, 2⅜" 400.00

China
Adams-Tunstall, white relief classical
Grecian scene, cobalt blue Wedgwood like ground, metal banded
neck, sgd 60.00
Royal Bayreuth, coal hod shape,
overhead handle
Corinthian pattern, black, satin finish 300.00
Tapestry, portrait of woman with a
horse 400.00

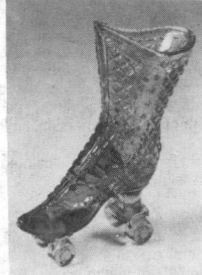

Figural, high-top button shoe, with roller skate, amber glass, dated 1886, $20.00.

Figural, glass
Chick, "Just Out," half egg shell,
frosted, sgd "Gillinder" inside base,
4¼" 75.00
Hand holding fan, milk glass 35.00
Military figures on each side, "Pre-
paredness" over crossed flags emb
across center well, clear 100.00
Top Hat, tooled curved edges, rough
pontil 55.00
Opalescent Glass
Beatty Honeycomb, white opal, blue
ground, Tiffin, OH, c1888 ...... 65.00
Chyrsanthemum, cranberry, white
opal stripes 85.00
Pattern Glass
Argonaut Shell, custard, dec 250.00
Cone, green opaque 65.00
Forget-Me-Not, pink opaque 60.00
Hearts, blue opaque 65.00
Millard, ruby stained 200.00
One-on-One, pink 45.00

TORTOISE SHELL ITEMS

History: For many years amber and mottled colored tortoise shell has been used in the manufacture of small items such as boxes, combs, dresser sets, and trinkets.

Note: Anyone dealing in the sale of tortoise shell objects should be familiar with the Endangered Species Act and Amendment in its entirety. As of November, 1978, antique tortoise shell objects can be legally imported and sold with some restrictions.

Bracelet, 3″ d, bangle, silver inlay, $30.00.

Bowl, 7¾" d, turned up back, applied
amber feet 110.00
Box, 4 x 11", cov, rect, fitted int. 150.00
Bracelet, 3", two silver inlaid animals . 30.00
Finger Bowl, 5⅝" d bowl, 6⅛" d under-
plate, ruffled rims, late 19th C 300.00
Hair Ornament, Art Nouveau
Back Comb, gilt brass, turquoise
glass accents 125.00
Side, applied metallic dec, simulated
gemstones 65.00
Hairpin, carved poppy blossom, heavy
shell 135.00
Inkstand, 8 x 16", three cut glass bottles,
brass inlay, shaped handles 400.00
Match Safe, pocket type, emb sides .. 65.00
Razor Case, sgd "Jefferson Steel" ... 15.00
Shaving Brush, handle with inlaid MOP
dec 40.00
Tea Caddy
4½" w, 4½" h, George III silver
mounts, MOP and ivory inlay, oblong ten sided body, hinged lid, late
19th C 1,600.00
5" w, 5½" h, George III silver mounts,
ivory inlay, late 18th C 1,375.00
6 x 8 x 5½", William IV, oblong top,
bread front outline, twin canisters,
conforming case resting on molded
base, second quarter 19th C 900.00
8" l, cov, ivory and tortoise shell, two
fitted compartments, English, 19th
C 900.00
Tobacco Humidor, 4½", rect, hinged lid 150.00
Vase, 8¾", flared top, pedestal base .. 150.00

TOYS

History: In America the first cast iron toys began to appear shortly after the Civil War. Leading 19th century manufacturers include Hubley, Dent, Kenton, and Schoenhut. In the first decades of the 20th century, Arcade, Buddy L, Marx, and Tootsie Toy joined the earlier firms. Wooden toys were made by George Brown and other manufacturers who did not sign or label their work.

In Europe, N:auurnberg, Germany, was the center for the toy industry from the late 18th through the mid 20th century. Companies such as Lehman and Marklin produced high quality toys.

Several auction houses, including Lloyd Ralston Toys and Phillips, have specialty auctions consisting entirely of toys.

Every toy is collectible. The key is the condition and working order if mechanical. Examples listed are considered to be in good to very good condition to mint condition unless otherwise specified.

References: Linda Baker, *Modern Toys, American Toys, 1930–1980*, Collector Books, 1985; Robert Carter and Eddy Rubinstein, *Yesterday's Yesteryears: Lesney "Matchbox" Models*, Haynes Publishing Group (London), 1986; Jurgen and Marianne Cieslik, *Lehmann Toys*, New Cavendish Books, 1982; Fred and Marilyn Fintel, *Yesterday's Toys With Today's Prices*, Wallace-Homestead, 1985; Gordon Gardiner and Alistair Morris, *The Illustrated Encyclopedia of Metal Toys*, Harmony Books, 1984; Gordon Gardiner and Alistair Morris, *The Price Guide To Metal Toys*, Antique Collectors' Club, 1980; Lillian Gottschalk, *American Toy Cars & Trucks*, Abbeville Press, 1985; Ernest & Ida Long, *Dictionary of Toys Sold in America*, 2 vols, published by author; David Longest, *Character Toys and Collectibles*, Collector Books, 1984; David Longest, *Character Toys and Collectibles, Second Series*, Collector Books, 1987; Albert W. McCollough, *The Complete Book of Buddy "L" Toys: A Greenberg Guide*, I. Greenberg Publishing Co., 1982; Brian Moran, *Battery Toys*, Schiffer Publishing, 1984; Richard O'Brien, *Collecting Toys: A Collectors Identification and Value Guide*, 4th Edition, Books Americana, 1985; Maxine A. Pinsky, *Greenberg's Guide To Marx Toys, Volume I*, Greenberg Publishing Co., 1988; Martyn L. Schorr, *The Guide To Mechanical Toy Collecting*, Performance Media, 1979; Peter Viemeister, *Micro Cars*, Hamilton's, 1982; Blair Whitton, *American Clockwork Toys, 1862–1900*, Schiffer Publishing Ltd, 1981; Blair Whitton, *Paper Toys of The World*, Hobby House Press, Inc., 1986; James Wieland and Dr. Edward Force, *Tootsie Toys, World's First Die Cast Models*, Motorbooks International, 1980; Blair Whitton, *The Knopf Collector's Guide to Amerian Toys*, Alfred A. Knopf, 1984.

Periodicals: *The Antique Toy World*, 4419 Irving Park Road, Chicago, IL 60618; *Professor Pug Frog's Newsletter*, 3 Hillside Avenue, Peabody, MA 01960.

Museums: American Museum of Automobile Miniatures, Andover, MA; Museum of the City of New York, New York, NY; Perelman Antique Toy Museum, Philadelphia, PA; Smithsonian Institution, Washington, D.C.; Margaret Woodbury Strong Museum, Rochester, NY; Toy Museum of Atlanta, Atlanta, GA.

Additional Listings: Disneyana and Schoenhut. Also see *Warman's Americana & Collectibles* for more examples.

Acme, American
Automobile, Oldsmobile, 11", light steelplate, windup, two seater, curved dash, red velveted seats, stenciled, black, white rubber tires 400.00
Delivery Wagon, 11" l, light steelplate, electric type, open truck, steel canopy, wind-up motor, rubber tires, red and black, c1898 .... 600.00
Arcade, Freeport, IL, 1893–1946
Cab, 7½", cast iron, yellow, molded cast iron spare tire, rubber tires, plated driver 650.00
Dump Truck, 12" l, Mack, painted red, replacement hoist mechanism, new axle 450.00
Greyhound Lines GMC, 10", painted cast iron, sightseeing bus 90.00
Arnold, German, 1906–Present
Coupe, 9½" l, litho tin, graffetti cov 1930s style car, driver and three passengers, c1953 .... 330.00
Ocean Liner, 10¼" l, litho tin windup, two decks, three stacks, and railings, red, blue, and cream 450.00
Gebrüder Bing, Nürenberg, Germany, 1880s–1934
Garage, 8", litho tin, two clockwork cars 265.00
Passenger Liner, *Leviathan*, 12¾" l, tinplate, windup, red and black, cream upper deck 600.00
Buddy L, American, 1921–Present
Coupe, Flivver, #210B, 11" l, black,

Buddy L, steam shovel, c1925, $250.00.

steering wheel controlled front
wheels, c1928 .... 275.00
Dump Truck, 23" l, crank lift, minor
rusting 300.00
Fire Hose and Water Pumper, 12" l,
red, two water pumps, one ladder,
MIB 160.00
Ice Truck, 26" l, canvas cov, open rear
bed, black and yellow, red solid disc
wheels, restored 500.00
International Harvester Truck, 24" l,
steelplate, enclosed cap, open
truck bed, spoke wheels, refinished
in red 1,100.00
Station Wagon, #371 .... 325.00

**Buffalo Toys, 12" l car, Silver Dash,
litho tin windup, silver body, red
wheels, two yellow figures, black hats,
Patent 1-20-25, $225.00.**

Buffalo Toys, American
Red Streak Racer, tinplate, red, yellow wheels, spiral spring pulled at
back propels car, c1925 .... 225.00
Silver Racer, tinplate, painted silver,
gold pipes, rubber bumper 150.00
Georges Carette & Cie, Nürenberg,
Germany, 1886–1917
Ferris Wheel, 15" h, painted tinplate,
manually operated, four seated figures, two flags, center label reads
"Caroussel Roundabout," c1900 . 2,250.00
Steam Launch, 14" l, painted tinplate,
white and red hull, tin canopy over
steam engine, three blade propeller, anchor, composition figure, tin
flag, c1911 .... 1,200.00
Touring Car #50, 8¼" l, painted tinplate, clockwork, open four seater,
twin headlights, trunk rack and
driver, passengers missing, c1906 2,750.00
C. E. Carter Mechanical Toys, Factory
Erie, PA
Pan-Gee The Funny Dancer, litho figure, green and red, hat, dancing on
box, keywind, marked on base "C.
E. Carter Co. Mechanical Toys,
Factory Erie, PA, Sales Office 200
Fifth Ave., NY" 300.00

Porter Pulling Wheelbarrow, 6½" l,
litho tin windup, Oriental figure, yellow and blue clothes, maroon two
wheeled open wheelbarrow 200.00

J. Chein & Co, Piano Ladeon, $250.00.

A. J. Chein, Harrison, NJ, c1930
Barnacle Bill, 7" h, litho tin, red hair,
wearing barrel 225.00
Bus, 9", blue, five windows per side,
litho curtains, marked "Junior Bus,
219" 110.00
Doughboy, 6" h, litho tin windup, walking World War I soldier 285.00
Popeye, 7" h, barrel walker, litho tin,
orig pipe 175.00
Roller Coaster, 20" l, litho tin windup 115.00
Santa, 6" h, litho tin windup, sack on
back, c1920 .... 300.00
Johann Distler, Nürenberg, Germany,
1887–World War II
Autobus, 7" l, litho tin windup, red,
black accents, yellow curved steps
to upper deck, orig driver at wheel 750.00
Coupe, 6" l, litho tin windup, blue and
black, red grille, orig driver and license plate 900.00
Durable Toy Corporation, USA, c1935,
pinball game, 23 x 14", Popeye, litho
tin 110.00
Ezra, American, steam shovel truck, 32"
l, steelplate, painted black and red,
operating shovel, Buddy L style ... 450.00
Fisher Price, East Aurora, NY, 1930–
Present
Big Pill Pelican, 9 x 7¾", white vinyl
head feathers, red plastic bill and
feet 8.50
Looky Push Car, 6½ x 8 x 7", 20"
handle with plastic steering wheel,
#875 .... 25.00
Jumbo Rollo, 9½ x 7 x 9", elephant,
legs pedal tricycle, beads roll in rattle cage, c1951 .... 18.00

Musical Duck, 12″ l, #795 . . . . . . **40.00**
Quacky Family, 13¼ x 5″, mother duck and three ducklings, yellow, red, and white, rubber connecting pcs, c1940 . . . . **25.00**
Xylophone Pull Toy
  9″, Mickey Mouse, #798 . . . . **80.00**
  11″, Donald Duck, #177 . . . . **75.00**

J. Fleishmann, Nürenberg, Germany, 1887–World War II
Battle Cruiser, 21″ l, tinplate, clockwork, upper section orig gray and black paint, refinished black hull, twelve gun enplacements, two stacks, two decks, two lifeboats, and anchor winch, Carette type ramrod bow, mid 1920s . . . **2,750.00**
Battleship, 17″ l, tinplate, clockwork, brown and gray, two stacks, three pivoting gun turrents, two flags, two lifeboards, two masts with crow's nests **850.00**
Ocean Liner, 20″ l, tinplate, white, blue trim, brown deck, single stack, masts, lifeboats, and flags missing **750.00**

Gama
Cadillac, 12¼″, sedan, tinplate, friction drive, light gray, blue top, chrome grill and piping, fully litho int., white walled tires **425.00**
Howitzer, 14″ l, trailer hitch, scissor mechanism **80.00**
Tank, German Panzer I, 4½″ l, litho tin windup, gray and green, Panzer officer in turret, orig box and key . **300.00**

Martin Gunthermann, Nürenberg, Germany, 1920–World War II
Felix, 7″ l, riding on scooter, keywind, three wheel vehicle **225.00**
Horse Drawn Carriage, 12″ l, litho tin, clockwork, two front lanterns, driver holding whip, four rubber tires, horse hair cov horse, c1895 . **1,550.00**
Phaeton, open, 9¼″ l, litho tin windup, red and black, tinplate driver, front wheels turn, c1915 . . . . **425.00**
Salto, 5″ l, litho tin windup, black and white bulldog, sits up, flips over . . **80.00**
Sedan, 14½″, tinplate, keywind, orig driver, cream and red, black trim, c1933 . . . . **1,700.00**

Hubley, Lancaster, PA, 1894–1965
Car Transport, 10″, painted cast iron, red, two cars **225.00**
Fire Pumper, 10″, red paint, silver trim, orig driver **250.00**
Plantation Wagon, 14½″, painted cast iron, repainted **100.00**
Yellow Cab, 7½″, painted and nickel plated cast iron, rubber tires **165.00**

Ives, Bridgeport, CT
Crawling Baby, 11½ x 5½″, mechan-ical, keywind, composition head with slight coating of wax, blonde mohair wig, composition limbs, torso with clockwork mechanism, white net cap, white cotton dress, patented March 14 and August 19, 1871 . . . . **500.00**
General Butler, mechanical walking man, wood, pot metal hair, cloth dressed, clockwork, Hotchkiss patent, 1870 . . . . **2,500.00**
Pull Toy, 6½″ l, walking horse, mounted on three wheels, orig straw tail **1,200.00**

Kenton, Kenton, OH
Chariot, 10″, cast iron, three horses, lady driver **475.00**
Fire Patrol Wagon, 20½″ l, cast iron, open orange passenger wagon stenciled "Fire Patrol," three seated helmeted firemen, one driver, two galloping black and white horses, double wheels, c1890 . . . . **750.00**
Overland Circus Wagon, 14″, painted cast iron, pressed steel, polar bear **450.00**
Ox Cart, 11″, painted cast iron **425.00**
Racing Trotter, 8″ l, cast iron, orig jockey seated between two large wheels, reining galloping horse, c1915 . . . . **180.00**
Yellow Kid, 7½″, standing in goat wagon, cast iron, yellow tunic, c1900 **400.00**

Lehman, Nürnberg, Germany, 1881–Present
Autobus, #590, 8″ l, litho tin windup, orig driver, red, yellow, and white, keywind sprung **500.00**
Cable Car #R161, 8″ h, litho tin, red, white, and blue, overhead pulleys, wheels, and wire, orig box **40.00**
New Century Cycle, 5″, litho tin, painted, clockwork **350.00**
Quack-Quack, 7½″, litho tin windup, duck and cart **250.00**
Tombo Jigger, 7″ h, dancing black man on litho platform box **200.00**
Tut Tut Auto, litho, mechanical, beige and red, red and green cowl lights, c1905 . . . . **450.00**

Linemar
Pluto Lantern, 7¼″ h, litho tin, battery operated, brilliant yellow, black and red features, orig tongue, ears, tail, bulb, and box **120.00**
Pluto Musician, 6″ h, litho tin windup, orig top hat, cane, bell, and megaphone **125.00**

Lionel, Irvington, NJ, 1906–Present
Handcar
  7″, Mickey Mouse, tinplate, red car,

composition Mickey and Minnie, one tail missing 300.00

10″ l, Donald Duck, tinplate and composition, long bill, bobbing head 350.00

Mobile, Peter Rabbit Chick, #1103, 10″ l, clockwork, three composition eggs and track, orig box, c1935 . . 600.00

Speedboat, 17″ l, competition type, tinplate, keywind, twin motors, dual drivers, cream and light green hull, orig Lionel cradle 750.00

Marklin, Goppingen, Germany, 1859– Present

Airplane, litho tin windup, D-A//LBA single motor, passenger, orig 21 x 12½″ box with individual pcs in orig positions, litho box cov, c1937, MIB 2,100.00

Battle Cruiser, 17″ l, tinplate, keywind, two tones of gray and dark brown, ten gun enplacements, two stacks, railings, and masts, c1925 . . . . . . 2,800.00

Doll Stroller, 6″, painted tin, cream and yellow, c1910 . . . . 825.00

Ocean Liner, 15″ l, painted tin, red, black, and white, deck with four lifeboats, bridge, three deck houses, masts and funnels, clockwork, marked on rudder, c1910 . . . . . . 1,550.00

Louis Marx & Co, Spic and Span, The Hams What Am, 10¼″ h, 6¼″ l base, litho tin windup, $275.00.

Louis Marx & Co., New York, 1921– Present

Airplane, Dagwood's Solo Flight, 8½″, litho tin windup, portraits of Dagwood, Blondie, Daisy, and Cookie, Dagwood as pilot 250.00

Car

Amos 'N' Andy Fresh Air Taxi, 7½″ l, litho tin, MIB 750.00

Learn to Drive, MIB 38.00

Milton Berle Crazy Car, 5½″ l, litho tin, twirling head, cowboy hat, MIB 275.00

Dairy Wagon, Toylands, horse drawn, litho tin, white and brown wagon, white horse, keywind mechanism missing 50.00

Dollhouse, metal, ranch style, complete with furniture, MIB 60.00

Fire Chief Car, 14″ l, painted red, yellow stenciling, windup, siren . . . 150.00

Tank, camouflage, litho, 9½″ 45.00

Oh Boy, American, bulldozer, 6″ l, cast iron, molded driver and controls, blue, red trim, rubber track wheels 475.00

Ohio Art, Bryan, OH, 1908–Present

Coast Guard Sea Plane, 10″ w wingspan, litho tin windup, red, white, and blue 100.00

Injun Chief, 8″ l, litho tin windup, tomohawk in hand, orig box 110.00

Washing machine, litho tin, hand crank on top, Mickey and Minnie Mouse doing laundry 160.00

Richter & Co., litho tin, clockwork, $1,760.00.

Schuco, trademark of Schreyer and Co., Germany, 1912–Present

Boy Scout, litho tin windup, playing violin 100.00

Donald Duck, 6″, litho tin windup, orig blue felt sailor shirt and hat 400.00

Race Car, 6″ l, keywind, blue, steerable front wheels, orig box, #1050 60.00

Sedan, 7½″, tinplate, battery operated, red, creamtone top, litho int., remote control steering system . . 90.00

Strauss, Ferdinand, New York City, 20th C

Inter-State Bus, double decker bus, brown and yellow, orig driver, c1926 . . . . 500.00

Mailplane, 12″, painted tin windup, red and blue 125.00

Travel-Chicks, 8″ l, litho tin windup, four chicks peck at bowl perched on moving railroad boxcar **275.00**

Zeppelin, *New York*, 10″ l, litho tin windup, gray ground, red and blue piping, wood simulated gondola, propeller missing, c1925 .... **425.00**

Unidentified Maker

American, pedal car, 80″ l, pressed steel, two passenger, twin side lights, front lamp, and horn **3,850.00**

German

Horse, 5½″ h, tinplate, keywind, Nazi soldier in full military uniform astride black and white speckled horse **1,000.00**

Lady with Parasol, 6½″ l, painted tinplate, friction, red dress, trimmed in black, early 1900s **1,350.00**

Pull Toy, 8½″ l, Admiral Dewey, articulated, bisque head and cap, painted facial features, waving American flag, wood platform and wheels, early 1900s **800.00**

Racing Car, 6½″ l, barrel hood, litho tin, friction drive, driver hunched over wheel, fully dressed, goggles, blue and cream, c1905 .. **500.00**

Wheel Wright, 6¼″ h, steam, tinplate, flywheel mechanism activates figure to hammer steel .. **275.00**

French, catastrophe racing car, 8″ l, litho tin, clockwork, driver and passenger, moving car splits in two, throwing headlamps and passengers, brick red, early 1880s **3,025.00**

Unique Art

Dancer, litho tin windup, black man dancing on roof of litho cabin **300.00**

G. I. Joe and His Joucing Jeep, 6¾″ l, litho tin, helmeted soldier bounces up and down **70.00**

Kiddy Cyclist, 9″, litho tin windup ... **100.00**

Li'l Abner Band, litho tin, keywind .. **350.00**

Rap & Tap In A Friendly Scrap, litho tin windup, 4″ h boxers, 5 x 4″ ring, 5 x 3 x 2″ base, c1925 .... **550.00**

Wilkins, Keene, NH, late 19th C

Consolidated Streetcar, 13″, painted cast iron **900.00**

Delivery Wagon, 10″ l, litho tin windup, dark blue, gold piping, yellow wheels, orig driver, c1915 ... **400.00**

Fire Wagon, 43″ l, cast iron, three black horses, red harness, large aerial fire hose apparatus, orig articulated driver, painted black, red piping, c1895 ..... **2,000.00**

Firehouse #8, 8½ x 18½″, litho tin windup, red, bell rings, doors open, some underneath rust **900.00**

Wyandotte, American

Airplane, stamped steel, rounded fuselage, painted red and black ... **225.00**

Garage-Service Center, 5 x 4″, litho tin, two car garage, service station, gas pumps, 1930s car on lift, two 4″ l metal cars, c1935 .... **175.00**

Sedan and House Trailer, 25½″, litho tin **150.00**

Toytown Estate Wagon, 20″, litho tin windup **125.00**

TRAINS, TOY

History: Railroading has always been an important part of childhood, largely because of the romance associated with the railroad and the emphasis on toy trains.

The first toy trains were cast iron and tin; windup motors added movement. The Golden Age of toy trains was 1920–1955 when electric powered units were available and names such as Ives, American Flyer, and Lionel were household words. The construction of the rolling stock was of high quality. The advent of plastic in the late 1950s lessened this quality considerably.

Toy trains were designated by a model scale or gauge. The most popular are HO, N, O and standard. Narrow gauge was a response to the modern capacity to miniaturize. Its popularity has lessened in the last few years.

Condition of trains is critical. Items in fair condition (scratched, chipped, dented, rusted or warped) and have generally have little value to a collector. Restoration is accepted, provided it is done accurately. It may enhance the price one or two grades. Prices listed below are for very good to mint condition unless noted.

References: John O. Bradshaw, *Greenberg's Guide To Kusan Trains*, Greenberg Publishing Co, 1987; Bruce Greenberg, (edited by Christian F. Rohlfing), *Greenberg's Guide To Lionel Trains: 1901–1942, Volume 1* (1988), *Volume 2* (1988), Greenberg Publishing Co.; Bruce Greenberg (edited by Roland La Voie and Steve Kimball), *Greenberg's Guide To Lionel Trains:1945-1969, Volume 1* (1987), *Volume 2* (1988), Greenberg Publishing Co.; John Hubbard, *The Story of Williams Electric Trains*, Greenberg Publishing Co., 1987; Steven H. Kimball, *Greenberg's Guide To American Flyer Prewar O Gauge*, Greenberg Publishing Co., 1987; Roland La Voie, *Greenberg's Guide To Lionel-Fundimensions Trains*, Greenberg Publishing Co., 1985; Dallas J. Mallerich, III, *Greenberg's Guide to Athearn Trains*, Greenberg Publishing Co., 1987; Eric J. Matzke, *Greenberg's Guide To Marx Trains*, Greenberg Publishing Co., 1985; Al McDuffie, et. al., *Greenberg Guide to Ives Trains*, 1901-1932, Greenberg Publishing Co, 1984; John R. Ottley, *Greenberg's Guide To LGB Trains*, Greenberg Publishing Co., 1986; James Patterson and Bruce C. Greenberg, *Greenberg's Guide To American Flyer S Gauge, Third Edition*, Greenberg Publishing Co., 1988; Vincent Rosa and George J. Horan, *Greenberg Guide To HO Trains*, Greenberg Publishing Co., 1986.

Note: Greenberg Publishing Company (7543 Main Street, Sykesville, MD 21784) is the leading publisher of toy train literature. Anyone interested in the subject should write for their catalog and ask to be put on their mailing list.

Collectors' Clubs: Lionel Collector's Club, P.O. Box 11851, Lexington, KY 40578; The National Model Railroad Association, P.O. Box 2186, Indianapolis, IN 46206; The Toy Train Operating Society, Inc., 25 West Walnut Street, Suite 305, Pasadena, CA 91103; The Train Collector's Association, P.O. Box 248, Strasburg, PA 17579.

Additional Listings: See *Warman's Americana & Collectibles* for more examples.

AMERICAN FLYER

Car
807, box car, Rio Grande, door opens	450.00
900, passenger car, Northern Pacific	125.00
979, caboose	25.00

Locomotive
263, Steam	425.00
3112, O gauge, baggage, Paul Revere on both sides, observation car with Paul Revere on one side and Lexington on other, orange with blue	400.00
4644, standard gauge, green and red, restored	125.00

Set
4637, locomotive, car 4018, 4017, 1010, 4022, and 4021, standard gauge	650.00
4680 locomotive, black and green, copper trim, 4693 tender, 4017 gondola, 4022 flat car, 4010 tank car, 4018 box car, 4021 caboose, standard gauge	750.00
9900, O gauge, Burlington Zephyr Streamline, diecast, chrome plated, two cars	350.00

IVES

Car
56, caboose, O gauge, Pennsylvania Lines, dark red wood litho sides, brown and black trim, stamped steel wheels, c1910	120.00
64387, freight car, O gauge, Canadian Pacific RR, yellow simulated wood litho, gray enameled roof, c1913	100.00

Locomotive
3235, standard gauge, bronze metallic, gold trim, restored	100.00

3241, standard gauge, red brass plate, cream trim, restored	225.00
3255R, O gauge, rusting and surface scratches	85.00

Lionel, set, No. 10 electric locomotive, #332 baggage car, #339 pullman, #341 observation, peacock illuminated cars, standard gauge, late 1920s, $375.00.

Set
3241, standard gauge, locomotive, eight cars, replaced whistle, white paint spots on locomotive	1,000.00

LIONEL

Car
212, Gondola, standard gauge, gray, three wood barrels	175.00
213, Cattle Car, standard gauge, terra cotta, green floor	250.00
214, Boxcar, standard gauge, yellow, orange roof, orig box	475.00
900, Trailer, 2 7/8 gauge, Metropolitan Express, maroon, black roof, 1904–05	3,400.00

Locomotive
10, standard gauge, green, orange Ives stripe, restored	150.00
42, standard gauge, black, NYC . . .	250.00
150, O gauge, maroon, green windows	160.00
2321, O gauge, Lackawanna, AB diesel	350.00
2360, O gauge, Pennsylvania GGI .	500.00
252, O gauge, peacock	90.00

Set, passenger, standard gauge
10E, locomotive, brown, altered roofs, restored	375.00
408E, locomotive, green, restored . .	1,100.00
384 locomotive, black with copper trim, 384 tender, 515 Sunoco tank car, 517 caboose, standard gauge	900.00
752E locomotive, 753 passenger, 754 observation, Union Pacific Streamline, diecast and tin, some rust . .	650.00

TRAMP ART

History: Tramp art was prevalent in the United States from 1875 to the 1930s. Items were made by itinerant artists who left no record of their identity. They used old cigar boxes and fruit and vegetable crates. The edges of items were chip-carved and layered, creating the "Tramp Art" effect. Finished items usually were given an overall stain. Today they are collected primarily as folk art.

Reference: Helaine Fendelman, *Tramp Art: An Itinerant's Folk Art Guide,* E. P. Dutton & Co., 1975.

Box, 7 x 8 x 5¼", hinged, red paper lining, with rabbit diecut pasted to lid interior, alternating layers of yellow and orange on pyramids, $90.00.

Box
- 8⅞" l, pedestal base, hinged lid, orig paper cigar label adv inside lid . . . 65.00
- 13½" l, whittled knob feet, natural patina . . . 150.00

Frame, 5¾ x 7¾", mirror . . . 45.00

Jewelry Box
- 10½ x 10½ x 9", brass trim and panels, red velvet insert top, lift out int. tray, hidden drawer, dated 1903 . . . 55.00
- 11 x 7 x 7" . . . 125.00
- Graduated, chip carved, mirror, hinged lid . . . 30.00

Magazine Rack, 15" w, hanging, orig dark finish, brass tacks . . . 40.00

Rocker, cut out curved sides, lyre-like splat, applied chip carved dec, alligator varnish and brown paint, two porcelain buttons in back, replaced wood seat . . . 175.00

Sewing Box, 9½" l, pin cushion frame top, drawer, orig dark finish . . . 25.00

Sewing Table, "Mother" on hinged lid . 850.00

Wall Pocket, 11 x 16½", hanging, applied strips . . . 80.00

TRUNKS

History: Trunks are portable containers that clasp shut for the storage or transportation of personal possessions. Normally "trunk" means the ribbed flat, or dome top models of the second half of the 19th century. Unrestored they sell between $50 and $150. Refinished and relined the price rises to $200 to $400, with decorators being a principal market.

Early trunks frequently were painted, stenciled, grained, or covered with wallpaper. These are collected for their folk art qualities and as such experience high prices.

Reference: Martin and Maryann Labuda, *Price & Identification Guide to Antique Trunks,* published by authors, 1980.

Dome top, 20¼ x 32 x 25", wood rim, wooden slats, int. shelf missing, much orig paint remains, $100.00.

DOME TOP

Grain Painted, 12¼" h, 30" l, black and red, simulated, plain int., early 19th C 300.00

Norwegian, painted
- 20" h, 40" l, pine, three plank top, "Aaid 1858" painted on front, white and yellow foliate swag borders, black ground, mounted loop handles . . . 600.00
- 29" h, 46⅕" l, yellow, green, blue, black, and white floral medallions and sprigs, plain int. with wrought iron strapwork, wrought iron loop handles, inscribed . . . 550.00

Pine, 21½" h, 41" l, painted green, plain int., wrought iron strap handles, inscribed "Adam Gates 1848 No. 1" . . 60.00

Sponge Painted
- 7" h, 15" l, black and brown, burled simulating, plain int., early 19th C 140.00
- 8⅛" h, 20" l, spotted red and brown, plain int., 19th C . . . 165.00

FLAT TOP

Grain Painted
11¾" h, 18½" l, red and brown raised molded plinth base, inscribed red "1856, PWS" **165.00**
16" h, 41" l, blue-green, plain white painted int., pierced handles, early 19th C **250.00**
Hide covered, 12" l, leather and brass tack trim, orig wallpaper int., loose handle **50.00**
Pine, 27½" l, dec, bowed side and lid, worn light blue repaint int., orig brown graining, orig wrought iron lock and hasp **175.00**
Stained, 7" h, 17½" l, red, raised rect panel top, plain int., metal handles, raised molded plinth base **75.00**

VAL SAINT-LAMBERT

History: Val Saint-Lambert, a twelfth century Cistercian abbey, was located during different historical periods in France, Netherlands, and Belgium (1930 to present). In 1822 Francois Kemlin and Auguste Lelievre, along with a group of financiers, bought the abbey and opened a glassworks. In 1846 Val Saint-Lambert merged with the Société Anonyme des Manufactures de Glaces, Verres à Vitre, Cristaux et Gobeletaries. The company bought many other glassworks.

Val Saint-Lambert developed a reputation for technological progress in the glass industry. In 1879 Val Saint-Lambert became an independent company employing 4,000 workers. Val Saint-Lambert concentrated on the export market making table glass, cut, engraved, etched, and molded pieces, and chandeliers. Some pieces were finished in other countries, e.g., silver mounts added in the United States.

Val Saint-Lambert executed many special commissions for the artists of the Art Nouveau and Art Deco periods. The tradition continues. The company also made cameo-etched vases, covered boxes, and bowls. The firm celebrated its 150th anniversary in 1975.

Decanter, 12½" h, cranberry cut to clear, sgd, orig paper label, orig stopper .. **165.00**
Goblet, 5⅜", clear, blown mold, applied foot and stem **25.00**
Plate
Van Dyck **65.00**
Van Gogh **65.00**

Powder Box, 7" d, 4" h, cameo glass, emb silver lid, cupids, gold, and green mums and leaf dec, $950.00.

Powder Jar, 2½", cov, clear, amber stain,sgd **50.00**
Toothbrush Holder, clear, amber stain, sgd **50.00**
Tumbler, 6", blue cut to clear, gilt cameo classical band, set of six **350.00**
Vase
6⅜" h, urn form, eight stylized molded corn cobs and silk tassels, amber glass, gray patina **175.00**
8½", craquelle, brass Art Nouveau applique, ruffled, sgd **65.00**

VALENTINES

History: Early cards were handmade, often containing both handwritten verses and hand drawn pictures. Many cards also were hand colored and contained cutwork.

Mass production of machine made cards featuring chromolithography began after 1840. In 1847 Esther Howland of Worcester, Massachusetts, established a company to make valentines which were hand decorated with paper lace and other materials imported from England. They had a small "H" stamped in red in the top left corner. Howland's company eventually became the New England Valentine Company (N.E.V. Co.).

George C. Whitney and his brother founded a company after the Civil War which dominated the market from the 1870's through the first decades of the twentieth century. They bought out several competitors, one of which was the New England Valentine Company.

Lace paper was invented in 1834. The 1835 to 1860 period is known as the "golden age" of lacy cards.

Embossed paper was used in England after 1800. Embossed lithographs and woodcuts developed between 1825–40, with early examples being hand colored.

References: Ruth Webb Lee, *A History of Valentines*, reprinted by National Valentine Collectors

Association; Frank Staff, *The Valentine And Its Origins*, out-of-print.

Collectors' Club: National Valentine Collectors Association, Box 1404, Santa Ana, CA 92702. *Newsletter*(quarterly).

Additional Listings: See *Warman's Americana & Collectibles* for more examples.

Advisor: Evalene Pulati.

German, 6¾ x 3¾", stand up, diecut, $8.00.

Cut-out, floral design and "Sue Bell," framed with bookmark and presentation card, 10¾ x 12⅝" 250.00

Easel Back, 8½", girl carrying red honeycomb paper parasol 50.00

Foldout
   5", cupid, c1920 . . . . 8.00
   13 x 10", diecut, lady, lacy border, c1890 . . . . 25.00

Layered, 5", hearts and flowers, c1860 15.00

Mechanical, black boy and girl, chicken and duck pop out of watermelon with cards in beaks 25.00

Sailor's, 23", octagonal, shells spell out "Love" and "Hopeful Seaman," geometric, whale, and floral designs, center painting sgd "Martha Cahoon" . . 3,900.00

Stand Up, diecut
   6¾", girl holding doves, German . . . 8.00
   9", adv, "If You Love Your Wife, Give Her A Woods," girl riding in Woods car 20.00

Tuck, Raphel
   Five double heart cards with little girls pictured, attached with pink ribbon, orig box 45.00
   Irish boy, 12½", green jacket, top hat, string moves jointed arms, legs . . 75.00

VALLERYSTAHL GLASS

History: Vallerystahl (Lorraine), France, has been a glass producing center for centuries. In 1872 two major factories, Vallerystahl glassworks and Portieux glassworks, merged and produced art glass until 1898. Later, pressed glass covered animal dishes were introduced. The factory continues operation today.

Salt, cov, 2½ x 1¾ x 2", hen on nest, pale pink, $42.50.

Animal Dish, cov
   Dog on rug, milk glass 90.00
   Fish, milk glass 85.00
   Hen on nest, blue 75.00
   Robin 110.00
   Swan, milk glass 100.00

Box
   3½ x 4", cov, blue milk glass 70.00
   5 x 3", cameo, dark green, applied and cut dec, sgd 950.00

Butter Dish, figural, radish 75.00

Candlestick, Grecian Girl, frosted 50.00

Candy Dish, 4⅛" d, white milk glass, basketweave, rope handles and finial 85.00

Cologne Bottle, 6¾", cameo, fuchsia flowers and leaves, frosted cranberry ground, gold colored collar and screw stopper, sgd "Cristaherie Le Gantin" 475.00

Goblet, ftd, blue 60.00

Lemon Dish, cov, figural, lemon, opaque yellow 50.00

Plate
   7½", floral dec, blue 35.00
   8", Thistle pattern, green 70.00

Tumbler, 4", cobalt blue 45.00

Vase
9½", cameo, budding branches, enameled insects, frosted ground, gilt highlights, c1900, sgd **600.00**
12", cameo, gold daffodils, amberina ground, sgd **3,500.00**

VAN BRIGGLE POTTERY

History: Artus Van Briggle, born in 1869, was a talented Ohio artist. He joined Rookwood in 1887 and studied in Paris under Rookwood's sponsorship from 1893 until 1896. In 1899 he moved to Colorado for his health and established his own pottery in Colorado Springs in 1901.

Van Briggle's work was influenced heavily by the Art Nouveau "school" he saw in France. He produced a great variety of matte glazed wares in this style. Colors varied.

The "AA" mark, a date, and "Van Briggle" were incised on all pieces prior to 1907 and sometimes into the 1910s and 20s. After 1920, "Colorado Springs, Colorado" or an abbreviation was added. Dated pieces are the most desirable.

Artus died in 1904. Anne Van Briggle continued the pottery until 1912.

References: Barbara Arnest (ed.), *Van Briggle Pottery: The Early Years,* The Colorado Springs Fine Art Center, 1975; Scott N. Nelson, Lois Crouch, Euphemia Demmin, and Robert Newton, *Collector's Guide To Van Briggle Pottery,* Halldin Publishing, 1986.

Collectors' Club: American Art Pottery Association, 270 Spangler Mill Road, New Cumberland, PA 17070.

Museum: Pioneer Museum, Colorado Springs, CO.

Reproduction Alert: Van Briggle pottery still is made today. These modern pieces often are confused for older examples. Among the glazes used are Moonglo (off white), Turquoise Ming, Russet, and Midnight (black).

1901–1920

Bookends, owl, green, 1910, pr **75.00**
Bowl
5¼ x 3", emb dragonflies, red, exposed clay, flowing powder blue matte glaze, 1906 .... **500.00**
7½", two tone maroon, semi-matte, 1918 .... **275.00**
Purple textured glaze, #776, dated 1918 .... **325.00**
Plate, 8", blue, green, and brown, 1903 **400.00**

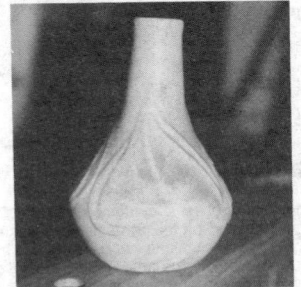

Vase, 8", light green, brown leaves, 1905, pattern 165, $450.00.

Tile, 6" sq, landscape, 1907–12 ..... **125.00**
Vase
3½", dark brown to medium speckled brown glaze, 1915 .... **310.00**
5 x 4¾", bulbous, diagonally incised collar rim, emb Indian geometric dec, insect, and bird's head, matte green finish, incised "Van Briggle," "1902," and "III," stamped "15" .. **950.00**
5 x 10¼", small collared rim tapering to bulbous base, double rows of emb stylized leaves, textured Persian rose matte, airbrushed green, 1903, incised "III" **1,500.00**
5½", semi-matte, maroon, marked "Ned Curtis, 1914" **215.00**
6¼ x 3", baluster, collar rim, relief bell flowers dec, medium blue matte finish, incised "Van Briggle, 1903, and III," die-stamped "197" **900.00**
7 x 3¾", bulging cylindrical, four emb violet and yellow Trifolium flower heads, green leaves and stems, khaki matte ground, incised "Van Briggle, 1903, and III," die-stamped "219" **2,100.00**

1921–1968

Bowl, 5", turquoise and dark blue, floral **35.00**
Figure
Cat, 15", brown glaze, 1955–68, marked "Anne Van Briggle" **65.00**
Elephant, 6", blue **40.00**
Vase
10" h, "Lorelei," Mountain Crag brown glaze, late 1920s, early 1930s, incised "Van Briggle-Colo. Spgs" **220.00**
12" h, matte pale blue, dark blue highlights, cylindrical form tapered to base, molded petal flowers, early 20th C, sgd **150.00**
13¼" h, dark blue on pale blue, elon-

gated form, iris swelling toward base, two loop handles, early 20th C, sgd **175.00**
Crag brown, c1920s **60.00**

Vasart

VASART

History: Vasart is a contemporary art glass made in Scotland by the Streathearn Glass Co. The colors are mottled, and sometimes shade from one hue to another. It is readily identified by and engraved signature on the base.

Bowl, 8″ d, green-gray ground, goldstone flakes, $75.00.

Basket, 8¼″ l, 5″ h, green shading to pink **90.00**
Bowl
  2″, mottled green, scalloped rim ... **30.00**
  5″, light green **35.00**
  5¾″, mottled gray, fold over rim, sgd **100.00**
Lamp, 10¼″ h, 5½″ d, flower form, bubble glass, pink, blue, and white, pink and white pulled swirls, five picked rims **300.00**
Mug, mottled blue and white **45.00**
Tray, 4 x 12″, mottled blue shading to green **75.00**
Tumbler, blue and white striped **75.00**
Vase
  4⅝″, mottled pink and white, sgd ... **65.00**
  6″, multicolored spatters, pink and blue flared top **90.00**

VENETIAN GLASS

History: Venetian glass has been made on the island of Morano, near Venice, since the 13th century. Most of the wares are thin walled. Many types

of decoration have been used: embedded gold dust, lace work, and applied fruits or flowers.
  Reproduction Alert: Venetian glass continues to be made today.

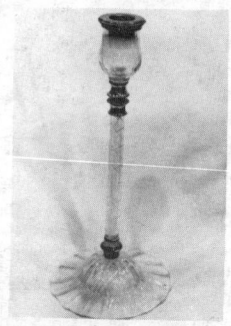

Candlestick, 11¼″ h, 5¼″ d base, opalescent ribbon twist stem, canary ground, brass fittings, $70.00

V.86

Basket, 6½″ d, 7½″ h, flared, notched rim, purple to clear, controlled bubbles, gold flecked base **75.00**
Candlesticks, pr, 10″ h, figural, yellow dragons **250.00**
Champagne, cranberry, clear dolphin stem **65.00**
Cologne Bottle, light green, paperweight type stopper **50.00**
Compote, 10″ d, ruffled, swan handles, clear, gold Aventurine **75.00**
Cruet, 8″, vertical blue, pink and yellow latticino bands **110.00**
Dish, 7″, alternating gold and red rays **45.00**
Figure, 6¼″ h, parrot, ruby body, amber head and tail, clear wings, gold dust trim, amber pedestal **30.00**
Finger Bowl, amber, threaded, matching underplate **65.00**
Goblet, frosted mauve, irid coinspots, clear amber stem, frosted base **45.00**
Jar, cov, amber, paperweight type finial **50.00**
Perfume Bottle, clear, gold spatter dec, orig stopper with long dauber **375.00**
Rose Bowl, ruffled, ftd, pink and gold flecks **100.00**
Vase
  4½″, butterscotch ground, applied black threading and dots, applied black handles **75.00**
  8″, bottle shape, frosted mauve, irid amber teardrops, amber ribbing on base, ruffled, c1895 .... **200.00**
Wine, latticino stripe, cranberry, clear, opal, and goldstone **75.00**

VERLYS GLASS

History: Verlys glass is an art glass originally made in France after 1930. For a period of a few months, Heisey Glass Co., Newark, Ohio, produced the identical glass, having obtained the rights and formula from the French factory.

The French-produced glass can be distinguished from the American product by the signature. The French is mold marked; the American is etched script signed.

Vase, 6½" maximum width, 4½" h, fan shape, Lovebirds pattern, script signature, $125.00.

Bowl
6" d		
	Cupid and Hearts pattern, clear	45.00
	Pine Cone pattern, three small feet	60.00
	Thistle pattern, cobalt blue	65.00
8½" d, Thistle pattern, three small feet		140.00
10" d, Chrysanthemum pattern, clear and frosted		125.00
11½" d, Frosted Tassel pattern, clear, sgd		110.00
Box, cov, 5¼" d, Chrysanthemum pattern, topaz		325.00
Charger, Water Lily pattern, clear		150.00
Console Bowl, 14" d, Butterfly pattern, clear		125.00
Figure, 4¼" h, pigeon, frosted		275.00
Planter, 10⅛", Chrysanthemum pattern, clear		85.00
Plate, 6¼" d, Pine Cone pattern, mold sgd		65.00
Soap Dish, 5⅜" l, 4" h, figural, fish, clear and frosted		65.00
Vase, 10" h, Thistle pattern, clear and frosted, sgd		240.00

VILLEROY & BOCH

History: Pierre Joseph Boch established a pottery near Luxemburg, Germany, in 1767. Jean Francis, his son, introduced the first coal-fired kiln in Europe and perfected a water-power-driven potter's wheel. Pierre's grandson, Eugene Boch, managed a pottery at Mettlach; Nicholas Villeroy also had a pottery nearby.

In 1841 the three potteries were merged into the firm of Villeroy & Boch. Early production included a hard paste earthenware comparable to English ironstone. The factory continues to use this hard paste formula for its modern tablewares.

Reference: Susan and Al Bagdade, *Warman's English & Continental Pottery & Porcelain, 1st Edition,* Warman Publishing Co., Inc., 1987.

Additional Listings: Mettlach.

Vases, 6¼" h, Art Deco, green and brown, white ground, gold outlines, pr, $200.00.

Bowl, 10½", blue floral dec, handled		165.00
Cruet, 8½", blue and white		75.00
Demitasse Cup and Saucer, Patermo		15.00
Mug, 3½", tan, leaf and twig dec, twig handle		50.00
Pitcher, 4¾ x 10⅝", six sided, white int., dark gray raised scrolls, leaves, pods, and birds, gray ground, beige crest mark		250.00
Plaque		
	12", woman and children in boat, P.U.G.	70.00
	13", Rheinstein castle	45.00
	16", Horse race, P.U.G., Dresden	150.00

Plate, 9", polychrome floral dec, gaudy
stick spatter **65.00**
Stein, 6½", five white figures, blue
ground, ½ liter, #171, Mercury mark
.... **225.00**
Teapot, 6¼", blue and white dec **130.00**
Tray
5 x 7½", Mettlach Abbey **70.00**
11 x 16", cavalier, P.U.G. **155.00**
Vase
7", white relief floral dec, yellow
ground **100.00**
12", bottle shape, sgraffito geometric
dec, Dresden **120.00**

WARWICK

WARWICK
CHINA

History: Warwick China Manufacturing Co.,
Wheeling, West Virginia, was incorporated in 1887
and continued until 1951. The company was one
of the first manufacturers of vitreous glazed wares
in the United States. Production was extensive and
included tableware, garden ornaments, and decorative and utilitarian items.

Pieces were hand painted or decorated by decals. Collectors seek portrait items and fraternal
pieces for groups such as the Elks, Eagles, and
Knights of Pythias.

Some experimental, eggshell-type porcelain
was made before 1887. A few examples are in the
market.

**Pitcher, 10½" h, brown ground, marked
"IOGA," $120.00.**

Ale Set, tankard pitcher, seven matching mugs, B.P.O.E. emblem and elk
dec, shaded brown ground **275.00**
Bone Dish, flow blue scenic dec,
marked **48.00**

Chocolate Pot, 10½", branches of orange thornapples, shaded brown to
creamy yellow and ivory ground, twig
handle, marked "Warwick China" .. **175.00**
Cream Soup, underplate, white, gold
trim **10.00**
Creamer, speckled blue and white, gold
trim on raised leaves around rim,
marked "Warwick China" **35.00**
Humidor, cov, portrait of woman, brown
ground, marked "IOGA" **200.00**
Pitcher
Cider, fruit dec, brown glaze **100.00**
Lemonade, portrait dec, brown glaze,
marked **165.00**
Tankard, 13" h, portrait of monk with
mug of ale **245.00**
Portrait Plate, 10", Indian, yellow shading to brown ground **65.00**
Vase
8", ftd, portrait of woman, large hat
with peacock feathers, holding rose
to her lips, shaded brown to cream
ground, marked "IOGA" **100.00**
10"
Amaryllis, orange blossoms, brown
ground, marked "IOGA" **70.00**
Orchid dec, red and brown **135.00**
10½", twig handles, Hibiscus pattern **150.00**

WATCHES, POCKET

History: Pocket watches can be found from flea
markets to the specialized jewelry sales at Butterfield's, Phillip's, and Sotheby's. Condition of movement is first priority; design and detailing of case
is second.

In pocket watches, listing aids are size (18/0 to
20), number of jewels in movement, open or
closed (hunter) face, and whether the case is gold,
gold filled, or some other metal. The movement is
the critical element since cases often were
switched. However, an elaborate case, especially
of gold, adds significantly to value.

Pocket watches designed to railroad specifica-
tions are desirable. They are 16 to 18 in size, have
a minimum of 17 jewels, adjust to at least five
positions, and conform to many other specifica-
tions. All are openfaced.

Study the field thoroughly before buying. The
literature is vast including books and newsletters
from clubs and collectors. Abbreviations: S = size;
gf = gold filled; yg = yellow gold; j = jewels.

References: Howard Brenner, *Collecting
Comic Character Clocks and Watches,* Books
Americana, 1987; Roy Ehrhardt & William Meg-
gers, *American Pocket Watches Identification And
Price Guide: Beginning To End...1830-1980,*
Heart of America Press, 1987; Cedric Jagger, *The
Artistry Of The English Watch,* Charles E. Tuttle
Co., 1988; Reinhard Meis, *Pocket Watches: From*

the Pendant Watch To The Tourbillon, Schiffer Publishing, 1987, orig published in German; Cooksey Shugart and Tom Engle, *The Official Price Guide To Watches, Eighth Edition,* House of Collectibles, 1988.

Collectors' Club: National Association of Watch & Clock Collectors, 514 Poplar Street, Box 33, Columbia, PA 17512. *Bulletin* (bi-monthly) and *Mart* (bi-monthly).

Museums: American Clock & Watch Museum, Bristol, CT; Hoffman Clock Museum, Newark, NY; National Association of Watch and Clock Collectors Museum, Columbia, PA; The Time Museum, Rockford, IL.

Character

Buck Rogers, lightning bolt hands, One-eyed Monster on reverse, Ingraham, 1935	210.00
Dizzy Dean, Dean with outstretched arm on dial, New Haven, 1935 . .	150.00
Donald Duck, silvered case, Ingersoll, 1939	240.00
Mickey Mouse, pocket, bright silver luster, white dial, orig strap, orig black, white, and red box with guarantee and price sticker	350.00
Tom Mix, Texas Longhorn steer head second hand, silvered case, "Always find time for a good deed, Tom Mix" on back, leather strap fob	200.00
Popeye, pocket, red, black, and blue on silver image, worn silver finish case, diecut arms points at minutes, hour arm missing, orig crystal	150.00

Railroad

American Waltham Watch Co, 17j, lever set, Model No. 1892	185.00
E. Howard Watch Co, 15j, stem wind, stem set gilded movement marked "E. Howard & Co, Boston L," sgd white enamel dial, Roman numerals, gf hunting case marked "Crescent"	160.00
Hamilton Watch Co, 21j, stem wind, lever set nickel movement marked "Hamilton 992B 21 jewels," sgd double sunk Montgomery dial, stainless steel case marked "Hamilton Watch Co," orig instructions and box	400.00
Hampden Watch Co, 23j, stem wind, lever set nickel movement marked "New Railway 23 jewels," sgd double sunk white enamel dial, Arabic numerals, gf case, c1900	125.00
Illinois Watch Co, 23j, stem wind, lever set nickel movement, sgd double sunk white enamel dial, Arabic numerals, nickel case marked "South Bend," c1925	250.00
South Bend Watch Co, 21j, stem	

wind, nickel movement, sgd silvered metal dial, Arabic numerals, 10K gf case marked "NAWCO Railroad Model," engraved locomotive on back, South Bend, IN, c1925 . **225.00**

Hampden, hunting case, lever set, gold fill, $185.00.

Regular

American Waltham Watch Co, Roadmaster, 17j, lever set, open face, gold jewel setting, Model No. 1899	250.00
Audemars Piguet, platinum, applied Arabic numerals, white cathedral hands, 19j lever movement, Swiss open face platinum case, gold Art Deco monogram "R.A.R.," c1930 .	850.00
Henry Benguelin & Son, hunter, lever nickel 21j bar pattern movement, 18K engine turned case	600.00
Charleton, lady's, yg and lapis, needs minor repair	150.00
E. Goldsmith, Liverpool movement, 18K yg, gold chain, seal, and key	650.00
Gruen, 17j, pentagon case, thin style, yellow gold filled	85.00
Hamilton Watch Co, 21j, stem wind, lever set nickel movement marked "Hamilton Watch Co, 21 jewels 992," sgd double sunk white enamel dial, Arabic numerals, silverode case marked "Hamilton," glass crystal, c1925	75.00
J. A. Hoddel and Co, 19½ ligne key wind, key set jeweled movement with gilded plates, sgd white enamel dial, Roman numerals, 18K engine turned case marked "Baldwin and Co," c1860	1,000.00
E. Howard & Co	
Hunting, Abbott Sure Time, 17j, open face, gold filled case	200.00
Lady's, 15j, stem wind, lever set gilded movement marked "E. Howard & Co, Boston, G," sgd white enamel dial, Roman numerals, 18K gold hunting scene case, engraved inside "From	

Father to M. Gertrude Curtis on her 18th Birthday Sept 9, 1875" **700.00**

Illinois Watch Co, gilt, 11j, key wind and key set movement marked "Columbia," white enamel dial, Roman numerals, engraved silver case marked "900," Springfield, IL, c1880 .... **90.00**

Patek Philippe, white enamel dial, radiating black Arabic numerals, 18j movement, wolf's tooth winding, 14K gold polished case, sgd "SJ #93709, c1910 .... **1,400.00**

Robert Toskell, 44 mm key wind key set gilded jeweled lever movement, fusee and chain, gilded brass dial, raised multicolored dec, Roman numerals, 18K raised gold case with hallmarks, bull's eye crystal, inscribed by maker **1,000.00**

Rockford Watch Co, 17j, stem wind, lever set nickel movement marked "Winnebago 17 jewels, adjusted five positions," sgd double sunk white enamel dial, Arabic numerals, silverode case marked "Keystone," engraved locomotive on back, orig glass crystal, c1910 ... **100.00**

Seth Thomas Watch Co, 17j stem wind, lever set nickel movement marked "Seth Thomas, adjusted and 17 jewels," sgd double sunk white enamel dial, Arabic numerals, gf case marked "B and B, 20 years," engraved ornate floral design on back, gilded hands, gf chain, c1895 .... **165.00**

Unknown Maker, gold case marked "750," engraved and enameled initials "H G C," c1900 .... **250.00**

WATCHES, WRIST

History: The definition of a wristwatch is simple: "a small watch that is attached to a bracelet or strap and is worn around the wrist." However, a watch on a bracelet is not necessarily a wristwatch. The key is the ability to read the time. A true wristwatch allows you to read the time at a glance, without making any other motions. Early watches on a bracelet that was worn on the arm had the axis of their dials, from 6 to 12, perpendicular to the band. Reading them required some extensive arm movement.

The first true wristwatch appeared about 1850. However, the key date is 1880 when the stylish decorative wristwatch appeared and almost universal acceptance occurred. The technology to create the wristwatch existed in the early nineteenth century with Brequet's shock-absorbing

"Parachute System" for automatic watches and Adrien Philipe's winding stem.

The wristwatch was a response to the needs of the entreprenuerial age with its emphasis on punctuality and planned free time. By approximately 1930 the sales of wristwatches surpassed that of pocket watches. Swiss and German manufacturers were quickly joined by American makers.

The wristwatch has undergone many technical advances during the twentieth century including self-winding (automatic), shock-resistance, electric operation, etc. It truly is the most significant and dominant clock of the century.

References: Howard S. Benner, *Identification and Value Guide Collecting Comic Character Clocks and Watches*, Books Americana, 1987; Kahlert MHe Brunner, *Wristwatches, History of A Century's Development*, Schiffer Publishing Ltd., 1986; Sherry and Roy Ehrhardt, Joe Demesy, and Ken Specht, *Vintage American & Europe Wrist Watch Price Guide, Book 2*, Heart of America Press, 1988; Sherry Ehrhardt and Peter Planes, *Vintage American & European Wrist Watch Price Guide*, Heart of America Press, 1984; Sherry Ehrhardt and Peter Planes, *Vintage American & European Wrist Watch Price Guide 1987 Values*, Heart of America Press, 1987; Cooksey Shugart and Tom Engle, *The Official Price Guide To Watches, Eighth Edition*, House of Collectibles, 1988.

Collectors' Club: National Association of Watch & Clock Collectors, 514 Poplar Street, Box 33, Columbia, PA 17512. *Bulletin* (bi-montly) and *Mart* (bi-montly).

Museums: American Clock & Watch Museum, Bristol, CT; Hoffman Clock Museum, Newark, NY; National Association of Watch and Clock Collectors Museum, Columbia, PA; The Time Museum, Rockford, IL.

Character

Alice In Wonderland, blue "Alice" dial, orig carton holds watch and 5" h ceramic figure **50.00**

Cinderella, pink dial, blue band, US Time, 1950 .... **50.00**

Dick Tracy, pistol moves back and forth, tan strap band **90.00**

Mary Marvel, silver finish, orig straps, box, and insert **100.00**

Snow White, blue strap band, orig box with movie scene inside lid, Ingersoll, 1939 .... **150.00**

Tom Corbett, leather strap band, rocket ship display card **125.00**

Lady's

Bulova, 14K gold case with diamonds, rect dial **200.00**

Ebel, off-white enamel dial, gold baton hands, jeweled quartz movement, brushed 18K case, waved

bracelet, diamond set bezel, presentation case, box, and guarantee **3,750.00**
Hamilton Watch Co, rect dial, 14K case **60.00**
Le Coultre, diamond, sq dial, trefoil marquise diamonds, scrolled bracelet, blued steel spade hands, backwound lever movement, platinum case, 1950s **2,750.00**
Lucien Piccard, bezel mounted with diamonds within caliber sapphire border, black Roman figured dial, 17j gilt lever movement, 14K white gold case #00179, dark blue suede strap **700.00**
Patek Philippe, rect, gold, sq silvered dial, baton hands, Swiss 18K Patek shape case, arched flint crystal, c1936 .... **4,250.00**
Universal, Geneve, 18K yg, rect dial, thin black band, c1938 .... **90.00**

Gruen Quadron, 14K gold fill, 17 jewel, $120.00.

Man's
Bulova, 17j, 14K gold case, rect dial **150.00**
Gruen, rect dial, 15j, gf **60.00**
Gubelin, silvered dial, applied gilt baton, gilt dauphine hands, 17j shock-resistant tonneau movement, 18K Swiss case, raised bezel, flint crystal, brown crocodile strap, c1960 . **1,500.00**
Hamilton Watch Co, 17j, round dial, stem wind and set, 14K gold case, leather band **125.00**
Illinois Watch Co, New Yorker, 17j, sq dial, 14K gold **175.00**
Patek Philippe, sq, silvered dial, applied gold baton hands and chapters, 18j caliber movement, shock protection, Swiss 18K gold two-piece case, mineral crystal, black Patek calfskin strap **2,250.00**
Perpetual Watch Co, 15j, gf, round

dial, Harwood movement, bezel, New York, 1930 .... **175.00**
Rolex, sq, silvered dial, raised gilt batons and hands, 28j Precision adjusted and shock protected caliber movement, rotor winding system, 18K rose gold Swiss case, flint crystal, black lizard strap, c1950 . **1,300.00**
Tiffany & Co, 17j, 14K polished yg, triple date, moon phase, 1940s .. **800.00**
Universal Watch, Compax, 17j, 18K polished yg, three dial chronograph, c1950 .... **250.00**
Waltham, 21j, 14K polished gf, c1940 **125.00**

WATERFORD

History: Waterford crystal is quality flint glass commonly decorated with cuttings. The original factory was established at Waterford, Ireland, in 1729. Glass made before 1830 is darker than the brilliantly clear glass of later production. The factory closed in 1852. After 100 years it reopened and continues in production.

Compote, 6¾" d, 5¾" h, turned down rim, pedestal, $275.00.

Butter, cov, ovoid, mushroom finial ... **250.00**
Candlestick, 7", pr, pear shape, hollow center, horizontal oval cuts on wafers between fluted top and rayed base, looped cross cuttings in two sizes, downward spray with star cut **150.00**
Decanter
 12", star base, paneled neck, stopper **75.00**
 15", allover geometric cutting, matching stopper **140.00**
Goblet
 Cameragh **30.00**
 Glengarett **35.00**
Jar, 7", cov, fan and diamond cuts ... **125.00**
Pitcher
 6¾", shaped spout, strap handle, Lismore **100.00**
 10", diamond cuts, applied handle .. **200.00**

Plate, 8", diamond cut center **90.00**
Salt, 3⅞", master, oval, diamond cut .. **65.00**
Vase, 7¼", bulbous, top to bottom vertical cuts separated by horizontal slash cuts, sgd **100.00**

WAVE CREST WARE

WAVE CREST

History: The C. F. Monroe Company of Meriden, Connecticut, produced the opal glassware known as wave crest from 1898 until World War I. The company bought the opaque, blown molded glass blanks for decoration from the Pairpoint Manufacturing Co. of New Bedford, Massachusetts, and other glass makers including European factories. Florals were the most common decorative motif. Trade names used were "Wave Crest Ware," "Kelva," and "Nakara."

References: Wilfred R. Cohen, *Wave Crest: The Glass of C.F. Monroe,* Collector Books, 1987; Elsa H. Grimmer, *Wave Crest Ware,* Wallace-Homestead, 1979.

Salt Shaker, 2¼" h, 1¾" w, Erie Twist, pink flowers, green leaves, blue highlights, (514) $85.00.

Biscuit Jar
  Helmschmied Swirl, hinged lid, beading, pastel wash **650.00**
  Pink wild roses, sq, 6" h, lid marked "C.F.M. Co." **110.00**
Bonbon, 1½ x 5¼", florals and scrolls, satin and shiny finish, handle **350.00**
Box
  3¾" d, 3" h, hp, house, pond, and trees scene, pale pink ground, orig lining, hinged lid **145.00**
  7" d, crystal, gold and paneled colors, nine storks and setting sun lid ... **1,500.00**
  7¼" d, Helmschmied Swirl mold, enameled florals, pale pink ground, lining, sgd **450.00**

Clock, triangular shape, easel, ormolu fitting **1,000.00**
Creamer and Sugar, pink rosebuds, tan and white swirls **635.00**
Dresser Box, 6½" l, 5" h, raised emb pink luster swirls, variegated color flowers, gold ormolu band and feet . **700.00**
Dresser Dish, ormolu engraved rim, bulbous swirl, pink, blue forget-me-not dec, enameling, Red Banner mark . **110.00**
Ferner, 7" sq, egg crate mold, enameled French blue florals, pale blue ground, ornate ormolu feet and rim **310.00**
Glove Box, 5½ x 10 x 4½", cobalt, lock, ftd **1,000.00**
Humidor, 6" h, Baroque shell mold, pink luster, robin's egg blue ground, hinged lid, sgd **495.00**
Jardiniere
  6½" h, rolled metal rim, ftd **600.00**
  7¼" h, 9" d, emb, Rococo mold, enameled spider chrysanthemums, shasta daisies, robin's egg blue ground, beaded ormolu rim **600.00**
Jewel Box, cov
  4" d, lavender crystal, blue flowers, white dotting on cov, sgd **500.00**
  5½ x 3", puffy, blue floral, lined, red banner mark **350.00**
Hair Receiver, 5¾", brass lid, floral base, emb, black mark **235.00**
Sugar Shaker, alternating yellow and pink panels **300.00**
Syrup, 5½" h, painted and enamel flowers surrounded by raised enamel dots dec, emb SP handle and hinged lid . **900.00**
Vase
  2¼ x 3¼", shell motif **400.00**
  3¾ x 4¼", squatty, multicolored, beaded rim, ftd **450.00**
  9 x 6½", hp, deep rust color, handle, ftd **900.00**
  10¾ x 4¾", hp, Mary had a little lamb scene, dark glossy green finish, ftd **1,200.00**
  11¼ x 4", hp, cobalt blue, chrysanthemum flowers on back, handled .. **1,200.00**
  15" h, birds in flight, ftd **750.00**
Wall Plaque
  5½" d, winter snow scene **800.00**
  8½ x 12", lovely lady surrounded by flowers **1,400.00**
  9¾" d
    Venetian scene, dark green border **1,000.00**
    Daisies and clover **850.00**

WEATHER VANES

History: A weather vane indicates wind direction. The earliest known examples were found on late 17th century structures in the Boston area. The vanes were handcrafted of wood, copper, or tin. By the last half of the 19th century, weather vanes adorned farms and houses throughout the nation. Mass produced vanes of cast iron, copper, and sheet metal were sold through mail order catalogs or at country stores.

The champion vane is the rooster. In fact, the name weathercock is synonymous with weather vane. The styles and patterns are endless. Weathering can affect the same vane differently. For this reason, patina is a critical element in collecting vanes.

Whirligigs are a variation of the weather vane. Constructed of wood and metal, often by unskilled craftsmen, whirligigs not only indicate the direction of the wind and its velocity, but their unique movements served as entertainment for children, neighbors, and passersby.

Reproduction Alert: Reproduction of early models exist, are being aged, and sold as originals.

Cast Iron, 32″ l, flat, Massachusetts, c1830, $1,500.00.

Angel, 35″ l, wood, tin trumpet, brown
  and yellow paint 2,000.00
Birds, 31″ l, two metal silhouettes, iron
  arrow, painted black, 20th C 85.00
Fish, 60″ l, old white paint traces, orig
  metal fins, made and used on Nan-
  tucket Island 2,500.00
Horse
  26″ h, prancing, painted tin, direc-
    tional arrow 400.00
  28½″ h, 33″ l, copper, full body, old
    brown paint, emb black mane,
    black tail, traces of gilt, soldered
    repairs 4,500.00
Indian, 39″ h, 40″ w, bow and arrow,
  copper, good detail, green patina,
  contemporary 700.00
Rooster
  11¾″ h, 15″ l, mounted on diamond
    shape wood base, orig, sgd, rect
    brand "A. E. Crowell/Maker/East
    Harwich/Mass" 7,000.00

26½″ h, 29″ l, copper, fine patina,
  traces of orig gold leaf beneath . . 5,500.00
29″ h, 27″ l, tin, painted, 19th C . . .   750.00
Rooster and Arrow, 46″ l, 31″ h, wood
  silhouette, weathered red paint, orig
  roof top mounting block, early 20th C   265.00
Schooner, 25½″ l, 18″ h, old black and
  white paint 325.00
Ship, 37″ h, sailing, copper 400.00
Windmill, 39½″, wood, teal green and
  dark red paint, replaced center spin-
  dle and arrow 150.00

WEBB, THOMAS & SONS

History: Thomas Webb & Sons was established in 1837 in Stourbridge, England. The company probably is best known for its very beautiful English cameo glass. However, many other types of colored glass were produced including enameled glass, iridescent glass, pieces with heavy glass ornamentation, cased glass, and other art glass besides cameo.

Additional Listings: Burmese, Cameo, and Peachblow.

Bowl
  7½ x 4⅞″, glossy peachblow, cream
    lining, gold prunus and bird dec,
    three applied amber reeded feet .   800.00
  12″, cased, fluted, folded top, opaque
    white ext., blush pink int., sgd . . .   225.00
  12½ x 5⅞ x 7″, oval, shaded blue,
    overlay, green and tan enamel
    leaves, yellow flowers, ruffled . . .   325.00
Bride's Bowl, 12″ d, enameled florals,
  pink shaded to strawberry red
  ground, sgd 215.00
Cologne, cameo, carved white florals,
  amber ground, SS top and mounting 1,250.00
Epergne, 9½ x 15″, orange to clear,
  threaded glass, four petal scalloped
  vases, clear branches 650.00
Goblet, 8½″ h, Alexandrite, circular
  wafer-thin base, twisted stem, four
  textured leaves applied to base of
  bowl, amber tulip shaped bowl shad-
  ing to fuchsia 1,750.00
Perfume Bottle, cameo, 3½″ h, squatty,
  carved white blossoms, blue satin
  ground, SS screw on cap 875.00
Pitcher, 5½″ h, scalloped top, gold
  shaded to white, applied frosted han-
  dle, sgd 225.00
Rose Bowl
  3¼″, gold flowers and insects, brown
    ground 125.00
  4⅜″, gold flower dec, peachblow
    ground 350.00
  5½″, Zipper pattern, MOP, brown
    shading to green, rose lining, sgd
    "Webb, RD #56693" 975.00

7½ x 7¼″, DQ, MOP, amberina shading **1,200.00**

Scent Bottle

1¼″ d, 4¼″ l, lay-down type, gold prunus dec, green shaded to yellow satin ground, SS screw on domed monogrammed cap **400.00**

2½″ d, 3½″ h, burmese, acid finish, gold leaves and berries, dec, hallmarked SS screw on dome cap .. **700.00**

Vase, 6¼″ h, peachblow, multicolored dec, unmarked, $175.00.

Vase

3½″, stick, gold flowers and insects, brown ground **175.00**

3¾ x 4¼″, Burmese, melon ribbed, ivy dec, acid finish, unsigned **400.00**

4⅛″, satin, squatty, gold, green, and brick red flowers and leaves **100.00**

5¼″, simulated ivory cameo, brown stain shading to ivory, flowers, leaves, and panel of three birds, scalloped top, sgd **850.00**

5¾″, glossy peachblow, cream lining, emb swirls, fancy crystal berries, leaves, and flowers applique and feet **550.00**

6″, gourd, gold flowers and insects, shaded brown ground **175.00**

8″, glossy peachblow, cream lining, gold floral and butterfly dec, blue highlights, cream applied handles **700.00**

9″, deep coral red overlay, white lining, heavy gold branch and flowers dec **350.00**

9¼″, gourd, gold flowers and insects, yellowish brown ground **275.00**

9⅜ x 5⅛″, flattened oval, glossy peachblow, gold and silver dec, propeller mark **675.00**

12 x 6½″, satin, shaded pink, bird, flowers, and fruit enamel dec, facing pr **1,100.00**

WEDGWOOD

WEDGWOOD

History: In 1754 Josiah Wedgwood entered into a partnership with Thomas Whieldon of Fenton Vivian, Staffordshire, England. Products included marbled, agate, tortoise shell, green glaze, and Egyptian black wares. In 1759 Wedgwood opened his own pottery at the Ivy House works, Burslem. In 1764 he moved to the Brick House (Bell Works) at Burslem. The pottery concentrated on utilitarian pieces.

Between 1766 and 1769 Wedgwood built the famous works at Etruria. Among the most renowned products of this plant were the Empress Catherina of Russia dinner service (1774) and the Portland Vase (1790s). Product lines were caneware, unglazed earthenwares (drabwares), piecrust wares, variegated and marbled wares, black basalt (developed in 1768), Queen's or creamware, Jasperware (perfected in 1774), and others.

Bone china was produced under the direction of Josiah Wedgwood II between 1812 and 1822 and revived in 1878. Moonlight lustre was made from 1805 to 1815. Fairyland lustre began in 1920. All lustre production ended in 1932.

A museum was established at the Etruria pottery in 1906. When Wedgwood moved to its modern plant at Barlaston, North Staffordshire, the museum was continued and expanded.

References: Susan and Al Bagdade, *Warman's English & Continental Pottery & Porcelain, 1st Edition,* Warman Publishing Co., Inc., 1987; David Buten and Jane Clancy, *Eighteenth-Century Wedgwood: A Guide For Collectors And Connoisseurs,* Main Street Press, 1980; Robin Reilly, *The Collector's Wedgwood,* Portfolio Press/A Robert Campbell Rowe Book, 1980; Robin Reilly and George Savage, *Dictionary Of Wedgwood,* Antique Collectors Club, 1980.

Collectors' Club: The Wedgwood Society, 246 N. Bowman Avenue, Merion, PA 19066; The Wedgwood Society, The Roman Villa, Rockbourne, Fordingbridge, Hents, England, SP 6 3PG.

Museum: Buten Museum, Merion, PA.

BASALT

Bust

8″ d, 11½″ h, Prior, marked "Wedgwood" **750.00**

10¼″ d, 17″ h, Mercury, marked "Wedgwood" **1,125.00**

13¾″ h, Venus, head turned to leaf, hair tied with ribbon, waisted circular socle, imp "Wedgwood," so-

Basalt, spill vase, 5″ h, Goddess of Music, $125.00.

cle also imp date cipher STZ (Sept 1871) **1,210.00**

Caddy Spoon, 2¼″ l, shell bowl, short handle, imp flowerhead, imp mark . . **275.00**

Candlesticks, pr
10¾″, figural, maiden in classical dress holding cornucopia surmounted by candle nozzle, fluted socle with laurel wreath, sq base with relief florette flanked by anthemia, imp "Wedgwood" and "C" **500.00**
10¹⁵⁄₁₆″, Triton, figural, mirman kneeling on rockwork base, whorled shell surmounted by floriform candle nozzle, imp mark, c1930 . . . . **825.00**

Miniature, 2³⁄₁₆″ h, teapot, cov, Capri dec, enameled floral sprays, orange line borders on spout, handle, and knob rims, imp mark **450.00**

Plaques, pr, 7³⁄₈″ h, high relief, Hercules strangling lion on one, other with Hercules supporting bound boar, imp marks **715.00**

Salt Spoon, 2⅝″, trifid terminal at base of curved handle, imp mark, late 18th C **225.00**

Vase
9″, painted enamel geometric motifs, brick-red, gray, and white, brick-red line borders, imp "Wedgwood" . . . **675.00**
9¼″, cov, The Dancing Hours, two foliate loop handles, fluted cov, acorn knob, engine turned flutes, sq base, imp "Wedgwood," pr **1,100.00**
10½″, Encaustic decoration, orange, white, and black, classical figure holding lyre and Scythian figure dancing, key fret border, leaf sprays on side, classical borders on neck, rim, and handles, imp "Wedgwood, M," incised number and potter's mark **2,250.00**

CANEWARE

Bulbpot, cov, pr, 8½″ l, D-shaped body, engine turned basketwork between ropework borders, glazed int., cov with three bulb holders surrounded by nine small circular apertures, imp mark, c1800 . . . . **1,450.00**

Solitaire Set, 5″ cov teapot, cov sugar bowl, milk jug, tea cup and saucer, tray, enameled garden flowers, blue line borders, glazed ints., imp mark, minor damage, c1820 . . . . **750.00**

Tea Service, partial, cov teapot with repaired silver tipped spout, cov sugar bowl, milk jug, waste bowl, two cups and saucers, relief dec of drab green ferns, daisies, and foliate borders, glazed ints., c1810 . . . . **1,210.00**

Teapot, cov, 3¾″
Circular, engine turned sides, bamboo stalks and horizontal bands, ends of stalks form stippled border at shoulder, engine turned cov, bamboo sprig knob, imp "Wedgwood," "M," and "5," c1780 . . . . . **1,650.00**
Pentagonal body, molded bamboo stalks, coiled bamboo sprig knob, imp "Wedgwood & Bentley," c1779 **3,400.00**

CREAMWARE

Footbath, 16″ l, oval, molded with three raised bands, two applied loop handles, imp mark, c1840 . . . . **1,000.00**

Jelly Mold, 9″ h, conical, painted, rose, purple, green, yellow, blue, and iron-red floral sprays and swags, brown line edge borders, four apertures on base, imp "Wedgwood, D," c1800, tip chipped **2,750.00**

Jug, 8½″ h, black transfer print, yellow and green enameled hunt scene inscribed "Stag Chase through the Thames," other side with drinking scene beneath banner inscribed "Sportsman Festival," hunting verse, imp "Wedgwood" and two potter's marks **1,550.00**

Plate
8⅛″, orange and black, Etruscan medallion of classical lady, anthemion and bound leaf border, imp "Wedgwood" and "II," c1800 . . . . **400.00**
9½″, fable, maroon, ochre, green, and yellow, two jugs floating down stream, Spanish shaped rim, ochre and brown edges, imp mark, sgd "E Lessore," c1865 . . . . **500.00**

Sock Block, 4¾″ h, molded as child's foot, imp "Wedgwood," letter "J," date cipher, c1890 . . . . **375.00**

Soup Plate, 9¾", armorial

Duke of Clarence Service, rim transfer printed in underglaze blue, border of scallops edged with gilded darts, multicolored center Royal Arms above motto, imp "Wedgwood" and "8," c1821 . . . . **715.00**

5th Earl of Shaftesbury service, rim of puce scallops edged with gilded darts, puce, iron-red, blue, black, green, and tan arms of Anthony Ashley-Cooper, imp "Wedgwood," potter's marks, c1790 . . . . **450.00**

Stand, 11⅜" l, orange and black, center lyre and torch, florette bands, basket molded rim, dash border, imp "Wedgwood" and "W-C," c1800 . . . . **275.00**

Supper Set, cov circular 8" d, dish, two fan shaped cov dishes, dessert plate, blue and sepia dec, unicorn and coronet crest of Marden of Hereford above monogram HM, wheat and flower border, imp "Wedgwood," letter and potter's mark, c1814 . . . . **500.00**

Vase, cov, 14¼", green, pink, blue, gray, and brown, Cupid and Psyche birdnesting on one side, blue, green, and brown bluebells and butterfly on other side, two figural flesh tinted women as handles, turquoise flutes on base and neck, bird knob with minor repairs, ochre line borders, modeled by Hugues Protat, painted by Pepin, imp "Wedgwood," potter's mark, date cipher JCD, c1875 . . . . **675.00**

Wine Cooler, rim of puce scallops edged with gilded darts, puce and gold, fluted handles, bacchic trophies, one handle repaired, imp "Wedgwood," "D" in gold, c1790 . . . . **450.00**

JASPERWARE

Biscuit Jar

4½ x 6", tricolor, lavender bands top and bottom, sage green center with raised white classical ladies and cupids, SP top, rim, and handle with engraved florals, acorn finial, marked Wedgwood only **700.00**

5 x 6⅞", tricolor, gold color top and bottom bands, black center band with white classical ladies and cupids, SP top, rim, and handle, marked Wedgwood only **700.00**

5⅛ x 6⅝", tricolor, gold top and bottom bands, wide black band, raised white figures, women, child, cupid, and floral garlands, SP top and handle, marked "Wedgwood" . . . **900.00**

Caddy Spoon, 3" l, solid white, shell form bowl, slender handle, scalloped border, imp mark, c1780–98 . . . . . . **675.00**

Chessmen, sage green queen modeled after Sarah Siddons on oct stepped base, imp "Wedgwood," blue and white rook modeled as crenellated turrets, blue and white knight on rearing horse, blue pawn modeled as man on rock, blue pawn modeled as warrior with shield, white pawn modeled as rock, and white pawn modeled as archer, late 18th C **1,200.00**

Creamer and Sugar, 3¾ x 7¼ x 6½", dark blue and white, classical figures, SP sugar rim, orig SP holder, marked "Wedgwood," pr **225.00**

Custard Cup, comma shape, finely potted, white relief trellis work, serrated rim, 2¼", pale blue solid jasper body, imp mark, late 18th C **350.00**

Hair Receiver, 3¼" d, 3½" h, dark blue and white, classical figures, lacy hearts, flowers, and leaves, marked "Wedgwood" only **150.00**

Jam Jar, 3¼ x 5¼", dark blue, white classical figures, SP lid, marked "Wedgwood" **120.00**

Medallion, portrait

3⅜" l, William Shakespeare, high relief white bust, yellow ground, imp name, two firing holes, imp "Wedgwood & Bentley," gilt wood frame, c1776–80 . . . . **1,450.00**

3⅞", Sir Joseph Banks, high white relief bust portrait, pale blue body dipped on either side in dark blue, two firing holes, imp "Wedgwood," late 18th C **350.00**

Pitcher, tankard

3¾" d, 6⅜" h, dark blue and white, classical ladies, grapes, and leaves border, marked "Wedgwood" only **110.00**

4" d, 5½" h, dark blue and white, three petal top, classical ladies and cherubs, marked "Wedgwood" only . . **165.00**

4½" d, 7½" h, dark blue and white, classical ladies, grapes and leaves border, marked "Wedgwood" only **145.00**

Plaque, 13⅜ x 7½", light blue and white, "Blindman's Bluff," orig black and gold frame **450.00**

Syrup, 3" d, 5¼", dark blue, white classical figures, grapes and grape leaves around top, pewter lid, white porcelain finial, marked "Wedgwood" only **150.00**

Vase, 2 x 3", dark blue, white classical figures, cylindrical, marked "Wedgwood, Made in England" **85.00**

LUSTERS

Butterfly

Bowl, 6" d, multcolored butterfly center **125.00**

Vase, 4⅛″ d, 8⅜″ h, MOP luster ext., multicolored gold outlined butterflies, gold rim, flame luster int., Portland vase mark **375.00**

Dragon

Bowl, 4½″ d, 2½″ h, mottled deep blue luster ext., gold dragons, Oriental motif, MOP luster int., Portland vase mark **175.00**

Box, cov

4 x 7 x 2⅝″, rect, mottled deep blue luster, gold dragons, MOP int. with dragons, Portland vase mark **400.00**

5⅜″ d, 5¼″ h, mottled green luster int., gold dragons **400.00**

Vase, 3⅞″ d, 8′ h, mottled deep blue luster ext., gold dragons, MOP int., Portland vase mark **275.00**

Fairyland

Bowl, 4 x 2″, York cup shape, elves playing leapfrog, gold stars in sky, flame luster ext., green luster int. on one, other with midnight luster ext. and MOP int., Portland vase mark, pr **500.00**

Melba Cup, 4⅞″ d, 3½″ h, green MOP luster int., two elves on branch in bottom, midnight blue luster ext., gold stars, green grass, leapfrogging elves and fairies, Portland vase mark **700.00**

Vase, 8″, Jeweled Tree, printed in gold, panels of Feng Hwang and Bridge, yellow, purple, blue, green, and crimson, MOP ground, MOP int. with Floating Fairies border, gold over black Portland Vase mark, c1920 . . . . **500.00**

Fruit Luster

Bowl

7⅝″ d, octagonal, copper-bronze ext., MOP int., printed gold, single and clustered lavender, blue, russet, green, and yellow fruits. gilt rope and Armagh borders, gold printed Portland Vase mark, c1930 . . . . **600.00**

8⅛ x 3⁵⁄₇″, mottled blue luster ext., mottled flame luster int., bunches of multicolored fruit, outlined in gold, marked "Wedgwood Porcelain" **550.00**

Hummingbird

Bowl, 5″, red-orange luster int., pale blue and cobalt blue ext., gold trim **245.00**

Vase

2½″ d, 5⅛″ h, mottled rich blue luster ext., mottled flame luster int., multicolored hummingbirds outlined in gold, gold trim, marked . **200.00**

3″ d, 6″ h, trumpet, mottled deep blue luster ext., multicolored gold outlined hummingbirds, flame luster int., Portland vase mark . **225.00**

5¾″ d, 11¾″ h, trumpet shape, deep mottled blue ext., flame luster int. **475.00**

Moonlight

Compote, 10¼″ l, matching 11¼″ l, bivalve stand, Nautilus pattern, splashed pink luster, touches of orange, ochre, and gray, imp mark, c1810 . . . . **1,450.00**

MAJOLICA

Bowl, 10½″, ftd, Cauliflower **235.00**

Match Striker, 5″, green and brown, sgd **200.00**

Toilet Box, cov, lady's, drab gray blue, brown, and ochre glacé, cov molded as medieval lady kneeling on pillow, tray forms jewel tray, two bowing page boys, removable tray fitted with three small pots and cov, imp "Wedgwood," date cipher GSA (September 1872), number "1263" and blue painted "X", minor damage **1,210.00**

Umbrella Stand, 22″, Aesthetic Movement, basket shape, modeled rows of alternating yellow and white plaited raffia, green, brown, and blue peacock feather, pale blue ribbon, bowknot ribbon tied at either end, turquoise glaze int., imp "Wedgwood," date cipher AJL (April 1883), registry mark of May 25, 1881, letters "L" and "K, pattern number 30073 painted in purple **1,925.00**

MISCELLANEOUS

Cheese Keeper, 8 x 9″, raised enamel, Oriental style dec, bamboo blossoms and fan shaped leaves, celadon type pale green ground, imp "Wedgwood" plus decorator marks and registry diamond **875.00**

Ladle, 5″ handle, blue acanthus leaf, white bowl with blue geometric pattern, incised mark **125.00**

Vase, cov

9½″ h, Victorian Ware, cerulean blue ground, gilt highlights, white relief floral swags, martial and bacchic trophies, foliate borders, gilt satyrhead heads, still leaf border on cov, sq base with anthemia border, base and foot imp "Wedgwood, H," base also imp "England," painted pattern number, c1900 . . . . **625.00**

9⅝″ h, 4¾″ d, pale cream ground, cobalt blue trim, gold handles and trim, hp pink roses, green leaves, Portland vase mark, c1900 . . . . . **425.00**

PEARLWARE

Bough Pot, 8½", urn shape, pierced cov, mottled brown, still leaves at pedestal base, marked 1,000.00

Box, 9", oblong, brown print and enameled birds, butterflies, and floral sprigs, gilt rim bands, imp Wedgwood, c1869 .... 160.00

Demitasse Cup and Saucer 175.00

Jelly Mold, cov, 9⅞" h, int. wedge shape, puce, yellow, purple, iron-red, green, and brown painted fruit clusters, bunch of grapes and strawberry vine on end, brown line edge border, circular base with four apertures, plain outer cov, base imp "Wedgwood" and two J form potter's marks, c1800, base chips 3,850.00

Jug, 5¼", botanical, black transfer print, green, yellow, puce and black spray of lilies on one side, flowering berry bush branch on other, neck , rim, and handle enriched with brown line border, imp and potter's marks, painted iron-red pattern number, c1810 .... 825.00

Plate, 8⅝", shell shape, shaded pink, imp "Wedgwood," c1871 .... 60.00

Soup Tureen, cov and ladle, blue dahlias, green foliage, black rope dec .. 400.00

QUEEN'S WARE

Box, cov, 4 x 5", round, light blue, relief berries and vine, marked "Queens Ware, Wedgwood, England" 100.00

Chocolate Pot, 4", green leaf dec 150.00

Condiment Set, 8½" 175.00

Platter, oval, reticulated, marked "Wedgwood" 450.00

Teapot, painted bamboo, 1860 ...... 85.00

ROSSO ANTICO

Jug, 3⅞", black relief grasses and flowers, glazed int., imp "Wedgwood" and potter's mark, c1810 .... 400.00

Sugar, cov, 6", crocodile finial, redware, black relief Egyptian dec, band of stylized key pattern 350.00

Teapot, 4¾" h, black relief band of hieroglyphs, key fret border, crocodile knob, glazed int., imp mark, c1810 . 600.00

TERRA COTTA WARE

Creamer, enameled florals, c1800 ... 120.00

Figure, 4¾" l, nude boy, sleeping, lying on rect draped base, canted corners, 19th C 1,100.00

Jug, 2¼ x 3½", miniature, dragon in relief, blue staining 30.00

Terra Cotta Ware, 5½" w, sucrier, black Egyptian motif, $825.00.

Spillholder Vase, 4½" h, modeled as clusters of four bamboo canes, oval rockwork base, c1840, pr 1,100.00

Sugar, cov, enameled florals 140.00

Teapot, cov, ribbed pumpkin shape, bamboo molded handle and spout . 350.00

Tobacco Jar, cov, round, classical figures, marked "Wedgwood Made in England," 20th C 200.00

Vase, 5¼", Portland, flaring rim, band of grass, angular handles, applied masks, black relief lilies and leaves . 275.00

WELLER POTTERY

History: In 1872 Samuel A. Weller opened a small factory in Fultonham, near Zanesville, Ohio, to produce utilitarian stoneware, such as milk pans and sewer tile. In 1882 he moved his facilities to Zanesville. In 1890 Weller built a new plant in the Putnam section of Zanesville along the tracks of the Cincinnati and Miskingum Railway. Additions followed in 1892 and 1894.

In 1894 Weller entered into an agreement with William A. Long to purchase the Lonhuda Faience Company, which had developed an art pottery line under the guidance of Laura A. Fry, formerly of Rookwood. Long left in 1895, but Weller continued to produce Lonhuda under a new name, Louwelsa. Replacing Long as art director was Charles Babcock Upjohn. He, along with Jacques Sicard, Frederick Hurten Rhead, and Gazo Fudji, developed Weller's art pottery lines.

At the end of World War I, many prestige lines were discontinued and Weller concentrated on commercial wares. Rudolph Lorber joined the staff and designed lines such as Roma, Forest, and Knifewood. In 1920 Weller purchased the plant of the Zanesville Art Pottery and claimed to be the largest pottery in the country.

Art pottery enjoyed a revival when the Hudson Line was introduced in the early 1920s. The 1930s saw Coopertone and Graystone Garden ware added. However, the Depression forced the closing of the Putnam plant and one on Marietta Street in Zanesville. After World War II, cheap Japanese imports took over Weller's market. In 1947 Essex Wire Company of Detroit bought the controlling stock. Early in 1948 operations ceased.

Reference: Sharon and Bob Huxford, *The Collectors Encyclopedia Of Weller Pottery*, Collector Books, 1979.

Collectors' Club: American Art Pottery Association, P. O. Box 714, Silver Spring, MD 20901.

Additional Listings: See *Warman's Americana & Collectibles* for more examples.

Ashtray, Coopertone, 4½″, figural, frog, ink stamp mark	65.00
Basket, Silvertone, 13″, molded grapes, ink stamp mark	200.00
Bowl, Kenova, 4½″, molded lily	125.00
Chalice, Rosemont	275.00
Clock, mantel, Louwelsa, branch of orange roses, green leaves, shaded rust to dark brown to orange and yellow ground, orig white ceramic face, hp blue and pink flowers, working, die stamped semi-circular mark	650.00
Console Set, Silvertone, round 12″ d bowl, 2¼″ h pr candlesticks, 4½″ d flower frog, 4 pcs	250.00
Ewer	
Floretta, 10½″, bisque ground, incised pears	375.00

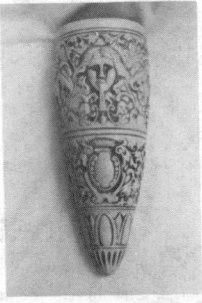

Wall Pocket, 10″ l, Ivory, sgd, $100.00.

Louwelsa, 7″, brown glaze, yellow daffodil, artist sgd, half circle mark	215.00
Wild Rose, aqua	30.00
Inkwell, 7 x 3¼″, figural, turtle, pottery insert and lid, frog handle	325.00
Jardiniere	
Aurelian, grape dec, 46″, 3 pc, sgd "K"	4,000.00
Hudson, 6 x 6″, multicolored floral dec, sgd "Pillsbury"	375.00
Mug, Dickensware, 4½″, brown, molded white lily-of-the-valley dec	350.00
Pitcher	
Dickensware, tankard, 12″, incised genie, multicolored dec, sgd "C J Upjohn 1902," second line	1,200.00
Louwelsa, tankard, 18″, sgd	1,000.00
Sicard, 22½″, four sided, straight walls, Art Nouveau woman with flowing gown and hair, whiplash curved vines and fruit, flowers and stems, figural stem handle, irid gold, purple, peacock blue, and green	1,800.00
Planter	
Forest, 6½ x 3½″	75.00
Souevo, 6½″, hanging, geometric design, pointed base	175.00
Tankard, Louwelsa, 11″, blackberries, artist sgd "HH"	265.00
Tobacco Jar, cov, Knifewood, 6½″, bird dogs, ducks, leaves, and trees, imp block mark	400.00
Vase	
Art Nouveau, 15½″, full figure woman	500.00
Burntwood, Three Wise Men, sgd	475.00
Dickensware	
7¾″, shades of gray and natural, Sam Weller, round disk on back "Sam Weller of Pickwick Papers," four open handles at shoulder, third line	1,200.00
10¼″, bulbous, incised and painted yellow flowers, red centers, intertwining celadon green stems and leaves, black ground, die stamped "Dickens Ware, Weller, 564 and 7″	425.00
Forest, 10½″	90.00
Greora, 6 x 9″, cylindrical	80.00
Hudson, 9 x 9″, bulbous, loop handles, blue, pink, and green floral, sgd "Timberlake"	975.00
Jap Birdmal, 9″, sgd "V. M. H."	525.00
Sicard	
11″, double gourd, four lobed base, swollen top, flowing petaled flowers, glowing irid violet, green, crimson, silver, and copper, painted "Sicard" mark	1,400.00
22½″, floor, blown out grapes and vines, irid purple, blue, green,	

and crimson glaze, painted "Weller Sicard" on side **5,000.00**

Wall Pocket
Dupont, 10" **90.00**
Woodcraft, squirrel **85.00**

WHALING

History: Whaling items are a specialized part of nautical collecting. Provenance is of prime importance since whaling collectors want assurances that their pieces are from a whaling voyage. Since ship's equipment seldom carries the ship's identification, some individuals have falsely attributed a whaling provenance to general nautical items. Know the dealer, auction house, or collector from whom you buy.

Special tools, e.g., knives, harpoons, lances, spades, etc., do not overlap the general nautical line. Makers' marks and condition determine value for these items.

Richard Bourne, Hyannis, Massachusetts, and Chuck DeLuca, York, Maine, regularly hold auctions featuring whaling material.

Reference: Thomas G. Lytle, *Harpoons And Other Whalecraft*, Old Dartmouth Historical Society, 1984.

Periodical: *Whalebone*, P. O. Box 2834, Fairfax, VA 22031.

Museums: Cold Spring Harbor Museum, Long Island, NY; Kendall Whaling Museum, Sharon, MA; Mystic Seaport Museum, Mystic, CT; National Maritime Museum, San Francisco, CA; Old Dartmouth Historical Society, New Bedford, MA; Whaling Museum, Nantucket, MA.

Additional Listings: Nautical Items and Scrimshaw.

Advisor: Bill Wheeler.

Bill of Sale, bark *Mars*, dated November 25, 1882, New Bedford artist Charles H Gifford appears as part owner ... **170.00**
Crew List, whaleship *Montpelier*, Sept 6, 1853, names, position, number of shares in voyages to be received .. **125.00**
Flag, whaleship *William S Henry*, 139½ x 76½", 37 stars, marked D B Greene **650.00**
Hand Pulls, two pair, 24 and 16½", used on gangways and hatchways, orig white paint **150.00**
Log Book
Bark *Manchester*, between Boston and New Orleans, c1884, orig marble paper covers, worn spine **125.00**
Bark *Pioneer*, Captain James S Hazard, departed New Bedford, August 5, 1869, held by US Consul at Mauritins, released and returned to New Bedford on December 1, 1872, sent home 232 barrels of sperm oil **3,500.00**

Quarterboard
Baltimore, 94¼" l, incised and painted, American emblem, 19th C **700.00**
Edith Nute, 84" l, orig gold lettering worn, old black paint traces, 19th C **200.00**
Registration Certificate, brig *Gold Hunter*, Edgartown, Mass, issued to Joseph Mayhew, dated August 31, 1837, framed **375.00**
Sailor's Valentine, 9½" d, words "Think of Me," 19th C **1,600.00**
Sextant, note attached to case reads "This sextant was used on the 1937/ MacMillan Expedition to Northern Labrador/and Affin Island by John H Halford, Jr '38" **325.00**
Speaking Trumpet, captain's, 18¼" l .. **300.00**

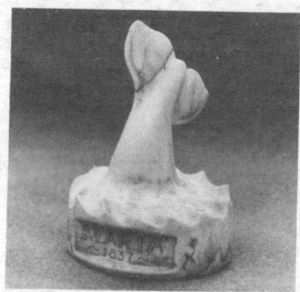

Whale Stamp, 1¼" d, 1¾" h, whale ivory, tail entering ocean, scrimshaw name and date, *Maria*, 1837, full whale stamp, $500.00.

Travel Desk, 14" w, lacquered finish, abalone and wood inlays, contains letters and cards, formerly owned by Captain Calvin Bradford, Middleboro, Mass, late 19th C **800.00**
Whalebone Products
Clothespin
Set of 6, 4¾" l, early 19th C **225.00**
Set of 11, 5" l, early 19th C **675.00**
Corset Busk, 13" l, mid 19th C **125.00**
Fid, 7⅜" l, turned rope, early 19th C **350.00**
Seam Rubber engraved "T D C," mid 19th C **300.00**
Wheel, 36", ship *Aria*, brass, made and sgd "Edison Mfg Co, Boston, Mass," dated 1903 .... **1,900.00**

WHIELDON

WHIELDON

History: The Staffordshire potter, Thomas Whieldon, established his shop in 1740. He is best known for his mottled ware, molded in forms of vegetables, fruits, and leaves. Josiah Spode and Josiah Wedgwood, in different capacities, had connections with Whieldon.

Whieldon ware is a generic term. His wares were never marked and other potters made similar items. Whieldon ware is agate-tortoise shell earthenware, in limited shades of green, brown, blue and yellow. Most pieces are utilitarian items, e.g., dinner ware and plates, but figurines and other decorative pieces are found.

Reference: Susan and Al Bagdade, *Warman's English & Continental Pottery & Porcelain, 1st Edition,* Warman Publishing Co., Inc., 1987.

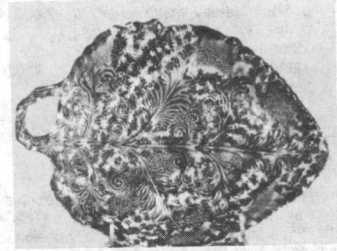

Dish, leaf shaped, c1760–70, $400.00.

Figure, pug dog, 3¼", seated, ochre, brown, and gray glaze	450.00
Miniature, pitcher, scalloped rim, green, orange, ochre, brown and buff tortoiseshell glaze	150.00
Plate	
9" d, molded rim with panels of teal-blue, green, and ochre glazed dot diaperwork separated by foliate cartouches, brown splashed ground, c1765, pr	650.00
9¼", emb scalloped rim, brown, gray, green, and ochre tortoiseshell glaze, brown and cream speckled back	250.00
Porringer, 4¾ x 2¾", creamware, sponged manganese, green and ochre brushed glaze, c1770	600.00
Stirrup Cup, 4¹⁵⁄₁₆", stag's head, creamware head, brown and green stripes heightened in brown and ochre dots, brown ears, incised eyelashes, and dimpled nose, ochre whorl-molded crest, c1780, minor repairs	4,125.00
Tea Caddy, 3¾", Cauliflower Ware, naturalistic colored glazes, SP cov, Wedgwood, c1765	350.00
Teapot, 4½" h, Pineapple Ware, green glazed leaves, ochre glazed lozenges, foliate spout, scaly dolphin	

handle, leaf cluster knob, green glaze, Wedgwood, c1760	1,800.00
Wall Pocket, 8½", cornucopia, cartouche with goddess, brown, ochre, and green glaze	1,350.00

WHIMSIES, GLASS

History: Glass workers occasionally spent time during lunch or after completing their regular work schedule creating whimsies (unusual glass objects), e.g., candy striped canes, darners, hats, paperweights, pipes, witch balls, etc. Whimsies were taken home and given as gifts to family and friends.

Because of their uniqueness and infinite variety, whimsies can rarely be attributed to a specific glass house or glass worker. Whimsies occurred wherever glass was made, from New Jersey to Ohio and westward. Some have suggested that style and color can be used to pinpoint region or factory, but no one has yet developed an identification key that is adequate.

One of the most collectible types of whimsey are witch balls. They are a hollow sphere of glass, often found with a matching glass vase type holder. Myths surround the origin and use of witch balls. Perhaps they were displayed by the fireplace to catch demon spirits as they descended the chimney, or they may have been used to store salt by the chimney to keep it dry.

Reference: Joyce E. Blake, *Glasshouse Whimsies,* published by author, 1984.

Additional Listings: See Glass, Early American and Sandwich Glass.

Ball, Portomania, New England, c1850	
9¼" d, aqua, free blown, contains several paper cut-outs of flowers, leaf, butterfly, and people, red, blue, green, and white int. powder	400.00
14½" d, aqua, free blown, contains several paper cut-outs of flowers, animals, and people, white powder ground, early glass stand	285.00
Bird Cage Fountain, 4½" h, clear, blown molded, vertical ribbed pattern, applied swirled finial, pontiled base	185.00
Bracelet, girl's, clear glass with delicate multicolored spirals entwining inner gold spiral, attributed to Sandwich, c1840	175.00
Cane, 50" l, clear glass with alternating close spirals of red, white, and blue	175.00
Flytrap	
5½" h, clear, round, free blown, sheared mouth, applied neck ring, three applied feet with hatch-marked dec	75.00
9¾" h, pale gray-blue, tooled neck ring, three applied feet, clear	

pressed stopper, factory ground
mouth **150.00**
Hand Cooler, 2½" h, egg shape, opaque
white, pink looping, pontil **160.00**
Hat
1¾" h, aqua, blown into 12 sided
medicine bottle mold, open pontil,
American, c1820–50, tiny rim flake **250.00**
2¼" h, brilliant deep-blue color, strong
geometric emb, pontil, Sandwich
Glassworks, c1840, McKearin GIII-
24 .... **850.00**
Pipe, 40" l, aqua, white stripes, spirals
extend from bowl to lip, blown, Philadelphia Exposition, 1876 .... **150.00**
Rolling Pin, 15" l, medium sapphire
blue, free blown, knobbed ends,
painted red floral dec and inscription
"A Present From Newcastle," c1850 **150.00**
String Holder, 4½" d, 4⅜" h, double cut
overlay, emerald green cut to clear,
Sandwich **300.00**
Trumpet, 9½" l, clear, blown, spiral ribbing **125.00**
Window Pane
4 x 8", light amethyst, daisy and
leaves motif, Addison Glass Co .. **75.00**
4⅞ x 6¹⁵⁄₁₆", lacy, clear, sgd "Bakewell" **700.00**
5 x 7", lacy, clear, rect shield with Ohio
riverboat, urns with florals and
large thistle, emb "J. & C. Ritchie,"
Wheeling, WV, c1833 .... **4,600.00**

**Witch Ball, matching vase holder, white
Nailsea type loopings, clear ground,
$650.00.**

Witch Ball
5" d, cranberry **200.00**
5¼" d, plum color **80.00**
Witch Ball and Matching Holder
4⅜" d, spatter glass, red, pink, and
green flecks, white ground **100.00**
4½" h, olive green, bulbous stand, attributed to Saratoga, mid 19th C,
ex-collection George S. McKearin **600.00**
4⅝" h, deep olive green, egg shaped
bowl, attributed to Saratoga **550.00**
9" h, 4" d blue opal ball, matching 5"
h pitcher base, applied handle .. **250.00**
11" h, amethyst ball, deep purple-blue
stand **800.00**
11½", large opaque white ball with
red and blue looping, clear stand,
South Jersey **550.00**
13¼" h, 4¾" d ball, amethyst with
white looping, matching 9¾" h
stand, solid white applied rim,
rough pontil **1,700.00**
13½", clear glass, opaque white looping, South Jersey, matched pr ... **2,000.00**
14⅞" h, 7¾" d ball, clear glass,
opaque white looping, matching 8"
h stand, attributed to Pittsburgh .. **750.00**

WHISKEY BOTTLES, EARLY

History: The earliest American whiskey bottles
were generic form bottles blown by pioneer glass
makers in the 18th century. The Biningers (1820–
1880s) were the first bottles specifically designed
for whiskey. After the 1860s distillers favored the
cylindrical 'fifth' form.

The first embossed brand name bottle was the
amber E. G. Booz Old Cabin Whiskey bottle which
was issued in 1860. Many stories have been told
about this classic bottle. Unfortunately, most are
not true. Research has proved that "booze" was
a corruption of the words "bouse" and "boosy"
from the 16th and 17th centuries. It was only a
coincidence that the Philadelphia distributor also
was named Booz. This bottle has been reproduced
extensively.

Prohibition (1920–1933) brought the legal whiskey industry to a standstill. Whiskey was marked
"medicinal purposes only" and distributed by private distillers in unmarked or paper label bottles.

The size and shape of whiskey bottles are standard. Colors are limited to amber, amethyst, clear,
green, and cobalt blue (rare). Corks were the common closure in the early period, with the inside
screw top being used in the 1880–1910 period.

Bottles made prior to 1880 are the most desirable. In purchasing a bottle with a label, condition
is a critical factor. In the 1950s distillers began to
issue collectors' special edition bottles to help increase sales.

References: Ralph & Terry Kovel, *The Kovels'
Bottle Price List, 7th Edition,* Crown Publishers,
1984; Carlo & Dot Sellari, *The Illustrated Price
Guide To Antique Bottles,* Country Beautiful Corp.,
1975.

Periodicals: *Antique Bottle and Glass Collector,* P.O. Box 187, East Greenville, PA, 18048.

Additional Listings: See *Warman's Americana & Collectibles* for a listing of Collectors' Special Editions Whiskey Bottles.

Warranted Flask, 6⅜" h, amber, molded, c1891–1900, $10.00.

Bear Creek, amber, cork stopper, dated 1868	25.00
Belle Of Anderson, milk glass, tooled mouth, 8⅛"	25.00
Bininger, NY, label, 1848	125.00
Casper's Whiskey, Made by Honset, North Carolina People, cobalt blue, 11⅞", 1870–90	225.00
Dutch Porter, long neck, open pontil	50.00
E.G. Booz's Old Cabin, Philadelphia, amber, 1840	60.00
Giffith Hyatt & Co, olive amber, label	475.00
Ginter Co, Importers, deep yellow green, 11", 1860–80	60.00
Hayner, clear, label, qt, 1916	10.00
Hodico, Hollenbach, Dietrien & Co, Reading, PA, amber, 11⅛" h	40.00
J.A. Gilka, Berlin, amber, 9½"	25.00
Jesse Moore, dark red amber	50.00
McKenna's, Nelson County, amber	100.00
N.B. Dursley, deep olive amber, qt, 1783	525.00
Nathans Bros 1863, Philadelphia, amber emb	125.00
Old Joe Gidoen, amber, ½ pt	10.00
Oxford Rye Whiskey, label, 11½", 1880s	20.00
Phoenix Old Bourbon, honey amber, bird and coffin, pt	115.00
Pride of Kentucky, yellow amber	750.00
Sour Mash 1867, amber, barrel shape, 8¼"	20.00
Spruance Stanley & Co, San Francisco, tooled top, 1869	25.00
Theodore Netter, barrel, clear	25.00
Turner Brothers, sq, olive green, 9¾", 1860–1900	65.00
William Maher, High Grade Liquors, Denver	80.00
Wormser Bros, San Francisco, amber, double ring, bubbles	90.00

WHITE PATTERNED IRONSTONE

History: White patterned ironstone is a heavy earthenware, first patented in 1813 by Charles Mason, Staffordshire, England, using the name "Patent Ironstone China." Other English potters soon began copying this opaque, feldspathic, white china.

All white ironstone dishes first became available in the American market in the early 1840s. The first patterns had simple Gothic lines similar to the shapes used in transfer wares. Pattern shapes were named New York, Union, and Atlantic, designed to appeal to the American housewife. Motifs, such as wheat, corn, oats, and poppies, were embossed on the forms as the American western prairie influenced design. Eventually over 200 shapes and patterns, with variations of finials and handles, were made.

White patterned ironstone is identified by shape names and pattern names. Many potters only named the shape in their catalogs. Pattern names usually refer to the decoration motif.

References: Jean Wetherbee, *A Look At White Ironstone*, Wallace-Homestead, 1980; Jean Wetherbee, *A Second Look At White Ironstone*, Wallace-Homestead, 1985.

Bowl, 7⅞", Leaf Fan, lid, Alcock	100.00
Butter Pats, set of 6, emb scrolled rims	40.00
Cake Plate, Cable and Ring, 12" l, reticulated handles, Anthony Shaw and Son, England	10.00
Chamber Pot, Johnson Bros	40.00
Coffeepot, Wheat and Blackberry, Clementson Bros	100.00
Compote, Pearl Sydenham, ftd, Meakin	175.00
Creamer	
Basketweave, 6" h, rect, marked "Opaque Stone China, Anthony Stone and Son, England"	30.00
Fuchsia, 5¼" h, unmarked	30.00
Wheat and Clover, Turner & Tomkinson	60.00
Cup and Saucer	
Acorn and Tiny Oak, Pankhurst	25.00
Grape and Medallion, Challinor	35.00
President, handleless, Edwards	45.00
Ewer, 12¾", Corn and Oats, Wedgwood	150.00
Gravy Boat	
Ceres, 5", unmarked	55.00
Vintage	25.00
Nappy, Prairie Flowers, Livesley Powell	15.00
Pancake Server, octagonal, Boote, 1851	40.00
Pitcher	
8½", Wheat, ribbed	30.00

Gravy Boat, underplate, 9 x 6½", marked "Richard Alcock," $65.00.

9¾" h, ribbed, marked "J W Pankhurst, Hanley"	80.00
10¾", Ceres, Elsmore & Forster	130.00
Plate	
7", Wheat and Clover, Turner & Tomkinson	15.00
8½", Prairie Flowers, Powell & Bishop	18.00
8¾", Corn and Oats, Wedgwood, 1863	20.00
9", Ceres Wheat, Elsmore & Forster	20.00
10½", Corn, Davenport	20.00
Platter	
Ceres, 16", Elsmore & Forster	55.00
Lily Of The Valley, 14½" l, Alfred Meakin	40.00
Rolling Star, octagonal, J Edwards	50.00
Relish Dish, parish shape, Alcock	20.00
Sauce Tureen	
Fluted Pearl, undertray, J Wedgwood	100.00
Wheat and Blackberry, Clementson Bros	60.00
Soap Dish, cov, Boote, 1851	25.00
Soup Plate	
8⅞", Paneled Grape, JF	18.00
9", Wheat and Clover, Turner & Tomkinson	25.00
Soup Tureen, Hyacinth, oval, ladle	220.00
Sugar	
Ceres, 8", Elsmore & Forster	70.00
Fuchsia, Meakin	40.00
Paneled, 8¼", T J & J Mayer	45.00
Syllabub Cup, Trumpet Vine	20.00
Teapot	
Forget-me-not, 8⅞" h, Wood, Rathbone and Co, Cobridge, Staffordshire	80.00
Laurel Wreath, luster trim	225.00
Toothbrush Holder	
Hyacinth, lid, Wedgwood	60.00
Wheat and Clover, underplate, Turner and Tomkinson	50.00
Vegetable, cov, Ceres, corn	125.00

Waste Bowl

Columbia, 4⅛ x 6⅜", unmarked	75.00
Morning Glory, Elsmore & Forster	60.00

WILLOW PATTERN CHINA

History: Josiah Spode developed the first "traditional" willow pattern in 1810. The components, all motifs taken from Chinese export china, are: a willow tree, "apple" tree, two pagodas, fence, two birds, and a three figures crossing a bridge. The legend, in its many versions, is an English invention based on the design components.

By 1830, there were over 200 plus makers of willow pattern china in England. The pattern has remained in continuous production. Some of the English firms that still produce willow pattern china are: Burleigh, Johnson Bros. (Wedgwood Group), Royal Doulton's continuation of the Booths pattern, and Wedgwood.

By the end of the 19th century, pattern production spread to France, Germany, Holland, Ireland, Sweden, and the United States. In the United States, Buffalo Pottery made the first willow pattern beginning in 1902. Many other companies followed, developing willow variants using rubberstamp simplified patterns as well as overglaze decals. The largest American manufacturers of the traditional willow pattern were Royal China and Homer Laughlin, usually preferred because it is dated. Shenango pieces are most desired among restaurant quality ware.

Japan began producing large quantities of willow pattern china in the early 20th century. Noritake began about 1902. Its early pieces used a Nippon "Royal Sometuke" mark. Most Japanese pieces are porous earthenware with dark blue pattern using the tradition willow design, usually with no inner border. Noritake did put the pattern on china bodies. Unusual forms include salt and pepper shakers, ¼ lb. butter dishes, and canisters. "Occupied Japan" may add a small percentage to the value of common table wares. Maruta and Moriyama marked pieces are especially valued. The most sought after Japanese willow is the fine quality NKT Co. ironstone with a copy of the old Booths pattern. Recent Japanese willow is a paler shade of blue on a porcelain body.

The most common dinnerware color is blue. However, pieces can also be found in black (with clear glaze or mustard-color glaze by Royal Doulton), brown, green, mulberry, pink (red), and polychrome. Although colors other than blue are hard to find, there is less demand; thus, prices may not necessarily be higher.

The popularity of the willow design has resulted in a large variety of willow-decorated products: candles, fabric, glass, graniteware, linens, needlepoint, plastic, tinware, stationery, watches, and wall coverings. All this material has collectible value.

References: Mary Frank Gaston, *Blue Willow: An Identification & Value Guide*, Collector Books, 1983 (revised prices, 1986); Veryl Marie Worth and Louise M. Loehr, *Willow Pattern China: Collector's Guide, 3rd Edition*, H. S. Worth Co, 1986.

Periodical: *American Willow Report*, 1733 Chase Street, Cincinnati, OH 45223.

Reproduction Alert: The Scio Pottery, Scio, Ohio, currently manufactures a willow pattern set sold in variety stores. The pieces have no marks or back stamps, and the transfer is of poor quality. The plates are flatter in shape than those of other manufacturers.

Additional Listings: Buffalo Pottery. See *Warman's Americana & Collectibles* for more examples.

Advisor: Connie Rogers.

Toothpick Holder, 1¾" h, border at top, English, unmarked, $45.00.

Bowl
6⅛" d, int. and ext. rim border, marked "Allertons, Made In England"	35.00
9" d, marked "Royal"	5.00
Butter Dish, cov, marked "Japan"	50.00
Cake Plate, flow blow pattern, pierced sides	55.00
Children's Dishes, dinner service, four plates, four cups and saucers, creamer, cov sugar, teapot, platter, cov casserole, and gravyboat, large size, marked "Japan"	225.00
Creamer, 2⅜" h, handle, pitcher style, marked "Shenango"	12.50
Egg Cup, 2¼" h, border on base, marked "England"	15.00
Gravy Boat, underplate, light blue, marked "Copeland"	45.00

Plate
8½", ivory ground, scalloped edge, light brown daisy border, blue all over willow pattern, gold bands on edge and base of border	50.00
9", pink, marked "Allerton"	4.50
10", pink, marked "Allerton"	6.00
Platter, 8 x 11", marked "Buffalo Pottery," c1908	46.00
Salad Bowl, 9¾" d, fork and spoon	35.00
Salt and Pepper Shakers, pr, 4" h, bulbous	18.00
Soup Plate, flanged, marked "Allerton"	20.00
Tea Cannister, chrome	38.00
Teapot, pink, marked "Royal"	25.00
Wash Bowl and Pitcher, Parrot pattern	350.00

WOODENWARE

History: Many utilitarian household objects and farm implements were made of wood. Although they were used heavily, these implements were made of the strongest woods and well taken care of by their owners.

This category serves as a catch-all for wood objects which do not fit into other categories.

Additional Listings: See *Warman's Americana & Collectibles* for more examples.

Apple Corer, 22 x 13½", attributed to Harrisburg, PA area, $200.00.

Ashtray, 8½" h, mahogany, carved hunter and dog, good detail, raccoons around base, varnish finish, sgd "Charles Williams 10-2-52"	100.00
Bowl, 6" w, 2" h, turned, old red ext.	285.00
Bread Board, round, carved edge	45.00
Butter Churn, 19½" h, stave constructed, old red paint	165.00

Butter Print
3¾" d, pineapple design, turned handle	65.00
4" d, deeply carved stylized eagle	185.00
4¼" d, carved star flower design, handle	135.00
Butter Wheel, 6½" l, flower designs	85.00
Candlesticks, 23" h, turned, tin sockets, painted black, pr	120.00

Chocolate Mold, six horse heads, 1½ x 11" **120.00**

Churn, 34" h, old red paint traces, pins and dasher **150.00**

Cranberry Scoop, 32" l, curved and bentwood handles, orig red paint, branded label "Cranberry Co" **225.00**

Dough Box, 42" l, poplar, old green paint traces **95.00**

Drying Rack, 27 x 42", accordion folded **35.00**

Foot Warmer, 8" h, oak, intricate "friesan" carving, carved Dutch inscription and date "1829" on door, brass bale, dark finish **250.00**

Keg, 23" h, stave constructed, porcelain knob lid, old red paint **50.00**

Knife Tray, 10 x 13½", mustard paint, slant sides, turned bar carrying handle **110.00**

Lantern, 10¾" h, mortised and pinned construction, hinged door, wire hinges and bail handle, replaced tin heat deflector **95.00**

Lemon Squeezer, carved, turned, two pcs **40.00**

Level, 62" l, wrought iron handle, adjustable ends, old dark patina **35.00**

Nutmeg Grater, 2½", bottle shape, rasp end handle **260.00**

Pantry Box, 9½" d, wire bail, wood handle, butter carrier **165.00**

Sausage Grinder, 42" l, red ground, black stenciled label "Coffman's Patent 1845, Coshocton County, Ohio" . **80.00**

Scoop
10" l, curly maple, rim hook bowl . . . **50.00**
16" l, open handle, whittled bowl, red stain **60.00**

Skimmer, pierced holes, tab handle, hole for hanging, 4½ x 6½", 18th C . **250.00**

Smoothing Board, 27½" l, chip carved and stamped, heart and circle design **135.00**

Snuff Box, 3¾" d, walnut, inlaid cherry circle, ink inscription "William Adolphus Donninton Smith 1859" **125.00**

Spice Box, round, seven labeled canisters **295.00**

Spoon, carved, smooth knob hook handle, 7" l, 18th C **150.00**

Sugar Bucket, staved construction
9¾", old varnish finish **85.00**
12" h, old dark finish **115.00**

Swift, 24" l, table clamp, orig yellow stain **125.00**

Tricycle, 44½" l, orig red paint, gold striping, leatherized upholstered seat with fringe, cast iron fittings, iron rimmed wheels **400.00**

Utensil Rack, 31" l, pine, scalloped crest, chip carved vertical bands, nine wrought iron holes **65.00**

Vise, 51" h, easel shape, chamfered detail, cutout star flower, old gray paint **45.00**

Wine Funnel, threaded tapered spout, removable copper screen, 6" h, 3½" d, early 1800s **110.00**

Yarn Reel, 53" h, chestnut and pine, dark patina, cross chamfered base, adjustable top reel **50.00**

WORLD'S FAIRS AND EXPOSITIONS

History: The Great Exhibition of 1851 in London marked the beginning of the World's Fair and Exposition movement. The fairs generally feature exhibitions from nations around the world displaying the best of their industrial and scientific achievements.

Many important technological advances have been introduced at world's fairs. Examples include the airplane, telephone, and electric lights. The ice cream cone, hot dog, and iced tea were products of vendors at fairs. Art movements often were closely connected to fairs with the Paris Exhibition of 1900 generally considered to have assembled the best of the works of the Art Nouveau artists.

References: Kurt Krueger, *Meet Me In St. Louis—The Exonumia Of The 1904 World's Fair*, Krause Publications, 1979; Howard Rossen and John Kaduck, *Columbia World's Fair Collectibles*, Wallace-Homestead, 1976, revised price list 1982.

Collectors' Clubs: ECHO, 1436 Killarney, Los Angeles, CA 90065; World's Fair, P. O. Box 339, Corte Madera, CA 94925.

Periodical: *World's Fair*, P.O. Box 339, Corte Madera, CA 94925.

1876 Centennial, 2" w, 3½" h, glass boot, orig top, $37.50.

1876, Philadelphia, Centennial
Paperweight, glass, exposition buildings **75.00**
Ribbon, Washington, framed **75.00**

1893, Chicago, Columbian
Bell, glass, engraved "World's Fair 1893" 150.00
Dish, bone, Bridgewood & Co 35.00
Paperweight, Kansas State Building, marked 25.00
Salt and Pepper Shaker, egg shape, black and white, "Columbian Exposition" on front 75.00
1901, Buffalo, Pan-American Exposition
Bookmark, celluloid 15.00
Hurricane Lamp, green, color symbol on globe, encircled name and date 350.00
Mug, transfer of buffalo and "Pan American Exposition 1901," Beaded Scroll pattern 45.00
Plate, bread and butter, photographic scenes, pastel colored border, gold edge, Haviland 60.00
Spoon, Columbus and ship, building and map handle 10.00
1904, St. Louis, Louisiana Purchase Exposition
Creamer, clear glass, Star of David pattern, ruby stained top, etched "World's Fair St. Louis, 1904" ... 125.00
Cup, porcelain 65.00
Fan, Keen Kutter Kutlery adv 35.00
Handkerchief, multicolored 20.00
Pin Tray, aluminum 15.00
Plate
China, blue transfer scene, floral border, Palace of Machinery ... 100.00
Metal, 7" 25.00
Spoon, SS, Palace of Electricity ... 55.00
Tray, 6½", brass 20.00
Vase, 6", ruffled top, handled, Electricity Building scene 150.00
1915, San Francisco, Panama-Pacific International Exposition
Book, *Red Book of Views of the Panama Intl. Exposition in San Francisco* 15.00
Napkin Ring, celluloid, pr 12.00
1933, Chicago, Century of Progress
Ashtray
Chrysler, copper 10.00
Firestone Tire, amber 35.00
Keychain, brass, Skyride 8.00
Plate, china, blue ground, Science Hall scene, Pickard 10.00
Tapestry, silk, ariel view, Zepplin and airplanes 80.00
Tissue Greeting with envelope, 4½" w, strip of toilet tissue-like stationary which unfolds to more then 72", printed humor letter with observations about sights and attractions, 5" sq red, white, and blue envelope 20.00
View Card, 53 views, boxed, stamped, unused 35.00
1939, New York, New York World's Fair

Cane, 34", blue-enameled wood, black and white composition head piece formed like die, top of hand with full color decal depicting Trylon, Perisphere, and fireworks, second decal giving year, steel tipped, orange and blue tassel cord 60.00
Hat, official, embroidered front, Trylon and Perisphere, worn by women employees 55.00
Lamp, Art Deco, Depression type glass, pink, Saturn 175.00
Letter Opener, logo handle, orig card 10.00
Map, fold-out type, fairground 25.00
Napkin Ring, bakelite, blue, Trylon and Perisphere 40.00
Pin, mother-of-pearl 15.00
1939, San Francisco, Golden Gate International Exposition
Ashtray, metal, white 15.00
Neckerchief 6.00
Plate, 10", marked "Homer Laughlin" 65.00
1964, New York, New York World's Fair
Apron, multicolored 18.00
Guide Book, *Official Guide New York World's Fair* 15.00
Tray, metal, Unisphere 6.00

YELLOW WARE

History: Yellow ware is a heavy earthenware of differing weight and strength which varies in color from a rich pumpkin to lighter shades which are more tan than yellow. Although plates, nappies, and custard cups are found, kitchen bowls and other cooking utensils are most prevalent.

The first American yellow ware was produced at Bennington, Vermont. English yellow ware has additional ingredients which make its body much harder. Derbyshire and Sharp's were foremost among the English manufacturers.

References: John Gallo, *Nineteenth and Twentieth Century Yellow Ware*, Heritage Press, 1985; Joan Leibowitz, *Yellow Ware: The Transitional Ceramic*, Schiffer Publishing, 1985.

Mixing Bowl, 11⅝" d, 4¾" h, pouring spout, emb dec, $75.00.

Bedpan, plain yellow 20.00
Bowl
   5¾" d, white band, brown stripes,
     mismatched lid 45.00
   8¼" d, 3⅝" h, emb ext., plume-like
     foliage, green and brown sponging 55.00
   11", Blue Bandit 35.00
Butter Crock, round, emb ribs 60.00
Chamberpot, 2½" h, miniature, black
   stripes, white band with blue sea
   weed dec, reglued handle 85.00
Colander, yellow bands, white int.,
   round 175.00
Desk Set, 8" l, white sanded finish, gilt,
   rabbit and stump 45.00
Footwarmer, wedge shape, yellow, cork
   plug 100.00
Mixing Bowl, 15" d, brown and white
   bands 45.00
Mug, 4⅞" h, raised blue bands 65.00
Nappy, plain, scalloped 55.00
Pitcher
   8" h, blue stripes 100.00
   8¾" h, basketweave, flower 85.00
   9" h, emb hunt scene, hanging game
     and "Miss Miria B. Handy, Marion,
     Mass", brown sponging, blue,
     green, and yellow ochre highlights,
     white slip int. with frog 65.00
Rolling Pin, wood handles 175.00
Wash Bowl, 12", plain, 1865 . . . . 75.00
Washboard, blue mottled glaze, pine
   frame mount, c1880 . . . . 475.00

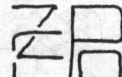

ZANE WARE
MADE IN U.S.A.

ZANE POTTERY

History: In 1921 Adam Reed and Harry Mc-
Clelland bought the Peters and Reed Pottery in
Zanesville, Ohio. The firm continued production of
garden wares and introduced several new art
lines: "Sheen," "Powder Blue," "Crystalline," and
"Drip." The factory was sold in 1941 to Lawton
Gonder.

Additonal Listings: Gonder and Peters and
Reed.

Bowl, 5", brown and blue 40.00
Figure, 10⅛" h, black cat, green eyes . 500.00
Jardiniere, 14½" h, variegated green
   semi-matte glaze, two handles, Mon-
   tene 125.00
Vase
   3½" h, sq, geometric design, rich
     green 65.00

**Jardiniere, 34" h, matching pedestal
base, green matte glaze, artist sgd
"Frank Ferreu," $300.00.**

7" h, flowing medium green, dark forest green ground, marked 90.00
Window Box, 12½ x 5 x 6", Moss Aztec,
   sgd "Ferrell" 125.00

LA MORO

ZANESVILLE POTTERY

History: Zanesville Art Pottery, one of several
potteries located in Zanesville, Ohio, began production in 1900. A line of utilitarian products was
first produced. Art pottery was introduced shortly
thereafter. The major line was La Moro which was
hand painted and decorated under glaze. The impressed block print mark La Moro appears on the
high glazed and matte glazed decorated ware. The
firm was bought by S. A. Weller in 1920 and became known as Weller Plant No. 3.

References: Louise and Evan Purviance and
Norris F. Schneider, *Zanesville Art Pottery In Color*,
Mid-America Book Company, 1968; Evan and
Louise Purviance, *Zanesville Art Tile In Color*, Wal-
lace-Homestead Book Co., 1972.

Bowl, 6½", mottled blue, fluted edge . . 40.00
Jardiniere, 9", brown and gold glaze . . 125.00
Paperweight, A. E. Tiling Co. Ltd, 1896
   calendar on back 25.00
Pitcher, tankard shape, floral dec, artist
   sgd 300.00
Tile, 24", sq, 16 tiles, elk, resembles
   needlepoint, "Mosaic" in oval and
   round circle mark 90.00
Vase, 8¾", cone top and neck, bulbous

Vase, 7″, bulbous, handled, circled collared neck with outward flaring rim, pansy dec, olive to brown, left to right glaze, marked "LaMoro," $150.00.

base, two handles, La Moro, marked
"2/802/4" **350.00**
Wine Decanter, monk **75.00**

ZSOLNAY POTTERY

History: Vilmos Zsolnay (1828–1900) assumed control of his brother's factory in Pécs, Hungary, in the mid-19th century. In 1899 Miklos, Vilmos's son, became manager. The firm still produces ceramic ware.

The early wares are highly ornamental, glazed, and have a cream color ground. "Eosin" glaze, a deep rich play of colors reminiscent of Tiffany's iridescent wares, received a gold medal at the 1900 Paris exhibition. Zsolnay Art Nouveau pieces show great creativity.

Originally no trademark was used. Beginning in 1878 a blue mark depicting the five towers of the cathedral at Pécs was used. The initials "TJM" represent the names of Miklos's three children.

Zsolnay's recent series of iridescent glazed figurines, which initially were inexpensive, now are being sought by collectors and show a steady increase in value.

Reference: Susan and Al Bagdade, *Warman's English & Continental Pottery & Porcelain, 1st Edition,* Warman Publishing Co., Inc., 1987.

Bowl, 9¾″, fan shape, reticulate, multicolored chrysanthemums, int. dec, rolled in sides, scrolled handle, cobalt ground, gold trim **320.00**

Salt, individual, cream ground, dark blue dec, sgd, $150.00.

Box, cov, irid glaze, molded band of chariots and soldiers on side **80.00**
Celery Tray, 13″ l, 7½″ w, diagonal band of piercing pastel floral dec, luster finish **175.00**
Dish, 8½ x 7½″, fan shape, beige, gold, and pink dec, reticulated, fold over border, steeple mark **180.00**
Ewer, 7½″, cream, yellow, and beige dec, gold reticulated neck band, ornate handle, gold around base **100.00**
Figure
  4¼ x 5¼″, Hungarian Sheep Dog, standing, beige **100.00**
  7″, dog, standing, irid, bronze and gold **55.00**
  10″ h, nude, standing, leaning on draped pedestal with urn, green irid high glaze, painted mark **675.00**
Jug, 9″, lustered, enameled flowers, cream ground, handles **200.00**
Plaque, 10″, portrait, gold foil ground . **250.00**
Plate, 8″, purple orchid, cobalt blue ground **75.00**
Puzzle Jug, 6¾″ h, multicolored jeweling and irid florals, reticulated roundels, three looped protrusions, pale beige ground, handled, blue castle mark **125.00**
Ring Tree, 3½″, irid gold **75.00**
Serving Dish, 8½″, pink and gold flowers, rolled reticulated side borders, beige ground **160.00**
Urn, 11″, floral dec, handled, marked "Zsolnay Pecs" **200.00**
Vase
  5½″, ovoid, alligator finish, irid red .. **140.00**
  6¾″ h, cobalt blue, irid glaze **200.00**
  9½″, baluster shape, reticulated, luster glaze and ivory flowers, gilt ground, wide shaped handles, ftd, printed factory mark **175.00**
Watering Can, 5″ h, floral dec **90.00**

PHOTO CREDITS

We wish to thank those who permitted us to photograph objects in their possession. Unfortunately, we are unable to identify the sources for all of our pictures; nevertheless, we are deeply appreciative for all who contributed to this and past editions, and to the editions of *Warman's Americana & Collectibles.*

California: Carlsbad, Dan Golden; Moor Park, Tony and Jackie Anello; Oceanside, Lois Misiewicz; San Francisco, Butterfields; Santa Ana, Evalene Pulati. **Connecticut**: New Canaan, Mildred Fishman; Stamford, Donna Schilero, West Hartford, Arnold Chase; Westport, Tom Gallagher. **Delaware**: Lewes, The Price's, Sea Gert Antiques. **Florida**: Cape Coral, The Calico Cat, Elizabeth Clancey, The Collector's Den, Sandra Martz, Country Closet Antiques; Clearwater Beach, Bill Wheeler, The Oar House; Ft. Myers, Ft. Myers Antique Mall, Mina Tinsley, Things Unlimited; Hollywood, Cynthia and Joseph Klein; Miami Beach, Estelle Zalkin; Orlando, Peg Harrison, Harrison's Antiques. **Georgia**: Atlanta, Walter Glenn, Geode Ltd., Jim Marin, Art Deco Atlanta. **Illinois**: Arlington Heights, T. Johnson; Mapleton, White's Antiques and Furniture Finishing; Northbrook, Al and Susan Bagdade; Peotone, Kathy Wojcie-chowski. **Iowa**: Spencer, Paul and Paula Brenner; Spirit Lake, Gaylord and Margaret Franken. **Maine**: Kennebunk, Richard W. Oliver Auction & Art Gallery; Oxford, Oxford Common; Topsham, Allan and Helen Smith, The Country House. **Maryland**: Laurel, Ken Cohen, Julie Rich; Temple Hills, John Rosenberg; **Massachusetts**: Cambridge, Stan Tillotson; Hyannis Port, Richard A. Bourne, Inc.

Michigan: Utica, Virgil Rogers and David Graves, Avant-Garde; West Bloomfield, Joan Collett Oates. **Missouri**: Sedalia, Crystal and Leyland Payton. **New Hampshire**: Salem, Bea and Bill Laycock, B & B Antiques & Collectibles. **New Jersey**: Bellmawr, Angie Ricciaardi Antiques; Demarest, Mimi Rudnick, The Salt Lady Antiques; Hackensack, Roz Albert; Madison, Don Fiore, The Toy Man; Magnolia, Carol Pollock, Custom Covers; Montclair, Susan Morse; Moorestown, Cindy and James Townes, Ladybug's Cupboard; Morris Plains, Elyce Litts; Old Bridge, Sue Theurich, Respectable Collectables; Paterson, Edward W. Leach; Stewartsville, Marcia and Bob Weissman, Neat Olde Things; Toms River, Shelley, Norman and Phyllis Galinkin; West Orange, Barbara and Melvin Alpern; Woodcliff Lake, Joan Raines Antiques. **New York**: Auburn, Lower Lake Collectibles; Elmsford, Gerald and Carol Newman; Fishkill, Robert A. Doyle; New Platz, Charlotte and Larry Settle; New York, John High, Sotheby's; Queens, Flamingoes; Valley Stream, Craig Dinner. **North Carolina**: Chapel Hill, Alda Horner, Whitehall Shop. **Ohio**: Beachwood, Rita Orons; Canton, Lewis Bettinger; Cincinnati, Connie Rogers; Newton Falls, Bob and Kathy Wujcik; Urbana, Parker's Antiques. **Oklahoma**: Tulsa, Phyllis Bess.

Pennsylvania: Adamstown, Dottie Freeman and Allan Teal; Allentown, The Borgmans, Wanamaker R.R. Depot Antiques, LeFevre's Antiques, Jim Lo Antiques, Phyllis and Alvin Kahn, The Pen Man's Antiques, Edna Stauffer, Today & Yesterday; Cabot, Clair Bargerstock; Coatesville, Chet Ramsay Antiques; Cogan Station, Roan Bros. Auction Gallery; Coopersburg, Neil and Clodogh Wotring; Danville, Lissa L. Bryan-Smith, Richard Smith, Holiday Antiques; Eagleville, Tyler's Antiques; Easton, Harold Mellor, Coach and Four Antiques; Hatfield, Sanford Alderfer Auction Co.; Lampeter, James S. Maxwell, Jr.; Lititz, Doug Flynn and Al Bolton, Holloway House; Montgomeryville, Clarence and Betty Maier, Burmese Cruet; Montoursville, M. Jeanne Foust, Jeanne's Glass House; New Freedom, George Theofiles, Miscellaneous Man; New Hope, Debby Bogdan, Ferry Hill, Ted and Linda Freed; Northampton, David and Sue Irons, Irons Antiques; Oley, Mrs. Lena Eyrich; Philadelphia, Shelly Hoffman, Ed Kelberg, Marcy Kula, Ed Volkrecht, Ed's Antiques, Inc., Murray and Selma Petersons; Pittsburgh, Regis and Mary Ferson, Edward Grzybowski; Pottsville, George and Tedi Hahn, Doorway To Glass; Whitehall, Herb and Nancy Hallman, The Churn Antiques; Wilkes-Barre, Al Sallitt Antiques, Golden Webb Antiques; Williamsport, Michael Rath; Yardley, Ellie Archer; York, Lookenbill's Antiques.

South Dakota: Huron, Joan Hull. **Tennessee**: Elaine J. Luartes, Athena Antiques. **Texas**: Dallas, Ted Birbilis; Euless, The Stevensons. **Vermont**: Cavendish, Henry and Doris Sigourney, Sigourney's Antiques. **Virginia**: Portsmouth, Whitney LeCompte. **Virginia**: Arlington, Carolyn Smith; Crozet, Betty L. Loba, Rose Valley Antiques; Hopewell, Carolyn R. Morris, Yestermorrow's Collectibles and More; Radford, Roy M. Collins. **Wisconsin**: Kaukauna, Ferill J. Rice.

INDEX

THE WARMAN'S READER REPORT

To: The Reader Report
    Warman Publishing Company
    P.O. Box 1112
    Willow Grove, PA 19090

Dear Publisher:
I have used the following Warman publication: _____
I would like to make the following ☐ suggestion, ☐ comment, ☐ criticism:

_____

_____

_____

_____

_____

_____

_____

_____

_____

_____

Thank you for taking the time to help us prepare better books.

From (name, optional): _____

Address: _____

City: _____ State: _____ ZIP: _____

Warman price guides are available from leading book stores and antiques booksellers, or they can be ordered directly from the publisher.

☐ **WARMAN'S ANTIQUES AND THEIR PRICES, 23rd Ed.,** edited by Harry L. Rinker. The standard price reference for the general antiques filed. 50,000 items, 1,000 photos, factory marks and illustrations, histories, references, 100's of American Pattern Glass designs, fully indexed. April 1989.

Paperback **$12.95**

☐ **WARMAN'S AMERICANA & COLLECTIBLES, 3rd Ed.,** edited by Harry L. Rinker. An all new edition of the best-selling price guide and reference in the collectibles field. 560 pages, 600 photos, 25,000 prices, histories, references, clubs. Fully indexed. January 1988. Paperback **$13.95**

☐ **WARMAN'S ENGLISH & CONTINENTAL POTTERY & PORCELAIN** by Susan and Al Bagdade. A price and reference guide to the entire field. 200 makers, 1,000's of items, 600 + photos and factory marks, plus histories, references and collecting hints.. Paperback **$18.95**

☐ **ZALKIN'S HANDBOOK OF THIMBLES & SEWING IMPLEMENTS** by Estelle Zalkin. A colorful new treasury of information covering 1,400 objects, 780 photographs and current prices. Useful histories and backgrounds on everything from thimbles and chatelaines to scissors and workboxes.

Hardback **$24.95**

Return with payment to:

Warman Publishing Co.
P.O. Box 1112, Dept. 23
Willow Grove, PA 19090

Prices are subject to change without notice. Allow 4-6 weeks for delivery.
Inquire about quantity discounts for dealers, schools, and clubs.
Phone (215) 657-1812

Qty.	Title	Price	Total
	Warman's Antiques and Their Prices, 23rd Ed.	$12.95	$
	Warman's Americana & Collectibles, 3rd Ed.	$13.95	$
	Warman's English & Continental Pottery & Porcelain	$18.95	$
	Zalkin's Handbook of Thimbles & Sewing Implements	$24.95	$
	TOTAL OF BOOKS ORDERED		$
	Pa. residents add 6% sales tax		$
	POSTAGE & HANDLING: $2.00 for first book, 50¢ each additional book		$
	TOTAL AMOUNT ENCLOSED		$

Send check or money order, no C.O.D.

Ship to:

NAME (please print) _____

ADDRESS _____

CITY _____

STATE _____ ZIP _____

23